THE OXFORD HANDBOO

POLITICAL
SCIENCE

THE
OXFORD
HANDBOOKS
OF
POLITICAL
SCIENCE

GENERAL EDITOR: ROBERT E. GOODIN

The *Oxford Handbooks of Political Science* is a ten-volume set of reference books offering authoritative and engaging critical overviews of all the main branches of political science.

The series as a whole is under the General Editorship of Robert E. Goodin, with each volume being edited by a distinguished international group of specialists in their respective fields:

POLITICAL THEORY
John S. Dryzek, Bonnie Honig & Anne Phillips

POLITICAL INSTITUTIONS
R. A. W. Rhodes, Sarah A. Binder & Bert A. Rockman

POLITICAL BEHAVIOR
Russell J. Dalton & Hans-Dieter Klingemann

COMPARATIVE POLITICS
Carles Boix & Susan C. Stokes

LAW & POLITICS
Keith E. Whittington, R. Daniel Kelemen & Gregory A. Caldeira

PUBLIC POLICY
Michael Moran, Martin Rein & Robert E. Goodin

POLITICAL ECONOMY
Barry R. Weingast & Donald A. Wittman

INTERNATIONAL RELATIONS
Christian Reus-Smit & Duncan Snidal

CONTEXTUAL POLITICAL ANALYSIS
Robert E. Goodin & Charles Tilly

POLITICAL METHODOLOGY
Janet M. Box-Steffensmeier, Henry E. Brady & David Collier

This series aspires to shape the discipline, not just to report on it. Like the Goodin–Klingemann *New Handbook of Political Science* upon which the series builds, each of these volumes will combine critical commentaries on where the field has been together with positive suggestions as to where it ought to be heading.

THE OXFORD HANDBOOK OF

POLITICAL SCIENCE

Edited by

ROBERT E. GOODIN

OXFORD
UNIVERSITY PRESS

OXFORD

UNIVERSITY PRESS

Great Clarendon Street, Oxford ox2 6DP

Oxford University Press is a department of the University of Oxford.
It furthers the University's objective of excellence in research, scholarship,
and education by publishing worldwide in

Oxford New York

Auckland Cape Town Dar es Salaam Hong Kong Karachi
Kuala Lumpur Madrid Melbourne Mexico City Nairobi
New Delhi Shanghai Taipei Toronto

With offices in

Argentina Austria Brazil Chile Czech Republic France Greece
Guatemala Hungary Italy Japan Poland Portugal Singapore
South Korea Switzerland Thailand Turkey Ukraine Vietnam

Oxford is a registered trade mark of Oxford University Press
in the UK and in certain other countries

Published in the United States
by Oxford University Press Inc., New York

British Library Cataloguing in Publication Data
Data available

Library of Congress Cataloging in Publication Data
Data available

Typeset by SPI Publisher Services, Pondicherry, India
Printed in Great Britain
on acid-free paper by
CPI Group (UK) Ltd, Croydon, CR0 4YY

ISBN 978–0–19–956295–4 (hbk.)
ISBN 978–0–19–960445–6 (pbk.)

5 7 9 10 8 6

PREFACE

....

Every book has a history. This one's begins with the XVIth World Congress of the International Political Science Association in Berlin, way back in 1994. I was scheduled to be its Program Chair; that was going to be a lot of work; I decided I'd be damned if the program booklet itself was all I'd have to show for my efforts. So Hans-Dieter Klingemann and I carved out a stream of "State of the Discipline" panels designed (with a few nips and tucks here and there) to feed into *A New Handbook of Political Science*, eventually published by Oxford University Press in 1996. That book did well for OUP. Indecently well, apparently. OUP editors ever since have been under orders to commission several such handbooks each year—doubtless cursing us as they do, for launching the handbook industry.

Publication of the *New Handbook* was overseen by Tim Barton, then OUP Politics Editor, and his then assistant, Dominic Byatt, whom I first met at the party for IPSA "State of the Discipline" panelists thrown by Hans-Dieter in the courtyard of James Stirling's wonderful Wissenschaftszentrum-Berlin. Passing through Oxford five years after the *New Handbook*'s publication, I joined Tim (by then Academic Director of OUP) and Dominic (risen to Politics Editor) for a drink in the Eagle and Child to celebrate its success. Tim was full of praise for the *New Handbook,* recounting how it had spawned a whole clutch of Oxford Handbooks across all academic disciplines. "Perhaps I ought get half a percent royalties on each of them, then," I replied. "I have an idea about that!" Tim shot back. And over the next pint or two, the scheme for the multi-volume series of "Oxford Handbooks of Political Science" was hatched.

There are of course all too many of handbooks of this and that, these days. (Apologies for whatever part our initial *New Handbook* might have played in that.) The ten-volume series of "Oxford Handbooks of Political Science" was supposed to be something different. It was not to be just another clutch of handbooks on random topics. Instead, the animating idea was to map political science systematically, sub-discipline by sub-discipline. The aim was nothing less than mapping of the genome of the discipline.

This was clearly going to be a massive undertaking: ten volumes, fifty chapters each. And while it would overload the production team to try to publish them all at the same time, OUP were rightly anxious that all ten volumes should be published within a very few years of one another (in the end, we managed to get all ten out in just three years). Clearly, I needed help. So I inveigled two dozen of the best political scientists in the world to edit the component volumes. My greatest debt is to them, whose names appear opposite the title page, for their gargantuan efforts in pulling this all off: conceptualizing their volume, talking demigods of the profession into writing for them (and chivvying them to deliver), working with authors to make strong chapters even stronger, and doing it all within a very tight timeframe. I co-edited the first two of the ten volumes myself and know just how much work was involved. So I thank them again, publicly and profusely, for their grace, their commitment, and above all for the excellent products of all their labors.

The present volume has been constructed by "mining" their ten volumes. When Tim, Dominic, and I conceived this plan over drinks seven years ago, it sounded like this step would be the easy one: a good way to produce, in effect, a replacement for the ageing (but still useful) *New Handbook*. That turned out to be an illusion. Editors of each of the ten sub-disciplinary handbooks had fifty chapters to play with; in the one-volume consolidation text, I had to represent all those fifty chapters with merely five per sub-discipline. Editors of the sub-disciplinary handbooks could orchestrate synergies among their chapters that I could not with so few chapters per sub-discipline. In the sub-disciplinary handbooks, many of the most outstanding chapters are detailed discussions of special topics, wonderful but ill-suited for the more general overview purposes of this consolidation text. So I apologize, firstly, to the many authors of truly excellent chapters that, for one reason or another, did not find their way into this volume. The tables of contents of all ten sub-disciplinary handbooks are printed at the back of the present book: I strongly encourage readers to check there to see what they are missing.

I apologize, secondly, to the editors of the ten other handbooks for giving them no hand in making the editorial selection for this volume. I suspect many of them might be relieved not to have had to make invidious comparisons among all the excellent chapters in their own volumes. But the real reason I did not ask them was that all they could tell me was what they thought the "best" chapters in their own handbooks were. This consolidation text is supposed to be more than the sum of its parts, however. While I hope to have chosen chapters that my fellow editors would agree are among the best in their own handbooks, even more than that I hope to have put together a set of chapters that makes organic sense as a collection in its own right, from the point of view of a general political science readership with only a passing acquaintance with many of the sub-disciplines represented. In doing that I have occasionally chosen chapters from handbooks other than that of the sub-discipline concerned: but let there be no implication that there were not plenty of great chapters in that sub-disciplinary handbook to choose from; it was just that some chapter from another of the handbooks better fitted the particular hole I needed to fill in *this* book.

In my opening chapter—which also is very much a personal statement from which many of my fellow handbook editors might well dissent in many places—I report the results of a rudimentary citation analysis operating on the ten-volume series as a whole, paralleling the one Hans-Dieter and I performed on the contents of the *New Handbook*. Take that with as many grains of salt as you deem appropriate: Bibliometrics are always wonky at the margins. Just know, however, that no one was told ahead of time that I was going to analyze other handbooks' indices in this way. Even if from the *New Handbook* precedent someone guessed that I might, there were so many different people writing chapters for the ten volumes overall that no one could, by strategic citation choices, do much to alter the overall outcome.

There are two overarching debts that remain for me to record. One is to my home institution: the Research School of Social Sciences at Australian National University. It is a truly remarkable hotbed of intellectual activity, across the whole range of social sciences. Looking at the map it may not seem so, but Canberra truly is the crossroads of the academic universe. Anyone who's anyone eventually visits, and when they come this far they come for a goodly period of time, so it is a genuinely useful interaction. I am proud to have had the chance to get to know so many talented people so well, thanks to the RSSS; and the fruits of all that networking have fed powerfully into the "Oxford Handbooks of Political Science" series and, through that, into this book. In addition to being a magnet for academic talent, I am also especially grateful to RSSS for relieving me from the need to teach students twenty-at-a-time, thus affording me the space to put together volumes like this that teach thousands-at-a-time.

My second overarching debt is to Oxford University Press and many fine people there. This volume is the culmination of a project of conceptualizing, commissioning, and cajoling that has been going on for some seven years; many people at Oxford University Press have helped at various points in the process, for which I'm grateful. But there are three people who have been there throughout, and who deserve far greater tribute than any I can possibly pay them here. Tim Barton as Academic Director for almost the entire period and Des King as the ever-present Politics Delegate were super-supportive from start to finish, always ready to wade in from on high when needed, always smoothing the way. But on a day-to-day (often many-times-a-day) basis it has been Dominic Byatt who has kept this show on the road. I have known many good editors, but I've never known a better one than Dominic: sensible, efficient, firm, unflappable, smart, judicious, funny. He has gone way beyond the call of duty to rescue us from more looming disasters, large and small, than either of us would care to count. He has been the source of as much good substantive advice as virtually any of my academic colleagues. Working with him has been a treat. So thanks, thanks, and thanks again, Dominic, for everything.

When proposing this consolidation volume as the de facto replacement for the *New Handbook of Political Science*, I jokingly suggested we entitle it *A Newer Handbook of Political Science*, so as to preserve my option of doing one more—to be entitled, of course, *The Newest Handbook of Political Science*. Now, at the end of this eleven-volume slog, I'm not sure . . . but give it five or ten years and another drink or two with the good people from OUP at the Eagle and Child, and who knows?

What I can say with some confidence is that the ten-volume mapping of the genome of the discipline truly feels to me like a once-in-a-generation undertaking, unlikely to be replicated anytime soon. I thank Oxford University Press for entrusting it to my General Editorship, and I thank my fellow editors and all the contributors to those volumes for pulling it off so magnificently.

Canberra
September 2008

Contents

PART IV LAW AND POLITICS

PART V POLITICAL BEHAVIOR

PART IX POLITICAL ECONOMY

PART X PUBLIC POLICY

PART XI POLITICAL METHODOLOGY

APPENDIX

About the Contributors

John H. Aldrich is Pfizer-Pratt University Professor in the Department of Political Science, Duke University.

Richard J. Arneson is Professor of Philosophy at the University of California, San Diego.

David Austen-Smith is Earl Dean Howard Distinguished Professor of Political Economy at Northwestern University.

Judith A. Baer is Professor of Political Science at Texas A&M University.

Eugene Bardach is Professor of Public Policy in the Richard and Rhoda Goldman School of Public Policy, University of California, Berkeley.

Michael Barnett is the Harold Stassen Chair of International Affairs at the Humphrey Institute of Public Affairs and Professor of Political Science at the University of Minnesota.

Jane Bennett is Professor of Political Science at Johns Hopkins University.

Davis B. Bobrow is Professor of Political Science and International Affairs at the University of Pittsburgh.

Carles Boix is Professor of Politics and Public Affairs, Princeton University.

Samuel Bowles is Research Professor and Director of the Behavioral Sciences Program of the Santa Fe Institute and Professor of Economics at the University of Siena.

Janet M. Box-Steffensmeier is Vernal Riffe Professor of Political Science and Sociology and Director of the Program in Statistics Methodology at Ohio State University.

Henry E. Brady is Class of 1941 Monroe Deutsche Professor in the Charles and Louise Travers Department of Political Science and the Goldman School of Public Policy, and Director of the Survey Research Center, UC DATA, and California Census Research Center, University of California, Berkeley.

John Braithwaite is Australian Research Council Federation Fellow in RetNet, Research School of Pacific and Asian Studies, Australian National University.

Gregory A. Caldeira is Distinguished University Professor and Chaired Professor of Political Science at the Ohio State University.

David Collier is Robson Professor in the Charles and Louise Travers Department of Political Science.

Josep M. Colomer is Research Professor in Political Science in the Higher Council of Scientific Research, Barcelona.

Russell J. Dalton is Professor of Political Science at the University of California, Irvine.

John S. Dryzek is Australian Research Council Federation Fellow in Political Science at the Research School of Social Sciences, Australian National University.

Tim Dunne is Professor of International Relations and Director of the Centre of Advanced International Studies at the University of Exeter.

James D. Fearon is Theodore and Frances Geballe Professor of Political Science, Stanford University.

Barbara Geddes is Professor of Political Science at the University of California, Los Angeles.

Alan S. Gerber is Professor of Political Science and Director of the Center for the Study of American Politics, Yale University.

John Gerring is Professor of Political Science at Boston University.

James L. Gibson is Sidney W. Souers Professor of Government at Washington University, St Louis.

Herbert Gintis is Emeritus Professor of Economics at the University of Massachusetts, Amherst, and a member of the External Faculty of the Santa Fe Institute.

Robert E. Goodin is Distinguished Professor of Social & Political Theory and of Philosophy in the Research School of Social Sciences, Australian National University.

Donald P. Green is A. Whitney Griswold Professor of Political Science and Director of the Institution for Social and Policy Studies, Yale University.

Russell Hardin is Professor in the Wilf Family Department of Political Science, New York University.

Colin Hay is Professor of Professor of Political Analysis at the University of Sheffield.

Ran Hirschl is Professor of Political Science and Canada Research Chair in Constitutionalism, Democracy and Development at the University of Toronto.

Bonnie Honig is Professor of Political Science at Northwestern University and Senior Research Fellow, American Bar Foundation.

John D. Huber is Professor of Political Science at Columbia University.

Torben Iversen is Harold Hitchings Burbank Professor of Political Economy at Harvard University.

R. Daniel Kelemen is Associate Professor of Political Science at Rutgers University.

Robert O. Keohane is Professor of International Affairs at Princeton University.

Herbert Kitschelt is George V. Allen Professor of International Relations in the Department of Political Science, Duke University.

Rudolf Klein is Professor of Social Policy Emeritus, University of Bath.

Hans-Dieter Klingemann is Emeritus Professor at the Wissenschaftszentrum, Berlin, where he was Director of the Research Unit for Institutions and Social Change.

David D. Laitin is James T. Watkins IV and Elsie V. Watkins Professor of Political Science, Stanford University.

James G. March is Professor of Education and Emeritus Jack Steele Parker Professor of International Management, of Political Science and of Sociology, Stanford University.

Theodore R. Marmor is Professor Emeritus of Public Policy and Management and Professor Emeritus of Political Science, Yale University.

Lynn Mather is Professor of Law and Political Science and Director of the Baldy Center for Law and Social Policy at the State University of New York at Buffalo.

Kenneth M. McElwain is a Post-Doctoral Fellow, Division of International, Comparative and Area Studies, Stanford University.

Michael Moran is W. J. M. Mackenzie Professor of Government, University of Manchester.

Andrew Moravcsik is Professor of Politics and Public Affairs at Princeton University.

Diana C. Mutz is Samuel A. Stouffer Professor of Political Science and Communication at the University of Pennsylvania, and serves as Director of the Institute for the Study of Citizens and Politics at The Annenberg Public Policy Center.

Johan P. Olsen is Professor Emeritus at ARENA, University of Oslo.

Anne Phillips is Professor of Gender Theory in the Department of Government and Gender Institute, London School of Economics.

J. G. A. Pocock is Henry C. Black Professor Emeritus of History, Johns Hopkins University.

Martin Rein is Professor of Sociology in the Department of Urban Studies and Planning, Massachusetts Institute of Technology.

Christian Reus-Smit is Professor of International Relations in the Research School of Pacific and Asian Studies, Australian National University.

R. A. W. Rhodes is Professor of Political Science at the University of Tasmania and at the Research School of Social Sciences, Australian National University.

Jeffrey A. Segal is Distinguished University Professor of Political Science at the State University of New York at Stony Brook.

Charles R. Shipan is the J. Ira and Nicki Harris Professor of Social Science and Professor of Public Policy at the University of Michigan.

Kathryn Sikkink is a Regents Professor and McKnight Distinguished University Professor of Political Science at the University of Minnesota.

Steve Smith is Vice-Chancellor and Professor of International Relations at the University of Exeter.

Duncan Snidal is Associate Professor in the Harris School, the Department of Political Science, and the College at the University of Chicago.

Hendrik Spruyt is Norman Dwight Harris Professor of International Relations, Department of Political Science, Northwestern University.

Susan C. Stokes is John S. Saden Professor of Political Science, Yale University.

Göran Therborn is a Director of the Swedish Collegium for Advanced Study in the Social Sciences, Uppsala.

Charles Tilly was Joseph L. Buttenwieser Professor of Social Science at Columbia University.

Eric M. Uslaner is Professor in the Department of Government and Politics, University of Maryland.

Barry R. Weingast is Senior Fellow, Hoover Institution, and the Ward C. Krebs Family Professor, Department of Political Science, Stanford University.

Keith E. Whittington is William Nelson Cromwell Professor of Politics at Princeton University.

Donald A. Wittman is Professor of Economics at the University of California, Santa Barbara.

Anne Wren is Assistant Professor of Political Science at Stanford University and Senior Research Fellow, Institute for International Integration Studies, Trinity College Dublin.

Thomas Zittel is Project Director, European Political Systems and their Integration at the University of Mannheim.

PART I

INTRODUCTION

CHAPTER 1

THE STATE OF THE DISCIPLINE, THE DISCIPLINE OF THE STATE

ROBERT E. GOODIN

A "handbook" is Germanic in both its origins and its ambitions. Handbooks invariably aspire to be comprehensive, systematic, exhaustive—and above all, in contemporary academic practice, *big*.[1] A handbook, at least in its academic instantiation, is definitely not a pocketbook. An editor of one particularly large volume of the *Oxford Handbooks of Political Science* wryly describes his as a "two-hand book."

Weighing in around 1,000 pages, such handbooks usually manage to be exhausting. But exhaustive is something else. Even with 1,000 pages, handbook editors soon come to realize just how selective they must nonetheless be in their choices of topics and treatments. When even ten volumes of that size prove not enough, it becomes clear just how ill conceived any aspiration to comprehensiveness and exhaustiveness must surely be.

The best any handbook can do is to offer a bird's-eye overview of the general shape of its subject, combined with some posthole exercises to show what riches might be found by probing deeper. That is the spirit in which this volume is offered. It is a schematic guide, and a sampler. There is much more by way of elaboration in

---

[1] Making academic usage deviant, judging from the *Oxford English Dictionary*'s definition of a "handbook" as "a small book or treatise, such as may conveniently be held in the hand."

the ten volumes upon which this one draws. There is, however, very much of great consequence that is left out, not only of this volume but also of those other ten as well.

So this book offers a glimpse of the breadth, the depth, and the excitement of political science. It is an invitation to delve deeper into the underlying ten volumes that constitute the series of *Oxford Handbooks of Political Science*.[2] It is an invitation to delve deeper into the discipline that even those ten volumes can merely skim. It hints at the wide range of topics that have recently been preoccupying political scientists, the wide range of theories that they have formulated about them, the wide range of techniques that they have deployed in systematically examining them.[3]

In short, this book does not tell you everything you need to know about political science. What hopefully it does do is give some indication of why you should want to know, and how you might go about finding out.

1 THE DISCIPLINE

....

1.1 A Mission Statement

Political science is a discipline with a mission. The main task of this chapter is to describe the former. Before turning to the state of the discipline, however, let me say a few words about how I conceive its mission.

The most oft-cited definition of "politics" is Lasswell's (1950): "who gets what, when, how."[4] Certainly that is a correct assessment of why we care about politics. If politics carried no consequences, if it made no material difference in the larger world, it would hardly merit serious study. At most, the study of politics would then amount to an exercise in purely aesthetic appreciation of courtly intrigues, deft maneuvers, clever gamesmanship, and such like: cute, but inconsequential.

We should, however, separate out "why politics matters" from "what it is." Lasswell's "who gets what, when and how"—broadly construed, per Lowi (1964)—is a good answer to the former question as to why politics matters. As to what politics is,

----

[2] And an eleventh not formally part of that series but very much a companion volume: Sears, Huddy, and Jervis's *Oxford Handbook of Political Psychology* (2003).

[3] My focus in this chapter is primarily on recent tendencies, glancing backwards to the discipline's past mostly just to ground prognostications as to its future. Those interested in more detail on the path to the present, particularly as regards some particular subject, can piece together the story from relevant chapters in the many handbooks surveying the discipline that have preceded this one. On the US discipline, which is this chapter's principal focus, see: Greenstein and Polsby 1975; Finifter 1983; 1993; Goodin and Klingemann 1996a; Katznelson and Milner 2002. On developments outside the US see the sources cited in n. 12, and on the discipline's history see those sources cited in n. 40.

[4] Followers of Arendt of course dissent (Calhoun and McGowan 1997).

however, I suggest a better answer would be this: politics is the constrained use of social power.[5]

Power of course takes many forms, and is constrained in many interestingly different ways (Lukes 1974/2005; Scott 1986; 1997). Systematically mapping all that is the fundamental task of political science.

Political scientists are often seen as handmaidens to power. Some cherish that role. Machiavelli and his modern-day heirs style themselves as counselors to princes and parties, advising on how to seize and wield power (Morgenthau 1948; Schultze 1992; Neustadt 2000). Other political scientists, taking their inspiration from Marx's eleventh thesis on Feuerbach, adopt a more critical stance toward the powers that be.[6] Self-styled policy scientists occupy points along the continuum, ranging from "accommodative" to "critical" (Wildavsky 1979; Dryzek 2006a).

Attempts at manipulating power always confront countervailing power and the constraints that come with that. Much though the strong might try to bend others to their will, their capacity to do so is inevitably limited. The weak have weapons of their own (Piven and Cloward 1979; Scott 1986). In politics, there is no such thing as a literally "irresistible force." Even the powerful cannot just dictate—they have to persuade as well (Majone 1989). As he was passing the US presidency on to a five-star general, Truman mused, "Poor Ike—it won't be a bit like the Army...He'll sit here and say, 'Do this, do that.' And nothing will happen" (Neustadt 1990, 10). But since the same is true even within a notionally hierarchical military chain of command, it turned out that Eisenhower already knew as much (Greenstein 1982). The essence of politics lies in strategic maneuvering (Riker 1986). Politics is a matter of pursuing your purposes as best you can, in the context of other purposeful agents doing the same, and with whom, through whom, or around whom you must work to accomplish your goals.

Mid-twentieth-century pluralists made much—perhaps too much—of the idea of polyarchy, of multiple centers of (implicitly, pretty nearly equal) power (Dahl 1961b; 1972; Polsby 1980). Critics rightly challenged their naivety in several respects (McCoy and Playford 1968; Bachrach and Baratz 1970; Lukes 1974/2005; Foucault 1991). They rightly emphasized how power might work behind the backs of agents, how structures channel agency (Wendt 1987; Jessop 1990), how social constructs enable and disable (Finnemore and Sikkink 2001), how ideas shape and obscure interests (Laclau and Mouffe 1985; Goldstein and Keohane 1993).[7] Useful correctives, all. But the cumulative effect is of course to expand, not contract, the list of ways in which power might be constrained as well as exercised.

---

[5] Tweaking Duverger's (1964/1966, ix) characterization of it as "organized power, the institutions of command and control."

[6] "The philosophers have only *interpreted* the world, in various ways; the point is, however to *change* it" (Marx 1845/1972, 109). That has long been the stance of the Caucus for a New Political Science, for example (Anon 2007).

[7] A propos the latter, Claus Offe tells me of a statue in the center of old East Berlin, with graffiti below depicting Marx saying to Engels, "It was just an idea..."

The general idea that politics is about the constrained use of power is not merely a pluralist preoccupation. It is endemic to liberalism more generally (Hume 1777), and to liberal democracy most particularly (Macpherson 1977).

Obviously, even in autocratic regimes it is of intense interest to the powerful how they can work around constraints to wield power effectively. Machiavelli envisioned himself advising a fairly ruthless Prince, after all. Politics has been studied in just that spirit in all sorts of societies for a very long time.

But it is no accident that political science as a discipline has grown up along-side and in the context of liberal democracy, with its very special emphasis upon checks and balances, separation of power, political accountability, and political competition.[8] It is in that setting that political science acquired its distinctive mission: to elucidate how social power is, can be, and should be exercised and constrained.

Power is constrained not only by countervailing power and social structures. Power is also constrained by purpose (Reus-Smit 1999)—not just by the powerholder's actual purposes, but also (and in certain respects more importantly) by what those purposes *should* be. A central plank of the mission statement of political science lies in the elucidation of proper purposes, of worthy goals, and of rightful ways of pursuing them.

Political philosophers have sometimes felt marginalized by the scientific turn of the discipline (Storing 1962; Wolin 1969; Dryzek, Honig, and Phillips, this volume). But that is just one more—albeit perhaps the most central—of the false dichotomies I shall be bemoaning in this chapter. Far from being peripheral to the main mission of political science, normative concerns are absolutely central to it.

Of course, values are different from facts, and anyone studying them had better keep those differences straight. That it would be good for some fact to be true does nothing to make it true. To suppose otherwise is just plain wishful thinking. That it is a fact that people think something is good or valuable does not make it truly so, except in the shallowest supply-and-demand sense. You do not establish the truths of morality, any more than those of mathematics, by taking a vote (or sampling opinion, either).[9]

While different methodologies are clearly required for exploring each of those two realms, it is equally clear that both must be pursued in tandem if political science is to accomplish its mission as I conceive it. Consider an analogy: moral philosophers tell us that ethics is supposed to be "action-guiding;" but clearly ethics must connect some facts about the world to the values it recommends, if it is to provide any guidance on how to act in the real world. Equally clearly, from the other side, political

---

[8] "For the greater part of its history, American political science has been tied to its political sibling, American reform liberalism" (Seidelman 1993, 311). Something similar was true in the UK (Collini, Winch, and Burrows 1983), although in continental Europe the emphases were more statist-modernizing ones (Wagner, Wittrock, and Whitley 1991; Heilbron, Magnusson, and Wittrock 1998; Wallerstein 1998, ch. 1). See more generally Easton, Gunnell, and Stein (1995).

[9] Useful though surveys of people's values are for the other quite distinct task of explaining and predicting their behavior, of course (Inglehart 1977).

science needs to connect up its empirical insights to some values in order to perform its own larger purpose.[10]

What is the point of finding out how things are, without wondering how they could and should be (Moore 1970; Geertz 1977)? Those are different questions, to be pursued in different ways perhaps by different people and certainly using different tool kits. Nonetheless, they are both clearly components of one and the same larger enterprise (Reus-Smit and Snidal, this volume). The mission of political science requires it to combine both.

1.2 The Discipline of a Discipline

When calling political science a "discipline," pause to ponder the broader associations of that term. According to the *Oxford English Dictionary*, "discipline" has all the following connotations (and more):

- A branch of instruction or education; a department of learning or knowledge; a science or art in its educational aspect.
- Instruction having for its aim to form the pupil to proper conduct and action; the training of scholars or subordinates to proper and orderly action by instructing and exercising them in the same; mental and moral training; also used *fig.* of the training effect of experience, adversity, etc.
- The orderly conduct and action which result from training; a trained condition.
- The order maintained and observed among pupils, or other persons under control or command, such as soldiers, sailors, the inmates of a religious house, a prison, etc.
- A system or method for the maintenance of order; a system of rules for conduct.
- *Eccl.* The system or method by which order is maintained in a church, and control exercised over the conduct of its members; the procedure whereby this is carried out; the exercise of the power of censure, admonition, excommunication, or other penal measures, by a Christian Church.
- Correction; chastisement; punishment inflicted by way of correction and training; in religious use, the mortification of the flesh by penance; also, in more general sense, a beating or other infliction (humorously) assumed to be salutary to the recipient. (In its monastic use, the earliest English sense.)

Running through all those definitions is this underlying thought: To subject yourself to some discipline is to be guided by a set of rules for doing certain things in an orderly fashion, rules that are shared among all others subject to the same discipline. Those who share the discipline take a critical reflective attitude toward those aspects of their conduct that fall under those standards (Hart 1961), judging their own conduct and that of others according to those standards (Hughes 1958; Caplow and McGee 1961; Parsons 1968; Sciulli 2007).

---

[10] The founding idea of American political science was one "of the discipline as a source of knowledge with practical significance" (Gunnell 2006, 485).

The discipline of political science is less fearsome than that of the church. "Mortification of the flesh by penance" is no part of standard induction into our discipline; and while some of its practitioners are denied tenure, few are literally banned from professing political science ever again. Still, it is an essential part of academic disciplines that they offer standards that can provide grounds for control, chastisement, and even occasional mortification. To discipline is to punish (Foucault 1977; Moran 2006), if only symbolically, if only occasionally or merely potentially.

Subjecting yourself to the discipline of a discipline is to accept constraints that are enabling in turn. A discipline imposes order. Its shared codes, traditions, standards, and practices give its practitioners something in common. A shared disciplinary framework channels the collective energies of the profession and facilitates collaborative attacks on common problems. It is what enables underlaborers to stand on the shoulders of giants, at the same time as enabling giants to stand on the accumulated product of underlaborers' efforts in turn. The division of the universe of knowledge into disciplines and sub-disciplines facilitates division of labor among practitioners who inevitably cannot be expert in all things (Abbott 1988). A shared disciplinary framework is what unobtrusively coordinates all our disparate research efforts and enables the discipline's findings to cumulate, after a fashion, into some larger synthesis.

An academic discipline is also, nowadays, a profession. But what our profession professes is, by and large, just its own professional competence. Professional associations serve to carve out an occupational niche for practitioners. So it was both with the American Political Science Association and many others around the world.[11] (In this chapter I shall concentrate primarily upon developments within the US discipline, which have such a powerful influence on how political science is practiced worldwide: developments elsewhere are canvassed in many other excellent collections.[12])

The sociology of work regards "professional" as a high-status occupational grade, access to which is typically controlled by existing members of the profession (Abbott 2002). Many bemoan the ritual practices of these self-replicating cartels, both in indoctrinating newcomers and in defending their turf against outsiders (Wallerstein 1998); and in their purely self-defensive modes, professions can indeed be conspiracies against the public interest, academically as surely as otherwise.

But academic professions have another side as well. They are self-organizing communities of scholars dedicated to trying to find progressively better answers to the problems around which they are organized. Anyone in doubt needs merely reflect

---

[11] Gunnell (2006). On the UK see Chester (1975); Barry (1999). For an intriguing mid-century assessment of developments around the world, see Macpherson (1954). Supranational associations serve rather different purposes (Coakley and Trent 2000; Rokkan 1979; Newton 1991).

[12] Schmitter (2002) is right that there are sometimes interesting local variations. See Easton, Gunnell, and Graziano (1991) for a wide-ranging comparative overview. For developments in Western Europe, see Newton and Vallès (1991), Dierkes and Biervert (1992), Quermonne (1996), and Klingemann (2007); and, in Eastern Europe, Kaase and Sparschuh (2002) and Klingemann, Kulesza, and Legutke (2002). For developments in specific countries, see Hayward, Barry, and Brown (1999) on the UK, Leca and Grawitz (1985) on France, Beyme (1986) on Germany, and Graziano (1987) on Italy.

upon the dilettantism of the American Social Science Association that preceded the American Political Science Association (Kaplan and Lewis 2001; see further Seidelman and Harpham 1985, 20; Seidelman 1993), and what passed for political science in the first third-century of the APSA's own existence (Sigelman 2006*b*, 473). Compared to that, the increasing professionalization of political science from the middle of the last century onward has surely greatly enhanced the discipline's collective capacity to bring a systematic body of theoretically integrated insights to bear on important problems of politics and society.[13]

Over a decade ago the *New Handbook of Political Science* offered a similarly rosy prognosis (Goodin and Klingemann 1996*b*; Almond 1996). Some scoffed at that as an unduly whiggish view of the discipline's history. Doubtless scoffers were right, in part. Progress comes in fits and starts, at different rates in different times, different sub-disciplines, and different countries (Dryzek and Leonard 1995; Sigelman 2006*b*, 473).[14] But there is movement in the right direction in most places. Let one example suffice. Writing in 1999, Barry (1999, 450–5) said he could see no evidence in the British discipline of the sort of professionalization the *New Handbook* described; less than a decade later, there has been a generational shift and a dramatic cross-fertilization of British political science from abroad (Goodin et al. 2007, 34–5; Goodin 2009).

1.3 Against Either–Or

There are many who think that the discipline of political science has, over the past half-century, taken wrong turns and gone up blind alleys, that too many eggs have been put in far too few methodological baskets. There are many who think that the disciplinary control exercised over the profession by certain sects has been far too tight.[15] That was the complaint of the Caucus for a New Political Science against behavioralism in the 1960s and 1970s (Easton 1969; Anon 2007) and of the Perestroika movement against rational choice in the 2000s (Schram 2003; Monroe 2005; Rudolph 2005).

To some extent those were movements targeted more at organizations than ideas. Reform of the professional association was high on the agendas of both insurgencies. In both cases, the American Political Science Association fobbed off the insurgents with a quintessentially organizational ploy: giving the dissidents an official new journal all their own (*PS* for the Caucus, *Perspectives on Politics* for Perestroika).[16] To a

---

[13] As I wrote in commenting on the state of the discipline in Britain, "I defy anyone hankering for a return to the pre-professional past to say in all honesty that they wish they had written any of the chapters in for example the (pre-Royal) Institute of Public Administration's survey of *British Government since 1918* (Campion et al. 1950)" (Goodin 2009).

[14] Sometimes in surprising ways: "how to become a dominant French philosopher" seems to be to get picked up by US comparative literature departments, judging from the case of Derrida (Lamont 1987).

[15] The problem is not peculiar to political science, of course. Deirdre McCloskey (2006, 55) delights in quoting back to contemporary economists Oliver Cromwell's words to the Scottish kirk: "I beseech you, in the bowel of Christ, think it possible you may be mistaken."

[16] Many would say they didn't remain "all their own" for long, with *PS* soon becoming an establishment organ and *Perspectives* soon moving to the rational-choice base camp (Rochester).

large extent, however, those movements were targeted at credos of the profession, the Caucus bemoaning its insistent value-neutrality, Perestroika bemoaning its narrowness of vision. Those issues are harder to resolve.[17]

Here, however, I want to focus on one characteristic feature of these periodic "great debates" within the profession: their Manichean, Good versus Evil form. Nor is it found in only those major episodes that traumatized the profession as a whole. Even as regards the more substantive "great debates" within each of the various subdisciplines, there is a remarkable penchant for representing the options in "either–or" fashion. Behavioralist or traditionalist, structure or agency, ideas or interests, realist or idealist, rationalist or interpretivist: you simply have to choose, or so we are constantly told.

On all those dimensions, and many others as well, the only proper response is to refuse to choose. Respond, insistently, "Both!" Both sides to the argument clearly have a point, both are clearly on to something. Elements of both need to be blended, in some judicious manner (not just any will do[18]), into a comprehensive overall account.[19]

The "tyranny of small differences" is a notorious hazard across all of life. Among academics on the make, the tendency to exaggerate the extent of their differences, so as to emphasize the novelty and distinctiveness of their own contribution, powerfully fuels that general phenomenon (Moran 2006). Still, those are the machinations of "youngsters in a hurry" (Cornford 1908, 5), not the settled judgements of seasoned practitioners confident of their place in the profession.[20]

That may seem a strong conclusion, but it has history on its side. Remember the equanimity with which the behavioral revolution was originally greeted by those then ruling the profession.

If the behavioral revolution's main tenets are behavior, science, pluralism and system, then "traditionalists" had little reason to oppose it. Research on behavior at the individual levels was already being done in the 1930s and 1940s ... —and those who did not do it had little

---

[17] Likewise the movement for a "public sociology" (Burawory 2005).

[18] As Barry (1970, 183) says, "there is no *intrinsic* advantage in mixing up opposed ideas ... the result can easily be a muddle."

[19] A point appreciated by writers as diverse as Bohman (1999; 2002), Hay (2002), and Katzenstein and Sil (2008). This is also the official ideology, if not always practice, of the Perestroika movement: "this new political science would not be one that is dedicated to replacing one method with another. Instead, such a discipline ... would encourage scholars to draw on a wide range of methods from a diversity of theoretical perspectives, combining theory and empirical work in different and reactive ways, all in dialogue with political actors in specific contexts" (Schram 2003, 837).

[20] Let me quote two. Russell Hardin (2006, 5) writes that "the small group who think there is a Methoden Streit that shakes many social scientists are largely ignored by the far—indeed, vastly—larger groups of active social scientists who more or less constructively pursue their highly varied methods. They are not shaken. They are not even stirred. And broadside dismissals will not bring them into this debate." Gabriel Almond's (1988, 840) phrase "separate tables" gave a name to a phenomenon he denies more than he decries; he insists that "mainstream political science is open to all methods that illuminate the world of politics and public policy. It will not turn its back on the illumination we get from our older methodologies just because it now can employ the powerful tools of statistics and mathematics."

objection to those who did. The commitment to science was of long standing. . . . Pluralism as empirical theory was hardly new—indeed, the "latent theory of the traditionalists as . . . [a] 'parallelogram of forces' . . ." sounds a lot like pluralism.   (Dryzek 2006*b*, 489–90)

Not until that revolution had been won was it seriously challenged, and even then in a way the mainstream studiously ignored. Leo Strauss's vituperative "Epilogue" to Storing's 1962 *Essays on the Scientific Study of Politics* constituted the challenge, but "the challenge was never officially accepted by the profession of political science." Other political theorists (Schaar and Wolin 1963) were left to "come to the defense of political science." And "political theorists . . . were left to squabble among themselves in their isolation from the discipline at large," which proceeded basically to ignore "both the accusations that had been made against them and the proffered defense" (Saxonhouse 2006, 847–8).

"Multi-perspectival approaches" are the embodiment of the refusal to succumb to the demands of "either–or."[21] The fruitfulness of such approaches, and the willingness of members of the profession not merely to tolerate but to embrace them, is evinced across the ten-volume series of *Oxford Handbooks of Political Science*. Constructivists co-edit and coauthor with rationalist-realists (Reus-Smit and Snidal, this volume), critical theorists with post-structuralists (Dryzek, Honig, and Phillips, this volume), qualitative methodologists with quantitative (Box-Steffensmeier, Brady, and Collier, this volume); and all of them celebrate the synergies. Nowadays very few sophisticated philosophers or social scientists believe in covering-law positivism anymore (Moon 1975; Kitcher 1981; Hay 2002). But instead of throwing their hands up in despair, they turn to whole other disciplines that systematically map the many other contextual factors upon which political outcomes depend (Tilly and Goodin, this volume; cf. Flyvbjerg 2001 and Laitin 2003).

For a brief worked example of how such a multi-perspectival approach might work, consider the "new institutionalism." Distinction-mongers divide that into multiple distinct "new institutionalisms" which they insist are incompatible in their fundamental epistemological and ontological assumptions: rational-choice, historical, constructivist, network (Rhodes, Binder, and Rockman 2006, chs. 2–5), discursive (Schmidt 2008). But it is not really all that hard to see coherent ways of synthesizing them all.

Of course, any attempt at synthesis has to start somewhere and in so doing will inevitably privilege some of those building blocks more than others. My own inclination is to start with a basically rational-choice account of intentional agents pursuing

---

[21] And they are commonplace among the wisest of the rational-choice modelers, so often accused of being narrow-mindedly hegemonic. Fiorina (1996, 88–9) observes that "when NASA put astronauts on the moon . . . its scientists and engineers did not rely on a single overarching model. They relied on literally hundreds of models and theories . . . No single model would have accounted for more than a few aspects of the total enterprise . . . [Likewise] I teach my students that [rational choice] models are most useful where stakes are high and numbers low, in recognition that it is not rational to go to the trouble to maximize if the consequences are trivial and/or your actions make no difference. . . . Thus, in work on mass behavior I utilize minimalist notions of rationality . . . whereas in work on elites I assume a higher order of rationality."

their projects through games of a slightly richer sort than ordinary game theory captures.[22] Out of the interplay of those interactions, institutionalized solutions to their common problems emerge and acquire normative force among those who want to rely on those institutionalized solutions for future dealings (the constructivist and network institutionalist insight). Some branches of the extensive form of the game end sooner and less satisfactorily than others, with all possibilities for further development having been played out; in those cases we must either resign ourselves to making do with nonideal arrangements or face the prospect of a sharp and costly renegotiation of our settled practices (the historical institutionalist point). Often however we can simply shift among a plurality of different institutions governed by different norms and involving different players to address different problems we encounter (constructivist, discursive, and network institutionalisms again). In short, thinking how intentional goal-seeking agents might operate on and through history, developing shared norms and institutions as an aid to doing so seems to me a tolerably good synthesis of the many ostensibly "very different" strands of the new institutionalism (Goodin 1996; 2000; see similarly Knight 1992; Hay and Richards 2000; Orren and Skowronek 2004; Offe 2006; Hertting 2007; and most especially Olsen 2009).

That seems a good example of the potential fruitfulness of judicious combinations of ostensibly either–or approaches within political science.[23] Such multi-perspectival accounts can come from collaboration via interdisciplinary or multidisciplinary research teams (Moran 2006). Or they might come from hybrid "border-crossing" scholars who themselves sit at the intersection of multiple different disciplines and move easily between them (Dogan and Pahre 1990; Dogan 1996; Rudolph 2002). Or they might come from collaborations across different sub-disciplines within political science, or from collaborations across some ostensible "great divide" within the same sub-discipline.

2 WHERE WE'RE AT

2.1 Revolutions We Have Known

Academics thrill at the thought of their disciplines having been racked by a series of "revolutions" (Kuhn 1962). It is the great aim of every aspiring academic to be at the forefront of the next revolution.

---

[22] Hay (2004) in contrast incorporates soft rational-choice style analyses within a broadly constructivist model, to address "what if" questions broadly after the fashion of Tetlock, Lebow, and Parker (2006) and Levy (2008).

[23] For others, see: Bendor and Hammond's (1992) masterly blending of Allison's (1971) three models; and attempts at blending rational choice and interpretivist approaches to culture by Bates et al. (1998) and Laitin and Weingast (2006; cf. Johnson 2002).

But of course revolutions rarely are quite as consequential as their advocates hope, or their opponents fear. Most things go on pretty much the same, on the other side of the revolution. Bismarck's social insurance legislation remained on the books under Hitler and afterwards in remarkably similar form in East and West Germany alike (US DHEW 1978). A revolution installs a new regime to which one is obliged to pay polite obeisance, and it genuinely gets in the way of some things you want to do. But generally you can work around it, to carry on much as before.

It is important to bear in mind not only how small the revolutionary avant-garde generally is, but also what a small proportion of the discipline are signed-up members of the ruling cadre even after a revolution has seemingly succeeded. As our International Benchmarking Panel reminded the UK Economic and Social Research Council:

> However monolithic the US discipline may seem from a distance, those working within it know fully well that it is internally highly diverse. From a distance, the US discipline may seem to be dominated by some hegemonic practice—"behaviouralism" in the previous generation or "rational choice" in the present one. But in fact, those supposedly "hegemonic" practices are actually practiced to any high degree by only perhaps 5% of the US discipline, even in many top departments.   (Goodin et al.[24] 2007, 9)

How "big" a revolution has to be to qualify as a revolution—how much of the territory it has to occupy, and just how much control it has to exercise over it—is a particularly open question when it comes to scientific revolutions (Dryzek 2006*b*, 487). I thus prefer to couch the next section's prognostications in terms of what might be the next "big thing," rather than the next "revolution." Still, the discipline's self-conception of its past is firmly organized around epochs punctuated by successful revolutionary takeovers, so let me begin by introducing the discipline in those, its own preferred terms.

According to the standard periodization, political science in the USA has been marked by three successful revolutions.[25] The first was that which founded the discipline at the very beginning of the twentieth century: the turn away from the dilettantish do-gooderism of the American Social Science Association and toward systematic and professionalized study of political processes. The second successful revolution shaping the US discipline was the behavioral revolution of the 1950s, a self-styled break away from the previous preoccupation with what is formally supposed to happen and toward how people actually behave politically. The third successful revolution shaping the US discipline was the rational choice revolution of the 1970s, promising a break from "mindless empiricism" and offering instead a tight set of theoretical propositions deduced from a Spartan set of fundamental assumptions.

Those are the "storylines" of the discipline, at least in the USA. Elsewhere, even in the anglophone world and certainly outside it, those revolutionary waves either

---

[24] My fellow members on that panel were James Der Derian, Kris Deschower, Friedrich Kratochwil, Audie Klotz, Brigid Laffan, Pippa Norris, B. Guy Peters, Joel Rosenthal, and Virginia Sapiro.

[25] Gunnell (2005) dissents in a way sufficiently contrived as to strike me as confirmation of the truth of that conventional wisdom.

came much later or passed political science there by altogether (Barry 1999). And even as regards the US discipline, those highlighted storylines are only part of the larger story. Much going on in each period was at best only loosely connected to (and much more was wholly apart from) the ostensibly dominant storyline. There were important subthemes and counterpoints in each period, some of which went on to form the basis of the next "revolutionary challenge." Some sub-disciplinary and sub-subdisciplinary and cross-disciplinary projects proceeded largely impervious to the imperial ambitions of the latest successful revolutionary cadre and were largely ignored by it: Public and Constitutional Law has always rather like that.[26] Others were definitely on the radar of people working across many different fields: The "new institutionalism" was certainly like that, having been widely embraced as the "next big thing" across the discipline as a whole over the past decade or more (Goodin and Klingemann 1996b, 11).

More will be said shortly about each of these various movements that have washed over the discipline. But that highly synoptic characterization will suffice to set up the principal point that I want to make at this stage. That point is simply that, by virtue of that self-conception of its past, the discipline has come to acquire an accumulated "core" body of knowledge that must be mastered by aspirants to the profession.

Professionals specialize as well, of course. Facilitating that, and marshaling specialization in collectively fruitful ways, is the whole point of a profession. So in much of their own work, disciplinary professionals will inevitably be engaged in ever more narrowly focused enquiries into arcane corners of some niche or another.

There have been complaints about political science saying "more and more about less and less" (Corwin 1929, 569) for the best part of a century. One measure of that, Sigelman (2006a, v–vi) notes half-jokingly, is the increasing frequency of colons in the titles of articles found in the premier journals.

But while the work of the profession becomes increasingly "fragmented," the profession as a whole need not. If there is a shared sense of what constitutes the core of the discipline (substantively even more than methodologically), and if professional training in the discipline insists upon mastering that as a condition of entry, then specialists however specialized have some common ground with one another. They have some sense, necessarily rudimentary, of where one another's specialty fits within the large scheme that they share.

Again, not all places in the world practice the profession of political science in this way. And not all that do necessarily would adopt exactly, or even roughly, the same canon as the "common core" to be communicated to aspiring members of the profession. Still, in the top US (and, increasingly, UK) graduate schools of political science, entry to the profession requires aspirants to have mastered at least after a fashion the "scope and methods" of the discipline, and that they have done so in broadly similar ways to those in pretty much any other top political science program.

---

[26] As Appendix 1.5 below shows.

As we put it in the introduction to the *New Handbook of Political Science*:

Few of those trained at any of the major [US] institutions from the 1970s [or UK ones from the 1990s on, I would now add] will be unduly intimidated (or unduly impressed either) by theories or techniques from behavioral psychology, empirical sociology or mathematical economics. Naturally, each will have his or her own predilections among them. But nowadays most will be perfectly conversant across all those methodological traditions, willing and able to borrow and steal, refute and repel, as the occasion requires.

(Goodin and Klingemann 1996*b*, 13)

In his introduction to its centenary issue, the editor of the *American Political Science Review* begged to differ. From where Sigelman (2006*b*, 473) sat, our "warm-and-fuzzy image of an increased empathetic capacity among adherents of different approaches to political science...seems oddly out of touch with the experience of a discipline wracked by periodic culture wars (as manifested in the Caucus for a New Political Science of the 1960s and 1970s and the Perestroika movement of the last few years)." He saw the discipline as being more "characterized by something closer to an armed truce—an agreement to disagree—among true believers of different disciplinary creeds than to an active, congenial engagement in a joint enterprise."

It is true that Klingemann and I did not see Perestroika coming. And from where I now sit I have to concede that, realistically, the profession probably has to undergo that sort of insurgency once every couple of generations, to remind itself of "things lost" over the course of its latest "revolution." I can well understand why those in the firing line—beseiged editors of the *American Political Science Review* preeminently among them—might see those as veritable "culture wars." But in academic politics as in real-world politics, trumped-up culture wars greatly exaggerate the depth of the disagreements and the extent of irreconcilability (Fiorina 2006). There is, I say again, no reason to accept the "either–or" straitjacket that cultural warriors would impose on us.

While I am sure some irreconcilables remain in each of the armed camps that Sigelman describes, I cannot help thinking that they are unrepresentative. The best talents in the profession are much less tempted to wallow in endless "meta" debates, and much more inclined to "just do it" (Dryzek 2005). The *Oxford Handbook of Contextual Analysis* (Goodin and Tilly 2006) is offered in evidence of just how productive it can be for mainstream political science to take those sorts of insights systematically on board, and as evidence of just how disciplined and systematic you can be in doing so—hopefully thereby allaying some of the mainstream's deepest concerns with the latest insurgency.

2.2 The Canon

What, then, is the core of the canon that practicing political scientists need to master in order to have mastered the discipline?

Of course, political science—like all the natural and many other social sciences[27]—is increasingly becoming an article-based discipline.[28] Some classic journal articles never grow into a book. Some whole debates are conducted on the pages of journals alone. And some whole subfields seem dominated by articles rather than books. Still, most lasting contributions to political science as a whole typically come in, or eventually get consolidated into, book form.[29]

The canon of political science can, therefore, be reasonably described in terms of a set of "core books" with which any competent professional must have at least a passing acquaintance. Any selection of "must read" classics is inevitably somewhat idiosyncratic, and inevitably there will be disagreement at the margins. But the list offered in Appendix 1.1 would, I think, command a reasonably broad consensus.[30]

I hasten to add that the Appendix 1.1 list is more by way of a report than of an evaluation. Those books are ones that are professionally prominent. Each of us might privately harbor doubts about just how good some of them really are. Still, those books truly are touchstones of the discipline, with which any serious practitioner needs to be competently acquainted.

There are other books that should be better known by political scientists than they actually are. I nominate a few of my personal favorites in Appendix 1.1, as well. Doubtless others will have their own. My list is offered in the spirit of "starting a conversation." Once we acknowledge that there is indeed a canon of the sort described in the first table in Appendix 1.1, the next logical thing we should do is have a conversation about what else ought to be included in it.

Where ought one to watch for new developments? Well, of course, much good work bubbles away below the surface for many years before breaking into high-profile places. But eventually important new trends will (and to become important discipline-wide, will have to) break into one or another of the truly major journals and book series that are the "outlets of record" for the profession as a whole. Among the journals serving that function are the *American Political Science Review*, the *American Journal of Political Science*, and the *British Journal of Political Science* and a raft of top-flight sub-disciplinary journals (such as *International Organization*, *Political Analysis*, *Studies in American Political Development*, *Politics & Society*, and so on). Among the book series serving that discipline-shaping function are CUP series on

---

[27] Note however that when mounting his spirited defense of postwar British empirical sociology, Marshall (1990) focuses on books rather than articles.

[28] A good guide to the "articles that have shaped the discipline" is found in the commentaries on the twenty most-cited articles in the *American Political Science Review* published in its Centennial Issue (Sigelman et al. 2006). For the British equivalent see Dunleavy, Kelly, and Moran (2000) and occasional online updates: <http://www3.interscience.wiley.com/journal/118510540/home>. Dewan, Dowding, and Shepsle (2008a) offer a similar list of classic articles in rational choice approaches to political science.

[29] Often the original article is a good substitute for (Axelrod 1981; 1984; Allison 1969; 1971), or occasionally much better than (March and Olsen 1984; 1989), the ensuing book. It also sometimes happens that the earlier editions of a book are much superior to subsequent ones (Allison 1971; Allison and Zeikow 1999; Neustadt 1960; 1990).

[30] Notice, for example, the strong overlap between the similar list produced for the *New Handbook of Political Science* (Goodin and Klingemann 1996a, 15–17) and the list of "40 classic books in political science" produced for rather different purposes by Hammond, Jen, and Maeda (2007, 437–4).

"Political Economy of Institutions & Decisions," "Cambridge Studies in International Relations," "Cambridge Studies in Comparative Politics," and the OUP "Oxford Political Theory" series.[31] All these developments are also ably surveyed in the *Annual Review of Political Science*, which serves, in effect, as the "annual supplement" to reference books such as the present one.

2.3 The Cast

The main players of the discipline can be identified through a bibliometric analysis of reference patterns across the ten volumes of *Oxford Handbooks of Political Science*. This exercise is akin to one conducted for the *New Handbook of Political Science* (Goodin and Klingemann 1996b, 27–43). It differs in counting index entries to authors, rather than the frequency of an author's appearance in reference lists alone.[32]

There is much information on citation rates already available (Masuoka, Grofman, and Feld 2007).[33] Standard citation counts based on citations in the journals indexed by the Thompson Scientific/ISI Web of Science are problematic in various ways. Coverage of non-anglophone journals is patchy (but decreasingly so as the database is expanded). Conventional citation rates traditionally count only journal-to-journal citations in journals, thus ignoring citations in and even to books—although unnecessarily so, since journal-to-book citations can (with effort) be extracted from information already in ISI databases (Butler 2006). Ordinary citation analyses tell us much of interest, and they would tell us even more if they were further enhanced in those ways.

There are, nonetheless, two compelling reasons to go on to conduct a citation analysis of the ten-volume *Oxford Handbooks of Political Science*. One reason relates to the nature of the works cited. Citations within reference books are much more likely to be laudatory citations, recommendations that these are publications that people in the profession really need to read. And because *Handbook* authors have to survey large literatures in a small space, their citations have furthermore to be highly selective.

The 1 percent of political scientists appearing most frequently in indices to the *Oxford Handbooks of Political Science* are listed in appendices to this chapter.[34] First that is done sub-discipline-by-sub-discipline, based on the index of each constituent sub-disciplinary volume. Appendix 1.2 lists "sub-disciplinary leaders" thus construed.

[31] In their editor's own immodest view, best relegated to a footnote, the *Journal of Political Philosophy* is almost certainly the most interesting political theory journal for a general political science audience, and the CUP series of books on "Theories of Institutional Design" is akin to those others listed.

[32] The latter strategy had the unfortunate effect, in the *New Handbook*, of treating authors identically whether they were referenced only once or multiple times in a chapter (Barry 1999, 452). The current strategy risks undercounting only insofar as authors are referenced multiple times on the same page.

[33] This, like most such studies, is however confined to scholars based in US departments of political science.

[34] And remember, those cited in the *Oxford Handbooks of Political Science* represent only a small fraction of all political scientists worldwide.

Table 1.1. Integration of the discipline

	Number of authors
Cited in 10 out of 10	7
9 out of 10	16
8 out of 10	20
7 out of 10	49
6 out of 10	93
Total	185

Appendix 1.3 then merges the indexes of all ten volumes of *Oxford Handbooks of Political Science*, to identify leaders of the discipline as a whole.

There is a second discipline-related reason to conduct a citation analysis on the ten volumes of *Oxford Handbooks of Political Science*. Doing so enables us to map the structure of the discipline. It allows us to assess how fragmented or integrated the discipline is, across its various sub-disciplines. Just how many people who are cited in one sub-discipline are also cited in others? And so on.

One measure of the extent to which the discipline as a whole is indeed well-integrated is the number of people whose work is used by several sub-disciplines in common. Following the *New Handbook of Political Science* (Goodin and Klingemann 1996a, 33–4), scholars whose names appear in more than half of the sub-disciplinary volumes of the *Oxford Handbooks of Political Science* are dubbed "integrators of the discipline." Appendix 1.4 names names. But what we most need to know to assess the state of the discipline are the frequency counts reported in Table 1.1.

There we see that only a handful of people—seven authors, to be precise—are influential across literally every sub-discipline. But from Table 1.1 we can also see that a fair few authors impact on more than half the sub-disciplines. Those 185 authors represent over 2 percent of all authors mentioned across the ten volumes of *Oxford Handbooks of Political Science*. Judged that way, it seems that the various sub-disciplines of political science do indeed have quite a few touchstones in common.

A second way of assessing the structure of the discipline is to map linkages between each of the sub-disciplines. We can do that by counting how often the scholars who appear in the index of one sub-disciplinary handbook also appear in the indexes of each of the other sub-disciplinary handbooks.[35] The larger the proportion of shared reference points, the "closer" one sub-discipline can be said to be to another. And the more other sub-disciplines that are "close" to it, the more "central" the sub-discipline can be said to be to the discipline as a whole.

---

[35] Admittedly, each sub-discipline is represented by a single *Oxford Handbook*; and a different set of editors would have chosen to emphasize different topics tapping different literatures. Still, each of those volumes contains chapters written by over fifty different people. Counting the overlaps between the references that two sets of fifty people employ is probably a fairly good basis upon which to assess linkages among the various sub-disciplines of political science.

Table 1.2. The structure of the discipline

	Law and pol.	Pol. econ.	Methodology	Pol. behavior	Comp. pol.	Pol. instns.	Context	Public policy	Internatl. rela.	Theory
Law and pol.	—	*			**	**				
Pol. econ.		—	**	*	***	***	*	*	*	
Methodology			—	**	***	**	*	*	*	
Pol. behavior				—	****	**	**	*		
Comp. pol.					—	***	**	**	**	
Pol. instns.						—	**	***	**	
Context							—	*	**	*
Public policy								—	*	*
Internatl. rela.									—	*
Theory										—

Notes: ****>25% authors shared; ***>20%; **>15%; *>10%.

The percentage of authors whose names appear in one sub-disciplinary volume's index also appear in the other's is reported in Appendix 1.5.[36] Table 1.2 represents those data in more summary manner. The more stars, the more shared references there are between the two sub-disciplines represented by that cell in Table 1.2.[37]

As we see from Table 1.2, the "core" of the discipline consists in Comparative Politics and Political Institutions. Political Behavior, Political Economy, and Political Methodology strands feed heavily into those. Law and Politics is connected to the Comparative Politics and Political Institutions core on the Political Economy side. Sub-disciplines of Public Policy and International Relations are connected to the Comparative Politics and Political Institutions core on the Contextual side. Political Theory dangles off the end of that latter cluster and is only very weakly connected to any of the rest of political science.

3 WHAT NEXT?

What is likely to be "the next big thing" to hit political science?[38] It is hard to say, of course. As Humphrey Lyttelton famously said of jazz, if we knew where political science was going we would be there already (Winch 1958, 94).

[36] Appendix 1.5 reports two slightly different numbers for each handbook pair. (The difference arises from the fact that the same number of overlapping authors is divided by the different total number of authors referenced in each of the handbooks concerned.) For purposes of Table 1.2, I simply average across those two numbers.

[37] I am grateful to Kieran Healy and Simon Niemeyer for advice on how this material might best be presented.

[38] I am indebted to Lee Sigelman for putting me in mind of this question.

What I can say, with a confidence born of reflection on the past bubbles that have punctuated the history of our discipline, is that the basic intellectual materials out of which the next big thing will be constructed already exist among us. The next big thing is something most of us will have bumped up against, something most of us will have mentioned in passing in writing or lectures. It is something we currently regard as an interesting curiosity, fitting awkwardly our current way of seeing things and doing business but not (as yet) occasioning any fundamental rethinking of them.

Having long been familiar with the next big thing as a minor curiosity, it will strike us as odd when a bubble suddenly arises around it, inflated by aspiring stars anxious to rise. Deeming it a perfectly worthy point or practice in its place, most of us will vaguely resent the exaggerated cure-all claims that will be made for the new snake oil. But that will be the modal tendency of a distribution whose two tails will inevitably go to war with one another, trying to force the sensible middle into taking sides.[39] Thus it was with the behavioral revolution, with systems theory and structural-functionalism, with rational choice, and so on.[40]

3.1 The Nature of "Big Things"

Those are the sorts of things I mean by a "big thing." They are not nearly so domineering as a *Weltanshaung* or a Kuhnian paradigm, necessarily, nor so overwhelming as a "revolution." "Big things" certainly set a research agenda and focus attention on "critical points" (Morgenstern 1972) or "unresolved problems" (Elster 1979, ch. 3) within it.[41]

In social science, a "big thing" is a simple idea that promises to pack a big explanatory punch, explaining much on the basis of a little. That, of course, is just what philosophers of science have long told us we ought be looking for: an explanation that is powerful and parsimonious at one and the same time (Carnap 1950, 3–8; Quine 1961, 16–17; Kitcher 1981).

"Big things" claim wide application, offering ways of reconceiving the discipline as a whole, or anyway some large portion of it. They promise something like "A Common Language for the Social Sciences" (the motto of the Harvard Department of Social Relations (Geertz 2000, 8)) or "a long-term program of scholarly activity which aims at no less than the unification of theory in all fields of the behavioral sciences" (as Talcott Parsons pitched it to Harvard's Faculty Committee on

---

[39] Merton (1973, ch. 3). The most vitriolic complaints come from those left behind: Straussians venting their spleen against then-orthodox behavioralism (Storing 1962; cf. Schaar and Wolin 1963); Green and Shapiro (1994; cf. Friedman 1996) venting theirs against the rational choice orthodoxy, after Mancur Olson's review panel berated their Yale department for having missed that boat.

[40] I limit my attention to post-Second World War developments, although there are interesting stories well told by others of developments earlier. See, e.g.: Easton, Gunnell, and Stein (1995); Farr, Dryzek, and Leonard (1995); Farr and Seidelman (1993); Heilbron, Magnusson, and Wittrock (1998); Wagner, Wittrock, and Whitley (1991); Collini, Winch, and Burrows (1983).

[41] They can, and often do, do that more in the spirit of "tying up loose ends" in the research program than of building protective belts to insulate it from falsification, necessarily (Quine 1961, 43; Kuhn 1962; Lakatos and Musgrave 1970).

Behavioralism (quoted in Rudolph 2005, 8)). David Truman pitched the behavioral revolution to the Social Science Research Council in similar terms, as have done countless advocates of other would-be "big things" in countless other venues.[42]

Alongside and within "big things" there are also many "medium-sized things"— "good gimmicks" (Mackenzie 1967, 111), tricks, tools, and mechanisms (Elster 1989; 2007; Hedström and Swedberg 1998), "theories of the middle range" (Merton 1968, ch. 2), and so on. These are loci of disciplinary feeding frenzies all their own. Recent examples include the new institutionalism (March and Olsen 1984; 1989) and ideas of social capital (Putnam 1993; 2000), path dependency (Pierson 2000; 2004), and deliberative democracy (Dryzek 2000). Those serve as ancillary theories, tricks or tools that can be mixed-and-matched with a variety of other things.[43]

Medium-sized things sometimes mushroom into big things, staging a takeover bid for the discipline as a whole. That happens as several cognate medium-sized things consolidate into "one big thing." Rational choice, for example, became a "big thing" in the 1970s by consolidating various previously unconnected strands: operations research in defense (Hitch and McKean 1960), game theory in international relations (Schelling 1960), and notions of "public goods" (Olson 1965) and "median voters" (Downs 1957). As late as 1967, so shrewd an observer as Mackenzie (1967, ch. 9) failed to foresee that consolidation coming, regarding all these instead as simply separate (albeit related) "partial theories" or "good gimmicks." Or for another example, the behavioral revolution consolidated realist skepticism about actual adherence to formal rules and ideal standards across several domains—constitution-writing (Beard 1913), policy-making (Bentley 1908/1967), public administration (Simon 1947, ch. 2), local governance (Lynd and Lynd 1929), international relations (Morgenthau 1948)— together with new experimental and observational methodologies and statistical techniques for assessing their findings (Merriam 1921; Key 1954). So too with all the other "big things" that have come and gone over the years: All have been conglomerations of medium-sized things with which we have long been familiar.

Finally, there are always research programs with "big thing" ambitions that have not (yet) succeeded in achieving hegemonic status across the profession as a whole. Political culture was one such, psychoanalytics another, biopolitics yet another. Although they once aspired to be more (and may still do), at least for now they remain middle-sized things available for mixing-and-matching with others. Likewise, failed "big things" never completely disappear but merely revert to the status of

---

[42] As Truman wrote in the 1951 SSRC newsletter, "Political behavior is not and should not be a specialty, for it . . . aims at stating all the phenomena of government in terms of the observed and observable behavior of men. To treat it as a 'field' coordinate with (and presumably isolated from) public law, state and local government, international relations, and so on, would be to defeat its major aim. That aim includes an eventual reworking and extension of most of the conventional 'fields' of political science" (quoted in Dahl 1961a, 767). Biopolitics similarly aspires to "effect a major transformation in political scientists' views and . . . instead of becoming a larger subfield of the discipline . . . disappear by total incorporation into it, as Christianity (to use Somit's metaphor) was enveloped by and incorporated into the Roman Empire" (Wahlke 1986, 872).

[43] Such medium-sized things predominate among the "advances in the social sciences" catalogued in Deutsch, Markovits, and Platt (1986; Deutsch 1979).

middle-sized things in the professional firmament, true so far as they go but definitely only part of the overall story.

3.2 The Next Big Thing: A Job Description

When scanning the horizon for the next big thing, it behooves us to recall the distinctive features of things that have formerly risen to become "big things."

3.2.1 *Simplicity*

"Big things" are, first and foremost, fundamentally simple ideas. They are capable of being expressed succinctly—stated in just a few words—yet they have wide ramifications.[44] Think of the catchcry of the behavioral revolutionaries: "don't just look at the formal rules, look at what people actually do." Think of the catchcry of structural-functionalists: "form fits function."[45] Think of the catchcry of systems theorists: "everything is connected; feedback matters." Think of the catchcry of the rational choice revolutionaries: "always remember, people pursue power and interest."[46] Think of the catchcry of new institutionalists: "institutions matter." Simple ideas, all.

3.2.2 *Broad Application*

"Big things" must have wide application to politics, across the board. That is why "consolidation" of medium-sized projects into "one big thing" is so important. To travel far, however, "big things" need to travel light: They need to be easily adaptable to the wide variety of circumstances and settings to which they aspire to apply. The same basic idea can, and should, play out differently in different contexts, without sacrificing its claim to simplicity and parsimony at some more fundamental level.

3.2.3 *Formalizable*

"Big things" must also admit of formalization of some sort or another.[47] That need not necessarily take the form of propositional logic or higher mathematics, as with rational choice theory. In the case of structural-functionalism, formalization amounted to little more than an elaborate conceptual schema and a few diagrammatic techniques borrowed from structural anthropology (Merton 1968, ch. 3). Proper input–output analysis and linear programming came later (Forrester 1971; Meadows

---

[44] The same feature characterizes what come to be regarded as a "great book that everyone must read" in political science (Barry 1974, 80) and, indeed, as Nobel-worthy economics (Alt, Levi, and Ostrom 1999, xvi).

[45] With apologies to the Bauhaus movement.   [46] With apologies to Shapiro (1999).

[47] Arguably the behavioral and rational choice revolutions were both method driven. The "next big thing" in political science might be similarly methodological—agent-based modeling or experimental or quasi-experimental methods or Bayesian rather than frequentist statistics. All these are surveyed at length in excellent chapters in the *Oxford Handbook of Political Methodology* (Box-Steffensmeier, Brady, and Collier 2008).

et al. 1972; cf. Shubik 1971*b*; Cole et al. 1973), but the early application of systems theory to political science consisted just in boxes connected by arrows (Easton 1957; 1965). So too with the early behavioral revolutionaries: Fancier techniques came later, but their initial formalism amounted to little more than cross-tabulations and chi-squares (Miller 1996, 301). Still, a "big thing" must always admit of formalization, be it heavy or light.

3.2.4 *Familiarity*

Like stars of the cinema, things that have subsequently become "big things" have generally been around for quite a while before they hit it big.[48] The raw materials of any "big thing"—what will subsequently come to be seen as its "classic texts"—were published long before it became big. Rational choice theory became a "big thing" in the mid-1970s (Sigelman 2006*b*, 469), but by then its seminal texts were all a decade or two old (Arrow 1951; Black 1958; Downs 1957; Riker 1962; Olson 1965). Likewise, by the time the behavioral revolution became a "big thing" in the 1950s (Dahl 1961*a*, 766; Sigelman 2006*b*, 469), its seminal texts were similarly antiquated (Merriam and Gosnell 1924; Tingsten 1937; Lazarsfeld, Berelson, and Gaudet 1944), and the intellectual materials out of which behavioralists built their models of politics were drawn from psychology of several decades previously (Lipset et al. 1954).[49] Similarly, the materials out of which post-Second World War structural-functionalists built their models were drawn from interwar anthropologists (Radcliffe-Brown 1935; Malinowski 1936/1976). And the materials out of which the new institutionalists of the 1980s built their models were drawn from decades-old organization theory and behavioral theories of the firm (Simon 1947; March and Simon 1958; March 1962; 1996; Cyert and March 1963).

3.2.5 *Marginality*

Finally, the materials out of which political science constructs its own "next big thing" tend to be leftover fragments from other disciplines.[50] From the point of view of political scientists, that makes it look like a takeover bid by some other discipline. But from the point of view of that other discipline, the raiders more often look like renegade bands operating at the margins of their home discipline.[51] The rational choice revolution in political science was spearheaded by scholars of social choice and of public finance, both far from the center of gravity of mainstream

---

[48] When leaders of the new revolution claim, with ostensive modesty, to be merely "standing on the shoulders of giants" (Merton 1965), what they are often really doing is claiming for themselves a lineage.

[49] As Hardin (2006, 4) remarks, "the [behavioral] movement had passed its peak in psychology when it became a dominant theoretical stance in political science."

[50] One wave of the future might be "intradisciplinarity," blending contributions from several of the discipline's increasingly differentiated sub-disciplines. For example, work on the European Union (and on multiple overlapping sovereignties more generally) blends Comparative Politics and International Relations (Moravcsik 1998; Héritier 2007; Olsen 2007). "Comparative political theory" blends Comparative Politics and Political Theory (Dallmayr 1999; 2004; Euben 1999).

[51] Perhaps because marginal scholars are, or are seen to be, more creative (Dogan and Pahre 1990).

economics.[52] The behavioral revolution in political science drew on social psychology, which again is a somewhat marginalized subfield within psychology proper. And political science borrowed the structural-functionalist model from sociology and anthropology at just the time those disciplines were repudiating it (Radcliffe-Brown 1949; Davis 1959; cf. Merton 1968, ch. 3).

3.3 Candidates for the Next Big Thing

I offer the following shortlist of candidate "next big things" with hesitation, knowing it is inevitably incomplete and that it almost certainly omits what will eventually win out. Still, interviewing several candidates is often the best way find out what job we really want to have done for us.

3.3.1 *Framing Models*

The basic idea of framing models is that of "choice under description" (Davidson 1980; 1984). Objects of choice always display a literal infinity of attributes. In choosing one thing over another, we focus in on some of those attributes whilst ignoring all the rest. We choose one under some description, picking out some features we see as particularly salient. Different frames lead to different choices, so shifting or imposing frames is an exercise of power: of the choosing agent, if done consciously and autonomously; of psychology over rationality, if it happens less consciously; of one person over another, if it happens less autonomously.

Part of the appeal of framing models is that they will provide a way of taking account of at least some of the crucial contextual effects to which Perestroikans point (Rudolph 2005). There are many ways in which "context matters," of course (Goodin and Tilly, this volume), and how we frame situations is only one; still, it looks like it might be a central one, connecting micro and macro. Another part of their appeal is that, in helping us see the choice situation from the actor's own point of view, framing models answer to the hermeneutic, interpretivist impulse.[53]

Within political science and political sociology, there is already a relatively rich array of forebears for this potential "next big thing" to build upon. Distinguished examples include: Allison's classic discussion of conceptual maps in connection with the Cuban Missile Crisis (Allison 1971; Allison and Zeitkow 1999); classic discussions of ways in which rhetoric and media frame political perceptions and shape reactions

---

[52] Judging from the "press release" under each of their entries in the archives of the Nobel Foundation (Royal Swedish Academy of Science 2005), Arrow's Nobel was awarded much more for his work on general equilibrium theory than for his impossibility theorem, and Sen's for his work on poverty measures and on famines as much as for his work on social choice. Only Buchanan's Nobel was awarded principally for work in work on "public choice" of the sort that the rational choice revolution brought to political science.

[53] Summarizing one of the "lessons" of his dissertation, off which he says he has been living ever since, Geertz (2000, 6) writes: "To discover who people think they are, what they think they are doing, and to what end they think they are doing it, it is necessary to gain a working familiarity with the frames of meaning within which they enact their lives." See further: Garfinkel 1967; Geertz 1973; Taylor 1985, volume 1, chs. 1, 3–4; Skinner 2002, volume 1.

(Gamson 1992; Riker 1986; Edelman 1988; Iyengar 1994; Chong and Druckman 2007); and more recent discussions of framing within social movements (Benford and Snow 2000), with echoes all the way back to Arendt's *Origins of Totalitarianism* (1951).

In adjacent disciplines, framing effects are central to the surprising findings of experimental economics and psychology. What these experiments systematically show is that people will differ dramatically in their reaction to objectively identical choice situations ("objectively identical," the sense that the same material effects will ensue from the same choices) depending just on the way the options are described and the choice thereby framed: whether as "saving lives" or "letting people die;" whether as a lost theater ticket or a lost bank note in the same value; whether as a gain or a loss, depending on how you describe the baseline; whether as being an issue of fairness or ordinary market behavior (Camerer 2002; Fehr and Fischbacher 2002; Güth, Schmittberger, and Schwarze 1982; Kahneman 2003; Kahneman, Knetsch, and Thaler 1986; Kahneman, Slovic, and Tversky 1982; Kahneman and Tversky 2000; Thaler 2000).

In trying to formalize notions of framing, one approach might be to extend Axelrod's (1973; 1976) work on the "structure of decision," mapping (literally: graphically) how people's beliefs hang together based on a close reading of texts. Another approach might be to work on the evidence in experimental psychology and experimental economics, trying to taxonomize the instances found there of framing and trying to tease out some generalizations about the various mechanisms that might lie behind them.

If people's decisions really are highly subject to framing and contextual effects, then we should obviously build that fact into our explanations of their actions and choices. We should do so with regret, however: normatively, because framing effects distort rationality and invite manipulation; empirically, because of the fundamental incompleteness of framing models. They must always be supplemented with some other account of what (or psychological forces of pattern recognition) causes people to see things one way rather than another. That crucial part of the explanation must come from outside the framing model itself.[54]

3.3.2 *Evolutionary Models*

The basic idea of evolutionary models is that society takes the shape it does because over time its elements have been subject to a repeated process of "selection for fitness" (Elster 1989, ch. 8). The elements subject to the selection mechanism can be genotypes, productive practices, game strategies, or whatever. The selection mechanism might involve differential reproductive success of biological organisms, differential bankruptcy rates of firms, social practices persisting or fading away, and so on (Witt 1993).

Part of the appeal of evolutionary models is that they offer a particularly rich account of dynamic aspects of social life. Furthermore, they do so by reference to

---

[54] And notice: it cannot stop with a story about other people manipulating you so as to see it that way; the question then arises as to how they came to see *their* choices in the way they did, leading them into that manipulation.

structural- or systemic- rather than individual-level mechanisms. For those who are suspicious of models of individual choice as the fundamental driver of social stability and change, these are great attractions.

Within political science, there is a long tradition of thinking in broadly bio-political terms. Some of those precedents, Social Darwinism and sociobiology most conspicuously, are unhappy ones (Dryzek and Schlosberg 1995); others make minimal reference to evolutionary dynamics as such.[55] But at least some of those models of biopolitics serve as important precursors to a systematic application of evolutionary modeling within political science (Somit and Peterson 2001; Alford and Hibbing 2008).

The greatest impetus for evolutionary models in political science, however, prob-ably lies in analyses of the "evolution of cooperation" in both experimental games and social settings. It was a "first" for our profession when Axelrod and Hamilton's (1981, 1396 n. 19) article in the prestigious journal *Science* referred readers for the proofs to the *American Political Science Review* (Axelrod 1981). Subsequent work by Axelrod (1986), Ostrom (1990), and myriad scholars following in their footsteps offer us important insights into "the evolution of institutions" for social cooperation and collective action.

Looking beyond our own discipline, economists have long noted the structural similarities between the equilibria reached as a great many selfish economic agents seek simultaneously to maximize their utility and the equilibria reached as a great many selfish genes seek simultaneously to maximize their inclusive fitness and hence survival (Hirschleifer 1977). In adapting evolutionary models to politics, we might therefore also turn to Nelson and Winter's classic 1982 *Evolutionary Theory of Eco-nomic Change* or to Bowles's work on evolutionary economics, combining experi-mental economics and anthropology with institutional factors (Bowles 2004; Bowles and Gintis, this volume).

Familiar models from population biology are an obvious, elaborate, and intricate source of off-the-shelf technologies for formalizing evolutionary models imported into other disciplines (Nowak 2006). Just how appropriate the borrowing is depends upon just how apt the analogy is between the biological and other borrowing disci-pline (more of which below). But there is a major industry working on the project.

Evolutionary models, like functional ones before them, must above all avoid reducing themselves to empty tautologies by saying "that something must be fit in some way simply because it exists. ... Most evolutionary theorists in biology or social science would accept" that notions of "fitness" must be given independent specifica-tion and selection mechanisms must "be specified in some detail ... if evolutionary theorizing is to explain anything" (Nelson 1994, 115).

Evolutionary modeling sometimes involves only a very loose analogy to processes modeled in evolutionary biology. Evolution of a Darwinian sort implies a very

---

[55] "Most writers on 'biopolitical' subjects," Wahlke (1979, 25) reports, "draw more heavily on modern ethology than on evolutionary biology per se," focusing on notions like "territoriality, dominance, submission and other concepts borrowed from biological disciplines" (Wahlke 1986, 871). Compare, e.g., Mackenzie (1967, ch. 11) and Masters (1989).

precise set of mechanisms: random mutation, natural selection, genetic transmission. Social science models purporting to be evolutionary often lack one or more of those features.

Sometimes there is nothing analogous to random mutation in the model. Thus for example models of "deterministic models employing complex nonlinear dynamic equations" are sometimes called "evolutionary" (Anderson, Arrow, and Pines 1988). Reflective evolutionary modelers, however, rightly insist that "the term 'evolutionary' is reserved for models that contain both systematic [selection] and random [stochastic] elements" (Nelson 1994, 114).

Social scientists typically call their models "evolutionary" primarily by virtue of the fact that some "selection process" is involved in producing a stable equilibrium, as in evolutionary game theory (Selten 1991; Skyrms 1996; Samuelson 1997; Binmore 1998). But the unit of selection and the mechanism of transmission are importantly different in those social applications compared to biological ones. The strategies played are sometimes treated as if they were themselves the players, and strategies in successive games as analogous to successive "generations" in biological selection. But of course what they really are, are successive choices of the same player who learns over time— which is more of a Lamarkian matter of transmission of acquired characteristics.

"The hallmark of standard biological evolutionary theory is," of course, "that only the genes, not any acquired characteristics or behavior, get passed on across the generations" (Nelson 1994, 116). Models of "cultural evolution" thus conspicuously differ in that crucial respect (Masters 1989; McElreath and Boyd 2007). Stories about cultural evolution concern the transmission of "memes" intragenerationally and intergenerationally, with replicator dynamics leading to evolutionary stable strategies.[56] This process is "conditioned by human biology but with cumulative force of its own" (Nelson 1994, 118).[57]

These models of "cultural evolution" are "tied to the genetical theory of natural selection no more than . . . to epidemiology" (Sober 1994, 479). They "do not attempt to specify the particular evolutionary mechanisms and 'cultural fitness' criteria operative. . . . Thus," Nelson (1994, 119)—himself a distinguished evolutionary economist— concludes, "these extensions . . . do not really come to grips with the kinds of evolutionary processes with which economists or other social scientists . . . have been concerned."

Before they can borrow with confidence the tools of evolutionary biology, social scientists thus have to assure themselves that the mechanisms at work are genuinely analogous in all respects that really matter. Until that has been done, "the biological concept of natural selection plays the role of a suggestive metaphor, and nothing more" (Sober 1994, 480).

---

[56] Maynard Smith's (1982) notion of an "evolutionary stable strategy" assumes organisms are pre-programmed to play one strategy, and evolutionary dynamics weeds ones programmed to play "wrong" strategies out of successive generations of the population, whereas Dawkins's (1976) model of "replicator dynamics" works through organisms each of which is choosing among various strategies.

[57] For example, "if characteristics were transmitted by parents teaching their children, a selection process could occur without the mediation of genes" (Sober 1994, 479).

3.3.3 *Network Models*

The basis idea behind network-based models is that of decentered governance. These are models with no strong central authority, where power is widely dispersed among many disparate agents who coordinate with one another via "partisan mutual adjustment" (Lindblom 1965). "Networks" are the communication channels—the "nerves" in Deutsch's (1963) old phrase—along which that business is transacted (Ansell 2006; Rhodes 2006).

Much of the appeal of these models lies in the fact that so much of the real political world is precisely like that. That is obviously so in the case of international relations, where there is no central authority: governance is inevitably via networking among sovereign states (Keohane 1984; 2001; Slaughter 2003). It is obviously so in weak federations, like the European Union, where the crab-dance of multiple overlapping sovereignties gives rise to notions like "subsidiarity" (Føllesdal 1998; van Kersbergen and Verbeek 2004) and "the open method of coordination" (Vandenbroucke 2002; Offe 2003; Olsen 2007, chs. 1, 5)—just as they did in pre-state Europe (Berman 1983; Spruyt 1994). But savvy observers know that even in "proper" states with notionally strong central authorities, the process of government involves an endless series of negotiations and networking with stakeholders with the power to exact tribute (Heclo 1978; Lehmbruch 1984; Rhodes 1988). Prudent authorities would naturally want to avoid showdowns with them, echoing the sentiments of Shaw's (1934, 1025) King Magnus: "Naturally I want to avert a conflict in which success would damage me and failure disable me."

Many of the sources upon which network models borrow are of course rooted in anthropology and sociology (Boissevain 1974; Mitchell 1974). Mark Granovetter's (1973; 1983) classic paper on "The strength of weak ties" would without doubt top anyone's reading list on the subject. But there is also a rich tradition within political science of thinking about matters in this way, as already alluded to. All the works on "the governmental process" (Bentley 1908/1967; Truman 1971) and the "iron triangles" and private-interest networking that are involved within it (Heclo 1978; Laumann and Knoke 1987; Heinz et al. 1993; Useem 1979; 1984) obviously serve as crucial professional touchstones for any subsequent elaboration of network-based models of politics. These models might also draw on studies of, for example, how "comity" used to work to bind Congressmen together (Matthews 1959; Uslaner 1991), how "epistemic communities" shape public policy (Haas 1992), how global power is mobilized (Grewal 2008), and how nongovernmental organizations mobilize transnational support for their causes (Keck and Sikkink 1998; Risse, Ropp, and Sikkink 1999).

Several "how-to" manuals have already been prepared for network analysis (Boissevain and Mitchell 1973; Burt and Minor 1983; Scott 1991; Wasserman and Faust 1994). And given its anthropological roots, much network analysis is inevitably going to be essentially ethnographic. But if it is genuine "formalization" we are after, the place to look is mathematical "graph theory." No doubt there remain more resources still to be tapped. But as an illustration of how graph-theoretic techniques can be put to social-scientific use, ponder Laumann and Pappi's (1976) microdescription of a small German town or Heinz and Laumann's (1982) mapping of networks among lawyers in Chicago.

Therein lies the rub, of course. Can those formalizations prove useful beyond small-scale networks, and if they cannot just how much insight into political life can they offer? The answer might still be "lots," if the governing elite is as small as some people suppose; but it might well be "not much," even if we live in only a moderately pluralist political world (of more than, say, a few hundred important actors).

3.3.4 An End to Big Things?

To ask "what will be the next big thing?" implies that there will be one. That begs a question that some hope and others believe is firmly closed in the negative. Perestroikans and postmodernists more generally, committed to a plurality of ways of understanding the world, suppose that the time of monolithic "grand narratives" and totalizing, hegemonic research programs is at an end (Monroe 2005; Rudolph 2005). Their view of "big things," like the Church of England's view of miracles, is that those are "something that had occurred in the past but could hardly be expected to happen nowadays" (Barry 1970, 1).

Sometimes that proposition is put as a sociological hypothesis, other times as a philosophical necessity. Sociologically, with the "fracturing of modernity" it becomes increasingly difficult to imagine ever finding one simple, overarching analysis capable of unifying all the fractured parts (Wagner 2008). Philosophically, world-making is seen as a process of social construction, with unlimited scope for human creativity and hence fundamentally unpredictable variability in social forms and practices.[58] Either alone, still more both together, make it difficult or impossible ever to come up with some single, unified "big thing" accounting for all social phenomena.

Those tempted by "big thing" ways of thinking, being of a more *a posteriori* cast of mind, will be undeterred by a priori demonstrations of the impossibility of their project. Their motto is, once again: "just do it" (Barry 1970, v; Dryzek 2005). If some "big thing" emerges that actually fills the bill, then the point is proven: The actual is *ipso facto* possible.

A raft of academic-political forces also push social science in "big thing" directions. "Big things" are hostile takeover bids, whereby outsiders seek to wrest control of the profession as a whole from its current management. The "next big thing" is the currency in which Young Turks bid to displace the Old Guard (Cornford 1908, 8; Moran 2006). It is the currency of department-builders and funding institutions trying to carve out a central rather than merely a niche role for themselves.[59]

"Big things" are also the terms in which whole disciplines compete with one another for power and influence. Economics is not so much queen of the social

---

[58] A position anticipated in Popper's *Poverty of Historicism* (1964) and at the forefront of today's "social epistemology" (Antony 2006).

[59] As the SSRC did with the behavioral revolution and the Ford Foundation did with area studies (Dahl 1961a, 764–5).

sciences as its hedgehog: It knows "one big thing" (Berlin 1953).[60] And as Shaw has his Prime Minister Proteus saying to cabinet a propos their struggle with the sovereign, "One man that has a mind and knows it can always beat ten men who havnt and dont" (Shaw 1934, 1016). If that is why economics has so much more influence than the other social sciences, then the other social sciences will need to find some "one big thing" of their own in order to compete with the hegemony of economics in the public sphere.

The competitive logic of individual careerism also drives "big thingism." Tempted though we may be to assimilate academic fads to mass frenzies like the South Sea Bubble and the Tulip Craze (Mackay 1841/1980), consider a couple of more rational sides to the story. In a world of imperfect and asymmetric information, price can serve as an indicator of quality. Other people know something you do not, and that is reflected in the higher price they are willing to pay or to demand for certain goods (Akerlof 1970; Stiglitz 1987). Further suppose the good in question is a "status good," requiring you to invest more heavily than your competitors in order to win (Shubik 1971a; Hirsch 1976). Academic distinction and the rewards of educational attainment are both famously like that (Boudon 1974; Bourdieu 1984); investments in the "next big thing," professionally, might be likewise, with the highest status rewards going to those who invest most. (Think of political methodologists investing ever more heavily in ever more rarified statistical techniques.) In that sort of scenario, everyone gets locked into a bidding war, with everyone investing ever more heavily in the good in question.

Alternatively (or perhaps equivalently), think of investing intellectual capital in the "next big thing" as akin to investing political capital in rising political stars. Bandwagons arise, arguably, from payoff structures, which derive in turn from the marginal increase in the probability of the candidate's winning caused by that supporter's joining the bandwagon. The marginal returns to the first comers are low, rising rapidly as support grows, and then drop off precipitously for late-comers (Brams 1978, ch. 2). Assume that payoffs (cabinet posts, good ambassador-ships, in the case of a nominating convention; credit for having been central to the "revolution," in the case of academic disciplines) are proportional to contribu-tions. It then follows that prudent people will want to get on board quick-smart once a bandwagon is really rolling, within the profession just as at a nominating convention.

"Big things" will always be with us, therefore—for better or worse. But what does it matter? Just how big a deal are those ostensibly "big things" in the workaday world of practicing political scientists? Are they ever more than merely loose "moods" (Dahl 1961a, 766) or "persuasions" (Eulau 1963)?

Clearly, for the committed cadre in the vanguard of the new revolution, they are a very big deal indeed. Their entire careers are oriented toward elaborating, extending, and advocating their particular "big thing." But the vast majority of political scientists

---

[60] And sociology knows three: Marx, Weber, and Durkheim.

whose main concerns lie elsewhere are generally nonplussed. They do obeisance to the reigning "big thing" in their opening paragraphs, but then they get down to business in pretty much the same way they would have done under any alternate regime.

Easy examples are found in structural-functionalism, which served (among political scientists anyway) largely just as a set of coding categories to facilitate comparison of "political systems differing radically in scale, structure and culture" (Almond 1960, 4; Mackenzie 1967, 317–21).[61] In *The Politics of the Developing Areas*, for example, Almond's introduction set out some functional categories and Coleman made light use of them in framing his conclusion; but those categories hardly impinged at all on the rest of the contributors, for whom they provided mostly just section headings and a framework for organizing material that, substantively, would have been very much the same if written to any other brief. Or for another example, notice how little "systems theory" actually impinges on Eisenstadt's fascinating account of *The Political Systems of Empires* (1963).

The same is true of all the other "big things" that have come along from time to time. Mid-century studies of Congress and the Presidency wore their behavioralism lightly: They were typically told in the manner of "contemporary history" without recourse to any of the technical apparatus of the behavioral sciences. Come the rational choice revolution, studies of Congress, the executive, voting, and such like began gesturing toward rational choice frameworks in their opening pages, but often without any very deep impact on the way the subsequent studies proceeded. Or again, after a cursory nod toward new institutionalism, contemporary studies typically just get down to the business of describing the workings of the institution at hand, without further reference to that or any other overarching theory.

So do "big things" not really matter? Certainly not as much as some hope, and others fear. Still, just as hypocrisy is the tribute that vice pays to virtue, so too might paying obeisance to some shared "big things" be the tribute that parochialism pays to professionalism.

"Big things" serve as a lingua franca—or for those more dismissively inclined, a pidgin—facilitating conversation across the disparate sub-disciplinary communities within the profession.[62] They help us see why something that matters to others maybe ought also matter to us, by showing us ways in which the two might be connected. They are what "bind us together into an intellectual community" (Stinchcombe 1982, 10).

---

[61] The same was true among sociologists (Parsons 1951: 3; cf. Barry 1970, 166). Structural-functionalists justified their functional specifications by reference to "system maintenance" at a pretty high level of abstraction, and analysis of any very particular practice or piece of behavior in those terms became terribly contrived and question-begging (Barry 1970, chs. 4, 8). See e.g. Birnbaum's (1955) critique of Shils and Young (1953).

[62] Milner (1998) for example comments on how rational choice institutionalism brought the American Politics and International Relations subfields into conversation with one another, in a way that had previously been rare.

4 DISCIPLINES WE HAVE KNOWN

Readers can judge for themselves the state of contemporary political science, after having perused the following chapters. Those constitute less a comprehensive survey than a select sample of what is currently under way within the discipline.

Still, even that small sample suffices—to my mind, at least—to illustrate both the unity and the diversity of contemporary political science. Much good work—interestingly different, yet powerfully complementary—is under way. Synergies abound. There is a genuine sense of excitement at forging research collaborations across long-standing divides. Different sub-disciplines are borrowing from, and contributing to, one another in ways and to extents not seen for years. Rejecting the illogic of "either–or," scholars are crafting judicious blends of different methodologies to give richer and more nuanced analyses of important political phenomena that are easily distorted or obscured when viewed through a single methodological lens alone.

What has made all this progress possible, I submit, is not any loosening of the discipline of political science. Rather, that progress is attributable to the strength of the discipline's discipline. If we were all freed from the discipline of the discipline merely to "go off and do our own thing," then very few of these extraordinarily fruitful collaborations would have come about. It is the obligation to talk together, the sense of shared purpose, of shared histories and shared touchstones in the professional literature, that brings political scientists—however different their particular concerns and approaches—together to read, critique, and profit from one another's work. The discipline is a pluralist one, but the plurality is contained within and disciplined by a discipline.[63] Diversity is a healthy attribute of a gene pool—but only if the carriers of those diverse genes actually interbreed. So too in the talent pools constituting an academic discipline (Aldrich, Alt, and Lupia 2008).

APPENDICES

Appendix 1.1 The Canon of Political Science

Table A1.1.1 lists classics of political science, divided by periods. The first column contains items first published prior to the watershed *American Voter* (Campbell et al. 1960). The second column items published between that and the seminal Greenstein–Polsby *Handbook of Political*

---

[63] Schram (2003, 837), describing the Perestroika vision of a "new political science," pauses at the work "discipline" to query "if that word is still appropriate." Perestroikans, I submit, were wildly wrong and wickedly pernicious ever to cast doubt on that.

Table A1.1.1. Classic texts in political science

Pre-1960	1960–75	1976–96	Post-1996
Arendt, *Origins of Totalitarianism* (1951)	Allison, *Essence of Decision* (1971)	Alt and Shepsle (eds.), *Perspectives on Positive Political Economy* (1990)	Acemoglu and Robinson, *Economic Origins of Dictatorship and Democracy* (2006)
Arrow, *Social Choice and Individual Values* (1951)	Almond and Verba, *Civic Culture* (1963)	Axelrod, *Evolution of Cooperation* (1984)	Boix, *Democracy and Redistribution* (2004)
Black, *Theory of Committees and Elections* (1958)	Banfield and Wilson, *City Politics* (1963)	Barnes and Kaase, *Political Action* (1979)	Bueno de Mesquita et al., *Logic of Political Survival* (2005)
Dahrendorf, *Class and Class Conflict in Industrial Society* (1959)	Barry, *Political Argument* (1965)	Bueno de Mesquita and Lahman, *War and Reason* (1992)	Cox, *Making Votes Count* (1997)
Downs, *Economic Theory of Democracy* (1957)	Burnham, *Critical Elections and the Mainsprings of American Politics* (1970)	Cox and McCubbins, *Legislative Leviathan* (1993)	Dryzek, *Deliberative Democracy and Beyond* (2000)
Duverger, *Political Parties* (1951)	Campbell et al., *American Voter* (1960)	Esping-Andersen, *Three Worlds of Welfare Capitalism* (1990)	Keck and Sikkink, *Activists beyond Borders* (1998)
Easton, *The Political System* (1953)	Campbell and Stanley, *Experimental and Quasi Experimental Designs for Research* (1963)	Fenno, *Home Style* (1978)	Krehbiel, *Pivotal Politics* (1998)
Hartz, *The Liberal Tradition in America* (1955)	Dahl, *Who Governs?* (1961)	Fiorina, *Retrospective Voting in American National Elections* (1981)	Lijphart, *Patterns of Democracy* (1999)
Key, *Politics, Parties and Pressure Groups* (1942)	Deutsch, *Nerves of Government* (1963)	Hood, *Tools of Government* (1983)	McAdam, Tarrow, and Tilly, *Dynamics of Contention* (2001)
Key, *Southern Politics in State and Nation* (1950)	Edelman, *The Symbolic Uses of Politics* (1964)	Inglehart, *The Silent Revolution* (1977)	Moravcsik, *Choice for Europe* (1998)
Luce and Raiffa, *Games and Decisions* (1957)	Ferejohn, *Pork Barrel Politics* (1974)	Jennings and Niemi, *Generations and Politics* (1981)	Pogge, *World Poverty and Human Rights* (2002)
March and Simon, *Organizations* (1958)	Hirschman, *Exit, Voice and Loyalty* (1970)	Jervis, *Perception and Misperception in International Politics* (1976)	Russett and Oneal, *Triangulating Peace* (2001)
Mills, *Power Elite* (1956)	Huntington, *Political Order in Changing Societies* (1968)	Kaase, Newton, and Scarbrough, *Beliefs in Government* (1995)	Scott, *Seeing Like a State* (1997)
Morgenthau, *Politics among Nations* (1948)	Kaufman, *The Forest Ranger* (1960)	Katznelson, *City Trenches* (1981)	Tsebelis, *Veto Players* (2002)
Schumpeter, *Capitalism, Socialism and Democracy* (1943)	Key, *Responsible Electorate* (1966)	Keohane, *After Hegemony* (1984)	Wendt, *Social Theory of International Politics* (1999)
Selznick, *TVA and the Grassroots* (1949)	Lane, *Political Ideology* (1962)	King, Keohane, and Verba, *Designing Social Inquiry* (1994)	
Simon, *Administrative Behavior* (1947)	Lijphart, *Politics of Accommodation* (1968)	Kymlicka, *Multicultural Citizenship* (1995)	
Waltz, *Man, the State and War* (1959)	Lindblom, *Intelligence of Democracy* (1965)	Lindblom, *Politics and Markets* (1977)	
	Lipset, *Political Man* (1960)	Lipsky, *Street Level Bureaucracy* (1980)	
	Lipset and Rokkan, *Party Systems and Voter Alignments* (1967)	March and Olsen, *Rediscovering Institutions* (1989)	
	Mayhew, *Congress: The Electoral Connection* (1974)		
	Moore, *Social Origins of Dictatorship and Democracy* (1966)		
	Neustadt, *Presidential Power* (1960)		
	Nozick, *Anarchy, State and Utopia* (1974)		

(cont.)

Table A1.1.1. (Continued)

Pre-1960	1960–75	1976–96	Post-1996
	Olson, Logic of Collective Action (1965)	Olson, Rise and Decline of Nations (1982)	
	Pateman, Participation and Democratic Theory (1970)	Orren, Belated Feudalism (1991)	
	Piven and Cloward, Regulating the Poor (1971)	Ostrom, Governing the Commons (1990)	
	Rawls, Theory of Justice (1971)	Pateman, Sexual Contract (1988)	
	Riker, Theory of Political Coalitions (1962)	Peterson, City Limits (1981)	
	Schattschneider, Semi-sovereign People (1960)	Popkin, The Reasoning Voter (1991)	
	Scheling, The Strategy of Conflict (1960)	Przeworski and Sprague, Paper Stones (1986)	
	Wildavsky, The Politics of the Budgetary Process (1964)	Putnam, Making Democracy Work (1993)	
	Wolin, Politics and Vision (1960)	Riker, Liberalism against Populism (1982)	
		Rogowski, Commerce and Coalitions (1989)	
		Schelling, Micromotives and Macrobehavior (1978)	
		Segal and Spaeth, Supreme Court and the Attitudinal Model (1993)	
		Skocpol, States and Social Revolution (1979)	
		Skocpol, Protecting Soldiers and Mothers (1992)	
		Skowronek, Politics Presidents Make (1993)	
		Sniderman, Brody, and Tetlock, Reasoning and Choice (1991)	
		Wildavsky, Speaking the Truth to Power (1979)	
		Wilson, Politics of Regulation (1980)	
		Young, Justice and the Politics of Difference (1990)	
		Zaller, Nature and Origins of Mass Public Opinion (1992)	

Science (1975). The third column items published between that and the *New Handbook of Political Science* (Goodin and Klingemann 1996a). The final column items published since then.

The lists in the four columns differ in length, not so much because some periods were more fruitful than others, but merely because they represent different lengths of time. The fact that the list in the last column is particularly short does not necessarily suggest that political science is running out of steam. That column covers the shortest period of time; and the list there is further truncated by fact that it takes time to see whether books, however good, actually start getting picked up by the profession at large.

There are other books, often already famous within their home discipline, that political scientists should know better than they do. Among those I would nominate are those listed in Table A1.1.2.

Table A1.1.2. Books political scientists should know better

Akerlof, *An Economic Theorist's Book of Tales* (1984)
Bates, de Figueiredo, and Weingast, *Analytical Narratives* (1998)
Berman, *Law and Revolution* (1983)
Braithwaite and Drahos, *Global Business Regulation* (2000)
Camerer, *Behavioral Game Theory* (2002)
Coleman, *Foundations of Social Theory* (1990)
Geertz, *The Interpretation of Cultures* (1973)
Hall and Soskice, *Varieties of Capitalism* (2001)
Sen, *Poverty and Famines* (1981)

Appendix 1.2 Sub-disciplinary Leaders

"Sub-disciplinary leaders" are defined as the 1 percent of people (ignoring pre-twentieth century authors) whose names appear most frequently in the index of the respective sub-disciplinary volume in the *Oxford Handbooks of Political Science* series.[64]

Conventional citation counts typically disregard self-citations. But it would be wrong to do so here. Authors were chosen to write for the *Oxford Handbooks of Political Science* because they are leaders in their field. Anyone writing a chapter on that topic would have referenced their work frequently, albeit perhaps not quite so frequently as they sometimes reference themselves. (In none of the cases listed below does any substantial proportion of the author's references come from self-referencing.)

I have therefore opted to include self-references in the counts reported in Table A1.2.1, and simply to flag the fact that the count might be inflated somewhat by setting an "A" against the count for people who authored a chapter in one of the volumes. Similar issues might arise with volume editors and with me as General Editor of the series; I flag that fact by setting an "E" against the count for any editor of the volume in question, and a "GE" against my name.

---

[64] References to the collective McNollgast are attributed to the individual authors, McCubbins, Noll, and Weingast.

Table A1.2.1. Sub-disciplinary leaders

Top 1%	Number of entries	Top 1%	Number of entries
Political theory (1,403 individuals cited)			
J. Rawls	86	H. Arendt	23
J. Habermas	50	B. Barry	23
M. Foucault	48	L. Strauss	23
I. M. Young	36	J. Waldron	22
R. Dworkin	35	S. Wolin	22
W. Kymlicka	34	*The next few*	
C. Taylor	30	J. Derrida	21
S. Benhabib	29	J. Dryzek	21 (E, A)
W. E. Connolly	28 (A)	J. Raz	21
D. Miller	24 (A)		
Political institutions (1,730 individuals cited)			
A. Lijphart	26	M. McCubbins	15
G. Cox	22	M. Duverger	14
R. A. W. Rhodes	22 (E, A)	P. Pierson	14
R. E. Goodin	20 (GE)	W. Riker	14
P. Hall	20	K. Strøm	14
J. P. Olsen	20 (A)	*The next few*	
G. Tsebelis	20	S. A. Binder	13 (E)
R. Keohane	19	G. Stoker	13 (A)
L. Martin	18 (A)	J. Braithwaite	12 (A)
B. G. Peters	16	C. Hay	11 (A)
K. Shepsle	16 (A)	G. B. Powell	11
J. M. Colomer	15 (A)		
Law and politics (1,693 individuals cited)			
M. Shapiro	40 (A)	M. A. Graber	17 (A)
J. A. Segal	34 (A)	L. A. Kornhauser	16 (A)
B. Weingast	34	C. R. Epp	15 (A)
L. Epstein	28 (A)	G. N. Rosenberg	15
H. Gillman	25 (A)	S. Silbey	15 (A)
J. Ferejohn	26	A. Stone Sweet	15
H. Spaeth	26 (A)	*The next few*	
K. E. Whittington	24 (E, A)	F. B. Cross	14 (A)
G. Caldiera	23 (E, A)	W. N. Eskridge, Jr.	14
M. McCann	21 (A)	J. Knight	14
R. Posner	20	M. McCubbins	14
A. Sarat	20	R. H. Pildes	14 (A)
S. Scheingold	20 (A)	C. R. Sunstein	14
R. Hirschl	18 (A)		
Political behavior (1,956 individuals cited)			
R. Inglehart	78 (A)	H.-D. Klingemann	44 (E, A)
R. Dalton	60 (E, A)	P. Converse	38 (A)
S. Verba	54	R. Rose	36 (A)
R. Putnam	53	W. Miller	28
P. Norris	50 (A)	P. M. Sniderman	27 (A)

(cont.)

Table A1.2.1. (*Continued*)

Top 1%	Number of entries	Top 1%	Number of entries
Political behavior (cont.)			
J. L. Gibson	26 (A)	M. Franklin	20
R. Huckfeldt	26 (A)	S. Huntington	20
W. Mishler	23	M. Kaase	20 (A)
D. Fuchs	22 (A)	*The next few*	
C. Welzel	22 (A)	S. Barnes	19
S. M. Lipset	21	A. Blais	19 (A)
J. Sprague	21	O. Knutsen	19 (A)
R. A. Dahl	20	J. Stimson	19 (A)
Contextual political analysis (2,056 individuals cited)			
C. Tilly	39 (E, A)	F. A. Polletta	11 (A)
C. Geertz	21	P. Bourdieu	10
C. Ginzburg	21	J. Goldstone	10
J. C. Scott	18	S. Jasanoff	10 (A)
T. Parsons	16	R. Keohane	10
W. Sewell	16	W. E. Bijker	9 (A)
P. Pettit	14 (A)	W. Gamson	9
S. Tarrow	14	A. Giddens	9
S. Verba	13	J. Habermas	9
G. A. Almond	12	T. Kuhn	9
P. Pierson	12	J. Mahoney	9 (A)
A. Wendt	12	T. Skocpol	9
D. McAdam	11	J. Wajcman	9 (A)
Comparative politics (1,778 individuals cited)			
A. Przeworski	57 (A)	R. M. Duch	23
C. Boix	39 (E, A)	J. A. Robinson	23
C. Tilly	32 (A)	T. Skocpol	23
G. Cox	30	A. Lijphart	22
H. Kitschelt	29 (A)	R. Stevenson	22
S. Verba	29	M. Laver	21
W. Riker	28	S. Tarrow	21 (A)
S. Stokes	27 (E, A)	*The next few*	
S. M. Lipset	25	D. Laitin	20
M. Shugart	25	D. C. North	19
B. R. Weingast	24	J. Ferejohn	18 (A)
International relations (1,219 individuals cited)			
R. O. Keohane	60 (A)	R. G. Gilpin	23
K. N. Waltz	48	P. Katzenstein	23 (A)
A. Wendt	40	D. S. Snidal	23 (E, A)
H. Bull	39	*The next few*	
A. Linklater	33	J. S. Nye, Jr.	22 (A)
C. Reus-Smit	33 (E, A)	D. Campbell	21
J. G. Ruggie	33	E. H. Carr	20
H. J. Morgenthau	28	A. Moravcsik	20 (A)
J. J. Mearsheimer	26	K. Sikkink	20 (A)

(cont.)

Table A1.2.1. (*Continued*)

Top 1%	Number of entries	Top 1%	Number of entries
Political economy (1,775 individuals cited)			
B. R. Weingast	57 (E, A)	K. Krehbiel	24 (A)
A. Alesina	49	J. Snyder	24
G. W. Cox	45 (A)	A. Downs	23
M. D. McCubbins	45 (A)	P. Ordeshook	23
K. A. Shepsle	39 (A)	T. R. Palfrey	23 (A)
J. Ferejohn	29	J. D. Fearon	22 (A)
R. McKelvey	29	*The next few*	
T. Perrson	28 (A)	J. Roemer	21 (A)
G. Tabellini	28 (A)	H. Rosenthal	21
D. Wittman	27 (E, A)	D. Austen-Smith	20 (A)
W. H. Riker	25	M. Laver	20 (A)
J. Buchanan	24 (A)	A. Przeworski	20 (A)
Public policy (1,986 individuals cited)			
A. Wildavsky	43	M. A. Hajer	16 (A)
J. G. March	33 (A)	E. Bardach	15 (A)
R. E. Goodin	31 (E, A, GE)	G. Esping-Andersen	15
J. P. Olsen	29 (A)	J. Pressman	15
M. Rein	29 (E, A)	R. A. Dahl	14
D. Schön	28	C. E. Lindblom	14
J. Forester	27 (A)	P. A. Sabatier	14
F. Fischer	24	*The next few*	
G. Majone	24 (A)	R. Neustadt	13
H. Heclo	22	J. W. Kingdon	12
C. Hood	22 (A)	M. Lipsky	12
H. D. Lasswell	22	C. Pollitt	12
B. G. Peters	19	J. C. Scott	12
R. A. W. Rhodes	18 (A)	H. Wagenaar	12
P. de Leon	16 (A)	R. J. Zeckhauser	12 (A)
Political methodology (1,642 individuals cited)			
G. King	36	J. Mahoney	17 (A)
N. Beck	33 (A)	A. George	16
D. Collier	29 (E, A)	S. Jackman	16 (A)
C. C. Ragin	29 (A)	D. P. Green	15 (A)
H. E. Brady	28 (E, A)	R. O. Keohane	15
C. H. Achen	22	T. Skocpol	15
J. Box-Steffensmeier	22 (E, A)	S. Verba	15
A. Bennett	21 (A)	*The next few*	
D. B. Rubin	21	J. N. Katz	14
L. M. Bartels	18	D. Campbell	13
B. Jones	18 (A)	D. A. Freedman	13
G. Goertz	17 (A)	J. M. Snyder	13

Appendix 1.3 Leaders of the Discipline

"Leaders of the discipline" are defined as the 1 percent of people (ignoring pre-twentieth century authors) whose names appear most frequently in the indices of the ten volumes of *Oxford Handbooks of Political Science* taken as a whole.

The same convention as in Appendix 1.2 is employed here, with an "A" indicating someone who authored a chapter in the volume in question; an "E" indicates someone who served as editor of the volume; and "GE" indicates the General Editor of the series as a whole.

The extent to which these results might be skewed by differences in citation practices across different sub-disciplines can be ascertained from Table A1.2. There is some difference across sub-disciplines in the frequency with which the very most frequently mentioned author is mentioned. But focusing on the last person among the 1 percent most referenced, that person gets around twenty mentions in all the established sub-disciplines. (The only exception is the less-established field of "Contextual Political Analysis.")

Table A1.3. Leaders of the discipline

Top 80 (~1%) Number of entries		Top 80 (~1%) cont.		Top 80 (~1%) cont.		The next few	
B. Weingast	138 (E, A)	J. G. March	65 (A)	B. M. Barry	47	N. Beck	40
R. Keohane	134 (A)	A. Alesina	64	R. Dworkin	47	C. Reus-Smit	40 (E, A)
J. Rawls	132	D. North	62 (A)	M. Fiorina	47	C. Taylor	40
S. Verba	124	A. Wendt	62	M. Duverger	46	I. Budge	39 (A)
G. W. Cox	109 (A)	H. E. Brady	61 (E, A)	H. Kitschelt	46 (A)	P. Katzenstein	39 (A)
R. Ingelhart	109 (A)	S. P. Huntington	59	S. Krasner	46	P. Sinderman	39 (A)
A. Przeworski	107 (A)	J. P. Olsen	59 (A)	M. Shapiro	46 (A)	I. M. Young	39
R. Dahl	98	K. N. Waltz	59	K. Sikkink	46 (A)	L. M. Bartels	38
J. Habermas	95	S. Tarrow	58 (A)	A. George	45	J. S. Dryzek	38 (E, A)
W. H. Riker	93	P. A. Hall	57	J. G. Ruggie	45	C. Geertz	38
R. D. Putnam	91	M. Olson	57	J. L. Gibson	44 (A)	R. Hardin	38 (A)
M. McCubbins	89 (A)	A. Wildavsky	57	W. E. Miller	44	W. Kymlicka	38
A. Lijphart	88	D. Collier	55 (E, A)	L. L. Martin	43 (A)	H. Rosenthal	38
C. Tilly	88 (E, A)	P. E. Converse	55 (A)	J. Elster	43	G. Sartori	38
T. Skocpol	85	C. Boix	54 (E, A)	R. Franzese	37 (A)	B. Simmons	38 (A)
M. Foucault	84	H.-D. Klingemann	54 (E, A)	J. J. Linz	43	J. M. Snyder	38
G. A. Almond	82	R. Rose	54 (A)	G. Tsebelis	43	J. Aldrich	37 (A)
J. Ferejohn	82 (A)	K. Strøm	54 (A)	J. A. Robinson	42 (A)	R. Axelrod	37
K. A. Shepsle	81 (A)	M. Shugart	53 (A)	G. Esping-Andersen	42	S. Benhabib	37
G. King	75	J. A. Segal	51 (A)	H. D. Lasswell	42	J. M. Buchanan	37 (A)
R. Dalton	74 (E, A)	J. C. Scott	50	P. Ordeshook	42	B. Bueno de Mesquita	37 (A)
P. Norris	71 (A)	T. Persson	50 (A)	D. Snidal	42 (E, A)	D. Diermeier	37 (A)
P. Pierson	71	G. Tabellini	50 (A)	C. Achen	41	J. S. Nye, Jr.	37 (A)
J. Fearon	69	D. Laitin	49 (A)	H. Bull	41	N. Schofield	37
S. M. Lipset	68	G. B. Powell	49 (A)	R. McKelvey	41		
A. Downs	68	J. Mahoney	48 (A)	J. A. Stimson	41 (A)		
R. E. Goodin	66 (GE, E, A)	C. C. Ragin	48 (A)				
M. Laver	65 (A)	A. Bennett	47 (A)				

Appendix 1.4 Integrators of the Discipline

"Integrators of the discipline" are defined as people whose work is influential across multiple branches of the discipline (Goodin and Klingemann 1996b, 33–4). Table A1.4 lists people whose name appears in the indexes of multiple volumes of the *Oxford Handbooks of Political Science*, according to the number of those ten volumes in which it appears.

Again, in deference to fears that self-referencing might have affected the results, an "E" indicates someone who edited one of the volumes and "GE" the General Editor of the series as a whole.

Appendix 1.5 Structure of the Discipline

This appendix maps relations among the sub-disciplines of political science, as represented by each of the ten component volumes of the *Oxford Handbooks of Political Science* series. The "closeness" of one sub-discipline to another will be adjudged by the proportion of authors who appear in the name indexes of both sub-disciplinary volumes.

Pre-twentieth-century authors are once again ignored. So too are the names of public figures not cited as authors (US Supreme Court justices whose written opinions are cited are treated as authors, however). It is sometimes unclear whether people with the same name are the same author or not; for those cases I have adopted the rule "when in doubt, count."

In Table A1.5, the total number of entries in the name index of each sub-disciplinary volume is reported below the name of the sub-discipline in the row and column headings. In each cell in the body of that table, two numbers appear: First, the total number of individuals whose name appears in the indexes of both volumes; and second, that expressed as a percentage of all names that appear in the handbook represented by that row. Since the total number of names indexed in different sub-disciplinary handbooks differs (the Context volume has 70 percent more names in its index than the one on International Relations), the two such percentages reported for the intersection of each pair of handbooks differs somewhat in the top-right and lower-left halves of Table A1.5.

The final column in Table A1.5 averages the interrelationships across the row representing the sub-discipline. From those averages, it would seem that—except for Political Theory and Law and Politics—the discipline as a whole is pretty uniformly integrated. Except for those two sub-disciplines, the average interrelationship between sub-disciplines ranges between 12 and 18 percent, with Comparative Politics and Political Institutions appearing as most central on average.

Table A1.4. Integrators of the discipline
Authors appearing in multiple subdisciplinary volumes (omitting pre-twentieth-century authors)

Influence 10 out of 10 sub-disciplines	Influence 7 out of 10 sub-disciplines	Influence 6 out of 10 sub-disciplines	Influence 6 out of 10 (cont.)
G. A. Almond	K. J. Arrow	B. Ackerman	J. J. Mansbridge
R. A. Dahl	P. Bachrach	T. Adorno	R. McKelvey
D. Laitin	R. H. Bates	J. E. Alt	R. K. Merton
A. Lijphart	P. Bordieu	R. M. Alvarez	J. W. Meyer
J. Rawls	J. M. Buchanan	C. Anderson	R. Niemi
W. H. Riker	I. Budge	L. Anderson	J. S. Nye, Jr.
T. Skocpol	T. Carothers	H. Arendt	C. Offe
	J. S. Coleman	U. Beck	P. C. Ordeshook
Influence 9 out of 10 sub-disciplines	J. Dewey	P. L. Berger	K. Orren
B. Barry	L. Diamond	I. Berlin	E. Ostrom
H. E. Brady (E)	D. Easton	B. Bueno de Mesquita	T. Persson
J. Elster	H. Eckstein	A. Campbell	K. T. Poole
D. P. Green	G. Esping-Andersen	F. G. Castles	D. Rae
P. A. Hall	J. Fearon	D. Collier (E)	C. Ragin
R. Hardin	E. Fehr	R. J. Dalton (E)	J. E. Roemer
S. P. Huntington	M. Fiorina	D. Diermeier	S. Rokkan
R. O. Keohane	F. Fukuyama	A. Downs	R. Rose
S. D. Krasner	W. A. Gamson	G. W. Downs	J. G. Ruggie
D. C. North	A. Giddens	J. N. Druckman	F. Scharpf
M. Olson	J. H. Goldthorp	P. B. Evans	E. E. Schattschneider
P. Pierson	J. R. Hibbing	R. Fenno	T. C. Schelling
A. Przeworski	A. O. Hirschman	M. Finnemore	T. Schwartz
I. Shapiro	R. Inglehart	M. Foucault	J. A. Segal
S. Verba	D. Kahneman	M. Friedman	C. R. Shipan
B. R. Weingast	T. S. Kuhn	G. Garrett	B. Simmons
	H. D. Lasswell	B. Geddes	N. J. Smelser
Influence 8 of 10 sub-disciplines	M. Levi	C. Geertz	J. McC. Smith
R. Axelrod	A. Lupia	A. Gramsci	J. Sprague
J. Ferejohn	C. W. Mills	B. Grofman	J. E. Stiglitz
C. J. Friedrich	B. Moore	T. R. Gurr	A. L. Stinchcombe
R. E. Goodin (E, GE)	A. Moravcsik	D. Held	D. E. Stokes
J. Habermas	R. A. Posner	S. Holmes	G. Tabellini
J. D. Huber	G. B. Powell	E. Huber	C. Taylor
P. Katzenstein	W. W. Powell	G. Jacobson	K. Thelen
G. King	R. Rogowski	R. Jervis	D. B. Truman
S. M. Lipset	G. Sartori	R. A. Kagan	A. Tversky
M. D. McCubbins	N. Schofield	T. L. Karl	E. M. Uslaner
T. Parsons	J. A. Schumpeter	R. S. Katz	J. L. Walker
R. Putnam	J. C. Scott	M. Keck	I. Wallerstein
C. Reus-Smit (E)	K. Sikkink	V. O. Key	M. Walzer
P. C. Schmitter	D. Snidal (E)	M. Laver	M. P. Wattenberg
A. K. Sen	J. Snyder	S. Levitsky	B. D. Wood
K. A. Shepsle	D. Soskice	C. E. Lindblom	O. R. Young
H. A. Simon	A. Stepan	J. J. Linz	J. Zaller
J. D. Stephens	C. R. Sunstein	T. Lowi	
G. Tsebelis	S. Tarrow	N. Luhmann	
A. Wildavsky	E. Theiss-Morse	S. Lukes	
	C. Tilly (E)	M. B. MacKuen	
	G. Tullock	G. Majone	

Table A1.5. The structure of the discipline (number and % of shared authors)

	Comp. pol. 1778	Pol. instns. 1730	Inter. rels. 1219	Pol. econ. 1775	Meth. 1642	Pol. beh. 1956	Context 2056	Public pol. 1986	Law & pol. 1693	Pol. th. 1403	Ave.
Comp. pol. 1778	–	404 = 22.72	211 = 11.87	516 = 29.02	390 = 21.93	506 = 28.46	348 = 19.57	255 = 14.34	204 = 11.47	134 = 7.54	18.55
Pol. instns. 1730	404 = 23.35	–	225 = 13.01	397 = 22.95	253 = 14.62	331 = 19.13	268 = 15.49	414 = 23.93	324 = 18.73	142 = 8.21	17.60
Inter. rels. 1219	211 = 17.31	225 = 18.46	–	150 = 12.31	190 = 15.59	127 = 10.42	233 = 19.11	192 = 15.75	139 = 11.40	163 = 13.37	14.86
Pol. econ. 1775	516 = 29.07	397 = 22.37	150 = 8.45	–	310 = 17.46	268 = 15.10	228 = 12.85	215 = 12.11	181 = 10.20	92 = 5.18	14.76
Meth. 1642	390 = 23.75	253 = 15.41	190 = 11.57	310 = 18.88	–	312 = 19.00	232 = 14.13	187 = 11.39	122 = 7.43	77 = 4.69	14.03
Pol. beh. 1956	506 = 25.87	331 = 16.92	127 = 6.49	268 = 13.70	312 = 15.95	–	326 = 16.67	236 = 12.07	137 = 7.00	130 = 6.65	13.48
Context 2056	348 = 16.93	268 = 13.04	233 = 11.33	228 = 11.09	232 = 11.28	326 = 15.86	–	294 = 14.30	162 = 7.88	202 = 9.82	12.39
Public pol. 1986	255 = 12.84	414 = 20.85	192 = 9.67	215 = 10.83	187 = 9.42	236 = 11.88	294 = 14.80	–	201 = 10.12	176 = 8.86	12.14
Law & pol. 1693	204 = 12.05	324 = 19.14	139 = 8.21	181 = 10.69	122 = 7.21	137 = 8.09	162 = 9.57	201 = 11.87	–	128 = 7.56	10.49
Pol. th. 1403	134 = 9.55	142 = 10.12	163 = 11.62	92 = 6.56	77 = 5.49	130 = 9.27	202 = 14.40	176 = 12.54	128 = 9.12	–	9.85

REFERENCES

ABBOTT, A. 1988. *The System of Professions*. Chicago: University of Chicago Press.

—— 2002. Sociology of professions. In *International Encyclopedia of the Social and Behavioral Sciences*, ed. P. Baltes and N. Smelser. Amsterdam: Elsevier.

ACEMOGLU, D. and ROBINSON, J. A. 2006. *Economic Origins of Dictatorship and Democracy*. Cambridge: Cambridge University Press.

AKERLOF, G. A. 1970. The market for "lemons:" qualitative uncertainty and the market mechanism. *Quarterly Journal of Economics*, 84: 488–500. Reprinted in Akerlof 1984, ch. 2.

—— 1984. *An Economic Theorist's Book of Tales*. Cambridge: Cambridge University Press.

ALDRICH, J., ALT, J., and LUPIA, A. 2008. The EIM apprach: origins and interpretations. Pp. 828–43. In Box-Steffensmeier, Brady, and Collier, *Oxford Handbook of Political Methodology*. Oxford: Oxford University Press, ed. 2008.

ALFORD, J. R. and HIBBING, J. R. 2008. The new empirical biopolitics. *Annual Review of Political Science*, 11: 183–204.

ALLISON, G. T. 1969. Conceptual models and the Cuban Missile Crisis. *American Political Science Review*, 63: 689–718.

—— 1971. *Essence of Decision*. Boston: Little, Brown.

—— and ZELIKOW, P. 1999. *The Essence of Decision*, 2nd edn. Reading, Mass.: Longman.

ALMOND, G. A. 1960. A functional approach to comparative politics. Pp. 3–66 in Almond and Coleman 1960.

—— 1988. Separate tables: schools and sects in political science. *PS: Political Science and Politics*, 21: 828–42.

—— 1996. Political science: the history of the discipline. Pp. 50–96 in Goodin and Klingemann 1996.

—— and COLEMAN, J. S. (eds.) 1960. *The Politics of the Developing Areas*. Princeton, NJ: Princeton University Press.

—— and VERBA, S. 1963. *The Civic Culture*. Princeton, NJ: Princeton University Press.

ALT, J. E., LEVI, M., and OSTROM, E. 1999. Introduction. In Alt, Levi, and Ostrom (eds.), *Competition and Cooperation: Conversations with Nobelists about Economics and Political Science*. New York: Russell Sage Foundation.

—— and SHEPSLE, K. A. (eds.) 1990. *Perspectives on Positive Political Economy*. Cambridge: Cambridge University Press.

ANDERSON, P., ARROW, K. J., and PINES, D. 1988. *The Economy as an Evolving Complex System*. Redwood City, Calif.: Addison-Wesley.

ANON. 2007. History of the caucus for a new political science. *New Political Science*, 29/4: 501–7.

ANSELL, C. 2006. Network institutionalism. Pp. 75–89 in Rhodes, Binder, and Rockman 2006.

ANTONY, L. 2006. The socialization of epistemology. Pp. 58–77 in Goodin and Tilly 2006.

ARENDT, H. 1951/1966. *The Origins of Totalitarianism*, 3rd edn. and London: Allen and Unwin.

ARROW, K. J. 1951/1963. *Social Choice and Individual Values*, 2nd edn. New Haven, Conn.: Yale University Press.

AXELROD, R. 1973. Schema theory: an information processing model of perception and cognition. *American Political Science Review*, 67: 1248–66.

—— (ed.) 1976. *The Structure of Decision*. Princeton, NJ: Princeton University Press.

—— 1981. Emergence of cooperation among egoists. *American Political Science Review*, 75: 306–18.

—— 1984. *The Evolution of Cooperation*. New York: Basic Books.

—— 1986. An evolutionary approach to norms. *American Political Science Review*, 80: 1095–112.

—— and HAMILTON, W. D. 1981. The evolution of cooperation. *Science*, 211: 1390–6.

BACHRACH, P. and BARATZ, M. 1970. *Power and Poverty*. New York: Oxford University Press.

BANFIELD, E. C. and WILSON, J. Q. 1963. *City Politics*. New York: Vintage.

BARNES, S., KAASE, M., et al. 1979. *Political Action: Mass Participation in Five Western Democracies*. Beverly Hills, Calif.: Sage.

BARRY, B. 1965. *Political Argument*. London: Routledge & Kegan Paul.

—— 1970. *Sociologists, Economists and Democracy*. London: Collier-Macmillan. 2nd edn. Chicago: University of Chicago Press, 1978.

—— 1974. Review article: exit, voice and loyalty. *British Journal of Political Science*, 4: 79–107.

—— 1999. The study of politics as a vocation. Pp. 425–67 in Hayward, Barry, and Brown 1999.

BATES, R. H., DE FIGUEIREDO, R. J. P., JR., and WEINGAST, B. R. 1998. The politics of interpretation: rationality, culture and transition. *Politics and Society*, 26: 603–42.

—— GREIF, A., LEVI, M., ROSENTHAL, J.-L., and WEINGAST, B. R. 1998. *Analytic Narratives*. Princeton, NJ: Princeton University Press.

BEARD, C. A. 1913. *An Economic Interpretation of the Constitution of the United States*. New York: Macmillan.

BENDOR, J. and HAMMOND, T. H. 1992. Rethinking Allison's models. *American Political Science Review*, 86: 301–22.

BENFORD, R. D. and SNOW, D. A. 2000. Framing processes and social movements: an overview and assessment. *Annual Review of Sociology*, 26: 611–39.

BENTLEY, A. F. 1908/1967. *The Process of Government*, ed. P. H. Odegard. Cambridge, Mass.: Harvard University Press. Originally published 1908.

BERLIN, I. 1953. *The Hedgehog and the Fox*. New York: Simon and Schuster.

BERMAN, H. J. 1983. *Law and Revolution: The Formation of the Western Legal Tradition*. Cambridge, Mass.: Harvard University Press.

BEYME, K. VON (ed.) 1986. Politikwissenschaft in der Bundesrepublik Deutschland. *Politische Vierteljahresschrift*, special issue 17. Opladen: Westdeutscher Verlag.

BINMORE, K. 1998. *Game Theory and Social Contract*. Volume 2: *Just Playing*. Cambridge, Mass.: MIT Press.

BIRNBAUM, N. 1955. Monarchs and sociologists. *Sociological Review*, 3: 5–23.

BLACK, D. 1958. *Theory of Committees & Elections*. Cambridge: Cambridge University Press.

BOHMAN, J. 1999. Democracy as inquiry, inquiry as democratic: pragmatism, social science and the cognitive division of labor. *American Journal of Political Science*, 43: 590–607.

—— 2002. How to make a social science practical: pragmatism, critical social science and multiperspectival theory. *Millennium*, 31: 499–524.

BOISSEVAIN, J. 1974. *Friends of Friends: Networks, Manipulators and Coalitions*. Oxford: Blackwell.

—— and MITCHELL, J. C. (eds.) 1973. *Network Analysis: Studies in Social Interaction*. The Hague: Mouton.

BOIX, C. 2004. *Democracy and Redistribution*. Cambridge: Cambridge University Press.

—— and STOKES, S. C. (eds.) 2007. *Oxford Handbook of Comparative Politics*. Oxford: Oxford University Press.

BOUDON, R. 1974. *Education, Opportunity, and Social Inequality*. New York: Wiley.

BOURDIEU, P. 1984. *Distinction*, trans. R. Nice. London: Routledge and Kegan Paul.

BOWLES, S. 2004. *Microeconomics: Behavior, Institutions and Evolution*. Princeton, NJ: Princeton University Press, for Russell Sage Foundation.

—— and GINTIS, H. 2006. The evolutionary basis of collective action. Pp. 951–70 in Weingast and Wittman 2006. Reprinted in this volume.

BOX-STEFFENSMEIER, J. M., BRADY, H. E., and COLLIER, D. (eds.) 2008. *Oxford Handbook of Political Methodology*. Oxford: Oxford University Press.

BRAITHWAITE, J. and DRAHOS, P. 2000. *Global Business Regulation*. Cambridge: Cambridge University Press.

BRAMS, S. J. 1978. *The Presidential Election Game*. New Haven, Conn.: Yale University Press.

BUENO DE MESQUITA, B. and LALMAN, D. 1992. *War and Reason: Domestic and International Imperatives*. New Haven, Conn.: Yale University Press.

——SMITH, A., SIVERSON, R. M., and MORROW, J. D. 2005. *The Logic of Political Survival*. Cambridge, Mass.: MIT Press.

BURAWORY, M. 2005. For public sociology. *American Sociological Review*, 70: 4–28.

BURNHAM, W. D. 1970. *Critical Elections and the Mainsprings of American Politics*. New York: Norton.

BURT, R. S. and MINOR, M. J. (eds.) 1983. *Applied Network Analysis: A Methodological Introduction*. Beverley Hills, Calif.: Sage.

BUTLER, L. 2006. RQF Pilot Study Project—History and Political Science Methodology for Citation Analysis. Briefing paper for CHASS Bibliometrics Project for the Department of Education, Science and Training, Commonwealth of Australia. Available at: <www.chass.org.au/papers/bibliometrics/CHASS_Methodology.pdf>.

CALHOUN, C. and MCGOWAN, J. (eds.) 1997. *Hannah Arendt and the Meaning of Politics*. Minneapolis: University of Minnesota Press.

CAMERER, C. F. 2002. *Behavioral Game Theory*. Princeton, NJ: Princeton University Press.

CAMPBELL, A., CONVERSE, P. E., MILLER, W., and STOKES, D. 1960. *The American Voter*. New York: Wiley.

CAMPBELL, D. T. and STANLEY, J. C. 1963. *Experimental and Quasi Experimental Designs for Research*. Boston: Houghton-Mifflin.

CAMPION, LORD, CHESTER, D. N., MACKENZIE, W. J. M., ROBSON, W. A., STREET, A., and WARREN, J. H. 1950. *British Government since 1918*. London: Allen and Unwin, for the Institute of Public Administration.

CAPLOW, T. and MCGEE, R. J. 1961. *The Academic Marketplace*. New York: Wiley.

CARNAP, R. 1950. *Logical Foundations of Probability*. Chicago: University of Chicago Press.

CHESTER, D. N. 1975. Political studies in Britain: recollections and comments. *Political Studies*, 23: 29–42.

CHONG, D. and DRUCKMAN, J. N. 2007. Framing theory. *Annual Review of Political Science*, 10: 103–26.

COAKLEY, J. and TRENT, J. 2000. *History of the International Political Science Association 1949–1999*. Dublin: International Political Science Association.

COLE, H. D. S., et al. (eds.) 1973. *Thinking about the Future*. London: Chatto and Windus, for Sussex University Press.

COLEMAN, J. S. 1990. *Foundations of Social Theory*. Cambridge, Mass.: Harvard University Press.

COLLINI, S., WINCH, D., and BURROWS, J. 1983. *That Noble Science of Politics*. Cambridge: Cambridge University Press.

CORNFORD, F. M. 1908. *Microcosmographia Academia*. Cambridge: Bowes and Bowes.

CORWIN, E. S. 1929. The democratic dogma and the future of political science. *American Political Science Review*, 23: 569–92.

COX, G. W. 1997. *Making Votes Count*. Cambridge: Cambridge University Press.

——and MCCUBBINS, M. D. 1993. *Legislative Leviathan: Party Government in the House*. Los Angeles: University of California Press; rev. edn. 2007.

CRICK, B. 1962. *In Defence of Politics*. London: Weidenfeld and Nicolson.

CYERT, R. M. and MARCH, J. G. 1963. *A Behavioral Theory of the Firm*. Englewood Cliffs, NJ: Prentice Hall.

DAHL, R. A. 1961a. The behavioral approach in political science: epitaph for a monument to a successful protest. *American Political Science Review*, 55: 763–72.

—— 1961b. *Who Governs?* New Haven, Conn.: Yale University Press.

—— 1972. *Polyarchy: Participation and Opposition*. New Haven, Conn.: Yale University Press.

DAHRENDORF, R. 1959. *Class and Class Conflict in Industrial Society*. Stanford, Calif.: Stanford University Press.

DALLMAYR, F. (ed.) 1999. *Border Crossings: Toward a Comparative Political Theory*. Lanham, Md.: Lexington Books.

—— 2004. Beyond monologue: for a comparative political theory. *Perspectives on Politics*, 2: 249–57.

DALTON, R. J. and KLINGEMANN, H.-D. (eds.) 2007. *Oxford Handbook of Political Behavior*. Oxford: Oxford University Press.

DAVIDSON, D. 1980. *Essays on Actions and Events*. Oxford: Clarendon Press.

—— 1984. *Inquiries into Truth and Interpretation*. Oxford: Clarendon Press.

DAVIS, K. 1959. The myth of functional analysis as a special method in sociology and anthropology. *American Sociological Review*, 24: 757–72.

DAWKINS, R. 1976. *The Selfish Gene*. Oxford: Oxford University Press.

DEUTSCH, K. W. 1963. *The Nerves of Government*. Glencoe, Ill.: Free Press.

—— 1979. Political science: major changes in the discipline. Pp. 157–80 in Rokkan 1979.

—— MARKOVITS, A. S., and PLATT, J. (eds.) 1986. *Advances in the Social Sciences*. New York: University Press of America.

DEWAN, T., DOWDING, K., and SHEPSLE, K. A. 2008a. Rational choice classics in political science. Ch. 1 in Dewan, Dowding, and Shepsle 2008b.

—— —— —— (eds.) 2008b. *Rational Choice Politics*. London: Sage.

DIERKES, M. and BIERVERT, B. (eds.) 1992. *European Social Science in Transition*. Frankfurt am Main: Campus Verlag.

DOGAN, M. 1996. Political science and the other social sciences. Pp. 97–130 in Goodin and Klingemann 1996a.

—— and PAHRE, R. 1990. *Creative Marginality*. Boulder, Colo.: Westview.

DOWNS, A. 1957. *An Economic Theory of Democracy*. New York: Harper.

DRYZEK, J. S. 2000. *Deliberative Democracy and Beyond*. Oxford: Oxford University Press.

—— 2005. A pox on perestroika, a hex on hegemony: toward a critical political science. In Monroe 2005.

—— 2006a. Policy analysis as critique. Pp. 190–203 in Moran, Rein, and Goodin 2006.

—— 2006b. Revolutions without enemies: key transformations in political science. *American Political Science Review*, 100: 487–92.

—— HONIG, B., and PHILLIPS, A. (eds.) 2006. *Oxford Handbook of Political Theory*. Oxford: Oxford University Press.

—— and LEONARD, S. T. 1995. History and discipline in political science. Pp. 27–48 in Easton, Gunnell, and Stein 1995.

—— and SCHLOSBERG, D. 1995. Disciplining Darwin: biology in the history of political science. Pp. 123–44 in Farr, Dryzek, and Leonard 1995.

DUNLEAVY, P., KELLY, P. J., and MORAN, M. (eds.) 2000. *British Political Science: Fifty Years of Political Studies*. Oxford: Blackwell.

DUVERGER, M. 1951/1954. *Political Parties*, trans. B. and R. North. London: Methuen.

—— 1964/1966. *The Idea of Politics: The Uses of Power in Society*, trans. R. North and R. Murphy. London: Methuen.

EASTON, D. 1953. *The Political System*. New York: Knopf.

—— 1957. An approach to the analysis of political systems. *World Politics*, 9: 383–406.

—— 1965. *A Systems Analysis of Political Life*. New York: Wiley.

—— 1969. The new revolution in political science. *American Political Science Review*, 63: 1051–61.

—— GUNNELL, J. G., and GRAZIANO, L. (eds.) 1995. *The Development of Political Science: A Comparative Survey*. London: Routledge.

—— —— and STEIN, M. B. (eds.) 1991. *Regime and Discipline: Democracy and the Development of Political Science*. Ann Arbor: University of Michigan Press.

EDELMAN, M. 1964. *The Symbolic Uses of Politics*. Urbana: University of Illinois Press.

—— 1988. *Constructing the Political Spectacle*. Chicago: University of Chicago Press.

EISENSTADT, S. N. 1963. *The Political Systems of Empires*. New York: Free Press.

ELSTER, J. 1979. Problematic rationality: some unresolved problems in the theory of rational behavior. Pp. 112–56 in Elster, *Ulysses and the Sirens*. Cambridge: Cambridge University Press.

—— 1989. *Nuts and Bolts for the Social Sciences*. Cambridge: Cambridge University Press.

—— 2007. *Explaining Social Behavior: More Nuts and Bolts for the Social Sciences*. Cambridge: Cambridge University Press.

ESPING-ANDERSEN, G. 1990. *The Three Worlds of Welfare Capitalism*. Cambridge: Cambridge University Press.

EUBEN, R. L. 1999. *Enemy in the Mirror: Islamic Fundamentalism and the Limits of Modern Rationalism, A Work of Comparative Political Theory*. Princeton, NJ: Princeton University Press.

EULAU, H. 1963. *The Behavioral Persuasion in Politics*. New York: Random House.

FARR, J. 1995. Remembering the revolution: behavioralism in American political science. Pp. 198–224 in Farr, Dryzek, and Leonard 1995.

—— DRYZEK, J. S., and LEONARD, S. T. (eds.) 1995. *Political Science in History: Research Programs and Political Traditions*. Cambridge: Cambridge University Press.

—— and SEIDELMAN, R. (eds.) 1993. *Discipline and History: Political Science in the United States*. Ann Arbor: University of Michigan Press.

FEHR, E. and FISCHBACHER, U. 2002. Why social preferences matter: the impact of non-selfish motives on competition, cooperation and incentives. *Economic Journal*, 112: C1–C33.

FENNO, R. 1978. *Home Style*. Boston: Little, Brown.

FEREJOHN, J. A. 1974. *Pork Barrel Politics*. Stanford, Calif.: Stanford University Press.

FINIFTER, A. W. (ed.) 1983. *Political Science: The State of the Discipline*. Washington, DC: American Political Science Association.

—— (ed.) 1993. *Political Science: The State of the Discipline II*. Washington, DC: American Political Science Association.

FINNEMORE, M. and SIKKINK, K. 2001. Taking stock: the constructivist research program in international relations and comparative politics. *Annual Review of Political Science*, 4: 391–416.

FIORINA, M. P. 1981. *Retrospective Voting in American National Elections*. New Haven, Conn.: Yale University Press.

FIORINA, M. P. 1996. Rational choice, empirical contributions and the scientific enterprise. Pp. 85–94 in Friedman 1996.

—— 2006. *Culture War? The Myth of a Polarized America*, 2nd edn. New York: Pearson Longman.

FLYVBJERG, B. 2001. *Making Social Science Matter*. Cambridge: Cambridge University Press.

FØLLESDAL, A. 1998. Subsidiarity. *Journal of Political Philosophy*, 6: 190–218.

FORRESTER, J. 1971. *World Dynamics*. Cambridge, Mass.: Wright-Allen Press.

FOUCAULT, M. 1977. *Discipline and Punish*, trans. A. Sheridan. Harmondsworth: Allen Lane.

FOUCAULT, M. 1991. Governmentality. Pp. 87–104 in *The Foucault Effect: Studies in Governmentality*, ed. G. Burchell et al. Hemel Hempstead: Harvester-Wheatsheaf.

FRIEDMAN, J. (ed.) 1996. *The Rational Choice Controversy: Economic Models of Politics Reconsidered*. New Haven, Conn.: Yale University Press.

GAMSON, W. A. 1992. *Talking Politics*. Cambridge: Cambridge University Press.

GARFINKEL, H. 1967. *Studies in Ethnomethodology*. Englewood Cliffs, NJ: Prentice Hall.

GEERTZ, C. 1973. *The Interpretation of Cultures*. New York: Basic Books.

—— 1977. The judging of nations. *Archives européennes de sociologie*, 18: 245–61.

—— 2000. *Available Light*. Princeton, NJ: Princeton University Press.

GOLDSTEIN, J. and KEOHANE, R. (eds.) 1993. *Ideas and Foreign Policy*. Ithaca, NY: Cornell University Press.

GOODIN, R. E. 1996. Institutions and their design. Pp. 1–53 in *The Theory of Institutional Design*, ed. R. E. Goodin. Cambridge: Cambridge University Press.

—— 2000. Institutional gaming. *Governance*, 13: 523–33.

—— 2009. The British study of politics: an assessment. In *Oxford Handbook of British Politics*, ed. M. Flinders, A. Gamble, C. Hay, and M. Kenny. Oxford: Oxford University Press.

—— and KLINGEMANN, H.-D. (eds.) 1996a. *A New Handbook of Political Science*. Oxford: Oxford University Press.

—— —— 1996b. Political science: the discipline. Pp. 3–49 in Goodin and Klingemann 1996a.

—— and TILLY, C. (eds.) 2006. *Oxford Handbook of Contextual Political Analysis*. Oxford: Oxford University Press.

—— et al. 2007. *International Benchmarking Review of UK Politics and International Studies*. London: Economic and Social Research Council in partnership with the British International Studies Association and the Political Studies Association.

GRANOVETTER, M. 1973. The strength of weak ties. *American Journal of Sociology*, 78: 1360–80.

—— 1983. The strength of weak ties: a network theory revisited. *Sociological Theory*, 1: 201–33.

GRAZIANO, L. (ed.) 1987. *La scienca politica italiana*. Milan: Feltrinelli.

GREEN, D. P. and SHAPIRO, I. 1994. *The Pathologies of Rational Choice*. New Haven, Conn.: Yale University Press.

GREENSTEIN, F. I. 1982. *The Hidden-Hand Presidency: Eisenhower as Leader*. New York: Basic Books.

—— and POLSBY, N. W. (eds.) 1975. *Handbook of Political Science*, 8 vols. Reading, Mass.: Addison-Wesley.

GREWAL, D. S. 2008. *Network Power: The Social Dynamics of Globalization*. New Haven, Conn.: Yale University Press.

GUNNELL, J. G. 2005. Political science on the cusp: recovering a discipline's past. *American Political Science Review*, 99: 597–609.

—— 2006. The founding of the American Political Science Association: discipline, profession, political theory and politics. *American Political Science Review*, 100: 479–86.

GÜTH, W., SCHMITTBERGER, R., and SCHWARZE, B. 1982. An experimental analysis of ultimatum bargaining. *Journal of Economic Behavior and Organization*, 3: 367–88.

HAAS, P. M. 1992. Epistemic communities and international policy coordination. *International Organization*, 46: 1–35.

HALL, P. A. and SOSKICE, D. (eds.) 2001. *Varieties of Capitalism*. Oxford: Oxford University Press.

HAMMOND, T. H., JEN. K. I., and MAEDA, K. 2007. Learning in hierarchies: an empirical test using library catalogues. *Journal of Theoretical Politics*, 19: 425–64.

HARDIN, R. 2006. Not shaken, not even stirred. *The Good Society*, 15: 1, 4–6.

HART, H. L. A. 1961. *The Concept of Law*. Oxford: Clarendon Press.

HARTZ, L. 1955. *The Liberal Tradition in America*. New York: Harcourt, Brace.

HAY, C. 2002. *Political Analysis*. London: Palgrave Macmillan.

——2004. Theory, stylized heuristic or self-fulfilling prophesy? The status of rational choice theory in public administration. *Public Administration*, 82: 39–62.

——and RICHARDS, D. 2000. The tangled webs of Westminster and Whitehall: the discourse, strategy and practice of networking within the British core executive. *Public Administration* 78: 1–28.

HAYWARD, J., BARRY, B., and BROWN, A. (eds.) 1999. *The British Study of Politics in the Twentieth Century*. Oxford: Oxford University Press, for the British Academy.

HECLO, H. 1978. Issue networks and the executive establishment. Pp. 87–124 in *The New American Political System,* ed. A. King. Washington, DC: American Enterprise Institute.

HEDSTRÖM, P. and SWEDBERG, R. (eds.) 1998. *Social Mechanisms*. Cambridge: Cambridge University Press.

HEILBRON, J., MAGNUSSON, L., and WITTROCK, B. (eds.) 1998. *The Rise of the Social Sciences and the Formation of Modernity*. Dordrecht: Kluwer.

HEINZ, J. P. and LAUMANN, E. O. 1982. *Chicago Lawyers: The Social Structure of the Bar*. New York: Russell Sage Foundation, for the American Bar Foundation.

————NELSON, R. L., and SALISBURY, R. H. 1993. *The Hollow Core: Private Interests in National Policymaking*. Cambridge, Mass.: Harvard University Press.

HÉRITIER, A. 2007. *Explaining Institutional Change in Europe*. Oxford: Oxford University Press.

HERTTING, N. 2007. Mechanisms of governance network formation: a contextual rational choice perspective. Pp. 43–60 in *Theories of Democratic Network Governance*, ed. E. Sørensen and J. Torfing. London: Palgrave Macmillan.

HIRSCH, F. 1976. *Social Limits to Growth*. Cambridge, Mass.: Harvard University Press.

HIRSCHLEIFER, J. 1977. Economics from a biological viewpoint. *Journal of Law and Economics*, 20: 1–52.

HIRSCHMAN, A. O. 1970. *Exit, Voice and Loyalty*. Cambridge, Mass.: Harvard University Press

HITCH, C. J. and MCKEAN, R. N. 1960. *The Economics of Defense in the Nuclear Age*. Cambridge, Mass.: Harvard University Press.

HOOD, C. C. 1983. *Tools of Government*. London: Macmillan.

HUGHES, E. C. 1958. *Men and their Work*. Glencoe, Ill.: Free Press.

HUME, D. 1777. That politics may be reduced to a science. Part I, Essay 3 in *Essays, Literary, Moral and Political*. London: A. Millar.

HUNTINGTON, S. P. 1968. *Political Order in Changing Societies*. New Haven, Conn.: Yale University Press.

INGLEHART, R. 1977. *The Silent Revolution*. Princeton, NJ: Princeton University Press.

IYENGAR, S. 1994. *Is Anyone Responsible? How Television Frames Political Issues*. Chicago: University of Chicago Press.

JENNINGS, M. K. and NIEMI, R. G. 1981. *Generations and Politics*. Princeton, NJ: Princeton University Press.

JERVIS, R. 1976. *Perception and Misperception in International Politics*. Princeton, NJ: Princeton University Press.

JESSOP, B. 1990. *State Theory*. Cambridge: Polity.

JOHNSON, J. 2002. How conceptual problems migrate: rational choice, interpretation and the hazards of pluralism. *Annual Review of Political Science*, 5: 223–48.

KAASE, M., NEWTON, K., and SCARBROUGH, E. (eds.) 1995. *Beliefs in Government*, 5 vols. Oxford: Oxford University Press.

KAASE, M., AND SPARSCHUH, V. 2002. *Three Social Science Disciplines in Central and Eastern Europe: Handbook on Economics, Political Science and Sociology (1989–2001)*. Bonn/Berlin/Budapest: GESIS/Social Science Information Centre and Collegium Budapest Institute for Advanced Study.

KAHNEMAN, D. 2003. Maps of bounded rationality: psychology for behavioral economics. *American Economics Review*, 93: 1449–75.

—— KNETSCH, J. L., and THALER, R. H. 1986. Fairness as a constraint on profit seeking: entitlements in the market. *American Economic Review*, 76: 728–41.

—— SLOVIC, P., and TVERSKY, A. (eds.) 1982. *Judgment under Uncertainty: Heuristics and Biases*. Cambridge: Cambridge University Press.

—— and TVERSKY, A. (eds.) 2000. *Choices, Values and Frames*. Cambridge: Cambridge University Press.

KAPLAN, D. E. and LEWIS, K. M. 2001. Guide to the American Social Science Association Records. New Haven, Conn.: Manuscripts and Archives, Yale University Library. <http://mssa.library.yale.edu/findaids/eadPDF/mssa.ms.1603.pdf>

KATZENSTEIN, P. and SIL, R. 2008. Eclectic theorizing in the study and practice of international relations. Ch. 6 in Reus-Smit and Snidal 2008.

KATZNELSON, I. 1981. *City Trenches*. Chicago: University of Chicago Press.

—— and MILNER, H. (eds.) 2002. *Political Science: The State of the Discipline III*. Washington, DC: American Political Science Association.

KAUFMAN, H. 1967. *The Forest Ranger*. Baltimore: Johns Hopkins University Press, for Resources for the Future.

KECK, M. and SIKKINK, K. 1998. *Activists beyond Borders: Advocacy Networks in International Politics*. Ithaca, NY: Cornell University Press.

KEOHANE, R. O. 1984. *After Hegemony*. Princeton, NJ: Princeton University Press.

—— 2001. Governance in a partially globalized world. *American Political Science Review*, 95: 1–14.

KEY, V. O., JR. 1942. *Politics, Parties and Pressure Groups*. New York: Crowell.

—— 1950. *Southern Politics in State and Nation*. New York: Knopf.

—— 1954. *A Primer of Statistics for Political Scientists*. New York: Crowell.

—— 1966. *The Responsible Electorate: Rationality in Presidential Voting, 1936–1960*. Cambridge, Mass.: Harvard University Press.

KING, G., KEOHANE, R., and VERBA, S. 1994. *Designing Social Inquiry*. Princeton, NJ: Princeton University Press.

KITCHER, P. 1981. Explanatory unification. *Philosophy of Science*, 48: 507–31.

KLINGEMANN, H.-D. (ed.) 2007. *The State of Political Science in Western Europe*. Opladen: Barbara Budrich.

—— KULESZA, E., and LEGUTKE, A. (eds.) 2002. *The State of Political Science in Central and Eastern Europe*. Berlin: Edition Sigma.

KNIGHT, J. 1992. *Political Institutions and Social Conflict*. Cambridge: Cambridge University Press.

KREHBIEL, K. 1998. *Pivotal Politics: A Theory of US Lawmaking*. Chicago: University of Chicago Press.

KUHN, T. 1962. *The Structure of Scientific Revolutions*. Chicago: University of Chicago Press.

KYMLICKA, W. 1995. *Multicultural Citizenship*. Oxford: Clarendon Press.

LACLAU, E. and MOUFFE, C. 1985. *Hegemony and Socialist Strategy*. London: Verso.

LAITIN, D. D. 2003. The Perestroikan challenge to social science. *Politics and Society*, 31: 163–84.

—— and WEINGAST, B. R. 2006. An equilibrium alternative to the study of culture. *The Good Society*, 15: 15–20.

LAKATOS, I. and MUSGRAVE, A. (eds.) 1970. *Criticism and the Growth of Knowledge*. Cambridge: Cambridge University Press.

LAMONT, M. 1987. How to become a dominant French philosopher: the case of Jacques Derrida. *American Journal of Sociology*, 93: 584–622.

LANE, R. E. 1962. *Political Ideology*. Glencoe, Ill.: Free Press.

LASSWELL, H. D. 1950. *Politics: Who Gets What, When, How?* New York: P. Smith.

LAUMANN, E. O. and KNOKE, D. 1987. *The Organizational State*. Madison: University of Wisconsin Press.

—— and. PAPPI, F. U. 1976. *Networks of Collective Action*. New York: Academic Press.

LAZARSFELD, P. F., BERELSON, B. R., and GAUDET, H. 1944. *The People's Choice*. New York: Columbia University Press.

LECA, J. and GRAWITZ, M. (eds.) 1985. *Traité de Science Politique*, 4 vols. Paris: Presses Universitaires de France.

LEHMBRUCH, G. 1984. Concertation and the structure of corporatist networks. Pp. 60–80 in *Order and Conflict in Contemporary Capitalism*, ed. J. H. Goldthorpe. Oxford: Clarendon Press.

LEVY, J. S. 2008. Counterfactuals and case studies. Pp. 627–44 in Box-Steffensmeier, Brady, and Collier 2008.

LIJPHART, A. 1968/1975. *The Politics of Accommodation: Pluralism and Democracy in the Netherlands*, 2nd edn. Berkeley: University of California Press.

—— 1999. *Patterns of Democracy*. New Haven, Conn.: Yale University Press.

LINDBLOM, C. E. 1965. *The Intelligence of Democracy*. New York: Free Press.

—— 1977. *Politics and Markets*. New York: Basic.

LINDZEY, G. (ed.) 1954. *Handbook of Social Psychology*. Cambridge, Mass.: Addison-Wesley.

LIPSET, S. M. 1960. *Political Man*. New York: Doubleday.

—— LAZARSFELD, P. F., BARTON, A. H., and LINZ, J. J. 1954. The psychology of voting: an analysis of political behavior. Pp. 1124–75 in Lindzey 1954.

—— and ROKKAN, S. (eds.) 1967. *Party Systems and Voter Alignments*. New York: Free Press.

LIPSKY, M. 1980. *Street Level Bureaucracy*. New York: Russell Sage.

LOWI, T. J. 1964. American business, public policy, case-studies and political theory. *World Politics*, 16: 676–715.

—— 1973. The politicization of political science. *American Politics Quarterly*, 1: 43–71.

LUCE, R. D. and RAIFFA, H. 1957. *Games and Decisions*. New York: Wiley.

LUKES, S. 1974/2005. *Power: A Radical View*, 2nd edn. London: Palgrave Macmillan.

LYND, R. S. and LYND, H. M. 1929. *Middletown*. New York: Houghton, Brace.

McADAM, D., TARROW, S., and TILLY, C. 2001. *Dynamics of Contention*. Cambridge: Cambridge University Press.

McCLOSKEY, D. 2006. *The Bourgeois Virtues: Ethics for an Age of Commerce*. Chicago: University of Chicago Press.

McCOY, C. A. and PLAYFORD, J. (eds.) 1968. *Apolitical Politics: A Critique of Behavioralism*. New York: Crowell.

McELREATH, R. and BOYD, R. 2007. *Mathematical Models of Social Evolution*. Chicago: University of Chicago Press.

MACKAY, C. 1841/1980. *Extraordinary Popular Delusions and the Madness of Crowds*. New York: Bonanza Books.

MACKENZIE, W. J. M. 1967. *Politics and Social Science*. Harmondsworth: Penguin.

MACPHERSON, C. B. 1954. World trends in political science research. *American Political Science Review*, 48: 427–49.

—— 1977. *The Life and Times of Liberal Democracy*. Oxford: Clarendon Press.

MAJONE, G. 1989. *Evidence, Argument and Persuasion in the Policy Process*. New Haven, Conn.: Yale University Press

—— and QUADE, E. S. (eds.) 1980. *Pitfalls of Analysis*. Chichester: Wiley, for International Institute for Applied Systems Analysis.

MALINOWSKI, B. 1936/1976. Functional anthropology. Pp. 511–24 in *Sociological Theory: A Book of Readings*, 4th edn., ed. L. A. Coser and B. Rosenberg. New York: Macmillan. Originally published as "Anthropology," *Encyclopedia Britannica*, first supplementary volume, 1936.

MARCH, J. G. 1962. Some recent substantive and methodological developments in the theory of organizational decision-making. Pp. 191–208 in *Essays on the Behavioral Study of Politics*, ed. A. Ranney. Urbana: University of Illinois Press.

—— 1996. Continuity and change in theories of organizational action. *Administrative Science Quarterly*, 41: 278–87.

—— and OLSEN, J. P. 1984. The new institutionalism: organizational factors in political life. *American Political Science Review*, 78: 734–49.

—— —— 1989. *Rediscovering Institutions*. New York: Free Press.

—— and SIMON, H. A. 1958. *Organizations*. New York: Wiley.

MARSHALL, G. 1990. *In Praise of Sociology*. London: Unwin Hyman.

MARX, K. 1845/1972. Theses on Feuerbach. Pp. 107–9 in *The Marx–Engels Reader*, ed. R. C. Tucker. New York: Norton.

MASTERS, R. D. 1989. *The Nature of Politics*. New Haven, Conn.: Yale University Press.

MASUOKA, N., GROFMAN, B., and FELD, S. 2007. The Political Science 400: a 20-year update. *PS: Political Science and Politics*, 40: 133–45.

MATTHEWS, D. R. 1959. The folkways of the United States Senate. *American Political Science Review*, 53: 1064–89.

MAYHEW, D. R. 1974. *Congress: The Electoral Connection*. New Haven, Conn.: Yale University Press.

MAYNARD SMITH, J. 1982. *Evolution and the Theory of Games*. Cambridge: Cambridge University Press.

MEADOWS, D. H., MEADOWS, D. L., RANDERS, J., and BEHRENS, W. W. III. 1972. *The Limits to Growth*. London: Earth Island.

MERRIAM, C. E. 1921. The present state of the study of politics. *American Political Science Review*, 15: 173–85.

—— and GOSNELL, H. F. 1924. *Non-voting*. Chicago: University of Chicago Press.

MERTON, R. K. 1965. *On the Shoulders of Giants*. Chicago: University of Chicago Press.

—— 1968. *Social Theory and Social Structure*, 3rd edn. New York: Free Press.

—— 1973. *The Sociology of Science*, ed. N. W. Storer. Chicago: University of Chicago Press.

MILLER, W. E. 1996. Political behavior, old and new. Pp. 294–305 in Goodin and Klingemann 1996a.

MILLS, C. W. 1956. *The Power Elite*. Oxford: Oxford University Press.

MILNER, H. V. 1998. Rationalizing politics: the emerging synthesis of international, American, and comparative politics. *International Organization*, 52: 759–86.

MITCHELL, J. C. 1974. Social networks. *Annual Review of Anthropology*, 3: S279–93.

MONROE, K. R. (ed.) 2005. *Perestroika! The Raucous Rebellion in Political Science*. New Haven, Conn.: Yale University Press.

MOON, J. D. 1975. The logic of political inquiry: a synthesis of opposed perspectives. Pp. 131–228 in Greenstein and Polsby 1975, vol. 1.

Moore, B., Jr. 1966. *The Social Origins of Dictatorship and Democracy*. Boston: Beacon.

—— 1970. *Reflections on the Causes of Human Misery*. Boston: Beacon.

Moran, M. 2006. Interdisciplinarity and political science. *Politics*, 26: 73–83.

—— Rein, M., and Goodin, R. E. (eds.) 2006. *Oxford Handbook of Public Policy*. Oxford: Oxford University Press.

Moravcsik, A. 1998. *The Choice for Europe*. Ithaca, NY: Cornell University Press.

Morgenstern, O. 1972. Thirteen critical points in contemporary economic theory. *Journal of Economic Literature*, 10: 1163–89.

Morgenthau, H. J. 1948/1973. *Politics among Nations*, 5th edn. New York: Knopf.

Nelson, R. R. 1994. Evolutionary theorizing about economic change. Pp. 108–36 in *Handbook of Economic Sociology*, ed. N. J. Smelser and R. Swedberg. Princeton, NJ: Princeton University Press.

—— and Winter, S. G. 1982. *An Evolutionary Theory of Economic Change*. Cambridge, Mass.: Harvard University Press.

Neustadt, R. E. 1960. *Presidential Power*. New York: Wiley.

—— 1990. *Presidential Power and the Modern Presidency*. New York: Free Press.

—— 2000. *Preparing to be President: The Memos of Richard E. Neustadt*, ed. C. O. Jones. Washington, DC: American Enterprise Institute, for Public Policy Research.

Newton, K. 1991. The European Consortium for Political Research. *European Journal of Political Research*, 20: 445–58.

—— and Vallès, J. M. (eds.) 1991. *Political Science in Western Europe, 1960–1990*. Special issue of *European Journal of Political Research*, 20: 225–466.

Nowak, M. A. 2006. *Evolutionary Dynamics*. Cambridge, Mass.: Harvard University Press.

Nozick, R. 1974. *Anarchy, State and Utopia*. Oxford: Blackwell.

Offe, C. 2003. The European model of "social" capitalism: can it survive European integration? *Journal of Political Philosophy*, 11: 437–69.

—— 2006. Political institutions and social power: conceptual explorations. Pp. 9–31 in *Rethinking Political Institutions: The Art of the State*, ed. I. Shapiro, S. Skowronek, and D. Galvin. New York: New York University Press.

Olsen, J. P. 2007. *Europe in Search of Political Order*. Oxford: Oxford University Press.

—— 2009. Change and continuity: an institutional approach to institutions of democratic government. *European Journal of Political Science*, 1.

Olson, M., Jr. 1965. *The Logic of Collective Action*. Cambridge, Mass.: Harvard University Press.

—— 1982. *The Rise and Decline of Nations*. New Haven, Conn.: Yale University Press.

Orren, K. 1991. *Belated Feudalism*. Cambridge: Cambridge University Press.

—— and Skowronek, S. 2004. *The Search for American Political Development*. New York: Cambridge University Press.

Ostrom, E. 1990. *Governing the Commons: The Evolution of Institutions for Collective Action*. New York: Cambridge University Press.

Parsons, T. 1951. *The Social System*. New York: Free Press.

Parsons, T. 1968. Professions. Volume 12, pp. 536–47 in *International Encyclopedia of the Social Sciences*, ed. D. L. Sills. London: Macmillan.

Pateman, C. 1970. *Participation and Democratic Theory*. Cambridge: Cambridge University Press.

—— 1988. *The Sexual Contract*. Oxford: Polity.

Peterson, P. E. 1981. *City Limits*. Chicago: University of Chicago Press.

Pierson, P. 2000. Increasing returns, path dependence and the study of politics. *American Political Science Review*, 94: 251–68.

PIERSON, P. 2004. *Politics in Time*. Princeton, NJ: Princeton University Press.

PIVEN, F. F. and CLOWARD, R. A. 1971. *Regulating the Poor*. New York: Pantheon.

——1979. *Poor People's Movements: Why They Succeed, How They Fail*. New York: Vintage.

POGGE, T. 2002. *World Poverty and Human Rights*. Cambridge: Polity.

POLSBY, N. W. 1980. *Community Power and Political Theory*, 2nd edn. New Haven, Conn.: Yale University Press.

POPKIN, S. L. 1991. *The Reasoning Voter*. Chicago: University of Chicago Press.

POPPER, K. 1964. *The Poverty of Historicism*, 3rd edn. New York: Harper and Row; originally published 1957.

PROULX, S. R., MORMISLOW, D. E. L., and PHILLIPS, P. C. 2005. Network thinking in ecology and evolution. *TRENDS in Ecology and Evolution*, 20: 345–53.

PRZEWORSKI, A. and SPRAGUE, J. 1986. *Paper Stones: A History of Electoral Socialism*. Chicago: University of Chicago Press.

PUTNAM, R. D. 1993. *Making Democracy Work*. Princeton, NJ: Princeton University Press.

——2000. *Bowling Alone*. New York: Simon and Schuster.

QUERMONNE, J.-L. (ed.) 1996. *La Science politique en Europe: formation, coopération, perspectives*. Rapport Final, Projet réalisé avec le soutien de la Commission Européenne (DG XII). Paris: Institut d'Études Politiques de Paris.

QUINE, W. v. O. 1961. *From a Logical Point of View*, 2nd edn. New York: Harper and Row.

RADCLIFFE-BROWN, A. R. 1935. On the concept of function in social science. *American Anthropologist*, 37: 394–402.

——1949. Functionalism: a protest. *American Anthropologist*, 51: 320–2.

RAWLS, J. 1971. *A Theory of Justice*. Cambridge, Mass.: Harvard University Press; rev. edn. 1999.

REUS-SMIT, C. 1999. *The Moral Purpose of the State*. Princeton, NJ: Princeton University Press.

——and SNIDAL, D. (eds.) 2008. *Oxford Handbook of International Relations*. Oxford: Oxford University Press.

RHODES, R. A. W. 1988. *Beyond Westminster and Whitehall*. London: Unwin Hyman.

——2006. Policy network analysis. Pp. 425–47 in Moran, Rein, and Goodin 2006.

——BINDER, S. A., and ROCKMAN, B. A. (eds.) 2006. *Oxford Handbook of Political Institutions*. Oxford: Oxford University Press.

RIKER, W. H. 1962. *Theory of Political Coalitions*. New Haven, Conn.: Yale University Press.

——1982. *Liberalism against Populism: A Confrontation between the Theory of Democracy and the Theory of Social Choice*. San Francisco: W. Freeman.

——1986. *The Art of Political Manipulation*. New Haven, Conn.: Yale University Press.

RISSE, T., ROPP, S. C., and SIKKINK, K. (eds.) 1999. *The Power of Human Rights: International Norms and Domestic Change*. Cambridge: Cambridge University Press.

ROGOWSKI, R. 1989. *Commerce and Coalitions*. Princeton, NJ: Princeton University Press.

ROKKAN, S. (ed.) 1979. *A Quarter Century of International Social Science*. New Delhi: Concept.

ROYAL SWEDISH ACADEMY OF SCIENCES 2005. The Bank of Sweden Prize in Economic Sciences in Memory of Alfred Nobel-Laureates. Available at: <http://nobelprize.org/economics/laureates> (accessed Jan. 3, 2008).

RUDOLPH, S. H. 2002. In defense of diverse forms of knowledge. *PS: Political Science and Politics*, 35: 193–5.

——2005. The imperialism of categories: situating knowledges in a globalizing world. *Perspectives on Politics*, 3: 5–14.

RUSSETT, B. M. and ONEAL, J. 2001. *Triangulating Peace: Democracy, Interdependence and International Organizations*. New York: Norton.

SAMUELSON, L. 1997. *Evolutionary Games and Equilibrium Selection*. Cambridge, Mass.: MIT Press.

SAXONHOUSE, A. W. 2006. Exile and re-entry: political theory yesterday and tomorrow. Pp. 844–58 in Dryzek, Honig, and Phillips 2006.

SCHAAR, J. and WOLIN, S. 1963. Essays on the scientific study of politics: a critique. *American Political Science Review*, 57: 125–50.

SCHATTSCHNEIDER, E. E. 1960. *The Semi-sovereign People*. New York: Holt, Rinehart and Winston.

SCHELLING, T. C. 1960. *The Strategy of Conflict*. Cambridge, Mass.: Harvard University Press.

—— 1978. *Micromotives and Macrobehavior*. New York: Norton.

SCHMIDT, V. A. 2008. Discursive institutionalism: the explanatory power of ideas and discourse. *Annual Reviews of Political Science*, 11: 303–26.

SCHMITTER, P. C. 2002. Seven (disputable) theses concerning the future of "trans-Atlanticized" or "globalized" political science. *European Political Science*, 1: 23–40.

SCHRAM, S. 2003. Return to politics: Perestroika and postparadigmatic political science. *Political Theory*, 31: 835–51.

SCHULTZE, C. 1992. *Memos to the President: A Guide through Macroeconmics for the Busy Policymaker*. Washington, DC: Brookings Institution.

SCHUMPETER, J. A. 1943. *Capitalism, Socialism, and Democracy*. London: Allen and Unwin.

SCIULLI, D. 2007. Professions before professionalism. *Archives européennes de sociologie*, 48: 121–47.

SCOTT, J. C. 1986. *Weapons of the Weak: Everyday Forms of Peasant Resistance*. New Haven, Conn.: Yale University Press.

—— 1991. *Social Network Analysis: A Handbook*. London: Sage.

—— 1997. *Seeing like a State*. New Haven, Conn.: Yale University Press.

SEARS, D. O., HUDDY, L., and JERVIS, R. (eds.) 2003. *Oxford Handbook of Political Psychology*. Oxford: Oxford University Press.

SEGAL, J. A. and SPAETH, H. J. 1993. *The Supreme Court and the Attitudinal Model*. Cambridge: Cambridge University Press.

SEIDELMAN, R. 1993. Political scientists, disenchanted realists and disappearing democrats. Pp. 311–25 in Farr and Seidelman 1993.

—— with HARPHAM, E. J. 1985. *Disenchanged Realists: Political Science and the American Crisis, 1884-1984*. Albany: State University of New York Press.

SELTEN, R. 1991. Evolution, learning and economic behavior. *Games and Economic Behavior*, 3: 3–24.

SELZNICK, P. 1949. *TVA and the Grassroots: A Study of Politics and Organization*. Los Angeles: University of California Press.

SEN, A. K. 1981. *Poverty and Famines*. Oxford: Clarendon Press.

SHAPIRO, I. 1999. Enough of deliberation: politics is about interests and power. Pp. 28–38 in *Deliberative Politics*, ed. S. Macedo. New York: Oxford University Press.

SHAPIRO, I. 2005. *The Flight from Reality in the Human Sciences*. Princeton, NJ: Princeton University Press.

SHAW, G. B. 1934. *The Apple Cart*. Pp. 1009–43 in *The Complete Plays of Bernard Shaw*. London: Odhams Press.

SHILS, E. and YOUNG, M. 1953. The meaning of the coronation. *Sociological Review*, 1: 63–81.

SHUBIK, M. 1971*a*. Games of status. *Behavioral Science*, 16: 117–29.

—— 1971*b*. Modelling on a grand scale. *Science*, 174: 1014–15.

SIGELMAN, L. 2006*a*. Introduction to the centennial issue. *American Political Science Review*, 100: v–xvi.

SIGELMAN, L. 2006b. The coevolution of American political science and the *American Political Science Review. American Political Science Review*, 100: 463–78.

—— et al. 2006. Top twenty commentaries. *American Political Science Review*, 100: 667–88.

SIMON, H. A. 1947. *Administrative Behavior.* New York: Free Press.

SKINNER, Q. 2002. *Visions of Politics.* Cambridge: Cambridge University Press.

SKOCPOL, T. 1979. *States and Social Revolutions.* Cambridge: Cambridge University Press.

—— 1992. *Protecting Soldiers and Mothers.* Cambridge, Mass.: Harvard University Press.

SKOWRONEK, S. 1993/1997. *The Politics Presidents Make*, 2nd edn. Cambridge, Mass.: Harvard University Press.

SKYRMS, B. 1996. *Evolution of the Social Contract.* Cambridge: Cambridge University Press.

SLAUGHTER, A.-M. 2003. Everyday global governance. *Daedalus*, 132: 83–91.

SNIDERMAN, P. M., BRODY, R. A., and TETLOCK, P. E. 1991. *Reasoning and Choice: Explorations in Political Psychology.* Cambridge: Cambridge University Press.

SOBER, E. 1994. Models of cultural evolution. Pp. 477–92 in *Conceptual Issues in Evolutionary Biology*, 2nd edn, ed. E. Sober. Cambridge, Mass.: MIT Press.

SOMIT, A. and PETERSON, S. A. 2001. Biopolitics in the year 2000. Pp. 181–202 in *Evolutionary Approaches to the Behavioral Sciences*, ed. S. A. Peterson and A. Somit. Amsterdam: JAI.

SPRUYT, H. 1994. *The Sovereign State and its Competitors.* Princeton, NJ: Princeton University Press.

STIGLITZ, J. E. 1987. The causes and consequences of the dependence of quality on price. *Journal of Economic Literature*, 25: 1–48.

STINCHCOMBE, A. 1982. Should sociologists forget their fathers and mothers? *American Sociologist*, 17: 2–11.

STORING, H. J. (ed.) 1962. *Essays on the Scientific Study of Politics.* New York: Holt, Rinehart and Winston.

TAYLOR, C. 1985. *Philosophy and the Human Sciences.* Cambridge: Cambridge University Press.

TETLOCK, P., LEBOW, R. N., and PARKER, N. G. (eds.) 2006. *Unmaking the West: "What If?" Scenarios that Rewrite World History.* Ann Arbor: University of Michigan Press.

THALER, R. H. 2000. From Homo Economicus to Homo Sapiens. *Journal of Economic Perspectives*, 14: 133–41.

TINGSTEN, H. 1937. *Political Behavior.* London: P. S. King.

TRUMAN, D. 1971. *The Governmental Process*, 2nd edn. New York: Knopf.

TSEBELIS, G. 2002. *Veto Players: How Political Institutions Work.* Princeton, NJ: Princeton University Press.

US DHEW (United States, Department of Health, Education and Welfare) 1978. *Social Security Programs Throughout the World 1977.* Social Security Administration, Office of Research and Statistics, Research Report no. 50. Washington, DC: Government Printing Office.

USEEM, M. 1979. The social organization of the American business elite and participation of corporation directors in the governance of American institutions. *American Sociological Review*, 44: 553–72.

—— 1984. *The Inner Circle: Large Corporations and the Rise of Political Activity in the US and UK.* New York: Oxford University Press.

USLANER, E. M. 1991. Comity in context. *British Journal of Political Science*, 21: 45–78.

VANDENBROUCKE, F. 2002. Foreword. In T. Atkinson, B. Cantillion, E. Marlier, and B. Nolan, *Social Indicators: The EU and Social Inclusion.* Oxford: Oxford University Press.

VAN KERSBERGEN, K. and VERBEEK, B. 2004. Subsidiarity as a principle of governance in the European Union. *Comparative European Politics*, 2: 142–62.

VERBA, S. and NIE, N. H. 1972. *Participation in America: Political Democracy and Social Equality.* New York: Harper and Row.

WAGNER, P. 2008. *Modernity as Experience and Interpretation.* Cambridge: Polity.

—— WITTROCK, B., and WHITLEY, R. 1991. *Discourses on Society: The Shaping of the Social Science Disciplines.* Dordrecht: Kluwer Academic.

WAHLKE, J. C. 1979. Pre-behavioralism in political science. *American Political Science Review,* 73: 9–31.

—— 1986. What does the biopolitical approach offer political science? *PS: Political Science and Politics,* 19: 871–2.

WALLERSTEIN, I. 1998. *Opening up the Social Sciences.* Report of the Gulbenkian Commission on the restructuring of the Social Sciences. Stanford, Calif.: Stanford University Press.

WALTZ, K. N. 1959. *Man, the State, and War: A Theoretical Analysis.* New York: Columbia University Press.

—— 1979. *Theory of International Politics.* New York: McGraw-Hill.

WASSERMAN, S. and FAUST, K. 1994. *Social Network Analysis: Methods and Applications.* Cambridge: Cambridge University Press.

WEINGAST, B. R. and WITTMAN, D. A. (eds.) 2006. *Oxford Handbook of Political Economy.* Oxford: Oxford University Press.

WENDT, A. E. 1987. The agent-structure problem in international relations theory. *International Organization,* 41: 335–70.

—— 1999. *Social Theory of International Politics.* Cambridge: Cambridge University Press.

WHITTINGTON, K. E., KELEMEN, R. D., and CALDEIRA, G. A. (eds.) 2008. *Oxford Handbook of Law and Politics.* Oxford: Oxford University Press.

WILDAVSKY, A. 1964. *Politics of the Budgetary Process.* Boston: Little, Brown.

—— 1979. *Speaking Truth to Power: The Art and Craft of Policy Analysis.* Boston: Little, Brown.

WILSON, J. Q. 1980. *The Politics of Regulation.* New York: Basic Books.

WINCH, P. 1958. *The Idea of a Social Science.* London: Routledge and Kegan Paul.

WITT, U. (ed.) 1993. *Evolutionary Economics.* Aldershot: Elgar.

WOLIN, S. 1960. *Politics and Vision.* Boston: Little, Brown. Expanded edn. Princeton, NJ: Princeton University Press, 2006.

—— 1969. Political theory as a vocation. *American Political Science Review,* 63: 1062–82.

YOUNG, I. M. 1990. *Justice and the Politics of Difference.* Princeton, NJ: Princeton University Press.

ZALLER, J. R. 1992. *The Nature and Origins of Mass Public Opinion.* New York: Cambridge University Press.

PART II

POLITICAL
THEORY

PART II

POLITICAL
THEORY

CHAPTER 2

OVERVIEW OF POLITICAL THEORY

JOHN S. DRYZEK

BONNIE HONIG

ANNE PHILLIPS

"What's your line of business, then?"
"I'm a scholar of the Enlightenment," said Nicholas.
"Oh Lord!" the young man said. "Another producer of useless graduates!"
Nicholas felt despondent.

(Lukes 1995, 199)

IN *The Curious Enlightenment of Professor Caritat*—Steven Lukes's fictionalized round-up of contemporary political theory—the hapless professor has been kidnapped by the resistance movement and sent off to search for grounds for optimism. In Utilitaria, he is asked to give a lecture on "Breaking Free from the Past;" in Communitaria, on "Why the Enlightenment Project Had to Fail." Neither topic is much to his taste, but it is only when he reaches Libertaria (not, as one of its gloomy inhabitants tells him, a good place to be unlucky, unemployed, or employed by the state) that he is made to recognize the limited purchase of his academic expertise. At the end of the book, the professor still has not found the mythical land of Egalitaria. But he has derived one important lesson from his adventures: In the pursuit of any one ideal, it is disastrous to lose sight of all the others.

The moral of that story is the need to accept both normative and methodological pluralism. As Lukes suggests, political theory has often been a battleground where competing theorists pursue their mutually exclusive positions, either ignoring or denying the insights they might derive from considering alternative approaches. Much of that mutual indifference and intolerance remains—political theorists are no more ideal citizens than anyone else—but there is also considerable evidence of pluralism and a marked capacity for borrowing from other traditions. We argue that this pluralism is a key feature and major strength of the field.

1 WHAT IS POLITICAL THEORY?

Political theory is an interdisciplinary endeavor whose center of gravity lies at the humanities end of the happily still undisciplined discipline of political science. Its traditions, approaches, and styles vary, but the field is united by a commitment to theorize, critique, and diagnose the norms, practices, and organization of political action in the past and present, in our own places and elsewhere. Across what sometimes seem chasms of difference, political theorists share a concern with the demands of justice and how to fulfill them, the presuppositions and promise of democracy, the divide between secular and religious ways of life, and the nature and identity of public goods, among many other topics.

Political theorists also share a commitment to the humanistic study of politics (although with considerable disagreement over what that means), and a skepticism towards the hegemony sometimes sought by our more self-consciously "scientific" colleagues. In recent years, and especially in the USA, the study of politics has become increasingly formal and quantitative. Indeed, there are those for whom political theory, properly understood, would be formal theory geared solely towards the *explanation* of political phenomena, where explanation is modeled on the natural sciences and takes the form of seeking patterns and offering causal explanations for events in the human world. Such approaches have been challenged—most recently by the Perestroika movement (Monroe 2005)—on behalf of more qualitative and interpretative approaches. Political theory is located at one remove from this quantitative vs. qualitative debate, sitting somewhere between the distanced universals of normative philosophy and the empirical world of politics.

For a long time, the challenge for the identity of political theory has been how to position itself productively in three sorts of location: in relation to the academic disciplines of political science, history, and philosophy; between the world of politics and the more abstract, ruminative register of theory; between canonical political and the newer resources (such as feminist and critical theory, discourse analyand film theory, popular and political culture, mass media studies, neuro-vironmental studies, behavioral science, and economics) on which political theorists increasingly draw. Political theorists engage with empirical work in politics, economics, sociology, and law to inform their reflections, and there have been plenty of productive associations between those who call themselves political scientists and those who call themselves political theorists. The connection to law is strongest when it comes to constitutional law and its normative foundations (for example, Sunstein 1993; Tully 1995; 2002).

Most of political theory has an irreducibly normative component—regardless of whether the theory is systematic or diagnostic in its approach, textual or cultural in its focus, analytic, critical, genealogical, or deconstructive in its method, ideal or piecemeal in its procedures, socialist, liberal, or conservative in its politics. The field welcomes all these approaches. It has a core canon, often referred to as Plato to NATO, although the canon is itself unstable, with the rediscovery of figures such as Sophocles, Thucydides, Baruch Spinoza, and Mary Wollstonecraft, previously treated as marginal, and the addition of new icons such as Hannah Arendt, John Rawls, Michel Foucault, and Jürgen Habermas. Moreover, the subject matter of political theory has always extended beyond this canon and its interpretations, as theorists bring their analytic tools to bear on novels, film, and other cultural artefacts, and on developments in other social sciences and even in natural science.

Political theory is an unapologetically mongrel sub-discipline, with no dominant methodology or approach. When asked to describe themselves, theorists will sometimes employ the shorthand of a key formative influence—as in "I'm a Deleuzean," or Rawlsian, or Habermasian, or Arendtian—although it is probably more common to be labeled in this way by others than to claim the description oneself. In contrast, however, to some neighboring producers of knowledge, political theorists do not readily position themselves by reference to three or four dominant schools that define their field. There is, for example, no parallel to the division between realists, liberals, and constructivists, recently joined by neoconservatives, that defines international relations theory. And there is certainly nothing like the old Marx–Weber–Durkheim triad that was the staple of courses in sociological theory up to the 1970s.

Because of this, political theory can sometimes seem to lack a core identity. Some practitioners seek to rectify the perceived lack, either by putting political theory back into what is said to be its proper role as arbiter of universal questions and explorer of timeless texts, or by returning the focus of political theory to history. The majority, however, have a strong sense of their vocation. Many see the internally riven and uncertain character of the field as reflective of the internally riven and uncertain character of the political world in which we live, bringing with it all the challenges and promises of that condition. In the last two decades of the twentieth century, liberal, critical, and post-structuralist theorists have (in their very different ways) responded to the breakdown of old assumptions about the unitary nature of nation-state identities. They have rethought the presuppositions and meanings of identity, often rejecting unitary conceptions and moving towards more pluralistic, diverse, or agonistic conceptions in their place. These reflections have had an impact on the field's own self-perception and understanding. Happily for political theory, the process has coincided with a movement within the academy to reconceive knowledge as more fundamentally *inter*disciplinary. This reconsideration of the function and role of the boundaries of the academic disciplines may help others, as well as political theorists, to see the field's pluralism as a virtue and a strength, rather than a weakness in need of rectification.

1.1 Relationship with Political Science

Political theory's relationship to the discipline of political science has not always been a happy one. Since the founding of the discipline in the late nineteenth century, there have been periodic proclamations of its newly scientific character. The "soft" other for the new science has sometimes been journalism, sometimes historical narrative, sometimes case-study methods. It has also, very often, been political theory. Beginning in the 1950s, behavioral revolutionaries tried to purge the ranks of theorists—and had some success at this in one or two large Midwestern departments of political science in the USA. The later impact of rational choice theory encouraged others, like William Riker (1982a, 753), to reject "belles letters, criticism, and philosophic speculation" along with "phenomenology and hermeneutics." For those driven by their scientific aspirations, it has always been important to distinguish the "true" scientific study of politics from more humanistic approaches—and political theory has sometimes borne the brunt of this.

Political theorists have noted, in response, that science and objectivity are steeped in a normativity that the self-proclaimed scientists wrongly disavow; and theorists have not been inclined to take the description of political "science" at face value. They have challenged the idea that their own work in normative theory lacks rigor, pointing to criteria *within* political theory that differentiate more from less rigorous work. While resisting the epistemic assumptions of empiricism, many also point out that much of what passes for political theory is profoundly engaged with empirical politics: What, after all, could be more "real", vital, and important than the symbols and categories that organize our lives and the frameworks of our understanding? The French have a word to describe what results when those elected as president and prime minister are representatives of two different political parties: *cohabitation*. The word connotes, variously, cooperation, toleration, sufferance, antagonism, and a sense of common enterprise. Cohabitation, in this sense, is a good way to cast the relationship between political theory and political science.

1.2 Relationship with History

History as a point of reference has also proven contentious, with recurrent debates about the extent to which theory is contained by its historical context and whether one can legitimately employ political principles from one era as a basis for criticizing political practice in another. When Quentin Skinner, famous for his commitment to historical contextualism, suggested that early principles of republican freedom might offer a telling alternative to the conceptions of liberty around today, he took care to distance himself from any suggestion that "intellectual historians should turn themselves into moralists" (Skinner 1998, 118). He still drew criticism for abandoning the historian's traditional caution.

In an essay published in 1989, Richard Ashcraft called upon political theorists to acknowledge the fundamentally historical character of their enterprise. While contemporary theorists recognize the "basic social/historical conditions which structure" their practice, "this recognition does not serve as a conscious guideline for their teaching and writing of political theory." Ashcraft continued: "On the contrary, political theory is taught and written about *as if* it were great philosophy rather than ideology" (Ashcraft 1989, 700). For Ashcraft, acknowledging the ideological character of political theory meant embracing its political character. The main objects of his critique were Leo Strauss and his followers, whom Ashcraft saw as seeking evidence of universally valid standards in canonical political theorists and calling on those standards to judge their works. For Straussians, the wisdom of the ancients and greats is outside history.

Ashcraft also criticized Sheldon Wolin, who shared Ashcraft's displeasure with Straussians, on the grounds of their inadequate attention to politics. Although Wolin acknowledged the historicity of the texts he had examined in his seminal *Politics and Vision* (1960), Ashcraft claimed that Wolin resisted the "wholesale transformation" that would result, in both his view and Ashcraft's, from putting that historicity at the center of his interpretative practice. Wolin is famous for championing what, in the style of Hannah Arendt, he termed "the political:" politics understood, not in its instrumental capacity (Harold Lasswell's (1961) "'Who gets what, when, and how'"), but rather in its orientation toward the public good coupled with a commitment to the "public happiness" of political participation. Contra Ashcraft, one might see Wolin's move to the political as a way of splitting the difference between a Straussian universalism and the thick contextualism of Ashcraft's preferred historicist approach.

"The political" is a conceptual category, itself outside of history, that rejects the idea that politics is about universal truths, while also rejecting the reduction of politics to interests. "The political" tends to connote, minimally, some form of individual or collective action that disrupts ordinary states of affairs, normal life, or routine patterns of behavior or governance. There are diverse conceptions of this notion. To take three as exemplary: The political takes its meaning from its figuration in Wolin's work by contrast primarily with statism, constitutionalism, and political apathy; in Arendt's work by contrast with private or natural spheres of human behavior; and in Rancière's (1999) work by contrast with the "police."

1.3 Relationship with Philosophy

The most unhistorical influence on political theory in recent decades has been John Rawls, whose work represents a close alliance with analytic philosophy. On one popular account, Rawls arrived from outside as political theory's foreign savior and rescued political theory from the doldrums with the publication in 1971 of *A Theory of Justice* (see Arneson, this volume). Rawls's book was an ambitious, normative, and systematic investigation of what political, economic, and social justice should look like in contemporary democracies. With the distancing mechanisms of a veil of ignorance and hypothetical social contract, Rawls followed Kant in looking to reason to adjudicate what he saw as the fundamental question of politics: the conflict between liberty and equality. Writing from within the discipline of philosophy, he returned political theory to one of its grand styles (Tocqueville's two-volume *Democracy in America*, also written by an outsider, would represent another). Much subsequent work on questions of justice and equality has continued in this vein, and while those who have followed Rawls have not necessarily shared his conclusions, they have often employed similar mind experiments to arrive at the appropriate relationship between equality and choice. The clamshell auction imagined by Ronald Dworkin (1981), where all the society's resources are up for sale and the participants employ their clamshells to bid for what best suits their own projects in life, is another classic illustration. Starting with what seems the remotest of scenarios, Dworkin claims to arrive at very specific recommendations for the contemporary welfare state.

One strand of current debates in political theory revolves around the relationship between the more abstracted or hypothetical register of analytic philosophy and approaches that stress the specificities of historical or contemporary contexts. Those working in close association with the traditions of analytic philosophy—and often preferring to call themselves political philosophers—have generated some of the most interesting and innovative work in recent decades. But they have also been repeatedly challenged. Communitarians and post-structuralists claim that the unencumbered individual of Rawlsian liberalism is not neutral but an ideological premiss with significant, unacknowledged political effects on its theoretical conclusions (Sandel 1982; Honig 1993). Feminists criticize the analytic abstraction from bodily difference as a move that reinforces heteronormative assumptions and gender inequalities (Okin 1989; Pateman 1988; Zerilli 2006). As we indicate later, analytic liberalism has made some considerable concessions in this regard. In *Political Liberalism*, for example, Rawls no longer represents his theory of justice as addressing what is right for all societies at all times, but is careful to present his arguments as reflecting the intuitions of contemporary liberal and pluralistic societies.

1.4 Relationship with "Real World" Politics

The way political theory positions itself in relation to political science, history, and philosophy can be read in part as reflections on the meaning of the political. It can also be read as reflections on the nature of theory, and what can—or cannot—be brought into existence through theoretical work. The possibilities are bounded on one side by utopianism. Political theorists have seemed at their most vulnerable to criticism by political scientists or economists when their normative explorations generate conclusions that cannot plausibly be implemented: principles of living, perhaps, that invoke the practices of small-scale face-to-face societies; or principles of distribution that ignore the implosion of Communism or the seemingly irresistible global spread of consumerist ideas (see Dunn 2000, for one such warning). There is an important strand in political theory that relishes the utopian label, regarding this as evidence of the capacity to think beyond current confines, the political theorist's version of blue-sky science. Ever since Aristotle, however, this has been challenged by an insistence on working within the parameters of the possible, an insistence often called "sober" by those who favor it. At issue here is not the status of political theory in relation to political science, but how theory engages with developments in the political world.

Some see it as failing to do so. John Gunnell (1986) has represented political theory as alienated from politics, while Jeffrey Isaac (1995) argues that a reader of political theory journals in the mid-1990s would have had no idea that the Berlin Wall had fallen. Against this, one could cite a flurry of studies employing empirical results to shed light on the real-world prospects for the kind of deliberative democracy currently advocated by democratic theorists (see for example the 2005 double issue of *Acta Politica*); or testing out theories of justice by reference to empirical studies of social mobility (Marshall, Swift, and Roberts 1997). Or one might take note of the rather large number of political theorists whose interest in contemporary political events such as the formation of a European identity, the new international human rights regime and the politics of immigration, the eschewal of the Geneva Conventions at the turn of the twentieth century, or the appropriate political response to natural disasters leads them to think about how to theorize these events. Concepts or figures of thought invoked here include Giorgio Agamben's (1998) "bare life" of the human being to whom anything can be done by the state, Michel Foucault's (1979) "disciplinary power" that conditions what people can think, Carl Schmitt's (1985) "state of exception" wherein the sovereign suspends the rule of law, Ronald Dworkin's (1977) superhuman judge "Hercules," Jacques Derrida's (2000) "unconditional hospitality" to the other, or Étienne Balibar's (2004) "marks of sovereignty" which signal the arrogation to themselves by political actors in civil society of rights and privileges of action historically assumed by states.

Political theorists take their cue from events around them, turning their attention to the challenges presented by ecological crisis; emergency or security politics; the impact of new technologies on the ways we think about privacy, justice, or the category of the human; the impact of new migrations on ideas of race, tolerance, and multiculturalism; the implications of growing global inequalities on the way we theorize liberty, equality, democracy, sovereignty, or hegemony. Indeed, in writing this overview of the current state of political theory, we have been struck by the strong sense of political engagement and the way this shapes the field.

1.5 Institutional Landscape

Institutionally, political theory is located in several disciplines, starting of course with political science, but continuing through philosophy and law, and including some representation in departments of history, sociology, and economics. This means that the professional associations and journals of these disciplines are hospitable (if to varying degrees) to work in political theory. Among the general political science journals, it is quite common to find political theory published in *Polity* and *Political Studies*, somewhat less so in the *American Journal of Political Science*, *British Journal of Political Science*, and *Journal of Politics*. On the face of it, the *American Political Science Review* publishes a substantial number of political theory articles, but the majority of these have been in the history of political thought, with Straussian authors especially well represented. In philosophy, *Ethics* and *Philosophy and Public Affairs* are the two high-profile journals most likely to publish political theory. Some of the more theoretically inclined law journals publish political theory, and so do some of the more politically inclined sociology journals.

Political theory's best-established journal of its own is *Political Theory*, founded in 1972. Prior to its establishment, the closest we had to a general political-theory academic periodical were two book series. The first was the sporadic *Philosophy, Politics and Society* series published by Basil Blackwell and always co-edited by Peter Laslett, beginning in 1956 and reaching its seventh volume in 2003. Far more regularly published have been the NOMOS yearbooks of the American Society for Political and Legal Philosophy, which began in 1958 and continue to this day. Recent years have seen an explosion in political theory journal titles: *History of Political Thought*; *Journal of Political Philosophy*; *The Good Society*; *Politics, Philosophy and Economics*; *Critical Review of International Social and Political Philosophy*; *European Journal of Political Theory*; *Contemporary Political Theory*; *Constellations*; and *Theory and Event* (an online journal). The *Review of Politics* has been publishing since 1939, although its coverage has been selective, with a Straussian emphasis for much of its history. Political theorists can often be found publishing in related areas such as feminism, law, international relations, or cultural studies. Journals that feature their work from these various interdisciplinary locations include *differences*; *Politics, Culture, and Society*; *Daedalus*; *Social Text*; *Logos*; *Strategies*; *Signs*; and *Millennium*. However, political theory is a field very much oriented to book publication (a fact which artificially depresses the standing of political theory journals when computed from citation indexes, for even journal articles in the field tend to cite books rather than other articles). All the major English-language academic presses publish political theory. Oxford University Press's *Oxford Political Theory* series is especially noteworthy.

Political theory is much in evidence at meetings of disciplinary associations. The Foundations of Political Theory section of the American Political Science Association is especially important, not just in organizing panels and lectures and sponsoring awards, but also in hosting what is for a couple of hours every year probably the largest number of political theorists in one room talking at once (the Foundations reception). The field also has associations of its own that sponsor conferences: the

Conference for the Study of Political Thought International, and the Association for Political Theory (both based in North America). In the UK, there is an annual Political Theory conference in Oxford; and though the European Consortium for Political Research has tended to focus more on comparative studies, it also provides an important context for workshops on political theory.

2 CONTEMPORARY THEMES AND DEVELOPMENTS

As befits a relentlessly critical field, political theory is prone to self-examination. We have already noted controversies over its relationship to various disciplinary and interdisciplinary landscapes. Occasionally the self-examination takes a morbid turn, with demise or death at issue; the most notorious example being when Laslett (1956) claimed in his introduction to the 1956 *Philosophy, Politics and Society* book series that the tradition of political theory was broken, and the practice dead. Even the field's defenders have at times detected only a faint pulse.

Concerns about the fate of theory peaked in the 1950s and 1960s with the ascendancy of behavioralism in US political science. Such worries were circumvented, but not finally ended, by the flurry of political and philosophical activity in the USA around the Berkeley Free Speech movement (with which Sheldon Wolin 1969, and John Schaar 1970, were associated), the Civil Rights movement (Arendt 1959), and protests against the Vietnam war and the US military draft (Walzer 1967; 1970). At that moment, the legitimacy of the state, the limits of obligation, the nature of justice, and the claims of conscience in politics were more than theoretical concerns. Civil disobedience was high on political theory's agenda.[1] Members of activist networks read and quoted Hannah Arendt, Herbert Marcuse, and others in support of their actions and visions of politics.

Throughout the 1960s, the struggle over the fate of theory was entwined with questions about what counted as politics and how to find a political-theoretical space between or outside liberalism and Marxism. It was against this political and theoretical background that John Rawls was developing the ideas gathered together in systematic form in *A Theory of Justice* (1971), a book devoted to the examination of themes that the turbulent 1960s had made so prominent: redistributive policies, conscientious objection, and the legitimacy of state power. Later in that decade Quentin Skinner and a new school of contextualist history of political thought (known as the Cambridge school) rose to prominence in the English-speaking world. Still other works of political theory from this period give the lie to the idea that political theory

---

[1] See notably Marcuse's "Repressive Tolerance" contribution in Wolff, Moore, and Marcuse (1965), Pitkin (1966), Dworkin (1968), the essay on "Civil Disobedience" in Arendt (1969), and Rawls (1969).

was in need of rescue or revivification. The following stand out, and in some cases remain influential: Leo Strauss's *Natural Right and History* (1953), Louis Hartz's *The Liberal Tradition in America* (1955), Karl Popper's *The Poverty of Historicism* (1957), Hannah Arendt's *The Human Condition* (1958) and *On Revolution* (1963), Sheldon Wolin's *Politics and Vision* (1960), Friedrich A. von Hayek's *The Constitution of Liberty* (1960), Michael Oakeshott's *Rationalism in Politics* (1962), James Buchanan and Gordon Tullock's *The Calculus of Consent* (1962), Judith Shklar's *Legalism* (1964), Herbert Marcuse's *One-Dimensional Man* (1964), Brian Barry's *Political Argument* (1965), and Isaiah Berlin's *Four Essays on Liberty* (1969).

2.1 Liberalism and its Critics

Looking at the field from the vantage point of the first years of the twenty-first century, there is certainly no indication of political theory failing in its vitality: This is a time of energetic and expansive debate, with new topics crowding into an already busy field. For many in political theory, including many critics of liberal theory, this pluralistic activity obscures a more important point: the dominance that has been achieved by liberalism, at least in the Anglo-American world. In its classic guise, liberalism assumes that individuals are for the most part motivated by self-interest, and regards them as the best judges of what this interest requires. In its most confident variants, it sees the material aspects of interest as best realized through exchange in a market economy, to the benefit of all. Politics enters when interests cannot be so met to mutual benefit. Politics is therefore largely about how to reconcile and aggregate individual interests, and takes place under a supposedly neutral set of constitutional rules. Given that powerful individuals organized politically into minorities or majorities can turn public power to their private benefit, checks across different centers of power are necessary, and constitutional rights are required to protect individuals against government and against one another. These rights are accompanied by obligations on the part of their holders to respect rights held by others, and duties to the government that establishes and protects rights. Liberalism so defined leaves plenty of scope for dispute concerning the boundaries of politics, political intervention in markets, political preference aggregation and conflict resolution mechanisms, and the content of rights, constitutions, obligations, and duties. There is, for example, substantial distance between the egalitarian disposition of Rawls and the ultra-individualistic libertarianism of Robert Nozick (1974).[2] Liberalism's conception of politics clearly differs, however, from the various conceptions of the political deployed by Arendt, Wolin, Rancière, and others, as well as from republican conceptions of freedom explored by Quentin Skinner (1998) or Philip Pettit (1997).

In earlier decades, liberalism had a clear comprehensive competitor in the form of Marxism, not just in the form of real-world governments claiming to be Marxist,

---

[2] Other important works in the vast liberal justice literature include Gauthier (1986), Barry (1995), and Scanlon (1998).

but also in political theory. Marxism scorned liberalism's individualist ontology, pointing instead to the centrality of social classes in political conflict. The market was seen not as a mechanism for meeting individual interests, but as a generator of oppression and inequality (as well as undeniable material progress). Marxism also rejected liberalism's static and ahistorical account of politics in favor of an analysis of history driven by material forces that determined what individuals were and could be in different historical epochs. Different versions of this were hotly debated in the 1970s, as theorists positioned themselves behind the "humanist" Marx, revealed in his earlier writings on alienation (McLellan 1970),[3] or the "Althusserian" Marx, dealing in social relations and forces of production (Althusser 1969; Althusser and Balibar 1970). Disagreements between these schools were intense, although both proclaimed the superiority of Marxist over liberal thought. In the period that followed, however, the influence of academic Marxism in the English-speaking world waned. The fortunes of Marxist theory were not helped by the demise of the Soviet bloc in 1989–91, and the determined pursuit of capitalism in China under the leadership of a nominally Marxist regime.

Questions remain about liberalism's success in defeating or replacing this rival. One way to think of subsequent developments is to see a strand from both liberalism and Marxism as being successfully appropriated by practitioners of analytic philosophy, such as Rawls and G. A. Cohen (1978). Focusing strictly on Marxism vs. liberalism, however, threatens to obscure the presence of other vigorous alternatives, from alternative liberalisms critical (sometimes implicitly) of Rawlsianism, such as those developed by Richard Flathman (1992), George Kateb (1992), Jeremy Waldron (1993), and William Galston (1991), to alternative Marxisms such as those explored by Jacques Rancière (1989) and Étienne Balibar and Immanuel Wallerstein (1991), and Nancy Hartsock (1983). Michael Rogin combined the insights of Marxism and Freudian psychoanalysis to generate work now considered canonical to American studies and cultural studies (though he himself was critical of that set of approaches; see Dean 2006). Rogin (1987) pressed for the centrality of race, class, property, and the unconscious to the study of American politics (on race, see also Mills 1997).

Liberal theory's assumptions about power and individualism were criticized or bypassed from still other perspectives through the 1970s, 1980s, and 1990s, a fecund period during which political theorists had a wide range of approaches and languages from which to choose in pursuit of their work. In France, social theorists writing in the 1970s (in the aftermath of May 1968) included, most famously, Michel Foucault, whose retheorization of power had a powerful influence on generations of American theorists. In Germany, a discursive account of politics developed by Jürgen Habermas (for example Habermas 1989, first published in German in 1962) captured the imaginations of a generation of critical theorists committed to developing normative standards through which to assess the claims of liberal democratic states to legitimacy. The 1970s Italian Autonomia movement inspired new Gramscian and

---

[3] See also the work of the US–Yugoslav Praxis group, and their now-defunct journal *Praxis International*.

Foucaultian reflections on equality, politics, violence, and state power (Virno 2004). For much of this period, feminism defined itself almost as an opposite of liberalism, drawing inspiration initially from Marxism, later from psychoanalytic theories of difference, and developing its own critique of the abstract individual. In Canada and at Oxford, Charles Taylor (1975) was thinking about politics through a rereading of Hegel that stressed the importance of community to political autonomy, influencing Michael Sandel (1982) and many subsequent theorists of multiculturalism. Deleuze and Guattari combined post-structuralism and psychoanalysis into a series of difficult ruminations on the spatial metaphors that organize our thinking at the ontological level about politics, nature, and life (1977; see also Patton 2006). Ranging from Freudian to Lacanian approaches, psychoanalysis has provided political theorists with a perspective from which to examine the politics of mass society, race and gender inequalities, and personal and political identity (Butler 1993; Laclau 2006; Zizek 2001; Irigaray 1985; Zerilli 1994; Glass 2006).

2.2 Liberal Egalitarianism

As the above suggests, alternatives to liberalism continue to proliferate, and yet, in many areas of political theory, liberalism has become the dominant position. Marxism has continued to inform debates on exploitation and equality, but in a shift that has been widely replayed through the last twenty-five years, reinvented itself to give more normative and analytic weight to the individual (Roemer 1982; 1986; Cohen 1995; 2000). There has been a particularly significant convergence, therefore, in the debates around equality, with socialists unexpectedly preoccupied with questions of individual responsibility and desert, liberals representing equality rather than liberty as the "sovereign virtue" (Dworkin 2000), and the two combining to make liberal egalitarianism almost the only remaining tradition of egalitarianism. One intriguing outcome is the literature on basic income or basic endowment, which all individuals would receive from government to facilitate their participation in an otherwise liberal society (van Parijs 1995; Ackerman and Alstott 1999).

For generations, liberalism had been taken to task for what was said to be its "formal" understanding of equality: its tendency to think that there were no particular resource implications attached to human equality. In the wake of Rawls's "difference principle" (see Arneson, this volume) or Dworkin's "equality of resources," this now seems a singularly inappropriate complaint. At the beginning of the 1980s, Amartya Sen posed a question that was to frame much of the literature on distributive justice through the next decade: equality of what? This generated a multiplicity of answers, ranging through welfare, resources, capabilities (Sen's preferred candidate), to the more cumbersome "equality of 'opportunity' for welfare," and "equality of access to advantage."[4] None of the answers could be dismissed as representing a merely formal

---

[4] Key contributions to this debate include Sen (1980; 1992); Dworkin (1981; 2000); Arneson (1989); and G. A. Cohen (1989).

understanding of equality, but all engaged with key liberal themes of individuality and responsibility. The subsequent explosion of liberal egalitarianism can be read as a radicalization of the liberal tradition. But the convergence between what were once distinctively liberal and socialist takes on equality can also be seen as demonstrating the new dominance of liberal theory. Much of the literature on equality is now resolutely individualist in form, running its arguments through thought experiments designed to tease out our intuitions of equality, and illustrating with stories of differently endowed individuals, exhibiting different degrees of aspiration and effort, whose entitlements we are then asked to assess. It is not always clear what purchase this discourse of individual variation (with a cast of characters including opera singers, wine buffs, surfers, and fishermen) has on the larger inequalities of the contemporary world. "What," as Elizabeth Anderson has asked, "has happened to the concerns of the politically oppressed? What about inequalities of race, gender, class, and caste?" (Anderson 1999, 288).

In the course of the 1990s, a number of theorists voiced concern about the way issues of redistribution were being displaced by issues of recognition, casting matters of economic inequality into the shade (Fraser 1997). There is considerable truth to this observation, but it would be misleading to say that no one now writes about economic inequality. There is, on the contrary, a large literature (and a useful website, The Equality Exchange[5]) dealing with these issues. The more telling point is that the egalitarian literature has become increasingly focused around questions of individual responsibility, opportunity, and endowment, thus less engaged with social structures of inequality, and less easily distinguishable from liberalism.

2.3 Communitarianism

One central axis of contention in the 1980s was what came to be known as the liberal–communitarian debate (for an overview, see Mulhall and Swift 1996). Communitarians like Michael Sandel (1982), influenced by both Arendt and Taylor, argued that in stressing abstract individuals and their rights as the building blocks for political theory, liberalism missed the importance of the community that creates individuals as they actually exist. For communitarians, individuals are always embedded in a network of social relationships, never the social isolates that liberalism assumes, and they have obligations to the community, not just to the political arrangements that facilitate their own interests. This opposition between the liberal's stripped-down, rights-bearing individual and the communitarian's socially embedded bearer of obligations seemed, for a period, *the* debate in political philosophy. But voices soon made themselves heard arguing that this was a storm in a teacup, a debate within liberalism rather than between liberalism and its critics, the main question being the degree to which holistic notions of community are instrumental to the rights and freedoms that both sides in the debate prized (Taylor 1989; Walzer 1990; Galston 1991).

---

[5] http://aran.univ-pau.fr/ee/index.html.

Liberalism, it is said, was misrepresented. Its conception of the individual was never as atomistic, abstracted, or self-interested as its critics tried to suggest.

2.4 Feminism

In the 1980s, feminists had mostly positioned themselves as critics of both schools. They shared much of the communitarian skepticism about disembedded individuals, and brought to this an even more compelling point about the abstract individual being disembodied, as if it made no difference whether "he" were female or male (Pateman 1988). But they also warned against the authoritarian potential in holistic notions of community, and the way these could be wielded against women (e.g. Frazer and Lacey 1993). Growing numbers challenged impartialist conceptions of justice, arguing for a contextual ethics that recognizes the responsibilities individuals have for one another and/or the differences in our social location (Gilligan 1982; Young 1990). Still others warned against treating the language of justice and rights as irredeemably masculine, and failing, as a result, to defend the rights of women (Okin 1989).

As the above suggests, feminism remained a highly diverse body of thought through the 1980s and 1990s; but to the extent that there was a consensus, it was largely critical of the liberal tradition, which was represented as overly individualistic, wedded to a strong public/private divide, and insufficiently alert to gender issues. There has since been a discernible softening in this critique, and this seems to reflect a growing conviction that liberalism is not as dependent on the socially isolated self as had been suggested. Nussbaum (1999, 62) argues that liberal individualism "does not entail either egoism or normative self-sufficiency;" and while feminists writing on autonomy have developed their own distinctive understanding of "relational autonomy," many now explicitly repudiate the picture of mainstream liberal theory as ignoring the social nature of the self (see essays in MacKenzie and Stoljar 2000). Some of the earlier feminist critiques overstated the points of difference from liberalism, misrepresenting the individual at the heart of the tradition as more self-contained, self-interested, and self-centered than was necessarily the case. But it also seems that liberalism made some important adjustments and in the process met at least part of the feminist critique. It would be churlish to complain of this (when you criticize a tradition, you presumably hope it will mend its ways), but one is left, once again, with a sense of a tradition mopping up its erstwhile opponents. Some forms of feminism are committed to a radical politics of sexual difference that it is hard to imagine liberalism ever wanting or claiming (see Zerilli 2006). But many brands of feminism that were once critical of liberalism have made peace with the liberal tradition.

2.5 Democracy and Critical Theory

In the literature on citizenship and democracy, liberalism has faced a number of critical challenges, but here, too, some of the vigor of that challenge seems to have dispersed. Republicanism pre-dates liberalism by two thousand years and emphasizes active citizenship, civic virtue, and the pursuit of public values, not the private interests associated more with the liberal tradition. Republicanism enjoyed a significant revival through the 1980s and 1990s as one of the main alternatives to liberal democracy (Sunstein 1990; Pettit 1997); indeed, it looked, for a time, as if it might substitute for socialism as *the* alternative to the liberal tradition. Nowadays, even the republican Richard Dagger (2004, 175) allows that "a republican polity must be able to count on a commitment to principles generally associated with liberalism, such as tolerance, fair play, and respect for the rights of others;" this is not, in other words, a total alternative. Deliberative democracy also emerged in the early 1990s as a challenge to established liberal models that regarded politics as the aggregation of preferences defined mostly in a private realm (J. Cohen 1989). For deliberative democrats, reflection upon preferences in a public forum was central; and again, it looked as though this would require innovative thinking about alternative institutional arrangements that would take democracies beyond the standard liberal repertoire (Dryzek 1990). By the late 1990s, however, the very institutions that deliberative democrats had once criticized became widely seen as the natural home for deliberation, with an emphasis on courts and legislatures. Prominent liberals such as Rawls (1997, 771–2) proclaimed themselves deliberative democrats, and while Bohman (1998) celebrates this transformation as "the coming of age of deliberative democracy," it also seems like another swallowing up of critical alternatives.

The recent history of critical theory—and more specifically, the work of Jürgen Habermas—is exemplary in this respect. Critical theory's ancestry extends back via the Frankfurt School to Marx. In the hands of Max Horkheimer and Theodor Adorno (1972; first published 1947) in particular, critique was directed at dominant forms of instrumental rationality that defined modern society. Habermas rescued this critique from a potential dead end by showing that a communicative conception of rationality could underwrite a more congenial political order and associated emancipatory projects. Habermas's theory of the state was originally that of a monolith under sway of instrumental reason in the service of capitalism, which had to be resisted. Yet come the 1990s, Habermas (1996) had redefined himself as a constitutionalist stressing the role of rights in establishing the conditions for open discourse in the public sphere, whose democratic task was to influence political institutions that could come straight from a liberal democratic textbook.

2.6 Green Political Theory

Green political theory began in the 1970s, generating creative proposals for ecologically defensible alternatives to liberal capitalism. The center of gravity was left-libertarianism verging on eco-anarchism (Bookchin 1982), although (at least in the 1970s) some more Hobbesian and authoritarian voices were raised (Ophuls 1977). All could agree that liberal individualism and capitalist economic growth were antithetical to any sustainable political ecology. More recently, we have seen the progress of "post-exuberant" ecological political theory, characterized by engagement with liberalism. Not all green theory has moved in this direction. For example, Bennett and Chaloupka (1993) work more in the traditions of Thoreau and Foucault, while Plumwood (2002) draws on radical ecology and feminism to criticize the dualisms and anthropocentric rationalism of liberalism.

2.7 Post-structuralism

Post-structuralism is often seen as merely critical rather than constructive. This mistaken impression comes from a focus on the intersections between post-structuralist theory and liberal theory. Some post-structuralist theorists seek to supplement rather than supplant liberalism, to correct its excesses, or even to give it a conscience that, in the opinion of many, it too often seems to lack. Hence Patton's suggestion (2006) that the distance between post-structuralist and liberal political theory may not be as unbridgeable as is commonly conceived. And some versions of liberal theory are more likely to be embraced or explored by post-structuralists than others: Isaiah Berlin, Richard Flathman, Jeremy Waldron, and Stuart Hampshire are all liberals whose work has been attended to in some detail by post-structuralist thinkers.

But post-structuralists have also developed alternative models of politics and ethics not directly addressed to liberal theory. One way to canvass those is with reference to the varying grand narratives on offer from this side of the field. Post-structuralism is often defined as intrinsically hostile to any sort of grand narrative, a claim attributed to Jean-Francois Lyotard (1984). This claim is belied by a great deal of work in the field that does not so much reject grand narrative as reimagine and reiterate it (Bennett 2002). Post-structuralists do reject foundational meta-narratives: those that present themselves as transcendentally true, for which nature or history has an intrinsic purpose, or that entail a two-world metaphysic. Those post-structuralists who do use meta-narratives tend to see themselves as writing in the tradition of social contract theorists like Hobbes, whose political arguments are animated by imaginary or speculative claims about the origins and trajectories of social life. Post-structuralists, however, are careful to represent their post-metaphysical views as an "onto-story whose persuasiveness is always at issue and can never be fully disentangled from an interpretation of present historical circumstances" (White 2000, 10–11; see also Deleuze and Guattari 1977).

What post-structuralists try to do without is not the origin story by means of which political theory has always motivated its readers, nor the wagers by way of which it offers hope. Rather, post-structuralists seek to do without the ends or guarantees (such as faith, or progress, or virtue) which have enabled some enviable achievements (such as the broadening of human rights), but in the name of which cruelties have also been committed (in the so-called "developing" world, or in the West against nonbelievers and nonconformists).[6] These ends or guarantees have

---

[6] On the role of progress in India, see Mehta (1999). On the fate of nonconformists in Rawls, for example, see Honig (1993).

sometimes enabled political theorists to evade full responsibility for the conclusions they seek, by claiming the goals or values in question are called for by some extra-human source, like god or nature.

3 POLITICAL THEORY AND THE GLOBAL TURN

Liberalism has demonstrated an almost unprecedented capacity for absorbing its competitors, aided by the collapse of its rival, Marxism, but also by its own virtuosity in reinventing itself and incorporating key elements from opposing traditions. Yet this is not a triumphalist liberalism, of the kind proclaimed in Fukuyama's (1989) "end of history," which celebrated the victory of liberal capitalism in the real-world competition of political-economic models. The paradox is that liberalism's absorption of some of its competitors has been accompanied by increasing anxiety about the way Western liberalism illegitimately centers itself. The much discussed shift in the work of Rawls is one classic illustration of this, for while the Rawls of *A Theory of Justice* (1971) seemed to be setting out "the" principles of justice that would be acceptable to any rational individual in any social context, the Rawls of *Political Liberalism* (1993) stressed the reasonableness of a variety of "comprehensive doctrines," including those that could be nonliberal, and the Rawls of *The Law of Peoples* (1999) encouraged us to recognize the "decency" of hierarchical, nonliberal societies that are nonetheless well ordered and respect a certain minimum of human rights.

Having won over many erstwhile critics in the metropolitan centers, liberals now more readily acknowledge that there are significant traditions of thought beyond those that helped form Western liberalism. They acknowledge, moreover, that the grounds for rejecting these other traditions are more slippery than previously conceived. The critique of "foundationalism" (for example, Rorty 1989) used to arouse heated debate among political theorists. Many were incensed at the suggestion that their claims about universal justice, equality, or human rights had no independent grounding, and accused the skeptics of abandoning normative political theory (see, for example, Benhabib et al. 1995). In the course of the 1990s, however, anti-foundationalism moved from being a contested minority position to something more like the consensus. Post-structuralist critiques of foundationalism led to liberalism's late twentieth-century announcement that it is "post-foundational" (Rawls 1993; Habermas 1996)—although with no fundamental rethinking of the key commitments of liberal theory. In the wake, however, of Rawls and Habermas disavowing metaphysical support for their (clearly normative) projects, Western political theorists have increasingly acknowledged the historical contingency of their own schools of thought; and this is generating some small increase in interest in alternative traditions. The awareness of these traditions does not, of itself, signal a crisis of confidence in liberal principles (arch antifoundationalist Richard Rorty certainly has no trouble declaring himself a liberal), but it does mean that political theory now grapples more extensively with questions of moral universalism and cultural or religious difference (e.g. Euben 1999; Parekh 2000; Honig 2001).

The explosion of writing on multiculturalism—largely from the 1990s—is particularly telling here. Multiculturalism is, by definition, concerned with the multiplicity of cultures: It deals with what may be radical differences in values, belief-systems, and practices, and has been especially preoccupied with the rights, if any, of nonliberal groups in liberal societies. The "problem" arises because liberalism is not the only doctrine on offer, and yet the way the problem is framed—as a question of toleration, or the rights of minorities, or whether groups as well as individuals can hold rights—remains quintessentially liberal. Will Kymlicka (1995) famously defended group rights for threatened cultural communities on the grounds that a secure cultural context is necessary to individual autonomy, such that the very importance liberals attach to individual autonomy requires them to support multicultural policies. His version of liberal multiculturalism has been widely criticized and many continue to see liberalism as at odds with multiculturalism (for example, Okin 1998; 2002; Barry 2001). But in analyzing the "problem" of multiculturalism through the paradigm of liberalism, Kymlicka very much exemplifies the field of debate. Liberalism simultaneously makes itself the defining tradition and notices the awkwardness in this. Its very dominance then seems to spawn an increasing awareness of traditions other than itself.

It is not entirely clear why this has happened now (liberalism, after all, has been around for many years) but that useful shorthand, globalization, must provide at least part of the explanation. It is difficult to sustain a belief in liberalism as the only tradition, or in secularism as the norm, when the majority of the world's population is patently unconvinced by either (Gray 1995; 1998). And although political theorists have drawn heavily on the liberal tradition in their explorations of human rights or global justice, the very topics they address require them to think about the specificity of Western political thought. Political theory now roams more widely than in the past, pondering accusations of ethno-centricity, questioning the significance of national borders, engaging in what one might almost term a denationalization of political theory. That description is an overstatement, for even in addressing explicitly global issues, political theory draws on concepts that are national in origin, and the assumptions written into them often linger into their more global phase. Terms like nation or state are not going to disappear from the vocabulary of political theory—but the kinds of shift Chris Brown (2006) discerns from international to global conceptions of justice are being played out in many corners of contemporary political thought.

It is hard to predict how this will develop, although the combination of a dominant liberalism with a concern that Western liberalism may have illegitimately centered itself looks unstable, and it seems probable that pockets of resistance and new alternatives to liberalism will therefore gain strength in future years. It seems certain that moves to reframe political theory in a more self-consciously global context will gather pace. This is already evident in the literature on equality, democracy, and social justice, where there is increasing attention to both international and global dimensions. It is also becoming evident in new ways of theorizing religion. Religion has been discussed so far in political theory mainly in the context of the "problem" of religious toleration, with little attention to the internal structure of religious beliefs. But other dimensions are now emerging, including new ways of understanding the politics of secularism, and closer examination of the normative arguments developed within different religions. It seems likely that new developments in science (particularly those associated with bio-genetics) will provide political theorists with difficult challenges in the coming decade, especially as regards our understanding of the boundaries between public and private, and the prospects for equality. And while the prospect of a more participatory or deliberative democracy remains elusive, we can perhaps anticipate an increasing focus on the role of pleasure and passion in political activism.

It is harder to predict what will happen in the continuing battle to incorporate issues of gender and "race" into mainstream political theory. Many of those who played significant roles in the development of feminist political theory no longer make feminism and/or gender so central to their work. The optimistic take on this is that gender is no longer a distinct and separate topic, but now a central component in political thought. The more pessimistic take is suggested in Zerilli (2006): that the attempt to think politics outside an exclusively gender-centered frame may end up reproducing the blind spots associated with the earlier canon of political thought. The likely developments as regards "race" are also unclear. We can anticipate that racial inequality will continue to figure in important ways in discussions of affirmative action or political representation, but the explosion of work on multiculturalism has focused more on "culture" or ethnicity, and political theory has not engaged in a thoroughgoing way with the legacies of colonialism or slavery.

4 Political Theory and Political Science: Current Trajectories

We noted earlier the sometimes difficult relationship between political theory and the rest of political science. We return to this here, but more with a view to areas of cooperation. In addition to its interdisciplinary locations, political theory has a place in the standard contemporary line-up of subfields in political science, alongside comparative politics, international relations, public policy, and the politics of one's own country. Here and there, methodology, public administration, political psychology, and public law might be added; and truly adventurous departments may stretch to political economy and environmental politics. All these subfields have a theoretical edge that potentially connects with the preoccupations of political theory. These connections confirm the importance of political theory to the rest of political science.

International relations has a well-defined sub-subfield of international relations (IR) theory, and we have noted that this is defined largely in terms of the three grand positions of realism, constructivism, and liberalism. Confusingly, liberalism in IR is not quite the same as liberalism in political theory. In IR theory, liberalism refers to the idea that actors can cooperate and build international institutions for the sake of mutual gains; it is therefore linked to a relatively hopeful view of the international system. Realism, in contrast, assumes that states maximize security in an anarchy where violent conflict is an ever-present possibility. Constructivism points to the degree to which actors, interests, norms, and systems are social constructions that can change over time and place. Each of these provides plenty of scope for engagement with political theory—even if these possibilities are not always realized. Despite its differences, IR liberalism connects with the liberalism of political theory in their shared Lockean view of how governing arrangements can be established, and when it comes to specifying principles for the construction of just and legitimate international institutions. Realism is explicitly grounded in the political theory of Thomas Hobbes, interpreting the international system in Hobbesian "state of nature" terms. Thucydides has also been an important if contestable resource for realism (Monoson and Loriaux 1998). Constructivism has been represented (for example, by Price and Reus-Smit 1998) as consistent with Habermasian critical theory. As Scheuerman (2006) points out, critical theory has reciprocated, in that it now sees the international system as the crucial testing ground for its democratic prescriptions. Normative theory is currently flourishing in international relations, and many of the resources for this are provided by political theory (Cochran 1999), with post-modernists, Rawlsian liberals, feminists, and critical theorists making particularly important contributions.[7]

The connections between comparative politics and political theory are harder to summarize because many of the practitioners of the former are area specialists with only a limited interest in theory. Those comparatists who use either large-n quantitative studies or small-n comparative case studies are often more interested in simple explanatory theory, one source of which is rational choice theory. But there are also points of engagement with political theory as we understand it. The comparative study of social movements and their relationships with the state has drawn upon the idea of the public sphere in democratic political theory, and vice versa. Accounts of the role of the state in political development have drawn upon liberal constitution-alist political theory. More critical accounts of the state in developing societies have drawn upon Marxist theory. In the last two decades democratization has been an important theme in comparative politics, and this work ought to have benefited from a dialogue with democratic theory. Unfortunately this has not happened. Studies of

---

[7] See, for example, Pogge (2002), Lynch (1999), Connolly (1991), der Derian (2001), Elshtain (2003), Walker (1993), Rawls (1999), and Habermas (2001a; 2001b).

democratization generally work with a minimalist account of democracy in terms of competitive elections, developed in the 1940s by Joseph Schumpeter (1942), ignoring the subsequent sixty years of democratic theory. Recent work on race and diaspora studies in a comparative context is perhaps a more promising site of connection, invoking Tocqueville (see also Bourdieu and Wacquant 1999; Hanchard 2003). And theorists working on multiculturalism and race have been especially attentive to comparative politics questions about the variety of governmental forms and their interaction with cultural difference (Carens 2000; Kymlicka 2001; Taylor 1994; Gilroy 2000).

Methodology might seem the subfield least likely to engage with political theory, and if methodology is thought of in terms of quantitative techniques alone, that might well be true. However, methodology is also home to reflection on what particular sorts of methods can do. Here, political theorists are in an especially good position to mediate between the philosophy of social science on the one hand, and particular methods on the other. Taylor (1979) and Ball (1987) point to the inevitable moment of interpretation in the application of all social science methods, questioning the positivist self-image of many of those who deploy quantitative methods. The interdisciplinarity that characterizes so much political theory provides especially fruitful material for methodological reflection.

Public policy is at the "applied" end of political science, but its focus on the relationship between disciplinary knowledge and political practice invites contribution from political theory; and many political theorists see themselves as clarifying the normative principles that underpin policy proposals. From Rawls and Dworkin onwards, work on principles of justice and equality has carried definite policy implications regarding taxation, public expenditure on health, the treatment of those with disabilities, and so on. While it has rarely been possible to translate the theories into specific recommendations (Dworkin's hypothetical insurance market and Amartya Sen's theory of capabilities are often said to be especially disappointing in this respect), they are undoubtedly directed at public policy. Normative reasoning applied to public policy largely defines the content of *Philosophy and Public Affairs*, though this reasoning involves moral philosophy as much as or more than political theory.[8] Political theorists working on questions of democracy and representation have also drawn direct policy conclusions regarding the nature of electoral systems or the use of gender quotas to modify patterns of representation (Phillips 1995).

Policy evaluation and design are important parts of the public policy subfield, and both require normative criteria to provide standards by which to evaluate actual or potential policies. Again, political theory is well placed to illuminate such criteria and how one might think about handling conflicts between them (for example, when efficiency and justice appear to point in different directions). It is also well placed to explore the discourse aspects of public policy, an aspect that has been an especial interest of the Theory, Policy, and Society group of the American Political Science Association. Among the linkages this group develops are those between

---

[8] See the compilations of Cohen, Nagel, and Scanlon (1974a; 1974b; 1977); also Goodin (1982).

deliberative democratic theory and policy analysis, between the logic of political argument and interventions by analysts and advocates in policy processes, and between interpretative philosophy of social science and policy evaluation (Hajer and Wagenaar 2003).

Cutting across all the subfields of political science in recent decades has been rational choice theory, grounded in microeconomic assumptions about the wellsprings of individual behavior. Indeed, to some of its practitioners, rational choice is what should truly be described as political theory. For these practitioners, rational choice theory is "positive" political theory, value free and geared toward explanation, not prescription. This claim does not hold up: As explanatory theory, rational choice theory is increasingly regarded as a failure (Green and Shapiro 1994). But many believe that it is very useful nevertheless. Game theory, for example, can clarify what rationality *is* in particular situations (Johnson 1991), thereby illuminating one of the perennial questions in political theory. And despite the frequent description of rational choice theory as value free, it has provided for plenty of normative theorizing among its practitioners. Arch-positivist Riker (1982*b*) deploys Arrow's social choice theory to argue that democracy is inherently unstable and meaningless in the outcomes it produces, and uses this to back a normative argument on behalf of a minimal liberal democracy that allows corrupt or incompetent rulers to be voted out—but nothing more. The conclusions of rational choice theory are often bad news for democracy (Barry and Hardin 1982); but it is possible to reinterpret this edifice in terms of critical theory, as showing what *would* happen if everyone behaved according to microeconomic assumptions. The political challenge then becomes one of how to curb this destructive behavioral proclivity (Dryzek 1992).

Leading comparativist Bo Rothstein (2005) has expressed the worry that the empirical arm of the discipline has lost its moral compass. To use his running example, its "technically competent barbarians" would have no defense against lining up in support of a political force like Nazism, should that be expedient. Rothstein himself sees the remedy in political theory: "The good news is that, unlike other disciplines, I think we have the solution within our own field of research. This, I believe, lies in reconnecting the normative side of the discipline—that is, political philosophy— with the positive/empirical side" (2005, 10). Despite the likelihood of some resistance to this from both sides of the divide, the examples discussed above suggest that such connection (or reconnection) is indeed possible.

We have argued that political theory is something of a mongrel sub-discipline, made up of many traditions, approaches, and styles of thought, and increasingly characterized by its borrowing from feminist and critical theory, film theory, popular culture, mass media, behavioral science, and economics. The current academy confronts two opposing trends. One draws the boundaries of each discipline ever more tightly, sometimes as part of a bid for higher status, sometimes in the (not totally implausible) belief that this is the route to deeper and more systematic knowledge. Another looks to the serendipitous inspirations that can come through cross-disciplinary and interdisciplinary work; or, more simply and modestly, realizes that there may be much to learn from other areas of study. It is hard to predict which of these will win out—and most likely, both will continue in uneasy combination for many years to come. We hope and believe that the second trend will turn out to be the dominant one.

References

ACKERMAN, B. and ALSTOTT, A. 1999. *The Stakeholder Society*. New Haven, Conn.: Yale University Press.

AGAMBEN, G. 1998. *Homo Sacer: Sovereign Power and Bare Life*, trans. D. Heller-Roazen. Stanford, Calif.: Stanford University Press.

ALTHUSSER, L. 1969. *For Marx*. London: Allen Lane.

—— and BALIBAR, E. 1970. *Reading Capital*. London: Verso.

ANDERSON, E. 1999. What is the point of equality? *Ethics*, 109: 287–337.

ARENDT, H. 1958. *The Human Condition*. Chicago: University of Chicago Press.

—— 1959. Reflections on Little Rock. *Dissent*, 6: 45–56.

—— 1963. *On Revolution*. New York: Viking.

—— 1969. *Crises of the Republic*. New York: Harcourt.

ARNESON, R. J. 1989. Equality and equal opportunity for welfare. *Philosophical Studies*, 56: 77–93.

ASHCRAFT, R. 1989. Political theory and the problem of ideology. *Journal of Politics*, 42: 687–705.

BALIBAR, É. 2004. *We the People of Europe? Reflections on Transnational Citizenship*, trans. J. Swenson. Princeton, NJ: Princeton University Press.

—— and WALLERSTEIN, I. 1991. *Race, Nation, Class: Ambiguous Identities*. New York: Verso.

BALL, T. 1987. Deadly hermeneutics: or *Sinn* and the social scientist. Pp. 95–112 in *Idioms of Inquiry: Critique and Renewal in Political Science*, ed. T. Ball. Albany: State University of New York Press.

BARRY, B. 1965. *Political Argument*. London: Routledge and Kegan Paul.

—— 1995. *Justice as Impartiality*. Oxford: Oxford University Press.

—— 2001. *Culture and Equality: An Egalitarian Critique of Multiculturalism*. Cambridge: Polity.

—— and HARDIN, R. (eds.) 1982. *Rational Man and Irrational Society?* Beverly Hills, Calif.: Sage.

BENHABIB, S., BUTLER, J., CORNELL, D., and FRASER, N. 1995. *Feminist Contentions: A Philosophical Exchange*. New York: Routledge.

BENNETT, J. 2002. The moraline drift. In *The Politics of Moralizing*, ed. J. Bennett and M. Shapiro. New York: Routledge.

—— and CHALOUPKA, W. (eds.) 1993. *In the Nature of Things: Language, Politics and the Environment*. Minneapolis: University of Minnesota Press.

BERLIN, I. 1969. *Four Essays on Liberty*. Oxford: Oxford University Press.

BOHMAN, J. 1998. The coming of age of deliberative democracy. *Journal of Political Philosophy*, 6: 399–423.

BOOKCHIN, M. 1982. *The Ecology of Freedom*. Palo Alto, Calif.: Cheshire.

BOURDIEU, P. and WACQUANT, L. 1999. On the cunning of imperialist reason. *Theory, Culture and Society*, 16: 41–58.

BROWN, C. 2006. From international to global justice? Pp. 621–35 in *Oxford Handbook of Political Theory*, ed. J. S. Dryzek, B. Honig, and A. Phillips. Oxford: Oxford University Press.

BUCHANAN, J. and TULLOCK, G. 1962. *The Calculus of Consent.* Ann Arbor: University of Michigan Press.

BUTLER, J. 1993. *Bodies that Matter: On the Discursive Limits of "Sex."* New York: Routledge.

CARENS, J. 2000. *Culture, Citizenship, and Community: A Contextual Exploration of Justice as Evenhandedness.* Oxford: Oxford University Press.

COCHRAN, M. 1999. *Normative Theory in International Relations.* Cambridge: Cambridge University Press.

COHEN, G. A. 1978. *Karl Marx's Theory of History: A Defence.* Princeton, NJ: Princeton University Press.

——1989. On the currency of egalitarian justice. *Ethics,* 99: 906–44.

——1995. *Self-Ownership, Freedom and Equality.* Cambridge: Cambridge University Press.

——2000. *If You're An Egalitarian, How Come You're So Rich?* Cambridge, Mass.: Harvard University Press.

COHEN, J. 1989. Deliberation and democratic legitimacy. Pp. 17–34 in *The Good Polity: Normative Analysis of the State,* ed. A. Hamlin and P. Pettit. Oxford: Basil Blackwell.

COHEN, M., NAGEL, T., and SCANLON, T. M. (eds.) 1974a. *War and Moral Responsibility.* Princeton, NJ: Princeton University Press.

—— —— —— 1974b. *The Rights and Wrongs of Abortion.* Princeton, NJ: Princeton University Press.

—— —— —— 1977. *Equality and Preferential Treatment.* Princeton, NJ: Princeton University Press.

CONNOLLY, W. 1974. *The Terms of Political Discourse.* Lexington, Mass.: Heath.

——1991. Democracy and territoriality. *Millennium,* 20: 463–84.

DAGGER, R. 2004. Communitarianism and republicanism. Pp. 167–79 in *Handbook of Political Theory,* ed. G. F. Gaus and C. Kukathas. London: Sage.

DEAN, J. 2006. Political theory and cultural studies. Pp. 751–72 in *Oxford Handbook of Political Theory,* ed. J. S. Dryzek, B. Honig, and A. Phillips. Oxford: Oxford University Press.

DELEUZE, G. and GUATTARI, F. 1977. *Anti-Oedipus: Capitalism and Schizophrenia.* New York: Viking.

DER DERIAN, J. 2001. *Virtuous War: Mapping the Military–Industrial–Media–Entertainment Network.* Boulder, Colo.: Westview.

DERRIDA, J. 2000. *Of Hospitality: Anne Dufourmantelle Invites Jacques Derrida to Respond,* trans. R. Bowlby. Stanford, Calif.: Stanford University Press.

DRYZEK, J. S. 1990. *Discursive Democracy: Politics, Policy, and Political Science.* New York: Cambridge University Press.

——1992. How far is it from Virginia and Rochester to Frankfurt? Public choice as critical theory. *British Journal of Political Science,* 22: 397–417.

DUNN, J. 2000. *The Cunning of Unreason: Making Sense of Politics.* New York: HarperCollins.

DWORKIN, R. 1968. On not prosecuting civil disobedience. *New York Review of Books,* 10 (10 June).

—— 1977. *Taking Rights Seriously.* Cambridge, Mass.: Harvard University Press.

——1981. What is equality? Part 1: equality of welfare; Part ii: equality of resources. *Philosophy and Public Affairs,* 10: 185–246; 283–345.

——2000. *Sovereign Virtue: The Theory and Practice of Equality.* Cambridge, Mass.: Harvard University Press.

ELSHTAIN, J. B. 2003. *Just War against Terror: The Burden of American Power in a Violent World.* New York: Basic Books.

EUBEN, R. 1999. *Enemy in the Mirror: Islamic Fundamentalism and the Limits of Modern Rationalism.* Princeton, NJ: Princeton University Press.

FLATHMAN, R. 1992. *Wilful Liberalism: Voluntarism and Individuality in Political Theory and Practice*. Ithaca, NY: Cornell University Press.

FOUCAULT, M. 1979. *Discipline and Punish: The Birth of the Prison*. New York: Vintage.

FRASER, N. 1997. *Justice Interruptus: Critical Reflections on the "Postsocialist" Condition*. New York: Routledge.

FRAZER, E. AND LACEY, N. 1993. *The Politics of Community: A Feminist Critique of the Liberal–Communitarian Debate*. Hemel Hempstead: Harvester.

FUKUYAMA, F. 1989. The end of history? *National Interest*, Summer: 3–18.

GALSTON, W. 1991. *Liberal Purposes: Goods, Virtues, and Diversity in the Liberal State*. Cambridge: Cambridge University Press.

GAUTHIER, D. 1986. *Morals by Agreement*. Oxford: Clarendon Press.

GILLIGAN, C. 1982. *In a Different Voice*. Cambridge, Mass.: Harvard University Press.

GILROY, P. 2000. *Against Race: Imagining Political Culture Beyond the Color Line*. Cambridge, Mass.: Belknap Press of Harvard University Press.

GLASS, J. 2006. Paranoia and political philosophy. Pp. 729–48 in *Oxford Handbook of Political Theory*, ed. J. S. Dryzek, B. Honig, and A. Phillips. Oxford: Oxford University Press.

GOODIN, R. E. 1982. *Political Theory and Public Policy*. Chicago: University of Chicago Press.

GRAY, J. 1995. *Enlightenment's Wake*. London: Routledge

—— 1998. *Endgames: Questions in Late Modern Political Thought*. Cambridge: Polity.

GREEN, D. P. and SHAPIRO, I. 1994. *Pathologies of Rational Choice Theory: A Critique of Applications in Political Science*. New Haven, Conn.: Yale University Press.

GUNNELL, J. G. 1986. *Between Philosophy and Politics: The Alienation of Political Theory*. Amherst: University of Massachusetts Press.

HABERMAS, J. 1989. *The Structural Transformation of the Public Sphere*, trans. T. Burger. Cambridge, Mass.: MIT Press.

—— 1996. *Between Facts and Norms: Contributions to a Discourse Theory of Law and Democracy*. Cambridge, Mass.: MIT Press.

—— 2001*a*. *The Postnational Constellation: Political Essays*. Cambridge, Mass.: MIT Press.

—— 2001*b*. Why Europe needs a constitution. *New Left Review*, 11: 5–26.

HAJER, M. and WAGENAAR, H. (eds.) 2003. *Deliberative Policy Analysis: Understanding Governance in the Network Society*. Cambridge: Cambridge University Press.

HANCHARD, M. 2003. Acts of misrecognition: transnational black politics, anti-imperialism and the ethnocentrisms of Pierre Bourdieu and Loïc Wacquant. *Theory, Culture and Society*, 20: 5–29.

HARTSOCK, N. 1983. *Money, Sex and Power: Towards a Feminist Historical Materialism*. New York: Longman.

HARTZ, L. 1955. *The Liberal Tradition in America*. New York: Harcourt, Brace.

HAYEK, F. A. VON 1960. *The Constitution of Liberty*. London: Routledge and Kegan Paul.

HONIG, B. 1993. *Political Theory and the Displacement of Politics*. Ithaca, NY: Cornell University Press.

—— 2001. *Democracy and the Foreigner*. Princeton, NJ: Princeton University Press.

HORKHEIMER, M. and ADORNO, T. 1972. *Dialectic of Enlightenment*. New York: Herder and Herder.

IRIGARAY, L. 1985. *Speculum of the Other Woman*, trans. G. C. Gill. Ithaca, NY: Cornell University Press.

ISAAC, J. C. 1995. The strange silence of political theory. *Political Theory*, 23: 636–52.

JOHNSON, J. 1991. Rational choice as a reconstructive theory. In *The Economic Approach to Politics*, ed. F. Monroe. New York: HarperCollins.

KATEB, G. 1992. *The Inner Ocean: Individualism and Democratic Culture*. Ithaca, NY: Cornell University Press.

KYMLICKA, W. 1995. *Multicultural Citizenship*. Oxford: Oxford University Press.

—— 2001. *Politics in the Vernacular: Nationalism, Multiculturalism, and Citizenship*. Oxford: Oxford University Press.

LACLAU, E. 2006. *The Populist Reason*. London: Verso.

LASLETT, P. 1956. Introduction. In *Philosophy, Politics and Society*, ed. P. Laslett. Oxford: Basil Blackwell.

LASSWELL, H. D. 1961. *Politics: Who Gets What, When and How*. Cleveland, Oh.: World.

LUKES, S. 1995. *The Curious Enlightenment of Professor Caritat*. London: Verso.

LYNCH, C. 1999. *Beyond Appeasement: Interpreting Interwar Peace Movements in World Politics*. Ithaca, NY: Cornell University Press.

LYONS, O. 1992. *Exiled in the Land of the Free: Democracy, Indian Nations, and the US Constitution*. Santa Fe, N. Mex.: Clear Light.

LYOTARD, J. F. 1984. *The Postmodern Condition: A Report on Knowledge*. Minneapolis: University of Minnesota Press.

MACKENZIE, C. and STOLJAR, N. (eds.) 2000. *Relational Autonomy: Feminist Perspectives on Autonomy, Agency, and the Social Self*. Oxford: Oxford University Press.

MCLELLAN, D. 1970. *Marx before Marxism*. London: Macmillan.

MARCUSE, H. 1964. *One-Dimensional Man*. Boston: Beacon.

MARSHALL, G., SWIFT, A., and ROBERTS, S. 1997. *Against the Odds? Social Class and Social Justice in Industrial Societies*. Oxford: Clarendon Press.

MEHTA, U. S. 1999. *Liberalism and Empire: A Study in Nineteenth-Century Liberal Thought*. Chicago: University of Chicago Press.

MILLS, C. W. 1997. *The Racial Contract*. Ithaca, NY: Cornell University Press.

MONOSON, S. S. and LORIAUX, M. 1998. The illusion of power and the disruption of moral norms: Thucydides' critique of Periclean policy. *American Political Science Review*, 92: 285–97.

MONROE, K. R. (ed.) 2005. *Perestroika! The Raucous Rebellion in Political Science*. New Haven, Conn.: Yale University Press.

MULHALL, S. and SWIFT, A. 1996. *Liberals and Communitarians*, 2nd edn. Oxford: Basil Blackwell.

NOZICK, R. 1974. *Anarchy, State and Utopia*. New York: Basic Books.

NUSSBAUM, M. 1999. The feminist critique of liberalism. Pp. 55–80 in *Sex and Social Justice*, ed. M. Nussbaum. Oxford: Oxford University Press.

OAKESHOTT, M. 1962. *Rationalism in Politics and Other Essays*. London: Methuen.

OKIN, S. M. 1989. *Justice, Gender and the Family*. New York: Basic Books.

—— 1998. Feminism and multiculturalism: some tensions. *Ethics*, 108: 661–84.

—— 2002. "Mistresses of their own destiny:" group rights, gender, and realistic rights of exit. *Ethics*, 112: 205–30.

OPHULS, W. 1977. *Ecology and the Politics of Scarcity*. San Francisco: W. H. Freeman.

PAREKH, B. 2000. *Rethinking Multiculturalism: Cultural Diversity and Political Theory*. London: Palgrave.

PATEMAN, C. 1988. *The Sexual Contract*. Cambridge: Polity.

PATTON, P. 2006. After the linguistic turn: post-structuralist and liberal pragmatist political theory. Pp. 125–41 in *Oxford Handbook of Political Theory*, ed. J. S. Dryzek, B. Honig, and A. Phillips. Oxford: Oxford University Press.

PETTIT, P. 1997. *Republicanism: A Theory of Freedom and Government*. Oxford: Oxford University Press.

PHILLIPS, A. 1995. *The Politics of Presence: The Political Representation of Gender, Ethnicity, and Race*. Oxford: Oxford University Press.

PITKIN, H. 1966. Obligation and consent II. *American Political Science Review*, 60: 39–52.

PLUMWOOD, V. 2002. *Environmental Culture: The Ecological Crisis of Reason*. New York: Routledge.

POGGE, T. W. 2002. *World Poverty and Human Rights: Cosmopolitan Responsibilities and Reforms*. Malden, Mass.: Basil Blackwell.

POPPER, K. R. 1957. *The Poverty of Historicism*. London: Routledge and Kegan Paul.

PRICE, R. and REUS-SMIT, C. 1998. Dangerous liaisons? Critical international theory and constructivism. *European Journal of International Relations*, 4: 259–94.

RANCIÈRE, J. 1989. *Nights of Labor: The Workers' Dream in 19th Century France*, trans. J. Drury. Philadelphia: Temple University Press.

—— 1999. *Dis-agreement*, trans. J. Rose. Minneapolis: University of Minnesota Press.

RAWLS, J. 1969. The justification of civil disobedience. Pp. 240–55 in *Civil Disobedience: Theory and Practice*, ed. H. A. Bedau. New York: Pegasus.

—— 1971. *A Theory of Justice*. Cambridge, Mass.: Harvard University Press.

—— 1993. *Political Liberalism*. New York: Columbia University Press.

—— 1997. The idea of public reason revisited. *University of Chicago Law Review*, 94: 765–807.

—— 1999. *The Law of Peoples*. Cambridge, Mass.: Harvard University Press.

RIKER, W. H. 1982a. The two-party system and Duverger's Law: an essay on the history of political science. *American Political Science Review*, 76: 753–66.

—— 1982b. *Liberalism against Populism: A Confrontation between the Theory of Democracy and the Theory of Social Choice*. San Francisco: W. H. Freeman.

ROEMER, J. E. 1982. *A General Theory of Exploitation and Class*. Cambridge, Mass.: Harvard University Press.

—— (ed.) 1986. *Analytical Marxism*. Cambridge: Cambridge University Press.

ROGIN, M. 1987. *Ronald Reagan the Movie and Other Episodes in Political Demonology*. Berkeley: University of California Press.

RORTY, R. 1983. Postmodern bourgeois liberalism. *Journal of Philosophy*, 80: 538–89.

—— 1989. *Contingency, Irony, and Solidarity*. Cambridge: Cambridge University Press.

ROTHSTEIN, B. 2005. Is political science producing technically competent barbarians? *European Political Science*, 4: 3–13.

SANDEL, M. 1982. *Liberalism and the Limits of Justice*. Cambridge: Cambridge University Press.

SCANLON, T. M. 1998. *What We Owe to Each Other*. Cambridge, Mass.: Harvard University Press.

SCHAAR, J. 1970. The Berkeley rebellion and beyond. In *Essays on Politics and Education in the Technological Society*, ed. J. Schaar and S. Wolin. New York: Vintage.

SCHEUERMAN, W. E. 2006. Critical theory beyond Habermas. Pp. 85–105 in *Oxford Handbook of Political Theory*, ed. J. S. Dryzek, B. Honig, and A. Phillips. Oxford: Oxford University Press.

SCHMITT, C. 1985. *Political Theology: Four Chapters on the Concept of Sovereignty*, trans. G. Schwab. Cambridge, Mass.: MIT Press.

SCHUMPETER, J. A. 1942. *Capitalism, Socialism and Democracy*. New York: Harper.

SEN, A. 1980. Equality of what? In *Tanner Lectures on Human Values*, ed. S. McMurrin. Cambridge: Cambridge University Press.

—— 1992. *Inequality Re-Examined*. Oxford: Oxford University Press.

SHKLAR, J. 1964. *Legalism*. Cambridge, Mass.: Harvard University Press.

SKINNER, Q. 1998. *Liberty before Liberalism*. Cambridge: Cambridge University Press.

STRAUSS, L. 1953. *Natural Right and History*. Chicago: University of Chicago Press.

SUNSTEIN, C. R. 1990. *After the Rights Revolution*. Cambridge, Mass.: Harvard University Press.
—— 1993. *The Partial Constitution*. Cambridge, Mass.: Harvard University Press.
TAYLOR, C. 1975. *Hegel*. New York: Cambridge University Press.
—— 1979. Interpretation and the sciences of man. In *Interpretive Social Science: A Reader*, ed. P. Rabinow and W. M. Bullivan. Los Angeles: University of California Press.
—— 1989. Cross-purposes: the liberal–communitarian debate. Pp. 159–82 in *Liberalism and the Moral Life*, ed. N. Rosenblum. Cambridge, Mass.: Harvard University Press.
—— 1994. The politics of recognition. In *Multiculturalism and "The Politics of Recognition,"* ed. A. Gutmann. Princeton, NJ: Princeton University Press.
TULLY, J. 1995. *Strange Multiplicity: Constitutionalism in an Age of Diversity*. Cambridge: Cambridge University Press.
—— 2002. The unfreedom of the moderns in relation to the ideals of constitutional democracy. *Modern Law Review*, 65: 204–28.
VAN PARIJS, P. 1995. *Real Freedom for All: What (If Anything) Can Justify Capitalism?* Oxford: Oxford University Press.
VIRNO, P. 2004. *A Grammar of the Multitude*. Cambridge, Mass.: Semiotext(e).
WALDRON, J. 1993. *Liberal Rights: Collected Papers 1981–1991*. Cambridge: Cambridge University Press.
WALKER, R. B. J. 1993. *Inside/Outside: International Relations as Political Theory*. Cambridge: Cambridge University Press.
WALZER, M. 1967. The obligation to disobey. *Ethics*, 77: 163–75.
—— 1970. *Obligations: Essays on Disobedience, War, and Citizenship*. Cambridge, Mass.: Harvard University Press.
—— 1990. The communitarian critique of liberalism. *Political Theory*, 18: 6–23.
WHITE, S. 2000. *Sustaining Affirmation: The Strengths of Weak Ontology in Political Theory*. Princeton, NJ: Princeton University Press.
WOLFF, R. P., MOORE, B., JR., and MARCUSE, H. 1965. *Repressive Tolerance*. Boston: Beacon.
WOLIN, S. 1960. *Politics and Vision*. Boston: Little, Brown.
—— 1969. Political theory as a vocation. *American Political Science Review*, 63: 1062–82.
YOUNG, I. M. 1990. *Justice and the Politics of Difference*. Princeton, NJ: Princeton University Press.
ZERILLI, L. 1994. *Signifying Woman: Culture and Chaos in Rousseau, Burke and Mill*. Ithaca, NY: Cornell University Press.
—— 2006. Feminist theory and the canon of political thought. Pp. 106–24 in *Oxford Handbook of Political Theory*, ed. J. S. Dryzek, B. Honig, and A. Phillips. Oxford: Oxford University Press.
ZIZEK, S. 2001. *Did Somebody Say Totalitarianism? Five Interventions into the (Mis)use of a Notion*. New York: Verso.

CHAPTER 3

....

NORMATIVE METHODOLOGY

....

RUSSELL HARDIN

MODERN political philosophy begins with Thomas Hobbes, David Hume, and others who train their focus on the individual and on interactions between individuals. The purpose of politics in their view is to regulate the behavior of individuals to enable them to be peaceful and productive. They treat of behavior and virtually ignore beliefs. They are interested in social order and its maintenance, not in the salvation of the soul, the creation of a heavenly city, or the ideal society. Hobbes's (1642; 1651) great works of political theory, *De Cive* and *Leviathan*, were published in the first and last years, respectively, of the English Civil Wars, one of the most devastating periods of English history. Against this background, his view of the role of political theory is the explanation and therefore the enablement of social order, a focus that continued through Locke and Hume, although they are increasingly concerned with the working of government and the nature of politics. If any of these three theorists were concerned with "the good society," they would have meant a society that is good for individuals. In an important sense, they are normatively behaviorist. That is to say, they attempt to explain rather than to justify political institutions and behavior. They are also forerunners of the modern self-interest and rational-choice schools of social thought. They are normative theorists only in the very limited sense of *explaining* what would get us to better states of affairs, in the sense of those states' being de facto in our interest or better for us by our own lights. From this vision, the main contemporary approaches to explanation derive. In contemporary normative social theory, there are three main schools—conflict, shared-value, and exchange theories—based, respectively, on interests, shared values, and agreement (as in contractarian theories of both explanation and justification).

The first move in much of normative social science, especially in normative political theory, is to establish a background of self-interested motivation and behavior. Indeed, the transformation of political theory by Hume in his *Treatise of Human Nature* is based on an account of normative issues that is not specifically a theory of those issues and how we should deal with them but is rather an account of how we see them and why we see them that way (Hume 2000 [1739–40], book 3; Hardin 2007, ch. 5). His account is essentially psychological. The way we see normative issues is to fit them to our interests. In keeping with their program to explain, not to justify, Hobbes and Hume are naturalists. Their explanations are grounded in the assumption that people are essentially self-interested and that their actions can be explained from this fact. From their time forward, the development of normative social science has depended heavily on the assumption that individuals are relatively self-interested.

1 SELF-INTEREST

One need not suppose that people are wholly self-interested, but a preponderance or a strong element of self-interest makes behavior explicable in fairly consistent terms. Consistency of individual motivations is central to the task of general explanation of behavior. Many normative or moral theories might yield explanations of behavior but only idiosyncratically, so that we can explain much of your behavior and commitments but not those of your neighbor. No standard moral theory comes close to the general applicability of self-interest as a motivation for large numbers of people.

Hobbes and Hume are not alone in this view. Bernard Mandeville,[1] Adam Smith, and Alexis de Tocqueville, among many others, conclude that self-seeking behavior in certain very important and pervasive contexts promotes the good of society in the—to them—only meaningful sense, which is promoting the good of individuals. Consider Tocqueville (1966 [1835 and 1840], ii, ch. 8) who, with his characteristic clarity, justifies the interest-based normative program in a forceful chapter on "Individualism and the doctrine of self-interest properly understood." He says that the doctrine of self-interest properly understood is *the best moral theory for our time*. He comes from a background in which French Catholic virtue theory was the dominant strain of moral judgment. He notes that in the United States, where he famously toured as de facto an ethnographer, there was no talk of virtue. Clearly he approves of this fact. In virtue theory, he says, one does good without self-interest. The American trick combines interest and charity because it is in the interest of each to work for the

---

[1] Mandeville's subtitle is "Private Vices, Publick Virtues."

good of all, although they need not know or intend this. This is Smith's argument from the invisible hand and it leads us to a resolution of the logic of collective action in the provision of large-scale public benefits. I seek my own good, you seek yours, and all together we promote the good of all. The happiness of all comes from the selfishness of each (ii. 376). Recall one of Smith's most quoted aphorisms, that it is "not from the benevolence of the butcher, the brewer, or the baker, that we expect our dinner, but from their regard to their own interest" (Smith 1976 [1776], 1.2.2, 26–7). Arguably, Tocqueville's central thesis is that, if you give democratic peoples education and freedom and leave them alone, they will extract from the world all the good things it has to offer (Tocqueville 1966 [1835 and 1840], ii. 543). This is, of course, a collective achievement based on individually motivated actions.

This view is not strictly only a modern vision. Aristotle states a partial version of it, in passing, in his praise of farmers as especially good citizens for democracy: "For the many strive for profit more than honor" (*Politics*, 1318b16–17). Aristotle says this with approval. If his claim were not true, he supposes that society would not cohere, because it is founded on the generality and stability of the motivations of farmers, whose productivity is fundamentally important for the good of all in the society. The scale of the contributions of farmers to the good of society remained relatively constant from the time of Aristotle until roughly two or three centuries ago in Europe when industrial production began to displace it as the main locus of employment. Today 2 or 3 percent of the workforce in the advanced economies suffices for agricultural production. It is an extraordinary fact that all of our main strands of political theory originate in the earlier era, when social structure was radically different.

A slight variant of the Aristotle–Hobbes–Hume view of the role of interest in the ordering of society is an assumption at the foundation of John Rawls's theory of justice. Rawls (1999, 112 [1971, 128]; see also Hardin 2003, 3–8) supposes that citizens are *mutually disinterested*. By this he means that my assessment of *my own benefits* from the social order established under his theory of justice does not depend on *your benefits* from that order. For example, I do not envy you and you do not envy me. Our social order has been established as just and there is no alternative that is similarly just and that would better serve my interests.[2] If we are mutually disinterested, then we have no direct concern with the aggregate outcome, but only with our own part or share in that outcome. This is a fundamentally important assumption in Rawls's theory, without which the theory would not go, but it is not often addressed in the massive literature on that theory. But even that theory, put forward in a nonagricultural world, builds on earlier visions of society.

---

[2] There could be two equally qualified just orderings, in one of which I am better off than I am in the other. It does not follow that a society of people who are committed to justice would rank the one of these equally qualified orderings in which I am better off above the other, because someone else will be worse off in that ordering. Hence, there would be no mutual advantage move that would make both of us better off.

2 THREE SCHOOLS OF SOCIAL THEORY

One can do normative political analysis without starting from rational choice principles and, indeed, such analysis is often done as an alternative to rational choice theories. But one cannot do very systematic, coherent political analysis without a clear delineation of basic principles on which the analyses are to be built. So for example, there are three grand theories—or schools of theory—on social order, each of which is based on a systematic set of theoretical assumptions. First are *conflict*, as represented by Thrasymachus (in Plato's *Republic*), Karl Marx, and Ralf Dahrendorf (1968; also see Wrong 1994). Hobbes is also commonly considered strictly a conflict theorist, but I think that this is wrong; that, as noted below, he is largely a coordination theorist. Conflict theories commonly turn to coercion or the threat of coercion to resolve issues. Hence, they almost inherently lead us into normative discussions of the justification of coercion in varied political contexts (Hardin 1990). They can also lead to debates about the nature of power and compliance as in Machiavelli, Marx, Gramsci, Nietzsche, or Foucault.

Second are *shared-value theories*, as represented by John Locke, Ibn Khaldun, and Talcott Parsons (1968 [1937], 89–94). Religious visions of social order are usually shared-value theories and, as Tocqueville notes, interest is the chief means used by religions to guide people. Religious and theological theories and justifications once held sway but are now of little import in Western social science. Now religious commitments and beliefs are merely social facts to be explained. Many contemporary shared-value theorists in the social sciences in the West are followers of Parsons. These followers are mostly sociologists and anthropologists—there are virtually no economists and there are now few political scientists in the Parsons camp. There was a grand Parsonian movement in political science from the 1950s through some time in the 1970s. The most notable and creative example of this movement is the civic culture of Gabriel Almond and Sidney Verba (1963) and others. Although there is not much of a grand-synthesis view of norms that remains in political science or even in much of sociology, there are still ad hoc theories of norms. For example, political scientists often explain the voting that occurs as public spirited, altruistic, or duty driven. And there is today a rising chorus of political scientists who take a more or less ad hoc stand on the importance of a value consensus, as represented by those concerned with the supposed declines in trust, family values, and community (e.g. Putnam 2000).

Contractarians in social theory are typically shared-value theorists. This may sound odd, because legal contracts typically govern exchanges. But social contract theory requires a motivation for fulfilling one's side of a contractual arrangement and a social contract is not analogous to a legal contract in this respect. Because there is no enforcer of it, a social contract is commonly therefore seen to require a normative commitment—essentially the same normative commitment from everyone (see Hardin 1999, ch. 3). For example, in the view of Thomas Scanlon (1982, 115 n.; 1999; see further Barry 1995 and Hardin 1998) the motivation to keep to a social contract is the desire to achieve reasonable agreement on cooperative arrangements. This appears to entail a straightforward factual issue about the existence of this desire. Is this desire prevalent? Because of the difficulty of defining reasonable agreement, it seems unlikely. The methodological task of demonstrating the prevalence of such a desire seems simple enough, but the reasonable agreement theorists have not bothered to test their assumption. It seems very unlikely that there is such a desire, so that Scanlon's contractualism cannot undergird social cooperation or, therefore, social theory. Contracts for ordinary exchanges are backed by various incentives to perform, especially by the threat of legal enforcement, by the interest the parties have in maintaining the relationship for future exchanges, or in maintaining their reputations. Social contracts have none of these to back them.

And, third, there are *exchange*, which are relatively more recent than the other two schools, with Bernard Mandeville and Adam Smith among the first major figures, and, in our time, George Homans and many social choice theorists and economists.[3] At the core of an exchange theory is individualism. Tocqueville (1966 [1835 and 1840], vol. ii. 506–08), writing in the 1830s, says "individualism" is a new term. It turns on the calm feeling that disposes each to isolate himself from the mass and to live among family and friends. It tends to isolate us from our past and our contemporaries. The rigorous, uncompromising focus on individuals is a distinctive contribution of Hobbes, the contribution that puts us on the track to modern political philosophy and that makes Hobbes at least partially an exchange theorist. For him, the assumption of individualism is de facto a method for focusing on what is central to social order. It is also, of course, a descriptive fact of the social world that he analyzes. It becomes Tocqueville's assumption in analyzing American society two centuries later, when it is also the basis for criticizing his own French society. He says that, at the head of any undertaking, where in France we would find government and in England some territorial magnate, in the United States we are sure to find an association (513). These associations are made up of individuals who voluntarily take on their roles; they are not appointed to these roles, which are not part of any official hierarchy. Tocqueville has a forceful method: go to the core of any activity to explain the form of its successes and failures. And when we do that for America in the 1830s, we find individuals motivated by their own interests. When we do it for France, we find government agents and regulations. Anyone who has lived in both France and the United States might reasonably conclude that the two societies have moved toward one another in this respect, but that they still differ in the way Tocqueville finds nearly two centuries ago.

Note that these three sets of assumptions—individualism, self-interest, and the collective benefits of self-seeking behavior—are the assumptions of both positive and normative theories. This should not be a surprise because the world we wish to judge normatively is the same world we wish to explain positively. Moreover, all of the normative theories we might address are likely to have positive elements that

---

[3] There are also many theories and assumptions, such as structural theories as represented by Marx and articulated by many structuralist sociologists in our time, that are much less broadly applicable, both positively and normatively.

we could analyze from the perspective of relevant positive theories. For example, to argue persuasively for shared-value theories we must be able to show that there are shared values. This is often not done very well or even at all, but is merely assumed as though it were obvious. A fully adequate normative theory must therefore fit both positive and normative assumptions and must depend on both positive and normative methodologies. Often this must mean that the methodological demands of normative claims are more stringent than the methodological demands of any parallel positive claims. Normative claims must pass muster on both positive and normative methodological standards.

Given the pervasiveness of shared-value theories in contemporary social and political theory, we should consider whether there are shared values of the relevant kind and force. This is, again, a positive issue and it should not be hard to handle. Once we establish that there are or are not relevant shared values, we can go on to discuss how they are constructed and what implications they might have for social theory, actual institutions, and political behavior.

3 SHARED VALUES

Suppose it is established that we do share some important set of political values, X, Y, and Z. What follows? Our shared values do not directly entail any particular actions because acting on those values might conflict with our interests in other things, and acting on our shared values might cost you heavily enough to block you from acting in our common interest. Superficially it might seem that interest, for example in the form of resources, is merely another value, or rather a proxy for values that could compare to X, Y, and Z. But this will commonly be wrong. For an important political example, suppose we are all or almost all patriotic. Your patriotism benefits me if it motivates you to act in certain ways, but acting in those ways likely has costs for you, so that although we share the value of patriotism we may not have incentives to act in ways that benefit each other. Given that we share the value of patriotism to a particular nation, we might want to ask on what that value commitment is founded. It could be founded on interests, identity, or bald commitment to our nation, right or wrong. It might not be easy to establish which, if any, of these plays a role. Tocqueville supposes that patriotism founded on interests must be fragile, because interests can change (Tocqueville 1966 [1835 and 1840], i. 373). We might also suppose that our interests in patriotism here could be compromised in favor of other interests.

Perhaps our commitment turns on our ethnic identity, as is commonly claimed for nationalist commitments. There can typically be no compromise on ethnicity and the costs of defending one's ethnicity may be discounted heavily for that reason. You cannot trade half of your ethnic commitments for half of mine. Of course, the next generation might do exactly that. They might marry across our ethnic divide, engage in joint corporate activities, and have friendship groups that straddle ethnic lines. Sadly, such actions and even merely their possibility might be sources of deep conflict between our groups. On economic issues, there commonly is some possibility of compromise that lets the parties split differences to allow all to gain from staying involved with each other, even cooperating together and coordinating on many fundamentally important activities. This is, for Smith and many other political economists, a major unintended benefit of the market for exchange.

Contract or agreement theories suggest a need or at least an urge to explain why we agree, and the answer often must be that it is in our interest to agree on some particular social arrangement or that we share the values on which we are to contract. Hence, agreement theories threaten to reduce to simple interest or to shared-value theories or explanations. But even then they have a strength that shared-value theories often lack. Once your interests, pro and con, are established, there is likely no further need to explain why you act in relevant ways. Motivations and interests tend to collapse into each other if they are fully defined. Unless someone's commitment to some value translates in standard terms into their interests (hence, the odd locution "can be cashed out" as), we still face the task of determining how that value commitment will motivate action, if at all. In sum, interest is both a value and a motivation. Shared-value theories must first establish what values are shared and then give an account of how commitment to them motivates action. Both steps here may be very difficult. Indeed, each of these steps might challenge some of our standard methodologies for establishing social and psychological facts.

An important subcategory of shared-value theory is the body of norms that regulate our behavior in social interaction. The category of norms is much broader than that for social order, but it is these that matter for political theory. We may parse the category of norms in many ways. The most common move is simply to list many norms and to apply them to particular problems, as with the putative norms on voting. In a far more systematic approach, Edna Ullmann-Margalit (1977) lays out several categories as based on the game-theoretic structure of the underlying problems that the norms help to resolve or at least address. Her deep insight is that norms must handle the strategic structure of the incentives people face if the norms are to get them to behave cooperatively. Her modal strategic categories are prisoner's dilemma, coordination and unequal coordination, and conflict. Some of Ullmann-Margalit's norms help us, respectively, to coordinate, to cooperate, or to manage conflict in these contexts.

It is striking that Ullmann-Margalit's book from only four decades ago is among the first serious efforts to bring strategic analysis systematically to bear on normative theory and problems. Indeed, we might well speak of the strategic turn in social theory, a turn that has been heavily influenced and even guided by game theory, which was invented roughly during the Second World War (Neumann and Morgenstern 1953 [1944]). That turn has influenced both positive and normative theory. There are standard norms that address all of Ullmann-Margalit's strategic categories and those norms have vernacular standing in ordinary life contexts. But Ullmann-Margalit shows that many norms are strategically related and thereby shows how they are grounded in incentives. In political theory, the norms that most interest us are those that regulate social order (Hardin 1995, chs. 4 and 5).

4 A FOURTH THEORY: COORDINATION

Because there generally is conflict in any moderately large society, coercion is a sine qua non for social order. But it is only one sine qua non. Two others are exchange and coordination. All are needed because the strategic structures of our potential interactions are quite varied, and we need devices for handling all of these reasonably well if we are to have desirable order and prosperity. In a subsistence agricultural society, coercion might be very nearly the only point of government. But in a complex society, coercion seems to be a minor element in the actual lives of most people, although the threat of it might stand behind more of our actions than we suppose. In such a society, exchange and coordination loom very large, radically larger than in the subsistence economy.

The three grand, broadly established schools of political thought—conflict, shared values, and agreement or exchange—are right about particular aspects of social order. But they miss the central mode of social order in a complex modern society, which is coordination (Lindblom 1977; Schelling 1960). We do not necessarily share values but we can coordinate to allow each of us to pursue our own values without destructive interaction or exchange. To grossly simplify much of the problem of social order in a complex society, consider the relatively trivial problem of maintaining order in traffic on roads. There are two main coordinations at stake. The first is the obvious one of merely getting all drivers to drive on the same side of the road—either all on their left or all on their right—in order to prevent constant accidents and difficult problems of negotiating who gets to go first. The second is the problem of controlling the flow of traffic at intersections, for which traffic signals and signs are used when the traffic is heavy enough. Two striking things about the collection of drivers are that *they are not genuinely in conflict* and that *they do not typically have to share any general social values* in order for these coordinations to work well. Furthermore, *there is no exchange* that they can make to solve the problems arising from their interactions. I have my purposes, you have yours, and we want merely to avoid getting in each other's way while going about our own affairs. The seeming miracle is that often we can do all of this spontaneously. For example, some coordinations can be managed by relying on focal points (Schelling 1960) that make a particular solution obvious or on institutions, which can define a resolution. Getting everyone to drive right is an instance of the first of these devices; managing traffic flow at intersections is an instance of the second.

As are conflict theories, coordination is an interest theory. Hobbes is perhaps the first major coordination theorist.[4] But David Hume (2000 [1739–40], book 3), Adam Smith (1976 [1776]), and C. E. Lindblom (1977) see much of social order as a matter of coordinating the disparate interests of many people. A shared-value theory could be essentially a coordination theory if the values motivate coordinated actions, but *coordination does not require broadly shared values*. This is the chief reason why coordination is fundamentally important in modern social and political theory. Shared-value theories typically make adherence to relevant values a matter of overriding one's interests and, when put into political power, overriding the interests of many citizens. For example, I help to defend my community despite the risks that such effort entails, I submerge my identity in the collective identity (whatever that might mean), or I vote despite the burden to me of doing so and despite the virtual irrelevance of the effect of my vote on my interests. But against the strenuous and implausible view of Parsons, a collection of quite diverse pluralists can coordinate on an order for the society in which they seek their diverse values. In sum, coordination interactions are especially important for politics and political theory and probably for sociology, although exchange relations might be most of economics, or at least of classical economics. In a sense, the residual Parsonians are right to claim that conflict relations are not the whole of political order, although not for reasons that they might recognize. They are right, again, because the core or modal character of social order is coordination.

While at a commonsense level the problem of coordination is typically not difficult to grasp, its general significance and its compelling nature have not been central understandings in the social sciences or in political philosophy. Hobbes had a nascent coordination theory in his vision of our coordinating on a single sovereign (Hardin 1991). Had he been more supple in his views, he might have recognized that the dreadful problem of civil war in his England was a matter of *multiple coordinations* of various groups in mortal conflict with each other. There was no war of all against all but only war between alternative factions for rule, each of which was well enough coordinated to wreak havoc on the others and on nonparticipant bystanders. Hume made the outstanding philosophical contribution to understanding coordination problems, but his insights were largely ignored for two centuries or more after he wrote and they are still commonly misread.[5] Thomas Schelling (1960, 54–8) gave the first insightful game-theoretic account of coordination problems and their strategic and incentive structures. But their pervasive importance in social life is still not a standard part of social scientific and philosophical understanding.

In social life, coordination occurs in two very different forms: spontaneously and institutionally. We can coordinate and we can be coordinated as in the two-part coordination of traffic. In Philadelphia in 1787 a small number of people coordinated spontaneously to create the framework to organize the new US nation institutionally.

---

[4] Not all Hobbes scholars would agree with this assessment. For an argument for understanding him as a coordination theorist, see Hardin (1991).

[5] Hume's arguments may have been overlooked because they are chiefly in a series of long footnotes in Hume (2000 [1739–40], 3.2.3.4 n–11 n).

Once they had drafted their constitution, its adoption was beneficial to enough of the politically significant groups in the thirteen states that, for them, it was mutually advantageous (Hardin 1999). Therefore, they were able to *coordinate spontaneously on that constitution* to subject themselves to being *coordinated institutionally by it* thereafter. This is the story of very many institutional structures that govern our social lives, and the more often this story plays out in varied realms, the more pervasively we can expect to see it carried over to other realms and to organize our institutions, practices, and even, finally, our preferences, tastes, and values. As it does so, it might be expected then to drive out or to dominate alternative ways to create and justify our social organization.

5 CONCLUDING REMARKS

In the era of Hobbes, writing during the English Civil War, the first focus of political theory was social order in which individuals might survive and prosper. Success in managing order has pushed worry about social order out of its formerly central place, even virtually out of concern altogether for many political theorists. The meaning of justice has changed to match this development. Through Hume's writings, justice is commonly conceived as "justice as order," as in Henry Sidgwick's (1907, 440) somewhat derisive term. This is more or less the justice that legal authorities and courts achieve in the management of criminal law and of the civil law of contracts and property relations. By Sidgwick's time, it begins to be conceived as, or at least to include, distributive justice, as in the theory of John Rawls (1999 [1971]). Hume and John Stuart Mill (1977 [1861]) also shift the focus toward the institutions of government, which in large modern societies entails representative government. This move brings back classical and Renaissance political thought. It also makes great demands on causal understandings and therefore on positive theory and methodology, again tying the normative and the positive tightly together in a single account. Rawls's theory also requires massive positive understandings when he says that now the task is to design institutions capable of delivering distributive justice, a task that he leaves to others, who have so far generally failed to take it up. Rawls's and Hobbes's theories are relatively holistic and general; Hume's and Mill's are relatively piecemeal and specific. Perhaps no methodology gives us serious entrée to handling holistic social and political theory at the level and scale required by Hobbes and Rawls. Eventually, therefore, we must want to break down the institutional moves entailed by Rawls's theory to make them piecemeal and manageable.

It is an interesting fact that normative methodologies have changed substantially over the past several decades. Methodologies in many fields of social theory and explanation have been refined extensively during that period, especially under the influence of rational choice and game theory but few if any of them have been dropped or developed *de novo*. Today's three leading normative methods have come into their own during that period, so much so that it is hard to imagine what normative theories would be like today without those methods driving their articulation and refinement. Developments have not been equally dramatic in all three methods. Two of the methods, shared-value and contractarian arguments, threaten to be narrowed down to use by academic moral theorists with little resonance beyond that narrow community. Any method that becomes as esoteric as much of contemporary moral theory has become is apt to be ignored and even dismissed by the overwhelming majority of social theorists as irrelevant. That would be a profoundly sad separation of normative from positive theory, the worst such separation in the history of social theory, worse than the separation of economic from utilitarian value theory wrought by G. E. Moore (1903, 84) a century ago, when he literally took utility into the vacuousness of outer space.

The theorists who work in the normative vineyard often seem to strive more for novelty than for comprehensiveness or even comprehension. Great novelty cannot generally be a worthy goal for us in social theory. The occasional major novel invention, such as Hobbes's all-powerful sovereign as a form of institutionally enforced coordination, Hume's convention as a form of spontaneously enforced coordination, Smith's classical economics, Vilfredo Pareto's (1971 [1927]) value theory, John von Neumann and Oskar Morgenstern's (1953 [1944]) game theory, or Schelling's (1960) coordination theory takes a long time to be incorporated into the main stream of theory and explanation of social institutions and practices. A flood of supposedly novel contributions is apt to be ignored or openly dismissed. Creativity in social theory is not likely to depend on such major innovations except on relatively rare occasions. *Most of the creativity we see is in the application of well-established innovations across many realms.*

Over the past four or five decades, rational-choice normative theory, the third major branch of contemporary normative methodology, has become a vast program that increasingly leaves the other two branches behind in its scope and sheer quantity of work. This development is made more readily possible by the clarity and systematic structure of game theory and game-theoretic rational choice. Game theory and rational choice methodology are very well laid out and easily put to use. Perhaps at least partially because of that fact, rational choice methods are taking over normative theorizing and theories. Early steps along the way in this seeming conquest include Richard Braithwaite's (1955) use of game theory in moral reasoning, David Lewis's (1969) analysis of convention in the spirit of Hume, Ullmann-Margalit's (1977) theory of norms, and a flood of other works from the 1980s on.

In this program, method and theory tend to merge. One might wonder whether this is a typical tendency for relatively developed theories and the methods successfully associated with them. Shared-value theory is perhaps becoming the most commonly asserted alternative to rational choice in our time as contractarian reasoning recedes from center stage in the face of challenges to the story of contracting that lies behind it and the difficulty of believing people actually think they have consciously agreed to their political order, as long ago noted by Hume (1985 [1748]). But it faces a harder task than rational-choice normative theory because it has barely begun at the basic level of establishing a set of demonstrably shared values other than own welfare. Own welfare is, of course, the shared value that shared-value theorists most want to reject, although one wonders how many of the most ardent opponents of that value as a general guiding principle in social theory would actually reject that value in their own lives.

References

ALMOND, G. and VERBA, S. 1963. *The Civic Culture: Political Attitudes and Democracy in Five Nations*. Boston: Little, Brown.

ARISTOTLE 1958 [4th century BC]. *Politics*, trans. E. Barker. New York: Oxford University Press.

BARRY, B. 1995. *Justice as Impartiality*. Oxford: Oxford University Press.

BRAITHWAITE, R. 1955. *Theory of Games as a Tool for the Moral Philosopher*. Oxford: Oxford University Press.

DAHRENDORF, R. 1968. In praise of Thrasymachus. Pp. 129–50 in Dahrendorf, *Essays in the Theory of Society*. Stanford, Calif.: Stanford University Press.

HARDIN, R. 1990. Rationally justifying political coercion. *Journal of Philosophical Research*, 15: 79–91.

—— 1991. Hobbesian political order. *Political Theory*, 19: 156–80.

—— 1995. *One for All: The Logic of Group Conflict*. Princeton, NJ: Princeton University Press.

—— 1998. Reasonable agreement: political not normative. Pp. 137–53 in *Impartiality, Neutrality and Justice: Re-Reading Brian Barry's* Justice as Impartiality, ed. P. J. Kelly. Edinburgh: Edinburgh University Press.

—— 1999. *Liberalism, Constitutionalism, and Democracy*. Oxford: Oxford University Press.

—— 2003. *Indeterminacy and Society*. Princeton, NJ: Princeton, University Press.

—— 2007. *David Hume: Moral and Political Theorist*. Oxford: Oxford University Press.

HOBBES, T. 1983 [1642]. *De Cive*, ed. H. Warrender, trans. from the Latin. Oxford: Oxford University Press.

—— 1994 [1651]. *Leviathan*, ed. E. Curley. Indianapolis: Hackett.

HUME, D. 2000 [1739–40]. *A Treatise of Human Nature*, ed. D. F. Norton and M. J. Norton. Oxford: Oxford University Press.

—— 1985 [1748]. Of the original contract. Pp. 465–87 in *David Hume: Essays Moral, Political, and Literary*, ed. E. F. Miller. Indianapolis: Liberty Classics.

LEWIS, D. K. 1969. *Convention*. Cambridge, Mass.: Harvard University Press.

LINDBLOM, C. E. 1977. *Politics and Markets: The World's Political-Economic Systems*. New York: Basic Books.

MILL, J. S. 1977 [1861]. *Considerations on Representative Government*. Pp. 376–613 in Mill, *Essays on Politics and Society*, vol. xix of *Collected Works of John Stuart Mill*, ed. J. M. Robson. Toronto: University of Toronto Press.

MOORE, G. E. 1903. *Principia Ethica*. Cambridge: Cambridge University Press.

NEUMANN, J. VON and MORGENSTERN, O. 1953 [1944]. *Theory of Games and Economic Behavior*, 3rd edn. Princeton, NJ: Princeton University Press.

PARETO, V. 1971 [1927]. *Manual of Political Economy*, trans. from French edition. New York: Kelley.

PARSONS, T. 1968 [1937]. *The Structure of Social Action*. New York: Free Press.

PUTNAM, R. D. 2000. *Bowling Alone: The Collapse and Revival of American Community.* New York: Simon and Schuster.

RAWLS, J. 1999 [1971]. *A Theory of Justice.* Cambridge, Mass.: Harvard University Press.

SCANLON, T. M. 1982. Contractualism and utilitarianism. Pp. 103–28 in *Utilitarianism and Beyond*, ed. A. Sen and B. Williams. Cambridge: Cambridge University Press.

—— 1999. *What We Owe to Each Other.* Cambridge, Mass.: Harvard University Press.

SCHELLING, T. C. 1960. *The Strategy of Conflict.* Cambridge, Mass.: Harvard University Press.

SIDGWICK, H. 1907. *The Methods of Ethics*, 7th edn. London: Macmillan.

SMITH, A. 1976 [1776]. *An Inquiry into the Nature and Causes of the Wealth of Nations.* Oxford: Oxford University Press.

TOCQUEVILLE, A. DE 1966 [1835 and 1840]. *Democracy in America*, trans. G. Lawrence. New York: Harper and Row.

ULLMANN-MARGALIT, E. 1977. *The Emergence of Norms.* Oxford: Oxford University Press.

WRONG, D. 1994. *The Problem of Order: What Unites and Divides Society.* New York: Free Press.

CHAPTER 4

THEORY IN HISTORY

PROBLEMS OF CONTEXT AND NARRATIVE

J. G. A. POCOCK

1 THE PROBLEMS OF TERMINOLOGY

To construct a study of the relations between "political theory" and "history"—as conceptualized phenomena or as disciplines we practice—it is necessary to study these terms and, if possible, to reduce them to manageable forms. The term "political theory" is imprecise; it has been used in a diversity of ways, and the contributors to this *Handbook* are probably not agreed on any single usage. From the standpoint from which this chapter is written, it is observable that "political theory" is often used as if it were interchangeable with "political thought," a term equally inexact. In the first half of the twentieth century, there were written a number of "histories of political thought," or of "political theory," of which the subject-matter and the method were practically indistinguishable. By "political thought" (and therefore "theory") were meant a number of intellectual disciplines—or alternatively, modes of rhetoric—which had from time to time been applied to a subject or subjects which it was agreed formed that of "politics." The "history" of these modes of discourse was agreed to form the "history of political thought" or "theory." They contained much that amounted to a "theoretical" treatment of an abstract concept of "politics," and each of them—at least in principle—had generated a second-order discourse which critically examined its conduct, and so amounted to "theory" in a further sense of that term.

These "histories" of political thought/theory were canonically constructed; that is, they arranged modes of discourse—and above all, the major texts that had acquired classical status and authority in each—in an order which it had come to be agreed formed the "history" being presented. Classically—and, it should be emphasized, for historical reasons, many of which were good—they began with the invention in fourth-century Athens of what was termed "political philosophy," so that "political philosophy" became a term of equal status (and imprecision) with "political thought" and "theory." A historical grand narrative emerged, in which "the history of political thought," "theory," or "philosophy" moved from Platonic or Aristotelian beginnings through a medieval period in which "philosophy" encountered Christian theology, into one in which this encounter was liquidated and replaced by modes of thought, theory, and philosophy it was agreed to term "modern."

It was a further characteristic of these "histories" that they were not written by historians so much as by "political theorists" and "philosophers" who held that the study of this "history" was in some way conducive to the enterprise or enquiry in which they were themselves engaged. To study "the history of political theory" was helpful to the practice of "political theory." This assumption came, at and after the middle of the twentieth century, to be attacked in two ways. There arose ways of conducting both the empirical and the normative study of politics which claimed to have no need of historical knowledge—still described in its canonical form—because they possessed means of validating, criticizing, verifying or falsifying, the statements that they made, which depended upon the method that they practiced and not upon historical circumstance or character. This may be considered one of the moments at which the term "political science" made its appearance. Concurrently—and in some ways in response to this development—historians appeared who proposed (often aggressively) to reduce "the history of political thought" to a rigorously autonomous mode of historical enquiry. The writing of texts, the slower formation of belief systems or "philosophies," were to be reduced to historical performances or "speech acts," the actions of historical actors in circumstances and with intentions that could be ascertained. They were not part of a "theory of politics;" or if they were, the processes by which they had come to be so, and the very existence of "political theories" themselves, were historical processes in the performance of acts and the formation of languages, to be studied as such.

Important claims can be made about the increase and intensification of historical knowledge which this revolution in method brings about. The theorist or philosopher is faced with the question of whether "political theory" is or is not to be reduced to the knowledge of its own history. A typical response has been to treat this question as itself a problem in theory or philosophy, and it can be observed that more has been written about Quentin Skinner—a leader in the historical revolution—as political theorist or philosopher than as historian. The author of this article, however, treats Skinner's work, and his own, as the construction of historical narratives, in which things happen (in this case the utterance of theoretical statements about politics), the conditions or "contexts" in which they happen exist and change, and processes occur in the history of these performances that can be narrated. In what follows, it will be presupposed that a "historian," interested in the question "what was it that was happening?", and a "political theorist," engaged in an enquiry possessing its own ways of self-validation, confront each other over the reading of a given text. I will bias my own enquiry by pointing out that the text will be a historical artifact, but that the theorist desires to make use of it for purposes other than establishing it as a historical phenomenon.

2 History and Theory: The Encounter

The activity of the mind called "political theory" will have been defined—probably, and properly, in more ways than one—by the contributors to this volume. For purposes of abbreviation, I will suppose that they have defined it as the construction of heuristic and normative statements, or systems of such statements, about an area of human experience and activity called "politics" or "the political." I will also suppose that the activity called "political theory" is a discipline possessing its own rules: that is to say, the statements it aims to construct acknowledge certain procedures according to which they are constructed and may be validated and criticized. There will instantly arise, however, a further activity of questioning how such procedures have been and are being constructed, to what capacities of the mind they make appeal, whether their claims to validity are or have been justifiable, and in short whether, and how, it is possible to construct a discipline called "political theory" at all. This activity of the second order may be called "political philosophy"—although this term has borne other meanings—and distinguished from "political theory" as carried on at levels confident enough of its procedures to dispense, at least provisionally, with the questioning of them at the levels called "philosophy." Having made this distinction, of course, we observe that the two activities continually intersect, although the distinction does not disappear.

It is valuable to imagine the "political theorist"—given that this term may have more than one meaning—confronted by a "historian of political thought," who regards "political theory," in any of its meanings, as one of many ways in which "thought," or rather "discourse," about "politics" has been going on. Even if we suppose our agonists to agree on a definition of the activity to be called "political theory," and to agree that this activity has had a continuous history of some duration, there will remain many senses in which they do not and perhaps should not have much to say to one another. The "theorist" is interested in the making of statements (hypotheses?) obedient to certain modes of validation; the "philosopher" in the question of how (and whether) it is possible to construct these (or any) modes of validation (or evaluation). The historian is not interested primarily, although perhaps secondarily, in any of these questions, but in the question "what happened?" (or was happening)—more broadly still, "what was it that was happening?"—when events or processes occurred in the past under study. One aims to characterize, to evaluate, to explicate (rather than explain), and therefore in the last analysis to narrate, actions performed in the recorded past; and if they were performed according to, or even in search of, certain modes of validation, one is interested in their performance rather than their validity, and in the validations to which they appealed as the context that renders them the happenings they were. The questions "is this statement valid?" and "what has happened when it is made?" are not identical, unless—and this is the issue—the theorist who asks the former can oblige the historian who asks the latter to admit that nothing has been going on except the practice of a certain mode of validation; and this the questions asked by the "philosopher" have already rendered somewhat uncertain.

The historian, then, may be thought of as scrutinizing the actions and activity of political theory, and asking questions about what it has been and done, answers to which will necessarily take the form of narratives of actions performed and their consequences. The historian's activity is clearly not identical with that of the political theorist. Before we go on to set these two activities in confrontation and interaction, it is desirable to ask whether "histories of political theory" have been or may be constructed, and what character they may possess. Here the focus of our enquiry shifts. A "history of political theory" would clearly move beyond the scrutiny of particular acts in the construction of such theory, and would suppose "political theory" to be and have been an ongoing activity, about which generalizations may be made and which can be said to have undergone changes in its general character over the course of time; changes which could be recounted in the form of a narrated history. There are, however, few such histories; few, that is, which are or may be called histories of political "theory" in any sense in which that term may be distinguished from, or isolated within, the "history of political thought" as the academic genre it has become. Histories of this kind are themselves indeterminate, in the sense that options exist and have been exercised as to what kinds of literature may or should be included in them, and it is a consequence that the terms "political thought" and "political theory" have often been used interchangeably, or with no precise attention to differences between them. The political theorist whose attention turns to history, therefore, is often confronted with historical narratives whose content bears little relation to the activity of "political theory" as it may have been defined. It is not unreasonable if such a theorist asks why such histories deserve attention.

3 Histories and their Purpose

In the last forty or fifty years, canonical histories of this kind have fallen into disfavor (although there have recently been some signs of a revival[1]). The best-known alternative in English, associated with the work of Quentin Skinner and others,[2] has taken

---

[1] For example, Coleman (2000); she might not accept the adjective "canonical."
[2] Skinner (2002, i); Tully and Skinner (1988); Palonen (2003); Pocock (1962, 1985, 1987).

the form of a close scrutiny of the history—a key word has been "context"—in which texts and patterns of political discourse may be situated and said to have happened. It will be seen that the distance, mentioned earlier, between the questions asked by the theorist or philosopher, and by the historian, has grown wider. Historians of this school look upon the political literature of any period as composed of acts of speech or writing, articulations performed by authors in the language or diversity of languages available to them. These languages have histories; they can be seen in formation and in change; the performances of authors act in and upon them; and this is the sense in which they can be termed the primary "context" in which texts and debates happen in history. There are of course further contexts, the political, religious, social, and historical situations in which authors and their publics were situated; and what these were is to be discovered as much from the implications of their languages as from the researches of historians. What actors thought was happening is of equal importance with what historians think was happening; history is the study of subjective behavior.

In this multiplicity of "contexts"—both linguistic and situational—historians pursue the interactions between an author's intentions, the language available for him or her to use, and the responses of those who read, or were informed concerning, the text and its author; the tensions between what an author "meant" to say and what a text "meant" to others, are often complex and productive of ambivalences. It may be the case that an author wrote in more than one "context" and was read in contexts other than those he intended. To give examples: *Leviathan* was written in both English and Latin, and one may differentiate between Hobbes's intention and reception in a circle of philosophers in Paris, the court of the exiled Stuarts, the pamphlet-reading public in London, and the Dutch and German universities. The works of Machiavelli were written in manuscript for discussion groups in the politics of Florence, and it was by others after his death that they were released on the print networks of Europe, where they were read and responded to by other groups and publics, in ways it is not immediately certain he intended. The happenings of communication and performance are of primary concern to the historian, but not to the political theorist. The former is interested in what an author "meant" and in what a text "meant" to actors in history; the latter in what it "means" to a theorist, in the context of the enquiry she or he is conducting.

Works on the history of political thought, written in the above manner, tend to be microhistories rather than macrohistories, studies of particular performances, actions, and compositions, focused on the immediate context of the action rather than its long-term consequences. If confined—as there is no reason why they should not be—to a particular text or group of texts, and to the state of the language culture at the time these were written, they will be synchronous rather than diachronous in their emphasis; and it has been asked whether the contextualist approach is capable of supplying a history of contexts. This, however, can be done in several ways. The text and its author can be shown innovating in and acting upon the language in which the text is written, obliging the language to say new things and modify or reverse its implications. The text can be studied as it is read and responded to by others, becoming what it means to them as distinct from what its author intended. Lastly, texts sometimes outlive both their authors and the contexts in which they are written, traveling both in space and in time to act and be acted upon in contexts of language and circumstance sharply unlike those in which they received their original meaning. There will now be the possibility of historical narrative, recounting both how the text underwent changes in use and meaning, perhaps and perhaps not continuing to convey its author's intentions in situations he cannot have foreseen, and how the language context underwent change for reasons not reducible to the intended performances of identifiable speech actors. It may even be possible—although it seems that it must be questionable—to supply unified "histories of political thought," in which one pattern of consensus and challenge is progressively replaced by another, although recent *Cambridge Histories* have tended to present several such histories going on concurrently in contexts distinguishable from one another.[3] If anything like the former canonical histories is restored, it will probably be the work of political theorists desirous of a usable past, rather than of historians not interested in supplying them with one.

4 THE ENCOUNTER RESUMED

To suppose a direct encounter between a political theorist and a historian, each engaged in studying the same text, we must make two assumptions. In the first place, we should suppose the theorist to be carrying out a programme of theoretical enquiry, possessing its own discipline and means of validating the statements it advances; this will enable us to juxtapose the theorist's propositions with those put forward by the historian, and enquire into any meeting or collision that may appear between them. In the second place—and here it is hard to avoid placing an additional burden on the theorist—we must suppose that the two actors are studying the same text, which has not been written by the theorist but by some other agent at some point in history. It is hard, although in principle not impossible, to imagine the historian studying a text written by a contemporary theorist as if it were a historical phenomenon. Historians are typically concerned with the past; they let time go by, during which evidence may assemble and perspectives emerge and alter. But once we suppose the theorist to be engaged with a text written by another hand, and itself a historical document, we must ask why this is happening, and what role a text written by another and— the historian instantly adds—in another context plays in the self-discipline and self-validating enterprise we have supposed the theorist to be conducting. The answer to our questions may emerge in literary and almost serendipitous terms. The theorist has, for whatever reason, read the historic text and finds its language to serve the purpose of some enterprise in political theory being conducted in the present; the

---

[3] Burns (1988); Burns with Goldie (1991); Goldie and Wokler (2006).

language of the text is therefore presented as a proposition to be evaluated in the terms and by the criteria of the present enterprise. The historian now appears, asking questions and making statements concerning the intentions of the text's author and the meaning (a two-faced term) of his words in the context or contexts he and they occupied in history. In what ways, if any, will the propositions advanced by theorist and historian affirm or deny one another?

The theorist may assert that the author in the past was engaged in a programme of political theorizing identical with, or very closely resembling, that being conducted by the theorist in the present; so that the author's language may be quoted, cited, or paraphrased as language employed in the theorist's enterprise. The historian will scrutinize this assertion. We will suppose her or him capable of understanding a programme of political theory conducted in the present, as well as of reconstructing the languages in which programs of a similar kind have been conducted in past historical contexts. Such a historian will therefore be capable of pronouncing the theorist's assertion valid or invalid. If the former, the past author's language can be employed in the present theorist's enterprise without doing violence to the former (with which the historian, as historian, is primarily concerned); that is without doing violence to the past author's intentions or the meanings of the words used in the text. It is not in principle impossible that this will be the outcome of the historian's enquiry.

But the historian's business is with then, not now; with what the author was doing,[4] with what was happening and happened when the text was written, published, read, and answered. The former's concern is with contexts, rather than programs; with the multiplicity of contexts in which the text may have had meaning and may have been intended; with the diversity of languages (or conceptual vocabularies) in which it will have been read and may even have been written (since authors are not incapable of recognizing multivalence and taking part in it). The theorist's reading of the text will therefore have been an act of selection, a decision to read the text as engaged in a particular program, even if the author proves to have made the same decision. The historian is interested in the multiplicity of the things that have happened and the contexts in which they happened, and will probably respond, even in the extreme case where it can be shown that an author wrote in only one language and was engaged in only one enterprise, by enquiring if that is the only way in which others read and have read that author's works. When texts outlive the historical situation in which they were first written and read, intended and understood, the likelihood of a diversity of effect becomes greater.

The theorist is performing an act of selection on grounds which are not those on which the historian acts. We have so far supposed a situation in which this selection raises no problems for the historian and is even acceptable as a historical statement about the text's or the author's "meaning," but it is methodologically interesting to move away from this supposition. Suppose instead that what the theorist is doing is less quotation than translation; a removal of the author's words from the meanings and implications they bore in a past historical context to those they may bear in a

---

[4] Skinner (1978, i, xiii).

present context—one, that is, defined by the enterprise the theorist is engaged in rather than by any other language situation. The last stipulation implies that the enterprise is purely theoretical and is not being carried on into practice, since practice takes place in a world of multiple contexts and history. Given this condition, however, the theorist may still be asked why the historically distant text has been chosen as the subject of this act of translation. The answer may be that it has happened accidentally; the theorist happens to have read this text, and it happens that its language lends itself to this theoretical purpose. The circumstance that the author had similar intentions, or alternatively that his or her language can be so interpreted, is itself accidental; we are in a situation where history is accidental, or incidental, to theory. These hypothetical circumstances, however, entail different historical statements; the former is about the author acting in her or his moment in history, the latter about the action and moment of the theorist. The latter claims to be acting now, making a statement whose validity does not depend upon the historical context in which it is performed. It may be called positivist in the sense that it offers its own conditions of validation and appeals only to them.

This is of course wholly justifiable; it is valuable to set up laboratories and construct hypotheses subject to validation under rigorously controlled conditions. A common consequence of falsification, however, is the discovery that something was present which the experiment did not foresee or succeed in excluding, and here our theorist's enterprise may be the better for knowing its own history; what exactly are the conditions it specifies, and why does it specify these and not others? This question becomes all the more pressing as we enter the realms of practice and history, where the conditions under which, and the contexts in which, we operate can never be defined with finality. Here we pass beyond the simple dialogue between theorist and historian, beyond the problem of congruence between a text's meaning in the present and those it has borne in pasts. The historian has begun to resemble a post-Burkean moderate conservative, reminding us that there is always more going on than we can comprehend at any one moment and convert into either theory or practice. One has become something of a political theorist in one's own right, advancing, and inviting others to explore, the proposition that political action and political society are always to be understood in a context of historical narrative. There is room therefore for consideration of historiography as itself a branch of political thought and theory, literature and discourse.

The theorist, however, may be imagined using historical information, making historical assumptions either explicit or implicit, or reflecting upon historical processes as these appear relevant to the enterprise in political theory being conducted.[5] The question now arises whether these operations are entailed by the method of framing and validating statements in which the theorist is engaged, or whether they are incidental or accidental to it. If the former, the theorist is claiming to make historical statements validated in either the same ways as those the historian practices, or in other ways which must be defined and defended. If the latter—and this the historian

---

[5] Schochet (1994).

finds easier to imagine—the distinction between "political theory" and "political thought" has begun to disappear: that is, the former has begun to coexist with other modes of political discourse, and we are re-entering the historical world in which discourses interact, modifying, changing, confusing, and distorting one another. There are historians who study and narrate what goes on in this world; it is possible that there may be a "political theory" which addresses the same phenomena.

References

Burns, J. H. (ed.) 1988. *The Cambridge History of Medieval Political Thought, c. 350–c. 1450*. Cambridge: Cambridge University Press.

—— and Goldie, M. (eds.) 1991. *The Cambridge History of Political Thought, 1450–1700*. Cambridge: Cambridge University Press.

Coleman, J. 2000. *A History of Political Thought from the Ancient Greeks to the Early Christians; A History of Political Thought from the Middle Ages to the Renaissance*. London: Athlone Press.

Goldie, M. and Wokler, R. (eds.) 2006. *The Cambridge History of Eighteenth Century Political Thought*. Cambridge: Cambridge University Press.

Palonen, K. 2003. *Quentin Skinner: History, Politics, Rhetoric*. Cambridge: Polity Press.

Pocock, J. G. A. 1962. The history of political thought: a methodological enquiry. In *Philosophy, Politics and Society: Second Series*, ed. P. Laslett and W. G. Runciman. Oxford: Basil Blackwell.

—— 1985. Introduction: the state of the art. In J. G. A. Pocock, *Virtue, Commerce and History: Essays on Political Thought and History, Chiefly in the Eighteenth Century*. Cambridge: Cambridge University Press.

—— 1987. Texts as events: reflections on the history of political thought. In *Politics of Discourse: The Literature and History of Seventeenth-Century England*, ed. K. Sharpe and S. N. Zwicker. Berkeley: University of California Press.

Schochet, G. J. 1994. Why should history matter? Political theory and the history of political discourse. In *The Varieties of British Political Thought, 1500–1800*, ed. J. G. A. Pocock, G. J. Schochet, and L. G. Schwoerer. Cambridge: Cambridge University Press.

Skinner, Q. 1978. *The Foundations of Modern Political Thought*. Cambridge: Cambridge University Press.

—— 2002. *Visions of Politics*. Cambridge: Cambridge University Press.

Tully, J. and Skinner, Q. (eds.) 1988. *Meaning and Context: Quentin Skinner and his Critics*. Princeton, NJ: Princeton University Press.

CHAPTER 5

JUSTICE AFTER RAWLS

RICHARD J. ARNESON

IN the mid-twentieth century John Rawls single-handedly revived Anglo-American political philosophy, which had not seen significant progress since the development and elaboration of utilitarianism in the nineteenth century. Rawls reinvented the discipline by revising the social contract tradition of Locke, Rousseau, and Kant. A series of essays starting with "Justice as Fairness" in 1958 culminated in a monumental treatise, *A Theory of Justice* (Rawls 1999a [originally published 1971]). That theory of justice was in turn qualified and set in a new framework by an account of legitimate political authority to which Rawls gave a definitive formulation in his second book, *Political Liberalism* (Rawls 1996 [originally published 1993]). Rawls also produced an important monograph on justice in international relations, *The Law of Peoples* (Rawls 1999c). Rawls's achievements continue to set the contemporary terms of debate on theories of social justice. This chapter comments on the present state of play in the political philosophy discussions that Rawls initiated and stimulated.

1 RAWLS'S THEORY OF JUSTICE IN A NUTSHELL

Rawls's theory consists in an egalitarian vision of justice, specified by two principles, and the original position, a method for comparing and justifying candidate principles of justice that is supposed to single out his proposed principles as uniquely reason-able. The vision is recognizably liberal in its striving to combine the values of equality and liberty in a single conception, and controversial both in the kind of equality that is espoused and in the particular freedoms that are given special priority. The principles are claimed to be ones that free and equal persons could accept as a fair basis for social cooperation.

The principles are as follows:

1. Each person has an equal claim to a fully adequate scheme of equal basic liberties, which scheme is compatible with the same scheme for all; and in this scheme the equal political liberties, and only those liberties, are to be guaranteed their fair value.
2. Social and economic inequalities are to satisfy two conditions: first, they are to be attached to positions and offices open to all under conditions of fair equality of opportunity; and second, they are to the greatest advantage of the least advantaged members of society (quoted from Rawls 1996, Lecture 1).

The first principle is called the *equal liberty principle*. In discussion, the second is often divided into its first part, *fair equality of opportunity*, and its second part, the *difference principle*.

The equal basic liberties protected by the first principle are given by a list: "political liberty (the right to vote and to hold public office) and freedom of speech and assembly; liberty of conscience and freedom of thought; freedom of the person, which includes freedom from psychological oppression and physical assault and dismemberment (integrity of the person), the right to hold personal property and freedom from arbitrary arrest and seizure as defined by the concept of the rule of law" (Rawls 1999a, 53). Roughly, the idea is to protect civil liberties of the sort that might well be entrenched in a political constitution.

The protection accorded to the basic liberties is augmented by the further stipulation that the first principle has strict lexical priority over the second. This means that one is not permitted to trade off basic liberties for gains in the other justice principle. In addition, fair equality of opportunity, the nondiscrimination principle, has strict lexical priority over the difference principle. The principles just stated make up Rawls's special conception of justice. This conception does not apply at all historical times, but only when economic growth produces a situation in which the basic liberties can be effectively exercised. Rawls's more general conception of justice holds that social and economic advantages must be arranged to be of greatest benefit to the least advantaged members of society.

The measure of individual benefits in Rawls's theory is the individual's holding of multi-purpose goods known as "primary social goods." In *A Theory of Justice* these goods are defined as those it is rational for a person to want more rather than less of, whatever else he wants. In later writings, primary social goods are defined as goods that any rational person would strive to have who gives priority to developing and exercising two moral powers, the capacity to adopt and pursue a conception of the good and the capacity to cooperate with others on fair terms (Rawls 1996, 106, 178). Primary social goods are held to consist mainly of "the basic rights and liberties covered by the first principle of justice, freedom of movement, and free choice of occupation protected by fair equality of opportunity of the first part of the second principle, and income and wealth and the social bases of self-respect" (Rawls 1996, 180).

According to Rawls, the primary subject of justice is the basic structure of society, the way that major institutions such as the political system, the economic system, and the family interact to shape people's life prospects. The principles of justice are intended to regulate the basic structure. The duties imposed by social justice on individuals are ancillary: Individuals have a duty to conform to the rules of just institutions, if they exist, and if they do not exist, to strive to some extent to bring them about.

Fair equality of opportunity may be contrasted with formal equality of opportunity or careers open to talents. The latter principle is satisfied if positions such as places in universities and desirable jobs and entrepreneurial opportunities (access to investment capital) are open to all who might wish to apply, positions being filled according to the relevant fitness of the candidates for the position in question. Formal equality of opportunity is violated if positions of advantage are passed out on any basis other than the relevant merits of the candidates. The more demanding fair equality of opportunity requires that institutions are arranged so that any individuals with the same native talent and the same ambition have the same chances for competitive success—success in competitions for positions that confer above-average shares of primary social goods. A society in which fair equality of opportunity is satisfied is, in a sense, a perfect meritocracy.

Why accept Rawls's principles? Rawls offers two arguments. One appeals to the implications of applying these principles in a modern setting. To the extent that the principles imply policies and outcomes for individuals that match our reflective judgments about these matters, the principles will appear reasonable. A second form of argument, a novelty introduced by Rawls, is the original position construction. The idea is to refine the social contract tradition. Justice is conceived to be what persons would agree to under conditions for choosing principles to regulate the basic structure of society that are ideally fair. The original position argument exemplifies a fair proceduralist standard of justification: What is right is what people following an ideal procedure would accept as right.

The original position argument carries the social contract idea to a higher level of abstraction. The object of the agreement is to be basic principles for regulating social life not actual social arrangements. The agreement is conceived to be hypothetical not actual. Actual contracts reached by people in ordinary life reflect their bargaining strength and other contingencies. Rawls's notable innovation is to try to ensure that the agreement that defines principles of justice is fair by depriving the parties who make the agreement of any information that might corrupt or bias the choice of principles. In Rawls's phrase, the parties are to choose under a veil of ignorance. Rawls urges a thick veil, with the result that parties in the original position know no particular facts about themselves, not even their own aims and values, but only general facts such as social science provides. The parties are assumed to prefer more rather than fewer primary social goods and choose principles according to their expectation of the primary social goods they would get in a society run according to the principles chosen in the original position.

Rawls conjectures that, in the original position so specified, the parties as defined would choose a maximin rule of choice (choose the policy that will make the worst possible outcome as good as possible) and on this basis would favor his principles.

The original position argument as Rawls presents it is significantly shaped by his conviction that to render his view plausible the formidable opponent that must be defeated is utilitarianism. According to Rawls, utilitarianism, although wrong, has received impressive formulation as a genuine normative theory of right conduct and institutions. A theory is a set of principles that specifies the facts relevant to social decision and that, once these relevant facts pertaining to any decision problem are known, determines what ought to be chosen in that decision problem without any further need for intuitive judgment. You cannot beat a theory except with a better theory, Rawls thinks. Rawls provides a partial theory, a theory of just institutions, that can stand as a rival to a utilitarian account. Rawls identifies utilitarianism with the view that one ought always to choose that action or policy that maximizes the aggregate (or average level) of informed desire satisfaction.

As Rawls sets up the original position argument, three arguments are prominent. One is that given the special circumstances of choice in the original position, it would be rational for the parties to choose to maximin and thus to adopt Rawls's principles. Another argument is that those in the individual position are choosing for a well-ordered society in which everyone accepts and complies with the principles chosen, so they cannot in the original position choose principles that they expect they might not be disposed to accept and follow in the society ruled by the principles chosen. A related argument or stipulation is that the parties are supposed to be choosing principles for a public conception of justice, so a choice of principles that could be successfully implemented only by being kept esoteric is ruled out.

Rawls adds to the original position argument a discussion of stability. He thinks his theory is only acceptable if it can be shown that in a society regulated by his principles of justice, people will embrace the principles and institutions satisfying their requirements and will be steadily motivated to comply with the principles and the institutions that realize them. Here in retrospect Rawls locates a pivotal mistake in *A Theory of Justice* (see Rawls 1996, "Introduction"). In later writings, culminating in *Political Liberalism* (1996), he maintains that he initially appealed to a comprehensive Kantian account of human autonomy and fundamental human aims to establish that people living under Rawlsian institutions will have good reason and sufficient motivation to comply with them. But he comes to believe this appeal was misguided. In any liberal society that sustains a clearly desirable freedom of speech, people will fan out into different and conflicting comprehensive views of morality and the good life, so any appeal to a narrow Kantian ideal of autonomy and the nature of persons is bound to be sectarian (Rawls 1996).

Political Liberalism affirms that a society that avoids sectarianism satisfies a liberal ideal of legitimacy: Basic political arrangements, the fundamental constitution of society, are justified by considerations that all reasonable persons, whatever their comprehensive views, have good and sufficient reason to accept.

2 Criticisms and Alternative Paths

From its first elaboration, Rawls's theory of justice has been scrutinized by an enormous amount of criticism. In my view, Rawls's theory has been broken on the rack of this critique. But the upshot is not a defeat for the theory of justice. New suggestions, not yet fully elaborated for the most part, point in a variety of promising, albeit opposed, directions.

2.1 Primary Social Goods and Sen's Critique

Rawls holds that just institutions distribute primary social goods fairly. Roughly, a fair distribution is identified with the distribution in which the worst off are as well off as possible according to the primary social goods measure. Amartya Sen objects that individuals born with different physical and psychological propensities will generally be unequally efficient transformers of resources such as primary social goods into whatever goals they might seek (Sen 1992). Consider two individuals with the same allotments of primary social goods. One is fit, hardy, and quick-witted; the other is lame, illness-prone, lacking in physical coordination, and slow-witted. In any terms that we care about, the condition of the two persons is unequal, but a primary social goods metric does not register the disparity. Sen proposes that we should look beyond the distribution of opportunities and income and other primary goods and see to what extent individuals are able to be and do with their primary goods allotments given their circumstances. The basis of interpersonal comparisons for a theory of justice should, according to Sen, be a measure of people's real freedom to achieve functionings they have reason to value.

A Rawlsian response is that the theory of justice assumes that all individuals are able to be fully contributing members of society throughout their adult life. Problems of disability and chronic debilitating illness are assumed away. Moreover, for those within the normal range of native talents and propensities, it is reasonable to hold individuals responsible for taking account of the primary goods shares they can expect and fashioning a reasonable plan of life on this basis. As Rawls says, justice as fairness "does not look beyond the use which persons make of the rights and opportunities available to them in order to measure, much less to maximize, the satisfactions they achieve" (Rawls 1999a, 80).

The response does not meet the difficulty. Differences in native talents and trait potentials exist among all persons, including those within whatever range is deemed to be normal. These differences strike many of us as relevant to what justice demands, what we owe to one another. Moreover, one can grant that a person endowed with poor traits would be well advised not to form unrealistic ambitions and to tailor his plan of life to what he can achieve. Expecting people to make such adjustments in their plan of life leaves entirely open whether compensation is owed to individuals to mitigate the freedom-reducing effect of poor natural endowment.

Although there is something salutary and correct about Sen's train of thought, it immediately runs into a puzzle. There are enormous numbers of capabilities to function, and they vary from the trivial to the momentously important. We need some way of ranking the significance of different freedoms if the capability approach is to yield a standard of interpersonal comparison (Arneson 1989; Nussbaum 1992). Viewed this way, carrying through Sen's critique would have to involve elaborating a theory of human good.

2.2 The Priority of the Right over the Good

A core ambition of Rawls's work on justice is to free the idea of what is right and just from the idea of what is good or advantageous for a person. This is a crucial part of the enterprise of constructing a theory that is a genuine alternative to utilitarianism. For the utilitarian, as Rawls correctly notes, the idea of what is good for a person is independent of moral notions; Robinson Crusoe alone on his island still has need of a notion of prudence, of what he needs to do to make his life go better rather than worse over the long haul. If we could get clear about what is really intrinsically good, the rest would be easy—what is morally right is maximizing, efficiently promoting the good. In contrast, Rawls aims to construct an account of rights that people have, specified by principles of justice, that is substantially independent of any particular notions of what is good, which are always bound to be disputable. Rawls's paradigm case of a dispute about how to live is religious controversy, which must end in stalemate. Reasonable people will persist in disagreeing about such matters. To reach objective consensus on issues of social justice, we must bracket these disagreements about God and more generally about the good, and in fact the willingness to set aside controversial conceptions of good in order to attain shared agreement on rules of social cooperation is for Rawls a prime mark of reasonableness.

But if the requirements of justice are conceived as disconnected in this way from human good, we have to countenance the possibility that in a perfectly just society people lead avoidably squalid lives. Perhaps they are even condemned to such lives; Rawlsian justice is no guarantee that your life goes well or has a good chance of going well. Moreover, the squalor might be pointless, in the sense that it is not that the misery of some is needed to avoid worse misery for others. Furthermore, the numbers do not count: If my small right is inviolable, then it must be respected, no matter the cost in the quality of human lives and in the number of persons who suffer such losses.

To the extent that we have an adequate conception of human good, that singles out what is truly worth caring about and what makes a life really go better for the person who is living it, it makes sense to hold that what people in a society fundamentally owe each other is a fair distribution of human good.[1] An adequate conception will surely be pluralistic, recognizing that there are many distinct goods and valuable ways of life, and will not claim more than the possibility or rough and partial commensurability of good across lives.

Many substantive claims about human good, such as that the list of valuable elements in a human life includes loyal friendship, reciprocal love, healthy family ties, systematic knowledge, pleasure, meaningful work, and significant cultural and scientific achievement, seem to me to be pretty uncontroversial, part of commonsense lore. But what is widely accepted is still sometimes disputed. Thinking straight about how to live is difficult, and we make mistakes. Prejudice, ignorance, superstition, and unthinking acceptance of convention play roles in rendering ethical knowledge controversial. Hence it does not offend against human dignity and respect for persons to endorse the implementation by a society of controversial but (by our best lights) correct conceptions of human good. The liberal legitimacy norm that Rawls embraces should be put in question if it is read as denying this. It all depends on what we mean by "reasonably" in the norm that one should treat people only according to principles that no one could reasonably reject. If "reasonably" refers to the ideal use of practical reason, then one reasonably rejects only incorrect principles and accepts correct ones. The norm is then unproblematic, but it allows imposition of views that are controversial in the ordinary sense of being contested among normal reasonable people (who may be making cognitive errors). But if "reasonably" is used in a weaker sense, so that one could reasonably make errors in judgment, then the weaker the standard of reasonableness that is invoked, the stronger and more constraining is the idea that one should not impose on people in the name of principles that are controversial among weakly reasonable people (but for a defense of Rawls, see Dreben 2003).

Here one might object that I am just pounding the table and dogmatically insisting that we can know the good, a controversial claim for which I have presented no argument. But I am just insisting on symmetry. Skepticism about knowledge of human good is a possible option, but by parity of reasoning, the grounds for that skepticism will carry over to claims about what is morally right and just as well. Only a sleight of hand would make it look plausible that reasonable people, if left uncoerced, will forever disagree about what is good but that all men and women of good will, if they are reasonable, will agree on principles of right such as the difference principle.

Restoring substantial claims about the content of human good to the theory of what is right and just does not necessarily lead back to utilitarianism. A good-based theory of justice asserts that we should choose actions and institutional

---

[1] Raz (1986, part II), Nussbaum (1992, 1999, 2000), Arneson (1989, 2000), Sher (1997), and Hurka (1993) (among others) advance arguments on this theme. Ackerman (1980), Larmore (1987), and Barry (1995, part II) defend versions of liberal neutrality on controversial conceptions of the good. On this issue, Nussbaum's current view appears in the final chapter of Nussbaum (2004).

arrangements to maximize some function of individual well-being, but maximizing aggregate or average well-being is just one option. In particular, more egalitarian principles beckon. In fact, Rawls has initiated an exploration of broadly egalitarian principles that is still ongoing.

2.3 The Difference Principle, Maximin, and the Original Position

The difference principle says that given the constraints imposed by the equal liberty and fair equality of opportunity principles, the social and economic primary social goods of the least advantaged should be maximized. Rawls's general conception of justice holds more simply that the basic structure of society should maximize the level of advantage, calculated in terms of primary social good holdings, of the least advantaged.

On its face, these principles assert an extreme priority weighting.[2] The principles insist that no gain, no matter how large, and no matter how large the number of already better off people to whom the gain accrues, should be pursued at the cost of any loss, no matter how tiny, and no matter how small the number of worse off persons who would suffer the loss (provided the change leaves intact people's status as belonging to the better off or worse off group). Rawls himself points out that this is counterintuitive (Rawls 1999a, 135–6) but remains unfazed on the ground that it is empirically wildly unlikely that in any actual society we would be faced with such a choice. But if this response is deemed satisfactory, this must mean the principles are no longer being pitched as fundamental moral principles but rather as practical policy guides, rules of thumb for constitution-makers and law-makers.

The claim that the strict lexical priority that the difference principle accords to the worst off, although admittedly too strict, will never lead to mistakes in practice, merits close scrutiny. To the extent this is plausible, its plausibility is entirely an artifact of the fact that Rawls would have us compare the condition of people only in terms of their primary goods allotments. If a possible policy would produce a huge gain in dollars for many better off people, surely some of that gain can be siphoned off to those worse off. But if we instead believe that the theory of justice should attend to people's actual overall quality of life over the entire life course, then we do face conflicts in which very tiny benefits for a few can be purchased only at huge cost in other people's lives. We could devote huge resources to the education of the barely educable or to extraordinary medical care that only slightly raises the life expectancy of those with grave medical conditions, and so on. Some of us are very inefficient transformers of resources into an enhanced quality of life. The hard issue of how much priority to accord to the achievement of gains for the worse off must be faced.

[2] This problem was first raised by Harsanyi (1975). A response that defends Rawls is in Freeman (2003, editor's introduction). A version of the original position idea appears in Harsanyi (1953), where it is used in an argument for utilitarianism. For discussion, see Roemer (1996, ch. 4; 2002); also Parfit (2004, 341–53).

The difference principle lies at the extreme end of a continuum of views that accord variously greater weight for achieving a gain of a given size for a person, depending on how badly off in absolute terms the person would be, absent receipt of this gain. At the other end lies utilitarianism, which accords no extra weight at all to achieving a gain for a person depending on the prior goodness or badness of her condition. The entire range between these end points corresponds to the prioritarian family of principles, according to which, the worse a person's lifetime condition, the morally more valuable it is to achieve a gain or avoid a loss for her. The distinction between valuing priority and valuing equality has been clarified in work by Derek Parfit (2000).

Counterintuitive or not, the difference principle and the broader maximin conception might be derivable by iron logic from undeniable premises. Rawls gestures at provision of this sort of support in his original position argument, but in the area in which Rawls is pointing I submit that no good argument is to be found (see the critical discussions cited in footnote 2). Suffice it to say that the innovation of the original position has not resonated in recent political philosophy in anything like the way that Rawls's powerful but controversial vision of justice as social democratic liberalism continues to shape the agenda of political philosophy for both proponents and opponents. In my view the underlying reason for the relative neglect of original position arguments is that the basic hunch that motivates the project is wrong. Recall that the idea of the original position is that the principles of justice are whatever would emerge from an ideally fair choice procedure for selecting principles of justice. The presupposition is that we have pretheoretic intuitions, which can be refined, concerning what are the fairest conditions for choosing basic moral principles. But why think this? Perhaps one should say that the fair set-up of a procedure for choosing principles of justice is whatever arrangement happens to produce the substantially best principles. We have commonsense beliefs about the conditions under which contracts and private deals are fairly negotiated, but there is no intuitive content to the idea of a fair procedure for choosing basic principles of social regulation. (If we knew that a particular person, Smith, was very wise and knew a lot about principles of justice and had thought more deeply about these matters than the rest of us, perhaps the "fairest" choice procedure would be, "Let Smith decide.")

This takes us back to a conflict of intuitions that needs to be clarified and perhaps resolved via theory. Some affirm equality: it is good if everyone has the same, or is treated the same, in some respect (Temkin 1993). Others affirm doing the best that can be done for the worst off. Priority weakens this strict maximin tilt in favor of the worst off. An unresolved Goldilocks issue arises here; how much priority arising from the badness of one's condition is too little, too much, or just enough? Another option worth mention is sufficientarianism: What matters morally and what justice requires is not that everyone has the same but that everyone has enough. Each should achieve, or be enabled to achieve, a threshold level of decent existence, the level being set by whatever we had better take to be the best standard of interpersonal comparison for a theory of justice (primary goods shares, or capabilities to function in valuable ways, or utility construed as pleasure or desire satisfaction, or well-being corresponding to achievement of the items on an objective list of goods, or whatever). Expressions of sufficientarian or quasi-sufficientarian opinion are common in recent political philosophy (Frankfurt 1987; Anderson 1999; D. Miller 2004; Nussbaum 2000), but the doctrines other than the difference principle mentioned in this paragraph need further elaboration and interpretation before we would be in a position definitively to gauge how compelling they are.

2.4 Nozick and Lockean Libertarianism

According to Rawls, the choice of economic systems—capitalist, socialist, or some other—need not reflect a fundamental moral commitment. At least, either a liberal capitalist or a liberal socialist regime could in principle implement the Rawlsian principles of egalitarian liberalism. Against this view Robert Nozick developed a powerful response of right-wing inspiration (Nozick 1974). His starting point is the idea that each person has the moral right to live as she chooses on any mutually agreed terms with others so long as she does not thereby harm nonconsenting other people in ways that violate their rights. These latter rights not to be harmed form a spare set. Each of us has the right not to be physically assaulted or menaced with the threat of physical assault, not to be imposed on by the actions of others in ways that cause physical harm to oneself or one's property, not to be defrauded, not to suffer theft or robbery. Nozick finds antecedents for these ideas in the writings of John Locke, who does not fully commit to them.[3] From this standpoint, the moral authority of the state to coerce people without their consent even just to maintain minimal public order appears problematic. The idea that society has the right and obligation to redistribute property to achieve a more fair distribution cannot find a place in Lockean natural rights theory. Property is owned by people, and the state, acting as agent of society, has no more right to take from some and give to others than a robber does.

The right of each person to act as she chooses has as its core a universal right of self-ownership: Each adult person is the full rightful owner of herself, possessing full property rights over her own person. The next question that arises here is how an individual may legitimately come to acquire rights to use or own particular pieces of the world. Without some such rights self-ownership would come to very little. The Lockean project is to specify how legitimate private ownership of property arises in a world in which objects are initially unowned, and what the terms and limits of such legitimate ownership are. The main stream of Lockean views defends the idea that private property ownership can be fully legitimate, given certain conditions, no matter how unequal the distribution of privately owned property. Left-wing Lockeans demur (Steiner 1994). They try to defend the view that each person is the full rightful owner of herself but that the distribution of ownership of the world must be roughly equal.

---

[3] See Locke (1980). See also the interpretation of Locke in Simmons (1992) and Waldron (1988, ch. 6) and developments of Lockean ideas in Simmons (2001).

Mainstream Lockean views concerning the legitimacy of private property owner-ship resonate strongly and positively with commonsense opinion in modern market societies, but the philosophical elaboration of these views is still a project that largely awaits completion. Nozick's arguments are sometimes brilliant but his views are sketchy. We are not yet in a good position definitively to compare Lockean versions of liberal justice with their more egalitarian rivals.

2.5 Desert, Responsibility, and Luck Egalitarianism

Surprisingly, Rawls rejects the platitude that justice is giving people what they deserve (Rawls 1999a). He argues against the idea that notions of desert belong in fundamen-tal principles of justice (although, of course, norms of desert might serve as means to implement justice goals). A notion of individual responsibility is implicit in Rawls's principles. The basic notion is that given a social context in which people's rights to access to primary social goods are assured, each person is responsible for deciding how to live, constructing a plan of life, and executing it. If one's choices have bad results and one has a poor quality of life, this fact does not trigger a valid moral claim to further compensation from others.

Some see problems in this picture (see Olsaretti, in *Oxford Handbook of Political Theory*, ed. J. S. Dryzek, B. Honig, and A. Phillips 2006. Oxford: Oxford University Press). One line of objection holds that a sharper line needs to be drawn between what we owe to one another and what each individual must do for herself. What we owe to each other is compensation for unchosen and uncourted bad luck. Some bad events just befall people in ways they have no reasonable opportunity to avoid, as when a meteor strikes. Some bad events are such that one does have reasonable opportunity to avoid them. A paradigm case would be losses that issue from volun-tarily undertaken high-stakes gambling. Social justice demands a differential response to bad luck, depending on how it arises. A complication here is that each person's initial genetic endowment of propensities to traits along with her early socialization is evidently a matter of unchosen and uncourted luck, good or bad. But my later, substantially voluntary choice to embrace bad values and make unwise decisions about how to live may simply express my initial unchosen bad luck in inherited traits and socialization experiences. Does justice then demand *some* compensation for courted bad luck traceable in part to uncourted earlier bad luck, paternalistic restriction of individual liberty to limit the harm to self that my lack of intelligence generates, or what? Ronald Dworkin has done the most to clarify these tangles and develop a coherent position concerning distributive justice on the basis of this line of thought (Dworkin 2000). Some sympathetic to this general line are trying to refine it (Roemer 1998). Others find the entire approach, labeled "luck egalitarianism" by critics, to be unpromising (Scanlon 1989; Fleurbaey 1995; Anderson 1999; Scheffler 2003). Luck egalitarianism is said to be too unforgiving to individuals who make bad choices. Its critics accuse it of exaggerating the significance of choice and of giving undue weight to the distribution-of-resources aspect of social justice.

A different but related line of thought finds that egalitarian principles of social justice inevitably must imply that individuals have moral duties to live their lives so that the principles are more rather than less fulfilled. How much more? If we must live our lives in ways that maximize justice fulfillment, the demands of justice on the conduct of individual lives will be very stringent and likely counterintuitive. Rawls suggested that the principles of justice for the basic structure of society are stringently egalitarian but that individuals are free to live their lives as they choose so long as they abide by the rules of just institutions. G. A. Cohen finds this position to be unstable (Cohen 2000). If well-off persons accept the difference principle (which holds that inequalities that are not to the maximal benefit of the least advantaged are unacceptable), they cannot benefit in good conscience from hard bargaining. Instead of threatening to strike for higher wages, already well-paid medical doctors, committed to the difference principle, could agree to work extra hours for no extra pay, or voluntarily to embrace pay cuts, for example. A large question arises here concerning the degree to which a modern liberal theory of justice can or should be libertarian in the sense of embracing some close relative of the principles defended by J. S. Mill in *On Liberty*.

2.6 Civil Liberties, Diversity, Democracy, and More-than-formal Equality of Opportunity

Liberalism in normative political theory is more an attitude or stance toward politics than a specific set of doctrines. Liberalism is strongly associated with strong protection of freedom of speech and assembly and related liberties. One argument is good-based: If what I fundamentally want is to lead a life that achieves truly worthwhile and valuable goals, I will want not just to satisfy whatever preferences I now have, but to enjoy a sound education and a culture of free speech, which has some tendency to undermine my false beliefs and bad values. (Of course free speech can also cause a person to abandon true beliefs and good values; the liberal position involves a broad faith that the free use of reason by ordinary persons will tend over time to lead to improvement rather than corruption.) Rawls appeals to the interest that persons as such are assumed to have in developing and exercising their moral powers to adopt conceptions of the good and to cooperate with others on reasonable terms (Rawls 1996). These arguments have some force, but they are also in some tension with each other, and it is not clear that either one or both can be worked into a doctrine that picks out privileged liberties and justifies according them strict priority.

Civil liberties traditionally understood strike some as insufficient to resolve problems of diversity in contemporary society. Women, members of minority ethnic groups and supposed races, people with nonheterosexual sexual orientation, and others who experience themselves as unfairly pushed to the margins of society seek recognition of their differences and common humanity (see Markell and Squires, both in *Oxford Handbook of Political Theory*, ed. J. S. Dryzek, B. Honig, and A. Phillips 2006. Oxford: Oxford University Press).

Another question is the place of democratic political rights in liberal theory (Christiano 1996). Democratic rights are not central in the Lockean tradition. One might suppose that egalitarian liberals will hold democratic rights to be of mainly instrumental value in securing other more fundamental rights. An egalitarian might hold that whatever political arrangements are most likely to achieve a fair distribution of good quality lives or opportunities for good quality lives to people should be instituted and upheld.

Advocates of democratic equality (e.g. Anderson 1999; J. Cohen 2003) hold a sharply contrasting view. They hold that the moral equality and equal dignity of persons rightly interpreted require above all equal fundamental liberty for all persons and that prominent among these liberties is the right to participate on equal terms with other members of one's society in collectively setting the laws that coercively regulate all members' lives.[4] In this perspective, the right to democracy can appear to be the right of rights, the crown jewel of individual rights.

A society can be more or less democratic along several dimensions of assessment. How democratic should society be? Rawls stakes out a demanding position in answer to this question. His final statement of his equal liberty principle states that the equal political liberties are to be guaranteed their "fair value." What he means is that any two citizens with equal political ability and equal ambition to influence political outcomes should have the same chances of influencing political outcomes. A kind of fair equality of opportunity is to operate in the political sphere that is close in spirit to the fair equality of opportunity that he holds should prevail in the competition for positions conferring economic and social advantages.

Rawlsian fair equality of opportunity is a strong, controversial doctrine. Rawls pushes to its logical limit an ideal that others either reject outright or hold should be constrained by conflicting values (Nozick 1974; Arneson 1999).

2.7 Global Justice

Do we owe more to fellow citizens than to distant needy strangers (Chatterjee 2004)? Should we embrace a two-tier theory of justice, which imposes demanding egalitarian requirements within each society but much less demanding requirements on members of one nation toward the members of other nations? A certain type of cosmopolitan view proposes a resounding "No" to both questions (Beitz 1979; Pogge 1989; Nagel 1991). This cosmopolitanism can take a right-wing form, which asserts that duties are minimal in both the national and the global context, and a left-wing form, which affirms strong duties within and across borders.

---

[4] Another aspect of democratic equality is what we have called "diversity"—how society must be arranged, in order to assure equality of the appropriate sort between members of groups, for example, between men and women and between members of different ethnicities or supposed races. On the former division, see Okin (1989). On the latter, see discussions of the rights of minority peoples in democratic society, for example, Kymlicka (1989, 1995) and Barry (2001).

This issue can be regarded as a part of the morality of special ties (Miller 1998; Scheffler 2001). Many of us intuitively feel that we have especially strong moral obligations to those who are near and dear to us, to family members, friends, members of our community, and perhaps fellow citizens, but it is unclear to what extent a sound theory of justice will vindicate or repudiate these pretheoretical feelings. And what about putative special obligations to fellow members of our own social class, ethnic group, or racial lineage?[5]

A related issue arises if we imagine a society that is just internally by our lights, and faces the task of choosing a just international relations policy. Should the just foreign policy of such a society press for ideal justice everywhere or rather extend strong sincere toleration and respect to any political regime that meets a threshold standard of decency?

Rawls's book *The Law of Peoples* (Rawls 1999c) adopts a conservative and somewhat anti-cosmopolitan stance toward the issues just mentioned. But the doctrine of egalitarianism within national borders and minimal duties across borders may ultimately prove to be unstable under examination. The arguments that urge minimal duties toward outsiders, if found acceptable, may undermine the case for egalitarian arrangements among insiders, and the arguments that urge egalitarian arrangements within borders, if found acceptable, may compel a similar egalitarianism across borders.

Thinking about global justice issues tends to unsettle one's prior convictions (see C. Brown, in *Oxford Handbook of Political Theory*, ed. J. S. Dryzek, B. Honig, and A. Phillips 2006. Oxford: Oxford University Press). A reflective equilibrium among our justice beliefs may be hard to achieve, and at any rate not within sight, in the present state of theory. This claim applies not just to global justice beliefs but to all beliefs about the content of social justice. The pot that Rawls has stirred up is still bubbling.

References

ACKERMAN, B. 1980. *Social Justice in the Liberal State*. New Haven, Conn.: Yale University Press.
ANDERSON, E. 1999. What is the point of equality? *Ethics*, 109: 287–337.
ARNESON, R. 1989. Equality and equal opportunity for welfare. *Philosophical Studies*, 56: 77–93.
—— 1999. Against Rawlsian equality of opportunity. *Philosophical Studies*, 93: 77–112.
—— 2000. Perfectionism and politics. *Ethics*, 111: 37–63.
BARRY, B. 1995. *Justice as Impartiality*. Oxford: Oxford University Press.
—— 2001. *Equality and Culture*. Cambridge, Mass.: Harvard University Press.
BEITZ, C. 1979. *Political Theory and International Relations*. Princeton, NJ: Princeton University Press.
CHATTERJEE, D. (ed.) 2004. *The Ethics of Assistance: Morality and the Distant Needy*. Cambridge: Cambridge University Press.
CHRISTIANO, T. 1996. *The Rule of the Many*. Boulder, Colo.: Westview Press.

---

[5] See the essays in McKim and McMahan (1997). Also Barry (2001) and Kymlicka (1995).

COHEN, G. A. 2000. *If You're an Egalitarian, How Come You're So Rich?* Cambridge, Mass.: Harvard University Press, lectures 8–9.

COHEN, J. 2003. For a democratic society. Pp. 86–138 in *The Cambridge Companion to Rawls*, ed. S. Freeman. Cambridge: Cambridge University Press.

DREBEN, B. 2003. On Rawls and political liberalism. Pp. 316–46 in *The Cambridge Companion to Rawls*, ed. S. Freeman. Cambridge: Cambridge University Press.

DWORKIN, R. 2000. *Sovereign Virtue: The Theory and Practice of Equality*. Cambridge, Mass.: Harvard University Press.

FLEURBAEY, M. 1995. Equal opportunity or equal social outcome? *Economics and Philosophy*, 11: 35–55.

FRANKFURT, H. 1987. Equality as a moral ideal. *Ethics*, 98: 21–43.

FREEMAN, S. (ed.) 2003. *The Cambridge Companion to Rawls*. Cambridge: Cambridge University Press.

HARSANYI, J. 1953. Cardinal utility in welfare economics and in the theory of risk-taking. *Journal of Political Economy*, 61: 434–5.

——1975. Can the maximin principle serve as a basis for morality? A critique of John Rawls's theory. *American Political Science Review*, 69: 594–606.

HURKA, T. 1993. *Perfectionism*. Oxford: Oxford University Press.

KAGAN, S. 1999. Equality and desert. Pp. 298–314 in *What Do We Deserve?*, ed. L. Pojman and O. McLeod. Oxford: Oxford University Press.

KYMLICKA, W. 1989. *Liberalism, Community, and Culture*. Oxford: Oxford University Press.

——1995. *Multicultural Citizenship*. Oxford: Oxford University Press.

LARMORE, C. 1987. *Patterns of Moral Complexity*. Cambridge: Cambridge University Press.

LOCKE, J. 1980. *Second Treatise of Government*, ed. C. Macpherson. Indianapolis: Hackett; originally published 1690.

MCKIM, R. and MCMAHAN, J. (eds.) 1997. *The Morality of Nationalism*. New York: Oxford University Press.

MILL, J. 1978. *On Liberty*, ed. E. Rapaport. Indianapolis: Hackett; originally published 1867.

MILLER, D. 2004. National responsibility and international justice. Pp. 123–43 in *The Ethics of Assistance: Morality and the Distant Needy*, ed. D. Chatterjee. Cambridge: Cambridge University Press.

MILLER, R. 1998. Cosmopolitan respect and patriotic concern. *Philosophy and Public Affairs*, 27: 202–24.

NAGEL, T. 1991. *Equality and Partiality*. New York: Oxford University Press.

NOZICK, R. 1974. *Anarchy, State, and Utopia*. New York: Basic Books.

NUSSBAUM, M. 1992. Human functioning and social justice: in defense of Aristotelian essentialism. *Political Theory*, 20: 202–46.

——1999. Women and cultural universals. In M. Nussbaum, *Sex and Social Justice*. Oxford: Oxford University Press.

——2000. *Women and Human Development: The Capabilities Approach*. Cambridge: Cambridge University Press.

——2004. *Hiding from Humanity: Disgust, Shame, and the Law*. Oxford: Princeton University Press.

OKIN, S. 1989. *Justice, Gender, and the Family*. New York: Basic Books.

PARFIT, D. 2000. Equality or priority? Pp. 81–125 in *The Ideal of Equality*, ed. M. Clayton and A. Williams. New York: St. Martin's Press.

—— 2004. What we could rationally will. Pp. 285–369 in *The Tanner Lectures on Human Values*, vol. 24, ed. G. Peterson. Salt Lake City: University of Utah Press.

POGGE, T. 1989. *Realizing Rawls*. Ithaca, NY: Cornell University Press.

RAWLS, J. 1958. Justice as fairness. Reprinted in J. Rawls, *Collected Papers*, pp. 47–72. Cambridge, Mass.: Harvard University Press.

—— 1996. *Political Liberalism*. New York: Columbia University Press.

—— 1999a. *A Theory of Justice*. Cambridge, Mass.: Harvard University Press; originally published 1971.

—— 1999b. *Collected Papers*, ed. S. Freeman, Cambridge, Mass.: Harvard University Press.

—— 1999c. *The Law of Peoples*. Cambridge, Mass.: Harvard University Press.

RAZ, J. 1986. *The Morality of Freedom*. Oxford: Oxford University Press.

ROEMER, J. 1996. *Theories of Distributive Justice*. Cambridge, Mass.: Harvard University Press.

—— 1998. *Equality of Opportunity*. Cambridge, Mass.: Harvard University Press.

—— 2002. Egalitarianism against the veil of ignorance. *Journal of Philosophy*, 99: 167–84.

SCANLON, T. 1989. The significance of choice. In *The Tanner Lectures on Human Values*, vol. 8, ed. S. McMurrin. Salt Lake City: University of Utah Press.

SCHEFFLER, S. 2001. *Boundaries and Allegiances: Problems of Justice and Responsibility in Liberal Thought*. Oxford: Oxford University Press.

—— 2003. What is egalitarianism? *Philosophy and Public Affairs*, 31: 5–39.

SEN, A. 1992. *Inequality Reexamined*. Cambridge, Mass.: Harvard University Press.

SHER, G. 1997. *Beyond Neutrality: Perfectionism and Politics*. Cambridge: Cambridge University Press.

SIMMONS, A. 1992. *The Lockean Theory of Rights*. Princeton, NJ: Princeton University Press.

—— 2001. *Justification and Legitimacy*. Cambridge: Cambridge University Press.

STEINER, H. 1994. *An Essay on Rights*. Oxford: Blackwell.

TEMKIN, L. 1993. *Inequality*. Oxford: Oxford University Press.

WALDRON, J. 1988. *The Right to Private Property*. Oxford: Oxford University Press.

CHAPTER 6

··

MODERNITY AND ITS CRITICS

··

JANE BENNETT

SEEKING insight into the political events and debates swarming around them, under-graduates enrolled in "Modern Political Thought" courses are often surprised to learn that the focus is on writers from the seventeenth, eighteenth, and nineteenth centuries. This is because, as part of the series ancient–medieval–modern–contemporary, "the modern" in political theory is that which has *already* passed, although its traces are said to remain in the background of today. The term "modernity" functions somewhat differently in the discipline: it names a *contemporary* condition. As I contend at the end of this chapter, modernity is alive and kicking even within a theoretical framework of *post*modernism.

In what does the condition of modernity consist? First, in a distinctive constellation of intellectual tendencies, including the propensity to subject established norms and practices to critical reflection, to seek physical causes for disease, to believe both in universal human rights and in cultural specificity, and to affirm oneself as an individual even while lamenting the lack of community. The condition of modernity refers, second, to a set of institutional structures associated with such a temper, including popular elections, rule by law, a secular bureaucracy, an independent judiciary and free press, public education, capitalism, and monogamous marriage.

"Modernity and Its Critics," therefore, is perhaps best approached as the *story* of this habit of mind and its institutional embodiments. In a version of the story that circulates widely in North America, Europe, and Australia, the plot goes something like this:

Once upon a time there was a (medieval Christian) world where nature was purposive, God was active in the details of human affairs, all things had a place in the order of things, social life was characterized by face-to-face relations, and political order took the form of an organic community experienced as the "prose of the world" (Foucault 1970). But this premodern cosmos gave way to forces of scientific and instrumental rationality, secularism, individualism, and the bureaucratic nation state.

"Modernity and Its Critics" is a tale of this epochal shift, of the secularization of a traditional order that had been imbued with divine or natural purpose. Some tellers of the tale celebrate secularization as the demise of superstition; others lament it as the loss of a meaningful moral universe. When placed against the backdrop of a dark and confused premodernity, modernity appears as a place of reason, freedom, and control; when it is compared to a premodern age of community and cosmological coherence, modernity becomes a place of dearth and alienation. Even the celebrators of modernity, however, share something of the sense of loss accentuated by its critics—and this is to be expected, given what seems to be the tale's prototype, the biblical story of the Fall.

As a cultural narrative or civilization fable, "Modernity and Its Critics" tells us who we are and are not, and it identifies the key ideals to guide us and the most important dangers and opportunities we confront. As such, the narrative serves less a historiographical than a therapeutic function. It helps to order the vast and variable field of experience, and thus to shape the actual world in which we live. Under its banner, a certain tradition of thought and a certain group of people try to make sense of themselves and their collective life.

But *which* tradition of thought, *which* group of people? The story of modernity is embedded in the history of seventeenth-, eighteenth-, and nineteenth-century Europe, in particular in its political struggles against totalizing forms of rule and unthinking forms of obedience. The twenty-first-century encounter between militant strains of Islamic fundamentalism and "Western culture" has been read by Michael Thompson, for example, as a recapitulation of Europe's own *internal* struggle between modern and anti-modern forces, between, that is, "Enlightenment notions of reason, secularism, universalism, civil society" on the one hand and "the *volkish* tendencies of cultural particularism, nativism, provincialism, and spiritualism" on the other (Thompson 2003, 1–2).

Bruno Latour has shown how the story of modernity portrays modern, Western culture as a *radical* break from all other modes of human thought, social organization, and inquiry into nature. Only the moderns, the story goes, have mastered the art of categorical purification, of distinguishing clearly between what is natural and what is cultural, between what is universal and true and what is particular and partial. Latour rejects this conceit, arguing that the difference between modern and other cultures is not qualitative but quantitative; that is, a matter of "lengthened networks." If modern critiques are more global, if modern self-consciousness is more explicit, if modern technologies are more masterful, it is only because of a difference in the "scope of mobilization," which, while important, "is hardly a reason to make such a great fuss" (Latour 1993, 124).

Other critics have noted that modernity, precisely *because* it is part of European history, cannot be exclusively European. Modernity cannot be divorced from the imperialist and colonialist projects of Europe or America, and thus is a product of the (psychic, linguistic, normative, bureaucratic, military) interactions between the West and the non-West. This means that multiple modernities exist side by side around the globe. Amit Chaudhuri makes a version of this point when he says that, "if Europe is a universal paradigm for modernity, we are all, European and non-European, to a degree inescapably Eurocentric. Europe is at once a means of intellectual dominance, an obfuscatory trope, and a constituent of self-knowledge, *in different ways for different peoples and histories*" (Chaudhuri 2004, 5; emphasis added). For Partha Chatterjee, too, because the cultural exchanges that generate modernity are not unidirectional, modernity must be understood as a multicultural production. Speaking in the context of India's modernity, he says that:

true modernity consists in determining the particular forms of modernity that are suitable in particular circumstances; that is, applying the methods of reason to identify or invent the specific technologies of modernity that are appropriate for our purposes.

(Chatterjee 1997, 8–9)

The postcolonial scholarship concerning non-Western or "alternative modernities" is rich and ongoing (see Gaonkar 2001; Chatterjee 2004). In insisting upon the geographical, cultural, and subcultural specificities of coterminous modernities, such work resists the idea that modernity has a single lineage or is a univocal practice. This resistance is also served by acknowledging that every version of modernity includes, right from the start, its critics. "There must be something in the very process of our becoming modern that continues to lead us, even in our acceptance of modernity, to a certain skepticism about its values and consequences" (Chatterjee 1997, 14). Although he writes from a position deep inside Europe, Max Weber helps reveal just what this something is, just how modernities of all kinds generate their own critics.

1 DISENCHANTMENT AND THE PROBLEM OF MEANINGLESSNESS

Max Weber (1864–1920) identified the central dynamic of modernity as *Entzauberung* or de-magification, usually translated into English as disenchantment. Disenchantment names the processes by which magic is gradually supplanted by calculation as the preferred means for enacting human ends. Disenchantment is itself an instance of a more general process of "rationalization," which in turn encompasses several related processes, each of which opts for the precise, regular, constant, and reliable over the wild, spectacular, idiosyncratic, and surprising. In addition to eschewing magic as a strategy of will ("scientizing" desire), rationalization also *systematizes* knowledge (pursues "increasing theoretical mastery of reality by means of increasingly precise and abstract concepts"); *instrumentalizes* thinking (methodically attains a "practical end by means of an increasingly precise calculation of adequate means"); *secularizes* metaphysical concerns (rejects "all non-utilitarian yardsticks"); and *demystifies* traditional social bonds in favor of those founded on the shared reason of all men (Weber 1981, 293).

Systematization, instrumentalization, secularization, demystification: the shared grammatical form of these terms emphasizes the fact that modernizing transformations are ever ongoing, never fully completed. There will always be some phenomena that remain resistant to full mathematical or social-scientific analysis. These remnants, in Weber's account, are to be left aside until such time as scientific knowledge has advanced further into the logic of nature and society, or they are relegated to (the distinctly modern invention of) the realm of private "values" and aesthetic, sexual, or mystical "experiences."

Weber acknowledges that the "modern" processes of rationalization predate modern times: attempts to displace magic were made, for example, by the ancient Hebrew prophets "in conjunction with Hellenistic scientific thought" (Weber 1958, 105; Jameson 1988, 26). But Weber describes the urge to demystify, pursued in fits and starts throughout history, as reaching its "logical conclusion" in seventeenth-century Puritanism. The ascetic ethic of Puritanism and its idea of a "calling" eventually became the entrepreneurship and acquisitiveness of modern capitalism (Weber 1958).

Whether directly or indirectly touched by Puritanism, any culture of modernity will encourage a distinctively *analytical* style of thinking. More specifically, to be modern is to be able to discern what things are "in principle" and not only what they are in current practice: one learns to relate to phenomena by seizing upon the *logic* of their structure, upon the *principle* of their organization, and this enables an even more careful and precise categorization of things. In a passage that also exemplifies how modernity is defined by way of contrast to an imagined primitivism, Weber describes this "in principle" logic:

Does...everyone sitting in this hall...have a greater knowledge of the conditions of life under which we exist than has an American Indian or a Hottentot? Hardly. Unless he is a physicist, one who rides on the streetcar has no idea how the car happened to get into motion.... The increasing intellectualization and rationalization do *not*, therefore, indicate an increased and general knowledge of the conditions under which one lives. It means something else, namely, the knowledge or belief that if one but wished one *could* learn it at any time. Hence, it means that principally there are no mysterious incalculable forces that come into play, but rather that one can, in principle, master all things by calculation. This means that the world is disenchanted.   (Weber 1981, 139)

Modernity produces a self skilled in the art of discerning the hidden logic of things. Key to Weber's story is the claim that while this skill is a laudable achievement, its cost is very high: a rationalized world stripped of all "mysterious incalculable forces" is a *meaningless* world. "The unity of the primitive image of the world, in which everything was concrete magic," gives way to "the mechanism of a world robbed of gods" (Weber 1981, 281). Or, as Charles Taylor puts the point:

People used to see themselves as part of a larger order. In some cases, this was a cosmic order, a "great chain of Being," in which humans figured in their proper place along with angels, heavenly bodies, and our fellow earthly creatures. This hierarchical order in the universe was reflected in the hierarchies of human society. . . . But at the same time as they restricted us, these orders gave meaning to the world and to the activities of social life. . . . The discrediting of these orders has been called the "disenchantment" of the world. With it, things lost some of their magic.   (Taylor 1991, 3)

Weber identified modern science as the "motive force" behind these disenchanting and discomforting effects: in defining nature as a mechanism of material parts, in defining materiality as deterministic and devoid of spirit, and in allowing spirit to retain its premodern definition as the exclusive locus of "meaning," science empties the lived, natural world of moral significance. What is more, the very logic of scientific *progress* also demoralizes. Because every piece of scientific knowledge must be understood merely as a temporary and soon-to-be-superseded truth, modern selves are denied the psychological satisfaction of closure, the pleasure of a fully accomplished goal:

civilized man, placed in the midst of the continuous enrichment of culture by ideas, knowledge and problems, . . . catches only the most minute part of what . . . life . . . brings forth ever anew, and what he seizes is always something provisional and not definitive, and therefore death for him is a meaningless occurrence. And because death is meaningless, civilized life as such is meaningless: by its very "progressiveness" it gives death the imprint of meaninglessness.

(Weber 1981, 140)

How, then, does Weber illuminate the link between modernity and self-critique? How does modernity necessarily engender radical repudiations of it? In subjecting norms to a demystification that weakens their efficacy without providing any critique-proof alternatives, in reducing nature to a calculable but heartless mechanism, and in celebrating a scientific progress that precludes the pleasure of completion, modernity *alienates*. One response, perhaps the most common one, is the demand for a return to a social whole exempt from relentless analysis and to a natural world restored to its cosmic purpose. Weber did not quite foresee the rise of Christian, Islamic, and Jewish fundamentalisms that would characterize the last years of the twentieth and beginning of the twenty-first centuries. But he did insist that rationalization inevitably generates a black hole of meaninglessness and a set of profoundly disaffected critics.

    To sum up the story that Weber recounts: modernity is now-time, positioned against a lost age of wholeness; moderns are swept up in accelerated processes of disenchantment, scientization, secularization, mathematization, bureaucratization, and alienation; as such, they bear the burden of a world without intrinsic meaning, although they also benefit from an unprecedented degree of critical acumen. The story ends, as do all fables, with some advice: do not resent the condition of modernity, counsels Weber, because a world devoid of intrinsic purpose positively overflows with opportunities for individuality and freedom. Modernity calls one to make one's own valuations, to choose for oneself among competing meanings:

So long as life remains immanent and is interpreted in its own terms, ... the ultimately possible attitudes toward life are irreconcilable, and hence their struggle can never be brought to a final conclusion. Thus it is necessary to make a decisive choice.   (Weber 1981, 152)

For Weber, the anti-modern project is futile because disenchantment, although never complete, is not a reversible historical trajectory. And so it is most profitably met by a heroic will to choose rather than by a cowardly slide into resentment.

The more recent work of Ulrich Beck, Anthony Giddens, and Scott Lash on "reflexive modernization" pursues a similar line of response. They argue that modernity is now:

a global society, not in the sense of a world society but as one of "indefinite space." It is one where social bonds have effectively to be made, rather than inherited from the past. ... It is decentred in terms of authorities, but recentred in terms of opportunities and dilemmas, because focused upon new forms of interdependence.   (Beck, Giddens, and Lash 1994, 107)

In its emphasis on the *inevitability* of the disenchantment process, Weber's tale distinguishes itself both from attempts to re-enchant modernity (Moore 1996; Sikorski 1993; Berman 1981) and from attempts to identify opportunities for wonder and enchantment in secular, counter-cultural, or even commercial sites within modernity (Bennett 2001; During 2002). Weber's version also diverges from Marx's story of modernity, which explores the possibility of a more radical escape.

2 COMMODITY FETISHISM

Karl Marx's (1818–1883) narrative of modernity focuses upon two linked social processes not emphasized by Weber: commodification and fetishization. A commodity is an article produced for market exchange rather than "for its own immediate consumption." In the commodity form, "the product becomes increasingly one-sided. ... [I]ts immediate use-value for the gratification of the needs of its producer appears wholly adventitious, immaterial, and inessential" (Marx 1977, 952–3). Commodification thus *homogenizes* objects, destroying their "sensuously varied objectivity as articles of utility" (Marx 1977, 166) and reduces them to equivalent units of exchange. Marx presents this alchemy, through which unequal things are made equal, as a sinister process (Jameson 1991, 233).

It is sinister not only because people are deprived of "sensuously varied objectivity," but also because, as commodified entities themselves, people (workers) come to be treated as mere objects. This objectification of labor is what makes profit possible: although a portion of labor is indeed "exchanged for the equivalent of the worker's wages; another portion is appropriated by the capitalist without any equivalent being paid" (Marx 1977, 953). The masking of this swindle is the most pernicious effect of modernity.

Second to that is its unnatural animation of artifacts. Marx compares the *tromp l'oeil* of commodification to the mystification perpetrated by religions:

> The mysterious character of the commodity-form consists...in the fact that the commodity reflects the social characteristics of men's own labour as objective characteristics of the products of labour themselves....In order...to find an analogy we must take flight into the misty realm of religion. There the products of the human brain appear as autonomous figures endowed with a life of their own.   (Marx 1977, 163–5)

In capitalism as in theism, nonhuman entities are empowered and humans are deadened.

Thus, commodity *fetishism*: the idolatry of consumption goods. This is an irrationality quite at home in the modern, rational self. Under its sway, the human suffering embedded in commodities (by virtue of their exploitative system of production) is obscured, and mere things gain hegemony as they dominate attention and determine desire. Commodity fetishism is modernity's relapse into primitivism, into the superstition that "an 'inanimate object' will give up its natural character in order to comply with [one's]...desires" (Marx 1975, 189).

Here again the Eurocentric tenor of the story comes to the fore: the negative force of the phrase "commodity fetishism" derives in part from an image of the repulsive non-European savage. More specifically, the primitive is aligned with the negro, the negro with pagan animism, animism with delusion and passivity, passivity with commodity culture. And this line of equivalences is contrasted with another, consisting of the modern, the light, the demystified, the debunking critical theorist. Here Marx highlights for us the central role played by the technique of demystification or "ideology critique"—what Weber called a rationalization process—within the narrative of modernity. For Marx, modernity is ideology; it is a narrative that maintains the existing structure of power by obscuring or defending as legitimate its inherent inequalities and injustices. The just response to modernity qua ideology is modernity qua critique; that is, the clear-eyed unmasking of inequities that reveals them to be products of social choices that could be otherwise.

3 IDEOLOGY CRITIQUE

An exemplary instance of ideology-critique is Max Horkheimer and Theodor Adorno's 1944 essay on "The Culture Industry" (see Horkheimer and Adorno 1972). This elaboration of Marx's analysis of commodity fetishism aims to awaken man's critical faculties, which have been blunted by a postwar world saturated with commercialism. Horkheimer and Adorno echo the calls of Friedrich Nietzsche (1844–1900), Ralph Waldo Emerson (1803–82), Henry Thoreau (1817–62), and others for a life lived *deliberately* and in opposition to the voices of conformity, normality, and respectability. Unlike Nietzsche and the American Transcendentalists (and the Adorno of *Aesthetic Theory* and *Negative Dialectics*), however, Horkheimer and Adorno are skeptical about the role that aesthetic experience might play in this project of wakefulness. They argue that even the senses have been colonized, rendered incapable of posing an effective challenge to the "iron system" of capital. "The culture industry can pride itself on having energetically executed the previously clumsy transposition of art into the sphere of consumption" (Horkheimer and Adorno 1972, 137). Despite its constant invocation of novelty, the culture industry serves up only formulaic amusements designed to produce a passive, consumeristic audience.

In the version of the story told by Horkheimer and Adorno, modernity is on the brink of no return. It has solidified into a system where commercial forces have almost wholly triumphed. Almost—for these heirs of Marx still harbor hope for a way out through the demystifying practice of radical critique. For Nietzsche, too, unmasking was a key strategy in the fight with modernity, a modernity that he identified with Christian and scientific asceticism. Nietzsche's practice of "genealogy," like ideology-critique, sought to uncover the violent, cruel, or simply contradictory elements within conventional ideals and concepts, including those constitutive of the modern self (e.g. moral responsibility, guilt, and conscience) (Nietzsche 1987, 1989)

Horkheimer and Adorno evinced a particularly strong faith in the power of ideology-critique, in, that is, the ability of human reason to expose the truth. Unlike Nietzsche, for whom reason required the supplement of aesthetic motivation, Horkheimer and Adorno imagine this truth as morally *compelling*, as capable of *enacting itself*. They reveal for us the extent to which the modern temper includes a belief in the efficacy of debunking, in the idea that insight into injustice carries with it its own impetus for undoing wrong and enacting right.

In invoking an independent and efficacious realm of critical reflection, Horkheimer and Adorno interrupt their own, more dominant, image of capitalist modernity as an *all-powerful* system of exploitation. In so doing, they display something of Gilles Deleuze's (1925–95) and Felix Guattari's (1930–92) sense that "there is always something that flows or flees, that escapes...the overcoding machine," that although "capitalists may be the master of surplus value and its distribution,...they do not dominate the flows from which surplus value derives" (Deleuze and Guattari 1986, 216, 226).

4 NATURE

Marx and the historical materialists indebted to him identify modernity with the exploitation of human labor and human sensibility. As in Weber's account, the abuse of *nonhuman* nature receives less attention. But associated with every cultural narrative of modernity is a particular image of nature. In general, the modern assumption is that nature is basically law-governed and predictable, "in principle" susceptible to rationalization.

Let us consider critics who contest this nature-picture. Martin Heidegger (1889–1976), for example, rejects modernity's "enframing" of the world, an institutional, mental, and bodily habit whose ultimate goal is to reduce the Earth to the abject status of "standing reserve." He calls instead for humans to become more receptive to nature and to let it be. Heidegger also contends that the rationalizing zeal of modernity will itself bring to light that which it cannot rationalize, that is, the "incalculable" or "that which, withdrawn from representation, is nevertheless manifest in whatever is, pointing to Being, which remains concealed" (Heidegger 1982, 154).

There is a sense in which Heidegger aims to re-enchant the world, to recapture a premodern sense of the universe as an encompassing whole that fades off into indefiniteness. There, nature and culture regain their primordial cooperation. Other critics of the picture of nature as calculable mechanism, however, eschew the serenity of Heidegger's counter-vision. They draw instead from "pagan" conceptions of materiality as turbulent, energetic, and surprising. For these vital materialists, nature is both the material of culture and an active force in its own right. Nietzsche is one such materialist. He describes nature as:

a monster of energy...that does not expend itself but only transforms itself.... [A] play of forces and waves of forces, at the same time one and many...; a sea of forces flowing and rushing together, eternally changing..., with an ebb and a flood of its forms; out of the simplest forms striving toward the most complex, out of the stillest, most rigid, coldest forms toward the hottest, most turbulent..., and then again returning home to the simple out of this abundance, out of the play of contradictions back to the joy of concord.

(Nietzsche 1987, 1067)

Political theorists described as postmodern or post-structuralist (see Foucault 1970, 1973, 1975, 1978; Butler 1993; Brown 1995; Ferguson 1991; Dumm 1996; Gatens 1996) also figure nature as resistant to human attempts to order it, although capable of emergent forms of *self*-organization. Like Marx and Nietzsche, they believe in the power of demystification: Foucaultian genealogies of madness, criminality, and sexuality; feminist and queer studies of gender and power; and postcolonial studies of race and nation all seek to expose the contingency of entities formerly considered universal, inevitable, or natural. But what is more, these exposés insist upon the *material recalcitrance* of contingent products. The mere fact that gender, sex, and race are cultural *artifacts* does not mean that they will yield readily to human understanding or control.

Nature appears in this work as neither imbued with divine purpose nor as disenchanted matter. Instead, all material formations—human and nonhuman—are described as processes with the periodic power to surprise, to metamorphosize at unexpected junctures. Drawing from discussions of nature in Spinoza (1632–1677) and Lucretius (*c.* 99–55 BCE), Deleuze and Guattari, for example, speak of nature as a perpetual "machine" for generating new and dynamic compositions, as "a pure plane of immanence...upon which everything is given, upon which unformed elements and materials dance" (Deleuze and Guattari 1987, 255).

For this "postmodern" set of critics of modernity, the nonlinearity of nature and culture retains a logic that can be modeled, despite the fact that the emergent causality of the system means that trajectories and patterns can often be discerned only retroactively, only after the fact of their emergence. Complexity theory, initially developed to describe a subset of chemical systems (Prigogine 1997), offers these political theorists the beginnings of a theoretical framework and methodology (see Serres 2001; Lyotard 1997; Bennett 2004; Latour 2004; Connolly 2002; Massumi 2002). Modern science is not rejected; on the contrary, one version of it is actively affirmed. And that is the one that understands nature as a turbulent system where small changes in background conditions can have big effects, where micro-shifts can produce macro-effects. However, the nature that consists of flows, becomings, and irreducible complexity is *not* a random set of fluctuations unrecognizable *as* a world. It remains, rather, a world "in which there is room for both the laws of nature and novelty and creativity" (Prigogine 1997, 16).

Within the rich and heterogeneous story of modernity, therefore, it is possible to identify three nodal points or attractors, each with its own image of nature and culture. At one point, we find a "Weberian" social order plagued by meaninglessness (or a "Marxist" world of economic injustice and alienating commodification), and a "dead, passive nature,...which, once programmed, continues to follow the rules inscribed in the program" (Prigogine and Stengers 1984, 6). At a second point, we find a "Heideggerian" modernity of ruthless enframing, accompanied by a nature that gestures darkly toward a higher purpose. At the third, "Nietzschean," point lays a world where creativity and novelty endlessly compete with the forces of regularization. All three versions, however, are infused with the *hope* that the world is susceptible to the critical reasoning, careful analysis, and practical interventions typical of modernity, and with the *will* to render that world more intelligible.

References

ASAD, T. 2003. *Formations of the Secular: Christianity, Islam, Modernity.* Stanford, Calif.: Stanford University Press.

BECK, U., GIDDENS, A., and LASH, S. 1994. *Reflexive Modernization: Politics, Tradition, and Aesthetics in the Modern Social Order.* London: Polity Press.

BENNETT, J. 2001. *The Enchantment of Modern Life.* Princeton, NJ: Princeton University Press.

—— 2004. The force of things: steps toward an ecology of matter. *Political Theory,* 32: 3.

BERMAN, M. 1981. *The Reenchantment of the World.* Ithaca, NY: Cornell University Press.

BLUMENBERG, H. 1983. *The Legitimacy of the Modern Age.* Cambridge, Mass.: MIT Press.

BROWN, W. 1995. *States of Injury: Power and Freedom in Late Modernity.* Princeton, NJ: Princeton University Press.

BUTLER, J. 1993. *Bodies That Matter: On the Discursive Limits of "Sex."* New York: Routledge.

CHATTERJEE, P. 1997. Our modernity. Sephis-Codestria Lecture No. 1. Dakar: South–South Exchange Programme for Research on the History of Development and the Council for the Development of Social Science Research in Africa.

—— 2004. *Politics of the Governed*. New York: Columbia University Press.

CHAUDHURI, A. 2004. In the waiting-room of history, review of Dipesh Chakrabarty's *Provincialising Europe: Postcolonial Thought and Historical Difference*. *London Review of Books*, 24 June.

CONNOLLY, W. 2000. *Why I Am Not a Secularist*. Minneapolis: University of Minnesota Press.

—— 2002. *Neuropolitics: Thinking, Culture, Speed*. Minneapolis: University of Minnesota Press.

DELEUZE, G. and GUATTARI, F. 1987. *A Thousand Plateaus*. Minneapolis: University of Minnesota Press.

DUMM, T. 1996. *Michel Foucault and the Politics of Freedom*. New York: Rowman and Littlefield.

DURING, S. 2002. *Modern Enchantments: The Cultural Power of Secular Magic*. Cambridge Mass.: Harvard University Press.

FERGUSON, K. E. 1991. *The Man Question: Visions of Subjectivity in Feminist Theory*. Berkeley: University of California Press.

FOUCAULT, M. 1970. *The Order of Things*. New York: Pantheon.

—— 1973. *Madness and Civilization*. New York: Vintage.

—— 1975. *Discipline and Punish*. New York: Penguin.

—— 1978. *The History of Sexuality, Vol. I*. New York: Pantheon.

GAONKAR, D. P. (ed.) 2001. *Alternative Modernities*. Durham, NC: Duke University Press.

GATENS, M. 1996. *Imaginary Bodies: Ethics, Power and Corporeality*. New York: Routledge.

HEIDEGGER, M. 1982. *The Question Concerning Technology and Other Essays*. New York: Perennial.

HORKHEIMER, M. and ADORNO, T. 1972. *Dialectic of Enlightenment*, trans. J. Cumming. New York: Herder and Herder.

JAMESON, F. 1988. The vanishing mediator; or Max Weber as storyteller. In *Ideologies of Theory, Essays 1971–1986, Volume 2: The Syntax of History*. Minneapolis: University of Minnesota Press.

—— 1991. *Postmodernism, or, the Cultural Logic of Late Capitalism*. Durham, NC: Duke University Press.

LATOUR, B. 1993. *We Have Never Been Modern*. Cambridge, Mass.: Harvard University Press.

—— 2004. *The Politics of Nature: How to Bring the Sciences into Democracy*. Cambridge, Mass.: Harvard University Press.

LYOTARD, J.-F. 1997. *Postmodern Fables*, trans. G. van den Abbeele. Minneapolis: University of Minnesota Press.

MARX, K. 1975. The leading article in No. 179 of the *Kolnische Zeitung*. In K. Marx and F. Engels, *Collected Works*, vol. 1, Karl Marx: 1835–43. New York: Lawrence and Wishart.

—— 1977. *Capital*, vols I and II, trans. B. Fowkes. New York: Vintage.

MASSUMI, B. 2002. *Parables for the Virtual*. Durham, NC: Duke University Press.

MOORE, T. 1996. *The Re-Enchantment of Everyday Life*. New York: HarperCollins.

NIETZSCHE, F. 1987. *The Will to Power*. New York: Random House.

—— 1989. On the *Genealogy of Morals*, trans. W. Kaufmann and R. J. Hollingdale. New York: Vintage.

PRIGOGINE, I. 1997. *The End of Certainty: Time, Chaos, and the New Laws of Nature*. New York: Free Press.

—— and STENGERS, I. 1984. *Order Out of Chaos: Man's New Dialogue with Nature*. New York: Bantam.

SERRES, M. 2001. *The Birth of Physics*. New York: Clinamen Press.

SIKORSKI, W. 1993. *Modernity and Technology: Harnessing the Earth to the Slavery of Man*. Tuscaloosa: University of Alabama Press.

TAYLOR, C. 1991. *The Malaise of Modernity*. Toronto: House of Anansi Press.

THOMPSON, M. J. (ed.) 2003. *Islam and the West: Critical Perspectives on Modernity*. New York: Rowman and Littlefield.

WEBER, M. 1958. *The Protestant Ethic and the Spirit of Capitalism*, trans. T. Parsons. New York: Charles Scribner's Sons.

—— 1981. *From Max Weber: Essays in Sociology*, ed. H. H. Gerth and C. Wright Mills. London: Oxford University Press.

PART III

POLITICAL INSTITUTIONS

C H A P T E R 7

OLD INSTITUTIONALISMS

AN OVERVIEW

R. A. W. RHODES

1 INTRODUCTION

Over the past decade, the narrative of the "new institutionalism" has been touted as the new paradigm for political science. For example, Goodin and Klingemann (1996) claim that political science has an overarching intellectual agenda based on rational choice analysis and the new institutionalism. That is one set of approaches, one research agenda, and specific to American political science. The focus of this chapter is broader; it looks at the study of political institutions, whenever, wherever. I define and give examples of four different traditions in the study of political institutions: modernist-empiricist, formal-legal, idealist, and socialist. My aims are simple: to show there are several long-standing traditions in the study of institutions in the Anglo-American world, and to illustrate that variety worldwide.

I have a second, equally important objective. It is a taken for granted assumption that the rise of the "new institutionalism" replaced the "old institutionalism." Old institutionalism is not limited to formal-legal analysis. It encompasses all the traditions discussed below. I argue there is life in all these old dogs. Moreover,

* I would like to thank Haleh Afsher, Mark Bevir, John Dryzek, Jenny Fleming, Bob Goodin, and John Wanna for either help, or advice, or criticism, and sometimes all three. I must record a special thank you to Robert Elgie for his thorough and detailed advice on French political science (personal correspondence, 6 June and 20 July 2005).

formal-legal analysis is not dead. Rather I argue it is a defining starting point in the study of *political* institutions. The distinctive contribution of political science to the study of institutions is the analysis of *the historical evolution of formal-legal institutions and the ideas embedded in them*. The "new institutionalisms" announced the rediscovery by American modernist-empiricist political scientists of this theme, and they offer sophisticated variations on it, but it is still the starting point.

I cannot cover the many traditions of political science worldwide, so I focus on the two most similar countries—the UK and the USA. If I can show different traditions in the Anglo-Saxon world, then my argument will travel well beyond it. To show that potential, I provide brief examples of the study of political institutions in Australia, France, and the Muslim world. I offer a narrative that is just one among several of possible narratives. I set my narrative of traditions side-by-side with the narratives elsewhere in Part II. The aim is to decenter the dominant Anglo-American tradition found in many "state of the art" assessments.

2 TRADITIONS IN THE STUDY OF POLITICAL INSTITUTIONS

A tradition is a set of understandings someone receives during socialization. A certain relationship should exist between beliefs and practices if they are to make up a tradition. First, the relevant beliefs and practices should have passed from generation to generation. Second, traditions should embody appropriate conceptual links. The beliefs and practices that one generation passes on to another should display minimal consistency.

This stress on the constructed nature of traditions should make us wary of essentialists who equate traditions with fixed essences to which they credit variations. For example, Greenleaf (1983, 15–20), following Dicey (1914, 62–9), describes the British political tradition as the dialectic between libertarianism and collectivism. But Greenleaf's categories of individualism and collectivism are too ahistorical. Although they come into being in the nineteenth century, after that they remain static. They act as fixed ideal types into which individual thinkers and texts are then forced. At the heart of the notion of tradition used in this chapter is the idea of agents using their reason to modify their contingent heritage (see Bevir and Rhodes 2003, 2006). So, tradition is a starting point for a historical story. This idea of tradition differs also from that of political scientists who associate the term with customary, unquestioned ways of behaving or with the entrenched folklore of premodern societies (cf. Oakeshott 1962, 123, 128–9).

Table 7.1 identifies four distinct traditions in the study of political institutions: formal-legal, idealist, modernist-empiricism, and socialist. Of course, these traditions are examples. The list is not exhaustive.

Table 7.1. Traditions in the study of political institutions

Traditions	Modernist-empiricist	Formal-legal	Idealist	Socialist
Definition of political institution	Formal rules, compliance procedures, and standard operating practices that structure relationships between individuals in various units of the polity and the economy Hall 1986: 19–20	Public laws that concern formal governmental organizations Eckstein 1979: 2	Institutions express...ideas about political authority...and embody a continuing approach to resolving the issues which arise in the relations between citizen and government Johnson 1975: 131, 112	The specific articulation of class struggle Miliband 1977: 19
Present-day examples Examples	USA: New institutionalisms March and Olsen 1989	French con-stitutionalism Chevallier 2002	UK: Conservative Idealism Johnson 2004	Pan-European post-Marxism Laclau 1990

3 Where are We Now—Modernist-Empiricism?

For many, the study of political institutions is the story of the "new institutionalism." In outline, the story goes that the new institutionalism was a reaction against behavioralism. Thus, for Thelen and Steinmo (1992, 3–5) both historical institutionalism and rational choice are a reaction against behavioralism just as behavioralism was a reaction against the old institutionalism. This reaction comes in three main guises, each rooted in one of the main social science disciplines. So, political science gave us historical institutionalism, economics gave us rational choice institutionalism, and sociology gave us sociological institutionalism (see Goodin 1996, 2–20; Hall and Taylor 1996, 936). Approaches proliferate (Lowndes 2002; Peters 1999). The labels vary—sociological institutionalism begat ideational institutionalism begat constructivism. The several proponents squabble. For aficionados of such debates, the several approaches, the key contributions, and their differences are clearly set out in Chapters 1–5. A further summary is unnecessary.

There are important differences between the several approaches; for example, between inductive and deductive methods. However, such differences are less important than their common ground in a modernist-empiricist epistemology. Thus, institutions such as legislatures, constitutions, and civil services are treated as discrete objects that can be compared, measured, and classified. If American concern with hypothesis testing and deductive methods raises the collective skeptical eyebrow of British political science, then Bryce's claim (1929, vol. 1, 13) that "[I]t is Facts that are needed: Facts, Facts, Facts" would resonate with many. British modernist empiricism has much in common with the positivism underpinning mainstream American political science; both believe in comparison, measurement, law-like generalization, and neutral evidence.

In so labeling the new institutionalism, I do not seek to criticize it, only to locate it in a broader tradition. Adcock et al. (2006) do this job admirably. They explore the diverse roots of the new institutionalism to dismiss the conventional narrative of a shared rejection of behavioralism. They dispute there is a shared research agenda or even the prospect of convergence. The new institutionalism is composed of diverse strands, building on different and probably incompatible intellectual traditions, united only in the study of political institutions and their commitment to modernist-empiricism. The new institutionalism may be a shared label but its divergent roots in incommensurable traditions mean the several strands have little else in common. When we move further afield, the divergence is even more marked.

At first glance, British political science took to historical institutionalism like a duck to water. However, many British political scientists denied any novelty to the new institutionalism. After all, in Britain, neither the behavioral revolution nor rational choice had swept the study of institutions away. Also, the new institutionalism is such a jumble of ideas and traditions that it can be raided for the bits that easily fit with other traditions. So, British political scientists could interpret the rise of the new institutionalism in America as a vindication of British modernist empiricism, with its skepticism toward both universal theory, and the scientism characterizing American political science. Thus, Marshall (1999, 284–5) observes we do not need "more or deeper conceptual theories" because "we have already have most of what we need" for "detailed description, classification and comparison" and the "explanatory problem is simply that of describing relevant segments of the system in sufficient detail to expose what happens or happened." Case studies of institutions can be dressed up as a revitalized institutionalism and British political scientists can claim they wear the latest fashionable clothes. But, if you look closely little has changed. Barry (1999, 450–5) concludes there is no shared intellectual agenda based on the new institutionalism, no shared methodological tool kit, and no band of synthesizers of the discipline. The new institutionalism is little more than a cloak with which Whigs and modernist-empiricists can pursue the kinds of work they long have done unruffled by the pretensions of behavioralism and rational choice.

The same argument can be made for Australian political science. Aitkin (1985, 4–6) notes the discipline was shaped by the strong intellectual links with Britain and the dominance of law, history, and philosophy in the universities. Formal-legal studies were alive, even dominant, well into the 1980s (see Jinks 1985). It is hard to discern the local impact of the new institutionalism (see McAllister et al. 2003, part 2) and the impact of rational choice was even less (see the locally influential critique by Stretton and Orchard 1994).

4 WHERE DID WE COME FROM—FORMAL-LEGAL ANALYSIS?

The study of political institutions is central to the identity of the discipline of political science. Eckstein (1963, 10–11) points out, "If there is any subject matter at all which political scientists can claim exclusively for their own, a subject matter that does not require acquisition of the analytical tools of sister-fields and that sustains their claim to autonomous existence, it is, of course, formal-legal political structure." Similarly, Greenleaf (1983, 7–9) argues that constitutional law, constitutional history, and the study of institutions form the "traditional" approach to political science, and he is commenting, not criticizing. Eckstein (1979, 2) succinctly defines this approach as "the study of public laws that concern formal governmental organizations."

The formal-legal approach treats rules in two ways. First, legal rules and procedures are the basic independent variable and the functioning and fate of democracies the dependent variable. For example, Duverger (1959) criticizes electoral laws on proportional representation because they fragment party systems and undermine representative democracy. Moreover, the term "constitution" can be narrowly confined to the constitutional documentation and attendant legal judgments. This use is too narrow. Finer (1932, 181), one of the doyens of the institutional approach, defines a constitution as "the system of fundamental political institutions." In other words, the formal-legal approach covers not only the study of written constitutional documents but also extends to the associated beliefs and practices or "customs" (Lowell 1908, 1–15). The distinction between constitution and custom recurs in many ways; for example, in the distinctions between formal and informal organization. Second, rules are prescriptions; that is, behavior occurs because of a particular rule. For example, local authorities limit local spending and taxes because they know the central government (or the prefect, or a state in a federation) can impose a legal ceiling or even directly run the local authority.

Eckstein (1979, 2) is a critic of formal-legal study, objecting that its practitioners were "almost entirely silent about all of their suppositions." Nonetheless, he recognizes its importance, preferring to call it a "science of the state"—*staatswissenschaft*—which should "not to be confused with 'political science'" (Eckstein 1979, 1). And here lies a crucial contrast with my argument. *Staatswissenschaft* is not distinct from political science; it is at its heart.

The formal-legal approach is comparative, historical, and inductive (Rhodes 1995, 43–6 and for the usual caricature see Thelen and Steinmo 1992, 3). Finer (1932) is a fine exponent of the comparative approach (and see Eckstein 1963, 18–23 and Bogdanor 1999 for more examples). In sharp contrast to many of his contemporaries, Finer did not adopt a country-by-country approach but compared institution-by-institution across countries. He locates his institutional analysis in a theory of the state. For Finer (1932, 20–2), the defining characteristic of the state is its legitimate monopoly of coercive power (see also Sait 1938, ch. 5). He surveys the main political institutions "not only in their legal form, but in their operation" (Finer 1932, viii), as they evolved. Political institutions are "instrumentalities" which embody the "power-relationship between [the state's] individual and associated constituents" (Finer 1932, 181). Then and only then does he begin to compare the political institutions of America, Britain, France, and Germany. His analysis covers the elements of state organization, including: democracy, separation of powers, constitutions, central-local territorial relations, and federalism. Finally, he turns to "the principal parts of modern political machinery, namely, the Electorate, the Parties, Parliament, the Cabinet, the Chief of State, the Civil Service and the Judiciary" (1932, 949). His approach is not narrow and formal. It is grounded in a theory of the state and explores both the evolution of the institutions and their operation. The critics of the institutional approach do not do justice to his sophisticated analysis.

Formal-legal analysis is also historical. It employs the techniques of the historian and explores specific events, eras, people, and institutions. History is extolled as "the great teacher of wisdom" because it "enlarges the horizon, improves the per-spective" and we "appreciate...that the roots of the present lie buried deep in the past, and...that history is past politics and politics is present history" (Sait 1938, 49). Because political institutions are "like coral reefs" which have been "erected without conscious design," and grow by "slow accretions," the historical approach is essential (Sait 1938, 16).

Finally, formal-legal analysis is inductive. The great virtue of institutions was that we could "turn to the *concreteness* of institutions, the *facts* of their existence, the character of their *actions* and the *exercise* of their power" (Landau 1979, 181; emphasis in the original). We can draw inferences from repeated observations of these objects by "letting the facts speak for themselves" (Landau 1979, 133).

In Britain and the USA, formal-legal analysis remains alive and well today in textbooks, handbooks, and encyclopedias too numerous to cite. Major works are still written in the idiom. Finer's (1997) three-volume history of government combines a sensitivity to history with a modernist-empiricist belief in comparisons across time and space, regularities, and neutral evidence. He attempts to explain how states came to be what they are with a specific emphasis on the modern European nation state. He searches for regularities across time and countries in an exercise in diachronic comparison. The *History* sets out to establish the distribution of the selected forms of government throughout history, and to compare their general character, strengths, and weaknesses using a standardized typology. It then provides a history of government from ancient monarchies (about 1700 BC) to 1875 AD. As Hayward (1999, 35) observes, Finer is either "the last trump reasserting an old institutionalism" or "the resounding affirmation of the potentialities of a new historical institutionalism within British political science." Given the lack of any variant of new institutional theory, the result has to be old institutionalism, and a fine example of an eclectic modernist-empiricism at work.

Formal-legal analysis is a dominant tradition in continental Europe. It was the dominant tradition in Germany, although challenged after 1945. The challenge is yet to succeed in, for example, Italy, France, and Spain. Here I can only give a flavor of the variety that is French political science and establish it as a distinctive endeavor that runs at times in a different direction to, and at times parallel with, Anglo-American political science.

There is a strong French tradition of constitutionalism. It is a species of the "old institutionalism" in that it is descriptive, normative, and legalistic. It focuses on the formal-legal aspects of institutions, but not on case law. It is another example of *staatswissenschaft*. For example, Chevallier (1996, 67) argues that "the growth of the French liberal state in the nineteenth century led to the predominance of the law and lawyers emphasizing the guarantee of citizen's rights and limits on state power." These jurists monopolized the field for nearly a century and it remains a major influence (see for example Chevallier 2002). So, despite various challenges, the 1980s witnessed "the resurgence" of "legal dogma" with its focus on the state's structures and functions (Chevallier 1996, 73).

Outside the tradition of constitutionalism, the French approach to the study of institutions remains distinctive and does not engage with the Anglo-American literature. An early example is Duverger (1954, 1980). Although his work on electoral systems and semi-presidentialism is probably better known outside France than inside, nonetheless it was a major challenge to the academic lawyers and influenced a younger generation of scholars. Latterly, "the strategic analysis of institutions" is an example of the new institutionalism before that term was invented. Its main proponents include, for example, Duhamel and Parodi (1985). Their heyday was the 1970s and 1980s but Parodi remains a major figure. The approach focuses on electoral systems, and core political institutions (such as the presidency), and tries to identify how institutions, singly and in combination, affect behavior (for citations see Elgie 1996). Parodi explains the changing nature of the Fifth Republic's political system by identifying how, for example, the direct election of the president with a majoritarian electoral system for the National Assembly bipolarized the party system. The approach is positivist and rigorous with some clear affinities to both rational choice and empirical institutionalism (see Peters 1999, ch. 5). However none of the proponents of the strategic analysis of institutions publish in English; none engage with the Anglo-American literature. Francophone and Anglophone traditions proceed in mutual ignorance. In short, French political science is rooted in constitutionalism or *staatswissenschaft* and, when it diverges from that tradition, it remains distinctive.

5 WHAT ARE THE COMPETING TRADITIONS—IDEALISM?

In British political science, the idealist tradition encompasses those who argue that social and political institutions do not exist apart from traditions or our theories (or ideas) of them (see Nicholson 1990). The major British idealist of recent times is Oakeshott (1991 and the citations on pp. xxiii–xvi). I concentrate on the application of his ideas to the study of political institutions.

The inheritors of idealism challenged behavioralism for its neglect of meanings, contexts, and history. Oakeshott (1962, 129–30) argued political education required the "genuine historical study" of a "political tradition, a concrete manner of behavior." The task of political science, although he would never use that label, is "to understand a tradition," which is "participation in a conversation," "initiation into an inheritance," and "an exploration of its intimations." For Oakeshott (1962, 126–7) a tradition is a "flow of sympathy" and in any political activity we "sail a boundless and bottomless sea" and "the enterprise is to keep afloat on an even keel." This is a conservative idealism that treats tradition as a resource to which one should typically feel allegiance (cf. Taylor 1985; Skinner 1969).

For Johnson (1989, 131, 112), political institutions "express...ideas about political authority...and embody a continuing approach to resolving the issues which arise in the relations between citizen and government." Institutions are also normative, "serv[ing] as means of communicating and transmitting values." They are the expression of human purpose, so political institutions necessarily contain a normative element (Johnson 1975, 276–7). The task of "political science," a term Johnson would abhor, is to study institutions using "the methods of historical research...to establish what is particular and specific rather than to formulate statements of regularity or generalisations claiming to apply universally." History is "the source of experience" while philosophy is "the means of its critical appraisal" (Johnson 1989, 122–3). Johnson's (1977, 30; emphasis in original) analysis of the British constitution is grounded in the "extraordinary and basically unbroken continuity of conventional political habits." The British "constitution *is* these political habits and little else" and the core notion is "the complete dominance" of the idea of parliamentary government. Johnson (2004) applies this idea of the customary constitution of practices "mysteriously handed down as the intimations of a tradition" and "inarticulate major premises" (the reference is, of course, to Oakeshott) to New Labour's constitutional reforms; for example, devolution. His detailed commentary is of little concern here. Of relevance is his "bias" towards "the customary constitution" because of its "remarkable record of adaptation to changing circumstances and challenges" (Johnson 2004, 5). However, a customary constitution depends on support from a society that is sympathetic to "habit, convention and tradition." Johnson fears there is a "crumbling respect for tradition" and ponders whether the current reforms move "beyond custom and practice," and "piecemeal adaptation may have its limits." The customary supports of the constitution may well have been "eroded beyond recall." Johnson (2004) ends on this interrogatory note.

The notion of institutions as embedded ideas and practices is central to Johnson's analysis. It also lies at the heart of the Islamic study of political institutions. Al-Buraey (1985, ch. 6) identifies a distinctive Islamic approach to the institutions and processes of administrative development. Its distinctive features include: its emphasis on Islamic values and ethical standards; prayers in an Islamic organization—*salah* five times a day is a duty because it is as necessary to feed the soul as to feed the body; bureaucracies that represent the groups they serve; and *shura* or the process of continuous dialogue between ruler and ruled until a consensus emerges. Also, as Omid (1994, 4) argues, Islam can produce two contrasting views of the role of the state. The state exists "only to protect and apply the laws as stated by God." The Saudi model means that you cannot have elections, leaders emerge by consensus and rule according to the teachings of the Koran. The Iranian model builds on the alternative view that Muslims have to abide by the rulings of Islam but that which is not prohibited is permitted. So, there can be elections, parliament, and legislation but the laws have to be subject to scrutiny by a council of guardians. I do not end on an interrogatory note, but stress the primacy of ideas in the study of political institutions (see also Blyth 2002; Campbell and Pederson 2001; Hay 2002).

6 WHAT ARE THE COMPETING TRADITIONS—SOCIALISM?

If historical materialism and economic determinism have been relegated to the dust-bin of history, what is left? I seek to show that the tradition persists and introduce briefly the Marxist theory of the state; the post-Marxists, whose work has been influenced by "the linguistic turn;" and the non-Marxists with their predilection for social engineering.

6.1 Marxist Political Economy

The specific area of concern to the student of political institutions is their analysis of the state. The literature burgeoned (see for example Hay 1996, 1999; Jessop 1990; and Chapter 7).

Jessop is a central figure. He argues against all those approaches to state theory predicated on a distinction between structure and agency. He treats structure and agency only as an analytical distinction; they do not exist apart from one another.

Rather we must look at the relationship of structure to action and action to structure. So, "structures are thereby treated analytically as strategic in their form, content and operation; and actions are thereby treated analytically as structured, more or less context sensitive, and structuring." This approach involves examining both "how a given structure may privilege some actors, some identities, some strategies ... some actions over others," and "the ways ... in which actors ... take account of this differential privileging through 'strategic-context analysis'" (Jessop 2001, 1223). In other words, individuals intending to realize certain objectives and outcomes make a strategic assessment of the context in which they find themselves. However that context is not neutral. It too is strategically selective in the sense that it privileges certain strategies over others. Individuals learn from their actions and adjust their strategies. The context is changed by their actions, so individuals have to adjust to a different context. Institutions or functions no longer define the state. It is a site of strategic selectivity; a "dialectic of structures and strategies" (Jessop 1990, 129).

According to Hay (1999, 170), Jessop's central achievement has been to transcend "more successfully than any other Marxist theorist past or present" the "artificial dualism of structure and agency." I do not want to demur from that judgment or attempt any critical assessment. For my purposes, I need to note only that Jessop's contribution is widely noticed in Continental Europe and substantially ignored by mainstream political science in America and Britain.

6.2 Post-Marxism

Ernesto Laclau is a leading figure in post-Marxism (Laclau 1990; Laclau and Mouffe 1985). His roots lie in Gramscian Marxism and with post-structuralist political philosophy, not with mainstream political science. Discourse theory has grown *without* engaging with mainstream political science. There is no specific critique of political science. Rather it is subsumed within a general critique of both modernism and naturalism in the social sciences (as in for example Winch 1990).

Discourse theory analyses "all the practices and meanings shaping a particular community of social actors." It assumes that "all objects and actions are meaningful" and that "their meaning is the product of historically specific systems of rules." Discourse analysis refers to the analysis of linguistic and non-linguistic material as "texts ... that enable subjects to experience the world of objects, words and practices" (Howarth 2000, 5, 8, 10). The "overall *aim* of social and political analysis from a discursive perspective is to describe, understand, interpret and evaluate carefully constructed objects of investigation." So, "instead of applying theory mechanically to empirical objects, or testing theories against empirical reality, discourse theorists argue for the *articulation* and *modification* of concepts and logics in each particular research context." At the heart of the approach is an analogy with language. Just as we understand the meaning of a word from its context, so we understand a political institution as sedimented beliefs within a particular discourse (and for commentary see Critchley and Marchant 2005).

If Laclau's debt to post-structuralism has undermined many of the characteristic themes of Marxist thinking—for example, his emphasis on the role of discourses and on historical contingency leaves little room for Marxist social analysis with its basic materialism—nonetheless he leaves us with the deconstruction of institutions as discourse.

6.3 Non-Marxists: Fabian Social Engineering

One strand in Fabian thought espoused social and administrative engineering: "disinterested inquiries into social problems that could be utilized by the leaders of either of the major parties." This "application of the scientific method or 'systematized common sense'" stressed such topics as public ownership in the guise of nationalizing industry and extending municipal enterprise (Pierson 1979, 314, 335). Its proponents range from Sydney and Beatrice Webb at the turn of the twentieth century, through postwar advocates such as William Robson and John Stewart, to the current heirs in such New Labour thinks tanks as Demos and the Institute for Public Policy Research. British political science differs sharply from American political science because it has a strong, differentiated socialist tradition.

Robson was "one of the Olympian Fabians, worthy company to the Webbs" (Hill 1986, 12) and a founder of public administration in Britain. His approach to the study of British government and public administration was formal-legal institutionalism and analyzed the history, structure, functions, powers, and relationships of government organizations. In Robson (1939, 1960), he fought for vigorous local democracy and he was a staunch defender of the public corporation. In the *festschrift* for Robson, Griffith (1976, 216) revisited Robson's (1928) *Justice and Administrative Law*, concluding that it was "a remarkable work of academic scholarship and political perception" that "challenged some major assumptions of the system, and not merely some defects which needed remedy." To modern eyes much of his work seems overly polemical. Robson took as self-evident, truths and propositions we would challenge today; for example, the positive relationship between increasing size and efficiency. It matters not. Robson typifies that blend of institutional description and reformism so typical of the British school.

I seek not to praise or bury Caesar, simply to point out that the Fabian social and administrative engineering tradition is alive and well and advising the New Labour government (see Perri 6, Leat, Seltzer, and Stoker 2002; and on the antecedents see Bevir 2005). And this conclusion applies to the several strands of the socialist tradition. It is long-standing, durable, varied, and still with us whether it is analyzing the state, deconstructing institutions as discourse, or advocating network governance reforms.

7 CONCLUSIONS

I address two questions. Were we right all along to focus on formal institutions? Where are we going in the study of political institutions?

7.1 Were We Right all Along?

My concern has been to identify and describe some of the many distinctive traditions in the study of political institutions. I have not even remotely exhausted the variety of such traditions. I have not attempted to pass judgment on their relative merits. I am wary of treating any one theoretical perspective as the valid one from which to judge all others, preferring to probe for neglected traditions. If there is a judgment, it is that we should not overlook them. For many readers, the formal-legal tradition may seem an anachronism, but if one looks at constitution making throughout developing countries, Eastern Europe, and the former Soviet Union, one has to conclude the tradition is alive and well.

When we look beyond Anglo-American institutionalism and cover at least some of the various traditions in the study of institutions we see there is a common core of ideas. The distinctive contribution of political science to the study of institutions lies in its emphasis on: *describing the written constitutional documents and their associated beliefs and practices, drawing on history and philosophy—the founding constituent disciplines of political science—to explore the historical evolution of political institutions.* Such texts and their allied customs constitute the governmental traditions that shape the practices of citizen, politician, administrator, and political scientists alike. Even for Anglo-American institutionalism such analysis provides the basic building blocks of analysis.

Of course modernist-empiricism adds two more ingredients to the pot: some permutation of the modernist-empiricist tool kit of hypothesis testing, deductive methods, atomization, classification, and measurement; and contemporary social and political theory, under the label "the new institutionalisms." For proponents of behavioralism and the new institutionalism alike, the kiss of death for formal-legal analysis is its atheoretical approach. Behavioralism found the study of political institutions wanting because of its "hyperfactualism," or "reverence for the fact," which meant that political scientists suffered from "theoretical malnutrition" and neglected "the general framework within which these facts could acquire meaning" (Easton 1971, 75, 77, 79). New institutionalism takes it for granted that the "old institutionalism" was "atheoretical" (see Thelen and Steinmo 1992, 4; and for a survey of the various criticisms and reply see Rhodes 1995).

Viewed from the modernist-empiricist tradition, these criticisms seem like the death knell. Proponents of the formal-legal approach do not spell out their causal theory. However, many would dispute the relevance of this criterion. If you are not persuaded of the merits of present-day social science, then you do not aspire to causal

theory but turn to the historical and philosophical analyses of formal-legal institutionalism. For example, Greenleaf (1983, 286) bluntly argues that although "the concept of a genuine social science has had its ups and downs, and it still survives, ... we
are as far from its achievement as we were when Spencer (or Bacon for that matter)
first put pen to paper." Indeed, he opines, these "continuous attempts ... serve only to
demonstrate ... the inherent futility of the enterprise." He holds a "determinedly old-
fashioned" view of the study of politics, with its focus on history, institutions, and the
interaction between ideas and institutions (Greenleaf 1983, xi). Moreover, Bogdanor
(1999, 149, 150, 175, 176–7, 178) is not about to apologize for his version of "political science." He has a profound aversion to "over-arching theory" and "positivism," opting
for "an indigenous British approach to politics, a definite intellectual tradition, and
one that is worth preserving." This is the tradition of Dicey, "who sought to discover
what it was that distinguished the British constitution from codified constitutions;"
and Bagehot, "who ... sought to understand political 'forms' through the analysis of
political 'forces'." Similarly, viewed from a constructivist standpoint, the absence of
the conventional battery of social science theories is also not a problem because its
proponents emphasize the meanings of rules for actors seeking the explanation of
their practices in the reasons they give. Null hypotheses and casual modeling play no
part. Formal-legal analysis has its own distinctive rationale and, understood as the
analysis of *the historical evolution of formal-legal institutions and the ideas embedded
in them*, it is the defining characteristic of the political science contribution to the
study of political institutions.

7.2 Where are We Going? History, Ethnography, and the Study of Political Institutions

A key concern in the formal-legal analysis of institutions, in idealism, in post-
Marxism, and in various species of the new institutionalism is the interplay of ideas
and institutions. In their different ways, all analyze the historical evolution of formal-
legal institutions and the ideas embedded in them. So, we read constitutions as text
for the beliefs they embed in institutions. We also explore the related customs by
observing politicians and public servants at work because observation is the prime
way of recovering ideas and their meanings. My argument for the continuing validity
of old institutionalism, therefore, stresses, not the provision of "facts, facts, facts," but
historical and philosophical analysis.

The focus on meanings is the defining characteristic of interpretive or constructivist approaches to the study of political institutions. So, an interpretive approach to
political institutions challenges us to decenter institutions; that is, to analyze the ways
in which they are produced, reproduced, and changed through the particular and
contingent beliefs, preferences, and actions of individuals. Even when an institution
maintains similar routines while personnel change, it does so mainly because the
successive personnel pass on similar beliefs and preferences. So, interpretive theory

rethinks the nature of institutions as sedimented products of contingent beliefs and preferences.

If institutions are to be understood through the beliefs and actions of individuals located in traditions, then historical analysis is the way to uncover the traditions that shape these stories and ethnographers reconstruct the meanings of social actors by recovering other people's stories (see for example Geertz 1973; Taylor 1985). The aim is "to see the world as they see it, to adopt their vantage point on politics" (Fenno 1990, 2). Ethnography encompasses many ways of collecting qualitative data about beliefs and practices. For example, Shore's (2000, 7–11) cultural analysis of how EU elites sought to build Europe uses participant observation, historical archives, textual analysis of official documents, biographies, oral histories, recorded interviews, and informal conversations as well as statistical and survey techniques. The techniques are many and varied but participant observation lies at the heart of ethnography and the aim is always to recover other people's meanings.

This "interpretive turn" is a controversial challenge to the mainstream. It is probably premature and certainly unwise to claim we are on the threshold of a post-modern political science. However, postmodernism does not refer only to debates about epistemology. It also refers to the postmodern epoch and the idea of a shift from Fordism, or a world characterized by mass production of consumer goods and large hierarchically structured business organizations, to flexible specialization, and customized production (see for example Clegg 1990, 19–22, 177–84). By extension, a postmodern political science may well be characterized by a Fordist heartland in the guise of rational choice institutionalism *and* customized political science rooted in national political traditions. And among these niches, old institutionalism will continue to thrive. Also, for the Fordist heartland, it will remain the starting point.

Pondering the aphorism "what goes around comes around," I conclude that old institutionalism has not only stayed around but that its focus on texts *and* custom and its commitment to historical and philosophical analysis make it increasingly relevant. Weighing the mounting criticism of rational choice institutionalism (as in for example Green and Shapiro 1994; Hay 2004), I expect to listen to a new generation of stories about actors and institutions. Interrogating the "interpretive turn," I conclude it is built on shifting sands because our notion of institutions is variously constructed within competing, non-commensurable traditions. So, we already live in a postmodern world with its tribes of political scientists. The key issue is whether we talk past one another or whether we have a reasoned engagement.

Bates et al. (1998) are distinguished proponents of rational choice who also argue for political anthropology and attempt to synthesize rational choice and interpretive theory. As Hay (2004, 58) argues, and Bates et al. acknowledge, "the post-positivist epistemology and post-naturalist ontology of interpretivism cannot be easily reconciled with the positivist epistemology and naturalist ontology of rational choice theory." Interpretive theory has not been assimilated to the rational choice mainstream. Rather, Bates et al. should be seen as "deploying rational choice *techniques* and *analytical strategies* in the service of an interpretivist *theory*" (Hay 2004, 58; emphasis in original). But, more important, their work is an example of reasoned engagement between the traditions.

Such engagement ought to be our future. I fear the professionalization of the political science discipline is the enemy of diversity; a case of *"vive la différence,"* but not too much.

REFERENCES

ADCOCK, R., BEVIR, M., and STIMSON, S. 2006. Historicizing the new institutionalisms. In *Modern Political Science: Anglo-American Exchanges since 1880*, ed. R. Adcock, M. Bevir, and S. Stimson. Princeton, NJ: Princeton University Press.

AITKIN, D. 1985. Political science in Australia: development and situation. Pp. 1–35 in *Surveys of Australian Political Science*, ed. D. Aitkin. Sydney: Allen and Unwin for the Academy of Social Sciences in Australia.

AL-BURAEY, M. A. 1985. *Administrative Development. An Islamic Perspective*. New York: Kegan Paul International.

BARRY, B. 1999. The study of politics as a vocation. Pp. 425–67 in *The British Study of Politics in the Twentieth Century*, ed. J. Hayward, B. Barry, and A. Brown. Oxford: Oxford University Press for the British Academy.

BATES, R. H., GREIF, A., LEVI, M., ROSENTHAL, J.-L., and WEINGAST, B. R. 1998. *Analytic Narratives*. Princeton, NJ: Princeton University Press.

BEVIR, M. 2005. *New Labour: A Critique*. London: Routledge.

—— and RHODES, R. A. W. 2003. *Interpreting British Governance*. London: Routledge.

—— —— 2006. *Governance Stories*. London: Routledge.

BLYTH, M. 2002. *The Great Transformations*. Cambridge: Cambridge University Press.

BOGDANOR, V. 1999. Comparative politics. Pp. 147–79 in *The British Study of Politics in the Twentieth Century*, ed. J. Hayward, B. Barry, and A. Brown. Oxford: Oxford University Press for the British Academy.

BRYCE, J. 1929. *Modern Democracies*, 2 vols. London: Macmillan.

CAMPBELL, J. L. and PEDERSEN, O. K. (eds.). 2001. *The Second Movement in Institutional Analysis*. Princeton, NJ: Princeton University Press.

CHEVALLIER, J. 1996. Public administration in statist France. *Public Administration Review*, 56 (1): 67–74.

—— 2002. *Science Administrative*, 3rd edn. Paris: PUF, Coll. Thémis.

CLEGG, S. 1990. *Modern Organizations: Organization Studies in a Postmodern World*. London: Sage.

CRITCHLEY, S. and MARCHANT, O. (eds.). 2005. *Laclau: A Critical Reader*. London: Routledge.

DICEY, A. V. 1914. *Lectures on the Relations between Law and Public Opinion During the Nineteenth Century*. London: Macmillan.

DUHAMEL, O. and PARODI, J.-L. (eds.). 1985. *La constitution de la Cinquième République*. Paris: Pressees de las FNSP.

DUVERGER, M. 1959 [1954]. *Political Parties*, 2nd rev. edn. London: Methuen.

—— 1980. A new political system model: semi-presidential government. *European Journal of Political Research*, 8: 165–87.

EASTON, D. 1971 [1953]. *The Political System. An Inquiry into the State of Political Science*, 2nd edn. New York: Alfred A Knopf.

ECKSTEIN, H. 1963. A perspective on comparative politics, past and present. Pp. 3–32 in *Comparative Politics: A Reader*, ed. H. Eckstein and D. E. Apter. London: Free Press of Glencoe.

—— 1979. On the "science" of the state. *Daedalus*, 108 (4): 1–20.

ELGIE, R. 1996. The French presidency: conceptualizing presidential power in the Fifth Republic. *Public Administration*, 74 (2): 275–91.

FARR, J., DRYZEK, J. S., and LEONARD, S. T. (eds.). 1995. *Political Science in History: Research Programs and Political Traditions*. New York: Cambridge University Press.

FENNO, R. F. 1990. *Watching Politicians: Essays on Participant Observation*. Berkeley: Institute of Governmental Studies, University of California.

FINER, H. 1932. *The Theory and Practice of Modern Government*, 2 vols. London: Methuen.

FINER, S. E. 1997. *The History of Government from the Earliest Times*, 3 vols. Oxford: Oxford University Press.

GEERTZ, C. 1973. *The Interpretation of Cultures*. New York: Basic Books.

GOODIN. R. E. 1996. Institutions and their design. Pp. 1–53 in *The Theory of Institutional Design*, ed. R. E. Goodin. Cambridge: Cambridge University Press.

—— and KLINGEMANN, H.-D. 1996. Political science: the discipline. Pp. 3–49 in *A New Handbook of Political Science*, ed. R. E. Goodin and H.-D. Klingemann. Oxford: Oxford University Press.

GREEN, D. P. and SHAPIRO, I. 1994. *Pathologies of Rational Choice*. New Haven, Conn.: Yale University Press.

GREENLEAF, W. H. 1983. *The British Political Tradition, Volume 1: The Rise of Collectivism*. London: Methuen.

GRIFFITH, J. A. G. 1976. Justice and administrative law revisited. Pp. 200–16 in *From Policy to Administration: Essays in Honour of William A. Robson*, ed. J. A. G. Griffith. London: Allen and Unwin.

GUNNELL, J. G. 2004. *Imagining the American Polity: Political Science and the Discourse of Democracy*. University Park: Pennsylvania State University Press.

HALL, P. 1986. *Governing the Economy: The Politics of State Intervention in Britain and France*. New York: Oxford University Press.

HALL, P. and TAYLOR, R. 1996. Political science and the three institutionalisms. *Political Studies*, 44: 936–57.

HAY, C. 1996. *Re-stating Social and Political Change*. Buckingham: Open University Press.

—— 1999. Marxism and the state. In *Marxism and Social Science*, ed. A. Gamble, D. Marsh, and T. Tant. London: Macmillan.

—— 2002. *Political Analysis*. Basingstoke: Palgrave.

—— 2004. Theory, stylised heuristic or self-fulfilling prophecy? The status of rational choice theory in public administration. *Public Administration*, 82 (1): 39–62.

HAYWARD J. 1999. British approaches to politics: The dawn of a self-deprecating discipline. Pp. 1–36 in *The British Study of Politics in the Twentieth Century*, ed. J. Hayward, B. Barry, and A. Brown. Oxford: Oxford University Press.

HILL, C. E. 1986. *A Bibliography of the Writings of W. A. Robson*. London: London School of Economics and Political Science, Greater London Paper No. 17.

HOWARTH, D. 2000. *Discourse*. Buckingham: Open University Press.

JESSOP, B. 1990. *State Theory: Putting Capitalist States in their Place*. University Park: Pennsylvania State University Press.

—— 2001. Bringing the state back in (yet again): reviews, revisions, rejections, redirections. *International Review of Sociology*, 11 (2): 149–73.

JINKS, B. 1985. Political institutions. Pp. 119–78 in *Surveys of Australian Political Science*, ed. D. Aitkin. Sydney: Allen and Unwin for the Academy of Social Sciences in Australia.

JOHNSON, N. 1975. The place of institutions in the study of politics. *Political Studies*, 25: 271–83.
—— 1977. *In Search of the Constitution*. Oxford: Perganon.
—— 1980. *In Search of the Constitution*. London: Methuen University Paperback.
—— 1989. *The Limits of Political Science*. Oxford: Clarendon Press.
—— 2004. *Reshaping the British Constitution: Essay in Political Interpretation*. Basingstoke: Palgrave Macmillan.
LACLAU, E. 1990. *New Reflections on the Revolution of Our Time*. London: Verso.
—— and MOUFFE, C. 1985. *Hegemony and Socialist Strategy: Towards a Radical Democratic Politics*. London: Verso.
LANDAU, M. 1979 [1972]. *Political Theory and Political Science: Studies in the Methodology of Political Inquiry*. Sussex: Harvester Press.
LEVI, M. 1988. *Of Rule and Revenue*. Berkeley: University of California Press.
LOWELL, A. L. (1908). *The Government of England*, 2 vols. New York: Macmillan.
LOWNDES, V. 2002. The institutional approach. Pp. 90–108 in *Theory and Methods in Political Science*, ed. D. Marsh and G. Stoker. Houndmills: Palgrave.
MCALLISTER, I., DOWRICK, S., and HASSAN, R. 2003. *The Cambridge Handbook of Social Sciences in Australia*. Melbourne: Cambridge University Press.
MARCH, J. G. and OLSEN, J. P. 1989. *Rediscovering Institutions: The Organizational Basis of Politics*. New York: Free Press.
MARSHALL, G. 1999. The analysis of British political institutions. Pp. 257–85 in *The British Study of Politics in the Twentieth Century*, ed. J. Hayward, B. Barry, and A. Brown. Oxford: Oxford University Press for the British Academy.
MILIBAND, R. 1977. *Marxism and Politics*. Oxford: Oxford University Press.
NICHOLSON, P. P. 1990. *The Political Philosophy of British Idealist: Selected Studies*. Cambridge: Cambridge University Press.
OAKESHOTT, M. 1991 [1962]. *Rationalism in Politics and Other Essays*, 2nd expanded edn. Indianapolis: Liberty Press.
OMID, H. 1994. *Islam and the Post-revolutionary State in Iran*. Basingstoke: Macmillan.
PERRI 6, LEAT, D., SELTZER, K., and STOKER, G. 2002. *Towards Holistic Governance: The New Reform Agenda*. Basingstoke: Palgrave.
PETERS, G. 1999. *Institutional Theory in Political Science: The "New Institutionalism."* London: Pinter.
PIERSON, S. 1979. *British Socialists: The Journey from Fantasy to Politics*. Cambridge, Mass.: Harvard University Press.
RHODES, R. A. W. 1995. The institutional approach. Pp. 42–57 in *Theories and Methods in Political Science*, ed. D. Marsh and G. Stoker. London: Macmillan.
—— 1997. *Understanding Governance*. Buckingham: Open University Press.
ROBSON, W. A. 1928. *Justice and Administrative Law*, 2nd edn 1947, 3rd edn 1951. London: Macmillan.
—— 1939. *The Government and Misgovernment of London*. London: Allen and Unwin.
—— 1962 [1960]. *Nationalized Industries and Public Ownership*, 2nd edn. London: Allen and Unwin.
SAIT, E. M. 1938. *Political Institutions: A Preface*. New York: Appleton-Century.
SHORE, C. 2000. *Building Europe: The Cultural Politics of European Integration*. London: Routledge.
SKINNER, Q. 1969. Meaning and understanding in the history of ideas. *History and Theory*, 8: 199–215.
STRETTON, H. and ORCHARD, L. 1994. *Public Goods, Public Enterprise, Public Choice*. Basingstoke: Macmillan.

TAYLOR, C. 1985. *Philosophical Papers, Volume 2: Philosophy and the Human Sciences.* Cambridge: Cambridge University Press.

THELEN, K. and STEINMO, S. 1992. Historical institutionalism in comparative politics. Pp. 1–32 in *Structuring Politics: Historical Institutionalism in Comparative Analysis*, ed. S. Steinmo, K. Thelen, and F. Longstreth. New York: Cambridge University Press.

WEINGAST, B. R. 2002. Rational choice institutionalism. Pp. 660–92 in *Political Science: The State of the Discipline*, ed. I. Katznelson and H. Milner. New York: W. W. Norton.

WINCH, P. 1990 [1958]. *The Idea of a Social Science and its Relation to Philosophy*, 2nd edn. London: Routledge.

CHAPTER 8

ELABORATING THE "NEW INSTITUTIONALISM"

JAMES G. MARCH

JOHAN P. OLSEN

1 AN INSTITUTIONAL PERSPECTIVE

An institution is a relatively enduring collection of rules and organized practices, embedded in structures of meaning and resources that are relatively invariant in the face of turnover of individuals and relatively resilient to the idiosyncratic preferences and expectations of individuals and changing external circumstances (March and Olsen 1989, 1995). There are constitutive rules and practices prescribing appropriate behavior for specific actors in specific situations. There are structures of meaning, embedded in identities and belongings: common purposes and accounts that give direction and meaning to behavior, and explain, justify, and legitimate behavioral codes. There are structures of resources that create capabilities for acting. Institutions empower and constrain actors differently and make them more or less capable of acting according to prescriptive rules of appropriateness. Institutions are also reinforced by third parties in enforcing rules and sanctioning non-compliance.*

While the concept of institution is central to much political analysis, there is wide diversity within and across disciplines in what kinds of rules and relations

---

* We thank Robert E. Goodin for constructive comments.

are construed as "institutions" (Goodin 1996, 20). Moreover, approaches to political institutions differ when it comes to how they understand (a) the nature of institutions, as the organized setting within which modern political actors most typically act; (b) the processes that translate structures and rules into political impacts; and (c) the processes that translate human behavior into structures and rules and establish, sustain, transform, or eliminate institutions.

Institutionalism, as that term is used here, connotes a general approach to the study of political institutions, a set of theoretical ideas and hypotheses concerning the relations between institutional characteristics and political agency, performance, and change. Institutionalism emphasizes the endogenous nature and social construction of political institutions. Institutions are not simply equilibrium contracts among self-seeking, calculating individual actors or arenas for contending social forces. They are collections of structures, rules, and standard operating procedures that have a partly autonomous role in political life.

Institutionalism comes in many flavors, but they are all perspectives for understanding and improving political systems. They supplement and compete with two other broad interpretations of politics. The first alternative is a *rational actor* perspective which sees political life as organized by exchange among calculating, self-interested actors. The second alternative is a *cultural community* perspective which sees political life as organized by shared values and world-views in a community of common culture, experience, and vision. The three perspectives—institutional, rational actors, and cultural community—are not exclusive. Most political systems can be interpreted as functioning through a mix of organizing principles. Nor are the perspectives always easy to distinguish. True believers in any one of the three can reduce each of the other two to the status of a "special case" of their preferred alternative. Pragmatically, however, the three perspectives are different. They focus attention on different aspects of political life, on different explanatory factors, and on different strategies for improving political systems.

The key distinctions are the extent to which a perspective views the rules and identities defined within political institutions as epiphenomena that mirror environmental circumstances or predetermined individual preferences and initial resources; and the extent to which a perspective pictures rules and identities as reproduced with some reliability that is, at least in part, independent of environmental stability or change.

Within an institutional perspective, a core assumption is that institutions create elements of order and predictability. They fashion, enable, and constrain political actors as they act within a logic of appropriate action. Institutions are carriers of identities and roles and they are markers of a polity's character, history, and visions. They provide bonds that tie citizens together in spite of the many things that divide them. They also impact institutional change, and create elements of "historical inefficiency".

Another core assumption is that the translation of structures into political action and action into institutional continuity and change, are generated by comprehensible and routine processes. These processes produce recurring modes of action and organizational patterns. A challenge for students of institutions is to explain how such processes are stabilized or destabilized, and which factors sustain or interrupt ongoing processes.

To sketch an institutional approach, this chapter elaborates ideas presented over twenty years ago in "The New Institutionalism: Organizational Factors in Political Life" (March and Olsen 1984). The intent of the article was to suggest some theoretical ideas that might shed light on particular aspects of the role of institutions in political life. The aspiration was not to present a full-blown theory of political institutions, and no such theory is currently available. The ideas have been challenged and elaborated over the last twenty years,[1] and we continue the elaboration, without making an effort to replace more comprehensive reviews of the different institutionalisms, their comparative advantages, and the controversies in the field.[2]

2 THEORIZING POLITICAL INSTITUTIONS

The status of institutionalism in political science has changed dramatically over the last fifty years—from an invective to the claim that "we are all institutionalists now" (Pierson and Skocpol 2002, 706). The behavioral revolution represented an attack upon a tradition where government and politics were primarily understood in formal-legal institutional terms. The focus on formal government institutions, constitutional issues, and public law was seen as "unpalatably formalistic and old-fashioned" (Drewry 1996, 191), and a standard complaint was that this approach was "relatively insensitive to the nonpolitical determinants of political behavior and hence to the nonpolitical bases of governmental institutions" (Macridis 1963, 47). The aspiration was to penetrate the formal surface of governmental institutions and describe and explain how politics "really works" (Eulau and March 1969, 16).

Theorizing political institutions, Polsby, for example, made a distinction between seeing a legislature as an "arena" and as "transformative." The distinction reflected variation in the significance of the legislature; its independence from outside influence and its capacity to mould and transform proposals from whatever source into decisions. In an arena-legislature, external forces were decisive; and one did not need to know anything about the internal characteristics of the legislature in order to account for processes and outcomes. In a transformative-legislature, internal structural factors were decisive. Polsby also suggested factors that made it more or less

---

[1] March and Olsen 1984, 1986, 1989, 1995, 1998, 2006. Some have categorized this approach as "normative" institutionalism (Lowndes 1996, 2002; Peters 1999; Thoenig 2003). "Normative" then refers to a concern with norms and values as explanatory variables, and not to normative theory in the sense of promoting particular norms (Lowndes 2002, 95).

[2] Goodin 1996; Peters 1996, 1999; Rothstein 1996; Thelen 1999; Pierson and Skocpol 2002; Weingast 2002; Thoenig 2003.

likely that a legislature would end up as an arena, or as a transformative institution (Polsby 1975, 281, 291–2).

More generally, students of politics have observed a great diversity of organized settings, collectivities, and social relationships within which political actors have operated. In modern society the polity is a configuration of many formally organized institutions that define the context within which politics and governance take place. Those configurations vary substantially; and although there are dissenters from the proposition, most political scientists probably would grant that the variation in institutions accounts for at least some of the observed variation in political processes and outcomes. For several centuries, the most important setting has been the territorial state; and political science has attended to concrete political institutions, such as the legislature, executive, bureaucracy, judiciary, and the electoral system.

Our 1984 article invited a reappraisal of how political institutions could be conceptualized, to what degree they have independent and endurable implications, the kinds of political phenomena they impact, and how institutions emerge, are maintained, and change:

First, we argued for the relative autonomy and independent effects of political institutions and for the importance of their organizational properties. We argued against understanding politics solely as reflections of society (contextualism) or as the macro aggregate consequences of individual actors (reductionism).

Second, we claimed that politics was organized around the interpretation of life and the development of meaning, purpose, and direction, and not only around policy-making and the allocation of resources (instrumentalism).

Third, we took an interest in the ways in which institutionalized rules, norms, and standard operating procedures impacted political behavior, and argued against seeing political action solely as the result of calculation and self-interested behavior (utilitarianism).

Fourth, we held that history is "inefficient" and criticized standard equilibrium models assuming that institutions reach a unique form conditional on current circumstances and thus independent of their historical path (functionalism).

In this view, a political order is created by a collection of institutions that fit more or less into a coherent system. The size of the sector of institutionalized activity changes over time and institutions are structured according to different principles (Berger and Luckmann 1967; Eisenstadt 1965). The varying scopes and modes of institutionalization affect what collectivities are *motivated* to do and what they are *able to do*. Political actors organize themselves and act in accordance with rules and practices which are socially constructed, publicly known, anticipated, and accepted. By virtue of these rules and practices, political institutions define basic rights and duties, shape or regulate how advantages, burdens, and life-chances are allocated in society, and create authority to settle issues and resolve conflicts.

Institutions give order to social relations, reduce flexibility and variability in behavior, and restrict the possibilities of a one-sided pursuit of self-interest or drives (Weber 1978, 40–3). The basic logic of action is rule following—prescriptions based on a logic of appropriateness and a sense of rights and obligations derived from an identity and membership in a political community and the ethos, practices, and expectations of its institutions.[3] Rules are followed because they are seen as natural, rightful, expected, and legitimate. Members of an institution are expected to obey, and be the guardians of, its constitutive principles and standards (March and Olsen 1989, 2006).

Institutions are not static; and institutionalization is not an inevitable process; nor is it unidirectional, monotonic, or irreversible (Weaver and Rockman 1993). In general, however, because institutions are defended by insiders and validated by outsiders, and because their histories are encoded into rules and routines, their internal structures and rules cannot be changed arbitrarily (March and Olsen 1989; Offe 2001). The changes that occur are more likely to reflect local adaptation to local experience and thus be both relatively myopic and meandering, rather than optimizing, as well as "inefficient," in the sense of not reaching a uniquely optimal arrangement (March 1981). Even when history is relatively "efficient," the rate of adaptation is likely to be inconsistent with the rate of change in the environment to which the institution is adapting.

3 INSTITUTIONAL IMPACTS ON POLITICAL ACTORS AND OUTCOMES

Although it is argued that much of the "established wisdom" about the effects of political institutions is very fragile (Rothstein 1996, 155), scholars who deal with political institutions are generally less concerned with *whether* institutions matter, than to what extent, in what respects, through what processes, under what conditions, and why institutions make a difference (Weaver and Rockman 1993; Egeberg 2003, 2004; Orren and Skowronek 2004). In this tradition, institutions are imagined to organize the polity and to have an ordering effect on how authority and power is constituted, exercised, legitimated, controlled, and redistributed. They affect how political actors are enabled or constrained and the governing capacities of a political system. Institutions simplify political life by ensuring that some things are taken as given. Institutions provide codes of appropriate behavior, affective ties, and a belief in a legitimate order. Rules and practices specify what is normal, what must be expected, what can be relied upon, and what makes sense in the community; that is, what a normal, reasonable, and responsible (yet fallible) citizen, elected representative, administrator, or judge, can be expected to do in various situations.

---

[3] "Appropriateness" refers to a specific culture. There is no assumption about normative superiority. A logic of appropriateness may produce truth telling, fairness, honesty, trust, and generosity, but also blood feuds, vendettas, and ethnic conflicts in different cultures (March and Olsen 2006).

It is commonplace to observe that the causal relation between institutional arrangements and substantive policy is complex. Usually, causal chains are indirect, long, and contingent (Weaver and Rockman 1993), so that political institutions can be expected to constrain and enable outcomes without being the immediate and direct cause of public policy. The same arrangement can have quite different consequences under different conditions. The disentanglement of institutional effects is particularly difficult in multilevel and multicentered institutional settings, characterized by inter-actions among multiple autonomous processes (Orren and Skowronek 2004; March and Olsen 2006).

One cluster of speculations about the effects of institutions focuses on rules and routines. The basic building blocks of institutions are rules, and rules are connected and sustained through identities, through senses of membership in groups and recog-nition of roles. Rules and repertoires of practices embody historical experience and stabilize norms, expectations, and resources; they provide explanations and justifi-cations for rules and standard ways of doing things (March and Olsen 1989, 1995). Subject to available resources and capabilities, rules regulate organizational action. That regulation, however, is shaped by constructive interpretations embedded in a history of language, experience, memory, and trust (Dworkin 1986; March and Olsen 1989). The openness in interpretation means that while institutions structure politics and governance and create a certain "bias" (Schattschneider 1960), they ordinarily do not determine political behavior or outcomes in detail. Individuals may, and may not, know what rules there are and what they prescribe for specific actors in specific situations. There may be competing rules and competing interpretations of rules and situations. Indeed, the legitimacy of democratic political institutions is partly based on the expectation that they will provide open-ended processes without deterministic outcomes (Pitkin 1967).

A central theme of organization theory is that identification and habituation are fundamental mechanisms in shaping behavior. In institutionalized worlds actors are socialized into culturally defined purposes to be sought, as well as modes of appropriate procedures for pursuing the purposes (Merton 1938, 676). Members of an organization tend to become imbued not only with their identities as belonging to the organization but also with the various identities associated with different roles in the organization. Because they define themselves in terms of those identities, they act to fulfill them rather than by calculating expected consequences (Simon 1965, 115, 136).

Observing that political actors sometimes deviate from what rules prescribe, insti-tutional scholars have distinguished between an institutional rule and its behavioral realization in a particular instance (Apter 1991). They have sought an improved understanding of the types of humans selected and formed by different types of institutions and processes, how and why different institutions achieve normative reli-ability (Kratochwil 1984), and under what institutional conditions political actors are likely to be motivated and capable of complying with codes of appropriate behavior. The coexistence of the logic of appropriateness and the logic of consequences, for example, also raises questions about how the two interact, which factors determine the salience of different logics, and the institutional conditions under which each logic is likely to dominate.[4]

With whom one identifies is affected by factors such as how activities are sub-divided in an organization, which positions individuals have and their responsibilities. It makes a difference how interaction, attention, experience, and memory are organized, the degree to which goals are shared, and the number of individual needs satisfied by the organization. Identification is also affected by tenure and turnover, the ratio of veterans to newcomers, opportunities for promotion and average time between promotions, job offers from outside, external belongings, and the prestige of different groups (March and Simon 1958; Lægreid and Olsen 1984).

Strong identification with a specific organization, institution, or role can threaten the coherence of the larger system. It has, in particular, been asked to what degree political order is achievable in multicultural societies where it is normatively problematic and probably impossible to create common identities through the traditional nation-building techniques (Weber 1977). For example, in the European Union, national identities are dominant. Identities are, nevertheless, increasingly influenced by issues and networks that cross national boundaries and there is no single center with control over education, socialization, and indoctrination (Herrmann, Risse, and Brewer 2004; Checkel 2005). The vision of "constitutional patriotism" reflects a belief in the forming capacity of shared institutions and that political participation will fashion a post-national civic European identity (Habermas 1994). Still, it is difficult to balance the development of common political institutions and the protection of cultural diversity. It is argued that the EU will face deadlock if governance aims at cultural homogeneity and that the EU needs institutions that protect cultural diversity as a foundation for political unity and collective identity, without excluding the possibility of transforming current identities (Kraus 2004).

Over the last few years, students of political institutions have learned more about the potential and the limitations of institutional impacts on policy and political actors. More is known about the processes through which individuals are transformed into office holders and rule followers with an ethos of self-discipline, impartiality, and integrity; into self-interested, utility maximizing actors; or into cooperating actors oriented towards the policy networks they participate in. More is also known about the processes through which senses of civic identities and roles are learned, lost, and redefined (March and Olsen 1995; Olsen 2005). Still, accomplishments are dwarfed by the number of unanswered questions about the processes that translate structures and rules into political impacts and the factors that impinge upon them under different conditions. This is also true for how institutional order impacts the dynamics of institutional change.

These interests in describing the effects of institutions are supplemented by interests in designing them, particularly in designing them for democratic political systems. The more difficult it is to specify or follow stable rules, the more

---

[4] March and Olsen 1998, 2006; Fehr and Gächter 1998; Isaac, Mathieu, and Zajac 1991; Olsen 2001, 2005.

democracies must rely on institutions that encourage collective interpretation through social processes of interaction, deliberation, and reasoning. Political debates and struggles then connect institutional principles and practices and relate them to the larger issues, how society can and ought to be organized and governed. Doing so, they fashion and refashion collective identities and defining features of the polity— its long-term normative commitments and causal beliefs, its concepts of the common good, justice, and reason, and its organizing principles and power relations.

Legitimacy depends not only on showing that actions accomplish appropriate objectives, but also that actors behave in accordance with legitimate procedures ingrained in a culture (Meyer and Rowan 1977; March and Olsen 1986). There is, furthermore, no perfect positive correlation between political effectiveness and normative validity. The legitimacy of structures, processes, and substantive efficiency do not necessarily coincide. There are illegitimate but technically efficient means, as well as legitimate but inefficient means (Merton 1938). In this perspective, institutions and forms of government are assessed partly according to their ability to foster the virtue and intelligence of the community. That is, how they impact citizens' identities, character, and preferences—the kind of person they are and want to be (Mill 1962, 30–5; Rawls 1993, 269).

4 INSTITUTIONAL ORDER AND CHANGE

The dynamics of institutional change include elements of design, competitive selection, and the accidents of external shocks (Goodin 1996, 24–5). Rules, routines, norms, and identities are both instruments of stability and arenas of change. Change is a constant feature of institutions and existing arrangements impact how institutions emerge and how they are reproduced and changed. Institutional arrangements can prescribe and proscribe, speed up and delay change; and a key to understanding the dynamics of change is a clarification of the role of institutions within standard processes of change.

Most contemporary theories assume that the mix of rules, routines, norms, and identities that describe institutions change over time in response to historical experience. The changes are neither instantaneous nor reliably desirable in the sense of moving the system closer to some optimum. As a result, assumptions of historical efficiency cannot be sustained (March and Olsen 1989; March 1994). By "historical efficiency" we mean the idea that institutions become in some sense "better" adapted to their environments and quickly achieve a uniquely optimum solution to the problem of surviving and thriving. The matching of institutions, behaviors, and contexts takes time and has multiple, path-dependent equilibria. Adaptation is less automatic, less continuous, and less precise than assumed by standard equilibrium models and it does not necessarily improve efficiency and survival.

The processes of change that have been considered in the literature are primarily processes of single-actor design (in which single individual actors or collectivities that act as single actors specify designs in an effort to achieve some fairly well-specified objectives), conflict design (in which multiple actors pursue conflicting objectives and create designs that reflect the outcomes of political trading and power), learning (in which actors adapt designs as a result of feedback from experience or by borrowing from others), or competitive selection (in which unvarying rules and the other elements of institutions compete for survival and reproduction so that the mix of rules changes over time).

Each of these is better understood theoretically than it is empirically. Institutions have shown considerable robustness even when facing radical social, economic, technical, and cultural change. It has often been assumed that the environment has a limited ability to select and eliminate political institutions and it has, for example, been asked whether governmental institutions are immortal (Kaufman 1976). In democracies political debate and competition has been assigned importance as sources of change. Yet, institutions seem sometimes to encourage and sometimes to obstruct reflection, criticism, and opposition. Even party structures in competitive systems can become "frozen" (Lipset and Rokkan 1967).

The ideal that citizens and their representatives should be able to design political institutions at will, making governing through organizing and reorganizing institutions an important aspect of political agency, has been prominent in both democratic ideology and the literature. Nevertheless, historically the role of deliberate design, and the conditions under which political actors can get beyond existing structures, have been questioned (Hamilton, Jay, and Madison 1787 [1964, 1]; Mill 1861 [1962, 1]). In spite of accounts of the role of heroic founders and constitutional moments, modern democracies also seem to have limited capacity for institutional design and reform and in particular for achieving intended effects of reorganizations (March and Olsen 1983; Goodin 1996; Offe 2001). Constitutions limit the *legitimacy* of design. The *need* for major intervention may be modest because routine processes of learning and adaptation work fairly well and the *capability* may be constrained by inadequate causal understanding, authority, and power (Olsen 1997).

The standard model of punctuated equilibrium assumes discontinuous change. Long periods of institutional continuity, where institutions are reproduced, are assumed to be interrupted only at critical junctures of radical change, where political agency (re)fashions institutional structures. In this view, institutions are the legacy of path dependencies, including political compromises and victories.[5] Massive failure is an important condition for change.

The assumption, that institutional structures persist unless there are external shocks, underestimates both intra- and interinstitutional dynamics and sources of change. Usually, there is an internal aspiration level pressure for change caused by enduring gaps between institutional ideals and institutional practices (Broderick 1970). Change can also be rule-governed, institutionalized in specific units or

---

[5] Krasner 1988; Thelen 1999; Pierson and Skocpol 2002; Orren and Skowronek 2004; Pierson 2004.

sub-units, or be generated by the routine interpretation and implementation of rules. Typically, an institution can be threatened by realities that are meaningless in terms of the normative and causal beliefs on which it is founded, and efforts to reduce inconsistency and generate a coherent interpretation are a possible source of change (Berger and Luckmann 1967, 103). As people gradually get or lose faith in institutional arrangements, there are routine switches between institutional repertoires of standard operating procedures and structures. Reallocation of resources also impacts the capability to follow and enforce different rules and therefore the relative significance of alternative structures (March and Olsen 1995).

Thus, a focus on "critical junctures" may underestimate how incremental steps can produce transformative results (Streeck and Thelen 2005). For example, in the post-Second World War period most Western democracies moved stepwise towards an intervening welfare state and a larger public sector. The Scandinavian countries, in particular, saw a "revolution in slow motion" (Olsen, Roness, and Sætren 1982). Since the end of the 1970s most Western democracies have moved incrementally in a neoliberal direction, emphasizing voluntary exchange, competitive markets, and private contracts rather than political authority and democratic politics. Suleiman, for example, argues that the reforms add up to a dismantling of the state. There has been a tendency to eliminate political belongings and ties and turn citizens into customers. To be a citizen requires a commitment and a responsibility beyond the self. To be a customer requires no such commitment and a responsibility only to oneself (Suleiman 2003, 52, 56).

Institutions face what is celebrated in theories of adaptation as the problem of balancing exploitation and exploration. Exploitation involves using existing knowledge, rules, and routines that are seen as encoding the lessons of history. Exploration involves exploring knowledge, rules, and routines that might come to be known (March 1991). Rules and routines are the carriers of accumulated knowledge and generally reflect a broader and a longer experience than the experience that informs any individual actor. By virtue of their long-term adaptive character, they yield outcome distributions that are characterized by relatively high means. By virtue of their short-term stability and their shaping of individual actions, they give those distributions relatively high reliability (low variability). In general, following the rules provides a higher average return and a lower variance on returns than does a random draw from a set of deviant actions proposed by individuals. The adaptive character of rules (and thus of institutions) is, however, threatened by their stability and reliability. Although violation of the rules is unlikely to be a good idea, it sometimes is; and without experimentation with that possibility, the effectiveness of the set of rules decays with time.

It is obvious that any system that engages only in exploitation will become obsolescent in a changing world, and that any system that engages only in exploration will never realize the potential gains of its discoveries. What is less obvious, indeed is ordinarily indeterminate, is the optimal balance between the two. The indeterminacy stems from the way in which the balance depends on trade-offs across time and space that are notoriously difficult to establish. Adaptation itself tends to be biased against exploration. Since the returns to exploitation are typically more certain, sooner, and more in the immediate neighborhood than are the returns to exploration, adaptive systems often extinguish exploratory options before accumulating sufficient experience with them to assess their value. As a result, one of the primary concerns in studies of institutional change is with the sources of exploration. How is the experimentation necessary to maintain effectiveness sustained in a system infused with the stability and reliability characteristic of exploitation (March 1991)?

Most theories of institutional change or adaptation, however, seem to be exquisitely simple relative to the reality of institutions that is observed. While the concept of institution assumes some internal coherence and consistency, conflict is also endemic in institutions. It cannot be assumed that conflict is solved through the terms of some prior agreement (constitution, coalition agreement, or employment contract) and that all participants agree to be bound by institutional rules. There are tensions, "institutional irritants," and antisystems, and the basic assumptions on which an institution is constituted are never fully accepted by the entire society (Eisenstadt 1965, 41; Goodin 1996, 39). There are also competing institutional and group belongings. For instance, diplomacy as an institution involves an inherent tension between being the carrier of the interests and policies of a specific state and the carrier of transnational principles, norms, and rules maintained and enacted by the representatives of the states in mutual interaction (Bátora 2005).

Institutions, furthermore, operate in an environment populated by other institutions organized according to different principles and logics. No contemporary democracy subscribes to a single set of principles, doctrines, and structures. While the concept "political system" suggests an integrated and coherent institutional configuration, political orders are never perfectly integrated. They routinely face institutional imbalances and collisions (Pierson and Skocpol 2002; Olsen 2004; Orren and Skowronek 2004) and "politics is eternally concerned with the achievement of unity from diversity" (Wheeler 1975, 4). Therefore, we have to go beyond a focus on how a specific institution affects change and attend to how the dynamics of change can be understood in terms of the organization, interaction, and collisions among competing institutional structures, norms, rules, identities, and practices.

Within a common set of generalized values and beliefs in society, modernity involved a large-scale institutional differentiation between institutional spheres with different organizational structures, normative and causal beliefs, vocabularies, resources, histories, and dynamics. Institutional interrelations varied and changed. Institutions came to be specialized, differentiated, autonomous, and autopoietic— self-referential and self-produced with closure against influence from the environment (Teubner 1993). There are strains and tensions and at transformative points in history institutions can come in direct confrontation. In different time periods the economy, politics, organized religion, science, etc. can all lead or be led and one cannot be completely reduced either to another or to some transcendent spirit (Gerth and Mills 1970, 328–57; Weber 1978).

A distinction, then, has to be made between change within fairly stable institutional and normative frameworks and change in the frameworks themselves. For example, there are routine tensions because modern society involves several criteria of truth and truth-finding. It makes a difference whether an issue is defined as a technical, economic, legal, moral, or political question and there are clashes between, for instance, legal and scientific conceptions of reality, their starting assumptions, and methods of truth-finding and interpretation (Nelken 1993, 151). Likewise, there are tensions between what is accepted as "rational," "just," and a "good argument" across institutional contexts. Different institutions are, for instance, based on different conceptions of both procedural fairness and outcome fairness and through their practices they generate different expectations about how interaction will be organized and different actors will be treated (Isaac, Mathieu, and Zajac 1991, 336, 339).

There are also situations where an institution has its *raison d'être*, mission, wisdom, integrity, organization, performance, moral foundation, justice, prestige, and resources questioned and it is asked whether the institution contributes to society what it is supposed to contribute. There are radical intrusions and attempts to achieve ideological hegemony and control over other institutional spheres, as well as stern defenses of institutional mandates and traditions against invasion of alien norms. An institution under serious attack is likely to reexamine its ethos, codes of behavior, primary allegiances, and pact with society (Merton 1942). There is rethinking, reorganization, refinancing, and possibly a new "constitutional" settlement, rebalancing core institutions. Typically, taken-for-granted beliefs and arrangements are challenged by new or increased contact between previously separated polities or institutional spheres based on different principles (Berger and Luckmann 1967, 107–8).

Contemporary systems cope with diversity in a variety of ways. Inconsistencies are buffered by institutional specialization, separation, autonomy, sequential attention, local rationality, and conflict avoidance (Cyert and March 1963). Inconsistencies are also debated in public and a well-functioning public sphere is seen as a prerequisite for coping with diversity (Habermas 1994). Modern citizens have lost some of the naive respect and emotional affection for traditional authorities and the legitimacy of competing principles and structures have to be based on communicative rationality and claims of validity. Their relative merits have to be tested and justified through collective reasoning, making them vulnerable to arguments, including demands for exceptions and exemptions that can restrict their scope (Kratochwil 1984, 701).

In general, the Enlightenment-inspired belief in institutional design in the name of progress is tempered by limited human capacity for understanding and control. The institutional frames within which political actors act impact their motivations and their capabilities, and reformers are often institutional gardeners more than institutional engineers (March and Olsen 1983, 1989; Olsen 2000). They can reinterpret rules and codes of behavior, impact causal and normative beliefs, foster civic and democratic identities and engagement, develop organized capabilities, and improve adaptability (March and Olsen 1995). Yet, they cannot do so arbitrarily and there is modest knowledge about the conditions under which they are likely to produce institutional changes that generate intended and desired substantive effects.

5 THE FRONTIER OF INSTITUTIONALISM

....

As the enthusiasm for "new institutional" approaches has flourished over the last twenty years, so also has the skepticism. It has been asked whether institutional accounts really present anything new; whether their empirical and theoretical claims can be sustained; whether their explanations are falsifiable; and whether institutional accounts can be differentiated from other accounts of politics (Jordan 1990; Peters 1999).

It has, however, turned out to be difficult to understand legislatures (Gamm and Huber 2002), public administration (Olsen 2005), courts of law (Clayton and Gillman 1999), and diplomacy (Bátora 2005) without taking into account their institutional characteristics. It has also been argued that the study of institutions in political science has been taken forward (Lowndes 2002, 97); that "there is a future for the institutional approach" (Rhodes 1995); and even that the variety of new institutionalisms have "great power to provide an integrative framework" and may represent the "next revolution" in political science (Goodin and Klingeman 1996, 25).

The "new institutionalism" tries to avoid unfeasible assumptions that require too much of political actors, in terms of normative commitments (virtue), cognitive abilities (bounded rationality), and social control (capabilities). The rules, routines, norms, and identities of an "institution," rather than micro-rational individuals or macro-social forces, are the basic units of analysis. Yet the spirit is to supplement rather than reject alternative approaches (March and Olsen 1998, 2006; Olsen 2001). Much remains, however, before the different conceptions of political institutions, action, and change can be reconciled meaningfully.

The fact that political practice in contemporary political systems now seems to precede understanding and justification may, however, permit new insights. Political science is to a large extent based upon the study of the sovereign, territorial state, and the Westphalian state-system. Yet the hierarchical role of the political center within each state and the "anarchic" relations between states are undergoing major transformations, for example in the European Union. An implication is that there is a need for new ways of describing how authority, rights, obligations, interaction, attention, experience, memory, and resources are organized, beyond hierarchies and markets (Brunsson and Olsen 1998). Network institutionalism is one candidate for understanding both intra- and interinstitutional relations (Lowndes 2002).

There is also a need to go beyond rational design and environmental dictates as the dominant logics of institutional change (Brunsson and Olsen 1998). There is a need for improved understanding of the processes that translate political action into institutional change, how an existing institutional order impacts the dynamics of change, and what other factors can be decisive. The list of questions is long, indeed (Thelen 1999; Orren and Skowronek 2004; Streeck and Thelen 2005). Which institutional characteristics favor change and which make institutions resistant to change? Which factors are likely to disrupt established patterns and processes of institutional maintenance and regeneration? What are the interrelations between change in some (parts of) institutions and continuity in others, and between incremental adaptation and periods of radical change? Under what conditions does incremental change give a consistent and discernable direction to change and how are the outcomes of critical junctures translated into lasting legacies? Which (parts of) political institutions are understood and controlled well enough to be designed and also to achieve anticipated and desired effects?

References

APTER, D. A. 1991. Institutionalism revisited. *International Social Science Journal*, August: 463–81.

BÁTORA, J. 2005. Does the European Union transform the institution of diplomacy? *Journal of European Public Policy*, 12 (1): 1–23.

BERGER, P. L. and LUCKMANN, T. 1967. *The Social Construction of Reality*. New York: Double-day/Anchor.

BRODERICK, A. (ed.) 1970. *The French Institutionalists. Maurice Hauriou, Georges Renard, Joseph Delos*. Cambridge, Mass.: Harvard University Press.

BRUNSSON, N. and OLSEN, J. P. 1998. Organization theory: thirty years of dismantling, and then…? Pp. 13–43 in *Organizing Organizations*, ed. N. Brunsson and J. P. Olsen. Bergen: Fagbokforlaget.

CHECKEL, J. T. 2005. International institutions and socialization in Europe: introduction and framework. *International Organization* (Special issue), 59(5).

CLAYTON, C. W. and GILLMAN, H. (eds.) 1999. *Supreme Court Decision-Making: New Institutionalist Approaches*. Chicago: University of Chicago Press.

CYERT, R. M. and MARCH, J. G. 1963. *A Behavioral Theory of the Firm*. Englewood Cliffs, NJ: Prentice Hall (2nd edn. 1992). Oxford: Basil Blackwell.

DREWRY, G. 1996. Political institutions: legal perspectives. Pp. 191–204 in *A New Handbook of Political Science*, ed. R. E. Goodin and H.-D. Klingemann. Oxford: Oxford University Press.

DWORKIN, R. 1986. *Law's Empire*. Cambridge, Mass.: Harvard University Press.

EGEBERG, M. 2003. How bureaucratic structure matters: an organizational perspective. Pp. 116–26 in *Handbook of Public Administration*, ed. B. G. Peters and J. Pierre. London: Sage.

—— 2004. An organizational approach to European integration: outline of a complementary perspective. *European Journal of Political Research*, 43 (2): 199–219.

EISENSTADT, S. 1965. *Essays on Comparative Institutions*. New York: Wiley.

EULAU, H. and MARCH, J. G. (eds.) 1969. *Political Science*. Englewood Cliffs, NJ: Prentice Hall.

FEHR, E. and GÄCHTER, S. 1998. Reciprocity and economics: the economic implications of *Homo Reciprocans. European Economic Review*, 42: 845–59.

GAMM, G. and HUBER, J. 2002. Legislatures as political institutions: beyond the contemporary Congress. Pp. 313–43 in *Political Science: State of the Discipline*, ed. I. Katznelson and H. V. Miller. New York: Norton.

GERTH, H. H. and WRIGHT MILLS, C. (eds.) 1970. *From Max Weber: Essays in Sociology*. London: Routledge and Kegan Paul.

GOODIN, R. E. 1996. Institutions and their design. Pp. 1–53 in *The Theory of Institutional Design*, ed. R. E. Goodin. Cambridge: Cambridge University Press.

—— and KLINGEMANN, H.-D. 1996. Political science: the discipline. Pp. 3–49 in *A New Handbook of Political Science*, ed. R. E. Goodin and H.-D. Klingemann. Oxford: Oxford University Press.

HABERMAS, J. 1994. Citizenship and national identity. Pp. 20–35 in *The Condition of Citizenship*, ed. B. van Steenbergen. London: Sage.

HAMILTON, A., JAY, J., and MADISON, J. 1964 [1787]. *The Federalist Papers*. New York: Pocket Books.

HERRMANN, R. K., RISSE, T., and BREWER, M. B. (eds.) 2004. *Transnational Identities: Becoming European in the EU*. Lanham, Md.: Rowman and Littlefield.

ISAAC, R. M., MATHIEU, D., and ZAJAC, E. E. 1991. Institutional framing and perceptions of fairness. *Constitutional Political Economy*, 2 (3): 329–70.

JORDAN, A. G. 1990. Policy community realism versus "new institutionalism" ambiguity. *Political Studies*, 38: 470–84.

KAUFMAN, H. 1976. *Are Government Organizations Immortal?* Washington, DC: Brookings Institution.

KRASNER, S. 1988. Sovereignty: an institutional perspective. *Comparative Political Studies*, 21 (1): 66–94.

KRATOCHWIL, F. 1984. The force of prescription. *International Organization*, 38 (4): 685–708.

KRAUS, P. A. 2004. A union of peoples? Diversity and the predicaments of a multinational polity. Pp. 40–4 in *Political Theory and the European Constitution*, ed. L. Dobson and A. Føllesdal. London: Routledge.

LÆGREID, P. and OLSEN, J. P. 1984. Top civil servants in Norway: key players—on different teams. Pp. 206–41 in *Bureaucrats & Policy Making*, ed. E. N. Suleiman. New York: Holmes and Meyer.

LIPSET, S. M. and ROKKAN, S. 1967. Cleavage structures, party systems, and voter alignments: an introduction. Pp. 1–64 in *Party Systems and Voter Alignments: Cross-National Perspectives*, ed. S. M. Lipset and S. Rokkan. New York: Free Press.

LOWNDES, V. 1996. Varieties of new institutionalism: a critical appraisal. *Public Administration*, 74 (2): 181–97.

—— 2002. Institutionalism. Pp. 90–108 in *Theory and Methods in Political Science*, ed. D. Marsh and G. Stoker (2nd edn.). Basingstoke: Palgrave Macmillan.

MACRIDIS, R. C. 1963. A survey of the field of comparative government. Pp. 43–52 in *Comparative Politics: A Reader*, ed. H. Eckstein and D. E. Apter. New York: Free Press of Glencoe.

MARCH, J. G. 1981. Footnotes to organizational change. *Administrative Science Quarterly*, 16: 563–77.

—— 1991. Exploration and exploitation in organizational learning. *Organization Science*, 2: 71–87.

—— 1994. *A Primer on Decision Making: How Decisions Happen*. New York: Free Press.

—— and OLSEN, J. P. 1983. Organizing political life: what administrative reorganization tells us about government. *American Political Science Review*, 77: 281–97.

—— —— 1984. The new institutionalism: organizational factors in political life. *American Political Science Review*, 78 (3): 734–49.

—— —— 1986. Institutional perspectives on political institutions. *Governance*, 9 (3): 247–64.

—— —— 1989. *Rediscovering Institutions*. New York: Free Press.

—— —— 1995. *Democratic Governance*. New York: Free Press.

—— —— 1998. The institutional dynamics of international political orders. *International Organization* 52: 943–69. Reprinted pp. 303–29 in P. J. Katzenstein, R. O. Keohane, and S. D. Krasner (eds.) 1999, *Exploration and Contestation in the Study of World Politics*. Cambridge, Mass.: MIT Press.

MARCH, J. G. and OLSEN, J. P. 2006. The logic of appropriateness. In *The Oxford Handbook of Public Policy*, ed. M. Moran, M. Rein, and R. E. Goodin. Oxford: Oxford University Press.

—— and SIMON, H. A. 1958. *Organizations*. New York: Wiley.

MERTON, R. K. 1938. Social structure and anomie. *American Sociological Review*, 3: 672–82.

—— 1942. Science and technology in a democratic order. *Journal of Legal and Political Sociology*, 1: 115–26.

MEYER, J. and ROWAN, B. 1977. Institutionalized organizations: formal structure as myth and ceremony. *American Journal of Sociology*, 83: 340–63.

MILL, J. S. 1962 [1861]. *Considerations on Representative Government*. South Bend, Ind.: Gateway.

NELKEN, D. 1993. The truth about law's truth. Pp. 87–160 in *European Yearbook in the Sociology of Law*, ed. A. Febbrajo and D. Nelken. Milan: Giuffrè.

OFFE, C. 2001. Institutional design. Pp. 363–9 in *Encyclopedia of Democratic Thought*, ed. P. B. Clarke and J. Foweraker. London: Routledge.

OLSEN, J. P. 1997. Institutional Design in Democratic Contexts. *Journal of Political Philosophy*, 5 (3): 203–29.

—— 2000. How, then, does one get there? An institutionalist response to Herr Fischer's vision of a European federation. Pp. 163–79 in *What Kind of Constitution for What Kind of Polity?* ed. C. Joerges, Y. Mény, and J. H. H. Weiler. Florence: EUI.

—— 2001. Garbage cans, new institutionalism, and the study of politics. *American Political Science Review*, 95 (1): 191–8.

—— 2004. Unity, diversity and democratic institutions: lessons from the European Union. *Journal of Political Philosophy*, 12 (4): 461–95.

—— 2005. Maybe it is time to rediscover bureaucracy. *Journal of Public Administration Research and Theory*, 16: 1–24.

—— RONESS, P. G., and SÆTREN, H. 1982. Norway: still peaceful coexistence and revolution in slow motion. Pp. 47–79 in *Policy Styles in Western Europe*, ed. J. J. Richardson. London: Allen and Unwin.

ORREN, K. and SKOWRONEK, S. 2004. *The Search for American Political Development*. Cambridge: Cambridge University Press.

PETERS, B. G. 1996. Political institutions: old and new. Pp. 205–20 in *A New Handbook of Political Science*, ed. R. E. Goodin and H.-D. Klingemann. Oxford: Oxford University Press.

—— 1999. *Institutional Theory in Political Science: The "New" Institutionalism*. London: Pinter.

PIERSON, P. 2004. *Politics in Time*. Princeton, NJ: Princeton University Press.

—— and SKOCPOL, T. 2002. Historical institutionalism in contemporary political science. Pp. 693–721 in *Political Science: State of the Discipline*, ed. I. Katznelson and H. V. Miller. New York: Norton.

PITKIN, H. 1967. *The Concept of Representation*. Berkeley: University of California Press.

POLSBY, N. W. 1975. Legislatures. Pp. 257–319 in *Handbook of Political Science*, vol. 5, ed. F. Greenstein and N. W. Polsby. Reading, Mass.: Addison-Wesley.

RAWLS, J. 1993. The basic structure as subject. Pp. 257–88 in *Political Liberalism*. New York: Columbia University Press.

RHODES, R. 1995. The institutional approach. Pp. 42–57 in *Theory and Methods in Political Science*, ed. D. Marsh and G. Stoker. London: Macmillan.

ROTHSTEIN, B. 1996. Political institutions: an overview. Pp. 133–66 in *A New Handbook of Political Science*, ed. H. E. Goodin and H.-D. Klingemann. Oxford: Oxford University Press.

SCHATTSCHNEIDER, E. E. 1960. *The Semi-Sovereign People*. New York: Holt, Rinehart and Winston.

SIMON, H. A. 1965. *Administrative Behavior* (2nd edn.). New York: Macmillan.

STREECK, W. and THELEN, K. 2005. Introduction: institutional change in advanced political economies. Pp. 1–39 in *Beyond Continuity: Institutional Change in Advanced Political Economies*, ed. W. Streeck and K. Thelen. Oxford: Oxford University Press.

SULEIMAN, E. 2003. *Dismantling Democratic States*. Princeton, NJ: Princeton University Press.

TEUBNER, G. 1993. *Law as an Autopoietic System*. Oxford: Blackwell.

THELEN, K. 1999. Historical institutionalism in comparative politics. Pp. 369–404 in *Annual Review of Political Science*, vol. 2, ed. N. Polsby. Palo Alto, Calif.: Annual Reviews.

THOENIG, J.-C. 2003. Institutional theories and public institutions: traditions and appropriateness. Pp. 127–37 in *Handbook of Public Administration*, ed. B. G. Peters and J. Pierre. London: Sage.

WEAVER, R. K. and ROCKMAN, B. A. (eds.) 1993. *Do Institutions Matter? Government Capabilities in the United States and Abroad*. Washington, DC: Brookings.

WEBER, M. 1977. *Peasants into Frenchmen: The Modernization of Rural France*. London: Chatto and Windus.

—— 1978. *Economy and Society*. Berkeley: University of California Press.

WEINGAST, B. R. 2002. Rational-choice institutionalism. Pp. 660–92 in *Political Science: State of the Discipline*, ed. I. Katznelson and H. V. Miller. New York: Norton.

WHEELER, H. 1975. Constitutionalism. Pp. 1–91 in *Handbook of Political Science: Governmental Institutions and Processes*, vol. 5, ed. F. I. Greenstein and N. W. Polsby. Reading, Mass.: Addison-Wesley.

CHAPTER 9

COMPARATIVE CONSTITUTIONS

JOSEP M. COLOMER

1 INTRODUCTION

Constitutions came earlier than democracy (Strong 1963). During the late Middle Ages and early modern times, constitutions were mainly devices for establishing rights and limiting powers, functions that are still emphasized in certain academic literature on constitutions (see, for example, North and Weingast 1989; North 1990; Buchanan 1990; Weingast 1995). But as the old powers to be limited were autocratic, constitutionalism advanced almost naturally, together with the expansion of suffrage rights and democratization.

A constitution is usually defined as "a set of rules" for making collective decisions (see, for example, Buchanan and Tullock 1962; Elster and Slagstad 1988; Mueller 1996). Enforceable decisions made by means of rules can solve human coordination and cooperation dilemmas (as discussed by Brennan and Buchanan 1985; Hardin 1989; Ordeshook 1992). However, different rules may favor different decisions with differently distributed benefits. Two sets of rules can be distinguished: (a) those "to regulate the allocation of functions, powers and duties among the various agencies and offices of government," and (b) those to "define the relationships between these and the public," which in democracy are based on elections (Finer 1988).

2 ORIGINS AND EVOLUTION OF CONSTITUTIONAL MODELS

2.1 Division of Powers

The first set of constitutional rules just mentioned regulates the division of powers among different institutions. Virtually all the political regimes in world history have been based on a dual formula: a one-person office combined with multiple-person offices (as remarked by Congleton 2001). The rationale for this dualism is that, while a one-person institution may be highly effective at decision-making and implementation, a multiple-person institution may be more representative of the different interests and values in the society. In modern times, a few basic constitutional models can be compared in the light of this dualism. They include: the old, transitional model of constitutional monarchy; the modern democratic models of parliamentary regime and checks-and-balances regime; and two variants of the latter usually called presidentialism and semi-presidentialism.

The model of constitutional monarchy reunites a one-person non-elected monarch with executive powers and a multiple-person elected assembly with legislative powers. This mixed formula was formally shaped by the French constitution of 1791, which, although ephemeral in its implementation, became a reference for many constitutions in other countries during the nineteenth century, including Austria, Belgium, Brazil, Germany, Norway, Portugal, Spain, and Sweden; in more recent times, similar formulas have been adopted in some Arab monarchies, such as Jordan and Morocco. With broadening suffrage and democratization, the non-elected monarch's powers were reduced, while those of the elected assembly expanded, especially regarding the control of executive ministers, thus moving towards formulas closer to the parliamentary regime.

The parliamentary regime is one of the two democratic formulas that can result from the process of enhancing the role of the electing assembly and limiting the monarch's executive powers. According to the English or "Westminster" model developed since the late seventeenth century, the parliament became the sovereign institution, also assuming the power of appointing and dismissing ministers, while the monarch remained a ceremonial though non-accountable figure. Not until the creation of the Third French Republic in 1871 did a parliamentary republic exist. Nowadays, there are parliamentary regimes in approximately half of the democratic countries in the world, including, with the British-style monarchical variant, Australia, Belgium, Canada, Denmark, Japan, the Netherlands, New Zealand, Norway, Spain, and Sweden, and with the republican variant, Austria, Czech Republic, Estonia, Finland, Germany, Greece, Hungary, India, Ireland, Italy, Latvia, Slovakia, Slovenia, South Africa, and Switzerland.

In this framework, the development of political parties was usually interpreted as a force eroding the central role of the parliament. In old constitutional studies, the British model was provocatively labeled rather than "parliamentary," a "cabinet" regime (see, for instance, Loewenstein 1957; Jennings 1959; Crossman 1963; Wheare 1963). However, it has more recently been remarked that the growth of party was instrumental in reducing the influence of the monarch but not necessarily that of the parliament. With the reduction of the monarch to a figurehead, the prime minister has indeed become the new one-person relevant figure, but the position of the cabinet has weakened. In contrast, the role of parliament has survived, and even, in a modest way, thrived. Despite long-standing concerns regarding the balance of power, "parliament has always remained the primary institution of the British polity" (Flinders 2002; see also Bogdanor 2003; Seaward and Silk 2003).

In the other democratic formula, which originated with the 1787 constitution of the United States, it is not only the multiple-person legislative assembly that is popularly elected but also the one-person chief executive. The non-elected monarch was replaced with an elected president with executive powers. This model of political regime implies, thus, separate elections and divided powers between the chief executive and the legislative branch. It was widely imitated in Latin American republics, but with the introduction of strong biases in favor of the presidency, as will be discussed below; other variants have also been adopted in a number of Asian countries under American influence, including Indonesia, South Korea, the Philippines, and Taiwan.

In the original US version, this model is a complex system of "checks and balances" or mutual controls between separately elected or appointed institutions (presidency, house, senate, court). They include term limits for the president, limited presidential veto of congressional legislation, senate rules permitting a qualified minority to block decisions, senatorial ratification of presidential appointments, congressional appointment of officers and control of administrative agencies, congressional impeachment of the president, and judicial revision of legislation.

Recent analyses have formally shown how these counter-weighting mechanisms play in favor of power sharing between institutions and as equivalent devices to supermajority rules for decision-making. The obstacles introduced by the numerous institutional checks may stabilize socially inefficient status quo policies, but they also guarantee that most important decisions are made by broad majorities able to prevent the imposition of a small, or minority, group's will. With similar analytical insight but a different evaluation, other analyses have remarked that separate elections and divided governments create a "dual legitimacy" prone to "deadlock;" that is, legislative paralysis and interinstitutional conflict (Hammond and Miller 1987; Riggs 1988; Neustadt 1990; Linz 1990a; Cox and Kernell 1991; Riker 1992; Krehbiel 1996, 1998; Brady and Volden 1998; Cameron 2000; Dahl 2002; Colomer 2005b).

Another two variants of political regime with separate elections for the presidency and the assembly have developed. The first, usually called "presidentialism," have eventually emerged in almost all twenty republics in Latin America from the mid- or late nineteenth century, including in particular Argentina, Brazil, Chile, Colombia, Costa Rica, Mexico, Peru, Uruguay, and Venezuela. As mentioned, some founding constitution makers in these countries claimed to be imitating the United States Constitution, but, in contrast to the preventions against one-person's expedient decisions introduced in the USA, some of them looked farther back to the absolutist monarchies preceding any division of powers and mixed regimes and aimed at having "elected kings with the name of presidents" (in Simón Bolívar's words). The distinction between US-style checks-and-balances, unified government in presidential regimes, and "presidentialism," which can be referred to Madison, Jefferson, and Hamilton, respectively (according to Burns 1965), was already remarked in old constitutional studies for Latin America (García Calderón 1914; Fitzgibbon 1945; Loewenstein 1949; Stokes 1959; Lambert 1963).

Presidential dominance has been attempted through the president's veto power over legislation and his control of the army, which also exist in the USA, supplemented with long presidential terms and re-elections, unconstrained powers to appoint and remove members of the cabinet and other highly-placed officers, legislative initiative, the capacity to dictate legislative decrees, fiscal and administrative authority, discretionary emergency powers, suspension of constitutional guarantees, and, in formally federal countries, the right to intervene in state affairs. The other side of this same coin is weak congresses, which are not usually given control over the cabinet and are frequently constrained by short session periods and a lack of resources (Linz 1990a; Shugart and Carey 1992; Linz and Valenzuela 1994; Aguilar 2000; Cox and Morgenstern 2002; Morgenstern and Nacif 2002). Proposals for reform have included moves towards all the other regime types, including semi-parliamentarism (Nino 1992), Westminster features (Mainwairing and Shugart 1997), US-style checks-and-balances (Ackerman 2000), and multiparty parliamentarism (Colomer and Negretto 2005).

The second variant, usually called a "semi-presidential" regime, but also "semi-parliamentary," "premier-presidential," or "dual-executive," had been experimented with in Finland and Germany after the First World War but was more consistently shaped with the 1958 constitution of France. Similar constitutional formulas have been recently adopted in a few countries in Eastern Europe, including Lithuania, Poland, Romania, and Russia, as well as a number of others in Africa. With this formula, the presidency and the assembly are elected separately, as in a checks-and-balances regime, but it is the assembly that appoints and can dismiss a prime minister, as in a parliamentary regime. The president and the prime minister share the executive powers in a "governmental diarchy" (Duverger 1970, 1978, 1980; Duhamel and Parodi 1988).

At the beginning of the French experience it was speculated that this constitutional model would produce an alternation between presidential and parliamentary phases, respectively favoring the president and the prime minister as a one-person dominant figure. The first phase of the alternation was indeed confirmed with presidents enjoying a compact party majority in the assembly. In these situations, "the president can become more powerful than in the classical presidential regimes," as well as more powerful than the British-style prime minister because he accumulates the latter's powers plus those of the monarch (Duverger 1998). The second, parliamentary phase was, in contrast, not confirmed, since, even if the president faces a prime minister, a cabinet, and an assembly majority with a different political orientation, he usually retains significant powers, including the dissolution of the assembly, as well as partial vetoes over legislation and executive appointments, among others, depending on the specific rules in each country. This makes the president certainly more powerful than any monarch or republican president in a parliamentary regime. (A gradual acknowledgment that a significant division of powers exists in the "cohabitation" phase can be followed in more recent works in French by Duverger 1986, 1996, 1998). There can, thus, indeed be two "phases," depending on whether the president's party has a majority in the assembly and can appoint the prime minister or not; however, the two phases are not properly presidential and parliamentary, but they rather produce an even higher concentration of power than in a presidential regime and a dual executive, respectively. (See also discussion in Bahro, Bayerlein, and Veser 1998; Sartori 1994; Elgie 1999).

2.2 Electoral Rules

The second set of constitutional rules mentioned above regulates the relationships between citizens and public officers by means of elections. A long tradition of empirical studies, usually focusing on democratic regimes during the second half of the twentieth century, has assumed that elections and electoral systems could be taken as an independent variable from which the formation of political parties and other features of a political system derive (Duverger 1951; Rae 1967; Grofman and Lijphart 1986; Taagepera and Shugart 1989; Lijphart 1994; Cox 1997; Katz 1997). But an alternative point of view emphasizes that it is the governments and parties that choose constitutional rules, including electoral systems, and, thus, the role of the dependent and the independent variables in the previous analytical framework could be upside down (Grumm 1958; Lipson 1964; Särlvick 1982; Boix 1999; Colomer 2004, 2005a).

Most modern electoral rules originated as alternatives to a traditional electoral system composed of multimember districts, open ballots permitting individual candidate voting, and plurality or majority rule. This understudied type of electoral system was used very widely in local and national assemblies in pre-democratic or early democratic periods before and during the nineteenth century; it is still probably the most common procedure in small community, condominium, school, university, professional organization, corporation board, and union assemblies and elections; and it has also been adopted in a small number of new democracies in recent times. It appears indeed as almost "natural" and "spontaneous" to many communities when they have to choose a procedure for collective decision-making based on votes, especially because it permits a varied representation of the community.

But while this set of rules can produce fair representation, at the same time it creates strong incentives for the formation of "factional" candidacies or voting coalitions, which are the most primitive form of political parties. In elections in multimember districts by plurality rule, factions or parties tend to induce "voting in bloc" for a closed list of candidates, which may provoke a single-party sweep. Once partisan candidacies, partisan voting in bloc, and partisan ballots emerged within the framework of traditional assemblies and elections, political leaders, activists, and politically motivated scholars began to search for alternative electoral systems able to reduce single-party sweeps and exclusionary victories (Duverger 1951; see also LaPalombara and Weiner 1966; and the survey by Scarrow 2002).

During the nineteenth and early twentieth centuries, new electoral procedures were invented and adopted as innovative variations of the traditional system mentioned above. They can be classified into three groups, depending on whether they changed the district magnitude, the ballot, or the rule. The first group implied a change of the district magnitude from multimember to single-member districts, of course keeping both individual candidate voting and majoritarian rules. With smaller single-member districts, a candidate that would have been defeated by a party sweep in a multimember district may be elected. This system, thus, tends to produce more varied representation than multimember districts with party closed lists, although less than the old system of multimember districts with an open, individual candidate ballot. The second group of electoral rules introduced new forms of ballot favoring individual candidate voting despite the existence of party candidacies, such as limited and cumulative voting, while maintaining the other two essential elements of the traditional system: multimember districts and majoritarian rules. Finally, the third group of new electoral rules implied the introduction of proportional representation formulas, which are compatible with multimember districts and also, in some variants, with individual candidate voting, and permit the development of multipartism (Colomer 2006).

Different electoral rules and procedures create different incentives to coordinate the appropriate number of candidacies (as has been emphasized by Cox 1997). However, coordination may fail, especially under restrictive formulas based on plurality rule that may require paramount efforts to concentrate numerous potential candidates into a few broad, potentially winning candidacies. By analyzing party systems and elections over long periods and, in some studies, within each country, it has been shown that electoral systems based on plurality or majority rules tend to remain in place only to the extent that two large parties are able to attract broad electoral support and alternate in government. But when multiple parties develop in spite of and against the incentives provided by the existing majoritarian system and through coordination failures, they tend to adopt more permissive electoral rules, especially proportional representation formulas.

Generally, the choice of electoral systems follows what can be called "Micro-mega's rule," by which the large prefer the small and the small prefer the large: a few large parties tend to prefer small assemblies, small district magnitudes, and rules based on small quotas of votes for allocating seats, such as plurality rule, while multiple small parties tend to prefer large assemblies, large district magnitudes, and large quotas such as those of proportional representation. Nowadays, more than 80 percent of democratic regimes in countries with more than one million inhabitants use electoral systems with proportional representation rules (Lijphart 1994; Blais and Massicotte 1997; Colomer 2004, 2005a).

The relevant implication of this discussion for constitutional analysis is that electoral systems are intertwined with party systems, which in turn shape the relations between the legislature and the executive. All these elements define different types of political regime.

3 CONSTITUTIONAL REGIME TYPOLOGIES

Traditional legalistic classifications of constitutional regimes focused, in addition to the distinction between autocracy and democracy, on the difference, within the latter, between "parliamentary" and "presidential" regimes (see, for example, Duverger 1955; Verney 1959; and the compilation by Lijphart 1992). The introduction of a second dimension, the electoral system, discussed in the previous section, makes the classification of democratic regimes more complex. In particular, within parliamentary regimes one can distinguish between those using majoritarian electoral rules, which typically imply that a single party is able to win an assembly majority and appoint the prime minister, and those using proportional representation, which correspond to multiparty systems and coalition cabinets. Presidential regimes and their variants, in contrast, are less affected by the electoral system dimension since at least one of the systems, the one for the election of the president, must be majoritarian and produce a single absolute winner.

What has possibly been the most influential political regime typology in recent comparative studies is based on the two institutional dimensions mentioned and the corresponding degrees of concentration of constitutional and party powers (Lijphart 1984, 1999). Lijphart primarily analyzes the "executives–parties" dimension; that is, the relation between cabinets and parliaments and the set of party and electoral systems, as well as a number of other highly-correlated variables (while another dimension not to be discussed here regards the degree of territorial centralization). By statistical correlations and factor analysis of the empirical data, he arrives at a dual political regime typology, organized around the "majoritarian" (or Westminster) and the "consensus" models of democracy, respectively characterized by high power concentration and broad power sharing.

This simple empirical dichotomy, however, seems to be a contingent result of the sample of countries considered, since very few have checks-and-balances, presidential, or semi-presidential regimes (1 percent in the first exercise with twenty-one countries, 17 percent in the second with thirty-six). Therefore, according to this widely used typology, such a diversity of political regimes as the parliamentary-majoritarian of the United Kingdom, the checks-and-balances of the United States, and semi-presidential of France, among others, are included in the "majoritarian" type, while the consensus type refers to parliamentary-proportional regimes, mostly located in continental Europe. (For methodological critiques and alternative operational proposals, see Bogaards 2000; Taagepera 2003.)

Other approaches to the way different constitutional regimes work do not focus on a priori analysis of institutions but give primacy to the role of political parties. Some authors have promoted broad uses of the categories of "unified" and "divided" government. This new dual typology was initially applied to the analysis of the United States, where a "unified government" with the president's party having a majority in both houses of Congress has existed for only 59 percent of the time from 1832 to 2006, while "divided government," which was very frequent during the second half of the twentieth century, implies that two different political party majorities exist in the presidency and Congress. However, US congressional rules have traditionally included the ability of 40 percent of senators to block any decision by filibustering, which has almost always made the president's party unable to impose its decisions on its own. This could explain why no significant differences in legislative performances between periods of "unified" and "divided" governments have been observed (as persistently reported by King and Ragsdale 1988; Mayhew 1991; Fiorina 1992; Cox and McCubbins 1993; Peterson and Greene 1993; Edwards, Barrett, and Peake 1997; Epstein and O'Halloran 1999; but see discussion in Howell, Adler, Caneron, and Riemann 2000; Conley 2003).

Assuming that, in order to prevent deadlock, a situation of divided government (and, in the United States, almost any real situation) may lead to negotiations between the president's and other parties to form a sufficient congressional majority to make laws, it has been postulated that the absence of a single-party parliamentary majority in a parliamentary regime should also be characterized as "divided government." The integration into the same category of both the congressional minority president in a regime of separation of powers and the typical multiparty coalition or minority government in a parliamentary-proportional regime would make the USA "not exceptional" (Laver and Shepsle 1991; Elgie 2001).

A related approach also integrating institutions and parties in the same count centers on so-called "veto-players" (Tsebelis 1995, 2002). In this approach, political regimes can be analyzed for how many veto-players exist, which may have significant consequences on the degree of complexity of policy decision-making. In the analysis of parliamentary systems, the number of veto-players turns out to be equivalent to the number of parties in government, thus not taking into account whether they are pivotal or superfluous to making the coalition a winning one (a subject largely discussed, in contrast, in the literature on coalition formation, as well as that on power indices, as revised by Felsenthal and Machover 1998; Leech 2002). In checks-and-balances and similar regimes, the number of veto-players increases with the number of "chambers" (including the presidency) with different partisan control. A single veto-player situation would be equivalent to "unified government" as defined above, thus also making parliamentary and checks-and-balances and related regimes equivalent when the decision-power is highly concentrated.

In contrast to other approaches, this may result in non-dual classifications, since not only one or two, but several numbers of veto-players can exist in a political system. However, this approach pretends to analyze how political institutions work in practice, not the a priori characteristics of different constitutional formulas, which does make it less appealing for constitutional choice, advice, or design. The exclusion of the electoral stage from the analysis tends even to blur the fundamental distinction between autocracy and democracy. From the perspective provided by the veto-player approach, single-party governments would work in the same way independently of whether they were autocratic or democratic (for methodological critiques, see Moser 1996; Ganghof 2005).

Taking into account the analyses of both the relations between the executive and the legislature and the electoral rules previously reviewed, a more complex five-fold typology of democratic constitutional regimes can be derived. The relatively high number of a priori, polar types here considered does not presume that there are always significant differences in the working and proximate outcomes of all of them, but it does not preclude potentially interesting empirical findings that more simple or dualistic typologies may make impossible to observe. Empirical analyses may reduce the number of relevant types when, for the purposes of the problem under scrutiny, some of them may appear to be collapsed into a single one. But this may be a result of the analysis rather than an a priori simplifying assumption. From lower to higher degrees of concentration of power, the types of constitutional regimes previously discussed are:

1. parliamentary-proportional (e.g. Germany, the Netherlands);
2. checks and balances (e.g. United States, Indonesia);
3. semi-presidential (e.g. France, Poland);
4. presidentialist (e.g. Argentina, Mexico);
5. parliamentary-majority (e.g. United Kingdom, Canada).

Note that types 1 and 5 correspond to the classical category of "parliamentary" regime, here drastically split for different party systems and electoral systems, while types 2, 3, and 4 are variants of the classical category of "presidential" regime as discussed in the previous section. Regarding the other typologies reviewed above, the "consensus" model would correspond to type 1, while the "majoritarian" model would include types 2, 3, 4, and 5; type 1 would usually be associated with "divided government," while types 2, 3, and 4 would alternate between "divided" and "unified" governments, and type 5 would usually be associated with "unified government;" there could be multiple veto-players in types 1, 2, 3, and 4, although not always, while type 5 would tend to have a single veto-player with higher frequency. Thus, the different typologies here reviewed only agree on considering types 1 and 5 as extreme, respectively implying diffuse and concentrated power, while types 2, 3, and 4 are differently classified, either together with any of the two extreme types or as intermediate ones.

4 CONSTITUTIONAL CONSEQUENCES

It has been repeatedly postulated that different constitutional formulas have different consequences on politics, policy, and the polity. The "proximate" political consequences of different constitutional arrangements regard mainly the type, party composition, and degree of stability of governments. The rest of the consequences should be considered relatively "remote," indirect, and perhaps identifiable in terms of constraints, limits, and opportunities, rather than determining specific decisions or outcomes. They may affect economic and other public policy-making, as well as the corresponding performance, but only partially. Also, different constitutional formulas may help democracy to endure or facilitate its shortening. On all of these levels, significant and interesting empirical correlations between different constitutional formulas and outcomes have been found. But these correlations do not always go together with the specification of the mechanisms by which they may exist; in particular, how different types of governments may be linked to different policy performances, and how the latter may be related to the duration of democratic regimes.

4.1 Government Formation

In parliamentary regimes with majoritarian electoral rules, a single party, even with minority electoral support, usually finds sufficient institutional levers to form a government. This tends to make these governments more internally consistent and more durable than multiparty coalition or minority governments typical of parliamentary regimes with proportional representation, which are more vulnerable to coalition splits, censure, or confidence-lost motions, and other events and strategies provoking anticipated elections (Grofman and Roozendaal 1997; Strom and Swindle 2002; Smith 2004).

However, relatively stable single-party parliamentary governments, as well as presidential governments with a president's party majority in the assembly and fixed terms, tend to produce more changing and unstable policies than those relying upon the support of multiple parties or interinstitutional agreements. To understand this, consider that a single-party government is the institutional result of an election that becomes decisive for all the multiple policy issues that may enter the government's agenda. As the "spatial theory" of voting can illuminate, the "single-package" outcome of political competition in a policy "space" formed by multiple issues and dimensions can be highly unpredictable. The election may be won on the basis of a small set of issues that become prominent during the campaign and in voters' information driving their vote. But the subsequent single-party government may have a free hand to approve and implement its preferred policies on many issues, even if they have not been salient in the previous debate and campaign.

In contrast, in multiparty elections producing coalition cabinets, as well as in interinstitutional relations involving different political majorities, each party can focus on a different set of issues, globally enlarging the electoral agenda and the corresponding debate. In the further institutional process, certain issues (typically including major domains such as macroeconomic policy, interior, and foreign affairs) are dealt with separately on single-issue "spaces." Each of them can usually be the subject of a broad multiparty or interinstitutional agreement around a moderate position, which precludes drastic changes and induces policy stability in the medium or long term. Other issues can be negotiated in such a way that the minority with more intense preferences on each issue may see its preferred policy approved, whether through the distribution of cabinet portfolios to parties focused on different domains (such as finance for liberals, education for Christian-democrats, social or labor policy for social-democrats, etc.) or through logrolling among different groups on different issues in congress. This second mechanism creates different but enduring political supports to the decisions on each issue and also tends to produce relative policy stability. (Some ideas of this sort can be found in Blondel and Müller-Rommel 1988, 1993; Budge and Keman 1990; Laver and Schofield 1990; Strom 1990; Laver and Shepsle 1994, 1996; Deheza 1998; Müller and Strom 2000).

4.2 Policy Performance

A seminal analysis of the policy effects of different constitutional regimes and the type of governments they produce emerged from the study of British politics (see early discussion in Finer 1975). As seen from this observatory, a parliamentary-majoritarian regime creating single-party governments on the basis of a minority of popular votes is the scene of "adversary politics." This implies two major consequences: first, electorally minority governments with a social bias are more prone to be captured by minority interest groups and to implement redistributive and protectionist policies hurting broad social interests; second, frequent alternation of socially and electorally minority parties in government produces policy reversal and instability (including changes in regulations of prices, the labor market, taxes), which depress investment incentives. The bases for sustained economic growth seemed, thus, to be damaged by the likely effects of Westminster-type constitutional rules on government formation and policy-making.

This kind of argument has been tested in a number of studies basically using the (Westminster) majoritarian/consensus dual typology reviewed in the previous section. Most empirical findings show no significant differences in the performance of the two types of political regimes regarding economic growth, although some of them indicate a slightly better record for consensus democracies on inflation and unemployment. Better results for the consensus model have been found regarding electoral participation, low levels of politically motivated violence, women's representation, and social and environmental policies (Powell 1982; Baylis 1989; Lijphart 1984, 1999; Crepaz 1996; Birchfield and Crepaz 1998; Eaton 2000).

Using a different approach, it has also been held that parliamentary regimes with proportional representation tend to develop broad programs benefiting a majority of the voters, including redistribution through social security and welfare policies, in contrast to narrower targets in both parliamentary regimes with majoritarian elections and presidential regimes. The parliamentary-proportional regimes appear to be associated with better growth-promoting policies, but they also have relatively high taxes and public spending, which do not necessarily favor growth (Persson and Tabellini 2003).

The weakness of empirical relations such as those reported here might reflect a relative remoteness of the independent variable (constitutional models) from the dependent one (economic and social performance). Economic growth, in particular, has indeed many more "proximate" causes than political institutions, such as capital formation, labor productivity, entrepreneurship, trade, technology availability, and education. The opposite of "proximate," which would correspond to the role of institutions, should be "remote," since the "proximate" causes just mentioned may in turn depend on institutions but also on other non-institutional variables such as climate and natural resources, population, and human capacities. Regarding institutions, those favoring state effectiveness and an effective judiciary, as well as those regulating property rights, contracts, and finances, might be more relevant to explaining economic growth than certain variants in constitutional formulas and not necessarily closely related to them. (For recent discussions, see Hammond and Butler 2003; Alesina and Glaeser 2004; Glaeser, La Porta, and Lopez-de-Silanes 2004; Przeworski 2004; Acemoglu, Johnson, and Robinson 2005).

A new way to research could be designed by analogy to some recent studies on the relation between electoral systems and party systems reported above. In both problems (the relation between electoral systems and party systems, and the relation between constitutional formulas and economic growth), the main tradition in empirical studies is comparative statics; that is, the comparison of different supposedly independent variables established in different countries. An alternative approach would compare different supposedly independent variables within the same country. In a similar way as changes in party systems have been identified before and after the change of electoral rules in each country, the rates of economic growth or other interesting variables could be compared for periods with different constitutional formulas in each country (including democracy or dictatorship). This may require difficult collection of data for very long periods. But it would permit a better identification of the specific effects of changing political-institutional variables over the background of presumably more constant variables for each country, such as natural resources and population.

4.3 Democracy Duration

Different constitutional formulas have also been linked to different rates of success of attempts at democratization and to the duration of democratic regimes. Recent analyses of political change have emphasized that strategic choices of different constitutional formulas are driven by actors' relative bargaining strength, electoral expectations, and attitudes to risk (Przeworski 1986, 1991; Elster 1996; Elster, Offe, and Preuss 1998; Colomer 1995, 2000; Geddes 1996; Goodin 1996; Voigt 1999). A common assumption is that citizens and political leaders tend to support those formulas producing satisfactory results for themselves and reject those making them permanently excluded and defeated. As a consequence, those constitutional formulas producing widely-distributed satisfactory outcomes should be more able to develop endogenous support and endure. In general, widely representative and effective political outcomes should feed social support for the corresponding institutions, while exclusionary, biased, arbitrary, or ineffective outcomes might foster citizens' and leaders' rejection of the institutions producing such results. In this approach, support for democracy is not necessarily linked to good economic performance, as discussed above, but to a broader notion of institutional satisfaction of citizens' political preferences. This is consistent with a rational notion of legitimacy (Rogowski 1974), it can modeled as a positive relation between institutional pluralism and democratic stability (Miller 1983), and it can be refined with the concepts of behavioral and institutional equilibrium (Shepsle 1986; Colomer 2001b, 2205a; Diermeier and Krehbiel 2003).

Citizens' political satisfaction with democratic outcomes has been estimated by means of measures of congruence between citizens' preferences and policy-makers' positions and through survey polls. From the first approach, it has been found that cabinets in parliamentary regimes with proportional representation include the median voter's preference with higher frequency than those using majoritarian electoral rules, in both parliamentary and presidential regimes; proportional representation and multiparties reduce, thus, the aggregate "distance" between citizens and rulers (Huber and Powell 1994; Powell 2000). Consistent with these findings, an analysis of survey polls in Western European countries show that political satisfaction with the way democracy works is more widely and evenly distributed in pluralistic regimes than in majoritarian ones (Anderson and Guillory 1997).

In general, constitutional democracies favoring power sharing and inclusiveness should be able to obtain higher endogenous support and have greater longevity than those favoring the concentration of power. Indeed, empirical accounts show that democratic regimes are the most peaceful ones, while semi-democratic or transitional regimes are most prone to conflict, even more than exclusionary dictatorships (basically because the latter increase the costs of rebellion) (Snyder 1996; Hegre, Ellingsen, Gates, and Gleditsch 2001). Among democracies, parliamentary regimes are more resilient to crises and more able to endure than presidential ones (Linz 1990b; Stepan and Skach 1993; Mainwaring 1993; Linz and Valenzuela 1994; Przeworski, Alvarez, Cheibub, and Limongi 2000; but see discussion by Power and Gasiorowski 1997; Cheibub and Limogi 2002). But by using a three-fold typology that, in consistency with the discussion above, also takes electoral systems into account, parliamentary majoritarian regimes appear to be associated with a higher frequency of ethnic and civil wars than presidential regimes, while parliamentary proportional regimes are the most peaceful ones (Reynal 2002, 2005). Proportional representation systems also experience fewer transnational terrorist incidents than majoritarian ones (Li 2005).

Actually, almost no new democracy established in the world during the broad "third wave" of democratization starting in 1974 has adopted the British-style constitutional model of parliamentary regime with a two-party system and majoritarian electoral rules. This may make comparisons based on the dual typology parliamentary/presidential less reductive for this period since the former type has become, in fact, largely identified with its variant of proportional representation elections. But the three-fold typology can illuminate the pitfalls of the British constitutional model in previous periods, when most new democracies having adopted this model eventually fell and were replaced with dictatorships.

The number of constitutional democracies rose enormously during the last quarter of the twentieth century, encompassing for the first time a majority of total world population since 1996. This has been the result of a very long-term evolution, which started in the so-called first and second "waves" of democratization (basically corresponding to the aftermaths of the First and Second World Wars), and accelerated in recent times with the end of the cold war. Thus, constitutionalism has been increasingly linked to democratization, as noted at the beginning of this survey.

Among democratic constitutions, there has been a trend in favor of formulas permitting relatively high levels of social inclusiveness, political pluralism, policy stability, and democracy endurance. This reflects the relatively greater capability of pluralistic formulas to generate endogenous support. Not only may citizens obtain relatively broad satisfaction of their expectations and demands from democratic institutional formulas requiring the formation of a broad majority to make collective decisions. Power-seeking politicians may also ultimately reject or abandon institutional formulas producing absolute losers and the total exclusion of relevant actors from power. Of the democratic countries with more than one million inhabitants, nowadays only less than one-sixth use parliamentary majority constitutional formulas, while about half are checks-and-balances regimes or its presidentialist and semi-presidential variants, and more than one-third are parliamentary-proportional representation regimes (updated from Colomer 2001*a*).

5 CONCLUSION

A number of questions addressed in the previous pages have become key questions in the political science literature on constitutions and may guide future research. There is still some room for discussion over the conceptual and empirical adequacy of the different political regime typologies. A clear distinction should be made between a priori institutional characteristics of the different models and the actual working of the samples of cases observed, which are always unavoidably limited and can thus induce biased inferences. The important role of party systems and electoral systems in shaping the relations between parliaments and governments is nowadays generally accepted, in contrast to narrower legalistic approaches that were typical of consti-tutional studies a few years ago. But other questions remain open to more accurate analysis in a comparative perspective. They include the differences between the US-style "checks-and-balances" model favoring power sharing, and the "presidentialist" model, diffused in Latin America and possibly other parts of the world, favoring the concentration of power and some exclusiveness. Also, it is not clear whether the so-called "semi-presidential" model should be conceived as an alternation between different phases corresponding to alternative constitutional models rather than as an intermediate type.

The scope of direct political consequences that have been attributed to different constitutional models also deserves to be revised. Fairly direct consequences may include different degrees of policy stability and instability, which seem to be asso-ciated, perhaps counter-intuitively, with complex and simple constitutional frame-works respectively. Regarding economic performance, it would probably be wise to consider that constitutional formulas may have only an indirect role that should be put in a broader framework of non-institutional variables. While the comparative method has been mostly applied to the hypothetical consequences of different consti-tutional formulas used in different countries, a temporal dimension may enhance the analysis. Rates of economic growth or other relevant variables could be compared not only for different countries with different regimes, but also for periods with different constitutional formulas in each country, including democracy and dictatorship.

Finally, theoretical and comparative analyses should help to improve constitutional choice, advice, and design. The present wide spread of democracy in the world raises new demands for constitutional formulas able to produce efficient decision-making and broad social satisfaction with the outcomes of government.

REFERENCES

ACEMOGLU, D., JOHNSON, S., and ROBINSON, J. 2005. Institutions as the fundamental cause of long-run growth. In *Handbook of Economic Growth*, ed. P. Aghion and S. Durlauf. Amsterdam: North-Holland.

ACKERMAN, B. 2000. The new separation of powers. *Harvard Law Review*, 113: 633–729.

AGUILAR RIVERA, J. A. 2000. *En pos de la quimera: Reflexiones sobre el experimento constitu-cional atlántico*. Mexico: Fondo de Cultura Económica.

ALESINA, A. and GLAESER, E. 2004. *Fighting Poverty in the U.S. and Europe*. Oxford: Oxford University Press.

ANDERSON, C. and GUILLOY. C. 1997. Political institutions and satisfaction with democracy. *American Political Science Review*, 91 (1): 66–81.

BAHRO, H., BAYERLEIN, B., and VESER, E. 1998. Duverger's concept: semi-presidential govern-ment revisited. *European Journal of Political Research*, 34: 201–24.

BAYLIS, T. 1989. *Governing by Committee*. Albany: State University of New York Press.

BIRCHFIELD, V. and CREPAZ, M. 1998. The impact of constitutional structures and collective and competitive veto points on income inequality in industrialized democracies. *European Journal of Political Research*, 34: 175–200.

BLAIS, A. and MASSICOTTE, L. 1997. Electoral formulas: a macroscopic perspective. *European Journal of Political Research*, 32: 107–29.

BLONDEL, J. and MÜLLER-ROMMEL, F. (eds.) 1988. *Cabinets in Western Europe*. New York: St Martin's Press.

—— —— 1993. *Governing Together*. London: Macmillan.

BOGAARDS, M. 2000. The uneasy relationship between empirical and normative types in consociational theory. *Journal of Theoretical Politics*, 12 (4): 395–423.

BOGDANOR, V. (ed.) 1988. *Constitutions in Democratic Politics*. Aldershot: Gower.

—— (ed.) 2003. *The British Constitution in the Twentieth Century*. Oxford: Oxford University Press.

—— and BUTLER, D. (eds.) *Democracy and Elections*. Cambridge: Cambridge University Press.

BOIX, C. 1999. Setting the rules of the game: the choice of electoral systems in advanced democracies. *American Political Science Review*, 93: 609–24.

BRADY, D. and VOLDEN, C. 1998. *Revolving Gridlock*. Boulder, Colo.: Westview Press.

BRENNAN, G. and BUCHANAN, J. 1985. *The Reason of Rules: Constitutional Political Economy*. Cambridge: Cambridge University Press.

BUCHANAN, J. 1990. The domain of constitutional economics. *Constitutional Political Economy*, 1 (1): 1–18.

—— and TULLOCK, G. 1962. *The Calculus of Consent: Logical Foundations of Constitutional Democracy*. Ann Arbor: University of Michigan Press.

BUDGE, I. and KEMAN, H. 1990. *Parties and Democracy*. Oxford: Oxford University Press.

BURNS, J. 1965. *Presidential Government*. Boston: Houghton Mifflin.

CAMERON, C. 2000. *Veto Bargaining*. Cambridge: Cambridge University Press.

CHEIBUB, J. A. and LIMOGI, F. 2002. Modes of government formation and the survival of presidential regimes. *Annual Review of Political Science*, 5: 151–79.

COLOMER, J. M. 1995. *Game Theory and the Transition to Democracy: The Spanish Model*. Cheltenham: Edward Elgar.

—— 2000. *Strategic Transitions*. Baltimore: Johns Hopkins University Press.

—— 2001a. *Political Institutions*. Oxford: Oxford University Press.

—— 2001b. The strategy of institutional change. *Journal of Theoretical Politics*, 13 (3): 235–48.

—— (ed.) 2004. *Handbook of Electoral System Choice*. New York: Palgrave-Macmillan.

—— 2005a. It's the parties that choose electoral systems (or Duverger's laws upside down). *Political Studies*, 53 (1): 1–21.

—— 2005b. Policy making in divided government. *Public Choice*, 125: 247–69.

—— 2006. On the origins of Electoral Systems and Political Parties. *Electoral Studies*, forthcoming. Available at: http://www.econ.upf.edu/cat/faculty/onefaculty.php?id=p261.

—— and NEGRETTO, G. 2005. Can presidentialism work like parliamentarism? *Government and Opposition*, 40 (1): 60–89.

CONGLETON, R. D. 2001. On the durability of king and council. *Constitutional Political Economy*, 12 (3): 193–215.

CONLEY, R. 2003. *The Presidency, Congress, and Divided Government*. College Station: Texas A&M University Press.

COX, G. 1997. *Making Votes Count*. Cambridge: Cambridge University Press.

—— and KERNELL, S. 1991. *The Politics of Divided Government*. Boulder, Colo.: Westview.

—— and McCUBBINS, M. 1993. *Legislative Leviathan*. Berkeley: University of California Press.

—— and MORGENSTERN, S. 2002. Latin America's Reactive Assemblies and Proactive Presidents. In *Legislative Politics in Latin America*, ed. S. Morgenstern and B. Nacif. Cambridge: Cambridge University Press.

CREPAZ, M. 1996. Consensus vs. majoritarian democracy: political institutions and their impact on macroeconomic performance and industrial disputes. *Comparative Political Studies*, 19 (1): 4–26.

CROSSMAN, R. H. 1963. Introduction. In Walter Bagehot, *The English Constitution*. Ithaca, NY: Cornell University Press.

DAHL, R. A. 2002. *How Democratic is the American Constitution?* New Haven, Conn.: Yale University Press.

DEHEZA, G. I. 1998. Gobiernos de coalición en el sistema presidencial: América del Sur. Pp. 151–69 in *El presidencialismo renovado*, ed. D. Nohlen and M. Fernández. Caracas: Nueva Sociedad.

DIERMEIER, D. and KREHBIEL, K. 2003. Institutionalism as a methodology. *Journal of Theoretical Politics*, 15 (2): 123–44.

DUHAMEL, O. and PARODI, J. L. (eds.) 1988. *La Constitution de la Vè République*. Paris: Fondation Nationale des Sciences Politiques.

DUVERGER, M. 1951. *Les parties politiques*. Paris: Seuil (English trans. *Political Parties*. New York: Wiley, 1954).

—— [1955] 1970. *Institutions politiques et droit constitutionnel*, 11th edn. Paris: Presses Universitaires de France.

—— 1978. *Échec au roi*. Paris: Albin Michel.

—— 1980. A New Political System Model: Semi-presidential Government. *European Journal of Political Research*, 8 (2): 168–83.

—— (ed.) 1986. *Les régimes semi-présidentiels*. Paris: Presses Universitaires de France.

—— 1996. *Le système politique français*, 21st edn. Paris: Presses Universitaires de France.

—— 1998. *Les constitutions de la France*, 14th edn. Paris: Presses Universitaires de France.

EATON, K. 2000. Parliamentarism versus presidentialism in the policy arena. *Comparative Politics*, 32: 355–76.

EDWARDS, G., BARRETT, A., and PEAKE, J. 1997. Legislative impact of divided government. *American Journal of Political Science*, 41 (2): 545–63.

ELGIE, R. (ed.) 1999. *Semi-presidentialism in Europe*. Oxford: Oxford University Press.

—— (ed.) 2001. *Divided Government in Comparative Perspective*. Oxford: Oxford University Press.

ELSTER, J. (ed.) 1996. *The Round Table Talks in Eastern Europe*. Chicago: University of Chicago Press.

—— and SLAGSTAD, R. (eds.) 1988. *Constitutionalism and Democracy*. Cambridge: Cambridge University Press.

—— OFFE, C., and PREUSS, U. (eds.) 1998. *Institutional Design in Post-Communist Societies*. Cambridge: Cambridge University Press.

EPSTEIN, D. and O'HALLORAN, S. 1999. *Delegating Powers*. Cambridge: Cambridge University Press.

FELSENTHAL, D. and MACHOVER, M. 1998. *The Measurement of Voting Power*. Cheltenham: Edward Elgar.

FINER, S. E. 1988. Notes towards a history of constitutions. Pp. 17–32 in *Constitutions in Democratic Politics*, ed. V. Bogdanor. Aldershot: Gower.

—— (ed.) 1975. *Adversary Politics and Electoral Reform*. London: Anthony Wigram.

FIORINA, M. 1992. *Divided Government*. New York: Macmillan.

FITZGIBBON, R. 1945. Constitutional development in Latin America: a synthesis. *American Political Science Review*, 39 (3): 511–22.

FLINDERS, M. 2002. Shifting the balance? Parliament, the executive and the British constitution. *Political Studies*, 50 (1): 23–42.

GANGHOF, S. forthcoming. Veto points and veto players: a skeptical view. In *Consequences of Democratic Institutions*, ed. H. Kitschelt.

GARCÍA CALDERÓN, F. 1914. *Les démocraties latines de l'Amérique*. Paris: Flammarion.

GEDDES, B. 1996. Initiation of new democratic institutions in Eastern Europe and Latin America. Pp. 15–42 in *Institutional Design in New Democracies*, ed. A. Lijphart and C. Waisman. Berkeley: University of California Press.

GLAESER, E., LA PORTA, R., and LOPEZ-DE-SILANES, F. 2004. Do Institutions Cause Growth? *Journal of Economic Growth*, 9 (3): 271–303.

GOODIN, R. E. (ed.) 1996. *The Theory of Institutional Design*. Cambridge: Cambridge University Press.

GROFMAN, B. (ed.) 1989. *The Federalist Papers and the New Institutionalism*. New York: Agathon.

—— and LIJPHART, A. (eds.) 1986. *Electoral Laws and their Political Consequences*. New York: Agathon.

—— and VAN ROOZENDAAL, P. 1997. Modeling cabinet durability and termination. *British Journal of Political Science*, 27: 419–51.

GRUMM, J. 1958. Theories of electoral systems. *Midwest Journal of Political Science*, 2 (4): 357–76.

HAMMOND, T. and BUTLER, C. 2003. Some complex answers to the simple question "Do institutions matter?" *Journal of Theoretical Politics*, 15 (2): 145–200.

—— and MILLER, G. 1987. The core of the constitution. *American Political Science Review*, 81: 1155–74.

HARDIN, R. 1989. Why a constitution? In *The Federalist Papers and the New Institutionalism*, ed. B. Grofman. New York: Agathon.

HEGRE, H., ELLINGSEN, T., GATES, S., and GLEDITSCH, N. 2001. Toward a democratic civil peace? *American Political Science Review*, 95 (1): 33–48.

HOWELL, W., ADLER, S., CAMERON, C., and RIEMANN, C. 2000. Divided government and the legislative productivity of Congress, 1945–94. *Legislative Studies Quarterly*, 25 (2): 285–312.

HUBER, J. and POWELL, G. B. 1994. Congruence between citizens and policymakers in two visions of liberal democracy. *World Politics*, 46 (3): 291–326.

JENNINGS, I. 1959. *Cabinet Government*. Cambridge: Cambridge University Press.

KATZ, R. 1997. *Democracy and Elections*. Oxford: Oxford University Press.

KING, G. and RAGSDALE, L. 1988. *The Elusive Executive*. Washington, DC: Congressional Quarterly.

KREHBIEL, K. 1996. Institutional and partisan sources of gridlock: a theory of divided and unified government. *Journal of Theoretical Politics*, 8: 7–40.

—— 1998. *Pivotal Politics*. Chicago: University of Chicago Press.

LAMBERT, J. 1963. *Amérique Latine: Structures sociales et institutions politiques*. Paris: Presses Universitaires de France.

LAPALOMBARA, J. and WEINER, M. (eds.) 1966. *Political Parties and Political Development*. Princeton, NJ: Princeton University Press.

LAVER, M. and SCHOFIELD, N. 1990. *Multiparty Government*. Oxford: Oxford University Press.

—— and SHEPSLE, K. 1991. Divided government: America is not exceptional. *Governance*, 4 (3): 250–69.

—— —— (eds.) 1994. *Cabinet Ministers and Parliamentary Government*. Cambridge: Cambridge University Press.

—— —— 1996. *Making and Breaking Governments*. Cambridge: Cambridge University Press.

LEECH, D. 2002. An empirical comparison of the performance of classical power indices. *Political Studies*, 50 (1): 1–22.

LI, Q. 2005. Does democracy promote or reduce transnational terrorrist incidents? *Journal of Conflict Resolution*, 49 (2): 278–97.

LIJPHART, A. 1984. *Democracies*. New Haven, Conn.: Yale University Press.

——(ed.) 1992. *Parliamentary versus Presidential Government*. Oxford: Oxford University Press.

——1994. *Electoral Systems and Party Systems*. Oxford: Oxford University Press.

——1999. *Patterns of Democracy*. New Haven, Conn.: Yale University Press.

——and GROFMAN, B. (eds.) 1988. *Choosing an Electoral System*. New York: Praeger.

LINZ, J. J. 1990a. The perils of presidentialism. *Journal of Democracy*, 1 (1): 51–69.

——1990b. The virtues of parliamentarism. *Journal of Democracy*, 1 (2): 84–91.

——and VALENZUELA, A. (eds.) 1994. *The Failure of Presidential Democracy*. Baltimore: Johns Hopkins University Press.

LIPSON, L. 1964. *The Democratic Civilization*. Oxford: Oxford University Press.

LOEWENSTEIN, K. 1949. The presidency outside the U.S. *Journal of Politics*, 11 (3): 447–96.

——1957. *Political Power and the Governmental Process*. Chicago: University of Chicago Press.

MAINWARING, S. 1993. Presidentialism, multipartism, and democracy: the difficult combination. *Comparative Political Studies*, 26: 198–228.

——and SHUGART, M. (eds.) 1997. *Presidentialism and Democracy in Latin America*. Cambridge: Cambridge University Press.

MAYHEW, D. 1991. *Divided We Govern*. New Haven, Conn.: Yale University Press.

MILLER, N. 1983. Pluralism and social choice. *American Political Science Review*, 21: 769–803.

MORGENSTERN, S. and NACIF, B. (eds.) 2002. *Legislative Politics in Latin America*. Cambridge: Cambridge University Press.

MOSER, P. 1996. The European Parliament as a conditional agenda setter. *American Political Science Review*, 90: 834–8.

MUELLER, D. 1996. *Constitutional Democracy*. Oxford: Oxford University Press.

MÜLLER, W. and STROM, K. 2000. *Coalition Governments in Western Europe*. Oxford: Oxford University Press.

NEUSTADT, R. 1990. *Presidential Powers and the Modern Presidents*. New York: Free Press.

NINO, C. 1992. *El presidencialismo puesto a prueba*. Madrid: Centro de Estudios Constitucionales.

NORTH, D. 1990. *Institutions, Institutional Change, and Economic Performance*. Cambridge: Cambridge University Press.

——and WEINGAST, B. 1989. Constitutions and commitment. *Journal of Economic History*, 49 (4): 803–32.

ORDESHOOK, P. 1992. Constitutional stability. *Constitutional Political Economy*, 3: 137–75.

PERSSON, T. and TABELLINI, G. 2003. *The Economic Effects of Constitutions*. Cambridge, Mass.: MIT Press.

PETERSON, P. and GREENE, J. 1993. Why executive–legislative conflict in the U.S. is dwindling. *British Journal of Political Science*, 24: 33–55.

POWELL, G. B. 1982. *Contemporary Democracies*. Cambridge, Mass.: Harvard University Press.

——2000. *Elections as Instruments of Democracy*. New Haven, Conn.: Yale University Press.

POWER, T. and GASIOROWSKI, M. 1997. Institutional design and democratic consolidation in the Third World. *Comparative Political Studies*, 30 (2): 123–55.

PRZEWORSKI, A. 1986. Some problems in the study of transitions to democracy. Pp. 47–63 in *Transitions from Authoritarian Rule*, ed. G. O'Donnell, P. Schmitter, and L. Whitehead. Baltimore: Johns Hopkins University Press.

——1991. *Democracy and the Market*. Cambridge: Cambridge University Press.

—— 2004. The last instance: are institutions a deeper cause of economic development? *Archives Européennes de Sociologie*, 45: 165–88.

—— ALVAREZ, M., CHEIBUB, J. A., and LIMONGI, F. 2000. *Democracy and Development*. Cambridge: Cambridge University Press.

RAE, D. 1967. *The Political Consequences of Electoral Laws*. New Haven, Conn.: Yale University Press.

REYNAL-QUEROL, M. 2002. Ethnicity, political systems and civil wars. *Journal of Conflict Resolution*, 46 (1): 29–54.

—— 2005. Does democracy preempt civil wars? *European Journal of Political Economy*, 21 (2): 445–65.

RIGGS, F. 1988. The survival of presidentialism in America. *International Political Science Review*, 9 (4): 247–78.

RIKER, W. H. 1992. The justification of bicameralism. *International Political Science Review*, 13 (1): 101–16.

ROGOWSKI, R. 1974. *Rational Legitimacy*. Princeton, NJ: Princeton University Press.

SÄRLVIK, B. 1982. Scandinavia. Pp. 123–48 in *Democracy and Elections*, ed. V. Bogdanor and D. Butler. Cambridge: Cambridge University Press.

SARTORI, G. 1994. *Comparative Constitutional Engineering*. London: Macmillan.

SCARROW, S. (ed.) 2002. *Perspectives on Political Parties*. New York: Palgrave-Macmillan.

SEAWARD, P. and SILK, P. 2003. The House of Commons. In *The British Constitution in the Twentieth Century*, ed. V. Bogdanor. Oxford: Oxford University Press.

SHEPSLE, K. 1986. Institutional equilibrium and equilibrium institutions. Pp. 51–81 in *Political Science: The Science of Politics*, ed. H. Weisberg. New York: Agathon.

SHUGART, M. S. and CAREY, J. 1992. *Presidents and Assemblies*. Cambridge: Cambridge University Press.

SMITH, A. 2004. *Election Timing*. Cambridge: Cambridge University Press.

SNYDER, J. 1996. *From Voting to Violence*. New York: Norton.

STEPAN, A. and SKACH, C. 1993. Constitutional Frameworks and Democratic Consolidation. *World Politics*, 44: 1–22.

STOKES, W. 1959. *Latin American Politics*. New York: Crowell.

STROM, K. 1990. *Minority Governments and Majority Rule*. Cambridge: Cambridge University Press.

—— and SWINDLE, S. 2002. Strategic parliamentary dissolution. *American Political Science Review*, 96: 579–91.

STRONG, C. F. 1963. *A History of Modern Political Constitutions*. New York: Capricorn.

TAAGEPERA, R. 2003. Arend Lijphart's dimensions of democracy. *Political Studies*, 51 (1): 1–19.

—— and SHUGART, M. S. 1989. *Seats and Votes*. New Haven, Conn.: Yale University Press.

TSEBELIS, G. 1995. Decision making in political systems. *British Journal of Political Science*, 25: 289–326.

—— 2002. *Veto Players*. Princeton, NJ: Princeton University Press.

VERNEY, D. 1959. *Analysis of Political Systems*. London: Routledge.

VOIGT, S. 1999. *Explaining Constitutional Change*. Cheltenham: Edward Elgar.

WEINGAST, B. 1995. The economic role of political institutions. *Journal of Law, Economics and Organization*, 7 (1): 1–31.

WHEARE, K. 1963. *Legislatures*. Oxford: Oxford University Press.

CHAPTER 10

....

POLITICAL PARTIES IN AND OUT OF LEGISLATURES

....

JOHN H. ALDRICH

RICHARD Fenno explained his career-long devotion to the study of the US Congress by saying that Congress is where democracy happens (pers. comm.). It is, metaphorically, the crossroads of democracy, where the public and politician, the lobbyist and petitioner meet. If legislatures are where democracy most visibly happens, political parties are the institutions that let us see *how* it happens. It may not be true that parties are literally necessary conditions for democracy to exist as Schattschneider (1942) famously wrote, but their ubiquity suggests that they are virtually, if not actually, a necessity for a democracy to be viable.

Political parties—in and out of legislatures—are the subjects of this chapter. As the chapter title suggests, we are to look at parties specifically here, but we cannot fully decouple parties from electoral systems (nor from other aspects of political institutions), and in particular from the virtually co-companion of electoral systems, party systems, nor can we decouple that from the study of parties as institutions. But we shall cover those extraordinarily rich literatures only to aid our focus on the specific questions considered here: how political parties mediate and integrate the goals and aspirations of the citizens with the often quite different goals and aspirations of politicians, and how these together shape policies adopted by government.

1 POLITICAL PARTIES AS INSTITUTIONS

The greatest scholar of twentieth-century American politics, V. O. Key Jr. (1964), led us to understand the American political party as organized around its three core activities. The party-in-the-electorate was the party of the campaign, the creation of the party's image and reputation in the public's mind, and the way the public used those sources as informational short-cuts and decision-making devices or aides. One of these "informational shortcuts" stands out as particularly important, creating a special role for political parties. Durable political parties develop long-term reputations that the personalities of particular politicians or variable agendas of policy concerns are generally unable to provide. While many things can go into these long-term reputations, the most important are the policy-based performances that create a partisan reputation and ideology. The party-in-government is the party that organizes the legislature and coordinates actions across the various institutions of national government, horizontally, and, for systems with vertical divisions of power, across the federal structures (Hofstadter 1969; Cox and McCubbins 1993; Haggard and McCubbins 2000). The party-as-organization is the party of its activists, resources, and campaign specialists; that is, those who negotiate between the public and government, sometimes rather invisibly, sometimes quite visibly, sometimes autonomously from the party-in-government, but often times as its external extension (Cotter, Gibson, Bibby, and Huckshorn 1984; Herrnnson 1988; Kitschelt 1989, 1999). This three-part structure applies to and certainly helps structure our thinking about political parties in all democracies, even if Key primarily writes about American politics.

Second, political parties differ from many other political institutions covered in this volume by virtue of being created, most often, external to the constitutional and, in some cases, developed largely external even to the legal order, per se. It is, for example, commonplace to note that the first parties, those in late eighteenth-century America (Hofstadter 1969; or early nineteenth-century America, depending upon one's point of view (e.g. Formisano 1981)), arose in spite of the wishes of their very founders and were unanticipated in writing the Constitution and early laws. Instead, political parties are organizations that are created by political actors themselves, whether emanating from the public (as, for instance in social movements that turn to electoral politics, such as social democratic parties: Lipset and Rokkan 1987; Przeworksi and Spraque 1986; and green parties, e.g. Kitschelt 1989) or, quite commonly, from the actions of current or hopeful political elites. The key point here is that, relative to most political institutions, political parties are shaped as institutions by political actors, often in the same timeframe and by the actions of the same figures who are shaping legislation or other political outcomes. They are, that is, unusually "endogenous" institutions, and we therefore must keep in mind that the party institutions (or at least organizations) can be changed with greater rapidity and ease than virtually any other political organization (Riker 1980; Aldrich 1995). To pick one simple example of the power of thinking about endogenous parties, consider the case of third parties in America. To be sure, there are the Duvergerian forces at work (1954; Cox 1997). But that explanation is only why two parties persist, not why the Democrat and Republican parties persist. The answer to the latter question is that they act in duopoly fashion so as to write rules that make entry and persistence by any contender to replace one or the other as a major party all but untenable (e.g. Rosenstone, Behr, and Lazarus 1996). Thus, the makeup of the party system is endogenously determined by the actors already in it. Indeed, the creation of the majority electoral system itself was the consequence of endogenous choice by partisan politicians in the USA (see Aldrich 1995).

2 PARTY SYSTEMS

Most of this chapter looks at the makeup of and/or actions taken in the name of the political party. It is, in that sense, a microscopic look inside the typical party. No democracy, however, has only one party. When there are two or more parties in competition over the same things—control over offices, over legislation, or over whatever—we should expect that each party will be shaped in part by its relationship to the other parties. How these parties form a system will not be assessed here, but we cannot look at the party in and out of the legislature without at least addressing two points.

The first is that a political system is not truly democratic unless its elections are genuinely competitive. Competition, in turn, does not exist without at least two parties with reasonable chances of electoral success. It is often thought that a fledgling democracy has not completed its transformation until there has been a free and competitive election that has peacefully replaced the incumbent party with one (or more) other parties. This happened, for example, in both Mexico and Taiwan in 2000, when erstwhile authoritarian one-party states transformed themselves into competitive democracies, and, in their respective elections, the erstwhile authoritarian party was voted out of office and peacefully surrendered power. Note that in Mexico, the long-reigning PRI had allowed the PAN to compete earlier, but did not allow free and open elections by virtue of restricting opposition-party access to the media before the 2000 election. This changed in 2000 and the PAN candidate, Vicente Fox, was elected president, marking the full democratic transition (see Aldrich, Magaloni, and Zechmeister 2005; Magaloni 2006).

Second, it could fairly be said that the central means of political representation is the political party. To be sure, individuals can be agents of representation as well, whether the chief executive or the individual legislator. But it is the political party that most systematically and durably represents the public in government. But representation is a relative thing, and as such it is a property of the party system, even more than it is a property of an individual or a single party. Thus, the question voters ask is not "how well does this party represent me, absolutely?" It is only relative both to the agenda that comes before the assembly and relative to the alternative or alternatives offered. Thus, it is rather more helpful to think of whether a member of party A voted (acted, spoke, etc.) more like any given constituent than did a member of party B, C, and so on.

The US Congress is often seen as exceptional. It is special by virtue of the nearly unique concatenation of having a two-party system with single-member districts and no formal party discipline. A two-party system exaggerates the limited range of feasible representation, compared to the more numerous choices faced in multiparty systems. Of all the myriad combinations of policy choices (let alone other matters of representation), the voters really have but two in front of them, and they grow accustomed to trying to decide which is the better choice—or, often, which is the "lesser of two evils." This is shared with most other Anglo-American democracies, among others (Lijphart 1984, 1999; Chhibber and Kollman 2004). Still, the range of choices is limited even in a multiparty system, and voters must decide which of this range is the best available, rather than search for the absolute best imaginable choice. The lack of formal party discipline means, on the one hand, that a party chosen to be representative may be sufficiently ineffective as to be able to enact its platform. On the other hand, the individual representative is often best understood, in the words of Gary Jacobson (2004), as responsive to the wishes of their constituents, but not responsible for outcomes. Limited choice and limited accountability tends to weaken if not undermine representation, perhaps uniquely in the USA.

Two-party parliaments with high party discipline can be more accountable. They are, however, just as limited to two effective options to present to the public. In some senses, the ability of the individual member of Congress to differentiate herself from her party provides the voters with a stronger sense of the range of feasible options in the USA than tends to be articulated in, say, England. But even there, there is growing attenuation of party discipline, and to that limited degree, two-party parliaments are at least slightly more like the USA—showing a marginal increase in the range of policy options coupled with a marginal decline in accountability.

Multiparty parliaments are often seen as much more representative bodies, especially so as the electoral rules are increasingly close approximations to purely proportional, and the resulting relatively high number of effective parties provides a closer approximation to representation of the various interests in society. That is, these systems are better at re-presenting the voices and preferences of the public inside the legislature. But this contrast between the two- and multiparty system should not be pushed too far, for two reasons.

First, while there may be many parties, their distribution of seats is often quite asymmetric (Laver and Budge 1992). Take Israel, for example (see, e.g., Aldrich, Blais, Indridiason, and Levine 2005; Blais, Aldrich, Indridiasan, and Levine forthcoming). As one of the more nearly proportional party systems (a single, nationwide district with low threshold for representation of 1.5 percent of the vote, soon to increase to 2 percent), it generally offers many choices to its voters, with a good fraction of them holding seats after the election. Thus, they are particularly strong in representing a relatively large fraction of the electoral views within the Knesset. Still, until Prime Minister Sharon broke with Likud while actually in office, Labor and Likud were invariably the two largest parties. One or both still is invariably in the government, meeting that their voice is heard where policy is really made (for theoretical views, see Laver and Shepsle 1996; Laver and Schofield 1990). And, of course, the strongest voice of all, the prime minister, always comes only from a major party, which in Israel's case was one of these two until very recently. Thus, "voice" and influence/power are quite differently distributed. Israel is far from unique in this regard. Governments are very far from random samples of members of the legislature, and prime ministers are not drawn as a simple random sample from the names of all legislators. This asymmetry in voice is in some sense parallel to the asymmetry in majoritarian electoral systems that results from the disproportionate translation of votes into seats in the two-party cases.

If there is asymmetry of one kind or another in both types of electoral systems, there is also a sort of accountability problem in multiparty systems, perhaps a stronger accountability problem than found in two-party systems. Take the case of Israel, again. In their election of 2003, everyone knew who would "win" the election (and where everyone understands that "winning the election" is quite different from merely winning a seat and thus a voice even in a multiparty parliament). It was clear from the outset that Likud would win and that their leader, Ariel Sharon, would become the prime minister. What was a mystery was what sort of government he would be able to form. Public discussion of alternative governments was commonplace in that campaign. Voters could—and some did—have preferences among the various coalitions that might form, and could—and some did—even condition their vote on those preferences over coalition governments rather than parties (Blais, Aldrich, Indridiason, and Levine forthcoming). But, the break in accountability is that there is little Sharon could do to bind himself to any promise about what sort of government would form and thus the range of policies he would make as prime minister. Therefore, voters could not really hold Likud or anyone else accountable on those grounds. In the event, the most popular coalition in the public view was rejected by Labor, and Sharon successfully formed a governing coalition consisting of an entirely different coalition than the ones considered in the campaign. There are no data about public preferences on this coalition, because no survey researcher imagined including it as a possible coalition, but it is reasonable to assume that it probably would have proved unpopular had it been considered in and by the public. The central lesson of this example is that accountability suffers dramatically. Post-election circumstances might, at least on occasion, force the selection of someone to be prime minister who deviates sharply from public opinion and perhaps even from the basis of voters' decisions. Even more commonly, negotiations over coalition governments might well force the outcome to be a government—and consequent set of policies—that differs sharply from the choices and preferences of the public.

In sum, both two- and multiparty systems generate problems over representation. This is true in terms of representation in two senses. It is true in interest articulation. That is, even the purest PR systems fail to create legislatures that mirror the preferences of the public, and this bias is systematic rather than random. It is also true in terms of accountability. Voters who wanted a Labor–Likud coalition in national unity could hardly hold Sharon and Likud, as winners of the election, accountable for Labor's refusal (announced during the campaign) to agree to enter any such coalition. And as it happens, they could not easily hold them accountable for the failure of his first coalition government, since it was replaced early in the electoral cycle. If there is going to be any voting on the basis of accountability (a.k.a. retrospective voting), it presumably will be based in the next election on the second, the lasting, and the more recent coalition.

In both two-party and multiparty coalition cases, then, the question is who or what can be held responsible? In the extreme US case, voters can basically hold their representatives accountable for failures to be responsive to their wishes, but not for failure to be responsible for the outcomes. In other two-party systems, voters can hold the majority party accountable, but typically only for failure to achieve a set of policies that the voters might have thought was not very close to their views in the first place. In the general multiparty case, one might hold a Sharon and Likud responsible (and if so, perhaps realistically, could turn to Labor as, in this case, the only responsible alternative), but who or what else? The party you voted for? The parties in the government?

In sum, the study of political parties necessarily entails two central aspects of the national party system, regardless of how focused one may be on the internal workings of a particular political party. First, the famous Schattschneiderian position on partisan necessity for democracy does not mean that it is this or that party that is necessary. Rather, it means that there must be a system of parties, and that every party forming or being in the government has to be at reasonable risk of electoral defeat in the next election. And for that to be true, there has to be a system of two or more parties. Second, it is equally true that representation requires not just a desirable option in the election for any particular citizen to choose. Rather, representation requires comparison between or among options, and thus also requires there to be a party system. Further, representation entails not only choices for the citizens as to how best to articulate their desires in government; it also requires the ability of the citizenry to hold the successful parties accountable for their actions in the government. The argument here is that both aspects of representation, first, require a party system, and, second, are not as different across the various types of party systems, two- or multiparty systems with greater or lesser degrees of party discipline, as often assumed. Indeed, in some ways, the accountability problem— how the public can try to ensure that their preferred choices really do represent them in government and in policy-making and not just on the campaign trail and in the manner needed to win votes—is greater in multiparty than in two-party systems.

3 THE PARTY OUTSIDE THE LEGISLATURE

In this and the following section, we consider the two major arenas of action for the political party. In this section, we look at the party as it is perceived by the public and as it thus helps the public negotiate the political process, make electorally relevant assessments, and take actions, particularly with respect to the turnout and vote decisions. In the next section, we examine the party as it operates in the legislative arena.

As was true above, so it is true here that a good place to start is with V. O. Key, Jr. In his magisterial account of *Southern Politics in State and Nation* (1949), he made the relevant comparison. Imagine the workings of a democracy with an established party system in comparison to the workings of a democracy without such a system. In this he was aided by the unique "natural experiment" of the embedding of a putative democracy in the American South, but one that had no party system throughout the sixty years of the "Jim Crow" system that Key was studying (that is the laws and practices that excluded blacks and poor whites from politics). The Jim Crow South was, however, also set within a functioning democracy with an established, durable two-party system at the national level. While this "natural experiment" happened to be found in the USA, he offers no reason, nor can I think of one fifty years later (Aldrich 2000), that makes his contrast less than fully general. The result of the experiment was clear, clean, and simple to convey. Politics was a perfectly reasonable real-world approximation of democracy as imagined in theory when found within an established and durable party system. Politics was extraordinarily undemocratic in the South, that is, it was undemocratic when not embedded in a competitive and durable party system, and Key was scathing in his description of the choices, such as they were, confronting voters.

The question of this section, then, is what role does the party play in furthering electoral democracy? Of the myriad aspects of parties-in-the-electorate, the core questions are "What does the party mean to potential and actual voters?" and "How does that meaning help shape their political decisions?" Here, I therefore address that core pair of questions.

The first question opens an apparent case of American exceptionalism, in that the theoretical understandings of party identification developed in the context of American survey research, are distinct and possibly theoretically unique to the USA. I suggest here that such a conclusion may be premature. The claim is that, if we can parse out the contemporaneous context of *voting* for, rather than assessing of, political parties, we may find beliefs akin to American party identification.

Campbell, Converse, Miller, and Stokes' classic accounts (1960, 1966) conceived party identification as an early-formed, durable, affectively-based loyalty to a political party. Their data showed that this conception was consistent with the beliefs and attitudes of a substantial majority in the American electorate, both in the 1950s and 1960s as they developed their theory, and again in recent years, as the (actually rather modest) attenuation of partisanship in the 1970s resurged to roughly the earlier levels (Bartels 2000). The key point was that this notion of partisan identification was relevant for understanding how ordinary citizens, with typically marginal interest in politics, were able to negotiate the complicated political world. This affect-centered view held that most people began with a bias in favor of their favored party (childhood socialization), they tend to hear things in a way biased toward their party (selective perception), and they are likely to further that bias even more by consuming information from sources that are themselves in favor of the citizen's preferred party (selective attention). Thus reinforced, partisan loyalty means that it is hard to change the minds of supporters of the opposing party, more so than it is to win over independents and apolitical citizens. In turn, it is harder to woo the uncommitted than to cement those already predisposed in one's favor.

An alternative view is due to Downs (1957), Key (1966), and Fiorina (1981). This view is of a more cognitively-based assessment. It assumes that voting and the partisanship that underlies those vote choices are based on assessments of outcomes, looking at past performance by partisan office holders to understand choices between partisan leaders for offices in the current election. The cognitive component to partisanship assesses how well or poorly politically induced outcomes—especially over economic and foreign affairs—have been under the management of one party compared to the other(s). Thus, unlike the affective account, partisanship is responsive to political events.

One might expect that these two contrasting views would be relatively easily distinguishable. Fiorina (1981) and Achen (1992) demonstrate, however, that both produce very similar empirical predictions. As a result, debate over these two understandings remains an active part of the contemporaneous research agenda within American politics (see especially Erikson, MacKuen, and Stimson 2002; Green, Palmquist, and Schickler 2002).

And, while the above two theories are often characterized as social-psychological vs. economic-rational views of politics, there is a third stream of research that looks at one large class of the uses to which partisanship (of whichever stripe) is put. While implicit in Campbell, Converse, Miller, and Stokes' (1960) account, it was Key (1966) again who first developed the notion of partisanship as a "standing decision." More recently, drawing from the "cognitive miser" approach in social psychology, scholars argued for the ability of extant partisanship to function as an aid in decision-making, reducing the costs of information processing and making of assessments in a complex world, and thus to serve variously as a schema, heuristic, or other decision-making short-cut. In the more economic and rational choice camps, scholars argued for, well, what is essentially the same thing. Popkin (1994) popularized this view for rationally negotiating the political world in general in what he called "gut-level rationality" (see Lupia and McCubbins 1998, for more formal development). Hinich and Munger (1994) put the idea of partisanship on ideological grounds, especially by looking at ideology as an informational short-cut, and developing scaling and related technologies to measure how partisan stances on ideology can operate much like the heuristics of the social-cognitive psychologist. In this, they were developing the ideas presented by Downs (1957) in which he argued that the political party was important by virtue of being consistent over time and therefore in aiding voters who are motivated to acquire information only incidentally. As a result, parties had incentives induced by voters to be consistent and moderately divergent on major dimensions of choice. Hinich and Munger (1994) developed the technology to make all of that estimable and to incorporate ideology into the account as the dimensions of divisions between parties and as the basis of choice by voters.

The important characteristic of all three of these conceptions is that partisanship is a property of the voters. That is, all view the political parties as they are perceived and employed by the voters, seeing parties as external objects to the electorate and as helping them negotiate the political process, especially the electoral system. Parties are objects about which beliefs and loyalties, preferences and assessments, are formed and used. They help lead the voters in making choices rather than being the objects of choice themselves. And, all of these are particularly American conceptions.

The authors of the Michigan model, to be sure, sought to develop the comparative extension of their ideas from the beginning. Perhaps the most extensive example is by Butler and Stokes (1974), in which they sought to use the ideas of *The American Voter* (Campbell, Converse, Miller, and Stokes 1960), including partisanship, to understand British politics. This was, of course, the obvious natural extension, given its similar continuity of an essentially two-party system with comparable continuity in stances of the major parties. Of course, the problem was that Britain differed from America in being a unitary parliamentary government with strict party loyalty, so that voters decided which party to vote for, rather than which nominee of a major party to support in their riding. To put it otherwise, voters typically said they voted for the party and not the person, the exact reverse of the claims of the American voter.

The great theorist of partisanship, Phil Converse, made a strong case for the general, comparative utility of partisanship, perhaps especially in his classic article, "Of Time and Partisan Stability" (1969). There, he demonstrated that the conception of partisanship was helpful for understanding major properties of party systems, and one might infer back that partisanship in the electorate is a function of the party system and not "just" of the properties of the parties themselves. He and Dupeux (1962) saw a surrogate identification to partisanship, what they called an ideologically based "tendence" in the then current French system with its diverse and highly variable cast of political parties contending for votes (see Converse and Pierce 1986 for a more modern view of French partisanship and voting). This "stand in" for partisanship suggested that voters thrived when they could find ways to hold matters sufficiently constant to provide structure to their conception of politics. Retrospective voting, for its part, is one of the most migratory of American-originated conceptions for understanding electoral politics. Fiorina's notion of party identification as a running tally has been applied metaphorically, although rarely in precise ways. The result, often, is a use of the term party identification or partisanship in comparative contexts, which lack precise and theoretical specification. Finally, it seems evident that if voters in stable two-party systems need heuristics to guide them through electoral decision-making, voters in less stable and/or in multiparty systems would be in far greater need of such informational short-cuts.

And yet, the concept of party identification did not travel particularly well as, say, retrospective voting did. The question for here is why? The answer I propose is not that there is no general value in these ideas. Rather, it is that the American electoral landscape has a unique configuration of attributes that highlights "parties-as-assessments," while in virtually all other systems, political parties are objects of actual *choices*, not just the basis for making assessments. Thus, the continuity of parties combined with a lack of rigorous party discipline in the legislature means that *choices* are and must be over candidates and not over parties. This is narrowly so, as in many systems votes are cast for political parties and not individual candidates, but it is also true more metaphorically. In Britain or other Anglo-American two-party systems, votes can (often *must*) be cast for individual candidates, but high party discipline dilutes the personal name-brand value any candidate may have, something of high value in the USA, and accentuates the value of the name brand of the party. As a result, vote decisions made in the name of a party naturally trump assessments of individual candidates, and that is reflected in responses to party-identification-like questions on an election survey. It does not follow from a concept being hard to measure that the concept is not relevant in those systems. It only follows that the concept is obscured—explaining, perhaps, why Converse could find the very abstract patterns so striking in the very same political systems where the micro-measures were difficult to observe.

The above is inferential. Historical evidence in America seems consistent with this set of claims. Voting in eighteenth century America was highly partisan, indeed as strongly so as in contemporary parliamentary systems. Historians of American elections naturally and correctly point to the form of ballot—non-secret voting, ballots made by the separate parties, etc.—and their interaction with institutions, notably partisan machines, to explain highly partisan elections (e.g. Hays 1980). While the move from open to secret balloting and other technical features of the voting process are important parts of the explanation of the decline of partisan elections in the USA, it is by now well understood that intervening between ballot reform and candidate-centered elections was the development of the individual office seeking motivation that these reforms and others made possible (Katz and Sala 1996; Price 1975). Thus, it was the increasingly candidate-centered campaigns of the late nineteenth and early twentieth centuries that generated the first level of decline in partisan elections, followed by the new technology of mid- to late-twentieth century politics that finalized the candidate-centered campaign as all but fully replacing the party-centered contests of the earlier era (Aldrich 1995). In short, the voters were responding to the possibilities of the electoral setting and especially to the nature of the campaigns they observed in generating first highly partisan and then highly candidate centered voting. Perhaps were party identification questions asked in nineteenth-century America, they would have been understood as asking vote intention.

In a comparative context, the above argument is also inferential. Several empirical observations might test the notion. For example, as party discipline is tending to erode in many nations' parliaments, those with single-member districts combined with durable parties dominating the system, or other systems (e.g. Japan) where candidate names have some value, the importance of party-as-assessment should be increasing, while as party discipline increases in the USA, party-as-choice should be more commonplace. Other convergences may be exploitable to examine whether party-as-assessment is, in fact, valuable for citizens in many nations as they seek to negotiate a complex political world. Indeed the Comparative Study of Electoral Systems (CSES) are making such explorations and convergences increasingly possible. Note, interestingly, that the question wording for "party identification" questions in the CSES (and, of course, that means as generated from comparative scholars from their own research traditions) are about how *close* one feels toward the various parties. Such a format leaves open the question of whether respondents mean they feel close to a party in the sense of identifying with it, or being close to what they *stand for*, and thus having a higher ideological proximity.

Partisanship, however defined and understood in the literature, focuses on the individual citizen. But the questions as to meaning have turned out to depend upon how they observe politicians and the parties they belong to. Thus, as Key taught us long ago, we can spend a good deal of time looking at, say, the party-in-the-electorate, but we cannot, in the final analysis, really understand it in isolation from the party-in-government or the party-as-organization. Our questions about what the party means to the voter have taken us to the party-in-government.

4 THE PARTY INSIDE THE LEGISLATURE

In this section we again ask two core questions, the two that emerged above. It should not be surprising that the core questions about the value of the political party for citizens and for politicians are closely related. That was Key's point. The questions are when and why do politicians support their party in the legislature—how united are parties—and when and why do parties align with, or oppose, one another? These questions have tended to be the focus of the literature on American parties and Congress, on the one hand, and on comparative parties and legislatures, on the other hand, and it is fair to say that the two party-and-legislature literatures are often close to dominated by their respective questions. Increasingly, new questions and new data are emerging especially within comparative politics, but we will only briefly touch on them. The core questions form the end points of a continuum, with the US two-party system candidate-centered elections at one end to a multiparty system with party-centered elections at the other.

Let us begin at the American exemplar end of the continuum. What forces shape the roll call vote? There has been considerable variation in the level of support the members gives their party. The post-Second World War era was particularly low, and the contemporary period (as in the nineteenth century) is considerably higher. Even at lowest ebb, however, party had by far the largest effect on the casting of the roll call vote (Weisberg 1978). He put the scholarly challenge to be to take party voting as the base line, with the theory tested by seeing how much it improved on party-line voting. This was at a point when the Democratic majority was divided, with nearly as many votes being cast with a "conservative coalition" (a majority of northern Democrats opposed by a majority of Southern Democrats and a majority of Republicans) as were being cast along party lines. To be sure, claiming a vote is a "party vote," when a simple majority of one opposes a simple majority of the other party, set a modest standard, even though the effect of party on the individual vote was stronger than that aggregate pattern suggested. Still, if congressional voting was primarily "party plus," it was nonetheless the case that party was much less consequential in shaping legislative choice than in virtually all other legislatures.

The above reflect, in effect, a parallelism between citizens' and legislators' voting choices. In both cases, party served as a strong base line, but there was more. In both cases, the role of party reached a low point at about 1970, climbing back to a more historically precedented high level more recently.

Congressional theory sought to explain the variation in levels of party voting and, at least indirectly, answering the question of why the US Congress lagged its European counterpart, even at its contemporary higher levels of party voting. The theoretical literature poses three explanations (for reviews see, e.g., Aldrich and Rohde 2000; Cox and McCubbins 2005). One is that the observed levels of party voting revealed very little to do with the role of party in Congress. Championed most vigorously by Krehbiel (1991, 1993), his argument is that the pattern of party voting in Congress mirroring that of party voting in the public is no coincidence. Legislators' votes reflect the wishes of the public as filtered through the goal of reelection. To be sure, legislators do not simply vote the views of their constituency, but the role of the party organization and leadership in Congress is, at best, marginal. And this makes a sharp contrast with their European brethren.

Cox and McCubbins take a different view (1993, 2005). In their view, party is the primary organizing device of Congress. Congress is thus organized to fulfill the collective interests of the majority party, and one important aspect of that is to ensure that the majority party structures Congress so that it does not put the reelection chances of the duly elected members of the majority at risk. The party thus shapes the agenda so that members can vote for what the majority party's members want without voting against their constituents' wishes often or on important matters. Thus, the majority party is pleased to have its members on committees that serve their constituents' concerns and can reward their constituents with distributive benefits. But while it provides room for its members to serve their constituents, it also provides room for its members to act on their collectively shared interests, all in the name of assisting their members' reelection chances. Circumstances dictate the kinds of power the majority will wield. When there were fewer collective interests to serve, the party was consequently less important to citizens, and it was better to be discrete in its use of power, typically by the use of negative agenda control. As polarization has led to more common interests and the party has thus become more important to the public, then it is increasingly satisfactory to exert more positive control over the agenda, to pass majority-preferred policies.

The third view is what Aldrich and Rohde call "conditional party government" (1997–98, 2000). If, they assert, there is variation in the influence of party in Congress, then we should investigate conditions under which it is at a higher and at a lower level. They argue that it is at a higher level when the electorate has selected members of the majority party with more homogenous preferences than at other times, and with preferences that are more clearly differentiated from the (typically also more homogenously distributed) preferences of the minority party. There is more for the majority party to win by acting together. And, when party preferences are more homogenous, there is less risk for the individual member of ceding authority to the party leadership than when their party is more heterogeneous. This view differs from that of, say, Krehbiel by virtue of its conditionality. That is, they agree that the electorate is the driving force. They differ in the role of the party in Congress. According to Krehbiel, it is epiphenomenal. In conditional party government, it magnifies the effect of the constituency at high levels, but not at low levels. It differs from the "party cartel" argument of Cox and McCubbins, if at all, by virtue of the latter's emphasis on the importance of negative agenda control (that is, blocking legislation from coming to a vote) when the majority party is heterogeneous, and emphasis on positive agenda control (that is seeking to pass legislation favored by the majority) otherwise. The conditional party government argument is simply that, instead of negative agenda control, a divided majority party exerts little control at all.

All three accounts argue that the driving force for explaining the observation of variation in levels of party voting in Congress are due to changes in the preferences of the electorate. Missing from all three accounts is an explanation of how and why those preferences change. Erikson, MacKuen, and Stimson (2002) argue that there is a thermostatic relationship or feedback between what the government does and how the electorate's partisan preferences and voting choices react. In particular, they find that the majority party tends to overshoot what the public wants, the Democratic Party acts too liberally, and a Republican Party too conservatively when in the majority. As a result, the public shifts back in the direction favored by the minority party, helping them work toward achieving majority status. Like a pendulum, parties in Congress sweep left and right farther than voters prefer and the public serves as counterweight, pulling the overly extreme policy choices back toward what the public as a whole desires. These propositions are new and still only lightly tested but seem both plausibly descriptive and enticing. The question then is why reelection minded officeholders would overshoot in this "macro polity." Two likely possibilities are that the politicians are personally more extreme in their policy beliefs than the public or that these politicians need resources from relative extreme partisan and interests groups for renomination and reelection. Of course, since many politicians were themselves once policy activists, both might be true. Further the public, in the aggregate, is generally moderate (indeed may literally be the definition of moderate) and so these activists may be only modestly "extreme." But, to answer the question of why party resources come from relative extremists is to ask a question about the party organization, a subject we will touch on in the conclusion. For now, note that findings that party activists are more extreme than the partisan identifiers in the electorate is not unique to the USA. It holds in many nations, and is one basis to begin to develop that general account that places the USA at one end and multiparty parliaments at the other end of the same continuum.

Whereas the traditional question asked of American legislative parties is whether they are ever united, the archetypical multiparty parliament finds the political party almost invariably united. Indeed, parties are often the unit of analysis, in virtual atom-as-billiard-ball fashion, rather than the American counterpart of party as atom-as-mostly-empty-space. In this tradition, the primary question is how parties form, maintain, or disband coalition governments, with the government and its ministers choosing policies for the parliament to ratify with strict party line voting. As Diermeier and Feddersen demonstrate (1998), the power of the no-confidence vote forces at least the parties in government into unity. It is only recently that the atom has been broken open, as it were, and non-lock-step unanimous behavior of party politicians considered.

The multiparty parliament inserts the extra step of government formation in the democratic crossroads of going from citizen preferences to policy (even when one party, majority or minority, see Strom, 1990, ends up forming the government). Technically, this is true in the US House, too, as its first action is to select from its own internal government by choosing a Speaker and a committee structure. All but invariably, that vote is also a strictly party-line vote, just as in, say, Britain. Perhaps the lack of a no-confidence vote in the Speaker undermines primarily party-line voting.

A substantial literature has sought to understand coalition formation in multiparty parliaments based on policy preferences. Thus, one beginning point would be with applications of Riker's (1962) minimal winning coalition hypothesis, with quite mixed empirical results. Axelrod (1970) added policy considerations per se by modifying minimal winning to "minimal winning connected coalition," and by "connected" he meant stand close or adjacent to each other on policy/ideology. The empirical findings were improved but still mixed. Then, Laver and Schofield (1990; see also Laver and Budge 1992) and Laver and Shepsle (1994, 1996) applied insights from social choice theory. In the first, Schofield developed a multi-dimensional analogue to the centrality of policy in the one-dimensional, median voter, and he and Laver applied this notion successfully in a number of empirical cases. Laver and Shepsle took a model that Shepsle (1979) had originally developed for the US Congress to describe how particular parties would form specific coalitions based on policy positions, even when there was no dominant majority outcome. Essentially, the coalition process strikes bargains in which party A is given control over policy x, party B over policy y, etc. It would be a different coalition with different policy outcome if party A controlled policy y and B policy x. They and others applied their model extensively to explain governments that formed (Laver and Shepsle 1994).

If the first question was which government formed, the second was how long would it last. Again, this literature moved toward alignment between theory and substance, but in this case, the literature unfolded in close dialogue between the two. A short version of this is that Browne, Frerdreis, and Gleiber (1986) developed a sophisticated statistical model of government duration that essentially showed how governments could handle exogenous shocks (or collapse in the face of them). King, Alt, Laver, and Burns (1990) developed this approach further. Lupia and Strom (1995) then began to develop a theoretical model that endogenized these events, followed by an increasingly sophisticated series of game theoretic models by Diermeier and associates (Diermeier and van Roozendaal 1998; Diermeier and Stevenson 1999) that moved toward testable implications to pit against and eventually extend the original statistical modeling of Browne, Frendreis, and Gleiber.

All of this increasingly precise, sophisticated, and empirically extensive research treats the parliamentary party as the unit of analysis. Two developments have moved towards treating the member of parliament as the unit of analysis. One thrust was due to the study of new democracies and therefore the study of the formation of parliaments and their practices, especially in Latin American (Morganstern and Nacif 2001) and former Soviet Union and Warsaw Pact nations. Smyth (2006), for example, examines early Russian Duma elections to study conditions under which candidates in their mixed system would choose to ally with a political party and when to run as an individual. Remington (2001) and Remington and Smith (2001) examine the formation of the Duma in the new era, looking at many of these same questions, while Andrews (2002) examines the policy formation process (or its failure!) in the early years of the post-Soviet Duma, finding precisely the kind of theoretical instability and policy chaos that underlies much of the theoretical work noted above. This study shows that the apparent stability of policy choices of most established legislatures, including the US Congress and the archetypal European multiparty parliament, needs to be derived—apparently from an established party system—rather than be assumed. Party instability occurs even in established parliaments, however. Heller and Mershon (2005) have examined the fluidity in MP partisan attachments after the reforms of the Italian parliamentary system. Here, unlike the Russian case, there seems to be reasonable policy stability within a great deal of partisan instability.

The second line of research inside the "black box" of the parliamentary party is to examine behavior in addition to roll call voting by which MPs can exert influence within and some degree of autonomy from their party. Martin and Vanberg (2004, 2005), for instance, examine means by which parliamentary committees and other devices can provide non-governing legislatures with influence over policy choices. As can be seen, "opening up" the black box of parliamentary parties is in its infancy, but these results imply that there is a good deal more legislative party politics of the kind ordinarily associated with American parties in their Congress to be found in multiparty parliaments. It may prove to be simply that the vote of confidence and electoral mechanisms that create party and government discipline have made it difficult to observe what Americans have thrust in front of them in much more public fashion.

5 CONCLUSION

There are a vast number of important themes that could direct a study of political parties in the legislature, out of the legislature, or both. This has focused on a small number of them. They were chosen because they have a common thread. That thread is one-half of the democratic process, looking at the role of political parties in shaping the beliefs and values of citizens and shaping their electoral decisions. Their choices, in turn, determined which parties and their candidates won legislative office. In some cases, a single party formed a majority, in others it required multiple parties to do so. In either case, the final step was how that majority governed, in terms of realizing (or deflecting) the wishes of the public who elected them.

This is but half the story, because the policies thus enacted shape the preferences and concerns of citizens going into the next election, repeating the process. This lacuna in coverage reflects the lacuna in analysis. However, ambitious politicians hoping to remain in office pick policies at least in part with an eye towards their best guess about public reaction, and so we, like they, anticipate voting for the next election, imperfectly embedding that anticipation into the policies chosen. As I hope this chapter made clear, there has been a great deal of scholarly progress on this Schattschneiderian role of the political party in shaping democratic politics in recent years, in the theoretical literature, in the substantive literature, and even more in their combination.

Examining how government actions might shape public preferences is one way to approach the problem of endogenous parties. A second is to consider seriously the relationship between the party system and the set of parties that make up that system. One theme has been the importance of a party system for the effective functioning of democracy. In general we define "party system" practically by the (effective) number of parties. The effective number tells us something about the case such as Israel, but perhaps better is to add to the effective number consideration of parties that serve as generators of prime ministerial candidates, or candidates for the major portfolios. In either case, the example above implies a sort of path dependency on the particular parties that make up the party system and on the height of barriers to entry to new parties and perhaps to achieving major party status.

Key's party-in-three-parts organized this chapter, but the reader may note that the third part, the party-as-organization, appeared on stage only briefly. Here it is appropriate to observe that one of the major components of the party organization, the activists and the resources in time, money, and effort that they control, is a critical component for synchronizing the party in the public's mind and the party in the legislature (see especially Aldrich 1995; Kitschelt 1989, 1999). There is an important regularity about party activists that cuts across the various types of party systems. In majoritarian and proportional, in two- and multiparty systems, in the US and European archetypical cases of this chapter, activists have turned out to be more extreme than the electoral members of their parties. Recently, Kedar (2005) has developed and tested a theory of this process, arguing that voters support parties with activists more extreme than they are, so that actual policy will be able to be moved in the direction of the activists, but, through the inertia created by the rest of the political system, almost assuredly less far than the activists would desire. The result is a change in policy much like the more-moderate voter actually desires. Aldrich and McGinnis (1989) offer a different but complementary story based on the US parties. Party activists can induce candidates and officeholders to move policy in their direction, but not as far in their direction (in this instance balancing their need for extremity to gather resources from activists to win votes and their need for moderation to retain support in the electorate). In either case, relatively more extreme activists are motivated to connect public and politician, pushing both to affect policy changes more to the activists' liking. Whatever the details, the activists are central party organization members for aggregating and articulating public desires and tying politicians to policy outcome. And, if Erikson, MacKuen, and Stimson (2002) have the dynamics right, they are the source of the swing of the policy pendulum.

Let me close with a fourth area which appears ripe for research breakthroughs. This chapter pointed towards a fully comparative political parties project. Instead of distinguishing between American political parties and the political parties of other (advanced, industrial, and postindustrial) democracies, we are beginning to see more clearly that political parties are common to all democracies, and they are so because democracy is, indeed, unthinkable save through the agency of the party. And it is through the theoretical unification of the party in and out of the legislature (perhaps accomplished through the party organization) that we can understand just how parties are necessary components of democracies. In this, American parties are not different, theoretically, from their European counterparts. We can explain apparent American exceptionalism as simply based on an unusual combination of empirical conditions, explainable through a common set of factors, and thus there is closer to a singular set of explanations of the party in and out of the legislature across at least the established democratic world.

References

ACHEN, C. H. 1992. Breaking the iron triangle: social psychology, demographic variables and linear regression in voting research. *Political Behavior*, 14 (3): 195–211.

ALDRICH, J. H. 1995. *Why Parties? The Origin and Transformation of Political Parties in the United States*. Chicago: University of Chicago Press.

—— 2000. Southern parties in state and nation. *Journal of Politics*, 62: 643–70.

—— and McGINNIS, M. D. 1989. A model of party constraints on optimal candidate positions. *Mathematical and Computer Modeling*, 12 (4–5): 437–50.

—— and ROHDE, D. W. 1997–98. Theories of party in the legislature and the transition to Republican rule in the House. *Political Science Quarterly*, 112 (4): 541–67.

—— —— 2000. The consequences of party organization in the House: the role of the majority and minority parties in conditional party government. Pp. 31–72 in *Polarized Politics: Congress and the President in a Partisan Era*, ed. J. R. Bond and R. Fleisher. Washington, DC: CQ Press.

——BLAIS, A., INDRIDIASON, I. H., and LEVINE, R. 2005. Coalition considerations and the vote. Pp. 143–66 in *The Elections in Israel—2003*, ed. A. Arian and M. Shamir. New Brunswick, NJ: Transaction.

——MAGALONI, B., and ZECHMEISTER, E. 2005. When Hegemonic Parties Lose: The 2000 elections in Mexico and Taiwan. Unpublished.

ANDREWS, J. T. 2002. *When Majorities Fail: The Russian Parliament, 1990–1993*. Cambridge: Cambridge University Press.

AUSTIN-SMITH, D. and BANKS, J. 1988. Elections, coalitions, and legislative outcomes. *American Political Science Review*, 82 (2): 405–22.

AXELROD, R. M. 1970. *Conflict of Interest: A Theory of Divergent Goals with Application to Politics*. Chicago: Markham.

BARTELS, L. M. 2000. Partisanship and voting behavior, 1952–1996. *American Journal of Political Science*, 44: 35–50.

BLAIS, A., ALDRICH, J., INDRIDIASON, I., and LEVINE, R. forthcoming. Voting for a coalition. *Party Politics*.

BROWNE, E., FRENDREIS, J., and GLEIBER, D. 1986. The process of cabinet dissolution: an exponential model of duration and stability in western democracies. *American Journal of Political Science*, 30: 628–50.

BUTLER, D. and STOKES, D. 1974 [1969]. *Political Change in Britain: The Evolution of Electoral Choice*, 2nd edn. New York: St. Martins Press.

CAMPBELL, A., CONVERSE, P. E., MILLER, W. E., and STOKES, D. E. 1960. *The American Voter*. New York: John Wiley.

————————1966. *Elections and the Political Order*. New York: John Wiley.

CHHIBBER, P. K. and KOLLMAN, K. 2004. *The Formation of National Party Systems: Federalism and Party Competition in Canada, Great Britain, India, and the United States*. Princeton, NJ: Princeton University Press.

CONVERSE, P. E. 1969. Of time and partisan stability. *Comparative Political Studies*, 2: 139–71.

——and DUPUEX, G. 1962. Politicization of the electorate in France and the United States. *Public Opinion Quarterly*, 26 (1): 1–23.

——and PIERCE, R. 1986. *Political Representation in France*. Cambridge, Mass.: Belknap Press of Harvard University Press.

COTTER, C. P., GIBSON, J. L., BIBBY, J. F., and HUCKSHORN, R. J. 1984. *Party Organizations in American Politics*. New York: Praeger.

COX, G. W. 1997. *Making Votes Count*. Cambridge: Cambridge University Press.

——and MCCUBBINS, M. D. 1993. *Legislative Leviathan: Party Government in the House*. Berkeley: University of California Press.

————2005. *Setting the Agenda: Responsible Party Government in the US House of Representatives*. Cambridge: Cambridge University Press.

DIERMEIER, D. and FEDDERSEN, T. J. 1998. Cohesion in legislatures and the vote of confidence procedure. *American Political Science Review*, 92 (3): 611–21.

——and STEVENSON, R. 1999. Cabinet terminations and critical events. *American Political Science Review*, 94: 627–40.

——and ROOZENDAAL, P. VAN 1998. The duration of cabinet formation processes in western multi-party democracies. *British Journal of Political Science*, 28 (4): 609–26.

DOWNS, A. 1957. *An Economic Theory of Democracy*. New York: Harper and Row.

DUVERGER, M. 1954. *Political Parties: Their Organization and Activities in the Modern State*. London: Methuen.

ERIKSON, R. S., MACKUEN, M. B., and STIMSON, J. A. 2002. *The Macro Polity*. Cambridge: Cambridge University Press.

FIORINA, M. P. 1976. The voting decision: instumental and expressive aspects. *Journal of Politics*, 38 (2): 390–415.

——1980. The decline in collective responsibility in American politics. *Daedalus*, 109 (3): 25–45.

——1981. *Retrospective Voting in American National Elections*. New Haven, Conn.: Yale University Press.

——1990. An era of divided government. Pp. 195–232 in *Developments in American Politics*, ed. B. Cain and G. Peele. London: Macmillan.

——1991. Divided governments in the states. Harvard University Center for American Political Studies Occasional Papers, January.

——1992. *Divided Government*. New York: Macmillan.

FORMISANO, R. P. 1981. Federalists and Republicans: parties, yes—system, no. Pp. 33–76 in *The Evolution of American Electoral Systems*, ed. P. Kleppner, W. D. Burnham, R. P. Formisano, S. P. Hays, R. Jensen, and W. G. Shade. Westport, Conn.: Greenwood Press.

GREEN, D., PALMQUIST, B., and SCHICKLER, E. 2002. *Partisan Hearts and Minds: Political Parties and the Social Identities of Voters*. New Haven, Conn.: Yale University Press.

HAGGARD, S. and McCUBBINS, M. D. (eds.) 2000. *Presidents, Parliaments, and Policy*. Cambridge: Cambridge University Press.

HAYS, S. 1980. *American Political History as Social Analysis*. Knoxville: University of Tennessee Press.

HELLER, W. B. and MERSHON, C. 2005. Party switching in the Italian Chamber of Deputies, 1996–2001. *Journal of Politics*, 67: 536–59.

HERRNSON, P. S. 1988. *Party Campaigning in the 1980s*. Cambridge, Mass.: Harvard University Press.

HINICH, M. J. and MUNGER, M. C. 1994. *Ideology and the Theory of Political Choice*. Ann Arbor: University of Michigan Press.

HOFSTADTER, R. 1969. *The Idea of a Party System: The Rise of Legitimate Opposition in the United States, 1780–1840*. Berkeley: University of California Press.

JACOBSON, G. C. 2004. *The Politics of Congressional Elections*, 6th edn. New York: Pearson Longman.

KATZ, J. N. and SALA, B. R. 1996. Careerism, committee assignments, and the electoral connection. *American Political Science Review*, 90 (1): 21–33.

KEDAR, O. 2005. When moderate voters prefer extreme parties: policy balancing in parliamentary elections. *American Political Science Review*, 99 (2): 185–99.

KEY, JR., V. O. 1949. *Southern Politics in States and Nation*. New York: Knopf.

——1964. *Politics, Parties, and Pressure Groups*, 5th edn. New York: Crowell.

——1966. *The Responsible Electorate: Rationality in Presidental Voting, 1936–1960*. Cambridge, Mass.: Harvard University Press.

KING, G., ALT, J., LAVER, M., and BURNS, N. 1990. A unified model of cabinet dissolution in parliamentary democracies. *American Journal of Political Science*, 34: 846–71.

KITSCHELT, H. 1989. *The Logics of Party Formation: Ecological Politics in Belgium and West Germany*. Ithaca, NY: Cornell University Press.

——1999. *Post-Communist Party Systems*. Cambridge: Cambridge University Press.

KREHBIEL, K. 1991. *Information and Legislative Organization*. Ann Arbor: University of Michigan Press.

——1993. Where's the party? *British Journal of Political Science*, 23: 235–66.

LAVER, M. J., and BUDGE, I. (eds.) 1992. *Party Policy and Government Coalitions*. New York: St Martin's Press.

——and SCHOFIELD, N. 1990. *Multiparty Government: The Politics of Coalition in Europe.* Oxford: Oxford University Press.

——and SHEPSLE, K. A. (eds.) 1994. *Cabinet Ministers and Parliamentary Government.* Cambridge: Cambridge University Press.

————1996. *Making and Breaking Governments: Cabinets and Legislatures in Parliamentary Democracies.* Cambridge: Cambridge University Press.

LIJPHART, A. 1984. *Democracies: Patterns of Majoritarian and Consensus Government in Twenty-one Countries.* New Haven, Conn.: Yale University Press.

——1999. *Patterns of Democracy: Government Forms and Performance in Thirty-six Countries.* New Haven, Conn.: Yale University Press.

LIPSET, S. M. and ROKKAN, S. (eds.) 1987. *Party Systems and Voter Alignments: Cross-National Perspectives.* New York: Free Press.

LUPIA, A. M. and McCUBBINS, M. D. 1998. *The Democratic Dilemma: Can Citizens Learn What They Need to Know?* Cambridge: Cambridge University Press.

——and STROM, K. 1995. Coalition termination and the strategic timing of parliamentary elections. *American Political Science Review*, 89: 648–65.

McCORMICK, R. P. 1982. *The Presidental Game: Origins of American Politics.* New York: Oxford University Press.

MAGALONI, B. 2006. *Voting for Autocracy: Hegemonic Party Survival and its Demise in Mexico.* Cambridge: Cambridge University Press.

MARTIN, L. and VANBERG, G. 2004. Policing the bargain: coalition government and parliamentary scrutiny. *American Journal of Political Science*, 48: 13–27.

————2005. Coalition policymaking and legislative review. *American Political Science Review*, 99: 93–106.

MORGENSTERN, S. and NACIF, B. (eds.) 2001. *Legislatures in Latin America.* Cambridge: Cambridge University Press.

PAGE, B. I. 1978. *Choices and Echoes in Presidential Elections: Rational Man and Electoral Democracy.* Chicago: University of Chicago Press.

POPKIN, S. L. 1994. *The Reasoning Voter: Communication and Persuasion in Presidential Campaigns*, 2nd edn. Chicago: University of Chicago Press.

PRICE, H. D. 1975. Congress and the evolution of legilsative "professionalism." Pp. 2–23 in *Congress in Change*, ed. N. J. Ornstein. New York: Praeger.

PRZEWORSKI, A. and SPRAGUE, J. 1986. *Paper Stones: A History of Electoral Socialism.* Chicago: University of Chicago Press.

REMINGTON, T. F. 2001. *The Russian Parliament: Institutional Evolution in a Transitional Regime, 1989–1999.* New Haven, Conn.: Yale University Press.

——and SMITH, S. S. 2001. *The Politics of Institutional Choice: Formation of the Russian State Duma.* Princeton, NJ: Princeton University Press.

RIKER, W. H. 1962. *The Theory of Political Coalitions.* New Haven, Conn.: Yale University Press.

——1980. Implications from the disequilibrium of majority rule for the study of institutions. *American Political Science Review*, 74 (2): 432–46.

——1982a. *Liberalism Against Populism: A Confrontation Between the Theory of Democracy and the Theory of Social Choice.* San Francisco: W. H. Freeman.

——1982b. The two-party system and Duverger's Law: An essay on the history of political science. *American Political Science Review*, 76 (4): 753–66.

ROSENSTONE, S. J., BEHR, R. L., and LAZARUS, E. H. 1996. *Third Parties in America*, 2nd edn. Princeton, NJ: Princeton University Press.

SCHATTSCHNEIDER, E. E. 1942. *Party Government.* New York: Rinehart.

SHEPSLE, K. A. 1979. Institutional arrangements and equilibrium in multidimensional voting models. *American Journal of Political Science*, 23 (1): 27–59.

SMYTH, R. 2006. *Candidate Strategies and Electoral Competition in the Russian Federation: Democracy without Foundation.* Cambridge: Cambridge University Press.

STROM, K. 1990. *Minority Government and Majority Rule.* Cambridge: Cambridge University Press.

WARWICK, P. 1992. Rising hazards: an underlying dynamic of parliamentary government. *American Journal of Political Science*, 36: 857–76.

WEISBERG, H. F. 1978. Evaluating theories of congressional roll-call voting. *American Journal of Political Science*, 22 (3): 554–77.

CHAPTER 11

···

THE REGULATORY
STATE?

···

JOHN BRAITHWAITE

1 REGULATION AND GOVERNANCE

···

States can be thought of as providing, distributing, and regulating. They bake cakes, slice them, and proffer pieces as inducements to steer events. Regulation is conceived as that large subset of governance that is about steering the flow of events, as opposed to providing and distributing. Of course when regulators regulate, they often steer the providing and distributing that regulated actors supply. Governance is a wider set of control activities than government. Students of the state noticed that government has shifted from "government of a unitary state to governance in and by networks" (Bevir and Rhodes 2003, 1; Rhodes 1997). But because the informal authority of networks in civil society not only supplements but also supplants the formal authority of government, Bevir, Rhodes, and others in the networked governance tradition (notably Castells 1996) see it as important to study networked governance for its own sake, rather than as simply a supplement to government. This chapter proceeds from the assumption that there has been a rise of networked governance and builds on Jacint Jordana and David Levi-Faur's (2003, 2004) systematic evidence that, since 1980, states have become rather more preoccupied with the regulation part of governance and less with providing. Yet non-state regulation has grown even more rapidly, so it

* My thanks to Rod Rhodes, Peter Grabosky, Jennifer Wood, Susanne Karstedt, Clifford Shearing, Christine Parker, and Peter Drahos for helpful comments on drafts of this chapter.

is not best to conceive of the era in which we live as one of the regulatory state, but of regulatory capitalism (Levi-Faur 2005).

The chapter sketches historical forces that have produced regulatory capitalism as a police economy that evolved from various feudal economies, the supplanting of police with an unregulable nineteenth-century liberal economy, then the state provider economy (rather than the "welfare state") that gives way to regulatory capitalism. In this era, more of the governance that shapes the daily lives of most citizens is corporate governance than state governance. The corporatization of the world is both a product of regulation and the key driver of regulatory growth, indeed of state growth more generally. The major conclusion of the chapter is that the reciprocal relationship between corporatization and regulation creates a world in which there is more governance of all kinds. 1984 did arrive. The interesting normative question then becomes whether this growth in hybrid governance contracts freedom, or expands positive liberty through an architecture of separated powers that check and balance state and corporate dominations. While that is the quandary of our time the chapter sets up, it does not answer it.

2 THE RISE OF REGULATORY STUDIES

In the 1970s and 1980s the Chicago School could lay claim to an extraordinary swag of Nobel Prize winners such as Milton Freidman and George Stigler (1988), and preeminent law and economics scholars such as Richard Posner, who made regulation a central topic in economics. The Keynesian orthodoxies of statist remedies to market failure were supplanted by what became a Chicago orthodoxy that state failure meant the cure was worse than the disease of market failure. While from within a Chicago framework this is an odd thing to say, it is nevertheless accurate that the Chicago School studied markets as the preeminent regulatory tool. Private property rights and the price mechanism would solve problems like excessive exploitation of resources. If something like pollution was a market externality, then the most efficient way to regulate it would be to create a market in tradable pollution rights. While the Chicago intellectual dominance of these decades crowded out regulation as a topic in political science, notions of regulatory capture by the regulated industry (Bernstein 1955), carved out by political scientists decades earlier, became central to the Chicago discourse.

The Chicago School captured the political imaginations of the Carter and Reagan administrations in the USA, the Thatcher government in the UK, and beyond from the late 1970s. But over time policy-makers became cynical that if whales were endangered, either the rising price of whale meat, or property rights in whales, or creating markets in whale killing rights, were smart or dependable solutions to the problem. By the 1990s, the Chicago School ascendancy had ended and the domination of regulatory studies by economics with it. Many political scientists, including Eugene Bardach and Robert Kagan (1982), John Scholz (1991), Margaret Levi (1988), James Q. Wilson (1980), Joseph Rees (1994), Michael Moran (2003), Christopher Hood (Hood et al. 1999), Giandomenico Majone (1994), Jacint Jordana and David Levi-Faur (2004), and Peter Grabosky (1994) became leading figures in an interdisciplinary field more or less equally populated also by sociologists, criminologists, economists, accountants, and lawyers with also some interest from other disciplines, with interdisciplinary chairs in regulatory studies becoming popular recently, especially in the UK and Australia.

Regulatory studies grew with the realization that neoliberal politics had not produced privatization and deregulation, but privatization and regulatory growth. The most dominant style of research became the study of the politics of particular state regulators and self-regulators, such as those of the nuclear industry (Rees 1994), in ways that revealed the connections among private and public governance networks. In Rees' (1994) case, it is revealed how the players in this governance network were "hostages of each other;" they feared another Three Mile Island, another Chernobyl, might bring them all down.

3 THE RISE OF THE REGULATORY STATE?

In the first two years of the Reagan presidency there was genuine deregulatory zealotry. But by the end of the first Reagan term, business regulatory agencies had resumed the long-run growth in the size of their budgets, the numbers of their staff, the toughness of their enforcement, and the numbers of pages of regulatory laws foisted upon business (Ayres and Braithwaite 1992, 7–12). Later in the Reagan administration financial deregulation came unstuck with a Savings and Loans debacle that cost American taxpayers over $200 billion (Rosoff, Pontell, and Tillman 2002, 255). In this domain, the Reagan and Thatcher governments actually reversed direction globally as well as nationally. The Federal Reserve (US) and Bank of England led the world down to financial deregulation in the early 1980s, then led global prudential standards back up through the G-10 after the banking crises of the mid-1980s for fear of the knock-on effects foreign bank collapses could have on American business (Braithwaite and Drahos 2000, 4). The current Republican administration has presided over a 42 percent increase in regulatory staffing levels since 2001, to 242,473 full-time equivalents by 2005. Admittedly 56,000 of the increase were airport screening agents in the Transportation Security Agency (Dudley and Warren 2005, 1).

In Britain, privatization proliferated in a way that created a need for new regulatory agencies. When British telecommunications was deregulated in 1984, Oftel was created to regulate it (now Ofcom); Ofgas was born for the regulation of a privatized gas industry in 1986, OFFER for electricity in 1989 (now combined in Ofgem), OfWat for water in 1990, and the Office of the Rail Regulator (mercifully not Ofrails!) appeared in 1993 (Baldwin, Scott, and Hood 1998, 14–21). Privatization combined with new regulatory institutions is the classic instantiation of Osborne and Gaebler's (1992) prescription for reinventing government to steer rather than row. Jordana and Levi-Faur (2003, 2004) show that the tendency for state regulation to grow with privatization is a global one. As privatization spreads, they find new regulatory agencies spread even faster, and they show how the diffusion of regulatory agencies moved from the West to take off in Latin America in the 1990s.

I used to describe the key transition as one from the liberal nightwatchman state, to the Keynesian welfare state, to the new regulatory state (after 1980) and a regulatory society (see also Majone 1994; Loughlin and Scott 1997; Parker 1999; Jayasuriya 2001; Midwinter and McGarvey 2001; Muller 2002; Moran 2003). The nub of the regulatory state idea is that power is deployed "through a regulatory framework, rather than through the monopolization of violence or the provision of welfare" (Walby 1999, 123). Now I prefer Levi-Faur's (2005) adaptation of the regulatory state idea into regulatory capitalism. According to Levi-Faur, we have seen since 1980 not only what Vogel (1996) found empirically to be *Freer Markets, More Rules*, but also "more capitalism, more regulation". Privatization is part of Levi-Faur's characterization of regulatory capitalism. But it sits alongside a proliferation of new technologies of regulation and meta-regulation (Parker 2002), or control of control (Power 1997), increased delegation to business and professional self-regulation and to civil society, to intra- and international networks of regulatory experts, and increased regulation of the state by the state, much of it regulation through and for competition (Hood et al. 1999). The regulatory capitalism framework theorizes the New Public Management post-1980 as a conscious separation of provider and regulator functions within the state, where sometimes the provider functions were privatized and regulated, and sometimes they were not privatized but nevertheless subjugated to the "audit society" and government by (audited) contract (Power 1997).

The Keynesian welfare state now seems a poor description of the institutional package that dominated until 1980. One reason is that Keynes is alive and well in his influence on policy processes. Second, it is not really true that states have hollowed out; they have continued to grow as regulators as they have contracted as providers. Nor has the welfare state atrophied. Welfare state spending by rich nations has not declined (Castles 2004). Finally, the state provider economy was not just about providing welfare; it was about states providing transport, industrial infrastructure, utilities, and much more beyond welfare, a deal of which was privatized in the transition to regulatory capitalism.

Even the idea of the nightwatchman state of the nineteenth century needs qualification. The prehistory of the institutional change summarized in this paper could be described as a transition from various feudalisms to a police economy. The sequence I will describe is a transition then from that police economy to the unregulable economy tending to laissez-faire after the collapse of police, to the "state provider economy" (rather than the "welfare state") to "regulatory capitalism" (rather than the "regulatory state").

4 THE POLICE ECONOMY

What does Tomlins (1993, 37–8) mean when he says that writing a history of the American state without a reference to the genealogy of "police" is "akin to writing a history of the American economy without discussing capitalism?" In white settler societies it is easier to see with clarity the police economy because it did not have to struggle to supplant the old economy of monopolies granted by the king to guilds, market towns, and trading companies like the Hudson Bay Company (even as the New World was partly constituted by the latter). That economy of monopoly domination granted by the king was not only an earlier development in the transition from feudalism to capitalism that was subsequently (de)regulated by police, it was also a development largely restricted to cities which were significant nodes of manufactures and long-distance trade.[1] Tiny agricultural communities that did not have a guild or a chartered corporation had a constable. The early modern idea of police differs from the contemporary notion of an organization devoted to fighting crime (Garland 2001). Police from the sixteenth to the nineteenth century in continental Europe meant institutions for the creation of an orderly environment, especially for trade and commerce. The historical origins of the term through German back to French is derived from the Greek notion of "policy" or "politics" in Aristotle (Smith 1978, 486; Neocleous 1998). It referred to all the institutions and processes of ordering that gave rise to prosperity, progress, and happiness, most notably the constitution of markets. Actually it referred to that subset of governance herein conceived as regulation.

Police certainly included the regulation of theft and violence, preventive security, regulation of labor, vagrancy, and the poor, but also of weights and measures and other forms of consumer protection, liquor licencing, health and safety, building, fire safety, road and traffic regulation, and early forms of environmental regulation. The institution was rather privatized, subject to considerable local control, relying mostly on volunteer constables and watches for implementation, heavily oriented to self-regulation, and infrequent (even if sometimes draconian) in its recourse to punishment. The *lieutenant de police* (a post established in Paris in 1667) came to have jurisdiction over the stock exchange, food supplies and standards, the regulation of prostitutes, and other markets in vice and virtue. Police and the "science of police" that in eighteenth-century German universities prefigured contemporary regulatory

---

[1] France was an exception that made guilds state organs and spread their regulatory authority out from towns across the entire countryside (Polanyi 1957, 66).

studies sought to establish a new source of order to replace the foundation laid by the estates in the feudal order that had broken down.

English country parishes and small market towns, as on the Continent, had constables and local watches under a Tudor system that for centuries beyond the Tudors regulated the post-feudal economic and social order. Yet there was an English aversion to conceptualizing this as police in the French, German, and Russian fashion. The office of the constable had initially been implanted into British common law and institutions by the Norman invasion of 1066. The office was in turn transplanted by the British to New England, with some New England communities then even requiring Native American villages to appoint constables. Eighteenth-century English, but not American, political instincts were to view Continental political theory of police as a threat to liberty and to seek a more confined role for the constable. Admittedly, Blackstone in his fourth volume of *Commentaries on the Laws of England* (1769 [1966]) adopts the Continental conception of police, and Adam Smith applauds it in his *Lectures on Jurisprudence* (1762–4 [1978]). But Neocleous (1998, 444) detects a shift from the Smith of the *Lectures* to the *Wealth of Nations*, both of which discuss police and the pin factory. The shift is from seeing:

police power contributing to the wealth-producing capacities of a *politically constituted* social order to being a site of autonomous social relations—the independent factory employing independent wage-labourers within a *laissez faire* economy.

Polanyi (1957, 66) quotes Montesquieu as sharing the early Smithian view of English police as constitutive of capitalism, when he says in the *Spirit of Laws* that "The English constrain the merchant, but it is in favor of commerce." Even as institutions of eighteenth-century police are to a considerable degree in place in the nations that become the cutting edge of capitalism (this is also true of the extremely effective policing of the Dutch Republic (Israel 1995, 677–84)), the leading interpreters of capitalism's success move from an interpretation of markets constituted by police to laissez-faire markets.

Peel's creation of the Metropolitan Police in London in 1829 and the subsequent creation of an even more internationally influential colonial model in Dublin were watersheds.

Uniformed paramilitary police, preoccupied with the punitive regulation of the poor to the almost total exclusion of any interest in the constitution of markets and the just regulation of commerce, became one of the most universal of globalized regulatory models. So what happened to the business regulation? From the mid-nineteenth century, factories inspectorates, mines inspectorates, liquor licensing boards, weights and measures inspectorates, health and sanitation, food inspectorates, and countless others were created to begin to fill the vacuum left by constables now concentrating only on crime. Business regulation became variegated into many different specialist regulatory branches. The nineteenth-century regulatory growth is more in the number of branches than in their size and power. Laissez-faire ideology underpinned this regulatory weakness. The regulators' feeble resourcing compared to the paramilitary police, and the comparative wealth of those they were regulating, made the early business regulators even more vulnerable to capture and corruption than the police, as we see with poorly resourced business regulators in developing economies today.

5 THE UNREGULABLE LIBERAL ECONOMY

Where problems were concentrated in space, nineteenth-century regulation secured some major successes. Coal mines became much safer workplaces from the latter years of the nineteenth century, as did large factories in cities (Braithwaite 1985), regulatory transitions that are yet to occur in China that today accounts for 80 percent of the world's coal mine fatalities. Rail travel was causing thousands of deaths annually in the USA late in the nineteenth century (McCraw 1984, 26); by the twentieth century it had become a very safe way to travel (Bradbury 2002). Regulation rendered ships safer and more humane transporters of exploited labor (slaves, convicts, indentured labor, refugees from the Irish famine) to corners of the empire suffering labor shortages (MacDonagh 1961). The paramilitary police were also successful in assisting cities like London, Stockholm, and Sydney to become much safer from crimes against persons and property for a century and a half from 1820 (Gurr, Grabosky, and Hula 1977). But it was only problems like these that were spatially concentrated where nineteenth-century regulation worked. In most domains it worked rather less effectively than eighteenth-century police. This was acceptable to political elites, who were mainly concerned to make protective regulation work where the dangerous classes might congregate to threaten the social order—in cities, convict ships, factories.

In addition to the general under-resourcing of nineteenth-century regulatory inspectorates, the failure to reach beyond large cities, the capture and corruption, there was the fact that the inspectorates were only beginning to invent their regulatory technologies for the first time. They were still learning. The final and largest limitation that made their challenge impossible was that in the nineteenth century almost all commerce was small business. It is harder for an inspector to check ten workplaces employing six people than one with sixty workers. This remains true today. We will see that the regulatory reach of contemporary capitalism would be impossible without the lumpiness of a commerce populated by big businesses that can be enrolled to regulate smaller businesses. Prior to the nineteenth century, it was possible to lever the self-regulatory capabilities of guilds in ways not dissimilar to twentieth-century capabilities to enrol industry associations and big business to regulate small business. But the well-ordered world of guilds had been one of the very things destroyed by the chaotic emergence of laissez-faire capitalism outside the control of such premodern institutions. Where guilds did retain control, capitalism did not flourish, because the guilds restricted competition.

While the nineteenth-century state was therefore mostly a laissez-faire state with limited reach in its capacity to regulate, it was a state learning to regulate. While the early nineteenth-century tension was between the decentralized police economy and laissez-faire liberalism, the late-century tension was between laissez-faire and the growth of an administrative state of office blocks in large cities.

6 THE UNREGULABLE LIBERAL ECONOMY CREATES THE PROVIDER STATE

A simple solution to the problem of private rail companies charging monopoly prices, bypassing poorer towns, failing to serve strategic national development objectives, and flouting safety standards, was to nationalize them. A remedy to unsanitary private hospitals was a public hospital system that would make it unnecessary for patients to resort to unsafe private providers. The challenge of coordinating national regulation of mail services with international regulation through the Universal Postal Union (established in 1863) rendered a state postal monopoly the simplest solution to the coordination that was otherwise beyond the unregulable nineteenth-century liberal economy. The spread of socialist ideas during the nineteenth century gave an ideological impetus to the provider state solution. Progressively, until the beginning of the second half of the twentieth century, the provider state model proliferated, especially in Europe, with airlines, steel, coal, nuclear power, urban public transport, electricity, water, gas, health insurance, retirement insurance, maternal and child welfare, firefighting, sewerage, and countless other things being provided by state monopolies.

Bismarck consciously pursued welfare state provision as a strategy for thwarting the growing popularity of the idea of a socialist revolution to replace capitalism entirely with a state that provided everything. Lloyd-George was impressed by Bismarck's diagnosis and the British Liberal Party also embraced the development of the welfare state, only to be supplanted by a Labour Party that outbid the Liberals with the state provision it was willing to provide to workers who now had votes and political organization.

While many of these state takeovers also occurred in the United States during the century and a half that preceded the arrival of regulatory capitalism, the scope of what was nationalized was narrower there. One reason was that trade unions and the parties and ideologies they spawned were weaker in the USA during the twentieth century. There were periods up to the first decade of the twentieth century when trade unions in the United States were actually numerically and politically stronger than in Europe. The big businesses that grew earlier in the United States used their legal and political capabilities to crush American unionism in the late nineteenth and early twentieth century, frequently through the murder of union officials and threats of violence (Braithwaite and Drahos 2000, 229). American big business could simply organize more effectively against the growth of trade unions and the provider state ideologies they sponsored than against the smaller family firms that predominated in Europe.

A paradox of the fact that American business culture moderated the growth of the provider state was that the regulatory state grew more vigorously in the USA, especially during the progressive era (1890–1913) (which saw the creation of the Federal Trade Commission, Food and Drug Administration, and Interstate Commerce Commission, among other agencies) and the New Deal (1930s) (which saw the creation of the Securities and Exchange Commission, the National Recovery Administration, the Federal Communications Commission, the Civil Aeronautics Board, among others) (McCraw 1984). Building paradox upon paradox, the growth in the sophistication of regulatory technologies in the USA showed that there were credible alternatives to the problems the provider state set out to solve. The New Deal also supplied an economic management rationale to an expansive state. Keynes' general theory was partly about increasing public spending to stimulate an economy when it was in recession, as it was at the time of the New Deal.

7 REGULATION CREATES BIG BUSINESS

Braithwaite and Drahos (2000) have described the corporatization and securitization of the world as among its most fundamental transformations of the last three centuries. I will summarize here how this was enabled by regulation, but then how corporatization in turn enabled regulatory capitalism to replace the provider state economy. Corporations existed for more than a millennium before securities. For our purposes, a security is a transferable instrument evidencing ownership or creditorship, as a stock or bond. The legal invention of the security in the seventeenth century was the most transformative movement in the history of corporations. It enabled the replacement of family firms with very large corporations based on pooled contributions of capital from thousands of shareholders and bondholders. These in turn enabled the great technological projects of eighteenth- and nineteenth-century capitalism—the railroads, the canals, the mines.

When it was first invented, however, the historical importance of the security had nothing to do with the corporatization of the world. Rather, it transformed state finances through bonds that created long-term national debts. While the idea of dividing the national debt into bonds was invented in Naples in the seventeenth century, it was England that managed by the eighteenth century to use the idea in a financial revolution that helped it gain an upper hand over its principal rival, France (Dickson 1993). England became an early provider state in a particularly strategic way by seizing full national control of public finance: formerly private tax and customs collecting were nationalized in the seventeenth century, a Treasury Board was established in the eighteenth, and finally the Bank of England was given national regulatory functions. The Treasury Board realized that the national debt could be made, in effect, self-liquidating and long-term, protecting the realm from extortionate interest rates at times of war and the kind of vulnerability that had brought the Spanish empire down when short-term loans had to be fully repaid after protracted war. Instead of making England hostage to Continental bankers, the national debt was divided into thousands of bonds, with new bond issues placed on the market to pay for old bonds that were due to be paid.

Securitization paid for the warships that allowed Britannia to rule the waves, to trade and colonize—to be a state provider of imperial administration and national as opposed to feudal security on a scale not imagined before. Today, of course, national debts can no longer be used to rule the world because they are regulated by other states through the Paris Club and the IMF (International Monetary Fund). The key thing here is that the early providers of state control of public finance in the process also induced a private bond market. This created the profession of stockbroking and the institution of the stock exchange. For most of the period when Amsterdam and London were the leading stock exchanges in the world, they were predominantly trading securities in the debts of nations. Gradually this created a market in private stocks and bonds. These enabled the English to create the Massachusetts Bay Company, the Hudson Bay Company, the British South Africa Company, the East India Company, and others that conquered the world, and the Dutch to create an even more powerful East India Company and the United New Netherland Company that built a New Amsterdam which was to succeed London as the next capital of the world.

State creation of a London market in the broking of securities fomented other kinds of securities exchanges as well, the most important of which was Lloyd's of London. Britannia's merchant fleet ruled the waves once an efficient market in spreading the lumpy risk of ships sinking with valuable cargos was created from a base in Lloyd's Coffee Shop. Lloyd's in turn became an important inventor of regulatory technologies that made regulatory capitalism possible in advance of the supplanting of the provider state with regulatory capitalism. For example, in building a global reinsurance market, it invented the plimsoll line that allowed insurers to check by simple observation at ports whether ships arrived overloaded.

But by far the most important impact of securitization was that it began a process, that only took off quite late in the nineteenth century, of replacing a capitalism of family firms with one of professional managers of securities put in their trust by thousands of shareholders. Even in New York, where the corporatization of the world was most advanced, it was not until the third decade of the twentieth century that the majority of litigants in appellate courts were corporations rather than individual persons and the majority of actors described on the front page of the *New York Times* were corporate rather than individual actors (Coleman 1982, 11).

8 Antitrust Globalizes American Mega-corporate Capitalism

In the 1880s, predominantly agrarian America became deeply troubled by the new threat to what they saw as their Jeffersonian agrarian republic from concentrations of corporate power that they called trusts. Farmers were especially concerned about the "robber barons" of railroads that transported their produce across the continent. But oil, steel, and other corporate concentrations of power in the northeast were also of concern. Because Jeffersonian republicanism also feared concentrations of state power in the northeast, the American solution was not to nationalize rail, oil, and steel. It was to break up the trusts. By 1890 at least ten US states had passed antitrust laws, at which point the Sherman Act was passed by a virtually unanimous vote of the US Congress.

The effect of enforcement of the Sherman Act by American courts was not exactly as intended by the progressive era social movement against the railroad, oil, steel, and tobacco trusts. Alfred Chandler (1977, 333–4) noted that "after 1899 lawyers were advising their corporate clients to abandon all agreements or alliances carried out through cartels or trade associations and to consolidate into single, legally defined enterprises." US antitrust laws thus actually encouraged mergers instead of inhibiting them, because they "tolerated that path to monopoly power while they more effectively outlawed the alternative pathway via cartels and restrictive practices" (Hannah 1991, 8). The Americans found that there were organizational efficiencies in managerially centralized, big corporations that made what Chandler (1990, 8) called a "three-pronged investment:" (1) "an investment in production facilities large enough to exploit a technology's potential economies of scale or scope;" (2) "an investment in a national and international marketing and distribution network, so that the volume of sales might keep pace with the new volume of production;" and (3) "to benefit fully from these two kinds of investment the entrepreneurs also had to invest in management."

According to Freyer's (1992) study in the Chandler tradition, the turn-of-the-century merger wave fostered by the Sherman Act thrust US long-term organization for economic efficiency ahead of Britain's for the next half-century, until Britain acquired its Monopolies Act 1948 and Restrictive Trade Practices Act 1956. Until the 1960s, the British economy continued to be dominated by family companies that did not mobilize Chandler's three-pronged investment. Non-existent antitrust enforcement in Britain for the first half of the twentieth century also left new small business entrepreneurs more at the mercy of the restrictive business practices of old money than in the USA. British commitment to freedom of contract was an inferior industrial policy to both the visible hand of American lawmakers' rule of reason and the administrative guidance of the German Cartel Courts. For the era of managerial capitalism, liberal deregulation of state monopolies formerly granted to Indies Companies and guilds was not enough. Simple-minded Smithean invocation of laissez-faire missed the point. A special kind of regulation for the deregulation of restrictive business practices was needed which tolerated bigness.

Ultimately, Braithwaite and Drahos (2000) show that this American model of competitive mega-corporate capitalism globalized under four influences:

1. Extension of the model throughout Europe after the Second World War under the leadership of the German anti-cartel authority, the *Bundeskartelamt*, a creation of the American occupation.
2. Cycles of Mergers and Acquisitions (M&A) mania in Europe catalyzed in part by M&A missionaries from American law firms.
3. Extension of the model to the dynamic Asian economies in the 1980s and 1990s, partly under pressure from bilateral trade negotiations with the USA and Europe (who demanded breaking the restrictive practices of Korean *chaebol*, for example).
4. Extension of the model to developing countries with technical assistance from organizations such as UNCTAD (United Nations Conference on Trade and Development), prodded by the IMF good governance agenda.

This history of a regulatory capitalism that promotes competition among large corporations dates from the 1880s for the US but is very recent for other states. Most of the world's competition regulators have been created since 1990. There were barely twenty in the 1980s; today there are approximately 100.

9 MEGA-CORPORATE CAPITALISM CREATES REGULATORY CAPITALISM

The regulatory state creates mega-corporations, but large corporations also enable regulatory states. We have seen that antitrust regulation is the primary driver of the first side of this reciprocal relationship. But other forms of regulation also prove impossible for small business to satisfy. In many industry sectors, regulation drives small firms that cannot meet regulatory demands into bankruptcy, enabling large corporates to take over their customers (see, for example, Braithwaite's (1994) account of how tougher regulation drove the "mom and pops" out of the US nursing home industry in favor of corporate chains). For this reason, large corporations often use their political clout to lobby for regulations they know they will easily satisfy but that small competitors will not be able to manage. They also lobby for ratcheting up regulation that benefits them directly (e.g. longer patent monopolies) but that are mainly a cost for small business (Braithwaite and Drahos 2000, 56–87).

To understand the second side of this reciprocal relationship more clearly—mega-corporates create regulatory capitalism—consider the minor example of the regulation of the prison industry (Harding 1997). It is minor because most countries have not taken the path of privatizing prisons, though in the USA, where prisons house more than two million inmates and employ about the same number, it is not such a minor business. In the 1990s many private prisons were created in Australia, a number of them owned by the largest American prison corporations. A question that immediately arose was how was the state to ensure that American corporations met Australia's national and international human rights obligations. When the state was the monopoly provider of prison places, it simply, if ineffectively, told its civil servants that they would lose their jobs if they did not fulfill their duty in respect of such standards. This requirement was put into contracts with the private prisons. But then the state has little choice but to invest in a new regulatory agency to monitor contract compliance.

As soon as it puts this in place, prisoner rights' advocates point out that in some respects the old state-run prisons are more abusive than the new private providers, so the prison inspectorate should monitor the public prisons. Moreover, it should make public its reports on the public prisons so that transparency is as real there as with private prisons (Harding 1997). Of course, the private corporations lobby for this as well to create a "level playing field" in their competition with the state. Hence, the corporatization of the prison industry creates not only a demand for the independent, publicly transparent regulation of the corporates, it also creates a potent political demand for regulation of the state itself. This is central to understanding why the regulatory state is not the correct descriptor of contemporary transformations; regulatory capitalism involves heightened regulation of the state as well as growth in regulation by the state (Hood et al. 1999). We have seen this in many other domains including the privatization of British nursing home provision described earlier which led to the inspection of public nursing homes.

Security generally has been a major domain of privatization. Most developed economies today have a ratio of more than three private police to one public police officer (Johnston and Shearing 2003). Under provider capitalism it was public police officers who would provide security at football stadiums, shopping complexes, universities, and airports. But today, as we move from airport to shops to leisure activity to work, we move from one bubble of private security to another (Shearing and Wood 2003; Johnston and Shearing 2003). If our purse is stolen at the shopping mall, it is a private security officer who will come to our aid, or who will detain us if we are caught shoplifting. The public police will only cover us as we move in the public spaces between bubbles of private security. As with prisons, public demand for regulation of the private security industry arises when high profile incidents occur, such as the recent death of one of Australia's most talented cricketers after a bouncer's punch outside a nightclub.

International security has also been privatized. Some of those allegedly leading the abuses at Abu-Grahib in Iraq were private security contractors. Many of these contractors carry automatic weapons, dress like soldiers, and are killed as soldiers by insurgents. In developing countries, particularly in Africa, military corporations have been hired to be the strike infantry against adversaries in civil wars. An estimated 70 per cent of the former KGB found employment in this industry (Singer 2002). This has led the British government to produce a White Paper on the need to regulate private military organizations and to the quip that the regulator be dubbed OfKill!

So the accumulation of political power into the hands of large private corporations creates public demand for regulation. Moreover, we have seen that the largest corporations often demand this themselves. In addition, the regulatory processes and (partly resultant) competitive imperatives that increase the scope and scale of corporations make what was unregulable in the nineteenth century, regulable in the twentieth. The chemicals/pharmaceuticals industry, for example, creates a huge public demand for regulation. Incidents like Bhopal with the manufacture of agricultural chemicals and thalidomide with pharmaceuticals, that kill thousands, galvanize mass concern. The nineteenth-century regulatory state could only respond to public outrage by scapegoating someone in the chemical firm and throwing them in prison. It was incapable of putting a regulatory regime in place that might prevent a recurrence by addressing the root causes of disasters. There were too many little chemical producers for state inspectors to monitor and it was impossible for them to keep up with technological change that constantly created new risks.

After the Bhopal disaster, which ultimately caused the demise of Union Carbide, the remaining large chemical producers put in place a global self-regulatory regime called "Responsible Care," with the objective of averting another such disaster that might cause a multinational to go under leaving a stain on the reputation of the entire industry (Moffet, Bregha, and Middelkoop 2004). That's all very well, the regulatory cynic notes, but it still remains the case today that most chemical risks are posed by small, local firms with poor self-regulatory standards, not by the multinationals. Yet the fact of mega-corporate capitalism that has evolved over the past century is that almost all small chemical firms are linked upstream or downstream to one multinational or another. They buy or sell chemical ingredients to or from the large corporates. This fact creates a mass tort risk for the multinationals. The multinationals are the ones with the deep pockets, the high public profile, and brand reputation; so they are more vulnerable to the irresponsibility of small chemical firms linked to them than are those firms themselves. So Responsible Care requires large firms to sustain a chain of stewardship for their chemicals upsteam and downstream. This has the effect of making large corporations the principal regulators of small chemical firms, not the state. This is especially so in developing countries where the temptations of state laissez-faire can make the headquarters' risks potentially most catastrophic.

State regulation and private regulation through tort creates larger chemical corporations. We see this especially in pharmaceuticals where the costs of testing new drugs now run to hundreds of millions of dollars. Global scandals that lead to demand for still tougher regulation creates a community of shared fate among large firms in the industry (note Rees's (1994) study of how the Three Mile Island disaster created a community of fate in the nuclear industry, a belief that another Three Mile Island could cripple the entire industry). Big business responds to finding itself in a community of fate in a risk society (Beck 1992) by industry-wide risk management. This implies managing upstream and downstream risks. Again we see that regulatory capitalism is not only about the regulatory state, though this is a big part of the chemicals, pharmaceuticals, and nuclear stories. It is also about regulation by industry associations of their large members and regulation of small producers by large producers who share the same chain of stewardship for a risk. At the end of the day, it is not only states (with technical assistance from international organizations like the World Health Organization and the OECD (Organization for Economic Co-operation and Development)) doing the regulating; it is global and national industry associations and large multinational firms. Not only does this ease some of the logistical burdens upon the regulatory state in monitoring a galaxy of small firms, it also eases some of the information problems that made chemicals unregulable in the nineteenth century. As partners in regulatory capitalism, state regulators can lean on Responsible Care, the OECD, and large multinationals that may know more than them about where new chemical risks are emerging. Of course there is debate about how well these private–public partnerships of regulatory capitalism work (Gunningham and Grabosky 1998).

Braithwaite and Drahos (2000) revealed the importance of yet other actors who are as important as non-state regulators. Ratings agencies like Moody's and Standards and Poors, having witnessed the bankrupting of imprudent chemical producers, downgrade the credit rating of firms with a record of sloppy risk management. This makes money more expensive for them to borrow. Reinsurers like Lloyd's also make their risks more expensive to reinsure. The cost and availability of lending and insurance also regulates small firms. Care homes (including nursing homes) frequently go bankrupt in the UK; these bankruptcies are often connected to the delivery of poor quality care. Reports of British government care home inspections are on the Internet. When homes approach banks for loans, it is good banking practice today to do an Internet check to see if the home has any looming quality of care problems. If it does, banks sometimes refuse loans until these problems are addressed. Banks have thence become important regulators of little and large British care home firms.

9.1 Corporatization, Tax, and the Constitution of Provider and Regulatory Capitalism

One effect of the corporatization of capitalism in the twentieth century was that it made it easier for the state to collect tax. This revenue made it possible to fund both the provider state and the regulatory state. State provision of things like welfare and transport, and state regulation are expensive activities. So taxpaying becoming regulable was decisive to the subsequent emergence of the provider state and regulatory capitalism. In most developing societies taxpaying remains unregulable and this has closed the door on credible state provision and state regulation.

Of course it is more cost-effective to collect tax from one large corporation than ten small ones and most corporate tax is collected from the largest 1 percent of corporations in wealthy nations. But this is not the main reason that corporatization created a wealthy state. More fundamentally, corporatization assisted the collectability of other taxes (see Braithwaite and Drahos 2000, ch. 9). As retailing organizations became larger corporates, as opposed to family-owned corner stores, the collection of indirect tax became more cost-effective. When most of the Australian working class was rural, itinerantly shearing sheep for graziers, cutting cane, or picking fruit, collecting taxes from them was difficult and costly. But as the working class became progressively more urban—in the employ of city-based corporations—income tax collections from workers became a goldmine, especially after the innovation of Pay As You Earn (withholding of tax from pay packets by employers, which started in Australia in 1944). The final contribution of mega-corporatization was financial institutions becoming more concentrated and computerized, making withholding on interest and dividends feasible. So tax on salary income, corporate tax, sales taxes, and tax on income from interest and dividends all became more collectable. The result was that, contrary to the fairytale of neoliberalism, the state grew and grew into a regulatory capitalism where the state both retained many of its provider functions and added many new regulatory ones.

Pay As You Earn was an innovative regulatory technology of wider relevance. PAYE taxpayers cannot cheat because it is not them, but their employers, who hand over the money. Theoretically of course the employer can cheat. But they have no incentive to do so, since only their employee benefits from the cheating, and the cheating is visible in the accounts. The regulatory strategy of general import here is to impose regulatory obligations on keepers of a gate that controls the flow of the regulated activity, where the gatekeepers do not benefit personally from opening and closing the gate. This not only separates the power from the incentive to cheat, it also economizes on surveillance. It is not necessary to monitor all the regulated actors at all times. The regulator must only monitor the gatekeeper at those points when gates can be unlocked.

10 THE REGULATED STATE

For 90 percent of the world's states there are large numbers of corporations with annual sales that exceed the state's GDP. The CEOs of the largest corporations typically are better networked into other fonts of power than the presidents of medium-sized states. Consequently large corporations do a lot of regulating of states. There are also some smaller global corporations like Moody's and Standard and Poors that have specialized regulatory functions over states—setting their credit ratings. More generally, finance capital holds sway over states. This is exercised through capital movements, but also through lobbying global institutions such as the IMF, the Basle Committee, World Trade Organization Panels, and the World Bank, who might have more direct control over a specific sphere of state activity. The most formidable regulator of debtor states is the IMF, as a result of its frequently used power to impose regulatory conditions upon debt repayment.

While states have formidable regulatory leverage over airlines, for example, airlines can enrol the International Civil Aviation Organization to regulate landing rights to and from states that fail to meet their obligations to the orderly conduct of international transport. While states regulate telecoms, they must submit to regulation by the ITU (International Telecommunication Union) if they want interconnectivity with telecoms in other states, and powerful corporations invest heavily in lobbying the ITU and in having their executives chair its technical committees.

Many states simply forfeit domains of regulation to global corporations that have superior technical capability and greater numbers of technically competent people on the ground. For example, in many developing nations the Big Four accounting firms effectively set national accounting standards. States are also regulated by international organizations (and bilaterally) to comply with legal obligations under treaties they have signed. Sanctions range from armed force to air and sea blockades, suspension of voting rights on international organizations, trade sanctions, and "smart sanctions" such as seizure of foreign assets and denial of visas to members of the regime and their families. Regional organizations such as the EU (European Union) and the African Union, of course, also have a degree of regulatory leverage over member states. Leverage tends to be greatest when states are applying for membership of an international club such as the World Trade Organization or EU from which they believe they would benefit.

One of the defining features of regulatory capitalism is that parts of states are set up with independent capacities to regulate other parts of the state. Since 1980 the globalization of the institution of the Ombudsman and the proliferation of audit offices has reached the point where some describe what Levi-Faur calls regulatory capitalism as *The Audit Society* (Power 1997). Finally, there is the development of independent inspectors of privatized industries moving their oversight back to public provision.

Of course the idea of a separation of powers where one branch of governance regulates another so that neither executive, judiciary, nor legislature can dominate governance is an old one, dating at least from the Spartan constitution and Montesquieu (Braithwaite 1997). But practice has become more variegated, especially in Asian constitutions such as those of Thailand and Taiwan that conceive of themselves as having more than three branches of governance, with branches such as the Election Commission, Ombudsman, Human Rights Commission, Counter Corruption

Commission, and Audit and Examination Offices enjoying constitutionally separated powers from the legislative, executive, and judicial branches. The theory as well as the practice of the doctrine of separation of powers under regulatory capitalism has also moved forward on how innovative separations of powers can deter abuse of power (see Braithwaite 1997). To the extent that there are richer, more plural separations within and between private and public powers in a polity, there is a prospect of moving toward a polity where no one power can dominate all the others and each power can exercise its regulatory functions semi-autonomously even against the most powerful branch of state or corporate power. As Durkheim began to see, the art of government "consists largely in coordinating the functions of the various self-regulating bodies in different spheres of the economy" (Schepel 2005, ch. 1; see also Cotterrell 1999; Durkheim 1930, preface).

11 CONCLUSION

The transitions since feudal structures of governance fell to incipient capitalist institutions have been from a police economy, to an unregulable nineteenth-century liberal economy that oscillated between laissez-faire, dismantling the decentralized police economy, and laying the bricks and mortar of an initially weak urban administrative state, to the provider state economy, to regulatory capitalism. Across all of these transitions, markets in fits and starts have tended to become progressively more vigorous, as has investment in the regulation of market externalities. Not only have markets, states, and state regulation become more formidable, so has non-state regulation by civil society, business, business associations, professions, and international organizations. Separations of powers within polities have become more variegated, with more private–public hybridity. This means political science conceived narrowly as a discipline specialized in the study of public governance to the exclusion of corporate governance, NGO governance, and the governance of transnational networks makes less sense than it once did. If we have entered an era of regulatory capitalism, regulation may be, in contrast, a fruitful topic around which to build intellectual communities and social science theory.

Interesting agendas implied by this perspective are empirical studies of how networked regulators like the Forest and Marine Stewardship Councils, Social Accountability International, and the Sustainable Agriculture Network (Courville 2003) operate, research on devolved regulatory technologies that harness local knowledge (Shearing and Wood 2003), Levi Faur's (2006) agenda of documenting and comparatively dissecting the *Varieties of Regulatory Capitalism*, the Hall and Soskice (2001), Stiglitz (2002), and Rodrik (2004) agendas of diagnosing the institutional mixes that make capitalism buzz and collapse in the context of specific states, the Dorf and Sabel (1998) agenda of evidence-based "democratic experimentalism," the Campbell Collaboration, and behavioral economics agendas for real policy experiments on the impacts of regulatory interventions. Important among these are experiments on meta-regulation—regulated self-regulation—as a form of social control that seems paradigmatic of regulatory capitalism (Parker 2002; Braithwaite 2005).

In seeing the separations among the periods posited in this chapter, it is also important to grasp the posited continuities. Both markets and the state become stronger, enlarged in scope and transaction density, at every stage. Elements of eighteenth-century police are retained in the creation of nineteenth-century paramilitary police and other specialized regulators. Post-1980 regulatory capitalism learns from and builds upon the weaknesses (and the strengths) of nineteenth- and early twentieth-century regulation—from twenty-first-century private security corporations learning from Peel's Metropolitan Police and the KGB, to state shipping regulators and the International Maritime Organization learning from regulatory technologies crafted in Lloyd's Coffee Shop. While many problems solved by state provision prior to 1980 are thence solved by privatization into contested, regulated markets, most of the state provision of the era of the provider state persists under regulatory capitalism. Even some re-nationalization of poorly conceived privatization has begun.

A contribution of this chapter has been to suggest that regulation, particularly antitrust and securitization of national debt, enabled the growth of both provider and regulatory states. Regulation did this through pushing the spread of large corporations that made Chandler's (1977, 1990) three-pronged investment. The corporatization of the world increased the efficacy of tax enforcement, funding provider and regulatory state growth. The corporatization of the world drove a globalization in which transnational networks, industry associations, professions, international organizations, NGOs, NGO/retailer hybrids like the Forest Stewardship Council, and most importantly corporations themselves (especially, but not limited to, stock exchanges, ratings agencies, the Big Four accounting firms, multinationals that specialize in doing states' regulation for them like Société Général de Surveillance,[2] and large corporates that regulate small upstream and downstream firms in the same industry) became important national, regional, and global regulators. This was a very different capitalism and a very different world of governance than existed in the early twentieth-century industrial capitalism of family firms. Hence the power of Levi-Faur's conceptualization of regulatory capitalism. While states are "decentred" under regulatory capitalism, the wealth it generates means that states have more capacity both to provide and to regulate than ever before.

---

[2] This is a large Swiss multinational that provides all manner of regulatory services for states from environmental inspection to collecting nations' customs duties for them in innovative ways (Braithwaite and Drahos 2000, 492–3).

REFERENCES

AYRES, I. and BRAITHWAITE, J. 1992. *Responsive Regulation: Transcending the Deregulation Debate*. New York: Oxford University Press.

BALDWIN, R., SCOTT, C., and HOOD, C. 1998. *A Reader on Regulation*. Oxford: Oxford University Press.

BARDACH, E. and KAGAN, R. A. 1982. *Going by the Book: The Problem of Regulatory Unreasonableness*. Philadelphia: Temple University Press.

BECK, U. 1992. *Risk Society: Towards a New Modernity*. Beverly Hills, Calif.: Sage.

BERNSTEIN, M. 1955. *Regulating Business by Independent Commission*. Princeton, NJ: Princeton University Press.

BEVIR, M. and RHODES, R. 2003. *Interpreting British Governance*. London: Routledge.

BLACKSTONE, W. 1966. *Commentaries on the Laws of England, Vol 4*. London: Dawsons.

BRADBURY, N. 2002. Face the facts on transport safety. *Railwatch*, November: 6–7.

BRAITHWAITE, J. 1985. *To Punish or Persuade: Enforcement of Coal Mine Safety*. Albany: State University of New York Press.

——1994. The nursing home industry. Pp. 11–54 in *Beyond the Law: Crime in Complex Organizations, Crime and Justice: A Review of Research*, ed. M. Tonny and A. J. Reiss. Chicago.: University of Chicago Press.

——1997. On speaking softly and carrying sticks: neglected dimensions of republican separation of powers. *University of Toronto Law Journal*, 47: 1–57.

——2005. *Markets in Vice, Markets in Virtue*. Oxford: Federation Press.

——and DRAHOS, P. 2000. *Global Business Regulation*. Melbourne: Cambridge University Press.

CASTELLS, M. 1996. *The Information Age: Economy, Society and Culture, Volume 1: The Rise of the Network Society*. Oxford: Blackwell.

CASTLES, F. G. 2004. *The Future of the Welfare State: Crisis Myths and Crisis Realities*. Cambridge: Cambridge University Press.

CHANDLER, A. D., JR. 1977. *The Visible Hand: The Managerial Revolution in American Business*. Cambridge, Mass.: Belknap Press.

——1990. *Scale and Scope: The Dynamics of Industrial Capitalism*. Cambridge, Mass.: Belknap Press.

COLEMAN, J. S. 1982. *The Asymmetric Society*. Syracuse, NY: Syracuse University Press.

COTTERRELL, R. 1999. *Emile Durkheim: Law in a Moral Domain*. Palo Alto, Calif.: Stanford University Press.

COURVILLE, S. 2003. Social accountability audits: challenging or defending democratic governance? *Law and Policy*, 25 (3): 267–97.

DICKSON, P. G. M. 1993 *The Financial Revolution in England: A Study in the Development of Public Credit, 1688–1756*. Brookfield, Vt.: Gregg Revivals.

DORF, M. and SABEL, C. 1998. A constitution of democratic experimentalism. *Columbia Law Review*, 98: 267–473.

DUDLEY, S. and WARREN, M. 2005. *Regulators' Budget Continues to Rise: An Analysis of the U.S. Budget for Fiscal Years 2004 and 2005*. St. Louis: Weidenbaum Center, Washington University.

DURKHEIM, E. 1930. *De la Division du Travail Social*, 2nd edn. Paris: PUF.

FREYER, T. 1992. *Regulating Big Business Antitrust in Great Britain and America, 1880–1990*. Cambridge: Cambridge University Press.

GARLAND, D. 2001. *The Culture of Control: Crime and Social Order in Contemporary Society*. Oxford: Oxford University Press.

GRABOSKY, P. N. 1994. Green markets: environmental regulation by the private sector. *Law and Policy*, 16: 419–48.

GUNNINGHAM, N. and GRABOSKY, P. 1998. *Smart Regulation: Designing Environmental Policy*. Oxford: Clarendon Press.

GURR, T. R., GRABOSKY, P. N., and HULA, R. C. 1977. *The Politics of Crime and Conflict*. Beverly Hills, Calif.: Sage.

HALL, P. A. and SOSKICE, D. (eds.) 2001. *Varieties of Capitalism: The Institutional Foundations of Comparative Advantage*. Oxford: Oxford University Press.

HANNAH, L. 1991. Mergers, cartels and concentration: legal factors in the US and European experience. Pp. 3–13 in *Antitrust and Regulation*, ed. G. H. Burgess, Jr. Aldershot: Edward Elgar.

HARDING, R. W. 1997. *Private Prisons and Public Accountability*. Buckingham: Open University Press.

HOOD, C., SCOTT, C., JAMES, O., JONES, G. W., and TRAVERS, A. J. 1999. *Regulation Inside Government: Waste-Watchers, Quality Police, and Sleaze-Busters*. Oxford: Oxford University Press.

ISRAEL, J. 1995. *The Dutch Republic: Its Rise, Greatness and Fall, 1477–1806*. Oxford: Clarendon Press.

JAYASURIYA, K. 2001. Globalization and the changing architecture of the state: the politics of the regulatory state and the politics of negative co-ordination. *Journal of European Public Policy*, 8 (1): 101–23.

JOHNSTON, L. and SHEARING, C. 2003. *Governing Security: Explorations in Policing and Justice*. London: Routledge.

JORDANA, J. and LEVI-FAUR, D. 2003. The rise of the regulatory state in Latin America: a study of the diffusion of regulatory reforms across countries and sectors. Paper to the Annual Meeting of the American Political Science Association, 28 August.

——— (eds.) 2004. *The Politics of Regulation: Examining Regulatory Institutions and Instruments in the Governance Age*. Cheltenham: Edward Elgar.

LEVI, M. 1988. *Of Rule and Revenue*. Berkeley: University of California Press.

LEVI-FAUR, D. 2005. The global diffusion of regulatory capitalism. *Annals of the American Academy of Political and Social Science*, 598: 12–32.

——— (ed.) 2006. Varieties of regulatory capitalism. From David Levi-Faur's homepage: My special issue on "Varieties of Regulatory Capitalism," published by *Governance*, May 2006.

LOUGHLIN, M. and SCOTT, C. 1997. The regulatory state. Pp. 205–19 in *Developments in British Politics 5*, ed. P. Dunleavy, I. Holliday, and G. Peele. London: Macmillan.

McCRAW, T. K. 1984. *Prophets of Regulation*. Cambridge, Mass.: Harvard University Press.

MACDONAGH, O. 1961. *A Pattern of Government Growth: The Passenger Acts and Their Enforcement*. London: Macgibbon and Kee.

MAJONE, G. 1994. The rise of the regulatory state in Europe. *West European Politics*, 17: 77–101.

MIDWINTER, A. and McGARVEY, N. 2001. In search of the regulatory state: evidence from Scotland. *Public Administration*, 79 (4): 825–49.

MOFFET, J., BREGHA, F., and MIDDELKOOP, M. J. 2004. Responsible care: a case study of a voluntary environmental initiative. Pp. 177–208 in *Voluntary Codes: Private Governance, the Public Interest and Innovation*, ed. K. Webb. Carleton: Carleton Research Unit on Innovation, Science and Environment.

MONTESQUIEU, C. DE SECONDAT 1989. *The Spirit of the Laws*, trans. and ed. A. M. Cohler and B. C. Miller. Cambridge: Cambridge University Press.

MORAN, M. 2003. *The British Regulatory State: High Modernism and Hyper-Innovation*. Oxford: Oxford University Press.

MULLER, M. M. 2002. *The New Regulatory State in Germany*. Birmingham: Birmingham University Press.

NEOCLEOUS, M. 1998. Policing and pin-making: Adam Smith, police and the state of prosperity. *Policing and Society*, 8: 425–49.

OSBORNE, D. and T. GAEBLER. 1992. *Reinventing Government: How the Entrepreneurial Spirit is Transforming the Public Sector*. Reading, Mass.: Addison-Wesley.

PARKER, C. 1999. *Just Lawyers*. Oxford: Oxford University Press.

—— 2002. *The Open Corporation*. Melbourne: Cambridge University Press.

POLANYI, K. 1957. *The Great Transformation*. Boston: Beacon Press.

POWER, M. 1997. *The Audit Society: Rituals of Verification*. Oxford: Oxford University Press.

REES, J. 1994. *Hostages of Each Other: The Transformation of Nuclear Safety Since Three Mile Island*. Chicago: University of Chicago Press.

RHODES, R. A. W. 1997. *Understanding Governance*. Buckingham: Open University Press.

RODRIK, D. 2004. *Rethinking Growth Policies in the Developing World*. Cambridge, Mass.: Harvard University Press.

ROSOFF, S. E., PONTELL, H. N., and TILLMAN, R. H. 2002. *Profit Without Honor: White-Collar Crime and the Looting of America*. Upper Saddle River, NJ: Prentice Hall.

SCHEPEL, H. 2005. *The Constitution of Private Governance*. Oxford: Hart.

SCHOLZ, J. T. 1991. Coperative regulatory enforcement and the politics of administrative effectiveness. *American Political Science Review*, 85: 115–36.

SHEARING, C. and WOOD, J. 2003. Nodal governance, democracy and the new "denizens." *Journal of Law and Society*, 30 (3): 400–19.

SINGER, P. W. 2002. Corporate warriors: the rise and ramifications of the privatised military industry. *International Security*, 26 (3): 186–220.

SMITH, A. 1978. *Lectures on Jurisprudence*, ed. R. L. Meek, D. D. Raphael, and P. G. Stein. Oxford: Clarendon Press.

—— 1979. *Inquiry into the Nature and Causes of the Wealth of Nations*, ed. R. H. Campbell, A. S. Skinner, and W. B. Todd. Indianapolis: Liberty Fund.

STIGLER, G. J. (ed.) 1988. *Chicago Studies in Political Economy*. Chicago: University of Chicago Press.

STIGLITZ, J. E. 2002. *Globalization and its Discontents*. New York: W. W. Norton.

TOMLINS, C. L. 1993. *Law, Labor, and Ideology in the Early American Republic*. New York: Cambridge University Press.

VOGEL, S. K. 1996. *Freer Markets, More Rules: Regulatory Reform in Advanced Industrial Societies*. London: Cornell University Press.

WALBY, S. 1999. The new regulatory state: the social powers of the European Union. *British Journal of Sociology*, 50 (1): 118–38.

WILSON J. Q. 1980. *The Politics of Regulation*. New York: Basic Books.

PART IV

··

LAW AND
POLITICS

··

PART IV

LAW AND
POLITICS

....

CHAPTER 12

OVERVIEW OF LAW AND POLITICS

THE STUDY OF LAW AND POLITICS

....

KEITH E. WHITTINGTON

R. DANIEL KELEMEN

GREGORY A. CALDEIRA

LAW is one of the central products of politics and the prize over which many political struggles are waged. The early American jurist James Wilson observed that law is the "great sinew of government" (Wilson 1896, 1, 314). It is the principal instrument by which the government exerts its will on society, and as such it might be thought to lie (at least indirectly) close to the heart of the study of politics. But law is also the means by which the government organizes itself. It is law in this second mode, sometimes called public law, that has attracted independent attention. Here law is not only the product of politics but also constitutive of politics.

The study of law and politics is a varied and multidisciplinary enterprise. From its starting point in political science of studying constitutional and administrative law, the field soon added courts, lawyers, and related legal actors to its purview. And the substantive scope of the field is broader now than it has ever been. Although the US Supreme Court has always been the center of gravity within the field in American political science, the politics of law and courts in the international arena and in other countries is receiving growing attention, and thriving communities of scholars continue to explore other aspects of law and courts beyond constitutional courts and peak appellate tribunals. The interdisciplinary connections of the study of law and politics have varied over time; but, like the discipline of political science, the field of law and courts has readily borrowed concepts and methods from other disciplines. Active scholarly communities concerned with various aspects of law and politics in various disciplines make this a particularly good time for cross-disciplinary conversations among those in political science, and those in the humanities, the other social sciences, and the law schools.

With increasing diversity comes specialization, and there is always the danger that specialist scholars who are broadly concerned with law and politics will nonetheless find themselves sitting at Gabriel Almond's (1990) "separate tables," having separate conversations and missing some of the productive cross-fertilization that can take place across the field as a whole. The range of scholars working in the field do not always talk effectively to one another. The field is fragmented along various cross-cutting fissures, including substantive area of interest, particular research question, and favored methodology. Too often, we have forgone productive exchanges across those boundaries as scholars focused on their own close-knit intellectual communities and ignored, or viewed with wary skepticism, the efforts of those working on related issues but on the other side of one of these divides.

Our starting point, however, is with the study of law *and* politics, or the political analysis of law and courts. Law, as an autonomous field of study as taught in schools of law, is centrally concerned with the substance of law and the practices of legal professionals. For the professional craft of law, the politics of law can often be bracketed. For scholars concerned with law and politics, it is the professional craft of law that is bracketed. We need not deny that legal reasoning and skill are real and matter in the determination and application of the law and in the actions of legal institutions. But the starting point for the study of law and politics is that politics is also important and that considerable analytical and empirical leverage over our understanding of law and legal institutions can be gained by placing politics in the foreground.

1 THE DEVELOPMENT OF THE STUDY OF LAW AND POLITICS

The study of law and politics held a prominent place within the discipline of political science as academic disciplines and departments developed in the late nineteenth century. It was the narrow professionalism of the law school that spurred Columbia University in 1880 to create a separate School of Political Science, the progenitor of the discipline, under John Burgess. The school was to develop and teach a "science of jurisprudence" that would provide better preparation for the new federal civil service. Within the school, a distinct Department of Public Law and Jurisprudence quickly emerged and was only decades later renamed the Department of Political Science. The first dissertations in political science, reflecting the strength of its faculty and the fact that most of its students had first passed through the law school, were dominated by constitutional and legal history (Hoxie et al. 1955; Somit and Tanenhaus 1967).

As the discipline developed internally, the study of law and politics, although prominent, became a distinct specialty within political science. The 1915 report of an American Political Science Association (APSA) committee on college instruction was chaired by Charles Grove Haines (1915, 356–7), one of the leading constitutional scholars of the period, and five of its twelve recommended core courses were on legal subjects (with a sixth dedicated to judicial administration and organization). Despite this endorsement, recommended courses such as commercial law and Roman law did not survive long in political science departments; and international law was soon crowded out by international relations, just as administrative law already had been by public administration. Constitutional law and jurisprudence became the core of the study of law and politics in political science, with legislation, administrative reports, and other legal materials the raw material of political science generally and other substantive areas of law being either absorbed into broader fields within the discipline or left entirely to the law schools.

The leading public law scholars prior to the Second World War were primarily constitutional scholars, often with an emphasis on history. With law schools by and large continuing to leave constitutional law in relative neglect, Edward Corwin, Charles Grove Haines, Thomas Reed Powell, and Robert E. Cushman were the leading constitutional scholars of their day, as well as leaders within the discipline (each served as president of the APSA). From 1917 to 1961, the association's flagship journal, the *American Political Science Review* (APSR), published an annual overview of the constitutional decisions of the US Supreme Court, written by Cushman during much of that period, often supplemented with a separate review of state constitutional law decisions.

Their constitutional scholarship and teaching was simultaneously realist and normative in its sensibilities. As Corwin (1929, 592) understood it, the purpose of political science was to cultivate an understanding of "the true ends of the state and how best they may be achieved." A 1922 *APSR* article on constitutional law teaching reported that law school classes in constitutional law were generally regarded as too technical and too focused on litigation to be suitable to the training of graduate students, who required a better grasp of the "historical, philosophical, and comparative aspects of the subject" and how "fundamental principles" of American constitutionalism evolved over time. The undergraduate classes in constitutional law brought political action and behavior to the political science curriculum. The formal and descriptive character of courses in American and comparative government might be the starting point for understanding American politics, but constitutional law was the class in

which students could see how principles, beliefs, actors, and social conditions interacted and developed; and a "problem method" of instruction could teach students
the valuable skill of how to draft legislation that could address a given social problem
while adhering to constitutional limitations (Hall 1922). In the context of a formal,
"old institutionalist" curriculum and scholarship that characterized the discipline,
constitutional law introduced realism and action.

Constitutional scholarship of this sort continued in political science after the
Second World War, but under increasing competitive pressure. A new generation of
constitutional lawyers in the law schools was more prominent and more sophisticated
than their predecessors. The *Harvard Law Review* began to provide an annual review
of the Supreme Court's decisions, with a focus on constitutional law. The foreword to
that issue became a prominent platform for constitutional law professors to speak to
the Court, as well as to the legal profession and academia. The University of Chicago
Law School created its own annual *Supreme Court Review*, featuring constitutional
law professors. The summary offered by the *American Political Science Review* had
long lost its preeminence before it was dropped from the journal. Political scientists
such as Carl Swisher, Alpheus Mason, David Fellman, and John Roche continued this
humanistic tradition of constitutional studies well into the 1960s, but their successors
were fewer and increasingly marginal to the discipline.[1] Others such as Martin Diamond, Herbert Storing, Walter Berns, and again Alpheus Mason drifted further into
political theory and American political thought. It is telling that in a 1958 volume on
the state of the discipline, two prominent constitutional scholars, Robert McCloskey
(1958) and Carl Friedrich (1958), were invited to discuss "political theory" rather than
public law.[2]

Within the discipline, the study of law and politics was generally shifting away
from constitutional law and thought and toward judicial politics. Although there were
some tentative earlier efforts to pursue quantitative studies of judicial behavior and to
consider the political and social influences on judicial decision-making, C. Herman
Pritchett (1948; 1954) pushed the field in a significant new direction with his statistical
studies of voting behavior on the Supreme Court in the 1930s and 1940s (Murphy
and Tanenhaus 1972, 17–20). Pritchett's studies reflected a new methodological and
analytical sensibility within the discipline, but they also reflected a new reality on
the Supreme Court. Counting votes both became analytically meaningful and took
on a new urgency as a political puzzle in the 1930s and 1940s when dissenting and
concurring opinions first became routine. But statistical analyses of voting behavior
did not wholly define the new movement within the field. With a different methodological and conceptual approach, Jack Peltason (1955; 1961) likewise sought to open
the field up by looking beyond constitutional decisions and the Supreme Court and

[1] Carl Swisher in 1960, Charles Hyneman in 1962, and Carl Friedrich in 1963 were the last
constitutionalists to be honored with the APSA presidency. The last law and politics scholar to serve as
APSA president was C. Herman Pritchett in 1964.

[2] Both McCloskey and Friedrich made their home at Harvard. Harvard did not hire or promote a
senior law and politics scholar to replace either of them after they departed.

focusing more broadly on the judicial process as it related the courts as policy-makers and administrators to one another, the broader political system, and the relevant political environment. These emerging works in judicial politics had in common a single-minded focus on the political behavior of judges and those with whom they interacted, analyzed as other political actors might be analyzed and largely stripped of substantive legal content, historical development, or philosophical implication. For Corwin, Haines, and their humanistic successors, the study of law and politics was concerned with marrying an understanding and appreciation of the substance of the law with an understanding of the process by which law developed over time. For the behavioralists who emerged in the postwar period, developing an understanding of the process by which law was created and implemented was a sufficient scholarly task.

Works on the political behavior of judges and associated actors proliferated in the 1960s and soon dominated the field (Pritchett 1968; Schubert 1966). Among others, Pritchett and Walter Murphy gave close study to the rising hostility in Congress to the federal judiciary and its decisions. David Danelski, Sheldon Goldman, and Joel Grossman unpacked the judicial recruitment and selection process. Martin Shapiro resuscitated administrative law and the policy-making role of the courts outside of constitutional law. Walter Murphy, Alpheus Mason, and J. Woodward Howard uncovered the internal operations of the courts. Clement Vose focused attention on litigants and the relevance of interest groups to the judiciary. In-depth studies of the implementation of and compliance with judicial decisions were undertaken. Glendon Schubert, Harold Spaeth, Sidney Ulmer, and a host of others followed directly on Pritchett and built sophisticated statistical analyses of judicial voting behavior. Several scholars made tentative efforts at public opinion research and comparative analysis. Although the use of statistical techniques received the most attention and was the most controversial—sparking debates between its practitioners and some humanists over whether "jurimetrics" provided valuable new insights into how the Court worked—the methodologies employed were varied and included archival research, judicial biographies, field studies, game theory, and more. This new wave of research ushered in a range of new methodological approaches that had not been common in the earlier scholarship, but what were equally notable were the types of focused questions being asked about many aspects of the judicial process. Broader syntheses that may have taken note of judicial selection or interest groups when examining an area of law gave way to detailed studies examining how those particular aspects of the judicial process worked and what consequences they might have.

Subsequent movements have deepened and broadened these currents in the study of law and politics in political science. The interdisciplinary law-and-society movement reinforced the behavioralist turn in political science but added a greater interest in the operation of law and courts closest to the ground—criminal justice, the operation of the trial courts, juries, dispute resolution, the behavior of lawyers, the informal penetration of law into the social, economic, and cultural spheres—and fostered new conversations about law and politics across the social sciences. In focusing on law as it is embedded in society, sociolegal scholars have attacked such problems as the nature of disputing, including how individuals recognize that they have a legal claim, decide whether to pursue that claim, and achieve success in addressing their injuries or changing policy (Mather 2008).

The empirical study of tribunals and law in the international arena and outside the United States has grown rapidly in recent years, fostering connections between the study of law and courts and the study of comparative politics and international relations. Law and courts have assumed new importance in both areas. International law and courts have gained increased prominence in recent decades, leading scholars to examine the forces that drive such institutions and the impact that they have on national and private actors. Courts have also become increasingly important in a large number of established and newly emergent democracies, and even in some non-democratic regimes. Many of these cases raise similar questions to those that can and have been explored in the American context. Perhaps more interesting, however, is the fact that many of these cases raise new puzzles about how law and courts fit into their political and social environments that either do not exist in the American context or cannot be readily examined in the American case. The struggle to establish independent judiciaries and the rule of law in countries undergoing democratization and economic development pose unique challenges and suggest a range of distinctive research questions and evidence to be examined (Chavez 2008; Ginsburg 2008; Vanberg 2008).

Historical institutionalist studies have recovered an interest in constitutional ideas and historical development and wedded it to the post-behavioralist concern with political action and the broader political system. Scholars working in this vein have been particularly interested in patterns and mechanisms of continuity and change in the American legal and constitutional systems. This work takes seriously the possibility that ideas matter within law and politics and that the ideational context within which judges and political actors operate is itself of interest and worthy of study. At the same time, historical institutionalist studies have examined how a range of political and judicial actors have sought to advance their perceived interests and commitments through legal and judicial means, respond to exercises of judicial power, and adjust to conflicting visions of legal and constitutional requirements (Smith 2008).

Game theoretic accounts of political strategy have come forth and provided new perspectives on judicial behavior and new approaches to linking courts with other political institutions. Such work has tended to emphasize the ways in which judges interact with various other actors in the political system, from legislators to litigators to other judges, and to detail the logic of those interactions. Although it is being increasingly integrated into all aspects of law and politics work, it has also brought an interdisciplinary component to the field and focused attention on questions relating to the development of doctrine and administrative law that had otherwise been overshadowed (Spiller and Gely 2008; Kornhauser 2008).

2 THE STRUCTURE OF THE FIELD

There is no single best way to divide up the field of law and politics. Literatures over-lap, and it is possible to view those literatures at different levels of aggregation or with different points of emphasis so as to highlight commonalities or differences. Indeed, the prior discussion suggests a basic bifurcation in the field, between constitutional law and jurisprudence on the one side and judicial process and politics on the other. But this basic bifurcation better reflects the historical evolution of the field than it does the current structure of the study of law and politics. We offer below one map of the field.

2.1 Jurisprudence and the Philosophy of Law

Jurisprudence and the philosophy of the law is the oldest aspect of the study of law and politics and stands conceptually at its foundation. Particularly as it emerged from the continuing debates over the work of H. L. A. Hart (1994), jurisprudence is concerned with the basic nature of law. It has sought to identify the essential elements of law, distinguishing the realm of law from other aspects of the social order and other forms of social control. In an older tradition, jurisprudence hoped to systematize legal knowledge, extracting and refining the central principles of the law and the logical coherence of the legal system as a whole. In this mode, jurisprudence was to be an essential tool of the legal teacher, scholar, and practitioner and the starting point of a legal science. When wedded to normative commitments and theories, jurisprudence was also a tool of legal reform, identifying where the law needed to be worked pure and how best to do so.

A primary task of jurisprudence is to answer the question: What is law? It seeks to identify the common features of a legal system and clarify the logical structure of law. To do so requires distinguishing law from other normative systems of social ordering, such as custom and religion. Basic to this enquiry has been the effort to identify the conditions that would render a norm legally valid. Two well-established schools of thought have developed around these questions, with natural lawyers contending that the legal validity of a rule depends in part on its substantive morality and legal positivists arguing that legal validity is potentially independent of morality and solely a function of social convention. Related to this issue are such concerns as clarifying the nature of legal concepts such as rights and duties, identifying the kinds of reasons by which legal authority is established and legal obligations are created, and explicating the process of legal reasoning. Supplementing analytical approaches to these issues are distinctively normative jurisprudential theories, which are concerned with which legal rights and obligations are most justified, how best to reason about the law, and the like.

These predominant branches of jurisprudence have been periodically challenged by self-consciously realist theories of law that attempt to ground the basic features of law in social conditions. From Roscoe Pound's sociological jurisprudence at the turn of the twentieth century (which urged judges to take greater account of the social conditions in which the law operated) onward, realist theorists have questioned whether law can be profitably analyzed in the abstract, apart from its relationship with external conditions, whether economic relations, human behavior, or something else. The linkage of legal theory with such empirical concerns has supported both critical theories aimed at subverting dominant jurisprudential models and more positive theories concerned with developing their own understandings of the law.

2.2 Constitutional Law, Politics, and Theory

Constitutional law is often paired with jurisprudence. The subfields share interests in the substance of law and ideas surrounding law. They also share an interest in normative aspects of law. But where jurisprudence is concerned with the conceptual underpinnings of law writ large, constitutional law is concerned with the legal and theoretical foundations of a particular, and a particular kind of, political order.

The subfield has long been concerned with constitutional law itself. In this vein, political scientists have, along with legal scholars, explored the doctrinal developments in particular areas of law. In addition, however, political scientists have been somewhat more likely to examine the intellectual history of constitutional concepts and modes of thought, the normative underpinnings of constitutional principles, the constitutional philosophies of individual justices or historical eras, and the relationship between constitutional law and broader political and social currents. Political scientists have been attracted to constitutional law as intellectual historians, normative political theorists, and social theorists, as well as legal doctrinalists.

In recent years, the study of constitutional law per se has been submerged within the broader subject of constitutional politics. Although there have been notable exceptions, constitutional law has traditionally been the particular subject area within which political scientists have explored the origin, development, and application of legal principles and the interaction of courts and judges with other institutions and actors on the political stage. Whether taking the form of individual case histories or broader analyses, the making of constitutional law can be studied like the making of other forms of public policy. Constitutional politics highlights the ways in which the creation of constitutional law is situated within a broader political, institutional, and intellectual context and the significance of actors other than judges in contributing to constitutional policy-making and implementing constitutional norms. More broadly still, understanding the design, founding, maintenance, and failure of constitutional systems requires looking far beyond courts and constitutional law.

2.3 Judicial Politics

The field within political science that studies law and politics was once widely known as "public law." For many, it is now known as "judicial politics." The behavioral revolution of the 1960s shifted the disciplinary center of gravity from the study of constitutional law and doctrine to the study of courts, judges, and company. The political process by which courts are constituted and legal decisions are made and implemented is central to the empirical research in the field (Segal 2008).

Originally, the study of the voting behavior of individual judges, in particular the justices on the Supreme Court, formed the core of the study of judicial politics: Why do judges vote as they do, as opposed to the how and the why of the reasons they give in opinions? What do the patterns of votes within the Court and other collegial courts tell us about these institutions as political actors? Now, judicial voting is but a part, albeit an important part, of the study of judicial politics. Scholars increasingly are taking a broader view, and are attempting to study the behavior of judges and courts in the political process, as just one more group or political actor among many others, including other courts and judges, executives, legislatures, interest groups, lawyers, and ordinary citizens.

An array of research questions has occupied scholarly attention within this rubric over time. Particularly prominent have been variations on the question of whether, to what degree, or how "law" matters to judicial decision-making. A particularly strong version of the political perspective would assert that judges are simply policy-makers, and, if sufficiently insulated from review or reprisal, will enact their policy preferences if given the opportunity. If so, we might expect that traditional "legal" factors such as textual language, established precedents, or judicial philosophies should have little independent significance in shaping judicial decisions, at least on courts such as the US Supreme Court. If such factors do matter, we would want to know how, under what circumstances, and with what significance. But scholars have also given attention to other concerns, including the internal decision-making processes within and between courts and the effects that various external factors such as the composition of the elected branches, the activities of interest groups, or public opinion might have on judicial decisions.

2.4 Law and Society

Law and society is not a subfield within political science, but rather an interdisciplinary enterprise that has long invited political scientists to explore a broader range of legal phenomena and to employ a broader range of methodologies. Law and society scholarship explores the reciprocal impact of law on society and of society on law—with some scholars focusing on the role of law as an instrument of social change or social control and others focusing on how social mobilization, culture, and legal consciousness determine the actual impact of law. With its roots in the legal realism scholarship of the 1950s, law and society scholarship proliferated in the 1960s with the founding of the Law and Society Association in the United States. Today the field of law and society includes a vibrant mix of scholars from political science, sociology, anthropology, history, and law who draw on a variety of methods and epistemological premisses.

Law and society scholarship has served as an important antidote to the tendency of most political scientists interested in law and courts to focus almost exclusively on the upper echelons of the judicial hierarchy and the storied battles between high courts and other branches of government. The law and society perspective has encouraged many political scientists to turn their gaze to the local level, to explore how law is mobilized, how it is experienced, and what impact it has across society in fields as diverse as criminal law, civil rights, and business regulation. Such contributions are perhaps most obvious in studies of legal mobilization and the impact of law, where law and society scholarship has shed light on the conditions under which social movements mobilize law in pursuit of their aims and the consequences of legal actions for those who are subject to the law. Such scholarship famously includes so-called "gap" studies, which frequently document the gap between "law on the books" and "law on the ground" and the inadequate or incomplete implementation of or compliance with court decisions or legal regulations. Law and society has also encouraged a comparative perspective, with the field shifting from its roots in studies of the American legal system to embrace an increasingly wide range of scholarship on comparative and transnational sociolegal issues. Some scholars (Provine 2007) suggest a growing rift between much of political science and the field of law and society, as the latter shifts away from an interest in formal institutions of law and government and from positivist social science. Given the fruitful engagement of political science and law and society over the past half-century, the growth of any such rift would be unfortunate.

2.5 Comparative and International Law and Courts

Until recently, the subfield of comparative politics largely ignored law and politics while the subfield of law and politics largely ignored law and courts outside the USA. Today change is coming from both directions. Comparatists are taking greater interest in the politics of law and courts, and scholars in the law and politics sub-field are increasingly doing comparative work. Current scholarship builds on the work of such pioneers as Murphy and Tanenhaus (1972), Schubert and Danelski (1969), Shapiro (1981), Kommers (1989), Stone (1992), and Volcansek (1992), who set out a research agenda, calling on others to examine and compare the influence of courts on politics and the influence of politics on courts across democracies. Although most of the early work focused exclusively on the politics of constitutional courts in established democracies, more recent work has expanded in two directions. First, the transitions to democracy in the 1980s and 1990s gave birth to a host of new constitutional courts in Latin America, Eastern Europe, and Asia which have spawned a new wave of scholarly research. Second, in studying the widespread "judicialization" of politics, comparatists have moved beyond an exclusive focus on constitutional courts to examine the role of the full range of administrative and civil courts in policy-making and implementation.

In the study of international law, the growing dialogue between legal scholars and political scientists has generated a rich literature. The institutionalist turn in international relations theory and the proliferation of international courts and law-based regimes have drawn more and more political scientists to the study of international law and legal institutions. Meanwhile, recognizing the limits of a strictly legal analysis, legal scholars have turned to international relations theory to help explain the design, operation, and impact of international rules and legal institutions. Finally, research on themes such as the globalization of law and European legal integration tie together comparative and international approaches, examining how international institutions and networks may spread legal norms and practices across jurisdictions.

The study of law and politics is as wide-ranging and diverse as it has ever been. Scholars in the field are exploring a greater number of research questions with a wider range of methods and across a wider array of subjects related to law and courts than has ever been the case. In doing so, they have built bridges between political science and other disciplines and between the particular study of law and politics and other subfields within political science. The field has long run the risk of internal balkanization, but the opportunities for dialogue and synthesis are particularly high at this point in the development of the field.

References

Almond, G. A. 1990. *A Discipline Divided: Schools and Sects in Political Science.* Newbury Park, Calif.: Sage.

Chavez, R. B. 2008. The rule of law and courts in democratizing regimes. In *Oxford Handbook of Law and Politics*, ed. K. E. Whittington, R. D. Kelemen, and G. A. Caldeira. New York: Oxford University Press.

Corwin, E. S. 1929. The democratic dogma and the future of political science. *American Political Science Review*, 23: 569–92.

Friedrich, C. J. 1958. Political philosophy and the science of politics. In *Approaches to the Study of Politics*, ed. R. Young. Evanston, Ill.: Northwestern University Press.

Ginsburg, T. 2008. The global spread of constitutional review. In *Oxford Handbook of Law and Politics*, ed. K. E. Whittington, R. D. Kelemen, and G. A. Caldeira. New York: Oxford University Press.

Haines, C. G. 1915. Report of the Committee of Seven on Instruction in Colleges and Universities. *American Political Science Review*, 9: 351–74.

Hall, A. B. 1922. The teaching of constitutional law. *American Political Science Review*, 16: 486–96.

Hart, H. L. A. 1994. *The Concept of Law*, 2nd edn. New York: Oxford University Press.

Hoxie, R. G., et al. 1955. *A History of the Faculty of Political Science, Columbia University.* New York: Columbia University Press.

Kommers, D. 1989. *The Constitutional Jurisprudence of the Federal Republic of Germany.* Durham, NC: Duke University Press.

Kornhauser, L. A. 2008. The analysis of courts in the economic analysis of law. In *Oxford Handbook of Law and Politics*, ed. K. E. Whittington, R. D. Kelemen, and G. A. Caldeira. New York: Oxford University Press.

McCloskey, R. G. 1958. American political thought and the study of politics. In *Approaches to the Study of Politics*, ed. R. Young. Evanston, Ill.: Northwestern University Press.

Mather, L. 2008. Law and society. In *Oxford Handbook of Law and Politics*, ed. K. E. Whittington, R. D. Kelemen, and G. A. Caldeira. New York: Oxford University Press.

Murphy, W. F. and Tanenhaus, J. 1972. *The Study of Public Law*. New York: Random House.

Peltason, J. W. 1955. *Federal Courts in the Political Process*. New York: Random House.

—— 1961. *Fifty-Eight Lonely Men*. New York: Harcourt, Brace and World.

Pritchett, C. H. 1948. *The Roosevelt Court*. New York: Macmillan.

—— 1954. *Civil Liberties and the Vinson Court*. Chicago: University of Chicago Press.

—— 1968. Public law and judicial behavior. *Journal of Politics*, 30: 480–509.

Provine, D. M. 2007. Law & society symposium: on separate paths. *Law and Courts*, Newsletter of the Law and Courts Section of the American Political Science Association, 17: 6–8.

Schubert, G. A. 1966. The future of public law. *George Washington Law Review*, 34: 591–614.

—— and Danelski, D. J. (eds.) 1969. *Comparative Judicial Behavior: Cross-Cultural Studies of Political Decision Making in East and West*. New York: Oxford University Press.

Segal, J. A. 2008. Judicial behavior. In *Oxford Handbook of Law and Politics*, ed. K. E. Whittington, R. D. Kelemen, and G. A. Caldeira. New York: Oxford University Press.

Shapiro, M. 1981. *Courts: A Comparative and Political Analysis*. Chicago: University of Chicago Press.

Smith, R. M. 2008. Historical institutionalism and the study of law. In *Oxford Handbook of Law and Politics*, ed. K. E. Whittington, R. D. Kelemen, and G. A. Caldeira. New York: Oxford University Press.

Somit, A. and Tanenhaus, J. 1967. *The Development of Political Science: From Burgess to Behavioralism*. Boston: Allyn and Bacon.

Spiller, P. T. and Gely, R. 2008. Strategic judicial decision-making. In *Oxford Handbook of Law and Politics*, ed. K. E. Whittington, R. D. Kelemen, and G. A. Caldeira. New York: Oxford University Press.

Stone, A. 1992. *The Birth of Judicial Politics in France*. New York: Oxford University Press.

Vanberg, G. 2008. Establishing and maintaining judicial independence. In *Oxford Handbook of Law and Politics*, ed. K. E. Whittington, R. D. Kelemen, and G. A. Caldeira. New York: Oxford University Press.

Volcansek, M. 1992. *Judicial Politics and Policy-Making in Western Europe*. London: Cass.

Wilson, J. 1896. *The Works of James Wilson*, ed. J. D. Andrews, 2 vols. Chicago: Callaghan.

CHAPTER 13

···

THE
JUDICIALIZATION
OF POLITICS

···

RAN HIRSCHL

THE judicialization of politics—the reliance on courts and judicial means for address-ing core moral predicaments, public policy questions, and political controversies—is arguably one of the most significant phenomena of late twentieth and early twenty-first century government. Armed with newly acquired judicial review procedures, national high courts worldwide have been frequently asked to resolve a range of issues, varying from the scope of expression and religious liberties, equality rights, privacy, and reproductive freedoms, to public policies pertaining to criminal justice, property, trade and commerce, education, immigration, labor, and environmental protection. Bold newspaper headlines reporting on landmark court rulings concerning hotly contested issues—same sex marriage, limits on campaign financing, and affirmative action, to give a few examples—have become a common phenomenon. This is evident in the United States, where the legacy of active judicial review recently marked its bicentennial anniversary; here, courts have long played a significant role in policy-making. And it is just as evident in younger constitutional democracies that have established active judicial review mechanisms only in the last few decades. Meanwhile, transnational tribunals have become the main loci for coordinating policies at the global or regional level, from trade and monetary issues to labor standards and environmental regulations.

However, the growing political significance of courts has not only become more globally widespread than ever before. It has also expanded its scope to become a manifold, multifaceted phenomenon that extends well beyond the now "standard" concept of judge-made policy-making, through ordinary rights jurisprudence and judicial redrawing of legislative boundaries between state organs. The judicialization of politics now includes the wholesale transfer to the courts of some of the most pertinent and polemical political controversies a democratic polity can contemplate. Recall such matters as the outcome of the American presidential election of 2000 or the Mexican presidential election in 2006, the war in Chechnya, the Pervez Musharraf-led military *coup d'état* in Pakistan, Germany's place in the EU, restorative justice dilemmas in post-authoritarian Latin America, post-Communist Europe, or post-apartheid South Africa, the secular nature of Turkey's political system, Israel's fundamental definition as a "Jewish and Democratic State," or the political future of Quebec and the Canadian federation: all of these and many other "existential" political controversies worldwide have been framed as constitutional issues. And this has been accompanied by the concomitant assumption that courts—not politicians or the demos itself—are the appropriate fora for making these key decisions.

Despite the increasing prevalence of this trend, academic discourse addressing the judicialization of politics worldwide remains surprisingly sketchy. With a few notable exceptions (e.g. Tate and Vallinder 1995; Goldstein et al. 2001; Hirschl 2002; 2004*a*; 2006; Ferejohn 2002; Shapiro and Stone Sweet 2002; Pildes 2004; Sieder et al. 2005), the judicialization of politics is often treated as an obvious byproduct of the global convergence toward constitutional supremacy and the prevalence of rights discourse. What is more, the judicialization of politics is often used indiscriminately to refer to what in fact are several distinct phenomena: these range from judicial activism and rights jurisprudence to debates over judicial appointments and the politicization of the judiciary—the inevitable flip side of judicialization.

This chapter presents a lucid vocabulary and a coherent framework for analyzing the scope, nature, and causes of the judicialization of politics as we now know it. I begin with a classification of the various categories and instances of the trend that is broadly referred to as the judicialization of politics. I illustrate the distinct characteristics of each of these groupings of judicialization through recent jurisprudence of courts and tribunals worldwide. Special attention is given to the judicialization of "mega" or "pure" politics—by this I mean the transfer to courts of contentious issues of an outright political nature and significance. In the chapter's second part, I explore the main theories that purport to identify the central institutional, societal, and political conditions that are conducive to the judicialization of politics.

1 WHAT IS THE JUDICIALIZATION OF POLITICS?

The "judicialization of politics" is an often umbrella-like term referring to what are really three interrelated processes. At the most abstract level, the term refers to the spread of legal discourse, jargon, rules, and procedures into the political sphere and policy-making fora and processes. The ascendancy of legal discourse and the popularization of legal jargon is evident in virtually every aspect of modern life. It is perhaps best illustrated by the subordination of almost every decision-making forum in modern rule-of-law polities to quasi-judicial norms and procedures. Matters that had previously been negotiated in an informal or nonjudicial fashion have now come to be dominated by legal rules and procedures (Sieder et al. 2005, 5). The proliferation of legalistic discourse and procedures seems to reflect the common translation of fundamental justice into what is predominantly procedural fairness. Judicialization of this type is inextricable from law's capture of social relationships and popular culture and its expropriation of social conflicts (Teubner 1987; Habermas 1988). Related aspects of this type of "juridification" of modern life have also been identified by early legal sociologists—for example, Henry Maine and Emile Durkheim's "from status to contract" thesis (Maine 2000 [1861]; Durkheim 1964 [1893]); or Max Weber's emphasis on the rise of a formal, unambiguous, and rational legal system in Western societies (Weber 1978 [1914]).

A second, more concrete aspect of the judicialization of politics is the expansion of the province of courts and judges in determining public policy outcomes, mainly through administrative review, judicial redrawing of bureaucratic boundaries between state organs, and "ordinary" rights jurisprudence. Not a single week passes by without a national high court somewhere in the world releasing a major judgment pertaining to the scope of constitutional rights protections or the limits on legislative or executive powers. Of these, the most common are cases dealing criminal due process rights and other aspects of procedural justice. Also common are rulings involving classic civil liberties, various aspects of the rights to privacy, and formal equality—all of which expand and fortify the boundaries of the constitutionally protected private sphere, often perceived as threatened by the long arm of the encroaching state and its regulatory laws (Hirschl 2004a, 103–18). This ever-expanding body of civil liberties jurisprudence has essentially redefined the boundaries of the private sphere in constitutional democracies, and has transformed numerous policy areas involving individual freedoms.

The proliferation of administrative agencies in the modern welfare state has expanded the scope of administrative review by courts. More often than not, such judicial involvement in public policy-making is confined to procedural aspects, focusing on process rather than substance. Drawing upon basic norms from contract law, constitutional law, and mainly administrative law, courts oversee and enforce the application of due process, equal opportunity, transparency, accountability, and reasonableness in public policy-making. It is therefore not surprising that judicialization of this type dominates the justice system itself, from civil procedure to criminal due process; it is particularly noticeable in other process-heavy policy areas such as immigration, taxation, or public tenders. But it is also clearly evident in countless other areas, from urban planning and public health to industrial relations and consumer protection. In short, whereas the first type of judicialization may be described as "juridification of social relations," judicialization of this second type manifests itself mainly in the domain of procedural justice and formal fairness in public policy-making processes.

Over the last two decades, the judicialization of public policy-making has also proliferated at the international level (Romano 1999; Slaughter 2000; Goldstein et al. 2001), with the establishment of numerous transnational courts and quasi-judicial tribunals, panels, and commissions dealing with human rights, transnational governance, trade, and monetary affairs. Perhaps nowhere is this process more evident than in Europe (e.g. Weiler 1999; Stone Sweet 2000). The European Court of Justice (ECJ) interprets the treaties upon which the European Union is founded and the enormous body of EU secondary legislation, and has been awarded an increasingly important status by legislators, executives, and judiciaries in the now eastward-expanded EU, particularly with respect to interstate legal and economic disputes. The European Court of Human Rights in Strasbourg, the judicial arm of the Council of Europe, has in effect become the final court of appeal on human-rights issues for most of Europe. The judgments of these courts (as well as of other supranational tribunals such as the Inter-American Court of Human Rights) carry great symbolic weight and have forced many countries to incorporate transnational legal standards into their domestic legal system.

A similar process has taken place with respect to international trade disputes. Decisions by the World Trade Organization's (WTO) dispute settlement mechanism have had far-reaching implications for trade and commerce policies at the national level. This is also the case even in the United States, where compliance with unfavorable rulings by foreign tribunals has always been a tough sell. The 1994 North America Free Trade Agreement (NAFTA) also establishes quasi-judicial dispute resolution processes regarding foreign investment, financial services, and antidumping and countervailing instances. Similar arrangements were established by the MERCO-SUR agreement in South America and ASEAN in the Asia-Pacific region. In short, a large-scale transfer of crucial policy-making prerogatives—from policy-making bodies and majoritarian decision-making arenas at the national level to relatively insulated transnational entities and tribunals—has been rapidly established over the last few decades. This trend has been described as nothing short of a new world order (Slaughter 2004).

A third emerging class of the judicialization of politics is the reliance on courts and judges for dealing with what we might call "mega-politics:" core political controversies that define (and often divide) whole polities. The judicialization of mega-politics includes a few subcategories: judicialization of electoral processes; judicial scrutiny of executive branch prerogatives in the realms of macroeconomic planning or national security matters (i.e. the demise of what is known in constitutional theory as the "political question" doctrine); fundamental restorative justice dilemmas; judicial corroboration of regime transformation; and above all, the judicialization of formative collective identity, nation-building processes and struggles over the very definition—or *raison d'etre*—of the polity as such—arguably the most problematic type of judicialization from a constitutional theory standpoint. These emerging areas of judicialized politics expand the boundaries of national high-court involvement in the political sphere beyond the ambit of constitutional rights or federalism jurisprudence, and take the judicialization of politics to a point that far exceeds any previous limit. More often than not, this trend is supported, either tacitly or explicitly, by powerful political stakeholders. The result has been the transformation of supreme courts worldwide into a crucial part of their respective countries' national policy-making apparatus. Elsewhere I have described this process as a transition to juristocracy (Hirschl 2004a).

It is difficult to overstate the profoundness of this transition. Whereas oversight of the procedural aspects of the democratic process—judicial monitoring of electoral procedures and regulations, for example—falls within the mandate of most constitutional courts, questions such as a regime's legitimacy, a nation's collective identity, or a polity's coming to terms with its often less than admirable past, reflect primarily deep moral and political dilemmas, not judicial ones. As such, they ought—at least as a matter of principle—to be contemplated and decided by the populace itself, through its elected and accountable representatives. Adjudicating such matters is an inherently and substantively political exercise that extends beyond the application of rights provisions or basic procedural justice norms to various public policy realms. Judicialization of this type involves instances where courts decide on watershed political questions that face the nation, despite the fact that the constitution of that nation does not speak to the contested issues directly, and despite the obvious recognition of the very high political stakes for the nation. It is precisely these instances of judicialization of watershed national questions involving the intersection of very high political stakes with little or no pertinent constitutional guidelines that make the democratic credentials of judicial review most questionable. For it is ultimately unclear what makes courts the most appropriate forum for deciding such purely political quandaries.

The difference between the second and third face of judicialization is subtle, but it is important. It lies in part in the qualitative distinction between mainly procedural justice issues on the one hand, and substantive moral dilemmas or watershed political quandaries that the entire nation faces on the other. In other words, there seems to be a difference between the political salience of judicialization of public policy-making and the judicialization of mega-politics. Ensuring procedural fairness in public tenders is an important element of corruption-free public administration. But its political salience is not nearly as significant as that of purely political issues such as the place of Germany in the European Union, the future of Quebec and the Canadian federation, the constitutionality of the post-apartheid political pact in South Africa, or that of the boundaries of the Jewish collective in Israel.

But the difference between the second and third level of judicialized politics goes beyond the question of political salience. It depends on our conceptualization of the "political." What counts as a "political" decision is not an easy question to answer. A political decision must affect the lives of many people. However, many cases that are not purely political (e.g. large class-action lawsuits) also affect the lives of many people. More importantly, since there is no plain and simple answer to the question "what is political?"—for many social theorists, the answer to that question would be "everything is political"—there cannot be a plain and simple definition of the judicialization of politics either. Likewise, what may be considered a controversial political issue in one polity (say, the right to have an abortion in the United States) may be framed as a clash between domestic law and supranational law in another country (e.g. Ireland), or may be a nonissue in yet another polity. That said, there seems to be a qualitative difference between the political salience of (for example) a court ruling refining the boundaries of the right to fair hearing or reviewing the validity of federal quotas on agricultural export, and a landmark judgment determining the legitimacy of a polity's regime or a nation's collective identity and membership boundaries. Indeed, few decisions may be considered more "political" than authoritatively defining a polity's very *raison d'être*. That elusive yet intuitive distinction is what differentiates the judicialization of mega-politics form the first two levels of judicialization. Consider the following examples—all are seldom addressed by American constitutional theory, often preoccupied with rights jurisprudence and with matters American.

2 A NEW FRONTIER: THE JUDICIALIZATION OF "MEGA-POLITICS"

The judicialization of mega-politics includes several different types of controversies, not all of which are equally problematic from the standpoint of canonical constitutional theory. One emerging subcategory of judicialized mega-politics is the increased judicial scrutiny of core prerogatives of legislatures and executives in foreign affairs, fiscal policy, and national security. The Supreme Court of Canada was quick to reject the "political question" doctrine (nonjusticiability of explicitly political questions) following the adoption of the Canadian Charter of Rights and Freedoms in 1982. In its landmark ruling in *Operation Dismantle* (1985)—a challenge to the constitutionality of U.S. missile testing on Canadian soil—the Supreme Court of Canada held unanimously that "[i]f a case raises the question of whether executive or legislative action violated the Constitution, then the question has to be answered by the Court, regardless of the political character of the controversy... [d]isputes of a political or foreign policy nature may be properly cognizable by the courts."

In the *Chechnya Case* (1995), the Russian Constitutional Court agreed to hear petitions by a number of opposition members of the Duma, who challenged the constitutionality of three presidential decrees ordering the Russian military invasion of Chechnya. Rejecting Chechnya's claim to independence and upholding the constitutionality of President Yeltsin's decrees as *intra vires*, the majority of the judges of this court stated that maintaining the territorial integrity and unity of Russia was "[a]n unshakable rule that excludes the possibility of an armed secession in any federative state." In a similar fashion, the Israeli Supreme Court ruled in 2004 on the constitutionality and compatibility with international law of the West Bank barrier—a controversial network of fences and walls separating Israel from Palestinian territory. It also heard arguments concerning the constitutionality of matters such as the Oslo Peace Accords or Israel's unilateral pullback from the Gaza Strip. In recent years, constitutional courts in many countries have also begun the scrutiny of "process-light" measures adopted by governments to combat terrorism in the so-called "war on terror" era. In 1999, the Israeli Supreme Court banned the use of torture in interrogations by Israel's General Security Services. In late 2006 it ordered the weighing of security considerations against potential harm to civilians in determining the legality of "targeted killings" (the controversial practice of assassinating suspected Palestinian terrorists by Israel's security forces).

A slightly different, yet equally telling manifestation of judicial scrutiny of core executive prerogatives—this time in the context of national fiscal and welfare policy—can be found in the 1995 *Austerity Package Decisions* (the so-called "Bokros cases") by the Hungarian Constitutional Court. Here, the Court drew upon the concepts of reliance interest and legal certainty to strike down twenty-six provisions of a comprehensive economic emergency plan introduced by the government, the major thrust of which was a substantial cut in the government's expenditures on welfare benefits, pension allowances, education, and health care in order to reduce Hungary's enormous budget deficit and foreign debt. An equally significant manifestation of the judicialization of contentious macroeconomic matters is the Supreme Court of Argentina's October 2004 ruling (the so-called *Corralito Case*) on the constitutionality of the government's "pesification" plan (total convergence of the Argentine economy into pesos) and the corresponding freezing of savings deposits nominated in U.S. dollars—a fall-out of Argentina's major economic crisis of 2001.

A second area of increased judicial involvement in mega-politics is the corroboration of regime change. The most obvious example here is the "constitutional certification" saga in South Africa: This was the first time a constitutional court refused to accept a national constitutional text drafted by a representative constitution-making body. Other recent manifestations of this type of judicialization of mega-politics include the 2004 dismissal by the Constitutional Court of South Korea of the impeachment of President Roh Moo-hyun by South Korea's National Assembly (the first time in the history of modern constitutionalism that a president impeached by a legislative body has been reinstated by a judicial body); the rarely acknowledged yet astonishing restoration of the 1997 Fijian constitution by the Fijian Court of Appeals in *Fiji v. Prasad* 2001 (the first time in the history of modern constitutionalism that a polity's high court restored a constitution and the democratic system of government created by it); and the crucial yet seldom recognized involvement of the Pakistan Supreme Court in political transformation in that country (since 1990 Pakistan has known five regime changes and the Pakistan Supreme Court has played a key role in each of these radical transitions).

The judicialization of mega-politics is also increasingly evident in a third area: judicial oversight of electoral processes, or what may be referred to as "the law of democracy" (Miller 2004). The most prevalent subcategory here is the judicial scrutiny of the pre-electoral process in virtually all countries where elections, referenda, or plebiscites take place. In some instances this is done via scrutiny, at times compulsory, of candidates and voter registry by electoral commissions that often comprise judges. In terms of jurisprudence, courts are frequently called upon to decide on matters such as party funding, campaign financing, and broadcast advertising during election campaigns; the redrawing of electoral districts; and the approval or disqualification of political parties and candidates. Over the last decade, courts in a number of countries, notably Bangladesh, Belgium, India, Israel, Spain, Thailand, and Turkey, have banned (or come close to banning) popular political parties from participating in national elections. During the last decade alone, constitutional courts in over twenty-five countries have been called upon to determine the political future of prominent leaders through impeachment or disqualification trials. Courts approved (or disapproved) the extension of Colombia's President Alvaro Uribe, Uganda's President Yoweri Museveni, and Russia's President Boris Yeltsin's terms in office. Pakistan's former prime ministers Benazir Bhutto and Nawaz Sharif, and the Philippines' President Joseph Estrada—to give a few examples—have all had their political fate determined by courts. To that list one could add corruption indictments against heads of state (e.g. Italy's Silvio Berlusconi, Peru's Alberto Fujimori, or Thailand's Thaksin Shinawatra), and "political trials," in which prominent opposition candidates and leaders have been disqualified or otherwise removed from the race by a politicized judiciary.

Courts have also become ultimate decision-makers in disputes over national election outcomes, for example in Taiwan (2004), Georgia (2004), Puerto Rico (2004), Ukraine (2005), Congo (2006), Italy (2006), where the Constitutional Court approved a win of fewer than 25,000 votes by center-left leader Romano Prodi in one of Italy's closest elections. Likewise, a series of election appeals and counter-appeals culminated in Mexico's Federal Electoral Court's dismissal of leftist runner-up Andres Manuel Lopez Obrador's claim for a massive fraud by right-wing candidate and election winner Felipe Calderon in the July 2006 presidential election in that country. Calderon won the election by a less than 0.6 percent margin. Constitutional courts have also played key roles in deciding election outcomes in states and provinces. Even the fate of elections in the exotic island nations of Madagascar and Trinidad and Tobago has been determined by judicial tribunals. Clearly, the *Bush v. Gore* courtroom struggle over the fate of the American presidency was anything but an idiosyncratic moment in the recent history of comparative constitutional politics.

A fourth emerging area of mega-politics that has been rapidly judicialized over the past few decades is that of transitional or restorative justice. Quasi-judicial "truth commissions" or special tribunals dealing with core issues of transitional justice have been established in dozens of countries from El Salvador to Ghana. Recall, for example, the judicialization of restorative justice in the early years of the post-apartheid era in South Africa: Here, the "amnesty-for-confession" formula had been given a green light by the South African Constitutional Court in *AZAPO* (1996) allowing establishment of the quasi-judicial Truth and Reconciliation Commission. Similarly, the Pinochet affair can be thought of as an example of the judicialization of restorative justice dilemmas in post-authoritarian Latin America. Another example would be the major role played by the newly established constitutional courts in post-Communist Europe: these courts have played a central role in confronting their respective countries' pasts through the trials of former officeholders who committed what are now considered to be human rights violations during the Communist era. A paradigmatic case here is the 1993 decision of the constitutional court of the Czech Republic to uphold a law that declared the entire Communist era in the former Czechoslovakia illegal. These courts also made landmark rulings pertaining to Holocaust-related reparative justice and restitution policies. Yet another example would be the wholesale judicialization of the battle over the status of indigenous peoples in so-called "settler societies," particularly Australia, Canada, and New Zealand.

The judicialization of restorative justice is also evident at the transnational level. Here too there are many examples. The International Criminal Court (ICC) (ratified by ninety countries as of 2006) was established in 1998 as a permanent international judicial body with potentially universal jurisdiction pertaining to genocide, crimes against humanity, war crimes, and so on. The International Criminal Tribunal for the former Yugoslavia (ICTY) in The Hague was established in 1993. Another example here is the International Criminal Tribunal for Rwanda (ICTR) in Arusha, Tanzania, established in 1995. Also included in this category are the "hybrid courts" in Cambodia, East Timor, Kosovo, and Sierra Leone, which are all tribunals working within the rules and regulations of the domestic legal system, and applying a compound of international and national, substantial and procedural, law. Notorious leaders such as Slobodan Milosevic, Charles G. Taylor, and Saddam Hussein, were all put to trial before this new nexus of war crime tribunals.

But the clearest manifestation of the wholesale judicialization of core political controversies—arguably, the type of judicialization of politics that is the hardest to reconcile with canonical constitutional theory concerning the role of courts in a democracy—is the growing reliance on courts for contemplating the very definition, or *raison d'être*, of the polity as such. This type of judicialized "mega-politics" is common in fragmented polities facing deep ethnic, linguistic, or religious cleavages. A few examples of this phenomenon include: the central role the Turkish Constitutional Court has played in preserving the strictly secular nature of Turkey's political system, by continually outlawing antisecularist political forces and parties; the landmark jurisprudence of the Supreme Court of India pertaining to the status of Muslim and Hindu religious personal laws; the crucial role of courts in Egypt, Pakistan, Malaysia, or Nigeria in determining the applicability of Islamic *Shari'a* law in public life; the wholesale transfer of the deep secular/religious cleavage in Israeli society to the Israeli judiciary through the judicialization of the question of "who is a Jew?" and the corresponding entanglement of the Israeli Supreme Court in interpreting Israel's fundamental definition as a "Jewish and Democratic State." An example here is the German Federal Constitutional Court's key role in the creation of the unified Germany, illustrated for example in the *Maastricht Case* (1993): here, the Court drew upon Basic Law provisions to determine the status of post-unification Germany vis-à-vis the emerging European supranational polity. Another "textbook" illustration is the unprecedented involvement of the Canadian judiciary in dealing with the status of bilingualism and the political future of Quebec and the Canadian federation, including the Supreme Court of Canada's landmark ruling in the *Quebec Secession Reference* (1998)—the first time a democratic country had ever tested in advance the legal terms of its own dissolution. Following a slim loss by the Quebecois secessionist movement in the 1995 referendum, the federal government was quick to draw upon the reference procedure to ask the Supreme Court to determine whether a hypothetical unilateral secession declaration by the Quebec government would be constitutional. The court accepted the challenge with open arms and took the liberty to articulate with authority the fundamental pillars of the Canadian polity in a way no other state organ has ever done before.

In short, "nothing falls beyond the purview of judicial review; the world is filled with law; anything and everything is justiciable," as Aharon Barak, the former Chief Justice of the Supreme Court of Israel, once said; and this appears to have become a widely accepted motto by courts worldwide. While many public policy matters still remain beyond the ambit of the courts (Graber 2004; Schauer 2006), in numerous countries throughout the world, there has been a growing legislative deference to the judiciary, an increasing (and often welcomed) intrusion of the judiciary into the prerogatives of legislatures and executives, and a corresponding acceleration of the process whereby political agendas have been judicialized. Together, these developments have helped to bring about a growing reliance on adjudicative means for clarifying and settling fundamental moral controversies and highly contentious political questions, and have transformed national high courts into major political decision-making bodies.

The wave of judicial activism that has swept the globe in the last few decades has not bypassed the most fundamental issues a democratic polity ought to address— whether it is the corroboration of new political regimes, coming to terms with its own (often not so admirable) past, or grappling with its embedded collective identity quandaries. Although foundational political questions of this nature may have certain important constitutional aspects, they are neither purely, or even primarily, legal dilemmas. As such, one would think, they ought to be resolved, at least on the level of principle, through public deliberation in the political sphere. Nonetheless, constitutional courts throughout the world have gradually become major decision-making bodies for dealing with precisely such dilemmas. Fundamental restorative justice, regime legitimacy, and collective identity questions have been framed in terms of constitutional claims (often for rights and entitlements), and as such have rapidly found their way to the courts.

3 Why the Judicialization of Politics?

Scholars have identified a number of possible reasons and explanations for the judicialization of politics. Akin to any other major sociolegal phenomenon, no simple or single explanation can account for its wide range of manifestations. Given that a confluence of elements must exist, it is most productive to consider the factors that are, *ceteris paribus*, conducive to the judicialization of politics. These may be grouped into three main categories: institutional features, judicial behavior, and political determinants.

3.1 Institutional Features

As a bare minimum, the judicialization of politics requires the existence of a reasonably independent judiciary, with a well-respected and fairly active apex court. It is also generally agreed that there is a close affinity between the existence of a constitutional catalogue of rights and viable judicial review mechanisms in a polity, and judicial activism on the part of that polity's judiciary. If the constitution does not list tangible and defensible rights that individuals hold against the state, then judicial review is based on limited *ultra vires* principles, and is generally confined to procedural matters. In these circumstances, intervention by the judiciary in fundamental moral controversies or in highly political or politicized issues is generally unlikely. On the other hand, the existence of a constitutional catalogue of rights and judicial review mechanisms not only provides the necessary institutional framework for courts to become more vigilant in their efforts to protect the fundamental rights and liberties of a given polity's residents; it also enables them to expand their jurisdiction to address vital moral dilemmas and political controversies of crucial significance to that polity.

What is more, the existence of a constitutional framework that facilitates judicial activism may provide political actors who are unable or unwilling to advance their policy preferences through majoritarian decision-making arenas with an alternative institutional channel (the courts) for accomplishing their policy goals. Likewise, the existence or adoption of a constitutional catalogue of rights is likely to increase the public's "rights awareness." It also allows for what may be referred to as "judicialization from below"—legal mobilization by groups and movements that aim to advance social change through constitutional rights litigation. Therefore, in countries where bills of rights and active judicial review procedures have been adopted, one can expect a significant growth in the frequency and scope of the exercise of judicial review, and a corresponding intrusion by the judiciary into the prerogatives of both legislatures and executives. Likewise, the adoption of multilateral treaties and international agreements that contain justiciable provisions, and the accompanying establishment of adjudication or arbitration tribunals at the supranational level, are preconditions for the judicialization of international trade disputes.

Models of judicial review employed by constitutional democracies vary significantly in their procedural characteristics—a fact that has important implications for
the scope and nature of judicial review in these countries. A pertinent distinction here
is between a priori or *abstract* review and a posteriori or *concrete* review—whether the
constitutionality of a law or administrative action is determined before or after it takes
effect, or whether a declaration of unconstitutionality can be made in the absence of
an actual case or controversy; in other words, the distinction is between hypothetical
"what if" scenarios ("abstract" review) and judicial review that may take place only
in the context of a specific legal dispute ("concrete" review). In the United States,
only a posteriori and *concrete* judicial review is allowed. Judicial review of legislation,
whether exercised by lower courts or by the Supreme Court, is a power that can only
be exercised by the courts within the context of concrete adversary litigation; i.e. when
the constitutional issue becomes relevant and requires resolution in the decision of
the case. In France, by contrast, judicial review is limited to an a priori and *abstract*
judicial review. The *Conseil Constitutionnel* has pre-enactment constitutional review
powers, but no power to nullify a law after it has been enacted by the legislature.

A number of leading democracies feature combined a priori/a posteriori, abstract
and concrete review systems. In the latter capacity, national high courts in such countries could outlaw a statute before it was formally enacted on the basis of hypothetical
constitutional arguments about its potential effect. Judicial review in Canada, for
example, is not limited to review within the context of concrete adversary litigation. The reference procedure allows both the federal and provincial governments
in Canada to refer proposed statutes or even questions concerning hypothetical legal
situations to the Supreme Court or the provincial courts of appeal for an advisory
(abstract) opinion on their constitutionality. It is hardly surprising therefore that
some of the most contentious issues in Canadian politics of the last few decades have
reached the Supreme Court through the reference procedure.

Moreover, unlike in the United States, most countries that employ an a priori and
abstract review model allow public officials, legislators, cabinet members, and heads
of state to initiate judicial scrutiny of proposed laws and hypothetical constitutional
scenarios, thereby providing a constitutional framework hospitable to the judicialization of politics and the accompanying politicization of the judiciary. In France
and Italy, for example, the initiation of constitutional litigation in constitutional
courts is limited to elected politicians. In other countries (Germany and Spain, for
example) elected officials may challenge proposed legislation through the abstract a
priori review. In short, a system that permits a priori and abstract review initiated
by politicians would appear to have a greater potential for generating high levels of
judicialized policy-making using the process of constitutional review (Stone 1992).
That said, scholars have correctly pointed out that "the apparently more restrictive
combination of *a posteriori* and concrete review has hardly relegated the U.S. Supreme
Court to a minor policy role" (Tate 1992, 6).

Another pertinent distinction is that which exists between *decentralized* (all courts)
and *centralized* (constitutional court) review. In a decentralized system (for example, in the U.S.), judicial review is an inherent competence of almost all courts in

nearly any type of case and controversy. The centralized judicial review system (often referred to as "constitutional review") is characterized by having only a single state organ (a separate judicial body in the court system or an extrajudicial body) acting as a constitutional tribunal. This model of judicial review has been adopted by many European countries that follow various branches of the civil law tradition (such as Germany, Austria, Italy, and Spain), as well as by almost all new democracies in post-Communist Europe. Some new constitutionalist countries (such as Portugal) employ a combined decentralized/centralized model of judicial/constitutional review.

Other variables being equal, the impact of the judiciary on public policy outcomes is likely to be more significant under a decentralized, all-court review system. As Tate points out, "restricting the power to declare legislation and regulations unconstitutional to a constitutional court ... sharply reduces the number of occasions and range of policy issues on which courts can be invited (or can invite themselves) to exercise judicial review" (1992, 7). That said, administrative review—however limited—is always available to the courts in most centralized review countries. Moreover, the symbolic importance of landmark high-court decisions in such countries is at least as significant as that of national high-court rulings in countries employing a decentralized review system. Germany's Federal Constitutional Court and the youthful Hungarian Constitutional Court are perhaps the most frequently mentioned examples of centralized judicial bodies that not only fulfill the sole function of judicial review in their respective countries, but have also become crucial policy-making bodies at the national level (Kommers 1997; Sólyom and Brunner 2000).

Another important aspect of judicial review that has implications for the judicialization of politics is the question of standing (*locus standi*) and access rights: Who may initiate a legal challenge to the constitutionality of legislation or official action; and at what stage of the process may a given polity's supreme court become involved. In the United States, standing rights have been traditionally limited to individuals who claim to have been affected by an allegedly unconstitutional legislation or official action. The U.S. Supreme Court will not hear a challenge to the constitutionality of legislation unless all other possible legal paths and remedies have been exhausted. Moreover, the Court has full discretion over which cases it will hear—its docket therefore consists of "discretionary leave" cases, rather than appeals by right. However, constitutional democracies that employ a priori and abstract judicial review (such as France) allow for, and even encourage, public officials and political actors to challenge the constitutionality of proposed legislation. Several polities authorize their constitutional court judges, in an *ex-officio* capacity, to initiate proceedings against an apparently unconstitutional law. Other countries (South Africa, for example) impose mandatory referrals of constitutional questions by lower courts to a constitutional tribunal. And yet other countries, most notably Israel and India, allow private-person constitutional grievances to be submitted directly to their respective high courts. In addition to legislative frameworks, constitutional courts in most liberal democracies have continuously liberalized the rules of standing and expanded intervener (e.g. *amicus curiae*) status. Other variables being equal, liberal standing and accessibility rights along with lowered barriers of nonjusticiability provides an important institutional channel through which ordinary citizens can challenge what they regard as infringements upon their constitutionally protected rights before a country's judicial system, thereby increasing the likelihood of judicial involvement in public policy-making.

3.2 Judicial Behavior

The rise of "philosopher king courts" cannot be attributed solely or even primarily to the existence of a constitutional framework conducive to the judicialization of politics. It depends to a large extent upon judicial willingness to engage in public policy-making. In that respect, an increasing number of scholars suggest that judges do not behave or reach decisions in a way that is fundamentally different from other branches of government. Courts are political institutions not merely because they are politically constructed, but also because the determinants of judicial behavior are not distinctly different from the determinants of decision-making by other public officials. Judicial behavior, especially by constitutional courts in cases involving politically charged issues, may be driven by adherence to national meta-narratives, responsiveness to public opinion, personal ideological preferences, collegial considerations, prevalent attitudes within the legal profession, or strategic considerations vis-à-vis other national decision-making bodies.

Of particular relevance to the judicialization of politics are some insights drawn from the strategic approach to the study of judicial behavior. Like most other institutions, courts and judges are strategic actors to the extent that they seek to maintain or enhance their institutional position vis-à-vis other major national decision-making bodies or simply expand the ambit of their political influence and international profile. Accordingly, constitutional court rulings may not only be analyzed as mere acts of professional, apolitical jurisprudence (as doctrinal legalistic explanations of court rulings often suggest), or reflections of judicial ideology (as "attitudinal" models of judicial behavior might suggest), but also a reflection of judges' own strategic choices (Epstein and Knight 1998; 2000).

Courts may realize that there are circumstances—such as the changing fates or preferences of other influential political actors, or gaps in the institutional context within which they operate—in which they may be able to strengthen their own position by extending the scope of their jurisprudence and fortifying their status as crucial national policy-making bodies. The establishment of a supranational rule of law in Europe, for example, was driven in no small part by national judges' attempts to enhance their independence, influence, and authority vis-à-vis other courts and political actors (Alter 2001), as well as by a corresponding and continuous judicial activism by the ECJ (Mattli and Slaughter 1998; Weiler 1999). Conversely, credible threats on the court's autonomy and harsh political responses to unwelcome activism or interventions on the part of the courts have chilling effects on judicial decision-making patterns (Epstein et al. 2001; Helmke 2005; Vanberg 2005). Courts must be responsive to the political environment in which they operate in other respects as well. Because justices do not have the institutional capacities to enforce their rulings, they must take into account the extent to which popular decision-makers will support their policy initiatives (McGuire and Stimson 2004). Judges seem to care about their reputation within their close social milieu, court colleagues, and the legal profession more generally (Baum 2006). And with the increasing internationalization of constitutional discourse, the judicialization of politics (primarily through constitutional rights litigation) may also support the interests of a supreme court seeking to increase its symbolic power and international prestige by fostering its alignment with a growing community of liberal democratic nations engaged in judicial review and rights-based discourses.

The centrality of judicial will in explaining the judicialization of politics is often emphasized by constitutional theorists critical of judicial activism. With a few exceptions, these critics often blame "power hungry" courts and judges for being too assertive and excessively entangled with moral and political decision-making, subsequently disregarding fundamental separation of powers and democratic governance principles. Even the more politically astute critics of the US Constitution's expropriation by the United States Supreme Court are more concerned with the Supreme Court's "imperialist" impulse than with the political conditions that promote the transition to juristocracy (e.g. Tushnet 1999; Bork 2001; Kramer 2004).

In my opinion, portraying courts and judges as the main source of judicialization is misguided. Courts are first and foremost political institutions. Like any other political institutions, they do not operate in an institutional or ideological vacuum. Their establishment does not develop and cannot be understood separately from the concrete social, political, and economic struggles that shape a given political system. Indeed, constitutionalization, political deference to the judiciary, and the expansion of judicial power more generally, are an integral part and an important manifestation of those struggles, and cannot be understood in isolation from them. And this brings us to the final category, political determinants of judicialization.

3.3 Political Determinants

A favorable constitutional framework and an active judiciary are important contributors to the judicialization of politics. However, this unprecedented level of political jurisprudence cannot develop, let alone be sustained, without the receptiveness and support, tacit or explicit, of the political sphere itself. Recent studies of comparative judicial politics propose a number of explanations for the expansion of judicial power and the corresponding judicialization of politics. These may be grouped into three subcategories: macro sociopolitical trends, the prevalence of rights discourse and litigation, and finally strategic maneuvering by powerful political stakeholders.

The proliferation of democracy worldwide is a main cause of judicialization and the expansion of judicial power more generally. By its very nature, the establishment of a democratic regime entails the establishment of some form of separation of powers among the major branches of government, as well as between the central

and provincial/regional legislatures. It also entails the presence of a set of procedural governing rules and decision-making processes to which all political actors are
required to adhere. The persistence and stability of such a system, in turn, requires
at least a semi-autonomous, supposedly apolitical judiciary to serve as an impartial
umpire in disputes concerning the scope and nature of the fundamental rules of
the political game. Active judicial review is both a prerequisite and a byproduct of
viable democratic governance in multilayered federalist countries (Shapiro 1999). In
other words, more democracy equals more courts. However, the "proliferation of
democracy" thesis cannot provide a full explanation for the significant variations in
levels of judicialization among new democracies. And it does not provide an adequate
explanation for increased levels of judicialization in polities that have not undergone
any apparent changes in their political regime.

From a functionalist standpoint, judicialization may emanate from the proliferation in levels of government and the corresponding emergence of a wide variety of
semi-autonomous administrative and regulatory state agencies as the main driving
forces behind the expansion of judicial power over the past few decades (Shapiro
and Stone Sweet 2002). According to this thesis, independent and active judiciaries
armed with judicial review practices are necessary for efficient monitoring of the ever-
expanding administrative state. Moreover, the modern administrative state embodies
notions of government as an active policy-maker, rather than a passive adjudicator
of conflicts. It therefore requires an active, policy-making judiciary (Feely and Rubin
1998). Along the same lines, the judicialization of politics may emanate from a general
waning of confidence in technocratic government and planning, and a consequent
desire to restrict the discretionary powers of the state, resulting in a diffusion of
judicial power (Shapiro 1999). It may also stem from the increasing complexity
and contingency of modern societies (Luhmann 1985), and/or from the creation
and expansion of the modern welfare state with its numerous regulatory agencies
(Teubner 1987; Habermas 1988). Some accounts of the rapid growth of judicialization
at the supranational judicial level portray it as an inevitable institutional response
to complex coordination problems deriving from the systemic need to adopt standardized legal norms and administrative regulations across member states in an era
of converging economic markets (Stone Sweet 2000). In some instances, economic
liberalization may be an important pro-judicialization factor. In the regulatory arena,
the combination of privatization and liberalization may encourage "juridical regulation" (Vogel 1998; Kelemen and Sibbitt 2004).

A second approach emphasizes the prevalence of rights discourse or greater awareness to rights issues, which is likely to yield what may be termed "judicialization
from below." Charles Epp (1998) suggests that the impact of constitutional catalogues
of rights may be limited by individuals' inability to invoke them through strategic
litigation. Hence bills of rights matter to the extent that a support structure for legal
mobilization—a nexus of rights-advocacy organizations, rights-supportive lawyers
and law schools, governmental rights-enforcement agencies, and legal-aid schemes—
is well developed. In other words, while the existence of written constitutional provisions is a necessary condition for the effective protection of rights and liberties, it

is certainly not a sufficient one. The effectiveness of rights provisions in planting the seeds of social change in a given polity is largely contingent upon the existence of a support structure for legal mobilization, and more generally, sociocultural conditions that are hospitable for "judicialization from below."

Legal mobilization from below is aided by the commonly held belief that judicially affirmed rights are self-implementing forces of social change removed from the constraints of political power. This belief has gained a near-sacred status in public discussion. The "myth of rights" as Stuart Scheingold (1974) termed it, contrasts the openness of judicial proceedings to the secret bargaining of interest group pluralism so as to underscore the integrity and incorruptibility of the judicial process. "The aim, of course, is to enhance the attractiveness of legal and constitutional solutions to political problems" (1974, 34). This is turn may lead a spread of populist "rights talk" and the corresponding impoverishment of political discourse (Glendon 1991).

Similarly, an authentic, "bottom up" judicialization is more likely to occur when judicial institutions are perceived by social movements, interest groups, and political activists as more reputable, impartial, and effective decision-making bodies than other bureaucracy-heavy government institutions or biased majoritarian decision-making arenas (Tate and Valinder 1995). An all-encompassing judicialization of politics is, *ceteris paribus*, less likely to occur in a polity featuring a unified, assertive political system that is capable of restraining the judiciary. In such polities, the political sphere may signal credible threats to an overactive judiciary that exert a chilling effect on courts. Conversely, the more dysfunctional or deadlocked the political system and its decision-making institutions are in a given rule-of-law polity, the greater the likelihood of expansive judicial power in that polity (Guarnieri et al. 2002, 160–81). Greater fragmentation of power among political branches reduces their ability to rein in courts, and correspondingly increases the likelihood of courts asserting themselves (Ferejohn 2002).

A more "realist" approach suggests that the judicialization of politics is largely a function of concrete choices, interests, or strategic considerations by self-interested political stakeholders. From the politicians' point of view, delegating policy-making authority to the courts may be an effective means of shifting responsibility, and thereby reducing the risks to themselves and to the institutional apparatus within which they operate. The calculus of the "blame deflection" strategy is quite intuitive. If the delegation of powers can increase credit or legitimacy, and/or reduce the blame placed on the politician as a result of the delegated body's policy decision, then such delegation can benefit the politician (Voigt and Salzberger 2002). At the very least, the transfer to the courts of contested political "hot potatoes" offers a convenient retreat for politicians who have been unwilling or unable to settle contentious public disputes in the political sphere. It may also offer refuge for politicians seeking to avoid difficult or "no win" decisions and/or avoid the collapse of deadlocked or fragile governing coalitions (Graber 1993). Conversely, political oppositions may seek to judicialize politics (for example, through petitions and injunctions against government policies) in order to harass and obstruct governments (Tate and Vallinder 1995). At times, opposition politicians may resort to litigation in an attempt to enhance their media exposure, regardless of the actual outcome of litigation (Dotan and Hofnung 2005). A political quest for legitimacy often stands behind the transfer of certain regime-change questions to courts. (Consider the aforementioned Pakistani Supreme Court legitimization of the 1999 military *coup d'état* in that country). Empirical studies confirm that national high courts in most constitutional democracies enjoy greater public legitimacy and support than virtually all other political institutions. This holds true even when courts engage in explicit manifestations of political jurisprudence (Gibson et al. 2003).

Judicial empowerment may also reflect the competitiveness of a polity's electoral market or governing politicians' time horizons. According to the "party alternation" thesis, for example, when a ruling party expects to win elections repeatedly, the likelihood of an independent and powerful judiciary is low. However, when a ruling party has a low expectation of remaining in power, it is more likely to support a powerful judiciary to ensure that the next ruling party cannot use the judiciary to achieve its policy goals (Ramseyer 1994; Ginsburg 2003). Likewise, judicial empowerment may be driven by "hegemonic preservation" attempts taken by influential sociopolitical groups fearful of losing their grip on political power (Hirschl 2004a). Such groups and their political representatives—who possess disproportionate access to, and influence over, the legal arena—are more likely to delegate power to the judiciary when they find strategic drawbacks in adhering to majoritartian decision-making processes or when their world-views and policy preferences are increasingly challenged in such arenas. For example, constitutional courts have become key guardians of secular or moderate interests against the increasing popularity of principles of theocratic governance (Hirschl 2008). Likewise, when elected politicians are obstructed from fully implementing their own policy agenda, they may favor the active exercise of constitutional review by a sympathetic judiciary to overcome those obstructions (Hirschl 2004b; Whittington 2005). Powerful national high courts may allow governments to impose a centralizing "one rule fits all" regime upon enormous and diverse polities (Morton 1995; Goldstein 2001). (Think of the standardizing effect of apex court jurisprudence in vast and exceptionally diverse polities such as the United States or the European Union).

Perhaps the clearest illustration of the necessity of political support for the judicialization of mega-politics is the political sphere's decisive reaction to instances of unwelcome judicial activism. Occasionally, courts may respond to counter-establishment challenges by releasing rulings that threaten to alter the political power relations in which the courts are embedded. However, as the recent history of comparative constitutional politics tells us, recurrent manifestations of unsolicited judicial intervention in the political sphere in general—and unwelcome judgments concerning contentious political issues in particular—have brought about significant political backlashes, targeted at clipping the wings of over-active courts. These include legislative overrides of controversial rulings, political tinkering with judicial appointment and tenure procedures to ensure the appointment of "compliant" judges and/or to block the appointment of "undesirable" judges, "court-packing" attempts by political power holders, disciplinary sanctions, impeachment or removal of "objectionable" or "over-active" judges, the introduction of jurisdictional constraints, or clipping jurisdictional boundaries and judicial review powers. In some instances (e.g. Russia in 1993, or Ecuador in 2004, or Pakistan in 2007) they have resulted in constitutional crises leading to the reconstruction or dissolution of high courts. To this we may add another political response to unwelcome rulings: more subtle, and possibly more lethal, sheer bureaucratic disregard for, or protracted or reluctant implementation of, unwanted rulings (Rosenberg 1991; 1992; Garrett et al. 1998; Conant 2002). In short, the judicialization of politics is derivative first and foremost of political, not judicial, factors.

In sum, over the last few decades the world has witnessed a profound transfer of power from representative institutions to judiciaries, whether domestic or supranational. One of the main outcomes of this trend has been the transformation of courts and tribunals worldwide into major political decision-making loci. Over the last two decades, the judicialization of politics has extended well beyond the now "standard" judicialization of policy-making, to encompass questions of pure politics—electoral processes and outcomes, restorative justice, regime legitimacy, executive prerogatives, collective identity, and nation-building. These developments reflect the demise of the "political question" doctrine, and mark a transition to what I have termed "juristocracy." Akin to any other transformation of that scope and magnitude, the judicialization of politics is not derivative of a single cause. Instead, a confluence of institutional, societal, and political factors hospitable to the judicialization of politics is necessary to create and sustain it. Of these factors, three stand out as being crucial: the existence of a constitutional framework that promotes the judicialization of politics; a relatively autonomous judiciary that is easily enticed to dive into deep political waters; and above all, a political environment that is conducive to the judicialization of politics.

References

ALTER, K. 2001. *Establishing the Supremacy of European Law*. Oxford: Oxford University Press.

BAUM, L. 2006. *Judges and Their Audiences: A Perspective on Judicial Behavior*. Princeton, NJ: Princeton University Press.

BORK, R. H. 2002. *Coercing Virtue: The Worldwide Rule of Judges*. Toronto: Vintage Canada.

CONANT, L. 2002. *Justice Contained: Law and Politics in the European Union*. Ithaca, NY: Cornell University Press.

DOTAN, Y. and HOFNUNG, M. 2005. Legal defeats—political wins: why do elected representatives go to court? *Comparative Political Studies*, 38: 75–103.

DURKHEIM, E. 1964 [1893]. *The Division of Labor in Society*. New York: Free Press.

EPP, C. 1998. *The Rights Revolution: Lawyers, Activists and Supreme Courts in Comparative Perspective*. Chicago: University of Chicago Press.

EPSTEIN, L. and KNIGHT, J. 1998. *The Choices Justices Make*. Washington, DC: CQ Press.

—————— 2000. Towards a strategic revolution in judicial politics: a look back, a look ahead. *Political Research Quarterly*, 53: 625–61.

EPSTEIN, L., KNIGHT, J. and SHVETSOVA, O. 2001. The role of constitutional courts in the establishment and maintenance of democratic systems of government. *Law and Society Review*, 35: 117–63.

FEELEY, M. and RUBIN, E. 1998. *Judicial Policy Making and the Modern State: How the Courts Reformed America's Prisons*. Cambridge: Cambridge University Press.

FEREJOHN, J. 2002. Judicializing politics, politicizing Law. *Law and Contemporary Problems*, 61: 41–68.

GARRETT, G. et al. 1998. The politics of judicial integration in the European Union. *International Organization*, 49: 171–81.

GIBSON, J. L., CALDEIRA, G., and SPENCE, L. K. 2003. The Supreme Court and the U. S. presidential election of 2000: wounds, self-inflicted or otherwise? *British Journal of Political Science*, 33: 535–56.

GINSBURG, T. 2003. *Judicial Review in New Democracies: Constitutional Courts in Asian Cases*. Cambridge: Cambridge University Press.

GLENDON, M. A. 1991. *Rights Talk: The Impoverishment of Political Discourse*. New York: Free Press.

GOLDSTEIN, J. et al. (eds.) 2001. *Legalization and World Politics*. Cambridge, Mass.: MIT Press.

GOLDSTEIN, L. 2001. *Constituting Federal Sovereignty: The European Union in Comparative Context*. Baltimore: Johns Hopkins University Press.

GRABER, M. 1993. The nonmajoritarian difficulty: legislative deference to the judiciary. *Studies in American Political Development*, 7: 35–73.

—— 2004. Resolving political questions into judicial questions: Tocqueville's thesis revisited. *Constitutional Commentary*, 21: 485–545.

GUARNIERI, C. and PEDERZOLI, P. 2002. *The Power of Judges: A Comparative Study of Courts and Democracy*. New York: Oxford University Press.

HABERMAS, J. 1988. Law as medium and law as institution. In *Dilemmas of Law in the Welfare State*, ed. G. Teubner. Berlin: Walter De Gruyter.

HELMKE, G. 2005. *Courts under Constraints: Judges, Generals, and Presidents in Argentina*. New York: Cambridge University Press.

HIRSCHL, R. 2002. Repositioning the judicialization of politics: *Bush v. Gore* as a global trend. *Canadian Journal of Law and Jurisprudence*, 15: 191–218.

—— 2004a. *Towards Juristocracy: The Origins and Consequences of the New Constitutionalism*. Cambridge, Mass.: Harvard University Press.

—— 2004b. Constitutional courts vs. religious fundamentalism: three Middle Eastern tales. *Texas Law Review*, 82: 1819–60.

—— 2006. The new constitutionalism and the judicialization of pure politics worldwide. *Fordham Law Review*, 75: 721–53.

—— 2008. Juristocracy vs. theocracy: constitutional courts and the containment of religious fundamentalism, *Middle East Law and Governance*.

KELEMEN, D. and SIBBITT, E. 2004. The globalization of American law. *International Organization*, 58: 103–36.

KOMMERS, D. 1997. *The Constitutional Jurisprudence of the Federal Republic of Germany*. Durham, NC: Duke University Press.

KRAMER, L. 2004. *The People Themselves: Popular Constitutionalism and Judicial Review*. New York: Oxford University Press.

LUHMANN, N. 1985. *A Sociological Theory of Law*. London: Routledge.

MAINE, H. 2000 [1861]. *Ancient Law*. Washington, DC: Beard Books.

MATTLI, W. and SLAUGHTER, A.-M. 1998. Law and politics in the European Union: a reply to Garrett. *International Organization*, 49: 182–90.

McGUIRE, K. and STIMSON, J. 2004. The least dangerous branch revisited: new evidence on Supreme Court responsiveness to public preferences. *Journal of Politics*, 66: 1018–35.

MILLER, R. A. 2004. Lords of democracy: the judicialization of "pure politics" in the United States and Germany. *Washington and Lee Law Review*, 61: 587–662.

MORTON, F. L. 1995. The effect of the Charter of Rights on Canadian federalism. *Publius*, 25: 173–88.

PILDES, R. 2004. The Supreme Court, 2003 term—foreword: the constitutionalization of democratic politics. *Harvard Law Review*, 118: 29–160.

RAMSEYER, J. M. 1994. The puzzling (in)dependence of courts: a comparative approach. *Journal of Legal Studies*, 23: 721–48.

ROMANO, C. 1999. The proliferation of international judicial bodies: the pieces of the puzzle. *New York University Journal of International Law and Politics*, 31: 709–51.

ROSENBERG, G. 1991. *The Hollow Hope: Can Courts Bring About Social Change?* Chicago: University of Chicago Press.

—— 1992. Judicial independence and the reality of political power. *Review of Politics*, 54: 369–98.

SCHAUER, F. 2006. The Supreme Court, 2005 Term-foreword: the Court's agenda—and the nation's. *Harvard Law Review*, 120: 4–64.

SCHEINGOLD, S. 1974. *The Politics of Rights: Lawyers, Public Policy, and Political Change.* New Haven, Conn.: Yale University Press.

SHAPIRO, M. 1999. The success of judicial review. In *Constitutional Dialogues in Comparative Perspective*, ed. S. Kenney. New York: Palgrave Macmillan.

—— and STONE SWEET, A. 2002. *On Law, Politics, and Judicialization.* New York: Oxford University Press.

SIEDER, R., SCHJOLDEN, L., and ANGELL, A. (eds.) 2005. *The Judicialization of Politics in Latin America.* New York: Palgrave Macmillan.

SLAUGHTER, A.-M. 2000. Judicial globalization. *Virginia Journal of International Law*, 40: 1103–24.

—— 2004. *The New World Order.* Princeton, NJ: Princeton University Press.

SÓLYOM, L. and BRUNNER, G. 2000. *Constitutional Judiciary in a New Democracy: The Hungarian Constitutional Court.* Ann Arbor: University of Michigan Press.

STONE, A. 1992 *The Birth of Judicial Politics in France: The Constitutional Council in Comparative Perspective.* New York: Oxford University Press.

STONE SWEET, A. 2000. *Governing with Judges: Constitutional Politics in Europe.* Oxford: Oxford University Press.

TATE, C. N. 1992. Comparative judicial review and public policy: concepts and overview. In *Comparative Judicial Review and Public Policy*, ed. D. Jackson and C. N. Tate. Westport, Conn.: Greenwood Press.

—— and VALLINDER, T. (eds.) 1995. *The Global Expansion of Judicial Power.* New York: New York University Press.

TEUBNER, G. 1987. *Juridification of the Social Spheres.* Berlin: Walter de Gruyter.

TUSHNET, M. 1999. *Taking the Constitution Away from the Courts.* Princeton, NJ: Princeton University Press.

VANBERG, G. 2005. *The Politics of Constitutional Review in Germany.* Cambridge: Cambridge University Press.

VOGEL, S. 1998. *Freer Markets, More Rules.* Ithaca, NY: Cornell University Press.

VOIGT, S. and SALZBERGER, E. 2002. Choosing not to choose: when politicians choose to delegate powers. *Kyklos*, 55: 289–310.

WEBER, M. 1978 [1914]. *Economy and Society: An Outline of Interpretive Sociology.* Berkeley: University of California Press.

WEILER, J. H. H. 1999. *The Constitution of Europe: Do the New Clothes Have an Emperor?* Cambridge: Cambridge University Press.

WHITTINGTON, K. E. 2005. "Interpose your friendly hand:" political supports for the exercise of judicial review by the United States Supreme Court. *American Political Science Review,* 99: 583–96.

CHAPTER 14

....

JUDICIAL BEHAVIOR

....

JEFFREY A. SEGAL

WHAT do judges do and why do they do it? The answers to these questions fall within the realm of judicial behavior, the study of which consists of systematic, empirical, theoretically based attempts to explain what courts and judges do. It is open to theoretical approach—legal, strategic, institutional, attitudinal, whatever—but excludes descriptive doctrinal approaches (i.e. what the law is), prescriptive normative approaches (what the law should be), and purely deductive formal approaches.[1]

So what then is it that judges do? Legal realists commonly assert that judges act like "single minded seekers of legal policy" (quoted in George and Epstein 1992, 325). Nevertheless, the extent to which judges *choose* to act in such a manner and the extent to which they *can realize their goals* by acting in such a manner is the subject of much debate. Thus, Gibson notes, "judges' decisions are a function of what they prefer to do, tempered by what they think they ought to do, but constrained by what they perceive is feasible to do" (1983, 7).

The extent to which judges choose to move beyond their policy preferences divides the field of law and politics. Normatively, influences over what judges ought to do include evaluating legal rules such as precedent or legislative intent, in an attempt to find the best answers to cases before them. Thus, in addition to the judges' own preferences, legal influences should be useful in explaining judicial behavior, though the extent to which it does undoubtedly varies throughout the judicial system.

* I thank Elyce Winters for research assistance.

[1] These approaches may, among other things, provide invaluable hypotheses, but any such work that provides formal proofs without more is not a study of judicial behavior.

Table 14.1. A typology of judicial decision-making models on the merits

Source of influence	Temporal influence	
	Past	Present
Legislators	Text and Intent	Separation of Powers
Judges	Horizontal or Vertical Precedent	Attitudinal Model

Similarly, strategic approaches deal with what is feasible for judges to do. Voting their sincere preferences may not, in many cases, further judges' policy goals. Because courts do not make policy in isolation from judicial superiors or other branches of government, strategic judges must temper their decisions by what they *can* do or else risk being overturned.

These models can be usefully depicted according to the schematic in Table 14.1. Sources of influence include legislators and judges. When judges rely on previous judicial decisions, whether vertically from hierarchical superiors, or horizontally, from courts at their own level, they are following legal precedent. But, when judges follow their own (present) preferences, they behave consistently with their political attitudes. When judges rely on the preferences of the lawmakers of the statutes and constitutional provisions under consideration, they follow legal text and intent. But, when they defer strategically to the constraints imposed by current legislative majorities, they behave consistently with the separation-of-powers model.

Judicial politics can be law or politics, but frequently it is both, with the mixture dependent on the type of court and the context of the case.

1 Modeling Law

Modeling law causes practical difficulties: we must be able to measure it. The arguments against empirically modeling law come from two sources: those who lacked the requisite imagination (e.g. Segal and Spaeth 1993, 33), and those philosophically opposed to the idea on the ground that legal decision-making is nothing more than "a sincere belief that their decision represents their best understanding of what the law requires" (Gillman 2001, 486).

Thus, under the latter approach, virtually any decision *can be* consistent with the legal model; and any decision *is* consistent with it so long as the judge has sincerely convinced herself that the decision is legally appropriate. The most basic problem with this approach is clear: the model is not falsifiable. Thus, by accepted standards of scientific research, the model cannot provide a valid explanation of what judges actually do.

It is impossible to know whether judges believe they are judging in good faith. The extensive psychological literature on motivated reasoning suggests that plausible arguments are all that decision-makers need to create an overlap between prior views and a subjective belief in correct results (Braman 2006), suggesting that good faith will not be all that difficult to come by.

Thus, those interested in modeling law must hold judges to a higher standard than "a sincere belief" in the appropriateness of their decisions; legal modelers must show that law has an independent and measurable influence. This does not, however, require a deterministic or mechanical approach to judicial decision-making and is not much different than viewing law as a gravitational force on decision-making.

To determine the impact of law is not much different to determining the impact of other social phenomena. Simply put, judges' decisions should change—not deterministically, but at the margins—as law changes, holding alternative phenomena constant.[2] This is easiest to see in the case of vertical *stare decisis*, where the strategic implications can be quite complex, but the essence of testing them requires little more than determining how lower court decisions change as higher court decisions change after controlling for other relevant factors such as case characteristics and the preferences of lower court judges. For example, it would not suffice simply to show that lower courts became more conservative during the Burger and Rehnquist courts, because Republican appointees during this era undoubtedly made both the upper and lower courts more conservative.

1.1 Stare Decisis

Despite early research showing substantial noncompliance with Supreme Court decisions (see Baum 1978), recent evidence indicates that judges on lower courts follow the preferences of judges on higher courts (Benesh and Martinek 2002). Overtly noncompliant decisions by Court of Appeals judges are exceedingly rare.

Why judges so frequently comply is a matter of dispute. According to legalistic accounts, the overwhelming number of lower court decisions that the Supreme Court must oversee, and the very few cases it chooses to hear, means that lower court judges have little fear of reversal. And to the extent that judicial decisions are binary, overturned outcomes are likely to be no worse than if the lower court had done the higher court's bidding in the first place. Thus judges presumably comply with the Supreme Court out of a belief that such behavior is legally appropriate (Cross 2005; Klein and Hume 2003). Strategic accounts, alternatively, argue that if judicial policy-making actually occurs over a continuous spectrum, the policy costs of reversal are real. Moreover, frequent reversal can limit the prospects for promotion. Since the likelihood of being reversed is a function of the lower court's level of compliance, fear of getting overturned can lead to a "compliance cascade" (Cross 2005) whereby lower courts compete to avoid being overturned by pushing their decisions closer and closer

---

[2] Nor should it change as legally irrelevant factors, such as the parties to a suit, change.

to the preferences of the higher court (Songer et al. 1994; McNollgast 1995). Certainly, the Supreme Court strategically uses both its certiorari jurisdiction (Cameron et al. 2000) and citations to its own precedents (Hansford and Spriggs 2006) as a means of obtaining compliance from lower courts.

One potential way through these competing explanations is with a thought experiment. What would happen if Congress denied the Supreme Court appellate jurisdiction over an issue? The legal reliance on Supreme Court precedent would arguably be the same, but the fear of override would literally be driven down to zero. If the issue area were abortion, would conservative lower court panels continue to uphold such rights? My hunch is that in salient issues such as this, the answer is no. In less salient areas, my hunch is still no, but with considerably less certainty.

Although tests for vertical *stare decisis* demonstrate compliance, testing for the horizontal impact of precedent poses substantially more difficulty. Once again, the task is to see how judges' behavior changes as law changes. Thus, we could try to determine how the behavior of Supreme Court judges changed on abortion rights following the massive change in law created by *Roe v. Wade* (1973). The problem, of course, is that we would be looking for this impact on the judges who created *Roe*. One way around this problem is to examine the impact of horizontal *stare decisis* on judges who dissented from the original ruling (cf. Gillman 2001). As Jerome Frank accurately stated, "Stare decisis has no bite when it means merely that a court adheres to a precedent that it considers correct. It is significant only when a court feels constrained to stick to a former ruling although the court has come to regard it as unwise or unjust" (*United States v. Shaughnessy* 1955, 719). This view equally applies to those who dissented on the original case but are faced with similar issues in subsequent cases. Thus, when Justice Stewart reversed his view in *Griswold v. Connecticut* (1965) and accepted the right to privacy in *Eisenstadt v. Baird* (1972), we have a *prima facie* case that *stare decisis* influenced the justice. Tests using this standard find that *stare decisis* influences the decisions of Supreme Court justices only about 10 percent of the time (Segal and Spaeth 1996; cf. Brenner and Stier 1996; Songer and Lindquist 1996), but it is worth noting that this percentage nearly doubles for the least salient of the Court's decisions (Spaeth and Segal 1999), suggesting the contingent nature of *stare decisis*, even within a court.

Alternatively, Richards and Kritzer (2002) proposed a "jurisprudential regime" approach to modeling law. This approach begins with fact-pattern analysis—using case stimuli to predict judicial decisions—to argue that certain cases create jurisprudential regimes that shift the manner in which the Supreme Court treats those stimuli. They show that the impact of different case stimuli, such as the level of government involved or the identity of the speaker, on the likelihood of a liberal decision vary before and after *Grayned v. City of Rockford* (1972), the First Amendment decision requiring content neutrality. Although the impact of First Amendment case stimuli vary significantly before and after 1972, the results also show that they vary before and after 1960, 1961, 1962 etc.; and the differences are higher in the years before *Grayned* than in the year of *Grayned*. Additionally, the authors do not test alternative functional forms for the change. That a case fact had a greater impact on the Court's decision after 1972 than before 1972 does not indicate that the change occurred in 1972, and indeed, it does not indicate that there was a discrete change at any time point. The impact of these case stimuli could be changing steadily over time, rather than abruptly, as required by their theory. Nevertheless, with further testing, this original line of research could readily answer questions about horizontal *stare decisis* that clearly need to be answered.

1.2 Text and Intent

Assessing the impact of text and intent, like the impact of precedent, poses difficulties, but not insurmountable ones. At least for text, we can start with the notion that judicial behavior should change as the text of law changes. This sounds trivial, but judicial behavior does not necessarily conform to obvious expectations.

Testing for the impact of text at the federal level poses certain problems, since many of the laws we are interested in have not changed in over 200 years. This problem makes the states a more natural laboratory to study such influence, and we could examine the impact of text either diachronically or cross-sectionally. Neither approach is without problems. Diachronically, judicial behavior should change over time as statutory or constitutional text changes, and cross-sectionally, judicial behavior should change over space as different jurisdictions have different laws.

Testing the impact of text across jurisdictions, Baldez, Epstein, and Martin (2006) find the presence of a state-level Equal Rights Amendment does not influence the likelihood of ruling in favor of litigants pressing sex-discrimination claims.[3] Moreover, there appears to be no impact of educational rights provisions in state constitutions on the decision of state supreme courts to strike down unequal funding provisions for public schools (Lundberg 2000). But constitutional rights to privacy significantly increase the likelihood that state supreme courts will nullify anti-abortion statutes (Brace, Hall, and Langer 1999).

Cross-sectional analyses cannot be conducted at the federal level, and diachronic analyses will not be very helpful for the sort of constitutional provisions that interest public law scholars. How, then, through *a priori* measures and falsifiable tests can we systematically assess, text and intent as potential explanations for the justices' behavior? One possibility is to measure *legal arguments* rather than "law." If, for example, Justice Scalia is truly a textualist, he should be more willing to support a litigant who makes an textual claim—e.g. an undisputed claim that the plain meaning of the statutory text supports his side—than a litigant who makes no such claim, *ceteris paribus*.

In fact, while Justices Scalia and Thomas support liberal textual claims in less than half of the cases (45.3 and 47.6 percent respectively), these numbers are higher than

---

[3] It does indirectly influence the probability that a court will use the strict-scrutiny standard by about .12.

their support for liberal parties lacking textual claims (Segal and Howard 2002). Similarly, Scalia and Thomas are more likely to support defendants' rights in criminal-justice disputes when those rights are supported by originalist arguments (Barkow 2006). For legislative or constitutional intent, though, Segal and Howard (2002) find little evidence that the justices respond to such claims.

Overall, though, these and other approaches have led to some conditional positive findings on the impact of law on judicial behavior, particularly in the lower courts. Yet, even where we would expect the influence of law to be the greatest, in vertical *stare decisis*, the results are mixed; and elsewhere, the impact has generally been minimal.

2 ATTITUDES

The attitudinal model holds that judges decide cases in light of their sincere ideological values juxtaposed against the factual stimuli presented by the case. Consider a search and seizure whose constitutionality the Court must determine. Assume that the police searched a person's house with a valid warrant supported by probable cause and there were no extenuating circumstances. The search uncovers an incriminating diary. Now imagine a second search, similar to the first in that probable cause existed, but in which the police failed to obtain a warrant.

We can place these searches in ideological space. Since the search with a warrant can be considered less intrusive than the search without the warrant, we place the first search to the left of the second search. This is diagrammed in Figure 14.1, where A represents the first search and B the second. Presumably, any search and seizure can be located on the line; the more invasive the search, the further to the right the search will fall. Points on the line where the searches lie are j-points.

Next, place the judges in ideological space. Consider three judges, 1, 2, and 3, respectively, liberal, moderate, and conservative. Judge 1 is so liberal that he would not even uphold the search in the first case. Thus we could place Judge 1 to the left

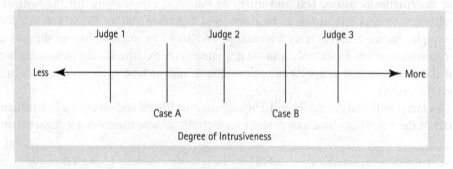

Fig. 14.1. Justices and cases in ideological space

of Case A. Judge 2 might not be quite so liberal as Judge 1; she would uphold the search of the home with a warrant, but would not uphold the warrantless search. Thus, we could place Judge 2 to the right of Case A but to the left of Case B. Finally, Judge 3 might find the warrant relatively unimportant and would uphold any search he considered reasonable, including Case B. Figure 14.1 places the justices in ideological space, with the markers for the judges representing their indifference points (i-points). Judges uphold all searches to the left of their indifference point, reject all searches to the right of their indifference point, and are indifferent about whether searches at that point are upheld or overturned.

Numerous behavioral implications follow from this model. At the case level, a court's decisions should depend in part on the factual stimuli in the case. This implication is consistent with, but not unique to, the attitudinal model. At the judge level, differences in judges' attitudes should influence aggregate and individual levels of ideological voting. Finally, the votes of particular judges in particular cases should depend on the interaction between the case stimuli and the judge's attitudes.

The likelihood of judges behaving consistently with the attitudinal model will depend on institutional incentives and disincentives for ideological behavior. Attitudinal behavior should be at its apogee for a court at the top of the judicial hierarchy and which therefore cannot be overruled by higher courts; where public opinion supports an independent judiciary, limiting legislative attempts to strike at the court; when the court has docket control and thus can weed out frivolous cases that no self-respecting judge could decide only on her ideology; when the judges enjoy life tenure; and when the judges lack ambition for higher office and thus have no incentive to placate others (Sisk, Heise, and Morriss 1998). Although legal realists might argue that discretion inheres in all judging, judges will have less discretion when judges can be overruled by higher courts, political culture disfavors judicial independence, legally determinate cases fill the docket, or when judges seek higher office, can be replaced by the electorate, or even assassinated by political enemies (Helmke 2002). "Your i-point or your life" should be an easy decision to make when threats are real.

2.1 The Supreme Court

The attitudinal model well fits behavior on the U.S. Supreme Court. At the case level, changes in case stimuli have repeatedly been shown to influence Court decisions (see Segal and Spaeth 2002, 312–20 for a review).

At the level of individual judges, the relationship between the justices' ideology (Segal and Cover 1989) and their behavior on the Court is quite strong. Ideally, the measure of the justices' behavior would be based on the policies they supported in the Court's written opinions, but such measures are not yet available (see Conclusion, below). Figure 14.2 thus shows the relationship between ideology and votes for all justices appointed since Earl Warren. The correlation coefficient, 0.78, demonstrates that the justices' ideology explains exceedingly well their aggregate voting behavior.

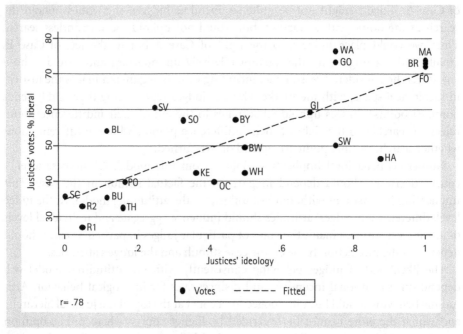

Fig. 14.2. Justices' votes by justices' ideology

As for the juxtaposition between the justices' ideology and case stimuli, the model well predicts the Court's search and seizure decisions. A model combining the justices' attitudes and a series of case stimuli predicts 71 percent of the justices' votes correctly (Segal and Spaeth 1992, ch. 8).

2.2 Lower Courts

For various reasons, attitudes are unlikely to have the same impact on lower court judges' decisions that they do on Supreme Court justices' decisions. Consider, for example, the U.S. Courts of Appeals. First, and foremost, Court of Appeals judges are undoubtedly influenced by the decisions and preferences of the U.S. Supreme Court. When Samuel Alito voted as a Court of Appeals judge to strike New Jersey's partial birth abortion law, he was undoubtedly expressing the Supreme Court's preference, not his own. Second, the Courts of Appeals have mandatory jurisdiction and undoubtedly hear many cases where they simply lack decisional discretion. Third, the composition of panels matters, i.e. Court of Appeal judges appear to be substantially influenced by those who sit with them on particular panels. Democrats (Republicans) sitting on a panel with a Republican (Democratic) majority are much more likely to vote conservatively (liberally) than they otherwise would, at least on less salient issues (Revesz 1997; Sunstein, Schkade, and Ellman 2004). Yet, in other situations, the minority on the panel, a "whistleblower," can

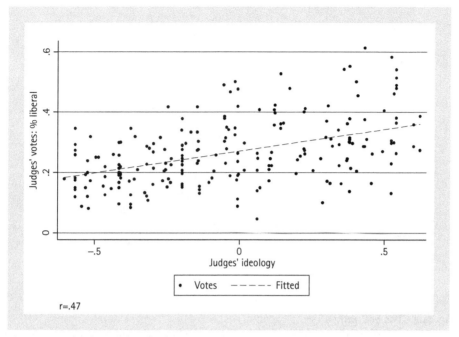

Fig. 14.3. Judges' votes by ideology

influence the majority by threatening to reveal doctrinal deviation to the higher court (Cross and Tiller 1998). And the presence of women and minorities on panels independently influences the decisions of those who sit with them (Farhang and Wawro 2004).

Figure 14.3 examines the relationship between ideology and liberal voting percentages on the U.S. Courts of Appeals. The data come from Songer's United States Court of Appeals database for all judges who voted in twenty or more civil liberties cases (criminal procedure, First Amendment, civil rights, due process and privacy). The ideology of judges on the Courts of Appeals comes from the well-validated scores created by Giles, Hettinger, and Peppers (2001), rescaled so that liberal scores have higher values and the predicted relationship between attitudes and votes is positive. Although the fit is pretty good—indeed, it would be hard to imagine any other variable that explains so substantial a proportion of the judges' voting behavior—obviously much more is at work on the Court of Appeals than just ideology.

Reliable measures of judges' attitudes are much more difficult to create for state courts, so partisanship is frequently used as a proxy for ideology (cf. Brace, Langer, and Hall 2000). Pinello's (1999) meta-analysis reports substantially lower relationships than reported here for federal courts, and indeed, at the state trial-court level, there appears to be no correlation between the judges' ideology and behavior (Gibson 1978; Narduli, Fleming, and Eisenstein 1984).

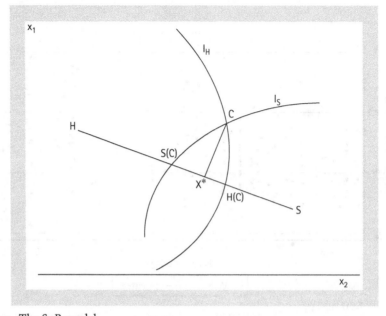

Fig. 14.4. The SoP model
H = House ideal point; S = Senate ideal point; C = Court ideal point; I_H = House indifference curve; I_S = Senate indifference curve; S(C) = Point on Set of Irreversible Decisions where Senate is indifferent to Court ideal point; H(C) = Point on Set of Irreversible Decisions where House is indifferent to Court ideal point; X^* = equilibrium.

3 SEPARATION OF POWERS

Separation of powers (SoP) models examine the degree to which courts must defer to legislative majorities in order to prevent overrides that result in a policy worse than what the court might have achieved through sophisticated behavior. Consider the example in Figure 14.4, where the Court must decide a case in two-dimensional policy space. The game is played as follows. First, the Court makes a decision in (x1, x2) policy space. Second, the House and Senate can override the Court's decision if they agree on an alternative. H, S, and C represent the ideal points of the House, Senate, and Court, respectively. The line segment HS represents the set of irreversible decisions, i.e. no decision on the line can be overturned by Congress because improving the position of one chamber by moving closer to its ideal point necessarily worsens the position of the other. Alternatively, any decision off of HS, call it x, can be overturned, because there will necessarily be at least one point on HS that H and S prefer to x. Imagine, for example, a decision at the Court's ideal point, C. The arc I_S represents those points where the Senate is indifferent to this decision, with the Senate preferring any point inside the arc to any point on or outside the arc. Similarly, I_H represents the points where the House is indifferent to the Court's decision. Thus, both the House and Senate prefer any point between S(C) (the point on the set of irreversible decisions where the Senate is indifferent to the Court's decision) and H(C) (the point on the set of irreversible decisions where the House is indifferent to the Court's decision) to a decision at C.

What, then, should a strategic Court do in this situation? If the Court rules at its ideal point or, indeed, any place off the set of irreversible decisions, Congress will overturn the Court's decision and replace it with something that is worse from the Court's perspective. For example, if the Court rules at C, then Congress's response will be someplace between S(C) and H(C). The trick for the Court is to find the point on the set of irreversible decisions closest to its ideal point. By the Pythagorean Theorem, the Court accomplishes this by dropping a perpendicular onto the line. Thus, rather than ruling sincerely at C and ending up with a policy between S(C) and H(C), the Court rules at X^*, the point between S(C) and H(C) it most prefers.

Separation-of-powers games vary in a variety of details, such as the number of issue dimensions, number of legislative chambers, influence of committees, existence of a presidential veto, etc. Regardless of the specific assumptions made, these models generally assume that the Court will construe legislation as close to its ideal point as possible without getting overturned by Congress (Ferejohn and Shipan 1990).

Despite its elegance, empirical support for the SoP model is not so clear-cut. Many articles on the SoP model are simply case studies—often selected on the dependent variable—that demonstrate examples of the Supreme Court acting strategically. Systematic analyses, though, report mixed results at best (Eskridge 1991), with the vast majority of studies reporting no impact (see Segal and Spaeth 2002, ch. 8 for a thorough review.)

Perhaps one reason the results typically do not work is that these studies typically examine the SoP model at the court that is perhaps most insulated from external influence: the U.S. Supreme Court. Judges on the Argentinian Supreme Court (Iaryczower, Spiller, and Tommasi 2006), Japanese lower court (Ramseyer and Rasmussen 2001), and U.S. state supreme courts (Brace and Hall 1990) appear more responsive to their political environments than justices on the U.S. Supreme Court.

Despite the lack of success in explaining the Supreme Court's statutory decisions as a function of congressional preferences, scholars have expanded the SoP model to include constitutional cases, at least theoretically (Rosenberg 1992). Empirically, although Whittington (2005) suggests that judicial review can be a tool of the dominant coalition, there is little systematic evidence to support strategic deference by the Court in constitutional cases. Friedman and Harvey (2003) argue that the increase in the number of federal laws declared unconstitutional after 1994 is evidence that a strategic, conservative Court found itself free to overturn legislation following the 1994 Congressional elections. But this increase in activism also came, with a short lag, after the Court gained a fifth vote for conservative activism with the appointment of Clarence Thomas in 1991. Thus, Segal and Westerland (2005) find that the conservatism of the Court, not its ideological distance from the current Congress, best explains the annual number of federal statutes that the Court struck down between 1949 and 2001.

4 CONCLUSION

There is of course much more to judicial behavior than covered in this chapter, which has focused on judges' decisions on the merits, with particular attention on four important models of judicial behavior. My focus has excluded important merits-related topics such as public opinion and the effect of the solicitor general, and broader studies on granting discretionary review (Caldeira, Wright, and Zorn 1999; Brenner 1979) and opinion writing (Epstein and Knight 1998; Hettinger, Linquist, and Martinek 2006; Maltzman, Spriggs, and Wahlbeck 2000).

A persistent complaint about virtually all of the "merits" work cited above is that it measures votes, e.g. a judge's decision to vote liberally or conservatively in a case or a series of cases, but what we're really interested in is the policy established by the judge or court (Friedman 2006). Nevertheless, there is a substantial relationship between the votes judges cast and the policies set forth in their opinions (Wenzel 1995). Yet Wenzel's findings are limited, and thus should not assuage us.

Recent work by McGuire and Vanberg (2005) opens up the possibility of more accurate and reliable recordings of judicial policy-making. Utilizing the computer-based Wordscore program, which has been used to map the ideology of political parties, McGuire and Vanberg have mapped the ideological positioning of Supreme Court opinions. The application of this technology should have a huge impact on our ability to better understand judicial behavior.

REFERENCES

BALDEZ, L., EPSTEIN, L., and MARTIN, A. D. 2006. Does the U.S. Constitution need an ERA? *Journal of Legal Studies*, 35: 243–83.

BARKOW, R. 2006. Originalists, politics, and criminal law on the Rehnquist Court. *George Washington Law Review*, 74: 1043–77.

BAUM, L. 1978. Lower court response to supreme court decisions: reconsidering a negative picture. *Justice System Journal*, 3: 208–19.

BENESH, S. C. and MARTINEK, W. L. 2002. State supreme court decision-making in confession cases. *Justice System Journal*, 23: 109–34.

BRACE, P. and HALL, M. G. 1990. Neo-institutionalism and dissent in state supreme courts. *Journal of Politics*, 52: 54–70.

——— and LANGER, L. 1999. Judicial choice and the politics of abortion: institutions, context, and the autonomy of courts. *Albany Law Review*, 62: 1265–300.

—— LANGER, L., and HALL, M. G. 2000. Measuring the preferences of state supreme court justices. *Journal of Politics*, 62: 387–413.

BRAMAN, E. 2006. Reasoning on the threshold: testing the separability of preferences in legal decision-making. *Journal of Politics*, 68: 308–21.

BRENNER, S. 1979. The new certiorari game. *Journal of Politics*, 41: 649–55.

—— and STIER, M. 1996. Retesting Segal and Spaeth's *stare decisis* model. *American Journal of Political Science*, 40: 1036–48.

CALDEIRA, G., WRIGHT, J. R., and ZORN, C. J. W. 1999. Strategic voting and gatekeeping in the Supreme Court. *Journal of Law, Economics and Organization*, 15: 549–72.

CAMERON, C. M., SEGAL, J. A., and SONGER, D. 2000. Strategic auditing in a political hierarchy: an informational model of the Supreme Court's certiorari decisions. *American Political Science Review*, 94: 101–16.

CROSS, F. B. 2005. Appellate court adherence to precedent. *Journal of Empirical Legal Studies*, 2: 369–405.

—— and TILLER, E. H. 1998. Judicial partisanship and obedience to legal doctrine: whistle-blowing on the federal courts of appeals. *Yale Law Journal*, 107: 2155–76.

EPSTEIN, L. and KNIGHT, J. 1998. *The Choices Justices Make.* Washington, DC: Congressional Quarterly Press.

ESKRIDGE, JR., W. N. 1991. Reneging on history? Playing the Court/Congress/President civil rights game. *California Law Review*, 79: 613–84.

FARHANG, S. and WAWRO, G. 2004. Institutional dynamics on the U.S. Court of Appeals: minority representation under panel decision-making. *Journal of Law, Economics and Organization*, 20: 299–330.

FEREJOHN, J. and SHIPAN, C. 1990. Congressional influence on bureaucracy. *Journal of Law, Economics and Organization*, 6: 1–20.

FRIEDMAN, B. 2006. Taking law seriously. *Perspectives on Politics*, 4: 261–76.

—— and HARVEY, A. 2003. Electing the Supreme Court. *Indiana Law Journal*, 78: 123–52

GEORGE, T. E. and EPSTEIN, L. 1992. On the nature of Supreme Court decision-making. *American Political Science Review*, 86: 323–37.

GIBSON, J. L. 1978. Judges' role orientations, attitudes, and decisions: an interactive model. *American Political Science Review*, 72: 911–24.

—— 1983. From simplicity to complexity: the development of theory in the study of judicial behavior. *Political Behavior*, 5: 7–49.

GILES, M. W., HETTINGER, V. A., and PEPPERS, T. 2001. Picking federal judges: a note on policy and partisan selection agendas. *Political Research Quarterly*, 54: 623–41.

GILLMAN, H. 2001. What's law got to do with it? Judicial behavioralists test the "legal model" of judicial decision-making. *Law and Social Inquiry*, 26: 465–504.

HANSFORD, T. G. and SPRIGGS, J. F. II 2006. *The Politics of Precedent on the U.S. Supreme Court.* Princeton, NJ: Princeton University Press.

HELMKE, G. 2002. The logic of strategic defection: court-executive relations in Argentina under dictatorship and democracy. *American Political Science Review*, 96: 291–303.

HETTINGER, V. A., LINDQUIST, S. A., and MARTINEK, W. L. 2006. *Judges on a Collegial Court: Influence on Federal Appellate Decision Making.* Charlottesville: University of Virginia Press.

IARYCZOWER, M., SPILLER, P. T., and TOMMASI, M. 2006. Judicial lobbying: the politics of labor law constitutional interpretation. *American Political Science Review*, 100: 85–97.

KLEIN, D. E. and HUME, R. J. 2003. Fear of reversal as an explanation of lower court compliance. *Law and Society Review*, 37: 579–606.

LUNDBERG, P. J. 2000. State courts and school funding: a fifty-state analysis. *Albany Law Review*, 63: 1101–46.

MALTZMAN, F., SPRIGGS, J. F. II, and WAHLBECK, P. J. 2000. *Crafting Law on the Supreme Court: The Collegial Game.* New York: Cambridge University Press.

McGUIRE, K. T. and VANBERG, G. 2005. Mapping the policies of the U.S. Supreme Court: data, opinions, and constitutional law. Presented at the annual meeting of the American Political Science Association.

McNOLLGAST 1995. A positive theory of judicial doctrine and the rule of law. *Southern California Law Review*, 68: 1631–89.

NARDULLI, P. F., FLEMMING, R. B., and EISENSTEIN, J. 1984. Unraveling the complexities of decision-making in face-to-face groups: a contextual analysis of plea bargained sentences. *American Political Science Review*, 78: 912–28.

PINELLO, D. R. 1999. Linking party to judicial ideology in American courts. *Justice System Journal*, 20: 219–54.

RAMSEYER, J. M. and RASMUSSEN, E. B. 2001. Why is the Japanese conviction rate so high? *Journal of Legal Studies*, 30: 53–88.

REVESZ, R. L. 1997. Environmental regulation, ideology, and the D.C. Circuit. *Virginia Law Review*, 83: 1717–72.

RICHARDS, M. J. and KRITZER, H. M. 2002. Jurisprudential regimes in Supreme Court decision-making. *American Political Science Review*, 96: 305–20.

ROSENBERG, G. N. 1992. Judicial independence and the reality of judicial power. *Review of Politics*, 54: 369–98.

SEGAL, J. A. and COVER, A. D. 1989. Ideological values and the votes of U.S. Supreme Court justices. *American Political Science Review*, 83: 557–65.

—— and HOWARD, R. M. 2002. An original look at originalism. *Law and Society Review*, 36: 113–38.

—— and SPAETH, H. J. 1993. *The Supreme Court and the Attitudinal Model*. New York: Cambridge University Press.

————1996. The influence of *stare decisis* on the votes of U.S. Supreme Court justices. *American Journal of Political Science*, 40: 971–1003.

————2002. *The Supreme Court and the Attitudinal Model Revisited*. New York: Cambridge University Press.

—— and WESTERLAND, C. 2005. The Supreme Court, Congress, and judicial review. *North Carolina Law Review*, 83: 101–66.

SISK, G. C., HEISE, M., and MORRISS, A. P. 1998. Charting the influences on the judicial mind: an empirical study of judicial reasoning. *New York University Law Review*, 73: 1377–1500.

SONGER, D. R. and LINDQUIST, S. A. 1996. Not the whole story: the impact of justices' values on Supreme Court decision-making. *American Journal of Political Science*, 40: 1049–63.

—— SEGAL, J. A., and CAMERON, C. M. 1994. The hierarchy of justice: testing a principal-agent model of Supreme Court–circuit court interactions. *American Journal of Political Science*, 38: 673–96.

SPAETH, H. J. and SEGAL, J. A. 1999. *Majority Rule vs. Minority Will: Adherence to Precedent on the U.S. Supreme Court*. New York: Cambridge University Press.

SUNSTEIN, C. R., SCHKADE, D., and ELLMAN, L. M. 2004. Ideological voting of federal courts of appeals: a preliminary investigation. *Virginia Law Review*, 90: 301–54.

WENZEL, J. P. 1995. Stability and change in the ideological values in Supreme Court decisions. Presented at the annual meeting of the Midwest Political Science Association.

WHITTINGTON, K. E. 2005. "Interpose your friendly hand:" political supports for the exercise of judicial review by the United States Supreme Court. *American Political Science Review*, 99: 583–96.

CASES

Eisenstadt v. Baird. 1972. 405 U.S. 438.
Grayned v. City of Rockford. 1972. 408 U.S. 104.
Roe v. Wade. 1973. 410 U.S. 113.
United States v. Shaughnessy. 1955. 234 F. 2d 715.

CHAPTER 15

....

LAW AND SOCIETY

....

LYNN MATHER

THE study of law and society rests on the belief that legal rules and decisions must be understood in context. Law is not autonomous, standing outside of the social world, but is deeply embedded within society. While political scientists recognize the fundamentally *political* nature of law, the law and society perspective takes this assumption several steps further by pointing to ways in which law is socially and historically constructed, how law both reflects and impacts culture, and how inequalities are reinforced through differential access to, and competence with, legal procedures and institutions.

The interdisciplinary field of law and society dates to the late 1950s/mid-1960s, and the story of its early development has been told before (e.g. Levine 1990; Schlegel 1995; Garth and Sterling 1998). Its philosophical roots lie in the jurisprudential writings of the legal realists, who saw law as a vehicle for social engineering and challenged depictions of law as apolitical and autonomous. Likewise, social scientists were highly optimistic and confident about the potential of their work to solve social problems. Law and society scholars of the 1960s were also responding to many of the burning issues (literally—from riots in Los Angeles, Detroit, and elsewhere) of the day. Dismayed and frustrated by the formalism of the legal academy and the irrelevance and narrowness of much social science, a number of legal scholars and social scientists sought to engage in research that would address current policy debates over racial discrimination, poverty, and crime. Substantial funding for empirical research on these topics from the Ford Foundation, Russell Sage, and others provided further impetus for studies that would combine social science and law. Responding to the availability of research funds and their own political and intellectual agendas, a multidisciplinary group of scholars created the Law and Society Association in 1964. Its members were drawn primarily from sociology, political science, and law, with some representation from anthropology, psychology, history, and occasionally economics.

The law and society field welcomed a wide range of subject areas for study. At the same time, President Lyndon Johnson's War on Poverty attempted to underscore the rule of law by creating federally funded legal aid programs to increase access to justice and address problems of the urban poor. Politicians and scholars recognized that what happened in local agencies or in trial courts could be as important as what happened in Washington, DC. This opened up new topics for empirical research on legal processes and resulted in law and society studies of public defender offices, legal aid, lower courts, administrative agencies, juries, police, and prosecutors. Political scientists authored many of these works and they enjoyed the feedback from sociologists and law professors they received in the law and society community. Constitutional law scholars who supported law and society in its early days had also turned their attention away from formal doctrinal analysis of Supreme Court decisions. They focused instead on interest groups and the lower courts in an effort to understand the political and organizational dynamics in test case litigation, the difficulties of implementing the decisions of the Supreme Court, the politics of administrative agencies, and the politics of judicial selection.

With this early history in mind, what are the key characteristics of a law and society perspective? What are some of the major research contributions of this field? And what recent developments in law and society hold particular promise for scholars of law and politics today?

1 KEY CHARACTERISTICS

Law and society scholarship has typically been *multidisciplinary* or *interdisciplinary*. Although most law and society scholars have been trained in one or another established discipline, they have frequently borrowed from other disciplines in their research. For example, early empirical analyses of plea bargaining in criminal courts reflected multiple methods and theories. The studies drew upon organization theory (Blumberg 1967; Eisenstein and Jacob 1977; Feeley 1979), social learning theory (Heumann 1978), ethnography (Mather 1979), ethnomethodology (Sudnow 1965), history (Alschuler 1979; Friedman 1979), and discourse analysis (Maynard 1984). As general law and society theories emerged, for example, to explain trial courts (Shapiro 1981; Boyum and Mather 1983), legal mobilization (McCann 1994), or "why the 'haves' come out ahead" (Galanter 1974), these theories sought to integrate the perspectives of different disciplines. Such interdisciplinary work has been more common in recent years. It reflects the maturity and growth of the field as well as the development of graduate and undergraduate programs in law and society.

Second, in terms of *epistemology and methodology*, law and society emerged during the 1960s, a time of the behavioral revolution in the social sciences and an optimistic embrace of positivism. Scholars focused their work on legal processes and individual and group decision-making. The study of rules was passé, as was the study of formal institutions. Empirical studies of behavior could be qualitative or quantitative, with the former defined broadly to encompass historical or anthropological methods. Methodological debates that were fierce in political science at this time were, by contrast, relatively muted within law and society. This tendency has continued to characterize the field, with greater focus on theory and substantive results than on sophistication of the methods or an insistence on the superiority of any particular method (Engel 1999).

By the 1980s, law and society critics of positivism raised serious challenges to the paradigm and articulated postrealist, interpretive, and constitutive approaches to law (Brigham and Harrington 1989; Harrington and Yngvesson 1990; Hunt 1993). Scholars reclaimed an interest in institutions (Smith 1988; Heydebrand and Seron 1990) as well as embracing an interest in legal ideology and legal discourse (Mather and Yngvesson 1980–1; Conley and O'Barr 1990; Merry 1990). Contemporary law and society scholarship encompasses a wide range of epistemological perspectives, from the cultural studies approach of law and humanities to empirical legal studies—and everything in between.

Third, *normative, policy-relevant* concerns for justice and equality that initially drove the field remain significant even as debate continues over the best way that scholars can realize that normative commitment. Sarat and Silbey (1988) urged law and society colleagues to reject the "pull of the policy audience" in order to produce broader, more critical scholarship and to avoid reinforcing the status quo. Levine (1990) noted the long history of tension between basic and applied research in sociolegal studies, but suggested that both could be realized; theoretical work can provide policy insights and studies of specific policy reforms can generate theory. In an important exchange over postmodernism and political change, Handler (1992) chastised the new postmodern scholarship for its inattention to power structures, collective identity, and the possibilities of transformative politics (but see responses by Calavita and Seron 1992; McCann 1992). A decade later, Munger (2001) called for renewed activism along with scholarly inquiry. He observed that as the law and society "field goes global, I see a reawakening of the earlier interest in justice and equality, and in power, class, race, ethnicity, and religion" (2001, 8).

Fourth, *comparative* approaches to research questions in law and society have been a long-standing commitment of the field, even as they have sometimes been honored in the breach more than the practice (Mather 2003). The very first volume of the *Law and Society Review* contained articles on comparative family law, one by a sociologist (Cicourel 1967) and the other by anthropologists (Bohannan and Huckleberry 1967). Other important sociolegal studies examined comparative disputing processes (Abel 1974; Moore 1978; Nader and Todd 1978), comparative lawyers (Abel and Lewis 1988; Epp 1998), comparative courts (Shapiro 1981; Jacob et al. 1996), comparative regulation (Hawkins 1992; Gunningham and Rees 1997; Kagan 2001), and comparative lay participation in legal decisions (Hans 2003).

One quarter of the membership of the Law and Society Association (LSA) is non-American, and the LSA leadership has been committed to holding its annual meetings in outside of the U.S. on a regular basis. Meetings in Amsterdam (1991), Glasgow

(1996), Budapest (2001), and Berlin (2007) were held jointly with the Research Committee on the Sociology of Law (the last meeting was also supported by three other non-U.S. associations). LSA meetings held in Vancouver (2002) and Montreal (2008) are cosponsored by the Canadian Law and Society Association. Political scientists in the United States regularly suggest that the field of "American politics" should really be a subset of "comparative politics," but old habits die hard. The American politics subfield operates quite independently and scholars infrequently cite across subfields. By contrast, the law and society field actively seeks connections to the empirical scholarship on law being done in other countries, connections that are facilitated by LSA networks.

Finally, while law is the central concern of law and society scholars, it is not seen as residing in a formal, separate sphere, apart from society. *Law is in society*, and most now agree with the argument Laura Nader made initially that the field should have been named "Law *in* Society" rather than law *and* society (Nader 1969). Just as political scientists have long recognized the political nature of law, sociolegal scholars add that law is also social, cultural, economic, linguistic, and ideological. Researchers engaged in empirical and theoretical work on law in society thus confront the extraordinarily messy (and some would say futile) question of how to say anything interesting or disciplined at all if in fact "the law is all over" (Sarat 1990). Scholars in the field do not agree in their response. But most identify a particular question or problem about the creation, maintenance, or change in law and seek to answer it wherever the question leads. What is important is to be self-aware in drawing the boundaries for study, as opposed to limiting a priori the scope, and to draw on other disciplines for relevant concepts, methods, or insights.

It is difficult to strictly define "the" law and society perspective for a political science audience. Some of what falls under this umbrella (e.g. courts and public policy, law and social change, regulation, judicial decision-making) is mainstream law and politics. Other law and society work may seem less so because of the individual topics studied (border patrol, divorce lawyers, film, science laboratories, lawyer jokes) or the methods used (narrative, experiments, network analysis, ethnography). Over the years law and society scholars have attempted to define the field through textbooks or edited collections; these underscore the editors' quite different perspectives on the field (Kidder 1983; Lempert and Sanders 1986; Macaulay, Friedman, and Stookey 1995; Sarat 2004).

2 MAJOR CONTRIBUTIONS TO LAW AND SOCIETY SCHOLARSHIP

A recent symposium of the *Law and Courts Newsletter* (Winter 2007) featured summaries of the law and society field and its relation to political science, written by seven political scientists who have long been active in this area. Readers should consult this issue for excellent descriptions of this large and robust field of study. I will concentrate on three broad areas of law and society scholarship: disputing; decision-making; and legal ideology and consciousness. I will then briefly mention other areas, while acknowledging that I am still omitting many others.

2.1 Disputing

Studies of *disputing* ask how disputes become court cases and what occurs to cases once they are in court. What are the alternatives to courts for resolving problems or disputes? Why do some conflicts become legal cases but most do not? How does understanding disputing help to explain conflict resolution and the impact of law? Both criminal and civil conflicts in the U.S. fill out a pyramid with vast numbers of grievances or injuries at the bottom, a smaller number that become disputes, even fewer that contain some kind of informal recourse to law (calling the police or a lawyer), an even smaller number with two-party legal activity (plea bargaining or negotiated settlement), and only a tiny fraction resolved by trial (Trubek 1980–1; Felstiner, Abel, and Sarat 1980–1). A large survey done in the late 1970s by the Civil Litigation Research Project (CLRP) showed that different types of civil grievances (e.g. post-divorce) were likelier than others (e.g. discrimination) to reach higher on the pyramid of legal action (Miller and Sarat 1980–1; Kritzer 1991). The empirical results of the CLRP scholars have been reported in myriad judicial process textbooks but this important, forty-year-old study has not been replicated.

Galanter's (1974) comprehensive theory exploring the use of courts by repeat players vs. one-shotters suggested multiple ways in which those experienced in legal procedures are advantaged in the legal process. Galanter also showed how disparities in the legal profession (specialization, relations with clients, legal training, etc.) further exacerbated the advantages of the repeat players. Galanter's study in the *Law and Society Review* is one of the most frequently cited law review articles of all time. A number of empirical studies since then have supported his theory (see Kritzer and Silbey 2003).

One aspect of Galanter's theory centers on the differential use of formal vs. informal mechanisms for dispute settlement by repeat players and one-shotters. That is, parties who are more familiar with legal processes know when to settle out of court and when to press on to formal trial, according to the likelihood of gain in the legal rule as opposed to a win or loss in the immediate conflict. This argument, powerfully supported by Albiston's (1999) research on litigation outcomes after the Family and Medical Leave Act, shows an important link between disputing and change in the law. Employers who were sued by employees seeking family leave ultimately "won" even when they "lost" by settling some cases out of court because employers gained important rule-making opportunities in other cases that ultimately weakened the legislation.

Another way in which disputing can be linked to change in law is through the expansion or reframing of a dispute into a new normative framework, and through the support for that expansion that parties may obtain. As Mather and Yngvesson (1980–1) suggest, legal cases are not objective events, but are socially constructed to reflect the interests of supporters of disputants, to appeal to a particular audience, and to incorporate the values and language of law. The language of law is inherently political, ordering facts and invoking norms to support one set of interests or another. By constructing claims in certain ways, one can expand the law and mobilize others in support of the new interpretation. Groups lacking in political power may succeed in attracting support for legal change through reframing issues and mobilizing support, as shown in litigation over comparable worth (McCann 1994), tobacco control (Mather 1998), and sexual harassment (Marshall 2005). A victory in litigation, even if later reversed on appeal, can aid in agenda setting and serve as a catalyst for further change.

The linkage among litigation, political order, and political change also emerges in empirical research on the use of courts over time. Filing disputes in court should be seen as an alternative to traditional forms of political participation, as Zemans (1983) argued, and indeed longitudinal study of court usage in the U.S. by McIntosh (1983) supports this view. Nevertheless, courts are not passive institutions waiting for disputes to percolate up the pyramid to become fodder for judicial decisions. Courts are institutions of the state and as such, they (or other arms of government) can and do exercise power to shape the nature and amount of litigation (Munger 1990; Harrington and Ward 1995). This general point about the power of institutions was made in law and society research some time ago. Recent battles over tort reform illustrate it well, as actions by state legislatures, Congress, and the U.S. Supreme Court have all sought to curb what business interests saw as an "explosion" of litigation.

2.2 Decision-making

A second major area of law and society research focuses on *decision-making*. Scholarship on judicial decision-making is hardly news to those interested in the politics of law, but those in law and society broadened the terrain in several ways. They examined decision-making by judges at *all* levels of court including nonlawyer judges on justice of the peace courts, those on small claims courts, misdemeanor and felony courts, civil courts, and occasionally appellate courts. Research revealed differences in sentencing severity across courts and in patterns of judicial interaction with prosecutors (Eisenstein and Jacob 1977; Eisenstein, Flemming, and Nardulli 1988). Questions about racial discrimination in trial court sentencing have been investigated numerous times, initially with some mixed results. More recently, an overview of forty different sentencing studies that controlled for offense and defendant's prior record showed clear evidence of significant race effects in judicial decisions in state and federal courts (Spohn 2000).

The impact of race has also been shown in numerous state studies of jury and prosecutorial decisions to recommend the death penalty. Jury decision-making has received a great deal of attention from sociolegal scholars. They have explored, for example, the impact of decision rules and jury size on verdicts, differences in evidence-driven vs. verdict-driven processes of deliberation, how juries compare to judges, juror assessments of credibility by race and gender of witnesses, jury assessments of corporate defendants, jury awards over time, and jury nullification (Levine 1992; Hans 2000; 2006; Sunstein et al. 2002).

Second, recognizing that over 95 percent of trial court cases settle through plea negotiations or settlement talks, without trial, sociolegal researchers examined decision-making by lawyers. They asked, for example, how, why, and when do prosecutors and defense attorneys engage in plea bargaining? Do decisions by defense attorneys vary according to whether they are privately employed or public defenders? How are lawyers' decisions to recommend particular dispositions affected by the views of their clients? The rich literature on these questions found in earlier research on plea bargaining would benefit from reexamination in order to see how legal changes on sentencing and jury selection, demographic changes in lower court personnel, increased punitiveness in the cultural and political climate, and the impact of federal anti-immigration measures on local officials, have affected the processes of negotiation in criminal courts.

Lawyers in civil cases also play important roles in dispute settlement and in the production of law. Research on lawyers representing personal injury plaintiffs (Rosenthal 1974; Genn 1987; Kritzer 2004) and divorce clients (Sarat and Felstiner 1995; Mather, McEwen, and Maiman 2001) has revealed much about lawyers' screening decisions in agreeing to represent clients, their interactions with clients, and their negotiating strategies and decisions on settlements. We also know a good deal about the strategies, problems, and goals of cause lawyers (Sarat and Scheingold 1998; Scheingold and Sarat 2004). By contrast, we know much less about decision-making in the work of corporate lawyers, and this is also an area that deserves more research.

Research that began by simply analyzing individual decision-making soon moved to consider (and to incorporate into theory building) the context in which those decisions were made. Relevant aspects of context include, for example, institutional features, legal rules, economic structures, social networks and organization, and shared cultural values. The literature thus moved from its original behavioral focus to reflect institutional and cultural theories. Understanding and explaining the work of lawyers involves studying them within their communities of practice, including the law firm as a community or important cultural space (Kelly 1994; Mather, McEwen, and Maiman 2001). Empirical research that has demonstrated collegial influence on lawyers' decisions has been done in the areas of divorce, personal injury, criminal defense, and most recently, occupational safety and health (Schmidt 2005).

Heinz and Laumann (1982) first reported the significant differences in lawyers according to what they called the two hemispheres of the legal profession: lawyers who represent organizations or corporate entities and those who represent individual clients (and see Heinz et al. 2005 for more recent findings). Lawyers representing organizations not only have higher incomes and prestige than those representing individuals, but they work in larger firms, have fewer clients, spend less time in court, and have different educational backgrounds, social characteristics, and political values. The bifurcated profession has enormous implications for the creation and enforcement of law. For example, law and politics scholars should examine how lawyers exercise influence on law through particular communities of legal practice (Mather forthcoming). Specialization by legal field, coupled with the social stratification of the profession (with disproportionate representation in different fields by gender, race, class, and religion) and observed differences in political values by field, provide rich data for political scientists who are willing to go to lawyers' offices, rather than to courts, to see where law is made.

Finally, sociolegal scholars broadened their scope beyond judges, juries, and lawyers to include the work of less visible legal actors such as court clerks (Yngvesson 1993), health and safety inspection officers (Hawkins 2002), immigration officials (Coutin 2000), probation officers, and police (Skolnick 1994; Bell 2002). Every decision of a low-level legal official helps to shape a pattern of law interpretation and enforcement, and to construct ideas about law for the public they encounter.

Even further, law and society researchers have explored the decisions and work of *private* actors, those without official legal status but who also contribute to lawmaking and law enforcement through private ordering. Who are some of these actors? They include: real estate agents and mortgage brokers who maintain a color line in urban housing; security guards with badges and uniforms who patrol malls and parking lots; human resource officers who define the parameters of civil rights laws through their routine advice and actions in employee disputes; mediators who help parties resolve conflicts without the expense of trial or the constraints of law. Political scientists studying the legislative process are accustomed to paying close attention to the role of private interest groups in lawmaking and administrative enforcement and have developed theories of specialized influence (e.g. the "iron triangle" for congressional subcommittees). Similarly, law and courts scholars should build on the empirical work on private ordering to better understand connections between powerful private interests and law (see e.g. Edelman and Suchman 1999).

2.3 Legal Ideology and Consciousness

Legal ideology and consciousness comprises a third major area of law and society scholarship. Decisions by the street-level bureaucrats, legal officials, and private actors discussed above matter in part because of the direct effect of their actions on people's lives: denying a mortgage; stopping and frisking a suspicious character; channeling personnel conflicts away from law. But from an ideological perspective, what is even more important for the law is the meaning conveyed by those decisions. What values reside in the categories of "suspicious" and "not suspicious" and how are they conveyed in each encounter? Law and society research reminds us that law is constructed through such categories for classification. When the clerk of a local court dismisses a citizen's grievance as not "really" a legal matter, he is making law for the court (Yngvesson 1993). Similarly, with every passage through airport security, government agents are communicating that the law of the U.S. border is different than it was before September 11; the state is more powerful, scrutinizing not only our passports and suitcases, but our belt buckles, toothpaste, and nail files.

Studies of the actuarial practices of insurance companies, for example, underline the power that comes from the rhetoric of granting or denying insurance (Simon 1988; Glenn 2000). Researchers have examined different areas of law to uncover the hidden assumptions, as in the racial bias of insurance, that privilege some people and interests over others. Numerous works document race and gender disparities that emerge from ostensibly neutral concepts or principles. As the title of one article says, "Is the 'reasonable person' a reasonable standard in a multicultural world?" (Minow and Rakoff 1998). Focus on legal ideology looks at the categories of law and how they are used, in order to reveal the process by which legal meaning is constructed. While political scientists readily acknowledge the ideology of constitutional constructs, law and society scholars analyze the narratives, taken for granted assumptions, and values in other areas of law—contracts and tort (Engel 1984), employment, property, family, and so forth.

If knowledge is power, then how do people obtain their knowledge of law? Examining the "litigation crisis" in tort law and the media coverage of the hot coffee and antitobacco lawsuits, Haltom and McCann (2004) found that the institutional conventions of news reporting combined with cultural values about the importance of personal responsibility to muffle the voices of litigation scholars and the plaintiffs' bar. Interest groups on different legal issues battle for the hearts and minds of jurors and the public. While the tort reformers played their hand in the mass media, the plaintiffs' bar chose an insider strategy of legislative and judicial lobbying. In addition to the newspapers' images of legal issues or cases, television and film provide ample material for the cultural production of law. The drama of trials, conflict between good and evil, guilt and innocence, chaos and order, all convey legal meaning that may find its way into law. Survey research on the "*CSI* effect," for example, has not revealed clear results, yet some trial attorneys are convinced that the TV show is shaping popular legal ideas. Prosecutors worry that avid watchers of *CSI*, when asked to serve on a jury, are more reluctant to convict unless there is scientific evidence.

Studies of legal consciousness explore how people's experiences and understandings of law translate into actions and how social action in turn constitutes their relation to law. For example, Ewick and Silbey (1998) conducted detailed interviews with people of diverse backgrounds and found three distinct narratives about law, each with its own normative value and structure: law as impartial, objective, and remote; law as a game shaped by self-interest and individual resources; law as a power to be resisted. Other research on legal consciousness, which examined people's experiences and understandings of how the law should respond to offensive public speech, found interesting variation in responses by race and gender (Nielsen 2004). Engel and Munger (2003) examined how people with disabilities understood and used the new rights conferred by the American for Disabilities Act. The authors concluded that individual identity was key to perceptions of, and experience with, legal rights. Scholars of law and politics should find intriguing material here to integrate with research on political participation, framing of issues, critical race theory, or feminist jurisprudence.

2.4 Other Areas of Law and Society Scholarship

Other areas of law and society scholarship may be more familiar to those in law and politics so I will mention them only briefly.

2.4.1 *Regulation and Compliance*

Studies of *regulation* and *compliance* have been a mainstay of law and society scholarship, encompassing research on compliance with Supreme Court decisions on prayer in schools, implementation of lower court orders on school busing, compliance with environmental, health and safety, or business regulations. Once a legal rule is announced, judicial decision is made, or new regulations go into effect, how do officials secure compliance? Whereas legal scholars try to draw a bright line between law and discretion, many sociolegal scholars would challenge the distinction. Law, it is argued, is constituted by the discretionary decisions that give it meaning. Instead of conceptualizing discretion as "the hole in a doughnut," surrounded by legal form, as Dworkin (1977) suggested, critics have challenged the very distinction between the two (Hawkins 1992; Pratt 1999).

Similarly, the notion of law as purely governmental regulation breaks down entirely with the proliferation of private and quasi-public actors whose support is critical for the success of any regulatory regime. In place of command and control models of regulation, some point to the empirical and normative advantages of self-regulation (Gunningham and Rees 1997). Important comparative work on regulation by Kagan (2001) identifies the very different approaches of Britain and the U.S. and critiques what he calls the "adversarial legalism" of the American system.

2.4.2 *Legal History*

One of the critical influences on the development of law and society was Willard Hurst and his focus on *legal history*. His view of law as deeply grounded in the social and economic context of its time shaped generations of scholars studying particular laws, judicial decisions, or legal movements (Simon 1999). The notion of law and society as mutually constitutive emerges clearly in much of the sociolegal historical scholarship (e.g. Gordon 1988; Hartog 2000), and especially in work on race and the law (Gomez 2004).

Friedman and Ladinsky's (1967) well-known account of the rise of workman's compensation law in the early twentieth century reflects a critical eye toward the autonomy of law. After charting the demise of the common law tort doctrine of the fellow-servant rule, they ask whether law was simply "lagging" behind society. Their answer, quite familiar to law and society scholars forty years later, was a resounding "NO." What was seen as "lag" to some was simply vested interests claiming their power. The old tort doctrine lasted as long as it did because there was no stable compromise behind its replacement. Many similar legal changes would benefit from reexamination by political scientists who have studied American political development and could bring new understandings of the political contexts for change as well as informing law and politics scholars about important areas of the common law they have overlooked.

2.4.3 Procedural Justice

Procedural justice questions have also been explored for decades by those interested in integrating philosophical questions of justice with psychological research and people's experiences with law. Applying the philosophical distinction between procedural and substantive justice to the legal system, psychologists hypothesized that providing fair and transparent court procedures would result in greater satisfaction and compliance regardless of the substantive outcome of their case. Tyler's (1990) work on *Why People Obey the Law* generated a large body of research testing this idea, and finding considerable support. Other researchers extended the research to litigant satisfaction in felony cases according to the perceived fairness of the procedures (Casper, Tyler, and Fisher 1988) and to acceptance of unpopular decisions of the U.S. Supreme Court (Gibson 1989; cf. Tyler and Rasinski 1991).

3 RECENT DEVELOPMENTS

Although the law and society field lacks clear boundaries to separate its interdisciplinary perspective from the other disciplines, it has significantly aided our understanding of law and politics through the various areas of research discussed here. I have already referred to some promising avenues for future research on law and politics. Let me just outline a few others.

1. Look beyond appellate courts. There has been little recent research on American trial courts, despite huge changes in the balance of federal to local legal power, a massive increase in incarceration, a wealth of quantitative data on state courts available from the National Center for State Courts, and the creation of new types of specialized courts for drugs or mental health. Further study of trial courts and tribunals in other countries would add greatly to our comparative knowledge of courts. Law and society work on international disputing through arbitration (Dezalay and Garth 1998) and on the international Tuna Court ("the world's premier fish market;" Feldman 2006, 313) show the potential for integrating norms, disputing, and law. Numerous other regional and international bodies could be studied as well to help us understand processes of law and globalization.

2. Broaden the range of legal actors to study beyond judges and beyond the arena of public law. Integrate studies of the legal profession with our understanding of courts and lawmaking. By combining the specialization of the bar with the sorting process of legal education that shapes the class, race, and gender of who enters (and remains) in corporate law, one might gain new understanding of the outcomes in different legal areas. The phrase "public law" is highly misleading given the range of public policy concerns and effects that emerge from areas of "private" law (Shapiro 1972). Private law areas of tort, property, contracts, labor, and family contain a wealth of interesting law and politics questions that would benefit from the scrutiny of political science. In punitive damages, for example, juries and trial judges were completely free (until very recent constitutional limits were imposed) to impose civil punishments for fraud or negligence. Why not do the same kind of rigorous investigation of damage awards that has been done for criminal sentencing to explore the determinants of punitive damages?

3. Examine how people use courts, harking back to a view of litigation as a form of political participation. Integrate perspectives from identity politics, legal consciousness, critical race theory, and feminist jurisprudence, with knowledge of legal institutions and processes. Examine test case litigation to see how changed conditions and new modes of communication have altered the strategies of interest groups.

4. Popular culture involves framing problems, events, and people. Law is increasingly seen as a set of visual images in popular culture. How do those visuals affect law? Political scientists with an interest in capital punishment should consider Haney's (2005) excellent book on the death penalty. Haney combines decades of psychological research on jury decision-making in death cases with research on popular culture and public opinion to present a disturbing look at the forces that maintain capital punishment in law.

In sum, the field of law and society continues to develop in response to new restarch questions and new scholars. Political scientists contribute to, and learn from, this interdisciplinary approach to law and politics.

REFERENCES

ABEL, R. L. 1974. A comparative theory of dispute institutions in society. *Law and Society Review*, 8: 217–347.

—— and LEWIS, P. S. C. (eds.) 1988. *Lawyers in Society*, 3 vols. Berkeley: University of California Press.

ALBISTON, C. 1999. The rule of law and the litigation process: the paradox of losing by winning. *Law and Society Review*, 33: 869–910.

ALSCHULER, A. 1979. Plea bargaining and its history. *Law and Society Review*, 13: 211–46.

BELL, J. 2002. *Policing Hatred: Law Enforcement, Civil Rights, and Hate Crime*. New York: New York University Press.

BLUMBERG, A. S. 1967. The practice of law as a confidence game: organizational cooptation of a profession. *Law and Society Review*, 1: 15–39.

Bohannan, P. and Huckleberry, K. 1967. Institutions of divorce, family and the law. *Law and Society Review*, 1: 81–102.

Boyum, K. O. and Mather, L. 1983. *Empirical Theories About Courts*. New York: Longman.

Brigham, J. and Harrington, C. 1989. Realism and its consequences: an inquiry into contemporary sociological research. *International Journal of the Sociology of Law*, 17: 41–62.

Calavita, K. and Seron, C. 1992. Postmodernism and protest: recovering the sociological imagination. *Law and Society Review*, 26: 765–72.

Casper, J. D., Tyler, T., and Fisher, B. 1988. Procedural justice in felony cases. *Law and Society Review*, 22: 483–507.

Cicourel, A. V. 1967. Kinship, marriage, and divorce in comparative family law. *Law and Society Review*, 1: 103–29.

Conley, J. M. and O'Barr, W. M. 1990. *Rules versus Relationships: The Ethnography of Legal Discourse*. Chicago: University of Chicago Press.

Coutin, S. B. 2000. *Legalizing Moves: Salvadoran Immigrants' Struggle for U.S. Residency*. Ann Arbor: University of Michigan Press.

Dezalay, Y. and Garth, B. G. 1998. *Dealing in Virtue: International Commercial Arbitration and the Construction of a Transnational Legal Order*. Chicago: University of Chicago Press.

Dworkin, R. 1977. *Taking Rights Seriously*. Cambridge, Mass.: Harvard University Press.

Edelman, L. and Suchman, M. 1999. When the "haves" hold court: speculations on the organizational internalization of law. *Law and Society Review*, 33: 941–92.

Eisenstein, J. B., Flemming, R. B., and Nardulli, P. F. 1988. *The Contours of Justice: Communities and Their Courts*. Boston: Little, Brown.

——and Jacob, H. 1977. *Felony Justice: An Organizational Analysis of Criminal Courts*. Boston: Little, Brown.

Engel, D. M. 1984. The oven bird's song: insiders, outsiders, and personal injuries in an American community. *Law and Society Review*, 18: 551–82.

——1999. Presidential Address—making connections: law and society researchers and their subjects. *Law and Society Review*, 33: 3–16.

——and Munger, F. W. 2003. *Rights of Inclusion: Law and Identity in the Life Stories of Americans with Disabilities*. Chicago: University of Chicago Press.

Epp, C. R. 1998. *The Rights Revolution: Lawyers, Activists, and Supreme Courts in Comparative Perspective*. Chicago: University of Chicago Press.

Ewick, P. and Silbey, S. S. 1998. *The Common Place of Law: Stories from Everyday Life*. Chicago: University of Chicago Press.

Feeley, M. M. 1979. *The Process is the Punishment*. New York: Russell Sage Foundation.

Feldman, E. A. 2006. The Tuna Court: law and norms in the world's premier fish market. *California Law Review*, 94: 313–70.

Felstiner, W. L. F., Abel, R. L., and Sarat, A. 1980–1. The emergence and tranformation of disputes: naming, blaming, claiming. . . . *Law and Society Review*, 15: 631–54.

Friedman, L. M. 1979. Plea bargaining in historical perspective. *Law and Society Review*, 13: 247–60.

——and Ladinsky, J. 1967. Social change and the law of industrial accidents. *Columbia Law Review*, 67: 50–82.

Galanter, M. 1974. Why the "haves" come out ahead: speculations on the limits of legal change. *Law and Society Review*, 9: 95–160.

Garth, B. and Sterling, J. 1998. From legal realism to law and society: reshaping law for the last stages of the social activist state. *Law and Society Review*, 32: 409–71.

Genn, H. 1987. *Hard Bargaining: Out of Court Settlement in Personal Injury Actions*. Oxford: Clarendon Press.

GIBSON, J. 1989. Understandings of justice: institutional legitimacy, procedural justice, and critical race theory. *Law and Society Review*, 23: 469–96.

GLENN, B. 2000. The shifting rhetoric of insurance denial. *Law and Society Review*, 34: 779–808.

GOMEZ, L. 2004. A tale of two genres: on the real and ideal links between law and society and critical race theory. Pp. 453–70 in Sarat 2004.

GORDON, R. W. 1988. The independence of lawyers. *Boston University Law Review*, 68: 1–83.

GUNNINGHAM, N. and REES, J. (eds.) 1997. Special issue. *Law and Policy*, 19 (4).

HALTOM, W. and McCANN, M. 2004. *Distorting the Law: Politics, the Media, and the Litigation Crisis*. Chicago: University of Chicago Press.

HANDLER, J. F. 1992. Presidential address—postmodernism, protest, and the new social movement. *Law and Society Review*, 26: 697–731.

HANEY, C. 2005. *Death by Design: Capital Punishment as a Social Psychological System*. New York: Oxford University Press.

HANS, V. P. 2000. *Business on Trial: The Civil Jury and Corporate Responsibility*. New Haven, Conn.: Yale University Press.

—— (ed.) 2003. Special issue on lay participation in legal decision making. *Law and Policy*, 25 (2).

—— (ed). 2006. *The Jury System: Contemporary Scholarship*. Aldershot: Ashgate.

HARRINGTON, C. B. and WARD, D. S. 1995. Patterns of appellate litigation, 1945–1990. Pp. 206–26 in *Contemplating Courts*, ed. L. Epstein. Washington, DC: Congressional Quarterly.

—— and YNGVESSON, B. 1990. Interpretive sociolegal research. *Law and Social Inquiry*, 15: 135–48.

HARTOG, H. 2000. *Man and Wife in America: A History*. Cambridge, Mass.: Harvard University Press.

HAWKINS, K. (ed.) 1992. *The Uses of Discretion*. New York: Oxford University Press.

—— 2002. *Law as Last Resort: Prosecution Decision-Making in a Regulatory Agency*. Oxford: Oxford University Press.

HEINZ, J. P. and LAUMANN, E. O. 1982. *Chicago Lawyers: The Social Structure of the Bar*. New York: Russell Sage Foundation.

—— NELSON, R. L., SANDEFUR, R. L., and LAUMANN, E. O. 2005. *Urban Lawyers: The New Social Structure of the Bar*. Chicago: University of Chicago Press.

HEUMANN, M. 1978. *Plea Bargaining: The Experiences of Prosecutors, Judges, and Defense Attorneys*. Chicago: University of Chicago Press.

HEYDEBRAND, W. and SERON, C. 1990. *Rationalizing Justice: The Political Economy of Federal District Courts*. Albany: State University of New York Press.

HUNT, A. 1993. *Explorations in Law and Society: Toward A Constitutive Theory of Law*. New York: Routledge.

JACOB, H. et al. 1996. *Courts, Law, and Politics in Comparative Perspective*. New Haven, Conn.: Yale University Press.

KAGAN, R. A. 2001. *Adversarial Legalism: The American Way of Law*. Cambridge, Mass.: Harvard University Press.

KELLY, M. J. 1994. *Lives of Lawyers*. Ann Arbor: University of Michigan Press.

KIDDER, R. I. 1983. *Connecting Law and Society: An Introduction to Research and Theory*. Englewood Cliffs, NJ: Prentice Hall.

KRITZER, H. M. 1991. *Let's Make A Deal*. Madison: University of Wisconsin Press.

—— 2004. *Risks, Reputations, and Rewards: Contingency Fee Legal Practice in the United States*. Stanford, Calif.: Stanford University Press.

—— and SILBEY, S. S. (eds.) 2003. *In Litigation: Do the "Haves" Still Come Out Ahead?* Stanford, Calif.: Stanford University Press.

LEMPERT, R. and SANDERS, J. 1986. *An Invitation to Law and Social Science*. New York: Longman.

LEVINE, F. J. 1990. Presidential address—goose bumps and "the search for signs of intelligent life" in sociolegal studies: after twenty-five years. *Law and Society Review*, 24: 7–33.

LEVINE, J. P. 1992. *Juries and Politics*. Belmont, Calif.: Brooks/Cole.

MACAULAY, S., FRIEDMAN, L. M., and STOOKEY, J. (eds.) 1995. *Law and Society: Readings on the Social Study of Law*. New York: W. W. Norton.

McCANN, M. W. 1992. Resistance, reconstruction, and romance in legal scholarship. *Law and Society Review*, 26: 733–50.

—— 1994. *Rights at Work*. Chicago: University of Chicago Press.

McINTOSH, W. 1983. Private use of a public forum: a long range view of the dispute processing role of courts. *American Political Science Review*, 77: 991–1010.

MARSHALL, A.-M. 2005. *Confronting Sexual Harassment: The Law and Politics of Everyday Life*. Burlington, Vt.: Ashgate.

MATHER, L. 1979. *Plea Bargaining or Trial? The Process of Criminal Case Disposition*. Lexington, Mass.: Lexington Press.

—— 1998. Theorizing about trial courts: lawyers, policymaking, and tobacco litigation. *Law and Social Inquiry*, 23: 897–940.

—— 2003. Presidential address—reflections on the reach of law (and society) post 9/11: an American superhero? *Law and Society Review*, 37: 263–82.

—— forthcoming. Bringing the lawyers back in. In *Exploring Judicial Politics*, ed. M. C. Miller. New York: Oxford University Press.

—— McEWEN, C. A., and MAIMAN, R. J. 2001. *Divorce Lawyers at Work: Varieties of Professionalism in Practice*. New York: Oxford University Press.

—— and YNGVESSON, B. 1980–1. Language, audience, and the transformation of disputes. *Law and Society Review*, 15: 775–822.

MAYNARD, D. 1984. *Inside Plea Bargaining: The Language of Negotiation*. New York: Plenum.

MERRY, S. E. 1990. *Getting Justice and Getting Even: Legal Consciousness Among Working-Class Americans*. Chicago: University of Chicago Press.

MILLER, R. E. and SARAT, A. 1980–1. Grievances, claims, and disputes: assessing the adversary culture. *Law and Society Review*, 15: 525–66.

MINOW, M. and RAKOFF, T. 1998. Is the "reasonable person" a reasonable standard in a multicultural world? Pp. 68–108 in *Everyday Practices and Trouble Cases: Fundamental Issues in Law and Society Research: Volume 2*, ed. A. Sarat, M. Constable, D. Engel, V. Hans, and S. Lawrence. Evanston, Ill.: Northwestern University Press.

MOORE, S. F. 1978. *Law as Process: An Anthropological Approach*. London: Routledge and Kegan Paul.

MUNGER, F. (ed.) 1990. Special issue on longitudinal studies of trial courts. *Law and Society Review*, 24 (2).

—— 2001. Presidential address: inquiry and activism in law and society. *Law and Society Review*, 35: 7–20.

NADER, L. 1969. Introduction. Pp. 1–10 in *Law in Culture and Society*, ed. L. Nader. Chicago: Aldine Press.

—— and TODD, H. 1978. *The Disputing Process: Law in Ten Societies*. New York: Columbia University Press.

NIELSEN, L. B. 2004. *License to Harass: Law, Hierarchy, and Offensive Public Speech*. Princeton, NJ: Princeton University Press.

PRATT, A. C. 1999. Dunking the doughnut: discretionary power, law and the administration of the Canadian Immigration Act. *Social and Legal Studies*, 8: 199–226.

ROSENTHAL, D. E. 1974. *Lawyer and Client: Who's In Charge?* New York: Russell Sage Foundation.

SARAT, A. 1990. "The law is all over:" power, resistance, and the legal consciousness of the welfare poor. *Yale Journal of Law and Humanities*, 2: 348–79.

—— 2004. *The Blackwell Companion to Law and Society*. Malden, Mass.: Blackwell.

—— and FELSTINER, W. L. F. 1995. *Divorce Lawyers and their Clients: Power and Meaning in the Legal Process*. New York: Oxford University Press.

—— and SCHEINGOLD, S. A. (eds.) 1998. *Cause Lawyering: Political Commitments and Professional Responsibilities*. New York: Oxford University Press.

—— and SILBEY, S. 1988. The pull of the policy audience. *Law and Policy*, 10: 97–166.

SCHEINGOLD, S. A. and SARAT, A. 2004. *Something to Believe In: Politics, Professionalism, and Cause Lawyering*. Stanford, Calif.: Stanford University Press.

SCHLEGEL, J. H. 1995. *American Legal Realism and Empirical Social Science*. Durham: University of North Carolina Press.

SCHMIDT, P. 2005. *Lawyers and Regulation: The Politics of the Administrative Process*. Cambridge: Cambridge University Press.

SHAPIRO, M. 1972. From public law to public policy, or the "public" in "public law." *PS*, 5: 410–18.

—— 1981. *Courts: A Comparative and Political Analysis*. Chicago: University of Chicago Press.

SIMON, J. 1988. The ideological effects of actuarial practices. *Law and Society Review*, 22: 771–800.

—— 1999. Law after society. *Law and Social Inquiry*, 24: 143–94.

SKOLNICK, J. H. 1994. *Justice Without Trial: Law Enforcement in Democractic Society*, 3rd edn. New York: Macmillan.

SMITH, R. M. 1988. Political jurisprudence, the "new institutionalism," and the future of public law. *American Political Science Review*, 82: 89–108.

SPOHN, C. C. 2000. Thirty years of sentencing reform: the quest for a racially neutral sentencing process. *Criminal Justice*, 3: 427–501.

SUDNOW, D. 1965. Normal crimes: sociological features of the penal code in a public defender office. *Social Problems*, 12: 255–76.

SUNSTEIN, C. R. et al. 2002. *Punitive Damages: How Juries Decide*. Chicago: University of Chicago Press.

TRUBEK, D. M. 1980–1. The construction and deconstruction of a disputes-focused approach: an afterword. *Law and Society Review*, 15: 485–501.

TYLER, T. R. 1990. *Why People Obey the Law*. New Haven, Conn.: Yale University Press.

—— and RASINSKI, K. 1991. Procedural justice, institutional legitimacy, and the acceptance of unpopular U.S. Supreme Court decisions: a reply to Gibson. *Law and Society Review*, 25: 621–30.

YNGVESSON, B. 1993. *Virtuous Citizens, Disruptive Subjects: Order and Complaint in a New England Court*. New York: Routledge.

ZEMANS, F. K. 1983. Legal mobilization: the neglected role of the law in the political system. *American Political Science Review*, 77: 690–703.

CHAPTER 16

....

FEMINIST THEORY AND THE LAW

....

JUDITH A. BAER

AMERICAN feminists have identified law as an instrument of male supremacy since their first national gathering at Seneca Falls, New York in 1848. Modeled on the Declaration of Independence, the conference's Declaration of Sentiments and Resolutions listed the denial of the vote, marriage law that made a wife "civilly dead," and divorce law "wholly regardless of the happiness of women" among the "injuries and usurpations on the part of man toward woman, having in direct object the establishment of an absolute tyranny over her" that had inspired the meeting (Commager 1963, 315–16). Critiques of law thus became an important part of the early feminist movement, which succeeded in eradicating the most blatant examples of legal sexism. The signers of the Seneca Falls document were acting not only as social activists but also as legal theorists. Their thesis that law was designed by men for the purpose of dominating women is not far from the arguments of some contemporary feminist jurists.

Feminist scholarship was a product of the second stage of feminism that began in the late 1960s. This feminism arose from women's growing recognition that earlier victories had not succeeded in establishing equality between the sexes. Yet the successes of the contemporary feminist movement might not have happened without one of those early successes: the opening of higher education to women. Campuses proved to be as fertile a ground for the women's movement as they were for the civil rights, antiwar, and student movements. The enactment in 1972 of Title IX of the Education Amendments to the Civil Rights Act of 1964, which extended the prohibition of sex-based discrimination to educational institutions receiving federal funds, enhanced women's opportunities for postgraduate education and helped enlarge the pool of potential feminist scholars.

Twenty-first century Americans disagree on whether second-stage feminism has succeeded or failed, is alive, dead, or merely sleeping, is in stasis, crisis, or disarray, or is a positive or negative force in society. What no thoughtful and knowledgeable person can dispute is that contemporary feminism has had a profound and lasting impact on intellectual discourse. Many young scholars focused on gender in their research, pursuing the feminist goal "to question everything" (Wishik 1986, 64). These scholars and their successors continue to realize the revolutionary potential of feminist thought. "Feminist jurisprudence," as it came to be called, is law's equivalent of feminist history, feminist psychology, feminist philosophy, and their counterparts. Feminist jurisprudence has borrowed freely and fruitfully from these cognate disciplines. Not only has feminist jurisprudence become an integral part of legal theory, but it has also contributed to real-world legal change.

This is not to imply that feminist jurisprudence has become law's equivalent of the pink-collar ghetto. Women legal scholars have made significant contributions in subfields that do not emphasize gender issues. No woman law professor, whatever her personal opinions about feminism, need choose feminist jurisprudence as her specialty; nor does the subfield exclude men.

Scholars who agree on little else agree that

> Feminists have tried to describe for the judiciary a theory of "special rights" for women which will fit the discrete, non-stereotypical, "real" differences between the sexes. And herein lies our mistake: We have let the debate become narrowed by accepting as correct those questions which seek to arrive at a definitive list of differences. In so doing, we have adopted the vocabulary, as well as the epistemology and political theory, of the law as it is.
>
> (Scales 1986, 1375)

Feminist theorists who distrust "the law as it is" share three fundamental premises. First, conventional legal doctrines, developed by men in a society dominated by men, have a fundamental male bias even when they are ostensibly gender-neutral. Secondly, women's lives, for whatever reasons, are so different from men's lives that theory developed by men does not fit women's concrete reality. Finally, the development of feminist theory requires that women produce theory from their own experience and perspective.

1 THE PREMISE AND PRESENCE OF BIAS

Feminist jurists who accept the premise of male bias insist on "asking the woman question...to identify the gender implications of rules and practices which might otherwise appear to be neutral or objective" (Bartlett 1990, 832). This approach to law is radical, if not revolutionary. Conventional jurisprudence requires that adjudication "must be genuinely principled, resting ... on analysis and reasons quite transcending the immediate result that is achieved" (Wechsler 1961, 5). The "woman question," on the other hand, exemplifies the result-oriented jurisprudence that conventional jurisprudence condemns. Feminists are not the first to reject law's claim to neutrality. Marxists and the Critical Legal Studies movement had a head start, not to mention Anatole France: "The law, in its majestic equality, forbids the rich as well as the poor to sleep under bridges, to beg in the streets, and to steal bread" (2002 [1894], ch. 7). Feminist scholars do not accept as equal "a scheme that affords extensive protection to the right to bear arms or to sell violent pornography, but not to control our reproductive lives" (Rhode 1990, 633).

Whether or not male decision-makers conspire to disadvantage women, policies designed for men have fit badly with women's lives. Some scholars have concluded that modern equal protection doctrine on sexual equality has benefited men at least as much as women; for example, by requiring gender-neutral spousal support laws (*Orr v. Orr* 1979) but permitting interpretations of divorce and child custody law that disadvantage ex-wives (Baer 1999, ch. 4). A specialist in contract law asserted that the law's refusal to enforce mutual agreements in nonmarital relationships injured the women plaintiffs by denying them compensation for homemaking and childrearing duties (Dalton 1985). When the second stage of feminism began, the law still allowed the defense to inquire into an alleged rape victim's sexual history.

The problem here is not so much that men are dominant and women subordinate, as that reality is gendered. This generalization, of course, is a restatement of the second premise of feminist jurisprudence that I have identified. Feminist jurists who accept this premise differ widely in their explanations of how and why reality is gendered.

2 FEMINIST JURISPRUDENCE AND GENDERED REALITY

Feminist jurisprudence has not been satisfied with pointing out the historical fact that law was created by men (more precisely, by all-male elites) and citing current examples of legal bias in favor of men (vis-à-vis women). These two observations have scant analytical value without connections between them. Making these connections became the first major project of feminist jurisprudence. Much of this early scholarship centered around what came to be called the "difference debate" (Goldstein 1992). There have been two overlapping versions of this discourse.

The first version, *sameness versus difference*, is essentially a dispute about the meaning of gender equality under law. Wendy Williams (1981; 1984–5; 1991 [1982]) and Ruth Bader Ginsburg (1978) advocated across-the-board gender equality with no special treatment for women.[1] Williams does not distinguish between invidious and benign sex discrimination. Therefore, she regards special benefits for women workers like pregnancy and childbearing leaves as no better than the once common, but now overruled, mandatory maternity leaves and the "fetal protection" policies that excluded women from jobs: "If we can't have it both ways, we need to think carefully about which way we want to have it" (1991 [1982], 26). Some feminist legal scholars regard male supremacist laws as anomalies within an essentially gender-neutral system. Nadine Strossen, for example, rejects the antipornography policies favored by many feminists: "We adamantly oppose any effort to restrict sexual speech not only because it would violate our cherished First Amendment freedoms . . . but also because it would undermine our equality, our status, our dignity, and our autonomy" (1995, 14.)

Scholars like Williams and Strossen comprise a distinct but vocal minority among feminist legal scholars. Most feminist jurists insist that gender equality cannot be equated with sameness, but demands the recognition of and adaptation to gendered realities like the childbearing function and women's economic disadvantages vis-à-vis men (Finley 1986; Kay 1985; Littleton 1987; West 1997; J. Williams 2000). Antipornography feminist Catharine MacKinnon insists that the First Amendment is one of several "abstract rights" that "authorize the male experience of the world" (1989, 248); giving constitutional protection to pornography effectively gives its consumers and producers license to brutalize and degrade women (1993). These responses to prevailing legal doctrines are among many feminist critiques of legal principles that feminist jurists have produced.

The second version of the debate, confusingly labeled *difference versus dominance*, consists of conflicting explanations of the bad fit between law and women's lives. Participants in this discourse use various labels for the two schools of thought, but the labels establish similar dichotomies. "Difference" or "cultural" feminists posit character differences between men and women that make masculinist theories inherently biased against women, whereas "dominance" or "radical" feminists hold that these differences result from "the perspective that has been forced on women" (MacKinnon 1989, 52). Difference feminism has been heavily influenced by the pathbreaking work of psychologist Carol Gilligan. Her study of moral psychology, *In a Different Voice*, maintains that, while men's moral development emphasizes "rights and noninterference," women's psychology is "distinctive in its greater orientation toward relationships and interdependence," valuing "attachment" to others over "separation" from them (1982, 2, 151).

---

[1] This characterization refers to Ruth Bader Ginsburg's work as a feminist lawyer and law professor, not to her performance on the U.S. Court of Appeals and the Supreme Court.

Robin West's application of these arguments to jurisprudence stresses physical gender differences. "Virtually all modern American legal theorists," she writes, accept "the 'separation thesis' of what it means to be a human being: a 'human being,' whatever else he is, is physically separate from all other human beings. . . . The cluster of claims that jointly constitute the 'separation thesis' . . . while usually true of men, are patently untrue of women." Why? Because women are "connected to life and to other human beings" through four "critical material experiences:" menstruation, heterosexual penetration, pregnancy, and breastfeeding (1988, 1–3). In an effort to unite care and justice, West criticizes conventional law for failing both "to protect and nurture the connections that sustain and enlarge women's lives" and "to intervene in those private and intimate "connections" that damage and injure" women (1997, 14).

The terms "connection thesis" and "ethic of care" have become familiar feminist concepts. The association of justice with men and care with women resonates with the observable reality that, other things being equal, women perform more caring activity than men do. The notion of a female ethic of care and nurturance may also appeal to those who share the belief of some nineteenth-century feminists that women are morally superior to men. Finally, the possibility of incorporating care into the concept of justice appeals to many feminist jurists who remain reluctant to associate care with women (Behuniak 1999). Linda McClain similarly argues for "recognizing and promoting care as a public value" that "should inform public deliberation about the meaning of personal responsibility and about the interplay of personal and public responsibility for social reproduction" and emphasizes "the indispensable role of care in fostering persons' capacities for democratic and personal self-government" (2001, 1730).

However, difference feminism and its focus on care have met with pervasive and persuasive criticism.[2] West's explanation for gender difference now seems simplistic, exclusionary, and illogical. While the experiences West mentions are unique to women, they are not common to all women; nor does she explain how these experiences connect women to people who are not connected to them. Feminist theorists have made no better case for gender differences than did pre-feminist or outright antifeminist theorists. Difference feminism reads too much like old arguments justifying male supremacy, such as the Supreme Court's opinion in *Muller v. Oregon* (1908), to gain universal feminist acceptance.

West distinguishes herself and other "cultural feminists" from radical feminists like MacKinnon. For cultural feminists, "the important difference between men and women is that women have children and men don't;" for radical feminists, "the important difference between men and women is that women get fucked and men fuck" (West 1988, 13). West does not exaggerate or distort. MacKinnon reasons by analogy with Karl Marx's theory of class struggle to argue that law is designed to facilitate men's sexual access to women: "Sexuality is to feminism what work is to

[2] Baer (1999, 40–56); MacKinnon (1987, 38–9); Schneider (1986, 589–652); Williams (1992, 41–98).

marxism: that which is most one's own, yet most taken away" (1989, 3). Radical feminism accepts the premise of the Seneca Falls delegates that men designed the legal system to establish, or at least to preserve, male power.

MacKinnon is by far the most controversial of today's feminist jurists. Her extreme position has provoked considerable feminist criticism.[3] She has been accused both of vilifying men by depicting them as sexual predators and of denigrating women by denying their agency and autonomy (Baer 1999, 58–62). But the fact that a position is extreme does not prove it wrong. The evidence MacKinnon advances to support her thesis includes the fact that the Supreme Court recognized rights to birth control and abortion years before it invalidated fetal protection policies barring women from well-paying blue collar jobs (1989, 190, 226). As we shall see, criticism has not persuaded MacKinnon to moderate either tone or content (MacKinnon; 2005; 2006; Jeffries 2006).

Feminist jurists need not believe that law's *purpose* is to entrench male supremacy in order to argue that law's *effect* is to do this. "Situation jurisprudence" (Baer 1999, 55–8), like radical feminism, emphasizes male power and privilege: men get to choose what they want to do, and women are stuck with whatever is left. Feminist jurists have subjected many ostensibly neutral legal concepts to reexamination and fresh analysis in terms of "what we know as women" (Baer 1999). One example of this type of analysis is Joan Williams's explanation of women's competitive disadvantage in employment. Williams argues that the workplace presumes an "ideal worker" whose other responsibilities take second place to the job. Since most women have greater domestic responsibilities, devoting more time and energy to care for households and dependents than do men, women are less likely to fit the description of the ideal worker (2000).

The difference versus dominance controversy continues in the face of—and in response to—the extensive and trenchant criticism both schools of thought have received. Ironically, feminist jurisprudence has received extensive criticism for doing what it criticizes conventional scholarship for doing. Authors who have asserted that conventional jurisprudence says "person" when it means "man" have been criticized by minority feminists for saying "woman" and meaning "woman plus modifiers:" Caucasian, heterosexual, Western woman.

Angela Harris criticizes both cultural and radical feminists for "gender essentialism—the notion that a unitary, 'essential' woman's experience can be isolated and described" (1990, 604). Harris maintains that race is a central component of the identities of women of color (in Europe and North America, at least), but not of white women. Therefore, the "critical material experiences" of cultural feminism and the sexual objectification of women emphasized by radical feminists are mediated through a racial context for some women but not for others. "Mainstream" Western feminist jurisprudence has encountered similar challenges made on behalf of lesbians (Brown 1990; Cain 1990) and disabled women (Baer 1999, 34–7).

---

[3] Cornell (1991, 139); "Feminist Discourse" (1985, 75); Smart (1989, 77).

No consensus exists within feminist theory about the possibility of locating a common essential identity. The same is true of the difference debate in its various manifestations. No one is forced to take sides, and many scholars choose to concentrate on other issues. But legal scholars on both sides and on neither side of these debates embrace the final premise of feminist jurisprudence: the need for scholarship based on women's experience.

3 FEMINIST LEGAL REASONING

The feminist premise of male bias applies as much to methods as to theories. Feminist critiques of method from the humanities and social sciences have influenced legal scholarship. These critiques have characterized conventional methodology as dichotomous, oppositional, hierarchical, abstract, reason-based, and emphasizing separation. Feminist alternative methodology is an intuitive/emotional, holistic, non-invasive, concrete, and contextualized epistemology of connection (Baer 1999, 72–8). It emphasizes "the distinctive features of women's situation in a gender-stratified society" (Harding 1990, 119), "the world of concrete particulars" to which many women are relegated (Smith 1990, 19), and "women's ways of knowing" (Belenky et al. 1986) which applies Gilligan's work to epistemology. For MacKinnon, women's way of knowing is through consciousness raising, "the process through which contemporary radical feminist analysis of the situation of women has been shaped and shared" (1989, 84). Consciousness raising is inductive, not deductive. It came out of the women's discussion groups that flourished in the early years of second-wave feminism. Many members of the founding generation of feminist theory participated in these groups. Feminist jurisprudence has applied the insights of feminist epistemology to the study of legal methods. One scholar credited Gilligan's book with helping her understand "why I felt so uncomfortable in law school" (Feminist Discourse 1985, 1). A study of law students at an Ivy League university discovered that women tended to do less well than comparable men and theorized that the Socratic method of law school teaching is an ordeal for many women (Guinier et al. 1997).

Feminist scholars' distinctions between male and female methods work better in theory than in practice. They do not stand up when applied to concrete, particular analysis of everyday legal decision-making. "Legal feeling" (Baer 1999, 84) is as omnipresent as "maternal thinking" (Ruddick 1989); any follower of the Supreme Court knows that appeals to emotion are a common feature of the justices' opinions. Consciousness raising combines inductive and deductive reasoning. The different versions of the process that developed encouraged participants to use concepts from feminist theory in interpreting their shared experiences. The case for a distinctively *female* epistemology has yet to be made. But *feminist* epistemology has had significant impact on theory and jurisprudence.

4 FROM THE "WOMAN QUESTION" TO "WOMAN ANSWERS"

Feminist jurisprudence has not stopped with pointing out ways in which existing law is hostile to women's interests. Scholars have shown remarkable creativity in devising woman-oriented alternative theories. Twenty-first-century legal doctrine shows the influence of feminist inquiry, although the nexus between cause and effect is neither clear nor simple. Some feminist contributions to legal theory have yet to be put into practice, but others have gained judicial recognition. Since a single article cannot present all of this scholarship, this chapter will focus on three important and controversial innovations. The first two of these, Martha Fineman's work on family law and Catharine MacKinnon's analysis of the law of rape, address specific gendered legal issues. The third innovation is the concept of the "reasonable woman," a theoretical construct that has guided decision-making in both civil and criminal law.

Martha Fineman's studies of family law reflected widespread feminist recognition that gender neutrality might not entail sexual equality. The gradual progression of American family law in the nineteenth and twentieth centuries from traditional male supremacy toward gender-neutrality coincided with, reinforced, and was reinforced by feminism. One major twentieth-century innovation that had some initial feminist support was "no-fault divorce." The old adversarial process of ending a marriage was replaced by "dissolution" premised on the assumption that the decision was mutual. At the same time, maternal preference in child custody decisions yielded to a neutral "best interests of the child" rule. But by the 1980s, feminists had discovered that the new rules often resulted in support judgments that impoverished women and children and custody arrangements that ignored or denied the fact that the mother was almost always the children's primary caregiver (Baer 2002, 134–58.)

Fineman perceives a connection between this legal undervaluing of the mother–child bond and widespread (though decreasing) public hostility toward single and lesbian mothers. She argues that family law presupposed a "sexual family" consisting of mother, father, and children. "The neutered mother" becomes one of two parents and only half of the parental unit; "marriage and family" become inseparable. Fineman proposes abolishing marriage as a legal category and replacing sex with care and dependency as the crucial family bond. This "newly redefined legal category of family" would include "inevitable dependents along with their caregivers. The caregiving family would...be entitled to special, preferred treatment by the state" (1995, 231). While the caregivers could be either women or men, the result of such a change would benefit many women and might even encourage caregiving behavior among men. It would also derail the controversy over same-sex marriage.

Catharine MacKinnon's most recent publications (2005; 2006) apply her theory of law's maleness to criminal law. The radical transformation in the law of sexual assault in the past thirty years represents a landmark victory for second-stage feminism. The modesty of the complainant's appearance, the prudence of her behavior, and the details of her sexual history are no longer before the court. Nonetheless, MacKinnon asserts, "The law of rape protects rapists and is written from their point of view to guarantee impunity for most rapes." She means, she tells an interviewer, "not that all the people who wrote [the law] were rapists, but that they are a member of the group who do." The interviewer continues:

She thinks consent in rape cases should be irrelevant. Women are so unfree that even if a woman is shown to have given consent to sex, that should never be enough to secure an acquittal. Why? "My view is that when there is force or substantially coercive circumstances between the parties, individual consent is beside the point; that if someone is forced into sex, that ought to be enough."   (Jeffries 2006)

The classic definition of rape is "carnal knowledge of a woman forcibly *and* (not *or*) without her consent." The prosecution must prove both the presence of force and the absence of consent. Nowhere does the law distinguish between a woman's consent (the commonest defense to a rape charge) and her submission (Schulhofer 1998, ch. 13). The elimination of consent as a defense to sexual assault, like the elimination of legal marriage, would be a change so extraordinary that it brings to mind Ruth Rosen's metaphor for the effects of feminism: "the world split open" (2000). Neither change is even remotely likely in the foreseeable future. But less dramatic developments are bringing both family law and criminal law closer to feminist ideals. Many jurisdictions have adopted a "primary caregiver" preference in child custody cases (Baer 2002, 156–8.) And rape law is showing the effect of the "reasonable woman" standard.

The concept of the "reasonable person" is a crucial component in the law of torts, and is found also in criminal law. To be at fault is to fail to act as a reasonable person would in the same situation. For example, a defendant in a negligence suit can avoid damages by showing by a preponderance of the evidence either that he or she had acted with the "reasonable care" that the context required or by showing that the plaintiff's failure to exercise reasonable care constituted contributory negligence (although statutes have limited or abolished this defense in some instances).

The "reasonable person" concept originated in the common law notion of the "reasonable man." Does the substitution render the concept gender-neutral? Kim Lane Scheppele (2004) insists that in many situations the reasonable person is in effect the reasonable man. She proposes a "reasonable woman" standard for gender-related civil and criminal law.

The question of whether "reasonable person" means "reasonable man" is integral to the criminal law of rape and domestic violence. Scheppele discusses the case of a man who got a ride home with a woman he had just met. He invited her to his apartment and snatched her car keys; she followed him because she feared being out on the street in an unfamiliar neighborhood. After much disagreement within the state appellate courts, the Maryland Supreme Court finally upheld the conviction (*State v. Rusk* 1981.) "Women don't sexualize situations as quickly as men do," Scheppele comments, "and so they may be slower to recognize danger in the first place" (2004, 460).

One tort, sexual harassment, is classified as sex discrimination by Title VII of the Civil Rights Act of 1964 (*Meritor v. Vinson* 1986). The law recognizes two types of sexual harassment. *Quid pro quo* harassment can be summarized as, "sleep with me or I'll fire you," or "sleep with me and I'll promote you." A more common form of harassment is the creation of a hostile environment in the workplace. The typical sexual harassment plaintiff is female; the typical defendant is male.

From the defendant's standpoint, the dispositive question in a hostile environment case becomes whether his behavior was that of a reasonable person or whether the plaintiff's reaction to his behavior met that standard. A defendant who pursues a co-worker after she has rebuffed him may well believe that his behavior is reasonable; after all, he is acting out the plot of countless works of fiction, drama, and comedy, and may even have seen this courtship technique work in real life. A defendant who tells dirty jokes or makes suggestive remarks may argue that the woman who complains about this behavior is unreasonably sensitive. Approaching sexual harassment litigation from these standpoints has the effect of authorizing men's experiences and attitudes.

But suppose that we approach hostile environment cases from the plaintiff's perspective. From her standpoint, the crucial questions become whether a reasonable woman would find the plaintiff's behavior objectionable or threatening enough to create a hostile environment in the workplace. The same year Scheppele published her article, an appellate court ruled in favor of a plaintiff who received unwelcome advances: "We adopt the perspective of a reasonable woman because a sex-blind reasonable person standard tends to be male-biased and tends to systematically ignore the experiences of women" (*Ellison v. Brady* 1991, 880). Plaintiffs who were asked "go to the Holiday Inn" to discuss pay raises, told to fish in the supervisor's pockets for change, or subjected to epithets like "dumb fucking broad" prevailed in court.

The reasonable woman doctrine is not without its defects and dangers. First, the concept conflates gender and role. As women gain power in the workplace, it is likely that some of them, like some men, will abuse their power. Asking what a reasonable woman might do will only confuse matters if aggressor and victim are the same sex (*Oncale v Sundowner Offshore Services* 1998). Might the law better adopt a "reasonable victim" rule? A second difficulty with a reasonable woman rule is that it could do real damage if applied in areas of law that are not overtly gender-sensitive. A jury in a negligence case, for example, might expect more caution and foresight from a reasonable woman than from her male counterpart. And think how a concept like "reasonable mother" might influence a jury!

The concept of the reasonable person has found yet another home in the area of domestic violence. Elizabeth Schneider (2000) points out that legal discourse has long been stuck on the question of why the battered women did not end the abusive relationship. This emphasis on the supposed unreasonableness of the victim's behavior became a rationale for law enforcement agencies and prosecutors to trivialize violence against women much as they once trivialized sexual assault. Feminist scholars have had much success in changing this official behavior.

Lenore Walker, a feminist sociologist, tried to explain victims' toleration of abuse by developing a concept that she labeled the "battered woman syndrome" (1984). Walker argued that long-term abuse taught many women that they were helpless to change their situation. Activists for battered women object that "the image that the concept of learned helplessness conveys...is one of passivity and lack of agency" (Downs 1966, 155–7). But the battered woman syndrome defense has won some acquittals in trials of women who kill their abusers, even though it applies the idea of learned helplessness to someone who has displayed considerable aggression. "BWS" is an uneasy combination of two defenses against homicide charges: self-defense and diminished capacity. These two doctrines do not mesh well; the first presumes a rational actor while the latter presumes the opposite.

Efforts to protect oneself, others, or property have long been recognized as exculpating factors in criminal cases. A defendant in a homicide case who pleads self-defense must convince the factfinder(s) that he or she perceived imminent danger of serious injury or death and that this belief was reasonable in the circumstances. Juries have been known to give defendants considerable latitude under the imminent danger rule. For instance, both a Louisiana man who fatally shot a stranger who rang his doorbell by mistake and a Virginia man who killed a neighbor who swore at him during an altercation were acquitted (Baer 1999, 207–8).

Feminists have questioned whether the imminent danger requirement is as neutral as it looks. The rule would lead us to expect a woman whose husband had abused her on numerous occasions to be acquitted after she killed him during yet another violent episode, even without recourse to the battered woman syndrome. When a woman was nonetheless convicted in such a case, the New Jersey Supreme Court ordered a new trial that would include testimony about BWS to show that that the woman could reasonably fear that her life was in danger during the episode (*State v. Kelly* 1984). But most battered women who kill do not do so during an attack, and BWS may have particular significance in those types of cases. The imminent danger rule that can respond so flexibly to male experience is unresponsive to their experience. The battered woman syndrome defense asks factfinders to consider whether the defendant might overreact to a perceived threat because her reasoning capacity is defective, in the same way that an insanity plea makes comparable demands. But, while the logic of the BWS defense is problematic, the defense has entered the legal repertoire.

5 CONCLUSION

Legal doctrine emerges from human experience. When women were excluded from the legal enterprise, man-made law was just that. The growth of feminist jurisprudence has coincided with the entry of more and more women into the lawyering, law-making, and judging professions. Relying on women's experiences and perspectives, the first generation of feminist legal scholars has progressed from incisive analyses of law's male bias to the creation of new doctrines, new methods, and new proposals for reform. Activists in the legal arena have changed law to embody these concepts, as the "reasonable person" example shows. The two groups of scholars and activists overlap, and each activity has infiltrated and influenced the other. But law's male bias remains pervasive enough to make legal doctrine more responsive to men's claims than to women's. Both scholars and practitioners know that much work remains for later generations to do.

REFERENCES

BAER, J. A. 1999. *Our Lives before the Law: Constructing a Feminist Jurisprudence*. Princeton, NJ: Princeton: University Press.

—— 2002. *Women in American Law: The Struggle for Equality from the New Deal to the Present*. New York: Holmes and Meier.

BARTLETT, K. T. 1990. Feminist legal methods. *Harvard Law Review*, 103: 829–88.

BEHUNIAK, S. M. 1999. *A Caring Jurisprudence: Listening to Patients at the Supreme Court*. Lanham, Md.: Rowman and Littlefield.

BELENKY, M., CLINCHY, B., GOLDBERGER, N., and TARULE, J. 1986. *Women's Ways of Knowing: The Development of Self, Voice, and Mind*. New York: Basic Books.

BROWN, W. 1990. Consciousness razing. *Nation*, 250: 61–4.

CAIN, P. A. 1991. Feminist jurisprudence: grounding the theories. Pp. 263–80 in *Feminist Legal Theory: Readings in Law and Gender*, ed. K. T. Bartlett and R. Kennedy. Boulder Colo.: Westview.

COMMAGER, H. S. (ed.) 1963. *Documents in American History*, 7th edn. New York: Appleton-Century-Crofts.

CORNELL, D. 1991. *Beyond Accommodation: Ethical Feminism, Deconstruction, and the Law*. New York: Routledge, Chapman and Hall.

DALTON, C. 1985. An essay in the deconstruction of contract doctrine. *Yale Law Journal*, 94: 997–1114.

DOWNS, D. A. 1996. *More Than Victims: Battered Women, the Syndrome Society, and the Law*. Chicago: University of Chicago Press.

DUBOIS, E. C., DUNLAP, M. C., GILLIGAN, C. J., MACKINNON, C. A., MARCUS, I., MENKEL-MEADOW, C. J., and SPIEGELMAN, P. J. 1985. Feminist discourse, moral values, and the law: a conversation. *Buffalo Law Review*, 34: 11–87.

FEMINIST DISCOURSE 1985. Moral values, and the law—a conversation. *Buffalo Law Review*, 55: 11–87.

FINEMAN, M. A. 1995. *The Neutered Mother, the Sexual Family, and other Twentieth Century Tragedies.* New York: Routledge.

FINLEY, L. 1986. Transcending equality theory: a way out of the maternity and the workplace debate. *Columbia Law Review*, 86: 1118–82.

FRANCE, A. 2002 [1894]. *The Red Lily.* Rockville, Md.: Wildside Press.

GILLIGAN, C. 1982. *In a Different Voice.* Cambridge, Mass.: Harvard University Press.

GINSBURG, R. B. 1978. Sex equality and the Constitution. *Tulane Law Review*, 52: 451–3.

GOLDSTEIN, L. F. (ed.) 1992. *Feminist Jurisprudence: The Difference Debate.* Lanham, Md: Rowman and Littlefield.

GUINIER, L., FINE, M., and BALIN, J. 1997. *Becoming Gentlemen: Women's Experience at One Ivy League Law School.* Boston: Beacon Press.

HARDING, S. 1990. *Whose Science? Whose Knowledge? Thinking from Women's Lives.* Ithaca, NY: Cornell University Press.

HARRIS, A. 1990. Race and essentialism in feminist legal theory. *Stanford Law Review*, 42: 581–616.

JEFFRIES, S. 2006. Are women human? Interview with Catharine MacKinnon. *Guardian*, April 12.

KAY, H. H. 1985. Equality and difference: the case of pregnancy. *Berkeley Women's Law Journal*, 1: 1–38.

LITTLETON, C. A. 1987. Reconstructing sexual equality. *California Law Review*, 75: 1279–337.

MacKINNON, C. A. 1987. *Feminism Unmodified.* Cambridge, Mass.: Harvard University Press.

—— 1989. *Toward a Feminist Theory of the State.* Cambridge, Mass.: Harvard University Press.

—— 1993. *Only Words.* Cambridge, Mass.: Harvard University Press.

—— 2005. *Women's Lives, Men's Laws.* Cambridge, Mass.: Harvard University Press.

—— 2006. *Are Women Human?* Cambridge, Mass.: Harvard University Press.

McCLAIN, L. C. 2001. Care as a public value: linking responsibility, resources, and republicanism. *Chicago-Kent Law Review*, 76: 1673–731.

RHODE, D. L. 1990. Feminist critical theories. *Stanford Law Review*, 42: 617–38.

ROSEN, R. 2000. *The World Split Open: How the Modern Women's Movement Changed America.* New York: Penguin.

RUDDICK, S. 1989. *Maternal Thinking: Toward a Politics of Peace.* New York: Ballantine.

SCALES, A. M. 1986. The emergence of feminist jurisprudence: an essay. *Yale Law Journal*, 95: 1373–403.

SCHEPPELE, K. L. 2004. The reasonable woman. Pp. 456–460 in *Philosophy of Law*, 7th edn., ed. J. Feinberg and J. Coleman. Belmont, Calif.: Wadsworth/Thomson Learning; originally published 1991.

SCHNEIDER, E. 1986. The dialectic of rights and politics: perespectives from the women's movement. *New York University Law Review*, 61: 589–615.

—— 2000. *Battered Women and Feminist Lawmaking.* New Haven, Conn.: Yale University Press.

SCHULHOFER, S. J. 1998. *Unwanted Sex: The Culture of Intimidation and the Failure of Law.* Cambridge, Mass.: Harvard University Press.

SMART, C. 1989. *Feminism and the Power of Law.* New York: Routledge.

SMITH, D. E. 1990. *The Conceptual Practices of Power: A Feminist Sociology of Knowledge.* Boston: Northeastern University Press.

STROSSEN, N. 1995. *Defending Pornography: Free Speech, Sex, and the Fight for Women's Rights.* New York: Anchor.

TRONTO, J. C. *Moral Boundaries: A Political Argument for an Ethic of Care.* New York: Routledge.

WALKER, L. 1984. *The Battered Woman Syndrome.* New York: Springer.

WECHSLER, H. 1961. *Principles, Politics, and Fundamental Law.* Cambridge, Mass.: Harvard University Press.

WEST, R. 1997. *Caring for Justice.* New York: New York University Press.

—— 1988. Jurisprudence and gender. *University of Chicago Law Review,* 55: 1–72.

WILLIAMS, J. 1992. Deconstructing gender. Pp. 41–98 in *Feminist Jurisprudence: The Difference Debate,* ed. L. F. Goldstein. Lanham, Md.: Rowman and Littlefield.

—— 2000. *Unbending Gender: Why Family and Work Conflict and What To Do about It.* New York: Oxford University Press.

WILLIAMS, W. 1981. Firing the woman to protect the fetus: the reconciliation of fetal protection with equal opportunity goals under Title VII. *Georgetown Law Journal,* 69: 641–704.

—— 1991 [1982]. The equality crisis: some reflections on culture, courts, and feminism. Pp. 15–34 in *Feminist Legal Theory,* ed. K. T. Bartlett and R. Kennedy. Boulder, Colo.: Westview.

—— 1984–5. Equality's riddle: pregnancy and equal treatment. *New York University Review of Law and Social Change,* 13: 325–80.

WISHIK, H. R. 1986. To question everything: the inquiries of feminist jurisprudence. *Berkeley Women's Law Journal,* 1: 64–77.

CASES

Ellison v. Brady. 1991. 924 F. 2d 872.

Meritor Savings Bank v. Vinson. 1986. 477 U.S. 57.

Muller v. Oregon. 1908. 208 U.S. 412.

Oncale v Sundowner Offshore Services. 1998. 523 U.S. 75.

Orr v. Orr. 1979. 440 U.S. 268.

State of Maryland v. Goldberg. 1978. 41 Md. App. 58.

State v. Kelly. 1984. 478 A.2d 364.

State v. Rusk. 1981. 424 A.2d 720.

PART V

POLITICAL BEHAVIOR

CHAPTER 17

....

OVERVIEW OF
POLITICAL
BEHAVIOR

POLITICAL BEHAVIOR
AND
CITIZEN POLITICS

....

RUSSELL J. DALTON
HANS-DIETER KLINGEMANN

THE behavioral revolution transformed research on American politics and then European politics in the 1960s and early 1970s. In the last two decades, this methodology has broadened to the field of comparative politics as the expansion of empirical research and the behavioral approach now have a near global reach. While a generation or two ago there was little systematic evidence on political processes outside the advanced industrial democracies, our knowledge base has expanded rapidly to provide an unprecedented storehouse of knowledge about the human condition. The

* We want to thank the authors in the *Oxford Handbook of Political Behavior* for their contributions to that volume, and we draw upon many of their findings and conclusions in this chapter.

world has changed when public opinion surveys in China (and other developing nations) are possibly more common than surveys of the American public in the early years of the behavioral revolution.

The behavioral revolution—or empirical research as a methodology—involves a range of political phenomena. Studies of political development have generated an impressive array of information about social and political conditions in the world. Policy studies are systematically expanding through the collection of comparable cross-national databases. These advances are seen in the chapters on institutions, legislative behavior, and other contributions to this volume.

This chapter summarizes our growing understanding of how contemporary publics think about politics, develop their basic political values, and participate in the political process. An expanding collection of public opinion data is one of the major accomplishments in comparative political behavior over the past several decades (see Kittilson 2007; Heath, Fisher, and Smith 2005). *The Civic Culture* (Almond and Verba 1963) was a dramatic step forward in comparative research by studying the publics in five nations. Today, institutionalized or semi-institutionalized cross-national surveys are repeated regularly, some with a near-global scope. The European Commission sponsors the Eurobarometer surveys in the member states of the European Union. A New Europe Barometer, Latinobarometer, Afrobarometer, East Asia Barometer, and AsiaBarometer survey citizens in these regions. Separate research consortiums regularly conduct the European Values Study (EVS), the International Social Survey Program (ISSP), the European Social Survey (ESS), and the Comparative Study of Electoral Systems (CSES). The largest number of nations is included in the World Values Surveys (WVS), which launched a fifth wave in 2005–7. In short, over the past few decades comparative political behavior has become a very "data-rich" field of research.

In addition, behavioral research has expanded during a period of tremendous political change in the world. Political behavior in advanced industrial democracies has shifted in fundamental ways during the latter half of the twentieth century. Social and political modernization is dramatically transforming much of the developing world. The third wave of democratization has reformed the political systems and the citizenry in the new democracies of Central and Eastern Europe, Asia, Africa, and Latin America.

These new developments provide distinctive opportunities to test old theories, expand the boundaries of knowledge, and develop new theories. We normally observe political systems in a state of equilibrium, when stability and incremental change dominate our findings. Now we can examine questions of political change and adaptation that often go to the heart of theoretical interests, but which we could seldom observe directly in earlier times.

This chapter reviews some of the major research debates and empirical findings in the study of citizen political behavior in broad cross-national terms, drawing upon the compilation in the *Oxford Handbook of Political Behavior* (Dalton and Klingemann 2007).

1 THE NATURE OF MASS BELIEF SYSTEMS

One of the enduring research debates in political behavior involves basic questions about the public's political abilities—their level of knowledge, understanding, and interest in political matters. For voters to make meaningful decisions, they must understand the options the polity faces. Citizens must have a sufficient knowledge of the workings of the political system if they intend to influence and control the actions of their representatives. Almond and Verba (1963), for example, considered cognition important in defining a political culture, and Dahl (1989, 307–8) stressed the quality of the political debate as a precondition to arrive at what he has called "enlightened understanding."

Debates about the political abilities of the public remain one of the major controversies in political behavior research. The early empirical surveys found that the public's political sophistication fell short of the theoretical ideal even in the established democracies (Campbell et al. 1960; Converse 1964; Butler and Stokes 1969). For most citizens, political interest and involvement barely seemed to extend beyond casting an occasional vote in national elections. Furthermore, people apparently brought very little understanding to their political participation. It was not clear that voting decisions were based on rational evaluations of candidates, parties, and their issue positions.

This image of the uninformed and unsophisticated voter reshaped the view of the citizenry and democratic politics (Campbell et al. 1960; Delli Carpini and Keeter 1996). Some experts argued that if the bulk of the public is unsophisticated, it is better for democracy that people remain politically uninvolved. And if this was beneficial to democracy, other scholars were anxious to argue the pitfalls of too excessive political mobilization and the benefits of political order in less developed nations (Zakaria 2006).

This debate has continued until the present (Lewis-Beck et al. 2008; Kuklinski and Peyton 2007; Converse 2007; Friedman 2006; Kinder 2006; Hibbing and Theiss-Morse 2002). Some research claims that political information and engagement remain limited even in Western democracies (Delli Carpini and Keeter 1996; Wattenberg 2006; Putnam 2000; Hardin 2006). If knowledge were limited in established democracies with affluent and educated publics, then the potential for active citizenship in developing nations would appear even more limited.

In contrast, a revisionist approach argues that contemporary publics have greater political sophistication than early research presumed, because either early measurement was flawed or sophistication has increased because of social modernization. Levels of political interest and cognitive mobilization are increasing over time in many established democracies, creating more informed and aware publics (Dalton 2007). Scholars also argue that the political context matters, and thus the interest and sophistication of mass publics partially reflect elite discourse. This contextual explanation is further supported by cross-national studies indicating that sophistication varies sharply across nations, with the relatively nonideological American system displaying one of the least ideological publics (Klingemann 1979; Stacy and Segura 1997).

In short, one school of research argues the glass is half empty, and going down; the opposite school argues the glass is half full, and going up. This political science prestidigitation—to have both things happen at once—is often based on analyses of the same public opinion surveys. The resolution of this question has fundamental implications for how we think about political behavior and the citizens' role in the democratic process. For instance, if one believes that the instruments of democracy should be expanded, this makes assumptions about the citizenry's ability to make informed political choices.

Other public opinion research suggests a different way of thinking about this question. Rather than asking if voters meet the ideal expectations of democratic theorists, which has often been the implicit standard, we should recognize that people regularly make political choices and ask how these choices are actually made. Bowler and Donovan (1998, 30 f.) aptly put it this way: "Voters, to use an analogy, may know very little about the workings of the internal combustion engine, but they do know how to drive. And while we might say that early voting studies focused on voter ignorance of the engine, the newer studies pay more attention to the ability to drive." Thus, many studies (such as Mutz, this volume; Sniderman and Levendusky 2007) ask the pragmatic question of how people make life decisions—including whom to vote for in the next election. Research on information cues argues that what citizens need to reach a meaningful political choice is less than once theorized. Quite naturally, citizens economize their investment in the information they need to make meaningful decisions and most of them optimize this investment in ways that keep democracies working (Lau and Redlawsk 2006; Lupia and McCubbins 1998; Popkin 1991). People in Western democracies now live in an information-rich environment which provides lots of cues on how people like oneself should vote or act on political issues. In short, citizens often use information shortcuts, cues, emotions, heuristics, and other methods to reach reasonable choices. Reasonable choices, when structured by institutions and cumulated across the electorate, lead to reasonable democratic outcomes (Surowiecki 2004). Admittedly cues and heuristics have limitations and are not the ideal way of making political choices, but they can be a sufficient method to make reasonable choices.

Furthermore, as public opinion studies have spread to developing nations and new democracies, they uncover higher levels of interest and awareness than was originally expected by the early political culture research (e.g. Bratton, Mattes, and Gyimah-Boadi 2004; Chu et al. 2008). In the modern world, more citizens are politically aware and interested in the affairs of government because those affairs affect their daily lives.

This continuing debate is a source of vitality in political behavior research, because it focuses attention on the question of what democracy expects of its citizens and whether they meet these expectations. The lofty ideals of classic democratic theory presumed a rational decision-making process by a fully informed electorate. Even given more positive judgements about the political sophistication of contemporary electorates, most voters (and even some political scientists) still fall short of the standards of classic democratic theory. However, we now understand that this maximalist definition of the prerequisites for informed decision-making is overly demanding. Instead, we should look at how citizens manage the complexities of politics and make reasonable decisions given their political interests and positions. Empirical research is emphasizing a satisficing approach to decision-making in which models ask: What are the pragmatic ways that individuals actually make their political choices.

2 MODERNIZATION AND DEMOCRATIZATION

One of the most powerful social science concepts to emerge in political behavior research—and one central to the study of citizen attitudes and behavior—is the concept of political culture. Almond and Verba's (1963) seminal study, *The Civic Culture*, contended that the institutions and patterns of action in a political system are closely linked to the political culture of the nation. The culture, in turn, is shaped by the historical, economic, and social conditions of a nation. Cultural studies are especially important in the study of democratization, as analysts try to identify the cultural requisites of democracy (Almond and Verba 1963; Pye and Verba 1965; Fuchs 2007).

Despite the heuristic and interpretative power of the concept of political culture, there are recurring questions about the precision and predictive power of the concept (Laitin 1995). Kaase (1983), for instance, said that measuring political culture is like "trying to nail jello to the wall." That is, the concept lacked precision and often became a subjective, stereotypic description of a nation rather than an empirically measurable concept. Some analysts saw political culture in virtually every feature of political life; others viewed it merely as a residual category that explained what remained unexplainable by other means. Even more problematic was the uneven evidence of culture's causal effect.

The 1990s witnessed a renaissance of political culture research and emphasized the link between modernization and political behavior. Inglehart demonstrated the congruence between broad political attitudes and democratic stability for twenty-two nations in the 1981 World Values Survey (Inglehart 1990). Putnam's (1993) study of regional governments in Italy provided even more impressive testimony in support of cultural theory. Putnam demonstrated that the cultural traditions of a region—roughly contrasting the cooperative political style of the North to the more hierarchic tradition of the South—were a potent predictor of the performance of contemporary governments. These studies generated counter-findings, and a new research debate emerged (e.g. Inglehart 1997; Reisinger 1995; Jackman and Miller 1996).

Moreover, the democratization wave of the 1990s focused attention on the connection between modernization and political culture. To what extent did political transformation in Central and Eastern Europe arise from gradual changes in the political culture? More important politically, to what extent can the prospects for democracy be judged by their public's support for democratic politics? Public opinion surveys of the Russian public initially found surprisingly high levels of support for basic democratic principles in the former Soviet Union (Miller, Reisinger, and Hesli 1993; Gibson, Duch, and Tedin 1992; Zimmerman 2002). Researchers in other Central and Eastern European nations examined the role of political culture in prompting the transitions and the consolidation of democracy (Rose, Haerpfer, and Mishler 1998; Rohrschneider 1999; Klingemann, Fuchs, and Zielonka 2006). Rather than the apathy or hostility that greeted democracy after transitions from right-wing authoritarian states, the cultural legacy of Communism in Central and Eastern Europe appears to be very different.

An equally rich series of studies is emerging for Asia, Africa, Latin America, and other developing regions. Despite the potential effects of conservative Confucian traditions and the government's hesitant support for democracy in many nations, the cultural foundations of democracy also are well developed in many Asian societies (Dalton and Shin 2006; Chu et al. 2008). Perhaps the most exciting evidence comes from studies of the People's Republic of China. Even in this hostile environment, there is surprising support for an array of democratic principles (Tang 2005). Similarly, the Afrobarometers provide the first systematic comparisons of public opinion on this continent, and the nature of political behavior in these developing nations (Bratton, Mattes, and Gyimah-Boadi 2004). New projects examine the political culture across Latin America (Booth and Seligson 2008; Lagos 1997). The breadth of support for democracy visible across a range of international survey projects—even in less than hospitable environments—is a surprising finding from this new wave of research (Shin 2007), and suggests that the aspiration for freedom, equality, and democratic rights is a common human value. One might question whether these opinions are sufficiently ingrained to constitute an enduring political culture in many developing nations, but even abstract endorsements of democratic norms are a positive sign about the prospects for democratic reform (van Beek 2005).

This research has also stimulated new debates on the broad course of human development. On the one hand, new versions of the social modernization thesis suggest a common pattern of social and political change as nations develop economically. This is most clearly seen in the analyses by Inglehart and Welzel (2005). On the other hand, others claim that historical experiences and national traditions produce different patterns of cultural development and distinct cultural regions—which may produce new sources of regional conflict (Huntington 1996). While this debate is ongoing, its very existence illustrates how the broadening of systematic opinion research to developing nations has renewed old debates about the courses and consequences of political culture.

As questions about political culture have grown in relevance for the democratizing nations, important cultural changes have also emerged within the advanced industrial democracies. Inglehart's (1977; 1990) thesis of postmaterial value change maintains that the socioeconomic forces transforming Western industrial societies are creating a new phase of human development. As affluent democracies have addressed many of the traditional "material" social goals, such as economic well-being and security, other political values are increasing attention toward new "postmaterial" goals of self-expression, personal freedom, social equality, self-fulfillment, and improving the quality of life. Inglehart's postmaterial thesis has gained considerable attention because of its potentially broad relevance to the politics of advanced industrial societies, although this thesis has also generated much scholarly debate (van Deth and Scarborough 1995).

Other studies examine whether a key element of a democratic political culture is changing in advanced industrial democracies: citizen orientations toward government. Almond and Verba (1963) maintained that democracy was based on a supportive public that endorsed a democratic system even in times of tumult. In the United States and many West European democracies, however, citizens are now less trustful of politicians, political parties, and democratic institutions (Dalton 2004; Pharr and Putnam 2000; Norris 1999; Nye, Zelikow, and King 1997). When coupled with evidence of changing orientations toward partisan politics and changing patterns of political participation (see below), this suggests that the ideals of a democratic political culture are changing among Western publics.

In summary, the study of modernization and democratization illustrates two major themes. First, research has made great progress in developing the empirical evidence that describes the political values for most nations in the world. Where once scientific empirical evidence of citizen orientations was quite thin and primarily limited to the large Western democracies, we now have rich evidence of how citizens think and act across nearly the entire globe. The growing empirical evidence has also reinforced the importance of key theoretical concepts that were developed during the early behavioral revolution. For example, Eckstein's (1966) concept of cultural congruence has provided a valuable framework for examining the interaction between citizen values and political processes. We now have a much richer and sounder theoretical and empirical knowledge about what are the significant attributes of a political culture.

Second, as the empirical evidence has grown, it is also apparent that we are living through a period of substantial political change—in both the advanced industrial democracies and the developing nations. This pattern presents several challenges for researchers. Normally, political institutions and the basic principles of a regime are constant; thus it is difficult to study the interaction between institutional and cultural change. However, the recent shifts in regime form in many nations create new opportunities to study the relationship between culture and institutional choices— and how congruence is established. Changing political norms enable us to study political culture as a dynamic process. Attempts to test theories of cultural change or theories on the nonpolitical origins of political culture are fertile research fields during this unusual period of political change.

Finally, the democratization process and changing democratic expectations in the West raise other questions. There is not just one "civic culture" that is congruent with the working of a democratic system. Experience suggests that there are various democratic cultures, as well as ways to define culture, that require mapping and further study. Just as the institutionalists have drawn our attention to the variations in the structure of the democratic politics and the implications of these differences (Rhodes, Binder, and Rockman 2006), we need to develop a comparable understanding of how citizen norms can create and sustain alternative democratic forms (Fuchs and Klingemann 2002).

3 ELECTORAL BEHAVIOR

One of the central roles of citizens in democracies and other political systems is to make decisions about political matters. In democracies, this involves decisions about which parties or candidates to support in an election, as well as decisions about which issue positions to hold, how to participate in politics, and so forth. In other political systems, the choices are different, but the task of making a choice remains. In an autocratic system, the choice might be between making an openly affirmative statement to a government declaration, remaining silent about it, or subtly even criticizing it. In any case, citizens make choices when political issues are brought to their attention, whether in an autocratic or a democratic system.

In democratic systems electoral choices are at the center of the political process. Thus, the study of electoral choice has quite naturally been a core theme in political behavior research, and past research has produced dramatic advances in our knowledge about how voters reach their decisions. Early electoral research presumed that many voters were ill prepared to deal with the complexities of politics; thus voters relied on shortcuts—such as group cues or affective partisan loyalties—to simplify political decision-making and guide their individual behavior (Campbell et al. 1960; Lipset and Rokkan 1967; Lewis-Beck et al. 2008). This approach also stressed the underlying stability of party competition because people supposedly based their political decisions on enduring social cleavages, and stable party–voter alignments were a focus of research.

During the 1980s, this model of stable cleavage-based or partisanship-based voting first came under challenge. Within a decade the dominant question changed from explaining the persistence of electoral politics to explaining electoral change (Dalton, Flanagan, and Beck 1984). Decreases in class and religious divisions were a first prominent indicator that electoral politics was changing. Franklin, Mackie, and Valen (1992) found that a set of social characteristics (including social class, education, income, religiosity, region, and gender) had a decreasing impact on partisan preferences in Western democracies over time. A general erosion of class voting occurred in most established democracies (Nieuwbeerta 1995; Knutsen 2006). Franklin concluded with the new "conventional wisdom" of comparative electoral research: "One thing that has by now become quite apparent is that almost all of the countries we have studied show a decline... in the ability of social cleavages to structure individual voting choice" (Franklin, Mackie, and Valen 1992, 385).

One of the major findings from the last generation of electoral research holds that social position no longer determines political positions as it did when social alignments were solidly frozen (cf. Evans 1999; Manza and Brooks 1999). In many Western democracies, the declining influence of group cleavages on electoral choice is paralleled by a weakening of affective party attachment that was the basis of the Michigan model of electoral choice. In nearly all the advanced industrial democracies for which long-term survey data are now available, partisan ties have weakened over the past generation (Dalton and Wattenberg 2000). Similarly, there has been a decrease in party-line voting and an increase in partisan volatility, split-ticket voting, and other phenomena showing that fewer citizens are voting according to a party or group-determined line (Thomassen 2005).

The decline of long-term predispositions based on social position or partisanship should shift the basis of electoral behavior research to factors such as candidate image and issue opinions. Thus, recent research focuses on candidate-centered voting choice (Poguntke and Webb 2005; Wattenberg 1991; Aarts, Blais, and Schmitt 2005). Furthermore, there are signs of a growing personalization of political campaigns in Western democracies: Photo opportunities, personalized interviews, walkabouts, and televised candidate debates are becoming standard electoral fare.

Electoral change also increases the potential for issue voting (Franklin, Mackie, and Valen 1992; Evans and Norris 1999; Dalton 2008). There appears to be a consensus that issue voting has become more important, but there is less consensus on a theoretical framework for understanding the role of issues in contemporary political behavior. A large part of the literature continues to work within the social-psychological approach, examining how specific issues affect party choice in specific elections, or how issue beliefs are formed. Other scholars focus on the systemic level, examining how aggregate electoral outcomes can be predicted by the issue stances of the parties (Budge and Farlie 1983; Adams, Merrill, and Grofman 2005). In a sense, this part of the research literature reminds us of the story of the blind men and the elephant: Several different research groups are making progress in explaining their part of the pachyderm, but there is not a holistic vision of the role of issues for contemporary electoral choice.

For advanced industrial democracies, the increase in candidate and issue voting has an uncertain impact on the democratic electoral process. It is unclear whether these changes will improve or weaken the "quality" of the democracy and the representation of the public's political interests. Public opinion is becoming more fluid and less predictable. This uncertainty forces parties and candidates to be more sensitive to public opinion, at least the opinions of those who vote. Motivated issue voters are more likely to have their voices heard, even if they are not accepted. Furthermore, the ability of politicians to have unmediated communications with voters can strengthen the link between politicians and the people. To some extent, the individualization of electoral choice revives earlier images of the informed voter classic democratic theory emphasized. Models of rational voter choice have thus gained in credibility.

At the same time, there is a potential dark side to these new patterns in electoral politics. The rise of single-issue politics handicaps a society's ability to deal with political issues that transcend specific interests and require trade-offs with other interests. In addition, elites who only cater to attentive publics can leave the electorally inactive without a voice. Too great an interest in a single issue, or too much emphasis on recent performance, can produce a narrow definition of rationality that is as harmful to democracy as "frozen" social cleavages. In addition, direct unmediated contact between politicians and citizens opens the potential for demagoguery and political extremism. Both extreme right-wing and left-wing political movements probably benefit from this new political environment, at least in the short term. At the same time as the electorate is less stable on the basis of established party alignments, it is also more susceptible to potential media manipulation.

In summary, comparative electoral studies have made major advances in our understanding of political behavior. This has in no way settled old debates. It has invigorated them. But they take place on a firmer base of evidence. This is another area in which research began with limited empirical evidence—national election studies were still quite rare in the 1960s and comparable cross-national analyses were exceedingly rare. Today, this literature on electoral behavior represents one of the largest fields of political behavior research. Moreover, as the empirical evidence has accumulated, it has become more apparent that the nature of electoral behavior is changing in advanced industrial democracies. The current research challenge is to define the nature of the new electoral order that is emerging.

3.1 Electoral Choice in Emerging Democracies

There is an apparent similarity between the portrait of voting choice we have just described and the situation in emerging democracies around the globe. Emerging party systems are unlikely to rest on stable group-based cleavages, especially when the democratic transition has occurred quite rapidly, as in Central and Eastern Europe. Thus, studies of these new democracies typically emphasize the high level of electoral volatility and fluidity in the party systems (Berglund, Hellén, and Aarebrot 1998; Mainwaring 1999; Mainwaring and Zoco 2007). Similarly, new electorates are unlikely to have long-term party attachments that might guide their behavior. Thus, with the exception of important sociocultural cleavages, such as ethnicity, electoral choice in many new democracies may involve the same short-term factors—candidate images and issue positions—that are emphasized in the electoral politics of advanced industrial democracies (e.g. Colton 2000; Rose, White, and McAllister 1997; Barnes and Simon 1998; Tucker 2005; Fuchs, Roller, and Zagórski 2006; Dalton, Shin, and Chu

2008). In addition, research is often preoccupied with the impact of economic voting in these systems as voters judge the new systems based on their performance (Tworzecki 2003; Tucker 2002).

These new democratic systems face the task of developing a relatively stable and institutionalized basis of party competition. This is largely a problem of the nature of elite politics, but also the lack of strong social bases for political parties. Without more structure, it is difficult for citizens to learn about the policy choices available to them, and translate this into meaningful electoral choices. Without more structure, it is difficult to ensure accountability in the democratic process. This situation presents the unique opportunity to study this process to examine how new party attachments take root, the relationships between social groups and parties form, party images develop, and citizens learn the process of representative democracy. However, the creation of party systems in the world of global television, greater knowledge about electoral politics (from the elite and public levels), and fundamentally different electorates are unlikely to follow the pattern of earlier democratization periods.

These questions require a dynamic perspective on the processes of electoral change. There has already been an impressive effort to develop the empirical research base in these new democracies (East Asian Barometer, Afrobarometer, Latinobarometer, and Comparative Study of Electoral Systems)—a development that took decades in most of the Western democracies. This research should lead to a new understanding of the positive and negative aspects of electoral development in these new democracies, and thus the prospects for further change.

4 POLITICAL PARTICIPATION

Democratic or not, all polities expect some public involvement in the political process, if only to obey political orders. Democracy, however, expects more active involvement than a nondemocratic order because democracy is designed to aggregate public preferences into binding collective decisions. Necessarily this requires an active citizenry, because it is through interest articulation, information, and deliberation that public preferences can be identified, shaped, and transformed into collective decisions that are considered legitimate. Autocratic regimes also engage the public in the political process, although this is primarily to indoctrinate the public to conform to decisions that elites have made. But even the control capacities of autocratic regimes are limited so that they have somehow to address what the citizenry wants and needs.

Empirical research has measured the levels of participation across nations and highlighted distinctions between different modes of political action. Verba and his colleagues (Verba, Nie, and Kim 1978; Verba, Schlozman, and Brady 1995) demonstrated that different forms of action vary in their political implications, and in the factors that stimulate individuals to act. This framework was extended to include the growth of unconventional political action that occurred since the 1960s (Barnes et al. 1979). This framework of participation modes is the common foundation of participation research.

Having identified the modes of action, researchers sought to explain patterns of participation. This was once an area intensely debated by rationalist and social-psychological theories of political behavior. The rationalist approach framed decisions to participate in simple cost–benefit terms, best represented in Olson's (1965) *Logic of Collective Action*. The charm of parsimony made this an attractive theoretical approach, but this parsimony created over-simplifications, false research paradoxes, and actually limited our understanding of citizen action. More productive is the behavioral model that stresses the influence of personal resources, attitudes, and institutional structures in explaining patterns of action (e.g. Verba, Nie, and Kim 1978; Verba, Schlozman, and Brady 1995).

For the past several years, the most intense debate has focused on whether the level of political participation is systematically changing in Western democracies. As supporting evidence, the long-standing "paradox of participation" has noted that turnout in the United States has decreased since the 1960s, even though educational levels and the affluence of the nation have dramatically increased (Brody 1978; Rosenstone and Hansen 1993).

Putnam (2000) provocatively argued that declining turnout is part of a broader trend that has us "bowling alone." Putnam claimed that social engagement is dropping in advanced industrial societies because of societal changes, such as changing labor patterns among women, rising television usage, urban sprawl, and the decline of traditional social institutions. These trends have supposedly led to a decline in social capital—the skills and values that facilitate democratic participation—and thereby to declines in the citizenry's participation in politics.

The study of social capital and the changes in the patterns of participation in contemporary democracies has been one of the most fertile areas of research for the past decade. On the one side is clear cross-national evidence of declining turnout in advanced industrial democracies (Blais 2000; Wattenberg 2002; Franklin 2004). Other measures of partisan activity, such as party membership, also show clear downward trends in most nations (Scarrow 2000). This might be part of a more general downturn in civic engagement because church attendance, union membership, and the engagement in several types of traditional voluntary associations are declining.

On the other side is a growing body of evidence that new forms of civic and political action—such as contacting, direct action, contentious politics, self-help groups, local initiatives, donations—are counterbalancing the decline in electoral participation and other traditional forms of civic engagement (Zukin et al. 2006; Pattie, Seyd, and Whiteley 2004; Cain, Dalton, and Scarrow 2003). In addition, social group membership and the formation of social capital seem to be increasing in many advanced industrial democracies, making the USA an atypical case (Stolle and Howard 2007; Putnam 2002). Moreover, modernization processes are changing the ways in which people interact and engage in the public sphere, transforming the character of social capital instead of eliminating it altogether: Loyalist forms of elite-guided engagement go down but spontaneous forms of self-driven engagement go up (Norris 2002; Van Deth, Montero, and Westholm 2006).

This controversy touches the vitality of the democratic process. Decreasing involvement in traditional social groups (such as unions and religious groups) and declining social capital from these group affiliations are generally seen in established democracies, but this might not indicate a general erosion of civic engagement and social capital. It might simply reflect a transformation of the ways in which citizens relate to each other and their communities (Skocpol 2003). The Internet and social networking sites are connecting individuals in new ways, and new forms of face-to-face groups are also developing. If one includes new forms of interaction and engagement, participation levels and the various methods of political action are generally expanding in most advanced industrial societies—even while participation in the traditional form of party membership and electoral politics is decreasing. New forms of engagement expand political participation beyond the boundaries of what it was conventionally viewed to be. These tendencies reflect a great flexibility of democracies, allowing forms of participation to adapt to changing societal conditions. The new style of citizen participation places more control over political activity in the hands of the citizenry as well as increasing public pressure on political elites.

However, the expanding repertoire of action also may raise potential problems. For example, some forms of participation can increase inequalities in involvement, which would bias the democratic process in ways that conflict with the ideal of "one (wo)man one vote" (Verba, Schlozman, and Brady 1995; Cain, Dalton, and Scarrow 2003; Parry, Moyser, and Day 1992). New forms of direct action are even more dependent on the skills and resources represented by social status, and thus may increase the participation gap between lower-status groups and higher-status individuals. These new forms of action also create new challenges for aggregating diverse political demands into coherent government policy. Ironically, overall increases in political involvement may mask a growing social-status bias in citizen participation and influence, which runs counter to democratic ideals.

The challenge for established democracies is to expand further the opportunities for citizens to participate and meaningfully influence the decisions affecting their lives. To meet this challenge means ensuring an equality of political rights and opportunities that will be even more difficult to guarantee with a wider variety of activities. However, a socially biased use of expanded political opportunities should not blame the opportunities but should blame the policies that fail to alleviate the social bias, such as unequal access to education and other social benefits that influence the citizens' resources to participate.

4.1 Participation in Emerging Democracies

The patterns of political participation are obviously different in emerging democracies and nondemocratic nations. In new democracies the challenge is to engage the citizenry in meaningful participation after years of ritualized action or prohibitions. In some cases this yields a mirror-image of old democracies: In old democracies citizens are moving from conventional to unconventional politics, in new democracies citizens often toppled autocratic regimes by revolutionary upheavals and now have to learn the routines of conventional participation.

Election turnout was often fairly high in the immediate post-transition elections in Eastern Europe, but has subsequently declined in most nations. Similarly, party activity has atrophied as democratic institutions have developed (Barnes and Simon 1998; van Biezen 2003). And while there was a popular lore claiming that a robust underground civil society prompted the democratization trend in Eastern Europe, post-transition research finds that social engagement is now limited (Howard 2003). Many East Europeans protested during the democratic transitions of the late 1980s and early 1990s, but these forms of action diminished after the transition in a kind of "post-honeymoon" effect (Inglehart and Catterberg 2003). Consequently, Eastern Europe still faces the challenge of integrating citizens into democratic politics and nurturing an understanding of the democratic process.

The challenges of citizen participation are, of course, even greater in nondemocratic nations. The advance of survey research has provided some unique insights into participation patterns in these nations. Shi's study of political participation in Beijing (1997), for example, found much more extensive public involvement than expected. Furthermore, political participation can occur in alternative forms in political systems where citizen input is not tolerated and encouraged through institutionalized channels (also see Jennings 1997). Similarly, Bratton, Mattes, and Gyimah-Boadi (2004) find a surprisingly large range of political activity across a set of African nations. If this occurs in these two settings, then we might expect citizens to be somewhat engaged even in transitional political systems.

The desire to participate in the decisions affecting one's life is common across the globe, but political institutions can shape whether these desires are expressed and how (Inglehart and Welzel 2005). Possessing the skills and resources to be politically active is an equally important factor. Research is now identifying how these two forces combine to shape the patterns of citizen action.

5 DOES PUBLIC OPINION MATTER

Another field of political behavior examines the impact of public opinion on policy-makers and governments—which is the ultimate question in the study of public opinion within a democracy. To what extent do the views of policy-makers and the outputs of government policy reflect the preferences that the public itself prefers (Uslaner and Zittel, this volume)?

The indirect effect of public opinion in a democracy, mediated through representative institutions, has created questions about the congruence of mass–elite outcomes, and the factors that affect this intermediation process. However, this process has had a difficult research history despite the theoretical and political importance of the topic.

The first empirical study of representation was the famous Miller–Stokes study of representation in America (Miller and Stokes 1963). This model and research approach were soon expanded to a host of other advanced industrial democracies (Barnes 1977; Converse and Pierce 1986; Thomassen 1994). This research examined one of the most important questions in research on democracy, but the findings were limited. The theoretical model developed in the United States did not seem to fit other democracies. In addition, it is difficult to assemble the resources required to conduct parallel studies of the citizenry. Thus, in the fifty years since the original Miller–Stokes study, their full research project has not been replicated in the United States.

Other studies in the United States have examined elements of the representation process; for instance, comparing the congruence between mass and elite opinions in the aggregate or the dynamics of mass opinion change (Erikson, McKuen, and Stimson 2002; Stimson 2004). Cross-national studies in Europe similarly indicate that the parties have not lost their capacity to represent their voters when judged in broad left–right terms (Schmitt and Thomassen 1999; Katz and Wessels 1999). This is an important measure of the working of the democratic process.

Researchers have also examined the congruence between public policy preferences and the outcomes of government (Page and Shapiro 1992). Gradually, this research has spread to other Western democracies, often adopted to national institutions or the structure of representation (Wlezien 2004; Wlezien and Soroka 2007). One important branch of this approach compares programmatic profiles of political parties and political preferences of their followers (Klingemann et al. 1994; Budge et al. 2001; Klingemann et al. 2006). In fact, based on a study comparing citizen spending preferences and government spending across different policy domains in the United States, Britain, and Canada, Stuart Soroka and Christopher Wlezien (2008) come to a simple but important conclusion: "democracy works."

As the number of these representation studies increases, research is now examining how institutional structures—such as the nature of electoral systems or the characteristics of the party systems—affect the representation of citizen preferences (Miller et al. 1999; Wessels 2007). The congruence between citizens and their government varies with the structure of institutions, increasing representation in some settings and accountability in others (Powell 2000).

The study of political representation is an area with great theoretical and empirical potential to understand the functioning of the democratic process through the mass–elite relationship. But it also remains one of the most challenging areas to study and compare across nations. Gradually research is yielding a better understanding of how the democratic process actually functions, which yields a positive view of the vitality of the process.

6 CHANGING PUBLICS: A CONCLUSION

We have recently experienced what are arguably the most significant political events of the last half-century: the collapse of the Soviet Empire and the global democratization wave of the 1990s. As advanced industrial societies are evolving into a new form of democratic politics, we are witnessing the initial development of democracy in a new set of nations. The democratization waves in Central and Eastern Europe, Asia, and Africa touch at the very core of many of our most basic questions about the nature of citizen politics and the working of the political process.

Normally we study democratic systems that are roughly at equilibrium and speculate on how this equilibrium was created (or how it changes in minor ways). Moreover, during the earlier waves of democratic transition the tools of empirical social science were not available to study political behavior directly. The current democratization wave thus provides a virtually unique opportunity to address questions on identity formation, the creation of political cultures (and possibly how cultural inheritances are changed), the establishment of an initial calculus of voting, and the dynamic processes linking political norms and behavior. These questions represent some of the fundamental research issues of our time. The answers will not only explain what has occurred during this democratization wave, but may aid us in better understanding the basic principles of how citizens function within the political process. There has never been a richer opportunity to study the choices of citizens across regime forms and between old and new democracies. The conditions to arrive at a theory of how citizens come to political choices depending on different political settings, and how these choices affect the settings, have never been better than they are today.

In each of the areas discussed in this chapter, research can be described in two terms. First, our empirical knowledge has expanded almost exponentially over the past generation. Until quite recently, a single national survey provided the basis for discussing the characteristics of citizen behavior; and such evidence was frequently limited to the larger advanced industrial democracies. Indeed, there were large parts of the world where our understanding of the citizenry, their attitudes, and behavior were based solely on the insights of political observers—which can be as fallible as the observer. Contemporary comparative research is now more likely to draw on cross-national and cross-temporal comparisons. Research has developed the foundations for the scientific study of the topic.

Second, it is ironic that our expanding empirical evidence has occurred during a time when many basic features of citizen attitudes and behaviors are changing in ways that may limit the value of past theories and models. In part, these trends reflect the tremendous social and political changes that have occurred in the world during the past half-century. Modernization has transformed living conditions in most nations, altered the skills and values of contemporary publics, and offered new technological advances that change the relationship between citizens and elites. Perhaps, this is the most interesting object worthy of study. For never before in history has the interaction between elites and people been shifted so much to the side of the people.

The global wave of democratization in the 1990s has dramatically increased the role of the citizenry in many of the new democracies in Central and Eastern Europe, Asia, Latin America, and Africa. This latter development makes our task as scholars of the citizen more relevant than ever before, but also more difficult. Even as our research skills and empirical evidence have expanded, the phenomena we study have been evolving—something that physicists and chemists do not have to deal with. These changes produce uncertainty about what new styles of political decision-making, or what new forms of political participation are developing. In addition, the nature of citizen politics is becoming more complex—or through our research we are now realizing that greater complexity exists. This produces a real irony: Even though we have greater scientific knowledge, our ability to predict and explain political behavior may actually be decreasing in some areas. For instance, we know much more about electoral behavior than we did in the 1950s, but simple sociodemographic models that were successful in predicting electoral behavior in the 1960s are much less potent in explaining contemporary voting behavior. So we have gained greater certainty about the uncertainty of voter decisions (Wren and McElwain, this volume).

Finally, we see broad outlines of what we think are some of the most productive areas for future research. Several aspects of research design offer exciting potential for the future. For instance, most studies use random surveys of individuals. This design focuses our attention on individuals as autonomous political actors and theories emphasizing the individualization of politics. However, people exist in a social, economic, and political context that can shape their political behavior. For example, limited political knowledge can be overcome by asking spouses, friends, or neighbors (Gunther, Ramón Montero, and Puhle 2006). Even more important, characteristics of the political context can alter the processes shaping citizen attitudes and behavior, such as exposure to supportive or dissonant information (Huckfeldt et al. 2004; Mutz 2006). Equally exciting are new research opportunities to study how the institutional structure of a polity interacts with citizen behavior (e.g. Anderson et al. 2005; Klingemann 2009). Thus, studying this complex of social and political interactions should yield new insights into how political behavior is shaped.

Another innovation is the introduction of experiments and quasi-experiments to our research tools. For example, Sniderman's (Sniderman and Piazza 1993; Sniderman et al. 2000) experiments in studying racial attitudes and prejudice illustrate how experiments and creative questionnaire design can provide unobtrusive measures of sensitive topics. Such experiments also provide leverage to study causality by manipulating choices presented to survey respondents, and analyze how opinions change. This innovation has tremendous potential that should be utilized more in future research.

An even more dramatic sign of the development of political behavior research is the increasing complexity of research designs. Once, a single national sample was the basis of extensive research because such evidence was still rare. However, as our knowledge has increased and our theories have become more complex, this calls for more complex research designs. Election studies, for instance, need to study individuals in context, including multiple and converging data collections: social context, media content, party actions, and other elements of the total process. Doing more of what we did in the past—more questions, more surveys, larger sample sizes—is not likely to generate the theoretical or empirical insights necessary to move the research field forward. Complex theories and complex processes require more complex research designs.

We also believe that research will engage a new set of theoretical issues as the field moves forward. It is more difficult to outline briefly the forefront for research, because theoretical questions are more diverse than the methodological innovations we have just outlined. However, several areas of potential enquiry stand out for their potential. While most research has focused on single nations, and typically Western democracies, the global expansion of research means that issues of social modernization and cross-national development are likely to be especially fruitful areas of study. This is a case where we have been theory rich and information poor—and now these theories will be tested, and undoubtedly new models developed in their place. Similarly, past theorizing has focused on explaining systems and behavior in equilibrium. Theories of political change seem an especially fruitful area for enquiry given the dynamic nature of contemporary politics.

Finally, one should not forget that because of the sheer number of countries for which survey data are available, we are for the first time able to study some of the basic assumptions underlying all research into mass belief systems: That variation in these belief systems has a true impact on a society's level of democracy and the outputs of government. Aggregate-level analysis of the correlates of democracy was usually left to political economists who could more easily correlate socioeconomic indicators to levels of democracy. But we can now test their models against political culture, examining whether socioeconomic factors or features of political culture have a stronger impact on democracy. As recent studies show (Inglehart and Welzel 2005), features of political culture have as strong an impact on levels of democracy as socioeconomic factors.

Our goal has been to introduce the readers to the research literature and the research questions that remain. We came away from this task with tremendous respect for what has been achieved since the onset of modern comparative research. At the same time, answering one question generates new questions, and cross-national research on political behavior is just entering its age of discovery.

REFERENCES

AARTS, K., BLAIS, A., and SCHMITT, H. (eds.) 2005. *Political Leaders and Democratic Elections.* Oxford: Oxford University Press.

ADAMS, J., MERRILL, S., and GROFMAN, B. 2005. *A Unified Theory of Party Competition: A Cross-National Analysis Integrating Spatial and Behavioral Factors.* New York: Cambridge University Press.

ALMOND, G. and VERBA, S. 1963. *The Civic Culture.* Princeton, NJ: Princeton University Press.

ANDERSON, C., et al. 2005. *Losers' Consent: Elections and Democratic Legitimacy.* New York: Oxford University Press.

BARNES, S. 1977. *Representation in Italy.* Chicago: University of Chicago Press.

—— and SIMON, J. (eds.) 1998. *The Postcommunist Citizen.* Budapest: Erasmus Foundation.

—— et al. (eds.) 1979. *Political Action.* Beverly Hills, Calif.: Sage.

BARTOLINI, S. and MAIR, P. 1990. *Identity, Competition, and Electoral Availability: The Stability of European Electorates, 1885–1985.* Cambridge: Cambridge University Press.

BERGLUND, S., HELLÉN, T., and AAREBROT, F. (eds.) 1998. *The Handbook of Political Change in Eastern Europe.* Cheltenham: Edward Elgar.

BLAIS, A. 2000. *To Vote or Not to Vote: The Merits and Limits of Rational Choice Theory.* Pittsburgh, Pa.: University of Pittsburgh Press.

BOOTH, J. and SELIGSON, M. 2008. *The Legitimacy Puzzle: Democracy and Political Support in Eight Latin American Nations.* Cambridge: Cambridge University Press.

BOWLER, S. and DONOVAN, T. 1998. *Demanding Choices: Opinion, Voting, and Direct Democracy.* Ann Arbor: University of Michigan Press.

BRATTON, M., MATTES, R., and GYIMAH-BOADI, E. 2004. *Public Opinion, Democracy, and Market Reform in Africa.* Cambridge: Cambridge University Press.

BRODY, R. 1978. The puzzle of political participation in America. In *The New American Political System,* ed. S. Beer. Washington, DC: American Enterprise Institute.

BUDGE, I. and FARLIE, D. 1983. *Explaining and Predicting Elections: Issue Effects and Party Strategies in Twenty-Three Democracies.* London: Allen and Unwin.

—— et al. 2001. *Mapping Policy Preferences: Estimates for Parties, Electors, and Governments 1945–1998.* Oxford: Oxford University Press.

BUTLER, D. and STOKES, D. 1969. *Political Change in Britain.* New York: St Martin's.

CAIN, B., DALTON, R., and SCARROW, S. (eds.) 2003. *Democracy Transformed? Expanding Political Opportunities in Advanced Industrial Democracies.* Oxford: Oxford University Press.

CAMPBELL, A., CONVERSE, P., MILLER, W., and STOKES, D. 1960. *The American Voter.* New York: Wiley.

CHU, Y., et al. (eds.) 2008. *How East Asians View Democracy.* New York: Columbia University Press.

COLTON, T. 2000. *Transitional Citizens: Voters and What Influences Them in the New Russia.* Cambridge, Mass.: Harvard University Press.

CONVERSE, P. 1964. The nature of belief systems in mass publics. Pp. 206–61 in *Ideology and Discontent,* ed. D. Apter. New York: Free Press.

—— 2007. Perspectives on mass belief systems and communication. In *Oxford Handbook of Political Behavior,* ed. R. J. Dalton and H.-D. Klingemann. Oxford: Oxford University Press.

—— and PIERCE, R. 1986. *Representation in France.* Cambridge, Mass.: Harvard University Press.

DAHL, R. A. 1989. *Democracy and its Critics.* New Haven, Conn.: Yale University Press.

DALTON, R. 2004. *Democratic Challenges, Democratic Choices.* Oxford: Oxford University Press.

DALTON, R. 2007. *The Good Citizen: How a Younger Generation is Transforming American Politics.* Washington, DC: CQ Press.

—— 2008. *Citizen Politics: Public Opinion and Political Parties in Advanced Industrial Democracies,* 5th edn. Washington, DC: CQ Press.

—— FLANAGAN, S., and BECK, P. (eds.) 1984. *Electoral Change in Advanced Industrial Democracies.* Princeton, NJ: Princeton University Press.

—— and KLINGEMANN, H.-D. (eds.) 2007. *Oxford Handbook of Political Behavior.* Oxford: Oxford University Press.

—— and SHIN, D. (eds.) 2006. *Citizens, Democracy, and Markets around the Pacific Rim.* Oxford: Oxford University Press.

—— —— and CHU, Y. (eds.) 2008. *Party Politics in East Asia: Citizens, Elections, and Democratic Development.* Boulder, Colo.: Lynne Rienner.

—— and WATTENBERG, M. (eds.) 2000. *Parties without Partisans: Political Change in Advanced Industrial Democracies.* Oxford: Oxford University Press.

DELLI CARPINI, M. and KEETER, S. 1996. *What Americans Know about Politics and Why it Matters.* New Haven, Conn.: Yale University Press.

DOWNS, A. 1957. *An Economic Theory of Democracy.* New York: Harper.

ERIKSON, R., McKUEN, M., and STIMSON, J. 2002. *The Macro Polity.* New York: Cambridge University Press.

EVANS, G. (ed.) 1999. *The End of Class Politics? Class Voting in Comparative Perspective.* Oxford: Oxford University Press.

—— and NORRIS, P. (eds.) 1999. *Critical Elections: British Parties and Voters in Long-Term Perspective.* Thousand Oaks, Calif.: Sage.

—— and WHITEFIELD, S. 1995. The politics and economics of democratic commitment. *British Journal of Political Science,* 25: 485–514.

FINIFTER, A. and MICKIEWICZ, E. 1992. Redefining the political system of the USSR. *American Political Science Review,* 86: 857–74.

FRANKLIN, M. 2004. *Voter Turnout and the Dynamics of Electoral Competition in Established Democracies since 1945.* New York: Cambridge University Press.

—— MACKIE, T., and VALEN, H. (eds.) 1992. *Electoral Change: Responses to Evolving Social and Attitudinal Structures in Western Countries.* New York: Cambridge University Press.

FREEDMAN, J. 2006. Democratic competence in normative and positive theory: neglected implications of "the nature of belief systems in mass publics." *Critical Reviews,* 18: 1–43.

FUCHS, D. 2007. The political culture paradigm. In *Oxford Handbook of Political Behavior,* ed. R. J. Dalton and H.-D. Klingemann. Oxford: Oxford University Press.

—— and KLINGEMANN, H. 2002. Eastward enlargement of the European Union and the identity of Europe. Pp. 58–80 in *The Enlarged European Union: Diversity and Adaptation,* ed. P. Mair and J. Zielonka. London: Frank Cass.

—— ROLLER, E., and ZAGÓRSKI, K. (eds.) 2006. The state of democracy in central and eastern Europe. Special issue of the *International Journal of Sociology,* 36.

GIBSON, J., DUCH, R., and TEDIN, K. 1992. Democratic values and the transformation of the Soviet Union. *Journal of Politics,* 54: 329–71.

GUNTHER, R., RAMÓN MONTERO, J., and PUHLE, H. (eds.) 2006. *Electoral Intermediation, Values, and Political Support in Old and New Democracies.* Oxford: Oxford University Press.

HARDIN, R. 2006. Ignorant democracy. *Critical Review,* 18: 179–95.

HEATH, A., FISHER, S., and SMITH, S. 2005. The globalization of public opinion research. *Annual Review of Political Science,* 8: 297–333.

HIBBING, J. and THEISS-MORSE, E. 2002. *Stealth Democracy: Americans' Beliefs about How Government Should Work.* New York: Cambridge University Press.

HOWARD, M. 2003. *The Weakness of Civil Society in Post-communist Europe*. New York: Cambridge University Press.

HUCKFELDT, R., et al. 2004. *Political Disagreement: The Survival of Diverse Opinions within Communication Networks*. New York: Cambridge University Press.

HUNTINGTON, S. 1996. *The Clash of Civilizations and the Remaking of World Order*. New York: Simon and Schuster.

INGLEHART, R. 1977. *The Silent Revolution*. Princeton, NJ: Princeton University Press.

—— 1990. *Culture Shift in Advanced Industrial Society*. Princeton, NJ: Princeton University Press.

—— 1997. *Modernization and Postmodernization*. Ann Arbor: University of Michigan.

—— and CATTERBERG, G. 2003. Trends in political action: the development trend and the post-honeymoon decline. Ch. 1 in *Islam, Gender, Culture, and Democracy*, ed. R. Inglehart. Willowdale: de Sitter.

—— and WELZEL, C. 2005. *Modernization, Cultural Change, and Democracy: The Human Development Sequence*. Cambridge: Cambridge University Press.

IVERSON, T. 1994. The logics of electoral politics: spatial, directional and mobilization effects. *Comparative Political Studies*, 27: 155–89.

JACKMAN, R. and MILLER, R. 1996. A renaissance of political culture. *American Journal of Political Science*, 40: 697–716.

JENNINGS, M. 1997. Political participation in the Chinese countryside. *American Political Science Review*, 91: 361–72.

KAASE, M. 1983. Sinn oder Unsinn des Konzepts "Politische Kultur" für die vergleichende Politikforschung. In *Wahlen und politisches System*, ed. M. Kaase and H. Klingemann. Opladen: Westdeutscher Verlag.

—— and NEWTON, K. (eds.) 1995. *Beliefs in Government*. Oxford: Oxford University Press.

KATZ, R. and WESSELS, B. (eds.) 1999. *The European Parliament, National Parliaments, and European Integration*. Oxford: Oxford University Press

KINDER, D. 2006. Belief systems today. *Critical Review*, 18: 197–216.

KITTILSON, M. 2007. Research resources in comparative political behavior. Pp. 865–95 in *Oxford Handbook of Political Behavior*, ed. R. J. Dalton and H.-D. Klingemann. Oxford: Oxford University Press.

KLINGEMANN, H. 1979. Measuring ideological conceptualization. Pp. 215–54 in Barnes et al. 1979.

—— (ed.) 2009. *The Comparative Study of Electoral Systems*. Oxford: Oxford University Press.

—— and FUCHS, D. (eds.) 1995. *Citizens and the State*. Oxford: Oxford University Press.

—— —— and ZIELONKA, J. (eds.) 2006. *Democracy and Political Culture in Eastern Europe*. London: Routledge.

—— VOLKENS, A., BARA, J., BUDGE, I., and MACDONALD, M. 2006. *Mapping Policy Preference II*. Oxford: Oxford University Press.

—— et al. 1994. *Parties, Policies, and Democracy*. Boulder, Colo.: Westview.

KNUTSEN, O. 2006. *Class Voting in Western Europe: A Comparative Longitudinal Study*. Lanham, Md.: Lexington Books.

KUKLINSKI, J. H. and PEYTON, B. 2007. Belief systems and political decision-making. Pp. 45–64 in *Oxford Handbook of Political Behavior*, ed. R. J. Dalton and H.-D. Klingemann. Oxford: Oxford University Press.

LAGOS, M. 1997. Latin America's smiling mask. *Journal of Democracy*, 8: 125–38.

LAITIN, D. 1995. "The Civic Culture" at thirty. *American Political Science Review*, 89: 168–73.

LAU, R. and REDLAWSK, D. 2006. *How Voters Decide: Information Processing during Election Campaigns*. New York: Cambridge University Press.

LEWIS-BECK, M., NORPOTH, H., JACOBY, W., and WEISBERG, H. 2008. *The American Voter Revisited*. Ann Arbor: University of Michigan Press.

LIPSET, S. and ROKKAN, S. (eds.) 1967. *Party Systems and Voter Alignments*. New York: Free Press.

LUPIA, A. and McCUBBINS, M. 1998. *The Democratic Dilemma: Can Citizens Learn What They Need to Know?* Cambridge: Cambridge University Press.

MAINWARING, S. 1999. *Rethinking Party Systems in the Third Wave of Democratization: The Case of Brazil*. Stanford, Calif.: Stanford University Press.

—— and ZOCO, E. 2007. The stabilization of interparty competition: electoral volatility in old and new democracies. *Party Politics*, 13: 155–78.

MANZA, J. and BROOKS, C. 1999. *Social Cleavages and Political Change: Voter Alignments and U.S. Party Coalitions*. New York: Oxford University Press.

MERRILL, S. and GROFMAN, B. 1999. *A Unified Theory of Voting: Directional and Proximity Spatial Models*. Cambridge: Cambridge University Press.

MILLER, A., REISINGER, W., and HESLI, V. (eds.) 1993. *Public Opinion and Regime Change: The New Politics of Post-Soviet Societies*. Boulder, Colo.: Westview.

MILLER, W. and SHANKS, M. 1996. *The New American Voter*. Cambridge, Mass.: Harvard University Press.

—— and STOKES, D. 1963. Constituency influence in Congress. *American Political Science Review*, 57: 45–56.

—— et al. 1999. *Policy Representation in Western Democracies*. Oxford: Oxford University Press.

MUTZ, D. 2006. *Hearing the Other Side: Deliberative versus Participatory Democracy*. New York: Cambridge University Press.

NIE, N., VERBA, S., and PETROCIK, J. 1976. *The Changing American Voter*. Cambridge, Mass.: Harvard University Press.

NIEUWBEERTA, P. 1995. *The Democratic Class Struggle in Twenty Countries, 1945–1990*. Amsterdam: Thesis.

NORRIS, P. (ed.) 1999. *Critical Citizens: Global Support for Democratic Government*. Oxford: Oxford University Press.

—— 2002. *Democratic Phoenix: Reinventing Political Activism*. Cambridge: Cambridge University Press.

NYE, J., ZELIKOW, P., and KING, D. (eds.) 1997. *Why Americans Mistrust Government*. Cambridge, Mass.: Harvard University Press.

OLSON, M. 1965. *The Logic of Collective Action*. Cambridge, Mass.: Harvard University Press.

PAGE, B. and SHAPIRO, R. 1992. *The Rational Public: Fifty Years of Trends in Americans' Policy Preferences*. Chicago: University of Chicago Press.

PARRY, G., MOYSER, G., and DAY, N. 1992. *Political Participation and Democracy in Britain*. Cambridge: Cambridge University Press.

PATTIE, C., SEYD, P., and WHITELEY, P. 2004. *Citizenship in Britain: Values, Participation and Democracy*. New York: Cambridge University Press.

PHARR, S. and PUTNAM, R. (eds.) 2000. *Discontented Democracies: What's Wrong with the Trilateral Democracies*. Princeton, NJ: Princeton University Press.

POGUNTKE, T. and WEBB, P. (eds.) 2005. *The Presidentialization of Politics: A Comparative Study of Modern Democracies*. New York: Oxford University Press.

POPKIN, S. 1991. *The Reasoning Voter*. Chicago: University of Chicago Press.

POWELL, G. 2000. *Elections as Instruments of Democracy*. New Haven, Conn.: Yale University Press.

PUTNAM, R. 1993. *Making Democracy Work*. Princeton, NJ: Princeton University Press.

—— 2000. *Bowling Alone: The Collapse and Revival of American Community*. New York: Simon and Schuster.

—— (ed.) 2002. *Democracies in Flux: The Evolution of Social Capital in Contemporary Society*. Oxford: Oxford University Press.

PYE, L. and VERBA, S. (eds.) 1965. *Political Culture and Political Development*. Princeton, NJ: Princeton University Press.

REISINGER, W. 1995. The renaissance of a rubric: political culture as concept and theory. *International Journal of Public Opinion Research*, 7: 328–52.

REMMER, K. 1991. The political economy of elections in Latin America. *American Political Science Review*, 87: 393–407.

RHODES, R., BINDER, S., and ROCKMAN, B. 2006. *Oxford Handbook of Political Institutions*. Oxford: Oxford University Press.

ROHRSCHNEIDER, R. 1999. *Learning Democracy: Democratic and Economic Values in Unified Germany*. Oxford: Oxford University Press.

ROSE, R., HAERPFER, C., and MISHLER, W. 1998. *Democracy and its Alternatives: Understanding Post–communist Societies*. Baltimore: Johns Hopkins University Press.

—— and MISHLER, W. 1998. Negative and positive party identification in post-communist countries. *Electoral Studies*, 17: 217–34.

—— WHITE, S., and MCALLISTER, I. 1997. *How Russia Votes*. Chatham, NJ: Chatham House.

ROSENSTONE, S. and HANSEN, J. 1993. *Mobilization, Participation, and American Democracy*. New York: Macmillan.

SCARROW, S. 2000. Parties without members? Pp. 79–102 in Dalton and Wattenberg 2000.

SCHMITT, H. and THOMASSEN, J. (eds.) 1999. *Political Representation and Legitimacy in the European Union*. Oxford: Oxford University Press.

SELIGSON, M. and BOOTH, J. 1993. Political culture and regime type: Nicaragua and Costa Rica. *Journal of Politics*, 55: 777–92.

SHI, T. 1997. *Political Participation in Beijing*. Cambridge, Mass.: Harvard University Press.

SHIN, D. 1999. *Mass Politics and Culture in Democratizing Korea*. Cambridge: Cambridge University Press.

—— 2007. Democratization perspectives from global citizenries. Pp. 259–282 in *Oxford Handbook of Political Behavior*, ed. R. J. Dalton and H.-D. Klingemann. Oxford: Oxford University Press.

SKOCPOL, T. 2003. *Diminished Democracy: From Membership to Management in American Civic Life*. Norman: University of Oklahoma Press.

SNIDERMAN, P. M. and LEVENDUSKY, M. 2007. An institutional theory of political choice. Pp. 437–456 in *Oxford Handbook of Political Behavior*, ed. R. J. Dalton and H.-D. Klingemann. Oxford: Oxford University Press.

—— and PIAZZA, T. 1993. *The Scar of Race*. Cambridge, Mass.: Harvard University Press.

—— et al. 2000. *The Outsider: Prejudice and Politics in Italy*. Princeton, NJ: Princeton University Press.

SOROKA, S. and WLEZIEN, C. 2008. Degrees of democracy: government institutions and the opinion–policy link. Presented at the annual meeting of the Midwest Political Science Association, Chicago, April.

STACY, G. and SEGURA, G. 1997. Cross-national variation in the political sophistication of individuals: capability or choice? *Journal of Politics*, 59: 126–47.

STIMSON, J. 2004. *Tides of Consent: How Public Opinion Shapes American Politics*. New York: Cambridge University Press.

STOLLE, D. and HOWARD, M. 2007. Symposium on civic engagement and civic attitudes in cross-national perspective. Special issue of *Political Studies*, 56: 1–259.

SUROWIECKI, J. 2004. *The Wisdom of Crowds: Why the Many Are Smarter than the Few and How Collective Wisdom Shapes Business, Economies, Societies and Nations.* New York: Doubleday.

TANG, W. 2005. *Public Opinion and Political Change in China.* Stanford, Calif.: Stanford University Press.

THOMASSEN, J. 1994. Empirical research into political representation. Pp. 237–64 in *Elections at Home and Abroad*, ed. M. K. Jennings and T. Mann. Ann Arbor: University of Michigan Press.

——(ed.) 2005. *The European Voter: A Comparative Study of Modern Democracies.* Oxford: Oxford University Press.

TUCKER, J. 2002. The first decade of post-communist elections and voting: what have we studied, and how have we studied it? *American Review of Political Science*, 5: 271–304.

——2005. *Regional Economic Voting.* New York: Cambridge University Press.

TWORZECKI, H. 2003. *Learning to Choose: Electoral Politics in East-Central Europe.* Stanford, Calif.: Stanford University Press.

VAN BEEK, U. 2005. *Democracy under Construction: Patterns from Four Continents.* Bloomfield Hills, Mich.: Barbara Budrich.

VAN BIEZEN, I. 2003. *Political Parties and New Democracies: Party Organization in Southern and East-Central Europe.* London: Palgrave.

VAN DETH, J., MONTERO, J., and WESTHOLM, A. (eds.) 2006. *Citizenship and Involvement in Europe.* London: Routledge.

——and SCARBOROUGH, E. (eds.) 1995. *The Impact of Values.* Oxford: Oxford University Press.

VERBA, S., NIE, N., and KIM, J. 1978. *Participation and Political Equality.* Cambridge: Cambridge University Press.

——SCHLOZMAN, K., and BRADY, H. 1995. *Voice and Political Equality.* Cambridge, Mass.: Harvard University Press.

WATTENBERG, M. 1991. *The Rise of Candidate Centered Politics.* Cambridge, Mass.: Harvard University Press.

——2002. *Where Have All the Voters Gone?* Cambridge, Mass.: Harvard University Press.

——2006. *Is Voting for Young People?* New York: Longman.

WESSELS, B. 2007. Political representation and democracy. Pp. 833–849 in *Oxford Handbook of Political Behavior*, ed. R. J. Dalton and H.-D. Klingemann. Oxford: Oxford University Press.

WLEZIEN, C. 2004. Patterns of representation: dynamics of public preferences and policy. *Journal of Politics*, 66: 1–24.

WLEZIEN, C. and SOROKA, S. N. 2007. The relationship between public opinion and policy. Pp. 799–817 in *Oxford Handbook of Political Behavior*, ed. R. J. Dalton and H.-D. Klingemann. Oxford: Oxford University Press.

ZAKARIA, F. 2006. *The Future of Freedom: Illiberal Democracy at Home and Abroad.* New York: Norton.

ZALLER, J. 1992. *The Nature and Origins of Mass Opinion.* Cambridge: Cambridge University Press.

ZIMMERMAN, W. 2002. *The Russian People and Foreign Policy: Russian Elite and Mass Perspectives, 1993–2000.* Princeton, NJ: Princeton University Press.

ZUKIN, C., KEETER, S., ANDOLINA, M., JENKINS, K., and DELLI CARPINI, M. 2006. *A New Engagement? Political Participation, Civic Life, and the Changing American Citizen.* New York: Oxford University Press.

CHAPTER 18

POLITICAL PSYCHOLOGY AND CHOICE

DIANA C. MUTZ

POLITICAL psychology is, at heart, concerned with the characteristics of individuals and of situations that are most conducive to a successful political system. For most political psychologists whose work is reviewed in this chapter, the ideal political system is a western-style democracy, with individual rights and responsibilities for self-governance, combined with varying degrees of protection of minority interests. For these reasons, the kinds of citizen choices that are most valued and most widely studied are ones that reflect these emphases. They include, but are not limited to, high levels of political information, active political participation, fair-minded evaluation of political alternatives, and so forth.

Given the sheer volume of work in this burgeoning area, I cannot hope to do a thorough review of the many contributions of political psychology in recent years. Moreover, another recent volume in this same series, the *Oxford Handbook of Political Psychology*, does an admirable job in summarizing the many developments in this field (see Sears, Huddy, and Jervis 2003). Thus, I have chosen to highlight three of the more recent trends and most promising new areas of investigation in political psychology that have emerged over the last few decades. I explore these particular themes not only because they are recent, but also because they hold some promise of changing, in some fundamental way, how we think about political psychology.

This chapter begins with an overview of the recent emphasis on the importance of emotion in understanding political choices. Next, I turn to research dealing with the ability of citizens to process information in an unbiased fashion. This category includes studies of motivated reasoning and selectivity, as well as research on the effects of partisanship and ideology on the processing of information. Third, I highlight the contributions of methodological innovations to our understanding of political psychology. While no one method is a cure-all, recent advances in the field of neuroscience are opening up new approaches with the potential to help us better understand the black box psychological processing of political stimuli.

Finally, I conclude by reflecting upon political psychologists' emphasis on the importance of information, cognition, and rationality in research over past decades, examining rationality's use as a standard (both empirical and normative) for judging the quality of decision-making processes. It is ironic that political psychology so often defines itself in opposition to rational choice approaches, and yet its standard for normative judgments is virtually the same.

1 THE ROLE OF EMOTION IN POLITICAL CHOICE

Over the last few decades, political psychologists have enriched our understanding of choice by incorporating emotion into models that were formerly almost exclusively cognitive in describing political decision-making processes. In order to describe the progress (and lack thereof) in this domain, it is useful to first discuss several terms that are used more or less interchangeably within contemporary political psychology, including mood, affect, feeling, and emotion. As Kuklinski (2001) has noted, the study of these concepts within political psychology is still in its infancy, and "[we] do not always adopt the same conception of identically labeled psychological phenomena." As a result, it is less clear than one might think what is and is not known about the role of emotion in political behavior. I begin by sorting through some of the most frequently used terms and operationalizations, and then turn to the difficulty of differentiating emotions from other phenomena.

Within political psychology, the term *affect* often is used to describe whether an individual likes or dislikes some political object, or whether it is positively or negatively valenced, or "affectively charged," to use a popular terminology. Common measurement techniques such as feeling thermometers or Likert scales are used to ascertain an individual's positive or negative evaluation of some political person, policy, or object.

Unfortunately, this operationalization of affect is often difficult or impossible to distinguish from political judgments and opinions more generally. Few doubt that affect influences political attitudes and the processing of political information, but as it is usually measured by political scientists, such positive or negative judgments need not necessarily result from emotional reactions. After all, one may feel positively or negatively toward a political object for reasons that are wholly cognitive in nature.

It has long been acknowledged, for example, that the strongest predictor of candidate choice in the American National Election Studies (ANES) comes from the feeling thermometer ratings of presidential candidates (see e.g. Bartels 1988). Such measures are often referred to as indicators of affect toward the candidates, and yet this evidence is a weak basis on which to claim that emotion plays an important role in political choice. Thermometer ratings may instead represent running tallies of respondents' likes and dislikes about the candidate over time, which is a far cry from the kind of visceral reaction to a political event that the study of emotion promises to help us understand.

Just as like or dislike for political objects and measures drawn from feeling thermometers should not be considered synonymous with emotion, another seemingly related concept—mood—is also frequently conflated with emotion. Whereas emotions tend to be fleetingly experienced in response to a specific stimulus, and then dissipate, mood refers to a much longer-lasting phenomenon. Moods are also less focused in their target than are emotional reactions (see Bless 2001).

Because of the inconsistent use of terms in the study of emotion and politics, and because of highly variable operationalizations of those same terms, it is difficult to draw a clear line between research on political attitudes and studies of political emotion. Researchers have proposed a variety of theories of emotion over the last century, but almost all define emotion in terms of physiological arousal, which is often (though not necessarily) combined with a cognitive label of some kind. To be consistent with most psychologists' definitions, political emotion should involve some kind of negative and/or positive reaction to a political object, along with a concurrent experience of arousal. This visceral reaction may occur below the level of conscious recognition, and is relatively automatic, that is, it need not be mediated by cognition.

Conceptually, emotions also are different from attitudes in that emotional reactions are relatively short-lived and highly focused. Perhaps because emotion involves well-known physiological symptoms, it is often assumed that people must know it when they feel it. But emotions need not be particularly pronounced or obvious to the person experiencing them. Although the natural tendency in studies of emotion and politics is to treat the political object that evokes the emotion as if it were the sole cause, the kind of cognitive label that people give to emotion is determined at least in part by cues present in the environment at the time. Likewise, when arousal is artificially induced unbeknownst to experimental subjects, they will nonetheless report experiencing an emotion and attribute it to something even though it was not the actual cause of their arousal.

A great deal of research within political science has focused on particular types of emotions, such as anxiety, anger, fear, or enthusiasm. This focus most likely results from the steady supply of self-report measures of these emotions in the ANES and other election surveys. Others have focused more on the extent to which emotional arousal occurs, without respect to the subspecies of emotion being experienced.

Both approaches are relevant so far as they lead to an understanding of how emotions are involved in political attitudes and behavior. Unfortunately, the traditional survey method has made it difficult to disentangle the experience of emotional arousal from the cognitive assessment of the object and the labeling of the specific emotion.

To date, the most prominent theory tying emotion to political psychology is Marcus, Neuman, and MacKuen's (2000) theory of affective intelligence, which posits that affect ultimately serves to make citizens more sophisticated. When anxious about how things are going in the political world, this generalized anxiety drives a search for more information, and for better use of existing information resources. Thus greater political "intelligence" is induced by emotion, at least this specific variety. Drawing on ANES data, Marcus and colleagues argue that generalized anxiety about politics causes people to engage in more effortful information gathering and processing. As a result, they are less likely to rely on default heuristics such as party identification in informing their vote preferences, and more likely to seek out and rely on substantive information. According to their formulation, emotion plays an indirect role in promoting more effortful processing by motivating citizens to seek out and use more information. In other words, emotion is the driving force behind a process that ultimately improves the quality of political decision making. More specifically, Marcus and colleagues argue that a specific positive emotion—enthusiasm—elicits greater participation, whereas the negative emotion labeled anxiety elicits an information search.

The theory of affective intelligence has undoubtedly played an important role in renewing consideration of emotion in a field that has been heavily cognitive throughout its brief history. Perhaps even more importantly, this work has brought about reconsideration of the normative perspective on emotion that is common to most political psychology. Much of political theory has disdained the role of emotion in political decision making and, until recently, political psychologists have largely followed suit. Psychologists have recognized the important role emotion plays in intelligent functioning, and how cognition alone leads to serious dysfunction. Political psychologists have been slower to take up the defense of emotion as a potentially positive force in political decision making.

The theory of affective intelligence is not without its critics. Although few argue with the general logic of the theoretical framework, nor that emotions may serve useful (as well as potentially harmful) purposes in the political world, the empirical evidence supporting affective intelligence has been criticized as limited and inconclusive. For one, evidence is limited to retrospective self-reports of emotional reactions. Evidence of affective intelligence hinges on the validity of survey questions asking respondents to tell the interviewer whether a given political figure has ever made them feel angry, afraid, anxious, enthusiastic, and so forth. While such measures have face validity, studies outside the political realm raise doubt that they provide accurate recall of previously experienced emotions. Without the presence of the emotion-inducing event or object, such reports tend to be heavily mediated by cognitions (Breckler 1984). Likewise, induced emotion is quite different from semantically activated reports of emotion. As Niedenthal and colleagues (2003, 327) suggest, "affect infusion . . . requires that the perceptual aspects of an emotion are experienced, not merely the semantic aspects."

In a related critique, Ladd and Lenz (2004) point out that while the theory of affective intelligence suggests that a *generalized* anxiety among members of the electorate drives greater engagement and the search for more information, empirical evidence is based on whether anxiety is reported to have been produced *by specific candidates*. Thus it is not a general emotional state that is operationally tapped in examinations of affective intelligence, but rather how one feels about a candidate or candidates. Using ANES data, Ladd and Lenz show, not surprisingly, that candidate preference and vote choice are related to comparative emotions toward the two candidates. The extent that one candidate produces more anxiety than another is strongly related to candidate preference. They argue that those reporting anxiety may, indeed, be more engaged, but only spuriously so, either because intensely held preferences drive both anxiety and engagement, or because political engagement leads to still stronger reactions to the campaign. As Ladd and Lenz note, the results seen thus far are consistent with evidence of affective intelligence, but they do not rule out other possible interpretations.

Clearly, some doubt exists regarding the specifics of affective intelligence, but few doubt that politics can be emotion provoking, nor that emotion matters to the political choices that people make. Although affective intelligence focuses our attention on the benefits of emotion for political behavior, emotion is also widely acknowledged to be potentially manipulative. As Brader and Corrigan (2005, 1) point out in their study of the emotional content of political advertisements, "The full significance of emotions for politics comes not because emotions influence the political behavior of citizens, but rather because political actors know that they do and try to capitalize on the power of emotions to achieve their goals." Most consultants believe in the importance of emotional appeals, though these lay theories have not been validated by empirical evidence (e.g. Kaid and Johnston 2001).

Methodologically, political scientists find it difficult to study emotion as distinct from cognition. Survey data alone cannot make a strong case for emotions as a cause of most politically relevant outcomes (e.g. Glaser and Salovey 1998; Isbell and Ottati 2002). But even in experimental settings, efforts to manipulate emotion without changing the informational content of messages prove quite difficult. For example, in two experiments on the role of emotion in political advertising, Brader (2005) compares the reactions of subjects exposed to ads that include emotional cues for enthusiasm and fear to those that do not. Operationally, he does this by comparing a relatively negative script to a similar one that includes evocatively fearful images and music, and a relatively positive ad to one that includes enthusiastic music and images. He suggests that imagery and music are critical to emotional appeals, whereas verbal content is processed in highly cognitive ways. While there is some evidence that pictures are particularly good at inducing emotional responses relative to words, like most scholars, Brader relied on the post hoc report of emotion.

It would be fairly simple to interpret the results of Brader's study if one could validate that information is entirely contained within the verbal content of communications, whereas changing the visual content and music alters only emotions. As psychological studies suggest, some words carry far more emotional content than others do, just as some pictures do (see Lang, Bradley, and Cuthbert 1997). But just as a picture is often said to be worth a thousand words, there is no clear way to change images and music within a presentation without also changing the information that viewers are given, and the context in which they are interpreting it. Within psychology, many researchers use standardized sets of words and pictures that allow them to roughly equate stimuli as strongly or weakly positive, negative or neutral in the emotions they elicit. But standardized stimuli like these have yet to be developed for political psychology. Moreover, to do so would be quite difficult. Whereas smiling babies and cute bunnies are consensually regarded as producers of positive affect in the psychology lab, George Bush could be one person's positive stimulus and another's strong negative one.

How else might researchers manipulate emotion without inadvertently changing other variables in their designs? In one study, subliminal cues were used to induce emotional reactions without viewer awareness and thus also without changing the visual or verbal information of which subjects were cognitively aware (see Weber, Lodge, and Taber 2005). This approach has the advantage of holding information constant, but it probably also mutes the potential effects that emotion might have relative to real world examples of emotion-inducing messages.

Furthermore, even if one does not seek to manipulate emotion, but instead measures it as an outcome, our usual methodological toolbox is limited in what it has to offer. The heavy reliance on emotion as reported by subjects after the fact casts serious doubts on the appropriate interpretation of many studies. If, as many psychologists suggest, affect is most often experienced extremely quickly and often in the absence of conscious cognitive awareness (see Zajonc 1980; Bargh and Chartrand 1999), then the usual approaches to measurement will not do. People only become aware of their emotions if they are very strong emotions, and most directed at the political world probably do not reach that level. As Alford and colleagues (2005, 20) summarize, "Emotion produces choices and behavior without much in the way of controlled cognitive deliberation that is introspectively transparent." Even if one trusts self-reports, there is the additional hurdle of getting subjects to accurately recall felt emotions. Civettini and Redlawsk (2005) find that when affect is reported immediately after a stimulus, and then recalled later in the same experiment, there are nonetheless high levels of error in their self-reports.

All of this is problematic for what we political scientists ask of our survey respondents and experimental subjects. There is no easy solution, but it seems doubtful that post hoc self-reports of emotion will continue to be defensible as the standard measure of emotional response. If political psychologists are convinced—as we seem to be—that automatic, preconscious emotional reactions precede and shape the kind of subsequent cognitive processing that transpires, then there is little choice but to pursue alternative approaches. If we are to further an understanding of emotion and politics that is more than simply a repackaging of studies of political cognition, then we need to sort out our terminological inconsistencies and improve methods of measurement. Despite progress, we know far too little about the extent to which emotions are involved in political judgment. At best we can say that we have studied the effects of some emotions that citizens are aware of and can label, and can respond to in some purposive way. But that points to a huge limitation on current knowledge.

2 THE PSYCHOLOGY OF BIASED PROCESSING

Because of the ever-increasing range of choice offered to citizens and consumers, one of the most active areas of political psychology research is the study of whether people are biased versus fair-minded processors of political information. Do people assimilate information in a rational way, or do they raise the bar for convincing evidence when new information contradicts their existing views? Are they simply rational updaters who take new information and add it to their existing mix in order to formulate a new opinion? Or are they selective in what they expose themselves to and to what extent they revise their views accordingly?

This research is triggered in part by renewed interest in parties and partisanship in American elections. The early research suggesting that partisanship was declining in the 1970s gave way to a consensus of "renewal" in the 1980s and 1990s (Fiorina 2002). The strength of the statistical relationship between party identification and vote choice rose continuously from 1972 to 1996, but this new consensus diffused relatively slowly throughout the discipline (see Bartels 2002). In addition, even widespread acceptance of the increased strength of this relationship has not necessarily meant that everyone agrees that party identification is now a stronger predictor of vote choice. As Fiorina (2002) points out, if party identification now works in concert with other determinants of vote choice that once predicted in opposite directions or not at all, then there may be good reason to call this new consensus into question.

More recently, Levendusky (2005) showed that party identification and ideology are much more tightly aligned now than in the 1970s. Whereas party ID and ideology were once largely orthogonal, liberals are now predominantly Democrats and conservatives are predominantly Republicans. This sorting process, he argues, has occurred as a result of elite polarization. When elites are ideologically polarized and send homogeneous signals about what it means to be a Democrat/Liberal and a Republican/Conservative, then the electorate "sorts" themselves into more consistent categories, largely by changing ideology to align with party identification.

Interestingly, what it means precisely to "identify" with a political party remains an unanswered question. Party identification is easily the most widely used concept in all of political psychology if not political science, but it has been reified to such an extent that its meaning is seldom questioned, except in comparative contexts.

Moreover, the extent to which people in various countries will self-identify with a party hinges precariously on how the question is asked. In a study comparing a variety of approaches to asking about party attachments in Canada, the US, and Britain, Blais and colleagues (2001) found that the extent of these publics willing to adopt these labels went from 76 percent to 48 percent, based on a minor change in the wording of the question.

Despite some skepticism about the newfound power of partisanship in the United States electorate, the strengthening of this statistical relationship has spawned a resurgence of interest in the extent to which partisanship biases the processing of political information. Whereas twenty-five years ago one was more likely to read about partisanship in the academic journals as a source of high levels of political knowledge, mobilization, and attitude consistency, many contemporary political psychologists study partisanship as a source of bias in the processing of political information. Political parties have been at the root of the debate over biased assimilation from the very beginning of election research. As Angus Campbell and colleagues (1960, 133) argued, "Identification with a party raises a perceptual screen through which an individual tends to see what is favorable to his partisan orientation." The theme of partisan resistance to new information persists in contemporary models of the vote, and it is argued to cause people to selectively consume information and/or selectively interpret the implications and importance of new information, so that it does not threaten their existing views.

Interest in selective perception and selective exposure has been with us since the earliest election studies (e.g. Lazarsfeld, Berelson, and Gaudet 1944), but only recently have these basic ideas taken root in more complex models of information processing. Selectivity and biased processing represent one of the most active areas of research in recent political psychology. As the number of avenues for obtaining political information has increased, political psychologists want to know whether citizens select sources that are more likely to reinforce their existing views. Further, to what extent is new information interpreted and processed so as to reinforce existing beliefs, and to what extent are citizens responsive to new information?

One prominent example of the emphasis on motivated reasoning is Lodge, Taber, and colleagues' work suggesting that all political concepts are affectively charged as positive or negative, and that this information is stored in long-term memory (see e.g. Taber, Lodge, and Glathar 2001; Lodge and Taber 2005). New information is not necessarily retained, but it is used to update the affective tags that are attached to these concepts in memory. When asked for an evaluation of a political concept, citizens are said to recall the affective tally attached to the concept. Feelings serve as a summary of information that is no longer accessible in memory. This model represents a relatively rational approach to choice, though not necessarily in the Bayesian sense of rational updating.

However, as Lodge, Taber, and colleagues (e.g. Taber, Lodge, and Glathar 2001) have pointed out, an accurate model of political reasoning must take into account that it is often motivated by goals other than accuracy. In their motivated reasoning model, the online tally is not simply an unbiased account of previously encountered information. Instead, directional goals continually alter the processing and integration of new information into the tally. To the extent that the goal is to maintain one's prior beliefs (as opposed to pursuing accuracy), people may ignore or devalue contrary information. They may also seek evidence selectively, biasing the considerations they draw from memory, exercising different levels of scrutiny for disconfirming evidence, and/or altering the weights attached to different criteria in a way that is less threatening to the prior belief. According to this model, directional goals "emerge spontaneously as the affective tags associated with elements of the problem represented in long-term memory are brought into working memory (hot cognition)."

According to this model, the direction and strength of affect toward a political person or idea will cause most citizens to be "biased reasoners" who fail to treat new evidence fairly: "Most citizens most of the time will be decidedly 'partisan' in what and how they think about and reason about political leaders, groups, events, and issues" (185). Interestingly, advocates of this model suggest that it is neither wholly a vice nor a virtue. On the one hand, an online tally provides a better summary of one's past evaluations than preferences based on the recollection of specific pros and cons that happen to come to mind at any given point in time. The online model thus implies that choices are based on more information than is evident in assessments of knowledge made at the time of the decision. On the other hand, that same affective tally biases the processing of subsequent information, and is, in that sense, normatively undesirable.

Lau and Redlawsk (2006) have constructed a closely related model of motivated reasoning based on behavioral decision theory. In their model of the vote choice, they focus on the process of decision making and how individual motivations influence the extent to which voters choose correctly. They begin by accepting the notion that pre-existing preferences bias subsequent assimilation of information, but they attempt to determine where such motivations enter into this process. Using an interactive information board/computer screen that allows people to seek out information in order to make decisions, they suggest that bias enters into information gathering and processing at many points along the way to decision-making. Surprisingly, voters who use a classically rational decision-making process, that is, one involving a deep and balanced information search, "were in many circumstances less likely to make a correct decision compared to voters using an intuitive or fast and frugal strategy" (Lau and Redlawsk 2005, 23). Barker and Hansen (2005) likewise question whether more information and deeper cognitive processing is the answer to what ails citizens. They found that subjects who engaged in systematic cognitive processing had weaker and less consistent attitudes than subjects in a control group.

Two recent studies stake out the ground on both sides of this important debate over whether citizens ultimately make good use of information. Gerber and Green (1999) use aggregate opinion data to argue that selectivity and perceptual bias are actually *not* the norm when citizens take in new information. Using over-time aggregate data, they argue that Republicans, Democrats, and Independents all basically change their views in the same direction and to the same extent as a result of new information.

Based on an analysis of presidential approval among Republicans, Democrats, and Independents, Gerber and Green (1999, 205) conclude that all three groups tend to go up and down together over time: "Only the faintest traces of selective perception are evidence from partisan tends in presidential approval. All three partisan groups move together—sometimes markedly—as party fortunes change." They applaud this pattern as rational in both the colloquial and Bayesian sense of the term. In other words, citizens appear to demonstrate Bayesian learning, with all groups making equally good use of new information as it comes along. If people were truly biased processors, they argue, their views would not move in parallel in response to ongoing political events.

If Gerber and Green's claim is correct, it has far-reaching consequences for some of the most widely believed tenets of mass political behavior. Partisanship, in this view, is simply a running tally of information and judgments that have occurred over time. It summarizes information efficiently but has no influence on choice independent of the information and value judgments that it encapsulates. This conceptualization stands in sharp contrast to the traditional idea of partisanship as a driving force in how people perceive, interpret, and respond to the political world. According to Gerber and Green, information is key to understanding the political fortunes of candidates and policies, and the public responds roughly as if it were updating its views accordingly.

For most political psychologists, Gerber and Green's conclusion is shocking if not implausible. How could so many studies, laboratory and otherwise, demonstrate findings of resistance to counter-attitudinal information, particularly in the context of political views that have been relatively stable throughout a person's lifetime? If prior views do, in fact, bias the processing of new information, one would expect this pattern to be observable in the realm of political decision making if it happens at all.

Interestingly, using the same standard model of Bayesian updating as the basis for his conclusion, Bartels (2000) suggests that biased processing is alive and well in the American public, with partisanship as its driving force. Bartels suggests that when oppositional partisan groups adjust their views in the same direction and to roughly the same extent over time, it is anything but evidence of Bayesian learning.

To help explain the basis for this difference of opinion, Figure 18.1 illustrates the same kind of over-time evidence that convinced Gerber and Green that political psychologists' assumptions about biased processing were greatly exaggerated. As new information becomes available to all three groups—say, for example, news that the economy has improved—all three partisan groups move toward higher levels of presidential approval. The trendlines in Figure 18.1 exemplify this parallel movement in presidential approval, though obviously from groups that began with very different attitudes toward a Republican president in this hypothetical example. Downturns due to bad news such as economic decline would cause all three groups' approval levels to plummet, as they do in this illustration between 1985 and 1988.

In contrast, Figure 18.2 provides an illustration of what Bartels thinks Bayesian learning should look like in over-time public opinion data. As new information

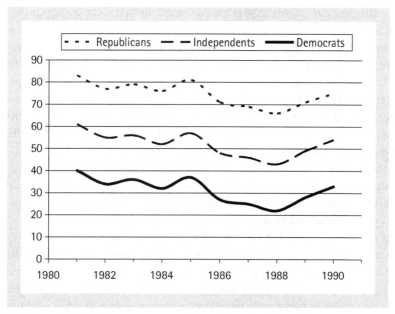

Fig. 18.1. Gerber/Green representation of Bayesian learning

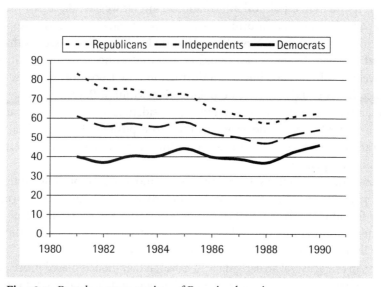

Fig. 18.2. Bartels representation of Bayesian learning

becomes available—perhaps news that the economy has worsened—the three groups of partisans update their presidential approval ratings in light of their initial views. In contrast to the Gerber/Green expectation, downward movement of approval due to negative information is not even across all groups, but is more pronounced in groups that begin with higher levels of approval. This occurs in a Bayesian model because the new information is more significant to the extent that it contradicts initial expectations. So, for example, in Figure 18.2 the decline in approval between 1981 and 1982 produces a shallower slope for Democrats, whose expectations for the Republican president were quite low to begin with. For Republicans, negative information of this kind is more of a surprise given their generally positive expectations, thus the extent of impact is greater for this group as shown by the steeper downward slope between 1981 and 1982. Most importantly, the net effect of Bayesian updating is some convergence of opinion. Whether the news is positive or negative, the three lines ultimately move closer and closer together over time. And even when the new information that citizens must incorporate is outside the range of expectation—better than even what the most supportive expect, or worse than what the most oppositional political group expects—the differential change in light of expectations should still bring the groups closer together if they are processing via Bayesian learning.

Thus Bartels suggests that we should not find real data that mimics Figure 18.1 particularly reassuring in its implications. It substantiates, rather than refutes, the hypothesis of biased processing. Moreover, Bartels's conclusion comports with the bulk of evidence in political psychology—that is, that partisans are indeed biased assimilators and that patterns of Bayesian convergence such as what is illustrated in Figure 18.2 are uncommon.

Neither model, however, takes us through the full range of possibilities for how citizens respond to new political information. Thus far we have discussed these models in terms of events and information with clear positive or negative implications that all citizens would share. News that pollution levels have increased, or that unemployment is down, for example, would be received as negative and positive news, respectively, by all citizens. But new information about position issues as opposed to valence issues could easily create polarization within a Bayesian framework. For instance, if the "new information" about the president is that he vetoed a gun control bill, then Republicans should move in the more positive direction, if at all, and Democrats in a more negative direction. In this scenario, Bayesian learners should, quite rationally, polarize.

Whatever their differences, biased processing models are typical of contemporary political psychology in that they share an underlying skepticism that information is the cure for all that ails the quality of political decisions. If people are not passive recipients of information, but rather active choosers, interpreters, and rationalizers, then the limitations of information become apparent.

We are, in one sense, at an early stage in research that models biased processing, still sorting out what qualifies as evidence and what does not. To understand this process more fully in the future, researchers must unpack the process of biased assimilation in order to understand how bias occurs in the selection of information sources, the credibility granted to those sources, the discounting of information, and the relative weights given to new information in updating preferences. These are all separate mechanisms by which new information could differentially affect partisan groups based on their initial predispositions.

3 BEYOND SELF-REPORT: NEW SOURCES OF THEORY AND EVIDENCE

Methodologically, political psychology has been criticized for relying too heavily on cross-sectional survey data (e.g. Krosnick 2002). Although this criticism seems valid with regard to much of the past work in this subfield, a greater level of methodological pluralism is difficult to find in any other subfield within political science. Burgeoning pluralism is evident in the kinds of methods political psychologists use as well as in the types of measures they now employ to operationalize key concepts.

In comparing early research in political psychology with today's studies, there is a striking difference in the extent to which political psychologists trust self-reports as a means of getting at the black box processes involved in formulating political choices. For example, when authors of classics such as *The People's Choice* wanted to know why people voted the way they did, they simply asked them. In contrast, the consensus view today is that the reasons people offer for their decisions "are better understood as justifications of a decision that has already been made" (12). (See also Lau 1982; McGraw 2000; Rahn, Krosnick, and Breuning 1994.)

For better or worse, humans appear to have little ability to introspect about the actual causes of their attitudes and actions. Nonetheless, they are disturbingly facile at rationalizing the choices and actions that they make. I say "disturbing" because as social scientists, we may be led on many a wild goose chase by people's abilities to rationalize their emotions and choices. In addition, it is disturbing to lose the comfort of believing that there is an accessible, transparent logic to individuals' political choices.

A dramatic example of the need to be skeptical of self-report and introspective accounts of behavior is illustrated by Wegner (2002) in a study in which electrical stimulation was used unbeknownst to experimental subjects to force them to react involuntarily by standing up. Despite the fact that their decision to stand was completely outside of their control, a large percentage reported a logical reason why they did so. Our brains are apparently compelled to offer deliberate, conscious reasons for our actions, but these rationalizations may have little to do with what actually happens. If we cannot understand the origins of our decision to sit or stand, how can we possibly understand the origins of a far more complex decision such as a vote choice?

What options do intrepid explorers of the black box psychological processes underlying political choices have to turn to? The good news is that the methodological repertoire for political psychology has undoubtedly expanded over the past fifty years. In addition to the survey data that served as the initial springboard for interest in the psychology of political choices, scholars now make regular use of laboratory experiments as well.

But the expansion in methodologies has not been exclusively toward imitating the internal validity of psychologists' laboratory studies. In addition, experimental designs embedded within surveys provide researchers with new insights into understanding the basis of sensitive and socially undesirable political opinions and behaviors such as non-voting (see Holbrook and Krosnick 2005) and negative attitudes toward racial minorities (Sniderman et al. 1991). What is more, field experiments have been brought back into the methodological mix as well, primarily by Green and his associates (see e.g. Green and Gerber 2002). Still others study the psychology of political decision making in the context of real world political choices, as Glaser (2002) did in his study of the effects of ballot structure on the outcome of school bond initiatives.

Recognizing that so much of what political psychologists want to know may transcend the realm of self-report or even self-awareness, scholars also increasingly pursue measures that do not require research participants' conscious awareness or introspection. Response times in answering questions, for example, are used to better understand respondents' associations between positive or negative attributes and racial groups. In the most sophisticated applications of these techniques, researchers use complex designs to understand the associative links that facilitate attitudes.

The two most widely used paradigms for evaluating implicit (as contrasted with explicit) attitudes, are the "implicit association test" (IAT; see Greenwald, McGhee, and Schwartz 1998), and the "bona fide pipeline" (BFP; see Fazio et al. 1995). The IAT measures the strength of an association between two target categories (e.g. black and white) and two attributes (e.g. good and bad) by having people categorize examples of the target and attribute categories at the same time. So, for example, respondents would be presented with a test stimulus (e.g. a picture of a flower), and asked to sort what they observe into one category if it is either Black or good, or a second category if the object is either White or bad. The speed with which they perform this task across a number of stimuli is then compared to the speed with which they perform the same task with the two groups switched so that they sort objects into either a Black/bad category or a White/good category. In this particular example, negative attitudes toward Blacks would be assessed by comparing response latencies on the Black-bad and White-good trials to the Black-good and White-bad trials. Interestingly, even when one knows how the test works and is aware of what is being measured, it is still next to impossible for respondents to falsify results by trying to respond more quickly to some pairings than others.

The BFP also measures implicit attitudes, but in this case a prime such as a Black or White face is presented before an adjective is shown. In this case, negative associations with Blacks would be demonstrated by faster latencies when Black faces and negative adjectives are shown, and slower latencies for Black faces followed by positive adjectives relative to the same latencies after the presentation of White faces.

Both techniques avoid the perils of self-report and solve social desirability biases. In studies of racial attitudes, they also predict race-related behaviors (Fazio and Olson 2003). Although these are controversial measures of racial prejudice and of negative attitudes toward groups (see e.g. Arkes and Tetlock 2004), they are uncontroversial as indicators of the associations that people maintain, whether they act on them or not. One might well ask whether they are really necessary to political psychology outside of a few particularly sensitive topics such as race. The answer to this question remains to be seen, but as political psychologists increasingly seek understandings of phenomena outside the realm of conscious awareness, techniques of this kind will undoubtedly become increasingly valuable.

Finally, another set of methods involving psycho-physiological approaches to political attitudes and behaviors has opened up new possibilities as political psychologists begin to see how social neuroscience and psycho-physiological measurement techniques may be useful for understanding political attitudes and behavior. Technological advances in our ability to observe physiological evidence of the processes underlying political choice have drawn a small group of scholars to incorporate the tools of neuroscience into their work. Although a thorough review of studies that employ psycho-physiological and social neuroscience approaches is beyond the scope of this chapter, a special issue of *Political Psychology* published in 2003 (Volume 24: 4) provides useful examples of how social neuroscience is increasingly incorporated into political psychology. Given the field's focus on understanding real world political events, these techniques are not likely to replace traditional methods within political psychology, but they are a very promising means of augmenting our limited access to people's internal states.

Recently political psychologists also have begun to draw on evolutionary psychology as a basis for understanding reactions to the political world. For example, Alford, Funk, and Hibbing (2005) use the results of twin studies to distinguish the environmental determinants of political attitudes from their inherited traits. They conclude that attitudes toward a wide variety of political issues, as well as affect toward the major parties, is significantly influenced by genetic predisposition. Likewise, Sidanius and colleagues' theory about the role of gender in social dominance orientation is rooted in evolutionary psychology. Mutz and Reeves (2005) also draw on evolutionary psychology to understand viewers' reactions to incivility in televised political discourse.

To be sure, the potential applications of these approaches to political choice are in their infancy, but they appear relevant to some of the very same questions political psychologists have been trying to answer for years. For example, brain imaging studies demonstrate that activity in one area of the brain can bias what goes on elsewhere in the brain, thus bolstering conclusions about biased processing. Moreover, there appears to be no centralized location in the brain for integrating information and making choices (see Alford, Hibbing, and Smith 2005). Thus there is unlikely to be any one calculus for political decision making.

To date, very little of this evidence is directed toward answering the kinds of questions that plague political psychology, but the implications are clear. For example, McClure et al. (2004) show that judgments made about immediate versus delayed gratification activate different areas of the brain. As Alford and colleagues explain, "the time element stimulated different parts of the brain that are associated with different functions. Specifically, the possibility of immediate gratification seems to activate the emotional part of the brain, but when immediate gratification is not an option, the more reflective and cognitive part of the brain is activated." As political scientists ponder how promises of tax cuts influence choice relative to long-term promises to protect the environment, such findings may well become applicable.

4 INFORMATION AS THE GOLD STANDARD

It is a profoundly erroneous truism...that we should cultivate the habit of thinking about what we are doing. The precise opposite is the case. Civilization advances by extending the number of operations which we can perform without thinking about them. Operations of thought are like cavalry charges in a battle—they are strictly limited in number, they require fresh horses, and must only be made at decisive moments.   (Alfred North Whitehead, 1911)

If an extraterrestrial took a cursory glance at the books published in political psychology over the past fifteen years, she would come away with the impression that what we earth people value in our citizens is information, reason, and rationality. Consider, for example, Ferejohn and Kuklinski's *Information and Democratic Processes* (1990), Popkin's *The Reasoning Voter* (1991), Sniderman, Brody, and Tetlock's *Reasoning and Choice* (1991), Lupia, McCubbins, and Popkin's *Elements of Reason: Cognition, Choice, and the Bounds of Rationality* (2000), Page and Shapiro's (1992) *The Rational Public,* and so forth. These books do not concur on all matters, but the desirability of rational, well-informed political choices resonates throughout all of these volumes.

A closer look would reveal that the bulk of studies concur that people do not have loads of information about politics—indeed, far from it. But this closer examination would nonetheless suggest that most political psychologists *wish* citizens had perfect information, and think the political process would be far better off if citizens could at least better approximate this goal. As Kuklinski (2002) has suggested, rational choice assumes citizens are even-handed processors of information, while political psychology tends to assume (and to find) that they are not, though it nonetheless argues that they should be.

In this respect, Whitehead's statement above may seem an anathema from the perspective of political psychology. What could be more sacred than the idea that good citizens should put a great deal of thought into the political choices they make? Are we, indeed, depleting citizens' resources by asking them to make too many political decisions? Or are we reaching the wrong conclusions by assuming that the best decisions are ones made based on the most information? It is worth remembering that the well-educated citizen was not always the gold standard in politics.

Contemporary political psychology is beginning to question whether a classic rational decision-making process is truly what political psychology should pursue as its gold standard. In all three of the areas discussed in this chapter, political psychologists are reconsidering the emphasis on information and cognition as the root of ideal political choice. Studies of emotion and politics suggest that emotion is equally, if not more, important to political choice than cognition, and they question whether that is necessarily a bad thing. Studies of information processing suggest that information is severely limited in its capacity to improve political choice given the extent of biased processing; moreover, rational decision making does not necessarily mean better choices. As new approaches to measurement are applied to political choice, they further suggest that much of human decision making—political or otherwise—may be driven by processes of which citizens are not aware.

Taken together, these trends suggest that one of the most long-lasting premises of political decision making—that information gathering, thinking, and reasoning make for superior political decisions relative to visceral, subconscious reactions—is being called into question. Whereas political psychologists in the past have thought of citizens as information processors, they are rapidly becoming seen as less purposeful and as having less conscious control over their preferences. Whether such a representation of citizen choice is more accurate than the citizen as rational processor and/or more normatively desirable remains to be seen. In an era when voters are being asked to make more individual political choices than ever before, the horses may indeed need rest.

REFERENCES

ALFORD, J., FUNK, C., and HIBBING, J. 2005. Are political orientations Genetically Transmitted? *American Political Science Review*, 99: 153–67.

—— HIBBING, J., and SMITH, K. 2005. The challenge evolutionary biology poses for rational choice. Paper presented at the Annual Meeting of the American Political Science Association, Washington, DC.

ARKES, H. and TETLOCK, P. 2004. Attributions of implicit prejudice, or "would Jesse Jackson 'fail' the implicit association test?" *Psychological Inquiry*, 15(4): 257–78.

BARGH, J. and CHARTRAND, T. 1999. The unbearable automaticity of being. *American Psychologist*, 54: 462–79.

BARKER, D. and HANSEN, S. 2005. All things considered: systematic cognitive processing and electoral decision making. *Journal of Politics*, 67 (2).

BARTELS, L. 1988. *Presidential Primaries and the Dynamics of Public Choice*. Princeton: Princeton University Press.

—— 2000. Partisanship and voting behavior, 1952–1996. *American Journal of Political Science*, 44: 35–50.

—— 2002. Beyond the running tally: partisan bias in political perceptions. *Political Behavior* 24: 117–50.

BLAIS, A., GIDENGIL, E., NADEAU, R., and NEVITTE, N. 2001. Measuring party identification: Britain, Canada and the United States. *Political Behavior*, 23 (1): 5–22.

BLESS, H. 2001. The consequences of mood on the processing of social information. Pp. 391–412 in *Blackwell Handbook of Sociology: Individual Processes*, ed. A. Tesser and N. Schwartz Malden, Mass.: Blackwell.

BRADER, T. 2005. Striking a responsive chord: how political ads motivate and persuade voters by appealing to emotions. *American Journal of Political Science*, 49: 388–405.

—— and CORRIGAN, B. 2005. Emotional cues and campaign dynamics in political advertising. Paper presented at the Annual Meeting of the American Political Science Association, Washington, DC.

BRECKLER, S. 1984. Empirical validation of affect, behavior and cognition as distinct components of attitude. *Journal of Personality and Social Psychology*, 47: 1191–205.

CACIOPPO, J. and VISSER, P. 2003. Political psychology and social neuroscience: strange bedfellows or comrades in arms? *Political Psychology*, 24: 647–56.

CAMPBELL, A., CONVERSE, P., MILLER, W., and STOKES, D. 1960. *The American Voter*. New York: Wiley.

CIVETTINI, A. and REDLAWSK, D. 2005. A feeling person's game: affect and voter information processing and learning in a campaign. Presented at the Annual Meeting of the American Political Science Association, Washington, DC.

FAZIO, R. H., JACKSON, J. R., DUNTON, B. C., and WILLIAMS, C. J. 1995. Variability in automatic activation as an obtrusive measure of racial attitudes: a bona fide pipeline? *Journal of Personality and Social Psychology*, 69: 1013–27.

—— and OLSON, M. A. 2003. Implicit measures in social cognition research: their meaning and use. *Annual Review of Psychology*, 54: 297–327.

FEREJOHN, J. and KUKLINSKI, J. (eds.) 1990. *Information and Democratic Processes*. Urbana: University of Illinois Press.

FIORINA, M. 2002. Parties and partisanship: a 40-year retrospective. *Political Behavior*, 24: 93–115.

GERBER, A. and GREEN, D. 1999. Misperceptions about perceptual bias. *Annual Review of Political Science*, 2: 189–210.

GLASER, J. 2002. White voters, black schools: structuring racial choices with a checklist ballot. *American Journal of Political Science*, 46: 35–46.

—— and SALOVEY, P. 1998. Affect in electoral politics. *Personality and Social Psychology Review*, 2: 156–72.

GREEN, D. and GERBER, A. 2002. Reclaiming the experimental tradition in political science. Pp. 805–32 in *Political Science: The State of the Discipline*, ed. H. V. Milner and I. Katznelson, 3rd edn. New York: W. W. Norton.

GREENWALD, A. G., McGHEE, D., and SCHWARTZ, J. L. K. 1998. Measuring individual differences in cognition: the implicit association task. *Journal of Personality and Social Psychology*, 74: 1469–80.

HOLBROOK, A. and KROSNICK, J. 2005. Vote over-reporting: testing the social desirability hypothesis in telephone and internet surveys. Paper presented at the 2005 Conference of the American Association for Public Opinion Research. Miami.

ISBELL, L. and OTTATI, V. 2002. The emotional voter. Pp. 55–74 in *The Social Psychology of Politics*, ed. V. C. Ottati, S. Tindale, et al. New York: Kluwer.

KAID, L. and JOHNSTON, A. 2001. *Videostyle in Presidential Campaigns*. Westport, Conn.: Praeger.

KROSNICK, J. 2002. Is political psychology sufficiently psychological? Distinguishing political psychology from psychological political science. Pp. 187–216 in Kuklinski 2002*b*.

KUKLINSKI, J. (ed.) 2001. *Citizens and Politics: Perspectives from Political Psychology*. New York: Cambridge University Press.

—— (ed.) 2002. *Thinking about Political Psychology*. New York: Cambridge University Press.

LADD, J. and LENZ, G. 2004. Emotions and voting behavior: a critique. Paper presented at the annual meeting of the Midwest Political Science Association, Chicago.

LANG, P. S., BRADLEY, L. M., and CUTHBERT, B. N. 1997. International Affective Picture System (IAPS): technical manual and affective ratings. NIMH Center for the Study of Emotion and Attention, retrieved on January 30, 2006 from www.unifesp.br/dpsicobio/adap/instructions.pdf

LAU, R. R. 1982. Negativity in political perception. *Political Behavior*, 4: 353–78.

—— and REDLAWSK, D. 2005. Toward a procedurally plausible model of the vote choice: decision strategies, information processing, and correct voting. Paper presented at the annual meeting of the American Political Science Association, Washington, DC.

———— 2006. *How Voters Decide: Information Processing during Election Campaigns.* New York: Cambridge University Press.

LAZARSFELD, P., BERELSON, B., and GAUDET, H. 1944. *The People's Choice.* New York: Duell, Sloan and Pearce.

LEVENDUSKY, M. 2005. Sorting, not polarization: understanding the dynamics of mass partisan change. Midwest Political Science Association Meetings, Chicago.

LODGE, M. and TABER, C. 2005. Implicit affect for candidates, parties and issues: an experimental test of the hot cognition hypothesis. *Political Psychology.*

LUPIA, A., MCCUBBINS, M., and POPKIN, S. (eds.) 2000. *Elements of Reason: Cognition, Choice, and the Bounds of Rationality.* New York: Cambridge University Press.

MCCLURE, S., LAIBSON, D., LOEWENSTEIN, G. and COHEN, J. 2004. Separate neural systems value immediate and delayed monetary rewards. *Science*, 306: 503–7.

MCGRAW, K. M. 2000. Contributions of the cognitive approach to political psychology. *Political Psychology*, 21: 805–32.

MARCUS, G., NEUMAN, W., and MACKUEN, M. 2000. *Affective Intelligence and Political Judgment.* Chicago: University of Chicago Press.

MUTZ, D. C. and REEVES, B. 2005. The new videomalaise: effects of televised incivility on political trust. *American Political Science Review*, 99 (1): 1–15.

NIEDENTHAL, P. M., ROHMAN, A., and DALLE, N. 2003. What is primed by emotion concepts and emotion words? Pp. 307–33 in *The Psychology of Evaluation: Affective Processes in Cognition and Emotion*, ed. J. Musch and K. C. Klauer. Mahwah, NJ: Erlbaum.

OLSON, M. and FAZIO, R. H. 2003. Relations between implicit measures of prejudice: what are we measuring? *Psychological Science*, 14 (6): 636–9.

PAGE, B. and SHAPIRO, R. 1992. *The Rational Public: Fifty Years of Trends in Americans' Policy Preferences.* Chicago: University of Chicago Press.

POPKIN, S. 1991. *The Reasoning Voter: Communication and Persuasion in Presidential Campaigns.* Chicago: University of Chicago Press.

RAHN, W., KROSNICK, J., and BREUNING, M. 1994. Rationalization and derivation process in survey studies of political candidate evaluation. *American Journal of Political Science*, 38: 582–600.

SEARS, D., HUDDY, L., and JERVIS, R. 2003. The psychologies underlying political psychology. Pp. 3–16 in *Oxford Handbook of Political Psychology*, ed. D. Sears, L. Huddy, and R. Jervis. Oxford: Oxford University Press.

SIDANIUS, J. and PRATTO, F. 2001. *Social Dominance: An Intergroup Theory of Social Hierarchy and Oppression.* Cambridge: Cambridge University Press.

SNIDERMAN, P., BRODY, R., and TETLOCK, P. 1991. *Reasoning and Choice: Explorations in Political Psychology.* New York: Cambridge.

—— PIAZZA, T., TETLOCK, P., and KENDRICK, A. 1991. The new racism. *American Journal of Political Science*, 35: 423–47.

Taber, C., Lodge, M., and Glathar, J. 2001. The motivated construction of political judgments. In *Citizens and Politics: Perspectives from Political Psychology*, ed. J. H. Kuklinski. New York: Cambridge University Press.

Weber, C., Lodge, M., and Taber, C. 2005. Subliminal priming and political campaigns: the impact of subliminally presented affective primes on campaign ad evaluations. Paper presented to the annual meetings of the American Political Science Association, Washington, DC, September.

Wegner, D. 2002. *The Illusion of Conscious Will*. Cambridge, Mass.: MIT Press.

Whitehead, A. 1911. *An Introduction to Mathematics*. New York: Holt.

Zajonc, R. 1980. Feeling and thinking: preferences need no inferences. *American Psychologist*, 35: 151–75.

CHAPTER 19

....

VOTERS AND PARTIES

....

ANNE WREN

KENNETH M. MCELWAIN

1 REALIGNMENT OR DEALIGNMENT IN THE PARTY–VOTER NEXUS

....

POLITICAL parties assume a prominent position in comparative studies of electoral and legislative behavior in advanced industrialized democracies. Unlike the electoral system, parliamentary committees, or other pervasive political institutions, parties are rarely defined—in either structure or function—by the national constitution.[1] Nevertheless, political parties can be found in essentially all democratic—and some autocratic—polities. Indeed, many studies of party politics lead with E. E. Schattschneider's famous quote, "Political parties created modern democracy and modern democracy is unthinkable save in terms of parties" (1942).

The reasons given for the relevance of political parties are manifold, but early studies focused on the parties' utility in the electoral process, particularly how they helped voters structure their preferences at the ballot box. As modern governments faced a widening and increasingly complex array of policy issues in both the pre-war and post-war periods, citizens were seen as being unwilling (or unable) to gather and process all the facts necessary to make an informed decision about which candidate to vote for (Campbell et al. 1960). Political parties—particularly those with

[1] There are notable exceptions, including Germany where the German Basic Law explicitly specifies the legal rights, functions, and structure of parties.

long legacies and organized bases of support—simplified this process by providing an informational heuristic about the policy platforms of those parties' candidates (Downs 1957). An American factory worker with strong labor union ties could infer how a Democratic Party candidate would vote in Congress without knowing very much about the candidate, herself. Again, in the words of Schattschneider, "The parties organize the electorate by reducing their alternatives to the extreme limit of simplification" (1960).

In addition to acting as informational cues, political parties played a crucial organizational and legislative role. Many parties—particularly on the left—maintained a large membership base, through which they recruited election candidates, distributed information, and aggregated interests to produce a coherent policy platform (Aldrich 1995; Dalton and Wattenberg 2000). They have also been the primary players in parliamentary decision making and coalition formation. Political parties coordinated like-minded members of parliament into cohesive legislative blocs, and, through the various carrots and sticks at their disposal, rewarded or sanctioned politicians based on their adherence to the party's long-term goals (Laver and Schofield 1990; Cox and McCubbins 1993; Bowler, Farrell, and Katz 1999).

In their classic treatment, Lipset and Rokkan (1967) describe the deeply embedded relationship which formed between voters and the early mass parties. Those parties which successfully organized in the period at, or before, the extension of mass suffrage enjoyed a first-mover advantage in the relationships which they built with the new electorates. The scale of this advantage was such that observed party systems in Western Europe displayed high levels of continuity between the 1920s and the 1960s, in spite of the turbulent political events which occurred in Europe during this period. As a result, these authors famously argue, the structure of electoral cleavages had become "frozen" so as to reflect the structure of ideological conflict in these countries at the time of the mass parties' foundation.

Parties' organizational strategies were particularly important in strengthening the affective relationships between parties and voters during this period. The incorporation of significant segments of the electorate into the grassroots networks of the main political parties, or into closely associated organizational groups such as trade unions, facilitated the inculcation of lasting political identities.[2] As a result, voters exhibited considerable stability in their voting behavior, as their decision making relied heavily on the informational shortcuts provided by trusted political organizations. Elections essentially became contests over which party could develop the largest mass organization, and the vote shares of established parties tended to be relatively stable.

Even as Lipset and Rokkan described this deeply embedded linkage between parties and voters, however, there were indications of upheaval in the electoral landscape. Figure 19.1 shows trends in the total vote shares of parties established before 1960—in other words, parties which were in existence during the peak periods of the "frozen

---

[2] See Przeworski and Sprague (1986) on the organizational strategies of electoral socialist parties and their relation to the trades union movement; see Kalyvas (1996) on the relationship between Christian Democratic parties and Catholic social organizations.

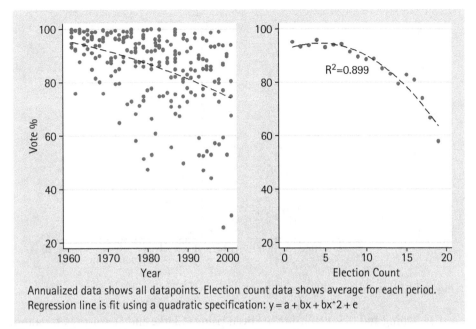

Annualized data shows all datapoints. Election count data shows average for each period.
Regression line is fit using a quadratic specification: y = a + bx + bx^2 + e

Fig. 19.1. Total vote % of parties established before 1960

cleavage" hypothesis—from the 1960s on.[3] The figure is composed of two panels, one containing annualized data and showing all data points; the second showing the average for each period between elections, or "election count," across all countries.[4] Using both year and election count allows us to differentiate between political outcomes that are a function of factors that affect countries contemporaneously (i.e. by year), or whether they vary by the frequency and natural cycle of electoral competition (i.e. by election count). Regardless of the measure, we can see that there is a strong quadratic relationship between time and the performance of established political parties.[5] The total vote share of these parties has declined at an increasing rate since the 1960s, indicating the stronger electoral presence of relatively new parties.

Additionally, numerous studies have found evidence of increasing instability in voter–party relationships. Panel surveys of individual voters show that the level of

[3] Electoral data here and in other figures are compiled from the following countries: Australia (1946–2004); Austria (1945–2002); Belgium (1946–2003); Denmark (1945–2001); Finland (1945–2003); French 5th Republic (1958–97); (West) Germany (1949–2002); Greece (1974–2004); Iceland (1946–2003); Ireland (1948–2002); Italy (1948–2001); Japan (1946–2003); Luxembourg (1954–2004); Malta (1947–2003); the Netherlands (1946–2003); Norway (1945–2001); Portugal (1976–2002); Spain (1977–2004); Sweden (1948–2002); and United Kingdom (1945–2005). Data taken from Gorvin (1989) and Caramani (2000).

[4] For example, the observation for election count "1" is the average vote share across all sampled countries in the first election held in the period under consideration. The election count figure restricts data to cases where election count is less than twenty; because only Australia, Denmark, and Japan have had that many elections in the post-war period, including those cases could bias results based on factors specific to those countries. All figures in this chapter restrict election count to less than twenty.

[5] The fitted values are quadratic predictions of total vote % based on a linear regression of total vote % on election count and election count squared. The quadratic prediction is calculated using the "twoway qfit" function on Stata 9.

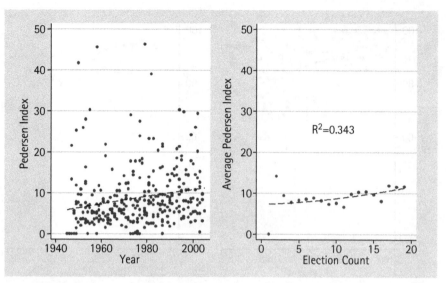

Fig. 19.2. Electoral volatility over time

party switching and ticket splitting has been rising (Clarke and Stewart 1998; Dalton, McAllister, and Wattenberg 2000). Similarly, formal membership in political parties has been falling in recent decades (Scarrow 2000), as has voter turnout—particularly in the 1990s (Wattenberg 2000). These changes have had a significant effect on election outcomes: there have been more new parties entering the political arena (Hug 2001; Tavits 2006), and, perhaps most significantly, fluctuations in the vote and seat shares of political parties have become more volatile (Mair 1997; Clarke and Stewart 1998; Dalton, McAllister, and Wattenberg 2000). Figure 19.2 displays trends in electoral volatility in the post-war period, using the Pedersen Index which measures net changes in parties' vote shares from election to election (Pedersen 1979).[6] The figure again uses two different time scales: one that plots every election by year, and a second that displays average volatility by election count. The scatter plots show that electoral volatility has increased over time at a fairly steady rate.[7]

These disparate trends in the data are indicative of changes in the nature of the relationship between parties and voters in advanced industrial democracies. The question is how we are to understand these transformations. A useful theoretical guideline is provided by Otto Kirchheimer (1966), who predicted three

---

[6] The Pedersen Index measures net changes in vote share using the formula: $0.5^* \sum(|V_{i,t} - V_{i,t-1}|)$, where V_i = vote share of each party i, and t = current election. There is some disagreement in the literature over how to calculate net vote share for new political parties. For example, if Party A and Party B merge to create Party C, should volatility be calculated as $V_{C,t} - V_{(A+B),t-1}$ or simply as V_C? Similarly, should fringe parties that are often tabulated in the "other" category be ignored altogether or treated as one bloc? In this chapter, we use the total vote share of Party C as the value of vote swing, and—following Lijphart 1994—ignore fringe parties altogether. This choice is motivated by the difficulty of keeping full track of which parties are merging/splitting in any given election, especially where different factions of the original party are amalgamated into separate parties.

[7] While the line of best fit is calculated using a quadratic regression, the slope appears to be constant over time, indicating that volatility is increasing linearly.

interconnected changes to the party–voter linkage: a reduction in the party's adherence to stringent ideologies, a de-emphasis in the party's electoral reliance on particular social classes or denominations, and the strengthening of the party leaders' organizational authority over individual party members. In recent years, the comparative politics literature has identified change along each of these dimensions. Here, we broadly group these indicators into two subcategories, each with different implications for the future.

On one side of the party–voter nexus is a gradual shift in the distribution and content of the electorate's *policy preferences*, and the powerful challenge that this poses to the continuing popularity of existing political parties. In Lipset and Rokkan's framework, the primary electoral cleavage which emerged in all states derived from the industrial revolution: the historical ideological confrontation between capitalism and socialism, and the class conflict between workers and the owners of capital.[8] In the electoral arena, this conflict focused increasingly on practical policy debates on the appropriateness and scope of government intervention in the economy, with parties of the left advocating high levels of welfare redistribution and state intervention in the economy, while parties of the right advocated the welfare-maximizing properties of free market outcomes.

In recent years, however, some authors have pointed to the increasing political salience of distributional conflicts which cannot be easily understood in traditional "left–right" terms, as the world's most economically developed democracies become more oriented towards service production, and more integrated into international economic networks (Rodrik 1997; Iversen and Wren 1998). Others argue that at high levels of economic development and security, the salience of distributional conflict itself declines, making way for "postmaterialistic" concerns about quality of life issues such as the environment and personal autonomy (Inglehart 1977, 1997). These changes in preference are forcing a transformation in the *expressive content* of political parties, particularly in the range of policies that governments pursue. Where parties cannot adjust their policy platforms to the evolving concerns of voters, we can expect electoral volatility to continue—at least until new parties emerge to take their place.

Of perhaps more significance in the long run, however, is the *organizational* and *institutional* transformation of political parties in general, and the fraying of the connective tissue binding voters to parties in particular. In the idealized form, the mass party model was once efficient because deeply embedded party–voter linkages benefited both sides of the transaction. Voters could rely on parties to inform them about current policy debates and simplify choices between candidates at the polls. Political parties could listen to their grassroots networks to get a sense of prevailing winds in public sentiment, and more importantly, benefit electorally from having a readily mobilized voting bloc. Two, largely exogenous changes in the electoral environment have challenged this mass party structure: improvements in the educational level of voters, and innovations in marketing and advertising technology, particularly

---

[8] The pattern of secondary cleavages, on the other hand—reflecting historical conflicts over religion, territorial issues, or rural–urban divides—varied from country to country depending on their individual history.

Table 19.1. Realignment vs. dealignment

Theory	Stimulus	Short-term implication	Response	Long-term implication
Realignment	Change in voter preferences	Growing ideological gap between voters and ESTABLISHED parties	Established parties adopt new policy platforms; Where slow, new parties take their place	Stabilization of vote fluctuations
Dealignment	Change in voter/party capabilities	Weaker affective and organizational ties between voters and ALL parties	Change in party organization: declining relevance of party activists and more "national" or centrist policies	Continuing vote fluctuations; declining voter turnout

public opinion polls and the television. Armed with these new tools, voters can now gather political information cheaply through non-party sources, and parties no longer have to maintain a massive grassroots organization to mount an effective national campaign (Dalton and Wattenberg 2000). In other words, it is argued that the usefulness of mass party organizational strategies has declined for both politicians and voters, creating incentives on both sides for their abandonment.

Although these two trends are not mutually exclusive, the primacy of either one draws different implications for the future of the party–voter linkage. Whereas the inability to match changes in the electorate's policy preferences is problematic for *existing parties*, changes in political capabilities represent a fundamental shift in the density of ties connecting voters to *all political parties*. The former leaves the door open for eventual ideological *re*alignment and long-term electoral stability, while the latter predicts greater fluidity in voter–party allegiances and permanent electoral *de*alignment. Table 19.1 depicts the causal logic and observable implications of both hypotheses in greater detail.

In this chapter, we re-evaluate the literature on re- vs. dealignment and offer our own predictions regarding the future of the party–voter linkage. In the next section, we discuss the argument that socioeconomic and demographic shifts are causing the worsening performance of traditional parties. The old guard has purportedly failed to adapt to the evolving concerns of voters, leaving them vulnerable to electoral attack from new entrants. Section 3 describes recent changes in parties' organizational structures and their implications for the electoral performance of traditional parties, and the stability of electoral outcomes more generally. In Section 4 we report the results of a statistical analysis designed to investigate the effects of electoral competition and organizational change on the performance of traditional mass parties. Section 5 presents our conclusions and some directions for future research.

To tip our hand early, we believe that the empirical ledger is tilted in favor of dealignment. The indications are that recent increases in electoral instability are symptomatic of more than a short-term readjustment of the party system to changing electoral preferences—although there is little doubt that such an adjustment is occurring. Rather they stem from underlying changes in the organizational structure of political parties themselves. We also note, however, that trends in electoral volatility do not seem to have much effect on the stability of government composition more generally. As such, the broader political implications of increased electoral instability may be less significant than is sometimes claimed.

2 Changes in the Policy Preferences of Voters

In standard theories of parliamentary behavior, voter preferences are assumed to be exogenous and fixed, while parties are reactive "second movers" who strategically choose policy platforms which maximize their political appeal. Early spatial models latched onto the idea of "issue congruence," wherein voters select political parties which advocate policies that are closest to their own preferences, and parties respond by crafting platforms which cater to the largest number of voters. Under certain conditions—most notably unimodal, left–right voter preferences and a first-past-the-post electoral system—parties should converge around the median voter and adopt centrist platforms (Downs 1957). More recent models of "directional" voting, on the other hand, assume that voters generally have vague policy preferences, and that their choices are determined by the direction and intensity of a party's promises—leading to ideological divergence, rather than convergence, among parties (Rabinowitz and Macdonald 1989; Iversen 1994). Under both models, however, the *mechanism* of ideological formation is identical: parties advocate policies which allow them to capture the largest segment of voters (Stokes 1999).

For much of the late nineteenth and twentieth centuries, the primary ideological cleavage in electoral competition formed along the left–right economic dimension. Socialist parties forged close alliances with labor unions and emphasized workers' interests—particularly lower unemployment and economic security—in their policy platforms. Conservative parties, on the other hand, maintained strong ties to capital owners and tended to advocate conditions better suited for business development and capital investment. While the ideological separation between the two groups was not hard and fast, numerous studies have found empirical evidence of distinctive partisan patterns in the policy outputs of governing parties which relate to the preferences of these parties' core constituencies (Hibbs 1977; Alesina and Rosenthal 1995).

Beginning in the 1970s, however, there has been a gradual shift in the distribution of policy preferences within the electorate. Most critical is the declining salience of the left–right economic cleavage as traditionally understood. This has occurred partially as a function of demographic changes. There is evidence that the social anchors of traditional partisanship have been eroding since the 1970s, with white-collar workers and a "new middle class" of service sector workers replacing farmers and laborers as the key socioeconomic segments of the electorate (Mair, Muller, and Plasser 2004). These changes have been associated with a decline in traditional class-based voting in many countries (Clark and Lipset 2001).

Alongside these demographic trends are changes in the debate over issues of economic organization, and in the range of alternatives under consideration. With the collapse of communism in Eastern Europe, debates over the relative merits of capitalism and socialism have been replaced by discussions as to how best to manage the national economy in an internationally integrated economic environment. The increased openness of capital markets in particular has placed significant restrictions on national governments' abilities to pursue independent fiscal and monetary policies (Simmons 1998; Boix 2000). In many countries, responsibility for monetary policy has been delegated to politically independent central banks in an effort to counteract inflationary pressures (Grilli, Masciandoro, and Tabellini 1991). For national governments in EU member states, meanwhile, the constraints on independent action have been made even tighter by the establishment of an independent European Central Bank and the adoption of a single currency. The balance of evidence from numerous empirical studies suggests that while these constraints have been insufficient to remove distinct patterns of partisanship in economic policy making, the size of these effects has declined in recent decades (Wren 2006).

Empirical evidence also suggests that on economic issues, party ideologies are showing signs of convergence. Using data from the Comparative Manifesto Project, Budge, Robertson, and Hearl (1987) posit that electoral manifestos are converging towards the center on the left–right economic scale. Caul and Gray (2000) find that the left–right distance between major parties has declined in ten out of fifteen advanced democracies, and that this centralization has been most pronounced in majoritarian electoral systems, where centripetal pressures on policy are most powerful. Closer analysis adds the important caveat that this trend is not unilinear: Volkens and Klingemann (2002) show that the ideological distance between parties decreased 1940–60, increased 1970–80, and has been decreasing again since the late 1980s. In general, however, both the degree of polarization (the salience of the left–right spectrum) and the range of ideology (distance between the leftmost and rightmost parties) appear to have been higher in the 1940s than in the 1990s. Ezrow (2005) suggests that this gradual centralization may be a vote-maximizing strategy, as centrist parties tended to win slightly more votes between 1984 and 1998.

As parties moderate their ideologies, the scope of policies offered to voters has narrowed. The moderation of party platforms has, in turn, led to more centrist *governments*. Figure 19.3 displays diachronic trends in the ideological composition of the first cabinet that forms after an election, relative to the last cabinet in power before the election. While government turnover also occurs between elections, examining ideological change *across* elections allows us to see how the initial shake-up in parliamentary seats affects which actors seize power. Governments are coded "1," "2," or "3," depending on whether a majority of the cabinet's portfolio is held by right-wing,

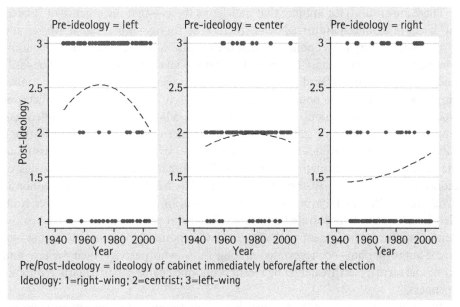

Fig. 19.3. Trends in cabinet ideology across elections

centrist, or left-wing parties, respectively.[9] The graphs on Figure 19.3 separate data points into cases where the government preceding the election was leftist, centrist, or rightist (pre-ideology), and tracks changes in the direction of the next government's ideology (post-ideology). The data indicate a clear trend towards more centrist governments, particularly since the 1970s. In other words, both conservative and socialist governments are veering to the center, while centrist governments are holding steady.

The decline in the salience of the left–right economic divide (as traditionally defined) has also allowed room for secondary cleavages to increase in electoral significance. This change was predicted by Inglehart (1977, 1987, 1997), whose early work identified a "value change" in advanced industrial societies associated with the increased prosperity and economic security in the post-Second World War era. With their material needs met by economic development and the expansion of the welfare state, younger generational cohorts are purportedly prioritizing "lifestyle" issues such as the environment and individual liberty over more traditional material concerns. Importantly, Inglehart's work with public opinion data shows that these value changes tended to persist even as the post-war cohort aged, indicating the existence of a permanent shift in the electoral landscape (1987, 1997).

---

[9] More formally, the ideological balance of cabinet is coded as: 1 = conservative parties control at least 51% or superplurality of cabinet positions; 2 = centrist parties control at least 51% OR there is a left–right alliance where each side controls at least 33% of cabinet; 3 = leftist parties control at least 51% or superplurality of cabinet. Superplurality is defined as holding more portfolio positions than the other two factions combined, e.g. not counting independents, % of left >% center +% right. Data on government composition and political party ideology are taken from Woldendorp, Keman, and Budge 2000 and the Comparative Political Data Set (Armingeon et al. 2005).

There are grounds for arguing that Inglehart's thesis—that the salience of "material" issues in advanced industrial democracies is declining—is overstated. Iversen and Wren (1998), for example, point out that the transition to a services-based economy confronts societies with stark new sets of distributional choices which cannot be easily understood in terms of traditional economic cleavages between "left" and "right." Similarly, several authors point to the increased significance of political conflict over globalization and, in particular, over perceived tradeoffs between economic openness, employment, and welfare state protection in Western democracies (Rodrik 1997). Kitschelt (1994, 1995) argues that electoral cleavages over "non-economic" issues of the environment or immigration are actually intimately linked with new sets of economic cleavages in post-industrial societies. The traditional left–right economic divide has shifted to incorporate this new dimension so that it now ranges from "left-libertarian"—concentrated among workers who are relatively sheltered in the new economic environment and who tend to espouse "postmaterial" values—to "right-authoritarian"—concentrated among those who perceive their welfare and economic security as threatened by recent economic changes, particularly economic openness.[10]

Traditional parties have been sluggish in their response to these socioeconomic changes, leaving open policy space for new parties to capture. While the entry of new parties into the political arena is by no means a novel trend, the proportion of elections with new parties has certainly been on the rise in recent decades. Of fifty-one elections during the 1950s, 27.5 percent saw at least one new party compete.[11] While this ratio held steady through the 1970s, it began to rise sharply in the 1980s, when 30.0 percent of elections had at least one new party, and even more in the 1990s, when 47.3 percent of elections saw new competition.

The new parties which have emerged in recent decades can be divided into three broad categories, centered around issues which were either new or neglected by existing parties. First are what Kitschelt (1994) calls left-libertarian parties, represented most notably by the Ecologists or Greens, whose emergence correlates with the rise of postmaterialist concerns over environmental degradation and nuclear energy.[12]

The second grouping is the New Radical Right, a mostly European phenomenon closely associated with emerging concerns over immigration from developing countries. The New Radical Right's electoral strategy is to capture policy space left empty by the increasing centralization of the traditional parties' platforms (Kitschelt 1995). While these parties—represented most (in)famously by Le Pen's Front National

---

[10] Benoit and Laver (forthcoming), in their recent expert survey covering forty-seven countries, also find evidence that the "left–right" dimension is increasingly interpreted in terms of ecological as well as economic issues in many countries.

[11] There is some disagreement in the literature over how to code a genuinely new party—particularly whether one should count the merger of two parties into one as a new entity (Hug 2001; Tavits 2006). Here, we do not discriminate between types of parties, and count all splits, mergers, and genuinely new parties. The one caveat is that we only count parties that win at least 1% of the vote or one seat in parliament.

[12] There are also several new socialist and communist parties, which are seen as competitors to traditional social democrats on both the left–right and libertarian–authoritarian dimensions.

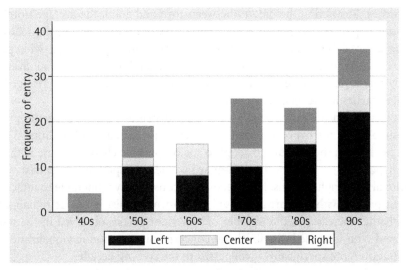

Fig. 19.4. Frequency of new party entry by ideology

in France, Haider's FPÖ in Austria, and Pim Fortuyn in the Netherlands—are best known for their xenophobic stance towards immigrants, their overall electoral strategy is more nuanced, as they adopt firm conservative principles in support of market liberalism which appeal to independent shop owners and conservative businessmen.

The third category is regionalist parties, which espouse greater political independence of their territories from the central government without necessarily staking ideological positions on the left–right debate. Found most commonly in fragmented polities, De Winter (1998) argues that the best predictor of regional party success is the level of linguistic fractionalization—think Belgium and Spain—and to some extent, regional wealth—richer regions generally want more autonomy.

Figure 19.4 shows diachronic trends in the entry of new political parties, looking at parties with discernible ideological trends that tilt left and right, as well as those that are largely centrist. The left–right categorization is based not only on traditional class conflicts, but also on a libertarian–authoritarian dimension including environmentalism on the left and immigration on the right. Regionalist parties with distinct positions on the left–right cleavage are included within this taxonomy, but those that primarily advocate regional autonomy are excluded, since the particulars of regional political competition tend to be very country specific.

Figure 19.4 offers some interesting insights. First, the steady increase in the number of left-libertarian parties is driving the rise in the total number of new parties. In the post-war period, leftist parties constituted 52 percent of new parties which entered electoral competition. This resonates with Inglehart's (1987) argument that postmaterialist voters tend to line up on the left side of the ideological spectrum, thereby prompting the entry of proportionately more leftist parties over time. Second, centrist parties show the least amount of diachronic fluctuation in the number of new entries. Restricting the data to between 1950 and 2000, the average number of new centrist parties per decade is 4.4, with a maximum of seven (in the 1960s) and a minimum of two (in the 1950s). The frequency of entry by new right-wing parties, on the other hand, displays the greatest level of instability. There was an average of 6.2 new conservative parties per decade between 1950 and 2000, but this ranged from zero new parties in the 1960s to eleven in the 1970s.

The increase in the number and ideological distribution of new parties provides some support for the hypothesis that the faltering performance of traditional parties stems partly from their failure to adapt to socioeconomic change. In line with Inglehart's hypotheses, it appears that old-guard parties, competing for centrist votes in traditional "left–right" terms, have been most consistently vulnerable to attack from new left parties with platforms focused on postmaterialist issues. It remains to be seen whether increases in the number of new right parties observed in the 1990s— associated with increased distributional concerns over economic globalization, and immigration more specifically—will persist in the coming decades.

Changes in vote preferences, however, cannot fully account for patterns of electoral volatility over the last few decades. Under the mass party model, the socialization of voters into enduring political identities ensured that changes in vote share would occur only when there were radical demographic shifts in the primary constituencies of the established parties. Given that shifts of this magnitude transpire slowly, we would expect the associated vote fluctuations to be relatively low and stable, at least to the extent that the voter–party linkage remains strong. At the same time, if new political parties have been successfully capturing disenfranchised voters, then their entry should lower volatility over time. However, as we saw from the scatter plots in Figure 19.2, electoral volatility has in fact increased at a fairly steady rate over the past forty years. This suggests that what we are observing is not simply preference divergence between voters and parties, but rather a more permanent *organizational* detachment between the two. In the next section, we discuss the more fundamental changes which are occurring in the nature of the party–voter linkage and their implications for the performance of the traditional parties.

3 ORGANIZATIONAL CHANGES TO THE PARTY–VOTER LINKAGE

The demographic explanation discussed in the last section cannot explain why existing parties cannot simply inculcate new members into their fold. The obstacles to this kind of strategic flexibility may be understood in terms of the *organizational rigidity* of the mass party model. If voters are tightly embedded into the institutional structure of specific political parties, the only question on polling day is which side can better coax their partisans to show up. In effect, election outcomes turn on shifting patterns in unionization or disparities in regional population growth. While the mass party organization may have been an effective means of political mobilization in an era where parties could not accurately monitor trends in popular sentiment and voters had little access to political information, this institutional structure severely limited the ideological flexibility of parties and the political choices of voters.[13]

Over time, however, the organizational structure of political parties, themselves, has begun to change. At the grassroots level, membership in political parties has been in steady decline in the last three decades (Katz and Mair 1992). Comparing fourteen advanced-industrialized democracies, Scarrow (2000) finds that most countries have seen a decline in party enrollment since 1960—both in absolute terms and as a ratio of the electorate—and that this downturn has been particularly pronounced since the 1990s. While parties often inflate membership figures for marketing purposes, Scarrow also cites public opinion poll data to demonstrate that self-reported party membership has experienced a steep fall.

These findings complement the literature on the diminishing affective ties between parties and voters. Using Eurobarometer surveys, Dalton, McAllister, and Wattenberg (2002) show that while the proportion of "very" and "fairly involved" partisans have stayed fairly constant over time, many "weak" sympathizers are turning into political independents. Examining majoritarian political systems, Clarke and Stewart (1998) detect what they call a "dealignment of degree:" while the percentage of voters with strong partisan ties is declining, they are turning into weak partisans or independents, not into supporters of other parties. On a broader comparative scale, Dalton, McAllister, and Wattenberg (2000) find an increase in the *reported* willingness of voters to split tickets between parties when there are multiple elections for different levels of government at stake. In general, the evidence points to voters abandoning partisan allegiances altogether, rather than permanently switching their allegiances to different parties.

This transformation is most pronounced among younger generations, who have grown up outside the mass party organization. Dalton (2000) makes the crucial point that the proportion of youths professing strong partisan attachments has been falling far faster than for older demographic groups. Inglehart (1987) argues that the strength of partisan attachments tend to increase with age, but only amongst voters who form attachments while they are young. If this is true, then the growing ranks of disaffected youth imply even weaker party–voter linkages down the road.

Underlying this transformation are two exogenous changes to the electoral marketplace—better education and new technology—which have allowed parties and voters to divest themselves of the mass party model. Both factors have altered the extent to which voters need parties to gain information about political events on the one hand, and how much parties rely on their grassroots membership on the other. While preference changes represent a shift in the ideological congruence between

[13] See Mair, Muller, and Plasser (2004) for more on country-specific causes and effects of party responses to increasing electoral volatility.

voters and parties, organizational changes are a function of shifts in the *capability* of the two actors, and the extent to which both sides depend on one another to maximize political goals.

From an organizational standpoint, the two key societal functions of parties have been to educate voters about policies (Duverger 1954) and simplify choices among candidates (Downs 1957). Whereas this role was valuable when workers lacked the means to gather and process political information, improvements in educational attainment and the proliferation of media outlets provide new, non-party sources of information to voters. With near-universal literacy in advanced industrialized democracies, almost everybody can follow events in newspapers, and even more easily through television, radio, and the internet. The growing pluralism in information dissemination frees voters from blindly following party cues, while also increasing the odds that voters will learn information which parties may prefer to edit out, such as poor government performance or bribery scandals.

In addition to voters no longer needing parties, parties can now mount effective national campaigns without being bound to the preferences of partisan activists. While grassroots party members once provided invaluable manpower during election campaigns (Aldrich 1995), the proliferation of television ownership since the 1970s and internet access more recently allows party elites to bypass these middlemen altogether and launch media advertisements to tap a wider audience (Farrell 2002). Indeed, Dalton, McAllister, and Wattenberg (2002) find that in almost all countries, fewer and fewer people are participating in actual campaign activities. This new organizational mobility allows parties to better adapt to the shifting ideological concerns of the electorate at large.

The influence of new technology is also reflected in the greater centralization of political parties, particularly in the coordination of electoral campaigns. One measure is the growing identification of the party label with the party *leader*. Looking at the ratio of mentions of candidates compared to parties, Dalton, McAllister, and Wattenberg (2000) find that the media now refers to leaders more frequently than to parties. Indeed, most countries now prominently feature televised party leader debates before the election (Farrell 2002).

A second change is the way in which policy platforms are crafted and disseminated during campaigns. Whereas the mass party organization used to be a crucial medium through which party elites gathered information about the policy preferences of voters, the increasing availability and reliability of opinion polls make it possible for parties to collect data from a wider segment of the electorate. The sophistication of advertising tools also allows parties to "sell" or "market" platforms based on the salient issues of the day, rather than articulating only those issues which have been popular in the past (Farrell and Webb 2000). The professionalization of campaign managers and the quantitative increase in staffers at party headquarters are symptoms of this evolution. Whereas mass parties once served as important networks connecting a vast membership organization to the elites, this more recent trend represents the transformation of parties into professional campaign agencies for individual political candidates, particularly the party leader.

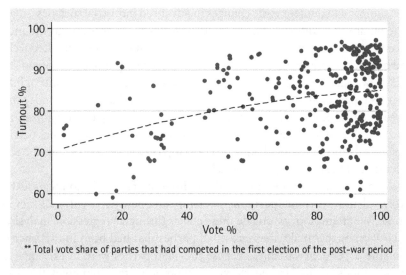

Fig. 19.5. Relationship between turnout and the vote share of established parties

One important side effect of the decline of the mass party model has been the decline in levels of voter turnout across advanced industrial democracies. Under the mass party model, party leaders could count on grassroots activists to drum up support and convince voters to show up on election day. There has, however, been a sharp decline in actual turnout figures, particularly since the 1980s. While turnout averaged 84.6 percent in the 1950s with a minimum of 71.3 percent, it has fallen to 77.3 percent since 2000 with a minimum of 59.5 percent. This drop-off stems in part from the declining mobilizational capacity of established parties. Figure 19.5 examines turnout as a function of the proportion of total votes garnered by political parties that had competed in that country's first post-war election. The correlation between turnout and the vote share of established parties is 0.293, and as the quadratic regression line indicates, there is a strong positive relationship between the two. Turnout tends to be higher when established parties dominate the electoral process; put differently, turnout is directly related to the electoral salience of these parties.

4 ELECTORAL COMPETITION, ORGANIZATIONAL CHANGE, AND THE PERFORMANCE OF TRADITIONAL PARTIES

The comparative politics literature thus provides us with two sets of hypotheses to account for the decline in vote share of traditional parties. The first focuses on socioeconomic and demographic changes in advanced industrial societies, suggesting that the failure of traditional parties to adapt to these changes and to the increased salience of new issues may be hampering their ability to compete effectively. The second highlights a more fundamental change in parties' political and organizational roles. As new technologies play an increasingly important role as conduits of information between parties and voters, and as voters' levels of education and independently acquired political knowledge increase, the need for mass party organizations has declined. In this view, the faltering electoral performance of traditional parties and increasing volatility in voting behavior are symptomatic of a generalized decline in the relevance of the existing party model.

Disentangling the causal weight of these disparate factors is no mean feat, given that vote volatility, turnout, party membership, and new party entry all vary closely with time. We attempt to investigate these effects through a regression analysis, using *Pre-1960 Vote*, or the total vote share of all parties that had been in existence before 1960, as the dependent variable. Because pre-1960 parties were in existence during the peak periods of the "frozen cleavage" hypothesis, they represent those parties that traditionally had the strongest mass organization base. The statistical model employed is a pooled OLS regression with panel-corrected standard errors and panel-specific AR1 (autoregressive process of order 1) autocorrelation.[14] Each case in the dataset is one election in a given country after 1960, which yields a total of 220 cases among twenty advanced-industrialized democracies. The model uses "country" and "election count" as the panel and time variables, respectively.

We include two lagged variables that pertain directly to changes in the electoral and organizational viability of pre-1960 parties. To capture electoral volatility, we include *Lag Pedersen*, which is the Pedersen Index measure for vote fluctuation in the *last* period. If electoral volatility is due to vote trading between established parties, then higher values of vote fluctuation should *not* affect the collective vote shares of pre-1960 parties. On the other hand, a negative coefficient would indicate that diachronic increases in electoral volatility are in fact due to post-1960 parties stealing votes from pre-1960 groups. *Lag turnout* is a continuous variable for the proportion of the total electorate which cast a ballot in the *previous* election. Because pre-1960 parties traditionally won votes by mobilizing their grassroots membership, lower turnout may indicate a decline in their organizational capacity. If turnout is not tied to the organizational capacity of any subset of parties, however, decreasing turnout should not adversely affect pre-1960 parties any more than it does post-1960 parties. We use the lagged rather than the contemporaneous measures for both *Pedersen* and *Turnout*, because of endogeneity concerns over cause and effect.[15]

Another important independent variable is *New party count*, a discrete measure which tabulates the number of new parties that entered that given election. If it is

---

[14] The AR1 specification indicates the inclusion of a lagged dependent variable.

[15] For example, vote swings of pre-1960 parties are direct, empirical components of the measure for current electoral performance, making contemporaneous values a "tainted" measure when explaining the dependent variable. The correlation between turnout and lagged turnout is 0.904, while the correlation between Pedersen and Lagged Pedersen is 0.218.

true that the decline in the electoral performance of traditional parties reflects, in part, their failure to adapt to socioeconomic change—i.e. if new parties are capturing voters that value new policy issues neglected by traditional parties—then we should see new party entry have a negative impact on the vote share of the established parties. On the other hand, if new parties generally have little influence on overall patterns of electoral competition or are simply trading votes with one another, then their entry should have insignificant effects on the old guard's performance.[16]

A series of other variables capture trends in electoral instability. We include the dichotomous variable *Coalition* which equals "1" when a coalition government immediately preceded the election. This follows a simple empirical observation by Rose and Mackie (1983) that parties in coalition governments generally do worse in the subsequent election than those in single-party governments. While all government parties lose votes on average, the effect is stronger for coalition parties, because their supporters often see the policy deals made to support coalition governments as an abandonment of the party's electoral manifesto. *Parliamentary turnover* is a discrete variable that counts the number of changes in cabinet composition between the last to current elections. We predict that government parties will be penalized by voters should they be unable to maintain a stable cabinet.

We also include two measures for political institutions. *Electoral change* is a dichotomous variable that equals "1" where the electoral system was altered prior to the election. This is recorded when there is a change in: (1) the electoral formula (e.g. switch from plurality to PR and vice versa, or changes in the type of PR rule); (2) the mean district magnitude (change of more than 10 percent); and (3) the legal threshold of representation. Changes to the electoral system alter the framework of electoral competition and, as such, should have a negative effect on *Pre-1960 vote*, as institutional change should disproportionately harm parties which have nurtured their organizational base to maximize efficiency under the status quo system.

Effective threshold is a continuous variable that measures the effective threshold of representation, a composite index of various electoral rules which represents the difficulty of winning a seat under that electoral configuration (Lijphart 1994).[17] One of the difficulties of winning votes in plurality systems (which have higher thresholds) is that voters tend to behave more strategically by not casting ballots in favor of doomed parties, even if they prefer the doomed party to more prominent, established alternatives (Duverger 1954; Cox 1997). In theory, a higher effective threshold should allow older parties to do better, since inertial effects in favor of the status quo party system are stronger.

---

[16] While models of strategic party entry generally predict that new parties should only compete when the odds of success are good, empirical studies have found that most new parties tend to do quite poorly. As of yet, there is no robust model on the correlates of initial party success (Hug 2001; Tavits 2006).

[17] The effective threshold is calculated by averaging (1) the threshold of exclusion, which is the maximum percentage of votes that a party can obtain without being able to win a seat, and (2) the threshold of inclusion, which is the minimum percentage of votes that a party can win and still gain a seat. The threshold of exclusion ($Texcl$) = $V/M + 1$, where V = vote share and M = number of seats in the district. The threshold of inclusion ($Tincl$) is the higher of either (1) the legal threshold of representation, or (2) $Tincl = 100/2M$, where M = average district magnitude (Lijphart 1994).

Table 19.2. Estimating the electoral performance of established political parties (1960–2002) (model: pooled OLS regression, correlated panels corrected standard errors (PCSEs))

Variable	Vote % of pre-1960 parties		Descriptive statistics		
	β	(SE)	Min/max	Mean	S.D.
New party count	-3.576^c	0.563	0/5	0.483	0.856
Lag Pedersen	-0.273^c	0.091	0/46.35	8.852	6.793
Lag turnout	0.149^a	0.089	59/97.2	83.583	8.880
Coalition	-2.585^b	1.316	0/1	0.562	0.497
Parliamentary turnover	0.535	0.435	0/6	0.727	1.080
Electoral change	-1.888^a	1.056	0/1	0.103	0.305
Electoral threshold	0.102^a	0.061	.67/35	11.074	11.319
1960s	11.925^c	2.748	# of cases:	45	
1970s	8.966^c	2.514		60	
1980s	7.239^c	2.589		60	
1990s	3.289	2.342		55	
Constant	70.988^c	7.711			
Wald	147.81				
N	220				
R^2	0.965				

Notes: Group variable: country (20); time variable: election count (1–24).
Panel-specific AR(1) auto-correlation; sigma computed by pairwise selection.
[a] $p < 0.1$.
[b] $p < 0.05$.
[c] $p < .01$.

Finally, dummy variables for *Decade* are also included in the model to distinguish between factors that affect all countries at the same point in time, and those that affect countries at certain periods in their political maturation (as captured by the *Election count* time factor). Crucially, *Decade* also allow us to disentangle the impact of the other independent variables from a simple time trend.

Table 19.2 displays the regression results from the pooled OLS regression. The overall model fit is excellent, with an R-squared of 0.97. The analysis yields some interesting observations regarding the electoral competition between new and older parties, as well as the organizational capacity of the older parties themselves.

First, we can see that the entry of new parties decreases the vote share of parties that had been around before 1960, suggesting that new entrants are indeed competing successfully on new issues. The coefficient on the *New party count* variable is negative, with each additional party lowering the vote share of pre-1960 parties by 3.58 percent.

Second, the increase in electoral volatility has been more damaging to traditional parties than to newer parties. The negative coefficient for *Lag Pedersen* indicates that electoral volatility has a negative effect on the vote share of traditional parties as a group. A one standard deviation increase in *Lag Pedersen* decreases *Pre-1960 vote* by

1.85 percent. These estimates indicate that instability in election outcomes is due to older parties losing voters to newer parties, rather than simple horse-trading between established parties.

Third, the *Lag turnout* variable has a positive coefficient, such that a 10 percent decrease in turnout in the previous period decreases the vote share of established parties by 1.5 percent. This finding again points to the significance of changes in the organizational structure of traditional parties. The implication is that older parties are losing votes faster than newer parties due to their declining ability to mobilize voters on election day.

Turning to the other variables, we can see that, as expected, *Coalition* is negative while *Parliamentary turnover* is positive, although only *Coalition* is statistically significant at conventional levels. The coefficients of both institutional variables—*Effective threshold* and *Electoral change* —have signs in the predicted direction, although their substantive impact is low. The difference between the most permissive and most restrictive thresholds—0.67 in the Dutch system of nationwide PR vs. 35 under British-style single-member plurality—only equates to an increase in the vote share of pre-1960 parties by 3.5 percent. The most likely explanation for the small coefficient is that the AR1 variable (lagged *Pre-1960 vote*) already incorporates the effects of electoral threshold on voter behavior in the previous time period, and because electoral threshold rarely changes over time, the lagged variable understates the true impact of this measure. Similarly, electoral rule change, which should theoretically wreak havoc on election outcomes, only decreases *Pre-1960 vote* by 1.89 percent. This may reflect the fact that electoral rules are generally altered at times and ways that favor incumbent government parties, many of which are pre-1960 groups (McElwain 2005). The decade dummies are all significant and positive, with the size of the coefficient becoming larger the further back one goes in time. Since there were fewer "new" parties in 1960 than in 1990, it is not surprising that older parties did progressively worse as the years wore on.

In sum, this simple analysis produces a few important findings. The entry of new parties has had a significant negative impact on the vote share of parties established before 1960. The traditional parties, as a group, appear to face a genuine electoral threat from the new competitors organized around new electoral issues, which we described in Section 3. Their faltering electoral performance, therefore, may be partly attributed to a failure to compete successfully on new policy dimensions. At the same time, the close relationship between the decline in voter turnout and the electoral performance of the established parties indicates that organizational change—and in particular the scaling back of the grassroots organizations of mass parties—has also had a critical role to play. Finally, and of considerable interest, is the finding that the increase in electoral volatility has not affected all parties proportionately, but rather has had a particularly negative impact on traditional parties.

How should we interpret these results? On the one hand, we might expect to observe increased electoral volatility as a side effect of electoral realignment. That is, if party systems are currently undergoing a period of adjustment in response to socioeconomic changes, then we should see a short period of increased volatility

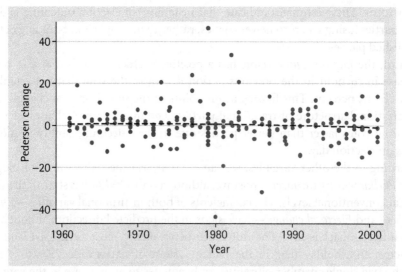

Fig. 19.6. Fluctuations in the Pedersen Index [Pedersen(t)–Pedersen(t−1)]

followed by a return to vote stability as the system returns to equilibrium, when once-established parties adjust their policy platforms or new parties take their place. On the other hand, if increased electoral volatility is in fact a symptom of more fundamental changes in party organizations, and in the nature of the voter–party relationship, then there is no reason to expect a reduction in volatility over time. Indeed, the statistical analysis shows support for both positions: new parties are entering the electoral arena and taking votes away from established parties, but at the same time, political mobilization—the hallmark of the "mass party model"—is declining overall and harming the electoral bottom line of the old guard.

Adjudicating between these two forces is a challenging task for future research, and lies beyond the scope of this essay. We can, however, investigate some empirical indicators which allow us to discern "trends within trends." Specifically, while electoral volatility may be on the rise, we can examine whether the *rate* of increase is high or low; put differently, are increases in volatility accelerating or holding steady? We conduct a simple test by comparing Pedersen Index values at time (t) with lagged Pedersen values at time (t − 1). The correlation between the contemporaneous and lagged values is only 0.218, indicating that vote fluctuations in one time period do not allow us to infer a great deal about fluctuations in the next period. The standard deviation for $Pedersen_{(t)} - Pedersen_{(t-1)}$ is much larger (8.553) than the mean (0.504), attesting to the high instability in electoral volatility. Figure 19.6 analyzes the rate of change in electoral volatility by displaying the difference between the contemporaneous and lagged measures, excluding elections that followed a major electoral rule change.[18] The data suggest that the rate of increase in electoral fluctuations is holding

---

[18] Including cases following electoral rule change does not significantly change results, but this operationalization better captures natural trends in electoral volatility independent of *institutional* volatility.

steady over time, giving us no reason to believe that electoral volatility will decline any time soon. Importantly, there is no indication of electoral stabilization *despite* the increasing number of new political parties (described in Figure 19.4). Based on the limited data available here, what we seem to be observing is steady *de*alignment, rather than cyclical realignment.

5 Conclusions

Parties play a crucial role in parliamentary politics, and its purported decline—operationalized here and in other works by an electoral volatility index—has been the focus of numerous studies of electoral and legislative behavior. Scholars have identified two parallel trends in the linkage between parties and voters. First, voters are showing weaker partisan identification with political parties, and there appears to be a widening gap between the policy preferences of voters and the electoral manifestos of parties. Second, improvements in educational attainment and innovations in media technology are strengthening the political capability of both parties and voters, making it unnecessary or undesirable for both groups to be locked into a mass party structure. These two changes are interconnected, one symptom of which is the increasing centralization of party platforms in favor of the median voter: the availability of advertising tools allows parties to tap a national audience for votes (capability change), but is also exacerbating the ideological distance between parties and voters (preference drift).

These two explanations have different implications for the future of the party–voter linkage. If preference change is the main culprit for electoral instability, we should see an eventual decline in vote volatility once existing parties realign and adapt to the evolving policy preferences of voters, or when new parties emerge to take their place. If electoral instability is driven by changes in the political capability of voters and parties, however, then the organizational ties between the two groups will continue to fray, and current vote fluctuations can be interpreted as a precursor to permanent partisan *dealignment*.

In this essay we have analyzed the causal weight of these divergent hypotheses. The literature suggests that new parties typically take advantage of ideological niches left unoccupied when older parties veer to the political center, leading to the proliferation of parties espousing "postmaterialist" values. Our statistical analysis confirms that older parties are progressively losing votes to newer groups, but equally important, that established parties are failing to ensure that their supporters turn out on polling day. Coupled with the fact that trends in electoral volatility—the rate of change in vote fluctuations—have held steady over time, the preponderance of evidence seems to point to long-term dealignment rather than temporary realignment.

While cross-national regressions are one way to study the effects of new parties on electoral competition, to truly understand the salience of new political parties, we must develop a better understanding of how they are structured internally. In theory, new parties should be organized in a way that best matches the preferences and capabilities of voters at the time of that party's inception; the organizational structure of older parties, on the other hand, may reflect historical baggage from the incentive structure of previous time periods. To play devil's advocate, if successful new parties develop a mass organization rather than a catch-all structure, we could infer that the full mobilization model of older parties is still relevant and that recent trends in electoral volatility do not necessarily indicate dealignment.

One way of settling this debate is to develop a "life-cycle model" of political parties. While there has been intriguing new research on *when* parties form, there is less information about what determines their initial success, how their organizational structure changes over time, and what factors explain their lifespan. This requires comprehensive data on the membership rolls, internal by-laws, ideological composition, and electoral strategies of new parties, but also of established parties which are currently dominant but were once young themselves. Most studies of electoral and party politics begin in the post-war period (as we do), but it is difficult to understand the evolution of new parties without knowing how parties which were small at their inception gradually became larger.

This distinction between small and large parties is more than just a matter of votes, since the organizational foundations of electoral success differ between parties of different size. Kirchheimer (1966), for example, argues that only large, nationally competitive political parties should adopt a catch-all structure, since smaller parties espousing relatively extreme or new ideological positions would be better off allying closely with the niche bloc of voters that care passionately about these issues. Maintaining a mass organization structure becomes problematic only when the ideological diversity within the party expands or the membership balloons to an unmanageable size, but new parties, particularly postmaterial groups, are still relatively small. As such, it is difficult to infer how they will adjust their organizational foundation should they become successful, especially if Inglehart is correct in predicting an expanding voter base with postmaterialist values.

Finally, while electoral volatility is an interesting phenomenon in its own right, it is by no means clear whether this should lead to a more fundamental change in party politics. On the one hand, the demobilization of mass parties, the increasing salience of postmaterialist values, and/or changes in the content of ideological debates over the economy may all change the issues discussed and policies legislated in parliament. On the other hand, instability in the electorate does not necessarily indicate instability in government composition and formation. The entry of new parties may diminish the electoral salience of established parties, but are these new parties increasingly entering government or causing more rapid turnovers in government composition?

This query lies at the heart of Peter Mair's distinction between party change and party *system* change. Party changes occur when the vote distribution between existing parties with similar ideological positions fluctuates, such as when socialist

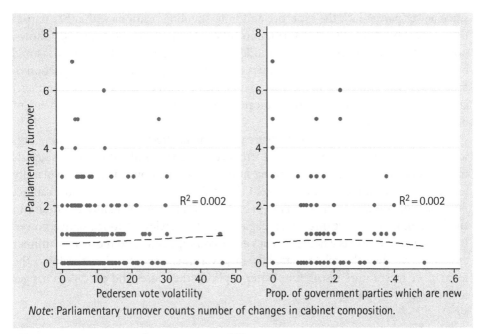

Fig. 19.7. Components of government stability

and communist parties trade votes. This does not change the overall pattern of political competition, however, since the left vs. right cleavage is preserved. Party *system* change, on the other hand, entails a shift in the cleavage structure of politics or in patterns of government formation. For example, if a dominant centrist party loses votes to both left- and right-wing parties, the ideological basis of political competition becomes more polarized. Alternatively, when a majoritarian party that competes against a coalition of smaller parties splits, creating a new system where two latent coalitions are vying for power, the basis of government formation is altered. A good example is Ireland in the late 1980s, when the Progressive Democrats split from Fianna Fáil, weakening the latter's claim of being a viable majoritarian party and setting up coalition alternatives of Fianna Fáil-PD vs. Fine Gael-Labour. In general, party change appears to be more frequent than party system change, leading Peter Mair to argue that electoral volatility is not fundamentally altering the foundation of political competition (Mair 1997; Mair and Mudde 1998).

Figure 19.7 gets at this distinction between party change and party system change by displaying trends in the frequency of cabinet turnover between elections.[19] Cabinets are far from stable in parliamentary systems: opposition parties can orchestrate a government coup by passing a vote of no confidence, or the cabinet may dissolve itself strategically to redistribute ministerial portfolios and spread the wealth among more MPs (Mershon 2002). One of the implications from the literature on electoral volatility is that the prevalence of new parties should decrease government longevity,

---

[19] Cabinet change is recorded whenever the executive is replaced or a new party enters/leaves the existing cabinet. This coding follows Woldendorp, Keman, and Budge (2000).

since newer parties lack the expertise and long-standing relations with other parties that make it possible to keep governments intact. The left panel of Figure 19.7 shows, however, that *government* stability is independent of *electoral* stability, as measured by vote volatility. The right panel depicts the relationship between the proportion of total government parties that are new (defined as never having been in government) and cabinet stability, and this, too, indicates that government stability is independent of new party entry.

While there are other ways to measure government effectiveness—examining policy outputs and macroeconomic performance come to mind—this figure suggests that the doom and gloom surrounding normative evaluations of electoral volatility may be overblown. Indeed, to the extent that older parties still occupy most cabinet positions, the decline in their relative vote shares may simply signify the desire to shed electoral fat, or organizational capacity that is irrelevant to legislative power. Restated, the question is whether parties are becoming leaner and meaner vs. thinner and weaker. While the relative stability in government composition speaks to the former, we trust future research to better explicate the causes and effects of changes to the party–voter linkage.

References

ALDRICH, J. H. 1995. *Why Parties? The Origin and Transformation of Political Parties in America*. Chicago: University of Chicago Press.

ALESINA, A. and ROSENTHAL, H. 1995. *Partisan Politics, Divided Government, and the Economy*. Cambridge: Cambridge University Press.

ARMINGEON, K., LEIMGRUBER, P., BEYELER, M., and MENEGALE, S. 2005. Comparative political data set 1960–2003. Institute of Political Science, University of Berne.

BENOIT, K. and LAVER, M. forthcoming. *Party Policy in Modern Democracies*. London: Routledge.

BOIX, C. 2000. Partisan governments, the international economy, and macroeconomic policies in OECD countries, 1964–93. *World Politics*, 53: 38–73.

BOWLER, S., FARRELL, D. M., and KATZ, R. S. 1999. Party cohesion, party discipline, and parliaments. Ch. 1 in *Party Discipline and Parliamentary Government*, ed. S. Bowler, D. M. Farrell, and R. S. Katz. Columbus: Ohio State University Press.

BUDGE, I., ROBERTSON, D., and HEARL, D. (eds.) 1987. *Ideology, Strategy, and Party Change: Spatial Analyses of Post-War Election Programmes in 19 Democracies*. Cambridge: Cambridge University Press.

CAMERON, D. 1984. Social democracy, corporatism, labor quiescence, and the representation of economic interest in advanced capitalist society. Pp. 143–78 in *Order and Conflict in Contemporary Capitalism*, ed. J. H. Goldthorpe. Oxford: Clarendon Press.

CAMPBELL, A., CONVERSE, P. E., MILLER, W. E., and STOKES, D. E. 1960. *The American Voter*. Chicago: University of Chicago Press.

CARAMANI, D. 2003. The end of silent elections: the birth of electoral competition, 1832–1915. *Party Politics*, 94: 411–43.

—— 2000. *The Societies of Europe: Elections in Western Europe since 1815*. London: Macmillan Reference.

CAUL, M. L. and GRAY, M. M. 2000. From platform declarations to policy outcomes: changing party profiles and partisan influence over policy. Pp. 208–37 in *Parties without Partisans: Political Change in Advanced Industrial Democracies*, ed. R. J. Dalton and M. P. Wattenberg. Oxford: Oxford University Press.

CLARK, T. N. and LIPSET, S. M. 2001. *The Breakdown of Class Politics: A Debate on Post-Industrial Stratification*. Baltimore: Johns Hopkins University Press.

CLARKE, H. D. and STEWART, M. C. 1998. The decline of parties in the minds of citizens. *Annual Review of Political Science*, 1: 357–78.

COX, G. 1987. *The Efficient Secret: The Cabinet and the Development of Political Parties in Victorian England*. Cambridge: Cambridge University Press.

—— 1997. *Making Votes Count: Strategic Coordination in the World's Electoral Systems*. Cambridge: Cambridge University Press.

—— and McCUBBINS, M. D. 1993. *Legislative Leviathan: Party Government in the House*. Los Angeles: University of California Press.

DALTON, R. J. 2000. The decline of party identifications. Pp. 19–36 in *Parties without Partisans: Political Change in Advanced Industrial Democracies*, ed. R. J. Dalton and M. P. Wattenberg. Oxford: Oxford University Press.

—— McALLISTER, I., and WATTENBERG, M. P. 2000. The consequences of partisan dealignment. Pp. 37–63 in *Parties without Partisans: Political Change in Advanced Industrial Democracies*, ed. R. J. Dalton and M. P. Wattenberg. Oxford: Oxford University Press.

—— —— —— 2002. Political parties and their publics. Pp. 19–42 in *Political Parties in the New Europe: Political and Analytical Challenges*, ed. K. R. Luther and F. Muller-Rommel. Oxford: Oxford University Press.

—— and WATTENBERG, M. P. 2000. Unthinkable democracy: political change in advanced industrial democracies. Pp. 3–18 in *Parties without Partisans: Political Change in Advanced Industrial Democracies*, ed. R. J. Dalton and M. P. Wattenberg. Oxford: Oxford University Press.

DE WINTER, L. 1998. Conclusion: a comparative analysis of the electoral, office and policy success of ethnoregionalist parties. Pp. 204–47 in *Regionalist Parties in Western Europe*, ed. L. De Winter and H. Tursan. New York: Routledge.

DOWNS, A. 1957. *An Economic Theory of Democracy*. New York: Harper and Row.

DUVERGER, M. 1954. *Political Parties: Their Organization and Activity in the Modern State*. New York: Wiley.

EZROW, L. 2005. Are moderate parties rewarded in multiparty systems? A pooled analysis of Western European elections, 1984–1998. *European Journal of Political Research*, 44: 881–98.

FARRELL, D. M. 2002. Campaign modernization and the west European party. Pp. 63–84 in *Political Parties in the New Europe: Political and Analytical Challenges*, ed. K. R. Luther and F. Muller-Rommel. Oxford: Oxford University Press.

—— and WEBB, P. 2000. Political parties as campaign organizations. Pp. 102–28 in *Parties without Partisans: Political Change in Advanced Industrial Democracies*, ed. R. J. Dalton and M. P. Wattenberg. Oxford: Oxford University Press.

GORVIN, I. (ed.) 1989. *Elections since 1945: A Worldwide Reference Compendium*. Chicago: St James Press.

GRILLI, V., MASCIANDORO, D., and TABELLINI, G. 1991. Political and monetary institutions and public financial policies in the industrialized countries. *Economic Policy*, 13: 341–92.

HIBBS, D. 1977. Political parties and macroeconomic policy. *American Political Science Review*, 71: 1467–87.

HUG, S. 2001. *Altering Party Systems: Strategic Behavior and the Emergence of New Political Parties in Western Democracies*. Ann Arbor: University of Michigan Press.

INGLEHART, R. 1977. *The Silent Revolution: Changing Values and Political Styles among Western Publics*. Princeton: Princeton University Press.

—— 1987. Value change in industrial societies. *American Political Science Review*, 814: 1289–303.

—— 1997. *Modernization and Postmodernization: Cultural, Economic, and Political Change in 43 Societies*. Princeton: Princeton University Press.

IVERSEN, T. 1994. The logics of electoral politics: spatial, directional, and mobilizational effects. *Comparative Political Studies*, 272: 155–89.

—— and WREN, A. 1998. Equality, employment, and budgetary restraint: the trilemma of the service economy. *World Politics*, 50: 242–56.

KALYVAS, S. N. 1996. *The Rise of Christian Democracy in Europe*. Ithaca, NY: Cornell University Press.

KATZ, R., and MAIR, P. (eds.) 1992. *Party Organizations: A Data Handbook on Party Organizations in Western Democracies, 1960–1990*. London: Sage.

—— —— 1995. Changing models of party organization and party democracy: the emergence of the cartel party. *Party Politics*, 11: 5–28.

KIRCHHEIMER, O. 1966. The transformation of the western European party systems. Pp. 177–200 in *Political Parties and Political Development*, ed. J. LaPalombara and M. Weiner. Princeton: Princeton University Press.

KITSCHELT, H. 1994. *The Transformation of European Social Democracy*. Cambridge: Cambridge University Press.

—— 1995. *The Radical Right in Western Europe: A Comparative Analysis*. Ann Arbor: University of Michigan Press.

KORPI, W. and SHALEV, M. 1979. Strikes, industrial-relations and class conflict in capitalist societies. *British Journal of Sociology*, 302: 164–87.

LANGE, P. and GARRETT, G. 1985. The politics of growth: strategic interaction and economic performance in the advanced industrial democracies, 1974–1980. *Journal of Politics*, 473: 792–827.

LAVER, M. and SCHOFIELD, N. 1990. *Multiparty Government: The Politics of Coalition in Europe*. Ann Arbor: University of Michigan Press.

LEWIS-BECK, M. 1988. *Economics and Elections: The Major Western Democracies*. Ann Arbor: University of Michigan Press.

—— and STEGMAIER, M. 2000. Economic determinants of electoral outcomes. *Annual Review of Political Science*, 3: 183–219.

LIJPHART, A. 1994. *Electoral Systems and Party Systems: A Study of Twenty-Seven Democracies 1945–1990*. Oxford: Oxford University Press.

LIPSET, S. M. and ROKKAN, S. (eds.) 1967. *Party Systems and Voter Alignments*. New York: Free Press.

MCELWAIN, K. M. 2005. Manipulating electoral rules: intra-party conflict, partisan interests, and constitutional thickness. Doctoral dissertation. Stanford University.

MACKUEN, M. B., ERICKSON, R. S., and STIMSON, J. A. 1992. Peasants or bankers? The American electorate and the US economy. *American Political Science Review*, 863: 597–611.

MAIR, P. 1990. Introduction. Pp. 1–22 in *The West European Party System*, ed. P. Mair. Oxford: Oxford University Press.

—— 1997. *Party System Change*. Oxford: Oxford University Press.

—— and MUDDE, C. 1998. The party family and its study. *Annual Review of Political Science*, 1: 211–29.

—— MULLER, W. C., and PLASSER, F. (eds.) 2004. *Political Parties and Electoral Change: Party Responses to Electoral Markets*. London: Sage.

MERSHON, C. 2002. *The Costs of Coalition*. Stanford, Calif.: Stanford University Press.

PEDERSEN, M. N. 1979. The dynamics of European party systems: changing patterns of electoral volatility. *European Journal of Political Research*, 71: 1–26.

POWELL, G. B. and WHITTEN, G. D. 1993. A cross-national analysis of economic voting: taking account of the political context. *American Journal of Political Science*, 372: 391–414.

PRZEWORSKI, A. and SPRAGUE, J. 1986. *Paper Stones: A History of Electoral Socialism*. Chicago: University of Chicago Press.

RABINOWITZ, G. and MACDONALD, S. E. 1989. A directional theory of issue voting. *American Political Science Review*, 83: 93–121.

RODRIK, D. 1997. *Has Globalization Gone Too Far?* Washington, DC: Institute for International Economics.

ROSE, R. and MACKIE, T. T. 1983. Incumbency in government: asset or liability? Pp. 115–37 in *Western European Party Systems: Continuity and Change*, ed. H. Daalder and P. Mair. Berkeley, Calif.: Sage.

SCARROW, S. E. 2000. Parties without members? Party organization in a changing electoral environment. Pp. 79–101 in *Parties without Partisans: Political Change in Advanced Industrial Democracies*, ed. R. J. Dalton and M. P. Wattenberg. Oxford: Oxford University Press.

SCHATTSCHNEIDER, E. E. 1942. *Party Government*. New York: Farrar and Rinehart.

——1960. *The Semisovereign People: A Realist's View of Democracy in America*. Fort Worth: Harcourt Brace Jovanovich College Publishers.

SIMMONS, B. 1998. The internationalization of capital. Pp. 36–69 in *Continuity and Change in Contemporary Capitalism*, ed. H. Kitschelt, P. Lange, G. Marks, and J. Stephens. Cambridge: Cambridge University Press.

STOKES, S. C. 1999. Political parties and democracy. *Annual Review of Political Science*, 2: 243–67.

STROM, K. 1990. *Minority Government and Majority Rule*. Cambridge: Cambridge University Press.

TAVITS, M. 2006. Party system change: testing a model of new party entry. *Party Politics*, 121: 99–119.

VOLKENS, A. and KLINGEMANN, H.-D. 2002. Parties, ideologies, and issues: stability and change in fifteen European party systems 1945–1998. Pp. 143–68 in *Political Parties in the New Europe: Political and Analytical Challenges*, ed. K. R. Luther and F. Muller-Rommel. Oxford: Oxford University Press.

WATTENBERG, M. P. 2000. The decline of party mobilization. Pp. 64–76 in *Parties without Partisans: Political Change in Advanced Industrial Democracies*, ed. R. J. Dalton and M. P. Wattenberg. Oxford: Oxford University Press.

WOLDENDORP, J., KEMAN, H., and BUDGE, I. 2000. *Party Government in 48 Democracies 1945–1998: Composition-Duration-Personnel*. Dordrecht: Kluwer Academic.

WREN, A. 2006. Comparative perspectives on the role of the state in the economy. In *Oxford Handbook of Political Economy*. Oxford: Oxford University Press.

CHAPTER 20

....

COMPARATIVE
LEGISLATIVE
BEHAVIOR

....

ERIC M. USLANER
THOMAS ZITTEL

PARLIAMENTARY legislative systems are orderly. Congressional legislative systems are disorderly. This claim may seem a bit odd when we think about the loudness, sometimes even the rowdiness, of debate in parliaments compared to the more flowery and civil language on the floor of the United States House of Representative and especially the Senate. The orderliness of parliamentary systems (and the disorderliness of congressional systems) refers not to language or style, but rather to how conflict is structured.

Parliamentary procedure is all about the power of political parties. Parliaments are the embodiment of collective responsibility of the prime minister and his/her governing party. In congressional systems, political parties play a much more limited—some would say a subsidiary—role. Individual members answer to their constituencies, their consciences, and especially their committees more than they do to their party leaders. Congressional procedure is disorderly because there is no centralized authority and no sense of collective responsiblity. Woodrow Wilson, the first modern student of Congress (1967, 59), argued in 1885: "It is this multiplicity of [committee] leaders, this many-headed leadership, which makes the organization of the House

* Eric M. Uslaner is grateful to the General Research Board, University of Maryland, College Park, for support on this and other projects.

too complex to afford uninformed people and unskilled observers any easy clue to its methods of rule. . . . There is no thought of acting in concert."

The standard explanation for these differences is institutional. Parliaments are majoritarian, centralizing power in party leaders who have the power to punish members who might dare to take an independent course. Congressional systems have weak parties and strong committees and leaders lack the power to discipline legislators who respond more to their constituents than to their parties. These explanations take us far, but in recent years we see growing power for congressional parties and weaker parties in parliametary systems—even as institutional structure remains constant. The critical changes seem to be behavioral—as legislators in the United States represent increasingly homogenous constituencies in polarized parties. Legislators in parliamentary systems have fought to become more independent of party leaders.

We now speak of increasing polarization and heightened partisanship in the United States Congress, where party leaders control the agenda with iron fists (at least in the House) and where voters in congressional elections are more likely than at any time in the past 100 years to divide along party lines. We also speak of greater attention to constituency demands in parliamentary systems. We focus on the changing role of political parties in legislative institutions, both parliamentary and congressional, in this chapter—and examine the structural and behavioral roots of legislative behavior. We examine the impact of different institutions, varying informal rules of the game, and the varying relations between legislators and constituents.

1 INSTITUTIONAL INFLUENCES ON PARTISANSHIP IN LEGISLATURES

A. Lawrence Lowell (1901, 332, 346), who pioneered the study of how legislators vote (in England and the United States), argued: "The parliamentary system is . . . the natural outgrowth and a rational expression of the division of the ruling chamber into two parties . . . since the ministry may be overturned at any moment, its life depends upon an unintermittent warfare and it must strive to keep its followers constantly in hand. . . . In America . . . the machinery of party has . . . been created outside of the regular organs of government and, hence, it is less effective and more irregular in its action." Almost three quarters of a century later, David R. Mayhew (1974, 27) wrote: "no theoretical treatment of the United States Congress that posits parties as analytic units will go very far." Philip Norton observed that for European parliamentary systems, "Political parties have served to . . . constrain the freedom of individual action by members of legislatures" (Norton 1990, 5).

The collective responsiblity of parliamentary systems binds legislators to their parties. If the government loses on a major bill, it will fall and there will be new elections. The parliamentary party can deny renomination to members who vote against the party. Constitutents vote overwhelmingly along party lines—members of parliament do not establish independent identities to gain "personal votes" as members of Congress do. Within the legislature, the only path to power is through the party organization. None of these factors hold within congressional systems. Members are independent entrepreneurs who serve on legislative committees that have been independent of party pressure—and often at odds with party goals. Members run for reelection with no fear that the national party can deny them renomination—or even cost them another term.

Even though roll calls are not frequent in many European parliaments, party cohesion in European national parliaments is very high. Beer (1969, 350) remarked about the British House of Commons by the end of the 1960s, that cohesion was so close to 100 percent that there was no longer any point in measuring it.

Parties were weaker in the United States. Yet, Lowell (1901, 336) noted at the turn of the twentieth century: "The amount of party voting varies much from one Congress, and even from one session, to another, and does not follow closely any fixed law of evolution." Later scholars would invest considerable effort in finding the patterns that eluded Lowell and in comparing the relative power of parties, committees, and constituencies across the House and the Senate. The larger House of Representatives with two-year terms was much more conducive to partisanship than the smaller Senate, where members served six-year terms and were not initially publicly elected.

Saalfeld's studies (1990, 1995) of the German Bundestag between 1949 and 1987 find strong levels of party voting for each of the three major parties. This finding is supported by other single-country studies for other European parliaments (Cowley and Norton 1999; Müller and Jenny 2000; Norton 1980).

The likelihood of defection is affected by the nature of an issue and the factor that moral as well as local issues are most likely to trigger the defection of single MPs from their party line (Skjaeveland 2001). Particularly in countries with a strong local tradition, such as Norway and Denmark, party leadership is reportedly understanding towards members dissenting for matters of local concern (Damgaard 1997). Other authors suggested that electoral factors such as a "mixed member voting system" (Burkett 1985) or the marginality of a seat (Norton 2002) might explain defections form the party line.

Power in parliamentary systems is centralized in the party leadership. In the German Bundestag party cohesion is the result of lobbying and arm twisting on the part of the party leadership (Saalfeld 1995). Similar conclusions have been reached for other European legislatures such as the Austrian Nationalrat (Müller and Jenny 2000). In the United States Congress, power has been decentralized to committees, which are often autonomous of the party leadership. Parliamentary parties' organizational clout can be measured in terms of budget, people, and rules. In most European legislatures, individual MPs have little staff support and budget resources to forge a strong link to their constituents and to establish a knowledge and information basis to participate effectively in the parliamentary process. In contrast to this, parliamentary party groups are well equipped in this respect with their own budgets and a sizeable staff. Party groups in European parliaments have developed a multitude of status positions that oversee and manage the decision process within the group.

The scope of party cohesion in European parliaments has been documented on the basis of measures that go beyond floor voting. Andeweg (1997, 118) found that 44 percent of Dutch MPs in 1990 reported asking for prior permission for a written question from the parliamentary party chairperson, even though this is a constitutional right of individual MPs.

Parliamentary parties also enjoy a preeminent legal status. In the German Bundestag, standing orders require that only groups comprising 5 percent of the whole—also the threshhold for a formal caucus—may introduce legislation. Individual members of parliament have few rights to participate such as introducing amendments on the floor or asking questions on the floor. In congressional systems, the individual has far more power.

In Europe and elsewhere, parliament possesses the power to make and break governments. These functions integrate particular groups of members of parliament (MPs) in the process of government formation and government breakdown. It defines MPs in the voters' perception and thus establishes collective responsibility. Parliamentary systems provide executives with resources such as ministerial appointments that can be used by party leaderships to induce MPs to go along with the policies of the government (Depauw 1999).

Beyond the simple dichtomy of parliamentary versus congressional systems other institutional features of the US Congress should lead to weaker partisanship as well. The president and members of each house of Congress run for election at different times and may not share a common fate, whereas a prime minister *comes from parliament and is responsible to it*. There is the possibility of divided control of the legislative and executive branches in the United States—and this makes assigning responsibility for legislation problematic. Senators serve six-year terms to insulate them from the whims of public opinion. Senators were initially appointed by state legislatures rather than elected. The upper chamber was designed, in George Washington's words, to "cool" the passions of the lower house. The House has long had procedures similar to those in parliamentary systems, where the majority, if it willed, could work its will.

The Senate's procedures have always been less majoritarian: In 1806, Senators eliminated a rule that allowed a majority to proceed to a vote and it was not until 1917 that the Senate had *any* procedure for calling the question. Unlimited debate, the filibuster, is a cherished tradition—now it takes sixty Senators to cut off debate. And most of the time, neither major party has sixty seats (or even when it does, sixty reliable votes). Krehbiel (1998) has argued that the potential for a filibuster means that legislative productivity in Congress does not simply reflect a "median voter" model. Instead, the capacity for enacting legislation depends upon where the "filibuster pivot" is—the positions of the member whose vote can break a filibuster in the Senate. The potential for gridlock (stalemate) is large and ordinarily it takes large majorities to enact major policy changes in the Senate (Krehbiel 1998, 47)—even more so under divided government. The existence of larger districts (states) of the Senate means that constituencies are more heterogeneous—so that it is more difficult for Senators to please their electorates than it is for members of the House. It also means that Senators' own ideologies will be more diverse, with more liberal Republicans and conservative Democrats than we find in the House. Party is not the common bond for ideology in the Senate as it is in the House—Senators from the same party and the same state are rivals for leadership and often try to distinguish themselves from each other ideologically to bolster claims to power (Schiller 2000). Finally, the Senate has a long tradition of strong bonds among members (what White 1956 called the "Inner Club"), which puts a premium on getting along rather than emphasizing party differences.

Parties have not always been weak in the USA: under Czar rule in 1890–1911, party leaders had extraordinary power: Speaker Thomas Reed (R, ME) chaired the powerful House Rules Committee, made all committee assignments himself, and had complete control over the House floor and the right of recognition. Members were regularly reassigned from one committee to another when they fell out of favor with the Speaker. A division within the Republican party—as Progressives became a more important force—led to the fall of Reed's successor, Clarence Cannon, on an obscure procedural vote in 1911 (when Progressives aligned with Democrats)—and to a decline in the role of parties in the US Congress.

The constitutional structure of the United States clearly shapes the lesser power of parties compared to parliamentary systems, especially in Europe. Yet students of Congress, from Woodrow Wilson to contemporary formal theorists, have focused more on an institutional feature of Congress that is extra-constitutional: the congressional committee system. The end of Czar rule led to the growth of a committee system that was independent of party pressures and that gave positions of authority to members based upon seniority (longevity on the committee) rather than party loyalty. Legislators seek committee assignments based upon the interests of their constituents and upon their own expertise. Once appointed to a committee, membership becomes a "property right" that cannot be abrogated (a reform enacted following the downfall of Czar rule).

Fenno (1973) stressed committee autonomy from the 1950s to the 1970s and emphasized how committees responded differently to their clienteles and their environments, rather than to a single master such as party leadership. Since conservative Southern Democrats were the most electorally secure, they dominated committee chair positions in both the House and the Senate and often blocked the agenda of the liberals who dominated the party's legislative contingent through the 1970s.

The new institutionalist perspective of Shepsle and Weingast (1994) focuses on committees as "preference outliers" from others in the chamber and argue that distributive policy-making stems from implicit logrolling among outlier committees (see also Wilson 1967, 121). These logrolls can occur *because committees are monopoly agenda setters—they operate under closed rules that prohibit others in the legislature from offering amendments*. Committees, then, have an extraordinary degree of power in these models.

An alternative institutionalist perspective focuses on committees as information providers (Krehbiel 1991). This informational power gives committees even greater power over legislation. They may not have monopoly agenda-setting power, but their greater knowledge of policy consequences implies that they can generally get their way within the legislature. Committees are *not* autonomous in this model—they must respond to the majority position within the legislature (regardless of party). But committees themselves are representative of the full chambers, not preference outliers. While these "new institutionalist" perspectives are at direct variance with each other, *both* downplay the role of parties in Congress.

Strong committees, under any account, lead to a policy-making arena that is very different from the party-dominated legislative process found in parliamentary systems. Parties in parliamentary systems promote policies *in order to get them adopted*. In European parliaments, parties control committee assignments and procedures (Damgaard 1995). In the United States, committees are designed to protect constituency interests and this often means *blocking rather than passing legislation*. The committee system is often seen as a "legislative graveyard" since only about 6 percent of bills introduced by members become law.

The institutional structure of the congressional system is thus insufficient to explain why bills get passed. Legislators rely upon *informal institutions (or norms)* to build cross-party coalitions. These norms—courtesy, reciprocity, legislative work, specialization, apprenticeship (members traditionally worked their way up from minor committees to more important ones), and institutional patriotism (respecting the rules and prerogatives of each chamber)—were key factors in securing bipartisan majorities for legislation (Matthews 1960). The norms waned during the period of heightened partisanship that took hold in the 1980s (Uslaner 1993). Since parliamentary systems do not depend upon the cooperation of the majority with the minority, a strong set of norms of collegiality never took hold.

2 THE BEHAVIORAL FOUNDATIONS OF PARTISANSHIP

The institutional structure of Congress laid the foundation for strong ties between legislators and their constituents. Members of the House faced election frequently and both House and Senate elections occurred in years when the president was not on the ballot. The weak parties meant that legislators were free to pay attention to the people who elected them—and committees were devoted to protection of constituency interests, even at the expense of party programs. Speaker of the House Thomas P. O'Neill (1977–1986) had a famous line that he told to junior members contemplating whether to support their party or their constituency: "All politics is local."

A large literature, developed mostly during the period of weak parties, posited that members of Congress were torn between serving two masters: their parties and their constituents. In the eighteenth century, British MP (and political philosopher) Edmund Burke told his electors in his Bristol constituency that he did not feel bound to abide by their views—that he would follow his own conscience and would accept the verdict of the voters as to whether they believed he was correct (they turned him out of office).

Burke's speech became the basis for *role theory* in the study of legislatures where legislators chose between the roles of *delegates*, who followed constituency opinion, or *trustees*, who followed their own conscience or their parties. Wahlke, Eulau, Buchanan, and Ferguson (1962) found, perhaps surprisingly, that most American state legislators in the five states they examined in the 1950s considered themselves trustees—with figures ranging from 55 percent in California to 81 percent in Tennessee. Only between 6 and 20 percent took on the pure "delegate" role, with the rest in between as "politicos." A decade later Davidson (1969) found similar results for members of the US Congress.

The Burkean distinction has been used in the European context as well (Barnes 1977; Converse and Pierce 1986; Searing 1994). Only a small minority of European MPs would consider themselves delegates. In the late 1970s only 3 percent of the members of the German Bundestag regarded themselves as instructed delegates (Farah 1980, 238). Compared to their American colleagues, many European MPs spend less time communicating with constituents. An analysis of the time budget of members of the German Bundestag found that about one quarter of an average member's time is devoted to "information and contact activities," a summary category which also includes time spent with constituency communication (Herzog et al. 1990, 83–92).

Searing (1994) interviewed 521 British MPs to distinguish between four preference roles (policy advocate, ministerial aspirant, constituency member, parliament man) and four position roles (parliamentary private secretary, whip, junior minister, minister). Searing found many policy advocates and few parliament men among the backbenchers he interviewed. While parliament men resemble the classical concept of an amateur who enjoys being a Member of Parliament and who is absorbed by the conduct of parliamentary business, policy advocates aim at influencing government policy and develop carrying degrees of issue familiarity and expertise.

Patzelt's (1997) interviews with German MPs from 1989 to 1992 demonstrated that MPs aim to reconcile and to synthesize the roles of trustee and delegate. European MPs are characterized by complex role sets that cannot be reduced to any single role type and that, at the same time, incorporate the notion of a partisan as a strong and predominant element within this role set (Müller and Saalfeld 1997).

In Europe, constituency has always taken a back seat to party. For the United States from the 1890s until 1911, partisanship reigned supreme and there was no conflict between party and constituency for legislators. Czar rule came to an end because of growing factionalism within the Republican Party, leading the Progressives in the House to side with the minority party (the Democrats) to defeat a routine procedural motion—marking the end of the strong Speaker. With the downfall of strong party leadership, members of Congress established committees with tenure not touchable by party leaders, and legislative authority of their own. Members looked more and more to their constituencies rather than to parties. Legislators were torn between which to support on the floor, as we saw as early as the 1920s, as shown by Julius Turner (later revised by Edward Schneier in Turner and Schneier 1970).

The parliamentary model of solidarity with one's party fell by the wayside in the United States: Some issues (states rights, legislative–executive relations, patronage) showing high levels of party conflict and others (foreign policy, business, agriculture, social welfare) dividing the parties less frequently. Clausen showed for the House (and Sinclair 1982 for both houses) that levels of voting along party lines depended heavily on the nature of the issue. Economic issues were the most heavily partisan and foreign policy and social issues were the least partisan.

Many of the least loyal Democrats were from the South and the least loyal Republicans were from the East. Southern Democrats often voted more frequently with Republicans than with Northern Democrats, forming an informal "conservative coalition." Yet, the very diversity of the Democratic Party may have been the key to the party's long-term electoral dominance.

Mayhew (1966) argued that House Democrats were the party of "inclusive compromise." The Republicans, with a much narrower ideological base, were the party of "exclusive compromise," destined to maintain minority status.

Miller and Stokes (1963) earlier showed that the connections between legislators' votes and constituency attitudes were frequently weak because members of Congress often misperceived public opinion. Most studies reported at best moderate correlations between legislators' votes and public opinion. Achen (1975) corrected the Miller–Stokes constituency opinions for measurement error and found much stronger correlations with legislators' votes.

Fenno (1978) argued that legislators focus not on just one constituency (the entire district), but have multiple masters. Of particular importance is the reelection constituency—mostly comprised of fellow partisans. Using data on public opinion derived from statewide exit polls in the states (Erikson, Wright, and McIver 1993) for both the full constituency (the state) and the reelection constituency (fellow state partisans), Uslaner (1999) showed that Senators respond primarily to their fellow partisans—and that there is generally a close correspondence between their own ideology and that of their reelection constituencies. His findings mirror Kingdon's (1973) analysis of House members' explanations for their voting behavior: the "field of forces" members face on roll calls—constituency opinion, interest group pressure, leadership mobilization, the administration, fellow members, their staff, and their own values—mostly have the bare minimum of conflict. This strikes a key blow at both the notion that legislators "shirk" their constituents in favor of their party or their own ideology—or that members must adopt either a delegate or a trustee role.

Yet, there remains tension between party and constituency demands. Members of Congress expanded their electoral base beyond their own partisans in the 1960s and 1970s by developing a strong "personal vote" apart from party identification. They attracted support across party lines through a combination of bringing back projects to the district, personal attention to constituents and their problems, and the ability to raise large amounts of money for their campaigns (Fiorina 1977; Jacobson and Kernell 1983). During the period of weak partisanship, the two major parties' constituencies were not ideologically polarized. However, even as the party coalitions began to diverge more sharply in presidential politics in the 1970s, the rise in candidate-centered (as opposed to party-centered) campaigns shielded congressional incumbents from national tides favoring one party or another (Brady and Hahn 2004).

Members of Congress focused on developing "home styles" to convince constituents that they were "one of them." Members use these "home styles" to broaden their bases of support—and they generally treat issues gingerly because ideological appeals may repel some constituents. Legislators do claim that they have power in Washington, but they are hardly above tearing down the institution to make themselves look good (Fenno 1978, 245–6). Much as Wilson feared a century earlier, "running for Congress by running against Congress" leads to a lack of concern for the collective good of the institution.

Members care more about their own electoral fates than about how well their party does—the reelection rates for the House now approach 100 percent while Senators fare less well but still prevail in about 85 percent of their races. Even in the Democratic debacle of 1994, when the party lost control of both houses (losing the House for the first time since 1954), 84 percent of Democratic Representatives seeking an additional term won (Jacobson 2004, 23). By developing home styles that focus on members' character and service to the district, incumbents have largely insulated themselves against national political tides—and even congressional performance. The level of gridlock (or stalemate) in Congress, Binder (2003, 110) reports, has little effect on the reelection prospects of incumbents.

3 THE RISE AND FALL IN PARTISANSHIP: INSTITUTIONAL AND BEHAVIORAL EXPLANATIONS

Cox and McCubbins (1993) argue that other "new institutionalists" have underestimated the impact of parties in Congress. Even during periods of strong committees, parties played a key role in shaping committee membership—and party leaders rarely lost votes on the floor when pitted against recalcitrant committee leaders. Poole and Rosenthal (1997) also argue that legislative voting has always been unidimensional. This single dimension encompasses both ideology and partisanship (Poole and Rosenthal 1997, 6)—so models focusing on ideology and models focusing on party are actually examining the same thing using different terms.

Most analysts still stand by the argument that American legislative parties were weak for much of the twentieth century, even as Brady and Hahn (2004) argue that American political life has normally been highly partisan and that the weak party era was exceptional rather than the norm. There is also general agreement that partisanship in the 1960s and especially the 1970s was much lower than normal. Beginning in 1981 with the inauguration of the Reagan administration, partisanship increased more dramatically and has continued to grow almost unabated (Rohde 1991, 51). Partisanship has now reached levels not seen in the Congress since the era of Czar rule (marked by an all-powerful Speaker) in the House at the turn of the century.

The major institutional explanations focus on structural reforms in the House of Representatives in the 1970s. The "Subcommittee Bill of Rights" transferred power from full committees to subcommittees. The initiation of electronic voting increased amending activity sharply. Party leaders also gained power at the expense of committees: the Speaker was given greater control over assigning members to committees and over referring bills to committees. There was also an expanded leadership system in the House that gave the Speaker and his aides more information. These reforms weakened most norms, especially courtesy, reciprocity, and institutional patriotism (Sinclair 1989; Smith 1989)—and placed greater power in the hands of both the party leaders and junior members. Three Southern committee chairs were removed from their positions in 1975 by the House Democratic caucus, one of the first steps in the move toward stronger parties. An even bigger boost in partisanship occcured in 1995, when the Republicans took control of Congress. Committees became much less independent of party leadership—the Speaker and his allies now control the committee appointment process, committee chairs are limited to three terms, and party renegades have found themselves relegated to minor committees and unable to advance within the party (Evans and Oleszek 1997). Recalcitrant committees faced the prospect that the leadership would take favored legislation out of their jurisdictions to be handled by special "task forces" appointed by the Speaker.

Strong party institutions and weaker committees, these institutional accounts argue, provide the foundation for greater partisanship on the part of the rank and file. Members of Congress will be more likely to toe the party line when parties are stronger. Demonstrating the effects of strong leadership on legislative voting is not so simple. Krehbiel (1993) argues that party influence in legislative voting is a mirage. Partisanship in legislative voting is simply a proxy for members' own ideologies—Democrats are more liberal, Republicans are more conservative. As each party becomes more homogenous, partisan polarization in the legislature increases. Finding an *independent effect for leadership mobilization* is elusive. On precisely those issues that are most important to the parties, the leaders make the greatest efforts to mobilize their bases. What appears to be strong mobilization by leaders is really little more than homogenous preferences among followers—real party pressure would involve voting for a bill favored by the leadership *even when the member does not agree with it*. Without information about members' "true preferences," there is no way to verify this claim.

There have been a few studies that attempt to get past this conondrum: Sinclair (2001) examines the selection of procedural rules in the House of Representatives from 1987 to 1996. She finds that majority party members are more likely to vote for the rule than for the bill—especially when the rule restricts the freedom of the minority. Ansolabehere, Snyder, and Stewart (2001) use surveys of candidate attitudes to obtain independent measures of policy preferences and show that the legislators' party shapes voting on roll calls even beyond the effect of member attitudes. Neither of these studies, however, measure leadership effects directly. Perhaps the only studies that get directly at leadership effects are Kingdon (1973) and Burden and Frisby (2004). Kingdon asked members of the House what factors shaped their roll call voting right after the legislators cast their ballots. He conducted his study in the weak party era (1969), so it is no surprise that he reported (Kingdon 1973, 121): "the sanctions [of party leaders] are not very effective, simply because many congressmen care more about voting as they see fit, either for ideological or political reasons, than about the risk of negative party sanctions. Members repeatedly voiced perfect willingness to defy the leadership and take whaetever consequences might come." Burden and Frisby examine previously private Democratic whip counts in 1971–2 (also the weak party era) to see if party pressure can switch votes. These data have preferences before party efforts and on the votes on the House floor. Only a small share of votes were changed. Consistent with Krehbiel's (1993) argument, there was general agreement within the Democratic Party (even during this period of relatively low cohesion) on the sixteen bills analyzed.

One key problem with these institutional approaches beyond the difficulty in establishing party leader effects is that the structural reforms that many posit as key to the rise in partisanship and polarization were restricted to the House of Representatives. Polarization increased *in both the House and the Senate* (Binder 2003; Brady and Hahn 2004; Poole and Rosenthal 1997; Uslaner 1993). The Senate was not the subject for widespread structural change at any point during the past fifty years—yet the trends in party polarization almost exactly mirror those of the House. This should not be so surprising: About 120 years ago Wilson (1967, 152–3) wrote (even as the Senate was still not directly elected): "there is a 'latent unity' between the Senate and the House, which makes continued antagonism between them next to impossible.... The Senate and the House are of different origins, but virtually of the same nature."

A more behavioral approach focuses on changes *outside the legislature—mostly in the electorate*. Cohesive floor voting as well as party driven role conceptions and institutional choices are seen as the result of common ideologies and shared values that become manifest in strong party structures at the social level. This, in turn, is seen as the result of historical and antecedent cultural factors such as the strength of localism in society or the pattern of cleavages underlying the party system.

Cooper and Brady (1981) argue that partisanship in the United States varies over time in a cylical fashion. When partisan and constituency ties overlap (as under Czar rule and from the 1980s to the present), parties will be strong. When they do not (as in the 1940s through the 1960s), parties will be weak. Rohde (1991) argues that the Voting Rights Act (VRA) of 1965 was the turning point leading to stronger parties in the United States. By enfranchising African-Americans in the South, the VRA pushed white Southern conservatives into the Republican Party (where they now predominate) and made the Southern Democratic Party largely African-American (and liberal). As the Republican Party moved right, the Democrats became dominant in formerly Republican areas such as the northeast and the parties polarized. Rohde's (1991, 35–6) argument, following upon Cooper and Brady, is called "conditional party government:" "instead of strong party leaders being the cause of high party cohesion, cohesive parties are the main precondition for strong leadership."

While American congressmen seem to move toward the European pattern of legislative behavior, there are signs that their European colleagues are focusing less on parties and more on individual member initiative. European legislatures have reallocated resources to the benefit of individual MPs. Personal staff has increased in many legislatures since the late 1960s. In 1969, the German Bundestag bestowed German members of parliament with a moderate budget that can be used to employ staff or to pay for office expenses. Since then the figure has increased substantially. When the number of districts in Germany was reduced from 328 to 298 prior to the 2002 election, parts of the savings were used to increase the budget of individual MPs (Saalfeld 2002, 59). Similar reallocations of resources have also been reported regarding other European legislatures (Gladdish 1990).

European MPs take constituency communication and constituency services more seriously. Cain, Ferejohn, and Fiorina (1984) showed over two decades ago that paying attention to constituencies through weekly surgeries (among other things) did have a payoff in a "personal vote" for British MPs. Norton reports more recently that newly elected British MPs increasingly took up residence in their constituencies and spent more time there compared to their older colleagues (Norton 2002, 25).

Carey and Shugart (1995) and Norris (2004, ch. 10), pinpoint the ballot structure as the most important incentive to cultivate a personal vote and to stress constituency rather than party. Some European countries such as the Netherlands and Sweden apply flexible list systems which provide incentives to forge a closer link between constituents and MPs. This ballot form allows voters to move candidates up the list and to ignore the rank order as determined by party elites. However, factors such as a large district size counter-balance the initial effect of the ballot structure towards personalization.

The UK has a single member district with plurality elections system that is similar to the one in the United States. It should act as an incentive to cultivate a direct bond between MPs and constituents, since there is greater accountability than in a multimember proportional representation system. This works regarding service responsiveness to some respect but it obviously does not affect party discipline in the House of Commons and the predominance of party structures in this parliament. One might assume that the British parliamentary system as well as the social environment counter-balances the effects of the electoral system. Bogdanor (1985, 193) sees this districting system as an empty vessel because it does not allow voters choices between different party candidates like in flexible list systems. An extra device is needed, such as the primary, if they are to provide for the choice of a candidate.

There are other signs of greater independence for legislators in parliamentary systems as well: European national parliaments have experienced increases in individual member initiatives such as questions to the government (Gladdish 1990). Patzelt (1997) argues that European MPs are no longer simply torn between party and constituency. Instead, they are increasingly using their new resources to assert their own influence within the party—and with independent policy networks. Legislators are now increasingly becoming policy specialists (Searing 1994).

4 CONSEQUENCES OF CHANGES IN PARTISANSHIP

We see two trends moving in opposite directions: stronger partisanship with a closer linkage between party and constituency in the United States; and declining partisanship and a weakening of historically strong bonds between parties and their followers in many other places, especially in Europe.

The polarization of constituents along partisan lines in the United States, together with the decline in competitive congressional districts, has heightened the level of partisan conflict in Congress. Even though voters began to sort themselves out ideologically (and by party) as early as the 1960s, it was not until the 1980s that voters' partisanship and ideological identification began to correlate strongly with their votes for Congress (Jacobson 2004, 248–52; Brady and Hahn 2004). As older members who were out of step with their constituents (especially Southern Democrats) retired, their replacements were much more ideologically in tune—and relied less on a "personal" than an ideological (party) vote to get reelected.

Wilson argued that the weakness of the American party system, especially in comparison to stronger parties in Europe, meant less governmental responsibility and a reduced capacity for informed policy-making. The stronger partisanship, measured by both roll call voting and the strength of congressional party leadership (especially at the expense of committee leaders), would have led a "resuscitated" Wilson to rejoice. He would see a political system that has a stronger capacity for policy-making.

Yet, there remain institutional obstacles to legislative productivity, even as congressional parties behave in the manner of their majoritarian counterparts in congressional systems. An institutional factor that observers from Wilson onward have long believed to hinder the enactment of legislation is divided government. Even as the electorate has become more polarized since the 1980s, it has also shown a tendency to give both parties at least some share of the legislative and executive branches. From 1981 to 2006, there has been divided control of government 77 percent of the time. *With high levels of polarization, this should be a recipe for legislative stalemate.* Yet, Mayhew (1991) argues that divided government does *not* affect the number of major laws passed in Congress. Binder (2003, ch. 4), however, argues that Mayhew's simple count of major laws does not take into account the size of the congressional agenda—and her measure of gridlock, which is the share of legislation on the nation's agenda (as determined by daily editorials in the *New York Times*) that does not pass, is strongly shaped by divided control of the legislative and executive branches. Conley (2003) provides a more nuanced view of structural factors: In the era of weak parties, divided government had no significant effect on the president's success in getting his agenda enacted by Congress. Only since party polarization has increased does divided government matter. As the level of partisanship has increased, the capacity for policy-making has *decreased*. Legislative stalemate became more frequent as party polarization rose (Binder 2003, 80). This polarization, among both elites and the public, has led to the waning of the norms that helped promote legislative policy-making in Congress (Uslaner 1993).

In European parliamentary systems, party voting remains as high as ever. The European Parliament is a different story: Members of the European Parliament (MEPs) overwhelmingly stick with their national parties, but are more likely to defect from their European party group. Even though this defection level is not high (about 13 percent from July 1999 to June 2000), voting contrary to one's European party was greatest when: (1) the electoral system for an MEP is candidate-centered and decentralized; and (2) there is policy conflict between European and the national party (Hix 2004).

Increased citizen demands for more responsiveness stimulated MPs to provide more opportunities for direct communication and interaction (Saalfeld 2002; Norton 2002, 180). Changes in technological opportunity structures decrease the costs of constituency communication and also remove practical obstacles in linking MPs and their constituents, bypassing political parties (Zittel 2003). Last but not least, the weakness of political parties themselves, their loss of membership, and the erosion of their social roots raises serious questions regarding the future of party government in European democracies.

Ironically, even though norms of cooperation have not been a major focus of parliamentary systems, there is at least anecdotal evidence (from British Labour MP Tony Colman to the senior author) that incivility has become a problem. In a chamber where booing and hissing have long been part of the legislative show, it is ironic that Europe and the United States are both experiencing more hostile legislative chambers, even as one becomes more partisan and the other less ruled by parties.

We know much about what American legislators do outside of Congress and what members in parliamentary systems (especially in Europe) do inside the legislature. Future research should help us understand what we don't know. In parliamentary systems, we should shift our emphasis away from roll calls toward behavior such as campaign strategies, constituency service, and constituency communication, or the use of parliamentary privileges such as asking questions to ministers. These are less visible and less consequential activities that will help us understand the weakening of parliamentary parties. In the United States, the key puzzle is over the "real" power of party leaders. Can leaders change members' votes in more than a handful of cases?

These questions, mixing quantitative research with the more intensive qualitative designs of Fenno (1973) and Kingdon (1973)—and perhaps also a greater focus on state legislatures—will help us understand why congressional parties are growing stronger and parliamentary parties are becoming weaker.

References

ACHEN, C. 1975. Mass political attitudes and the survey response, *American Political Science Review*, 69: 1218–31.

ANDEWEG, R. B. 1997. Role specialisation or role switching? Dutch MPs between electorate and executive. Pp. 110–27 in *Members of Parliament in Western Europe: Roles and Behavior*, ed. W. C. Müller and T. Saalfeld. Portland, Oreg.: Frank Cass.

ANSOLABEHERE, S., SNYDER, J. M., JR., and STEWART, C., III 2001. The effect of party and preferences on Congressional roll-call voting, *Legislative Studies Quarterly*, 26: 815–31.

BARNES, S. 1977. *Representation in Italy: Institutionalized Tradition and Electoral Choice*. Chicago: University of Chicago Press.

BEER, S. H. 1969. *British Politics*. London: Faber.

BENDINER, R. 1964. *Obstacle Course on Capitol Hill*. New York: McGraw-Hill.

BINDER, S. 2003. *Stalemate*. Washington, DC: Brookings Institution.

BOGDANOR, V. 1985. Conclusion. Pp. 1–12 in *Representatives of the People? Parliamentarians and Constituents in Western Democracies*, ed. V. Bogdanor. Aldershot: Gower.

BRADY, D. W. and HAHN, H. 2004. An extended historical view of Congressional party polarization. Unpublished paper, Stanford University.

BURDEN, B. C. and FRISBY, T. M. 2004. Preferences, partisanship, and whip activity in the U.S. House of Representatives. *Legislative Studies Quarterly*, 29: 569–91.

BURKETT, T. 1985. The West German Deputy. Pp. 117–31 in *Representatives of the People? Parliamentarians and Constituents in Western Democracies*, ed. V. Bogdanor. Aldershot: Gower.

CAIN, B., FEREJOHN, J., and FIORINA, M. 1984. *The Personal Vote*. Cambridge, Mass.: Harvard University Press.

CAREY, J. M. and SHUGART, M. 1995. Incentives to cultivate a personal vote: a rank ordering of electoral formulas. *Electoral Studies*, 14: 417–39.

CLAUSEN, A. R. 1973. *How Congressmen Decide: A Policy Focus*. New York: St. Martin's Press.

CONLEY, R. S. 2003. *The President, Congress, and Divided Government*. College Station: Texas A&M University Press.

CONVERSE, P. E. and PIERCE, R. 1986. *Political Representation in France*. Cambridge, Mass.: Cambridge University Press.

COOPER, J. and BRADY, D. W. 1981. Institutional context and leadership style. *American Political Science Review*, 75: 411–25.

COWLEY, P. and NORTON, P. 1999. Rebels and rebellions: Conservative MPs in the 1992 parliament. *British Journal of Politics and International Relations*, 1: 81–105.

COX, G. W. and MCCUBBINS, M. D. 1993. *Legislative Leviathan*. Berkeley: University of California Press.

DAMGAARD, E. 1995. How parties control committee members. Pp. 308–25 in *Parliaments and Majority Rule in Western Europe*, ed. H. Döring. Frankfurt: Campus Verlag.

—— 1997. The political roles of Danish MPs. Pp. 79–90 in *Members of Parliament in Western Europe: Roles and Behavior*, ed. W. C. Müller and T. Saalfeld. London: Frank Cass.

DAVIDSON, R. 1969. *The Role of the Congressman*. New York: Pegasus.

DEPAUW, S. 1999. Parliamentary party cohesion and the scarcity of sanctions in the Belgian Chamber of Representatives (1991–1995). *Res Publica*, 41: 15–39.

ERIKSON, R. S. 1978. Constituency opinion and Congressional behavior: a reexamination of the Miller–Stokes representation data. *American Journal of Political Science*, 22: 511–35.

——WRIGHT, G. C., and MacIVER, J. P. 1993. *Statehouse Democracy*. New York: Cambridge University Press.

EVANS, C. L. and OLESZEK, W. 1997. *Congress Under Fire*. Boston: Houghton-Mifflin.

FARAH, B. G. 1980. Political representation in West Germany. Ph.D. dissertation, University of Michigan.

FENNO, R. F., JR. 1973. *Congressmen in Committees*. Boston: Little, Brown.

——1978. *Home Style*. Boston: Little, Brown.

FIORINA, M. P. 1977. *Congress: Keystone of the Washington Establishment*. New Haven, Conn.: Yale University Press.

GLADDISH, K. 1990. Parliamentary activism and legitimacy in the Netherlands. Pp. 103–19 in *Parliaments in Western Europe*, ed. P. Norton. Portland, Oreg.: Frank Cass.

HEIDAR, K. 1997. Rules, structures and behavior: Norwegian parlamentarians in the nineties. Pp. 91–109 in *Members of Parliament in Western Europe: Roles and Behavior*, ed. W. C. Müller and T. Saalfeld. Portland, Oreg.: Frank Cass.

HERZOG, D., REBENSTORF, H., and WESSELS, B. 1990, *Abgeordnete und Büvger*. Opladen: Westdeutscher Verlago.

HIX, S. 2004. Electoral institutions and legislative behavior: explaining voting defection in the European Parliament. *World Politics*, 56: 194–223.

JACOBSON, G. C. 2004. *The Politics of Congressional Elections*, 6th edn. New York: Longman.

——and KERNELL, S. 1983. *Strategy and Choice in Congressional Elections*, 2nd edn. New Haven, Conn.: Yale University Press.

KINGDON, J. W. 1973. *Congressmen's Voting Decisions*. New York: Harper and Row.

KREHBIEL, K. 1991. *Information and Legislative Organization*. Ann Arbor: University of Michigan Press.

——1993. Where's the party? *British Journal of Political Science*, 23: 235–66.

——1998. *Pivotal Politics*. Princeton, NJ: Princeton University Press.

LOWELL, A. L. 1901. The influence of party upon legislation in England and America. *Annual Report of the American Historical Association for 1901*, 1: 319–542.

MATTHEWS, D. R. 1960. *U.S. Senators and Their World*. Chapel Hill: University of North Carolina Press.

MAYHEW, D. R. 1966. *Party Loyalty Among Congressmen*. Cambridge, Mass.: Harvard University Press.

——1974. *Congress: The Electoral Connection*. New Haven, Conn.: Yale University Press.

——1991. *Divided We Govern*. New Haven, Conn.: Yale University Press.

MÜLLER, W. C. and JENNY, M. 2000. Abgeordnete, parteien und koalitionspolitik: individuelle präferenzen und politisches handeln im Nationalrat. *Österreichische Zeitschrift für Politikwissenschaft*, 29: 137–56.

——and SAALFELD, T. (eds.) 1997. *Members of Parliament in Western Europe: Roles and Behavior*. Portland, Oreg.: Frank Cass.

NORRIS, P. 2004. *Electoral Engineering: Voting Rules and Political Behavior*. Cambridge: Cambridge University Press.

NORTON, P. 1980. *Dissension in the House of Commons 1974–1979*. Oxford: Clarendon Press.

——(ed.) 1990. *Parliaments in Western Europe*. Portland, Oreg.: Frank Cass.

NORTON, P. 2002. Introduction. Pp. 1–18 in *Parliaments and Citizens in Western Europe*, ed. P. Norton. London: Frank Cass.

PATZELT, W. J. 1997. German MPs and their role. Pp. 55–78 in *Members of Parliament in Western Europe: Roles and Behavior*, ed. W. C. Müller and T. Saalfeld. London: Frank Cass.

POOLE, K. T. and ROSENTHAL, H. 1997. *Congress: A Political-Economic History of Roll Call Voting*. New York: Oxford University Press.

ROHDE, D. W. 1991. *Parties and Leaders in the Postreform House*. Chicago: University of Chicago Press.

SAALFELD, T. 1990. The West German Bundestag after 40 years: the role of parliament in a "party democracy." Pp. 43–65 in *Parliaments in Western Europe*, ed. P. Norton. Portland, Oreg.: Frank Cass.

—— 1995. *Parteisoldaten und Rebellen: Eine Untersuchung zur Geschlossenheit der Fraktionen im Deutschen Bundestag (1949–1990)*. Opladen: Leske u. Budrich.

—— 2002. Parliament and citizens in Germany: reconciling conflicting pressures. In *Parliaments and Citizens in Western Europe*, ed. P. Norton. London: Frank Cass.

SCHILLER, W. J. 2000. *Partners and Rivals*. Princeton, NJ: Princeton University Press.

SEARING, D. D. 1994. *Westminster's World: Understanding Political Roles*. Cambridge, Mass.: Cambridge University Press.

SHEPSLE, K. and WEINGAST, B. 1994. Positive theories of congressional institutions. *Legislative Studies Quarterly*, 19: 149–80.

SINCLAIR, B. 1982. *Congressional Realignment, 1925–1978*. Austin: University of Texas Press.

—— 1989. The transformation of the U.S. Senate. Baltimore: Johns Hopkins University Press.

—— 2001. Do parties matter? Pp. 36–63 in *Party, Process, and Political Change: New Perspectives on the History of Congress*, ed. D. Brady and M. McCubbins. Stanford, Calif.: Stanford University Press.

SKJAEVELAND, A. 2001. Party cohesion in the Danish parliament. *Journal of Legislative Studies*, 7: 35–56.

SMITH, S. S. 1989. *Call to Order: Floor Politics in the House and Senate*. Washington, DC: Brookings Institution.

TURNER, J. and SCHNEIER, E. V., JR. 1970. *Party and Constituency*, rev. edn. Baltimore: Johns Hopkins University Press.

USLANER, E. M. 1993. *The Decline of Comity in Congress*. Ann Arbor: University of Michigan Press.

—— 1999. *The Movers and the Shirkers*. Ann Arbor: University of Michigan Press.

WAHLKE, J., EULAU, H., BUCHANAN, W., and FERGUSON, L. 1962. *The Legislative System*. New York: John Wiley.

WHITE, W. S. 1956. *The Citadel*. New York: Harper and Brothers.

WILSON, W. 1967. *Congressional Government*. Cleveland, Ohio: Meridian; orig. pub. 1885.

ZITTEL, T. 2003. Political representation in the networked society: the Americanisation of European systems of responsible party government? *Journal of Legislative Studies*, 9: 32–53.

CHAPTER 21

....

POLITICAL INTOLERANCE IN THE CONTEXT OF DEMOCRATIC THEORY

....

JAMES L. GIBSON

IN 1954, in the midst of the infamous McCarthy-led Red Scare in the United States, Samuel Stouffer initiated the modern study of political intolerance with a major survey of both the American mass public and local community leaders. Stouffer, like many others, observed the widespread political repression being undertaken in the name of protecting America and its values from the godless communists, and wondered whether such repression was supported by ordinary people. The results were unequivocal when it comes to the mass public: Of 4,933 respondents interviewed, only 113 people—a paltry 2.3 percent—would not restrict the activities and rights of an admitted communist in some way.[1] Local community leaders, on the other hand, expressed considerably less appetite for intolerance. Out of Stouffer's research

---

* I acknowledge the helpful comments of Jessica Flanigan on an earlier version of this chapter.

[1] Stouffer asked his respondents nine questions about placing restrictions on the activities of an admitted communist. The responses ranged from the 89.6 percent who would fire the communist from a job working in a defense plant (and the 89.4% who would fire the communist from a job teaching in a university) to a "low" of 35.5 percent who would stop buying a brand of soap that was plugged by a communist on a radio show.

emerged highly influential "elitist" theories of democracy (e.g. Bachrach 1967), as well as an intellectual concern that has persisted for fifty years about the causes and consequences of the intolerance of ordinary citizens (e.g. for a study of British elites and masses see Barnum and Sullivan 1989; on Canadian elites and masses see Sniderman et al. 1996; on Nicaragua see Stein 1999; for contrary findings on elite–mass differences see Rohrschneider 1996).

Intolerance—the unwillingness to put up with disagreeable ideas and groups—has thus become a staple of research on the democratic orientations of citizens throughout the world. The topic is today no less important than it was in the days of Joseph McCarthy (the Republican Senator from Wisconsin who led the Red Scare of the 1950s), since intolerance in one form or another fuels the conflicts in Northern Ireland, the Middle East, Rwanda, and many other areas of the world. And even where intolerance does not directly produce political violence, the failure of democratizing regimes to embrace political freedom for all, even those in the opposition, has become one of the most important impediments to the consolidation of democratic reform throughout the world (as in the so-called illiberal democracies—see Zakaria 2003). Thus, it is important to assess what fifty years of social scientific research have taught us about the causes and consequences of political intolerance. That is the purpose of this chapter.[2]

This chapter begins with an overview of democratic theory, since the meaning of political tolerance (like all concepts) can best be understood within the context of theory. Because tolerance is often confused with other fellow travelers such as permissiveness, it is useful to carefully explicate the concept. The definition of concepts is of course arbitrary, but all concepts acquire their meaning from theory. In the case of political tolerance, the relevant body of thought is democratic theory, and perhaps even more precisely, theories of liberal democracy.[3]

1 THE ROLE OF TOLERANCE IN DEMOCRATIC THEORY

Democracy is of course a system of procedures by which majorities tend to have their way: the majority rules. Liberal democracies require mechanisms of aggregating citizen preferences within majoritarian institutions and this is perhaps the essence of the concept of democracy (e.g. Dahl 1989). But democracy is also a system in

---

[2] For an earlier useful review of the tolerance literature see Sullivan and Transue (1999).

[3] This is not to imply that the only legitimate conceptualization of tolerance is that connected to liberal democratic theory (for various theories of tolerance, see Sullivan, Piereson, and Marcus 1982). Indeed, Gibson (2004a) conceptualizes tolerance as an element of "reconciliation" (as in the South African truth and reconciliation process). That conceptualization is not incompatible with liberal democratic theory, even if it places emphasis on a slightly different theoretical approach.

which institutionalized respect for the rights of political minorities to try to become a majority must exist. In particular, political minorities in a liberal democracy must be given the means of contestation—the right to try to convince others of the rightness of their positions. Setting up institutions of majority rule turns out to be a comparatively simple task; ensuring the right of unpopular political minorities to compete for political power turns out to be far more difficult.

Without guarantees of the right of all to participate in politics, the "marketplace of ideas" cannot function effectively. The idea of a marketplace is that anyone can put forth a product—an idea—for political "consumers" to consider. The success of the idea is determined by the level of support freely given in the market. The market encourages deliberation, through which superior ideas are found to be superior, and through which the flaws of bad ideas are exposed for all to see (almost as if guided by an invisible hand).[4] Liberal political philosophers (like J. S. Mill) have long been attracted to this marketplace notion, and many consider it an essential element of democratic governance.

Many instances exist in which lack of confidence in the effectiveness of the marketplace of ideas has stimulated governments to place restrictions on the potential entrants to the arena. Some political systems prohibit, for instance, political parties based on religion, others ban all political parties not based on a particular religion. "Extremist" ideas are banned in some systems (as in laws prohibiting Holocaust denials), just as "radical" political parties are prohibited from participating in other systems (e.g. fascist parties in Germany). American policy makers in 1954 (and policy makers throughout much of the world as well) apparently had so little confidence in the ability of ordinary people to consider and reject communism that they banned communists from putting their ideas forward for consideration.[5] Perhaps most common throughout the world today, governments that have become accustomed to political power often seek to prohibit opposition groups from participating in the marketplace of ideas.[6] Without a willingness to put up with all ideologies seeking to compete for the hearts and minds of the citizenry the market is likely to fail. Thus, a fairly simple theory is that democracies require the free and open debate of political differences, and such debate can only take place where political tolerance prevails.

Political tolerance in a democracy requires that all political ideas (and the groups holding them) get the same access to the marketplace of ideas as the access legally extended to the ideas dominating the system. This definition obviously precludes any form of violence and therefore I make no claim that political tolerance extends

---

[4] I do not discount the value of simply allowing all ideas—right and wrong—to have their say, to have what procedural justice scholars refer to as "voice" (e.g. Tyler and Mitchell 1994; Tyler et al. 1997). Procedural justice theories posit that allowing groups voice enhances the legitimacy of the democratic process, especially among those unable to win within majoritarian arenas.

[5] See Gibson (1988) for examples of the types of restrictions put on Communists in the US during the 1940s and 1950s. See also Goldstein (1978).

[6] In the early party of the twenty-first century, examples of this phenomenon are too numerous to catalog. The efforts of Robert Mugabe to maintain his power in Zimbabwe provide an excellent exemplar.

to the right of terrorists to engage in terror. It may, however, protect the speech rights of terrorists, or, more precisely, those who advocate terrorism (e.g. defenders or advocates of suicide bombing).[7] The liberal democratic theory of political tolerance does not protect many forms of non-political expression, such as pornography (except as enlisted in the service of politics) and most types of commercial speech. It does however extend the right of contestation to deeply unpopular ideas, such as the need for a violent revolution or racism or Communism or radical Islam.

Whenever the definition of tolerance is considered, critics question whether certain types of "extreme" speech must be protected. These discussions are useful in principle, but not in practice. From the point-of-view of empirical research on tolerance, the controversies that emerge do not have to do with the most extreme and unusual forms of speech, but rather with the contestation rights of relatively innocuous ideas. In the case of the United States, for instance, even in the twenty-first century, 48 percent of the American people prefer that atheists (someone who is against all religion and churches) be denied the right to hold a public demonstration (see Gibson 2005c). Similar findings have been reported from a Polish survey in 1993 (Karpov 1999, 1536). Only after ordinary people come to tolerate a range of even slightly unorthodox ideas should research then focus on tolerance of the views of the most extreme members of society.

Liberal democratic theory also provides some guidance as to what sorts of activities must be guaranteed to political minorities: Actions and behaviors related to efforts to persuade people and to compete for political power must be put up with. This might include giving public speeches, running candidates for public office, or even publicizing a group by removing trash from the freeways (and claiming credit for doing with so with a publicly erected sign). Obviously, illegal activity need not be countenanced, even if I acknowledge that the line between legal and illegal is often thin, given the power and propensity of majorities to criminalize political activities by the minority.[8]

This theory of the marketplace of ideas anticipates two important (and interconnected) restraints on freedom. First, as I have already mentioned, many fear that the government, typically under the guise of regulation, will usurp power and deny the expression of ideas threatening to the status quo (i.e. the power of the government of the day). Examples of such abuses of minority rights to participation are too widespread to even begin to catalog.

A second constraint on freedom is more subtle: It originates in the political culture of a polity—the beliefs, values, attitudes, and behaviors of ordinary citizens.

---

[7] As I write this, the British are considering new proposals to ban pure speech in support of such activities as suicide bombing. It remains to be seen whether such legislation will be acceptable to British judges and the British people.

[8] This issue is actually a bit more complicated given that political minorities typically need access to specific tactics (e.g. public demonstrations) that the majority does not require or find useful. Thus, regimes sometimes invoke political equality when they ban all demonstrations, even if the effect of such bans falls quite disproportionately on different segments of the political community.

Restraints on freedom can certainly emanate from public policy; but they can also be found in subtle demands for conformity within a society's culture. To the extent that ordinary citizens are intolerant of views challenging mainstream thought, the expression of such viewpoints is likely to generate sanctions and costs. This can in turn create what Noelle-Neumann (1984) has referred to as a "spiral of silence:" A dynamic process in which those holding minority viewpoints increasingly learn about how rare their views are, thereby leading to silence, which in turn makes the ideas seem to be even less widely held, and therefore more dangerous or costly to express. Perhaps the most significant legacy of McCarthyism in the United States was not the limitations imposed on communists and their fellow travelers—legal limitations that were often severe and included imprisonment—but instead was the creation of a "Silent Generation," a cohort unwilling to express views that might be considered controversial or unpopular. And, to complete the circle, mass political intolerance can be a useful form of political capital for those who would in turn enact repressive legislation. To the extent that a political culture emphasizes conformity and penalizes those with contrarian ideas, little tolerance exists, and the likelihood of political repression is high.

1.1 Measuring Political Intolerance

Tolerance thus requires that citizens and governments put up with ideas that are thought to be objectionable. Two components of this definition require further consideration: Which ideas must be put up with, and which activities must be allowed? The answers to both of these questions are intimately related not just to the conceptualization of tolerance, but to its operationalization as well. From the viewpoint of empirical studies of political tolerance, measurement issues of whom and what have become concerns of great importance.[9]

In Stouffer's era, the nature of the perceived threat to the dominant ideology of the time was clear: It came from communists, and their "fellow travelers."[10] Consequently, tolerance questions were framed around the right of communists to compete for political power. To the extent that it is obvious which groups are objects of intolerance in a society, then at least part of the job of measuring mass political intolerance is easy.

For instance, the largest amount of data on political tolerance has been collected by the General Social Survey (GSS) in the United States. This survey, begun in the early 1970s and continuing through today, routinely asks about five groups: someone who is against all churches and religion (atheists), a man who admits he is a communist, a man who admits he is a homosexual, a person who advocates doing away with elections and letting the military run the country, and a person who believes that

---

[9] On the measurement of tolerance and other democratic values see Finkel, Sigelman, and Humphries (1999).

[10] Sullivan et al. (1985) make the same argument about Israel.

blacks are genetically inferior. These particular groups are derived from Stouffer's research and are assumed to be representative today of the fringes of the American ideological continua.

The obvious limitation of these questions is that the replies of those who are themselves atheists, homosexuals, communists, racists, and militarists cannot be treated as valid measures of political tolerance.[11] The flaw with the Stouffer approach to measuring political intolerance was discovered by John Sullivan and his colleagues. Tolerance is putting up with that with which one disagrees. Consequently, it makes no sense to ask one who is a communist whether communists should be allowed to make speeches, etc.[12] Sullivan, Piereson, and Marcus (1982) argued that a valid measure of intolerance requires an "objection precondition," by which they meant that the stimulus presented to every respondent (the ideology or group representing the ideology) must be objectionable. To achieve this, the respondents must be allowed to name a highly disliked group; the researcher does not specify which groups are asked about; rather the respondent must be allowed to designate the group. So as to introduce some degree of comparability across respondents, each is asked to identify the group he or she *dislikes the most*; tolerance questions are then asked about this group. The technique has been named the "least-liked" measurement approach, even though this is a slight misnomer in that the group asked about is actually the most disliked, not, strictly speaking, the least liked.[13]

Some controversies continue to plague the measurement literature, however. Not everyone is convinced of the value of the least-liked approach, at least as it was initially developed by Sullivan, Piereson, and Marcus (see, for examples, McClosky and Brill 1983; Gibson 1986; Sniderman et al. 1989; Chong 1993; and Hurwitz and Mondak 2002). Perhaps the most potent critique of the approach is that it fails to tell us much about the "breadth" of intolerance, by which I mean the range of differences in ideas that is not tolerated. Perhaps many people can name a particular group/idea that they find uniquely offensive (in the twentieth century context, the Ku Klux Klan or Nazis, for instance), and owing to the extraordinary nature of the group/idea, they would not tolerate it. At the same time, however, the category of not-tolerated-ideas/groups is limited to this most extreme instance. Other citizens express intolerance for their most disliked group, but are also willing not to tolerate many other groups that are disliked less than the most disliked. This gives these citizens a broad range of groups, perhaps covering a considerable expanse of ideological territory, that they will not put up with. Most Americans in the 1950s would not tolerate political activity by communists; but most also would not tolerate political activity by socialists, atheists,

---

[11] Note that Kuklinski and Cobb (1997) argue on the basis of a "list experiment" that roughly one-half of white males in the American South are racist.

[12] Scholars have tried innovative methods for correcting for such bias (e.g. Wilson 1994; Mondak and Sanders 2003), but it seems likely that the utility of asking questions about these groups will continue to diminish over time.

[13] One important drawback of the least-liked technology is that it is quite costly in terms of questions and interview time and is difficult to administer via telephone interviews.

and even "integrationists."[14] The "breadth" of intolerance signifies the minimum amount of antipathy that must exist before a respondent is willing not to tolerate. Unfortunately, we know little about the breadth of intolerance of individuals or countries throughout the world.[15]

Another measurement issue has recently been raised by Mondak and Sanders (2003), who have argued that it is useful under some circumstances to conceptualize tolerance as a dichotomy: people are either tolerant (perfectly so, allowing everything by everyone), or they are intolerant (although Mondak and Sanders recognize that the degree of *intolerance* may vary). Their argument is part of an effort to rescue the tolerance measures employed in the General Social Survey (GSS) and elsewhere (e.g. the Polish General Social Survey—see Karpov 1999). Gibson (2005a, 2005b) has shown that this argument is neither conceptually nor empirically useful, primarily because nearly all people can imagine a group or an activity that they would prefer not be allowed. The number of perfectly tolerant people (allow all groups all activities) is too small to be of any empirical consequence. Moreover, extant cross-national research has shown that most countries are in no danger whatsoever of approaching extreme levels of tolerance! For example, Peffley and Rohrschneider (2003) refer to levels of tolerance in the seventeen countries they study as "a scarce commodity" (248) and "abysmally low" (254), and generally conclude that "intolerance is the norm, tolerance the exception" (248). Most scholars seem to believe that tolerance is a continuum that varies from those who would place fewer restrictions of objectionable ideas and actions to those who would place greater restrictions.

The least-liked approach to measuring intolerance serves well those who are primarily interested in investigating individual differences among people. The technique is less well suited for studying the politics of civil liberties in a society. It one wants to know, for instance, whether there is widespread support for banning a particular idea from the marketplace of ideas, then establishing an objection precondition for each respondent may not be necessary (e.g. Barnum and Sullivan 1989). And, as I have noted, in some societies (e.g. Israel) there is little ambiguity about who the enemy of the status quo is; in such cases, the least-liked technology may not be necessary.[16]

---

[14] See Stouffer (1955). For an engaging and insightful analysis of how race and anti-communism got conflated in Texas in the 1950s (and in Houston in particular) see Carleton (1985).

[15] To address this issue, one must ask questions about not just the most disliked group, but many different groups. So, for instance, the World Values Survey asked about only a single group, thus providing no information on breadth (Peffley and Rohrschneider 2003). Gibson and Gouws (2003), on the other hand, asked about several groups, giving the authors at least some purchase on the breadth question. Providing a spatial analysis of the breadth of ideological difference deemed legitimate in a society (the breadth of the "loyal opposition") seems to be an important but difficult research question for the field.

[16] Perhaps the only systematic comparison of the least-liked measures of intolerance with the fixed-group approach is the analysis of Gibson 1992b. The general conclusion of that research is that, at least under the circumstances of the United States in 1987, the two approaches generate similarly valid and reliable measures.

1.2 Pluralistic Intolerance

The least-liked measurement approach is closely connected to one of the most important ideas to emerge from the tolerance literature: the theory of pluralistic intolerance.
Sullivan, Pierson, and Marcus (1982) have argued that lack of consensus on who
the enemy is—pluralistic intolerance—can neutralize even widespread intolerance.
When everyone picks a different "least-liked" group, it may mean that there is insufficient agreement for intolerance to be mobilized into political repression. When
intolerance is pluralistic, it is dispersed and may be benign. Indeed, their theory
strongly emphasizes the need to identify the factors contributing to the *focusing* of
intolerance, for it is focused intolerance that is dangerous and pernicious (see Sullivan
et al. 1985).

Unfortunately, little rigorous research at the system level (either over time or cross-
nationally) has investigated the theory of pluralistic intolerance. In their research
on South Africa, Gibson and Gouws (2003) discovered that intolerance can be both
focused and pluralistic, in the sense that many groups, of various ideological affinities,
may not be tolerated by people. Gibson (1998a), on the other hand, asserts that
intolerance is focused on the far right wing in Russia (see also Gibson and Duch
1993). More research needs to be conducted to determine the "breadth" of tolerance
in different societies—the range of ideas that people believe can be legitimately
expressed in a society.

1.3 What Tolerance is Not: Intolerance and Intergroup Prejudice

One might naturally expect that intolerance and prejudice are simply different sides of
the same coin, and that the literatures on political tolerance and intergroup conflict
and prejudice are closely integrated.[17] In fact, that is not so. To an amazing degree,
these two bodies of research rarely intersect. That this is so is one of the major enigmas
in the tolerance literature (see Gibson 2006).

Stenner has strongly argued that intolerance and prejudice are cut from the same
cloth. She asserts: "This work began with the conviction that racial, political and
moral intolerance, normally studied in isolation, are really kindred spirits: primarily driven by the same fundamental predispositions, fueled by the same motives,
exacerbated by the same fears" (2005, 325). Yet, to date, only partial and inconclusive data have been produced specifically documenting that political intolerance
(especially as measured by the least-liked technology) and intergroup prejudice are
intercorrelated to any significant degree. For instance, Gibson (2006a) has shown
that the two concepts are entirely unrelated in both Russia and South Africa. Gibson's
argument is that expressing prejudice toward one's political enemies is simply not

---

[17] For a useful study of interethnic intolerance see Massey, Hodson, and Sekulić? 1999. See also
Gibson 2004a.

a precondition for political intolerance. What groups stand for is a sociotropic factor, which differs greatly from the perceived characteristics of the individual members of the group. For many, it is not necessary to ascribe a series of negative stereotypes to those with whom political disagreements are severe.[18] It is therefore important not to *assume* that intolerance and prejudice are necessarily cut from the same cloth, and to investigate the relationship carefully in future empirical research.

As I have noted, perhaps one reason why intolerance and prejudice are not always interconnected has to do with the highly influential role of threat perceptions in shaping political intolerance. The strongest predictor of intolerance is the feeling that a group is threatening. Perceptions of threat may be based upon prejudice, but they need not be, and one can well imagine that many perceptions of group threat are based on objective and realistic perceptions that have nothing to do with prejudice. One might find some strains of Islam threatening, for instance, not out of mistaken generalizations about Muslims but rather out of opposition to those who would not put a wall of separation between religion and politics (e.g. Sniderman and Hagendoorn 2007). Secularists and atheists may view a variety of religious groups as threatening, without any degree of prejudice. And conversely, one can easily hold prejudiced views toward groups seen as impotent, and hence not threatening. For instance, it would not be surprising to find that many hold prejudiced views of members of the neo-Nazis today, while believing that the group poses little threat directly owing to the ascribed characteristics (e.g. "neo-Nazis are too stupid to be threatening").

Finally, political tolerance has to do with what one expects of the state, not of oneself. It is easy to imagine the citizen who would fight strongly to protect the rights of a despised political minority, while at the same time being unwilling to share a meal with a member of the group or have her daughter marry a group member. In a democratic society, keeping a great deal of social distance from a group is not incompatible with tolerating its political activities.

Thus, extant theory provides many insights into how political tolerance can be conceptualized and operationalized. Tolerance requires putting up with political activity by groups whose ideas are repugnant. It does so under the liberal democratic theory that all ideas must be free to compete within the marketplace. The intolerance of ordinary people is important not just because it can fuel repressive legislation, but also because it can contribute to a climate of conformity that sanctions the expression of minority viewpoints. As a consequence, social scientists have devoted considerable resources to measuring mass political intolerance, and then to investigating its origins. It is to this last point of emphasis that I turn next.

---

[18] Conversely, Sullivan, Piereson, and Marcus (1982, 4) argue that: "Tolerance...is not merely the absence of prejudice... The prejudiced person may in fact be tolerant, if he understands his prejudices and proceeds to permit the expression of those things toward which he is prejudiced." They conclude: "Thus, the prejudiced person may be either tolerant or intolerant, depending on what action he or she is prepared to take politically" (1982, 5).

2 WHAT CAUSES SOME CITIZENS TO BE TOLERANT BUT OTHERS NOT?

Perhaps one of the most widely investigated questions in the tolerance literature has to do with the etiology of intolerance at the individual level. Many have contributed to identifying predictors of intolerance, ranging from Sniderman's work (1975) on self-esteem and social learning, to Sullivan, Piereson, and Marcus (1982) on threat perceptions, democratic values, and psychological insecurity, to Stenner's book (2005) on the personality trait authoritarianism. Nearly all agree that some sort of closed-mindedness or psychological rigidity contributes to intolerance, even if the precise label attached to the concept varies across researchers.

In virtually all studies, threat perceptions are one of the strongest predictors of intolerance. Not surprisingly, those who are more threatened by their political enemies are less likely to tolerate them. However, a number of surprises are associated with the threat–tolerance relationship. The strongest predictor of intolerance is the feeling that a group is threatening, but, ironically perhaps, it is not the direct threat to one's own personal well-being (egocentric threat perceptions) that is crucial, but instead perceived threat to the group and/or society (sociotropic threat perceptions) that is so likely to generate intolerance (e.g. Gibson and Gouws 2003; Davis and Silver 2004). Moreover, several studies have now reported that the perceived efficacy of a group (its power or potential for power) has few implications for the other aspects of threat perceptions or for political intolerance (e.g. Marcus et al. 1995; Gibson and Gouws 2003). It seems natural to suggest that intolerance flourishes where the threat of groups and ideas is highest, yet the various processes involved have been found to be fairly complex and the simple relationship does not typically exist.[19]

It is also paradoxical that, even though one might expect perceptions of threat to be shaped by personality characteristics, in fact little convincing evidence has been adduced on this point. The most concentrated effort to identify the personality precursors to threat is the work of Marcus et al. (1995), although many scholars have worked on this problem. If in fact threat perceptions are based on realistic factors (e.g. realistic group conflict) then there is no necessary requirement for psychological variables to be implicated. On the other hand, to the extent that groups represent sociotropic threats, one might well hypothesize that individual personality character-istics (e.g. authoritarianism and chauvinistic nationalism) are activated. Unraveling these relationships—or lack of relationships—is a research problem of considerable importance for the field.

---

[19] That sociotropic threat perceptions are the most influential type of threat implies that social identity concerns may play an important role in this process. That hypothesis has been investigated, but the results are too complicated to consider in this essay. For research on the role of group attachments in shaping identities see Gibson and Gouws (2000), and Gibson (2006b).

Some of the most interesting work on this score posits an interactive effect of psychological attributes and external environmental factors. No research better demonstrates this effect than that of Feldman (e.g. Feldman and Stenner 1997; Feldman 2003), who has shown that authoritarianism and perceptions of environmental stress interact in creating intolerance. Similarly, Gibson (2002) has shown that Russian intolerance reacts to their perceptions of political and economic stress, and crime in particular. Gibson and Gouws (2003) have also documented that perceptions of an out-of-control crime rate among South Africans can fuel the anxiety that gives rise to enhanced perceptions of threat (see also Huddy et al. 2005). On the other hand, this process is far from automatic—Gibson and Howard (2007) have demonstrated that despite all of the factors being in alignment for Jews to be scapegoated in Russia during the 1990s, in fact anti-Semitic attacks on Jews (formal or informal) failed to materialize. Learning who the enemy is requires a theory of blame, and under many social and political circumstances it is not at all clear who is to blame. The whole process of attributing blame and calculating threat from groups is at present poorly understood.

In the original model of the origins of intolerance, Sullivan, Piereson, and Marcus (1982) demonstrate that tolerance is connected to a more general set of beliefs about democracy (even though the slippage between general commitments to democracy and specific applications to the rights of disliked groups is considerable). Gibson, Duch, and Tedin (1992, see also Gibson 1995) have expanded this research to consider more specifically the connection between tolerance and support for democratic institutions and processes (see also Finkel and Ernst 2005). At least in Russia, such interrelationships are not strong, largely owing to the difficulty of embracing tolerance of hated groups and ideas. In formerly dictatorial systems, people were denied majority rule; consequently, the majoritarian aspects of democracy are readily embraced since they lead to the empowerment of the people. Extending these rights to unpopular minorities requires more intellectual effort than many can muster. Tolerance may be the most difficult democratic value of all; only among those with a fully articulated democratic belief system—which is especially uncommon among people not repeatedly exposed to democratic institutions and processes—do we see close connections between tolerance and the other democratic values.

2.1 Can Intolerance Be Changed?

Little research has directly investigated change in political tolerance over time. A couple of studies have shown intolerance to be sensitive to exogenous environmental stress such as crime and social unrest (e.g. Gibson and Gouws 2003; Gibson 2002; Feldman and Stenner 1997), but micro-level analysis of change is as rare as it is important. One of the most interesting findings to emerge from this limited literature is that, while it is clear that threat perceptions cause intolerance, it may also be the case that intolerance causes threat perceptions (Gibson forthcoming). That is, because tolerant people are in some sense more secure, they are not predisposed to see their political competitors as particularly threatening. It may be that a "spiral of tolerance" can be created in the sense that tolerance breeds lower perceptions of group threat, which breeds more tolerance, etc.

A sizeable body of literature exists on "civic education" (e.g. Nie, Junn, and Stehlik-Barry 1996), and tolerance is one value that researchers seek to foster through education and training programs. Successes (based on rigorous data analysis) have been few and far beyond (e.g. Avery et al. 1993). Recently, efforts have been made to evaluate the programs of the United States government to enhance support for democratic institutions and processes, including political tolerance, but the early results have not been very promising, especially as concerns tolerance (e.g. Finkel 2002, 2003; Finkel and Ernest 2005). It may well be that basic orientations toward foreign and threatening ideas are shaped at an early age, and, although environmental conditions can ameliorate or exacerbate such propensities, core attitudes and values are fairly resistant to change.

One other way in which scholars have studied change in intolerance is through the so-called sober second thought experiment (e.g. Gibson 1998b). Stouffer (1955) long ago theorized that tolerance is a difficult and cognitively demanding position to adopt (see also McClosky and Brill 1983). Indeed, the conventional view among scholars is that tolerance requires deliberation and that in the absence of such deliberation, intolerance likely results, owing to the emotional basis of the response to threatening stimuli (but see Kuklinski et al. 1991). When people take the time and energy to deliberate, they often can discern the costs of intolerance, in addition to the benefits of intolerance that are usually so readily calculable. Thus, one knows immediately that "bad ideas must be repressed," but determining that such repression may actually backfire (e.g. by making the bad ideas more attractive simply because they are forbidden) is a more arduous task. Thus, the conventional hypothesis is that deliberation enhances tolerance. Much of the contemporary literature on deliberative democracy makes this assumption, either implicitly or explicitly.

Empirical research has not been especially kind to this expectation. Perhaps most interesting is the finding that tolerance is considerably more pliable than intolerance. For instance, Gibson (1998b) and others (e.g. Peffley, Knigge, and Hurwitz 2001; Sniderman et al. 1996; Marcus et al. 1995; and Kuklinski et al. 1991) have shown that tolerance and intolerance differ in their pliability—the tolerant can be more readily persuaded to abandon their tolerance than can the intolerant be convinced to become tolerant. For instance, based on the Sober Second Thought Experiment, Gibson reports (1998b, 828) that, while 74.1 percent of intolerant Russians did not budge from their intolerance when presented with three reasons to tolerate, only 44.8 percent of the tolerant remained tolerant when exposed to three pro-intolerance counter-arguments. Other research reports similar asymmetries. This finding has been replicated in both South Africa (Gibson and Gouws 2003) and the United States (Gibson 1996). The susceptibility of tolerance to being trumped by other values is apparently high since democratic belief systems (within which tolerance is embedded) often contain values that conflict. For instance, the desire to protect innocent and weak groups from slander may override a commitment to free speech for all political ideas.[20] Unfortunately, research to date has not been very successful in identifying ideas and arguments that might convert the intolerant into embracing political tolerance. In any event, this asymmetry in the potency of tolerance and intolerance is a finding so important that it warrants considerable additional investigation.[21]

As in so many areas of the social sciences, static research dominates. Scholars use cross-sectional analysis to make inferences about change, and macro-level analysis (e.g. cohort analysis and pooled cross-sections) provide additional inferential leverage. However, such analyses can also be highly misleading in that micro-level change is often obscured by macro-level appearance of stasis. The tolerance subfield is almost entirely dominated by cross-sectional research. Until more dynamic theories and data sets are produced, a full understanding of the origins of intolerance will remain elusive and incomplete.

3 WHAT ARE THE CONSEQUENCES OF MASS POLITICAL INTOLERANCE?

Does intolerance matter? This question is difficult to address since it is bound up in complex theories about the role of public opinion in shaping public policy. Moreover, intolerance probably matters most within the context of specific disputes, as in the dispute in Skokie, Illinois, over the rights of American Nazis to hold a demonstration (e.g. Gibson and Bingham 1985). Indeed, one tradition in research on the consequences of intolerance is to pursue what Sniderman (1993) calls "firehouse studies:" studies that respond to specific civil liberties controversies (e.g. Gibson 1987, Gibson and Tedin 1988). Such research is difficult to mount, however, since disputes over civil liberties rarely develop with the periodicity or predictability of other political events, such as elections. As a consequence, some research relies upon hypothetical scenarios to investigate the behavioral implications of intolerance (e.g. Marcus et al. 1995) and to consider the role of contextual factors in shaping intolerance (e.g. Gibson and Gouws 2001).

Another line of research involves determining whether intolerant opinion has the sort of characteristics likely to make it pernicious. Gibson's (1998a) study of

---

[20] An obvious example of free speech concerns being trumped is legislation and policy against so-called hate speech. For a very interesting study of the impact of hate speech legislation on the intolerance of college students, see Chong (2006).

[21] This asymmetry may also extend to the connection between attitudes and actual behavior, with intolerance more likely than tolerance to produce action. See Gibson and Bingham (1985); Barnum and Sullivan (1990); Marcus et al. (1995); and Gibson (2006a). Since studies of actual behavior are relatively rare, however, less confidence should be vested in this finding, as compared to the findings on persuadability.

Russian opinion adopts this perspective, focusing on whether intolerance is principled (bound up within an ideology), focused, "empowered" in the sense that the intolerant believe their views are in the majority, and common among the more politically relevant subsection of the mass public ("opinion leaders"). In the Russian case, Gibson concludes that mass political intolerance is in fact potentially consequential for the rights of unpopular political minorities.

Connecting mass political intolerance to specific public policies has proven difficult. Gibson, for instance, has shown (1988; see also Page and Shapiro 1983) that repressive state policies against Communists adopted in the 1950s were not a direct consequence of mass public opinion (even if policy was related to elite opinion). On the other hand, there was a connection between mass intolerance and repressive policies during the era of Vietnam War dissent, but the relationship is not as expected. States with opinion that was more tolerant were *more likely* to adopt repressive legislation (Gibson 1989). Gibson shows that tolerance was related to the prevalence of protest, and that protest generated a repressive response. Thus, these relationships are complicated.

As I suggested, a key process by which intolerance affects political freedom in a polity may have to do with cultural norms that encourage or discourage political disagreement. Gibson (1992a) has shown that intolerance within a family does indeed constrain political discussion and affect the extent to which people feel free to express their political views. And a growing body of literature suggests that political homogeneity in social networks reinforces political intolerance (Mutz 2002). Indeed, because networks tend so commonly to be homogeneous, many of the key assumptions of theories of deliberative democracy turn out to be challenged by the empirical evidence available (but see Huckfeldt, Johnson, and Sprague 2005).

3.1 Political Intolerance in Times of Crisis

The attack on the United States on 9/11/2001 by Muslim fanatics ushered in a new, but not entirely unfamiliar, era in American politics. Throughout American history, during times of crisis, civil liberties have been either suspended or limited in important ways (e.g. Epstein et al. 2005). No better chronicling of these episodes has been reported than the encyclopedic work of Goldstein (1978).

The policy response to the 9/11 attack is therefore not unprecedented. What is new, however, is the ability of scholars to launch systematic research efforts to understand how citizens come to balance expectations of personal and societal security with the demands of tolerance and individual liberty. Davis and Silver (2004), for instance, show that people make tradeoffs between liberty and order in arriving at positions on civil liberties policies, and that these tradeoffs are sensitive to several moderating influences (e.g. the degree of trust in government). Undoubtedly, the nature of the tradeoffs varies over time, as external threats wax and wane. Unfortunately, little is understood about the details of this dynamic process.

A familiar complaint against all subfields in public opinion is that attitudes are not important because they do not influence actual behavior (e.g. Weissberg 1998). In general, meta-analyses routinely show this charge to be false (Kraus 1995). The limited research addressing this issue in the tolerance literature also suggests that civil liberties attitudes do indeed influence citizens' political behavior in actual civil liberties conflicts (e.g. Gibson and Bingham 1985). Nonetheless, the political tolerance subfield would undoubtedly profit from greater attention to the consequences of mass political intolerance. In doing so, we ought to cast our nets broadly, remembering that the failure of citizens to put up with views with which they do not agree can influence feelings of political freedom and willingness to discuss and debate (Gibson 1992a), as well as public policy at both the local and national levels.

4 Concluding Comments

The study of political intolerance is a vast enterprise at both the micro- and macro-levels, and research on political tolerance constitutes a subfield much too large to be able to be comprehensively surveyed in a short chapter such as this. I have barely mentioned philosophical or normative studies of intolerance (e.g. Bollinger 1986), detailed studies of how individuals select their targets have not been considered (e.g. stereotype threat, Golebiowska 1996), many case studies of outbreaks of intolerance have not been addressed here (e.g. Strum 1999); and studies of intolerance in nations outside the United States have been slighted (e.g. Sullivan et al. 1985). Nor have I reviewed important issues such as how and why members of the mass public and elites differ on issues of tolerance (see Sullivan et al. 1993), or issues such as whether religion and religiosity and intolerance are inextricably interconnected (e.g. see Karpov 1999). Furthermore, new issues are constantly emerging: It appears inevitable that the neurology of threat perceptions and intolerance will be a hot topic for future research (e.g. Marcus, Wood, and Theiss-Morse 1998). Those interested in pursuing research on the myriad dimensions of political tolerance will find a fresh and vibrant literature on nearly all specific research questions, even if many such questions are beyond the scope of this chapter.

Instead, in this chapter, I have attempted three things. First, I have tried to show that, as a concept, political tolerance derives its rigor and specificity from liberal democratic theory. Political tolerance does not require that everything be put up with under all circumstances; instead, it only requires free and unfettered entry for all views to the marketplace of ideas. Second, I have demonstrated that the origins of intolerance at the micro-level are reasonably well understood, even if some very important enigmas still exist. Intolerance flows most regularly from perceptions of group threat, even if we understand little about how some groups become threatening while others are not. Finally, intolerance has important political consequences.

The simplistic view that intolerance directly fuels repressive public policy does not warrant much support, even if intolerance, when having characteristics rendering it pernicious, can on occasion be mobilized by political entrepreneurs. The intolerance of citizens can also affect the nature of deliberation and disagreement in society, and therefore constrain the market even without direct government intervention.

Even if we understand something of the etiology of intolerance and something of the consequence it has for democratic development, a host of important unanswered questions exist. My hope is that some might be stimulated by this chapter to pursue these questions further, and thereby contribute to creating a more tolerant world.

References

AVERY, P. et al. 1993. *Tolerance For Diversity of Beliefs: A Secondary Curriculum Unit.* Boulder, Colo.: Social Science Education Consortium.

BACHRACH, P. 1967. *The Theory of Democratic Elitism: A Critique.* Boston: Little, Brown.

BARNUM, D. and SULLIVAN, J. 1989. Attitudinal tolerance and political freedom in Britain. *British Journal of Political Science,* 19 (1): 136–46.

———— 1990. The elusive foundations of political freedom in Britain and the United States. *Journal of Politics,* 52 (3): 719–39.

BOLLINGER, L. 1986. *The Tolerant Society: Freedom of Speech and Extremist Speech in America.* New York: Oxford University Press.

CARLETON, D. 1985. *Read Scare!: Right-Wing Hysteria, Fifties Fanaticism, and their Legacy in Texas.* Austin: Texas Monthly Press.

CHONG, D. 1993. How people think, reason and feel about rights and liberties. *American Journal of Political Science,* 37 (3): 867–99.

—— 2006. Free speech and multiculturalism in and out of the academy. *Political Psychology,* 27 (1): 29–54.

DAHL, R. A. 1989. *Democracy and Its Critics.* New Haven: Yale University Press.

DAVIS, D. and SILVER, B. 2004. Civil liberties vs. security: public opinion in the context of the terrorist attacks on America. *American Journal of Political Science,* 48 (1): 28–46.

EPSTEIN, L., Ho, D., KING, G., and SEGAL, J. 2005. The Supreme Court during times of crisis: how war affects only non-war cases. *New York University Law Review,* 80 (1): 1–116.

FELDMAN, S. 2003. Enforcing social conformity: a theory of authoritarianism. *Political Psychology,* 24 (1): 41–74.

—— and STENNER, K. 1997. Perceived threat and authoritarianism. *Political Psychology,* 18 (4): 741–70.

FINKEL, S. 2002. Civic education and the mobilization of political participation in developing democracies. *Journal of Politics,* 64 (4): 994–1020.

—— 2003. Can democracy be taught? *Journal of Democracy,* 14 (4): 137–51.

—— and ERNST, H. 2005. Civic education in post-Apartheid South Africa: alternative paths to the development of knowledge and democratic values. *Political Psychology,* 26 (3): 333–64.

—— SIGELMAN, L., and HUMPHRIES, S. 1999. Democratic values and political tolerance. Pp. 203–96 in *Measures of Political Attitudes,* ed. J. Robinson et al. New York: Academic Press.

GIBSON, J. 1986. Pluralistic intolerance in America: a reconsideration. *American Politics Quarterly*, 14: 267–93.

——1987. Homosexuals and the Ku Klux Klan: a contextual analysis of political intolerance. *Western Political Quarterly*, 40 (3): 427–48.

——1988. Political intolerance and political repression during the McCarthy Red Scare. *American Political Science Review*, 82 (2): 511–29.

——1989. The policy consequences of political intolerance: political repression during the Vietnam War era. *Journal of Politics*, 51 (1): 13–35.

——1992*a*. The political consequences of intolerance: cultural conformity and political freedom. *American Political Science Review*, 86 (2): 338–56.

——1992*b*. Alternative measures of political tolerance: must tolerance be 'least-liked'? *American Journal of Political Science*, 36: 560–77.

——1995. The resilience of mass support for democratic institutions and processes in the nascent Russian and Ukrainian democracies. Pp. 53–111 in *Political Culture and Civil Society in Russia and the New States of Eurasia*, ed. V. Tismaneanu. Armonk, NY: M. E. Sharpe.

——1996. The paradoxes of political tolerance in processes of democratisation. *Politikon: South African Journal of Political Studies* 23 (2): 5–21.

——1998*a*. Putting up with fellow Russians: an analysis of political tolerance in the fledgling Russian democracy. *Political Research Quarterly*, 51 (1): 37–68.

——1998*b*. A sober second thought: an experiment in persuading Russians to tolerate. *American Journal of Political Science*, 42: 819–50.

——2002. Becoming tolerant? Short-term changes in Russian political culture. *British Journal of Political Science*, 32: 309–34.

——2004. *Overcoming Apartheid: Can Truth Reconcile a Divided Nation?* New York: Russell Sage Foundation.

——2005*a*. On the nature of tolerance: dichotomous or continuous? *Political Behavior*, 27 (4): 313–23.

——2005*b*. Parsimony in the study of tolerance and intolerance. *Political Behavior*, 27 (4): 339–45.

——2005*c*. Political intolerance in the United States, 2005. Unpublished paper, Washington University in St Louis.

——2006*a*. Enigmas of intolerance: fifty years after Stouffer's *Communism, Conformity, and Civil Liberties*. *Perspectives on Politics*, 4 (1): 21–34.

——2006*b*. Do strong group identities fuel intolerance? Evidence from the South African Case. *Political Psychology*, 27 (5): 665–705.

——forthcoming. Is intolerance incorrigible? An analysis of change among Russians. In *Toleration on Trial*, ed. I. Creppell, R. Hardin, and S. Macedo. Lanham, Md.: Lexington Books.

——and BINGHAM, R. 1985. *Civil Liberties and Nazis: The Skokie Free Speech Controversy*. New York: Praeger.

——and DUCH, R. 1993. Political intolerance in the USSR: the distribution and etiology of mass opinion. *Comparative Political Studies*, 26: 286–329.

————and TEDIN, K. 1992. Democratic values and the transformation of the Soviet Union. *Journal of Politics*, 54 (2): 329–71.

——and GOUWS, A. 2000. Social identities and political intolerance: linkages within the South African mass public. *American Journal of Political Science*, 44 (2): 278–92.

————2001. Making tolerance judgments: the effects of context, local and national. *Journal of Politics*, 63 (4): 1067–90.

GIBSON, J. and GOUWS, A. 2003. *Overcoming Intolerance in South Africa: Experiments in Democratic Persuasion.* New York: Cambridge University Press.

—— and HOWARD, M. M. 2007. Russian anti-Semitism and the scapegoating of Jews: The Dog That Didn't Bark? *British Journal of Political Science,* 37 (2, April): 193–224.

—— and TEDIN, K. 1988. The etiology of intolerance of homosexual politics. *Social Science Quarterly,* 69 (3): 587–604.

GOLEBIOWSKA, E. 1996. The "pictures in our heads" and individual-targeted tolerance. *Journal of Politics,* 58 (4): 1010–34.

GOLDSTEIN, R. 1978. *Political Repression in Modern America.* Cambridge, Mass.: Schenkman.

HUCKFELDT, R., JOHNSON, P., and SPRAGUE, J. 2005. *Political Disagreement: The Survival of Diverse Opinions within Communications Networks.* New York: Cambridge University Press

HUDDY, L., FELDMAN, S., TABER, C., and LAHAV, G. 2005. Threat, anxiety, and support of antiterrorism policies. *American Journal of Political Science,* 49 (3): 593–608.

HURWITZ, J. and MONDAK, J. 2002. Democratic principles, discrimination and political intolerance. *British Journal of Political Science,* 32 (1): 93–118.

KARPOV, V. 1999. Religiosity and political tolerance in Poland. *Sociology of Religion,* 60 (4): 387–402.

KRAUS, S. 1995. Attitudes and the prediction of behavior: a meta-analysis of the empirical literature. *Personality and Social Psychology Bulletin,* 21: 58–75.

KUKLINSKI, J. and COBB, M. 1997. Racial attitudes and the "New South". *American Journal of Political Science,* 59 (2): 323–49.

—— RIGGLE, E., OTTATI, V., SCHWARZ, N., and WYER, R. JR. 1991. The cognitive and affective bases of political tolerance judgments. *American Journal of Political Science,* 35 (1): 1–27.

MCCLOSKY, H. and BRILL, A. 1983. *Dimensions of Tolerance: What Americans Think about Civil Liberties.* New York: Russell Sage Foundation.

MARCUS, G., WOOD, S., and THEISS-MORSE, E. 1998. Linking neuroscience to political intolerance and political judgment. *Politics and the Life Sciences* 17 (2): 165–78.

—— SULLIVAN, J., THEISS-MORSE, E., and WOOD, S. 1995. *With Malice Toward Some: How People Make Civil Liberties Judgments.* New York: Cambridge University Press.

MASSEY, G., HODSON, R., and SEKULIĆ, D. 1999. Ethnic enclaves and intolerance: the case of Yugoslavia. *Social Forces,* 78 (2): 669–91.

MONDAK, J. and SANDERS, M. 2003. Tolerance and intolerance, 1976–1998. *American Journal of Political Science,* 47 (3): 492–502.

MUTZ, D. 2002. Cross-cutting social networks: testing democratic theory in practice. *American Political Science Review,* 96 (1): 111–26.

NIE, N., JUNN, J., and STEHLIK-BARRY, K. 1996. *Education and Democratic Citizenship in America.* Chicago: University of Chicago Press.

NOELLE-NEUMANN, E. 1984. *The Spiral of Silence: Public Opinion, our Social Skin.* Chicago: University of Chicago Press.

PAGE, B. and SHAPIRO, R. 1983. Effects of public opinion on public policy. *American Political Science Review,* 77: 175–90.

PEFFLEY, M., KNIGGE, P., and HURWITZ, J. 2001. A multiple values model of political tolerance. *Political Research Quarterly,* 54 (2): 379–406.

—— and ROHRSCHNEIDER, R. 2003. Democratization and political tolerance in seventeen countries: a multi-level model of democratic learning. *Political Research Quarterly,* 56 (3): 243–57.

ROHRSCHNEIDER, R. 1996. Institutional learning versus value diffusion: the evolution of democratic values among parliamentarians in Eastern and Western Germany. *Journal of Politics*, 68: 442–66.

SNIDERMAN, P. 1975. *Personality and Democratic Politics*. Berkeley: University of California Press.

——1993. The new look in public opinion research. Pp. 219–45 in *Political Science: The State of the Discipline II*, ed. A. Finifter. Washington, DC: The American Political Science Association.

——and HAGENDOORN, L. 2007. *When Ways of Life Collide: Multiculturalism and Its Discontents in the Netherlands*. Princeton: Princeton University Press.

——TETLOCK, P., GLASER, J., GREEN, D., and HOUT, M. 1989. Principled tolerance and the American mass public. *British Journal of Political Science*, 19 (1): 25–45.

——FLETCHER, J., RUSSELL, P., and TETLOCK, P. 1996. *The Clash of Rights: Liberty, Equality, and Legitimacy in Pluralist Democracy*. New Haven: Yale University Press.

STEIN, A. 1999. The consequences of the Nicaraguan revolution for political tolerance: explaining differences among the mass public, Catholic priests, and secular elites. *Comparative Politics*, 30 (3): 335–53.

STENNER, K. 2005. *The Authoritarian Dynamic*. New York: Cambridge University Press.

STOUFFER, S. 1955. *Communism, Conformity and Civil Liberties*. New York: Doubleday.

STRUM, P. 1999. *When the Nazis Came to Skokie: Freedom for Speech We Hate*. Lawrence: University Press of Kansas.

SULLIVAN, J., PIERESON, J., and MARCUS, G. 1982. *Political Tolerance and American Democracy*. Chicago: University of Chicago Press.

——and TRANSUE, J. 1999. The psychological underpinnings of democracy: a selective review of research on political tolerance, interpersonal trust, and social capital. *Annual Review of Psychology*, 50: 625–50.

——SHAMIR, M., WALSH, P., and ROBERTS, N. 1985. *Political Tolerance in Context: Support for Unpopular Minorities in Israel, New Zealand, and the United States*. Boulder, Colo.: Westview.

——WALSH, P., SHAMIR, M., BARNUM, D., and GIBSON, J. 1993. Why politicians are more tolerant: selective recruitment and socialization among political elites in Britain, Israel, New Zealand and the United States. *British Journal of Political Science*, 23: 51–76.

TYLER, T. and MITCHELL, G. 1994. Legitimacy and the empowerment of discretionary legal authority: The United States Supreme Court and abortion rights. *Duke Law Journal*, 43: 703–815.

——BOECKMANN, R., SMITH, H., and HUO, Y. 1997. *Social Justice in a Diverse Society*. Boulder, Colo.: Westview.

WEISSBERG, R. 1998. *Political Tolerance: Balancing Community and Diversity*. Thousand Oaks, Calif.: Sage.

WILSON, T. 1994. Trends in tolerance toward rightist and leftist groups, 1976–1988: effects of attitude change and cohort succession. *Public Opinion Quarterly*, 58 (4): 539–56.

ZAKARIA, F. 2003. *The Future of Freedom: Illiberal Democracy at Home and Abroad*. New York: W. W. Norton.

PART VI

CONTEXTUAL POLITICAL ANALYSIS

....

CHAPTER 22

OVERVIEW OF CONTEXTUAL POLITICAL ANALYSIS

IT DEPENDS

CHARLES TILLY
ROBERT E. GOODIN

....

1 OVERTURE

....

CAST of characters:

- Sivu, pseudonym for a peasant in Aurel Vlaicu (Vlaicu for short), a Transylvanian village of about 820 people living in 274 houses
- Agron, the local land commission's agronomist
- Map, the land commission's surveyor
- Com't, a member of the land commission from Vlaicu
- Katherine Verdery, American anthropologist and long-time observer of life in Vlaicu

Time: Spring 1994.

In 1994, the Romanian government and the people of Vlaicu faced a knotty problem: how to privatize the village collective farm set up under Romania's state socialism. Before socialism, Vlaicu had maintained its own form of private property with some collective controls over land, animals, and agricultural products. That system lasted until the Russian takeover of 1945. Between then and 1959, however, Romania's socialist authorities went from organizing cooperatives to coercing collectivization; they created both a state farm and a collective farm. In contrast to the government-owned and centrally managed state farm, Vlaicu's households acquired provisional shares of the collective farm's lands, on condition of using its facilities and producing their quotas of its crops.

Over the thirty years between 1959 and the collapse of Romanian socialism in 1989, numerous villagers whose families had previously held land left for city jobs, families that stayed in the village waxed or waned, and shares in the collective farm shifted accordingly. As the old regime collapsed, villagers often claimed the land they were then working, sold it, shared it with other family members, or passed it on to heirs. In 1994, then, the land commission had to decide which rights, whose rights, and as of what date, established claims to the land now being privatized. Hence the drama, as recorded in Verdery's field notes:

Sivu comes in and is very noisy about what terrible things he's going to do if his case isn't settled. He has a piece in Filigore, claims it must be measured, Map says it already has been—they repeat this several times. Map gets mad because people want remeasuring: "We'll never finish this job if people make us remeasure all the time!" One woman wants him to go measure in Lunca; he says, "We already did it there, if we have to go back we won't get out for two weeks." Sivu says loudly, "I don't want anything except what's *mine*!" He accosts Com't: "Look into my eyes, you're my godfather, I'm not asking for anything except what's *mine*. I bought it from Gheorghe, it's next to Ana and to Constantin. If you don't give it to me, I'll . . . I'll do what no one's done in all of Vlaicu." (Verdery 2003, 117)

The village drama enacts politics as most ordinary people experience politics most of the time: not as grand clashes of political theories or institutions, but as a local struggle for rights, redress, protection, and advantage in relation to local officials. Here, as elsewhere, how political processes actually work and what outcomes they produce depend heavily on the contexts in which they occur.

Property figured centrally in the Vlaicu drama, but not as the abstract property of constitutions and treatises. Sivu bought Gheorghe's plot, which neighbored those of Ana and Constantin; he wanted the authorities to record and legitimize his right to exactly that piece of land. He insisted that the surveyor and the agronomist set down the land's boundaries so that Ana and Constantin (who may well have been encroaching on Gheorghe's parcel as they plowed) would recognize where their fields ended and his began. Looking on, professional political analysts witness an encounter about which they often theorize: between state-defined rights and obligations, on one side, and local social relations, on the other.

Political analysts are not, however, simply observing the clash of two discordant principles; they are watching the continuous creation and re-creation of rights through struggle. As Verdery (2003, 19) puts it, "I have proposed treating property as simultaneously a cultural system, a set of social relations, and an organization of power. They all come together in social processes." Verdery reports that in reckoning rights to collectivized property the Romanian government adopted a formal, genealogical conception of rights in land, ignoring who had actually worked various plots under socialism, who had invested care in older former proprietors, and so on. From the government's perspective, any individuals who occupied similar positions within the genealogy—two brothers, two cousins, two aunts—had equal rights to shares in privatizing property over which a household or kin group had a legal claim. That formalistic reasoning clashed with local moral codes. According to Verdery:

Villagers, however, had not understood kinship that way; for them, it was performative. To be kin meant *behaving* like kin. It meant cooperating to create marriage, baptismal and death rituals; putting flowers on relatives' graves; helping out with money or other favors; and caring for the elderly (who might not even be one's parents) in exchange for inheriting their land.

(Verdery 2003, 165)

When Sivu demanded what was rightfully his, he appealed to his godfather, the local commissioner, for confirmation of his rights. He was calling on a different code from the one written into Romanian national law.

In the case at hand, Verdery found that—to the dismay of most villagers—the actual distribution of privatized land reproduced the local hierarchy prevailing at the terminus of the socialist regime. The pyramid of land ownership ended up "with state farm directors at the top, collective farm staff below them, and village households at the bottom, holding very few resources for surviving in the new environment" (Verdery 2003, 11). As happened widely elsewhere in the collapse of state socialist regimes, people used their knowledge of the expiring system to capture their pieces of what remained (Solnick 1998). That fact offered tremendous advantages to people who had already been running factories, bureaucracies, security services, or state farms under socialism. But ordinary peasants also used memories, connections, arguments, and threats as best they could.

2 CONTEXT MATTERS

Note the immediate importance of context. No one who imagined that privatization simply followed the laws of the market—or of the jungle—could describe or explain what actually happened. Through incessant negotiation, resources that had existed (or had come into being) under governmental control became private property. The negotiation, the character of the contested resources, the privatization process, Verdery's collection of evidence on all three, and our own capacity to describe and explain what was going on in Vlaicu at the time all depend on local and national context.

The context immediately in question here consisted chiefly of previously established relations between villagers and a variety of state officials. But as we step back from Vlaicu's local disputes toward the more general problem of relations between political power and property at large, we begin to see the relevance of other contexts: historical, institutional, cultural, demographic, technological, psychological, ideological, ontological, and epistemological. We cannot dismiss the question "What is property?" with Pierre-Joseph Proudhon's famous reply: "Property is theft." As analysts of political processes, we have no choice: We must place rights to resources in context.

Property obviously does not stand alone in this regard. Political scientists' enquiries into democratization and de-democratization, civil and international war, revolution and rebellion, nationalism, ethnic mobilization, political participation, parliamentary behavior, and effective government all raise contextual questions: when, where, in what settings, on what premises, with what understandings of the processes under investigation? Viable answers to questions of this sort require serious attention to the contexts in which the crucial political processes operate.

The *Oxford Handbook of Contextual Political Analysis* provides a survey of relevant contexts. Against the most reductive versions of parsimony, it argues that attention to context does not clutter the description and explanation of political processes, but, on the contrary, promotes systematic knowledge. Against the most exaggerated versions of postmodernism, it argues that context and contextual effects lend themselves to systematic description and explanation, hence their proper understanding facilitates discovery of true regularities in political processes. Between those extreme positions, it examines the multiple ways in which context affects analysts' understanding of political processes, the extent and sort of evidence available concerning political processes, and the very operation of political processes. In this brief chapter, we concentrate on showing the importance for systematic political knowledge of getting context right.

Here is another way of putting our main point: In response to each big question of political science, we reply "It depends." Valid answers depend on the context in which the political processes under study occur. Valid answers depend triply on context, with regard to understandings built into the questions, with regard to the evidence available for answering the questions, and with regard to the actual operation of the political processes. We take this position not as a counsel of despair, but as a beacon of hope. We pursue the hope that political processes depend on context in ways that are themselves susceptible to systematic exploration and elaboration.

The hope applies both to description and to explanation. On the side of description, political scientists make significant contributions to knowledge simply by getting things right—developing reliable means of identifying the major actors in political conflicts, clarifying where and when different sorts of electoral systems succeed or fail, verifying the factual premises of governmental doctrines, and so on. On the side of explanation, superior cause–effect accounts of political processes not only serve the advance of political science as a discipline but also permit more accurate forecasts of the effects likely to result from a given political intervention. Better description and explanation improve both theory and practice.

We therefore organized the *Oxford Handbook of Contextual Political Analysis* to show how and why a variety of contexts matter to systematic description and explanation of political processes. The contexts examined range from abstractly philosophical to concretely local. Together they allow us to distinguish three classes of contextual effects:

1. On analysts' understanding of political processes.
2. On the evidence available for empirical examination of political processes.
3. On the processes themselves.

Thus an analyst's understanding of electoral campaigns derives in part from the analyst's own involvement or lack of involvement in electoral campaigns, evidence concerning electoral campaigns comes in part from campaign participants' public declarations of who they are, and electoral campaigns vary significantly in form as a function of their locations in time and space. To be sure, the three interact: Participant observation of electoral campaigns not only shapes the analyst's understanding and gives the analyst access to certain sorts of evidence other analysts can rarely acquire, but also makes the analyst a cause, however slight, of what actually happens in the election. Nevertheless, we will do well to maintain broad distinctions among the three kinds of contextual effects. Writings on contextual political analysis typically deal with one or two of them, but not all three at once.

2.1 Alternative Approaches

Although any reflective political analyst makes some allowances for context, two extreme positions on context have received surprisingly respectful attention from political scientists during recent decades: the search for general laws, and postmodern skepticism.

2.1.1 *The Search for General Laws*

On one side, we have context as noise, as interference in transmission of the signal we are searching for. In that view, we must clear away the effects of context in order to discover the true regularities in political processes. In a spirited, influential, and deftly conciliatory synthesis of quantitative and qualitative approaches to social science, Gary King, Robert Keohane, and Sidney Verba begin by making multiple concessions to complexity and interpretation, but end up arguing that the final test for good social science is its identification of casual effects, defined as:

the difference between the systematic component of observations made when the explanatory variable takes one value and the systematic component of comparable observations when the explanatory variable takes on another value.   (King, Keohane, and Verba 1994, 82)

This seemingly bland claim turns out to be the thin edge of the wedge, the camel's nose under the tent, or the elephant in the room—choose your metaphor. It initiates a remarkable series of moves including the assimilation of scientific inference to the world-view contained in statistics based on the general linear model, the assumption that the fundamental causes of political processes do, indeed, consist of variables, the consequent rejection of mechanisms as causes, and advice for making small-n studies look more like large-n studies—all of which commit the authors more firmly to explanation as the identification of general laws that encompass particular cases.

2.1.2 *Postmodern Skepticism*

On the other side, we have context as the very object of political analysis, the complex, elusive phenomenon we must interpret as best we can. In this second view, the first view's "regularities" become illusions experienced by political interpreters who have not yet realized that systematic knowledge is impossible and that they only think otherwise because they have fallen victim to their own immersion in a particular context. Anthropologist Clifford Geertz has written some of the most eloquent and influential statements of the view; indeed, King, Keohane, and Verba (1994, 38–40) quote Geertz's ideas as an often-cited but even more often misunderstood objection to their own approach. Here is Geertz on how law works:

Law, I have been saying, somewhat against the pretensions encoded in woolsack rhetoric, is local knowledge; local not just as to place, time, class and variety of issue, but as to accent— vernacular characterizations of what happens connected to vernacular imaginings of what can. It is this complex of characterizations and imaginings, stories about events cast in imagery about principles, that I have been calling a legal sensibility. This is doubtless more than a little vague, but as Wittgenstein, the patron saint of what is going on here, remarked, a veridical picture of an indistinct object is not after all a clear one but an indistinct one. Better to paint the sea like Turner than attempt to make of it a Constable cow.   (Geertz 1983, 215)

Much more fun than the "systematic component of comparable observations," Geertz's argument comes close to saying that the systematic component does not exist, and would not be worth looking for if it did. Like the King–Keohane–Verba manual, the *Oxford Handbook of Contextual Political Analysis* came into existence largely because political analysts steeped in Geertzian skepticism have offered serious objections to standard social scientific portrayals of political processes, but have not—sometimes on principle—systematized their knowledge of context, cultural variability, and social construction (Hacking 1999). It ends up, however, much more concerned about those objections than King, Keohane, and Verba.

2.1.3 *Something In-between*

Political scientists rarely line up in disciplined armies under the banners of General Laws and Skepticism to do open battle with each other. Yet the two flags define the limits of a terrain across which political analysts regularly deploy their forces. From differing bases within the terrain, polemicists often venture out for struggle to control one piece or another of the territory. Some observers speak of choices between positivism and constructivism, between covering laws and hermeneutics, between general and local knowledge, or between reductionism and holism. Regardless of the terminology, at one end of the range we find claims for universal principles that cut across particular social contexts, at the other claims that attempts to describe and explain political phenomena have no means of escaping particular social contexts.

Certainly limiting cases exist in which each approach applies in a relatively extreme form. On the one hand, seekers of General Laws can sometimes find fairly robust lawlike regularities. Consider the relationship between inflation and unemployment traced by the Phillips Curve (at least the shape of that curve seems constant, even if its actual values have to be recalibrated in every period: Friedman 1977). Another might be Duverger's Law: how plurality voting rules give rise to and sustain two-party electoral systems (Riker 1982). We can also sometimes find clear cases where the acts in question are literally constituted by speech and the shared understandings embodied in it; constitution writing provides a compelling example (Searle 1969; 1995; Skinner 1969; 2002; Tully 1988). Political actors weave legal fictions like sovereignty of just such stuff (Walker 1993; Krasner 1999; Wendt 1999). Around them, distinctive "standpoints," perspectives, and discourses of different social groupings coalesce.[1] If part of what exists in our world, ontologically, comes into being through these sorts of social construction, then we need an epistemology suited to understanding those mechanisms of social construction—the "how" of constructivism rather than merely the "if...then" of positivism, "knowing how" rather than merely "knowing that" (Ryle 1949; Foucault 1981; Rose and Miller 1992).

Although we can clearly find cases where one or the other approach captures the whole story, more typically some mixed strategy is required (Archer et al. 1998; Hay 2002, ch. 3). Most of the chapters of the *Oxford Handbook of Contextual Political Analysis* offer arguments, at least implicitly, in defense of one position within the range and against others. Readers who consult the *Oxford Handbook of Contextual Political Analysis* on the way to pursuing their own descriptions and explanations of political processes face the same choices. But we hope that having been duly sensitized to the effects of context, none of that book's readers will ever again find themselves in the position of Ashford's (1992, 27) "analyst of French communal budgets [who], laboring to extend a data bank to 1871, was mystified [by the paucity of data] until someone told him of the Franco-Prussian War."

2.2 Ontologies

Leaving much finer distinctions aside for present purposes, we can distinguish three aspects of the unavoidable choices: ontology, explanatory logic, and mechanisms. Within political science, major *ontological* choices concern the sorts of social entities whose coherent existence analysts can reasonably assume. Major alternatives include

---

[1] See e.g. Smith (1987); Antony and Witt (1993); Hajer (1995); Finnemore and Sikkink (2001); Jackson (2004).

holism, methodological individualism, phenomenological individualism, and relational realism. *Holism* is the doctrine that social structures have their own self-sustaining logics. In its extreme form—once quite common in political science but now unfashionable—a whole civilization, society, or culture undergoes a life of its own. Less extreme versions attribute self-reproducing powers to major institutions, treat certain segments of society as subordinating the rest to their interests, represent dominant mentalities, traditions, values, or cultural forms as regulators of social life, or assign inherent self-reproducing logics to industrialism, capitalism, feudalism, and other distinguishable varieties of social organization.

Methodological individualism insists on human individuals as the basic or unique social reality. It not only focuses on persons, one at a time, but imputes to each person a set of intentions that cause the person's behavior. In more economistic versions of methodological individualism, the person in question contains a utility schedule and a set of assets, which interact to generate choices within well-defined constraints. In every such analysis, to be sure, figures a market-like allocative structure that operates externally to the choice-making individual—but it is astonishing how rarely methodological individualists examine by what means those allocative structures actually do their work.

The less familiar term *phenomenological individualism* refers to the doctrine that individual consciousness is the primary or exclusive site of social life. Phenomenological individualism veers into solipsism when its adherents argue that adjacent minds have no access to each other's contents, therefore no observer can escape the prison of her own awareness. Even short of that analytically self-destructive position, phenomenological individualists tend to regard states of body and mind—impulses, reflexes, desires, ideas, or programs—as the chief motors of social action. In principle, they have two ways to account for large-scale political structures and processes: (1) as summed individual responses to similar situations; (2) as distributions and/or connections among individual actions.

In the first case, political scientists sometimes constitute collective actors consisting of all the individuals within a category such as peasant or woman. In the second case, they take a leaf from those political scientists who see national political life as a meeting place, synthesis, and outcome of that shifting distribution of attitudes we call public opinion or from the social psychologists who see individual X's action as providing a stimulus for individual Y's action. Even there, they hold to the conception of human consciousness as the basic site of social life.

Relational realism, the doctrine that transactions, interactions, social ties, and conversations constitute the central stuff of social life, once predominated in social science. Classical economists, Karl Marx, Max Weber, and Georg Simmel all emphasized social relations, regarding both individuals and complex social structures as products of regularities in social relations. During the twentieth century, however, relational realism lost much of its ground to individualism and holism. Only in American pragmatism, various versions of network analysis, and some corners of organizational or labor economics did it prevail continuously. Only with the breakdown of structural Marxism has it once again come to the fore elsewhere. Relational realism concentrates on connections that concatenate, aggregate, and disaggregate readily, forming organizational structures at the same time as they shape individual behavior. Relational analysts follow flows of communication, patron–client chains, employment networks, conversational connections, and power relations from the small scale to the large and back. A case in point is the way in which democracy emerged through networks of workers forming and re-forming effervescent "workers commissions" in the interstices of the rigid, formal mechanisms of corporatist intermediation in Franco's Spain (Foweraker 1989).

Intellectual genetic engineers can, of course, create hybrids of the four basic ontologies. A standard combination of phenomenological individualism and holism portrays a person in confrontation with society, each of the elements and their very confrontation having its own laws. Methodological individualists usually assume the presence of a self-regulating market or other allocative institution. Individualists vary in how much they allow for emergents—structures that result from individual actions but once in existence exert independent effects on individual actions, much as music-lovers enter a concert hall one by one, only to see the audience's distribution through the hall affect both the orchestra's performance and their own reactions to it. Relational analysts commonly allow for partly autonomous individual processes as well as strong effects on interaction by such collectively created structures as social categories and centralized organizations. Nevertheless, the four ontologies lead to rather different accounts of political processes.

They also suggest distinctive starting points for analysis. A holist may eventually work her way to the individuals that live within a given system or the social relations that connect individuals with the system, but her starting point is likely to be some observation of the system as a whole. Methodological individualists can treat social ties as products of individual calculation, but above all they must specify relevant individual actors before launching their analyses. Phenomenological individualists likewise give priority to individuals, with the two qualifications that (1) their individuals are sites of consciousness rather than of calculating intentions; and (2) they frequently move rapidly to shared states of awareness, at the limit attributing shared orientations to all members of a population. Relational realists may begin with existing social ties, but to be consistent and effective they should actually start with transactions among social sites, then watch when and how transactions bundle into more durable, substantial, and/or consequential relations among sites.

2.3 Explanatory Strategies

Some of political science's fiercest disagreements involve *logics of explanation*. At the risk of fierce disagreement, let us distinguish five competing positions: skepticism, law-seeking accounts, propensity analyses, systemic analyses, and mechanism-based accounts.

Skepticism considers political processes to be so complex, contingent, impenetrable, or particular as to defy explanation. Short of an extreme position, however, even a skeptic can hope to describe, interpret, or assign meaning to processes that are complex, contingent, particular, and relatively impenetrable. Thus political science skeptics continue to describe, interpret, and assign meaning to the Soviet Union's collapse without claiming to have explained that momentous process.

Law-seeking accounts consider explanation to consist of subjecting robust empirical generalizations to higher and higher-level generalizations, the most general of all standing as laws. In such accounts models are invariant, i.e. work the same in all conditions. Investigators search for necessary and sufficient conditions of stipulated outcomes, those outcomes often conceived as "dependent variables." Studies of covariation among presumed causes and presumed effects therefore serve as validity tests for proposed explanations; investigators in this tradition sometimes invoke John Stuart Mill's (1843) Methods of Agreement, Differences, Residues, and Concomitant Variation, despite Mill's own doubts of their applicability to human affairs. Thus some students of democratization hope to state the general conditions under which any nondemocratic polity whatsoever becomes democratic.

In contemporary political science, however, few analysts propose flat laws in the form "All Xs are Y." Instead, two modified versions of law-seeking explanations predominate. The first lays out a principle of variation, often stated as a probability. The proposed law often takes the form "The more X, the more Y"—for example, the higher national income the more prevalent and irreversible is democracy.[2] In this case, the empirical demonstration often rests on identifying a partial derivative that stands up robustly to "controls" for such contextual matters as region and predominant religion. The second common version of law-seeking explanations consists instead of identifying necessary and/or sufficient conditions for some outcome such as revolution, democracy, or civil war, typically through comparison of otherwise similar positive and negative cases (Ragin 1994).

Propensity accounts consider explanation to consist of reconstructing a given actor's state at the threshold of action, with that state variously stipulated as motivation, consciousness, need, organization, or momentum. The actors in question may be individuals, but analysts often construct propensity accounts of organizations or other collective actors. Explanatory methods of choice then range from sympathetic interpretation to reductionism, psychological or otherwise. Thus some students of contentious politics compare the experiences of different social groupings with structural adjustment in an effort to explain why some groupings resist, others suffer in silence, and still others disintegrate under pressure (Auyero 2003; Walton and Seddon 1994).

Although authors of law-seeking and propensity accounts sometimes talk of systems, *systemic* explanations strictly speaking consist of specifying a place for some event, structure, or process within a larger self-maintaining set of interdependent elements, showing how the event, structure, or process in question serves and/or results from interactions among the larger set of elements. Functional explanations typically qualify, since they account for the presence or persistence of some element

---

[2] As argued, variously, by Burkhart and Lewis-Beck (1994); Muller (1995); Przeworski et al. (2000).

by its functions—its positive consequences for some coherent larger set of social relations or processes. Nevertheless, systemic accounts can avoid functionalism by making more straightforward arguments about the effects of certain kinds of relations to larger systems. Thus some students of peasant revolt explain its presence or absence by peasants' degree of integration into society as a whole.

Mechanism-based accounts select salient features of episodes, or significant differences among episodes, and explain them by identifying within those episodes robust mechanisms of relatively general scope. As compared with law-seeking, propensity, and system approaches, mechanism-based explanations aim at modest ends: selective explanation of salient features by means of partial causal analogies. Thus some students of nationalism try relating its intensity to the extent and character of competition among ethnic entrepreneurs. In such accounts, the entrepreneurs' competition for political constituencies becomes a central (but not exclusive or sufficient) mechanism in the generation of nationalism.

Systemic explanations still recur in international relations, where the views called "realism" generally attribute great causal efficacy to locations of individual states within the international system. Otherwise, they have lost ground in political science since the heyday of David Easton's *Political System* (1953). When today's political scientists fight about explanation, however, they generally pit law-seeking against propensity accounts, with the first often donning the costume of Science and the second the garb of Interpretation. (Nevertheless, the search for microfoundations in rational choice approaches to political science involves a deliberate attempt to locate general laws in the choice-making propensities of individuals.) Explanation by means of robust causal mechanisms has received much less self-conscious attention from social science methodologists than have law-seeking, propensity, and systemic explanations. Let us therefore say a bit more about mechanistic explanations.

2.4 Mechanisms

Satisfactory law-seeking accounts require not only broad empirical uniformities but also mechanisms that cause those uniformities.[3] For all its everyday employment in natural science, the term "mechanism" rarely appears in social-scientific explanations. Its rarity probably results partly from the term's disquieting suggestion that social processes operate like clockwork, but mainly from its uneasy coexistence with its explanatory competitors: skepticism, law-seeking accounts, propensity analyses, and systemic analyses.

Without much self-conscious justification, most political scientists recognize one or another of these—especially individual or group dispositions—as genuine explanations. They grow uneasy when someone identifies mechanisms as explanations. Even sympathetic analysts often distinguish between mechanisms as "how" social

---

[3] As emphasized in different ways by: Brady (1995); Laitin (1995); Tilly (2000; 2001); Elster (2007); cf. King, Keohane, and Verba (1994).

processes work and dispositions as "why" they work. As a practical matter, however, social scientists often refer to mechanisms as they construct partial explanations of complex structures or processes. Mechanisms often make anonymous appearances when political scientists identify parallels within classes of complex structures or processes. In the study of contentious politics, for example, analysts frequently invoke the mechanisms of brokerage and coalition formation (McAdam, Tarrow, and Tilly 2001). If those mechanisms appear in essentially the same form with the same small-scale consequences across a wide range of circumstances, we can call them "robust."

How will we know them when we see them? We choose a level of observation: individual thoughts, individual actions, social interactions, clusters of interactions, durable social ties, or something else. At that level of observation, we can recognize as robust social mechanisms those events that:

1. Involve indistinguishably similar transfers of energy among stipulated social elements.
2. Produce indistinguishably similar rearrangements of those social elements.
3. Do so across a wide range of circumstances.

The "elements" in question may be persons, but they also include aspects of persons (e.g. their jobs), recurrent actions of persons (e.g. their amusements), transactions among persons (e.g. Internet communications between colleagues), and configurations of interaction among persons (e.g. shifting networks of friendship).

To the extent that mechanisms become uniform and universal, their identification starts to resemble a search for general laws. Yet two big differences intervene between law-seeking and mechanism-based explanations. First, practitioners of mechanistic explanation generally deny that any strong, interesting recurrences of large-scale social structures and processes occur.[4] They therefore deny that it advances enquiry to seek lawlike empirical generalizations—at whatever level of abstraction—by comparing big chunks of history. Second, while mechanisms have uniform immediate effects by definition, depending on initial conditions and combinations with other mechanisms, their aggregate, cumulative, and longer-term effects vary considerably. Thus brokerage operates uniformly by definition, always connecting at least two social sites more directly than they were previously connected. Yet the activation of brokerage does not in itself guarantee more effective coordination of action at the connected sites; that depends on initial conditions and combinations with other mechanisms.

Let us adopt a simple distinction among mechanisms, processes, and episodes:

- *Mechanisms* form a delimited class of events that change relations among specified sets of elements in identical or closely similar ways over a variety of situations.
- *Processes* are frequently occurring combinations or sequences of mechanisms.
- *Episodes* are continuous streams of social life.

---

[4] See e.g. Bunge (1997); Elster (1999); Hedström and Swedberg (1998); Little (1998); Stinchcombe (1991); Tilly (2000).

Social mechanisms concatenate into social processes: combinations and sequences of mechanisms producing relatively similar effects. A process we might call identity enlargement, for example, consists of broadening and increasing uniformity in the collective answers given by some set of persons to the question, "Who are you?" Identity enlargement typically results from interaction of two mechanisms: brokerage and social appropriation—the latter activating previously existing connections among subsets of the persons in question. Thus in collective action, enlargement of relevant identities from neighborhood membership to city-wide solidarity emerges from the concatenation of brokerage with social appropriation.

Mechanisms and processes compound into episodes, bounded and connected sequences of social action. Episodes sometimes acquire social significance as such because participants or observers construct names, boundaries, and stories corresponding to them: this revolution, that emigration, and so on. More often, however, analysts chop continuous streams of social life into episodes according to conventions of their own making, thus delineating generations, social movements, fads, and the like. The manner in which episodes acquire shared meanings deserves close study. But we have no a priori warrant to believe that episodes grouped by similar criteria spring from similar causes. In general, analysts of mechanisms and processes begin with the opposite assumption. For them, uniformly identified episodes provide convenient frames for comparison, but with an eye to detecting crucial mechanisms and processes within them. Choice of episodes, however, crucially affects the effectiveness of such a search. It makes a large difference, for example, whether students of generational effects distinguish generations by means of arbitrary time periods or presumably critical events.

Mechanisms, too, entail choices. A rough classification identifies three sorts of mechanism: environmental, cognitive, and relational:

- *Environmental mechanisms* mean externally generated influences on conditions affecting social life; words like "disappear," "enrich," "expand," and "disintegrate"—applied not to actors but their settings—suggest the sorts of cause–effect relations in question.
- *Cognitive mechanisms* operate through alterations of individual and collective perception; words like "recognize," "understand," "reinterpret," and "classify" characterize such mechanisms.
- *Relational mechanisms* alter connections among people, groups, and interpersonal networks; words like "ally," "attack," "subordinate," and "appease" give a sense of relational mechanisms.

Here we begin to detect affinities among ontologies, explanatory strategies, and preferred mechanisms. Methodological individualists, for example, commonly adopt propensity accounts of social behavior and privilege cognitive mechanisms as they do so. Holists lean toward environmental mechanisms, as relational realists give special attention to relational mechanisms. Those affinities are far from absolute, however. Many a phenomenological individualist, for example, weaves accounts in which environmental mechanisms such as social disintegration generate cognitive mechanisms having relational consequences in their turn. In principle, many permutations of ontology, explanatory strategy, and preferred mechanisms should be feasible.

Review of mechanisms identifies some peculiarities of rational choice theory's claims to constitute a—or even *the*—general explanation of social life. Rational choice theory centers on situations of choice among relatively well-defined alternative actions with more or less known costs and consequences according to previously established schedules of preference. It focuses attention on mental processes, and therefore on cognitive mechanisms.

From that focus stem three problems: upstream, midstream, and downstream. Upstream, rational choice theory lacks a plausible account of how preferences, available resources, choice situations, and knowledge of consequences form or change. Midstream, the theory incorporates a dubious account of how people make decisions when they actually confront situations of choice among relatively well-defined alternative actions with more or less known costs and consequences according to previously established schedules of preference. Both observational and experimental evidence challenge the rational choice midstream account, confining its scope to very special conditions (Kahneman 2003). Those special conditions rest on historically developed knowledge, preferences, practices, and institutions (Kuran 1991; 1995). They depend on context.

Downstream, the theory lacks an account of consequences, in two senses of the word. First, considering how rarely we human beings execute actions with the flair we would prefer, the theory leaves unclear what happens between a person's choice to do something and the same person's action in response to that choice. Second, considering how rarely we human beings anticipate precisely the effects of our less-than-perfect actions, it likewise remains unclear what links the theory's rationally chosen actions to concrete consequences in social life. In fact, error, unintended consequences, cumulative but relatively invisible effects, indirect effects, and environmental reverberations occur widely in social life. Any theory that fails to show how such effects of human action occur loses its claim to generality.

3 THE NATURE OF SOCIAL EXPLANATION

3.1 Explanatory Stories

In dealing with social life in general and political processes in particular, we face a circumstance that distinguishes most of social science from most other scientific enquiries: the prominent place of explanatory stories in social life (Ryan 1970; Tilly 2007). Explanatory stories provide simplified cause–effect accounts of puzzling, unexpected, dramatic, problematic, or exemplary events. Relying on widely available knowledge rather than technical expertise, they help make the world intelligible. They often carry an edge of justification or condemnation. They qualify as a special sort of narrative, which a standard manual on narrative defines as "the representation of an event or a series of events" (Abbott 2002, 12). This particular variety of narrative includes actors, their actions, and effects produced by those actions. The story usually gives pride of place to human actors. When the leading characters are not human—for example, when they are animals, spirits, organizations, or features of the physical environment such as storms—they still behave mostly like humans. The story they enact accordingly often conveys credit or blame.

Political science's explanatory stories generally reify collective agents and artifacts—states (Allison and Zelikow 1999), parties (Lawson 1990; Strøm 2001), classes, societies, and corporations. They treat them as if they were unified intentional agents, with goals of their own and the capacity to pursue them, who therefore should be held to the same standards of credit and blame. The ubiquity of explanatory stories in everyday life makes the logical slippage all the easier.

Of course, even natural scientists resort to explanatory stories, at least in telling their tales to lay audiences: This ball hit that, and then that in turn; this electron got excited and jumped into a higher shell; this infectious agent penetrated that cell's membrane. And in those explanatory stories that natural scientists tell lay audiences, objects in the story are anthropomorphized and ascribed a sort of quasi-agency. Sophisticated observers might balk at that way of talking about objects they know to be inanimate or with no will of their own. But couching our explanations in terms of such stories comes quite naturally in the human sciences, where we are confident that the actors are genuine agents with wills of their own, however constrained they may be in acting on them.

Aristotle's *Poetics* presented one of the West's first great analyses of explanatory stories. Speaking of tragedy, which he singled out as the noblest form of creative writing, Aristotle described the two versions of a proper plot:

> Plots are either simple or complex, since the actions they represent are naturally of this twofold description. The action, proceeding in the way defined, as one continuous whole, I call simple, when the change in the hero's fortunes takes place without Peripety or Discovery; and complex, when it involves one or the other, or both. These should each of them arise out of the structure of the Plot itself, so as to be the consequence, necessary or probable, of the antecedents. There is a great difference between a thing happening *propter hoc* and *post hoc*.   (Aristotle 1984, 1452a)

A "peripety," for Aristotle, was a complete reversal of a state, as when the messenger who comes to comfort Oedipus actually reveals to him the identities of his father and mother. A "discovery" was a fateful change from ignorance to knowledge, an awful or wonderful recognition of something previously concealed; in the story of Oedipus, a discovery (the messenger's announcement) produced a peripety (Oedipus' unmasking as a man who killed his father and bedded his mother). Aristotle caught the genius of the explanatory story: one or a few actors, a limited number of actions that cause further actions through altered states of awareness, continuity in space and time, an overall structure leading to some outcome or lesson.

By attributing their main effects to specific actors (even when those actors are unseen and/or divine), explanatory stories follow common rules of individual responsibility: X did it, and therefore deserves the praise or blame for what happened as a result. Their dramatic structure separates them from conventional giving of reasons: Traffic was heavy, my watch stopped, I have a bad cold, today's my lucky day, and so on. In fact, explanatory stories more closely resemble classical dramas. They generally maintain unity of time and place instead of jumping among temporal and geographic settings. They involve limited casts of characters whose visible actions cause all the subsequent actions and their major effects. They often have a moral. On the whole, however, they represent causal processes very badly: They radically reify and simplify the relevant actors, actions, causes, and effects while disregarding indirect effects, environmental effects, incremental effects, errors, unanticipated consequences, and simultaneous causation (Mills 1940; Scott and Lyman 1968; Ross 1977).

Many political scientists implicitly recognize the inadequacy of explanatory stories for political phenomena by adopting formal representations whose causal logics break decisively with the logic of storytelling: multidimensional scaling, simultaneous equations, input–output tables, syntactic analyses of texts, and much more. These non-narrative models, however, prevail much more regularly in the processing of evidence than in either the initial framing of arguments or the final interpretation of results. At those two ends, explanatory stories continue to predominate.

Explanatory stories matter visibly, even vitally to our study of context. They intervene in all three sorts of contextual effect:

- Analysts' understanding of political processes commonly takes the form of stories; as teachers of formal modeling soon learn, it takes heroic efforts to produce students who do not customarily cast descriptions and explanations as stories and who habitually recognize simultaneous equations or flow charts as helpful representations of political processes.
- Evidence concerning political processes arrives in the form of stories told by participants, observers, respondents, journalists, historians, or other political analysts; even survey research regularly transforms respondents' stories into a questionnaire's fixed alternatives.
- Storytelling frequently looms large within important political processes; just think of how nationalists, revolutionaries, and candidates for public office wield stories about who they are and what they are doing.

Thus one important element of getting context right consists of identifying, describing, and explaining the operation of explanatory stories.

3.2 Other Elements of Context

Of course, other influences than the prevalence of explanatory stories produce contextual effects on our knowledge of political processes. As contributors to this volume show in detail, assumptions built into nonstory models likewise deeply affect political scientists' acquisition of knowledge. The bulk of the statistics routinely used by political scientists, for example, assume a world of linear relationships among discrete variables that in nature conform to regular distributions. Once again the influence of those assumptions appears in all three varieties of contextual effect: shaping analysts' understandings of how the world works, pervading the practices of data collection and measurement employed by analysts, and fitting political phenomena themselves with widely varying degrees of appropriateness (Jackson 1996; Jervis 1997; Kuran 1991; 1995).

Other contributors alert us to a quite different source of contextual effects: the fact that political structures and processes have constraining histories. Participants in revolutions emulate earlier revolutions, acquire legitimacy or illegitimacy from those earlier revolutions, and use institutions, ideas, organizations, and social relations set in place by those earlier revolutions. Electoral contests generate laws, memories, rifts, and alliances that affect subsequent elections. Property rights gain historical force through long use even when they originate in outright predation or deceit.

Our stress on context meshes badly with the view that the ultimate aim of political science is to identify general laws of political process that cut across the details of time, place, circumstance, and previous history. Often political scientists seek to specify extremely general necessary or sufficient conditions for some phenomenon such as democracy or polarization. The specification often concerns covariation: How X varies as a function of Y.

On that issue, we take three provisional positions (not necessarily shared by all of the contributors to the *Oxford Handbook of Contextual Political Analysis*):

- *First*, the program of identifying simple general laws concerning political structures and processes has so far yielded meager results. It has most likely done so because its logical underpinnings and routine practices conform badly to the way politics actually works.
- *Second*, what strength that program of seeking simple general laws has achieved lies in its identification of empirical regularities to be explained, not in its provision or verification of explanations.
- *Third*, regularities certainly occur in political life, but not at the scale of whole structures and processes. Political scientists should shift their attention away from empirically grounded general laws to repeated processes, and toward efficacious causal mechanisms that operate at multiple scales but produce their aggregate effects through their concatenation, sequences, and interaction with initial conditions.

4 CONTEXT AS PIECES OF A PUZZLE

Explanatory stories are offered in response to puzzlement. Why do South-East Asian peasants refuse to plant "wonder rice," when its average yield is so much greater? Because the variability of yield is also greater, and peasants living at the margins of subsistence cannot afford a bad harvest in even a single year (Scott 1976). Why did Margaret Thatcher retain her popularity while presiding over a period of unprecedented economic decline? Because Britons had expected the decline to be even more severe (Alt 1979). Why did Gorbachev do so little to stop the collapse of Communism in Eastern Europe? Perhaps because he was incompetent or the world was just too complicated; but more plausibly because "decisive inaction" was an effective way to shed the Soviet Union's strategically irrelevant and economically costly client states, despite the internal factions that profited from them (Anderson 2001).

As actors, when choosing our own actions, we are highly sensitive to the peculiarities of our own particular desires and the rich particulars of our own mental processes. But in trying to make sense of the social world, we tend (at least as a first approximation) to impute to others broadly the same sort of psychology, broadly the same sorts of beliefs and desires, that we ourselves possess. Not only are we "folk psychologists" (Jackson and Pettit 1990; Pettit 1996); we are also "folk situationalists," assuming (until further investigation reveals otherwise) that the context in which others are acting is broadly the same as our own.[5] When that model fails to fit, we go looking for which bits are to blame: in what ways the actors, or situations, are peculiar. We "make sense" of an otherwise puzzling phenomenon by finding some special features about it which, when taken into account, allow us to assimilate that case to our standard model of how the world works (Grofman 2001).

Sometimes what we need to solve the puzzle is a relatively simple piece of information. To understand why politics takes the peculiar form it does in Senegal, we need to understand that the primary connotation of "demokaraasi" is not so much competition as solidarity (Schaffer 1998). To understand why Kerala is so far ahead of the rest of India, and indeed the whole developing world, when it comes to female literacy and related aspects of social progress (Drèze and Sen 1995), it helps to know that Kerala was historically a matrilineal society. To understand why there was so little take-up of Keynesianism in interwar France, we need to understand that there was already a rich "tradition of government measures to alleviate unemployment that went back to at least 1848 ... closely related to the self-understanding of the republican order in general" (Wagner 2003; see further Rosanvallon 1989).

---

[5] The latter is one source (among many: see Gilbert and Malone 1995) of what social psychologists know as the "fundamental attribution bias." Experimental subjects are much more likely to attribute other people's "odd" behavior to discreditable attitudes and dispositions, rather than to assume that there must have been some peculiar situational factors at work, in the absence of any particular information about those other people. When subjects are told of the particular constraints under which others' "odd" behavior was generated, they are much more mixed in that judgement (Jones and Harris 1967, 6; Gilbert, Pelham, and Krull 1988).

Sometimes what we need to appreciate is how the situation looks from the actor's perspective, the actor's "frame" or "standpoint."[6] Other times what we need to appreciate are the options and constraints on action, structures thus channeling agency (Wendt 1987; Hay 2002, ch. 3). Those structures themselves often represent the accretion of past practice, ways of doing things and ways of seeing things that have grown up over time, under the intentional or unintentional influence of agents who stood to benefit from those ways of doing or seeing things (Bourdieu 1977; Foucault 1981).

Yet other times what we have to understand is "agency gone wrong." Sometimes the explanation is simply that intentional actors did something stupid, or something that seemed like a good idea but that backfired, perhaps because of misinformation, miscommunication, or the contrary intentions of other intentional agents. Stories couched in terms of the "unintended consequences of purposive social action" (Merton 1936) are very much explanatory stories with human intention at their heart. We cannot understand what "went wrong" without understanding what they were *trying* to do.

In the process of puzzle-solving, generalists and contextualists proceed in surprisingly similar and ultimately complementary ways. Where one starts leaves a residue, and it shapes one's presentation at the margins. Those who start from the more formal, abstract end of the continuum couch their discussion in one language, that of technical terminology and formal representations (Bates, de Figueiredo, and Weingast 1998; Bates et al. 1998; Strøm 2001); those who start from the more nuanced end of the continuum tend more toward "thick description" (Geertz 1973, ch. 1). But neither type of craft can do its work without at least *some* of the other's kit.

Popkin's (1979) account of peasant behavior, however "rationalist," nonetheless needs to be firmly rooted in situational aspects of South-East Asian peasant existence. Equally, Scott's (1976) competing account of peasant behavior, however rooted in particulars of South-East Asian peasant culture, nevertheless must appeal to general ways of understanding the world that we too share. Contextualist narratives must be "analytical" in that minimal sense, if they are to be intelligible to us at all. Conversely, rational choice theorists must "acknowledge that their approach requires a complete political anthropology" and that they "must 'soak and poke' and acquire much the same depth of understanding as that achieved by those who offer 'thick' descriptions" (Bates, de Figueiredo, and Weingast 1998, 628; see further Bates et al. 1998; Ferejohn 1991, 281). In that sense, at least, the "rational choice wars" within political science seem considerably overblown, however problematic we otherwise might find the bolder claims of rational choice modelers.[7]

Some advocates anxiously seek explanations that are *simple* in form, others ones that are *general* in their applicability. Concrete explanation, however, typically requires compromise. We might be able to find a valid law that is relatively simple in form (in the sense that it has few subordinate clauses), provided we confine its range

---

[6] On "frames" see: Goffman (1975); Kahneman (2003); Kahneman and Tversky (2000); Kahneman, Slovic, and Tversky (1982). On "standpoints" see Smith (1987); Antony and Witt (1993).

[7] Key texts in that controversy are Green and Shapiro (1994); Friedman (1996); Monroe (2004).

of application sufficiently narrowly; alternatively, we might be able to find some valid law that is relatively general in its applicability, provided we are prepared to make it sufficiently complex by writing lots of "if" clauses into it. Naturally, if we go too far down the latter track, writing *all* the particulars of the case at hand into our "if" clauses, we end up not with an explanation of the phenomenon but rather with a mere redescription of the same phenomenon. That is a pointless exercise; if that is all social science can do, then it becomes intellectually redundant and socially ineffectual (Walby 1992; cf. Flyvbjerg 2001). But we must not be overly fond of Occam's razor, either. Explanatory accounts that are too stark, providing too little insight into the actual mechanisms at work, might predict but they cannot truly explain (cf. Friedman 1953). If we want explanations that are of general applicability, then we simply must be prepared to complicate our explanations a little by indexing more to context as necessary. Any sensible social scientist should surely agree (King, Keohane, and Verba 1994, 20, 29–30, 104).

5 CONTEXT IN ITS PLACE

The variety of different contexts in which political action occurs is, for some, a cherished part of the rich tapestry of political life. For others bent on the pursuit of parsimonious generalizations, contextual effects subvert their ambitions toward austerity. Still, account for them they must. They can do so in either of two ways: by designing their studies in such a way as to "control for context," in effect eliminating contextual variability in their studies; or they can try to "correct for context," taking systematic account of how different contexts might actually matter to the phenomena under study. The latter is obviously a more ambitious strategy. But even the former requires rich contextual knowledge, if only of what contexts might matter in order to bracket them out in the research design.

5.1 Controlling for Context

Some wit described the field of study known as "American politics" as "area studies for the linguistically challenged." It can also be a refuge for the contextually tone-deaf. It is not as if American politics is context-free, of course. It is merely that, operating within a large internal market where broadly the same context is widely shared, context can by and large be taken for granted and pushed into the background.

Of course, even within a single country and a single period, context matters. In generalizing about *The American Voter*, Campbell et al. (1960, ch. 15) had to admit that farmers were different—the best predictor of their votes being, not party identification like the rest of Americans, but rather the price received for last year's crop.

So too were Southern politics different, at least in the era of the one-party South (Key 1949). And of course even in country contexts that we think we know well, we are still capable of being surprised: American political development looks very different once you notice the lingering effects there of the feudal law of masters and servants (Orren 1991; Steinfeld 2001).

Still, by focusing on a country where so much of the context is familiar to both writers and readers, most of the context can remain unspoken most of the time. Comparative US state politics is often said to be a wonderful natural experiment, in that sense, in which federalism means that a few things vary while so much of the background is held constant.

Controlling for context does not mean ignoring context, though. We need to know what aspects of context might matter, to make sure that they do indeed hold constant in the situation under study. What things have to be controlled for, in order to get the limited sorts of generalizations in which social scientists such as Campbell et al. (1960) pride themselves? Well, all those covered in the *Oxford Handbook of Contextual Political Analysis*: philosophical self-understandings of society, psychology, culture, history, demography, technology, and so on. As long as none of those things actually vary among the cases you are considering, then you are safe to ignore them.

Ideally, you should use that as a diagnostic checklist in advance. But you can also use it as a troubleshooting guide, after the fact. If generalizations fail you, running down that checklist might be a good place to start in trying to figure out why. Which bit of the contextual ground has shifted under your feet?

In many interesting cases, those factors are pretty well held constant. But even in single-country studies of limited duration, there are cultural differences, rooted in history, that matter. Remember V. O. Key on *Southern Politics* (1949). Every time we put an "urban/rural" variable into an equation predicting voting behavior we are gesturing toward a contextual factor (demographic or perhaps technological) that affects the phenomenon under study.

In cross-national and/or cross-time comparisons, especially, contextual variation always forms a large part of the explanation. Different cleavages have been frozen into different party systems, over time (Lipset and Rokkan 1967). There are different levels of technological development, different demographic divisions that are socially salient (Patterson 1975).

5.2 Correcting for Context

Where context varies, we have to take those differences into account, as systematically as possible. We do not have, and cannot realistically aspire to, any perfectly general laws telling us fully when and how each of those contextual factors will affect the life of a society. But we can aspire to "theories of the middle range" (Merton 1957) explicating in a fairly systematic way the workings of at least some of the key mechanisms. We do have at least partial understandings of how many of these contextual effects work: theories, for example, about the "demographic transition" from high birth rates in developing countries to much lower ones, as infant mortality declines and female education increases (Caldwell, Reddy, and Caldwell 1989; Drèze and Sen 1995).

So context matters, and context often varies. But these contextual effects are not random. There are patterns to be picked out, and understood from within each distinct historical, cultural, and technological setting. That understanding itself may or may not lend itself to generalization in ways that will allow them to be fit into over-arching "laws." Sometimes it might; often it will not. But contrary to the assumptions of more extreme skeptics, there are "rules of the game" within each of those contextual milieux to which such skeptics quite rightly say our explanations need to be indexed. Skeptics are right that our generalizations need to be indexed to particular contexts; they are wrong to deny that, once those indexicals are in place, we can have something that might approximate "systematic understanding" of the situation.

Besides, we do not need a completely comprehensive account of context to use it as a corrective; in this regard, contextual analysis differs fundamentally from the search for general laws. Contextualist accounts typically work by helping us get a grip on some puzzling phenomenon. The contextualist account provides one or two keys, given which someone coming to the story from the outside will say, "Of course: *now* I get it!" In the story of property rights in transition with which we began, the thing you need to realize is that in Vlaicu kinship is a social and not merely a blood relation: Someone who took care of your grandmother in her old age is kin, whatever the blood tie may be. To understand how social power is exercised you need to understand both technology (Mann 1986; 1993; Wittfogel 1957; Wajcman 1991) and ideas or strategy (Freedman 1981; Scott 1998). To understand why certain social forms are widely acceptable in one time and place but not another, you may need to understand differing social ontologies—things like "the king's two bodies" (Kantorowicz 1957) or "the West" (Jackson 2004)—and you need to understand the way different languages code and embody them (Bernstein 1974; Bourdieu 1977; Foucault 1981; Laitin 1992; Wagner 2003).

6 STRUCTURING THE SUBJECT

Remember the three kinds of contextual effects we are seeking to analyze:

1. On analysts' understanding of political processes.
2. On the evidence available for empirical examination of political processes.
3. On the processes themselves.

We take broad views of these effects. Instead, for example, of concentrating on how local knowledge (Geertz 1983; Scott 1998) shapes understandings, evidence, and political processes, the *Oxford Handbook of Contextual Political Analysis* offers a commonsense division of contextual areas: philosophy, psychology, ideas, culture, history, place, population, and technology. For a full listing of chapters under each heading, see the table of contents reproduced in the appendix to the present volume.

6.1 Philosophy Matters

Outside of political theory, political scientists often tremble at the injection of philosophical issues into what had seemed concrete comparisons of arguments and evidence. But so many disputes and confusions in political analysis actually pivot on epistemology, ontology, logic, and general conceptions of argument that philosophy demanded its place at the contextual table. Political science could benefit from a band of philosophical ethnographers who would observe the ways that specialists in political processes make arguments, analyze evidence, and draw inferences about causes. The chapters in this section of the *Oxford Handbook of Contextual Political Analysis* provide a foretaste of what those ethnographers would report.

6.2 Psychology Matters

Political scientists often speak of psychological matters as "microfoundations." We have not used that term for two reasons. First, the term itself suggests a preference for methodological individualism and analogies with economic analysis—serious presences in political science, but by no means the only regards in which psychology matters to political analysis. Second, enough political analysts employ conceptions of collective psychology (for example, collective memory) that readers deserve serious reflection on relations between individual psychological processes and those collective phenomena.

6.3 Ideas Matter

Some readers will suppose that together philosophy and psychology exhaust the analysis of ideas as contexts for political analysis. The three topics certainly overlap. The *Oxford Handbook of Contextual Political Analysis* gives ideas separate standing because so many political analysts attribute autonomous importance, influence, and histories to ideas as such: ideas of justice, of democracy, of social order, and much more. The chapters in this section of the *Oxford Handbook of Contextual Political Analysis* help us see how to take ideas into account as contexts for analysts' understanding of political processes, evidence available for empirical examination of political processes, and influences on or components of the processes themselves.

6.4 Culture Matters

Many objections to broad inferences and comparisons across polities rest on the argument that culturally embedded ideas, relations, and practices profoundly affect the operation of superficially similar political processes. Even within the same polities, analysts sometimes object that linguistic, ethnic, religious, and regional cultures differ so dramatically that all efforts to detect general political principles in those polities must fail. Instead of brushing aside such objections by pointing to empirical generalizations that do hold widely, contributors in this section of the *Oxford Handbook of Contextual Political Analysis* look seriously at culture, asking how political analysts can take it into account without abandoning the search for systematic knowledge.

6.5 History Matters

One of us (Tilly) elaborates on this topic in Chapter 26 below, and we need not anticipate his more detailed arguments here. Suffice it to say that in all three types of contextual effects—on analysts' understanding of political processes, on the evidence available for empirical examination of political processes, and on the processes themselves—history figures significantly. We do not claim that those who fail to study history are condemned to repeat it, but we do claim that knowledge of historical context provides a means of producing more systematic knowledge of political processes.

6.6 Place Matters

In some definitions, history as location in space and time exhausts the influence of place. Yet geographically attuned political analysts detect effects of adjacency, distance, environment, and climate that easily escape historians who deal with the same times and places. This section of the *Oxford Handbook of Contextual Political Analysis* gathers analysts of political processes who have worked seriously on just such effects generally, comparatively, and/or in particular time–place settings. They provide guidance for taking place into account without succumbing entirely to the charms of localism.

6.7 Population Matters

This section of the *Oxford Handbook of Contextual Political Analysis* may surprise readers. One might turn to it for inventories of demographic tools that can advance political analysis. The discipline of demography does indeed offer a number of formal techniques such as life tables and migration-stream analyses that bear directly on political processes and suggest valuable analogies for political analysis. But we have pointed our contributors in rather a different direction: toward reflection on how population processes affect or constitute political processes. Thus they look hard at demographic change and variation as contexts for politics.

6.8 Technology Matters

In contemporary political analysis, technology often appears as a black box, a demonic force, or an exogenous variable that somehow affects politics but does not belong to politics as such. Such a view is hard to sustain, however, when the subject is war or economic imperialism. In fact, technologies of communication, of production, of distribution, of organization, and of rule pervade political processes, and receive insufficient attention for their special properties. In this section, skilled analysts of different technologies and technological processes offer ideas on how political scientists can (and must) take technological contexts into account.

Here, as in the *Oxford Handbook of Contextual Political Analysis*, we deliberately avoid giving ourselves the last word about the subject. In very open-ended spirit of this enterprise, we offer no last word at all. Instead of syntheses and conclusions from the individual chapters, our book's final section contained more general reflections on context and political processes from two distinguished senior practitioners, David Apter and Lucian Pye, who raised old and new questions for readers to take up for themselves. Our fondest hope is that the materials in the *Oxford Handbook of Contextual Political Analysis*—of which the following chapters are but a small sample— might in that way help readers accomplish new work that takes better account of the contexts in which political processes unfold.

REFERENCES

ABBOTT, H. P. 2002. *The Cambridge Introduction to Narrative*. Cambridge: Cambridge University Press.

ALLISON, G. T. and ZELIKOW, P. 1999. *The Essence of Decision*, 2nd edn. Reading, Mass.: Longman.

ALT, J. E. 1979. *The Politics of Economic Decline*. Cambridge: Cambridge University Press.

ANDERSON, R. D., JR. 2001. Why did the socialist empire collapse so fast—and why was the collapse a surprise? Pp. 85–102 in Grofman 2001.

ANTONY, L. and WITT, C. (eds.) 1993. *A Mind of One's Own: Feminist Essays on Reason and Objectivity*. Boulder, Colo.: Westview.

ARCHER, M., BASHKAR, R., COLLIER, A., LAWSON, T., and NORRIE, A. (eds.) 1998. *Critical Realism: Essential Readings*. London: Routledge.

ARISTOTLE 1984. *Poetics*. Volume 2, pp. 2316–40 in *The Complete Works of Aristotle*, ed. J. Barnes. Princeton, NJ: Princeton University Press.

ASHFORD, D. E. 1992. Historical context and policy studies. Pp. 27–38 in *History and Context in Comparative Public Policy*, ed. D. E. Ashford. Pittsburgh, Pa.: University of Pittsburgh Press.

AUYERO, J. 2003. Relational riot: austerity and corruption protest in the neoliberal era. *Social Movement Studies*, 2: 117–46.

BATES, R. H., DE FIGUEIREDO, JR., R. J. P., and WEINGAST, B. R. 1998b. The politics of interpretation: rationality, culture and transition. *Politics and Society*, 26: 603–42.

—— GREIF, A., LEVI, M., ROSENTHAL, J.-L., and WEINGAST, B. R. 1998a. *Analytic Narratives*. Princeton, NJ: Princeton University Press.

BERNSTEIN, B. B. 1974. *Class, Codes and Control*. London: Routledge and Kegan Paul.

BOURDIEU, P. 1977. *Outline of a Theory of Practice*. Cambridge: Cambridge University Press.

BRADY, H. 1995. Doing good and doing better. *Political Methodology*, 6: 11–19.

BUNGE, M. 1997. Mechanism and explanation. *Philosophy of the Social Sciences*, 27: 410–65.

BURKHART, R. E. and LEWIS-BECK, M. S. 1994. Comparative democracy: the economic development thesis. *American Political Science Review*, 88: 903–10.

CALDWELL, J. C., REDDY, P. H., and CALDWELL, P. 1989. *The Causes of Demographic Change*. Madison: University of Wisconsin Press.

CAMPBELL, A., CONVERSE, P. E., MILLER, W., and STOKES, D. 1960. *The American Voter*. New York: Wiley.

DRÈZE, J. and SEN, A. 1995. *India: Economic Development and Social Opportunity*. Delhi: Oxford University Press.

EASTON, D. 1953. *The Political System: An Inquiry into the State of Political Science*. New York: Knopf.

ELSTER, J. 1999. *Alchemies of the Mind: Rationality and the Emotions*. Cambridge: Cambridge University Press.

—— 2007. *Explaining Social Behavior: More Nuts and Bolts for the Social Sciences*. Cambridge: Cambridge University Press.

FEREJOHN, J. A. 1991. Rationality and interpretation: parliamentary elections in early Stuart England. Pp. 279–305 in *The Economic Approach to Politics*, ed. K. R. Monroe. New York: HarperCollins.

FINNEMORE, M. and SIKKINK, K. 2001. Taking stock: the constructivist research program in international relations and comparative politics. *Annual Review of Political Science*, 4: 391–416.

FLYVBJERG, B. 2001. *Making Social Science Matter: Why Social Inquiry Fails and How it Can Succeed Again*. New York: Cambridge University Press.

FOUCAULT, M. 1981. *Power/Knowledge*. New York: Pantheon.

FOWERAKER, J. 1989. *Making Democracy in Spain: Grass-roots Struggle in the South, 1955–1975*. Cambridge: Cambridge University Press.

FREEDMAN, L. 1981. *The Evolution of Nuclear Strategy*. London: Macmillan.

FRIEDMAN, J. (ed.) 1996. *The Rational Choice Controversy: Economic Models of Politics Reconsidered*. New Haven, Conn.: Yale University Press.

FRIEDMAN, M. 1953. *Essays in the Methodology of Positive Economics*. Chicago: University of Chicago Press.

—— 1977. Nobel lecture: inflation and unemployment. *Journal of Political Economy*, 85: 451–72.

GEERTZ, C. 1973. *The Interpretation of Cultures*. New York: Basic Books.

—— 1983. *Local Knowledge*. New York: Basic Books.

GILBERT, D. T. and MALONE, P. S. 1995. The correspondence bias. *Psychological Bulletin*, 117: 21–38.

—— PELHAM, B. W., and KRULL, D. S. 1988. On cognitive business: when person perceivers meet persons perceived. *Journal of Personality and Social Psychology*, 54: 733–40.

GOFFMAN, E. 1975. *Frame Analysis*. Harmondsworth: Penguin.

GREEN, D. P. and SHAPIRO, I. 1994. *The Pathologies of Rational Choice*. New Haven, Conn.: Yale University Press.

GROFMAN, B. (ed.) 2001. *Political Science as Puzzle Solving*. Ann Arbor: University of Michigan Press.

HACKING, I. 1999. *Social Construction of What?* Cambridge, Mass.: Harvard University Press.

HAJER, M. A. 1995. *The Politics of Environmental Discourse*. Oxford: Clarendon Press.

HAY, C. 2002. *Political Analysis*. Basingstoke: Palgrave.

HEDSTRÖM, P. and SWEDBERG, R. (eds.) 1998. *Social Mechanisms*. Cambridge: Cambridge University Press.

JACKSON, F. and PETTIT, P. 1990. In defence of folk psychology. *Philosophical Studies*, 57: 7–30.

JACKSON, J. E. 1996. Political methodology: an overview. Pp. 717–48 in *A New Handbook of Political Science*, ed. R. E. Goodin and H.-D. Klingemann. Oxford: Oxford University Press.

JACKSON, P. T. 2004. Defending the West: occidentalism and the formation of NATO. *Journal of Political Philosophy*, 11: 223–52.

JERVIS, R. 1997. *System Effects: Complexity in Political and Social Life*. Princeton, NJ: Princeton University Press.

JONES, E. E. and HARRIS, V. A. 1967. The attribution of attitudes. *Journal of Experimental Social Psychology*, 3: 1–24.

KAHNEMAN, D. 2003. Nobel lecture: maps of bounded rationality: psychology for behavioral economics. *American Economic Review*, 93: 1449–75.

——SLOVIC, P., and TVERSKY, A. (eds.) 1982. *Judgment under Uncertainty: Heuristics and Biases*. Cambridge: Cambridge University Press.

—— and TVERSKY, A. (eds.) 2000. *Choices, Values and Frames*. Cambridge: Cambridge University Press.

KANTOROWICZ, E. 1957. *The King's Two Bodies*. Princeton, NJ: Princeton Univeristy Press.

KEY, V. O., JR. 1949. *Southern Politics*. New York: Knopf.

KING, G., KEOHANE, R. O., and VERBA, S. 1994. *Designing Social Inquiry: Scientific Inference in Qualitative Research*. Princeton, NJ: Princeton University Press.

KRASNER, S. D. 1999. *Sovereignty: Organized Hypocrisy*. Princeton, NJ: Princeton University Press.

KURAN, T. 1991. Now out of never: the element of surprise in the East European revolution of 1989. *World Politics*, 44: 7–48.

——1995. The inevitability of future revolutionary surprises. *American Journal of Sociology*, 100: 1528–51.

LAITIN, D. D. 1992. *Language Repertoires and State Construction in Africa*. Cambridge: Cambridge University Press.

——1995. Disciplining political science. *American Political Science Review*, 89: 454–6.

LAWSON, K. 1990. Political parties: inside and out. *Comparative Politics*, 23: 105–19.

LIPSET, S. M. and ROKKAN, S. (eds.) 1967. *Party Systems and Voter Alignments*. New York: Free Press.

LITTLE, D. 1998. *On the Philosophy of the Social Sciences: Microfoundations, Method, and Causation*. New Brunswick, NJ: Transaction.

MCADAM, D., TARROW, S., and TILLY, C. 2001. *Dynamics of Contention*. Cambridge: Cambridge University Press.

MANN, M. 1986; 1993. *The Sources of Social Power*, 2 vols. Cambridge: Cambridge University Press.

MERTON, R. K. 1936. The unintended consequences of purposive social action. *American Sociological Review*, 1: 894–904.

——1957. *Social Theory and Social Structure*. Glencoe, Ill.: Free Press.

MILL, J. S. 1843. *A System of Logic*. London: Parker.

MILLS, C. W. 1940. Situated actions and vocabularies of motive. *American Sociological Review*, 5: 904–13.

MONROE, K. R. (ed.) 2004. *Perestroika, Methodological Pluralism, Governance and Diversity in Contemporary American Political Science*. New Haven, Conn.: Yale University Press.

MULLER, E. N. 1995. Economic determinants of democracy. *American Sociological Review*, 60: 966–82.

ORREN, K. 1991. *Belated Feudalism: Labor, the Law and Liberal Development in the United States*. Cambridge: Cambridge University Press.

PATTERSON, O. 1975. Context and choice in ethnic allegiance: a theoretical framework and Caribbean case study. Pp. 305–49 in *Ethnicity*, ed. N. Glazer and D. P. Moynihan. Cambridge, Mass.: Harvard University Press.

PETTIT, P. 1996. *The Common Mind*, 2nd edn. New York: Oxford University Press.

POPKIN, S. L. 1979. *The Rational Peasant*. Berkeley: University of California Press.

PRZEWORSKI, A., ALVAREZ, M. E., CHEIBUB, J. A., and LIMONGI, F. 2000. *Democracy and Development. Political Institutions and Well-Being in the World, 1950–1990*. Cambridge: Cambridge University Press.

RAGIN, C. C. 1994. *Constructing Social Research: The Unity and Diversity of Method*. Thousand Oaks, Calif.: Pine Forge.

RIKER, W. 1982. The two-party system and Duverger's law: an essay on the history of political science. *American Political Science Review*, 76: 753–66.

ROSANVALLON, P. 1989. The development of Keynesianism in France. Pp. 171–93 in *The Political Power of Economic Ideas: Keynesianism across Nations*, ed. P. Hall. Princeton, NJ: Princeton University Press.

ROSE, N. and MILLER, P. 1992. Political power beyond the state: problematics of government. *British Journal of Sociology*, 43: 172–205.

ROSS, L. 1977. The intuitive psychologist and his shortcomings. Volume 10, pp. 173–220 in *Advances in Experimental Social Psychology*, ed. L. Berkowitz. San Diego: Academic Press.

RYAN, A. 1970. *The Philosophy of the Social Sciences*. London: Macmillan.

RYLE, G. 1949. *The Concept of Mind*. London: Hutchinson.

SCHAFFER, F. C. 1998. *Democracy in Translation: Understanding Politics in an Unfamiliar Culture*. Ithaca, NY: Cornell University Press.

SCOTT, J. C. 1976. *The Moral Economy of the Peasant*. New Haven, Conn.: Yale University Press.

—— 1998. *Seeing Like a State*. New Haven, Conn.: Yale University Press.

SCOTT, M. B. and LYMAN, S. M. 1968. Accounts. *American Sociological Review*, 33: 46–63.

SEARLE, J. R. 1969. *Speech Acts*. Cambridge: Cambridge University Press.

—— 1995. *The Construction of Social Reality*. New York: Free Press.

SKINNER, Q. 1969. Meaning and understanding in the history of ideas. *History and Theory*, 8: 1–53.

—— 2002. *Visions of Politics*. Cambridge: Cambridge University Press.

SMITH, D. E. 1987. *The Everyday World as Problematic: A Feminist Sociology*. Boston: Northeastern University Press.

SOLNICK, S. L. 1998. *Stealing the State: Control and Collapse in Soviet Institutions*. Cambridge, Mass.: Harvard University Press.

STEINFELD, R. J. 2001. *Coercion, Contract, and Free Labor in the Nineteenth Century*. Cambridge: Cambridge University Press.

STINCHCOMBE, A. L. 1991. The conditions of fruitfulness of theorizing about mechanisms in social science. *Philosophy of the Social Sciences*, 21: 367–88.

STRØM, K. 2001. Why did the Norwegian Conservative Party shoot itself in the foot? Pp. 13–42 in Grofman 2001.

TILLY, C. 2000. Processes and mechanisms of democratization. *Sociological Theory*, 18: 1–16.

—— 2001. Mechanisms in political processes. *Annual Review of Political Science*, 4: 21–41.

—— 2007. *Why?* Princeton, NJ: Princeton University Press.

TULLY, J. (ed.) 1988. *Meaning and Context: Quentin Skinner and his Critics.* Princeton, NJ: Princeton University Press.

VERDERY, K. 2003. *The Vanishing Hectare: Property and Value in Postsocialist Transylvania.* Ithaca, NY: Cornell University Press.

WAGNER, P. 2003. As intellectual history meets historical sociology: historical sociology after the linguistic turn. In *Handbook of Historical Sociology*, ed. G. Delanty, E. Isin, and M. Somers. London: Sage.

WAJCMAN, J. 1991. *Feminism Confronts Technology.* Oxford: Polity.

WALBY, S. 1992. Post-post-modernism: theorizing social complexity. Pp. 31–52 in *Destabilizing Theory*, ed. M. Barratt and A. Phillips. Oxford: Polity.

WALKER, R. B. J. 1993. *Inside/Outside: International Relations as Political Theory.* Cambridge: Cambridge University Press.

WALTON, J. and SEDDON, D. 1994. *Free Markets and Food Riots: The Politics of Global Adjustment.* Oxford: Blackwell.

WENDT, A. E. 1987. The agent–structure problem in international relations theory. *International Organization*, 41: 335–70.

—— 1999. *Social Theory of International Politics.* Cambridge: Cambridge University Press.

WITTFOGEL, K. A. 1957. *Oriental Despotism.* New Haven, Conn.: Yale University Press.

···

POLITICAL ONTOLOGY

···

COLIN HAY

> The problems of pure philosophical ontology have seemed so deep or con-
> fused that philosophers who concentrate primarily on the concept of being
> as such have acquired an occasionally deserved reputation for obscurity and
> even incoherence.   (Jacquette 2002, xi)

THE terms "political" and "ontology" have, until recently, rarely gone together and,
given the above comments, it might seem desirable to maintain that separation.
Political scientists, for the most part, have tended to leave ontological issues to
philosophers and to those social scientists less encumbered by substantive empirical
concerns. Yet as the discipline has become more reflexive and perhaps rather less
confident than once it was at the ease with which it might claim a scientific license
for the knowledge it generates, so ontological concerns have increasingly come to
the fore. In addressing such issues, as I shall argue, political analysts have no so
much moved into novel terrain as acknowledged, reflected upon, challenged, and,
in some cases, rethought the tacit assumptions on which their analytical enterprises
were always premised. No political analysis has ever been ontologically neutral; rather
fewer political analysts are prepared to proceed today on the basis of this once unacknowledged and unchallenged presumption.

Consequently, however tempting it might well be to leave ontology to others, that
option may not be available to us. The principal aim of the present chapter is to
explain why this is so. The argument is, in essence, simple. Ontological assumptions
(relating to the nature of the political reality that is the focus of our analytical attentions) are logically antecedent to the epistemological and methodological choices
more usually identified as the source of paradigmatic divergence in political science

(cf. King, Keohane, and Verba 1994; Monroe 2004). Two points almost immediately follow from this. First, often unacknowledged ontological choices underpin major theoretical disputes within political analysis. Second, whilst such disagreements are likely to be manifest in epistemological and methodological choices, these are merely epiphenomena of more ultimately determinate ontological assumptions. Accordingly, they cannot be fully appreciated in the absence of sustained ontological reflection and debate.

This is all very well in the abstract, but it remains decidedly abstract. The second challenge of this chapter is to demonstrate that "ontology matters" in substantive terms. This may sound like a tall order. However, it is in fact rather more straightforward that might be assumed. First, we might note that political ontology is intimately associated with adjudicating the categories to which legitimate appeal might be made in political analysis. As Charles Tilly and Robert E. Goodin note, "ontological choices concern the sorts of social entities whose consistent existence analysts can reasonably assume" (2006). In other words, whether we choose to conduct our analysis in terms of identities, individuals, social collectivities, states, regimes, systems, or some combination of the above, reflects a prior set of ontological choices and assumptions—most obviously about the character, nature, and, indeed, "reality" of each as ontological entities and (potential) dramatis personae on the political stage.

Second, even where we can agree upon common categories of actors, mechanisms, or processes to which legitimate appeal can be made, ontological choices affect substantively the content of our theories about such entities (and hence our expectations about how the political drama will unfold). A shared commitment to ontological individualism (the view that human individuals are the sole, unique, and ultimate constituents of social reality to which all else is reducible) is no guarantee of a common approach to political analysis, far less to a common account of a specific political drama or context. The substantive content of our ontological individualism will vary dramatically if we regard actors to be self-serving instrumental utility maximizers, on the one hand, or altruistic communitarians, on the other, just as our view of the strategies appropriate to the emancipation of women will vary significantly depending on our (ontological) view as to the biological and/or social character of seemingly "essential" gender differences (compare, for instance, Brownmiller 1975; Daly 1978; Elshtain 1981; Wolf 1993; Young 1990). In these, and innumerable other ways, our ontological choices—whether acknowledged or unacknowledged—have profound epistemological, methodological, and practical political consequences.

Given this, it is pleasing to be able to report that contemporary political analysts are rather more reflexive, ontologically, than many of their immediate predecessors. Representative of contemporary trends in this respect is Alexander Wendt. Ontology, he suggests,

is not something that most international relations (IR) scholars spend much time thinking about. Nor should they. The primary task of IR social science is to help to understand world politics, not to ruminate about issues more properly the concern of philosophers. Yet even the most empirically minded students of international politics must "do" ontology.   (1999, 370)

In the brief survey that follows, my aim is to indicate in outline form what "doing" political ontology entails. But it is first important to establish, in somewhat greater detail, what it is and why it is important.

1 POLITICAL ONTOLOGY: WHAT IS IT?

Most standard philosophical treatments of ontology differentiate between two, albeit closely related, senses of the term.[1] The first, and more abstract, is concerned with the nature of "being" itself—what is it to exist, whether (and, if so, why) there exists something rather than nothing, and whether (and, if so, why) there exists one logically contingent actual world. The second sense of the term is concerned with the (specific) set of assumptions made about the nature, essence, and characteristics (in short, the reality) of an object or set of objects of analytical inquiry. However ethereal such issues may nonetheless seem, political analysts have principally concerned themselves with the latter, philosophically more prosaic, set of concerns. In Benton and Craib's (2001) terms, political ontology is a "regional ontology." This chapter replicates that focus.

Thus, whilst ontology is defined, literally, as the 'science' or 'philosophy' of being, within political analysis it has tended to be defined in more narrow and specific terms. Norman Blaikie's definition is here representative. Ontology, he suggests, "refers to the claims or assumptions that a particular approach to social [or, by extension, political] enquiry makes about the nature of social [or political] reality—claims about what exists, what it looks like, what units make it up and how these units interact with one another" (1993, 6). Ontology relates to *being*, to what *is*, to what *exists*, to the constituent units of reality; political ontology, by extension, relates to *political being*, to what *is* politically, to what *exists politically*, and to the units that comprise political reality.

The analyst's ontological position is, then, her answer to the question: What is the nature of the social and political reality to be investigated? Alternatively, what exists that we might acquire knowledge of? As this already implies, ontology logically precedes epistemology. However put, these are rather significant questions whose answers may determine, to a considerable extent, the content of the political analysis we are likely to engage in and, indeed, what we regard as an (adequate) political explanation. Thus, for "ontological atomists," convinced in Hobbesian terms that "basic human needs, capacities and motivations arise in each individual without regard to any specific feature of social groups or social interactions" (Fay 1996, 31), there can be no appeal in political explanation to social interactions, processes or structures. For "ontological structuralists," by contrast, it is the appeal to human needs and capacities that is ruled inadmissible in the court of political analysis. Similarly, for

[1] See e.g. Grossmann 1992; Honderich 1995, 634–5; Jacquette 2002; Schmitt 2003; see also Benton and Craib 2001, 183.

those convinced of a separation of appearance and reality—such that we cannot trust our senses to reveal to us that which is real as distinct from that which merely presents itself to us *as if* it were real—political analysis is likely to be a rather more complex and methodologically exacting process than for those prepared to accept that reality presents itself to us in a direct and unmediated fashion.

Working from this simple definition, a great variety of issues of political ontology can be identified. Adapting Uskali Mäki's thoughtful (and pioneering) reflections on economic ontology (2001, 3; see also Mäki 2002, 15–22) to the political realm, we might identify all of the following as ontological questions:

What is the polity made of? What are its constituents and how do they hang together? What kinds of general principles govern its functioning, and its change? Are they causal principles and, if so, what is the nature of political causation? What drives political actors and what mental capacities do they possess? Do individual preferences and social institutions exist, and in what sense? Are (any of) these things historically and culturally invariant universals, or are they relative to context?

Such questions readily establish a simple analytical agenda for political ontology. They also serve to indicate that no political analysis can proceed in the absence of assumptions about political ontology. That such assumptions are rarely explicit hardly makes them less consequential. Presented more thematically, amongst the ontological issues on which political analysts formulate consequential assumptions are the following:

1. The relationship between structure and agency, context, and conduct.
2. The extent of the causal and/or constitutive role of ideas in the determination of political outcomes.
3. The extent to which social and political systems exhibit organic qualities or are reducible in all characteristics to the sum of their constituent units/parts.
4. The (dualistic or dialectical) relationship between mind and body.
5. The nature of the human (political) subject and its behavioural motivations.
6. The extent to which causal dynamics are culturally/contextually specific or generalizable.
7. The respective characteristics of the objects of the natural and social sciences.
8. Perhaps most fundamentally of all, the extent (if any) of the separation of appearance and reality—the extent to which the social and political world presents itself to us as really it is such that what is real is observable.

Whilst interest in, and reflexivity with respect to, such ontological issues has certainly risen considerably in recent years, coverage of such issues is very uneven. Indeed, it is really only some of these issues—principally the first, second, third, and, to some extent, the fifth—that have prompted sustained ontological reflection to date.[2] It is on these issues that this chapter will concentrate principally.

---

[2] Whilst the appropriate preference function(s) and behavioral assumptions that we should adopt in, for instance, game-theoretic modeling has been a focus of considerable attention, the vast majority of that reflection has failed to acknowledge the ontological character of the issue.

The crucial point, for now, to note about each of these issues is that none of them can be resolved empirically. Ultimately, no amount of empirical evidence can refute the (ontological) claims of the atomist or the structuralist; neither can it confirm or reject the assumption that there is no separation of appearance and reality.[3] This is all rather disconcerting and perhaps explains the characteristic reluctance of political analysts to venture into debate on, and thereby to lay bare, their ontological assumptions. For to acknowledge an ontological dependence, and hence a reliance upon assumptions that are in principle untestable, may be seen to undermine the rightly cherished and long-fought-for authority of the analyst and the analytical traditions in which her contribution is constructed. Yet, on any sustained reflection, silence is not a very attractive option either. For, whether we like it or not, and whether we choose to acknowledge it or not, we *make* ontological assumptions—in Wendt's terms, we "do" ontology. These assumptions profoundly shape our approach to political analysis and cannot simply be justified by appeal to an evidential base. It is to the consequences of such choices that we now turn.

2 ... And Why Is It Important?

However significant they may be in their own terms, ontological assumptions find themselves increasingly the subject of the political analyst's attentions largely for their epistemological and methodological consequences.

Again it is important to be precise about our terminology, for confusions abound in the literature.[4]

Epistemology, again defined literally, is the "science" or "philosophy" of knowledge. In Blaikie's terms, it refers "to the claims or assumptions made about the ways in which it is possible to gain knowledge of reality" (1993, 6–7). In short, if the ontologist asks "what exists to be known?", then the epistemologist asks "what are the conditions of acquiring knowledge of that which exists?" Epistemology concerns itself with such

---

[3] For, clearly, what counts as evidence in the first place depends on one's view of the relationship between that which is observed and experienced, on the one hand, and that which is real, on the other. Where the (archetypal) pluralist sees an open and democratic decision-making process, the (similarly archetypal) elite theorist sees the work of covert agenda-setting processes behind the scenes, and the (no less archetypal) Marxist, evidence of preference-shaping ideological indoctrination.

[4] In the much-lauded second edition of their highly respected and influential text on *Theory and Methods in Political Science*, for instance, the editors and contributors display a marked lack of consistency in defining ontology and epistemology. Given that theirs is practically the only entry-level introduction to these topics currently available to students of political science, this is all the more tragic. Thus, in their introductory essay, David Marsh and Gerry Stoker suggest, quite remarkably, that "ontology is concerned with what we can know and epistemology with how we can know it" (2002, 11). Yet in the first substantive chapter of the volume, David Marsh, this time with Paul Furlong, defines ontology (correctly) as "a theory of being" and suggests that epistemology relates to "what we can know about the world" and (more problematically) "how we can know it" (2002, 18–19). Of these, only the second definition of ontology is entirely unproblematic.

issues as the degree of certainty we might legitimately claim for the conclusions
we are tempted to draw from our analyses, the extent to which specific knowledge
claims might be generalized beyond the immediate context in which our observations
were made, and, in general terms, how we might adjudicate and defend a preference between contending political explanations. As this indicates, epistemological
assumptions are invariably ontologically loaded—whether knowledge is transferable
between different settings for political analysis and hence whether we can legitimately
generalize between "cases" (an epistemological consideration) depends on (prior)
assumptions about the ontological specificity of such settings.

Yet the implications of ontological choices are not confined to epistemology; they
are also methodological.

Methodology relates to the choice of analytical strategy and research design which
underpins substantive research. Although methodology establishes the principles
which might guide the choice of method, it should not be confused with the methods
and techniques of research themselves. Indeed, methodologists frequently draw the
distinction between the two, emphasizing the extent of the gulf between what they
regard as established methodological principles and perhaps equally well-established
methodological practices. What they invariably fail to do is to acknowledge and
reflect upon the ontological dependence of methodological choices. For our purposes
methodology is best understood as the means by which we reflect upon the methods
appropriate to realize fully our potential to acquire knowledge of that which exists.

What this brief discussion hopefully serves to demonstrate is that ontology, epistemology, and methodology, though closely related, are irreducible. Ontology relates to
the nature of the social and political world, epistemology to what we can know about
it, and methodology to how we might go about acquiring that knowledge.

As this perhaps already serves to indicate, their relationship is also directional—
ontology logically precedes epistemology which logically precedes methodology (see
also Archer 1998; Bhaskar 1989, 49; Gilbert 1989, 440; though cf. Smith 1990, 18).
We cannot know what we are capable of knowing (epistemology) until such time
as we have settled on (a set of assumptions about) the nature of the context in which
that knowledge must be acquired (ontology). Similarly, we cannot decide upon an
appropriate set of strategies for interrogating political processes (methodology) until
we have settled upon the limits of our capacity to acquire knowledge of such processes
(epistemology) and, indeed, the nature of such processes themselves (ontology).

The directional dependence of this relationship is presented schematically and
illustrated with respect to postmodernism in Figure 23.1. As this already serves to
indicate, to suggest that ontological consideration are both irreducible and logically
prior to those of epistemology is most definitely not to suggest that they are unrelated.
The degree of confidence that we might have for the claims we make about political
phenomena, for instance, is likely to vary significantly depending on our view of the
relationship between the ideas we formulate on the one hand and the political referents of those ideas, on the other. In this way, our ontology may shape our epistemology; moreover, both are likely to have methodological implications. If we are happy
to conceive of ourselves as disinterested and dispassionate observers of an external

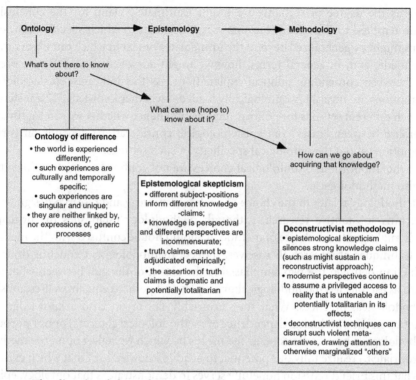

Fig. 23.1. The directional dependence of ontology, epistemology, and methodology: the case of postmodernism
Source: Hay (2002: 227).

(political) reality existing independently of our conceptions of it, then we are likely to be rather more confident epistemologically than if we are prepared to concede that: (1) we are, at best, partisan participant observers; (2) that there is no neutral vantage-point from which the political can be viewed objectively; and that (3) the ideas we fashion of the political context we inhabit influence our behavior and hence the unfolding dynamics of that political context.[5] Such ontological assumptions and their epistemological implications are, in turn, likely to influence significantly the type of evidence we consider and the techniques we deploy to interrogate that evidence. If, for instance, we are keen to acknowledge (ontologically) an independent causal role for ideas in determining the developmental trajectory of political institutions, then we are likely to devote our methodological energies to gauging the understandings of political subjects. If, by contrast, we see ideas as merely epiphenomenal of ultimately determinant material bases (for instance, the self-interest of the actors who hold such ideas), then our methodological attentions will be focused elsewhere.

[5] To suggest that our ideas influence our conduct and that our conduct has, in turn, the capacity to reshape our environment is not, of course, to insist that it necessarily does so in any given setting over any particular time-horizon. It is to suggest, however, that insofar as conduct serves to shape and reshape a given political landscape, the ideas held by actors about that context are crucial to any understanding of such a process of political change (see also Rueschemeyer, in *Oxford Handbook of Contextual Political Analysis*, ed. R. E. Goodin and C. Tilly 2006. Oxford: Oxford University Press).

3 The Status of Ontological Claims

Given the sheer volume of literature devoted in recent years to questions of ontology (principally the structure–agency and material–ideational relationships) in political science and international relations, it might be tempting to assume that the need for a series of reflections on this question is relatively undisputed. The reality, however, it somewhat different. For even in sociology, perhaps the natural home of reflection on such issues, there are dissenting voices. In making the case for the centrality of such concerns to political analysis it is perhaps appropriate that we first deal with the potential objections. Among the most vociferous of critics of the "craze" for abstract ontological reflection is Steve Fuller. His central argument is simply stated:

> Given the supposedly abortive attempts at solving the structure–agency problem, one is tempted to conclude that sociologists are not smart enough to solve the problem or that the problem itself is spurious.   (Fuller 1998, 104)

The case is certainly well made, and might be extended to almost all ontological reflection within the social sciences. There would seem to be little to be gained by political analysts in following their sociological forebears into an ontological cul-de-sac of obfuscation and meaningless abstraction.

Yet Fuller's remarks are not quite as devastating as they might first appear. For, in certain crucial respects, they reveal a systematic, if widespread, misinterpretation of the nature of ontological disputes of this kind. In this respect they prove quite useful in helping us establish what is—and what is not—at stake in debates about the relative significance of ideational and material, or structural and agential factors. Put most simply, ontological issues such as these are not "problems" to which there is, or can be, definitive solutions.

To appeal to the issue of structure and agency, for instance, as a "problem" with a potential "solution" is effectively to claim that the issue is an empirical one that can be resolved definitively. Yet, claims as to the relative significance of structural and agential factors are founded on ontological assumptions as to the nature of a social and political reality. To insist that such claims can be resolved by appeal to the evidence is, then, to conflate the empirical and the ontological. To put this in more practical and prosaic terms, any given and agreed set of empirical observations can be accounted for in more or less agential, more or less structural terms. We might, for instance, agree on the precise chain of events leading up to the French Revolution of 1789 whilst disagreeing vehemently over the relative significance of structural and agential factors in the explanation of the event itself. Evidence alone is not ontologically discriminating, though it is often presented as such.[6]

---

[6] This is largely because the process of presenting evidence is invariably one which situates it ontologically (with respect to often tacit ontological assumptions, such as the extent, if any, of a separation of appearance and reality).

Two important implications follow directly from the above discussion. First, if the relative significance of structural and agential, ideational, and material factors cannot be established empirically, then we must seek to avoid all claims which suggest that it might. Sadly, such claims are commonplace. Even Wendt himself, doyen both of the "structure–agency problematique" and of constructivism in international relations theory, is not above such conceptual confusions. Consider the following passage from an otherwise exemplary discussion co-written with Ian Shapiro:

The differences among ... "realist" models of agency and structure—and among them and their individualist and holist rivals—are differences about where the important causal mechanisms lie in social life. As such, *we can settle them only by wrestling with the empirical merits of their claims about human agency and social structure ... These are in substantial part empirical questions.*   (Wendt and Shapiro 1997, 181, emphasis added)

Wendt and Shapiro are surely right to note that ontological differences such as those between, say, more agency-centered and more structure-centered accounts, tend to resolve themselves into differences about where to look for and, indeed, what counts as important causal mechanisms in the first place. This implies that ontology precedes epistemology. Such a view is entirely consistent with the argument of the previous section—we must decide what exists out there to know about (ontology) before we can consider what knowledge we might acquire of it (epistemology), let alone how we might go about acquiring that knowledge (methodology). Yet having noted this, Wendt and Shapiro almost immediately abandon the logic it implies, suggesting that we might choose between contending ontologies on the basis of what we observe empirically. Surely this now implies that epistemology precedes ontology. If our ontology informs where we look for causal mechanisms and what we see in the first place (as they contend), then how can we rely upon what we observe to adjudicate between contending ontologies?

Wendt and Shapiro's confusion is further compounded in the passage which immediately follows, in which a Popperian logic of falisifiability is invoked:

The advocates of individualism, structuralism and structuration theory have all done a poor job of specifying the conditions under which their claims about the relationship of agency and social structure would be falsified.   (Wendt and Shapiro 1997, 181)

Here again we see direct appeal to the possibility of an epistemological refutation of ontological propositions. The point is that, as ontological positions, individualism, structuralism, and structuration theory *cannot* be falsified—our preference between them has to be adjudicated differently. A similar conflation underpins Wendt's recent prescriptive suggestion that "ontology talk is necessary, but we should also be looking for ways to translate it into propositions that might be adjudicated empirically" (1999, 37). If only this were possible. When, as Wendt himself notes, ontological sensitivities inform what is "seen" in the first place and, for (philosophical) realists like himself, provide the key to peering through the mists of the ephemeral and the superficial to the structured reality beneath, the idea that ontological claims as to what exists can be adjudicated empirically is rendered deeply suspect. Quite simply, perspectives on the question of structure and agency, or any other ontological issue for that matter, cannot be falsified—for they make no necessary empirical claim. It is for precisely this reason that logical positivists (like Popper) reject as meaningless ontological claims such as those upon which realism and structuration theory are premised.[7]

It is important, then, that we avoid claiming empirical license for ontological claims and assumptions. Yet arguably more important still is that we resist the temptation to present positions on, say, the structure–agency question as universal solutions for all social scientific dilemmas. In particular, social ontologies cannot be brought in to resolve substantive empirical disputes. Giddens' structuration theory can no more tell me who will win the next US presidential election than the theory of predestination can tell me whether my train will arrive on time tomorrow. The latter might be able to tell me that the movements of trains is etched into the archaeology of historical time itself, just as the structuration theorist might tell me the next US presidential election will be won and lost in the interaction between political actors and the context in which they find themselves. Neither is likely to be of much practical use to me, nor is it likely to provide much consolation if my train is late and my preferred candidate loses. It is important, then, that we do not expect too much from "solutions" to ontological "problems."

4 ONTOLOGICAL DISPUTES IN POLITICAL ANALYSIS

Of all issues in political ontology, it is the related though by no means interchangeable (see Pettit 1993) questions of the relationship between individuals and social collectivities and between structure and agency that have undoubtedly attracted the most sustained attention and reflection over the longest period of time. A rather more recent set of concerns relates to the question of the relationship between the material and the ideational as (related or independent) dimensions of political reality. In the brief sections which follow, I consider each set of issues in turn.

4.1 The Individual–Group Relationship

In political analysis and the philosophy of the social sciences more broadly there is no more hardy perennial than the question of the relationship between individuals and

---

[7] However tempting this strategy may seem, however, it does not provide an escape from ontological issues and choices. For, as indicated earlier, whether we choose to acknowledge them or nor, political analysis necessarily proceeds on the basis of ontological assumptions.

social collectivities or groups (see Fay 1996, ch. 3; Gilbert 1989; Hollis 1994; Pettit 1993; Ryan 1970, ch. 8). Can collective actors (states, political parties, social movements, classes, and so forth) realistically, or indeed just usefully, be said to exist? If so, do they exhibit organic qualities, such that their character or nature is not simply reducible to the aggregation of the constituent units (generally individual actors) from which they are forged? Are such entities (if that is indeed what they are) appropriate subjects of political analysis and, if so, what if any behavioural characteristics can be attributed to them?

These and other related ontological questions have divided political analysts, and will no doubt continue to divide political analysts, as they have divided philosophers, for centuries. Generally speaking the controversy they have generated has seen protagonists resolve themselves with one of two mutually exclusive positions. These are usually labeled "individualism" and "holism" and they are often defined in mutually antagonistic terms. As Margaret Gilbert explains, ontological individualism is simply the doctrine that "social groups are nothing over and above the individuals who are their members" (1989, 428). It tends to be associated with a further, analytical set of claims, namely that what she terms "everyday collectivity concepts" (states, classes, parties, and other groups) "are analysable without remainder in terms of concepts other than collectivity concepts, in particular, in terms of the concept of an individual person, his [sic] goals, beliefs and so on" (1989, 434–5).

Holism, by contrast, is invariably understood as the simple denial of individualism, the doctrine that "social groups exist in their own right" (1989, 428) or, in Brian Fay's more applied terms, that "the theories which explain social phenomena are not reducible to theories about the individuals which perform them" (1996, 50). In its more extreme variants, however, holism is less a belief in the organic nature of social and political reality than the dogmatic assertion that the task of social and political analysts is exclusively to document the (causal) role of social, i.e. holistic, phenomena, processes, and dynamics (cf. Ryan 1970, 172). In this form, holism, though very much in vogue in the 1970s, is now little more than a term of abuse within contemporary political science. It might be tempting, then, to see the dispute having been resolved in favor of individualism. This, however, would be too rash an inference to draw. For although most analytical routes in political science today lead from individualism, many make considerable concessions, as we shall see, to holism.

The dispute, as already indicated, is a timeless one, with perhaps the most eloquent defender of ontological (and, indeed, methodological) individualism being John Stuart Mill:

The laws of the phenomena of society are, and can be, nothing but the laws of the actions and passions of human being united together in the social state... Men [sic] are not, when brought together, converted into another kind of substance, with different properties... Human beings in society have no properties but those which are derived from, and may be resolved into, the laws of nature of individual man.   (1970 [1843], 573; cited in Hollis 1994, 10)

Though, as is often noted, Mill was by no means consistent in keeping to the strictures of such an individualism and can be found at various times on the other side of the fence, he is a seemingly obligatory first citation for those asserting or defending their (ontological) individualism.

Unremarkably, the most dogged contemporary defence of individualism is found in rational choice theory. Jon Elster is characteristically incisive in claiming that "the elementary unit of social life is the individual human action." Consequently "to explain social institutions and social change is to show how they arise as the result of the action and interaction of individuals" (1989, 13). What is unusual about this comment is that, unlike most rational choice theory, it seeks to present and defend individualism in ontological, rather than in more narrowly methodological, terms. Yet even rational choice theory, resolutely committed as it remains to methodological individualism, has made significant concessions to the organic qualities of social and political collectivities identified by holists. Indeed, in this respect, the developmental trajectory of rational choice in recent years is suggestive of something of an emerging ontological consensus amongst political analysts. Two points might here be made. First, whilst there have always been those who have presented rational choice theory in such terms (most notably, Friedman 1953, 14–15), many more contemporary rational choice theorists seem prepared to accept the ontological irrealism of rational choice assumptions, defending such premises in terms of their analytical utility not their correspondence to an external reality (for a more sustained discussion, see Hay 2004). Second, the move by many rational choice theorists, particularly so-called rational choice institutionalists, from an absolute towards a "bounded," i.e. context-dependent, conception of rationality significantly qualifies and arguably violates any purist defence of ontological or, indeed, methodological individualism. For, put simply, if the stylized rational actor's utility- and/or preference-function is a product of her context, role, or systemic function (as in much contemporary rational choice institutionalism), then to explain her behavior or to predict the consequences of her behavior in terms of such a utility/preference-function is no longer to subscribe to a methodological individualism.

As this perhaps suggests, however seemingly entrenched holism and individualism have, on occasions, become, a commonsense ground between such antagonistic extremes exists and is inhabited by a growing number of political analysts. Such a position accepts, ontologically, the following: (1) that a social whole is "not merely the sum of its parts"; (2) that there are "holistic properties" of such social wholes; (3) that these "can sensibly be said to belong to the whole and not to any of the parts"; and yet (4) that dismantle the whole and we are left with the parts and "not them and some mysterious property which formerly held the whole thing together" (Ryan 1970, 181).

4.2 The Structure–Agency Relationship

No less classical or disputed an issue in the philosophy of the social sciences is the question of the structure–agency relationship. Though closely related, it is by no means irreducible to the question of the relationship between groups and individuals and has been far more hotly contested than the latter in recent years.

Though space does not permit a detailed review of the literature, the key trends can nonetheless be established relatively simply (for more sustained discussion see Hay 1995; 2002, 89–134):

- The proliferation of interest in the relationship between structure and agency has in fact been remarkably consensual, with scholars in political science and international relations rounding on both structuralist and intentionalist tendencies.[8]
- In so doing they have come to champion a range of perspectives from social theory, notably Giddens' (1984) structuration theory and the critical realists' strategic-relational approach (Bhaskar 1979; 1989; Jessop 1990; 1996).
- What each of these perspectives shares is the attempt to explore the dynamic interplay of structure and agency.

In short, and almost without exception, those who have reflected in a sustained fashion upon the question of structure and agency have done so with an increasing sense of frustration at the tacit intentionalism or, more usually, structuralism of existing mainstream approaches to political analysis. In particular they have found structuralism lurking in some apparently unlikely places. Chief amongst these is rational choice theory.

As a perspective which emphasizes the rationality exhibited by conscious and reflective actors in the process of making choices, it is difficult to imagine an approach that is seemingly more attentive to agency. However, impressions can be deceptive. For, within any rational choice model, we know one thing above all: that the actor will behave rationally, maximizing his or her personal utility. Consequently, any rational actor in a given context will choose precisely the same (optimal) course of action. Actors are essentially interchangeable (Tsebelis 1990, 43). Moreover, where there is more than one optimal course of action (where, in short, there are multiple equilibria), we can expect actors' behavior to be distributed predictably between— and only between—such optima. What this implies is that the agent's "choice" is rendered predictable (and, in the absence of multiple equilbria, entirely predictable) given the context. The implications of this are clear. We need know nothing about the actor to predict the outcome of political behavior. For it is independent of the actor in question. Indeed, it is precisely this which gives rational choice modes of explanation their (much cherished) predictive capacity.

In short, it is only the substitution of a fixed preference function for an indeterminate actor that allows a spurious and naturalist notion of prediction to be retained in rational choice (see also Hay 2004). Render the analytical assumptions about the individual actor more complex and realistic (by recognizing some element of contingency) and rational choice models become indeterminate.

This raises a final and important point, something of a leitmotif of this chapter. The rise of political ontology has increasingly led to a series of challenges to naturalism (a belief in the possibility of a unity of method between the natural and social sciences)

---

[8] See, for instance, Adler 1997; Carlsnaes 1992; Cerny 1990; Dessler 1989; Kenny and Smith 1997; Smith 1998; 1999; Suganami 1999; Wendt 1987. For a review, see Hay 1995.

and to naturalistic political science more specifically. The above paragraphs provide but one example. As they suggest, rational choice theory can deliver a naturalist science of politics only by virtue of the implausible (ontological) assumptions it makes about the universally instrumental, self-serving, and utility-maximizing character of human conduct. These serve, in effect, to empty agency of any content such that the actor becomes a mere relay for delivering a series of imperatives inherent in the context itself. In short, a naturalist science of politics is only possible if we assume what we elsewhere deny—that all actors, in any given context, will act in a manner rendered predictable (in many cases fully determinate) by the context in which they find themselves. Soften the assumptions, or even the universality of the assumptions, and the fragile edifice of naturalism crumbles. With it must go the universal pretensions of much rational choice theory and, indeed, the very possibility of a predictive science of the political.

4.3 The Ideational–Material Relationship

Very similar themes emerge in the burgeoning literature on the relationship between the ideational and the material and the extent to which ideas may be accorded a causal and/or constitutive role in the determination of political outcomes.[9] Here, once more, the key question relates to the limits of naturalism. In particular, it is suggested, the existence of an irredeemably cognitive dimension to the social and political world for which there is no direct equivalent or analogue in the natural world, presents profound ontological impediments to a naturalist social science.

Once again there has been a considerable degree of harmony and consensus amongst those who have addressed these issues in ontological terms. The result is a convergence upon, and consolidation of, a position usually labeled constructivism in international relations theory, and usually seen as a development of historical institutionalism in political science (for a useful review see Blyth 2003). It defines itself in opposition to the materialist and naturalist rump of mainstream political science and international relations.

Like the qualified materialism of many contemporary rational choice institutionalists and neo-realists,[10] constructivists start from the recognition that we cannot hope to understand political behavior without understanding the ideas actors hold about the environment in which they find themselves. Yet here the materialists and the constructivists part company, with the latter refusing to see such ideas as themselves reducible to ultimately determinant material factors (such as contextually given interests). Consequently, they accord ideas an independent causal role in political explanation. Nonetheless, whilst it is important not simply to reduce the ideational to a reflection, say, of underlying material interests, it is equally important not to subscribe to a voluntarist idealism in which political outcomes might be read off, more

---

[9] See Hay (2002, 194–215) for a more sustained discussion.
[10] See, for instance, Denzau and North 1994; Goldstein and Keohane 1993; North 1990.

or less directly, from the desires, motivations, and cognitions of the immediate actors themselves. What is required, instead, is a recognition of the complex interaction of material and ideational factors. Political outcomes are, in short, neither a simple reflection of actors' intentions and understandings nor of the contexts which give rise to such intentions and understandings. Rather, they are a product of the impact of the strategies actors devise as means to realize their intentions upon a context which favors certain strategies over others and does so irrespective of the intentions of the actors themselves.

Constructivism is, however, a broad church, encompassing a diverse range of positions. At the idealist end of the spectrum we find varieties of "thick" constructivism keen to privilege the constitutive role of ideas whilst not entirely denying the significance of material factors. At the other end of the spectrum we find varieties of critical realism whose rather "thinner" constructivism tends to emphasize instead the constraints the material world places on such discursive constructions.[11] What each of these positions shares, however, is a complex or dialectical view of the relationship between the ideational and the material and a rejection of the possibility of a naturalist social science.

5 CONCLUSION

As the previous sections have sought to demonstrate, the proliferation of literature on political ontology in recent years has produced (or perhaps reflected and reinforced) a remarkable consensus. The vast majority of authors who have interrogated systematically the relationships between structure and agency and the material and the ideational *as ontological issues*, have, for instance, come subsequently to promote a post-naturalist, post-positivist approach to social and political analysis premised upon the acknowledgement of the dynamic interplay of structure and agency and material and ideational factors. In so doing they have pointed to a consistent disparity between the often tacit and normalized analytical assumptions of existing mainstream approaches to political analysis and those which emerge from sustained ontological reflection.

In particular they have challenged the often parsimonious and self-confessedly unrealistic analytical assumptions which invariably make naturalist approaches to political science possible. This is undoubtedly a useful exercise and has already given rise to genuinely novel approaches to political analysis and a series of important insights (the contributions of the new constructivist–institutionalist synthesis being a case in point). Yet it can be taken too far. In one sense it is unremarkable that political ontologists, interested principally in the extent to which the complexity and

---

[11] For a variety of different positions within this spectrum compare the various contributions to Christiansen, Jørgensen, and Wiener (2001).

contingency of the "real world" of social and political interaction might be captured, encourage us to choose complex, credible, and realistic analytical assumptions. Yet this is not a costless move. Simple, elegant, and parsimonious analytical assumptions are unlikely to satisfy the political ontologist, but this may not be sufficient reason to jettison them. However unrealistic they may be, they have an appeal and can certainly be defended in the kind of pragmatic terms that are unlikely to feature prominently in the ontologist's deliberations. Here, as elsewhere, clear trade-offs are involved. Political ontology can certainly help us to appreciate what is at stake in such choices, providing something of a counterbalance to the mainstream's characteristic silence on its most central assumptions, but it cannot be allowed to dictate such choices alone.

REFERENCES

ADLER, E. 1997. Seizing the middle ground: constructivism in world politics. *European Journal of International Relations*, 3: 319–63.

ARCHER, M. S. 1998. Social theory and the analysis of society. Pp. 69–85 in *Knowing the Social World*, ed. T. May and M. Williams. Buckingham: Open University Press.

BENTON, T. and CRAIB, I. 2001. *Philosophy of Social Science: The Philosophical Foundations of Social Thought*. Buckingham: Open University Press.

BHASKAR, R. 1979. *The Limits of Naturalism*. Brighton: Harvester Wheatsheaf.

—— 1989. *Reclaiming Reality*. London: Verso.

BLAIKIE, N. 1993. *Approaches to Social Enquiry*. Cambridge: Polity.

BLYTH, M. 2003. Structures do not come with an instruction sheet: interests, ideas and progress in political science. *Perspectives on Politics*, 1: 695–706.

BROWNMILLER, S. 1975. *Against Our Will: Men, Women and Rape*. London: Secker and Warburg.

CARLSNAES, W. 1992. The agent–structure problem in foreign policy analysis. *International Studies Quarterly*, 6: 245–70.

CERNY, P. G. 1990. *The Changing Architecture of Politics: Structure, Agency and the Future of the State*. London: Sage.

CHRISTIANSEN, T., JØRGENSEN, K. E., and WIENER, A. 2001. Introduction. Pp. 1–21 in *The Social Construction of Europe*, ed. T. Christiansen et al. London: Sage.

DALY, M. 1978. *Gyn/Ecology: The Metaethics of Radical Feminism*. Boston: Beacon Press.

DENZAU, A. T. and NORTH, D. C. 1994. Shared mental models: ideologies and institutions. *Kyklos*, 47: 3–31

DESSLER, D. 1989. What's at stake in the agent-structure debate? *International Organization*, 43: 441–73.

ELSHTAIN, J. B. 1981. *Public Man, Private Woman: Women in Social and Political Thought*. Princeton, NJ: Princeton University Press.

ELSTER, J. 1989. *Nuts and Bolts for the Social Sciences*. Cambridge: Cambridge University Press.

FAY, B. 1996. *Contemporary Philosophy of Social Science: A Multicultural Approach*. Oxford: Blackwell.

FRIEDMAN, M. 1953. *Essays in Positive Economics*. Chicago: University of Chicago Press.

FULLER, S. 1998. From content to context: a social epistemology of the structure–agency craze. Pp. 92–117 in *What is Social Theory? The Philosophical Debates*, ed. A. Sica. Oxford: Blackwell.

GIDDENS, A. 1984. *The Constitution of Society*. Cambridge: Polity.

GILBERT, M. 1989. *On Social Facts*. Princeton, NJ: Princeton University Press.

GOLDSTEIN, J. and KEOHANE, R. O. (eds.) 1993. *Ideas and Foreign Policy: Beliefs, Institutions and Political Change*. Ithaca, NY: Cornell University Press.

GROSSMANN, R. 1992. *The Existence of the World: An Introduction to Ontology*. London: Routledge.

HAY, C. 1995. Structure and agency. Pp. 189–206 in *Theory and Methods in Political Science*, ed. D. Marsh and G. Stoker. London: Macmillan.

—— 2002. *Political Analysis*. Basingstoke: Palgrave.

—— 2004. Theory, stylised heuristic or self-fulfilling prophecy? The status of rational choice theory in public administration. *Public Administration*, 82: 39–61.

HOLLIS, M. 1994. *The Philosophy of Social Science*. Cambridge: Cambridge University Press.

HONDERICH, T. (ed.) 1995. *The Oxford Companion to Philosophy*. Oxford: Oxford University Press.

JACQUETTE, D. 2002. *Ontology*. Chesham: Acumen.

JESSOP, B. 1990. *State Theory: Putting Capitalist States in their Place*. Cambridge: Polity.

—— 1996. Interpretative sociology and the dialectic of structure and agency. *Theory, Culture and Society*, 13 (1): 119–28.

KING, G., KEOHANE, R. O., and VERBA, S. (eds.) 1994. *Designing Social Inquiry: Scientific Inference in Qualitative Research*. Princeton, NJ: Princeton University Press.

KENNY, M. and SMITH, M. J. 1997. (Mis)Understanding Blair. *Political Quarterly*, 68: 220–30.

MÄKI, U. 2001. Economic ontology: what? why? how? Pp. 3–14 in *The Economic Worldview: Studies in the Ontology of Economics*, ed. U. Mäki. Cambridge: Cambridge University Press.

—— 2002. The dismal queen of the social sciences. Pp. 3–32 in *Fact and Fiction in Economics: Models, Realism and Social Construction*, ed. U. Mäki. Cambridge: Cambridge University Press.

MARSH, D. and FURLONG, P. 2002. A skin not a sweater: ontology and epistemology in political science. Pp. 17–41 in *Theory and Methods in Political Science*, ed. D. Marsh and G. Stoker, 2nd edn. Basingstoke: Palgrave.

—— and STOKER, G. 2002. Introduction. Pp. 1–16 in *Theory and Methods in Political Science*, ed. D. Marsh and G. Stoker, 2nd edn. Basingstoke: Palgrave.

MILL, J. S. 1970. *A System of Logic*. London: Longman; originally published 1843.

MONROE, K. R. (ed.) 2004. *Perestroika, Methodological Pluralism, Governance and Diversity in Contemporary American Political Science*. New Haven, Conn.: Yale University Press.

NORTH, D. C. 1990. *Institutions, Institutional Change and Economic Performance*. Cambridge: Cambridge University Press.

PETTIT, P. 1993. *The Common Mind: An Essay on Psychology, Society and Politics*. Oxford: Oxford University Press.

RYAN, R. 1970. *The Philosophy of the Social Sciences*. Basingstoke: Macmillan.

SCHMITT, F. F. 2003. Socialising metaphysics: an introduction. Pp. 1–37 in *Socialising Metaphysics*, ed. F. F. Schmitt. Boulder, Colo.: Rowman and Littlefield.

SMITH, M. J. 1998. Reconceptualising the British state: theoretical and empirical challenges to central government. *Public Administration*, 76: 45–72.

—— 1999. *The Core Executive in Britain*. London: Macmillan.

SMITH, S. 1990. Positivism and beyond. Pp. 11–46 in *International Theory: Positivism and Beyond*, ed. S. Smith, K. Booth, and M. Zalewski. Cambridge: Cambridge University Press.

SUGANAMI, H. 1999. Agents, structures, narratives. *European Journal of International Relations*, 5: 365–86.

Tilly, C. and Goodin, R. E. 2006. It depends. Pp. 3–32 in *The Oxford Handbook of Contextual Political Analysis.*, ed. R. E Goodin and C. Tilly. Oxford: Oxford University Press.

Tsebelis, G. 1990. *Nested Games: Rational Choice in Comparative Politics.* Berkeley: University of California Press.

Wendt, A. 1999. *Social Theory of International Politics.* Cambridge: Cambridge University Press.

——and Shapiro, I. 1997. The misunderstood promise of realist social theory. Pp. 166–90 in *Contemporary Empirical Political Theory*, ed. K. R. Monroe. Berkeley: University of California Press.

Wolf, N. 1993. *Fire With Fire: The New Female Power and How to Use It.* New York: Fawcett Combine.

Young, I. M. 1990. *Throwing Like a Girl and Other Essays in Feminist Philosophy and Social Theory.* Bloomington: Indiana University Press.

CHAPTER 24

THE LOGIC OF APPROPRIATENESS

JAMES G. MARCH

JOHAN P. OLSEN

THE logic of appropriateness is a perspective on how human action is to be interpreted. Action, policy making included, is seen as driven by rules of appropriate or exemplary behavior, organized into institutions. The appropriateness of rules includes both cognitive and normative components (March and Olsen 1995, 30–1). Rules are followed because they are seen as natural, rightful, expected, and legitimate. Actors seek to fulfill the obligations encapsulated in a role, an identity, a membership in a political community or group, and the ethos, practices, and expectations of its institutions. Embedded in a social collectivity, they do what they see as appropriate for themselves in a specific type of situation.

The present chapter focuses particularly on rules of appropriateness in the context of formally organized political institutions and democratic political orders. We ask how an understanding of the role of rule-driven behavior in life might illuminate thinking about political life, how the codification of experience into rules, institutional memories, and information processing is shaped in, and shapes a democratic political system. *First*, we sketch the basic ideas of rule-based action. *Second*, we describe some characteristics of contemporary democratic settings. *Third*, we attend to the relations between rules and action, the elements of slippage in executing rules. *Fourth*, we examine the dynamics of rules and standards of appropriateness. And, *fifth*, we discuss a possible reconciliation of different logics of action, as part of a future research agenda for students of democratic politics and policy making.

* We thank Jeffrey T. Checkel, Robert E. Goodin, Anne-Mette Magnussen, Michael Moran, and Ulf I. Sverdrup for constructive comments.

1 THE BASIC IDEAS

A vision of actors following internalized prescriptions of what is socially defined as normal, true, right, or good, without, or in spite of calculation of consequences and expected utility, is of ancient origin. The idea was, for example, dramatized by Sophocles more than 2,000 years ago in Antigone's confrontation with King Creon and by Martin Luther facing the Diet of Worms in 1521: "Here I stand, I can do no other." The tendency to develop rules, codes, and principles of conduct to justify and prescribe action in terms of something more than expected consequences seems to be fairly universal (Elias 1982/1939), and echoes of the ancient perspectives are found in many modern discussions of the importance of rules and identities in guiding human life.

The exact formulation of the ideas varies somewhat from one disciplinary domain to the other, but the core intuition is that humans maintain a repertoire of roles and identities, each providing rules of appropriate behavior in situations for which they are relevant. Following rules of a role or identity is a relatively complicated cognitive process involving thoughtful, reasoning behavior; but the processes of reasoning are not primarily connected to the anticipation of future consequences as they are in most contemporary conceptions of rationality. Actors use criteria of similarity and congruence, rather than likelihood and value. To act appropriately is to proceed according to the institutionalized practices of a collectivity, based on mutual, and often tacit understandings of what is true, reasonable, natural, right, and good. The term "logic of appropriateness" has overtones of morality, but rules of appropriateness underlie atrocities of action, such as ethnic cleansing and blood feuds, as well as moral heroism. The fact that a rule of action is defined as appropriate by an individual or a collectivity may reflect learning of some sort from history, but it does not guarantee technical efficiency or moral acceptability.

The matching of identities, situations, and behavioral rules may be based on experience, expert knowledge, or intuition, in which case it is often called "recognition" to emphasize the cognitive process of pairing problem-solving action correctly to a problem situation (March and Simon 1993, 10–13). The match may be based on role expectations (Sarbin and Allen 1968, 550). The match may also carry with it a connotation of essence, so that appropriate attitudes, behaviors, feelings, or preferences for a citizen, official, or expert are those that are essential to being a citizen, official, or expert—essential not in the instrumental sense of being necessary to perform a task or socially expected, nor in the sense of being an arbitrary definitional convention, but in the sense of that without which one cannot claim to be a proper citizen, official, or expert (MacIntyre 1988).

The simple behavioral proposition is that, most of the time humans take reasoned action by trying to answer three elementary questions: What kind of a situation is this? What kind of a person am I? What does a person such as I do in a situation such as this (March and Olsen 1989; March 1994)?

2 THE SETTING: INSTITUTIONS OF DEMOCRATIC GOVERNANCE

Democratic political life is ordered by institutions. The polity is a configuration of formally organized institutions that defines the setting within which governance and policy making take place. An institution is a relatively stable collection of rules and practices, embedded in structures of *resources* that make action possible—organizational, financial and staff capabilities, and structures of *meaning* that explain and justify behavior—roles, identities and belongings, common purposes, and causal and normative beliefs (March and Olsen 1989, 1995).

Institutions are organizational arrangements that link roles/identities, accounts of situations, resources, and prescriptive rules and practices. They create actors and meeting places and organize the relations and interactions among actors. They guide behavior and stabilize expectations. Specific institutional settings also provide vocabularies that frame thought and understandings and define what are legitimate arguments and standards of justification and criticism in different situations (Mills 1940). Institutions, furthermore, allocate resources and empower and constrain actors differently and make them more or less capable of acting according to prescribed rules. They affect whose justice and what rationality has primacy (MacIntyre 1988) and who becomes winners and losers. *Political* institutionalization signifies the development of distinct political rules, practices, and procedures partly independent of other institutions and social groupings (Huntington 1965). Political orders are, however, more or less institutionalized and they are structured according to different principles (Eisenstadt 1965).

This institutional perspective stands in contrast to current interpretations of politics that assume self-interested and rationally calculating actors, instrumentalism, and consequentialism. In the latter perspective rules simply reflect interests and powers, or they are irrelevant.[1] It can never be better to follow a rule that requires actions other than those that are optimal under given circumstances (Rowe 1989, vii); and the idea that society is governed by a written constitution and rules of appropriateness is seen as a possible reflection of the naive optimism of the eighteenth century (Loewenstein 1951). The logic of appropriateness, in contrast, harks back to an older conception that sees politics as rule driven and brands the use of public institutions and power for private purposes as the corruption and degeneration of politics (Viroli 1992, 71).

---

[1] Following the logic of consequentiality implies treating possible rules and interpretations as alternatives in a rational choice problem and it is usually assumed that "man's natural proclivity is to pursue his own interests" (Brennan and Buchanan 1985, ix). To act on the basis of the logic of consequentiality or anticipatory action includes the following steps: (*a*) What are my alternatives? (*b*) What are my values? (*c*) What are the consequences of my alternatives for my values? (*d*) Choose the alternative that has the best expected consequences. To act in conformity with rules that constrain conduct is then based on rational calculation and contracts, and is motivated by incentives and personal advantage.

Rules of appropriateness are also embodied in the foundational norms of contemporary democracies. Subjecting human conduct to constitutive rules has been portrayed as part of processes of democratization and civilization; and legitimacy has come to depend on *how* things are done, not solely on substantive performance (Merton 1938; Elias 1982/1939). For example, an important part of the modern democratic creed is that impersonal, fairly stable, publicly known, and understandable rules that are neither contradictory nor retroactive are supposed to shield citizens from the arbitrary power of authorities and the unaccountable power of those with exchangeable resources. Self-given laws are assumed to be accepted as binding for citizens. A spirit of citizenship is seen to imply a willingness to think and act as members of the community as a whole, not solely as self-interested individuals or as members of particular interest groups (Arblaster 1987, 77). Judges, bureaucrats, ministers, and legislators are expected to follow rules and act with integrity and competence within the democratic spirit. Officialness is supposed to imply stewardship and an affirmation of the values and norms inherent in offices and institutions (Heclo 2002).

In short, actors are expected to behave according to distinct democratic norms and rules and the democratic quality of a polity depends on properties of its citizens and officials. If they are not law-abiding, enlightened, active, civic-minded, and acting with self-restraint and a distance from individual interests, passions, and drives, genuine democratic government is impossible (Mill 1962/1861, 30). Yet, as observed by Aristotle, humans are not born with such predispositions. They have to be learned (Aristotle 1980, 299).

Democratic governance, then, is more than an instrument for implementing predetermined preferences and rights. Identities are assumed to be reflexive and political, not inherited and pre-political (Habermas 1998), and institutions are imagined to provide a framework for fashioning democrats by developing and transmitting democratic beliefs. A democratic identity also includes accepting responsibility for providing an institutional context within which continuous political discourse and change can take place and the roles, identities, accounts, rules, practices, and capabilities that construct political life can be crafted (March and Olsen 1995).

3 RULES OF APPROPRIATENESS IN ACTION

The impact of rules and standard operating procedures in routine situations is well known (March and Simon 1958; Cyert and March 1963). The relevance of the logic of appropriateness, however, is not limited to repetitive, routine worlds, and rule prescriptions are not necessarily conservative. Civil unrest, demands for comprehensive redistribution of political power and welfare, as well as political revolutions and major reforms often follow from identity-driven conceptions of appropriateness more than conscious calculations of costs and benefits (Scott 1976; Lefort 1988; Elster 1989).

Rules prescribe, more or less precisely, what is appropriate action. They also, more or less precisely, tell actors where to look for precedents, who are the authoritative interpreters of different types of rules, and what the key interpretative traditions are. Still, the unambiguous authority of rules cannot be taken as given—it cannot be assumed that rules always dictate or guide behavior. Rather, it is necessary to understand the processes through which rules are translated into actual behavior and the factors that may strengthen or weaken the relation between rules and actions. How do actors discover the lessons of the past through experience and how do they store, retrieve, and act upon those lessons? How do actors cope with impediments to learning and resolve ambiguities and conflicts of what the situation is and what experience is relevant; what the relevant role, identity, and rule are and what they mean; and what the appropriate match and action are?

Sometimes action reflects in a straightforward way prescriptions embedded in the rules, habits of thought, "best practice," and standard operating procedures of a community, an institution, organization, profession, or group. A socially valid rule creates an abstraction that applies to a number of concrete situations. Most actors, most of the time, then, take the rule as a "fact." There is no felt need to "go behind it" and explain or justify action and discuss its likely consequences (Stinchcombe 2001, 2).

A straightforward and almost automatic relation between rules and action is most likely in a polity with legitimate, stable, well-defined, and integrated institutions. Action is then governed by a dominant institution that provides clear prescriptions and adequate resources, i.e. prescribes doable action in an unambiguous way. The system consists of a multitude of institutions, each based on different principles. Yet, each institution has some degree of autonomy and controls a specified action sphere. The (living) constitution prescribes when, how, and why rules are to be acted upon. It gives clear principles of division of labor, maintains internal consistency among rules, prevents collisions between divergent institutional prescriptions, and makes the political order a coherent whole with predictable outcomes. Together, a variety of rules give specific content in specific situations both to such heroic identities as statesman or patriot and to such everyday identities as those of an accountant, police officer, or citizen (Kaufman 1960; Van Maanen 1973).

In other contexts actors have problems in resolving ambiguities and conflicts among alternative concepts of the self, accounts of a situation, and prescriptions of appropriateness. They struggle with how to classify themselves and others—who they are, and what they are—and what these classifications imply in a specific situation. The prescriptive clarity and consistency of identities are variables, and so are the familiarity with situations and the obviousness of matching rules. Fulfilling an identity through following appropriate rules often involves matching a changing and ambiguous set of contingent rules to a changing and ambiguous set of situations.

A focus on rules and identities therefore assures neither simplicity nor consistency (Biddle 1986; Berscheid 1994). It is a non-trivial task to predict behavior from knowledge about roles, identities, rules, situations, and institutions, and describing action as rule following is only the first step in understanding how rules affect behavior. As a result, a distinction is made between a rule and its behavioral realization in a particular situation in the study of formal organizations (Scott 1992, 304; March, Schulz, and Zhou 2000, 23), institutions (Apter 1991), and the law (Tyler 1990). The possible indeterminacy of roles, identities, rules, and situations requires detailed observations of the processes through which rules are translated into actual behavior through constructive interpretation and available resources (March and Olsen 1995). We need to attend to the interaction between rules and purposeful behavior and the factors that enhance or counteract rule following and mediate the impact rules have on behavior (Checkel 2001).

Defining a role or identity and achieving it require time and energy, thought and capability. In order to understand the impact of rules upon action, we need to study such (imperfect) processes as attention directing, interpretation of rules, the validation of evidence, codification of experiences into rules, memory building and retrieval, and the mechanisms through which institutions distribute resources and enable actors to follow rules, across a variety of settings and situations.

For example, individuals have multiple roles and identities and the number and variety of alternative rules assures that only a fraction of the relevant rules are evoked in a particular place at a particular time. One of the primary factors affecting behavior, therefore, is the process by which some of those rules rather than others, are attended to in a particular situation, and how identities and situations are interpreted (March and Olsen 1989, 22). Fitting a rule to a situation is an exercise in establishing appropriateness, where rules and situations are related by criteria of similarity or difference through reasoning by analogy and metaphor. The process is mediated by language, by the ways in which participants come to be able to talk about one situation as similar to or different from another, and assign situations to rules. The process maintains consistency in action primarily through the creation of typologies of similarity, rather than through a derivation of action from stable interests or wants.[2]

Individuals may also have a difficult time interpreting which historical experiences and accounts are relevant for current situations, and situations can be defined in different ways that call forth different legitimate rules, actors, and arguments (Ugland 2002). Where more than one potentially relevant rule or account is evoked, the problem is to apply criteria of similarity in order to use the most appropriate rule or account. In some cases, higher-order rules are used to differentiate between lower-order rules, but democratic institutions and orders are not always monolithic, coordinated, and consistent. Some action spheres are weakly institutionalized. In others

---

[2] Processes of constructive interpretation, criticism, justification, and application of rules and identities are more familiar to the intellectual traditions of law than economics. Lawyers argue about what the rules are, what the facts are, and what who have to do when (Dworkin 1986, vii). Law in action—the realization of law—involves legal institutions and procedures, legal values, and legal concepts and ways of thought, as well as legal rules (Berman 1983, 4).

institutionalized rule sets compete. Rules and identities collide routinely (Orren and Skowronek 1994), making prescriptions less obvious. Actors sometimes disobey and challenge some rules because they adhere to other rules. Potential conflict among rules is, however, partly coped with by incomplete attention. For instance, rules that are more familiar are more likely to be evoked, thus recently used or recently revised rules come to attention.

In general, actors may find the rules and situations they encounter to be obscure. What is true and right and therefore what should be done may be ambiguous. Sometimes they may know what to do but not be able to do it because prescriptive rules and capabilities are incompatible. Actors are limited by the complexities of the demands upon them and by the distribution and regulation of resources, competencies, and organizing capacities; that is, by the institutionalized capability for acting appropriately. A separation between substantive policy making and budgeting is, for example, likely to create a gap between prescribed policy rules and targets and the capabilities to implement the rules and reach the targets.

Rules, then, potentially have several types of consequences but it can be difficult to say exactly how rules manifest themselves, to isolate their effects under varying circumstances and specify when knowledge about rules is decisive for understanding political behavior. While rules guide behavior and make some actions more likely than others, they ordinarily do not determine political behavior or policy outcomes precisely. Rules, laws, identities, and institutions provide parameters for action rather than dictate a specific action, and sometimes actors show considerable ability to accommodate shifting circumstances by changing behavior without changing core rules and structures (Olsen 2003).

Over the last decades focus has (again) been on the pathologies and negative effects of rule following, in the literature as well as in public debate in many countries. The ubiquity of rules, precedents, and routines often makes political institutions appear to be bureaucratic, stupid, insensitive, dogmatic, or rigid. The simplification provided by rules is clearly imperfect, and the imperfection is often manifest, especially after the fact. Nevertheless, some of the major capabilities of modern institutions come from their effectiveness in substituting rule-bound behavior for individually autonomous behavior.

Rules, for example, increase action capabilities and efficiency—the ability to solve policy problems and produce services. Yet the consequences of rules go beyond regulating strategic behavior by providing incentive structures and impacting transaction costs. Rules provide codes of meaning that facilitate interpretation of ambiguous worlds. They embody collective and individual roles, identities, rights, obligations, interests, values, world-views, and memory, thus constrain the allocation of attention, standards of evaluation, priorities, perceptions, and resources. Rules make it possible to coordinate many simultaneous activities in a way that makes them mutually consistent and reduces uncertainty, for example by creating predictable time rhythms through election and budget cycles (Sverdrup 2000). They constrain bargaining within comprehensible terms and enforce agreements and help avoid destructive conflicts. Still, the blessing of rules may be mixed. Detailed rules and rigid rule following may under some conditions make policy making and implementation more effective, but a well-working system may also need discretion and flexibility. Consequently, short-term and long-term consequences of rules may differ. Rules may, furthermore, make public debate obligatory, but rule following may also hamper reason giving and discourse.

A one-sided focus on policy consequences may furthermore hide a broader range of effects. Logics of action are used to describe, explain, justify, and criticize behavior and sometimes the primary reason for rules is to proclaim virtue rather than to control behavior directly, making the implementation of rules less important (Meyer and Rowan 1977; Brunsson 1989; March 1994, 76). Rules and institutions of government are, in addition, potentially transformative. More or less successfully, they turn individuals into citizens and officials by shaping their identities and mentalities and making them observe the *normative* power of rules (Mill 1962/1861; Fuller 1971; Joerges 1996).

An important aspect of rules, then, is their possible consequences for the development of a community of rule, based on a common identity and sense of belonging. A key issue of political organization is how to combine unity and diversity and craft a cooperative system out of a conflictual one; and the democratic aspiration has been to hold society together without eliminating diversity—that is, to develop and maintain a system of rules, institutions, and identities that makes it possible to rule a divided society without undue violence (Wheeler 1975, 4; Crick 1983, 25).

The growth and decay of institutions, roles, and identities, with their different logics of action, are therefore key indicators of political change (Eisenstadt 1965; Huntington 1965). Rules also help realize flexibility and adaptiveness as well as order and stability. This is so because part of the democratic commitment is the institutionalization of self-reflection and procedures through which existing rules can legitimately be examined, criticized, and changed.

4 The Dynamics of Rules of Appropriateness

Why are the rules of appropriateness what they are? Why are specific behavioral prescriptions believed to be natural or exemplary and why do rules vary across polities and institutions? Through which processes and why do rules of appropriateness change? A conception of human behavior as rule and identity based invites a conception of the mechanisms by which rules and identities evolve and become legitimized, reproduced, modified, and replaced. Key behavioral mechanisms are history-dependent processes of adaptation such as learning or selection. Rules of appropriateness are seen as carriers of lessons from experience as those lessons are encoded either by individuals and collectivities drawing inferences from their own and others' experiences, or by differential survival and reproduction of institu- tions, roles, and identities based on particular rules. Rule-driven behavior associated with successes or survival is likely to be repeated. Rules associated with failures are not.

A common interpretation of rules, institutions, roles, and identities is that they exist because they work well and provide better solutions than their alternatives (Goodin 1996; Hechter, Opp, and Wippler 1990; Stinchcombe 1997, 2001). They are, at least under some conditions, functional and consistent with people's values and moral commitments. In contemporary democracies, this interpretation is reflected in high learning aspirations. Appropriate rules, in both technical and normative terms, are assumed to evolve over time as new experiences are interpreted and coded into rules, or less attractive alternatives are eliminated through competition. Lessons from experience are assumed to improve the intelligence, effectiveness, and adaptability of the polity and be a source of wisdom and progress. The key democratic institution for ensuring rational adaptation of rules is free debate where actors have to explain and justify their behavior in public through reason-based argumentation, within a set of rules defining appropriate debates and arguments.

In practice, however, the willingness and ability of democracies to learn, adapt rules, and improve performance on the basis of experience is limited (Neustadt and May 1986; March 1999). Rules are transmitted from one generation to another or from one set of identity holders through child rearing, education, training, socializa- tion, and habitualization. Rules are maintained and changed through contact with others and exposure to experiences and information. Rules spread through social networks and their diffusion is constrained by borders and distances. They compete for attention. They change in concert with other rules, interfere with or support each other, and they are transformed while being transferred (Czarniawska and Joerges 1995; March, Schulz, and Zhou 2000). Change also takes place as a result of public dis- course and deliberate interventions. These dynamics reflect both the effects of change induced by the environment and endogenous changes produced by the operation of the rule system itself.

Yet, as is well known from modern investigations, such processes are not perfect. For example, the encoding of history, either through experiential learning or through evolutionary selection, does not necessarily imply intelligence, improvement, or increased adaptive value. There is no guarantee that relevant observations will be made, correct inferences and lessons derived, proper actions taken, or that imper- fections will be eliminated. Rules encode history, but the coding procedures and the processes by which the coded interpretations are themselves decoded are filled with behavioral surprises.[3]

We assume that new experiences may lead to change in rules, institutions, roles, and identities and yet we are not committed to a belief in historical efficiency, i.e.

---

[3] March and Olsen 1975, 1989, 1995, 1998; Levitt and March 1988; March 1994, 1999; March, Schulz, and Zhou 2000; Olsen and Peters 1996.

rapid and costless rule adaptation to functional and normative environments and deliberate political reform attempts, and therefore to the functional or moral necessity of observed rules (March and Olsen 1989, 1995, 1998). Democratic institutions, for example, are arranged to both speed up and slow down learning from experience and adaptation. Democracies value continuity and predictability as well as flexibility and change, and usually there are attempts to balance the desire to keep the basic rules of governance stable and the desire to adapt rules due to new experience. The main picture is also one of renewal and continuity, path departures and path dependencies. Different rules, roles, and identities are evoked in different situations and when circumstances fluctuate fast, there may be rapid shifts within existing repertoires of behavioral rules based on institutionalized switching rules. However, the basic repertoire of rules and standard operating procedures change more slowly.

Change in constitutive rules usually requires time-consuming processes and a strong majority, a fact that is likely to slow down change. The same is true when the basic rules express the historical collective identity of a community and embody shared understandings of what counts as truth, right, and good. Deliberate reform then has to be explained and justified in value-rational terms; that is, in terms of their appropriateness and not solely in efficiency terms (Olsen 1997); and change in entrenched interpretative traditions and who are defined as the authoritative interpreters of different types of rules, are also likely to change relatively slowly.

Core political identities are not primordial and constant. Nevertheless, barring severe crises, processes of identity formation and reinterpretation are likely to be slow. All political rulers try to transfer naked power into authority. Civic virtue and shared internalized principles of rights and obligations[4] and identities are to some degree accessible to political experience, reasoning, and action. They can, for example, be affected through policies of nation building, mass education, and mass media, even if the causal chains are long and indirect. In democracies, where the authority of law is well established, identities may also be fashioned through political and legal debates and decisions (Habermas 1996). Legalization may in some settings be a prelude to internalization of rules of appropriateness, even if they in other settings may substitute for internalized rules.

There is, however, modest knowledge about the factors that govern targets of political identification and codes of appropriate behavior, and where, when, and how different types of actors obtain their identities and codes—for example the relative importance of specific political ideologies, institutions, professions, and educations, and belonging to larger social categories such as nation, gender, class, race, religion, and ethnicity (Herrmann, Risse, and Brewer 2004). Neither is it obvious how well different institutions today embody and encourage democratic identities and make it more likely that citizens and officials act in accordance with internalized democratic

---

[4] As observed by Rousseau: "the strongest man is never strong enough to be always master unless he transforms his power into right, and obedience into duty" (Rousseau 1967/1762/1755, 10). In modern society, Weber argued, the belief in legality—the acceptance of the authority of law, legal actors, reasoning, precedents, and institutions—is the most common form for legitimacy (Weber 1978, 37).

principles and ideals. Furthermore, an improved understanding of rule dynamics may require better insight into how the dynamics of change may be related to normal, new, and extraordinary experience in different institutional settings.

Consider normal experience and routine learning. Experiences are routinely coded into rules, rules into principles, and principles into systems of thought in many spheres of life. Routine refinement of rules can be imagined to improve their fit to the environment, and one study showed that the stability of rules is related positively to their age at the time of last revision. However, changes in rules can also create problems that destabilize rules, and the current stability of rules is related negatively to the number of times they have been revised in the past (March, Schulz, and Zhou 2000).

In some spheres, i.e. Weberian bureaucracies and court systems, these processes are systematic and institutionalized (Weber 1978; Berman 1983); in other spheres they are less so. Conflict between competing situational accounts, conceptions of truth and justice, and interpretations of appropriate behavior is also routine in contemporary democracies. Democracies are at best only *partly* communities of shared experiences, communication, interpretative traditions, and memory that give direction and meaning to citizens. They are glued together by shared debates, controversies, and contestations and by fairly broad agreement on some basic rules for coping with conflicts.

In fragmented, or loosely coupled systems, competing rules of appropriateness may be maintained over long time periods due to their separateness. As long as rule following meets targets and aspiration levels, rules are unlikely to be challenged, even if they are not in any sense "optimal." Reduced slack resources may, however, call attention to inconsistencies in rules and produce demands for more coordination and consistency across institutional spheres and social groups (Cyert and March 1963). Comparison across previously segmented institutional spheres or groups with different traditions, rules of appropriateness, and taken-for-granted beliefs, may then trigger processes of search and reconciliation or dominance and coercion.

Consider new experience and settings. Processes of search and change may also be triggered when an existing order, its institutions, rules of appropriateness, and collective self-understandings, are challenged by new experiences that are difficult to account for in terms of existing conceptions (Berger and Luckmann 1967, 103). Entrenched accounts and narratives then do not make sense. They no longer provide adequate answers to what is true or false, right or wrong, good or bad, and what is appropriate behavior; and there is search for new conceptions and legitimizations that can produce a more coherent shared account (Eder 1999, 208–9).

Account and concepts may be challenged because new institutions and meeting places have developed. An example of a new institutional setting generating increased contact and challenging national traditions is the integration of sovereign nation-states into the European Union. Challenges may also follow from institutional collisions between previously separated or segmented traditions, for example the invading of market rules of appropriateness into institutional spheres traditionally based on different conceptions, such as democratic politics, science, and sport. Increased mobility or massive migration across large geographical and cultural distances may likewise create collisions that challenge established frames of reference and institutionalized routines. Such collisions may generate destructive conflicts, but they may also generate rethinking, search, learning, and adaptation by changing the participants' reference groups, aspiration levels, and causal understandings.

Consider the unacceptability of the past and institutional emancipation. Actors are likely to learn from disasters, crises, and system breakdowns—transformative periods where established orders are delegitimized, are challenged, or collapse. Then, institutions and their constitutive rules are discredited as unworkable and intolerable and change initiatives are presented as emancipation from an order that is a dysfunctional, unfair, or tyrannical relic of an unacceptable past, as was, for example, the case when Communist regimes in central and eastern Europe collapsed (Offe 1996; Wollmann 2006).

In situations of disorientation, crisis, and search for meaning, actors are in particular likely to rethink who and what they and others are, and may become; what communities they belong to, and want to belong to; and how power should be redistributed. Often the search for legitimate models and accounts is extended far back to possible glorious periods in own history, or they are copied from political systems that can be accepted as exemplary. Short of revolution or civil war, there may be shifts in cognitive and normative frames, in who are defined as legitimate interpreters of appropriateness, in interpretative traditions, and in the system for collecting, communicating, and organizing knowledge (Eder 1999), as well as in resource distributions and power relations.

In sum, an improved theoretical understanding of the dynamics of rules, institutions, roles, and identities requires attention to several 'imperfect' processes of change, not a focus on a single mechanism. Change is not likely to be governed by a single coherent and dominant process. Except under special circumstances, rules of appropriateness develop and change through a myriad of disjointed processes and experiences in a variety of places and situations, even when the result is normatively justified post hoc by rational accounts (Eder 1999, 203). For example, decrees, command, and coercion have a limited role in developing and maintaining legitimate rules, roles, and identities. The internalization of rules and identities is usually not a case of willful entering into an explicit contract either. In practice, processes such as learning, socialization, diffusion, regeneration, deliberate design, and competitive selection all have their imperfections, and an improved understanding of these imperfections may provide a key to a better understanding of the dynamics of rules (March 1981).

Required then is the exploration of the scope conditions and interaction of such processes as purposeful reform, institutional abilities to adapt spontaneously to changing circumstances, and environmental effectiveness in eliminating suboptimal rules, institutions, and identities (Olsen 2001). In the final part, we explore how an adequate understanding of politics may also require attention to the scope conditions and interaction of different logics of behavior.

5 RECONCILING LOGICS OF ACTION

Action is rule based, but only partly so. There is a great diversity in human motivation and modes of action. Behavior is driven by habit, emotion, coercion, and calculated expected utility, as well as interpretation of internalized rules and principles. Here, focus is on the potential tension, in the first instance, between the role- or identity-based logic of appropriateness and the preference-based consequential logic; and in the second instance, between the claims of citizenship and officialdom and the claims of particularistic roles or identities.

Democratic governance involves balancing the enduring tensions between different logics of action, for instance between the demands and obligations of offices and roles and individual calculated interests (Tussman 1960, 18). Political actors are also likely to be held accountable for both the appropriateness and the consequences of their actions. A dilemma is that proper behavior sometimes is associated with bad consequences and improper behavior sometimes is associated with good consequences. From time to time, democratic actors will get 'dirty hands.' That is, they achieve desirable outcomes through methods that they recognize as inappropriate. Or, they follow prescribed rules and procedures at the cost of producing outcomes they recognize to be undesirable (Merton 1938; Thompson 1987, 11).

Partly as a result of the tensions between them, there are cycles between logics of action. Compared to the *Rechtsstaat*, with its traditions and rhetoric tied to the logic of appropriateness, twentieth-century democracies (particularly the welfare states of Europe) embraced practices and rhetoric that were more tied to the logic of consequentiality. Consequence-oriented professions replaced process-oriented ones, and effectiveness and substantive results were emphasized more than the principles and procedures to be followed. Governance came to assume a community of shared objectives rather than a community of shared rules, principles, and procedures (March and Olsen 1995).

More recent reforms have continued that trend. Governments in the 1980s generally tried to change concepts of accountability even more toward emphasis upon results and away from an emphasis on the rules and procedures (Olsen and Peters 1996). While several reforms were processual in character, rules were often seen as instrumental rather than having a legitimacy of their own. In particular, they aimed at binding and controlling elected politicians and experts. One reason for the reforms was the conviction that individuals needed better protection against political interventions. A second reason was the conviction that consequence-oriented professions such as medical doctors and teachers in welfare states were ineffectively subjected to public accountability and that obligations to report and being subject to audit had to be expanded (Power 1994).

Nevertheless, there is no uniform and linear trend making rules of appropriateness outdated. Scandals in both the private and public sector have triggered demands for legal and ethical rules and an ethos of responsibility. The European Union is to a large extent a polity based on rules and legal integration; and in world politics there is a trend towards legal rules and institutions, including an emphasis on human rights, even if the trend may be neither even nor irreversible (Goldstein et al. 2000).

Political systems deal with the multitude of behavioral motivations in a variety of ways and one is separating different logics by locating them in different institutions and roles (Weber 1978). Different logics of action are also observed within single institutions. Individual institutions, on the one hand, separate logics by prescribing different logics for different roles. For instance, in courts of law the judge, the prosecutor, the attorney, the witness, and the accused legitimately follow different logics of action. The credence of their arguments, data, and conclusions is also expected to vary. On the other hand, logics also compete within single institutions. In public administration, for example, there have been cycles of trust in control of behavior through manipulation of incentive structures and individual cost–benefit calculations, and trust in an ethos of internal-normative responsibility and willingness to act in accordance with rules of appropriateness. Historically, the two have interacted. Their relative importance, as well as the definition of appropriateness, have changed over time and varied across institutional settings (deLeon 2003).

A theoretical challenge is to fit different motivations and logics of action into a single framework. Specific logics, such as following rules of appropriateness and calculating individual expected utility, can be good approximations under specific conditions. It is difficult to deny the importance of each of them (and others) and inadequate to rely exclusively on one of them. Therefore, a theory of purposeful human behavior must take into consideration the diversity of human motivations and modes of behavior and account for the relationship and interaction between different logics in different institutional settings. A beginning is to explore behavioral logics as complementary, rather than to assume a single dominant behavioral logic (March and Olsen 1998; Olsen 2001).

If it is assumed that no single model, and the assumptions upon which it is based, is more fruitful than all the others under all conditions and that different models are not necessarily mutually exclusive, we can examine their variations, shifting significance, scope conditions, prerequisites, and interplay, and explore ideas that can reconcile and synthesize different models. We may enquire how and where different logics of actions are developed, lost, and redefined. We may examine the conditions under which each logic is invoked. We may ask how logics interact, how they may support or counteract each other, and which logics are reconcilable. We may also specify through what processes different logics of action may become dominant.

We may, in particular, explore how different logics of action are formally prescribed, authorized, and allowed, or how they are defined as illegitimate and proscribed, in different institutional settings, for different actors, under different circumstances. We may enquire how institutional settings in practice are likely to prompt individuals to evoke different logics. We may also study which settings in practice enable the dominance of one logic over all others, for example under what conditions rules of appropriateness may overpower or redefine self-interest, or the

logic of consequentiality may overpower rules and an entrenched definition of appropriateness (March and Olsen 1998; Olsen 2001).[5]

In the following, focus is on some possible relationships between the logic of
appropriateness and the logic of consequentiality. An unsatisfactory approach is to
subsume one logic as a special case of the other. Within the logic-of-appropriateness
perspective, consequential choice is then seen as one of many possible rules that actors
may come to believe is exemplary for specific roles in specific settings and situations.
From the logic-of-consequentiality perspective, rules of appropriateness may be seen
as the result of higher-level or prior utility calculations, choice, and explicit contracts.
We see this approach as unsatisfactory because it denies the distinctiveness of different
logics.

An alternative is to assume a *hierarchy* between logics. The logic of appropriateness
may be used subject to constraints of extreme consequences, or rules of appropriateness are seen as one of several constraints within which the logic of consequentiality
operates. One version of the hierarchy notion is that one logic is used for major
decisions and the other for refinements of those decisions, or one logic governs the
behavior of politically important actors and another the behavior of less important
actors. It is, for example, often suggested that politics follows the logic of consequentiality, while public administrators and judges follow the logic of appropriateness.
The suggestion of a stable hierarchy between logics and between types of decisions
and actors is, however, not well supported by empirical findings.

A more promising route may be to differentiate logics of action in terms of their
prescriptive clarity and hypothesize that a clear logic will dominate a less clear logic.
Rules of appropriateness are defined with varying precision and provide more or
less clear prescriptions in different settings and situations. For instance, rules are in
varying degrees precise, consistent, obligatory, and legally binding. There are more
or less specified exceptions from the rules and varying agreement about who the
authoritative interpreter of a rule is. Likewise, the clarity of (self-)interests, preferences, choice alternatives, and their consequences varies. Bureaucrats, for example,
are influenced by the rules and structural settings in which they act, yet they may face
ambiguous rules as well as situations where no direct personal interest is involved
(Egeberg 1995, 2003). In brief, rules and interests give actors more or less clear behavioral guidance and make it more or less likely that the logic of appropriateness or the
logic of consequentiality will dominate.

Even when actors are able to figure out what to do, a clear logic can only be followed when available resources make it possible to obey its prescriptions. Following
rules of appropriateness, compared to predicting the future, clarifying alternatives
and their expected utility, partly requires different abilities and resources. Therefore,
variation and change in the relative importance of the two logics may follow from
variation and change in the resources available for acting in accordance with rules of
appropriateness and calculated (self-)interest.

---

[5] Such questions are raised in several disciplines and subdisciplines, for example by Fehr and Gächter
1998, 848; Finnemore and Sikkink 1998, 912; Clayton and Gillman 1999; van den Bergh and Stagl 2003, 26;
Jupille, Caporaso, and Checkel 2003.

Examples are shifting mixes of public and private resources, budgetary allocations to institutions that traditionally have promoted different logics, and changes
in recruitment from professions that are carriers of one logic to professions that
promote the other logic. Tight deadlines are also likely to promote rule following
rather than the more time- and resource-demanding calculation of expected utility
(March and Simon 1993, 11). The relation between level of societal conflict and logics
of action is not obvious, however. In democratic settings, confrontations and conflicts usually challenge existing rules and possibly the logic of appropriateness. But
protracted conflicts also tend to generate demands for compromises and constitutive
rules that can dampen the level of conflict.

Lack of resources and understanding may also be one reason why different logics
of action are used for different *purposes*, such as making policies and justifying
policies. In institutional spheres and societies where policy making is prescribed to
follow the logic of appropriateness, the rule of law, traditions, and precedents, and
the prescriptions are difficult to implement, the logic of appropriateness is likely
to be used to justify decisions also when it is not used to make them. Likewise, in
institutional spheres and societies where policy making is prescribed to follow the
logic of consequentiality, rational calculation, and an orientation towards the future,
and where following the prescription is difficult, the logic of consequentiality is likely
to be used for justifying decisions, whatever the underlying logic of making them. We
hypothesize, however, that rationality and the logic of consequentiality is more easily
used to justify decisions. This is so because consequentiality is behaviorally more
indeterminate in its implications than rule following and the logic of appropriateness
in situations of even moderate ambiguity and complexity. It is easier to rationalize
behavior in terms of one interest or another, than to interpret behavior as appropriate,
simply because rules of appropriateness are collective, publicly known, and fairly
stable.

The time dimension is also important. A polity may institutionalize a *sequential*
ordering of logics of action, so that different phases follow different logics and
the basis of action changes over time in a predictable way. In democracies, an
example is the vision of an institutionalized demand for expert information and
advice as a precondition for informed political decision, followed by technical-logical
implementation, monitoring, and adjudication of decisions. Another example is the
Habermasian vision of an institutionalized public sphere, providing an ideal speech
situation that makes it necessary even for self-interested, utility-calculating actors
to argue in universal rather than particularistic terms. Over time deliberation and
reasoned arguments become habitualized and normatively accepted, turning egoists
into citizens (Habermas 1989). More generally, Mills (1940: 908) hypothesized that
the long acting out of a role or rule of appropriateness 'will often induce a man to
become what at first he merely sought to appear.'

Finally, change between logics of action may be the result of *specific experiences*.
Rules of appropriateness are likely to evolve as a result of accumulated experience with
a specific situation over extended time periods. Therefore, rules and standard operating procedures are most likely to dominate when actors have long tenure, frequent

interaction, and shared experiences and information; when they share accounts and institutionalized memories; and when environments are fairly stable. Consequences are fed back into rules and rules are likely to be abandoned and possibly replaced by the logic of consequentiality, when rule following is defined as unsatisfactory in terms of established targets and aspiration levels.

In particular, rules are likely to be abandoned when rule following creates catastrophic outcomes, and in periods of radical environmental change, where past arrangements and rules are defined as irrelevant or unacceptable. Similarly, recourse to rules and standard operating procedures is likely when consequential calculations are seen as having produced catastrophes. In particular, rational calculation of consequences is easiest when problems are of modest complexity and time perspectives are short. When applied to more complex problems and longer time perspectives they are more likely to create big mistakes, afterwards seen as horror stories (Neustadt and May 1986).

As these speculations show, the scope conditions and interaction of different logics of action and types of reason are not well understood. Accomplishments are dwarfed by the large number of unanswered questions. Nevertheless, the gap may also be seen as providing a future research agenda for students of democratic politics and policy making.

References

APTER, D. A. 1991. Institutionalism reconsidered. *International Social Science Journal*, 43: 463–81.

ARBLASTER, A. 1987. *Democracy*. Milton Keynes: Open University Press.

ARISTOTLE. 1980. *Politics*. Harmondsworth: Penguin.

BERGER, P. L. and LUCKMANN, T. 1967. *The Social Construction of Reality*. New York: Doubleday, Anchor.

BERMAN, H. J. 1983. *Law and Revolution: The Formation of the Western Legal Tradition*. Cambridge, Mass.: Harvard University Press.

BERSCHEID, E. 1994. Interpersonal relationships. *Annual Review of Psychology*, 45: 79–129.

BIDDLE, B. J. 1986. Recent developments in role theory. *Annual Review of Sociology*, 12: 67–92.

BRENNAN, G. AND BUCHANAN, J. M. 1985. *The Reason of Rules: Constitutional Political Economy*. Cambridge: Cambridge University Press.

BRUNSSON, N. 1989. *The Organization of Hypocrisy*. Chichester: Wiley.

CHECKEL, J. T. 2001. Why comply? Social learning and European identity change. *International Organization*, 55: 553–88.

CLAYTON, C. W. and GILLMAN, H. 1999. *Supreme Court Decision-Making: New Institutionalist Approaches*. Chicago: University of Chicago Press.

CRICK, B. 1983. *In Defense of Politics*, 2nd edn. Harmondsworth: Penguin.

CYERT, R. M. and MARCH, J. G. 1963. *A Behavioral Theory of the Firm*. Englewood Cliffs, NJ: Prentice Hall. 2nd edn. 1992.

CZARNIAWSKA, B. and JOERGES, B. 1995. Winds of organizational change: how ideas translate into objects and action. *Research in the Sociology of Organizations*, 13: 171–209.

DeLEON, P. 2003. On acting responsibly in a disorderly world: individual ethics and administrative responsibility. Pp. 569–80 in *The Handbook of Public Administration*, ed. B. G. Peters and J. Pierre. London: Sage.

DWORKIN, R. 1986. *Law's Empire*. Cambridge, Mass.: Belknap, Harvard University Press.

EDER, K. 1999. Societies learn and yet the world is hard to change. *European Journal of Social Theory*, 2: 195–215.

EGEBERG, M. 1995. Bureaucrats as public policy-makers and their self-interest. *Journal of Theoretical Politics*, 7: 157–67.

——— 2003. How bureaucratic structure matters: an organizational perspective. Pp. 116–26 in *The Handbook of Public Administration*, ed. B. G. Peters and J. Pierre. London: Sage.

EISENSTADT, S. 1965. *Essays on Comparative Institutions*. New York: Wiley.

ELIAS, N. 1982/1939. *The Civilizing Process: State Formation and Civilization*, 2nd edn. Oxford: Basil Blackwell.

ELSTER, J. 1989. Demokratiets verdigrunnlag og verdikonflikter. Pp. 77–93 in *Vitenskap og politikk*. Oslo: Universitetsforlaget.

FEHR, E. and GÄCHTER, S. 1998. Reciprocity and economics: the economic implications of *homo reciprocans*. *European Economic Review*, 42: 845–59.

FINNEMORE, M. and SIKKINK, K. 1998. International norm dynamics and political change. *International Organization*, 52 (4): 887–917.

FULLER, L. L. 1971. *The Morality of Law*. New Haven, Conn.: Yale University Press.

GOLDSTEIN, J. L., KAHLER, M., KEOHANE, R. O., and SLAUGHTER, A.-M. (eds.) 2000. Legalization and world politics. *International Organization* (Special Issue). Reprinted Cambridge, Mass.: MIT Press, 2001.

GOODIN, R. E. (ed.) 1996. *The Theory of Institutional Design*. Cambridge: Cambridge University Press.

HABERMAS, J. 1989. *The Structural Transformation of the Public Sphere*. Cambridge, Mass.: MIT Press.

——— 1996. *Between Facts and Norms*. Cambridge, Mass.: MIT Press.

——— 1998. *The Inclusion of the Other: Studies in Political Theory*, ed. C. Cronin and P. de Greiff. Cambridge, Mass.: MIT Press.

HECHTER, M., OPP, K. D., and WIPPLER, R. 1990. *Social Institutions: Their Emergence, Maintenance and Effects*. New York: de Gruyter.

HECLO, H. 2002. The spirit of public administration. *PS: Political Science & Politics*, 35: 689–94.

HERRMANN, R. K., RISSE, T., and BREWER, M. B. (eds.) 2004. *Transnational Identities: Becoming European in the EU*. Lanham, Md.: Rowman and Littlefield.

HUNTINGTON, S. P. 1965. Political development and political decay. *World Politics*, 17: 386–430.

JOERGES, C. 1996. Taking the law seriously: on political science and the role of law in integration. *European Law Journal*, 2: 105–35.

JUPILLE, J., CAPORASO, J. A., and CHECKEL, J. T. 2003. Integrating institutions: rationalism, constructivism, and the study of the European Union. *Comparative Political Studies*, 36: 7–41.

KAUFMAN, H. 1960. *The Forest Ranger*. Baltimore: Johns Hopkins University Press.

LEFORT, C. 1988. *Democracy and Political Theory*. Minneapolis: University of Minnesota Press.

LEVITT, B. and MARCH, J. G. 1988. Organizational learning. *Annual Review of Sociology*, 14: 319–40.

LOEWENSTEIN, K. 1951. Reflections on the value of constitutions in our revolutionary age. Pp. 191–224 in *Constitutions and Constitutional Trends since World War II*, ed. A. Z. Zurcher. New York: New York University Press.

MACINTYRE, A. 1988. *Whose Justice? Which Rationality?* 2nd edn. Notre Dame, Ind.: University of Notre Dame Press.

MARCH, J. G. 1981. Footnotes to organizational change. *Administrative Science Quarterly*, 16: 563–77.

—— 1994. *A Primer on Decision Making: How Decisions Happen.* New York: Free Press.

—— 1999. *The Pursuit of Organizational Intelligence.* Oxford: Blackwell.

—— and OLSEN, J. P. 1975. The uncertainty of the past: organizational learning under ambiguity. *European Journal of Political Research*, 3: 147–71.

—— —— 1989. *Rediscovering Institutions.* New York: Free Press.

—— —— 1995. *Democratic Governance.* New York: Free Press.

—— —— 1998. The institutional dynamics of international political orders. *International Organization*, 52: 943–69.

—— SCHULZ, M., and ZHOU, X. 2000. *The Dynamics of Rules: Change in Written Organizational Codes.* Stanford, Calif.: Stanford University Press.

—— and SIMON, H. A. 1958. *Organizations.* New York: Wiley.

—— —— 1993. *Organizations*, 2nd edn. New York: Wiley.

MERTON, R. K. 1938. Social structure and anomie. *American Sociological Review*, 3: 672–82.

MEYER, J. and ROWAN, B. 1977. Institutionalized organizations: formal structure as myth and ceremony. *American Journal of Sociology*, 83: 340–63.

MILL, J. S. 1962/1861. *Considerations on Representative Government.* South Bend, Ind.: Gateway Editions.

MILLS, C. W. 1940. Situated actions and vocabularies of motive. *American Sociological Review*, 5 (6): 904–13.

NEUSTADT, R. E. and MAY, E. R. 1986, *Thinking in Time: The Uses of History for Decision-Makers.* New York: Free Press.

OFFE, C. 1996. Designing institutions in East European transitions. Pp. 199–226 in *The Theory of Institutional Design*, ed. R. E. Goodin. Cambridge: Cambridge University Press.

OLSEN, J. P. 1997. Institutional design in democratic contexts. *Journal of Political Philosophy*, 5: 203–29.

—— 2001. Garbage cans, New Institutionalism, and the study of politics. *American Political Science Review*, 95: 191–8.

—— 2003. Towards a European administrative space? *Journal of European Public Policy*, 10: 506–31.

—— and PETERS, B. G. (eds.) 1996. *Lessons from Experience: Experiential Learning in Administrative Reforms in Eight Countries.* Oslo: Scandinavian University Press.

ORREN, K. and SKOWRONEK, S. 1994. Beyond the iconography of order: notes for a "new" institutionalism. Pp. 311–30 in *The Dynamics of American Politics: Approaches and Interpretations*, ed. L. Dodd and C. Jillson. Boulder, Colo.: Westview.

POWER, M. 1994. *The Audit Explosion.* London: Demos.

ROUSSEAU, J.-J. 1967/1762/1755. *The Social Contract and Discourses on the Origin of Inequality*, ed. and introd. L. G. Crocker. New York: Washington Square Press.

ROWE, N. 1989. *Rules and Institutions.* New York: Philip Allan.

SARBIN, T. R. and ALLEN, V. L. 1968. Role theory. Pp. 488–567 in *The Handbook of Social Psychology*, ed. G. Lindzey and E. Aronson, 2nd edn. Reading, Mass.: Addison-Wesley.

SCOTT, J. C. 1976. *The Moral Economy of the Peasant: Rebellion and Subsistence in Southeast Asia.* New Haven, Conn.: Yale University Press.

SCOTT, W. R. 1992. *Organizations: Rational, Natural, and Open Systems*, 3rd edn. Englewood Cliffs, NJ: Prentice Hall.

STINCHCOMBE, A. L. 1997. On the virtues of the old institutionalism. *Annual Review of Sociology*, 23: 1–18.

——2001. *When Formality Works: Authority and Abstraction in Law and Organizations*. Chicago: University of Chicago Press.

SVERDRUP, U. I. 2000. Precedents and present events in the European Union: an institutional perspective on Treaty reform. Pp. 241–65 in *European Integration after Amsterdam*, ed. K. Neunreither and A. Wiener. Oxford: Oxford University Press.

THOMPSON, D. F. 1987. *Political Ethics and Public Office*. Cambridge, Mass.: Harvard University Press.

TUSSMAN, J. 1960. *Obligation and the Body Politic*. London: Oxford University Press.

TYLER, T. R. 1990. *Why People Obey the Law*. New Haven, Conn.: Yale University Press.

UGLAND, T. 2002. *Policy Recategorization and Integration: Europeanization of Nordic Alcohol Policies*. Oslo: Arena Report 02/3.

VAN DEN BERGH, J. C. J. M. and STAGL, S. 2003. Co-evolution of economic behavior and institutions: towards a theory of institutional change. *Journal of Evolutionary Economics*, 13: 289–317.

VAN MAANEN, J. 1973. Observations on the making of policemen. *Human Organization*, 32: 407–18.

VIROLI, M. 1992. *From Politics to Reason of State: The Acquisition and Transformation of the Language of Politics 1250–1600*. Cambridge: Cambridge University Press.

WEBER, M. 1978. *Economy and Society*, ed. G. Roth and C. Wittich. Berkeley: University of California Press.

WHEELER, H. 1975. Constitutionalism. Pp. 1–91 in *The Handbook of Political Science: Governmental Institutions and Processes*, vol. v, ed. F. I. Greenstein and N. W. Polsby. Reading, Mass.: Addison-Wesley.

WOLLMANN, H. 2006. Executive trajectories compared. In *Governing after Communism: Institutions and Policies*, ed. V. Dimitrov, K. H. Goetz, and H. Wollmann. Lanham, Md.: Rowman and Littlefield.

CHAPTER 25

WHY AND HOW PLACE MATTERS

GÖRAN THERBORN

1 PLACE AND POLITICS

POLITICS begins with place. The Western notion of politics derives from a particular place and the concerns of its inhabitants, from *polis*, the Ancient Greek city(-state). The Roman Empire, for all its territorial extension (from today's Iraq to today's Scotland) was a very place-conscious rule, in which *urbs*, the city (Rome), was the crucial center of power. *Civitas*—whence current key concepts of politics, like citizen(ship/ry), civic, and civil originate, directly or indirectly—was in classical Latin not only a concept but also a designation of place and its inhabitants. *Civitas aureliana*, for instance, was today's German Baden-Baden and French Orléans, *Civitas augusta* today's Italian Aosta. Place was an important notion to classical European social and political theory, such as in Aristotle's *Politics* of the fourth century BCE, and place and motion were key concepts of his *Physics* (Casey 1997; Morison 2002).

The polity with which Aristotle was concerned was the *polis*, the city-state (with an agricultural surrounding), not an empire like that of his pupil Alexander. Book 7 of *Politics* is largely devoted to its ideal location and size, the lay-out of streets and buildings. "[T]he land as well as the inhabitants... should be taken in at a single view" (Aristotle 1988, 164). His main concern is security against enemy assault, so cities should not be built along straight lines, for instance (172); but he also stipulates an elevated site for religious worship and beneath it an *agora* for free men, free of trade, artisans, farmers, and "any such person" (173)

Place politics is not Eurocentric. Ancient Chinese conceptions of government, for instance, were also concerned with place and location. Here the focus was not on the city and empowered male citizens, but on the sovereign ruler, the Son of Heaven, and his mediation between the human and the natural worlds. This central mediation task of kingship, of empire, was tied to a concrete location: the *Ming Tang* (the Hall of Light), which later developed into the central *locus* of imperial power, the "Forbidden City," the imperial Palace City in the center of the capital of the Central Kingdom of the World. The construction of a capital city was a key element of legitimate power, and codified in rules of place-based power in *Kao Gong Ji* (*Code Book of Work*, a Confucian classic from the "Spring and Autumn Period," 6–8 centuries BCE) (Dutt et al. 1994, 31 ff.; Sit 1995, 12 ff.). The rules were spread all over the area of Sinic civilization, stretching from Vietnam to Korea and Japan. They are still very prominent in today's Beijing. The Chinese also developed a more general knowledge about the right place and spatial orientation of construction (*feng shui*, or "geomancy" in Latin English).

In the Americas, pre-Columbian places of power, like Machu Picchu in today's Peru and Tenochtitlán in current Mexico, are still conveying their majestic importance to latter-day tourists.

So much for origins and traditions. But how much of place is there in the current world of broadcasting, globalization, Internet, virtuality? Has place become "abstracted from power," because it is now organized in a "space of flows," and not of places, as Manuel Castells (1996, ch. 6) has argued in a great work? A perusal of the main journals of political science for the new century hardly yields any hint of politics of place, although there are geographers who bring their disciplinary expertise of space to political questions (most recently Jones, Jones, and Wood 2004) and devoted journals like *Hérodote* (situated by Claval 2000; Hepple 2000) and *Political Geography*. Is place becoming something of the past only, or just an academic special interest?

Some reflection will show that place is still crucial today to power and politics, in some respect arguably even more than before. Above all, it matters in three kinds of politics: democratic, military (war), and symbolic. But before entering into hot contemporary empirical issues, let us take a circumspect theoretical look.

2 THE PLACE, THE UNIVERSE, AND THE GLOBE

Place has three decisive aspects of social being. First, it means a fixity in space. A place is a fixed location, a stable spot on a map. This means that place is something you can go to, leave, and return to—after a week, a year, a decade, a century, a millennium. A place can be destroyed and disappear, true, but it is always a good bet that it will be there across the vicissitudes of time, in some shape or other.

Second, place means contiguity. A place is where people can meet, can come and can be close to each other, where buildings can relate, where vehicles meet frequently. In this respect, the importance of place varies, positively with contiguous social ties or with local networks, and negatively with the significance of extra-local networks. Place is the site of face-to-face communication, opposite to letter-writing, calling, and Internet chatting.

Third, place means distinctiveness. A place is something different from another place, from anywhere, and from nowhere. A node is defined only by its connectivity, and a position by its relations; but a place is defined by its characteristics. The Norwegian architectural historian and theorist Christian Norberg-Schulz (1982) has referred to this distinctiveness as "*genius loci*," the spirit of character of place, manifested both in the built environment and in the landscape.

Place matters to the extent that the universal does not. Universal laws rule regardless of place; they rule in all places without distinction. After Aristotle (who accorded a particular priority to place and to the question "where?") universe and space came to obliterate place in Western philosophy and science (Casey 1997). It re-emerged in the mid-1930s in Heidegger's philosophy, to which postmodernist and post-structuralist thought have paid close attention.

In other words, in so far as there are universal laws of social science—of economics, of politics, of sociology—place is irrelevant. Now, social scientists agree to having few if any universal laws. Does that mean that place is recognized as important? Not necessarily, because the non-universal may be specific instead to class, gender, ethnicity, culture, or any other non-place features. American-style identity politics, and studies of it, have hardly highlighted place-based identity (cf. Calhoun 1994).

The global is different. While the universe overshadows all places, the globe reveals them and connections among them. In contrast to the universal, the global denotes interconnection, interaction, interlinkage, as opposed not only to unit isolation but also to boundless universality. And global connectivity further implies global difference, global variability, the very opposite of universalistic invariance.

However, there is a tension between connectivity and variability, and a competition for attention and recognition. The main thrust of global studies has been on connectivity and its consequences of interdependence, influence, and hybridization. Much less analytical energy has been devoted to the global variability of places. The discourse on globalization has focused more on the connection, and less on what is being connected.

Globality, in this sense, has important epistemological consequences, too. In contrast to the one-way gaze of universalism and its privileged vantage-point, globality points to the importance of cross-cultural intercommunication as the infrastructure of the global knowledge of difference and connectivity.

In brief, places have competitors in space, the universe, the network position, flows, processes of connection and linkage, as well as from time, social character, and rational choice. To go further, we had better try to grasp the positive potential of place.

3 PLACE AND SOCIAL ACTION

Politics is a kind of social action, a kind having direct collective implications and involving some choice of course within a wider set of rules. Individual pursuits are not politics. Neither is the adjudication or implementation of rules—tasks of judges and bureaucrats, rather than of politicians or political activists.

Looked at from the general perspective of social action, place may be important for any one or more of five fundamental reasons:

- place is the forming mould of actors;
- place is a compass of meaning to the actions of actors;
- place is the immediate setting in which action occurs, or "takes place";
- place crucially affects the consequences of action;
- and finally (the character of a) place is an eminent outcome of action.

The last aspect means that there is an important feedback loop between place and action. In other words, place is both a crucial explanatory or "independent" variable," an "intermediary" variable of setting or "locale" (Giddens 1994, 118–19), and a significant "dependent" variable. Place is thus an example of the dialectics of structure and agency.

"Place," then, is taken as multiply defined, on a scale ranging from the globe to an office building. One definition is civic-political: being within a certain state, being within a certain political or cultural region, having a particular political or cultural (for instance, religious) history. Another is socioeconomic: having a particular socioeconomic structure (agrarian, industrial, commercial, for example), and being prosperous or poor. Still another we may label sociospatial or geosocial: including geopolitical, geoeconomic, geocultural; being central or peripheral, large or small in social space; or on a continuum of social density, of rurality and urbanity, or of communication, from centrality to isolation. A fourth dimension of place refers to its natural location: for example, coastal or inland, plain or mountainous, and with regard to the quality of the soil and the character of the climate. The first two definitions of place refer to contingent spatial effects from outcomes of past action; the latter two to the intrinsic weight of social and natural space upon social action.

To argue comprehensively and to exemplify adequately these modalities of place significance would require at least a handbook of its own. Within the constraints of this chapter, the approach will be to attempt a systematic outline and a set of illustrations. These are drawn largely, but far from exclusively, from my own work in progress on capital cities.[1]

The capital cities of nation states are of note in this context as places of consequential significance and as places of meaning. Capitals are places where crucial decisions are made, on war and peace, on legislation and taxation, on the final adjudication of crime and litigation. They are places where governments are installed, and where

---

[1] For a preliminary publication, see Therborn (2002).

governments lose their power. They are the centers of political debate about the orientation of the country. National capitals are also the locations where decisive reactions to external events have to be made: where ultimata of foreign governments and of fateful organizations like the IMF have to be answered, where pressures and threats from states or transnational corporations have to be either yielded to or resisted. Issues of this sort are decided, not in "global cities" like New York, Los Angeles, or Hong Kong, but in Washington, DC, in Accra, Bangkok, Brasilia, Buenos Aires, Beijing, and other national capitals. Capital cities are places where national differences are made. The capital is therefore often used metaphorically, referring to complex processes of government. "Paris says no"—for instance to an invasion of Iraq—is a way of summing up a whole process of democratic decision-making.

As seats of power, capital cities owe their site to the spatiality of power. Most elementarily, capitals develop with territorial polities—ancient developments in the West (Mesopotamia, Persia) and East Asia (China), but developing very unevenly across the world—and, secondly, with the permanent location of territorial power. The latter phenomenon is also ancient, but disappeared for many centuries in the early European Middle Ages, for instance, and remained rudimentary at least up to the Renaissance. The Central European German *Reich* never managed to get a proper capital in its almost thousand years of existence, until its dissolution in 1806 (Berges 1953; Schultz 1993)—and the capital has been a "problem" in German history at least into the 1990s

3.1 The Formation of Actors

The state you grow up in tends to mold you as a political actor. Your experiences, your successes, defeats, or traumas as a citizen affect your trust or mistrust in institutions and people, your views of government and of politicians. As a Scandinavian in the year 2000 there is a two-thirds chance that you would think that most people can trusted, but if you were Brazilian the probability would only be three in a hundred. A good third of Britons had confidence in their Parliament in 2000, but only 7 percent of Macedonians had. The same year, 9 percent of Americans, 17 percent of Poles, 20 percent of Indians, and 96 percent of Indonesians held that army rule would be "good" or "fairly good" for the country (Inglehart et al. 2004, tables A165, E75, and E116).

A classical idea of place molding actors was the urban–rural difference. The United States of America, for instance, were provided with a strong ruralistic, anti-urban message by one of their Founding Fathers, Thomas Jefferson. Appalled by the big cities of Europe, Jefferson held big cities injurious to "the morals, the health and the liberty of man," that is, to the formation of civic actors (in a letter to Benjamin Rush of September 23, 1800, quoted in Yarborough 1998, 84). Big cities have remained in conflict with state politics throughout American history. A recent overview of US local government emphasizes that "one of the most persistent themes in state–local relations has been the conflict between state legislatures and the largest cities" (Berman 2003, 53; cf. Ching and Creed 1997).

More naturalistic but also more vague has been the counter-position of coastal cultural openness and sensuality against inland closure and austerity, a stereotype often invoked with respect to rival cities such as St. Petersburg and Moscow, Barcelona and Madrid, Beirut and Damascus, Shanghai and Beijing, Guyaquil and Quito.

When three eminent American urban scholars, Peter Dreier, John Mollenkopf, and Todd Swanstrom (2001) argue that *Place Matters*, they bring out differences among three Congressional districts, the New York 16th (South Bronx), the Ohio 10th (Westside Cleveland and adjacent suburbs), and the Illinois 13th (a suburbia west of Chicago). What they want to show is the "big difference in the quality of life" between these three metropolitan areas, from poor, staunchly Democratic South Bronx, to affluent, solidly Republican Chicago suburbs, via socioeconomically mixed, politically swinging Westside Cleveland. Economic segregation is making these place differences larger, and the distance between their supply of life chances wider.

Voters in different places of the same country tend to vote differently. Electoral geography was pioneered in France, by André Siegfried just before the First World War, focusing on the regional formation of actors. Territorial effects (ranging from provincial to municipal) could account for 75 percent or more of the party vote variation in eleven of sixteen Western European countries in elections of the 1970s. In Belgium they account for over 90 percent of the variance, and in Austria, Ireland, Sweden, and the UK close to that (Lane and Ersson 1999, 118). Those calculations do not include any controls for other factors, though. If you do control, not only for the social composition of actors but also for constituency characteristics and for political attitudes, little regional variation was found even in Britain (McAllister and Studlar 1992). The more interesting analyses lie between these poles.

Every democratic country exhibits a spatial pattern of voting, with classes, genders, age groups, or religious and secular people, for example, voting differently in different places or regions. But the reasons for this are still controversial among electoral researchers.[2] In this context we shall pay attention to place-voting from the general angles of actor-formation, action-setting, and consequences of action.

Center versus periphery is a spatial dimension of actor-formation, an important cleavage of party systems as well as of voters. In Europe, it was put into focus by the Norwegian political scientist Stein Rokkan (1970; Rokkan and Urwin 1982). The peripheries of a Great Britain centered on the south of England, for example, tend to favor the oppositional left-of-center. The strong north–south polarization in the 1994 Finnish, Swedish, and Norwegian referenda on EU membership combined space and class effects. In favor of EU membership was the affluent, more bourgeois center in the south; and against it was the somewhat less affluent, more working class or small farmer northern periphery.

---

[2] Recent useful overviews are given by: Johnston and Pattie 2004; Marsh 2002; Johnson, Shively, and Stein 2002.

For the US, Walter Dean Burnham (1970) has argued that the American party system from 1896 to 1932 was hung up on a polarity primarily between an industrial "metropole" in the Northeast supporting the Republicans and "colonial" areas in the West and the South supporting the Democrats. The defeated Confederacy states of the American South established for long a one-party system, throughout the national vicissitudes of the national Democratic label.

But while it has a capacity for hibernation, place politics is not fixed in time. There was, for instance, a significant correlation between the Spanish Socialist vote in 1933 and in the first post-Fascist elections of 1977: strong in Andalucia, Madrid, and Murcia; weak in Castilia-León, Galicia, Navarra, and Aragon (Tezanos 2004, 57). "Critical" elections and gradual sociopolitical processes can change traditions. American politics became more class-based with the New Deal, and class- and culture-based after the end of the Democratic one-party system in the South. Southern culture and traditions still matter, but in different political ways than before (cf. Lind 2003). Indeed, from recent presidential elections a pattern the reverse of the 1896–1920s alignment seems to have emerged. Now Democrats are concentrated in the Northeast (and on the West Coast), while the Republican bases are in the South and the West (Kim, Elliott, and Wang 2004). In France, the regional electoral cleavages going back to mid-nineteenthth century have been reshuffled. In the regional elections of 1986, the right gained even the old left Republican (part of the) south; and in 2004, the left captured Britanny and Vendée in the west, the bastion of the right since the French Revolution.

Since the nineteenth or early twentieth century Western European democratic electoral politics has undergone a process of nationalization, more affected by class and less by locality. However, after the First World War place effects have tended to stabilize. In a few countries, the end of the century saw an increase of the place-formation of voters, in Belgium above all, but also in Italy (Caramani 2004).

Place effects on the formation of political elites have been little studied. But other things being equal (which they rarely are), under democratic conditions—with politicians more rooted in powerful peripheries—the politics of specifically political capitals are likely be less socially cohesive and to be more insulated from economic and cultural elites, as well from popular forces and politicians. To the extent that that is true, it should imply more "log-rolling" or "horse-trading" among legislators. Its governments are more likely to be "governments of strangers" (to borrow a title from a shrewd observer of American public policy—Heclo 1977—who nevertheless paid no attention at all to the peculiar place of Washington). To the extent that it holds, this would imply policy conflict and policy inconsistency, among government incumbents as well as between governments. This sort of capital tends to occur in federal states, with their de-centered domestic politics.

"Total capitals," dominant culturally and economically as well as politically, should be expected (other things being equal) to favor socially and culturally cohesive political elites, and through them more consistent public policies. But the total capital may also harbor—nay, be the center of—all the conflicts of the country. This has certainly been the record of Paris, from the Revolution on. Then at least a common culture or political style may ensue, amidst polarizations of policy. The intellectual character of French national politics and the *pantouflage*, the moving between top positions in the bureaucracy and in business manifest common a Parisian culture of elite schools and literary milieux. But even a centralized country with an overwhelming capital may push provincial power-brokers, "notables," onto the central political stage: as the French Third Republic increasingly did, up to the First World War; and as can still happen, as shown by the current French Prime Minister Raffarin (Corbin 1992, 810 ff.).

The extent to which capital office may be a catapult to national leadership is remarkably small. In so far as there is a capital electoral politics, it may be ill-representative of the country as a whole: that was the case with heavily social democratic Berlin in Wilhelmine Germany, while Paris voted right throughout the twentieth century. Another reason is that an incumbent government tends to be concerned with keeping the capital city under its own control. In Europe, the current French President Jacques Chirac is an exception, in getting to the presidency from being mayor of the capital. In Latin America, though, several capital mayors have recently become presidents, from Tabaré Vázquez in Uruguay to Arnoldo Alemán in Nicaragua.

3.2 Compass of Meaning

Inherent in the distinctiveness of places is their meaning, to inhabitants, to former inhabitants, to visitors, to onlookers, to anyone thinking about them and discussing them. Places vary not only in their size, their topography, their connectivity, or their kind of inhabitants. They have also different meanings, to different people. Places are invested with meaning. As such, places provide compasses of action. Places indicate attachment, belonging, attraction, revulsion; objects of identification, of ambition, and of desire. Their direction of action includes the radiation of meaning by places— such as "global cities" or other sites of power, money, and glory—as well as the pull of place roots. The geographer and architectural theorist Edwatd Relph (1976) distinguishes seven kinds of place-orientation, around the dichotomy of the insider and outsider:

- existential insideness, a close habitual relation;
- empathetic insideness, a reflective relation;
- behavioral insideness, a pragmatically navigating relation;
- vicarious insideness, a relation by identification from afar;
- accidental outsideness, the visitor's look, the tourist gaze;
- objective outsideness, the vision of the deliberately distant observer;
- existential outsideness, alienation from the place.

From historians we have recently learned much about "places of memory," the places where "memory crystallises and takes refuge" (Nora 1984, xvii). "Places," there, are taken in an explicitly metaphorical sense (François and Schulze 2001, 1: 18); the historical inventories include persons, words, inheritance, invested with collective meaning, as well as places (Nora 1984–92; Francois and Schulze 2001).

In order to get at compasses of meaning in a theory of social and political action, we had better take a somewhat different track. In this vein we may focus on:

1. places to be in, to strive to remain in, to go to, or at the very least to follow from afar;
2. places to defend, or to liberate;
3. places to visit: to see; to commemorate; to pay pilgrimage to; alternatively, to avoid;
4. places of discursive reference.

1. *Places to be in.* There are two kinds of places that occupy most of our minds in this respect. One is home—village, town, region—wherever it is. But the positive meaning varies strongly, not only among persons but also over the lifetime of the same person. Centers are the other main kind—centers of action, of wealth, power, and culture.

Comprehensive capital cities—such as Buenos Aires, London, Paris ("the soul of France, its head and its heart": Jordan 1995, 171), Vienna, Cairo, Bangkok, Tokyo, and many others—have this attraction to ambitious people in most walks of life (cf., Charle and Roche 2002). As sites of authority, capital cities also have as a key function to provide compass of meaning to the population of the state. In the Confucian classic on statecraft, the capital should form "a moral yardstick to which his [i.e. the sovereign's] people may look" (Sit 1995, 25). This maxim is echoed more than 2,000 years later in the official 1987 Strategic Long-term Study of Beijing, then characterized as "the nerve center that links the hearts of the people and the Party together... [and as] the 'model district' for guiding the nation in modernisation" (Sit 1995, 321).

Colonial city planning was oriented to conveying the majesty of imperial power. The most ambitious modern example is the construction in the 1910s of a new capital for British India, New Delhi. "First and foremost it is the spirit of British sovereignty which must appreciated in its stone and bronze," one of the two chief architects, Herbert Baker (1944, 219) wrote in a commissioned letter to the *Times* in 1912. To his colleague Edwin Lutyens he stressed that Delhi "must not be Indian, nor English, nor Roman, but it must be Imperial" (Metcalf 1989, 222). A grand imperial design ensued, combining European and Mughal elements, centered on an enormous Vice-regal Palace by Lutyens, flanked by two competing impressive administrative buildings by Baker, up on a hill, at the end of a long and wide avenue-cum-parade ground, Kingsway. Here, as so often, most of the colonial heritage survived decolonization by national recycling. The Vice-regal palace has become the Presidential Palace, and Kingsway has been renamed Rajpath.

The United States built a new capital mainly because of the rivalry among existing cities. From 1774 to 1789 Congress met in eight different places. Washington was laid out by a French engineer, L'Enfant, who had rallied to the American cause and acquired American citizenship. Having grown up in the shadow of Versailles, L'Enfant put forward a daring plan "proportional to the greatness which... the Capital of a great Empire ought to manifest," as he wrote to President Washington (Sonne 2003, 50). L'Enfant soon fell out with the federal commission, but by and large and over time his monumental design for the American capital was realized, with its bipolar political layout, huge diagonals overtowering any civic space (although the Mall has lately become a national rallying-point), and its central Washington Monument.

In Europe a French author in the Age of Absolutism, Alexandre Le Maître in 1682, highlighted three crucial functions of a capital: to be the site of authority; to be the pivot of all exchanges; and to "concentrate the values and the force of a country" (Zeller 2003, 633). An intensive debate about the values and the force of nation represented by competing capitals broke out in Germany with the reunification of the country in 1990. Bonn (the post-Second World War capital of West Germany) and Berlin were invested with very different meanings: Bonn was presented as symbolizing the Western and the European orientation of a post-national Germany, a capital of *Gemütlichkeit*; Berlin was seen as a symbol of German unification and as the normal metropolis of a normal nation, freed of the historical inferiority complexes of the Bonn Republic (Richie 1998: 850 ff.; Keiderling 2004; von Beyme 1991). The vote was close, and cut through traditional party and cultural cleavages. In the end Berlin won with 337 parliamentary votes to 320.

2. *Places to defend or liberate*. Places to defend are often peripheral, which may have been the reason why they were attacked. The Falklands islands at the bottom of the South Atlantic are one of the most peripheral places on the planet from the center of London, but their defense was seen by a large part of the metropolitan population as well as by the government as worthwhile regardless of cost, human and financial. From the other side, opponents as well as supporters of Argentina's then-military regime saw the Malvinas as a natural part of the country, robbed by the British in the heyday of imperialism. To both parties, the value was symbolic only, but high enough to go to war for.

Modern nationalism has led to a remarkable sacralization of national territory, with a great many places that have to be liberated or defended. The Caucasus region has a number of them, and so have former Yugoslavia and the Horn of Africa. Jerusalem/al Qods is not only a sacred place to three religions, but has also become overloaded with contested meanings to two nations in conflict.

3. *Places to visit*. Travel to interesting or beautiful places is ancient, and so is pilgrimage to sacred sites. But places to visit have become much more important in current times. Nation-building has brought national places into focus. "One cannot be fully Indonesian until one has seen Jakarta," Indonesia's greatest writer, Pramoedya Ananta Toer wrote in 1955 (Kusno 2001, 15). Tourism has become a major industry, and tourism politics and policy have become important political tasks. Secondly, there has also evolved a political practice of deliberately investing places with heavy symbolic meaning, as sites of commemoration. This is most developed in Europe, mainly with reference to events of the Second World War and the Nazi terror. Former concentration camps and death camps, like Buchenwald and Auschwitz, and former Jewish ghettoes in many cities have become meaningful places to visit.

Places may also have a meaning of repulsion, places not to be visited. The German war cemetery of Bittburg was such a place in the eyes of many, on the occasion of an official visit there by President Reagan and Chancellor Kohl, because SS men are also buried there. Every time a senior Japanese politician visits the Yasakuni shrine in Tokyo there is a Chinese protest, because Japanese war criminals have been laid at rest there.

4. *Places of discursive reference.* Places of meaning may orient our minds and discourse. The little Belgian town of Waterloo, where Napoleon was fatally beaten in 1815, has become synonymous with defeat to such an extent that it has entered the world of late twentieth-century pop hits. "Munich" in international politics stands for accommodation to violent dictators, after the British and French Prime Ministers agreed to Nazi German demands on Czechoslovakia in a summit in 1938. "Vichy" (the small-town site of the pro-German government of France in 1940–4) in European political discourse denotes collaboration with an occupying enemy (cf. Watkins 2004). "Pearl Harbour" in American politics means perfidious attack, and "Sèvres" in Turkish discourse refers to splitting the country (after the Paris suburb where the Ottoman empire was subjected to a humiliating peace treaty in 1920). In Chile during the left-wing government of Allende in the early 1970s, right-wing graffiti painted the name of "Jakarta," the Indonesian capital, where an anti-communist massacre—of probably more than half a million people—was unleashed in 1965.

3.3 Settings of Action

Almost all social action, except for telephonic or electronic communication, takes place somewhere, in some local setting. Capital cities are settings of power, exercise, and contest, truly "landscapes of power" in a phrase that Sharon Zukin (1991) uses primarily to refer to New York. A famous case of city planning as a setting for political action is the transformation of Paris in the third quarter of the nineteenth century. It was carried out for Emperor Napoleon III by his prefect, Baron Haussmann. There were several reasons for changing old, rapidly grown Paris; above all hygienic ones, as the city had become very insalubrious. Imperial aesthetics was also an important concern. Whatever the controversial priority order, a major task of Haussmann was to make government power safe from rebellion by the people of densely populated, labyrinthine east-central Paris. By time of the June 1848 violent repression of insurrectionary Paris, barricades had been put up eight times since 1827; and twice revolutions had succeeded, in July 1830 and February 1848. The solution was to raze a number of poor neighborhoods, to open up a set of big boulevards, difficult to barricade and easy to move troops in, and to locate army barracks close to places of popular gathering. Most affected by this strategic plan were the areas between what are now the Places de la République and de la Nation on the Right Bank, and on the Left from the new Boulevard Saint Michel to Mount St. Geneviève (Jordan 1995). As a counter-insurgency strategy all this was hardly successful, and did not prevent the revolutionary Paris Commune of 1871, but the setting of urban life in Paris had been lastingly transformed.

In the colonial cities, racial segregation was the primary rule, as manifestations of power and for reasons of security, epidemic as well as political (Georg and de Lemps 2003). The most ambitious governors built new European cities outside indigenous ones, as the French governor Lyautey did in Morocco (Abu-Lughod 1980; Rabinow 1989), or as the British did in New Delhi, which was laid out spaciously as a tree-shadowed garden city just opposite the crowded Old Delhi. Like other cities of the British Empire, it also had its layout segregated not only between the rulers and the natives, but also between the military "cantonments" and the administrative "civil lines." Not quite 5 percent of the new city area was intended as "Native Residential" (Hussey 1950, 263). These colonial military cantonments or "Defense Colonies" still contribute to the configurations of urban life in cities of Bangladesh, India, and Pakistan.

But capitals can also be or provide spaces of civic representation. A powerful citizenry is manifested in a civic space, a public space where people can meet as citizens and as individuals with varied tastes. The ancient Greek *agora* and the Roman forum are classical examples. The tradition was revived by the autonomous High Medieval cities of Europe, in particular along the city belt from Italy to the Low Countries. Italian Siena's *Piazza del Campo* is arguably one of the most beautiful examples (cf. Rowe 1997, ch. 1), but it may be followed by the *Grande Place* of Brussels. In the Americas, the Boston Common (Hackett Fischer 2000) is perhaps a paradigmatic example. But all colonial Latin American cities had and still have a central square where people met and assembled. True, it was also used for displays of power, such as military parades, and in Hispanic America it was often called *Plaza de Armas* (Place of Arms).

Security considerations seem to render futile the idea of the architects of the new Berlin government quarter, Schultes and Frank, of a "Federal and Civic Forum" between the Chancellors's Office and the parliament building, although there is still some open, accessible space there. The civic space of Chandigarh, the capital of Indian Punjab and later also of the Indian state of Haryana, was laid out by the great modernist architect Le Corbusier, relating the three branches of government through open squares, provided with abstract civic sculptures. The insecurity situation—with the Punjabi Chief Minister assassinated in the 1990s—has led to a closing off to the public of the whole governmental area. However, in democratized Seoul, the area in front of City Hall has been changed from just a traffic circus to a lawn accessible to pedestrians where people gather, for small outdoor concerts as well as for expressing political opinion.

The classical Chinese concept of political space was in a sense the opposite of the civic one, centered on a closed space of power, the imperial palace as the "Forbidden City." On its south side, was an opening onto an outer court for petitions and for public announcements (Sit 1995, 56 ff.). The Javanese *kraton* or royal palace was laid out on the basis of similar principles, as a closed, central site of power, with a public space (*alun-alun*) for royal announcements and for public celebrations and festivities (Tjahjono 1998, 90). In Muslim cities the mosques and their large courtyards are places of assembly, but of members of the *umma* (the religious community) rather than of a political citizenry, who were usually facing an overtowering, fortified site of power, from the Red Fort of Mughal Delhi to the Topkapi of Ottoman Istanbul. But sometimes the Muslim city could include a big central square, a *meidan*, in front of a palace or and/of the main mosque. In this respect, the center of Isfahan resembled that of Lima or Quito, with a meeting-place and a place of public recreation. In other respects, the East as well as the West Asian cities were dominated by private, family space, of compounds around a walled-in courtyard connected only by meandering alleys, very different from the Ancient European street grid that was later exported to the Americas.

Another kind of political space is the space for political rallies. Nationalism was the first major wave of popular mobilization, and it could often make new use of absolutist parade grounds: the *Champs de Mars* in Paris, where the Revolution held its first mass rallies; or the *Heldenplatz* in Vienna, the "Heroes Square" in front of the imperial palace, where the coming of the First World War in 1914 and of Adolf Hitler in 1938 were fêted. The Communist rulers paid serious attention to places of mass rally. In Moscow the old Red Square outside the Kremlin was a natural site, focused by the Lenin Mausoleum of 1924. The East Germans tore down the war-damaged imperial castle to make room for a large rallying-point, the *Marx-Engels-Platz*. Mao Zedong and the Chinese comrades were duly impressed by Red Square upon their visit to Moscow in 1950, and set upon enlarging the Tian An Men, just south of the imperial Forbidden City, into the largest political parade ground in the world (Webb 1990).

The world religions have also realized the significance of places of mass assembly, as manifested by the place around the *Kaaba* in Mecca or outside the church of St. Peter in Rome.

The settings of voting behavior may be viewed in various ways. At one end, there is the structural context, presumably perceived by the voter. For instance, according to British census polls for the period of 1991–2001, the percentage voting Conservative or Labour varied strongly with the structural socioeconomic disadvantage of the neighborhood. In the most advantaged areas 77 percent of the "higher service class" of professionals and managers voted Tory, and 68 percent of skilled manual workers; whereas in the least advantaged neighbourhoods 48 and 19 percent did, respectively (Johnston et al. 2004, table 4.).

From another angle, the setting of voting is social interaction, local campaigning, groups or networks of political discussions. There is no unanimity among electoral specialists on the importance of these interactive effects, but they clearly exist (Huckfeldt and Sprague 1995; Whiteley and Seyd 2003).

3.4 Places and Consequences of Action

"Being in the right place at the right time" (or "in the wrong place at the wrong time") are well-known words of wisdom, applying to sexual as well as to political life. In politics, it applies both to aspiring leaders and, especially, to ordinary people.

When police and military round-ups are being made, you had better not be in the wrong place. Otherwise you may, in present times, land in Guantánamo or in some other concentration camp. In order to make a successful bid for power, you have to be in the right place at the decisive moment

Wars, geopolitical or world systems, and democratic elections are all examples of the importance of place for consequences of action. And capital cities are by definition the place where consequential state action is taken.

Maps have always been crucial to modern warfare. Why? Because it is crucial to locate where your enemy is, what possibilities of movement he has, and where to hit him hardest. Knowing where to do battle, and when, is a key demand on a successful commander. Recent supposedly "precision bombing" has raised the stakes, rather than making place trivial.

To stay, in the face of encirclement, and fight was a fatal mistake of the Nazi Germans in Stalingrad and of the colonial French at Dien Bien Phu. The decision of the US Clinton administration in the 1990s to concentrate military interventions in the Balkans—where Secretary of State Albright was well connected—and to leave Rwanda to its fate, made possible the genocide of Tutsi people by Hutu people, and substituted Croatian and Albanian ethnic cleansing for Serbian in the former Yugoslavia. But it did bring about the desired regime toppling in Serbia. The decision of the Bush administration to make war in Iraq has been successful in "regime change," but again at the cost of large-scale destruction and killings, of about 12,000 to 13,000 civilian Iraqis according to estimates reported by CNN on September 8, 2004. A large part of the death and destruction does not seem to have been intended, but followed from the violent logic of the place, which the bombers and invaders never bothered to learn about. To both US governments, the dynamics of place seems to have been fatally neglected.

In the heyday of inter-imperialist rivalry about a century ago, a geographical theory of politics and power, *geopolitics*, was developed by Rudolf Kjellén (the Swedish professor of geography and political science who coined the term), Harold Mackinder (Oxford geographer and LSE Director), and Friedrich Ratzel (the German geographer). States struggling for space was their common vision, and spatial parameters of this big-power rivalry their main concern (Heffernan 2000). The characteristic confluence of the emerging academic discipline of geography, the climate of Social Darwinism, and the peak of intra-European imperialist rivalry, carried forward by the German Nazis, discredited the idea of geopolitics for a while after the Second World War. But the thesis by Frederick Jackson Turner of the sociopolitical importance of the American frontier and of its closing around 1890 is also an influential example of geopolitical thought. De facto, the cold war strategists on both sides were clearly very geographically conscious, in negotiating and pressuring their respective territorial "spheres of influence."

Geopolitics made an interesting comeback in the 1990s. It did so intellectually, in a culturalist mutation: as part of a postmodern geography, focusing on imaginations of space, on bodies in places, and on non-state politics, by institutions, cities, or movements of resistance to power (Agnew 1999; Ó Tuathail and Dalby 1998; Soja 1996).

It did so politically, in a more direct return to classical strategic geopolitics as part of a new assertiveness of American world power. The most eloquent and significant example is Zbigniew Brzezinski (1997), National Security Adviser to President Carter and a key architect of the Islamic counter-revolution in Afghanistan.

To Brzezinski, control of Euarasia is the "chief geopolitical prize" for the United States, and the decisive strategic question to be addressed is how that "preponderance on the Eurasian continent" can be sustained (1997, 30). The answer is sought in seeing Eurasia as a "grand chessboard" on which the struggle for global primacy is played. The approach is explicitly geopolitical, as "geographic location still tends to determine the immediate priorities of a state" (38). The key units are "geostrategic players"—"the states that have the capacity and national will to exercise power or influence beyond their borders in order to alter... the existing geopolitical state of affairs" (40)—and "geopolitical pivots," "states whose importance is derived... from their sensitive location" (41).

In this neoclassical as well as in classical geopolitical thought, state actors are shaped by their place in the world, but the main emphasis is on the risks and the opportunities for state power that the control—by ego or by alter—of places and territories offer, and on the best strategies of states under given geopolitical conditions. A more economic than military–political view of geopolitics, befitting a Japan-centered perspective, is provided by Rumley et al. (1998). A less imperial, more objective view of contemporary geopolitics is given by its American academic doyen, S. B. Cohen (2003, 3) as "the analysis of the interaction between geographical settings and perspectives, and international politics."

Place also matters in the world system of Immanuel Wallerstein (1974), his associates, and followers. Economic and social development, in this influential perspective, is not primarily a matter of individual countries taking off. They follow from a world system of division of labor, established by Western European powers in the sixteenth century, and the location of countries within it: in the advantaged core, in the exploited periphery, or in the intermediate semi-periphery. The dynamics of the systemic logic may be argued about, but world system analysis is a prominent example of place-matters analysis.

World system analysis is basically a kind of geoeconomics, both related to and rivalling geopolitics. The recent "global cities" perspective gives this global geoeconomics an urban twist. Here commanding and pace-setting action is portrayed as being concentrated into a hierarchy of "global cities," headed by London and New York (Sassen 1991; Taylor 2004). In this perspective, states—and their capacity to tax, to control borders, and to wage wars—tend to disappear from view, being of secondary significance at most. Places matter in this view to the extent that they are the sites of transnational corporate headquarters, in particular of firms of business services. Washington, DC, then appears as a "medium"-sized "global command center," similar to Amsterdam (Taylor 2004, 90).

In most electoral democracies, the decisive thing is not just how many votes you get. It matters also, and sometimes crucially, where you get your votes. Above all, this is important in the Anglo-Saxon first-past-the-post system, which in theory always and in practice sometimes can produce an elective majority for a party backed by a minority of voters. Most recently, this was the case in the US in 2000, when the Electoral College of state representatives elected George W. Bush President of the United States with 47.9 percent of the votes against 48.4 percent for Al Gore. In American history a minority President had been inaugurated three times before, but all in the nineteenth century (John Quincy Adams in 1824, Rutherford Hayes in 1876, and Benjamin Harrison in 1888). In 1951, Winston Churchill and the British Conservatives won a very consequential election, opening a thirteen-year period of Tory rule, with less votes than the Labour Party, 48.0 to 48.8 percent, yielding a seat majority of 51.4 to 47.2 (Flora 1983, 151, 188).

Electoral strategists in countries with this electoral system are, of course, always primarily preoccupied with "swing" constituencies or, in American presidential elections, swing states.

The electoral importance of place also means that the drawing up of electoral districts has become a major political art. In its (normal) biased form it has even been given a name, "gerrymandering," after the early nineteenth-century governor of Massachusetts, Gerry, who according to a contemporary cartoonist, created salamander-like constituencies. In most, but far from all American states this is a partisan task, carried out by the majority of the state legislature where the votes are cast.

3.5 Places as Outcomes of Action

Places are not fixed in time, in spite of their inherent inertia. They may go up and down in terms of population and of relative centrality or prosperity. Some of these changes are governed by nature: by volcanoes and earthquakes, by climate changes, by the wanderings of fish shoals, by the silting of rivers. But most tend to be outcomes of human action, by the discovery/exploitation or the depletion of natural resources, by the building and obsolescence of transport routes (mountain passes, bridges, canals, ports, and railways, for example), by policies of territorial exploitation, neglect, or support, or by direct place construction or destruction.

About eighty years ago, a British historian (Cornish 1923) tried to grasp the location of what he called *The Great Capitals*, by which he meant "Imperial" capitals or capitals of "Great Powers." Most important in his view was their location as the "Storehouse" of the wealth of the empire; secondly, there was transport connectivity, "Crossways"; and thirdly, considerations of war, "Strongholds." Under these constraints, the fact that the foreign relations of the empire are conducted from the capital propels the capital into a "Forward position," relatively close to the exterior. More often than not the national capital is the most cosmopolitan, or the most "globalized" part of the nation.

However, the place of the capital is not determined only by national dimensions. Capital cities are made up of a triangle of relations: between the local and the national, the national and the global, and the global and the local. As places they constitute the habitat of a local population with their everyday needs and habits. Like all places, capital cities have their *genii loci*, their local "spirits of place," given by their location, and their local social and political relations. The river and the hill provide the parameters of Prague, the sea and the islands of Stockholm and Helsinki, for instance. Local Washington is actually largely black and poor, very different from the national and the global radiations from the White House, the Pentagon, and Capitol Hill. In Helsinki, the City Council has determined the sites of national buildings and monuments, separating the Republican Parliament from the ex-imperial government area, for instance. In many other countries, from the UK to China, the capital city is largely directly under central government control.

While Cornish is a good starting-point, situating social action in natural settings, later experience testifies to other springs of capital action as well. This is seen most easily and clearly in the modern history of deliberately created capitals.

Why have new capitals been constructed, as alternatives not only to remaining in the historical place but also to moving to some other city in existence, an ancient political practice?

Starting with St Petersburg, begun in 1703, officially a capital (or "throne") city in 1712, with the transfer of the imperial court to it, and continuing up to the first years of the twenty-first century, we may distinguish a limited set of reasons for such major political displacement.

St Petersburg was a product of monarchical absolutism, and its rationale was reactive modernization. The founding of a new capital was part of an effort from above to modernize the country, then conceived more in cultural than in economic terms. From its "forward" location at the western edge of the empire, St Petersburg was built as a fortified gateway to more developed Western Europe, and as a vanguard of Russian modernization. Dutch city planning, Italian architects, and French culture were resorted to for this purpose, and made possible by a massive use of coerced labor (Lemberg 1993; Jangfeldt 1998; Tjekanova et al. 2000; Zeller 2003, 666 ff.). The modernist thrust of Tsar Peter I was to remain unrivalled for a long time. Edo/Tokyo was already a major city, perhaps the largest in the world in the eighteenth century, although it became the imperial capital only with the Meiji Restoration of 1868 (Seidensticker 1985, ch. 1). Ankara was also in existence, although at a modest level, before chosen as the capital of Turkey in the 1920s (Sen and Aydin 2000).

Chronologically, Washington was the next novel capital. It was to set a pattern for the rest of the white settlements of the British Empire as well as for the USA. The main picture of this capital history is one of places of political exchange.

The location of US capital cities were often bargaining chips in political games, or interest compromises. The federal capital owes its site on the Potomac to a deal brokered by Alexander Hamilton, whereby the union took over all public debt in exchange for Northern support for a Southern site for the capital (Cummings and Price 1993, 216 ff.). The world had experienced the founding of new capitals before in modern times. But the conception of a specifically political center, separated from the economic and demographic one—which was then Philadelphia—was new, although adumbrated in the role of the Hague in the Dutch United Provinces as the meeting village of the Estates-General. It set an American pattern, followed already in 1797 when the state government of New York moved to Albany and in 1799, when that of

Pennsylvania went to Lancaster. In 1857, Abraham Lincoln put together an infrastructural package of railway and canal construction with a relocation of the Illinois capital to Springfield (Johannsen 2000, 186 ff.). An anti-urban animus has played a significant part in the widespread American practice of making relatively small cities state political capitals, from Albany, New York, and Harrisburg, Pennsylvania, to Sacramento, California, via Lansing, Michigan, and Springfield, Illinois (cf. Dye 1988; Berman 2003).

The Washington principle of territorial political balance was followed in Canada in 1867, when Queen Victoria conferred capital status to the town of Ottawa, on the border of Anglophone Ontario and Francophone Quebec. It was further followed in Australia, placing the capital Canberra between the major capitals of the states of Victoria and New South Wales; in New Zealand, placing the capital Wellington between the North and the South Island; and in South Africa, where the capital functions were divided between the government in Transvaal Boer Pretoria, parliament in Anglo Cape Town, and the Supreme Court in Boer Oranje Bloemfontein. But the US anti-urban animus did not spread.

The new capitals of recent times have a different rationale. The most spectacular is Brasilia, built in the late 1950s on the high plateau wilderness of interior Brazil. Brasilia was built as a project of national development, opening up a previously undeveloped interior. Owing to its master planner (Lucio Costa) and its master architect (Oscar Niemayer), Brasilia has become an icon of mid-twentieth-century urban modernity, daring and controversial (cf. Kubitschek 1975; Holston 1989)

The Nigerian move from Lagos to the new Abuja, while spatially similar to the Brazilian move to Brasilia was more motivated by reasons of ethnic balance and political security. Lagos, the inherited colonial capital, was de facto a mainly Yoruba city, and as such impregnated by one the three major ethnicities of multiethnic Nigeria. The official criteria for choosing a new capital for Nigeria were as shown in Table 25.1.

The relocation was actually decided by a military dictatorship, under mounting pressure from popular protests as well as from assassination attempts. It should not be assumed that these official criteria were de facto strictly abided by. Nevertheless, at least they provide an insight into an important contemporary political discourse on place.

In recent years, there has been a growing concern in several parts of the world with too much centrality, with overgrown capitals suffering from congestion and overpopulation. The most advanced example is in Malaysia, where the capital is moving to a new city, Putrajaya, already well under way—with a palatial Prime Minister's Office and a nearby large mosque as their most impressive constructions. The Malaysian capital move is also related to a vision of electronic information development— both similar to and different from the Brazilian interior development program with Brasilia—and includes the building of a parallel high-tech city, Cyberjaya.

The current Korean president is committed to locating out of Seoul for similar reasons. There is a parliamentary decision supporting the move, and the selection of a preliminary site by mid-2004, but this is still on the drawing board. Discussions along

Table 25.1. Official criteria for choosing the Nigerian capital

Criterion	Proportional weight
Centrality	22
Health and Climate	12
Land Availability and Use	10
Water Supply	10
Multi-Access Possibility	7
Security	6
Existence of Local Bldg. Materials	6
Low Population Density	6
Power Resources	5
Drainage	5
Soil	4
Physical Planning Convenience	4
Ethnic Accord	3

Source: Eyinla 2000, 250

the same lines are being held in several Asian countries: China, Japan, Indonesia. But plans may get stuck, as in Argentina in the 1980s, or the realization stalled, as in Tanzania or Côte d'Ivoire.

4 PLACES IN HISTORY AND TODAY

While increasingly mobile, human beings still locate themselves in places, fixed, contiguous, distinctive. Places mold actors, structuring their life chances, providing them with identities and traditions of social and political action. Places direct actors, by attraction or repulsion, providing compasses of action, contribute to the meaning of life by orienting civic action, supporting action, subject action, consuming action, celebration, remembrance, mourning, non-action. Social action almost always takes place in a specific location. Places are strategic sites of action, very much affecting outcomes of success, victory, and power—and their opposites. The creation, development, or destruction of places form an important part of political agendas.

Are these effects and implications of place mainly a legacy of the past, largely being overcome in the current age of electronic networking and global satellite communication? The evidence is ambiguous, but three conclusions seem to be warranted. First and foremost, place has not disappeared, but is still important. Secondly, it is less important than a century ago. Thirdly, the evidence for a recent major change is flimsy, and most probably untenable.

Institutions of formal education clearly mitigate the effects of place of birth, although the latter still weighs heavily on your channels to schooling. Faster means of transport (automobiles, airplanes, fast trains) have made distances shrink. There is currently as much inter-national migration as a century ago, but it is today much easier to keep up ties to places of origin—by satellite TV, telephone, e-mail, and bank remittances—than previously. Intra-national migration, on the other hand, has increased enormously, in Africa, Asia, and Latin America. Place voting declined before the First World War, but little after, and some very recent tendencies of Europe and America go both up and down.

Geopolitics was always controversial, its relevance always contested. But it is a noteworthy sign, that it has recently staged a discursive comeback. Military technology is undoubtedly much less place-dependent than previously. Intercontinental nuclear missiles make up the aces, rather than defensive or controlling locations. More doubtful is whether current concerns with "global governance" have moved beyond the "great games" of rival imperialisms 100 years ago, and its interimperial conferences, like that in Berlin of 1884.

The cities versus state literature remains within the field of place. The gist of this business-focused literature is the emphasis on central or "commanding" places versus others. The current tendencies towards a regionalization of trade and of interstate cooperation point to a mounting significance of place and contiguity. The European Union, the NAFTA, the Mercosur, the ASEAN, the Asian extensions of ASEAN to the east (China, Japan, and South Korea) and recently to the west (India), the African Union: all indicate an increasing importance of place, albeit a move from nation state to region. The classical centre–periphery distinction, with regard to all kinds of action, does not seem to be disappearing.

While there is some (contradictory) evidence of a diminishing importance of place in the formation of actors and in affecting the consequences of action, no such tendency can be detected with respect to place as the meaning of action. Places of meaning are invented all the time. A noteworthy example is the Garden of Diana of Wales put up in Revolutionary Republican Havana in the late 1990s. While there is no hard quantitative evidence, it seems plausible that the number of meaningful places is increasing. There is in any case quite an entrepreneurship around to invent such places.

This is being written in the shadow of American elections. In 2000, the US presidential election was decided in Miami-Dade county, in 2004 in the state of Ohio. Few spots of the planet are likely to be unaffected by who wins the legitimate power of the United States.

REFERENCES

ABU-LUGHOD, J. 1980. *Rabat: Urban Apartheid in Morocco*. Princeton, NJ: Princeton University Press.

AGNEW, J. 1999. The new geopolitics of power. Pp. 173–93 in *Human Geography Today*, ed. D. Massey, J. Allen, and P. Sarre. Cambridge: Polity.

ARISTOTLE 1988. *The Politics*, ed. S. Eveson, trans. B. Jowitt. Cambridge: Cambridge University Press.

BAKER, H. 1944. *Architecture and Personalities*. London: Country Life.

BERGES, W. 1953. Das Reich ohne Hauptstadt. Pp. 1–30 in *Das Hauptstadtproblem in der Geschichte*, ed. Friedrich-Meinecke-Institut. Tübingen: Max Niemeyer Verlag.

BERMAN, D. R. 2003. *Local Government and the States*. Armonk, NY: M. E. Sharpe.

BEYME, K. VON 1991. *Hauptstadtsuche*. Frankfurt: Suhrkamp.

BRZEZINSKI, Z. 1997. *The Grand Chessboard*. New York: Basic Books.

BURNHAM, W. D. 1970. *Critical Elections and the Mainsprings of American Politics*. New York: Norton.

CALHOUN, C. 1994. *Social Theory and the Politics of Identity*. Oxford: Blackwell.

CARAMANI, D. 2004. *The Nationalization of Politics*. Cambridge: Cambridge University Press.

CASTELLS, M. 1996. *The Rise of the Network Society*. Oxford: Blackwell.

CASEY, E. C. 1997. *The Fate of Place: A Philosophical History*. Berkeley: University of California Press.

CHARLE, C. and ROCHE, D. (eds.) 2002. *Capitales culturelles Capitales symboliques: Paris et les expérience européennes*. Paris: Publications de la Sorbonne.

CHING, B. and CREED, G. M. 1997. Recognizing rusticity: identity and the power of place. Pp. 1–38 in *Knowing Your Place: Rural Identity and Cultural Hierarchy*, ed. B. Ching and G. M. Creed. London: Routledge.

CLAVAL, P. 2000. *Hérodote* and the French Left. In Dodds and Atkinson 2000, 239–67.

COHEN, S. B. 2003. Geopolitical realities and United States foreign policy. *Political Geography*, 22: 1–33.

CORBIN, A. 1992. Paris–province. Pp. 777–823 in *Les lieux de mémoire III: 1 Les Frances*, ed. P. Nora. Paris: Gallimard.

CORNISH, V. 1923. *The Great Capitals: An Historical Geography*. London: Methuen.

CUMMINGS, M. C., JR., and PRICE, M. C. 1993. The creation of Washington, DC. In Taylor et al. 1993, 213–29.

DODDS, K. and ATKINSON, D. (eds.) 2000. *Geopolitical Traditions*. London: Routledge.

DREIER, P., MOLLENKOP, J., and SWANSTROM, T. 2001. *Place Matters: Metropolitics for the Twenty-first Century*. Lawrence: University Press of Kansas.

DUTT, A., COSTA, F., AGGARWAL, S., and NOBLE, A. 1994 *The Asian City: Processes of Development, Characteristics and Planning*. Dordrecht: Kluwer.

DYE, T. R. 1988. *Politics in States and Communities*. Englewood Cliffs, NJ: Prentice Hall.

EYINLA, B. M. 2000. From Lagos to Abuja: the domestic politics and international implications of relocating Nigeria's capital city. In Sohn and Weber 2000, 239–68.

FLORA, P. 1983. *State, Economy, and Society in Western Europe, 1815–1975*. Vol. 1. Frankfurt: Campus.

FRANÇOIS, E. and SCHULZE, H. 2001. *Deutsche Erinnerungsorte*, 3 vols. München: C. H. Beck.

GEORG, O., and DE LEMPS, X. H. 2003. La ville européenne outre-mer. Vol. 2: 279–544 in *Histoire de l'Europe urbaine*, ed. J.-L. Pinol. Paris: Seuil.

GIDDENS, A. 1994. *The Constitution of Society*. Cambridge: Polity Press.

HACKETT FISCHER, D. 2000. Boston Common. Pp. 125–43 in *American Places*, ed. W. E. Leuchtenburg. Oxford: Oxford University Press.

HECLO, H. 1977. *Government of Strangers*. Washington, DC: Brookings Institution.

HEFFERNAN, M. 2000. On the origins of European geopolitics, 1890–1920. In Dodds and Atkinson 2000, 27–51.

HEPPLE, L. 2000. Yves Lacoste, *Hérodote* and French radical geography. In Dodds and Atkinson 2000, 268–301.

HOLSTON, J. 1989. *The Modernist City: An Anthropological Critique of Brasilia*. Chicago: University of Chicago Press.

HUCKFELDT, R. and SPRAGUE, J. 1995. *Citizens, Politics, and Social Communication*. Cambridge: Cambridge University Press.

HUSSEY, C. 1950. *The Life of Sir Edwin Lutyens*. London: Country Life.

INGLEHART, R., BASÁÑÑEZ, M., DÍEZ-MEDRANO, J., HALMAN, L., and LUIJKS, R. (eds.) 2004. *Human Beliefs and Values*. México: Siglo XXI.

JANGFELDT, B. 1998. *Svenska vägar till Sankt Petersburg*. Stockholm: Wahlström & Widstrand.

JOHANNSEN, R. W. 2000. Illinois old capitol. Pp. 185–99 in *American Places*, ed. W. E. Leuchtenburg. Oxford: Oxford University Press.

JOHNSON, M., SHIVELY, P., and STEIN, R. M. 2002. Contextual data and the study of elections and voting behaviour: connecting individuals to environments. *Electoral Studies*, 21: 219–33.

JOHNSTON, R. and PATTIE, C. 2004. Electoral geography in electoral studies: putting voters in their place. Pp. 45–66 in *Spaces of Democracy*, ed. C. Barnett and M. Low. London: Sage.

JOHNSTON, R. K., JONES, R., SARKER, PROPPER, C., BURGESS, S., and BOLSTER, A. 2004. Party support and the neighbourhood effect: spatial polarization and the British electorate. *Political Geography*, 23: 367–402.

JONES, M., JONES, R., and WOODS, M. 2004. *An Introduction to Political Geography*. London: Routledge.

JORDAN, D. 1995. *Transforming Paris: The Life and Labour of Baron Hauussmann*. New York: Free Press.

KEIDERLING, G. 2004. *Der Umgang mit der Haupstadt*. Berlin: Verlag am Park.

KIM, J., ELLIOTT, E., and WANG, D.-M. 2003. A spatial analysis of county level outcomes in US presidential elections 1988–2000. *Electoral Studies*, 22: 741–61.

KUBITSCHEK, J. 1975. *Por Que Construí Brasilia*. Rio de Janeiro: Bloch Editores.

KUSNO, A. 2001. Violence of categories: urban design and the making of Indonesian modernity. Pp. 15–50 in *City and Nation. Rethinking Place and Identity*, ed. M. P. Smith and T. Bender. New BRUNSWICK, NJ: Transaction.

LANE, J.-E. and ERSSON, S. 1999. *Politics and Society in Western Europe*, 4th edn. London: Sage.

LEMBERG, H. 1993. Moskau und St. Petersburg: Die Frage der Nationalhaupstadt in Russland: Eine Skizze. Pp. 103–13 in *Hauptstädte in europäischen Nationalstaaten*, ed. T. Schieder and G. Brunn. Munich: Oldenbourg.

LIND, M. 2003. *Made in Texas*. New York: Basic Books.

McALLISTER, I. and STUDLAR, D. 1992. Regional voting in Britain: territorial polarisation or artefact? *American Journal of Political Science*, 3: 168–99.

MARSH, M. 202. Electoral context. *Electoral Studies*, 21: 207–18.

METCALF, T. R. 1989. *An Imperial Vision: Indian Architecture and the British Raj*. Oxford: Oxford University Press.

MORISON, B. 2002. *On Location*. Oxford: Clarendon Press.

NORA, P. (ed.) 1984–92. *Les lieux de mémoire*, 7 vols. Paris Gallimard.

NORBERG-SCHULZ, C. 1982. *Genius loci: Landschaft, Lebensraum, Baukunst*. Stuttgart: Klett-Cotta.

Ó TUATHAIL, G. and DALBY, S. (eds.) 1998. *Rethinking Geopolitics: Towards A Critical Geopolitics*. London: Routledge.

RABINOW, P. 1989. *French Modern*. Cambridge, Mass.: MIT Press.

RELPH, E. 1976. *Place and Placelessness*. London: Pion.

RICHIE, A. 1998. *Faust's Metropolis*. London: HarperCollins.

ROKKAN, S. 1970. *Citizens, Elections, Parties*. Oslo: Universitetsforlaget.

—— and URWIN, D. 1982. *The Politics of Territorial Identity*. London: Sage.

Rowe, P. G. 1997. *Civic Realism*. Cambridge, Mass.: MIT Press.

Rumley, D., Chiba, T., Takaghi, A., and Fukushima, Y. (eds.) 1998. *Global Geopolitics and the Asia-Pacific*. Aldershot: Ashgate.

Sassen, S. 1991. *The Global City*. Princeton, NJ: Princeton University Press.

Schulz, U. (ed.) 1993. *Die Hauptstädte der Deutschen*. Munich: C. H. Beck.

Seidensticker, E. 1985 *Low City, High City*. San Francisco: Donald S. Ellis

Sen, F. and Aydoin, H. 2000. Ankara: Vom Dorf zur Hauptstadt. Pp. 161–81 in A. Sohn and H. Weber (eds.), *Hauptstaädte und Global Cities an der Schwelle zum 21. Jahrhundert*. Bochum: Winkler.

Sit, V. F. S. 1995. *Beijing*. Chichester: Wiley.

Soja, E. W. 1996. *Thirdspace: Journeys to Los Angeles and Other Real-and-Imagined Places*. Oxford: Blackwell.

Sohn, A. and Weber, H. (eds.) 2000. *Hauptstädte und Global Cities an der Schwelle zum 21: Jahrhundert*. Bochum: Winkler.

Sonne, W. 2003. *Representing the State: Capital City Planning in the Early Twentieth Century*. Munich: Prestel

Taylor, J., Lengellé, J. G., and Andrew, C. (eds.) 1993. *Capital Cities: Les Capitales*. Ottawa: Carlton University Press.

Taylor, P. J. 2004. *World City Network*. London: Routledge.

Tezanos, J. F. 2004. El PSOE en la democracia. *Temas para el debate*, 117–18: 55–60.

Therborn, G. 2000. *Die Gesellschaften Europas 1945–2000*. Frankfurt: Campus.

—— 2002. Monumental Europe: the national years. *Housing, Theory and Society*, 19, 1: 26–47.

Tjahjono, G. 1998. Palace and city. Pp. 90–3 in *Indonesian Heritage: Architecture*, ed. G. Tjahjono. Singapore: Editions Didier Millet.

Tjekanova, O., Urusova, G., and Prijamurski, G. 2000. *Det kejserliga St: Petersburg*. Jyväskylä: Gummerus.

Wallerstein, I. 1974. *The Modern World Systems*. New York: Academic Press.

Watkins, S. 2004. Vichy on the Tigris. *New Left Review*, 28: 5–17.

Webb, M. 1990. *The City Square*. London: Thames and Hudson.

Whiteley, P. and Seyd, P. 2003. How to win a landslide election by really trying: the effects of local campaigning on voting in the 1997 British general election. *Electoral Studies*, 22: 301–24.

Yarborough, J. M. 1998. *American Virtues: Thomas Jefferson and the Character of a Free People*. Lawrence: University Press of Kansas.

Zeller, O. 2003. La Ville Moderne. Vol. 2: 595–860 in *Histoire de l'Europe urbaine*, ed. J.-L.Pinol. Paris: Seuil.

Zukin, S. 1991. *Landscapes of Power: From Detroit to Disneyworld*. Berkeley: University of California Press.

CHAPTER 26

WHY AND HOW HISTORY MATTERS

CHARLES TILLY

Do you suppose that historians labor dumbly in deep trenches, digging up facts so that political scientists can order and explain them? Do you imagine that political scientists, those skilled intellectual surgeons, slice through the fat of history to get at the sinews of rational choice or political economy? Do you claim that political scientists can avoid peering into the mists of history by clear-eyed examination of the contemporary world that lies within their view? On the contrary: this chapter gives reasons for thinking that explanatory political science can hardly get anywhere without relying on careful historical analysis.

Let us begin, appropriately, with a historical experience. Early in 1969, Stanford political scientist Gabriel Almond proposed that the (US) Social Science Research Council use Ford Foundation funds to support a study of state formation in Western Europe. Thus began an adventure. For fifteen years before then, the SSRC's Committee on Comparative Politics had been looking at what it called "political development in the new states." By then, committee members Almond, Leonard Binder, Philip Converse, Samuel Huntington, Joseph LaPalombara, Lucian Pye, Sidney Verba, Robert Ward, Myron Weiner, and Aristide Zolberg had converged on the idea that new states faced a standard and roughly sequential series of crises, challenges, and problems. Resolution of those problems, they argued, permitted states to move on to the next stage en route to a fully effective political regime. In a phrase that reflected their project's normative and policy aspirations, they often called the whole process state- and nation-building. The SSRC committee labeled its crises PIPILD: Penetration, Integration, Participation, Identity, Legitimacy, and Distribution.

Committee members theorized that (*a*) all new states confronted the six crises in approximately this order, (*b*) the more these crises concentrated in time, the greater the social stress and therefore the higher the likelihood of conflict, breakdown, and disintegration, (*c*) in general, new states faced far greater bunching of the crises than had their Western counterparts, hence became more prone to breakdown than Western states had been. The violence, victimization, and venality of new states' public politics stemmed from cumulation of crises. Presumably superior political science knowledge would not only explain those ill effects but also help national or international authorities steer fragile new states through unavoidable crises.

The SSRC scheme rested on one strong historical premise and two weak ones. On the strong side, the theorists assumed that Western states had, on the whole, created effective national institutions gradually, in a slow process of trial, error, compromise, and consolidation. More hesitantly, these analysts assumed both that political development everywhere followed roughly the same course and that the course's end point would yield states resembling those currently prevailing in the Western world.

Since theorists of political development actually drew regularly on Western historical analogies (see, e.g., Almond and Powell 1966), SSRC committee members naturally wondered whether a closer look at Western history would confirm their scheme. It could do so by showing that the same crises appeared recognizably in the historical record, that they occurred more discretely and over longer periods in older states, that later-developing states experienced greater accumulations of crises, and that bunched crises did, indeed, generate stress, conflict, breakdown, and disintegration. In my guise as a European historian, they therefore asked me to recruit a group of fellow European historians who had the necessary knowledge, imagination, and synthetic verve to do the job. (As we will see later, they were also sponsoring a rival team of European historians, no doubt to check the reliability of my team's conclusions.)

Our assignment: to meet, deliberate, do the necessary research, report our results, criticize each other's accounts, and write a collective book. A remarkable set of talented scholars accepted the challenge: Gabriel Ardant, David Bayley, Rudolf Braun, Samuel Finer, Wolfram Fischer, Peter Lundgreen, and Stein Rokkan. We spent the summer of 1970 together at the Center for Advanced Study in the Behavioral Sciences (Stanford, California), frequently calling in critics such as Gabriel Almond, Val Lorwin, and G. William Skinner. We presented draft chapters to each other and a few sympathetic critics in Bellagio, Italy, during a strenuous week the following year. After multiple exchanges and painstaking editing, we finally published our book in 1975.

Before we began the enterprise, I had produced several essays dissenting from the sorts of breakdown theories that formed the midsection of the committee's scheme (e.g. Tilly 1969). Some committee members may therefore have hoped to convert me to the committee's views. Or perhaps secret skeptics within the committee wanted to raise their colleagues' doubts about the committee's political development scheme.[1] In either case, they got more than they bargained for. Looked at closely,

---

[1] For hints in that direction, see Verba 1971.

the relevant Western European history revealed repeated crises, constant struggle, numerous collapses, far more states that disappeared than survived, and a process of state transformation driven largely by extraction, control, and coalition formation as parts or byproducts of rulers' efforts not to build states but to make war and survive.

In an abortive effort to counter the intentionality and teleology of such terms as "state-building" and "political development," my co-authors and I self-consciously substituted what we thought to be the more neutral term "state formation." The term itself caught on surprisingly fast. Unfortunately, it also soon took on teleological tones in the literature on political change.[2] Contrary to our intentions, students of state formation in Latin America, Africa, the Middle East, or Asia began taking the European experience as a model, and asking why their regions had failed to form proper states.[3] Nevertheless, many readers saw the book as a serious challenge to existing ideas about political development (Skocpol 1985).

What is more, our historical reflections raised the distinct possibility that the processes of state formation were far more contingent, transitory, and reversible than analysts of political development then supposed. Hoping to write the final sentence of the final volume in the SSRC's series of books on political development, I therefore ended my concluding essay with these words:

> But remember the definition of a state as an organization, controlling the principal means of coercion within a given territory, which is differentiated from other organizations operating in the same territory, autonomous, centralized, and formally coordinated. If there is something to the trends we have described, they threaten almost every single one of these defining features of the state: the monopoly of coercion, the exclusiveness of control within the territory, the autonomy, the centralization, the formal coordination; even the differentiation from other organizations begins to fall away in such compacts as the European Common Market. One last perhaps, then: perhaps, as is so often the case, we only begin to understand this momentous historical process—the formation of national states—when it begins to lose its universal significance. Perhaps, unknowing, we are writing obituaries for the state.   (Tilly 1975, 638)

I lost, alas, my rhetorical bet: a parallel SSRC group of historians working on direct applications of the crisis scheme to the United Kingdom, Belgium, Scandinavia, the United States, Spain, Portugal, France, Italy, Germany, Russia, and Poland under Raymond Grew's leadership took even longer to publish their volume than we did. Editor Grew closed his presentation of the book's findings with words more cautious than my own:

> Models of political development should not tempt us to explain too much, nor be allowed to stimulate too many ingenious answers before the questions are clear. Today's heuristic device must not become tomorrow's assumption. One of the strengths of these essays is that they do not attempt to create a closed system; another is their recognition of many paths to political survival—and of many higher goals. A next step should be the careful formulation of historical (and therefore not just developmental) problems, followed by the comparison of realities rather than abstractions. The Committee's broad categories of political development,

---

[2] See, e.g., Biggs 1999; Braddick 2000; Corrigan and Sayer 1985.
[3] For critiques, see Barkey and Parikh 1991; Centeno 2002.

like photographs of the earth taken from space, remind us that familiar terrain is part of a larger system, and urge us to compare diverse features that from a distance appear similar. They do not obviate the need for a closer look.   (Grew 1978, 37)

In short, according to Grew, the crisis-and-sequence scheme may raise some interesting historical questions, but it certainly does not answer them.

Differences between the Tilly and Grew conclusions mark an important choice for historical analysts of political processes.[4] On one side (Grew), we can stress the obdurate particularity of historical experiences, hoping at most to arrive at rough, useful empirical generalizations through close analysis of specific cases. On the other (Tilly), we can use history to build more adequate explanations of politics past and present. Unsurprisingly, this chapter recommends the theoretically more ambitious second course, while heartily agreeing with Grew that it requires expert historical knowledge. Not only do all political processes occur in history and therefore call for knowledge of their historical contexts, but also where and when political processes occur influence *how* they occur. History thus becomes an essential element of sound explanations for political processes.

1 WHY HISTORY MATTERS

Several different paths lead to that conclusion. Here are the main ones:

- At least for large-scale political processes, explanations always make implicit or explicit assumptions concerning historical origins of the phenomenon and time–place scope conditions for the claimed explanation. Those assumptions remain open to historical verification and falsification. Example: students of international relations commonly assume that some time between the treaty of Augsburg (1555) and the treaties of Westphalia (1648), Europeans supplanted a web of overlapping jurisdictions with a system of clearly bounded sovereign states that then provided the context for war and diplomacy up to the present.
- In the case of long-term processes, some or all features of the process occur outside the observations of any connected cohort of human analysts, and therefore require historical reconstruction. Example: displacement of personal armies, feudal levies, militias, and mercenary bands by centrally controlled national standing armies took several centuries to occur.
- Most or all political processes incorporate locally available cultural materials such as language, social categories, and widely shared beliefs; they therefore vary

[4] Here and hereafter, "historical" means locating the phenomenon meaningfully in time and place relative to other times and places, "political" means involving at least one coercion-wielding organization as participant or influential third party, and "process" means a connected stream of causes and effects; see Pierson 2004, Tilly 2001a.

as a function of historically determined local cultural accumulations. Example: economically, linguistically, ethnically, racially, and religiously segmented regions create significantly different configurations of state–citizen relations.

- Processes occurring in adjacent places such as neighboring countries influence local political processes, hence historically variable adjacencies alter the operation of those processes. Example: the Swiss Confederation survived as a loosely connected but distinct political entity after 1500 in part precisely because much larger but competing Austrian, Savoyard, French, and German states formed around its perimeter.

- Path dependency prevails in political processes, such that events occurring at one stage in a sequence constrain the range of events that is possible at later stages. Example: for all its service of privilege, the entrenchment of the assembly that became England's Parliament by the barons' rebellion of 1215 set limits on arbitrary royal power in England from that point forward.

- Once a process (e.g. a revolution) has occurred and acquired a name, both the name and one or more representations of the process become available as signals, models, threats, and/or aspirations for later actors. Example: the creation of an elected national assembly in the France of 1789 to 1792 provided a model for subsequent political programs in France and elsewhere.

In all these ways, history matters. In the case of state transformation, there is no way to create comprehensive, plausible, and verifiable explanations without taking history seriously into account.

Apparently political scientists have learned that lesson since the 1960s. Now and then an economist, sociologist, geographer, or anthropologist does come up with a transhistorical model of state transformation.[5] Rare, however, is the political scientist that follows their lead (exceptions include Midlarsky 1999, Taagepera 1997). To be sure, the historicists could be wrong and the unhistorical modelers right. I hope, however, to persuade you that historical context matters inescapably, at least for all but the most fleeting and localized political processes.

Whether the importance of history seems obvious or implausible, however, depends subtly on competing conceptions of explanation. As a first cut, let us distinguish:

1. Proposal of covering laws for complex structures and processes.
2. The special case of covering law accounts featuring the capacity of predictors within mathematical models to exhaust the variance in a "dependent variable" across some set of differing but comparable cases.
3. Specification of necessary and sufficient conditions for concrete instances of the same complex structures and processes.
4. Location of structures and processes within larger systems they supposedly serve or express.

---

[5] E.g. Batchelder and Freudenberger 1983; Bourdieu 1994; Clark and Dear 1984; Earle 1997; Friedmann 1977; Gledhill, Bender, and Larson 1988; Li 2002.

5. Identification of individual or group dispositions just before the point of action as causes of that action.

6. Reduction of complex episodes, or certain features of those episodes, to their component mechanisms and processes.

In an earlier day, political scientists also explained political processes by means of "7. Stage models in which placement within an invariant sequence accounted for the episode at hand." That understanding of explanation vanished with the passing of political development.

History *can*, of course, figure in any of these explanatory conceptions. In a covering law account, for example, one can incorporate history as a scope condition (e.g. prior to the Chinese invention of gunpowder, war conformed to generalization X) or as an abstract variable (e.g. time elapsed or distance covered since the beginning of an episode[6]). Nevertheless, covering-law, necessary-sufficient condition, and system accounts generally resist history as they deny the influence of particular times and places. Propensity accounts respond to history ambivalently, since in the version represented by rational choice they depend on transhistorical rules of decision-making, while in the versions represented by cultural and phenomenological reductionism they treat history as infinitely particular.

Mechanism-process accounts, in contrast, positively welcome history, because their explanatory program couples a search for mechanisms of very general scope with arguments that initial conditions, sequences, and combinations of mechanisms concatenate into processes having explicable but variable overall outcomes. Mechanism-process accounts reject covering-law regularities for large structures such as international systems and for vast sequences such as democratization. Instead, they lend themselves to "local theory" in which the explanatory mechanisms and processes operate quite broadly, but combine locally as a function of initial conditions and adjacent processes to produce distinctive trajectories and outcomes.[7]

2 HISTORY AND PROCESSES OF STATE TRANSFORMATION

Across a wide range of state transformation, for example, a robust process recurrently shapes state–citizen relations: the extraction–resistance–settlement cycle. In that process:

- Some authority tries to extract resources (e.g. military manpower) to support its own activities from populations living under its jurisdiction.
- Those resources (e.g. young men's labor) are already committed to competing activities that matter to the subordinate population's survival.

[6] See Roehner and Syme 2002.   [7] McAdam, Tarrow, and Tilly 2001; Tilly 2001b.

- Local people resist agents of the authority (e.g. press gangs) who arrive to seize the demanded resources.
- Struggle ensues.
- A settlement ends the struggle.

Clearly the overall outcome of the process varies from citizens' full compliance to fierce rejection of the authorities' demands (Levi 1988; 1997). Clearly that outcome depends not only on the process's internal dynamic but also on historically determined initial conditions (e.g. previous relations between local and national authorities) and on adjacent processes (e.g. intervention of competing authorities or threatened neighboring populations). But in all cases the settlement casts a significant shadow toward the next encounter between citizens and authorities. The settlement mechanism alters relations between citizens and authorities, locking those relations into place for a time.

Over several centuries of European state transformation, authorities commonly won the battle for conscripts, taxes, food, and means of transportation. Yet the settlement of the local struggle implicitly or explicitly sealed a bargain concerning the terms under which the next round of extraction could begin (Tilly 1992, chs. 3–4). Individual mechanisms of extraction, resistance, struggle, and settlement compound into a process that occurs widely, with variable but historically significant outcomes. From beginning to end, the process belongs to history.

Consider a second robust process of state transformation: subordination of armed forces to civilian control. Over most of human history, substantial groups of armed men—almost exclusively men!—have bent to no authority outside of their own number. Wielders of coercion have run governments across the world. Yet recurrently, from Mesopotamian city-states to contemporary Africa, priests, merchants, aristocrats, bureaucrats, and even elected officials who did not themselves specialize in deployment of armed force have somehow managed to exert effective control over military specialists.[8]

That process has taken two closely related forms. In the first, the course of military conquest itself brought conquerors to state power. Then administration of conquered territories involved rulers so heavily in extraction, control, and mediation within those territories that they began simultaneously to create civilian staffs, to gather resources for military activity by means of those staffs, and thus to make the military dependent for their own livelihoods on the effectiveness of those staffs. In the process, tax-granting legislatures and budget-making bureaucrats gained the upper hand.

In the second variant, a group of priests or merchants drew riches from their priestly or mercantile activity, staffed the higher levels of their governments with priests, merchants, or other civilians, and hired military specialists to carry out war and policing. In both versions of the subordination process, the crucial mechanisms inhibited direct military control over the supply of resources required for the reproduction of military organization.

---

[8] Bratton and van de Walle 1997; Briant et al. 2002; Creveld 1999; Huters, Wong, and Yu 1997; Khazanov 1993; López-Alves 2000; Wong 1997.

As in the case of extraction–resistance–settlement processes, the actual outcomes depended not only on internal dynamics but also on initial conditions and adjacent processes. In Latin America, for example, military specialists who had participated extensively in domestic political control recurrently overthrew civilian rule (Centeno 2002). Military men retained more leverage where they had direct access to sustaining resources, notably when they actually served as hired guns for landed elites and when they could sell or tax lootable resources such as diamonds and drugs. Again, a similar process occurs across a wide range of historical experience, but its exact consequences depend intimately on historical context.

3 SOCIAL MOVEMENTS AS POLITICAL INNOVATIONS

State transformation may seem too easy a case for my argument. After all, since the fading of political development models most political scientists have conducted contemporary studies of state changes against the backdrop of explicit references to historical experience. The same does not hold for the study of social movements. By and large, students of contemporary social movements fail to recognize that they are analyzing an evolving set of historically derived political practices. Either they assume that social movements have always existed in some form or they treat social movements as contemporary political forms without inquiring into their historical transformations.

Nevertheless, sophisticated treatments of social movements generally assume a broad historical connection between democratization and social movement expansion.[9] One of the more important open questions in social movement studies, indeed, concerns the causal connections between social movement activity and democratization—surely two-way, but what and how (Ibarra 2003; Tilly 2004, ch. 6)?

Social movements illustrate all the major arguments for taking the history of political processes seriously:

- Existing explanations of social movements always make implicit or explicit assumptions concerning historical origins of the phenomenon and time–place scope conditions for the claimed explanation.
- Some features of social movements occurred outside the direct observations of any connected cohort of human analysts, and therefore require historical reconstruction.

---

[9] Costain and McFarland 1998; Edelman 2001; Foweraker and Landman 1997; Hoffmann 2003; Meyer and Tarrow 1998; Walker 1991.

- Social movements incorporate locally available cultural materials such as language, social categories, and widely shared beliefs; they therefore vary as a function of historically determined local cultural accumulations.
- Social movements occurring in adjacent places such as neighboring countries influence local social movements, hence historically variable adjacencies alter the kinds of social movements that appear in any particular place.
- Path dependency prevails in social movements as in other political processes, such that events occurring at one stage in a sequence constrain the range of events that is possible at later stages.
- Once social movements had occurred and acquired names, both the name and competing representations of social movements became available as signals, models, threats, and/or aspirations for later actors.

None of these observations condemns students of social movements to historical particularism. Regularities in social movement activity depend on and incorporate historical context, which means that effective explanations of social movement activity must systematically take historical context into account. Like anti-tax rebellions, religious risings, elections, publicity campaigns, special interest lobbying, and political propaganda, social movements consist of standard means by which interested or aggrieved citizens make collective claims on other people, including political authorities. Like all these other forms of politics, the social movement emerges only in some kinds of political settings, waxes and wanes in response to its political surroundings, undergoes significant change over the course of its history, and yet where it prevails offers a clear set of opportunities for interested or aggrieved citizens.

Consider just two historically conditioned aspects of social movements: their repertoires of claim-making performances and their signaling systems. History shapes the availability of means for making collective claims, from the humble petition received by a Chinese emperor to the *pronunciamiento* of a nineteenth-century Spanish military faction. Those means always involve interactive performances of some sort, preferably following established scripts sufficiently to be recognizable but not so slavishly as to become pure ritual. They therefore draw heavily on historically accumulated and shared understandings with regard to meanings, claims, legitimate claimants, and proper objects of claims.

In any given historical period, available claim-making performances group linking various pairs of claimants, and objects of claims clump into restricted *repertoires*: arrays of known alternative performances. In Great Britain of the 1750s, for example, the contentious repertoire widely available to ordinary people included:

- *attacks on coercive authorities*: liberation of prisoners; resistance to police intervention in gatherings and entertainments; resistance to press gangs; fights between hunters and gamekeepers; battles between smugglers and royal officers; forcible opposition to evictions; military mutinies
- *attacks on popularly-designated offenses and offenders*: Rough Music; ridicule and/or destruction of symbols, effigies, and/or property of public figures and moral offenders; verbal and physical attacks on malefactors seen in public places;

pulling down and/or sacking of dangerous or offensive houses, including work-houses and brothels; smashing of shops and bars whose proprietors are accused of unfair dealing or of violating public morality; collective seizures of food, often coupled with sacking the merchant's premises and/or public sale of the food below current market price; blockage or diversion of food shipments; destruction of tollgates; collective invasions of enclosed land, often including destruction of fences or hedges

- *celebrations and other popularly-initiated gatherings*: collective cheering, jeering, or stoning of public figures or their conveyances; popularly-initiated public celebrations of major events (e.g. John Wilkes' elections of the 1760s), with cheering, drinking, display of partisan symbols, fireworks, etc., sometimes with forced participation of reluctant persons; forced illuminations, including attacks on windows of householders who fail to illuminate; faction fights (e.g. Irish vs. English, rival groups of military)
- *workers' sanctions over members of their trades*: turnouts by workers in multiple shops of a local trade; workers' marches to public authorities in trade disputes; donkeying, or otherwise humiliating, workers who violated collective agreements; destroying goods (e.g. silk in looms and/or the looms themselves) of workers or masters who violate collective agreements
- *claim-making within authorized public assemblies* (e.g. Lord Mayor's Day): taking of positions by means of cheers, jeers, attacks, and displays of symbols; attacks on supporters of electoral candidates; parading and chairing of candidates; taking sides at public executions; attacks or professions of support for pilloried prisoners; salutation or deprecation of public figures (e.g. royalty) at theater; collective response to lines and characters in plays or other entertainments; breaking up of theaters at unsatisfactory performances.

Not all British claim-makers, to be sure, had access to all these performances; some of the performances linked workers to masters, others market regulars to local merchants, and so on. In any case, the repertoire available to ordinary Britons during the 1750s did not include electoral campaigns, formal public meetings, street marches, demonstrations, petition drives, or the formation of special-interest associations, all of which became quite common ways of pressing claims during the nineteenth century. As these newer performances became common, the older ones disappeared.

That is where the social movement repertoire comes in. Originating in Great Britain and North America during the later eighteenth century, a distinctive array of claim-making performances formed that marked off social movements from other varieties of politics, underwent a series of mutations from the eighteenth century to the present, and spread widely through the world during the nineteenth and (especially) twentieth centuries. Social movements constituted sustained claims on well-identified objects by self-declared interested or aggrieved parties through performances dramatizing not only their support for or opposition to a program, person, or group, but also their worthiness, unity, numbers, and commitment. (Social movement participants always claim to represent some wider public, and sometimes claim to speak for non-participants such as fetuses, slaves, or trees.) The array of performances constituting social movement repertoires has shifted historically, but from the earliest days it included formation of named special-interest associations and coalitions, holding of public meetings, statements in and to the press, pamphleteering, and petitioning.

Social movement repertoires amply illustrate the importance of history. Although the British–American eighteenth century repertoire brought new elements together, each element had some sort of available precedent. British governments repressed popular, private, non-religious associations that took public stands as threats to the rights of Parliament. Yet they had accepted or even promoted religious congregations, authorized parish assemblies, grudgingly allowed workers' mutual-aid societies that refrained from striking and other public claim-making. Authorities had also long tolerated clubs of aristocrats and wealthy city-dwellers. (The term "club" itself derives from the practice of clubbing together for shared expenses, and thus taking on a resemblance to a knotted stick.) More rarely and indirectly, social movement repertoires also drew on authorized parades of artisans' corporations, militias, and fraternal orders. Adaptations of such parades figured extensively in Irish conflicts from the eighteenth century to the present.[10]

Eighteenth-century innovations broadened those practices in two different directions, converting authorized religious and local assemblies into bases for campaigns and creating popular special-purpose associations devoted to public claim-making rather than (or in addition to) private enjoyment, improvement, and mutual aid. The broadening occurred through struggle, but also through patronage by sympathetic or dissident members of the elite. More generally, the internal histories of particular forms of claim-making, changing relations between potential claimants and objects of claims, innovations by political entrepreneurs, and overall transformations of the political context combined to produce cumulative alterations of social movement repertoires (Tilly 1993).

The formation of the social movement repertoire included substantial losses as well as considerable gains. Many of the avenging, redressing, and humiliating actions that had worked intermittently to impose popular justice before 1800—seizures of high-priced food, attacks on press gangs, donkey-riding of workers who violated local customs, and others—became illegal. Authorities whose predecessors had mostly looked the other way so long as participants localized their actions and refrained from attacking elite persons or property, began to treat all such actions as "riots," and to prosecute their perpetrators. Establishment of crowd-control police as substitutes for constables, militias, and regular troops in containment of demonstrations and marches temporarily increased the frequency of violent confrontations between police and demonstrators. Over the long run, however, it narrowed the range of actions open to street protestors, promoted prior negotiation between social movement activists and police, encouraged organizers themselves to exclude unruly

[10] Bryan 2000; Farrell 2000; Jarman 1997; Kinealy 2003; Mac Suibhne 2000.

elements from their supporters, and channeled claim-making toward non-violent interaction. Path dependence prevailed, as early innovations in the social movement repertoire greatly constrained later possibilities.

Social movement *signaling systems* similarly illustrate the importance of history. From the start, social movements centered on campaigns in support of or in opposition to publicly articulated programs by means of associations, meetings, demonstrations, petitions, electoral participation, strikes, and related means of coordinated action. Unlike many of its predecessors, the social movement form provided opportunities to offer sustained challenges directed at powerful figures and institutions without necessarily attacking them physically. It said, in effect, "We are here, we support this cause, there are lots of us, we know how to act together, and we could cause trouble if we wanted to."

As compared with the many forms of direct action that ordinary people had employed earlier, social movement performances almost never achieved in a single iteration what they asked for: passage of legislation, removal of an official, punishment of a villain, distribution of benefits, and so on. Only cumulatively, and usually only in part, did some movements realize their claims. But individual performances such as meetings and marches did not simply signal that a certain number of people had certain complaints or demands. They signaled that those people had created internal connections, that they had backing, that they commanded pooled resources, and that they therefore had the capacity to act collectively, even disruptively, elsewhere and in the future.

More exactly, from early on social movement performances broadcast WUNC: worthiness, unity, numbers, and commitment. How they broadcast those attributes varied historically, but in early stages the signaling had something like this character:

- *Worthiness:* sober demeanor, neat clothing, presence of dignitaries
- *Unity:* matching badges, armbands, or costumes, marching in ranks, singing and chanting
- *Numbers:* headcounts, signatures on petitions, messages from constituents
- *Commitment:* mutual defense, resistance to repression, ostentatious sacrifice, subscription and benefaction

If any of these elements—worthiness, unity, numbers, or commitment—visibly fell to a low level, the social movement lost impact. This signaling system helps explain two centuries of dispute between authorities and participants over whether pleasure-seekers or vandals had joined a performance, how many of the people present happened to be on the premises for other purposes or out of idle curiosity, how many people actually took part in the performance, and whether the police used undue brutality. Social movement performances challenge authorities and other political actors to accept or reject both a set of claims and the existence of a distinctive collective political actor. But the relevant signaling systems change and vary historically.

4 SOCIAL MOVEMENTS IN HISTORY

With these lessons in mind, let us look more closely at the early development of social movement claim-making. We can usefully begin a history of social movements as distinctive forms of political action in the 1760s, when after the Seven Years War (1756–1763) critics of royal policy in England and its North American colonies began assembling, marching, and associating to protest heightened taxation and arbitrary rule (Tilly 1977). Braving or evading repression, they reshaped existing practices such as middle-class clubs, petition marches, parish assemblies, and celebratory banquets into new instruments of political criticism. Although social movement activity waxed and waned with state toleration and repression, from the later eighteenth century the social movement model spread through Western Europe and North America, becoming a major vehicle of popular claim-making.

In the British Isles, for example, by the 1820s popular leaders were organizing effective social movements against the slave trade, for the political rights of Catholics, and for freedom of association among workers. In the United States, anti-slavery was becoming a major social movement not much later. American workers' movements proliferated during the first half of the nineteenth century. By the 1850s social movements were starting to displace older forms of popular politics through much of Western Europe and North America.

Throughout the world since 1850, social movements have generally flourished where and when contested elections became central to politics. Contested elections promote social movements in several different ways:

- First, they provide a model of public support for rival programs, as embodied in competing candidates; once governments have authorized public discussion of major issues during electoral campaigns, it becomes harder to silence that discussion outside of electoral campaigns.
- Second, they legalize and protect assemblies of citizens for campaigning and voting. Citizens allowed to gather in support of candidates and parties easily take up other issues that concern them.
- Third, elections magnify the importance of numbers; with contested elections, any group receiving disciplined support from large numbers of followers becomes a possible ally or enemy at the polls.
- Finally, some expansion of rights to speak, communicate, and assemble publicly almost inevitably accompanies the establishment of contested elections. Even people who lack the vote can disrupt elections, march in support of popular candidates, and use rights of assembly, communication, and speech.

Once social movements existed, nevertheless, they became available for politics well outside the electoral arena. Take temperance: opposition to the sale and public consumption of alcohol. In Britain and America, organized temperance enthusiasts sometimes swayed elections. American anti-alcohol activists formed a Prohibition Party in 1869. But temperance advocates also engaged in direct moral intervention by organizing religious campaigns, holding public meetings, circulating pledges of abstinence, and getting educators to teach the evils of alcohol. In both Great Britain and the United States, the Salvation Army (founded in London, 1865) carried on street crusades against alcohol and for the rescue of alcoholics without engaging directly in electoral politics. American agitator Carrie Nation got herself arrested thirty times during the 1890s and 1900s as she physically attacked bars in states that had passed, but not enforced, bans on the sale of alcohol. Social movements expanded with electoral politics, but soon operated quite outside the realm of parties and elections.

Anti-slavery action in the United States and Britain (that is, England, Wales, Scotland) illustrates the social movement's rise.[11] Mobilization against slavery and increasing salience of national elections—with slavery itself an electoral issue—reinforced each other in the two countries. The timing of anti-slavery mobilization is surprising. Both the abolition of the slave trade and the later emancipation of slaves occurred when slave-based production was still expanding across much of North and South America. The Atlantic slave trade fed captive labor mainly into production of sugar, coffee, and cotton for European consumption. North and South American slave labor provided 70 percent of the cotton processed by British mills in 1787 and 90 percent in 1838. Although slave production of sugar, coffee, and cotton continued to expand past the mid-nineteenth century, transatlantic traffic in slaves reached its peak between 1781 and 1790, held steady for a few decades, then declined rapidly after 1840.

Outlawing of slavery itself proceeded fitfully for a century, from Haiti's spectacular slave rebellion (1790 onward) to Brazil's reluctant emancipation (1888). Argentina, for example, outlawed both slavery and the slave trade in its constitution of 1853. Between the 1840s and 1888, then, the Atlantic slave trade was disappearing and slavery itself was ending country by country. Yet slave-based production of cotton and other commodities continued to increase until the 1860s. How was that possible? Increases in slave-based commodity production depended partly on rising labor productivity and partly on population growth within the remaining slave population. Slavery did not disappear because it had lost its profitability. Movements against the slave trade, then against slavery itself, overturned economically viable systems.

How did that happen? Although heroic activists sometimes campaigned publicly against slavery in major regions of slave-based production, crucial campaigns first took place mostly where slaves were rare but beneficiaries of their production were prominent. For the most part, anti-slavery support arose in populations that benefited no more than indirectly from slave production. The English version of the story begins in 1787. English Quakers, Methodists, and other anti-establishment Protestants joined with more secular advocates of working-class freedoms to oppose all forms of coerced labor. A Society for the Abolition of the Slave Trade, organized in 1787, coordinated a vast national campaign, an early social movement.

During the next two decades, British activists rounded out the social movement repertoire with two crucial additions: the lobby and the demonstration. Lobbying began literally as talking to Members of Parliament in the lobby of the Parliament

---

[11] d'Anjou 1996; Drescher 1986; 1994; Eltis 1993; Grimsted 1998; Klein 1999, ch. 8.

building on their way to or from sessions. Later the word generalized to mean any direct intervention with legislators to influence their votes. British activists also created the two forms of the demonstration we still know today: the disciplined march through streets and the organized assembly in a symbolically significant public space, both accompanied by coordinated displays of support for a shared program. Of course all the forms of social movement activism had precedents, including public meetings, formal presentations of petitions, and the committees of correspondence that played so important a part in American resistance to royal demands during the 1760s and 1770s. But between the 1780s and the 1820s British activists created a new synthesis. From then to the present, social movements regularly combined associations, meetings, demonstrations, petitions, electoral participation, lobbying, strikes, and related means of coordinated action.

Within Great Britain, Parliament began responding to popular pressure almost immediately, with partial regulation of the slave trade in 1788. By 1806, abolition of the slave trade had become a major issue in parliamentary elections. In 1807, Parliament declared illegal the shipping of slaves to Britain's colonies, effective at the start of the following year. From that point on, British activists demanded that their government act against other slave-trading countries. Great Britain then pressed for withdrawal of other European powers from the slave trade. At the end of the Napoleonic Wars in 1815, the major European powers except for Spain and Portugal agreed to abolition of the trade. Under economic and diplomatic pressure from Britain, Spain and Portugal reluctantly withdrew from officially sanctioned slave trading step by step between 1815 and 1867. From 1867 onward, only outlaws shipped slaves across the Atlantic.

Soon after 1815, British activists were moving successfully to restrict the powers of slave owners in British colonies, and finally—in 1834—to end slavery itself. Although French revolutionaries outlawed both the slave trade and slavery throughout France and its colonies in 1794, Napoleon's regime restored them ten years later. France did not again abolish slavery and the slave trade until the Revolution of 1848. With Brazil's abolition of slavery in 1888, legal slavery finally disappeared from Europe and the Americas. Backed aggressively by state power, British social movement pressure had brought about a momentous change.

As of the later nineteenth century, social movements had become widely available in Western countries as bases of popular claim-making. They served repeatedly in drives for suffrage, workers' rights, restrictions on discrimination, temperance, and political reform.[12] During the twentieth century, they proliferated, attached themselves more firmly to the mass media, and gained followings in a wider variety of class, ethnic, religious, and political categories. More frequently than before, social movements also supported conservative or reactionary programs—either on their own or (more often) in reaction to left movements. Italian and German fascists, after all, employed anti-leftist social movement strategies on their ways to power (Anheier, Neidhardt, and Vortkamp 1998). As a result of incessant negotiation and

---

[12] Buechler 1990; Calhoun 1995; Gamson 1990; McCammon and Campbell 2002; McCammon et al. 2001; Tarrow 1998.

confrontation, relations between social movement activists and authorities, especially police, changed significantly.[13]

Regularities in social movements, then, depended heavily on their historical contexts. Eighteenth-century social movement pioneers adapted and combined forms of political interaction that were already available in their contexts: the special-purpose association, the petition drive, the parish meeting, and so on. They thereby created new varieties of politics. Forms of social movement activity mutated in part as a consequence of changes in their political environments and in part as a result of innovations within the form itself on the part of activists, authorities, and objects of claims (Tilly and Wood 2003). Early innovations stuck and constrained later innovations not only because widespread familiarity with such routines as demonstrating facilitated organizing the next round of claim-making, but also because each innovation altered relations among authorities, police, troops, activists, their targets, their rivals, their opponents, and the public at large. When movement repertoires diffused, they always changed as a function of differences and connections between the old setting and the new (Chabot and Duyvendak 2002). Social movement politics has a history.

5 CONCLUDING REFLECTIONS

So does the rest of politics. We could pursue the same sort of argument across a great many other historically grounded political phenomena: democratization and de-democratization, revolution, electoral systems, clientelism, terror, ethnic mobilization, interstate war, civic participation, and more. The conclusion would come out the same: every significant political phenomenon lives in history, and requires historically grounded analysis for its explanation. Political scientists ignore historical context at their peril.

So should political science quietly dissolve into history? Must professional political scientists turn in their badges for those of professional historians? No, at least not entirely. I would, it is true, welcome company in the thinly populated no man's land at the frontiers of history and political science. But history as a discipline has its own peculiarities. Historians do not merely take serious account of time and place. They revel in time and place, defining problems in terms of specific times and places, even when doing world history. One ordinarily becomes a professional historian by mastering the sources, languages, institutions, culture, and historiography of some particular time and place, then using that knowledge to solve some problem posed by the time and place. The problems may in some sense be universal: how people coped with disaster, what caused brutal wars, under what conditions diverse populations managed to live together. The proposed solutions may also partake of universality:

---

[13] Fillieule 1997; della Porta 1995; della Porta and Reiter 1998.

one step in the evolution of humanity, persistent traits of human nature, the tragedy of vain belief. But the questions pursued belong to the time and place, and adhere to the conversation among students of the time and place.

Although we might make exceptions for area specialists and students of domestic politics, on the whole political scientists' analytic conversations do not concern times and places so much as certain processes, institutions, and kinds of events. Let me therefore rephrase my sermon. As the analysis of state transformations and social movements illustrates, political scientists should continue to work at explaining processes, institutions, and kinds of events. To do so more effectively, however, they should take history seriously, but in their own distinctive way.

References

ALMOND, G. and POWELL, G. B., JR. 1966. *Comparative Politics: A Developmental Approach.* Boston: Little, Brown.

ANHEIER, H. K., NEIDHARDT, F., and VORTKAMP, W. 1998. Movement cycles and the Nazi Party: activities of the Munich NSDAP, 1925–1930. *American Behavioral Scientist*, 41: 1262–81.

D'ANJOU, L. 1996. *Social Movements and Cultural Change: The First Abolition Campaign Revisited.* New York: Aldine de Gruyter.

BARKEY, K. and PARIKH, S. 1991. Comparative perspectives on the state. *Annual Review of Sociology*, 17: 523–49.

BATCHELDER, R. W. and FREUDENBERGER, H. 1983. On the rational origins of the modern centralized state. *Explorations in Economic History*, 20: 1–13.

BIGGS, M. 1999. Putting the state on the map: cartography, territory and European state formation. *Comparative Studies in Society and History*, 41: 374–405.

BOURDIEU, P. 1994. Rethinking the state: genesis and structure of the bureaucratic field. *Sociological Theory*, 12: 1–18.

BRADDICK, M. 2000. *State Formation in Early Modern England c. 1550–1700.* Cambridge: Cambridge University Press.

BRATTON, M. and VAN DE WALLE, N. 1997. *Democratic Experiments in Africa: Regime Transitions in Comparative Perspective.* Cambridge: Cambridge University Press.

BRIANT, P., GASCHE, H., TANRET, M., COLE, S. W., VERHOEVEN, K., CHARPIN, D., DURAND, J.-M., JOANNÈS, F., MANNING, J. G., FRANCFORT, H.-P., and LECOMTE, O. 2002. Politique et contrôle de l'eau dans le Moyen-Orient ancien. *Annales. Histoire, Sciences Sociales*, 57: 517–664.

BRYAN, D. 2000. *Orange Parades: The Politics of Ritual, Tradition and Control.* London: Pluto Press.

BUECHLER, S. M. 1990. *Women's Movements in the United States: Woman Suffrage, Equal Rights and Beyond.* New Brunswick, NJ: Rutgers University Press.

CALHOUN, C. 1995. New social movements of the early nineteenth century. Pp. 173–216 in *Repertoires and Cycles of Collective Action*, ed. M. Traugott. Durham, NC: Duke University Press.

CENTENO, M. 2002. *Blood and Debt: War and the Nation-State in Latin America.* University Park: Pennsylvania State University Press.

CHABOT, S. and DUYVENDAK, J. W. 2002. Globalization and transnational diffusion between social movements: reconceptualizing the dissemination of the Gandhian repertoire and the "coming out" routine. *Theory and Society*, 31: 697–740.

CLARK, G. L. and DEAR, M. 1984. *State Apparatus: Structures and Language of Legitimacy.* Boston: Allen and Unwin.

CORRIGAN, P. and SAYER, D. 1985. *The Great Arch: English State Formation as Cultural Revolution.* Oxford: Blackwell.

COSTAIN, A. N. and MCFARLAND, A. S. (eds.) 1998. *Social Movements and American Political Institutions.* Lanham, Md.: Rowman and Littlefield.

CREVELD, M. VAN. 1999. *The Rise and Decline of the State.* Cambridge: Cambridge University Press.

DRESCHER, S. 1986. *Capitalism and Antislavery: British Mobilization in Comparative Perspective.* London: Macmillan.

——1994. Whose abolition? Popular pressure and the ending of the British slave trade. *Past and Present*, 143: 136–66.

EARLE, T. 1997. *How Chiefs Come to Power: The Political Economy in Prehistory.* Stanford, Calif.: Stanford University Press.

EDELMAN, M. 2001. Social movements: changing paradigms and forms of politics. *Annual Review of Anthropology*, 30: 285–317.

ELTIS, D. 1993. Europeans and the rise and fall of African slavery in the Americas: an interpretation. *American Historical Review*, 98: 1399–423.

FARRELL, S. 2000. *Rituals and Riots. Sectarian Violence and Political Culture in Ulster, 1784–1886.* Lexington: University Press of Kentucky.

FILLIEULE, O. (ed.) 1997. Maintien de l'ordre. Special issue of *Cahiers de la Sécurité Intérieure.*

FOWERAKER, J. and LANDMAN, T. 1997. *Citizenship Rights and Social Movements: A Comparative and Statistical Analysis.* Oxford: Oxford University Press.

FRIEDMANN, D. 1977. A theory of the size and shape of nations. *Journal of Political Economy*, 85: 59–78.

GAMSON, W. A. 1990. *The Strategy of Social Protest*, rev. edn. Belmont, Calif.: Wadsworth.

GLEDHILL, J., BENDER, B., and LARSEN, M. T. (eds.) 1988. *State and Society: The Emergence and Development of Social Hierarchy and Political Centralization.* London: Unwin Hyman.

GREW, R. (ed.) 1978. *Crises of Political Development in Europe and the United States.* Princeton, NJ: Princeton University Press.

GRIMSTED, D. 1998. *American Mobbing, 1828–1861: Toward Civil War.* New York: Oxford University Press.

HOFFMANN, S.-L. 2003. Democracy and associations in the long nineteenth century: toward a transnational perspective. *Journal of Modern History*, 75: 269–99.

HUTERS, T., WONG, R. B., and YU, P. (eds.) 1997. *Culture and State in Chinese History. Conventions, Accommodations and Critiques.* Stanford, Calif.: Stanford University Press.

IBARRA, P. (ed.) 2003. *Social Movements and Democracy.* New York: Palgrave.

JARMAN, N. 1997. *Material Conflicts: Parades and Visual Displays in Northern Ireland.* Oxford: Berg.

KHAZANOV, A. M. 1993. Muhammad and Jenghiz Khan compared: the religious factor in world empire building. *Comparative Studies in Society and History*, 35: 461–479.

KINEALY, C. 2003. Les marches orangistes en Irlande du Nord: Histoire d'un droit. *Le Mouvement Social*, 202: 165–82.

KLEIN, H. S. 1999. *The Atlantic Slave Trade.* Cambridge: Cambridge University Press.

LEVI, M. 1988. *Of Rule and Revenue.* Berkeley: University of California Press.

——1997. *Consent, Dissent and Patriotism.* Cambridge: Cambridge University Press.

LI, J. 2002. State fragmentation: toward a theoretical understanding of the territorial power of the state. *Sociological Theory*, 20: 139–56.

LÓPEZ-ALVES, F. 2000. *State Formation and Democracy in Latin America, 1810–1900*. Durham, NC: Duke University Press

MAC SUIBHNE, B. 2000. Whiskey, potatoes and paddies: volunteering and the construction of the Irish nation in northwest Ulster, 1778–1782. Pp. 45–82 in *Crowds in Ireland c. 1720–1920*, ed. P. Jupp and E. Magennis. London: Macmillan.

McADAM, D., TARROW, S., and TILLY, C. 2001. *Dynamics of Contention*. Cambridge: Cambridge University Press.

McCAMMON, H. J. and CAMPBELL, K. E. 2002. Allies on the road to victory: coalition formation between the suffragists and the Women's Christian Temperance Union. *Mobilization*, 7: 231–52.

————— GRANBERG, E. M., and MOWERY, C. 2001. How movements win: gendered opportunity structures and U.S. women's suffrage movements, 1866 to 1919. *American Sociological Review*, 66: 49–70.

MEYER, D. S. and TARROW, S. (eds.) 1998. *The Social Movement Society: Contentious Politics for a New Century*. Lanham, Md.: Rowman and Littlefield.

MIDLARSKY, M. I. 1999. *The Evolution of Inequality. War, State Survival and Democracy in Comparative Perspective*. Stanford, Calif.: Stanford University Press.

PIERSON, P. 2004. *Politics in Time*. Princeton, NJ: Princeton University Press.

DELLA PORTA, D. 1995. *Social Movements, Political Violence and the State: A Comparative Analysis of Italy and Germany*. Cambridge: Cambridge University Press.

———— and REITER, H. (eds.) 1998. *Policing Protest: The Control of Mass Demonstrations in Western Democracies*. Minneapolis: University of Minnesota Press.

PORTER, B. 1994. *War and the Rise of the State*. New York: Free Press.

ROEHNER, B. M. and SYME, T. 2002. *Pattern and Repertoire in History*. Cambridge, Mass.: Harvard University Press.

SKOCPOL, T. 1985. Bringing the state back in: strategies of analysis in current research. Pp. 3–43 in *Bringing the State Back In*, ed. P. B. Evans, D. Rueschemeyer, and T. Skocpol. Cambridge: Cambridge University Press.

TAAGEPERA, R. 1997. Expansion and contraction patterns of large polities: context for Russia. *International Studies Quarterly*, 41: 475–504.

TARROW, S. 1998. *Power in Movement: Social Movements and Contentious Politics*. Cambridge: Cambridge University Press.

TILLY, C. 1969. Collective violence in European perspective. Pp. 5–34 in vol. 1 of *Violence in America*, ed. H. D. Graham and T. R. Gurr. Washington, DC: U.S. Government Printing Office.

———— 1975. Western state-making and theories of political transformation. Pp. 601–38 in *The Formation of National States in Western Europe*, ed. C. Tilly. Princeton, NJ: Princeton University Press.

———— 1977. Collective action in England and America, 1765–1775. Pp. 45–72 in *Tradition, Conflict and Modernization: Perspectives on the American Revolution*, ed. R. M. Brown and D. Fehrenbacher. New York: Academic Press.

———— 1992. *Coercion, Capital and European States, AD 990–1992*, rev. edn. Oxford: Blackwell.

———— 1993. Contentious repertoires in Great Britain, 1758–1834. *Social Science History*, 17: 253–80.

———— 2001a. Historical analysis of political processes. Pp. 567–88 in *Handbook of Sociological Theory*, ed. J. H. Turner. New York: Kluwer/Plenum.

———— 2001b. Mechanisms in political processes. *Annual Review of Political Science*, 4: 21–41.

TILLY, C. 2004. *Social Movements, 1768–2004*. Boulder, Colo.: Paradigm Press.

—— and WOOD, L. 2003. Contentious connections in Great Britain, 1828–1834. Pp. 147–72 in *Social Movements and Networks: Relational Approaches to Collective Action*, ed. M. Diani and D. McAdam. New York: Oxford University Press.

VERBA, S. 1971. Sequences and development. Pp. 283–316 in *Crises and Sequences in Political Development*, ed. L. Binder et al. Princeton, NJ: Princeton University Press.

WALKER, J. L. 1991. *Mobilizing Interest Groups in America: Patrons, Professions and Social Movements*. Ann Arbor: University of Michigan Press.

WONG, R. B. 1997. *China Transformed: Historical Change and the Limits of European Experience*. Ithaca, NY: Cornell University Press.

PART VII

COMPARATIVE POLITICS

CHAPTER 27

OVERVIEW OF COMPARATIVE POLITICS

CARLES BOIX

SUSAN C. STOKES

Why do authoritarian states democratize? What accounts for the contours, dynamics, and ideologies of the nation state? Under what conditions do civil wars and revolutions erupt? Why is political representation channeled through political parties in contemporary democracies? Why do some parties run on policy programs, others on patronage? Can citizens use elections and courts to hold governments accountable?

These are some of the crucial questions that the subfield of comparative politics addresses. And they are the questions, among others, around which we organized the *Oxford Handbook of Comparative Politics* (Boix and Stokes 2007). We asked a set of top scholars in comparative politics to write critical surveys of areas of scholarship in which they are expert. We assembled the volume with two guiding principles. First, we were committed to the possibility (and desirability) of generating a systematic body of theoretical knowledge about politics. The discipline advances, we believe, through theoretical discovery and innovation. Second, we embraced a catholic approach to comparative methodology.

1 COMPARATIVE POLITICS AS (EMPIRICAL) POLITICAL SCIENCE

In the last few decades, the discipline of comparative politics has experienced three main and defining changes: in its object of enquiry; in the methods it now deploys to gather data and test its empirical findings; and in the assumptions (about human and political behavior) it employs to build any theoretical propositions. In doing so, comparative politics has come of age, becoming a key contributor to empirical (as opposed to normative or philosophical) political enquiry. For organizational and administrative reasons, comparative politics is likely to remain a separate field in the discipline and in US departments (where most of today's political research takes place) in the near future. But from an epistemological point of view, comparative politics is turning into a true science of politics—in the same way economic theory replaced the study of national economies at some point in the past.

Most graduate students in comparative politics who studied in leading depart-ments in the 1960s through the 1980s were trained to conduct research in a single region or country. Indeed, the very term *comparative* was in most cases misleading. Comparative politics frequently entailed not making comparisons but studying the politics of a foreign country. This methodological choice came hand in hand with an epistemological one. The researcher had to show a deep understanding and a detailed analysis of the political intricacies of a particular polity. That descriptive work often came at the expense of any of the theoretical ambitions that had populated most classical political thinkers from Aristotle to Mill. With slight exaggeration one could think of that state of affairs as the State Department approach to comparative politics, where one scholar staffs the "Japan desk," another the "Chile desk," and so on. Of course there were extremely important exceptions. Almond and Verba's *The Civic Culture* compared citizens' attitudes in five countries. Barrington Moore's *Social Origins of Democracy and Dictatorship* embarked in a parallel examination of the political and economic evolution of great powers since the early modern period.

The first way in which the field of comparative politics has changed has been epistemological. Even without abandoning the study of particular cases or countries, most comparatists have endorsed the construction and testing of causal theoretical models as the central task of the field. That shift in the object of research has had many progenitors. In part it came from realizing the limits of writing single case studies: Looking at one observation point in a plane will never tell us what forces brought it there. In part it was fed by a few yet very influential comparative pieces written by some modernization and political-development scholars (such as, again, Almond, Lipset, Moore, Rokkan, or Verba). Finally, the gradual introduction of statistical techniques and the mere exercise of data gathering spurred a general interest in cross-national comparisons.

Jointly with a growing acceptance among most researchers about the need to develop broad, general propositions about politics, comparative politics has also embraced the use of standard scientific practices to provisionally validate any theoretical claims. Large-n cross-national studies are now a prominent feature in the (comparative) study of politics—something that would have been hard to predict circa 1970s or even 1980s. But more important than the size of data-sets, what characterizes comparatists today (and rightly so, in our opinion) is a concern for a research design that makes it possible to test theoretical propositions. Provided there are enough degrees of freedom, this should be possible (at least in principle) to accomplish even with very few (but well-chosen) data points or cases. Interestingly, this growing consensus has come with an equally increasing and valuable skepticism about how much it can be accomplished by employing quasi-experimental methods of the kind comparatists usually employ. (In this, comparative politics is not alone: For good or ill, the debate over proper instrumentation has also taken over empirical economists. We will deal over this skepticism in more detail at the end of this chapter.)

In addition to a growing acceptance of the endeavors of theory-building and theory-testing through standard scientific procedures, the scientific enquiry of comparative politics has also shifted in the last decades or, one may say, over the course of the last three generations of scholars devoted to this field, in a third and probably more controversial way—namely, in the way in which theory is built. Probably influenced by the then-dominant approaches of structural sociology and Marxism, in the past comparatists relied on systemic, broad explanations to explain political outcomes. Just think of the initial theories of political modernization, the first articles relating democracy to development or the work on party formation laid out in the 1960s. Today, theory-building very often proceeds (or, perhaps more modestly, claims to proceed) from "microfoundations;" that is, it starts from the individual, and her interests and beliefs, to then make predictions about aggregate outcomes. We find this to constitute an advance in political science. Making us think hard about the final unit of analysis of the model, that is, about each individual (and his motives and actions), allows us to have theories that are more transparent (i.e. where one can truly probe the consistency and plausibility of assumptions) and easier to falsify.

At this point it is important, however, to pause to stress that embracing the principle of methodological individualism does not necessarily mean accepting a purely instrumental or rationalist model of human action. Nor does it mean that the interests and preferences of individuals are not shaped by social and political forces. Recent work in comparative politics has stressed that partisan, ethnic, national, and class identities are in important ways inculcated in individuals by parties, states, and other political actors. As is well known, our increasing reliance on microfoundations has been triggered to a considerable degree by an influx of mathematical and game-theoretic tools and by the influence of economic models in the discipline. But as Moon discussed in the Greenstein–Polsby handbook thirty years ago, models built on propositions about how individual actors will behave under certain circumstances may well employ a variegated set of assumptions about the interests and beliefs of the actors themselves. In fact, his claim (and our hunch) is that the only way to show that rationalistic assumptions do not work is to build models that are populated by intentional actors (with goals that are not strictly instrumental) and that these models perform better than those developed by rational choice theorists. To sum up, building theories of intentional actors and constructing models of (strictly) rationalist individuals are two different enterprises. The latter needs the former but the reverse is not true. Realizing that difference should save for all of us what has been a considerable source of conflict and confusion.

The growing emphasis on building broadly valid theoretical propositions (the first transformation of the field) together with the growing appreciation of the role of individuals and their motives (the third change of the field) have had a beneficial effect on comparative politics and, by definition, on political science. In a way, they have moved the study of politics much closer to our historical predecessors in the discipline. Classical political thinkers, from Aristotle and Machiavelli to Hobbes, Locke, and Rousseau, made an effort to construct a set of theoretical propositions that could explain political life; that is, the foundations of political obligation and its consequences. Even Tocqueville's celebrated study of America has weathered the passage of time due to the universal theoretical implications it develops in the discussion of a single case. What's more, each classical political theory started with a particular conception of human nature. With different tools and with a different data-set (for one, we have some information about how real democracies work in practice), all these different (micro) models are, in the end, grounded on specific assumptions about human behavior. These assumptions are still deeply contested in comparative politics: They span from a purely instrumental conception of political actors intent on securing survival and maximizing power to a notion of individuals that may consent to particular structures contingent on others cooperating to, finally, visions of politics that appeal to the inherent sociability of humans. This contestation is unavoidable and healthy. Our guess is that as we move to build intentional models of politics, it should become easier to adjudicate among different points of departure.

2 States, State Formation, and Political Consent

The foundations of power and the sources of political obligation are without much doubt the two main building blocks of any theoretical inquiry in politics. Hence it is not surprising that contractarian theorists paid considerable attention to the mechanisms underlying the formation of states—although they did so mainly for normative reasons. From an empirical or positive point of view, the effort to build theories of state formation happened much later in time. When they appeared, they divided into neoclassical models, which stressed the construction of a coercive structure as part of a voluntary agreement between individuals specialized in coercion and individuals in need of protection, and Marxian models, which portrayed the state as an invention of an elite intent on the exploitation of the masses. Today, mostly as a result of neoinstitutionalist contributions from authors such as North and Olson, the formation of states is seen as a historical turning point in which those agents who specialize in the exercise of violence acquire the right incentives to shift from plundering a population of producers to protecting them from other plunderers. In other words, the founders of states were mostly bandits who, under the proper material and military circumstances, had the incentive to pacify and control a given territory and population in a systematic and orderly manner.

That last theoretical insight has had important empirical implications. It can be actually related to specific historical circumstances that began to take place 10,000 to 8,000 years ago, when agriculture was invented and states followed suit. And it probably explains why stateless societies, where permanent protection mechanisms are absent, have fared much worse in economic terms than human communities governed by state structures.

Still, the theoretical and empirical underdevelopment of the current theories of state formation calls for further scholarly research. Let us just mention two potential avenues of analysis. In the first place, neoinstitutionalists have reduced the foundation of states to a single cause: the transformation of bandits into lords. Yet that conclusion does not seem convincing on both historical and formal grounds. States may form (from a strictly logical point of view) and indeed were formed whenever some producers decided to join forces (that is, whenever they decided to accept a common, binding authority) to respond in some coordinated fashion to (internal or external) plunderers. In fact, in the absence of this second formative path, it seems impossible to explain why noncoercive types have been successful at constructing and maintaining states—a democratic transition, for example, should be seen as an instance of state formation since the problem of political obligation reappears, now in a new light (i.e. with different subjects and sovereigns), as political authority is transferred from one or a few to many. In the second place, theories of state formation have offered some plausible conjectures on the impact of states on economic growth (indeed most of them were mainly built to explain the latter). But they still have little to say about the distributive and social consequences of the emergence of political authority.[1]

The monopoly of coercion and authority has grown exponentially in both scope and scale in the last half-millennium—it is probably appropriate to think about the modern state as a very different species from the ancient state. In an essay that is reproduced in this volume, Hendrik Spruyt provides a bird's-eye overview of recent contributions to our understanding of modern state formation, an area of research that has grown substantially in the last three decades. He reviews the ways in which the modern state, with its absolute claims of sovereignty over a particular territory and population, formed and displaced all other forms of governance. This change came in response to a shift in war technology, the growth of commercial capitalism, and new ideas about legitimate government. Spruyt also examines several influential and still-unsettled debates about what caused the emergence of distinct types of constitutional and administrative regimes in the modern period. Most studies of state-building have focused on Europe in the modern period. The recent

---

[1] For an attempt to deal with some of these questions, see Boix (2009).

emergence of independent states outside of Europe in the last centuries is not adequately explained by these accounts. As Spruyt notes, state formation in the twentieth
century allows us to evaluate the extent to which the international system, the economy, and the colonial legacy affect how sovereignty and legitimacy have expanded
across the globe.

As conveyed by the dominant, Weberian definition of state, political authority
relies both on coercion and on some form of legitimization. Accordingly, comparative
politics has also considered the ideological dimensions of state formation and of
intrastate identity conflict.[2] Research on the ideological underpinnings of the modern state has focused on the formation of national identities. Although the debate
on the sources, structure, and dimensions of national adscription and nationalism
is far from settled, the scholarly community now sees nations as mostly "modern
constructs," i.e. as separate communities to whom individuals perceive themselves
as belonging with particular moral attachments and political obligations. Here a,
or perhaps the, fundamental point of contention among scholars results from disagreements about the ultimate trigger that caused the appearance of national sentiments. For some, nationalism is the functional response in the political sphere to
the demands of industrialization. For others, it derives from the decline of traditional
mindsets and the emergence of print capitalism and media markets. Yet for others,
nationalism arose in modern times as a response to an upsetting of traditional hierarchies which led, in turn, to a reinterpretation of everyone's political position as one
of belonging to a nation of equals.[3]

3 POLITICAL REGIMES AND TRANSITIONS

Given the democratic revolution of the past quarter-century, it is scarcely surprising
that democracy has been a central concern—perhaps *the* central concern—of comparative politics.

Over the last fifty years, democratization theory has developed several, at times
overlapping, at times contradictory, insights and models. Empirically, there seems to
be a strong correlation between levels of development and democracy (Lipset 1959;
Przeworski and Limongi 1997; Boix and Stokes 2003). Theoretically, the initial structural explanations (Moore 1966) gave way to game-theory models stripped of any
sociological foundations—either employed in a metaphorical way, e.g. O'Donnell,
Schmitter, and Whitehead (1986), or in a strict, analytical manner, e.g. Przeworski
(1990). Those two theoretical approaches have recently been combined to point out
why the political consequences of different constitutional institutions account for

---

[2] See in particular the chapters by Hardin (2007) and Greenfeld and Eastwood (2007) in the *Oxford
Handbook of Comparative Politics*.
[3] See, for example, Gellner (1983), Anderson (1983), and Greenfeld and Eastwood (2007).

the social and economic underpinnings of democratic regimes (e.g. Boix 2003). In a chapter reproduced in this volume, Barbara Geddes reviews these theories. She claims that we still have few firm and uncontested conclusions about democracy's causes and that our empirical results are less robust than one would like, changing with the sample of countries studied, the timeframe considered, and the specification of estimations. The problem is not an absence of theory. Our theories of democratization have become increasingly sophisticated and explicit. Rather, Geddes suggests, the problem may lie in the heterogeneity of the explanandum, democratization. Transitions from absolutist monarchy to constitutional monarchy or to republics may be fundamentally different than transitions from modern military dictatorship to mass democracy. Separating these distinct phenomena, analyzing them—and, more to the point, developing distinct theories of them—is the key, in her view, to gaining firmer knowledge of why countries democratize.

Although behavioral studies and the use of mass surveys spearheaded the transformation of political science into a more *comparative* and hence more scientific endeavor, the examination of opinion surveys has been somewhat of a laggard in the field of democratization studies. In the volume we edited, Welzel and Inglehart partly correct that imbalance. Reporting findings from a series of recent cross-national studies that have analyzed the effects of mass beliefs on the broadest possible basis, they show that the process of socioeconomic modernization nurtures liberal mass orientations which have, in turn, a positive effect on democracy.

With the exception of Hobbes, the relationship between civic culture and political regimes has been one of the central preoccupations of all modern political theorists. Embracing the new methods that characterized the self-consciously empirical political science that emerged after the Second World War, Almond and Verba in the 1960s tackled this secular concern in their highly influential book on civic culture. Yet this attempt to put the study of the relationship on solid empirical grounds proved unsuccessful.[4] The problem with this research agenda had less to do with the (still) very contentious notion of culture than with the ways in which researchers categorized democracy and political culture. They entertained too limited a conception of democracy, restricted to the institutional mechanisms that determine governance at the national level. They thus disregarded the vast number of democratic practices that operate at the local level and in intermediate social bodies. They defined political culture, in turn, as a set of beliefs and dispositions toward certain political objects. But this notion proved to be unsatisfactory: The role that these beliefs and attitudes played in sustaining democratic life and practices was unclear; their origins remained unknown; and, from a purely empirical point, there was no clear proof that democratic stability was bolstered by a particular democratic culture. Nonetheless, it was precisely at the time when the political culture approach had gone down a "degenerative path" that researchers rescued the concept of culture and hence the problem of its political effects by stressing its eminently relational nature. In the late 1980s, Gambetta put trust back into the research agenda. Several researchers emphasized the

[4] See Sabetti (2007) in the *Oxford Handbook of Comparative Politics*.

need to understand interpersonal networks to explain particular behavior. Coleman drew on game-theoretic concepts to develop the notion of social capital. And Putnam then transformed our way of understanding governance and culture in his famous study of Italian regional politics. This new approach is still in its infancy: We know little (both theoretically and empirically) about the mechanisms that go from social capital to good governance, and next to nothing about the dynamics that create, sustain, or deplete civic virtue. And some of us may doubt that trust, as opposed to an engaged skepticism, is the appropriate posture of citizens in democratic polities. But the new approach may well be putting us in the right path to "untangle the complex relationship between democracy and civic culture" (Sabetti 2007, 357).

More than thirty years ago, Juan Linz wrote a highly influential piece on dictatorships for the *Handbook of Political Science*, edited by Fred Greenstein and Nelson Polsby. Linz's approach was mostly conceptual and sociological and drew on the literature on totalitarianism and authoritarianism that had been developing since the Second World War. Nondemocratic regimes, according to Linz, could be defined by their degree of internal pluralism, their ideology, and the level of political mobilization which they demanded of their subject populations. Typological approaches have limited empirical purchase, however. Realizing that no single principle can accommodate all the variety of autocracies in place, researchers responded by building a sprawling and mostly ad hoc list of types, such as military dictatorships, traditional absolutist monarchies, one-party states, totalitarian and post-totalitarian systems, parliamentary democracies, city-state oligarchies, "sultanistic" principalities, and so on. These ideal types have turned out to be scarcely informative about the mechanisms through which autocracies work. In this scientific tradition, researchers describe the traits of each type—in other words, they engage in the process of tallying the most frequent elements of each ideal model. But they hardly explain the mechanisms through which power is maintained and the consequences those different institutional structures may have on political stability, citizen compliance, and economic development.

After a period of relative neglect (perhaps a result of the third wave of democratization), the literature on dictatorships has experienced a notable transformation in recent years. Several political economists have started to abandon the strict typological tradition and have instead examined the incentives and mechanisms that structure power and the process of governance in authoritarian systems. Wintrobe (2007), for example, in an essay in the volume we edited, offers an account of dictatorships that starts from rationalist assumptions. To rule, dictators have to combine some degree of repression with the construction of political loyalty. Given the two variables— repression and loyalty—and the objective functions dictators may have, Wintrobe distinguishes between tinpot dictators (who maximize consumption and minimize repression levels), totalitarian dictators (intent on maximizing power), tyrants (who repress without achieving much "loyalty"), and timocrats (who invest in creating loyalty and gaining their citizens' love). Besides Wintrobe's work, other scholars have made important contributions to our understanding of electoral autocracies (Magalone 2006), the use of parties and legislatures in authoritarian regimes (Geddes 1999; Wright 2008; Gandhi 2008), or the dynamics of conflict within authoritarian elites (Svolik 2007).

4 POLITICAL INSTABILITY, POLITICAL CONFLICT

In a vibrant and by now classic debate, scholars argued first that revolutions occur exclusively as a result of social and economic modernization (Moore, Skocpol, Huntington). More recently, an influential line of argument, brought forth by Goldstone, has framed revolutions as the outbreak that follows a Malthusian imbalance between a growing population and its environment. In an important essay published in the *Oxford Handbook of Comparative Politics*, Steve Pincus claims that the necessary prerequisite for revolution was always state modernization. State modernization programs simultaneously bring new social groups and new regions into direct contact with the state, and legitimize ideologies of change. These two developments create a social basis and a language on which to build revolutionary movements. Revolutions lead to very different political outcomes. In part following in the steps of Barrington Moore, Jr., Pincus argues that revolutions lead to open, democratic regimes when the state relies on merchant communities and foreign trade. Absent the latter, however, revolutions typically result in the imposition of an authoritarian regime.

In the last decades reality has put civil wars in a central place on the agenda of comparatists. Research on the sources of modern political violence (in the form of civil wars and guerrilla warfare) has gone through several theoretical turns since its inception as a comparative endeavor almost fifty years ago. Modernization scholars explained rebellions as a function of economic inequality (Russett 1964; Paige 1975; Midlarsky 1988; Muller 1985), the impact of social and economic development, and the status and political claims of particular social groups (Huntington 1968; Wolf 1969; Gurr 1973). That strand of enquiry was joined by a second line of research relating violent conflict to ethnic nationalism and the distribution of resources along ethnic lines (Horowitz 1985; Connor 1994). In recent years almost all scholars have de-emphasized the role of economic factors, existing social grievances, or political ideologies in igniting violent conflicts, to stress instead the context of economic and political opportunities in which potential rebels may decide to engage in violent action. Collier and Hoeffler (2004) link the emergence of rebellious activities to the availability of both finance—namely, abundant natural resources—and potential recruits—individuals with reduced prospects of material advancement through peaceful activities. Fearon and Laitin hypothesize that civil wars happen in "fragile states with limited administrative control of their peripheries" (2003, 88). Writing from a different angle, rooted in the examination of the micrologic of violence deployed in civil wars, Kalyvas downplays the presence of single, sociologically unique motivations and describes civil wars as "imperfect, mulilayered, and fluid aggregations of highly complex, partially overlapping, diverse, and localized civil wars with pronounced differences from region to region and valley to valley" (Kalyvas 2006, 371). In the volume we edited, Kalyvas insists as well that war-driven conditions are themselves likely to shape the outcomes of interest: Much changes as civil wars unfold, including the distribution of populations, the preferences of key actors, and the value of resources over which combatants seek control. The exploration of political conflict has also generated an important literature on contentious politics (episodic public collective action) and social movements (sustained challenge to holders of power). Modernization and the spread of democracy spawned the invention of social movements. Yet at the same time, the time and location of social movements (that is, their interaction with political institutions, society, and cultural practices) determined the form in which they emerged (Tarrow and Tilly 2007; Lichbach and deVries 2007).

5 MASS POLITICAL MOBILIZATION

Modern democracies are representative democracies. As such they are also party democracies: Political representatives generally coordinate in stable organizations for the purposes of contesting elections and governing. In a chapter reproduced in this volume, Herbert Kitschelt offers of a broad review of the questions that scholars ask about party systems and the way they answer them. Why do democracies feature parties in the first place, as almost all do? Why do many parties compete in some democracies whereas in others competition is restricted to two major parties (or two major ones and a minor one)? Why do some parties compete with the currency of programs, others with valence issues, and still others with clientelism and patronage? Why are elections perennially close in some systems, lopsided in others? Kitschelt reviews the measures that scholars find helpful in answering these questions—party-system fractionalization, the effective number of parties, electoral volatility, and cleavages. The problems afflicting party politics are regionally specific: Whereas scholars of advanced industrial systems worry, as Kitschelt notes, about the decay of party–voter linkages, scholars of new democracies worry about whether such linkages will ever take shape.

Beyond the systemic or functional elements of parties and party systems, and starting with Lipset and Rokkan's (1967) seminal contribution, researchers have also devoted considerable efforts to understanding why parties formed in the way they did; why and how parties and party systems developed in Western Europe and North America from rather loose networks of politicians, catering to small and strictly delimited electorates, in the early nineteenth century to mass-based, well-organized electoral machines in the twentieth century; and why the number and ideologies of parties varied across countries. As shown in Boix (2007), the nature of parties and party systems can be traced to the underlying structures of preferences, which could be either uni- or multidimensional. But these preferences or political dimensions were mobilized as a function of several additional key factors: the parties' beliefs about which electoral strategy would maximize their chances of winning, and the electoral institutions that mediate between voters' choices and the distribution of seats in national parliaments. (These electoral institutions, as shown in Boix 1999, were themselves the product of strategic action by parties.) In a way, that chapter may be read as a response to two types of dominant approaches in the discipline: those institutionalist models that describe political outcomes as equilibria and that, somehow trapped in static applications of game theory, hardly reflect on the origins of the institutions that they claim constrain political actors; and those narratives that stress the contingency and path dependency of all political phenomena while refusing to impose any theoretical structure on them. By contrast, we think it should be possible to build historical accounts in which we reveal (1) how political actors make strategic choices according to a general set of assumptions about their beliefs and interests and (2) how their choices in turn shape the choice set of future political actors.

One of the central contentions of the comparative work done in the 1960s was that partisan attachments and party systems had remained frozen since the advent of democracy in the West. Yet in the last forty years party–voter linkages have substantially thawed (Wren and McElwain 2007). Economic growth, the decline of class differences, and the emergence of postmaterialist values lie in part behind this transformation. In the wake of changes in the electorate and its preferences, it took party bureaucracies some time to adjust. Taking advantage of the slow rate of adjustment of the older parties, new parties sprang up to lure away dissatisfied voters.

Yet party dealignment and electoral volatility have not diminished, even after new parties that should have stabilized the electoral market have entered these party systems. Therefore, to explain continued volatility, we must look beyond changes in the structure of voter preferences. Weakening party–voter ties must be put in the context of a shift in the educational level of the population and new technologies (radios and TV). As parties became less important as informational shortcuts, politics has grown more candidate centered and party elites have been able to pursue electoral campaigns without relying on the old party machinery. If Wren and McElwain are right, our old models of, and intuitions about, party-centered democracy should give way to a more "Americanized" notion of democracies, where personal candidacies and television campaigns determine how politicians are elected and policy made.

In the last two decades, democracy has become the dominant system of government across the world, both as a normative ideal and as a fact. But not all nominal democracies generate accountable, clean governments. In a chapter reproduced in this volume, Susan Stokes addresses one of the possible causes of malfunctioning democracies by looking at the practices, causes, and consequences of clientelism. Clientelism, or the "proffering of material goods [by the patron] in return for electoral support [by the client]," was a hot topic of research in the 1960s and 1970s, buoyed by the emergence of new nations. Shaped by a sociological approach, researchers at that time explained clientelism as a practice underpinned by a set of norms of reciprocity. Yet, as Stokes claims, clientelism must rather be seen as a game in which patrons and clients behave strategically and in which they understand that, given certain external conditions (such as a certain level of development and the organizational conditions that allow for the effective monitoring of the other side), they are better off sustaining a pattern of exchange over the long run. Such a theoretical account then allows us to make predictions, which are beginning to be tested empirically, about the institutions underpinning clientelistic practices, the electoral strategies pursued by patrons, and the potential economic and political effects of clientelism: whether it depresses economic development and political competition.

Political activism has also spawned a large body of research. In her chapter in the *Oxford Handbook of Comparative Politics*, Pippa Norris (2007) reviews the social and psychological model of participation developed by Verba and Nie, as well as the critiques generated from a rational choice perspective. She then examines how key developments in the research community and the political world have affected the ways in which we evaluate this subfield. She notes a growing interest in the role of institutions in shaping participation in general and turnout in particular. Echoing Wren and McElwain, she draws our attention to changes in party membership, which was widespread and hence instrumental in many advanced democracies but has progressively shrunk, with consequences that are still widely debated among scholars. The constructs of trust and social capital, pioneered by Coleman and Putnam, are also relevant to our expectations about levels of participation. Norris also identifies cause-oriented forms of activism as a distinct type of participation, activism that includes demonstrations and protests, consumer politics, professional interest groups, and more diffuse "new" social movements and transnational advocacy networks. All of these, she notes, have expanded and in a way marginalized the more institutionalized, party- and union-based mechanisms of participation that dominated in the past.

6 PROCESSING POLITICAL DEMANDS

In the magisterial five-volume *Handbook of Political Science* published thirty years ago by Greenstein and Polsby, the term *accountability* appears not once. The term *representation* appears sporadically and, outside of the volume on political theory, only a handful of times. Thirty years later, accountability has emerged as an organizing concept in comparative politics, with representation not far behind.

In democracies, how do citizens' preferences get translated into demands for one public policy over another? If everyone in a society had the same preferences, the problem would not be a problem at all. But never is this the case. And scholarship on preference aggregation must come to grips with social choice theory, which should lead us to doubt that citizens in any setting in which politics is multidimensional can evince any stable set of policy preferences. The dominant strains of research, some of which come to grips with the social choice challenge and others of which ignore it, include examinations of the congruence (between preferences and outcomes) of various sorts (Powell 2007). One kind of congruence study looks at the fit between constituents' preferences and the issue positions of their representatives. Another looks at the fit between electoral outcomes and the allocation of elected offices, treating citizens' policy preferences as though they were fully expressed by their votes. Another sort of congruence study examines the coherence of issue positions among co-partisans, both political elites and citizens who identify with parties, and tends to find a good deal more coherence among the former than among the latter. Yet another deals with the congruence between electoral platforms and campaign promises, and government policy. Given the role institutions play in aggregating preferences, a big chunk of political science is again devoted to the study of the former—we say "again" because institutions were a key part of the study of politics until the sociological and survey revolution that gripped the discipline in the 1930s and 1940s. Neoinstitutional scholars have focused their attention on electoral rules, executives, legislatures, federalism and, more recently, the judiciary.

Since Duverger's seminal work, research on electoral rules has focused on the ways (mechanical and psychological) in which electoral systems affect the voting behavior of electors and, as a result, the election of candidates, the structure of parties and party systems, and the politics of coalition-building in democracies (Duverger 1954; Cox 1997; Taagapera 2007).

The existing work on executives and legislatures has centered on two broad topics. First, what is the effect of a constitutional structure based on the separation of powers? Second, what determines the patterns of coalition-making in governments? In the volume we edited, Samuels (2007) reviews what we know about the impact of the separation of powers on accountability. The conventional view in the United States is that a separation of powers is so central to democratic accountability that this separation is nearly definitional of democracy. Samuels evaluates this proposition empirically. His own research and that of other authors which he reviews address questions of accountability and representation, as well as the effects of a separation of powers on the policy process and on regime stability. Among his central findings is that presidentialism has several deleterious effects; a separation of executive from legislative powers increases the chances for policy deadlock and for the breakdown of democracy. In turn, Strom and Nyblade (2007) critically assess the literature on coalition-making, particularly regarding the formation of governments in parliamentary democracies. Drawing on neoinstitutionalism and, more specifically, on the transaction costs literature, they show how the costs of negotiation and the demands of the electorate, interested in monitoring parties' performance, reduce cycles and push politicians to strike relatively stable pacts. They note that theories of coalition formation began with William Riker's application of the "size principle," which predicted that parties would try to minimize the number of actors in a coalition. Although influential theoretically, this approach proved to be rather unsatisfactory empirically. In response, Strom and Nyblade relax Riker's fundamental assumptions about payoffs, about the role of information, and about the effects of decision rules and institutions, to reach a much richer theory, and one that fits the data more closely.

As discussed by Pablo Beramendi in a thought-provoking chapter, we know far less than we should about federalism. Our theories on the origins of federalism are still sketchy—security threats, the level of heterogeneity, and the evolution of the world economy (in terms of its level of integration) shape the extent of decentralization in a critical manner. The study of the consequences of federalism is slightly more advanced. The relationship between democracy and federalism seems to be conditional, as far as we know, on the particular internal structure of federalism. The effects on the economy of having a federal structure, in turn, depend on how the federal institutions allocate power and responsibilities between the center and regional governments.

The study of the judiciary was traditionally reserved to legal scholars. In their chapter in the *Oxford Handbook of Comparative Politics*, John Ferejohn, Frances Rosenbluth, and Charles Shipan (2007) remind us why that is not the case any more. After examining the conditions under which courts attain independence, especially from executives but also from legislatures (an independence which O'Donnell and others consider a necessary condition for vertical accountability), they also explain other aspects of cross-national variation, such as why courts everywhere are not enabled to carry out judicial review and why courts are sometimes more active in the legislative process, other times less.

Assessing judicial independence, as these authors acknowledge, is not always straightforward. They advocate two measures: the frequency with which courts reverse governments, and the frequency with which they reverse governments that nationalize parts of the economy (or attempt to do so). The authors note that a drawback of either approach is that courts, which seek (among other objectives) not to have their decisions reversed, may rule against governments only when they anticipate not being reversed, in which case these measures would tend to overestimate their independence. Another difficulty is that courts may rule in favor of governments when they find governments' actions to be lawful or when they spontaneously agree with governments' actions. Hence, whereas rulings against governments probably indicate independence, rulings in their favor are less certain indications of dependence (see Helmke 2002; 2005).

7 GOVERNANCE IN COMPARATIVE PERSPECTIVE

....

It was in the 1970s, that is, about two decades after comparative politics started to develop causal, testable theories, that political scientists ventured in a systematic way

into the effects of politics on economic outcomes (and vice versa). Part of that growing interest in political economics started with the analysis by political sociologists
of voting and, particularly, of economic voting. The first models presented a simple
rule of thumb that voters could—and did—apply when deciding whether to vote
for incumbents: If the economy had performed well on their watch, retain them; if
it hadn't, turn them out. Recent scholarly developments place economic voting in
institutional contexts and present more nuanced stories about what voters need to
know to carry off "simple" economic voting. Raymond Duch's chapter in our volume
reflects and advances this new agenda. Duch (2007) develops a series of propositions
about how varying institutional contexts, coalition governments, and informational
settings will mediate between economic conditions and voters' appraisal of them. Factors that Duch suggests will influence economic voting include party-system size, the
size of government, coalition governments, trade openness, and the relative strength
of governing and opposition parties in the legislature.

At the same time that a few scholars studied how voters react to economic conditions, other researchers began exploring how politicians affect the economy (and
therefore voting decisions). After Nordhaus published a seminal paper in 1975 on
electoral business cycles, the scholarly literature has evolved in three (complementary) directions. A first set of studies has examined the impact of electoral cycles on
the economy. Scholars now tend to agree that the presence of politically induced economic cycles is rather irregular. But, of course, this opens up an important question
(particularly from the point of view of democratic representation): Why should voters accept policy manipulation and leave governments unpunished? In our volume,
James Alt and Shanna Rose (2007) argue that political business cycles must be understood as a particular instance of the broader phenomenon of political accountability
in democratic regimes. Political business cycles are not merely the result of a signaling
game in which politicians try to build their reputation as competent policy-makers.
Rather, the manipulation of economic policy and outcomes is an inevitable result
of voters' willingness to accept the transfer of some rents to politicians in exchange
for the election of competent policy-makers. A second set of studies has focused on
the effect that parties, mostly as congealed preferences, may have on macroeconomic
policies. Here scholars detect some, generally mild and mostly transitory, effect on
macroeconomic factors: Left-wing governments tend to get lower unemployment
than right-wing governments for a while, at the cost of permanently higher (and even
accelerating) inflation (Alesina et al. 1997). Yet these effects are mostly conditional on
the institutional setup (of central banks and wage bargaining institutions) in which
governments operate: This last insight has generated the third set of works in the
political economics literature (Hall and Franzese 1998; Alvarez, Garrett, and Lange
1991).

After the first papers and books on the topic were written within the framework
of modernization theory, welfare state scholars moved to assess the impact of power
politics (through parties and unions) on the construction of different types of welfare states. That class-based orientation, however, had limited validity beyond some
archetypical cases with high levels of union mobilization and strong left-wing parties.

Accordingly, researchers switched to explore the impact of cross-class coalitions—hence dwelling on the role of middle classes, agricultural producers, and employers. In doing so, they have shifted our attention from the pure redistributive components of the welfare state, which were the keystone of pure class-based, power politics accounts, to social policies as insurance tools that address the problem of risk and volatility in the economy. Related to this change in perspective, welfare state scholars have progressively spent more time mulling over the impact of the international economy on social policy. Two path-breaking pieces by Cameron and Katzenstein showing economic openness and the welfare state to be positively correlated have been followed by an exciting scholarly debate that has alternatively related the result to a governmental response to higher risk (due to more economic volatility in open economies), denied the correlation completely, or called for models that take openness and social policy as jointly determined. As Carnes and Mares (2007) discuss in the essay we edited, the welfare state literature has indeed traveled a long way from its inception. Yet it still has a very exciting research agenda ahead of it: First, it should become truly global and extend the insights (and problems) of a field built around Europe and North America to the whole world; second, it should offer analytical models that combine the different parameters of the successive generations of research in the area; third, it should take seriously the preferences and beliefs of voters across the world (and the cultural differences we observe about the proper role of the state); and, finally, it ought to integrate the consequences of welfare states (something about which we know much less than we should) with the forces that erect them.

Whether the transition to democracy in many developing countries in recent decades has meant a shift to accountable, effective government is a question that has concerned many scholars of comparative politics. Although both the number of researchers and the theories on the topic have multiplied considerably, we still know little about the relationship between growth and political regimes. We know that policy and performance vary considerably across democracies. Poor democracies show lower growth rates and worse public policies than rich democracies. In a nutshell, in spite of having formal mechanisms that should have increased political accountability and the welfare of the population in poor democracies, the provision of public goods and economic performance remain thoroughly deficient in those countries. In our edited volume, Keefer (2007) claims that, since the key parameters of democracy and redistribution (inequality and the struggle for political control between elites and nonelites) cannot explain that outcome (since low development and democratization are cast as contradictory), it must be political market imperfections that explain the failure of governments to deliver in democracies. In young, poor democracies, politicians lack the credibility to run campaigns that promise the delivery of universal benefits and public goods. Accordingly, they shift to building personal networks and delivering particular goods. This type of electoral connection, compounded by low levels of information among voters, who can scarcely monitor politicians, results in extreme levels of corruption and bad governance.

The promise of economic voting was that voters would be able to use economic conditions as a measure of the success or failure of governments; the anticipation of being thus measured would induce politicians to improve economic conditions on their watch. Economic voting would enforce accountability. Yet, as José María Maravall shows in his contribution to our edited volume, "in parliamentary democracies losses of office by prime ministers depend in one half of the cases on decisions by politicians, not by voters" (2007, 935). This fact would not be so dire if prime ministers were removed from office by colleagues who anticipated bad electoral outcomes—if, as Maravall puts it, "voters and politicians ... share the same criteria for punishing prime ministers." But they do not. Whereas prime ministers are more likely to be turned out by voters when economic times are bad, they are more likely to be turned out by their colleagues when economic times are good. Hence politicians who hold their comrades to account seem to practice a reverse kind of "economic voting." Maravall's chapter cautions us against excessive optimism regarding democracy, accountability, and economic voting. If (as economic voting implies) officeholders who produce bad economic outcomes will face the wrath of voters, why would they ever risk a costly transition to a liberalized economy? Whether asked in the context of post-Communist countries undertaking a "leap to the market" or in developing countries elsewhere in the world under pressure to move away from statist policies, the question has preoccupied comparative politics and political economy for more than a decade. Reviewing the literature on economic transitions in Eastern Europe, Timothy Frye identifies a number of factors, from the quality of domestic governance to membership in the European Union, that make governments more likely to undertake reforms and then stick with them (Frye 2007). Yet serious gaps remain in our understanding of the determinants of market reforms, including what role is played by institutional legacies from the past, and by contemporary social institutions—networks, business associations, reputational mechanisms—state institutions—courts, bureaucracies, legislatures—and the interaction of the two.

8 THEORY AND METHODS

The questions posed above and others that our contributors raise are too complex, and too important, to restrict ourselves to one or another methodology in our attempts to answer them. It is not that, methodologically speaking, "anything goes;" some research designs and methods for gathering and analyzing evidence are not fruitful. But the contributors to the *Oxford Handbook of Comparative Politics* explain the advantages and pitfalls of a wide range of techniques deployed by comparatists, from econometric analysis of cross-national data-sets and observational data to extended stints of fieldwork. They employ a variegated tool kit to make sense of political processes and outcomes.

The volume we edited includes several studies that take stock of what we would lose should the traditional comparative enterprise, with its emphasis on close knowledge of the language, history, and culture of a country or region, be abandoned altogether, and should the activity supporting that approach, the extended period of work in the field, be lost along with it. John Gerring (2007) contends that neither case studies nor large-n comparisons are an unalloyed good; rather, both entail trade-offs, and we are therefore well advised as a discipline to retain both approaches in our collective repertoire. Where case studies are good for building theory and developing insights, Gerring argues, large-n research is good for confirming or refuting theory. Where case studies offer internal validity, large-n studies offer external validity. Where case studies allow scholars to explore causal mechanisms, large-n comparisons allow them to identify causal effects. Elisabeth Wood's chapter alerts us to what we are in danger of losing should we as a profession give up on field research (Wood 2007). To the rhetorical question, "Why ever leave one's office?" she gives several answers. Interacting personally with subjects in their own setting may be the only way to get a handle on many crucial research questions, such as which of many potential political identities subjects embrace and what their self-defined interests are. Fieldwork is not without perils, Wood explains, both intellectual and personal. Interview subjects may be evasive and even strategically dissimulating; field researchers may have strong personal reactions, positive or negative, to their subjects, reactions that may then color their conclusions; and fieldwork is a lonely endeavor, with predictable highs and lows. Wood suggests strategies for dealing with these pitfalls. James Mahoney and Celso Villegas (2007) discuss another variant of qualitative research: comparative historical studies. The aims of this research differ from those of cross-national studies, they contend. Comparative historical scholars "ask questions about the causes of major outcomes in particular cases," and hence seek to explain "each and every case that falls within their argument's scope." By contrast, large-n researchers "are concerned with generalizing about average causal effects for large populations and ... do not ordinarily seek to explain specific outcomes in particular cases."

Robert Franzese's chapter defends, in turn, large-n, quantitative techniques against some of the critiques that other contributors level against them (Franzese 2007). Comparative political scientists, like empirically oriented sociologists and economists, are bedeviled by four problems: a trade-off between quantity and quality in the collection of data; multicausality; context-conditionality, that is, the fact all the effects of our variables are conditional on other variables; and endogeneity. Yet as Franzese argues, these obstacles, which are in fact inherent to our trade, should not lead us to dodge quantitative strategies of research. On the contrary, a simple back-of-the-envelope calculation shows that the plausible loss of precision involved in measuring large numbers of observations does not justify retreating to qualitative studies of a few cases—even if we attain very precise knowledge about small samples, they fail to yield robust inferences. Similarly, the presence of multiple and conditional causality cannot be solved easily by case studies (although good process tracing may alleviate these problems). Finally, qualitative case-study research does not necessarily escape problems of endogeneity. To move from correlational analysis to causal propositions, Franzese contends, we need to employ more sophisticated techniques, such as variable instrumentation, matching, or vector autoregression. But even these techniques are not sufficient. Here we would like to add that, influenced by a few macroeconomists and political economists, part of the discipline seems on the verge of uncritically embracing the use of instrumentation to deflect all the critiques that are leveraged against any work on the grounds that the latter suffer from endogeneity. It turns out that there are very few, if any, instruments that are truly exogenous—basically, geography. Their use has extraordinary theoretical implications that researchers have either hardly thought about (for example, that weather determines regime, in a sort of Montesquieuian manner) or simply dodge (when they posit that the instrument is simply a statistical artefact with no theoretical value on its own and then insist that it is the right one to substitute for the variable of interest). Thus, we want to stress with Franzese that only theory-building can truly help us in reducing the problem of endogenous causation.

Adam Przeworski (2007) offers a less optimistic perspective on observational research, large-n or otherwise. Observational studies, ones that do not (and cannot fully) ensure that the cases we compare are matched in all respects other than the "treatment," cannot deal adequately with problems of endogeneity. "We need to study the causes of effects," he writes, "as well as the effects of causes." Some covariates (traits a unit has prior to the application of a treatment) are unobserved. These unobserved covariates may determine both the likelihood of a unit's being subjected to the treatment and the likelihood of its evincing the effect. Because these covariates are unobserved, we cannot test the proposition that they, rather than the treatment or putative cause, are actually responsible for the effect.

Przeworski discusses traditional as well as more novel approaches to dealing with endogeneity, but his chapter leans toward pessimism. "To identify causal effects we need assumptions and some of these assumptions are untestable." His chapter will be must reading for comparatists as they assess the promise and limitations of observational versus experimental or quasi-experimental designs.

But perhaps the mood of the chapter is more pessimistic than it need be. Theory should help us distinguish cases in which endogeneity is plausibly present from ones in which it is not. One way of reading Przeworski's chapter is that a crucial research task is to shift key covariates from the unobserved to the observed category. This task is implied by a hypothetical example that Przeworski offers. A researcher wishes to assess the impact of governing regime on economic growth. Future leaders of some countries study at universities where they become pro-democratic and learn how to manage economies, whereas others study at universities that make them pro-dictatorial and teach them nothing about economic management. Both kinds return home to become leaders and govern their societies and economies in the manner consistent with their training. It therefore appears that democracy produces economic growth. The training of leaders is a variable that we cannot observe systematically, in Przeworski's view. But there is a difference between unobserved and unobser*vable*. It is not obvious to us why this variable could never be systematically observed, should our theory—and, perhaps, our close, case-study-informed knowledge—tell us that we should worry about it.

Whether one studies a large or small number of cases, and whether one employs econometrics or other techniques, Robert Bates's chapter in the *Oxford Handbook of Comparative Politics* argues that one should do theoretically sophisticated work informed by game theory (Bates 2007). Indeed, the use of game-theoretical models, of varying degrees of formalization, is a strong recent trend in comparative politics. Illustrating his methodological claims with his recent research on the politics of coffee production and commercialization, Bates offers a comprehensive strategy for comparative study. The first step of research is apprehension: a detailed study and understanding of a particular time and place. *Verstehen* is then followed by explanation: The researcher apportions the things she knows "between causes or consequences" and attempts to develop "lines of logic to link them." In Bates's view, the explanatory drive should begin with the assumption (or principle) of rationality and use game theory to impose a structure on the phenomena we observe. The structure of the game allows us to push from the particular to the construction of broader theories, themselves susceptible of validation. The construction of theoretical explanations must then be subject to the test of confirmation: This implies progressively moving from small-n comparisons to much larger data-sets in which researchers can evaluate their theories against a broad set of alternatives and controls.

An analysis of the methodological foundations of contemporary political research would be incomplete without an exploration of the role of rationalist assumptions in the discipline. Eleanor Ostrom (2007) takes as her point of departure the proposition that "the theory of collective action is *the* central subject of political science" and that the problem of collective action is rooted in a social dilemma (or, in game theory terms, a prisoner's dilemma) in which, as is well known, rational individuals in pursuit of their optimal outcome may end up not cooperating even if it was in their interest to do so. Ostrom assesses the first generation of studies of collective action, which stress the structural conditions (number of players, type of benefits, heterogeneity of players, the degree of communication among them, and the iteration of games) that may increase the likelihood of achieving cooperation. She finds these studies wanting. Ostrom recognizes that the rationalist model only explains part of human behavior. Hence she calls for a shift toward a theory of boundedly rational, norm-based human behavior. Instead of positing a rationalistic individual, we should consider agents who are inherently living in a situation of informational uncertainty and who structure their actions, adopt their norms of behavior, and acquire their knowledge from the social and institutional context in which they live. In this broader theory of human behavior, humans are "adaptive creatures who attempt to do as well as they can given the constraints of the situations in which they find themselves (or the ones that they seek out)." They "learn norms, heuristics, and full analytical strategies from one another, from feedback from the world, and from their own capacity to engage in self-reflection. They are capable of designing new tools—including institutions—that can change the structure of the worlds they face for good or evil purposes. They adopt both short-term and long-term perspectives dependent on the structure of opportunities they face." All in all, Ostrom's approach encompasses a broader range of types of human action—from individuals who are fully "rational" (normally in those environments in which they live in repetitive, highly competitive situations) to "sociological agents" (whose behavior simply follows shared social norms). To some extent, the discipline seems to come full circle with this contribution: moving from cultural approaches under the aegis of modernization theory to the rationalist assumptions of institutionalist scholars and now back to a richer (perhaps looser but certainly closer to the way our classical thinkers thought about human nature) understanding of human agency. This journey has not been useless. On the contrary, as we traveled from one point to the other we have learned that a good theory of politics must be based on solid microfoundations; that is, on a plausible characterization of the interests, beliefs, and actions of individuals.

9 LOOKING AHEAD

When we pause to take stock of the evolution of empirical political science in the last three decades, we think we should be pleased with the progress we have made as a community of scholars. The discipline has moved forward substantially in modeling certain political outcomes. We can offer the first inklings of theories of state formation and democratization. We are in a position to understand how power is sustained and exercised in dictatorships. We have fruitful models of the impact of institutions in preference aggregation and electoral behavior. We are beginning to tackle with some analytical precision the problem of political accountability. As we argued at the beginning of the chapter, we think this progress has been brought about by three conceptual engines: a renewed commitment to solve the central theoretical problems already debated by our forefathers; the decision to harness our empirical work (be it cases or cross-country regressions) to standard scientific practices; and a commitment to build "transparent" theoretical propositions; that is, propositions based on assumptions which can in turn be debated and from which we can derive results in a logical way.

There may be a hundred different things that need to be changed, improved, or altogether invented in our discipline. We will only stress one here. Many of our most successful models are simply equilibria. The gains from that type of methodological choice are clear. But we still know little about the ways in which political institutions, social practices, norms, and arrays of political interests originate and collapse. History was important in the broad, sociological literature written a few decades ago. Yet the way in which it was tackled was messy or unsystematic. Institutionalists altogether abandoned historical work. We think that, with the new tools we have in our hands, the right time has come to deal with that question again. To some extent, given the problems of endogenous causation we are confronted with, engaging in this type of work is now becoming inevitable.

REFERENCES

ALESINA, A. et al. 1997. *Political Cycles and the Macroeconomy*. Cambridge, Mass.: MIT Press.

ALT, J. E. and ROSE, S. S. 2007. Context-conditional political budget cycles. Ch. 34 in Boix and Stokes 2007.

ALVAREZ, R. M., GARRETT, G., and LANGE, P. 1991. Government partisanship, labor organization and macroeconomic performance, 1967–1984. *American Political Science Review*, 85: 539–56.

ANDERSON, B. 1983. *Imagined Communities: Reflections on the Origin and Spread of Nationalism*. New York: Verso.

BATES, R. H. 2007. From case studies to social science: a strategy for political research. Ch. 7 in Boix and Stokes 2007.

BOIX, C. 1999. Setting the rules of the game: the choice of electoral systems in advanced democracies. *American Political Science Review*, 93: 609–24.

—— 2003. *Democracy and Redistribution*. New York: Cambridge University Press.

—— 2007. The emergence of parties and party systems. Ch. 21 in Boix and Stokes 2007.

—— 2009. Some thoughts on the origins of inequality. Unpublished manuscript, Princeton University.

—— and STOKES, S. 2003. Endogenous democratization. *World Politics*, 55: 517–49.

———— (eds.) 2007. *Oxford Handbook of Comparative Politics*. New York: Oxford University Press.

CARNES, M. and MARES, I. 2007. The welfare state in global perspective. Ch. 35 in Boix and Stokes 2007.

COLLIER, P. and HOEFFLER, A. 2004. Greed and grievance in civil war. *Oxford Economic Papers*, 56: 563–95.

CONNOR, W. 1994. *Ethnonationalism: The Quest for Understanding*. Princeton, NJ: Princeton University Press.

COX, G. 1997. *Making Votes Count*. New York: Cambridge University Press.

DUCH, R. 2007. Comparative studies of the economy and the vote. Ch. 33 in Boix and Stokes 2007.

DUVERGER, M. 1954. *Political Parties*. New York: Wiley.

FEARON, J. and LAITIN, D. 2003. Ethnicity, insurgency, and civil war. *American Political Science Review*, 97: 75–90.

FEREJOHN, J., ROSENBLUTH, F., and SHIPAN, C. 2007. Comparative judicial politics. Ch. 30 in Boix and Stokes 2007.

FRANZESE, R. J. 2007. Multicausality, context-conditionality, and endogeneity. Ch. 2 in Boix and Stokes 2007.

FRYE, T. 2007. Economic transformation and comparative politics. Ch. 38 in Boix and Stokes 2007.

GANDHI, J. 2008. *Political Institutions under Dictatorship*. New York: Cambridge University Press.

GEDDES, B. 1999. Authoritarian breakdown: empirical test of a game theoretic argument. Unpublished manuscript, UCLA.

—— 2007. What causes democratization? Ch. 14 in Boix and Stokes 2007.

GELLNER, E. 1983. *Nations and Nationalism*. Ithaca, NY: Cornell University Press.

GERRING, J. 2007. The case study: what it is and what it does. Ch. 4 in Boix and Stokes 2007.

GREENFELD, L. and EASTWOOD, J. 2007. National identity. Ch. 11 in Boix and Stokes 2007.

GURR, T. 1973. The revolution–social change nexus. *Comparative Politics*, 5: 359–92.

HALL, P. A. and FRANZESE, R. J., JR. 1998. Mixed signals: central bank independence, coordinated wage bargaining, and European Monetary Union, *International Organization*, 52: 505–35.

HARDIN, R. 2007. Compliance, consent, and legitimacy. Ch. 10 in Boix and Stokes 2007.

HELMKE, G. 2001. The logic of strategic defection: judicial decision-making in Argentina under dictatorship and democracy. *American Political Science Review*, 96: 291–330.

—— 2005. *Courts under Constraints: Judges, Generals, and Presidents in Argentina*. Cambridge: Cambridge University Press.

HOROWITZ, D. L. 1985. *Ethnic Groups in Conflict*. Los Angeles: University of California Press.

HUNTINGTON, S. 1968. *Political Order in Changing Societies*. New Haven, Conn.: Yale University Press.

KALYVAS, S. 2006. *The Logic of Violence in Civil War*. New York: Cambridge University Press.

—— 2007. Civil wars. Ch. 18 in Boix and Stokes 2007.

KEEFER, P. 2007. The poor performance of poor democracies Ch. 36 in Boix and Stokes 2007.

LICHBACH, M. I. and DEVRIES, H. G. E. 2007. Mechanisms of globalized protest movements. Ch. 20 in Boix and Stokes 2007.

LIPSET, S. M. 1959. Some social requisites of democracy: economic development and political legitimacy. *American Political Science Review*, 53: 69–105.

—— and ROKKAN, S. 1967. Cleavage structures, party systems, and voter alignments. Pp. 1–56 in *Party Systems and Voter Alignments*, ed. S. M. Lipset and S. Rokkan. New York: Free Press.

MAGALONE, B. 2006. *Voting for Autocracy: Hegemonic Party Survival and its Demise in Mexico*. New York: Cambridge University Press.

MAHONEY, J. and VILLEGAS, C. M. 2007. Historical enquiry and comparative politics. Ch. 3 in Boix and Stokes 2007.

MARAVALL, J. M. 2007. Accountability and the survival of governments. Ch. 37 in Boix and Stokes 2007.

MIDLARSKY, M. I. 1988. Rulers and the ruled: patterned inequality and the onset of mass political violence. *American Political Science Review*, 82: 491–509.

MOORE, B. 1966. *Social Origins of Dictatorship and Democracy: Lord and Peasant in the Making of the Modern World*. Boston: Beacon.

MULLER, E. N. 1985. Income inequality, regime repressiveness, and political violence. *American Sociological Review*, 50: 47–61.

NORDHAUS, W. 1975. The political business cycle. *Review of Economic Studies*, 42: 169–90.

NORRIS, P. 2007. Political activism: new challenges, new opportunities. Ch. 26 in Boix and Stokes 2007.

O'DONNELL, G., SCHMITTER, P. C., and WHITEHEAD, L. (eds.) 1986. *Transitions from Authoritarian Rule: Comparative Perspectives*, Volume 4: *Tentative Conclusions and Uncertain Democracies*. Baltimore: Johns Hopkins University Press.

OSTROM, E. 2007. Collective action theory. Ch. 8 in Boix and Stokes 2007.

PAIGE, J. M. 1975. *Agrarian Revolution*. New York: Free Press.

POWELL, G. B. 2007. Aggregating and representing political preferences. Ch. 27 in Boix and Stokes 2007.

PRZEWORSKI, A. 1990. *Democracy and the Market*. New York: Cambridge University Press.

—— 2007. Is the science of comparative politics possible? Ch. 6 in Boix and Stokes 2007.

—— and LIMONGI, F. 1997. Modernization: theories and facts. *World Politics*, 49: 155–83.

RUSSETT, B. M. 1964. Inequality and instability. *World Politics*, 16: 442–54.

SABETTI, F. 2007. Democracy and civic culture. Ch. 15 in Boix and Stokes 2007.

SAMUELS, D. 2007. Separation of powers. Ch. 27 in Boix and Stokes 2007.

STROM, K., and NYBLADE, B. 2007. Coalition theory and government formation. Ch. 32 in Boix and Stokes 2007.

SVOLIK, M. 2007. Power-sharing and leadership dynamics in authoritarian regimes. Unpublished manuscript, UIUC.

TAAGAPERA, R. 2007. Electoral systems. Ch. 28 in Boix and Stokes 2007.

TARROW, S. and TILLY, C. 2007. Contentious politics and social movements. Ch. 19 in Boix and Stokes 2007.

WINTROBE, R. 2007. Dictatorship: analytical approaches. Ch. 16 in Boix and Stokes 2007.

WOLF, E. R. 1969. *Peasant Wars in the Twentieth Century*. New York: Harper and Row.

WOOD, E. J. 2007. Field research. Ch. 5 in Boix and Stokes 2007.

WREN, A. and McELWAIN, K. M. 2007. Voters and parties. Ch. 23 in Boix and Stokes 2007.

WRIGHT, J. 2008. Do authoritarian institutions constrain? How legislatures impact economic growth and foreign aid effectiveness. *American Journal of Political Science*, 52.

CHAPTER 28

WAR, TRADE, AND STATE FORMATION

HENDRIK SPRUYT

1 INTRODUCTION

ONLY a few decades ago the study of the state lay moribund in political science, banished to the realm of historical scholarship. Behavioralism, methodologically individualist in its epistemological approach, sought to understand the political process by micro-level analyses. Pluralism in turn extolled the virtues of an American polity in which social actors rather than governmental action accounted for political outcomes.

In reaction to those dominant perspectives some scholars called for a renewed interest in the role of the state and state formation (Nettl 1968; Tilly 1975). Political science, and particularly the subfields of comparative politics and international relations, embraced those calls with vigor. The scholarship examining the causal connections between state formation, regime type, and state failure is today so vast that any discussion must, by necessity, constitute a bird's eye overview.

The scholarship on state formation has concentrated on several key features of the modern state, particularly its immense capacity to mobilize and tap into societal resources, and its ability to wield coercive force. In classic Weberian parlance, the state is that "compulsory political organization" which controls a territorial area in which "the administrative staff successfully upholds the claim to the monopoly of the legitimate use of physical force in the enforcement of its order," (Weber 1978, i. 54). Inevitably accounts stressing this feature of modern statehood focus on the importance of warfare and the monopolization of warfare by the state.

The Weberian definition also draws attention to related but distinct dimensions of state formation: the formation of a rationalized-legal administration; the rise of extractive capacity by a central government; and the legitimacy of such authority. The modern state transformed personalistic rule and ad hoc justification of authority to depersonalized, public governance based on the rule of law (Collins 1986). With this transformation came the claim that government could, far more intrusively than pre-modern governments, regulate many aspects of social and political life. Its ability to mobilize populations for economic growth and warfare went thus hand in hand with its ability to raise revenue (Levi 1988; Webber and Wildavsky 1986). Logically, scholars who adopt those economic and administrative foci are particularly interested in tracing how the institutional structures of the state were affected by economic changes, such as trade and the advent of capitalism, and how the state in turn influenced class structure, capitalist development, and the provision of public goods (North 1981).

The formation of the modern state inevitably involved the creation of new legitimizations of authority and power. Nascent political elites in early states either displaced or sought to control kinship structures, ethnic ties, and religious authority and to forge a new identification with the authority of the state and the holder of public office (Anderson 1991). Modern states recast and channeled individual loyalties to the extent that modern states could affect every level of individual and social life—unlike the capstone governments of older polities which extended over vast geographic areas without affecting their societies in any great measure (Gellner 1983).

Besides an exponential increase in governmental capacity, modern states differ from precursors in another important way: modern state authority is defined uniquely as territorial rule with fixed geographic boundaries. Thus, at the crossroads of the study of international relations and comparative politics, another body of literature has focused particularly on the territorial aspects of modern authority (Kratochwil 1986; Ruggie 1986; Spruyt 1994). How did the notion of territorial, sovereign states displace authority structures that were universalistic in ambition (empires), based on theocratic justification (as the aspirations to forge a unified Christian Europe), or based purely on market exchanges (as trading city-networks)? This territorial aspect of statehood arguably preceded the other characteristics associated with modern states, as rational administration, fiscal ability, and national loyalty. Indeed, from purely a territorial perspective, states preceded nations and high-capacity modern administrations by several centuries.[1]

Inevitably the study of any one of these features of state formation will implicate other aspects. Monopolization of violence can only occur if governments are deemed at least partially legitimate. Moreover, the successful monopolization of violence itself will correlate with the ability of central governments to establish some modicum of efficient administration as well as the ability to raise revenue. Thus, while each aspect of statehood may be studied in its individual form as an ideal type,

---

[1]   The territorial aspect of statehood is thus closely connected to the notion of sovereignty. See Benn (1967); Hinsley (1986). For a recent critique that the importance of sovereignty has been overstated, see Krasner (1999).

any analysis must involve other dimensions of state formation. As a consequence, regardless of the particular feature of the state that one wishes to study, causal explanations will inevitably have to account for the specific dynamics of warfare, economic transformation wrought by trade and finance, and ideological aspects of state legitimization.

The particular modalities of state formation, in terms of its twin features (governmental capacity and territorial definition), will determine the type of regime. Some governments will try to mobilize their societies by contractual agreement or vest their claims to legitimacy in popular approval. Others might seek alternative modes of mobilization and support.

This essay makes several claims. First, a serious student of state formation, regardless of the geographic area of interest, should take European state formation as its referent point.[2] It is that particular conceptualization of authority that succeeded in displacing rival forms of political organization in Europe and which was then transplanted globally (Giddens 1987; Strang 1991). Moreover, methodologically, such a comparative study serves to demonstrate maximum contrast in values on the causal variable (van Evera 1997). State formation outside of Europe was greatly affected by external pressure, a vastly different international milieu (both in term of security and economics), and proceeded in a highly compressed chronology. Highlighting the key causal dynamics in the European case will thus serve to demonstrate how the external and the internal aspects of state development interacted in a vastly different manner outside of Europe.

Second, the study of European state formation serves as a useful template to generate causal hypotheses regarding regime development in general. Understanding how European state formation influenced the propensity for absolutist or constitutionalist forms of government will shed light on regime transitions elsewhere, particularly given the variation in historical trajectories. The variation on the independent variables, obvious when contrasting European and non-European cases, allows us to deductively generate rival expectations about state formation and regime type. For example, Lisa Anderson (1987) has taken such an approach to study state formation in North Africa and the Middle East. Victoria Tin-bor Hui has compared early imperial Chinese state formation with the European experience (2004).

Jeffrey Herbst (2000) is undoubtedly correct in asserting that the literature on state formation has focused excessively on the European experience. But even he bases his account of state construction in Africa by juxtaposing the African experience with European trajectories, and by utilizing theories of European state formation, such as those of Charles Tilly.

This chapter thus starts with a brief account of European state formation. It distinguishes the generative factors behind the transformation of late medieval forms of government to new types of authority from the selection and convergence among these distinct types.[3]

---

[2] Two of the best overviews of European state formation are Badie and Birnbaum (1983) and Poggi (1978). For a more extensive discussion of state formation and regime type, see Bendix (1978).

[3] For a more extensive discussion, see Spruyt (1994); Tilly (1990).

The essay then turns to a discussion of how the process of state formation had effects on the type of regime that emerged in various states. That is, while the next section of this chapter provides for an overview of how sovereignty and territoriality were established as key features of authority in Europe, the following section discusses how state formation implicated the rise of absolutist or constitutionalist forms of rule. The fourth part highlights how accounts of state formation in Europe currently inform the study of state development in newly emerging countries, and identifies particularly intriguing avenues for further enquiry. The manner in which non-European regions diverged from the European experience profoundly affects their contemporary status as effective or failed states, and the likelihood that democratic transitions will be successful.

2 CAUSAL DYNAMICS OF STATE FORMATION

2.1 War Making as Generative Cause

Early state formation in Europe correlated with changes in the frequency and modes of warfare (Bean 1973; Tilly 1975). Starting roughly in the early fourteenth century, military developments began to disadvantage the mounted cavalry and challenge the social and political organization of feudalism.

First, massed infantry (at battles such as Courtrai) and English longbow archers (as at Agincourt) booked resounding successes against heavy cavalry. Thus, relatively unskilled troops of socially low position could, with the right organization and if sufficient in number, defeat more highly skilled knights. The result was a shift to the greater use of infantry soldiers which individually were less expensive to equip than mounted knights. By some calculations, the costs of equipping a knight with armor and horse required roughly the labor of 500 commoners. However, given the larger aggregations of fighting men that were required for successful combat, the new military style required overall greater outlay. Whereas armed feudal service was based on personal ties (resembling a form of artificial kinship) and for a relatively short period of time (forty days per year was the norm), the emerging style of warfare called for larger numbers of paid troops. At the end of the Hundred Years War, the French thus moved towards a standing army.

The successful deployment of massed infantry was followed by the introduction of gunpowder. Given the rudimentary arms of the time, its effects were first felt with the introduction of siege artillery (McNeill 1982). Even in its nascent form such artillery proved capable of destroying the most advanced fortifications of that time, as demonstrated by the Ottoman conquest of Constantinople in 1453. Advances in artillery thus sparked a defensive reaction towards building ever more advanced and thus more expensive fortifications, employing the *trace italienne*.

All these developments in military technology in turn necessitated greater centralization, administration, and central revenue.[4] Such revenue could be gained by internal mobilization and taxation. Alternatively, rulers could pursue territorial conquest and geographic efficiencies of scale.

Military developments thus begot institutional innovation. Institutional innovation in turn corresponded with greater effectiveness on the battlefield and the opportunity to expand one's realm. This in turn ratcheted up competition among rival lords and kings making the successful conduct of war the key feature of early modern administration. Between 1500 and 1700 many of the great powers were continuously at war or on a war footing (Parker 1979, 1988).

Charles Tilly (1985) has compared this process of state formation to a protection racket. While various lords competed for the loyalty (and thus revenue) of their subjects, kings tended to be the most efficient providers of protection and thus displaced lesser lords, leading to the Weberian characterization of the state as having a monopoly on violence. Tilly's account thus melds a description of a broad exogenous change—the change in the nature of warfare—with a contractarian explanation for the rise of central authority. Central authority provided protection in exchange for revenue.

Tilly is no doubt correct in arguing that early states devoted most of their revenue to waging war (see, for example, Brewer 1989). Moreover, his account is particularly appealing in providing a methodological individualist explanation, a micro-level account, for a larger structural, macro-level phenomenon. Many other accounts working in a similar vein have contented themselves with descriptive narratives chronicling the evolutionary progress to the modern state. Not only does Tilly's account provide for a plausible explanation it also logically entails that the modalities of contracting between subjects and ruling elites should lead to different forms of authority, which Tilly rightly noted in his earlier work (1975) and for which he tried to account in his later book (1990).

Yet several problems remain with accounts stressing solely the importance of warfare. Some historians, particularly those associated with the Princeton school pioneered by Joseph Strayer, locate institutional innovation before the great revolutions in military technology (Strayer 1965). Norman administrative structures and French royal practices met with considerable success during the thirteenth century. Clearly the subsequent process of state development had many more centuries to come, but it does raise questions regarding military changes as the primary or only dynamic.

Second, the contractarian account does not fully convince. Tilly argues that kings were the most efficient providers of protection, but if subjects (consumers) were indifferent between the providers for protection, one would expect many warlords to have been able to rise to kingship given the weak position of kings. (If kings were already more powerful than the other lords, the explanation would be tautological

[4] The historical record is clear on this point; for a brief synopsis, Ames and Rapp (1977); Bean (1973). Rasler and Thompson (1985) demonstrate how war making led to state expansion in the modern era.

and insufficient.) Yet historically this seldom occurred. Dynastic lineages were quite durable. In other words it leaves the attraction of the king as contractarian party to provide protection or other public goods unexplained.

Finally, Tilly alternates between an explanation based on relative factor endowments and a coalitional explanation of political strategy. Polities endowed with capital (urban centers) forced political elites to enter into contractual arrangements with the cities. Towns were not inclined to surrender their liberties and revenues to authoritarian rule, and thus capital-intensive mobilization occurred in north-western Europe and northern Italy. Tilly then classifies mobilization in areas lacking rich capital endowments as coercive. In so doing he assumes that areas rich in either labor or land would both show a similar political strategy of mobilization along authoritarian lines. Empirically, it might be the case that aspiring political elites forged alliances with landowning aristocracy, as happened with the Prussian Second Serfdom (Rosenberg 1943–4). Theoretically, however, one need not a priori preclude an elite–peasant bargain against landowners if labor were abundant. Indeed, to some extent North and Thomas's (1973) and North's (1981) account of the decline of the feudal order is based on a shift in relative factor endowments diminishing the ability of landowners to coerce the peasantry. Put another way, concluding that capital abundance might correlate with constitutionalist government, does not logically require one to conclude that capital scarcity must correlate with coercive forms of rule.

2.2 Economic Transitions and the Rise of Trade as a Generative Factor

A rival account acknowledges the changes in the military milieu of the late medieval period, but stresses instead the economic changes that marked the end of feudalism and the gradual emergence of politically consolidated states and incipient capitalism. These economic changes pre-dated the military revolution of this period, and made possible the subsequent emergence of large-scale mercenary warfare. This economic perspective on the rise of the territorial state can in turn be distinguished in neo-Marxist views and neo-institutionalist analyses.

Neo-Marxists and neo-institutionalists are in broad agreement with regard to economic change being the causal factor behind the demise of personalized feudalistic rule. From the eleventh century on, a variety of factors eroded the economic foundations of feudalism and precipitated the beginning of early (merchant) capitalism. They differ, however, in the role played by the state in this process.

(Neo-)Marxist analyses and neo-institutionalists concur on the rise of trade as a harbinger of early capitalism (Anderson 1974a, 1974b; North and Thomas 1973).[5] Urbanization and the growth of trade led to the emergence of a social group that was politically and socially disadvantaged in the feudal structure. These burghers

---

[5] In historical scholarship, this argument was popularized as the Pirenne thesis (Pirenne 1952).

(burg dwellers, from which bourgeoisie) made their living by production and trade and thus stood outside the traditional barter, personalized exchange that formed the basis of the feudal economy. Indeed, burghers were politically free from servile bonds unlike the peasantry (city air makes free, as the medieval adage had it).

In the neo-Marxist account, however, the state performed the role of arbiter of class tensions. The advent of early capitalism thus dovetailed and necessitated the growth of a state apparatus. A royal–urban alliance, and in some cases a royal–peasant alliance, brought the feudal, decentralized order to its end.

Neo-institutionalists recognize the role of urbanization and the emergence of new economic groups that opposed the existing feudal order. However, the state does not act in a predatory fashion, as an agent of the ruling class (the emerging bourgeoisie), but emerges out of contracts between ruler and subject, and the ruler's desire for personal gain, by maximizing societal welfare.

Douglas North and Robert Thomas (1973) pioneered such explanations, suggesting that changes in weather, agricultural innovations (such as crop rotation and the deep plough), increased trade flows, diminished invasions, and demographic shifts altered the relative power of social groups possessing land, labor, and capital. These environmental shifts thus transformed the balance between the factors of production. The resulting change in relative bargaining power of the various factors in turn influenced political outcomes. Thus, the decline of population following the plague of 1353 (and there were numerous outbreaks of the disease) created a supply shortage of labor, enhancing the bargaining position of the peasantry vis-à-vis the possessors of land (the aristocracy). This eroded the feudal economy based on indentured agriculture.

A more fully articulated neo-institutionalist perspective emerges in North's later work (1981, 1990). This perspective takes an explicitly contractarian approach. The ruler exchanges protection for revenue. Efficiencies of scale in the provision of this public good lead to consolidation in one provider. Secondly, the ruler acting in this monopoly position allocates property rights to maximize the revenue of society at large, and, by taxation, thus yield more revenue for the individual ruler. However, the ruler's monopoly is not absolute. Rivals within the state might emerge as more efficient (or less extortionist) providers of public goods. Or rival states might provide exit options to the constituents (North 1981, 23).

Neo-institutional explanations thus emphasize a potential communality of economic interests between the monarchy and the emerging mercantile groups. As far as military protection goes mercantile groups would be indifferent between who provided protection. However, kings were more attractive as contracting parties than local feudal lords, given efficiencies of scale. Moreover, mercantile groups favored greater standardization of weights, measures, and coinage; the weakening of feudal obligations; clearer definition of property rights; and written legal codes. Given royal interests in maximizing revenue, such standardization, monetization of the economy, and legalization of royal rule (by the introduction of Roman law) were as dear to the king as they were to urban interests.

Neo-institutional accounts, therefore, share the neo-Marxist interpretation of a royal–urban alliance as a key explanation for the emergence of more rationalized, centralized, and territorially defined rule. It differs in placing less emphasis on the state as a coercive mechanism to remedy the inefficiencies of feudalism and repress the labor force. It stresses instead the role of the state as an institutional solution to the transaction and informational hurdles that hampered the feudal economy.

2.3 The State as Ideological Revolution

A third account of early state formation places particular emphasis on ideology. The move towards depersonalized, rationalized administration could only occur against the backdrop of a dramatic shift in collective beliefs.[6] On the one hand this entailed the emergence of a sense of individuality. Thus Macfarlane's (1978) observation regarding the emergence of individualism in twelfth-century England has an important bearing on the rise of early capitalism (and the early state). John Ruggie (1993) has similarly noted the changes in perception giving rise to a sense of mechanical, ordered structure. Changes in artistic perception coincided with, and were indicative of, changes in perceptions of right political order—an order which could emerge by rational design rather than religious mandate. Rather than presuppose a contractarian environment, an examination of ideological shifts clarifies the conditions under which humans came to understand themselves as atomistic individuals (rather than members of larger social entities), and how they came to see themselves as contracting parties of ruler and subject (rather than being part of some preordained order).[7] What methodological individualist accounts take as a given (in either seeing war or economic changes as altering the terms of the contract between rulers and ruled), ideological reflections pry apart and problematize.

The emergence of the early state, consequently, meant that the feudal collective consciousness was abandoned. In classical feudal theory, political order was modeled on that of heaven (Duby 1978). As such, a tri-level political order was the most desirable. At the pinnacle stood "those that prayed." Those that fought, the military aristocracy, should serve those that prayed. Peasants and commoners, "those who worked," in turn were inferior to both of the other castes and occupied the lowest rung. The notion of territorial authority based on contract challenged such concepts of preordained station.

The emergence of individual states also challenged the notion that Europe, being the domain of Christianity, should constitute one political community. In the feudal

---

[6] See, for example, Corrigan and Sayer (1991). Pizzorno (1987) suggests the state assumed many of the ideological roles claimed by institutionalized religion.

[7] Neo-institutionalists as North (1981, 45–58) also draw attention to ideology, but do so largely from a functional perspective, seeing ideology as a device to overcome collective action problems, rather than as creating preferences and identity.

perspective the pope as its leader would be served by the vicar of God, the emperor, who formed the sword and right hand of the spiritual elements.

In practice, however, the centuries-long conflict between emperor and pope, and the subsequent victory of monarchy over either of those two conceptualizations, meant that the religious views of a theocratic imperial Europe came to naught. The territorial conceptualization of authority won out over alternative logics of legitimization. States emerged out of the stalemate for European dominance of emperors and popes.[8]

3 DIVERSITY AND SELECTION

Any generative account of institutional change runs the risk of functionally linking, in a post hoc manner, causal explanations of institutional demise to the specific institutional outcome that is the focus of that particular scholar. But in liminal moments when old orders are shattered and space opens up for institutional innovation, agents rarely agree on the type of innovation they should bring about. Individuals have diverse preferences. They might be risk averse, or ignorant of the long-term consequences of their choices. Initial choices might have unintended consequences in the long run (Thelen 2004).

Thus generative accounts of state formation require some account for selection among the diversity of agent choices. At the sunset of the feudal order various alternative forms for structuring political authority were possible, as Tilly (1975) noted. The imperial claim to reconstitute a hierarchically governed European space surfaced in various guises. German emperors claimed to revive the Roman Empire. Later, Spanish rulers sought to expand their authority under the imperial banner with similar theocratic ambitions. Such theocratic claims were only gradually set aside by agreements as the Treaty of Augsburg (1555) and the Peace of Westphalia (1648).

Additionally, city-states, city-leagues, loose confederal entities (such as the Swiss federation), and odd hybrid states (such as the Dutch United Provinces) held center stage throughout late medieval and early modern European history.[9] Such authorities often held competing claims to rule over a given geographic space. For example, many

---

[8] Not coincidentally the Investiture Struggle empowered territorial kings (Tierney 1964).

[9] In an interesting article Knudsen and Rothstein 1994 argued that Denmark and Scandinavia differed from both the "Western" mode of state formation (based on strong urban centers and free peasantry) and the "Eastern" mode (based on weak towns and serfdom), presenting us with two hybrid types. In a bold claim Putnam (1983) argues that the medieval development of Italian city-states explains many of the institutional features of the Italian landscape today, suggesting that scrutiny of past state development sheds light on the present.

cities throughout northern Europe held dual allegiance to the territorial lord in their vicinity and the city-leagues of which they were members.

The explanations for the convergence to a system of sovereign entities, which claimed exclusive jurisdiction within recognized borders, tend to parallel the analytic approaches of the end of feudalism. Accounts focusing on changes in military affairs tend to emphasize selection. Neo-institutionalists in turn stress the efficiency of institutional design, combining selection mechanisms with individual preferences. Those stressing ideational changes draw attention to sovereignty as a social construct.

Thus, accounts that stress the importance of war emphasize selective mechanisms in Darwinian terms. Indeed, some of these views lean towards strong-form selection. Given a particular environment selection will be harsh, trending towards convergence on a singular surviving type. Sovereign, territorially defined organization with strong central administrations thus defeated and eliminated less efficient and less effective forms of governance. In the study of international relations, realists tend to favor this view of environmental selection, although they may blend such agent-less accounts with intentional mimicry of successful practice and socialization (Waltz 1979).

Strong-form selection, however, is a rarity even in biology. Odd types and less efficient designs often continue to exist in niches. So too, multiple institutional forms often exist side by side in the political realm. Path dependence, entrenched interests, and jury-rigged institutional solutions that agents devise in the face of challenges to the existing institutions, all militate against simple selective mechanisms.

Consequently, neo-institutionalists often blend selective mechanisms and deliberate agent choices. Rather than simply note the competitive advantage of states they ask why such advantages existed in the first place, or why certain polities did not opt for more efficient arrangements, as, for example, by changing manifestly inefficient property rights. Neo-institutional explanations thus account for the advantage of sovereign territorial organization in terms of its success in reducing transaction and information costs, and the provision of public goods in general (North 1981; Spruyt 1994). The system of sovereign, territorial states did not emerge simply by blind selection but equally by individual choices. Rulers were cognizant of their limitations to rule, given exit options for their constituents. Internal and external rivalry also led rulers to opt for more efficient designs. They made conscious decisions to delimit spheres of jurisdiction in domestic and international realms.

Finally, perspectives that emphasize sovereign territoriality as an ideational construct tend to sociological and anthropological explanations for why this form displaced rival types. Sociological institutionalism, in particular, sees the convergence toward the state as a process of mimicry and social imprinting (Thomas et al. 1987). Polities tend to interact with like types of government. At the same time newly emerging polities will style themselves self-consciously to conform to the existing "organizational field" (DiMaggio and Powell 1983). The existing set of practices is taken for granted by those wishing to be deemed legitimate states.

4 STATE FORMATION AND REGIME TYPE

Competition, individual strategic choice and mimicry affected not only the displacement of non-territorial forms of rule, but they also had a direct bearing on the types of regimes that emerged. Variation in intensity and modes of warfare, as well as the differential impact of trade and modernization, affected the development of absolutism and constitutionalism.

As Otto Hintze (1975) noted, frequent and intense warfare will tend to correlate with authoritarian government. The need to mobilize resources by the state will lead to a high degree of government intervention in society. Frequent geopolitical conflict will require manpower and financial resources in order to secure the survival of the polity. Rather than rely on militias and incidental service, the state will prefer to develop standing military forces.

Those military forces, however, can serve a dual purpose. Not only will they serve to protect the state from external enemies, they can be used to repress internal dissent. Thus, frequent and intense warfare will give birth to a garrison state, justified by external threats, but equally capable of stifling constitutionalist movements. The Prussian Great Elector and the Junkers forged their alliance in reaction to the mortal threats posed by Sweden, Austria, and Russia, but equally used this coalition to establish a Second Serfdom without constitutional guarantees (Rosenberg 1943–4).

Hintze also noted that land-based forces had different internal effects than naval forces. Those polities that were fortunate enough to have geographic advantages and who could rely on maritime power for their external defense (such as Britain) need not suffer the same fate as countries that needed to maintain large standing armies. Although the government might still require considerable burdens from the population in terms of taxation, naval forces could not be as easily deployed for internal repressive purposes. Heavy taxation would thus have to be obtained by consent rather than coercion.

Charles Tilly (1990) and Brian Downing (1992) have expanded on these insights. Tilly observed that the ready availability of financial resources might mitigate the tendency towards absolutism. Although all European states were heavily involved with frequent, organized warfare from roughly the late fifteenth century onward (Parker 1988), garrison states only emerged where urban centers were poorly developed. Although, as noted earlier, Tilly confuses his descriptions of political strategies with a description of relative factor endowments, he is correct in noting the relative absence of absolutist forms of government on the European core axis that ran roughly from the European north-west to northern Italy. The states that formed this core axis had strong urban communities whose consent was required for war. Thus, these polities emerged as constitutionalist forms of government.

Downing rightly adds that other intervening variables might affect the causal relation between war and regime type. The availability of external capital (through colonies, or allies), as well as geographic features that facilitate defense (the Swiss mountains, for example), may complicate the picture. Defense of the state, even if surrounded by belligerent actors, need not necessarily lead to a garrison state. Rather than internal mobilization the state may secure its existence by judicious management of its external relations.

Downing's account thus draws attention to how warfare and economic milieu intertwine to affect regime type. Where trade flourished urban centers were vibrant. This allowed the state to raise large sums of capital for warfare, while at the same time the strong urban centers demanded participation in how this money would be allocated.

War making and economic transition interacted also with the creation of early capitalism by mercantilist practices. Although Machiavelli realized (and before him Cicero) that money was the sinews of power, power in turn provided one with markets and commodities. War making and economic change thus pointed towards greater government intervention and absolutist rule in the classical mercantilist style. Indeed, all states, including Britain and the Netherlands (the later champions of liberal trade), engaged in such mercantilist practices during their formative phase.

The particular timing of state development may further affect the impact of external competition on regime type. Taking Germany and Russia as templates, Gerschenkron argued that late state formation required not merely the centralization of political authority and definition of territorial boundaries, but also an activist government to catch up with more advanced economies (Gerschenkron 1962). Modernization from the "top down" thus correlated with authoritarianism.

Taking his cue from Gerschenkron and Hintze, Thomas Ertman (1997) submits that geopolitical competition, combined with the periodization of state building, sheds light not only on regime type but also on the state's administrative infrastructure. The latter can be patrimonial or administrative-bureaucratic. The timing of the onset of competition and the pre-existing strength of local assemblies affect subsequent outcomes on regime type and administrative structure.

All things being equal geopolitical competition prior to 1450 should lead to patrimonial administration and absolutism in Latin Europe, but constitutionalism and patrimonialism in Britain, due to the strength of local assemblies. With the later onset of geopolitical competition and strong local assemblies in Hungary and Poland, we should expect bureaucratic constitutionalism in Eastern Europe. However, this did not happen, says Ertman, due to the independent effect of parliament, reversing the expected outcomes in the British and East European cases.

His discussion usefully opens up the analysis beyond regime type or administrative structures. However, one may wonder whether the account succeeds. Thus whereas Tilly, Hintze, Downing, each in their own way, try to account for the relative strength of local assemblies, Ertman takes this variation as a starting point, and then argues that this variation in turn had subsequent effects on the emergence of absolutism versus constitutionalism. However, when he introduces the strength of parliament as having an independent effect on the outcomes observed the account gains a tautological flavor.

Finally, neo-institutional accounts of state formation have also weighed in the discussion of state formation and regime type. Neo-institutionalists suggest that less hierarchical regimes have salutary internal and external consequences. Internally, less hierarchical governments tend to foster economic development when the government has credibly tied its own hands (North and Weingast 1989). Since entrepreneurs need not fear government predation, their private incentives to pursue economic gain parallel public objectives. Externally, governments that tie their own hands can more credibly commit to international obligations. Since the sovereign is accountable to its domestic public it cannot retreat from international agreements (Cowhey 1993; Martin 2000). Democratically accountable governments thus have a competitive advantage over rival types.

Neo-institutionalists in a sense thus reverse, and alter, the causal linkage of conflict and regime type. Whereas Hintze, Downing, and others focus on the consequences of warfare on regime type, neo-institutionalists might well concentrate on the effect that regimes have on rulers' ability to mobilize society for war. Thus rulers that are constitutionally bound might be more able to raise revenue from their population, or from other states, in times of war (D'Lugo and Rogowski 1993). Similarly, given audience costs and their ability to credibly commit, democratic regimes make states more attractive as allies and trading partners.[10]

5 State Formation and State Failure in the Modern Era

The literature on state formation in Europe thus presents a variety of analytic angles to clarify how sovereign territoriality became the constitutive rule for the modern state system, why some states developed as constitutional or absolutist regimes, and how some states created rational administrative structures which others lacked. However reflecting on the European historical trajectory generates theoretical lenses through which to view contemporary developments elsewhere. Nowhere is this more pertinent than in the newly independent states that emerged in the latter part of the twentieth century.[11]

Indeed, since the end of the Second World War the number of independent states has multiplied almost fourfold. Decolonization in Africa and Asia created new entities

---

[10] On the relevance of audience costs for credibility, see Fearon (1994).

[11] There is also a growing body of literature that has started to examine non-European state formation prior to European colonial expansion. Tin-bor Hui (2004) thus argues that state formation during China's Warring States period (656–221 BC) looked markedly different than war making and state making in Europe. Carolyn Warner notes how some states in West Africa had emerged as viable territorial entities with considerable state capacity before European encroachment (Warner 1998).

in the shadow of erstwhile maritime empires while the end of communist domination in Eastern Europe and the fragmentation of the USSR added another two dozen polities in the 1990s. While the new polities have emerged in a state system in which the adherence to the principle of sovereign territoriality is a sine qua non for international recognition, these new states face a dramatically different environment than the early European actors.

Consequently, most of the independent states that emerged in the twentieth century readily accept territorial sovereignty as a constitutive rule of international relations (although it is perhaps challenged by certain religious principles in Islam). State capacity and rational, bureaucratic administration, however, have been found critically wanting, burdened as many of these states are by patrimonialism, weak economies, and rampant organized corruption. This weak administrative infrastructure has affected their ability to monopolize the means of violence within their borders; their ability to develop viable domestic economies; and their ability to provide public goods to their populace. Combined with borders that have been superimposed on heterogeneous populations, rulers inevitably lack legitimacy.

5.1 The Changed Security Environment

The new states of the post-1945 era emerged in a completely different security environment than the states of early modern Europe. Rather than emerge out of the cauldron of geopolitical conflict that for centuries typified the European landscape most of these entities gained independent status by fiat. Even in the USSR, conflicts that emerged in the wake of the Union's collapse were primarily conflicts within the newly independent states, secessionist conflicts, not inter-republic wars.[12]

Many of these states consequently acquired independence after colonial powers withdrew and by subsequent international recognition, but they did not undergo the process that accompanied traditional state formation (Jackson 1987). Although some colonies fought wars of liberation, compared to the centuries of European geopolitical strife, these wars did not require long-term mobilizational strategies. As a result, these nationalist conflicts did not enhance state capacity. In the words of Joel Migdal, while the governments of such newly independent countries affect many spheres of social life, they lack the ability to direct these societies. Weak states confront strong societies (Migdal 1988).

Interstate war, in general, is increasingly considered an aberration. The international community considers war an illegal means of pursuing foreign policy objectives (Zacher 2001). Thus, the United Nations only legitimizes force under specific conditions. Furthermore, for much of the Cold War the bipolar environment stifled conflict. Many wars of the post-1945 era were internal conflicts, or conflicts between the lesser powers. In addition, nuclear weapons and the balance of power made great power conflict unwinnable. Finally, territorial aggrandizement has become

---

[12] The former Yugoslavia or India and Pakistan might be construed as exceptions.

more difficult and is no longer a prerequisite for the accumulation of wealth (Spruyt 2005).

For these reasons, warfare has declined in frequency and has become virtually obsolete in Europe and the Americas. Arguably, the likelihood of interstate war, although not improbable in Asia and Africa, has declined even there. The lack of frequent, intense conflict has retarded the development of strong states in regions such as Africa (Herbst 1989). Given a low population density and high costs of creating an administrative infrastructure, pre-colonial African states largely concentrated state resources in a key core area with state control receding further away from the core. Boundaries were permeable. The current international system, however, recognizes the imperially imposed borders to mark the extent of (ascribed) state authority. African political elites have embraced these borders in an attempt to expand their own power and mediate external pressures. Tellingly, Herbst criticizes this artificiality: "the fundamental problem with the boundaries in Africa is not that they are too weak but that they are too strong" (Herbst 2000, 253).

In some areas the state lacks a monopoly of violence altogether. Instead, multiple groups vie with each other for internal control of the state (Reno 1998). Some of these groups might provide some public goods, resembling the beginnings of proto-states in late medieval Europe. "Shadow states" thus emerge in lieu of recognized public authority. In many cases, however, rulers tend to pursue more particularistic gains favoring narrow clienteles or ethnic communities. Warlordism, trafficking in drugs or conflict diamonds, and ethnic conflicts emerge in their wake.

The absence of an actor who holds a monopoly on the legitimate exercise of force has led to the introduction of private actors who possess means of violence (Singer 2003). As Avant (2005) points out, the consumers and suppliers for these private actors come from a wide array of actors. Thus, whereas European states saw a gradual monopolization of violence and the gradual eradication of armed private actors (Thomson 1989, 1990), some areas in Africa are witnessing the opposite trend.

The internal features of weak and failed states might contradict some expectations from international relations. Whereas this literature has largely studied patterns of international interaction by examining developed states, weaker states in the developing world might not follow expected patterns of balancing and bandwagoning (David 1991; Lemke 2003).

5.2 The Economic Environment and Late State Formation

These newly emerging states also face a different economic environment than early European states. Not only has the direct link between warfare and state making been severed, but it has weakened the traditional mercantilist junction of state making and modernization. The barriers to interstate war thus hinder the ability of emerging states to create, and mobilize, consolidated internal markets, and at the same time pursue state revenue by external aggrandizement.

Mercantilist state making has been further impeded by the spread of liberal capitalism. American hegemony explicitly yoked the creation of the Bretton Woods system to the denunciation of mercantilist practice and imperial preference. While primarily intended to delimit the protectionist and interventionist practices of the European great powers, this subsequently had consequences for their erstwhile colonies.

Globalization of trade and capital markets has also led to pressures for convergence. If strong states, such as France, had to give way due to international capital flight in the early 1980s (Garrett 1992), such constraints must hold a fortiori for less developed countries. How much latitude states still have to pursue neo-mercantilist strategies and thus link economic development and state making, as late developing European states could (Gerschenkron 1962; Hall 1986), is an ongoing matter of debate. Arguably the East Asian states succeeded in state development because they found means to utilize protectionist measures and industrial policy to their benefit (Johnson 1982; Amsden 1989; Deyo 1987). Richard Stubbs (1999) submits that the East Asian states managed to develop during the Cold War by a classical linking of preparation for war (due to the communist threat) and economic development (partially with support of American capital and aid.). Neo-mercantilist economic policy, state development, and authoritarian government went hand in hand. Indeed, there is some evidence that the more successful developing states in the 1990s, such as China, resisted the "Washington consensus" that preached the virtues of less government intervention and liberal trade (Wade 2003).

Given the apparent success of the East Asian "tigers" one inevitably must ask why state making and interventionist economic policy making did not lead to state capture and rent seeking by elites in that region, and why the developmental state has had less success elsewhere (Haggard and Kaufman 1995). In comparing two Middle Eastern states (Turkey and Syria) with South Korea and Taiwan, David Waldner claims that premature incorporation of popular classes during the state-building process had an adverse effect on economic development (Waldner 1999). South Korea and Taiwan, by contrast, managed to hold back participation and distributive pressures. Thus rather than see differential external factors as causes for successful economic takeoff and state formation, this alternative line of enquiry explains variation by different internal trajectories of coalition building.

Other newly emerging states have followed alternative paths of economic mobilization. In the standard European developmental path, internal mobilization for war and economic development often meant a tradeoff for the ruler between mobilization and participation. In common parlance, taxation required representation. Absolutist rulers could only circumvent the connection by making potential opponents of royal centralization tax exempt. The lack of taxation of the aristocracy thus correlated with the absence of effective parliamentary oversight in pre-revolutionary France, Spain, and Prussia.

Some of the newly independent states that possess considerable natural resources, however, can obtain resources without making such tradeoffs. Rents accruing from natural resources, particularly in natural gas and oil, allow governments to provide essential public goods, or side payments to potential dissidents, without having to make concessions. The rentier state literature thus argues that rentier economies show an inverse correlation with democracy (Anderson 1986; Chaudhry 1997; Dillman 2000; Karl 1997; Vandewalle 1998). The standard rentier argument was developed with particular reference to the Middle East, but the argument has been applied to other states as well. Intriguingly, the notion of rents might also be extended to other export commodities, or even foreign aid.[13]

But there is some debate whether rentier states inevitably lead to societal acquiescence. In one perspective, rentier economies might generate the very conditions that precipitate dissidence. Because governments selectively allocate rents to select groups, the presence of considerable financial resources makes it worthwhile for the excluded group to mobilize its constituency to challenge the existing authority (Okruhlik 1999).

In another intriguing line of enquiry, some scholars have examined the relation between economic context and the state through formal models. This has yielded interesting observations with regards to efficient state size and the number of states in the international system. Alesina and Spolaore (1997) start from the premiss that public goods provision is more efficient in larger units. Thus, a fictitious social planner could maximize world average utility by designing states of optimal size with an equilibrium number of units. Several factors, however, will offset the benefits of large jurisdictions. First, heterogeneous populations will make uniform public goods provision more costly. Second, given diverse preferences and the declining efficiency of provision the further one resides from the center of the country, democratic rulers will not be able to create optimal redistributive systems as efficiently as rulers who can unilaterally maximize utility. Third, an international liberal trading scheme will decrease the costs for small jurisdictions.

They have extended this line of analysis to the provision of security as a public good (Alesina and Spolaore 2005). A geopolitical hostile environment creates benefits for large jurisdictions, as security provision will be more efficient. With declining international competition such benefits will recede and the number of nations will expand.

International relations scholars have made similar observations, albeit from different analytic perspectives. Michael Desch (1996) thus argued, following realist views in international relations scholarship, that the durability of alliances and territorial integrity were heavily dependent on the presence of external threat. Events since the end of the Cold War seem to have borne such expectations out. Moreover, if Alesina and Spolaore are correct, the attempts to foster democratic regimes in many of the new states will not necessarily lead to economically efficient outcomes. Finally, their analysis comports well with Herbst's (2000) argument. The artificial borders of many African states, which thus comprise many diverse ethnic communities, have coincided with inefficient economic outcomes and the suboptimal provision of public goods.

---

[13] For a good overview of some of this literature, see Cooley (2001).

5.3 Legitimizing the State in Newly Emerging Polities

The preceding observations have serious consequences for rulers seeking to legitimize their rule and the existing territorial borders. The ideological legitimation of the sovereign, territorial state in Europe involved a threefold process. First, it required the triumph of rule based on territoriality. The idea of a theocratic, universalist non-territorial organization based on a Christian community had to be displaced in favor of territorial identification. Already by the fourteenth century kings had started to challenge papal claims to rule. And by the sixteenth century, by the principle *cuius regio, eius religio*, territorial rulers came to determine the dominant religious identification of their state.

Second, the state had to contend with alternative forms of identification and loyalty—ethnic community, clans, kinship structures, and trans-territorial loyalties (as with feudal obligations). National language, public education, compulsory military service, and other strategies were enlisted to "forge peasants into Frenchmen" (Weber 1979; Posen 1993). The emergence of national armies and citizenship went hand in hand. In exchange for public goods provision and protection, citizens had to do more than pay taxes; they had to serve with life and limb to defend the national community (Levi 1998). The creation of a nation to identify with the particular territorial space, consequently, involved a destruction of local variation and identification and a reconstruction of a national citizen.

Third, in the process of contractual bargaining or even by coercive imposition of authority over time, the state acquired a taken-for-granted character. The greater the contractarian nature of the state, the greater the ability of the state to acquire legitimacy. But even authoritarian states, once they had attached legitimate rule to the disembodied state, rather than a particular dynastic lineage, could count on popular support in moments of crisis, such as war.

Few of these processes are at work in the newly independent states of the last decades. Territorial identification has not uniformly displaced trans-territorial affinity based on language and religion. For example, whether the idea of territorially demarcated authority is compatible with theocratic organization in the Muslim world still remains a matter of debate (Piscatori 1986). The interplay of trans-territorial claims to rule varies by historical legacy, the particular manifestation of the dominant religion on the ground, and even individual rulers' calculations. Even within the same country territorial rulers themselves have at particular junctures championed trans-territorial affinities while their successors denied such claims. In Egypt, Nasser invoked pan-Arab loyalties, while Sadat proved more an Egyptian nationalist. While many Middle East rulers (Gause 1992) have largely abjured the trans-territorial claims of their early independence, the legitimacy of their authority remains contested.

The newly independent states of the former Soviet Union have not been immune either. Some scholars have suggested an attraction of pan-Turkic identification (Mandelbaum 1994). Others see legitimization problems which look similar to those of the Middle Eastern states given the tensions between secular rulers, often the direct heirs of the Communist Party cadres, and religious authorities.

In many newly independent states local affinities of tribe, ethnic community, clan, and kin dominate any sense of national citizenship. In the Middle East and North Africa, states such as Tunisia and Egypt, which were historically relatively autonomous entities prior to colonial subjugation, have had a longer track record of melding local identity with territory (Anderson 1987). Other states, such as on the Arabian peninsula, have had to contend with various alternate loci of identification, some of which were fostered by colonial rule. Similarly, in the newly independent states of Central Asia, traditional loyalties, like clan networks, continue to provide means of representation vis-à-vis state authorities as well as means for demanding state distribution towards such networks (Collins 2004).

This pattern holds equally in Africa as in many states of Asia. Even where nationalist elites gained their independence by force of arms rather than by metropolitan retreat, these elites have not always been successful in creating a national identity. For instance, although the Indonesian army obtained considerable popular support in its struggles with the Dutch, the national project has largely been seen as a Javanese one. Ethnic and regional tensions have thus resurfaced in such places as Borneo, Atjeh, and Ambon.

In Eastern Europe and the former Soviet area as well, nationalist elites have had mixed success. Czechoslovakia and Yugoslavia dissolved altogether, while Romania, Hungary, and many of the former Union republics continue to face multiple challenges. Within the former Soviet Union, the Baltics, who could fall back on a prior historical legacy of independence, have fared better in muting virulent tensions.

As said, these states emerged due to a mixture of imperial collapse, metropolitan withdrawal, international delegitimization of empire, and nationalist resistance. In very few instances were elites involved in contractarian bargaining with social actors. Nationalist alliances were often agreements of convenience rather than durable quid pro quo exchanges as in European state formation. The internal features of successful state making were absent and thus logically the means through which rulers could justify their authority.

This is not to say that national elites in all newly emerged states are doomed to failure. Although public goods provision might be suboptimal in heterogeneous populations, and although there are reasons to fear deleterious overall effects of ethnic diversity on economic growth, strategic choices to mitigate the effects of ethnic cleavages can bear fruit. For example, there is some evidence that nation-building efforts in Tanzania, despite a highly heterogeneous population, and despite limited resources, have met with considerable success. In Tanzania, the government chose a national language policy, reformed local governments following independence, distributed public expenditures equitably, and adopted a national school curriculum. As a result public school expenditures show far less correlation with ethnicity and the nation-building project as a whole has been relatively successful. In Kenya, conversely, public goods have been distributed far less equitably and nation building has stalled (Miguel 2004). Taking Tanzania as a "less likely case" for successful nation building, given its low level of economic development and its ethnic diversity, suggests that deliberate state strategies might yield modest success even under difficult circumstances.

6 Institutional Legacies of Empire

There is, given the observations above, a broad consensus that late state formation outside of the Western experience, and particularly in the developing countries, occurs in a vastly different environment and will thus diverge from the European model. In addition to a different geopolitical and economic milieu, the newly independent states differ from the European trajectory in that many of them emerged in the wake of imperial disintegration and retreat. The study of emerging states thus sparked enquiry into the institutional consequences of imperial rule.

The former Soviet space and Eastern Europe have proven particularly fertile ground for comparative political studies. Given the relative similarity of background conditions (particularly in the former USSR), these states lend themselves to cross-case analyses regarding institutional choice and the consequences of institutional type (Laitin 1991; Elster 1997). What kinds of institutions emerged during this third wave of democratization? With scarcely more than a decade gone by, it appears evident that many polities in Eastern Europe and the former Soviet Union have opted for strong presidential systems (Easter 1997).

One hardly needs to mention that the consequences of presidential and parliamentary systems remain a matter of debate within the comparative politics literature. Those in favor of parliamentary forms of government argue that presidential systems lend themselves to abuse of power and are poorly equipped to deal with multiethnic societies (Lijphart 1977; Linz 1996; Skach and Stepan). Presidential systems will thus be prone to eroding democratic rights and to limiting parliamentarian opposition. Conversely, others argue that parliamentary systems might be as prone to abuse and winner-take-all policies as presidential systems (Mainwaring and Shugart 1997). Comparative study of these states in the years ahead will be a fruitful avenue of enquiry to test these rival arguments.

Eastern Europe and the former Soviet republics also provide a laboratory for the study of economic transition. Shortly after independence, proponents of "shock therapy" held sway.[14] Economists suggested that a successful, rapid transition to a capitalist system was feasible. Subsequent analysis, partially on the basis of comparisons with Western European state formation and economic development, remained far more skeptical. Political and social conditions that had accompanied takeoff in Western Europe seemed absent. Paradoxically, states which seemed to have inherited fewer institutional and material resources from the USSR, such as the Ukraine, proved

---

[14] One such proponent was Anders Aslund (1995).

to be more successful in their transition than Russia itself, which could build on the state capacity left from the USSR (Motyl 1997).

Finally, this region has provided generalizable theoretical insights about institutional arrangements and territorial fragmentation. Valerie Bunce suggests in her comparative analysis of Czechoslovakia, Yugoslavia, and the USSR that civil–military relations and ethnofederal institutions are key elements that may contribute to territorial dissolution (Bunce 1999).[15] More recent research, however, suggests that ethnofederal solutions might not have such adverse consequences and might be able to deal with heterogeneous populations. A balance between the core region and other units might be critical for the stability of the ethnofederal arrangement (Hale 2004).

The Soviet ethnofederal system also had some unique features that contributed to its demise. The Soviet titular elite policy officially linked particular nationalities to territorial entities but also created incentives for the agents (the titular elites) to disregard commands from the principal (the Communist Party), particularly when oversight mechanisms declined while at the same time rewards from the center diminished. Steven Solnick utilizes such a principal–agent framework to contrast Chinese territorial integrity during its economic transition with the collapse of the USSR (Solnick 1996).[16] Randall Stone (1996) has argued that lack of oversight and information problems plagued principal (USSR) and agents (the East European states) as well—seriously distorting their pattern of trade.

Finally, scholarship has also turned to the question whether colonial legacies show commonalities across time and space, despite widely divergent historical and cultural trajectories. A growing body of research has started to compare the states of Central Asia and African states (Beissinger and Young 2002; Jones-Luong 2002). These states share various features in common that do not bode well for their subsequent development. They share poverty, a history of institutionalized corruption, patrimonial institutions, and weak state development due to imperial domination. Nevertheless some of these states have embarked on modest democratic trajectories (such as Kyrgyzstan) while others remain authoritarian (such as Uzbekistan). Similarly, some sub-Saharan states show modest economic success (such as Botswana) while others evince abject failure (such as Zimbabwe). Cross-regional comparison, therefore, might allow greater specification of the causal variables for state failure, economic takeoff, and democratic reform.

To conclude, the study of the state is alive and well. Indeed, there has been a dramatic revival of studies of state formation, the linkage between state formation and regime type, as well as of state failure. It is also clear that subfield boundaries fade into the background in the study of such substantive macro-level questions. While the integration of subfields has been most manifest within comparative politics and international relations, other subfields may contribute greatly as well. American politics, in its nuanced understanding of institutional choices and their consequences, can shed light on how electoral reforms might enable or constrain economic growth

---

[15] Other accounts that look at the particular nature of Soviet ethnofederalism are Brubaker (1994); Roeder (1991); Suny (1993).

[16] For another account using a neo-institutionalist logic, see Nee and Lian (1994).

and democratic reform. Questions of citizenship, identity politics, and legitimacy inevitably involve political philosophy.

Aside from multidisciplinarity, the study of the state must be historical. For better or for worse, it is the European state system which has been superimposed on the rest of the world. The differences in historical environment and the divergent trajectories not only shed light on the problems confronting the newly independent states of the last half-century, but possibly point the way to remedies which might start to address the dire effects of state failure.

REFERENCES

ALESINA, A. and SPOLAORE, E. 1997. On the number and size of nations. *Quarterly Journal of Economics*, 112 (4): 1027–56.

——— 2005. War, peace, and the size of countries. *Journal of Public Economics*, 89: 1333–54.

AMES, E. and RAPP, R. 1977. The birth and death of taxes: a hypothesis. *Journal of Economic History*, 37: 161–78.

AMSDEN, A. 1989. *Asia's Next Giant: South Korea and Late Industrialization*. New York: Oxford University Press.

ANDERSON, B. 1991. *Imagined Communities*. New York: Verso.

ANDERSON, L. 1986. *The State and Social Transformation in Tunisia and Libya, 1830–1980*. Princeton: Princeton University Press.

——— 1987. The state in the Middle East and North Africa. *Comparative Politics*, 20 (1): 1–18.

ANDERSON, P. 1974a. *Passages from Antiquity to Feudalism*. London: Verso.

——— 1974b. *Lineages of the Absolutist State*. London: Verso.

ASLUND, A. 1995. *How Russia Became a Market Economy*. Washington, DC: Brookings Institution.

AVANT, D. 2005. *The Market for Force: The Consequences of Privatizing Security*. New York: Cambridge University Press.

BADIE, B. and BIRNBAUM, P. 1983. *The Sociology of the State*. Chicago: University of Chicago Press, 1983.

BEAN, R. 1973. War and the birth of the nation state. *Journal of Economic History*, 33 (1): 203–21.

BEISSINGER, M. and YOUNG, C. (eds.) 2002. *Beyond State Crisis? Postcolonial Africa and Post-Soviet Eurasia in Comparative Perspective*. Washington, DC: Woodrow Wilson Center Press.

BENDIX, R. 1978. *Kings or People*. Berkeley and Los Angeles: University of California Press.

BENN, S. 1967. Sovereignty. Pp. 501–5 in *The Encyclopedia of Philosophy*, vol. vii/viii. New York: Macmillan.

BREWER, J. 1989. *The Sinews of Power*. New York: Alfred Knopf.

BRUBAKER, R. 1994. Nationhood and the national question in the Soviet Union and post-Soviet Eurasia: an institutionalist account. *Theory and Society*, 23: 47–78.

BUNCE, V. 1999. *Subversive Institutions*. New York: Cambridge University Press.

CHAUDHRY, K. 1997. *The Price of Wealth: Economies and Institutions in the Middle East*. Ithaca, NY: Cornell University Press.

COLLINS, K. 2004. The logic of clan politics: evidence from Central Asian trajectories. *World Politics*, 56 (2): 224–61.

COLLINS, R. 1986. *Weberian Sociological Theory*. Cambridge: Cambridge University Press.

COOLEY, A. 2001. Booms and busts: theorizing institutional formation and change in oil states. *Review of International Political Economy*, 8 (1): 163–80.

CORRIGAN, P. and SAYER, D. 1991. *The Great Arch*. New York: Blackwell.

COWHEY, P. 1993. Elect locally—order globally: domestic politics and multilateral cooperation. Pp. 157–200 in *Multilateralism Matters*, ed. J. Ruggie. New York: Columbia University Press.

DAVID, S. 1991. Explaining Third World alignment. *World Politics*, 43 (2): 233–56.

DESCH, M. 1996. War and strong states, peace and weak states? *International Organization*, 50 (2): 237–68.

DEYO, F. (ed.) 1987. *The Political Economy of the New Asian Industrialism*. Ithaca, NY: Cornell University Press.

DILLMAN, B. 2000. *State and Private Sector in Algeria*. Boulder, Colo.: Westview Press.

DIMAGGIO, P. and POWELL, W. 1983. The iron cage revisited: institutional isomorphism and collective rationality in organizational fields. *American Sociological Review*, 48: 147–60.

D'LUGO, D. and ROGOWSKI, R. 1993. The Anglo-German naval race as a study in grand strategy. In *The Domestic Bases of Grand Strategy*, ed. R. Rosecrance and A. Stein. Ithaca, NY: Cornell University Press.

DOWNING, B. 1992. *The Military Revolution and Political Change*. Princeton: Princeton University Press.

DUBY, G. 1978. *The Three Orders*. Chicago: University of Chicago Press.

EASTER, G. 1997. Preference for presidentialism: postcommunist regime change in Russia and the NIS. *World Politics*, 49 (2): 184–211.

ELSTER, J. 1997. Afterword: the making of postcommunist presidencies. Pp. 225–37 in *Postcommunist Presidents*, ed. R. Taras. New York: Cambridge University Press.

ERTMAN, T. 1997. *Birth of the Leviathan*. New York: Cambridge University Press.

FEARON, J. 1994. Domestic political audiences and the escalation of international disputes. *American Political Science Review*, 88: 577–92.

GARRETT, G. 1992. International cooperation and institutional choice: the European Community's internal market. *International Organization*, 46 (2): 533–60.

GAUSE, G. 1992. Sovereignty, statecraft and stability in the Middle East. *Journal of International Affairs*, 45 (2): 441–69.

GELLNER, E. 1983. *Nations and Nationalism*. Ithaca, NY: Cornell University Press.

GERSCHENKRON, A. 1962. *Economic Backwardness in Historical Perspective*. Cambridge, Mass.: Harvard University Press.

GIDDENS, A. 1987. *The Nation-State and Violence*. Berkeley and Los Angeles: University of California Press.

HAGGARD, S. and KAUFMANN, R. 1995. *The Political Economy of Democratic Transitions*. Princeton, NJ: Princeton University Press.

HALE, H. 2004. Divided we stand: institutional sources of ethnofederal state survival and collapse. *World Politics*, 56 (2): 165–93.

HALL, P. 1986. *Governing the Economy*. Cambridge: Polity.

HERBST, J. 1989. The creation and maintenance of national boundaries in Africa. *International Organization*, 43 (4): 673–92.

—— 2000. *States and Power in Africa*. Princeton: Princeton University Press.

HERZ, J. 1976. *The Nation-State and the Crisis of World Politics*. New York: David McKay.

HINSLEY, F. H. 1986. *Sovereignty*. Cambridge: Cambridge University Press.

HINTZE, O. 1975. *The Historical Essays of Otto Hintze*, ed. Felix Gilbert. New York: Oxford University Press.

HUI, V. 2004. Toward a dynamic theory of international politics: insights from comparing ancient China and early modern Europe. *International Organization*, 58 (1): 175–205.

JACKSON, R. 1987. Quasi states, dual regimes, and neo-classical theory: international jurisprudence and the Third World. *International Organization*, 41 (4): 519–49.

JOHNSON, C. 1982. *MITI and the Japanese Miracle*. Stanford, Calif.: Stanford University Press.

JONES-LUONG, P. 2002. *Institutional Change and Political Community in Post Soviet Central Asia*. New York: Cambridge University Press.

KARL, T. 1997. *The Paradox of Plenty: Oil Booms and Petro States*. Berkeley and Los Angeles: University of California Press.

KNUDSEN, T. and ROTHSTEIN, B. 1994. State building in Scandinavia. *Comparative Politics*, 26 (2): 203–20.

KRASNER, S. 1999. *Sovereignty: Organized Hypocrisy*. Princeton: Princeton University Press.

KRATOCHWIL, F. 1986. Of systems, boundaries and territoriality: an inquiry into the formation of the state system. *World Politics*, 39 (1): 27–52.

LAITIN, D. 1991. The national uprisings in the Soviet Union. *World Politics*, 44 (1): 139–77.

LEMKE, D. 2003. African lessons for international relations research. *World Politics*, 56 (1): 114–38.

LEVI, M. 1988. *Of Rule and Revenue*. Berkeley and Los Angeles: University of California Press.

—— 1998. Conscription: the price of citizenship. Pp. 109–47 in *Analytic Narratives*, ed. R. Bates, A. Greif, M. Levi, J. Rosenthal, and B. Weingast. Princeton: Princeton University Press.

LIJPHART, A. 1977. *Democracy in Plural Societies*. New Haven: Yale University Press.

LINZ, J. 1996. The perils of presidentialism. Pp. 124–42 in *The Global Resurgence of Democracy*, ed. L. Diamond and M. Plattner. Baltimore: Johns Hopkins University Press.

MACFARLANE, A. 1978. *The Origins of English Individualism*. Oxford: Blackwell.

MCNEILL, W. 1982. *The Pursuit of Power*. Chicago: University of Chicago Press.

MAINWARING, S. and SHUGART, M. 1997. Juan Linz, presidentialism, and democracy: a critical appraisal. *Comparative Politics*, 29 (4): 449–71.

MANDELBAUM, M. (ed.) 1994. *Central Asia and the World*. New York: Council on Foreign Relations Press.

MARTIN, L. L. 2000. *Democratic Commitments: Legislatures and International Cooperation*. Princeton: Princeton University Press.

MIGDAL, J. 1988. *Strong Societies and Weak States*. Princeton: Princeton University Press.

MIGUEL, E. 2004. Tribe or nation? Nation building and public goods in Kenya versus Tanzania. *World Politics*, 56 (3): 327–62.

MOTYL, A. 1997. Structural constraints and starting points: the logic of systemic change in Ukraine and Russia. *Comparative Politics*, 29 (4): 433–47.

NEE, V. and LIAN, P. 1994. Sleeping with the enemy: a dynamic modeling of declining political commitment in state socialism. *Theory and Society*, 23 (2): 253–96.

NETTL, J. P. 1968. The state as a conceptual variable. *World Politics*, 20 (4): 559–92.

NORTH, D. 1979. A framework for analyzing the state in economic history. *Explorations in Economic History*, 16: 249–59.

—— 1981. *Structure and Change in Economic History*. New York: W. W. Norton, 1981.

—— 1990. *Institutions, Institutional Change and Economic Performance*. Cambridge: Cambridge University Press.

—— and THOMAS, R. 1973. *The Rise of the Western World*. Cambridge: Cambridge University Press.

—— and WEINGAST, B. 1989. Constitutions and commitment: the evolution of institutions governing public choice in 17th century England. *Journal of Economic History*, 49: 803–32.

OKRUHLIK, G. 1999. Rentier wealth, unruly law, and the rise of opposition: the political economy of oil states. *Comparative Politics*, 31 (3): 295–315.

PARKER, G. 1979. Warfare. Ch. 7 in *New Cambridge Modern History*, vol. xiii, ed. P. Burke. Cambridge: Cambridge University Press.

—— 1988. *The Military Revolution*. New York: Cambridge University Press.

PIRENNE, H. 1952/1925. *Medieval Cities*. Princeton: Princeton University Press.

PISCATORI, J. 1986. *Islam in a World of Nation-States*. New York: Cambridge University Press.

PIZZORNO, A. 1987. Politics unbound. Pp. 26–62 in *Changing Boundaries of the Political*, ed. C. Maier. Cambridge: Cambridge University Press.

POGGI, G. 1978. *The Development of the Modern State*. Stanford, Calif.: Stanford University Press.

POSEN, B. 1993. Nationalism, the mass army, and military power. *International Security*, 18 (2): 80–124.

PUTNAM, R. 1983. Explaining institutional success: the case of Italian regional government. *American Political Science Review*, 77 (1): 55–74.

RASLER, K. and THOMPSON, W. 1985. War making and state making: governmental expenditures, tax revenues and global war. *American Political Science Review*, 79 (2): 491–507.

RENO, W. 1998. *Warlord Politics and African States*. Boulder, Colo.: Lynne Rienner.

ROEDER, P. 1991. Soviet federalism and ethnic mobilization. *World Politics*, 43 (2): 196–232.

ROSENBERG, H. 1943–4. The rise of the Junkers in Brandenburg-Prussia, 1410–1653. *American Historical Review*, Part I, 49 (1): 1–22; and Part II, 49 (2): 228–42.

RUGGIE, J. 1986. Continuity and transformation in the world polity. Ch. 6 in *Neorealism and its Critics*, ed. R. Keohane. New York: Columbia University Press.

—— 1993. Territoriality and beyond: problematizing modernity in international relations. *International Organization*, 47 (1): 139–74.

SINGER, P. 2003. *Corporate Warriors: The Rise of the Privatized Security Industry*. Ithaca, NY: Cornell University Press.

SKACH, C. and STEPAN, A. 1993. Constitutional frameworks and democratic consolidation: parliamentarism versus presidentialism. *World Politics*, 46 (1): 1–22.

SOLNICK, S. 1996. The breakdown of hierarchies in the Soviet Union and China: a neoinstitutional perspective. *World Politics*, 48 (2): 209–38.

SPRUYT, H. 1994. *The Sovereign State and its Competitors*. Princeton: Princeton University Press.

—— 2005. *Ending Empire: Contested Sovereignty and Territorial Partition*. Ithaca, NY: Cornell University Press.

STONE, R. 1996. *Satellites and Commissars*. Princeton: Princeton University Press.

STRANG, D. 1991. Anomaly and commonplace in European political expansion: realist and institutionalist accounts. *International Organization*, 45 (2): 143–62.

STRAYER, J. 1965. *Feudalism*. New York: Van Nostrand Reinhold.

STUBBS, R. 1999. War and economic development: export-oriented industrialization in East and Southeast Asia. *Comparative Politics*, 31 (3): 337–55.

SUNY, R. 1993. *The Revenge of the Past*. Stanford, Calif.: Stanford University Press.

THELEN, K. 2004. *How Institutions Evolve: The Political Economy of Skills in Germany, Britain, the United States, and Japan*. New York: Cambridge University Press.

THOMAS, G., MEYER, J., RAMIREZ, F., and BOLI, J. 1987. *Institutional Structure: Constituting State, Society and the Individual*. Beverly Hills, Calif.: Sage.

THOMSON, J. 1989. Sovereignty in historical perspective: the evolution of state control over extraterritorial violence. Pp. 227–54 in *The Elusive State*, ed. J. Caporaso. Newbury Park, Calif.: Sage.

—— 1990. State practices, international norms, and the decline of mercenarism. *International Studies Quarterly*, 34 (1): 23–48.

TIERNEY, B. 1964. *The Crisis of Church and State, 1050–1300*. Englewood Cliffs, NJ: Prentice Hall.

TILLY, C. 1975. *The Formation of National States in Western Europe*. Princeton: Princeton University Press.

——1985. War making and state making as organized crime. Pp. 169–87 in *Bringing the State Back in*, ed. P. Evans, D. Rueschemeyer, and T. Skocpol. Cambridge: Cambridge University Press.

——1990. *Coercion, Capital and European States, AD 990–1990*. Cambridge: Basil Blackwell.

VAN EVERA, S. 1997. *Guide to Methods for Students of Political Science*. Ithaca, NY: Cornell University Press.

VANDEWALLE, D. 1998. *Libya since Independence: Oil and State-Building*. Ithaca, NY: Cornell University Press.

WADE, R. 2003. What strategies are viable for developing countries today? The WTO and the shrinking of development space. *Review of International Political Economy*, 10 (4): 621–44.

WALDNER, D. 1999. *State Building and Late Development*. Ithaca, NY: Cornell University Press.

WALTZ, K. 1979. *Theory of International Politics*. New York: Random House.

WARNER, C. 1998. Sovereign states and their prey: the new institutionalist economics and state destruction in 19th-century West Africa. *Review of International Political Economy*, 5 (3): 508–33.

WEBBER, C. and WILDAVSKY, A. 1986. *A History of Taxation and Expenditure in the Western World*. New York: Simon and Schuster.

WEBER, E. 1979. *Peasants into Frenchmen: The Modernization of Rural France, 1870–1914*. Stanford, Calif.: Stanford University Press.

WEBER, M. 1978. *Economy and Society*, 2 vols. Berkeley and Los Angeles: University of California Press.

ZACHER, M. 2001. The territorial integrity norm: international boundaries and the use of force. *International Organization*, 55 (2): 215–50.

CHAPTER 29

WHAT CAUSES DEMOCRATIZATION

BARBARA GEDDES

RESEARCH on democratization has become increasingly sophisticated during the last decade. With the completion and sharing of new datasets and the ratcheting up of training in statistics and modeling, approaches to studying democratization have changed greatly since the mid-1990s. Economic models of democratization and large-N statistical investigations of its causes play an ever larger role in its study. What we think we know about democratization has changed much less, though we have some intriguing new ideas to think about. Recent research has confirmed what we thought we knew several decades ago: richer countries are more likely to be democratic. Controversy continues about whether economic development increases the likelihood of transitions to democracy. Przeworski and his co-authors (2000) have argued emphatically that development does not cause democratization; rather, development reduces the likelihood of democratic breakdown, thus increasing the number of rich democratic countries even though it has no causal effect on transitions *to* democracy. Other careful analyses of regime change, however, continue to find a relationship between development and transitions to democracy (e.g., Boix and Stokes 2003; Epstein et al. forthcoming).

Several other empirical regularities have achieved the status of stylized facts, though all have also been challenged. Reliance on oil, and perhaps other mineral exports, reduces the likelihood of democracy (Barro 1996; Ross 2001; Fish 2002). Countries with large Muslim populations are less likely to be democratic (Fish 2002). Weiner (1987) and Payne (1993) among others have suggested that British colonial heritage contributes to better prospects for democracy later, and Barro (1996) finds support for their claims.[1]

As with the relationship between development and democracy, controversy continues about whether these are causal relationships or correlations explained by something else. Among those who believe relationships are causal, there are disagreements about the processes through which the causes produce the outcome. Middle East experts explain the correlation between oil wealth and dictatorship as a consequence of a rentier state that can use its rents from the sale of natural resources to distribute subsidies to large parts of the population and thus to maintain popular compliance with the regime (Anderson 1987; Crystal 1995). In a parallel argument, Dunning (2006) argues that oil rents can in some circumstances be used to sustain democracy. Herb (2005), however, shows that when a measure of development that excludes the effect of oil on the economy is used in place of GDP per capita in statistical analysis of the causes of democratization, oil-rich countries fit the same patterns as other countries. The proxy measure of development has a strong positive effect on changes in democracy scores, and rent dependence, measured separately, has no effect. In short, he challenges the existence of a relationship between oil wealth and regime type. Some observers have suggested an affinity between Muslim doctrine or the attitudes of believers and authoritarianism, but Fish (2002) suggests that Muslim countries tend to be authoritarian not for the reasons usually mentioned but because of the suppression of women's rights in these countries.

In 1959, Seymour Martin Lipset argued that modernization caused democracy. He supported his claim with what was then a state-of-the-art quantitative test, a table showing a relationship between various measures of development and democracy in a cross-section of countries. In succeeding decades, analytic techniques have become much more sophisticated, more data have become available, and scholars have developed more nuanced measures of democracy. In ever more sophisticated ways, analysts have confirmed the existence of a correlation between democracy and development (Bollen and Jackman 1985; Burkhart and Lewis-Beck 1994; Gasiorowski 1995; Barro 1996; Przeworski et al. 2000).[2] Without denigrating their contribution, which has been very great, it is still possible to note that little beyond greater certainty about that original claim has been added to the pile of knowledge we can be reasonably sure we know.

In trying to understand democratization, we have traditionally relied on descriptions of transitions in individual countries and small groups of countries or large-N statistical studies. The case studies have been very useful in providing information about particular transitions. Large-N studies typically include all countries for which information about proposed causes is available. These studies have built the current accumulation of knowledge about the relationship between development and democracy. The authors of the large-N studies have suggested various processes through

---

[1]   But Fish (2002) finds no relationship between British colonial heritage and democracy.
[2]   But see Acemoglu et al. (2005) for an empirical challenge. Acemoglu and Robinson's (2001) deductive model, however, could easily lead to a correlation between democracy and development.

which growth and the related spread of education, urbanization, and individual mobility might lead to demands for democracy, and many of these arguments have been tested. A correlation between education, especially primary education, and democracy is well established (Barro 1996). Some studies have found a relationship between the income share of the middle class and democracy (Barro 1996). The results on urbanization are mixed, with some showing a negative effect on democracy. These studies have not actually modeled the process of democratization via these avenues, however. They all seem to assume that if citizens want democracy and have the required skills, they can achieve it.

Given the quality and amount of effort expended on understanding democratization, it is frustrating to understand so little. Scholars have responded by pushing the research frontier in two intriguing directions. Some have taken up Robert Barro's (1996) challenge: "Given the strength of the Lipset/Aristotle hypothesis as an empirical regularity, it is surprising that convincing theoretical models of the relation do not exist. Thus development of such a theory is a priority for future research (S182)." Modeling and testing interactions between elites, who may not want to share power, and citizens, who may want to influence distribution and therefore demand democracy as a means of gaining influence, have now moved to the top of the research agenda. Several scholars have proposed plausible deductive arguments that identify underlying causes of democratization, most of which are correlated with development, and that therefore explain the correlation. The next section discusses recent models of the process of democratization and the evidence supporting them.

A different direction has been taken by other analysts, who claim that international factors have played a much larger role in explaining democratization than earlier observers had realized. If international forces have a major effect on democratization, and especially if there is an interaction between international and domestic factors, their exclusion from statistical tests may explain some of the limited and contradictory results obtained in these tests. International influences have barely figured in the historical literature on democratization, but studies including them have produced interesting results in the last few years. The second section below summarizes recent findings about international effects on transitions to democracy.

In response to the mix of success and failure to which the study of democratization has led, I suggest that the reason results have been somewhat limited so far is that the phenomenon we label democratization actually includes several different causal processes. If the large-N studies have lumped multiple causal processes into the same statistical models, it is not surprising that only the most basic relationships have emerged. Similarly, if the models that have been proposed fit democratization in some contexts but not others, then it is also not surprising that empirical support for the models has been modest. A different approach to understanding democratization would begin by disaggregating into several distinct processes or subgroups and then theorizing different transition processes separately. In the third section I discuss some different ways to think about theoretically useful disaggregations of the process of democratization.

1 INVESTIGATING THE PROCESS: WHAT CAUSES THE CORRELATION BETWEEN DEVELOPMENT AND DEMOCRACY?

In a very influential book and article, Przeworski and co-authors (1997, 2000) have argued that there is no relationship between levels of economic development and transitions to democracy. They note that transitions can occur for many reasons, not all of which are systematic. They claim that the apparent relationship results from the political stability of rich democracies. Although poor democracies sometimes collapse and return to dictatorship, rich democracies never do, which over time leads to a high proportion of rich countries among democracies. Using a different measure of democracy and a dataset covering a much longer period of time, Gleditsch and Choun (2004) also find no relationship between development and transitions to democracy after controlling for characteristics of countries' neighbors.[3]

Other analysts, however, have been unpersuaded by Przeworski et al.'s argument. In a very careful reanalysis that extends the time period back to 1850, Boix and Stokes (2003) show that development does contribute to democratic transitions, though the average effect for the whole period is small relative to the effect of development on maintaining democracy. In fact, they note that a careful reading of *Democracy and Development* shows that even Przeworski et al. (2000) find a small statistically significant effect of development on the likelihood of transitions to democracy. Boix and Stokes (2003) show that when the dataset is divided by time periods, economic development is an extremely important predictor of transition prior to 1950, but has only a small (though statistically significant) effect in the post-1950 period. Epstein et al. (forthcoming) also challenge the Przeworski et al. (2000) findings. They show that results are changed by using a trichotomous measure of democracy rather than a dichotomous one, as Przeworski et al. did. They find that development has strong predictive power for transitions into and out of the category they call partial democracy, but less effect on transitions from full autocracy to full democracy. Epstein et al.'s (forthcoming) findings should probably be interpreted as meaning that development is a good predictor of the softening or routinization of authoritarian regimes, though not necessarily of regime change.

Economic development is correlated with many other trends, and one or more of those may be the causal mechanism that accounts for the apparent relationship

---

[3] Pevehouse (2002) also finds no relationship between development and democratization after controlling for the average level of democracy in the members of regional international organizations that countries belong to. These findings are open to different interpretations. Since development tends to vary by region, level of development is likely to be collinear with average democraticness in neighboring countries or regional international organizations. It might be that development in a region causes democraticness in a region, thus accounting for the correlation between neighbors' regime type and the likelihood of democratization, even if neighbors have no direct influence. Alternatively, it might be that neighbors' influence is the reason for the correlation between development and democracy.

between development and democracy. Lipset and other modernization theorists suggested that increasing education, equality, urbanization, experience of working in factories, and the weakening of traditional loyalties to tribe and village—all correlates of economic development—would result in citizens with more tolerant and participatory attitudes who would demand a say in government (Lipset 1959; Inkeles and Smith 1974). These arguments stressed the experiences and values of ordinary citizens as the bases for democracy without specifying the process through which transitions might occur or giving much attention to the possible reluctance of elites to give up power. Scholars influenced by Marx expect the middle class—which tends to grow as the economy develops—to be the carrier of the demand for democracy: "no bourgeoisie, no democracy."[4] Zak and Feng (2003) have modeled a process through which this relationship might unfold, but have not tested it.

Boix (2003), Acemoglu and Robinson (2001, 2005), and Zak and Feng (2003) argue that democratization is more likely when the income distribution—which tends to even out as countries reach high levels of development—is more equal. Boix and Acemoglu/Robinson argue that elites fear redistribution less when income distribution is relatively equal because the median voter's preference with regard to taxes will then be less confiscatory. Elites, according to Acemoglu and Robinson (2001), are willing to cede some power rather than risk the costs of revolution when they expect democracy not to lead to extremely redistributive taxation. Boix (2003) expects a linear relationship between equality and the likelihood of democratization. Acemoglu and Robinson's (2001) model suggests a non-monotonic relationship: at low levels of inequality, an increase can promote democracy by increasing the threat of revolution, but at higher levels of inequality, elites will repress rather than offering concessions because of their fear of the redistributive consequences of democratization. An empirical challenge to these arguments is that evidence of more equal income distributions in democracies is at best mixed (Bollen and Jackman 1985). There is little evidence that the current set of recalcitrant dictatorships is made up of countries with especially unequal income distributions. In the post-Second World War period, longer-lived dictatorships (excluding monarchies) have more equal income distributions than brief ones.

Boix (2003) and Rogowski (1998) argue that capital mobility, which also tends to rise with development, also contributes to democratization. When capital is mobile, it can flee in response to high taxes. Knowing that, democratic governments are expected to refrain from taxing heavily; so elites need not fear democracy. In the Boix (2003) model, elites' interests can be protected either by a relatively equal income distribution or by capital mobility. Where capital mobility is low, as in countries with predominantly agricultural economies, and income unequal, however, elites should be unwilling to negotiate democratization. The Boix and Acemoglu/Robinson arguments are discussed in more detail below.

---

[4] This is Barrington Moore's summary of Marx (1966, 416).

2 MODELS OF DEMOCRATIZATION AS
STRATEGIC INTERACTIONS BETWEEN ELITES
AND CITIZENS

Models of the interactions between ruling elites and others that may lead to democratization can be divided into two categories depending on their basic assumptions about who the relevant actors are and what their goals are. The Boix (2003) and Acemoglu/Robinson (2001) models described above assume that the most important division within society is between rich and poor, and that the rich form and maintain dictatorships in order to protect their assets. They also assume, as do many economic models of authoritarian politics, that the key policy decision that determines the level of redistribution is the level of taxation on domestic capital. It is assumed that the median voter, who is poor, prefers high taxes in order to redistribute wealth. The more unequal the income distribution, the poorer the median voter and thus the more confiscatory the tax rate can be expected to be in a democracy. In short, the median voter in these models has never met "Homer."[5] Elites consider changing the rules, however, because of the threat of violence or revolution. In these models politicians are perfect agents of societal interests, and political leaders do not maximize their own revenue distinct from the revenue of the elite group they represent.

An alternative conception of autocracy assumes that the most important division in society is between the rulers (sometimes simplified to a single dictator) and the ruled. They assume that rulers maximize their own income from tax revenue at the expense of both rich and poor ruled. Rulers thus set taxes at the highest rate that does not deter economic effort by citizens. In these models, rulers offer increments of democracy when doing so can increase the credibility of their promises to provide public goods and other policies that will increase economic growth and thus benefit both rulers and ruled (North and Weingast 1989; Weingast 1997; Escriba Folch 2003). Alternatively, democratic institutions may be offered as a means of directly increasing revenues (Levi 1988; Bates and Lien 1985; Rogowski 1998). Bueno de Mesquita et al. (2003) propose a more complicated set of societal divisions and actors: a leader; a ruling coalition; a "selectorate" that includes those citizens who can affect the composition of the ruling coalition; and residents, those who are taxed but politically marginal. In all these models, the ruled care about growth and the share of their own production they are allowed to keep. Taxation is not seen as a means of redistribution in favor of the poor, but rather as a means of enriching rulers. Rulers become rich by ruling; they do not rule because they were rich before achieving power. They cling to power in order to continue collecting revenue from the productive population under their control, not to protect themselves from redistributive taxation. The main

---

[5] Larry Bartels (2005) has christened the real-life low-income voter who favors more social spending but who nevertheless opposes the estate tax Homer after the famous Homer Simpson.

constraint on rulers' pursuit of wealth for themselves is the threat of declining revenue caused by capital flight or reduction in economic effort.

Both of these approaches offer some insights into the process of democratization. The Boix (2003) and Acemoglu/Robinson (2001) models are plausible simplifications of early democratizations in Western Europe and of many transitions in Latin America, but models emphasizing the conflict between rulers and ruled are more plausible when applied to recent struggles over democratization in Africa, Eastern Europe, the Middle East, and parts of Asia. These models, like large-N studies of democratization to date, have implicitly assumed that a single model will explain democratization in all times and all circumstances.

2.1 Rich Rulers versus Poor Ruled

As noted above, Boix (2003) argues that income equality and capital mobility reduce elite fears of democracy, the first because it reduces expected redistribution by popular governments and the second because it provides capital holders with an exit option if taxes become confiscatory. This is a seminal contribution to the literature on democratization because it provides plausible microfoundations for the observed correlation between development and democracy. Other laudable aspects of the research include a serious effort to test the argument and the inclusion of nineteenth- and early twentieth-century democratizations in the analysis. Virtually all other quantitative studies of democratization have looked only at the post-Second World War period because of data limitations. Boix has made a huge effort to overcome those limitations.

The Boix (2003) study has not resolved all debates, however, in part because the empirical support for the argument is somewhat ambiguous. On the positive side, income inequality has a substantial effect on the likelihood of democratization in a dataset that covers 1950–90 and thus excludes most African democratizations. We do not know if the result would change if a number of transitions in poor African countries were added. The percentage of family farms, used as a proxy for inequality in the historical tests, has a negative effect on the probability of transition, contrary to expectations. One of the measures of capital mobility, average share of agriculture as a percentage of GDP, fails to produce expected results. Other indicators used to measure capital mobility have strong effects but ambiguous interpretations.

The ratio of fuel exports to total exports, for example, is a plausible indicator of capital mobility. The correlation between reliance on oil and authoritarianism, however, is usually attributed to the oil-producing government's ability to provide transfers to large parts of the population *without* relying on taxation.[6] So how can we tell whether the reported relationship between oil dependence and democratization

---

[6] For rentier state arguments, see Anderson 1987 and Crystal (1995).

is caused by reduced capital mobility or the strategic use of resources by dictators to buy popular support?

Average years of schooling is used as a measure of human capital, which is more mobile than physical capital, and Boix finds a positive relationship between education and democratization. Many other analysts have found this relationship, however, and attributed it to the propensity of more-educated citizens to demand democracy. In short, although Boix's argument is plausible and attractively simple, the empirical investigation is not definitive. The argument fits well with the stylized facts of West European democratization, however, and redistributive changes followed democratization in Western Europe as this argument would predict (Lindert 1994). Further tests of this argument deserve to be important items on the research agenda of students of democratization.

Acemoglu and Robinson's (2001) argument begins with many of the same basic assumptions about the way the world works as Boix's. It also gives a central role in resistance to democratization to elites' fear of redistribution when the starting income distribution is unequal. Its predictions are complicated, however, by limiting the threat of revolution to periods of recession. In this argument, when the rich are threatened by revolution (which only occurs during recession), they can grant redistribution without changing the political system, grant democracy as a way of making the commitment to redistribution credible, or repress. Redistribution without regime change is not credible to the poor because they know that they cannot maintain the threat of revolution after the recession is over. According to Acemoglu and Robinson, democratization is a more credible commitment to maintaining redistribution over a longer time period. (Why the poor should accept democratization as credible when even the model allows the rich to stage coups if they are dissatisfied by the later tax rate is not clear.)

The introduction of recessions, which vary in both intensity and frequency, substantially complicates making predictions about the effects of inequality on elite behavior. Equality makes democratization less threatening to elites, but how they react to inequality depends on the seriousness of the threat of revolution and the cost of repression. In this model, the likelihood of revolution depends on inequality (which increases the threat of revolution) and the intensity of recession (which decreases revolution's cost to the poor). Frequent recessions, however, increase the likelihood that the elite can credibly offer redistribution without democratization because frequent recessions allow the poor to threaten revolution often, thus enforcing the bargain. So intense recessions destabilize dictatorships leading to democratization, revolution, or repression, but frequent recessions lead paradoxically to stable authoritarianism with redistribution. The bottom line, according to Acemoglu and Robinson (2001, 957), is that "democracy is more likely to be consolidated if the level of inequality is limited, whereas high inequality is likely to lead to political instability, either in the form of frequent regime changes or repression of social unrest."

In contrast to the Boix argument, Acemoglu and Robinson expect income inequality to lead to unstable regime changes, not continued authoritarianism. One of the attractive features of the Acemoglu and Robinson model is that it explains repeated transitions between democracy and dictatorship, a phenomenon that has characterized some parts of the developing world since the middle of the twentieth century. The model seems to be a plausible simplification of events in much of Latin America and in a few other developing countries. It does not fit most of the Middle East, Eastern Europe, Africa, or Asia, where fear of redistributive taxation is not a plausible reason for resistance to democratization since substantial portions of productive assets were state or foreign owned for much of the late twentieth century. State elites who control a large portion of productive assets may certainly fear loss of power since it will dispossess them, but they will not suffer less dispossession because the income distribution is more equal. Acemoglu and Robinson do not offer systematic empirical tests of their arguments so we cannot assess their fit with the real world.

Models linking democratization to inequality seem highly plausible initially, but the empirical investigation of the relationship between regime type and income inequality does not offer strong support for their basic assumptions. Nor does empirical investigation of the relationship between democracy and redistribution. If these arguments were correct, we would expect to find the remaining dictatorships in the world more unequal on average than democracies, but Bollen and Jackman (1985) find no relationship between democracy and inequality. Przeworski et al. (2000) find a positive relationship between only one of three measures of inequality tried and transitions to democracy. They find a stronger relationship between inequality (in democracies) and democratic breakdown, which might explain any relationship that exists between democracy and equality (if one does exist), but does not support the idea that equality makes democratization more likely.

The models also assume that the main reason elites fear democracy and ordinary citizens want it is that they expect it to lead to redistribution. LIndert (1994) has shown that the expected redistribution occurred in Western Europe after the first steps toward democratization were taken, but Mulligan, Sala-i-Martin, and Gil (2003) show that contemporary democracies do not on average distribute more than dictatorships.[7] We should not be surprised by this result. Income distribution varied greatly among late twentieth-century dictatorships. Many, both communist and noncommunist, expropriated traditional elites and redistributed income and opportunities through land reform, much increased public education, and industrialization policies that led to the movement of large numbers of people out of agriculture and into factories. It is hard to imagine that elites in these kinds of authoritarian regimes would be motivated by a fear of greater redistribution. They would fear loss of their own power and wealth, but not via redistributive taxation. Income equality would not reassure them.

---

[7] Boix (2003) challenges this result.

2.2 Revenue Maximizing Rulers versus Politically Powerless Citizens

This approach to the study of democratization, which owes much to seminal articles by North and Weingast (1989) and Olson (1993), sees rulers as maximizing their own individual revenue via taxation and citizens as sharing a desire for productivity-enhancing policies and public goods, regardless of whether they are rich or poor. In this image of politics, taxes redistribute wealth from citizens to rulers, not from rich to poor. Rulers may want revenue in order to pursue wars, to buy support in order to stay in power, or for personal consumption; their reason does not affect the logic of the argument. Rulers are motivated by their desire for revenue to offer public goods and a tax rate that does not reduce investment or effort.

In some versions of this approach, societal elites or holders of capital are most affected by the ruler's policies and can do most to destabilize his rule if they are dissatisfied. Consequently, they are the ones most likely to be accommodated when the ruler offers an institutionalized form of participation in return for their cooperation. Rulers may offer representative institutions as a means of offering a credible commitment to supply desired public goods (Levi 1988; North and Weingast 1989; Escriba Folch 2003) or simply in exchange for wealth holders' contingent consent to the taxation of mobile capital (Bates and Lien 1985). As in the Boix (2003) argument, democratization becomes more likely as capital becomes more mobile, but the reason for the relationship changes. The more mobile capital, according to Bates and Lien (1985), the harder it is to tax without contingent consent and thus the more likely the ruler will offer representative institutions. Rogowski (1998) suggests a more general form of this logic in which citizens' ability to move away increases the likelihood that rulers will offer them representative institutions or good government in order to induce them to remain, along with their productive capacity, within the ruler's territory.[8] Thus these models often explain the first small steps toward democratization from absolutist monarchy.

Bueno de Mesquita et al. (2003) suggest a more complicated general framework for understanding politics in both democracy and autocracy. Their model, to reiterate, includes: a ruler supported by a winning coalition; a "selectorate," meaning those citizens who have some influence on who can join the winning coalition; and residents who play no role in selecting rulers. In democracies, the selectorate is the enfranchised population, and the winning coalition is made up of those who voted for the winning party or coalition, that is, roughly 50 percent of the selectorate. In single-party authoritarian regimes, the winning coalition is the small group of actual rulers, and the selectorate is made up of all members of the ruling party. In military regimes, the winning coalition is the junta and the selectorate is the officer corps. They do not discuss reasons for different authoritarian institutional choices.

---

[8] But see Bravo (2006) for evidence that the exit of those citizens most dissatisfied with a ruler's policies may increase the probability that he survives in office—thus giving the ruler a reason to provide policies that induce the exit of those citizens most likely to join the opposition.

Rulers maximize personal revenue via taxation but are constrained by the need to provide private and public goods in order to maintain the support of the winning coalition. If enough members of the ruling coalition defect because they are dissatisfied with their share, the ruler is overthrown. Citizens outside the winning coalition benefit only from the public goods provided when the winning coalition is too large to be maintained by private goods alone.

Residents and sometimes members of the selectorate may hold demonstrations or join rebellions to challenge rulers who tax them too heavily or provide insufficient public goods, but rulers in this model always respond with repression. If revolutionary challengers win despite repression, the new rulers face the same incentives that other rulers do to narrow the winning coalition and keep resources for themselves. In other words, revolutions and popular uprisings in this model do not threaten redistribution or lead to democracy. Instead they lead to a seizure of power by a new leader and winning coalition who maximize their own wealth at the expense of those they exclude. One of the most useful and empirically realistic points made by Bueno de Mesquita et al. is that participation in a coup, uprising, or revolution does not guarantee the participant an improved share of power or wealth after the fall of the old regime because those who lead such movements have incentives after they win to renege on earlier promises.

Thus democracy cannot arise as a response to popular uprising in this model. Instead, it arises when the members of the winning coalition can benefit themselves by expanding its size. Members of winning coalitions are cross-pressured when it comes to the size of coalition they prefer to be part of. Their individual share of private goods is larger when the coalition is smaller, but the ruler keeps less for himself and provides more public and total private goods when the coalition is larger. In the model, the winning coalition has a tipping point at the size at which it prefers to increase further. Once that happens, democracy will eventually follow. This model, like those described above, portrays democratization as elite led. In the Bueno de Mesquita et al. (2003) model, however, winning coalition elites are motivated simply by wanting to improve their own welfare relative to that of the ruler. They are not responding either to a challenge from the excluded or to the threat of capital strike.

Models that emphasize conflict between revenue-maximizing rulers and politically powerless citizens capture elements of reality in many recent transitions in developing countries. Once the changes in the international economy provoked by the debt crisis had rendered state interventionist development strategies unsustainable, many authoritarian governments were forced to begin liberalizing their economies. In order to attract private investment to replace state investment that could not be sustained without foreign inflows, governments had to offer more predictable policies and certain public goods conducive to private investment (Roberts 2006). Like democrats, dictators' survival in office is threatened by poor economic performance. As noted by North and Weingast (1989), Acemoglu and Robinson (2001), Escriba Folch (2003), and others, policy promises made by dictators inherently lack credibility. Dictators can increase the credibility of these promises by creating institutions that give capital holders a say in policy making and that increase the constraints on the dictator's arbitrary power. Democratic institutions such as legislatures and multiparty electoral competition can create those constraints if the commitment to the institutional change is itself considered credible. If the institutions benefit both the ruler, by increasing revenues, and the ruled, by increasing productivity or welfare, then the institutional bargain is self-enforcing and thus credible. These models, in other words, provide a reason for expecting institutional bargains to be more credible than offers to provide desired policies in the absence of institutional change, which the Acemoglu and Robinson (2001) model does not.

These models thus suggest intuitions about why democratization and economic liberalization tended to vary together in the late twentieth century (Hellman 1998). Prior to the debt crisis of the 1980s, governments had a choice between relying primarily on state investment or private investment. Those that chose state investment did not have to offer credible commitments to provide public goods, predictable economic policy, or policies favorable to private investors in order to secure revenue flows, and thus the economic pressure to initiate institutional constraints on rulers' arbitrary powers was low. Since the 1980s, the state investment strategy has become unworkable except possibly in countries reliant on the export of oil or other high-priced natural resources. Consequently, governments have sought to attract private investment via capital-friendly policies, and political institutions that constrain the dictator's discretion help to make those policies credible to investors (Roberts 2006).

The emphasis on the interest differences between rulers and ruled and on redistribution in favor of rulers as a central fact of dictatorship fits well with what we know about many of the dictatorships referred to as personalistic, sultanistic, or patrimonial by different authors. These models do not accommodate the role that popular uprisings have played in many late twentieth-century democratizations, however. Moreover, most of these models are very abstract, and most tests of them have been narrowly focused or open to multiple interpretations.

Some features of late twentieth-century democratization have not found their way into models, though they have been included in large-N statistical studies. The correlation between reliance on oil exports and authoritarianism, for example, has been found repeatedly. In developing countries, oil is usually state owned or owned by foreign multinationals and taxed heavily. Whether it is state owned or not, the government draws its revenues largely from natural resource production, not from taxation on domestic wealth holders. A large mostly descriptive literature on the effects of oil on politics exists (Karl 1997; Chaudhry 1997; Anderson 1987; Crystal 1995). Yet, I know of no model that has grappled seriously with state ownership of productive resources and its effect on the struggle over democratization. All models assume a capitalist economy with private domestic investors as important actors. During the third wave of democratization, however, most transitions affected authoritarian regimes in which state investment was high. In many, foreign investment also played a large role, and revenue from foreign aid was more important than revenues from taxation in some.

International factors have also been largely absent from models of democratization. Many observers have suggested that international forces, such as the diffusion of democratic ideas and pressure from international financial institutions to democratize, have affected transitions, especially since the 1980s. Earlier quantitative studies found it hard to document these influences, but Gasiorowski (1995) and Gleditsch and Choun (2004) show that the proportion of democratic neighbors increases the likelihood of transitions to democracy in neighboring countries, lending some support to the diffusion argument. Jon Pevehouse (2002) shows that membership in regional international organizations in which most other members are democratic increases the likelihood of democratization. Since membership in democratic regional international organizations is likely to be correlated with having democratic neighbors, however, we cannot be sure whether organizations have an independent effect beyond the effect of living in a "good" neighborhood. Bueno de Mesquita, Siverson, and Woller (1992; Bueno de Mesquita and Siverson 1995) show that war affects the survival of both political leaders and regimes. Gleditsch and Choun (2004) show that wars increase the likelihood of transition from one authoritarian government to another, but neither Gleditsch and Choun (2004) nor Pevehouse (2002) shows strong evidence that wars in the neighborhood decrease the likelihood of democratization, as some have suggested. Marinov (2005) shows that although sanctions are effective at bringing down democratic leaders, they have little effect on the survival of dictators and therefore we can infer little effect on authoritarian regimes.[9] Theoretical treatments of democratization, however, continue to focus on domestic causes. It may be that the focus on domestic causes is appropriate when explaining democratizations before the Second World War, but that international influences—both economic and political—have become more pronounced over time.

3 DISAGGREGATING DEMOCRATIZATION

Assuming that there is one explanation of democratization may be the reason that scholars continue to disagree about its causes. Different analysts have deeper knowledge about some sets of cases than others, and naturally their intuitions formalized in models fit the cases they know best better than those they know less well. The findings of large-N studies differ from each other depending on specification, time period included, and cases used, leaving very basic ideas contested. Such varying results should be expected if single statistical models are being imposed on a set of

---

[9] He does not test the effect of sanctions on economic performance, and growth is included as a control variable in the test of the effect of sanctions, so it is quite possible that sanctions do affect authoritarian survival through their effect on growth. In democracies, though, sanctions affect leadership survival even with growth controlled for.

disparate processes without efforts to specify how the process might differ over time or in different kinds of transitions.[10] I suggest that it would be useful to consider the possibility that processes of democratization might be different in different contexts, that these differences might be systematic, and that developing a theoretical understanding of these differences would lead to useful empirical results and a better understanding of how transitions really take place.

Two context differences that might influence the democratization process are the historical period in which it takes place and the type of regime that democracy replaces. Early democratizations took place in capitalist economies in which the rich usually held political power. Later democratizations have also occurred in countries with high levels of state ownership of productive assets, especially natural resources. State ownership makes possible both the accumulation of wealth by political leaders and also the distribution of benefits to supporters, and in some cases citizens, without the need for high taxation of private wealth holders. Rulers who have acquired wealth through access to state resources, in contrast to those who hold political power because they own private wealth, have to fear losing most of their assets if they are deposed, regardless of the income distribution or other factors that might affect future taxation.

Most transitions before the Second World War were transitions from some form of oligarchic government; many were gradual transitions from very limited suffrage to nearly universal. Post-Second World War democratizations have occurred in several quite different ways, but nearly all have involved a transition to immediate universal suffrage democracy. These have included the transition from colonial rule to universal suffrage democracy at independence; transitions from universal suffrage authoritarianism to universal suffrage democracy; and redemocratizations in which most of the parties and political institutions of a prior democracy are reinstated at the conclusion of an authoritarian interlude. Gradual transitions from limited to almost universal suffrage have been rare during the last fifty years (cf. Huntington 1991).

If elite opposition to democracy is motivated by fear of redistributive taxation, gradual increases in suffrage should be easier than rapid ones because the median voter after a limited enfranchisement would be richer and thus demand less redistribution. Such institutional choices are often made during bargaining over the conditions of transition. We might expect authoritarian rulers concerned about redistributive taxation to negotiate incremental enfranchisement, but dictators with different fears might not consider universal suffrage threatening.

Various international influences on democratization have arguably had greater effects since the Second World War and perhaps greater still since the 1980s. The differences in the sources of dictators' wealth before and after the Second World War

---

[10]   Besides the exceptions noted in the text above, a number of large-N studies have modeled factors that have changed over time. Gleditsch and Choun (2004), for example, show that the predominance of Catholicism in countries has a negative effect on prospects for democratization before Vatican II and a positive effect afterward. Gasiorowski (1995) shows that economic crisis has different effects on the likelihood of democratization during different time periods.

noted above are associated with a change in economic strategy that swept through the developing world between about 1930 and 1970. Nearly all developing countries initiated development strategies that increased state investment, ownership, and regulation of their economies. These strategies reduced governments' dependence on private investors and created non-tax sources of revenue, which could then be distributed along with monopolies and subsidies of various kinds in exchange for support. The ability to use state resources to expropriate traditional and foreign wealth holders and create new elites beholden to the government may have reduced pressures for democratization during the decades when this strategy remained viable.

A second change in the international economy, beginning around 1980 with the debt crisis, brought that period to an end. When foreign lending was no longer available to cover the trade and budget deficits characteristic of the state interventionist development strategy, developing country governments faced intense pressure to adopt policies conducive to attracting investment. Attracting investments depends on credible policy commitments and secure property rights. If, as various analysts have argued, dictators can use legislatures and other quasi-democratic institutions to make their policy commitments credible, the economic strategy changes brought about by the debt crisis of the 1980s should have created strong incentives toward some degree of democratization. In the post-1980 period, we see an increase in both democratizations and also the adoption of quasi-democratic institutions by authoritarian regimes (Levitsky and Way 2006).

The end of the Cold War has also changed the process of democratization. Before 1990, authoritarian regimes were supported with extensive aid and other help from both superpowers. Such aid both increased the regimes' repressive capacity (Boix 2003, 29–30) and also added to dictators' ability to buy support without redistributing from domestic producers. Since 1990, Levitsky and Way (2006) show that those authoritarian regimes with the closest linkages to the USA and Western Europe are the most likely to have democratic-looking institutions such as multiparty elections in which some real competition is allowed. Such regimes may be easier to dislodge since opposition is usually less risky and costly in them. The reduction in foreign support for dictatorships since the end of the Cold War also contributed to the increase in democratizations in the late twentieth century.

Thus, for both domestic and international reasons, we might think that a model of the early process of democratization would be different from a model of the later process. The finding by Boix and Stokes (2003) that economic development and income distribution have much stronger effects on the likelihood of democratization before 1950 than after lends support to the idea that modeling separate processes for the two time periods would be fruitful.

These cross-time differences in the causes of democratization may be caused in part by differences in the kinds of regimes from which democracies emerge. Pre-Second World War democratizations, which occurred primarily in Europe and Latin America, generally replaced governments controlled by the rich, whether these were planter oligarchies or monarchies, through electoral systems with very limited suf-frage. In most of these non-democratic regimes, legislatures existed, elite parties or proto-parties competed for office, and struggles by legislatures to limit the power of monarchs or executives had played an important role in determining the shape of political institutions. Democratization tended to occur through the extension of suffrage to new groups without other large institutional changes. More citizens voted, sometimes new parties formed to attract the votes of the newly enfranchised, and elections became fairer, but parliamentary systems in Europe and separation of powers systems in Latin America accommodated the inclusion of new voters and parties.

We cannot make the same kinds of generalizations about late twentieth-century transitions. The authoritarian regimes from which late twentieth-century democ-ratizations emerged differed from the stylized portrait in the paragraph above. Few of their rulers were born to wealthy families. Most came to prominence via either a military career or a rise to leadership in a revolutionary or nationalist party. Some contemporary authoritarian regimes have repressed all political activ-ity, but many have held regular elections with universal suffrage. Competition for control of government has been limited by restrictions on opposition parties or manipulation of voters and playing field, not restrictions on suffrage. Some con-temporary authoritarian regimes have protected the interests of the rich, but oth-ers have redistributed land, nationalized natural resources, and expropriated other wealth. Sometimes these expropriations have led to more equal income distribu-tions and other times to an altered but equally uneven distribution with wealth concentrated in the hands of the dictator's family and supporters. In the former situation, regime supporters fear the loss of power entailed by more competitive politics, not redistribution. In the latter, they fear confiscation, being brought to trial for corruption and human rights abuses, prison, and execution (Kaminski, Nalepa, and O'Neill 2006), but these dangers are not lessened by a relatively equal income distribution.

Because of these differences, late twentieth- and twenty-first-century democra-tizations may not only be different from earlier ones but also different from each other. If wealthy private sector elites rule countries, then they may indeed resist democratization when they expect more redistributive taxation, and their fears may be allayed by a relatively equal income distribution or capital mobility (Boix 2003). Incremental suffrage extensions may be especially easy for them to endure. If, how-ever, ruling elites came to power either through election or revolution as the leaders of movements determined to overthrow traditional elites, then regardless of whether they actually carried out their promises or have simply stolen in their turn, their fears of being deposed seem unlikely to be allayed by factors that reduce future taxation. Instead, their fears might be allayed by enforceable bargains not to prosecute them for corruption and human rights abuses (i.e. allowing them to go into friendly exile) or institutional bargains that give them a good chance of returning to office in competitive elections in the future.

These differences do not imply a return to case studies or within-region comparisons as the main way of studying democratization, however.[11] Rather, they suggest the possibility that there are theoretically relevant differences among authoritarian governments themselves and in the ways that they interact with the ruled that may require different explanations of how transitions from them occur. As Diamond (2002, 33) notes, contemporary authoritarian regimes differ from each other "and if we are to understand the contemporary dynamics, causes, limits, and possibilities of regime change (including future democratization), we must understand the different, and in some respects new, types of authoritarian rule." His attempt at classification, however, simply relies on drawing lines between scores on the Freedom House scale to create categories. If the relevant differences are in degrees of "not democraticness," then we do not need to theorize processes separately; we can simply include a measure of democracy in statistical models, as a number of analysts have. Unsurprisingly, they find that countries that are more democratic at time one are likely to be even more democratic at time two. We cannot tell, however, whether the analysis means that less repressive forms of authoritarianism are less stable or that democratization is often incremental, and dictatorships that have liberalized somewhat in one year often continue on that path in subsequent years. A more fruitful approach to classification would begin by thinking about how the causes of democratization seem to vary from one context to another. Then classification could be based on expectations about how those differences would be likely to unfold.[12]

Linz and Stepan (1996) take a first step toward the kind of theoretically based classification that might help explain differences in democratization processes with their classification of some authoritarian regimes as "sultanistic," meaning one individual has discretion over all important personnel and policy decisions, some as "neo-totalitarian," meaning, in effect, post-Stalinist, and so on. They expect the usual characteristics of these different kinds of authoritarian regime to have systematic effects on different aspects of democratic consolidation. These arguments have not been tested, but they do suggest plausible links between characteristics of particular kinds of authoritarianism and expected outcomes.

If post-Second World War authoritarian regimes with different kinds of leadership tend to have different institutional structures and different relationships with supporters and ordinary citizens, then we would expect them to break down differently because different institutions privilege and disadvantage different groups. A simple

[11] Mainwaring and Pérez-Liñán (2003) argue that democratization in Latin America differed from the general path shown by Przeworski et al. (2000). Different models could be appropriate for different regions, as they argue, but we would only know it by comparing regions with each other. Stokes (2004) provides a thoughtful discussion of why regional differences in democratization processes might occur.

[12] Some early descriptions of democratization classified transition processes themselves using categories such as from above, from below, by transaction, and so on. What I suggest here might build on these earlier ideas but differs from them in that the classifications of differences would be rooted in basic features of authoritarian regimes.

and intuitive way to categorize these different kinds of leadership and institutions is as professionalized military, hegemonic party, and personalistic. These regime types emerge from struggles among elite contenders with different backgrounds, support bases, and resources after seizures of power. They do not derive in an obvious way from underlying social or economic structures, and all have been compatible with a wide range of economic ideologies. All types were common in the late twentieth century, so understanding something about how they break down might help to explain why post-1950 democratizations have been different from those that came before. In the real world, there are of course lots of borderline cases, but we can use the simple types to develop theories and empirical expectations.

On average, governments ruled by the professionalized military are more fragile than other kinds of authoritarianism (Gasiorowrski 1995; Geddes 2003).[13] They are more easily destabilized by poor economic performance because factionalization over how to respond to crisis causes many officers to want to return to the barracks in order to reunify the armed forces. Because of officers' dread of factionalism, the first moves toward liberalization often arise within the military elite, as noted by O'Donnell, Schmitter, and Whitehead (1986). Since military rulers usually decide to return to the barracks rather than being forced out, transitions from military rule tend to be negotiated and orderly. Negotiation is more likely to lead to democracy than is violent overthrow, and the successors to professionalized military regimes are nearly always elected in competitive elections. Thus the fall of a military regime usually results in a democracy, though it may not last.

In contrast to the military, several scholars have noted the robustness of hegemonic party regimes. Geddes (2003) shows that regimes ruled by dominant parties last substantially longer than other non-monarchic forms of authoritarianism.[14] Gandhi and Przeworski (2006) argue that dictators supported by single parties survive longer in office. When dominant or single-party regimes face severe challenges, they try to hang on by changing institutions to allow some participation by moderate opponents— thus isolating and rendering less threatening more extreme opponents (Lust-Okar 2005; Magaloni 2006). When they see the writing on the wall, they put great effort into negotiating electoral institutions that will benefit them when they become ex-authoritarians competing in fair elections (Geddes 1995; Magaloni 2006). If members of a dominant party regime cannot maintain their monopoly on power, they prefer to be replaced by a democracy since they have a good chance of being able to continue their political careers as democratic politicians. Replacement by an opposing authoritarian regime is likely to exclude them from the political game at best. Consequently dominant party governments negotiate their extrications through elections. The elections that end the rule of hegemonic parties most often initiate a democracy,

[13] For the logic underlying this argument and some of the evidence supporting it, see Geddes (2003).
[14] Hadenius and Teorell (2005) find different survival rates than do most other scholars because their coding rules do not allow them to distinguish between what most other analysts would identify as a regime change and smaller institutional changes that occur while a regime, in the usual sense of the word, remains in power.

but sometimes they result in a new hegemonic party regime. This happens because the new ruling party can sometimes make use of institutions originally devised to help the previous ruling party.

Regimes in which power has been personalized under one individual, however, are more likely to be replaced by a new dictatorship than by a democracy (Hadenius and Teorell 2005). Personalistic dictators are less willing to negotiate leaving office because they face a greater likelihood of assassination, prosecution, confiscation, or exile than do the leaders of other kinds of authoritarianism. Transitions from personalist dictatorship are seldom initiated by regime insiders; instead, popular opposition, strikes, and demonstrations often force dictators to consider allowing multiparty elections (Bratton and van de Walle 1997). Personalistic dictators are more likely to be overthrown in revolutions, civil wars, popular uprisings, or invasions (Skocpol and Goodwin 1994; Geddes 2003). Linz and Chehabi (1998) have described the difficulties of democratization following what they call sultanistic regimes. Several observers have suggested that transitions from personalist rule are more affected by international factors, such as pressures from international financial institutions and invasion by neighboring or ex-colonial countries, than are other kinds of authoritarianism. International financial institutions pressured a number of African dictators to agree to multiparty elections (Bratton and van de Walle 1997).

For these reasons, the process of transition from personalized dictatorship should not be modeled as an elite-led bargain. Transitions from personalized dictatorship are less likely to result in democracy, but sometimes they do. A model that focused on such transitions would help us to understand the special circumstances that lead to this outcome. Neeman and Wantchekon (2002) have proposed that democracy occurs when neither of two contending forces can defeat the other. They address situations in which opposition to dictatorship has developed into civil war, but the model might be generalizable to non-violent forms of political conflict. Models that explain transitions to democracy from personalized dictatorship should be on the democratization research agenda, as should models that include foreign pressures.

There may be other fruitful ways of disaggregating the democratization process. My point in this section has not been to argue that there is one true way to break the process into theorizable parts, but rather that we have considerable evidence that not all democratizations occur in the same way and that these differences are systematic not random. The identification of democratization as one "thing" is an artifact of our use of normal language to describe the process. If the current state of empirical knowledge allows us to see that there are theoretically important differences in democratization processes depending on when they happened, what kinds of dictatorship were being replaced, or something else, we should not expect a single model to capture all the processes well. Nor should we combine all democratizations in the same statistical tests without making an effort to specify cross-time or other theoretically relevant differences.

4 CONCLUSION

Recent empirical research on democratization has confirmed the relationship between economic development and democracy. Most research also agrees that countries with oil and mostly Muslim populations are less likely to be democratic, though these conclusions have been challenged by some analysts. It has also confirmed that countries with highly educated populations are more likely to be democratic. The explanations for these correlations remain contested. Przeworski et al. (2000) argue that economic development causes democratic stability not democratization. Boix and Stokes (2003), however, show that economic development had a substantial impact on democratization before the Second World War and continues to have a smaller effect. Middle East scholars have described a process through which oil rents are translated into popular acquiescence to authoritarianism, but Herb (2005) argues that oil wealth leads to a misspecification of statistical tests of the effect of economic development on democratization in oil-rich countries, not to a special kind of rentier authoritarianism. Most observers have attributed the apparent affinity between Islam and authoritarianism to traditional values widely held by individual Muslims, but Fish (2002) claims that the treatment of women in Muslim societies hinders democratization.

These empirical regularities with contested interpretations bring two tasks to the forefront of the research agenda in the study of democratization: empirical studies aimed explicitly at testing different causal mechanisms; and the creation of carefully specified models to explain democratization. Some progress is being made on both fronts. Fish (2002) tests his argument about the treatment of women. Herb (2005) attempts to disaggregate the effects of rentierism from the effect of economic development as a way of testing the rentier state argument. Boix (2003) tests his argument that income equality and capital mobility increase the likelihood of democratization. None of these tests is fully persuasive, but they are very useful steps in the direction of identifying causal mechanisms. Boix (2003), Acemoglu and Robinson (2001, 2005), Zak and Feng (2003), North and Weingast (1989), Weingast (1997), Bates and Lien (1985), Neeman and Wantchekon (2002), and others have proposed formal models of democratization that offer a number of useful insights. Most of these models have been proposed as universal explanations of democratization, but when examined carefully, most turn out to be useful simplifications of democratization or elements of it in one specific context.

I suggest that we take seriously our own research showing systematic differences in the process of democratization across time and type of authoritarianism. Other differences in the process may also be theoretically important. We might make progress faster, both empirically and theoretically, if we identified clear domains for our arguments about the causes of democratization rather than assuming that just because we cover many processes of democratization with one word we should also uncritically model it as one process regardless of what we know about historical and other differences.

REFERENCES

ACEMOGLU, D. and ROBINSON, J. 2001. A theory of political transitions. *American Economic Review*, 91: 938–63.

————2005. *Economic Origins of Dictatorship and Democracy*. New York: Cambridge University Press.

——JOHNSON, S., ROBINSON, J. and YARED, P. 2005. Income and democracy. NBER Working Paper 11205.

ANDERSON, L. 1987. The state in the Middle East and North Africa. *Comparative Politics*, 20: 1–18.

BARRO, R. 1996. Determinants of democracy. *Journal of Political Economy*, 107: S158–S183.

BARTELS, L. 2005. Homer gets a tax cut: inequality and public policy in the American mind. *Perspectives on Politics*, 3: 15–31.

BATES, R. and LIEN, D. 1985. A note on taxation, development, and representative government. *Politics and Society*, 14: 53–70.

BOIX, C. 2003. *Democracy and Redistribution*. Cambridge: Cambridge University Press.

——and STOKES, S. 2003. Endogenous democratization. *World Politics*, 55: 517–49.

BOLLEN, K. and JACKMAN, R. 1985. Economic and non-economic determinants of political democracy in the 1960s. Pp. 27–48 in *Research in Political Sociology*, ed. R. G. Braungart and M. M. Braungart. Greenwich, Conn.: JAI Press.

BRATTON, M. and VAN DE WALLE, N. 1997. *Democratic Experiments in Africa: Regime Transitions in Comparative Perspective*. Cambridge: Cambridge University Press.

BRAVO, J. 2006. The political economy of recent Mexico–U.S. migration: a view into Mexican sub-national politics. Ph.D. dissertation. Duke University.

BUENO DE MESQUITA, B. and SIVERSON, R. M. 1995. War and the survival of political leaders: a comparative study of regime types and political accountability. *American Political Science Review*, 89: 841–55.

————and WOLLER, G. 1992. War and the fate of regimes: a comparative analysis. *American Political Science Review*, 86 (3): 638–46.

——SMITH, A., SIVERSON, R. M. and MORROW, J. D. 2003. *The Logic of Political Survival*. Cambridge, Mass.: MIT Press.

BURKHART, R. and LEWIS-BECK, M. 1994. Comparative democracy: the economic development thesis. *American Political Science Review*, 88: 903–10.

CHAUDHRY, K. 1997. *The Price of Wealth: Economies and Institutions in the Middle East*. Ithaca, NY: Cornell University Press.

CRYSTAL, J. 1995. *Oil and Politics in the Gulf: Rulers and Merchants in Kuwait and Qatar*. Cambridge: Cambridge University Press.

DIAMOND, L. 2002. Thinking about hybrid regimes. *Journal of Democracy*, 13: 21–35.

DUNNING, T. 2006. Does oil promote democracy? Regime change in rentier states. Presented at Annual Conference of the International Society for New Institutional Economics, Boulder, Colo.

EPSTEIN, D., BATES, R., GOLDSTONE, J., DRISTENSEN, I., and O'HALLORAN, S. Forthcoming. Democratic transitions. *American Journal of Political Science*.

ESCRIBA FOLCH, A. 2003. Legislatures in authoritarian regimes. Working Paper 196, Instituto Juan March de Estudios e Investigaciones.

FISH, M. S. 2002. Islam and authoritarianism. *World Politics*, 55: 4–37.

GANDHI, J. and PRZEWORSKI, A. 2006. Authoritarian institutions and the survival of autocrats. Unpublished manuscript. Emory University.

GASIOROWSKI, M. 1995. Economic crisis and political regime change: an event history analysis. *American Political Science Review*, 89: 882–97.

GEDDES, B. 1996. The initiation of new democratic institutions in Eastern Europe and Latin America. In *Institutional Design in New Democracies*, ed. A. Lijphart and C. Waisman. Boulder, Colo.: Westview.

——2003. *Paradigms and Sand Castles: Theory Building and Research Design in Comparative Politics*. Ann Arbor: University of Michigan Press.

GLEDITSCH, K. S. and CHOUN, J. L. 2004. Autocratic transitions and democratization. Prepared for presentation at the International Studies Association, Montreal.

HADENIUS, A. and TEORELL, J. 2005. Learning more about democratization: persistence and fall of authoritarian regimes 1972–2003. Prepared for presentation at the APSA.

HELLMAN, J. 1998. Winner take all: the politics of partial reform in postcommunist transitions. *World Politics*, 50: 203–34.

HERB, M. 2005. No representation without taxation? Rents, development and democracy. *Comparative Politics*, 37: 297–317.

HUNTINGTON, S. 1991. *The Third Wave: Democratization in the Late Twentieth Century*. Norman: Oklahoma University Press.

INKELES, A. and SMITH, D. H. 1974. *Becoming Modern: Individual Change in Six Developing Countries*. Cambridge, Mass.: Harvard University Press.

KAMINSKI, M., NALEPA, M., and O'NEILL, B. 2006. Normative and strategic aspects of transitional justice. *Journal of Conflict Resolution*, 50: 292–302.

KARL, T. 1997. *The Paradox of Plenty: Oil Booms and Petro-States*. Berkeley and Los Angeles: University of California Press.

LEVI, M. 1988. *Of Rule and Revenue*. Berkeley and Los Angeles: University of California Press.

LEVITSKY, S. and WAY, L. 2006. Competitive authoritarianism: origins and evolution of hybrid regimes in the post-Cold War era. Presented at APSA, Philadelphia.

LINDERT, P. 1994. The rise of social spending, 1880–1930. *Explorations in Economic History*, 31: 1–37.

LINZ, J. and CHEHABI, H. E. eds. 1998. *Sultanistic Regimes*. Baltimore: Johns Hopkins University Press.

——and STEPAN, A. 1996. *Problems of Democratic Transition and Consolidation: Southern Europe, South America, and Post-Communist Europe*. Baltimore: Johns Hopkins University Press.

LIPSET, S. M. 1959. Some social requisites of democracy: economic development and political legitimacy. *American Political Science Review*, 53: 69–105.

LUST-OKAR, E. 2005 *Structuring Conflict in the Arab World: Incumbents, Opponents and Institutions*. Cambridge: Cambridge University Press.

MAGALONI, B. 2006. *Voting for Autocracy: The Politics of Party Hegemony and its Decline*. Cambridge: Cambridge University Press.

MAINWARING, S. and PÉREZ-LIÑÁN, A. 2003. Levels of development and democracy: Latin American exceptionalism, 1945–1996. *Comparative Political Studies*, 36: 1031–67.

MARINOV, N. 2005. Do economic sanctions destabilize country leaders? *American Journal of Political Science*, 49: 564–76.

MOORE, B. 1966. *Social Origins of Dictatorship and Democracy: Lord and Peasant in the Making of the Modern World*. Boston: Beacon Press.

MULLIGAN, C., SALA-I-MARTIN, X., and GIL, R. 2003. Do democracies have different public policies than non-democracies? National Bureau of Economic Research.

NEEMAN, Z. and WANTCHEKON, L. 2002. A theory of post Civil-War democratization. *Journal of Theoretical Politics*, 14: 439–64.

NORTH, D. and WEINGAST, B. 1989. Constitutions and commitment: evolution of the institutions governing public choice in 17th century England. *Journal of Economic History*, 49: 803–32.

O'DONNELL, G., SCHMITTER, P., and WHITEHEAD, L. 1986. *Transitions from Authoritarian Rule: Tentative Conclusions about Uncertain Democracies*. Baltimore: Johns Hopkins University Press.

OLSON, M. 1993. Dictatorship, democracy, and development. *American Political Science Review*, 83: 567–76.

PAYNE, A. 1993. Westminster adapted: the political order of the Commonwealth Caribbean. In *Democracy in the Caribbean*, ed. J. Dominguez, R. Pastor, and R. DeLisle Worrell. Baltimore: Johns Hopkins University Press.

PEVEHOUSE, J. 2002. Democracy from the outside-in? International organizations and democratization. *International Organization*, 56: 515–49.

PRZEWORSKI, A. and LIMONGI, F. 1997. Modernization: theories and facts. *World Politics*, 49: 155–83.

——ALVAREZ, M. E., CHEIBUB, J. A. and LIMONGI, F. 2000. *Democracy and Development: Political Institutions and Well-Being in the World, 1950–1990*. Princeton: Princeton University Press.

ROBERTS, T. 2006. An international political economy theory of democratic transition. Unpublished MS. UCLA.

ROGOWSKI, R. 1998. Democracy, capital, skill, and country size: effects of asset mobility and regime monopoly on the odds of democratic rule. Ch. 4 in *The Origins of Liberty: Political and Economic Liberalization in the Modern World*, ed. P. Drake and M. McCubbins. Princeton: Princeton University Press.

ROSS, M. 2001. Does oil hinder democracy? *World Politics*, 53: 325–61.

SKOCPOL, T. and GOODWIN, J. 1994. Explaining revolutions in the contemporary Third World. Pp. 301–44 in *Social Revolutions in the Modern World*, ed. T. Skocpol. Cambridge: Cambridge University Press.

SMITH, B. 2004. Oil wealth and regime survival in the developing world. *American Journal of Political Science*, 48: 232–46.

STOKES, S. 2004. Region, contingency, and democratization. Presented at Conference on Contingency in the Study of Politics, Yale University.

WEINER, M. 1987. Empirical democratic theory. Pp. 3–34 in *Competitive Elections in Developing Countries*, ed. M. Weiner and E. Ozbudun. Durham: University of North Carolina Press.

WEINGAST, B. 1997. The political foundations of democracy and the rule of law. *American Political Science Review*, 91: 245–63.

WHITEHEAD, L. 1996. Three international dimensions of democratization. Pp. 3–25 in *The International Dimensions of Democratization: Europe and the Americas*, ed. L. Whitehead. Oxford: Oxford University Press.

ZAK, P. and FENG, Y. 2003. A dynamic theory of the transition to democracy. *Journal of Economic Behavior and Organization*, 52: 1–25.

CHAPTER 30

....

PARTY SYSTEMS

....

HERBERT KITSCHELT

THE concept of party system, while ubiquitous in political science texts, hardly receives systematic treatment, if handbooks by Greenstein and Polsby (1975) and Goodin and Klingemann (1996) are the reference points (cf. Epstein 1975; Pappi 1996). In a similar vein, all editions of the American Political Science Association's *Political Science: The State of the Discipline* (1983, 1993, 2002) discuss parties only within the micro-political context of individual political behavior and preference formation, but have no room for party systems. In the most recent volume, party systems appear only in Fiorina's (2002) article centered exclusively on US parties.

The subject of political party systems may be too complex and heterogeneous to deserve coherent treatment in key political science handbooks. Therefore entire handbooks have been devoted to the study of parties and party systems (cf. Katz and Crotty 2006). Or the proliferation of party system typologies in the 1950s and 1960s may have led to a "confusion and profusion" (Sartori 1976, 119) not even resolved by Sartori's own last-ditch effort. Or comparative politics at least in America has turned its attention so decisively toward comparative political economy, political regime change, and ethnocultural identity politics as to ignore the study of parties and party systems.[1] Nevertheless, party system attributes continue to play a critical role in treatments of political economy and public policy. The substantive alignments of interests and the competitiveness of party systems representing such interests are critical variables in studies of political economy, public policy, and democratic regime survival.

In this article, I first conceptualize party systems separate from parties in analogy to Waltz's (1954, 1979) treatment of international systems separate from states

---

[1] Not by chance, these are the three prominent themes of comparative politics singled out by Laitin 2002 in his overview of the comparative politics subfield.

(Section 1). I then identify systemic properties of party systems for the comparative-static analysis of competition (Section 2). Subsequently, I probe into the historical-evolutionary competitive dynamic of party systems (Section 3). Here historical-comparative analysis comes into its own beyond the study of formal properties of party systems and competition. My contribution refrains from discussing party systems as independent variables that may account for outputs and outcomes of democratic politics, as this subject is covered in other handbook chapters.

1 THE CONCEPT OF PARTY SYSTEM

Waltz (1954) distinguished three analytical levels or "images" of international politics. The first deals with human behavior, the motivations and actions of individual policy makers and members of societies. The second focuses on processes of group decision making internal to state organizations, as they produce binding collective decisions about foreign policy. The third examines state strategies as a consequence of "systemic" features. The system is conceived as a set of interacting units (Waltz 1979, 40). In a system, the action of *each* participant entity is affected by the actions of *all others*. Systemic theory must hence "show how the systems level, or structure, is distinct from the level of interacting units" (ibid.). In game-theoretic language, systemic features map the structure of the game, as defined by actors' resources, preference schedules, and feasible moves that translate into positive or negative outcomes contingent upon the other players' moves. If preferences are fixed and exogenous, equilibrium states of a system are entirely determined by systemic features concerning the numbers of players, the rules of movement, and resources distributed among the actors. As in economic markets, hegemonic or oligopolistic configurations permit actors to coordinate around different equilibria (relative prices, states of war and peace in the system) than competitive markets with many suppliers and purchasers.

Also party system theory identifies numbers of players, distributions of resources and capabilities among them, and permissible rules of movement to arrive at predictions that hold true regardless of internal idiosyncrasies of the individual elements. Equilibria concern the number of sustainable players, their profile of payoffs, and their relations of alliance and conflict among each other. These then translate into practices of creating and maintaining government executives, extracting and allocating scarce resources to constituencies, and maintaining or abandoning democracy more generally. Even if such systemic propositions are successful, however, they may require qualifications and further specifications based on knowledge about the internal behavior of individual parties, thus setting limits to a purely systemic analysis.

At least tacitly the "three images" of international relations theory have always been a staple also of comparative party system theory, as Sorauf's (1964) distinction between "party in the electorate" (individual behavior and orientations), "party as organization" (polities as organizations), and "party systems" suggests. Party systems theory is driven by a particular parsimony of focus: Net of idiosyncrasies characterizing individual actors (citizens, politicians) and modes of intra-party decision making, does the structure and dynamics of party systems causally account for identifiable outputs and outcomes of the political process?

Let me begin by outlining first and second image assumptions without which no useful hypotheses about third image (systemic) features and processes can be derived. Just as international systems presuppose historically distinctive first and second image features (cf. Ruggie 1989; Spruyt 1994), also party "systemness" and "systemic processes" take place only when certain lower order conditions are satisfied.

First image assumptions about individual actors (citizens, politicians). Systemic strategic interactions among parties presuppose that at least some citizens compare candidates and parties for electoral office with respect to some of the rewards they offer citizens. If all citizens abstain from voting, vote in a random fashion, or vote based on immutable affective collective group affiliations rather than the comparative alignment of principals' and potential agents' preferences, then there can be no systemic processes. In the sense of Lupia and McCubbins (1998) or Erickson, MacKuen, and Stimson (2002), at least some voters must be "rational information misers" whose strategic choices (voting or non-voting, supporting one candidate/party rather than another) are contingent upon the expected behavior of other voters and of electoral candidates who offer to serve as their agents in legislatures and executives.

In a similar vein, the candidate agents ("politicians") in the electoral polity must strategically act so as to take the preferences and strategic options of at least some principals (voters) and rival candidates into account in their own choice of a course of action. Just as states in international relations theory are postulated to seek survival, politicians seek (re)election to political office—executive office, and as a second best legislative office—as the baseline objective, whatever other goals they may pursue beyond that (personal rents, glory, policy, or targeted benefits for constituencies). Whether and how they pursue these higher-order objectives is endogenous to the competitive situation, characterized by the rules of the game, the stances of their competitors, and the demands of the voters. It is these constraints that prevent politicians in some circumstances from becoming just utterly cynical self-regarding rent maximizers and predators.[2] In some circumstances, the pursuit of executive office may presuppose that politicians credibly commit to collective goods producing public policies.

Systemic processes in electoral democracies presuppose the *existence of an "electoral market"* in which choices of principals and agents are contingent upon each other. There must be some "elasticities" between supply and demand. Where empirically this condition is not met, systemic party theory is inapplicable. Principals may lack material and cognitive resources to participate in an electoral market, e.g. in extremely poor countries, or they may be so committed to a particular political agent

---

[2] On systemic conditions for the choice of parties' and politicians' preferences, see Strom 1990a.

("party identification") as to pre-empt systemic processes, e.g. in ethnically highly divided polities.

Second image assumptions about constituent entities of the party system (collective agents). In mass democracies with universal franchise, principals and agents can act effectively in electoral markets only through intermediary vehicles of coordination that help them to overcome collective action problems, to facilitate the flow of information in the market, and to simplify the range of service options based on which principals and politicians may enter direct or indirect contracts with each other. Political parties, the constituent elements of a party system, may provide some or all of such services (Aldrich 1995). Party is here used in a generic sense as a set of politicians pooling resources, not necessarily the label that demarcates parties in a legal-institutional sense. The effective locus of coordination may sometimes be factions within party labels or coalitions combining party labels (Morgenstern 2004). To simplify matters, parties are henceforth the effective collective agents, not necessarily the legal labels.

Parties may help to overcome collective action problems by reducing voters' costs of information gathering and candidates' costs of information distribution in the run-up to the electoral choice. Parties may also reduce problems of "social choice" that surface in unstable and cycling majority decisions in legislatures and governments by bundling and binding sets of politicians with different individual preference schedules to work together in pursuit of a single collective preference schedule ("party program").[3] There may be other vehicles of collective mobilization that contribute to the articulation and aggregation of interests, such as social movements and interest groups. Only in a very few limitational empirical cases, such as Papua New Guinea, does democracy appear to exist without parties in the generic sense of a system of collective agents intermediating in the electoral process. At the other end of the spectrum, where most parties exhibit some durability and capacity to coordinate citizens and politicians time and again, we speak of party system institutionalization (Huntington 1968, ch. 7; Mainwaring and Scully 1995). It is akin to what Sartori (1968, 288–97; 1986, 55–6) has called a "structured" party system and Mair (1997, 213–14) refers to as "systemness" through "closure," namely the identity of interacting corporate units (parties) over some extended time period.

2 VARIETIES OF PARTY SYSTEMS

Party system theory aims at predicting strategies of the competitors and preferably identifying equilibria of such strategies. The critical elements are the number of

---

[3] On the theory of party formation, see especially Aldrich (1995); Cox and McCubbins (1993, chs. 4 and 5); and Snyder and Ting (2002). Whether or not they solve collective action and social choice problems, as Aldrich 1995 postulates, however, is a contingent process (see below).

competitors and the "currency" of competition for voter support, namely the policy issues and issue bundles politicians promise to enact to shore up electoral support. Theories typically assume an indirect exchange between voters and politicians. Citizens surrender their vote at the beginning of the electoral term in exchange for the winning politicians implementing campaign promises during the electoral term. Democratic accountability operates indirectly because of (1) the time elapsed between election and policy delivery; (2) the benefits and costs of policy accruing to all voters, regardless of whether they supported winners; and (3) voters speaking their verdict over the record of governing politicians (and the opposition) retrospectively at the end of the electoral term and taking that evaluation into account in their prospective assessment of politicians' promises for the subsequent electoral term.

The policy-based "responsible partisan" model, however, is only one special case of principal–agent relations within a broader set of mechanisms expressing democratic accountability. Before turning to the key elements of the common models of party competition—numbers of competitors and numbers of dimensions of competition— let us therefore distinguish modes of democratic accountability in terms of different principal–agent exchanges (Section 2.1). Moreover, and related to this point, critics have argued that responsible partisan models home in on a highly constrained view of the currency of competition, namely policy positions rather than a variety of valence goods broadly conceived (Section 2.2). Once the special place of positional issue competition has been characterized, we then can turn to numbers of players and dimensions of policy issues as structural properties of party systems (Sections 2.3 and 2.4). Finally, for all party systems we can distinguish greater or lesser intensity of competition or "competitiveness" (Section 2.5).

2.1 Modes of Democratic Accountability

Why do voters support parties and how can politicians in calculated fashion appeal to voters for support? Party systems theories focus on mechanisms that involve rational deliberation, as opposed to affective psychological attachments, such as party identification, voter identification with the objective traits of candidates (gender, ethnicity), or the personal inspirational ("charismatic") qualities of a candidate. Inasmuch as support based on such criteria treats them as tracers of candidates' cumulative policy records and policy commitments, such as in Fiorina's (1977, 1997) felicitous phrase of party identification as the "running tally" of a party's past record, of course, they are incorporated into theories of party competition.

Among rational modes of accountability, let us distinguish between indirect and direct exchange between voters (as principals) and politicians (as their agents). In the indirect policy exchange, citizens surrender their vote in accordance with the responsible partisan model. The exchange is indirect because it involves an intertemporally long drawn out process between the principal delivering the vote and the agent putting authoritative measures into place that allocate costs of benefits to all members of abstract categories of voters, regardless of whether individual members of each category actually voted for the decision maker or not. Politicians may have only a general sense of where their supporters are located in society. They are unable to pinpoint, monitor, or sanction their voters. In contrast to this indirect "policy" exchange, in direct, targeted, "clientelistic" exchange, individuals and small groups of voters obtain immediate gratification in exchange for their vote or suffer negative consequences in case of supporting the loser. The currency of exchange here involves gifts or money, public sector jobs, public housing, privileged access to social policy transfers, favorable regulatory rulings, or procurement contracts that allow firms to hire workers who supported the winning party and candidate.[4] Clientelistic politics comes with direct or indirect social mechanisms permitting politicians to monitor and even sanction the electoral behavior exhibited by small groups.

Numerous theories have tried to account for the relative prominence of clientelistic exchange relations in party competition (cf. Scott 1969; Schmidt et al. 1977; Shefter 1994; Kitschelt 2000a; Piattoni 2001; Keefer 2005; Kitschelt and Wilkinson 2006). Increasing affluence and eradication of poverty may make the relative value of clientelistic inducements meaningless for voters and heightens their sensitivity to the opportunity costs of such practices, e.g. in political production of collective goods. Net of development, clientelism hinges upon the economic viability of state-owned, state-subsidized, or state-regulated firms and entire sectors. Eonomic entities operating under a state-provided "soft budget" umbrella are more amenable to crony appointments and thus clientelism. The presence of mobilized and electorally vocal ethnocultural groups in divided societies furthermore tends to fuel clientelistic practices (cf. Horowitz 1985; Chandra 2004; Wilkinson 2004). Furthermore, all these factors may interact with the competitiveness of a party system (see below). Greater competitiveness may fuel more intensive efforts by politicians to engage in either clientelistic and/or programmatic policy competition.

Whether electoral and executive institutions affect the balance of clientelistic and programmatic competition in party systems, however, is a matter of disagreement. Electoral rules that require candidates to carve out narrowly circumscribed electoral constituencies with whom candidates have direct dealings may induce clientelistic exchange (cf. Katz 1980; Ames 2001). But it is easy to find examples of closed-list multi-member district electoral systems where most parties have practiced clientelism, such as Venezuela (–1999) and Austria, or programmatic parties in open list preference voting systems (cf. Samuels 2004).

2.2 Valence or Positional Competition

Critics of conventional theories of party competition have introduced another useful distinction that can be related to modes of democratic accountability: that between

---

[4] Clientelism always involves material incentives to turn out the vote, not just a monetary transfer by a rich citizen to a party in exchange for economic favors. Such material provisions, of course, make it easier for politicians to establish clientelism.

valence and positional issues or party offers (Stokes 1963). Citizens' preference distribution over some salient, prized good is highly skewed so that most citizens want more rather than less of a good (honest politicians, competent management of the economy...). Parties do not take "positional" stances over whether or not to supply some good, but whether they can credibly supply that good better or to a greater extent than their rivals. Each party claims to have "more" attractive candidates and technical advisers, demonstrate "greater" competence in producing collective goods (such as facilitating economic stability and growth, protecting the environment, preventing terrorism), and/or distribute "more copious" targeted benefits to anyone who is asking for them.

Positional competition, by contrast, assumes a broad distribution of voter preferences over the merits of the parties' offers of goods or services. Parties may then promise different things to different voters on the same dimension (see Section 2.3). Positional offers mostly concern policy issues and bundles thereof. But critics of positional theory claim that for voters valence issues trump positional issues most of the time. Retrospective economic voting, for example, has to do with the perceived "competence" of a party's politicians in delivering good economic performance, such as low inflation and high growth. Moreover, non-policy modes of principal–agent relations also operate in the realm of valence competition. In clientelistic politics, parties compete for votes by advertising themselves as suppliers of the most copious, reliable, and expediently delivered targeted benefits. And competition with a candidate's personal charisma may turn on widely desired qualities such as leadership, compassion, or youthful dynamism.

Nevertheless, there is no one-to-one relationship between modes of democratic accountability and the prevalence of valence or positional offers in party competition. With respect to candidate qualities, while no voter would want incompetent politicians, some citizens may prefer compassion and careful deliberation as a quality of political leadership over decisiveness and expedient action. In a similar vein, descriptive representation of electoral constituencies (by means of the candidate's gender or ethnicity) may be a "positional" strategic move in diverse constituencies where candidates with different ethnocultural markers are competing for political office. Also clientelistic exchange may evolve according to a positional dynamic. There may be electoral situations with highly diversified constituencies that make it attractive for some parties to embrace clientelism and imply that one of its correlates, corruption, should be treated leniently, whereas other parties take the opposite position.

Most importantly, however, one might directly contradict Stokes (1963) and actually assert that most policy issue appeals are at least implicitly positional rather than valence based. Whereas many ultimate objectives in political life may be of the valence type, politics is about the choice of means to obtain those ends, and here one may be firmly in the realm of positional competition because of cognitive and evaluative disagreements. People may have different assessments about the causal efficacy of a policy means to reach an end, given the complexity and uncertainty surrounding causal relations in social life. People may also disagree on the distributive

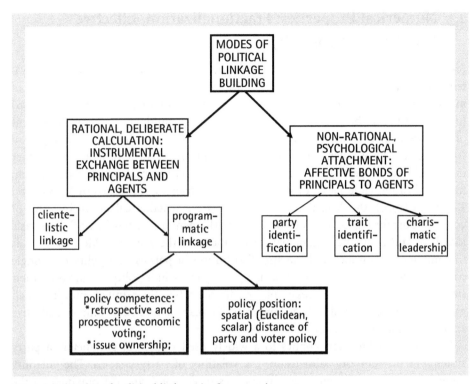

Fig. 30.1. Modes of political linkage in democracies

implications that the choice of policy means involves. Politicians may use valence codes—such as fighting crime, reducing inflation, or creating jobs—to pursue a distributive agenda. For politicians it is part of the art of heresthetics (Riker 1986) to conceal the distributive implications of their own appeal to valence issues, but to highlight those of their opponents' valence issue frames. It is important to realize the limits of valence competition because the *Party Manifestoes Project*, as the most comprehensive and systematic enterprise to register the programmatic appeals of political parties, was at least initially based on the supremacy of a valence-based characterization of party competition (cf. Budge, Robertson, and Hearl 1987; Budge et al. 2001).

Figure 30.1 summarizes the relationship between accountability mechanisms and the prevalence of valence or positional competition. Empirically, I claim the following testable regularities. Political candidate appeals play out in most instances into valence competition and only rarely as positional competition. Clientelistic accountability works mostly as valence competition among parties (who can deliver the most and most reliably? alternatively: Who is the "cleanest" in rejecting clientelistic inducements?). Under certain conditions of economically highly stratified constituencies with great disparities of income, clientelism may become a matter of positional competition, with some parties defending and others attacking it.

2.3 Numerical Properties: Fractionalization, Effective Number, and Volatility

From early on, party systems have been divided into two-party and multiparty systems (cf. Duverger 1954; Downs 1957), ultimately giving way to a proliferation of numerical criteria (Mair 1997, 200–6). Most prominent may have been Sartori's (1976) further distinction between moderate and polarized multiparty systems dependent on the presence of "anti-system" spoiler parties. But since the 1970s typologies of party systems have fallen out of favor to the advantage of a variable-based, finer instrument to gauge the size of party systems. It is the measure of party system fractionalization (Rae 1967), or its mathematical inversion proposed by Laakso and Taagepera (1979), the "effective number of parties," whether calculated in terms of voter support for parties (ENVP) or size of parliamentary parties (ENPP). The basic idea here and in further mathematical iterations of the measure (Molinar 1991) is to combine the number and the size distribution of parties in a polity in a single coefficient of fragmentation that sums up the parties in a polity weighted by their size. Fractionalization measures employ partisan labels as their unit of counting. Such measures are meaningful only as long as parties can be treated as unitary collective actors (cf. Morgenstern 2004).

The same qualification applies to a widely used structural parameter of party systems in the temporal dimension, the volatility of party systems. The volatility index summarizes the percentage differences of electoral support obtained by the same parties in two subsequent elections (usually divided by two to give a maximum value of 100) (cf. Pedersen 1983). It is almost self-evident that fractionalization and volatility are closely related. But where several parties are close to each other and operate as one "bloc" in legislatures and elections, a party-based volatility index may seriously overstate volatility by not focusing on the "inter-bloc" volatility of party systems (cf. Bartolini and Mair 1990). The differential conceptualization of volatility may have major consequences, if one employs the concept to gauge the stability and consolidation of party systems over time (e.g. Mainwaring and Scully 1995; Roberts and Wibbels 1999).

2.4 Policy-based Programmatic Party Systems: Social and Political Divides, Cleavages, Competitive Dimensions

In addition to numbers of players, spatial-positional theories of programmatic party systems consider the number of dimensions on which parties compete, something that empirical comparative analysis often refers to as "cleavages." Because of the variability of language that prevails in this literature, it is important to draw clear terminological distinctions. There are lines of division running through every society generated by social, political, economic, and cultural group interests and sentiments of deprivation. If such divides of traits, affiliations, and opinions are durable we may call them *cleavages* (Rae and Taylor 1970), particularly if they mutually reinforce each other (Bartolini and Mair 1990). They are separate from mere "divisions" that denote more fleeting group divides typically associated with a single point decision (e.g. to take an example from Europe: driving on the left or the right side of the road). Cleavages tend to have the qualities of social *entrapment and closure*. Individuals face costly barriers to enter and to exit a social or political category and the rewards and deprivations associated with membership. Therefore they tend to organize as that category in order to acquire or defend certain economic, political, or cultural resources, rights, and privileges.

Only few of these divides ever translate into collective action to change the allocation of gratifications, let alone the very specific and challenging form of party politics. A *political partisan divide* appears where parties represent different sides of a social divide. Statistically, such partisan mapping of divides can be detected with techniques of factor and discriminant analysis as well as regression analysis, with party choice as the dependent variable, especially multinomial logistic models. The number of social divides that map onto the party system may be larger than the number of partisan divides, if there are several reinforcing divides captured by the same party alternatives. Thus, if all working-class voters are also secular and all non-working-class voters are religious, there will be no separate religious and class partisan political divides, even if parties map both issues onto the party system. Conversely, where group memberships on social divides cross-cut each other *and* are mapped onto parties, they tend to generate multiple partisan divides.

From the perspective of office-seeking strategic politicians, what matters for their strategic moves to win elections may be neither social nor even partisan divides, but only the minimal set of *competitive divides or "competitive dimensions"* in a party system. These are only those divides on which voters display some *elasticity of partisan choices,* responding to modifications of the competing parties' appeals and offers. By contrast many political divides are a matter of political identification rather than competition (cf. Sani and Sartori 1983). In this instance, group membership predicts the propensity to favor a party, but there is no open electoral market in which voters would change their partisan choice, were competing parties to modify their appeals on the given political dimension. In case of a competitive dimension, a critical subset of rational voters is responsive to parties' changing electoral appeals. These elasticities are elusive to measure, as they would require a panel data design. A weak tracer of the competitive status of a dimension is the salience of the underlying issues for voters and parties.

Table 30.1 summarizes the terminological conventions introduced in the preceding paragraphs. An example might illustrate the usefulness of the distinctions in anticipation of the stylized historical sketch provided later (Section 2.4). In Belgium, until the 1950s, there were two cross-cutting political partisan divides that were both competitive, a social class-based one pitting the working-class socialists, at one extreme, against the cross-class Christian Democrats in the center and the business-oriented liberals at the other extreme, and a religious divide separating a secular socialist-liberal sector from a Catholic Christian Democratic camp. Over time, the

Table 30.1. The organization of issue opinions in democratic party competition

CENTRALITY OF DIVISIONS FOR THE ORGANIZATION OF THE PARTY SYSTEM?	DURABILITY OF ISSUE DIVISIONS?	
	LOW: "DIVIDES"	HIGH: "CLEAVAGES"
LOW: IDEOLOGICAL DIVISIONS AT THE SOCIETAL LEVEL	SOCIAL and "IDEOLOGICAL" DIVIDES	SOCIAL and "IDEOLOGICAL" CLEAVAGES
INTERMEDIATE: PARTISAN DIVISIONS AT THE POLITICAL LEVEL	POLITICAL PARTISAN DIVIDES (transitory)	POLITICAL PARTISAN CLEAVAGES
HIGH: COMPETITIVE DIMENSIONS	COMPETITIVE DIVIDES (transitory)	COMPETITIVE CLEAVAGES

religious divide lost its competitiveness and became a pure partisan identification divide. As a parallel movement since the 1950s a hitherto politically unmapped, but long-standing ethnocultural divide over language and region began to articulate itself on the plane of party competition, but much more so in Flanders than in Wallonia. By the 1990s, a realigned socioeconomic distributive divide, the ethnolinguistic divide, and a newly arising libertarian-authoritarian divide over political governance all surface in Belgian party competition, particularly in Flanders. At the same time, the old socioeconomic working class versus business divide as well as the religious divide had lost their capacity not only to shape party competition, but even to maintain a partisan identification divide.

Does the number of parties reflect the number of cleavages in a party system (Taagepera and Grofman 1985; Lijphart 1999, 81–3)? While there may be some tendency that a proliferation of societal divides boosts the number of political partisan divides and the latter boosts the number of competitive dimensions, this is far from a foregone conclusion. The relationship between numbers of parties and positional divides in a polity is theoretically problematic and empirically untested because existing research has taken insufficient care in conceptualizing political divides and competitive dimensions.

In many instances, but not in the Belgian example above, political parties reduce the number of active dimensions of electoral competition to one or two only. The literature offers several not necessarily exclusive reasons for a reduction in the dimensionality in party competition. In all instances, the baseline assumption is that parties cannot simply cherry-pick issues and refrain from taking a stance on the full scope of salient issues, except if they are very small niche parties. This is so because party politicians are elected in territorial districts to represent constituencies over an uncertain and unlimited range of issues in legislatures where they have only very limited agenda control, as is evidenced by the necessity to vote on a state budget that covers a bewildering range of issues.

First, where institutional barriers to entry favor a two-party system, politicians in the established parties have powerful incentives to prevent internal party divisions through cross-cutting issues and therefore map positions on new and salient issues on the existing divides (Stimson 2005). Second, general cognitive limits of politicians' and citizens' information processing of political alternatives give a strong advantage to parties that can articulate their positions in a very low-dimensional space of ideological alternatives (cf. Downs 1957; Hinich and Munger 1994; Lupia and McCubbins 1998). Third, the evolution of social structure and the effects of policies, such as the growth of the welfare state, on the distribution of preferences in society might facilitate a bundling of political preferences around a very low-dimensional space (Kitschelt 1994). None of these hypotheses suggests that there is a logically compelling constraint according to which particular issue positions fit together.

2.5 The Competitiveness of Party Systems

Party systems are more "competitive," when (1) there is great uncertainty of electoral outcomes and (2) uncertainty matters, i.e. small variances in parties' electoral support translate into large variance in their legislative representation and/or bargaining power over executive appointments, patronage, or policy. Where competitiveness is intense, politicians make greater efforts to mobilize support and voters pay more attention to politics (campaign contributions, turnout, information processing).

In two-party systems, competitiveness has often been measured as the ex-ante closeness of two candidates in the electoral race, i.e. the expected margin of victory. But this operationalization is not sufficiently general and does not take the "stakes" of the electoral contest into account. Do voters and candidates make a great effort, if the alternatives on offer are essentially the same?

Competitiveness of a party system is intense, if the following five conditions prevail (see Figure 30.2).[5] (1) For strategic politicians, marginally greater support translates into large increases in bargaining power over legislative majorities (coalitions) and executive office appointments. "Majoritarian" democracy with single-member districts and plurality formula that tend to manufacture single-party unified majority government, at least under parliamentarism, and lack of outside institutional veto points, thus giving high institutional leverage to legislative or executive coalitions, tends to increase the competitiveness of elections (cf. Lijphart 1999; Powell 2000; Tsebelis 2002). (2) Where more than two effective contenders prevail, politicians shore up competitiveness if they configure around *identifiable alternative parties or party blocs* vying for political power.[6] On the side of voters, preference distribution must make all actors perceive the outcome as both (3) close (low margin of victory

---

[5] For a related discussion of electoral competitiveness, also there referred to as "executive responsiveness," see now Franklin (2004, 112–14).

[6] For a discussion of identifiability and its operationalization see Strom (1990b, 47, 73–5).

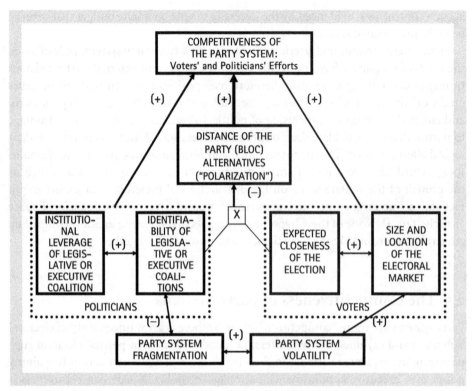

Fig. 30.2. Variables influencing the competitiveness of party systems

between party blocs) and (4) open in the sense that there is a sizeable electoral market of floating voters situated between the electoral alternatives and responsive to small modulations of candidates' appeals.

Even if these four conditions are met, competitiveness is intense, however, only if also (5) the "stakes" of the competition are high, i.e. the disparity of the cost–benefit allocation by rival camps of politicians is great. Politicians raise or lower the stakes in part as a function of conditions (1) through (4), but as the next section will show, these relations are far from unambiguous. On the face of it, one might expect the median voter theorem to hold: Where two identifiable blocs compete to win majority status that endows great institutional leverage on the winner and there is an electoral market between the competitors in a close race, both camps of politicians actually *reduce* the stakes by offering *similar* cost–benefit allocations in case of victory, and these commitments are most pleasing to the median voter. As we shall see, there are complications that contradict this logic of countervailing forces between strong competitiveness at the level of majority formation and weak competitiveness of majority action ("stakes").

Given the complexity of the conditions that affect the competitiveness of elections both from the perspective of politicians' as well as voters' incentives to make an effort in the electoral contest, simple measures such as party system fragmentation and volatility cannot serve as empirical tracers of competitiveness. Nevertheless, they have often been employed for such purposes, although they only indirectly affect some of the conditions that determine competitiveness. Moreover, the causal links attributed to such measures are debatable at best. While party system fragmentation has often been considered to boost electoral competitiveness by increasing uncertainty of electoral victory, the opposite may be true because fragmentation tends to reduce the identifiability of governing coalitions. Party system volatility may be a tracer of the size of the electoral market, but not necessarily of its location (between rival camps?). Moreover, following Bartolini and Mair (1990) for the task of predicting politicians' and voters' strategic choices in the party competition, volatility would have to be measured at the level of party blocs rather than individual labels, a practice rarely followed in the literature.

3 COMPARATIVE STATICS: STRATEGIC CHOICE IN PARTY SYSTEMS

Most theories of party system competition work with the assumption that (1) principal–agent relations concern indirect programmatic exchange about (2) positional issues and offers. Strategic choices vary according to the number of competitors and the relevant competitive dimensions of party systems only. The key objective is to find equilibria contingent upon numbers and dimensions of competition such that no strategic actor could alter her choice without lowering her payoff. Because formal research over half a century has found that the identification of equilibria under such conditions is elusive, more recent theorizing has relaxed model assumptions, including those about principal–agent relations and positional issues, to obtain equilibrium predictions. Alternatively, the quest for equilibria has been abandoned altogether and been replaced by agent-based modeling in computer simulations.

3.1 Simple Spatial Theory: The Elusiveness of Equilibria

The most simple case and the starting point of the literature is Downs's (1957) median voter theorem according to which two parties will both choose policy appeals proximate to the position of the median voter. To derive this equilibrium, one must postulate among many other things (1) office-motivated politicians with (2) perfect knowledge of the situation (including voter preferences), (3) not having to fear the entry of additional competitors, (4) relying on the selfless support of political activists whose objectives are perfectly aligned with that of the candidates, (5) competing in a unidimensional space of voter distribution for the support of rational voters who (6) have explicit preference schedules and knowledge of the situation, (7) must not abstain, and (8) cast their vote for the party whose announced position is closest to their personal ideal point (9) at the very moment of the election. In a similar vein, under highly restrictive conditions of unidimensional competition, some formal theories can show that in systems with four or more candidates rivals disperse over the competitive space and generate an equilibrium distribution.[7]

Relaxing any one or several of the numerous assumptions necessary to derive the median voter theorem, however, reveals its fragility (for an overview: Grofman 2004). This dovetails with the empirical observation that even in unidimensional two-party competition often enough the positions of the competitors diverge rather than converge. Also equilibrium conditions in multiparty and/or multidimensional competition are fragile and elusive. Shepsle (1991) sees no promise to find equilibria when both more than one competitive dimension or more than two candidates are allowed and certain other reasonable assumptions apply. In a survey, one of the most prolific contributors to spatial theorizing of party competition concludes "that simple theoretical generalizations about the structure of competition are unlikely to be forthcoming" (Ordeshook 1997, 266). Theories that try to gain empirical relevance have therefore made additional assumptions or abandoned the search for equilibria. In both instances, the key aspiration is to account for both conditions of party dispersion as well as stability, even if the size of electoral districts (M) and the electoral formula would permit larger party systems with more entry (cf. Cox 1997: $M + 1$ as outer bounds of the size of party systems).

3.2 Complex Spatial Theory: Equilibria under Special Conditions

Because of the proliferating literature, I confine myself to listing a few prominent proposals to relax spatial-positional theories of competition. I sidestep valence-based issue theories of competition (Budge and Farlie 1983), as I am convinced that issues are always positional, when choices are properly framed. "Valence" comes into play, however, through non-issue considerations of candidate attractiveness, party identification, including the competence of both to deliver selective benefits or "good" public policy, and here we get to two prominent recent proposals to account for stability and dispersion of party positions in two- and N-party systems.

First, Adams, Merrill, and Grofman (2005) develop a spatial model in which ingredients of (1) voters' non-policy partisan predilections (including identification), (2) discounting of the candidates' credibility or effectiveness in delivering on their promises, and (3) voters' ability to abstain bring about stable equilibria of programmatically dispersed parties in unidimensional or multidimensional spaces. The non-policy partisan preferences are key, while discounting and the option to abstain only amplify their effect on the dispersal of the partisan vote. The logic is clear. If voters identify with a party for non-policy reasons, they support it even if its current issue positions are further removed from the voter's ideal point than those of a competitor.

---

[7] See especially Enelow and Hinich (1990) and Shepsle (1991).

While plausible, the trouble with this argument is that "non-policy" factors involve a whole host of variables that must be unpacked and that indirectly often may have a subtle policy base, for example when the influence of people's occupation or party identification may amount to a long-term assessment of a party's policy commitments.

Second, Schofield (2003, 2004) has refined a valence model of competition in which strategic parties disperse over a programmatic issue space so long as their advantage or disadvantage in capturing voters on an additional valence dimension, incorporating their candidates' reputation for competence and leadership, gives them flexibility in their programmatic appeals. While formally elegant, in empirical terms this proposal may generate a post hoc opportunistic account of party system strategic dispersal. Just as in Adams et al.'s (2005) investigation, given the flexibility of the key independent variable, researchers will always be able to locate some sort of valence factor, if dispersal of parties occurs.

Third, starting with May (1973) and Robertson (1976) through Aldrich (1983) and Schlesinger (1984) to McGann (2002) and Miller and Schofield (2003), theorists have introduced preference heterogeneity among the principals who select a party's electoral candidates and office holders. If such candidates rely not only on voters, but also on party "activists" who contribute labor and capital to mobilize voters without being candidates themselves, then the aspirations and preferences of the latter may matter for the strategic appeals of the former. To preserve the electoral credibility of their party, leaders may need to give activists some voice in the strategic decision-making process, thus demonstrating that unity around a set of objectives is more than tactical lip service of a few leaders, but a broadly shared commitment (Caillaud and Tirole 2002). But party activists tend to be ideologs who join a party to express programmatic preferences rather than to win elections (cf. Panebianco 1988). To secure indispensable activist input, candidates may be compelled to adopt issue positions distinctly removed from their optimal voter issue appeal. Whether or not activists hold such radicalizing positions, however, may depend on the format of the party system and on societal preference mobilization around a class of issues (cf. Kitschelt 1989a). In multiparty systems where dissatisfied activists can join competing party labels it is less likely that activists express systematically different views than instrumental for the pursuit of votes and office.

Fourth, a long line of modeling has postulated that electoral candidates are not just office, but also policy seeking, and therefore diverge from their spatially optimal vote-getting programmatic appeal. The most encompassing and complex elaboration of that perspective can be found in Roemer (2001) who shows that even in the two-party case the presence of policy-motivated candidates, faced with uncertainty over voters' preferences in a two-dimensional policy space and the task to build a winning coalition among three different intra-party factions around a winning joint electoral strategy, will yield equilibrium positions that clearly set the competitors apart from each other.

Fifth, voters may be strategic and not vote based on the proximity between their own policy ideal points and that of individual parties, but that of likely future partisan coalitions (Kedar 2005). In that case more extreme parties may gain larger shares of votes and yield a more polarized spectrum of alternatives. Voters support more radical parties than is warranted by their own policy ideal points in the expectation that these have to bargain policy compromises with moderate collaborators that ultimately bring the center of policy gravity of a coalition government close to the voters' sincere ideal points. A further modification of this point may be a model of lexical voting (Kitschelt and Rehm 2005). If parties, constrained by their past record of action, do not substantially diverge from each other on a highly salient policy dimension so that voters are basically indifferent between the partisan alternatives, in a manner of "lexical" ordering in their choice among parties voters may focus on a second, third, or n-th dimension of competition just as long as partisan alternatives on that dimension are stark and salient for the voters.

Sixth, voters may not act on a simple spatial rationale in which they gauge the Euclidean distance, weighted by salience, between their own ideal policy schedules and those of the partisan competitors, but support parties in a "directional" fashion based on whether they take a pronounced position on the "correct" side of a political issue, thus giving parties an incentive to disperse their issue positions (cf. Rabinowitz and McDonald 1989). A huge theoretical and empirical literature surrounds this proposal that ultimately appears to conclude that both spatial and directional elements enter voters' calculation, but that empirically the directional component only adds a vanishingly small modification to the basic spatial set-up of voting behavior (cf. Merrill and Grofman 1999).

3.3 Agent-based Modeling of Party Competition

As a backlash against formal theory, but also voicing unease with purely historical narratives of party competition, a new computational approach of agent-based modeling of political behavior has tried to gain theoretical insights in the comparative statics and dynamics of party systems (cf. Kollman, Miller, and Page 1992, 1998). Critical assumptions are here that voters and politicians have very limited knowledge-processing capacity and therefore act on simple rules rather than on a survey of everyone's preferences and strategic options. Because voters vote spatially, but process little information, parties can only slowly move in the issue space without wrecking their reputation. Following Laver (2005), parties act on simple rules of thumb, such as that of "hunter" who repeats appeals that have increased electoral support recently and modifies them, if elections were lost, or that of "predator" who always moves toward the electorally strongest party. In a two-dimensional space with randomly distributed voters, such conduct may yield a gradual gravitation of the partisan actors to the center region of the space, but with no party moving directly dead center and continuous oscillation of positions that prevents stable equilibria.

The advantage, but also downside, of agent-based computational models is that an infinite number of modifications and complications can be introduced without knowing the epistemological advantage of each move in the enterprise. Do we achieve a theoretical explanation of observable behavior if the simulation results of a certain model specification coincide with empirical patterns? What if many different specifications reproduce the same empirical patterns? What this suggests is that agent-based modeling must be combined with empirical research that lends robustness to the behavioral assumptions employed in the computer simulations. In this sense, Laver's model could be enriched by a simple calculus of voters' abstention or participation in elections, contingent upon the observed parties in the vicinity of voters.

3.4 Entry of New Parties

Formal spatial theories have scored only very limited success in accounting for party entry (for a critique, see Laver and Schilperoord 2005, 8–9). More promising may be a recent non-spatial game-theoretical model with incomplete information where a potential entrant interacts with an established party, although it makes questionable assumptions about the distribution of incumbent and challenger (private) knowledge in the game and generates rather mixed empirical results (Hug 2001).

The informal, empirical literature has implicitly been driven by a behaviorally constrained quasi-spatial framework of competition in which the entry and exit of parties is seen as a result of an interplay between demand and supply (cf. Hauss and Rayside 1978; Harmel and Robertson 1984; Kitschelt 1988, 1995a). Induced by sociological and political-economic developments, new political demands become salient that established political parties are not willing to service. This intransigence may result from an interaction of (1) the reputation of an established party that can be changed only slowly at considerable electoral cost combined with (2) the electoral tradeoffs involved in modified programmatic appeals. While a new issue appeal may attract new electoral constituencies only gradually, established voters may be alienated quickly, plunging an established party into an electoral crisis. Barriers of entry to new challengers, as erected by electoral systems, mass media access, or party finance, may make it more or less comfortable for existing parties to ignore new political demands. Computational models can capture both the strategic immobility of established parties as well as the barriers to entry encountered by new parties (cf. Laver and Schilperoord 2005).

While much of the informal and computational literature on party entry implicitly subscribes to a spatial model of party competition, though with relaxed rationality endowments for voters and politicians, critics have modified this perspective through salience models. Meguid (2005) argues that new niche parties may arise if a party antagonistic to its claims nevertheless raises the salience of the issue by engaging in an adversarial strategy in the hope to hurt an existing competitor who prefers to dismiss the issue because it might internally divide and make it lose some of its current party constituencies, if the issue were to become salient. Meguid tries to endogenize the dimensions of party competition itself. In a more radical fashion this was anticipated by Riker's (1982, 213–32) theory that a permanent loser party on an existing dimension of party competition may try to create a new competitive dimension in the party system that internally divides the hegemonic party and creates an opening for a new party or an old loser to displace it electorally. Riker's historical reference point is the rise of the Republicans with the slavery issue. The example also shows, however, the limits of a voluntarist theory in which strategic politicians can "manufacture" salient issue dimensions. As Weingast's (1998) alternative account of the slavery issue in party competition suggests, politicians may create new parties and alignments only when political-economic conditions enable them to count on an exogenous process in which sufficiently large constituencies develop new political claims that are not mapped onto the existing party system.

4 HISTORICAL DYNAMICS OF PARTY SYSTEMS

Students of the historical dynamics of party systems, the trailblazer of which was Lipset and Rokkan's (1967) article about the emergence and persistence of political cleavages in Western Europe, implicitly build on and apply many elements explicitly modeled in spatial theories of party competition and in models of party entry and exit. Thus there is no contradiction between the formal or informal general analytical literature on party competition, on one side, and the comparative-historical analysis of party system evolution. As socioeconomic, political, and cultural conditions create new divides of interests and values in society, different issue bundles will be mapped onto the arena of party competition, contingent upon the institutional constraints and strategic opportunities politicians see in the game of jockeying for votes, political office, and control of public policy. Ideally, the general analytical and the historical-comparative literatures on party systems complement and cross-fertilize each other. Whereas the former is mostly a comparative-static analysis of strategic moves when the political preferences of voters and party politicians are given, but the number of partisan players is either exogenous or endogenous, the latter fills this ahistorical framework with flesh and blood by identifying the sociological, political-economic, and cultural developments that shape preferences as well as the institutional and strategic conditions that influence the set of political strategies seen as feasible by the political actors.

4.1 Classical Analysis of Party System Formation in Western Europe

Lipset and Rokkan (1967) analyze the development of European party systems from the nineteenth to the mid-twentieth century against the backdrop of the twin challenges of the national and industrial revolutions that began to take place since the seventeenth century. But in no way is their analysis one of sociological determinism (Sartori 1968). First of all, the historical conditions that shaped the mobilization of societal divisions were shot through with political action. The development of parties and party systems takes place against the backdrop of strategic political choices and interactions among conflicting elites in the process of building territorial states, subduing religious associations under state authority, coping with the reticence of agrarian elites against relinquishing political control, and including the growing working-class movements in institutionalized politics. Second, they emphasize the complex and varied political process of electoral enfranchisement and institution building both as consequence and as cause of party system formation. Agrarian and religious divides therefore do not naturally flow from sociological conditions, but result from a complex strategic interaction among political elites.

The finest examples of post-Lipset–Rokkan comparative historical analysis capturing the interrelations of demand and supply conditions in the formation and realignment of European party systems are probably the works of Luebbert (1991), Kalyvas (1996), and Bartolini (2000). Luebbert emphasizes the different strategic conflict between socialist, liberal, and conservative parties in the mobilization of agrarian constituencies to account for different pathways of party systems in the interwar period. Kalyvas (1996) highlights the strategic calculations of the Catholic Church and of Catholic lay politicians involved in the formation of confessional parties since the late nineteenth century. And Bartolini (2000) develops an all-inclusive landscape of demand and supply conditions that have shaped the mobilization of the class cleavage in European politics as the last and therefore residual line of conflict strategic politicians had to wedge into already party systems already constituted along other divides.

These books render a more subtle and empirically plausible picture of party formation than two analytically leaner, but historically far less insightful perspectives. Przeworski and Sprague's (1986) intentionally voluntarist account of partisan class politics emphasizes strategic politicians and their capacity to shape the terms of working-class formation, although the empirical analysis is compelled to concede the powerful role of pre-existing cross-nationally varying cultural diversity, corporatist interest intermediation, and socioeconomic development of blue-collar electoral constituencies. At the opposite end of the spectrum, Rogowski (1989) offers an economically determinist account of political coalitions and partisan cleavages in Europe and around the world based on relative scarcities of domestic land, labor, and capital in world markets and resulting group interests over trade openness or protectionism under conditions of an expanding or a contracting world economy. While yielding important novel insights, the analysis overstates the importance of external economic exposure for the formation of political divides and competitive dimensions, probably because it lacks an analysis of the conditions under which collective mobilization of economic interests and their translation into party competition takes place.

4.2 The Transformation of Party Politics in Post-industrial Democracies

Lipset and Rokkan's (1967) famous dictum about the "freezing" of European party systems in the 1920s was hugely overrated in the literature. What started out as a simple observational suggestion in the conclusion to a lengthy comparative-historical analysis of European political cleavage formation was subsequently blown up into a fundamental theoretical and empirical claim about the nature of mature, institutionalized party systems. The empirical observation of relative party system stability in Europe over some period of time, however, did not compel Lipset and Rokkan to deny that such systems may get caught up in a profound process of systemic dealignment and realignment (cf. Mair 1997, 4). At least three different themes in the comparative literature about the transformation of party systems in affluent post-industrial democracies deserve highlighting.

First, inspired by Lipset and Rokkan's work, many scholars have probed into continuity or decline of existing European political cleavage structures. Studies of aggregate party system volatility usually found only moderate increases (cf. Maguire 1983; Shamir 1984; Bartolini and Mair 1990). But individual-level voting analysis shows a strong, though cross-nationally variable decline in conventional class voting (cf. Franklin, Mackie, and Valen 1992). On the one hand, this gave rise to a perspective that postulates a "dealignment" of voters from parties (Dalton, Flanagan, and Beck 1984; Dalton 2004). Post-industrialization has made especially educated citizens distrustful of parties and prepared to engage in a variety of forms of political interest mobilization that sidestep the electoral process. That trend is associated with declining voter turnout, disjointed single-issue voting, and vanishing partisan identification, resulting in a detachment of economic and social structures of conflict from partisan-level divides.

As a second theme contradicting the dealignment perspective, other scholars have emphasized the emergence of new partisan divides and competitive dimensions with post-industrial economic structure. Realignments of political-economic interests with the implosion of the manual working class, the differentiation of educational-professional skills, and the rise of a vast non-profit sector of social services, often configured around the welfare state, create new opportunities for political parties to realign political divides and competitive dimensions (cf. Brooks, Nieuwbeerta, and Manza 2006; Evans 1999; Knutsen 2006; Manza and Brooks 1999). Again, partisan divides and competitive dimensions are no direct reflection of underlying social change, but result from the strategic positioning of parties and their ability to craft electoral coalitions (cf. Kitschelt 1994; Kitschelt and Rehm 2005). These party system changes may not so much signal a demise of economic-distributive politics, as diagnosed in the postmaterialism literature (Inglehart 1990, 1997), as a novel fusion of economic interest alignments and demands about political and cultural governance.

The combination of economic and non-economic interests by entrepreneurial politicians faced with cross-nationally varying strategic configurations among existing parties is also at the heart of a burgeoning literature on new party formation and success in post-industrial democracies. While this literature initially focused on a libertarian left (cf. Kitschelt 1988, 1989b; Redding and Viterna 1999), much more attention has recently been devoted to the rise of extreme rightist parties in many European polities and Anglo-Saxon settler democracies. While there is widespread agreement on the socioeconomic transformations that bring about electoral con- stituencies available for such parties (primarily manual laborers at different skill levels and traditional small business owners, such as farmers, craftsmen and shopkeepers, men with low skills more generally) and pit them against other groups impervious to rightist political appeals (primarily highly trained professionals, particularly women and especially in the social service sector), it is more contentious how political opportunity structures have affected the nature of the radical right's appeals and its electoral success (cf. Kitschelt 1995a; Lubbers, Gilsberts, and Scheepers 2002; Norris 2005). Central controversies concern the extent to which the radical right incorporates liberal market economics into its menu of political appeals (cf. Cole 2005; Ivarsflaten 2005; Kitschelt 1995a; Schain, Zolbergi and Hossau 2002), the causal efficacy of electoral laws in promoting or preventing the rise of new radical rightist parties (Carter 2005; Golder 2003; Jackman and Volpert 1996; Norris 2005; Veugelers and Magnan 2005) and the role the convergence and similarity among conventional left and right parties in their policies and governing practices has played for the success of new rightist parties (Carter 2005; Ignazi 2003; Kitschelt 1995a; Meguid 2005; Norris 2005; van der Brug, Fennema, and Tillie 2005; Veugelers and Magnan 2005).

A further interesting question of realignment concerns the way divisions over European integration have inserted themselves into national party systems (cf. Gabel 1998; Hix 1999; Marks and Wilson 2000; Marks, Wilson, and Ray 2002; Marks and Steenbergen 2004). In many countries, it is unlikely that European integration becomes a competitive dimension in the sense specified above (cf. Mair 2000). Beyond that, contextual conditions related to the perceived and anticipated conse- quences of EU integration for national political economies may bring about a rather diverse insertion of the EU issue into domestic politics (cf. Bringar, Jolly, and Kitschelt 2004; Ray 2004; Scheve 2000).

A third and final theme concerns the extent to which citizen–politician relations in contemporary post-industrial polities can still be conceived within a principal– agent framework. Some have argued that the transition to capital-intensive campaign strategies with an overwhelming role for the mass media and increasingly funded by public party finance has created unaccountable "party cartels" impervious to voter demands (Blyth and Katz 2005; Katz and Mair 1995, reprinted in Mair 1997), while others have invoked the power of competition and voter exit to contradict that thesis (Kitschelt 2000b). In other words, does the undeniable tendency of voters to express greater dissatisfaction with parties than in previous decades indicate that there is a crisis of political representation precipitated by unaccountable elites, or are these misgivings by-products of weaker economic performance and structural economic change that opens opportunities for partisan realignment?

4.3 Party Systems in New Democracies of the Developing World

Whereas comparative literature on Western OECD polities worries about the erosion of relations of democratic accountability, students of democracy in developing countries are preoccupied with the reverse question of whether accountability relations and "institutionalized" party systems will ever emerge in the first place. Particularly students of Latin American and post-communist politics have been impressed by the high volatility of many parties and party systems signaling difficulty in establishing lasting relations between voters and political agents (cf. Mainwaring and Scully 1995; Mair 1997, ch. 8; Roberts and Wibbels 1999; Rose and Munro 2003). In countries where party systems have developed some staying power, it is not programmatic politics based on indirect exchange, but clientelistic principal–agent relations that appear to dominate the scene and adapt to new constituencies and political challenges, whether in South and South-East Asia (cf. Kohli 1990; Chandra 2004; Chhibber 1998; Krishna 2002; Sachsenröder 1998; Wilkinson 2006), in Latin America (Fox 1994; Gibson 1997; Levitsky 2003) or post-communist Eastern Europe (Hale 2006; Kitschelt et al. 1999). The persistence or demise of clientelistic conditions does not simply depend on economic poverty and unequal asset distribution in a polity, but also on the strategic incentives generated within the arena of party competition to switch to a different accountability relationship (cf. Kitschelt and Wilkinson 2006). Also weak performance of public sector enterprises or of publicly regulated companies that are often shot through with clientelistic exchange relations may affect how democratic political accountability relations evolve.

Upon closer inspection, within each region of the developing world the current state of party system consolidation and the practices of principal–agent relations varies widely. Both in post-communist Europe as well as in Latin America a number of party systems have quite clearly structured programmatic political cleavages and rather stable competitive partisan divides, particularly if we follow Bartolini and Mair's (1990) focus not on the volatility of individual parties, but on party blocs with roughly similar appeals within a cleavage system. A growing literature has examined the extent and the nature of political cleavages and competitive party divides in the post-communist region (cf. Bielasiak 2002; de Waele 2004; Evans and Whitefield 1993, 2000; Kitschelt 1992, 1995b; Lewis 2000; Pridham and Lewis 1996; Tavits 2005; Whitefield 2002). Particular attention has been devoted to the insertion of the former communist ruling parties into democratic partisan politicis (cf. Bozoki and Ishiyama 2002; Grzymala-Busse 2002). Controversies surround both the descriptive characterization of the political divides and competitive dimensions as well as the explanation for more or less programmatic structuring. Is it a consequence of political experiences of the past ("legacies") in each country, of democratic institutions (such as electoral systems and relations between the executive and the legislature), or of the momentous political-economic reforms that generate new divides between interests?

Comparative scholarship on Latin America has asked closely parallel questions. Some authors have ventured to identify the historical origins, profile, and durability of political cleavages in at least some party systems (Dix 1989; Coller and Collier 1991; Coppedge 1998). Others have focused on general patterns of stability and change in Latin American party systems in order to explore the causes of democratic party system institutionalization (cf. Dix 1992; Mainwaring and Scully 1995; Geddes 2003). In Latin America, just as in Eastern Europe, those party systems appear more consolidated and structured around mechanisms of programmatic accountability in which there had been other episodes of democratic competition before the current spell of democratic competition beginning in the 1980s. Such episodes of broad political mobilization enabled people to gain political experience and sometimes even to "lock in" certain political economic achievements, such as the beginnings of a welfare state, that provided a focal point to crystallize electorates around programmatic alternatives, particularly in an era of conomic reform and market liberalization.

There is a curious asymmetry, however, when comparing Eastern Europe and Latin America. In Latin America party system consolidation and programmatic structuring tend to have undergone the greatest erosion in the 1990s and since 2000 precisely in countries with historically more established party systems. This erosion is greatest in Venezuela, followed by Argentina, but also present to a lesser extent even in Costa Rica, Uruguay, Mexico, and Chile. At the same time, Latin American countries with always inchoate party systems show few signs of changing that state of affairs. In Eastern Europe, by contrast, the polities with the most promising historical priors for party system institutionalization around programmatic accountability are also those that have achieved the comparatively greatest institutionalization. But even many less hospitable places have shown signs of moving toward patterns of programmatic accountability.

In Eastern Europe and also in South and South-East Asia sustained economic growth for at least the past decade and often longer has most certainly benefited the gradual establishment of robust structures of representation. In Latin America, by contrast, the demise of import-substituting industrialization strategies in the 1980s and the inability of political elites to embrace a definite new strategy of political-economic development, as evidenced by anemic growth and repeated monetary stabilization crises, may have contributed not only to the region's continuing economic hardship, but also the fragility of its democratic party systems.

5 CONCLUSION

My review of the party system literature has been highly selective, driven by my personal research interests in the area and an effort to stress certain agenda points for future research. Thus I believe more emphasis has to be placed on the comparative study of the varieties of mechanisms that may govern the relationship between principals and agents in democratic party systems. I also believe that in the study of the "dimensionality" of party competition, more attention needs to be paid to the distinction between social, political, and competitive partisan divides. Third, and intimately linked to the previous point, the competitiveness of party systems deserves better conceptualization and more intensive study than in the past. Conversely, I submit that too much significance has been attached to certain relatively easily measured macro-level properties of party systems, such as party system fragmentation, polarization, and volatility, none of which are good measures of party system competitiveness.

My treatment of party systems has ignored, however, any discussion of the concept as independent variable. After all, we might develop concepts and theorems of party systems not for their own sake, but as fruitful tools to study the consequences of party competition for a variety of political and economic processes. Among them I would count the formation of legislative and executive majorities, the resulting process of policy formation and implementation, and ultimately the consequences of party system dynamics for the stability and survival of the political regime form itself. Since these topics are treated elsewhere in this volume, I could do without a detailed discussion in this entry on party systems. At the same time, a more sophisticated conceptualization of party systems, particularly of mechanisms of democratic accountability and partisan competitiveness, may perform wonders in improving the causal efficacy of explanations that employ party system attributes to predict political economic developments and political regime trajectories.

References

ADAMS, J., MERRILL, S., III, and GROFMAN, A. 2005. *A Unified Theory of Party Competition*. Cambridge: Cambridge University Press.

ALDRICH, J. 1983. A Downsian spatial model with party activism. *American Political Science Review*, 77: 974–90.

——1995. *Why Parties? The Origin and Transformation of Party Politics in America*. Chicago: Chicago University Press.

AMERICAN POLITICAL SCIENCE ASSOCIATION 1983. *Political Science: The State of the Discipline. 1983*, ed. S. M. Lipset. Washington, DC: APSA.

—— 1993. *Political Science: The State of the Discipline. 1993*, ed. A. W. Finifter. Washington, DC: APSA.

—— 2002. *Political Science: The State of the Discipline. 2002*, ed. I. Katznelson and H. Milner. New York: W. W. Norton.

AMES, B. 2001. *The Deadlock of Democracy in Brazil*. Ann Arbor: University of Michigan Press.

BARTOLINI, S. 2000. *The Political Mobilization of the European Left, 1860–1980: The Class Cleavage*. Cambridge: Cambridge University Press.

—— and MAIR, P. 1990. *Identity, Competition and Electoral Availability. The Stability of European Electorates 1885–1985*. Cambridge: Cambridge University Press.

BIELASIAK, J. 2002. The institutionalization of electoral and party systems in postcommunist states. *Comparative Politics*, 34: 189–210.

BLYTH, M. and KATZ, R. 2005. From catch-all politics to cartelisation. *West European Politics*, 28: 33–60.

BOZOKI, A. and ISHIYAMA, J. (eds.) 2002. *The Communist Successor Parties of Central and Eastern Europe*. Armonk, NY: M. E. Sharpe.

BRINEGAR, A., JOLLY, S., and KITSCHELT, H. 2004. Varieties of capitalism and political divisions over European integration. Pp. 62–89 in *Dimensions of Contestation in the European Union*, ed. G. Marks and M. Steenbergen. Cambridge: Cambridge University Press.

BROOKS, C., NIEUWBEERTA, P., and MANZA, J. 2006. Cleavage-based voting behavior in cross-national perspective: evidence from six postwar democracies. *Social Science Research*, 35: 88–128.

BUDGE, I. and FARLIE, D. 1983. *Explaining and Predicting Elections*. London: Allen and Unwin.

—— ROBERTSON, D., and HEARL, D. (eds.) 1987. *Ideology, Strategy and Party Change: Spatial Analyses of Post-War Election Programmes in Nineteen Democracies*. Cambridge: Cambridge University Press.

—— KLINGEMANN, H.-D., VOLKENS, A., BARA, J., and TANENBAUM, A. (with group of further co-authors) 2001. *Mapping Policy Preferences: Estimates for Parties, Electors, and Governments 1945–1998*. Oxford: Oxford University Press.

CAILLAUD, D. and TIROLE, J. 2002. Parties as political intermediaries. *Quarterly Journal of Economics*, 117: 1453–89.

CARTER, E. 2005. *The Extreme Right in Western Europe: Success or Failure?* Manchester: Manchester University Press.

CHANDRA, K. 2004. *Why Ethnic Parties Succeed: Patronage and Ethnic Headcounts in India*. Cambridge: Cambridge University Press.

CHHIBBER, P. K. 1998. *Democracy without Associations*. Ann Arbor: Michigan University Press.

COLE, A. 2005. Old right or new right? The ideological positioning of parties of the far right. *European Journal of Political Research*, 44: 203–30.

COLLIER, D. and COLLIER, R. 1991. *Shaping the Political Arena*. Princeton: Princeton University Press.

COPPEDGE, M. 1998. The evolution of Latin American party systems. Pp. 171–96 in *Politics, Society, and Democracy*, ed. S. Mainwaring and A. Valenzuela. Boulder, Colo.: Westview Press.

COX, G. 1997. *Making Votes Count*. Cambridge: Cambridge University Press.

—— and McCUBBINS, M. 1993. *Legislative Leviathan: Party Government in the House*. Berkeley and Los Angeles: University of California Press.

DALTON, R. J. 2004. *Parties without Partisans: Political Change in Advanced Industrial Democracies*. Oxford: Oxford University Press.

—— FLANAGAN, S., and BECK, P. A. 1984. *Electoral Change in Advanced Industrial Democracies: Realignment or Dealignment?* Princeton: Princeton University Press.

DE WAELE, J.-M. (ed.) 2004. *Les Clivages politiques en Europe centrale et orientale*. Brussels: Édition de l'Université de Bruxelles.

DIX, R. 1989. Cleavage structures and party systems in Latin America. *Comparative Politics*, 22: 23–37.

—— 1992. Democratization and the institutionalization of Latin American political parties. *Comparative Political Studies*, 24: 488–511.

DOWNS, A. 1957. *An Economic Theory of Democracy*. New York: Harper and Row.

DUVERGER, M. 1954. *Political Parties*. London: Methuen.

ENELOW, J. M. and HINICH, M. (eds.) 1990. *Advances in the Spatial Theory of Voting*. Cambridge, Mass.: Cambridge University Press.

EPSTEIN, L. D. 1975. Political parties. Pp. 229–78 in *Handbook of Political Science, iv: Non-Governmental Politics*, ed. F. I. Greenstein and N. W. Polsby. Reading, Mass.: Addison-Wesley.

ERICKSON, R. S., MacKUEN, M. B., and STIMSON, J. A. 2002. *The Macro-Polity.* Cambridge: Cambridge University Press.

EVANS, G. (ed.) 1999. *The End of Class Politics? Class Voting in Comparative Context.* Oxford: Oxford University Press.

—— and WHITEFIELD, S. 1993. Identifying the bases of party competition in eastern Europe. *British Journal of Political Science,* 23: 521–48.

—————— 2000. Explaining the formation of electoral cleavages in post-communist democracies. Pp. 36–68 in *Elections in Central and Eastern Europe: The First Wave,* ed. H. D. Klingemann, E. Mochmann, and K. Newton. Berlin: Edition Sigma.

FIORINA, M. 1977. An outline for a model of party choice. *American Journal of Political Science,* 21: 601–25.

—— 1997. Voting behavior. Pp. 391–414 in *Perspectives on Public Choice,* ed. D. C. Mueller. Cambridge: Cambridge University Press.

—— 2002. Parties, participation, and representation in America: old theories face new realities. Pp. 511–41 in *Political Science: The State of the Discipline,* ed. H. V. Milner and I. Katznelson. New York: Norton.

FOX, J. 1994. The difficult transition from clientelism to citizenship. *World Politics,* 46: 151–84.

FRANKLIN, M. 2004. *Voter Turnout and the Dynamics of Electoral Competition in Established Democracies since 1945.* Cambridge: Cambridge University Press.

—— MACKIE, T., and VALEN, H. (eds.) 1992. *Electoral Change: Responses to Evolving Social and Attitudinal Structures in Western Democracies.* Cambridge: Cambridge University Press.

GABEL, M. 1998. Political support for European integration: an empirical test of five theories. *Journal of Politics,* 60 (2): 333–54.

GEDDES, B. 2003. *Paradigms and Sandcastles.* Ann Arbor: University of Michigan Press.

GIBSON, E. 1997. The populist road to market reform: policy and electoral coalitions in Mexico and Argentina. *World Politics,* 49: 339–70.

GOLDER, M. 2003. Explaining variation in the success of extreme right parties in Western Europe. *Comparative Political Studies,* 36 (4): 432–66.

GOODIN, R. E. and KLINGEMANN, H.-D. (eds.) 1996. *A New Handbook of Political Science.* Oxford: Oxford University Press.

GREENSTEIN, F. I. and POLSBY, N. W. (eds.) 1975. *Handbook of Political Science,* iv: *Non-Governmental Politics.* Reading, Mass.: Addison-Wesley.

GROFMAN, B. 2004. Downs and two-party convergence. *Annual Review of Politics,* 7: 25–46.

GRZYMALA-BUSSE, A. M. 2002. *Redeeming the Communist Past: The Regeneration of Communist Parties in East Central Europe.* Cambridge: Cambridge University Press.

—— 2003. Redeeming the past: communist successor parties after 1989. Pp. 157–81 in *Capitalism and Democracy in Central and Eastern Europe,* ed. G. Ekiert and S. E. Hanson. Cambridge: Cambridge University Press.

HALE, H. 2006. Correlates of clientelism: political economy, politicized ethnicity, and post-communist transition. Forthcoming in *Patrons, Clients, and Policies: Patterns of Democratic Accountability and Political Competition,* ed. H. Kitschelt and S. Wilkinson. Cambridge: Cambridge University Press.

HARMEL, R. and ROBERTSON, J. D. 1984. Formation and success of new parties: a cross-analysis. *International Political Science Review,* 6: 501–23.

HAUSS, C. and RAYSIDE, D. 1978. The development of new parties in western democracies since 1945. Pp. 31–57 in *Political Parties: Development and Decay,* ed. L. Maisel and J. Cooper. Beverly Hills, Calif.: Sage.

HINICH, M. and MUNGER, M. 1994. *Ideology and the Theory of Political Choice.* Ann Arbor: Michigan University Press.

HIX, S. 1999. Dimensions and alignments in European Union politics: cognitive constraints and partisan responses. *European Journal of Political Research*, 35: 69–125.

HOROWITZ, D. 1985. *Ethnic Groups in Conflict*. Berkeley and Los Angeles: University of California Press.

HUG, S. 2001. *Altering Party Systems: Strategic Behavior and the Emergence of New Political Parties in Western Democracies*. Ann Arbor: University of Michigan Press.

HUNTINGTON, S. P. 1968. *Political Order in Changing Societies*. New Haven: Yale University Press.

IGNAZI, P. 2003. *Extreme Right Parties in Western Europe*. Oxford: Oxford University Press.

INGLEHART, R. 1990. *Culture Shift*. Princeton: Princeton University Press.

——1997. *Modernization and Postmodernization*. Princeton: Princeton University Press.

IVARSFLATEN, E. 2005. The vulnerable populist right parties: no economic realignment fuelling their electoral success. *European Journal of Political Research*, 44: 465–92.

JACKMAN, R. and VOLPERT, K. 1996. Conditions favouring parties of the extreme right in Western Europe. *British Journal of Political Science*, 26: 501–22.

KALYVAS, S. 1996. *The Rise of Christian Democracy in Europe*. Ithaca, NY: Cornell University Press.

KATZ, R. S. 1980. *A Theory of Parties and Electoral Systems*. Baltimore: Johns Hopkins University Press.

——and CROTTY, W. (eds.) 2006. *Handbook of Party Politics*. London: Sage Publications.

——and MAIR, P. 1995. Changing models of party organization and party democracy: the emergence of the cartel party. *Party Politics*, 1 (1): 5–28. Reprinted in P. Mair, *Party System Change: Approaches and Interpretations*. Oxford: Oxford University Press, 1997.

KEDAR, O. 2005. When moderate voters prefer extreme parties: policy balancing in parliamentary elections. *American Political Science Review*, 99: 185–200.

KEEFER, P. 2005. Democratization and clientelism: why are young democracies badly governed? World Bank Policy Research Paper 3594.

KITSCHELT, H. 1988. The rise of left-libertarian parties in western democracies: explaining innovation in competitive party systems. *World Politics*, 40: 194–234.

——1989a. The internal politics of parties: the law of curvilinear disparity revisited. *Political Studies*, 37: 400–21.

——1989b. *The Logics of Party Formation*. Ithaca, NY: Cornell University Press.

——1992. The formation of party systems in east central Europe. *Politics and Society*, 20: 7–50.

——1994. *The Transformation of European Social Democracy*. Cambridge: Cambridge University Press.

——(in collaboration with A. J. McGANN) 1995a. *The Radical Right in Western Europe*. Ann Arbor: University of Michigan Press.

——1995b. The formation of party cleavages in post-communist democracies: theoretical propositions. *Party Politics*, 1: 447–72.

——2000a. Linkages between citizens and politicians in democratic polities. *Comparative Political Studies*, 33: 845–79.

——2000b. Citizens, politicians, and party cartellization: political representation and state failure in post-industrial democracies. *European Journal of Political Research*, 37: 149–79.

——HAWKINS, K., ROSAS, G., and ZECHMEISTER, L. forthcoming. *Latin American Party Systems*.

——and REHM, P. 2005. Work, family, and politics: foundations of electoral partisan alignments in postindustrial democracies. Paper prepared for delivery at the Annual Meeting of the American Political Science Association, Washington, DC.

KITSCHELT, H. and WILKINSON, S. (eds.) 2006. *Patrons, Clients and Policies: Patterns of Democratic Accountability and Political Competition.* Cambridge: Cambridge University Press.

—— and ZECHMEISTER, E. 2003. Patterns of party competition and political accountability in Latin America. Paper prepared for delivery at the 2003 Annual Meeting of the American Political Science Association, Philadelphia.

—— MANSFELDOVA, Z., MARKOWSKI, R., and TOKA, G. 1999. *Post-Communist Party Systems: Competition, Representation, and Inter-Party Cooperation.* Cambridge: Cambridge University Press.

KNUTSEN, O. 2006. *Social Class and Party Choice in Eight Countries: A Comparative Longitudinal Study.* Boulder, Colo.: Westview.

KOHLI, A. 1990. *Democracy and Discontent: India's Growing Crisis of Governability.* Cambridge: Cambridge University Press.

KOLLMAN, K., MILLER, J., and PAGE, S. 1992. Adaptive parties in spatial elections. *American Political Science Review,* 86: 929–37.

————— 1998. Political parties and electoral landscapes. *British Journal of Political Science,* 28: 139–58.

KRISHNA, A. 2002. *Active Social Capital: Tracing the Roots of Democracy and Development.* New York: Columbia University Press.

LAAKSO, M. and TAAGEPERA, R. 1979. Effective number of parties: a measure with application to western Europe. *European Journal of Political Research,* 12: 3–27.

LAITIN, D. 2003. Comparative politics: the state of the subdiscipline. Pp. 630–59 in *Political Science: The State of the Discipline,* ed. H. V. Milner and I. Katznelson. New York: W. W. Norton.

LAVER, M. 2005. Policy and the dynamics of party competition. *American Political Science Review,* 99: 263–82.

—— and HUNT, B. W. 1992. *Policy and Party Competition.* London: Routledge.

—— and SCHILPEROORD, M. 2005. The birth and death of political parties. Draft prepared for *Philosophical Transactions of the Royal Society B.* Edinburgh, 30 July–5 August.

LEVITSKY, S. 2003. *Transforming Labor-Based Parties in Latin America.* Cambridge: Cambridge University Press.

LEWIS, P. G. 2000. *Political Parties in Post-Communist Eastern Europe.* London: Routledge.

LIJPHART, A. 1999. *Patterns of Democracy.* New Haven: Yale University Press.

LIPSET, S. M. and ROKKAN, S. 1967. Cleavage structures, party systems, and voter alignments: an introduction. Pp. 1–64 in *Party Systems and Voter Alignments: Cross-National Perspectives,* ed. S. M. Lipset and S. Rokkan. New York: Free Press.

LUBBERS, M., GIJSBERTS, M., and SCHEEPERS, P. 2002. Extreme right-wing voting in Western Europe. *European Journal of Political Research,* 41: 345–78.

LUEBBERT, G. 1991. *Liberalism, Fascism, or Social Democracy: Social Classes and the Political Origins of Regimes in Interwar Europe.* New York: Oxford University Press.

LUPIA, A. and MCCUBBINS, M. 1998. *The Democratic Dilemma: Can Citizens Learn What They Need to Know?* Cambridge: Cambridge University Press.

MCGANN, A. J. 2002. The advantages of ideological cohesion: a model of constituency representation and electoral competition in multi-party democracies. *Journal of Theoretical Politics,* 14: 37–70.

MAGUIRE, M. 1983. Is there still persistence? Electoral change in western Europe, 1948–1979. Pp. 67–94 in *Western European Party Systems: Continuity and Change,* ed. H. Daalder and P. Mair. Beverly Hills, Calif.: Sage.

MAINWARING, S. and SCULLY, T. 1995. Introduction: party systems in Latin America. Pp. 1–35 in *Building Democratic Institutions: Party Systems in Latin America,* ed. S. Mainwaring and T. Scully. Stanford, Calif.: Stanford University Press.

Mair, P. 1997. *Party System Change: Approaches and Interpretations.* Oxford: Oxford University Press, 1997.

—— 2000. The limited impact of Europe on national party systems. *West European Politics*, 23: 27–51.

Manza, J. and Brooks, C. 1999. *Social Cleavages and Political Change: Voter Alignments and U.S. Party Coalitions.* Oxford: Oxford University Press.

Marks, G. and Steenbergen, M. (eds.) 2004. *European Integration and Political Conflict.* Cambridge: Cambridge University Press.

—— and Wilson, C. 2000. The past in the present: a cleavage theory of party response to European integration. *British Journal of Political Science*, 30: 433–59.

—— —— and Ray, L. 2002. National political parties and European integration. *American Journal of Political Science*, 46: 585–94.

May, J. D. 1973. Opinion structure and political parties: the special law of curvilinear disparity. *Political Studies*, 21: 135–51.

Mayhew, D. R. 2000. Electoral realignments. *Annual Review of Political Science*, 3: 449–74.

Meguid, B. 2005. Competition between unequals: the role of mainstream party strategy in niche party success. *American Political Science Review*, 99: 347–60.

Merrill, S., III, and Grofman, B. 1999. *A Unified Theory of Voting: Directional and Proximity Spatial Models.* Cambridge: Cambridge University Press.

Miller, G. and Schofield, N. 2003. Activists and partisan realignment in the United States. *American Political Science Review*, 97 (2): 245–60.

Molinar, J. 1991. Counting the number of parties: an alternative index. *American Political Science Review*, 85: 1383–91.

Morgenstern, S. 2004. *Patterns of Legislative Politics.* Cambridge: Cambridge University Press.

Norris, P. 2005. *Radical Right: Voters and Parties in the Electoral Market.* Cambridge: Cambridge University Press.

Ordeshook, P. 1997. The spatial analysis of elections and committees: four decades of research. Pp. 247–70 in *Perspectives on Public Choice*, ed. D. C. Mueller. Cambridge: Cambridge University Press.

Panebianco, A. 1988. *Political Parties: Organization and Power.* Cambridge: Cambridge University Press.

Pappi, F. U. 1996. Political behavior: reasoning voters in multi-party systems. Pp. 255–74 in *A New Handbook of Political Science*, ed. R. E. Goodin and H.-D. Klingemann. Oxford: Oxford University Press.

Pedersen, M. 1983. Changing patterns of electoral volatility in European party systems, 1948–1977: explorations in explanation. Pp. 29–66 in *Western European Party Systems: Continuity and Change*, ed. H. Daalder and P. Mair. Beverly Hills, Calif.: Sage.

Piattoni, S. (ed.) 2001. *Clientelism, Interests, and Democratic Representation.* Cambridge: Cambridge University Press.

Powell, G. B. 2000. *Elections as Instruments of Democracy: Majoritarian and Proportional Visions.* New Haven: Yale University Press.

Pridham, G. and Lewis, P. (eds.) 1996. *Stabilizing Fragile Democracies: Comparing New Party Systems in Southern and Eastern Europe.* London: Routledge.

Przeworski, A. and Sprague, J. 1986. *Paper Stones.* Chicago: University of Chicago Press.

Rabinowitz, G. and McDonald, S. E. 1989. A directional theory of issue voting. *American Political Science Review*, 83: 93–121.

Rae, D. W. 1967. *The Political Consequences of Electoral Laws.* New Haven: Yale University Press.

—— and Taylor, M. 1970. *The Analysis of Cleavages.* New Haven: Yale University Press.

RAY, L. 2004. Don't rock the boat: expectations, fears, and opposition to EU level policy-making. Pp. 51–61 in *Dimensions of Contestation in the European Union*, ed. G. Marks and M. Steenbergen. Cambridge: Cambridge University Press.

REDDING, K. and VITERNA, J. 1999. Political demands, political opportunities: explaining the differential success of left-libertarian parties. *Social Forces*, 78: 491–510.

RIKER, W. 1982. *Liberalism versus Populism*. San Francisco: Freeman.

——1986. *The Art of Political Manipulation*. New Haven: Yale University Press.

ROBERTS, K. and WIBBELS, E. 1999. Party systems and electoral volatility in Latin America: a test of economic, institutional, and structural explanations. *American Political Science Review*, 93: 575–90.

ROBERTSON, D. 1976. *A Theory of Party Competition*. New York: Wiley.

ROEMER, J. 2001. *Political Competition: Theory and Applications*. Cambridge, Mass.: Harvard University Press.

ROGOWSKI, R. 1989. *Commerce and Coalitions*. Princeton: Princeton University Press.

ROSE, R. and MUNRO, R. 2003. *Elections and Parties in New European Democracies*. Washington, DC: Congressional Quarterly Press.

RUGGIE, J. G. 1989. International structure and international transformation: space, time, and method. Pp. 21–35 in *Global Changes and Theoretical Challenges*, ed. E.-O. Czempiel and J. Rosenau. Lexington, Mass.: D. C. Heath.

——1993. Territoriality and beyond: problematizing modernity in international relations. *International Organization*, 47: 139–74.

SACHSENRÖDER, W. 1998. Party politics and democratic development in East and Southeast Asia: a comparative view. Pp. 1–35 in *Political Party Systems and Democratic Development in East and Southeast Asia*, vol. i, ed. W. Sachsenröder and U. E. Frings. Ashgate: Aldershot.

SAMUELS, D. 2004. From socialism to social democracy: party organization and the transformation of the Workers' Party in Brazil. *Comparative Political Studies*, 37: 999–1024.

SANI, G. and SARTORI, G. 1983. Polarization, fragmentation and competition in western democracies. Pp. 307–340 in *Western European Party Systems. Continuity and Change*, ed. H. Daalder and P. Mair. Beverly Hills, Calif.: Sage.

SARTORI, G. 1968. The sociology of parties: a critical review. Pp. 1–25 in *Party Systems, Party Organisation and the Politics of the New Masses*, ed. O. Stammer. Berlin: Institut für Politische Wissenschaften.

——1976. *Parties and Party Systems: A Framework for Analysis*. Cambridge: Cambridge University Press.

——1986. The influence of electoral systems: faulty laws or faulty method? Pp. 43–68 in *Electoral Laws and their Political Consequences*, ed. B. Grofman and A. Lijphart. New York: Agathon Press.

SCHAIN, M., ZOLBERG, A., and HOSSAU, P. (eds.) 2002. *Shadows over Europe: The Development and Impact of the Extreme Right in Western Europe*. Houndmills: Palgrave Macmillan.

SCHEVE, K. 2000. Comparative context and public preferences over regional economic integration. Paper presented at the Annual Meeting of the American Political Science Association. Washington, DC.

SCHLESINGER, J. 1984. On the theory of party organization. *Journal of Politics*, 46: 369–400.

SCHMIDT, S. W., GUASTI, L., LAND, C. H., and SCOTT, J. C. eds. 1977. *Friends, Followers, and Factions*. Berkeley and Los Angeles: University of California Press.

SCHOFIELD, N. 2003. Valence competition in the spatial stochastic model. *Journal of Theoretical Politics*, 15: 371–83.

——2004. Equilibrium in the spatial "valence" model of politics. *Journal of Theoretical Politics*, 16: 447–81.

SCOTT, J. C. 1969. Corruption, machine politics, and political change. *American Political Science Review*, 62: 1142–58.

SHAMIR, M. 1984. Are western party systems "frozen?" A comparative dynamic analysis. *Comparative Political Studies*, 12: 35–79.

SHEFTER, M. 1994. *Political Parties and the State: The American Historical Experience*. Princeton University Press.

SHEPSLE, K. 1991. *Models of Multiparty Electoral Competition*. Chur: Harwood Academic Publishers.

SNYDER, J. M., JR. and TING, M. M. 2002. An informational rationale for political parties. *American Journal of Political Science*, 46: 90–110.

SORAUF, F. J. 1964. *Party Politics in America*. Boston: Little, Brown.

SPRUYT, H. 1994. *The Sovereign State and its Competitors*. Princeton: Princeton University Press.

STIMSON, J. 2005. *Tides of Consent: How Public Opinion Shapes American Politics*. Cambridge: Cambridge University Press.

STOKES, D. 1963. Spatial models of party competition. *American Political Science Review*, 57: 368–77.

STROM, K. 1990a. A behavioral theory of competitive political parties. *American Journal of Political Science*, 34: 565–98.

——1990b. *Minority Government and Majority Control*. Cambridge: Cambridge University Press.

TAAGEPERA, R. and GROFMAN, B. 1985. Rethinking Duverger's law: predicting the effective number of parties in plurality and PR systems: parties minus issues equals one. *European Journal of Political Research*, 13: 341–53.

TAVITS, M. 2005. The development of stable party support: electoral dynamics in post-communist Europe. *American Journal of Political Science*, 49 (2): 283–98.

——2006. Party systems in the making. the emergence and success of new parties in new democracies. *British Journal of Political Science* (forthcoming).

TSEBELIS, G. 2002. *Veto Players*. Princeton: Princeton University Press.

VAN DER BRUG, W., FENNEMA, M., and TILLIE, J. 2005. Why some anti-immigrant parties fail and others succeed: a two-step model of aggregate electoral support. *Comparative Political Studies*, 38: 537–73.

VEUGELERS, J. and MAGNAN, A. 2005. Conditions of far-right strength in contemporary Western Europe: an application of Kitschelt's theory. *European Journal of Political Research*, 44: 837–60.

WALTZ, K. 1954. *Man, the State, and War: A Theoretical Analysis*. New York: Columbia University Press.

——1979. *Theory of International Politics*. Reading, Mass.: Addison-Wesley.

WEINGAST, B. 1998. Political stability and civil war: institutions, commitments, and American democracy. Pp. 148–93 in *Analytical Narratives*, ed. R. H. Bates, A. Greif, M. Levi, J.-L. Rosenthal, and B. R. Weingast. Princeton: Princeton University Press.

WHITEFIELD, S. 2002. Political cleavages and post-communist politics. *Annual Review of Political Science*, 5: 181–200.

WILKINSON, S. I. 2004. *Votes and Violence: Electoral Competition and Ethnic Riots in India*. Cambridge: Cambridge University Press.

——2006. Explaining changing patterns of party–voter linkages in India. Pp. 110–40 in *Patrons, Clients and Policies*, ed. H. Kitschelt and S. I. Wilkinson. Cambridge: Cambridge University Press.

CHAPTER 31

....

POLITICAL CLIENTELISM

....

SUSAN C. STOKES

IF most scholars of the topic are right, political clientelism slows economic development, vitiates democracy, and allows dictators to hold onto power longer than they otherwise would. It slows economic development by discouraging governments from providing public goods and by creating an interest in the ongoing poverty and dependency of constituents. Its vitiates democracy by undermining the equality of the ballot, allowing some voters to use their votes to communicate policy preferences while others use their votes only as an exchange for minor side payments. And it keeps dictators in power by allowing them to stage elections in which competition is stifled in which voters who would prefer to vote against the regime are kept from doing so by fear of retaliation. Given these critical effects, we need to understand clientelism's internal dynamics, its causes, and its consequences.

1 DEFINITIONS

....

1.1 Clientelism

The concept of clientelism suffers more than most from a lack of consensus about its meaning. Focusing on clientelism as a method of electoral mobilization, I define it

* I thank Carles Boix, Valeria Brusco, Noam Lupu, and Marcelo Nazareno for their comments.

as *the proffering of material goods in return for electoral support, where the criterion of distribution that the patron uses is simply: did you (will you) support me?*[1]

It is worth noting that "proffering of material goods" in reality sometimes takes the form of threats rather than inducements. We have the government of Singapore threatening to withhold improvements of housing in districts that elect opposition legislators (Tam 2005), Christian Democratic operatives in Naples and Palermo threatening to cite opposition-supporting grocers for health violations (Chubb 1982), and the local magnate threatening to fire citizens who vote against his favored candidates in Misiones, Argentina (Urquiza 2006), to cite just a few examples.

It is the distributive criterion of electoral support that distinguishes clientelism from other materially oriented political strategies. Consider, by contrast, what is known in the USA as *pork barrel politics*, in which benefits are paid to one or a few districts while costs are shared across all districts (Aldrich 1995, 30).[2] The implicit criterion for the distribution of pork is: do you live in my district? Or consider *programmatic redistributive politics*, in which parties in government emit public policies that withdraw resources from some groups and distribute them to others, almost always with electoral considerations in mind. The criterion for who will benefit from redistributive programs is: do you occupy a given class of beneficiaries (those who are unemployed, or have retired, or fall into a given tax bracket, etc.)?[3] Programmatic benefits therefore have a public good quality: they redistribute resources from classes of non-beneficiaries to classes of beneficiaries, but within a class of beneficiaries, particular people who qualify cannot be excluded. By contrast there is a quid pro quo aspect to clientelist redistribution: it is only available on condition that the client complies by providing political support.

My definition is not worlds apart from Kitschelt and Wilkinson's, who note that citizen–politician linkages are often "based on direct material inducements targeted to individuals and small groups of citizens whom politicians know to be highly responsive to such side-payments and willing to surrender their vote for the right price." This they call a "patronage-based, voter-party linkage" (2007, 10). But alternative (or at least different) definitions abound. One defines "patron–client relationships" more generically as a "vertical dyadic alliance...between two persons of unequal status, power or resources each of whom finds it useful to have as an ally someone superior or inferior to himself (Landé 1977, p. xx). The "dyadic" part of the definition underscores the face-to-face quality of clientelism; the "alliance" part emphasizes the repeated character of the relationship.

---

[1] A different phenomenon, which would be labeled *campaign finance* or *corruption* (depending on a country's laws), is when private actors give money to politicians and parties in exchange for legislative concessions and other favors. In this relation, the flow of money is the reverse of the flow in clientelism: it goes not from politician to private actor but from private actor to politician.

[2] Safire notes that the phase "probably is derived from the pre-Civil War practice of periodically distributing salt pork to the slaves from huge barrels" (1993).

[3] These distinctions are conceptual, not empirical: a politician who deploys clientelist strategies may simultaneously provide public and programmatic-redistributive goods (see Magaloni, Diaz-Cayeros, and Estérez 2006).

Other students of clientelism define it narrowly as an exchange of a public sector job for political support (see e.g. Robinson and Verdier 2003, 2)—what many call *patronage*. Still others define it in terms of what it is that patrons and clients exchange. According to James Scott, the relation is an "instrumental friendship in which an individual of higher socioeconomic status (patron) uses his own influence and resources to provide *protection or benefits*, or both, for a person of lower status (client) who, for his part, reciprocates by offering *general support and assistance*, including personal services, to the patron" (1972, 92, emphasis mine). Whitaker makes a similar point in his discussion of politics in emirates, writing that in clientelist relations, "patronage, economic security, and protection can be exchanged for personal loyalty and obedience" (cited in Lemarchand 1977, 102).

Scott's definition raises the question: under what conditions would a client not simply purchase protections and benefits in the market, rather than eliciting them from someone whom he knows personally and who is of a higher status than he? Markets may not exist or be well developed for the kinds of protections or benefits sought. Or these protections and benefits may be available on the market but their potential consumer (the client) has insufficiently plentiful resources (income) to secure them from an impersonal seller. The low-income, limited-assets client has other resources in greater abundance: time, a vote, insertion into networks of other potential supporters whom he can influence, and the like. We do not have to get very far into definitions of clientelism before we are reminded of the material poverty of the client.

Scott's definition also focuses our attention on the clients' interest in securing security and protection. In many polities security and protection are provided by the state as a public good. Hence, taking Scott's two points together, all else equal we would expect patron–client ties to be prevalent in societies with widespread poverty and with a relatively weak and ineffective state apparatus.

1.2 Vote Buying and Patronage

Having explored definitions of clientelism (and offered my own), I now do the same for the related concepts of patronage and vote buying. In my usage, patronage and vote buying are subclasses of clientelism. Whereas clientelism involves the dyad's inferior member giving electoral support broadly construed, including her own vote and efforts to secure for the patron the votes of others, vote buying is a more narrow *exchange of goods (benefits, protections) for one's own vote*. In contrast, again, to pork and programmatic redistribution, the criterion for selecting vote sellers is: did you (will you) vote for me?

Patronage, in turn, is *the proffering of public resources (most typically, public employment) by office holders in return for electoral support*, where the criterion of distribution is again the clientelist one: did you—will you—vote for me? Hence patronage is distinct from the broader category of clientelism. In clientelism, the more powerful political actor may or may not hold public office, and therefore may or may not be able to credibly promise to secure public resources (as opposed to, say, party resources) for the client. In patronage, the patron holds public office and distributes state resources. This definition concurs with those of others, such as Mainwaring, who defines patronage as "the use or distribution of state resources on a nonmeritocratic basis for political gain" (1999, 177). The clientelism–patronage distinction corresponds to Medina and Stokes's (2007) one between *economic monopoly* over goods which the patron controls independent of the outcome of an election, and *political monopoly* over goods that he controls only if he retains office. An example of an economic monopoly is a grain elevator in a rural community, access to which its owner can limit to those who voted or will vote for him, whether or not he wins the election. An example of a political monopoly is public employment, which a patron can use to reward or punish voters only in the case that he wins.

Whether a relationship is of more general clientelism or of patronage—whether it is based on an economic or a political monopoly—is consequential. Under a political monopoly, voters who wish to throw a patron out of office may face a collective action problem: his exit represents a public good, yet the voter who votes against him when a majority of others does not risks suffering the patron's retaliation. Each voter minimizes her risk and maximizes her payoff when she votes for the unpopular patron but all other voters (or at least a majority) vote against him. Yet because all voters face this same incentive, the unpopular patron remains in power.

An implication is that, in polities in which patronage or political monopoly is widespread, one cannot infer a party's (or its program's) popularity from its electoral successes. Mexico's PRI offers an example of a ruling party that remained in power and continued to win elections, probably long after its underlying popularity had been severely eroded (see Magaloni 2006).

2 Two Waves of Studies of Clientelism

The post-war literature on clientelism comes basically in two waves, the first one inspired by the emergence of new nations, the second by the democratization of large swaths of the developing world. The papers gathered and reissued in Schmidt, Scott, Landé, and Gausti's influential 1977 reader, *Friends, Followers, and Factions*, had first appeared in print between 1950 and 1974, the bulk of them during the ten years after 1964. Important monographs appeared in the 1980s (such as Judith Chubb's studies of clientelism and patronage in southern Italy), and the theoretical ground for studies of clientelism began to shift in the late 1980s and 1990s.

After a hiatus of several decades, studies of political clientelism are again legion. In addition to reappearance in journals and monographs, after 2007 we will have not one but three major new collections on related topics.[4] The two waves of writings differ in many ways: in the political regimes studied (the early wave was indifferent to regimes, the second focused mainly on clientelism under democracy); in the basic conceptual categories employed; in the modes of analysis used; and in their disciplinary influences. The early wave was inspired mainly by anthropology and secondarily by sociology, the later one by economics.

2.1 The Paradox of Clientelism

Relations of patron and client present us with a paradox. They entail unequal actors—slave and master, serf and lord, sharecropper and landowner, worker and manager, voter and party boss—who enter into a relationship that is both voluntary and, from the less-powerful member's vantage point, exploitative. In Kitschelt's words, clientelism "involves reciprocity and voluntarism but also exploitation and domination" (2000, 849). By extension, we would expect clientelist relations to be full of opportunities for defection and betrayal. Why does the relationship persist, even though the client might be better off severing the link? We look, then, for some social cement to keep the client and patron together.

In many early (and even some more recent) studies, the cement is a *norm*. A norm is a consequential and broadly held idea that takes the form: "*do x*" (Elster 1989). Gouldner claimed as universal a "moral norm of reciprocity" that makes two demands: "(1) people should help those who have helped them, and (2) people should not injure those who have helped them" (1960, 171). Under clientelism, superior members of dyads reinforce the norm of reciprocity by giving their inferiors ceremonial gifts, which, like spontaneous and useful gifts, (presumably) create a sense of obligation that the gift must be reciprocated. Scott reflects on the normative and psychological tenor of relations that are personalized and ongoing. The patron–client dyad is distinguished by

the *face-to-face*, personal quality of the relationship. The continuing pattern of reciprocity that establishes and solidifies a patron–client bond often creates trust and affection between the partners. When a client needs a small loan or someone to intercede for him with the authorities, he knows he can rely on his patron; the patron knows, in turn, that "his men" will assist him in his designs when he needs them. Furthermore, the mutual expectations of the partners are backed by community values and rituals.   (1972, 94; emphasis in the original)

According to many norms-oriented students of clientelism, norms of reciprocity have the effect of pushing obligations from one sphere of a relationship into others. "Reciprocities that were once restricted to a specific type of exchange have thus led to cumulative or alternative exchanges among parties" (Lemarchand 1977, 106). Lemarchand cites as examples the overflow of patron–client ties in Senegal from spheres of feudal and religious obligations into clan politics; the generalizing of patron–client

---

[4] They are Piattoni (2001); Schaffer (2007); Kitschelt and Wilkinson (2007).

ties between Hutu and Tutsi in Rwanda from land ownership into cattle ownership; and the spillover of mercantile clientelism into local politics in Ibadan, Nigeria. This generalized set of obligations also spills over into relations between patron-politicians and voter-clients. Citing Wurfel, Scott notes that a Filipino politician "does favors *individually* rather than collectively because he wishes to create a personal obligation of clientship" (1972). In sum, if the emphasis on social norms as a cement of clientelism is not ill placed, their effect is not only to keep the subordinate member of the dyad from rebelling but also to generalize his subordination.

A very different way of thinking about clientelist exchanges is that they tie the client to the patron not by encouraging a norm of reciprocity but by encouraging a fear that the flow of benefits will be cut off. Such a perspective is more consistent with turn-of-the-century (twentieth to twenty-first) sensibilities than with the sensibilities of students of clientelism in the 1960s and 1970s. But it was by no means absent from the first-wave literature. In his classic monograph *Political Leadership among the Swat Pathans*, Frederick Barth insisted that "gifts can be cancelled out by an equivalent return, and do not imply any authority of the giver over the receiver...Unilateral gift-giving...does not effectively put the recipient under an obligation to respond to the command of the giver, as does the payment of bribes or salaries." Instead, he explained, "gift-giving and hospitality are potent means of controlling others, not because of the debts they create, but because of the recipient's dependence on their continuation. A continuous flow of gifts creates needs and fosters dependence and the threat of its being cut off becomes a powerful disciplinary device" (1959, 77).

Barth's interest-oriented explanation is nearly identical to the one put forth forty years later by Brusco and her co-authors, that voters (in Argentina) comply with an implicit clientelist contract "because they anticipate that, should they not comply, they would be cut off from the flow of minor payoffs in the future" (2004, 76). (The only difference is that "satisfied men" among the Swat Pathan have incomes hundreds of times greater than those of the "hungry men" to whom they give gifts, which are therefore, from the latter's perspective, by no means "minor.")

Just as some first-wave studies posited that the cement binding clients to patrons was the client's fear of the patron's cutting off of rewards, so some second-wave studies continue to emphasize the client's normative sense of obligation to the patron. A Filipino observer explains the power of campaign gifts thus: "Once a person has granted us something, a favor, we would do everything to pay that favor back to him or her, sometimes even at the expense of ourselves" (cited in Schaffer and Schedler 2006, 32).

In a similar vein, a client of the Argentine Peronist party responded in the following way to a question about whether a local party broker asked her to attend rallies in exchange for free medicines:

No...I know that I have to go with her instead of with someone else. Because she gave me medicine, or some milk, or a packet of yerba or sugar, I know that I have to go to her rally in order to fulfill my obligation to her, to show my gratitude.   (Auyero 2001, 160)

The brokers use these feelings of friendship and gratitude to harvest votes. Following a long day of handing out goods and favors at Children's Day celebrations, a Peronist broker remarked: "After what you just saw ... votes will come. I don't have to go and look for them ... votes will come anyway" (Auyero 2001, 82).

Yet Auyero's research shows that, in the minds of clients, the instrumentalism underlying the friendship is never far below the surface. The same client who attended rallies out of gratitude for medicine, milk, and sugar added that "if I do not go to [the Peronist broker's] rally, then, when I need something, she won't give it to me. [She would say,] 'go ask the person who went to the rally with you' " (cited in Auyero 2001, 160).

Generally, scholars have fallen into the norms or self-interest camp without subjecting their inclinations to anything like an empirical test. An exception is the study by Brusco, Nazareno, and Stokes (2004). We asked our Argentine samples whether people who received targeted goods during election campaigns felt obliged to vote for the party who had proffered the goods. Not many more answered that recipients do feel an obligation than that they do not (51 percent to 43 percent). But those who said, as a factual matter, that people do feel obliged tended to be the kind who would never receive such a handout: compared to the means for our samples they were wealthy, non-Peronist, and came from big cities. They seemed to be interpreting other people's experiences, not their own. We also asked whether people who receive goods *should* feel an obligation to reciprocate with their vote. If there is a norm of political reciprocity in Argentina saying that "gifts" demand a response, this norm has far-from-widespread acceptance: nine out of ten people whom we sampled said that recipients of campaign handouts should not feel obliged to return the favor of a handout with a vote (2004, 81). We cannot be sure that these results are not country and time specific, but they do suggest that norms of political reciprocity are not universal and are perhaps vulnerable to political mobilization against them.

3 CLIENTELISM AND COMMITMENT

The second-wave shift away from norms and toward fear of retaliation draws on economics and political economy. A series of papers in the 1980s and 1990s explained formally how parties could use individualized or targeted inducements to mobilize electoral support. The basic idea was that, rather than using public policies to effect transfers from some classes of voters to others, parties could deliver inducements to individual voters and thus bolster the parties' electoral prospects. Dixit and Londregan (1996) call this "tactical" as opposed to "programmatic" redistribution.[5] A

[5] Their distinction does not exactly follow the one I offer above. By programmatic redistribution they mean redistribution grounded in ideological visions of redistributive justice and implemented through

central finding of this formal literature was that, when parties knew their constituents well and could efficiently deliver goods to those who would be most likely to return the favor with their vote, then doing so could be cost effective. Parties that practiced this strategy would target *core constituents*: voters whose needs (Dixit and Londregan 1996) or electoral predispositions (Cox and McCubbins 1986) were well known to the party and hence who presented little risk that the party would waste resources on them. (See also Lindbeck and Weibull 1987.)

Following these theoretical leads, Magaloni, Diaz-Cayeros, and Estévez (2006) posited that risk aversion is a variable quality, even of a single party over time; varying tolerance for risk could explain the mix of strategies—programmatic in some constituencies and in some periods, clientelistic in others—that parties deployed.

A difficulty with this line of theorizing about clientelism as an electoral strategy is that it deals inadequately with problems of commitment.[6] A voter who receives a bag of food with the understanding (implicit or explicit) that she will return the favor with a vote can easily renege on the deal on election day, especially when she is protected by the secret ballot. Indeed, the secret ballot was introduced to free voters of the kind of tacit coercion that vote buying entails. And the commitment problem runs in both directions: a party that before an election promises patronage in exchange for votes may well forget its promise afterwards.

To illustrate, consider a *patronage game*: members of a favored group enjoy the tactically redistributed goods, following Dixit and Londregan, only when the patronage party wins. First the voter decides whether to comply and vote for this party or defect and vote against it. Then nature makes the party either win or lose the election. If the party wins it then chooses whether to reward the voter or withhold a reward. If the party loses it cannot disburse rewards and the game ends. Figure 31.1 is the extensive form of the game. The sequence laid out there implies that the voter chooses whether to comply or defect before the outcome of the election is known (the party, if it gets to act, obviously knows that it has won).

The party gains v when the voter votes for it and assumes a loss of $-r_p$ whenever it pays a reward. By assumption, $v > r_p$: the best outcome for the party is to gain a vote without paying for it but it prefers to pay and get the vote than not to pay and forgo the vote. In this game the voter is mildly ideologically predisposed against the patronage party: its most preferred outcome is to win the reward and vote against the party but it would vote for it if necessary to win the reward. Thus it prefers the outcomes in the following order: $(r_v + d) > (r_v + c) > d > c$.

If the party wins, its dominant strategy is to withhold a reward from the voter. Whether the voter has complied or defected, the party does better denying him a reward. Knowing that the party, even if it wins, will not give a reward, the voter is always better off defecting and voting for the party which, on ideological grounds,

income (and, less commonly, wealth) taxes. Tactical redistribution (which they also refer to as "pork") is in a sense between classes of people: the examples they offer are subsidies to some industries and the location of military bases in some districts. Hence they shy away from truly individualized benefits, although their "machine case" would seem to involve individualized distribution and monitoring.

[6] For an exception, see Robinson and Verdier (2003).

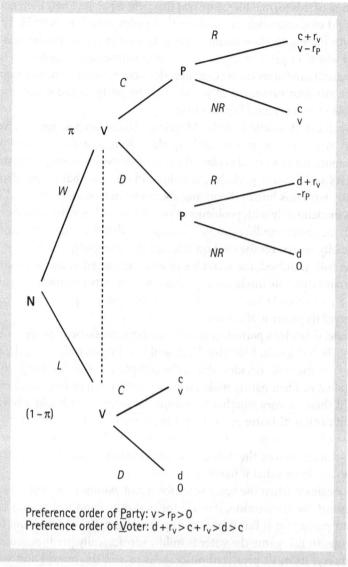

Preference order of P̲arty: v > r_P > 0
Preference order of V̲oter: d + r_v > c + r_v > d > c

Fig. 31.1. A one-shot game between a voter and a would-be patron (rewards dependent on incumbency)

he prefers. Hence the party never offers a reward and the voter's decision is entirely driven by its pre-redistributive preference for or against the party.

Even if the voter were ideologically inclined to vote for the patronage party, this preference, rather than the promise of patronage, would motivate the vote. The party still would do better reneging on its promise. Therefore the voter would ignore the promise and vote purely on ideology. Again, no patronage is meted out and its promise does not motivate electoral choices.

But we know that patronage and vote buying do occur and hence we need to rethink the model. Rather than the one-shot games developed in the literature, we do well to return to the insights of many students of clientelism that the relationships involved are face to face and ongoing. The "gift giving" of clientelism and patronage does not only motivate people to vote for the patron's party directly but also reinforces a social network in which patron and client are embedded. That clientelist relationships are ongoing—that the dyad is embedded in a social network—is theoretically important for several reasons. Networks provide information about their members to other members: we know whether our neighbor or co-worker votes or abstains, voices support for one party or another, and comes from a family of communists or Christian Democrats (Democrats or Republicans, Peronists or Radicals, etc.), none of which we know about strangers. Clientelist parties use operatives who are embedded in these networks and, like the Taiwanese campaign managers described by Wang and Kurzman, are "walking encyclopedia[s] of local knowledge" (2007, 94). This local knowledge allows them to make informed guesses about whether a voter to whom the party gave goods or employment actually followed through and supported the party or defected to another. Networks allow clientelist parties to sidestep the secret ballot.

The party can then use this information to reward the voter who has cooperated and punish the voter who has defected—it can hold the voter accountable for his or her vote. Yet in contrast to the kind of accountability celebrated in democratic theory, this is "perverse accountability," in which *voters* are held accountable for their actions by *parties* (Stokes 2005).

Given that patrons and clients are embedded in networks, we can model clientelism as a repeated game. The voters' preferences are given by

$$u_i = -\frac{1}{2}(v_i - x_i)^2 + r_{vi}$$

where $v_i = \{x_1, x_2\}$ is a vote for either the clientelist party or the opposition, x_i is voter i's position on the ideological spectrum, and $r_{vi} = \{0, r\}$ is the value to the voter of the reward offered by the machine in exchange for votes, relative to the value of voting according to the voter's preferences. Thus $-\frac{1}{2}(v_i - x_i)^2$ is the expressive value of voting for one of the two parties.

Table 31.1 presents the normal form of the game, and Table 31.2 simplifies the payoffs. Consider the case of a voter who is mildly opposed, on ideological or pro-

Table 31.1. Normal form of a game between the clientelist party and a voter

Voter	Party	
	Reward	No reward
Comply	$\frac{1}{2}(x_i - x_i)^2 + r, v - r$	$\frac{1}{2}(x_i - x_i)^2, v$
Defect	$\frac{1}{2}(x_i - x_2)^2 + r, -r$	$\frac{1}{2}(x_i - x_2)^2, 0$

Table 31.2. Normal form of the game between the clientelist party and a weakly opposed voter with simplified payoffs

Voter	Party	
	Reward	No reward
Comply	3, 3	1, 4
Defect	4, 1	2, 2

grammatic grounds, to the clientelist party. Without any inducements she will vote for its opponent, but it can offer her a reward (r) that would improve her payoff over voting against the clientelist party and not receiving the reward. That is, her preference order is:

$$\frac{1}{2}(x_i - x_2)^2 + r > -\frac{1}{2}(x_i - x_1)^2 + r > -\frac{1}{2}(x_i - x_2)^2 > \pm(x_i - x_1)^2$$

The clientelist party, in turn, would most like to receive her vote without having to pay a reward but is willing to pay for the vote if necessary. Hence its preference order is:

$$v > v - r > 0 > -r$$

Table 31.2 makes clear that the clientelist party and the mildly opposed voter are in a prisoner's dilemma. Both would like to "cooperate" in a vote-buying arrangement, with the party paying a reward and the voter supporting the party. But if the voter supports the party then the party does better by withholding the reward, and if the party withholds the reward then the voter does better voting against it.

In the one-shot game, vote buying fails. But in the repeated game, they can cooperate to traffic in votes. They can do so by playing a grim-trigger strategy, with either side responding to a defection from the pair of strategies vote for the clientelist, pay reward by punishing the other side in every subsequent election in the future. The voter's minmax value, the lowest payoff that the clientelist party can hold her to, is $-\frac{1}{2}(x_i - x_2)^2$: even if she is forced to forgo the reward, she can always vote for the opposition party. The party's minmax value is 0: in response to the voter who defects, the party can at least always withhold a reward.

These minmax values allow us to define the feasible and individually rational payoffs of the two players, as illustrated in Figure 31.2. Among these payoffs is the pair that results when vote buying occurs: $-\frac{1}{2}(x_i - x_1)^2 + r, v - r$. By the folk theorems, in a repeated-play setting, if the players are patient then all feasible and individually rational payoffs enforce an equilibrium. The reason is that "when players are patient, any finite one-period gain from deviation is outweighed by even a small loss in utility in every future period" (Fudenberg and Tirole 2002, 153). Yet note also in Figure 31.2 that the vote-buying equilibrium is only one of several possible; the entire shaded area consists of feasible and individually rational payoffs.

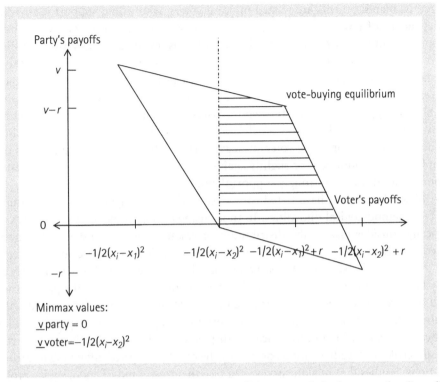

Fig. 31.2. Feasible and individually rational payoffs in repeated play between the clientelist party and a weakly opposed voter

The game outlined above generates several hypotheses:

- the greater a clientelist party's ability to directly observe an individual's vote, the more likely vote buying is to occur;
- the closer the vote comes to being fully opaque and anonymous, the less likely vote buying is to occur;
- the closer parties are to one another ideologically, the more likely vote buying is to occur;
- the more valuable the reward or private inducement is to the voter, the more likely vote buying is to occur (Stokes 2005).

4 ARE CLIENTS CORE SUPPORTERS OR SWING VOTERS?

Clientelism as a repeated game between voters and parties embedded in social networks also tells us something about the kind of voter whom clientelist parties target. Its blandishments are wasted on loyal voters, who would support it anyway, independent of rewards, and hence cannot credibly commit to withdrawing their support should the flow of rewards be cut. Blandishments are also wasted on die-hard opposition voters. In contrast to the mild opponents discussed earlier, these die-hards' ideological distaste for the party outweighs the value of the reward; they therefore cannot credibly commit to vote for it.[7] Indifferent voters, and those who are slightly opposed to the party—whose distaste for voting for it is outweighed by the value of the reward—are the ideal targets of vote-buying efforts. The model thus predicts a marginal or swing voter strategy: parties will shower targeted rewards on people who are indifferent or slightly against them on ideological or programmatic grounds, not those who strongly support them.

A handful of studies have tested core versus swing voter hypotheses. These studies face methodological difficulties. In those using ecological data, the investigators typically consider bias in the distribution of resources toward districts that have voted heavily for the governing party in the past as evidence of a core voter strategy. Yet the voters who support the party and are then showered with public resources may have supported the party in the past because they were also, in the past, showered with resources. Hence the term "core" or "loyal" should be interpreted with caution. "Loyal" voters are those with a proven receptiveness to targeted goodies rather than those with an ideological predisposition in favor of the clientelist party. Ideally, ecological studies would control for the effect of targeted gift giving in earlier elections. Studies that rely on survey data face their own kind of endogeneity problem: does a person's self-reported friendliness toward a party cause him or her to receive handouts, or do handouts make him or her friendly? For that matter, are self-reported indifferent voters actually opponents whose opposition has been mitigated by rewards?

With these caveats in mind, empirical studies paint a mixed picture. Ansolabehere and Snyder (2002) find that US counties that traditionally provide high levels of support for the governor's party receive larger transfers from the state to local governments. They also find that a change in which party controls state government is followed by a shift in the distribution of these transfers in favor of counties that vote heavily for the new governing party.

Elsewhere in the hemisphere, several studies test core versus swing voter hypotheses with ecological data. Studying Mexico, Magaloni (2006) finds that the PRI spent lightly on social programs in regions controlled by the opposition, and spent heavily in regions in which voters would be most likely to defect by abstaining, again suggesting a marginal voter strategy. By contrast, Pérez Yarahuan (2006) finds that the ruling party favored its own electoral strongholds in the distribution of social programs and discriminated against opposition strongholds, suggesting a core strategy, at least in the 1994 election (see also Hiskey 1999). In a study of political manipulation of expenditures on an anti-poverty program in Peru, Schady (2000) finds that the

---

[7] Hence the preference order of the clientelist party's mild opponent is: $-1/2(x_i - x_2)^2 + b > -1/2(x_i - x_1)^2 + b > -1/2(x_i - x_2)^2 > -1/2(x_i - x_1)^2$. The preference order of the die-hard opponent is: $-1/2(x_i - x_2)^2 + b > -1/2(x_i - x_2)^2 > -1/2(x_i - x_1)^2 + b > -1/2(x_i - x_1)^2$.

Fujimori government favored "marginal" districts, ones in which the president had come close to winning or losing in his first election and in a referendum.

In Argentina, the evidence is also mixed. Weitz-Shapiro (2006) finds that toward the end of Carlos Menem's time in power and at the beginning of the De la Rúa administration (1999–2001), the distribution of unemployment compensation funds was biased in favor of swing districts—those where margins of victory of one party or another were thin. Nazareno, Brusco, and Stokes (2006), also using ecological data, show that the smaller a party's margin of victory in past elections (or, sometimes, soon-to-occur future elections), the greater the proportion of its budget that went to expenditures on personnel. Employing survey data on campaign handouts, Stokes (2005) finds the evidence to be less decisive. Although she finds that the Argentine Peronists withheld campaign handouts from strong opponents (handouts which, according to her model, would have been a wasted on these kinds of voters), the Peronists gave inducements indifferent or marginal voters but also voters who favored the party. She speculates that clientelist parties often combine clientelist gift giving with ideological appeals: the ward-heeler who appears at a person's door with a bag of food or the offer of employment will also explain the party's programmatic advantages. Alongside their face-to-face material mobilization the parties also proselytize, and the once-indifferent voter begins to look more like a loyal constituent.

In sum, the bulk of the empirical data points toward clientelist parties targeting marginal or swing voters, but a few important exceptions find that they target core constituents. No one has accounted for this variation. Following Dixit and Londregan, Cox and McCubbins, and Magaloni and her co-authors, it may be that the key variable is risk: when politicians face ideologically diverse groups and wish to minimize their risk of wasting goodies, or when the politicians are themselves risk averse, they deploy a core voter strategy. Recent work that focuses not (following Cox's 2006 terminology) on "persuasion" (changing voters' minds about whom to vote for) but on "mobilization" (including them to vote, rather than to abstain) may shed further light on this matter.

5 Causes and Consequences

5.1 Why does Poverty Encourage Clientelism?

We saw that the very definition of clientelism points toward the poverty of the client. Indeed, it is impossible to survey the qualitative literature on political clientelism without concluding that it is a feature disproportionately of poor countries. It gets studied in the contexts of eighteenth-century Holland (Randeraad and Wolffram 2001), eighteenth- and nineteenth-century England (O'Gorman 2001), inter-war Greece (Mavrogordatos 1983), US cities in the late nineteenth century through the 1950s (Wilson and Banfield 1963; Reynolds 1988), Iceland in the 1940s and 1950s (Kristinsson 2001), southern Italy in the 1950s and 1960s (Graziano 1977; Chubb 1981, 1982), South Asia (Weiner 1967; Chandra 2004, 2007; Wilkinson 2006; Krishna 2007), South-East Asia (Landé 1965; Scott 1972), Africa (Lemarchand 1977; Wantchekon 2003; van de Walle 2007), Bulgaria (Kitschelt et al. 1999); and in Latin America from Mexico (Fox 1994; Magaloni 2006, Magaloni, Diaz-Cayeros, and Estévez 2007) to Argentina (Levitsky 2003; Calvo and Murillo 2004; Brusco, Nazareno, and Stokes 2004) and everywhere in between. We lack quantitative cross-national studies of the subject—it is hard to develop cross-nationally comparable quantitative measures of clientelism—but a mere glance at the qualitative literature shows that, while it is not an exclusive feature of the developing world (yesterday's or today's), one is much more likely to encounter it there than in the advanced democracies.[8]

Less obvious is why this is so. Without noticing that they are doing so, scholars have posited two distinct explanations for the link between clientelism and poverty. In the first and more common account, poor people value a handout more highly than do wealthy people; hence, if one is going to hand out goodies, one will target the poor (diminishing marginal utility of income—see e.g. Dixit and Londregan 1996; Calvo and Murillo 2004). In the second account, poor people are risk averse and hence value more highly a bag of goodies in hand today than the promise of a redistributive public policy tomorrow (see e.g. Desposato 2007; Wantchekon 2003; Kitschelt 2000; Scott 1976). As Kitschelt explains, "poor and uneducated citizens discount the future, rely on short causal chains, and prize instant advantages such that the appeal of direct, clientelist exchanges always trumps that of indirect, programmatic linkages promising uncertain and distant rewards to voters" (2000, 857).

Data emerging from one study cast doubt on the risk aversion explanation. Brusco, Nazareno, and Stokes (2006) find that poor Argentines were indeed more risk averse than were their wealthier compatriots. But risk aversion had no independent effect on one's propensity to sell one's vote. Comparing two equally poor voters, the more risk-averse one was no more likely to sell her vote than was the less risk-averse one.

A third account, slightly different from the others, is that not poverty per se but income inequality encourages clientelism (see e.g. Hicken 2007; Stokes 2007; Robinson and Verdier 2003). If the resources available for vote buying rise at the same rate as a country's average income, then development will not make it too expensive. But if clientelism must be paid for by a growing (upper) middle class and if its targets are themselves increasingly from the (lower) middle class, then the transfer will increasingly be as painful for those on the giving side as they are profitable for those on the receiving side, and one should encounter more resistance from the givers.

---

[8] Although the quantitative research has not been cross-national, we have learned much from systematic data generated by field studies (see Wantchekon 2003) and from survey research (see Brusco, Nazareno, and Stokes 2004). The latter study shows that parties were substantially more likely to try to buy the votes of poor than of wealthy Argentines.

Furthermore, middle-class citizens have higher opportunity costs for monitoring the activities of other voters; parties will find it more difficult to retain a presence in social networks and hence to monitor individuals' voting behavior when the distribution of voters by incomes is dense in the middle and thinner at the lower end.

Another perspective altogether is that, rather than poverty generating clientelism, clientelism generates poverty. As a strategy to stay in power, clientelist parties may develop an interest in holding back income growth. Chubb blamed underdevelopment in Italy's Mezzogiorno on clientelism and patronage carried out by the Christian Democratic Party, which wished to keep its constituents poor and dependent. Other accounts point toward the underprovision of development-enhancing public goods in polities in which office holders focus on the provision of private goods (see e.g. Robinson and Verdier 2003), and on the declining relative productivity of, and dependence on, monopolized-goods sectors as countries undergo economic development (Medina and Stokes 2007; see also Lyne 2006). Of course it may be true both that poverty causes clientelism and that clientelism causes poverty.

5.2 Institutions

Electoral rules. Some analysts find it intuitive that electoral systems that encourage the personal vote also encourage clientelism (see e.g. Hicken 2007; Kitschelt 2000). Kitschelt reasons that

Personalized contests permit candidates and constituencies to organize, monitor, and enforce direct trades of support for favors flowing from office. In multimember electoral districts, personal preference votes for individual candidates rather than entire party lists make possible personalized trades. Politicians' incentives to pursue clientelism further increase when the votes that different candidates for the same party receive individually are not pooled to calculate the seats won by the entire party and/or when the party leadership does not control the nomination of list candidates.   (2000, 859)

The flaw in this account is that it elides the personalist appeal of candidates with personalized, face-to-face voter mobilization. Although the two have in common a downplaying of issues and programs, they are in other ways quite distinct. A campaign that focuses on the personal qualities of the candidate may invest in mass media appeals and rely on a highly centralized party structure. By contrast, clientelist parties and campaigns rely on an army of brokers, intermediaries, and campaign workers to monitor the actions of voters at a fine-grained level. Clientelist parties in fact are decentralized parties, and decentralization is the price that the party leadership has to pay if it is to sustain an army of brokers to, in effect, spy on voters. Were the centralized leadership, or an individual charismatic leader, able to circumvent these decentralized brokers—were they able to replace decentralized vote buying with rousing oratory or compelling ideology—they would gladly do so. The personalization of electoral campaigns is hence at odds with clientelism, and we may be on the wrong track when we link personalizing electoral rules with the prevalence of clientelism. Again, however, this dispute remains theoretical in nature, and probably will until we discover a cross-nationally robust measure of clientelism that allows us to assess the impact of electoral rules on the phenomenon.

Legal restrictions on patronage and vote buying. Today, the vast majority of democracies place legal restrictions on patronage and vote buying. They enact laws and regulations regarding the recruitment of personnel into the bureaucracy, and they prohibit vote trafficking. According to Shefter's (1977, 1994) influential analysis, patronage was strictly limited in polities in which the civil service was professionalized before the franchise was broadened, but was more widespread in polities in which mass enfranchisement pre-dated any serious efforts at civil service reform. In the latter, parties were freer to mobilize mass support by offering public employment.

Shefter's account leaves some questions unanswered. Why do civil servants professionalize early in some places and later in others? In some settings where a professionalized civil service is in place, ambitious politicians mount an effective assault on it, reversing its autonomy and turning it into a source of patronage. This was the experience, for instance, of Pakistan under Zulfikar Ali Bhutto: the country inherited an autonomous and professionalized civil service from British India but Bhutto's 1973 reform turned the Pakistani civil service into a patronage machine for his party, the PPP (see Baxter et al. 2002). In this and other instances like it, laws and regulations limiting patronage and vote buying appear malleable in the hands of politicians.

Ballots. The technology that governments and parties allow voters to use to express their electoral choices also influences clientelism. The main reason is that clientelism is greatly aided by less-than-opaque and -anonymous voting; ballots that facilitate the monitoring of voters' choices also facilitate clientelism. By the early twentieth century most countries that were independent and had democratic intervals had eliminated voice voting and gone over to the secret ballot, greatly reducing the scope for vote trafficking. Nevertheless, some ballots and balloting systems still in use today help parties infer the vote choices of individual voters. Spain, for instance, combines ticket ballots—ones containing only the names of candidates from one party's list—with the option of voting semi-publicly: Spanish voters have a choice of placing their preferred party list in an envelope in a curtained booth or doing so openly. (France and some former French colonies, as well as several other democracies, also use ticket ballots.) A handful of countries, among them Argentina, Panama, and Uruguay, use party ballots, ballots that political parties produce and in which individual candidates (for executive offices) or party lists appear on separate ballots.

Ticket and party ballots are both distinct from Australian ballots, in which all candidates or lists of candidates for a given office appear listed in the same format, and in which public agencies produce and distribute the ballots on the day before or day of the election, under controlled conditions (Converse 1972). Reynolds and Steenbergen (2005) calculate that 85 percent of countries today use Australian ballots, 15 percent what I am calling ticket and party ballots.

Party ballots may particularly facilitate vote buying not because of the format of the ballot but because parties produce them and usually can distribute them well before the election. The distribution of ballots becomes part of the process of mobilizing voters, and when parties distribute ballots along with bags of food, building materials, or other individualized inducements, the message comes across especially clearly that the favors are expected to be reciprocated with a vote. Brusco, Nazareno, and Stokes (2004) find that Argentine voters who received their ballots directly from party representatives are significantly more likely to have received campaign handouts and to report that these handouts influenced their vote.

Because it is politicians who write regulations discouraging patronage and design ballots that work against vote buying, one wonders whether these rules have an independent effect of reducing clientelism or whether they are brought to life only after other factors, such as economic development, have made clientelism less effective and hence less tempting for politicians. Still, in some settings parties compete against one another by shining a light on vote buying and electoral corruption, creating electoral incentives to carry out ballot and other institutional reforms. This dynamic has been observed in Mexico, in Taiwan, and in Argentina; in all three countries, opposition politicians admonish voters, as an Argentine politician put it, to "receive with one hand and vote with the other" (quoted in Szwarcberg 2001).

Accounts of transitions from clientelist to programmatic politics offer clues about the factors encouraging clientelism. Lehoucq and Molina (2002) attribute the decline of vote buying in Costa Rica in the 1940s to the introduction of the secret ballot and the increasing costliness of payments to voters, the latter suggestive of development as a cause of this decline.

Recall that, as illustrated in Figure 31.2, the clientelist equilibrium is only one of many possible equilibria. Schaffer and Schedler point out that, whereas markets in consumer goods are generally considered morally legitimate, "the explicit purchase of votes runs counter to present norms of democratic liberty and equality" (2006, 6). It is therefore vulnerable to ideological attacks. In Peru, a progressive military regime, followed by leftist organizers and radical clergy, encouraged people to think of themselves as citizens who should receive public services in exchange for their taxes, rather than as clients who needed to plead for special favors (Stokes 1995).

Several authors note a decline in clientelism and vote buying in Mexico with that country's gradual democratization, which culminated in 2000. A Mitofsky poll found that 5 percent of voters received a handout before the 2000 elections; the *Mexico 2000* panel study put the number at just under 15 percent (see Cornelius 2004).[9] He interprets both numbers as a decline over past practice. Lehoucq (2006) and Cornelius give credit to Mexico's Federal Electoral Institute (the Instituto Federal Electoral, IFE), overhauled in 1994, for reducing clientelism and vote buying. Magaloni concurs, but goes a step further and analyzes the reasons why the PRI, Mexico's ruling party, was

---

[9] Yet during the 2006 presidential campaign, "millions of poor Mexicans have been threatened with exclusion from health care and social assistance programs if they do not vote for various candidates [and] others, mostly in rural areas, have been given cash payoffs of $40 to $60 for their votes" (Alianza Civica, cited in *Washington Post* 2006).

willing to grant the IFE independence. It granted this independence, in her analysis, as a way of inducing the opposition to endorse the legitimacy of elections. Fair elections with the possibility of losing were a better outcome for the PRI than illegitimate elections and the social instability that followed.

Institutional consequences of clientelism. Little research has delved into the institutional causes of clientelism, but even less into its institutional *consequences.* But in a highly original paper, Desposato (2007) studies clientelism's effects on political parties in legislatures. He reasons that parties that use clientelist strategies will behave differently in the legislature than parties that mobilize electoral support by providing public goods. Clientelist parties will work determinedly to secure public resources for distribution throughout their personal networks; when they are in opposition, they will display little legislative cohesion. Public-goods oriented parties will work determinedly to provide these goods and claim credit for their provision, and will display more legislative cohesion, whether in government or in opposition. Desposato compares two state legislatures in Brazil, one in a state (Piauí) where clientelism is widespread, the other in a state (Brasília) in which it is nearly absent. He finds differences in the behaviors of the legislative parties—greater frequency of roll-calls in Brasília, less cohesion of opposition parties in Piauí—that accord with his theory.

5.3 The Effectiveness of Clientelism and Patronage

Most students and casual observers of clientelism assume that it *works* as an electoral strategy—that, all else equal, a party that disburses clientelist benefits will win more votes than it would have had it not pursued this strategy. In general we do not expect parties to pursue strategies that are ineffective. And yet we have some theoretical reasons for believing that conditions are not always ripe for clientelism. In the repeated game outlined earlier, the vote-buying equilibrium is just one of many possible equilibria.

Voters who are offered patronage by an unpopular incumbent may find ways to overcome the collective action problem of voting against him or her, as they eventually did in Mexico (Magaloni 2006). And if we assume that parties sometimes lack information about the consequences of their strategies, particularly in new democracies, then we should not be surprised that they sometimes undermine themselves.[10]

A few studies have explored the electoral consequences of clientelism, most of them in the Americas. In the USA, Levitt and Snyder (1997) study the effect of pork-barrel spending (by the definition offered above) on subsequent elections for the House of Representatives. They find that an additional $100 in federal spending can increase

---

[10] Strategic debates within parties, in the present context over whether, for instance, to pursue "air" (advertising, propaganda) or "ground" (vote buying, face-to-face mobilization) strategies, are an indication of some uncertainty about what will work and what will not.

the popular vote of the incumbent by as much as 2 percent.[11] In Peru, Roberts and Arce (1998) find a positive correlation between the Fujimori government's per capita expenditures by department on anti-poverty programs in 1994 and early 1995 and Fujimori's vote share in his 1995 (re)election.

But clientelism and patronage are not always a plus. In Argentina, Calvo and Murillo (2004) find that, in provinces governed by the Peronist party, the larger the number of public employees per thousand, the greater the Peronist vote share in subsequent elections. But in provinces governed by Argentina's other main political party, the Radicals, public employment has no significant effect on Radical vote shares. Using more disaggregated (municipal) data, Nazareno, Brusco, and Stokes (2006) find similar—and even starker—results: patronage spending by Radical mayors *depresses* their party's vote share. The same is true of spending by the federal government (controlled by the Peronists) on targeted unemployment relief programs in the late 1990s. Controlling for other factors (such as poverty), Peronist mayors could expect to receive about twice as much funding per capita as Radicals, and spending in Radical-controlled municipalities significantly *reduced* the Radical vote share in the next election. In contrast, when these same targeted funds were distributed in Peronist municipalities, local Peronists increased their vote share in subsequent elections.

Like Levitt and Snyder, Nazareno and his associates reason that mayors who knew they were in trouble heading into an election might spend more; even if the extra spending enhanced their vote share over the level it would have stayed at had they not intensified their patronage efforts, the patronage would appear, misleadingly, to depress the incumbent's support. We thus face a possible endogeneity problem: (anticipated) poor electoral performance might cause more spending, rather than spending causing poor electoral performance. To deal with this possibility, Nazareno and his co-authors employ an instrument: spending in an earlier election. Still, even correcting for endogeneity, the results hold: Radical patronage depresses the Radical vote.

Why would clientelist spending ever be bad for the party that does the spending? For some kinds of constituents—especially wealthier, more autonomous constituents—such spending may indicate inefficient, pandering governments. It is highly suggestive that the best case we have of such negative effects is spending by the Argentine Radical Party, a party of relatively middle-class constituents.

6 CONCLUSIONS

Political clientelism, the giving of material resources as a quid pro quo for political support, is best understood as part of an ongoing exchange between patron and

---

[11] An important feature of their paper is that it deals with the fact that effort to attract federal dollars by House members is a potential omitted variable. The authors deal with this problem by introducing federal expenditures in other districts in the same state as an instrumental variable.

client, with threats of defection instead of, or perhaps in addition to, norms of reciprocity sustaining it. Incorporating the old observation that patron–client linkages are face to face and ongoing allows us to model the exchange as a repeated game, and hence one that can overcome problems of commitment and defection on either side. Theoretical and empirical studies identify conditions under which both core and marginal voters will be the targets (or beneficiaries) of clientelist parties. Clientelism is intimately linked to poverty and inequality, of which it is probably both a cause and a consequence. Institutions such as personalized campaigns, ballot design, and legal restrictions may also influence whether parties deploy clientelist or programmatic strategies.

Much theoretical work and empirical research remain to be done. The affinity between poverty (inequality) and clientelism is settled fact, but the mechanisms linking the two, and the direction of causality, are not. We tend to treat clientelism as involving a dyadic link between patron and client, in an electoral context, between party and voter. But really the strategic interactions of at least three actors should be considered: party leaders, party brokers, and voters. We have some detailed empirical information on brokers, such as Wang and Kurzman's (2006) fascinating study of Kuomintang brokers in Taiwan, but the implications of their presence for theory have not been sufficiently worked out. Furthermore, we would like to know more about the interactions between parties as they strategize about which methods to pursue. Finally, our understanding of the relationship between clientelism and institutions— from macro institutions such as electoral systems to micro institutions such as ballot design—is in its infancy. Not until we achieve fuller theoretical accounts and test them with more systematically comparative data will we have the tools to tame political clientelism.

References

Aldrich, J. H. 1995 *Why Parties? The Origin and Transformation of Political Parties in America.* Chicago: University of Chicago Press.

Ansolabehere, S. and Snyder, J. M., Jr. 2002. Party control of state government and the distribution of party expenditures. Typescript. Massachusetts Institute of Technology.

Auyero, J. 2001. *Poor People's Politics: Peronist Survival Networks and the Legacy of Evita.* Durham, NC: Duke University Press.

Barth, F. 1959. *Political Leadership among the Swat Pathans.* London: Athlone.

Baxter, C., Malik, Y. K., Kennedy, C. H., and Oberst, R. C. 2002. *Government and Politics in South Asia.* Boulder, Colo.: Westview Press.

Brusco, V., Nazareno, M., and Stokes, S. 2004. Vote buying in Argentina. *Latin American Research Review,* 39 (2): 66–88.

———————— 2006. Clientelism and risk. Typescript. Yale University.

Calvo, E. and Murillo, M. V. 2004. Who delivers? Partisan clients in the Argentine electoral market. *American Journal of Political Science,* 48 (4): 742–57.

CHANDRA, K. 2004. *Why Ethnic Parties Succeed: Patronage and Ethnic Head Counts in India*. Cambridge: Cambridge University Press.

—— 2007. Counting heads: a theory of voter and elite behavior in patronage democracies. Pp. 183–239 in *Patrons, Clients, and Policies: Patterns of Democratic Accountability and Political Competition*, ed. H. Kitschelt and S. Wilkinson. Cambridge: Cambridge University Press.

CHUBB, J. 1981. The social bases of an urban political machine: the case of Palermo. *Political Science Quarterly*, 96 (1): 107–25.

—— 1982. *Patronage, Power, and Poverty in Southern Italy*. Cambridge: Cambridge University Press.

CONVERSE, P. E. 1972. Change in the American electorate. Pp. 263–337 in *The Human Meaning of Social Change*, ed. A. Campbell. New York: Russell Sage Foundation.

CORNELIUS, W. A. 2004. Mobilized voting in the 2000 elections: the changing efficacy of vote buying and coercion in Mexican electoral politics. Pp. 47–65 in *Mexico's Pivotal Democratic Election: Candidates, Voters, and the Presidential Campaign of 2000*, ed. J. I. Domínguez and C. Lawson. Stanford, Calif.: Stanford University Press.

COX, G. 2006. Voters, core voters, and distributive politics. Typescript, University of California, San Diego.

COX, G. W. and McCUBBINS, M. D. 1986. Electoral politics as a redistributive game. *Journal of Politics*, 48 (2): 370–89.

DESPOSATO, S. W. 2006. How does vote buying shape the legislative arena? Pp. 144–79 in *Elections for Sale: The Causes and Consequences of Vote Buying*, ed. F. C. Schaffer. Boulder, Colo.: Lynne Rienner.

DIXIT, A. and LONDREGAN, J. 1996. The determinants of success of special interests in redistributive politics. *Journal of Politics*, 58: 1132–55.

ELSTER, J. 1989. *Nuts and Bolts for the Social Sciences*. Cambridge: Cambridge University Press.

Fox, J. 1994. The difficult transition from clientelism to citizenship: lessons from Mexico. *World Politics*, 46: 151–84.

FUDENBERG, D. and TIROLE, J. 2002. *Game Theory*, 8th edn. Cambridge, Mass.: MIT Press.

GOULDNER, A. 1960. The norm of reciprocity: a preliminary statement. *American Sociological Review*, 25 (2): 161–78.

GRAZIANO, L. 1977. Patron–client relationships in southern Italy. Pp. 360–78 in *Friends, Followers, and Factions: A Reader in Political Clientelism*, ed. S. W. Schmidt, J. C. Scott, C. Landé, and L. Guasti. Berkeley and Los Angeles: University of California Press.

HICKEN, A. 2007. How do rules and institutions encourage vote buying? Pp. 68–89 in *Elections for Sale: The Causes and Consequences of Vote Buying*, ed. F. C. Schaffer. Boulder, Colo.: Lynne Rienner.

HISKEY, J. 1999. Does democracy matter? Electoral competition and local development in Mexico. Ph.D. dissertation. University of Pittsburgh.

KITSCHELT, H. 2000. Linkages between citizens and politicians in democratic polities. *Comparative Political Studies*, 33 (6–7): 845–79.

—— and WILKINSON, S. (eds.) 2007. Citizen–politician linkages: an introduction. In *Patrons, Clients, and Policies: Patterns of Democratic Accountability and Political Competition*. Cambridge: Cambridge University Press.

—— MANSFELDOVA, Z., MARKOWSKI, R., and TOKA, G. 1999. *Post-Communist Party Systems: Competition, Representation, and Inter-party Cooperation*. Cambridge: Cambridge University Press.

KRISHNA, A. 2007. Politics in the middle: mediating relationships between citizens and the state in rural north India. Pp. 298–383 in *Patrons, Clients, and Policies: Patterns of Democratic*

Accountability and Political Competition, ed. H. Kitschelt and S. Wilkinson. Cambridge: Cambridge University Press.

KRISTINSSON, G. H. 2001. Clientelism in a cold climate: the case of Iceland. Pp. 172–92 in *Clientelism, Interests, and Representation: The European Experience in Comparative Perspective*, ed. S. Piattoni. Cambridge: Cambridge University Press.

LANDÉ, C. H. 1965. *Leaders, Factions, and Parties: The Structure of Philippine Politics*. Yale Southeast Asia Monograph Series 6. New Haven: Yale University Press.

—— 1977. Introduction: the dyadic basis of clientelism. Pp. xiii–xxxvii in *Friends, Followers, and Factions: A Reader in Political Clientelism*, ed. S. W. Schmidt, J. C. Scott, C. Landé, and L. Guasti. Berkeley and Los Angeles: University of California Press.

LEHOUCQ, F. E. 2007. When does a market for votes emerge? Theoretical and empirical perspectives. Pp. 48–67 in *Elections for Sale: The Causes and Consequences of Vote Buying*, ed. F. C. Schaffer. Boulder, Colo.: Lynne Rienner.

—— and MOLINA, I. 2002. *Stuffing the Ballot Box: Fraud, Electoral Reform, and Democratization in Costa Rica*. Cambridge: Cambridge University Press.

LEMARCHAND, R. 1977. Political clientelism and ethnicity in tropical Africa: competing solidarities in nation-building. Pp. 100–23 in *Friends, Followers, and Factions: A Reader in Political Clientelism*, ed. S. W. Schmidt, J. C. Scott, C. Landé, and L. Guasti. Berkeley and Los Angeles: University of California Press.

LEVITSKY, S. 2003. *Transforming Labor-Based Parties in Latin America: Argentine Peronism in Comparative Perspective*. Cambridge: Cambridge University Press.

LEVITT, S. D. and SNYDER, J. M., JR. 1997. The impact of federal spending on House election outcomes. *Journal of Political Economy*, 105 (1): 30–53.

LINDBECK, A. and WEIBULL, J. 1987. Balanced budget redistribution as the outcome of political competition. *Public Choice*, 52 (3): 273–97.

LYNE, M. 2007. Rethinking economics and institutions: the voter's dilemma and democratic accountability. Pp. 335–80 in *Patrons, Clients, and Policies: Patterns of Democratic Accountability and Political Competition*, ed. H. Kitschelt and S. Wilkinson. Cambridge: Cambridge University Press.

MAGALONI, B. 2006. *Voting for Autocracy: Hegemonic Party Survival and its Demise in Mexico*. Cambridge: Cambridge University Press.

—— DIAZ-CAYEROS, A., and ESTÉVEZ, F. 2007. Clientelism and portfolio diversification: a model of electoral investment with applications to Mexico. Pp. 381–429 in *Patrons, Clients, and Policies: Patterns of Democratic Accountability and Political Competition*, ed. H. Kitschelt and S. Wilkinson. Cambridge: Cambridge University Press.

MAINWARING, S. P. 1999. *Rethinking Party Systems in the Third Wave of Democratization: The Case of Brazil*. Stanford, Calif.: Stanford University Press.

MAVROGORDATOS, G. T. 1983. *Still-Born Republic: Social Coalitions and Party Strategies, 1922–1936*. Berkeley: University of California Press.

MEDINA, L. F. and STOKES, S. 2007. Monopoly and monitoring: an approach to political clientelism. Pp. 150–82 in *Patrons, Clients, and Policies: Patterns of Democratic Accountability and Political Competition*, ed. H. Kitschelt and S. Wilkinson. Cambridge: Cambridge University Press.

NAZARENO, M., BRUSCO, V., and STOKES, S. C. 2006. Réditos y peligros electorales del gasto público en Argentina. *Desarrollo económico*, 46 (181): 63–86.

O'GORMAN, F. 2001. Patronage and the reform of the state in England, 1700–1860. Pp. 54–76 in *Clientelism, Interests, and Representation: The European Experience in Comparative Perspective*, ed. S. Piattoni. Cambridge: Cambridge University Press.

Pérez Yarahuan, G. 2006. Policy making and electoral politics: three essays on the political determinants of social welfare spending in Mexico, 1988–2003. Ph.D. dissertation. University of Chicago.

Piattoni, S. (ed.) 2001. *Clientelism, Interests, and Representation: The European Experience in Comparative Perspective*. Cambridge: Cambridge University Press.

Randeraad, N. and Wolffram, D. J. 2001. Constraints on clientelism: the Dutch path to modern politics, 1848–1917. Pp. 101–21 in *Clientelism, Interests, and Representation: The European Experience in Comparative Perspective*, ed. S. Piattoni. Cambridge: Cambridge University Press.

Reynolds, A. and Steenbergen, M. 2005. How the world votes: the political consequences of ballot design, innovation, and manipulation. *Electoral Studies*, 25 (4).

Reynolds, J. 1988. *Testing Democracy: Electoral Behavior and Progressive Reform in New Jersey, 1880–1920*. Chapel Hill: University of North Carolina Press.

Roberts, K. and Arce, M. 1998. Neoliberalism and lower-class voting behavior in Peru. *Comparative Political Studies*, 31 (2): 217–46.

Robinson, J. and Verdier, T. 2003. The political economy of clientelism. Typescript. University of California, Berkeley.

Safire, W. 1993. *Safire's New Political Dictionary*. London: Random House.

Schady, N. 2000. The political economy of expenditures by the Peruvian social fund (FONCODES), 1991–1995. *American Political Science Review*, 94 (2): 289–304.

Schaffer, F. C. (ed.) 2007. *Elections for Sale: The Causes and Consequences of Vote Buying*. Boulder, Colo.: Lynne Rienner.

——and Schedler, A. 2007. What is vote buying? Pp. 24–47 in *Elections for Sale: The Causes and Consequences of Vote Buying*, ed. F. C. Shaffer. Boulder, Colo.: Lynne Rienner.

Schmidt, S. W., Scott, J. C., Landé, C., and Guasti, L. (eds.) 1977. *Friends, Followers, and Factions: A Reader in Political Clientelism*. Berkeley and Los Angeles: University of California Press.

Scott, J. C. 1969. Corruption, machine politics, and political change. *American Political Science Review*, 63: 1142–58.

——1972. Patron–client politics and political change in Southeast Asia. *American Political Science Review*, 66: 91–113.

——1976. *The Moral Economy of the Peasant: Rebellion and Subsistence in Southeast Asia*. New Haven: Yale University Press.

Shefter, M. 1977. Party and patronage: Germany, England, and Italy. *Politics and Society*, 7: 403–51.

——1994. *Political Parties and the State: The American Historical Experience*. Princeton: Princeton University Press.

Stokes, S. C. 1995. *Cultures in Conflict: Social Movements and the State in Peru*. Berkeley and Los Angeles: University of California Press.

——2005. Perverse accountability: a formal model of machine politics with evidence from Argentina. *American Political Science Review*, 99 (3): 315–25.

——2007. Is vote buying undemocratic? Pp. 117–43 in *Elections for Sale: The Causes and Consequences of Vote Buying*, ed. F. C. Schaffer. Boulder, Colo.: Lynne Rienner.

Szwarcberg, M. L. 2001. Feeding loyalties: an analysis of clientelism, the case of the Manzaneras. Typescript. Universidad Torcuato di Tella.

Tam, W. 2005. Political insecurity and clientelist politics: the case of Singapore. Typescript. University of Chicago.

URQUIZA, E. Y. 2006. Las eternas internas: política y faccionalismo en un municipio radical, 1983–1999. Pp. 57–80 in *Democracia local: clientelismo, capital social, e innovación política en Argentina*, ed. S. Amaral and S. Stokes. Buenos Aires: Eduntref.

VAN DE WALLE, N. 2007. Meet the new boss, same as the old boss? The evolution of political clientelism in Africa. Pp. 112–49 in *Patrons, Clients, and Policies: Patterns of Democratic Accountability and Political Competition*, ed. H. Kitschelt and S. Wilkinson. Cambridge: Cambridge University Press.

WANG, C.-S. and KURZMAN, C. 2007. Logistics: how to buy votes. Pp. 90–116 in *Elections for Sale: The Causes and Consequences of Vote Buying*, ed. F. C. Schaffer. Boulder, Colo.: Lynne Rienner.

WANTCHEKON, L. 2003. Clientelism and voting behavior: evidence from a field experiment in Benin. *World Politics*, 55: 399–422.

WASHINGTON POST FOREIGN SERVICE 2006. Dirty politics "ingrained" in Mexico. June 26, p. A16.

WEINER, M. 1967. *Party Building in a New Nation*. Chicago: University of Chicago Press.

WEITZ-SHAPIRO, R. 2006. Partisanship and protest: the politics of workfare distribution in Argentina. Typescript. Columbia University.

WILKINSON, S. I. 2007. Explaining changing patterns of party–voter linkages in India. Pp. 238–97 in *Patrons, Clients, and Policies: Patterns of Democratic Accountability and Political Competition*, ed. H. Kitschelt and S. Wilkinson. Cambridge: Cambridge University Press.

WILSON, J. Q. and BANFIELD, E. 1963. *City Politics*. Cambridge, Mass.: Harvard University Press.

PART VIII

INTERNATIONAL RELATIONS

CHAPTER 32

OVERVIEW OF
INTERNATIONAL
RELATIONS

BETWEEN UTOPIA AND REALITY

CHRISTIAN REUS-SMIT

DUNCAN SNIDAL

THIS chapter advances a series of arguments about the nature of International Relations as a field, informed by our experience in commissioning and reading the many fine chapters in the *Oxford Handbook of International Relations*.[1] We are concerned, in particular, with three interrelated questions: What is the nature of the theoretical endeavor in International Relations? How have the empirical and the normative aspects of theories interacted to shape individual theories and the debates between them? And, finally, has there been progress in the study of international relations, and if so in what sense?

* We thank Greg Fry, Robert Goodin, Richard Price, Heather Rae, and Alexander Wendt for their insightful comments on the penultimate draft of this chapter.

[1] This chapter, and the other chapters in this part, employ the convention of using upper case when referring to the academic discipline of "International Relations" and lower case when referring to "international relations" as a realm of social and political practice.

Although there is no singular answer to these questions, the contributors to the *Oxford Handbook of International Relations* have led us to a number of general conclusions. First, they have encouraged us to formulate a distinctive understanding of the theoretical enterprise, one broad enough to encompass the diverse forms of theorizing that populate the field. We argue that the art of theorizing about international relations has come to integrate three components: questions, assumptions, and logical arguments. Second, International Relations theories are best conceived as contending "practical discourses" that despite their significant differences are all, implicitly or explicitly, animated by the question "how should we act?" This abiding feature of International Relations theories explains the persistence of both empirical and normative aspects in all of them. Finally, our contributors' discussions of diverse theories, methods, and problems in International Relations invite comment on the question of progress in the field. Across the board their chapters report increased sophistication in theory and method, greater communication and learning across theoretical boundaries, and more artful borrowing of ideas from other fields. However, progress within different areas remains heavily influenced by contestation among theoretical perspectives. Harnessed properly, such contestation is an engine of increased understanding even as it simultaneously explains the sometimes seeming lack of progress for the field as a whole.

1 Our Approach

There is no shortage of overviews and introductions to international relations and global politics, either as a field or as a realm of political practice. New introductions—more or less advanced—appear each year, and this is not the first "handbook" on the subject. With few exceptions, however, these all adopt variations on a common approach. A choice is made by authors and editors about the topics worthy of discussion (a choice we too have made), and chapters are crafted to do these topics justice. Seldom, though, do these volumes have a "voice" of their own, above and beyond that of their individual, constituent chapters. The most recent handbook to appear, for example, has neither an introductory framing chapter nor a general conclusion (Carlsnaes, Risse, and Simmons 2002). Although an excellent volume, it has nothing to say or conclude about the field it has surveyed. Our goal was to step beyond this general approach to give the *Oxford Handbook of International Relations* a voice of its own.

The first thing to note about the *Handbook* is its emphasis on theory, on conceptions of International Relations as a discipline, on contending ideas of theoretical progress, on different theoretical perspectives, and on the methodological ideas that drive the study of world politics. We adopted this emphasis not because we value theoretical over empirical enquiry or the pursuit of abstract ideas over more "practical" forms of scholarship. We did so because we believe that theoretical assumptions (and debates surrounding them) determine the contours of the field and inform even the most empirical research. An enquiry into the field of International Relations ought, first and foremost, to be an enquiry into the ideas that animate it—the ideas that distinguish international relations (or global politics) as a domain of social and political life, the ideas that determine what constitutes knowledge of this political realm, the ideas that dictate the questions that merit answers, and the ideas that shape the field's relations with other disciplines. Without these ideas, International Relations would have neither identity, skeleton, nor pulse.

One consequence of this emphasis is our decision not to devote specific chapters to empirical issue areas, such as great power competition, weapons proliferation, environmental protection, human rights, nationalism, and international trade and finance. Again, this does not reflect a lack of interest in such issues; to the contrary. Rather, it reflects our belief that it is the ideas and debates canvassed in this volume that have informed and structured analyses of these issues. Theoretical and methodological ideas have determined which issues are legitimate focuses of enquiry for international relations scholars, and they have provided the intellectual tools that scholars have taken up in the pursuit of understanding. The complexities of particular issue areas—especially new ones—do, of course, serve as catalysts for theoretical innovation, and grappling with them has often driven international relations scholars to conscript new ideas from other fields of enquiry. Our strategy, however, was to concentrate on International Relations as a milieu of ideas, and to ask our contributors to draw on their diverse empirical expertise to illustrate their arguments and propositions. This choice of strategy was reinforced by our sense that the literature is now saturated by survey chapters on new and old issue areas, and yet another compendium is unwarranted.

The most distinctive feature of the *Oxford Handbook of International Relations* was not its focus on theory but our reading of theory as *both* empirical *and* normative. Most surveys of international relations theory concentrate on empirical (and/or positive) theory; if normative theory receives any attention, it is left for a final chapter or two on "ethics and international affairs." Interestingly, this is as true of surveys originating outside the United States as from within (see Baylis and Smith 2005; Burchill et al. 2005; Carlsnaes, Risse, and Simmons 2002). The assumptions appear to be that empirical and normative enquiry can be segregated and that international relations theory is almost exclusively an empirical or positive project. Although it is acknowledged (in some limited fashion) that there is another body of theory—normative theory—that treats the international as its subject, this is the preserve of philosophers or political theorists. Thus the default position is that International Relations is an explanatory endeavor, concerned with the "is" of world politics not the "ought."

We find this segregation both unsustainable and unhelpful. All theories of international relations and global politics have important empirical *and* normative dimensions, and their deep interconnection is unavoidable. When realists criticize national governments for acting in ways inconsistent with the national interest, or for acting in ways that destabilize international order, they base their criticisms on values of interest and order that can only be defended normatively. When postmodernists recommend a scholarly stance of relentless critique and deconstruction, they do so not for interpretative reasons (though this is in part their motive) but because this constitutes a practice of resistance against structures of power and domination. Indeed, as the authors in the *Oxford Handbook of International Relations* demonstrated, every International Relations theory is simultaneously about what the world is like and about what it ought to be like. One of the axes of diversity in our field is the different orientations scholars, and their attendant theoretical traditions, have had to the relationship between the normative and empirical aspects of theory. Some have embraced the intersection, many have sought to purge their theories of normative traits, and still others have gone in the opposite direction, privileging philosophical reflection over empirical. But the terrain between the empirical and the normative is one trodden by all theorists, explicitly or implicitly.

The conventional explanation for why our theories all exhibit empirical and normative aspects is epistemological. Critical theorists have long argued that our values enter our enquiries from the moment we ask questions about the world, from the moment we make choices about what we will study to answer those questions, and from the moment we decide how we will study whatever it is we have chosen (for a classic statement, see Taylor 1979). Nothing we say here challenges this line of argument. Our explanation is different.

From the outset International Relations theory has been a practical discourse. We don't mean this in any deep Habermasian sense of the word, or say this to promote simplistic notions of the practical over the theoretical. Rather, as anticipated in the introduction, we mean that all International Relations theories, in one form or another, have at some level been concerned with the question "how should we act?" This is true for realists and liberals, Marxists and feminists. It is true of those who congregate under the umbrella of critical theory as well as those who pursue problem-solving theory. Different perspectives emphasize different issues that demand action, and arrive at different conclusions about types of action required. But whether they are concerned with the promotion of peace, order, institutional development, economic well-being, social empowerment, or ending global forms of discrimination, or whether they recommend the balancing of power, the promotion of free trade, the intensification of social contradictions, or resistance to all institutions and discourses of social power, they are nonetheless animated by the practical question of how we should act.[2]

This abiding nature of International Relations theory as a practical discourse explains (above and beyond the epistemological reasons) the persistence of *both* the empirical *and* the normative in all of our theories. We cannot answer the question of how we should act without some appreciation of the world in which we seek to act (the empirical) and some sense of what the goals are that we seek to achieve (the normative). This was E. H. Carr's central proposition in *The Twenty Years' Crisis*,

---

[2] The same is true for the field of public policy of course. See Goodin, Rein, and Moran (2006).

that neither unadulterated realism nor idealism could sustain International Relations if it were to be a practical discourse—without idealism, realism was sterile, devoid of purpose; without realism, idealism was naive, devoid of understanding of the world in which one seeks to act. For Carr, International Relations had to be a political science that brought the "is" and the "ought" together—"Utopia and reality are thus the two facets of political science. Sound political thought and sound political life will be found only where both have their place" (Carr 1946, 10).

Carr was appealing to the emergent field of International Relations when he made this claim, appealing for it to take a particular form and direction. Our claim is not that his vision has guided the evolution of the field. For one thing, his message has been consistently lost in the misinterpretation of his work. Rather, our claim is that Carr identified a truth about all discourses with practical ambitions: that once this ambition exists, however subterranean and unacknowledged it may be, theorists are forced onto the difficult terrain between the empirical and the normative. This is clearly the case for scholars who wish their work to have direct relevance to the question of action whether in the form of policy advice or in the form of political resistance. But even those whose concerns are mainly "scholarly" must tiptoe beyond the bounds of either empirical or normative theory to engage subject matter that is intrinsically intertwined with practical problems and so cannot be neatly partitioned. The field has never been able to reside comfortably in pure empirical or normative enquiry, and this is destined to continue.

Instead of suppressing this duality of International Relations theory, we have chosen to highlight it, to draw it out into full view. Our motive is not simply that this promises to be a particularly interesting and illuminating way to read the field, although we have certainly found this. We believe that it is important for International Relations scholars to reflect on the status of International Relations theory as a practical discourse and its consequences for what we do. As many of our contributors (from diverse quarters of the field) reinforce, we want International Relations to be a field that ultimately speaks to the most pressing problems of political action in the contemporary world, even if we always speak with diverse voices, from diverse perspectives. But accepting this as an ambition means accepting that as a field we have to navigate the difficult terrain between empirical and normative theory. Understanding how this terrain has been navigated to date—by realists and postmodernists, Marxists and constructivists—is an instructive first step. Furthermore, highlighting the empirical and normative aspects of all theories has the advantage of unsettling many of our established assumptions and conceits about the field. It challenges us to see different perspectives in different lights, and to reconsider the theoretical terrain of the field in different ways.

The second organizing theme of the *Oxford Handbook of International Relations* was the dynamic interplay between different theoretical and methodological perspectives. Again, this is a departure from established practice. Most surveys, introductions, and compendia treat perspectives as isolated bodies of thought—this is realism, this is liberalism, this is constructivism, and so on. Individual chapters almost always cast their subject theory against theoretical "others," but the purpose is usually to highlight what is distinctive about a particular theory and only secondarily its evolution as part of a wider theoretical milieu. There have, of course, been many attempts to see the evolution of the field as the product of debate, the most frequently invoked being the tale of recurrent great debates: realism versus idealism, classicism versus scientism, and reflectivism versus rationalism (Lapid 1989). But whatever the merits of such accounts (and over the years they have helped acclimatize many students to the field) they work at a macro-level, obscuring much of the detailed interplay, conversation, and contestation between different perspectives. It is this level of interplay that interests us. How have the limitations of existing approaches prompted the development of new ones? How have established perspectives responded to new challengers? How have the ensuing debates and contestations shaped the nature of contending approaches? How have theories borrowed from each other to bolster their heuristic, interpretative, or critical power? Is the field, in the end, one marked by interchange and co-constitution or territoriality and mutual incomprehension?

These two organizing themes ran through the *Oxford Handbook of International Relations*, serving both as structuring devices and reference points for our contributors. The broad organization of the volume reflects our judgement about where the major debates over ideas are taking place. We opened with a series of contending perspectives on what the central empirical focus of International Relations ought to be: Should its central concern be relations between sovereign states (Lake 2008), or should it address the wider constellation of political relationships operating at the global level (Barnett and Sikkink, this volume)? More provocatively, are the very ideas of "international relations" or "global politics" misplaced, ontological frameworks that privilege certain standpoints over others (Cox 2008; Darby 2008)?

Having considered these questions, our attention shifted to the volume's largest section, that addressing the field's principal substantive theories and their ethics: realism, Marxism, neoliberal institutionalism, new liberalism, the English School, critical theory, postmodernism, and feminism.[3] It is here that our concern with the empirical and normative aspects of theory is most apparent. Instead of having one chapter on each of these theories, which is the established practice, the *Oxford Handbook of International Relations* had two: the first providing a general overview of, and engagement with, the theory in question; the second drawing out its underlying ethical standpoint and propositions. We opened this section with an essay on the merits on eclectic theorizing by Peter Katzenstein and Rudra Sil (2008). There appears to be a greater interest today in bridge-building across the theoretical traditions of the field, and it is appropriate to lead with a piece that explores systematically the merits of such dialogue.

Next our *Handbook* addressed ideas about method. Our conception of method is broad and eclectic. For some, method is a positivist preserve, a preoccupation only of those who see International Relations as a social science modeled on the natural

---

[3] These are complex and contested categories so we do not offer thumbnail sketches of them here but refer readers to the respective chapters of the *Oxford Handbook of International Relations*. Table 32.1 characterizes the different approaches in terms of three key dimensions of particular relevance to this chapter.

sciences. But method, like theory, is unavoidable. Every table of contents betrays a method, a set of choices the author has made about how best to go about answering the question that animates his or her research. Sometimes this is the product of systematic reflection, at other times intuition. But just as method is unavoidable, there is no "one size fits all" method—different questions demand different methods. Some questions are best answerable through quantitative methods, some through qualitative, some through historical, some through philosophical, deconstructive, and genealogical methods, and some through artful combinations of two or more of these.[4]

We next turned to the borderlands of the field: the internal borders between International Relations' subfields, and the external borders between International Relations and its near neighbors. As the "international" issues animating scholarship have multiplied—from an initial focus on questions of war and peace to a contemporary agenda that encompasses everything from global finance to population movements—two tendencies have been apparent. On the one hand, there has been the proliferation of distinct communities under the broad umbrella of "International Relations." Some of these are so self-contained that their relationship to the broad umbrella is an active topic of debate: Are strategic studies, foreign policy studies, or international ethics subfields of International Relations or distinctive fields of study? On the other hand, there has been a tendency for International Relations scholars to push out towards other disciplines, most notably economics, law, and continental social theory. In some cases this has involved reengagement with realms of scholarship that were once seen as integral to the nascent field of International Relations, international law being the prime example.[5]

Alongside debates over the substantive focus of the field, the nature of theoretical progress, the relative merits of various "isms," the appropriateness of particular methods, and the integrity of individual subfields, persistent anxiety has surrounded the appropriate relationship between the scholar and the policy-maker. For some, the scholar's role is "to speak truth to power," a stance reinforced by Robert Keohane (in this volume). For others, policy relevance and engagement with government is the true test of scholarship. And for yet others, it is the very pretence of speaking truth that makes International Relations scholars so easily complicit in practices of power and domination. At the heart of these debates are issues of scholarly identity, the relationship between power and knowledge, the nature of social and political engagement, and the relationship between "science" and objectivity. These issues are

---

[4] *Handbook* contributors explored the principal methodological approaches—rational choice (Kydd 2008), sociological and interpretative (Kratochwil 2008), psychological (Goldgeier and Tetlock 2008), quantitative (Mansfield and Pevehouse 2008), qualitative (Bennett and Elman 2008), and historical (Quirk 2008) methods—privileged by the substantive schools of thought examined in the previous section, although we readily acknowledge that our selection was not exhaustive.

[5] Thus, Part V of the *Oxford Handbook of International Relations* investigates the dynamics of these borderlands, paying particular attention to developments within international political economy (Ravenhill 2008), strategic studies (Ayson 2008), foreign policy analysis (Stuart 2008), international ethics (Nardin 2008), and international law (Byers 2008).

taken up by various authors in the *Oxford Handbook of International Relations*, but most directly by Henry Nau (2008) and Joseph Nye (2008).

Consider, next, the field's diversity, or lack thereof. Within the USA it is often assumed (often subconsciously) that the theoretical, methodological, and substantive concerns of American scholars define the nature and contours of International Relations as a field of political enquiry—"American IR is the field." Outside the USA, this chauvinism is frequently observed and linked to a widespread concern that the American academy exerts a hegemonic influence on the field, privileging those concerns, perspectives, and methods favored by American scholars and publishers—"International Relations is an American social science." But while the American academy exerts an undeniable centripetal pull on the field, a pull characterized by clear relations of power, the actual diversity of international relations scholarship globally deserves recognition. International relations scholarship in Britain, Canada, Australia, China, India, France, and Germany varies greatly, and none of it is identical to that conducted within the American academy. It is these issues of the field's homogeneity or heterogeneity—of the potential for diversity within hegemony—that our contributors addressed, focusing in particular on the "subaltern" view of International Relations "from below" (Blaney and Inayatullah 2008), and on the perspective of International Relations from within Great Britain, a former Great Power (Little 2008).

So where has the field been and, more importantly, where ought it to be going? For much of its history, International Relations has been a male-dominated field, and by some measures it remains so today. But in the past twenty years a significant demographic change has occurred, one that has seen the number of women undergraduates, graduate students, and faculty in International Relations grow dramatically. Women's voices are central to multiple debates in the field, and often they are at the leading edge of conceptual, theoretical, and analytical innovation. We sought to acknowledge and reflect this changing demographic by seeking the views not only of three eminent men—Keohane (this volume), Steve Smith (this volume), and Richard Rosecrance (2008)—whose work has been influential in shaping the field, but also those of two women—Janice Bially Mattern (2008) from the USA, and Toni Erskine (2008) from Britain—who have established themselves as significant new voices.

2 Theorizing in International Relations

Our understandings of international relations are organized by theory—and our multiplicity of understandings is reflected in the broad range of contending theoretical approaches canvassed in the *Oxford Handbook of International Relations*. Some of these approaches are closely connected and largely complementary to one another (for example, rationalism and liberal institutionalism; feminism and critical theory), whereas other approaches are usually seen as competitive or even mutually hostile to one another (for example, realism and liberalism; rationalism and postmodernism). International Relations further embraces a wide range of substantive topics and questions, some of which have an elective affinity with particular theoretical approaches. This cacophony of theoretical approaches reflects its subject matter and is key to understanding how the field has developed.

The tendency has been for International Relations scholars to think divisively about theorizing, about the nature of theory in general, and about particular theories. In a field centrally concerned with territoriality, fence-building is a prized craft. But our fellow contributors have encouraged us to think expansively about theorizing, to seek a conception of the theoretical endeavor that is broad enough to encompass a wide variety of theoretical projects without homogenizing them. Not only do many of our contributors advocate bridge-building, but we see in their work as many commonalities as differences.

The definition of theory is contested, and resolving that issue, even if it were possible, would be against the spirit of our enterprise of examining how the interactions of theories organize and drive the field. We have chosen, therefore, to focus on the art of theorizing in International Relations rather than the nature of theory. We propose here that theorizing in International Relations—in all of its diverse manifestations—has come to exhibit three principal components and the dynamic interplay between them.

First, theorizing takes place in relation to the questions (empirical and normative) we ask about the "international" political universe. On the one hand, we construct theories to answer questions. These questions might be highly abstract—such as those animating formal theorizing—or very empirical. They might be broad in scope, or narrowly focused. But International Relations theory always presupposes a referent question about the world we live in or could live in. On the other hand, theorizing often generates questions. For instance, theories which assume that anarchy generates like politics encourage questions about political variations across anarchic systems (Reus-Smit 1999). Second, theorizing rests on assumptions we make about what matters (empirically and normatively) in the "international" political universe, assumptions such as "states are the most important actors," "agents are rational utility maximizers," "norms constitute identities and interests," "discourses are politically constitutive," "truth statements condition power relations," "human rights are universal," "community is the source of all value." A distinction is often made between our ontological, normative, and epistemological assumptions (Price and Reus-Smit 1998). But in reality these are often inextricably linked. Postmodernists do not reject the ontological assumption that states are the most important actors, or the normative assumption that human rights are universal, because they are empirically false, but because they are epistemologically unsustainable (George 1994). Third, theorizing necessarily involves logical argument. It is through argument that we mobilize our assumptions in relation to our questions to infer new conclusions. Arguments are the creative medium through which we combine, enliven, hierarchize, and give meaning to our assumptions, and we do this in the process of answering our questions.

Logical coherence with heuristic or deductive power is the one criterion that all theoretical approaches accept and give pride of place to: Logical contradictions and non sequiturs are no more tolerated by feminists than by neoliberal institutionalists. Good theory is distinguished by how well its internal logic leads us to new insights and conclusions. Like a good story, theory has an internal logic that drives the argument. Once certain elements are specified, conclusions begin to follow, new lines of argument develop, and other elements emerge as logical candidates for inclusion in the theory. This internal dynamic leads to new implications and arguments about the world. Indeed, when a theoretical logic is especially powerful it not only drives the research but can even change and shape the very questions that are asked and create its own inward-looking theoretical "world." Good theory also opens up our assumptions and understandings about what is fixed and what can be changed—both in the theory and as a guide to action in the world.

This conception of the theoretical endeavor encompasses the wide spectrum of theoretical approaches in International Relations. It is as applicable to ostensibly normative theories as empirical ones. Charles Beitz's (1979) classic argument for a cosmopolitan ethic is concerned with the central question of what principles of justice ought to apply globally and rests on the primary assumption that practical interdependence (an empirical idea he draws from Keohane and Nye 1977) necessarily leads to moral interdependence. It is also as applicable to critical theories as problem-solving. Andrew Linklater (1998) has been centrally concerned with understanding patterns of inclusion and exclusion in world politics, and his argument about the expansion of moral community globally rests on assumptions about the logic of communicative action. Similarly, Keohane (1984) has focused on the question of explaining patterns of international institutional cooperation, with his arguments building on assumptions about rational state action under conditions of interdependence. Finally, this conception is as applicable to theories addressing interpretative "how" questions as those concerned with explanatory "why" questions. The scholar who asks how chemical weapons have come to attract such high moral disapprobation (Price 1997) will build logically on the basis of assumptions about the international political universe as readily as the scholar who asks why states engage in balance-of-power politics (Kaplan 1957; Waltz 1979; Mearsheimer 2001).

Because International Relations theory addresses questions about the world, it necessarily has empirical content. Even our normative questions have empirical referents—the nature of the use of force between states, patterns of global inequality, the subordination of women, the hierarchy of cultures. Although the boundaries of International Relations are fluid and contested, the field is defined in large part by its evolving empirical domain and the questions we ask of this domain. Questions of security and order are enduring, but changing interrelations at the global level from transnationalism to interdependence have expanded the set of enduring issues to include prosperity and growth (Risse-Kappen 1995; Gilpin 2001) and, increasingly, rights and freedoms (Risse, Ropp, and Sikkink 1999). This evolution has been punctuated by important events including world wars, decolonization, the oil crisis, the end of the cold war, and the attacks of September 11, events that have shaped and directed International Relations scholarship. Of course, different theories and areas of International Relations emphasize different aspects of the empirical domain, and even different aspects of the "same" empirics. Security and international political economy define themselves in terms of different though partially overlapping substantive problems, which lead them to contending understandings of world politics and possibilities. Differences reign even within areas. The meaning and origins of "security" are contested (Wæver 1995), as are the important questions and theoretical constructs—interdependence or dependency or globalization—of political economy (Ravenhill 2008). Even specific empirical "facts" are contested—is the world unipolar (Brooks and Wohlforth 2002)? Is globalization homogenizing or fragmenting (Scholte 2005)? Does free trade alleviate or accentuate global inequality (Rodrik 1997)? Often these disagreements provide the puzzles to be explained and the inspiration for introducing new elements into theory.

Most International Relations theorizing relies on empirical evidence to distinguish good arguments from crazy ideas. While this position is most often identified with positivism, it undergirds most International Relations scholarship. To take a seemingly hard example, postmodernists make the signature claim that texts are open to multiple interpretations, and that there is no Archimedean standpoint from which to determine the truth of one reading over another. But their increasingly sophisticated analyses of diverse political discourses nevertheless rest on the assumption that texts and events are amenable to better and worse interpretations (Price and Reus-Smit 1998; Hansen 2006). Pointing out that a broad spectrum of International Relations theories rely on empirical evidence to support their arguments is not the same, however, as treating falsification as a paramount value. Insofar as positivism gives unreflective primacy to falsification, or treats theory only as a hook upon which to hang empirical results, it misses the fact that theory can be important even when it cannot be empirically validated or falsified. This is as true of positive theorizing such as the Arrow (1951) theorem which establishes that every international voting or decision rule must fail to meet certain democratic aspirations,[6] as it is of normative theorizing, such as the claim that human rights are universal (Donnelly 2003)—neither can be validated or falsified empirically. Conceptual theorizing is also vitally important but not empirically verifiable. Thus while theorizing is never independent of empirical things, International Relations theory has an autonomy from, and must take priority over, empirical analysis.

---

[6] The Arrow theorem is also an excellent example that positive theory can be deeply normative. Some of Arrow's conditions (for example, nondictatorship, Pareto) are directly motivated on normative grounds while others (for example, independence of irrelevant alternatives, universal domain) raise implicit normative questions about what we desire in a "democratic" social choice process—the very desirability of which is itself a normative question.

While many different stripes of International Relations theory peacefully coexist, disagreements are the most prominent feature of the landscape. Two axes of division stand out. The first is between critical and problem-solving theories. Robert Cox famously argued that the latter "takes the world as it finds it, with the prevailing social and political power relationships and the institutions into which they are organized, as the given framework of action," while the former "allows for a normative choice in favor of a social and political order different from the prevailing order; but it limits the range of choice to alternative orders which are feasible transformations of the existing order" (Cox 1986, 208, 210). This distinction remains an important one, pointing us to the crucial difference between theorizing that focuses on the emancipatory transformation of the "social and political complex as a whole" and that which concentrates on the technical management of particular aspects of that complex. The following chapters suggest, however, that it may no longer be a straightforward guide to differentiating particular International Relations theories. As Richard Shapcott (2008) explains, one of critical theory's contributions to the field is that concern with the normatively oriented transformation of world politics is no longer the sole preserve of self-identified critical theorists: In different ways, constructivists, liberals, and English School scholars are all plowing this field. Equally importantly, it is now clear that theoretical approaches not traditionally associated with the critical project may fruitfully be conscripted to its aid. Notable here is the contribution methodological individualists have made to understanding the origins of the contemporary system of sovereign states (Spruyt 1994; 2007).

The second axis of division is between verbal and formal mathematical theory. Proponents see the formal approach as the highest form of theory whereas critics see it as the ultimate in abstract irrelevance. Neither position is correct. A theory that can be modeled mathematically engages a particularly powerful form of deductive power. But even here the art is in the "modeling dialog" (Myerson 1992) which entails the pursuit of substantive as well as mathematical arguments. Moreover, many problems which cannot be modeled productively through mathematics are amenable to verbal theory as a means of advancing our theoretical understanding. Defining our questions by our techniques misses the point of developing theory about the world we care about. To reduce the field to what can be mathematically modeled would narrow it to a barren landscape; conversely, not to take advantage of formal deduction when possible is to risk missing important theoretical insights and possibly allowing inconsistent arguments to stand.[7]

It is often contended that different International Relations theories are fundamentally incompatible with one another. Approaches such as postmodernism and liberalism often seem irreconcilable while others, such as psychological (Goldgeier

---

[7] Relevant examples are myriad. Some involve fairly technical mathematical presentations (Powell 1999; Downs and Rocke 1995; Kydd 2008), but many other ideas founded in technical analysis have entered International Relations through more accessible translations. Examples of the latter category include James Fearon's (1995) discussion of rational war, the widespread use of Mancur Olson's (1965) collective action analysis (based on Paul Samuelson's quite technical analysis of public goods), or Thomas Schelling's (1960) discussion of credibility and deterrence.

and Tetlock 2008) and sociological approaches (Kratochwil 2008), may just have little to say to each other. Unfortunately, the field has a tendency to exaggerate and even glorify these differences: One purpose of theory is to clarify fundamental from nonfundamental differences and, where possible, to establish common ground. This has been occurring, for example, in the much discussed and somewhat overblown debate between rationalism and constructivism. There has already been some convergence with regard to the role of ideas (to which rationalists pay increasing attention: Goldstein and Keohane 1993; Snidal 2002) and of strategic rationality (which constructivists are increasingly incorporating into their accounts: Keck and Sikkink 1998). Even the purported differences (Wendt 1999) between the causal theory of rationalism and the constitutive theory of constructivism are exaggerated. After all, rational choice's central equilibrium concept is a constitutive statement that a set of elements are in harmony with each other; equilibrium analysis only becomes causal by asking what happens when one element is displaced and harmony disrupted. Conversely, constructivist theorizing about norms has been increasingly used as the theoretical underpinning for causal relations and empirical testing (Checkel 1999; Ruggie 2005). Even where common ground does not exist, lessons can migrate across perspectives as, for example, has happened with the critical theory challenge to the positivist ideal of value-free research. This is not to argue that deep incompatibilities do not exist, only that International Relations theorizing at its best serves to clarify which differences are fundamental and which can be bridged.

3 The Empirical and Normative Faces of Theory

Security studies has long been driven by the impetus to understand war so we can control and reduce it; human rights analysis is motivated by the desire to stop atrocities ranging from genocide to slavery to torture; international political economy is ultimately about promoting mutually beneficial economic interactions among states, firms, and individuals; and we study institutions like the World Health Organization and the Food and Agriculture Organization to understand how to improve global health and food, respectively. Although International Relations theories often present themselves as scientific and even objective, the underlying choice of assumptions is never objective and neither are values that animate them. All theories contain significant normative elements through the questions they ask, the concepts they use, the factors they exclude or hold constant, and the values they seek to further. Nevertheless, much of contemporary International Relations neglects and even denies its normative underpinnings out of concern that it will impede intellectual progress.

In this section we argue the opposite position—so long as International Relations remains a practical discourse, one ultimately (though often implicitly) concerned with the question of "how we should act," scholars will be compelled to occupy the difficult terrain between the empirical and the normative. Furthermore, closer attention to the variety of ethical underpinnings in the field can strengthen our understanding of what we do and, channeled properly, can motivate research progress as it enhances our ability, individually or collectively, to speak to the most pressing issue of political action in contemporary world politics.

The normative component has been falsely suppressed in International Relations for a combination of substantive, methodological, and theoretical reasons. The traditional realist emphasis on national security as a seemingly uncontroversial goal, and the state as the uncontroversial actor, eliminated any need to problematize the goals of action. Early English School (Cochran 2008) and liberal American approaches (Richardson 2008) echoed this neglect of normative concerns in their emphasis on equally uncontroversial goals of order and efficiency, respectively. Of course, as Jack Donnelly (2008) shows, even the most hardcore security realism entails some ethical content; the English School has also invested heavily in normative theorizing and liberals are increasingly aware of the shortcoming of efficiency as its singular normative concept. And questions of just war, treatment of foreigners, and fair exchange have long been with us. Currently, the changing and expanding range of questions of international politics—including new dimensions of security such as terrorism and ethnic conflict, new twists on long-standing North–South issues and new political economy issues such as regulation that penetrate into the domestic workplace and home, and deepened concern for issues such as human rights, the global environment, and effects beyond the great powers—all present issues where goals are contested and the myth of normative consensus is unsustainable.

Behavioralism, positivism, and the effort to create a "science" of International Relations provided a second motivation for the neglect of ethical considerations. Although most positivists accept that normative considerations are relevant to what questions to ask and to the uses to which those answers are put, "science" is seen as the intermediate stage involving production of knowledge which is ostensibly value-free.[8] However, normative considerations are deeply, though often implicitly, embedded in this scientific stage itself. Thus quantitative International Relations now pays close attention to selection bias within its analyses but quantitative analysis itself is an important form of selection bias driven by measurability and data availability (Mansfield and Pevehouse 2008). Further value judgements are necessarily lodged in the definition of contested concepts such as power, liberty, or equality. These normative assumptions can be varied through alternative conceptualizations and measurements but they cannot be eliminated. Perversely, the choice to limit research to questions where it is (falsely) believed that value-free assessment is possible can have the unfortunate byproduct of limiting the questions asked—itself an implicit value judgement.

---

[8] We thank Alex Wendt for suggesting this formulation.

An outside example that has had profound effects on international relations is the "ordinalist revolution" of economics in the 1930s in which economists discovered that they could derive key market results without recourse to cardinal individual utility or interpersonal comparisons of utility—both of which raise thorny normative issues (Blaug 1985). This reorientation allowed economics to make important and fundamental progress—but at the cost of largely abandoning the social welfare questions which had been central to the discipline up to that time. The heritage of this methodological move is reflected within International Relations in the emphasis on Pareto-efficiency rather than distribution in liberal institutionalism which, in turn, implicitly gives the status quo normative pride of place. Liberals are well aware of this bias but their analytic tools are not as powerful for addressing other values, which are therefore slighted. Of course, the procedures of science—especially its efforts at being systematic, comparable, and transparent—provide means to highlight these normative elements and perhaps evaluate their implications. But at best they can illuminate, not eliminate, the normative element.

The tendency to set aside ethical considerations has been reinforced by misleading efforts fully to substitute logic for values. This underlying impetus is well captured in the rational choice adoption of the distinction between "normative" theory as being about "ought" and "positive" theory as being about "is." Positive theory analyzes the consequences that logically follow from interactions among a set of actors, given their goals and their capacities, without any evaluation or judgement of those goals. Of course, the assumptions regarding the actors, their goals, and their capacities are themselves partly normative assertions, while the normative content of the predictions is what motivates our interest in the analysis in the first place. More importantly, rational choice short-changes itself by denying its normative heritage and possibilities. In addition to emanating from the distinctively normative utilitarian tradition, rational choice can be viewed as a normative theory about what actors should do given their circumstance—what is rational action?—as much as an empirical prediction about what actors will do. This is especially important insofar as rationality is often impaired so that actors cannot be assumed to be fully capable of achieving their goals (Levy 1997). Moreover, much of rational choice is directed toward understanding how to ameliorate the adverse consequences of individual rationality (as evidenced in problems such as the prisoner's dilemma, collective action; or principal–agent relations) and how to achieve better outcomes either through individual remedies such as precommitment (Martin 2000) or reputation (Tomz 2007), or through collective remedies such as arms control or institutional design (Koremenos, Lipson, and Snidal 2001). Such solutions are justified in terms of efficiency as the primary normative value in rational choice and one which is typically presented as a neutral or even "scientific" value. But efficiency claims can mask other values such as distribution or rights (Gruber 2000). Andrew Kydd (2008) argues more generally that rational choice is premised on liberal normative biases, including respect for the individual, and that it has an elective affinity for specific substantive outcomes such as free exchange and decentralized power. Thus, far from being a purely logical rather than a partially normative theory, rational choice is a logical theory based on normative premisses that provides guidance regarding how to further our normative goals.

The problem of separating empirical from normative analysis has been reinforced by the tendency of scholars who do take normative considerations seriously to distance themselves from social scientific approaches. This is most pronounced among those whose central concern is philosophical, determining what constitutes right conduct in a variety of international situations, from global aid provision to humanitarian intervention. Very often the process of ethical reasoning is defined narrowly, to encompass only the logical determination of ethical principles. But ethical reasoning is in practice much broader than this, combining empirical propositions and assumptions with philosophical speculation (Reus-Smit 2008). Defining it narrowly, however, encourages a neglect of empirical enquiry and the theories and methods it necessarily entails. This tendency is also apparent, though to a lesser extent, among approaches that take normative concerns seriously but shun more "scientific" approaches to empirical enquiry. Until recently, this has been a weakness of the English School, whose critically important meditations on the relationship between order and justice have historically been limited by its unsystematic approach to the nature of social and institutional relations among states (Reus-Smit 2005). Instead of a proper engagement between normative and scientific positions, we typically see either mutual neglect or mutual critiques that fall on deaf ears. The result is a divide with "science" on one side and "normative" on the other.

This separation severely impairs the ability of International Relations to speak to practical concerns. On the one hand, the unwillingness of "scientists" to tackle ethical and seemingly unscientific problems means it often has little to say on the important problems of the day; on the other hand, insofar as normative International Relations is insufficiently well grounded in empirical knowledge, it is not competent to say what we should do in specific cases. Advice on whether or not to intervene in the next Rwanda or Darfur, for example, rests both on an analysis of what is possible (do sanctions work? can military intervention be effective?), and on a judgement as to who has the right or obligation to do so. In order to connect International Relations theory back to the practical questions that motivate it, both normative and empirical legs of the analysis must be firmly in place. This is the long-standing position of critical theorists such as Cox and Linklater, who seek normatively compelling transformations of international order that are "realistic" and consistent with the empirical dynamics of the global system (Cox 1986, 208; Linklater 1998). It is also the position advocated more recently by Keohane (2001; see also Buchanan and Keohane 2004), who has called on International Relations scholars to help bring about a new international institutional order, a project that demands the integration of empirical and normative theory.

Our purpose here, however, is not simply to encourage greater interaction and integration between empirical and normative theorizing; it is to show that all International Relations theories already have empirical and normative dimensions. There are two reasons why this is necessarily so. The first, and most commonly observed, is that we as scholars can never escape our values; they permeate the questions we ask, the puzzles we seek to fathom, the assumptions we make, and the methods we adopt. There is, however, a second reason that we wish to highlight here. As explained in the first section, International Relations has always been a practical discourse, in the sense that the question of "how we should act" has undergirded and informed scholarship across the field. This is no less true of postmodern scholarship—concerned as it is with how to respond to structures of domination—than realist scholarship with its concern for the effective prosecution of the national interest under conditions of anarchy. Because their practical questions exist as a motive force, however implicitly, scholars are drawn onto the difficult terrain between the empirical and the normative. Answering the question of "how we should act" in terms of the values we seek to realize demands an appreciation of "how we can act" in terms of the context of action we face.

This interconnection between empirical and normative theorizing exists not just at the stages of the questions we ask and the purposes for which we use theory but also at the intermediate stage of knowledge production. We made the point earlier that normative biases permeate this stage. But with practical discourses the empirical and the normative are even more deeply entwined in processes of knowledge production. Answering the question of how we should act requires empirical knowledge production that examines the causal, constitutive, and discursive structures and processes that frame political action. But it also requires normative knowledge production that examines who the "we" is that seeks to act, what principles we seek to realize, and what resources we are prepared to sacrifice to achieve our ends (such as the loss of compatriots to save strangers) (Reus-Smit 2008). With practical discourses, therefore, knowledge production cannot be confined to the "scientific" realm of empirical theory; it is necessarily more expansive, encompassing normative enquiry just as centrally.

One of our central goals in the *Oxford Handbook of International Relations* was to draw out these empirical and normative dimensions of International Relations theories, and this has been done most systemically in our survey of the principal substantive theories. In the remainder of this section, we draw on our contributors' insights to map these theories' empirical and normative aspects, leading we hope to a markedly different characterization of the field than is common. We have found it illuminating to map them against three empirical and two normative axes, though others are no doubt possible.

With regard to their empirical-theoretic aspects, we have focused on their assumptions regarding agency and structure, ideas and materiality, and the nature of power. With the first of these, we have distinguished between theories that are agential (emphasizing individual choice in determining political outcomes), structural (emphasizing the opportunities and constraints that social structures place on individual choice), structurationist (emphasizing the mutually constitutive relationship between agents and structures), and post-structuralist (stressing the way in which systems of signification and meaning constitute subjectivities). With the second, we have differentiated between theories that are ideational (attributing constitutive power to intersubjective ideas and meanings), rational institutionalist (emphasizing the role of ideas in mediating the relationship between material or other interests and political outcomes), and materialist (highlighting the causal force of material factors). With the third set of assumptions, we distinguish between four different conceptions of "power" in different International Relations theories. We have conscripted Michael Barnett and Raymond Duvall's (2005, 3, emphasis in original) typology where:

Compulsory power refers to relations of interaction that allow one actor to have direct control over another...*Institutional power* is in effect when actors exercise indirect control over others...*Structural power* concerns the constitution of social capacities and interests of actors in direct relation to one another...*Productive power* is the socially diffuse production of subjectivity in systems of meaning and signification.

When it comes to the normative-theoretic aspects of theories, we have concentrated on two axes of variation: value commitments and orientation toward change.[9] The first refers to the values or purposes that theories seek to realize, implicitly or explicitly. Drawing on our contributors, we have identified five distinct value commitments: (1) the prudent pursuit of the national interest; (2) international cooperation (ranging from order through minimal norms of sovereignty to achievement of higher-order social values through international governance); (3) individual freedom (including negative freedom through the removal of constraints on individual liberty as well as positive freedom through the protection of individuals' basic rights); (4) inclusivity and self-reflexivity; and (5) responsibility to otherness. Our second axis—orientation toward change—refers to theorists' general inclinations to the question of moral and practical change: Are they (implicitly or explicitly) optimistic or skeptical? The normative aspects of International Relations theories are not only determined by the values scholars embrace, but by their willingness to entertain that moral change is possible. We have treated this as a separate axis on which to map theories, as the orientations toward change of different theories are reducible neither to their empirical understandings nor to their substantive value commitments—are realists generally skeptical about moral change because of the empirical assumptions they make, or do they favor these assumptions because they are moral pessimists?

Table 32.1 maps nine substantive theories of international relations against these empirical and normative dimensions. Our purpose here is not to reify these theories, reducing their complexities to singular, homogeneous, forms.[10] Nor is it to suggest that our chosen axes of comparison are the only relevant dimensions of similarity or

---

[9] These are not the only axes of variation that could have been chosen here. For instance, we could have disaggregated value commitments into deontological and consequentialist subcategories, and we could have added an axis categorizing theories according to how they treat the relationship between means and ends.

[10] Such categorizations are necessarily vulgar and disguise important internal variations within approaches. For example, some realists are optimists and some constructivists are pessimists. Elements of the English School are more structural than strucurationist while institutionalism might sometimes handle compulsory as well as institutional power. While our categorizations are necessarily imperfect, we believe they capture the general tendencies. The exceptions suggest other overlaps and intersections among perspectives.

Table 32.1. Empirical and normative faces of theory

| Theories | Empirical aspects | | Conception of power | Normative aspects | | Orientation toward change |
	Agency–structure	Ideational–material		Value commitment	
Realism	Structural (Anarchy)	Material	Compulsory	National interest	Skeptical
Marxism	Structural (Capitalism)	Material	Structural	Individual freedom (Negative–Emancipation)	Skeptical
Neoliberal Institutionalism	Agential (States)	Rational-institutionalist	Institutional	International cooperation	Optimistic
New Liberalism	Agential (Individuals)	Rational-institutionalist	Institutional	Individual freedom (Negative–Liberty)	Optimistic
English School					
(ES-Pluralists)	Structural (Anarchy)	Rational-institutionalist	Institutional	International cooperation	Skeptical
(ES-Solidarists)	Structurationist	Ideational	Structural	Individual freedom (Positive–Universal human rights)	Optimistic
Constructivism	Structurationist	Ideational	Structural	Individual positive freedom/International cooperation	Optimistic
Critical Theory	Structurationist	Ideational/material	Structural	Individual freedom (Negative–Emancipation)	Optimistic
Postmodernism	Structurationist	Ideational	Productive	Responsibility to otherness	Skeptical
Feminism	Structurationist	Ideational	Productive	Inclusivity/Self-reflexivity	Skeptical

difference. Our goal is to show(a) that indeed all theories of International Relations entail empirical and normative dimensions, and (b) that a number of interesting patterns and overlaps emerge when theories are viewed in this way. Among other things, this reveals that a number of ritual characterizations that are used to divide the field are vastly overworked. The most notable is the much brandished distinction between realists and idealists, scientists and utopians: a distinction that rests on the purported ability to quarantine empirical theories from normative influence. A second is that the field is fundamentally riven by epistemological differences, by differences over what constitutes true knowledge. But while these differences are all too apparent, and their implications for how we conduct our scholarship important, they obscure multiple other significant points of convergence between theoretical approaches.

Our comparison reveals three patterns of note. The first is that of value resonance across seemingly opposed theories. This is perhaps most striking between critical theorists and new liberals. As Robyn Eckersley (2008) explains in her chapter on the ethics of critical theory, at the level of "normative ethics, critical theory's overriding ethical goal is to promote emancipation, or remove constraints on human auton- omy, by means of ever more inclusive and less distorted dialogue." The similarity between this normative standpoint and the priority given to individual liberty by new liberals is difficult to ignore. For both, the good of human individuals has ethical primacy, and for both the removal of constraints on their freedom is prioritized. This is not to obscure important differences between these theories' ethical positions, but their similarities should not be surprising given their common Enlightenment origins. Value resonance is also apparent between English School solidarists and constructivists, both evincing a central concern for clarifying the conditions under which sovereignty can be compromised to better promote the positive freedom of individuals, particularly in the form of international human rights. Again, important differences should not be obscured, particularly over methodology and the prior- ity given to philosophical enquiry, but convergence at the level of values is all too apparent.

Second, our comparison reveals a strong correlation between the orientations toward change of theories that adopt a compulsory conception of power and those that embrace a productive one. The prime example of this is the relation between realism and postmodernism. Both are skeptical of the possibility of moral change in international relations. For realists this is because the politics of morality is always eclipsed by the politics of power; for postmodernists it is because moral discourses are necessary for the production of power: All processes of moral signification produce relations of domination. Peter Lawler (2008) observes correctly that the postmodernists' critique of moral universalism does not lead them to the "moral despair" of realists, only to a preference "for localized, contingent responses to eth- ically troubling cases." However, theories that embrace compulsory or productive conceptions of power share a view of power as ubiquitous to international relations. For realists this is because it is the struggle for power that defines politics; for post- modernists it is that all processes of signification are constitutive of power. Both ultimately encourage a position of moral skepticism, even if this does not amount to despair.

The third pattern of note is the consistent correlation between structural theories and skepticism and between agential or structurationist theories and optimism. Realists, Marxists, and English School pluralists are all structural, in the sense that they see either the structure of anarchy or of capitalism providing the incentives and constraints for social actors. Not surprisingly their relative neglect of the role such actors can play in the constitution of social structures leaves little room for the possibility of moral change in international relations—with the partial exception of the Marxist view of the structure itself being unstable in the long term (Teschke 2008). Conversely, theories that are agential or structurationist—such as new liberalism, solidarism within the English School, or constructivism—leave greater space for the creative power of individual or collective human agency, providing the social theoretic foundations for more optimistic positions on the question of both moral and practical change. Of course, agency can work to bad ends as well—neoliberal institutionalists understand that cooperation can be aimed against third parties while constructivists recognize the possibility of bad norms leading to pathological consequences (Rae 2002). Finally, postmodernism and feminism are exceptions in being structurationist and skeptical, possibly because their emphasis on productive power overwhelms the impact of structurationism, encouraging skepticism not optimism.

4 THE QUESTION OF PROGRESS

While the above comparison reveals the diversity of contemporary theorizing in International Relations, as well as diverse ways in which theories have traversed the difficult terrain between the empirical and the normative, has such diversity led to progress in the field? It is unfashionable to speak of progress in International Relations, but it is also the case that some notion of progress informs all of our scholarship. If we don't believe that our work makes some contribution to improving our understanding of world politics, and that our collective endeavors as a field yield some knowledge gains, what justifies our research? For this reason, we believe that progress in International Relations can be evaluated in terms of the extent to which we have expanded our understanding of the subject matter—viewed broadly to include explanatory, interpretative, normative, and other approaches to understanding—and whether this has improved our ability to act effectively in international affairs. Simply put, can we do things better now than before in these two related spheres? An important distinction here is between progress within sub-areas of International Relations—defined by substantive topic, methodology, or theoretical approach—versus progress of the field as a whole. We argue that the seeming lack of progress in the field as a whole is intimately related to the nature of progress within its sub-fields.

Evaluating progress is difficult for several reasons. We have no agreed criteria by which to measure what we know or how effectively it has been (or could be) applied to real-world action. International relations' dynamic character makes it a moving target as both an object of enquiry and a field of study. Although some questions are enduring, others are changing with both world events and intellectual fashions. Most importantly, the field is inherently political and contested so that any measure of progress is inherently value laden and depends significantly on beliefs regarding what is possible and what is desirable.

Nevertheless, the contributions to this volume clearly document multiple ways in which progress has been made. Conceptually, the field is much more rigorous; even where it comes to no settled consensus, it is clearer about its differences. Fundamental concepts like power remain "essentially contested," but in differentiating types of power (Barnett and Duvall 2005) we have substantially advanced our understanding of its different facets. Similarly, the presumption of state-centrism has been increasingly challenged by analyses incorporating transnational and sub-national actors (Moravscik, this volume), but the theoretical sophistication of both state-centric approaches and their competitors has advanced considerably. William Wohlforth (2008) shows how realism has flourished and multiplied in terms of more finely tuned arguments and debates, such as those between offensive and defensive realism; Ian Hurd (2008) and Friedrich Kratochwil (2008) show how constructivism has incorporated philosophical and sociological arguments to develop a novel ideational theory and norm-based explanations as a counterpoint to overly materialist traditional theory based solely on power and interests. Postmodernism, for all its skepticism about progress, has also developed ever more sophisticated methods of deconstruction, discourse analysis, and genealogical enquiry, yielding important insights into the discursive construction of post-cold war international relations (Burke 2008).

Other important aspects of the field's progress have been the incorporation of new approaches to long-standing questions, the opening of new areas of enquiry, and the asking of questions that are either new or have been neglected. These shifts have sometimes been prompted by emerging problems in the world, sometimes by the internal logic of theoretical approaches, sometimes by changing intellectual forces, and usually by a combination of all of these. For example, post-cold war and post-September 11 security research has shifted to new concerns with ethnic conflict and terrorism, and its logics of assurance and deterrence have been adapted in light of the new challenges these problems present. The concept and boundaries of security (Buzan, Wæver, and de Wilde 1998) have been contested and seen to involve much deeper elements of personal security rather than simply military matters or state interests. International political economy has moved beyond its traditional concerns with trade and money, though those remain important, to look at emerging issues of standard-setting, transnational business regulation, and money-laundering

(Abbott and Snidal 2001; Drezner 2007; Mattli and Büthe 2003). Institutions have been reconceptualized with increasing attention paid to their different forms and specific properties (Koremenos, Lipson, and Snidal 2001). Similarly, the emergence of global warming as an issue and new regard for human rights around the globe have challenged traditional theories and sparked increased interest in new ones.

The field, or at least part of it, has become less complacent about the questions being asked. The proliferation of questions and approaches has been connected to a greater appreciation that questions asked are never neutral but always reflect underlying values and power relations. Critical approaches and feminism have challenged long-standing biases of "mainstream" realism and liberalism while interpretativist and more historically oriented work have challenged the more universalistic ambitions of positivism. Ironically, some of these differences emerge because realism can also be criticized for being substantively less ambitious in assuming that the fundamental nature of international politics is unchanging, whereas liberals see possibilities for change within the system that need to be explained and more radical approaches problematize the existing international system to open up the need to explain large-scale system change.

The continuing relative neglect of Third World issues reminds us that the biases of our intellectual community, which remains a Northern and a Western one, continue to shape our discipline and limit its progress in at least some areas. Phillip Darby's (2008) critique of International Relations as a discipline, Anthony Burke's (2008) discussion of postmodernism, and David Blaney and Naeem Inayatullah's (2008) "view from below" all argue that International Relations theory excludes the questions and analyses most relevant to the Third World and continues to define progress in Western terms. Postcolonialism, postmodernism, and feminism all challenge the predominant focus on states and sovereignty, as well as the neglect of non-Western cultures and issues such as global injustice that receive little more than lip service in the North. Blaney and Inayatullah (2008; see also Gilroy 2006) propose that such approaches need to engage "IR from above" to expose their hidden assumptions and political purposes.

Progress in the use of increasingly sophisticated methodology is easy to document. Statistical and formal mathematical approaches have both become more widespread and more carefully tailored to substantive problems of international relations (Mansfield and Pevehouse 2008). There has been a continuing development of improved data-sets on an expanding set of questions, now including human rights (Hathaway 2002; Hafner-Burton 2005), environment (Sprinz 2004), domestic institutions (Howell and Pevehouse 2007; Mansfield, Milner, and Rosendorff 2002), and democracy (Russett and Oneal 2001; Pevehouse and Russett 2006). Formal models (Snidal 2004) have become more common and more complicated and have driven theory in certain areas such as deterrence and cooperation. These approaches have also become better at recognizing and dealing with their limits—as reflected in increased attention to selection and identification problems in quantitative work (Drezner 2003; von Stein 2005; Vreeland 2003) or the use of agent models

(Cederman 2003) to address problems not amenable to closed-form mathematical analysis.

Importantly, methodological progress has not been limited to these more technical approaches. Case study methods have advanced significantly not only in their use of historical and interpretative methods but also in the use of techniques such as process tracing to combine careful causal analysis with close attention to underlying mechanisms (Bennett and Elman 2008). Postmodernism has advanced in its argumentation as reflected in its genealogical analysis of discourses of security (Hansen 2006) and its practices and, more generally but perhaps also more controversially, in its closer attention to historical events and contemporary policy (Burke 2008). The different methods have also interacted to their mutual benefit. Statistical analysis of selection problems spurred considerable attention to selection problems in qualitative research, which in turn has led to a richer understanding of selection issues and research designs that go beyond the pure statistical models (Signorino 2002). The complementarity of different approaches has also been revealed by the widespread use of combinations of case studies and large-n analysis, which has almost become formulaic in some areas. In this vein, whereas early constructivist work was criticized by positivists as not being testable, constructivists have more than demonstrated their capacity to produce methodologically rigorous, empirical research (for a recent example see Acharya and Johnston 2007)—and positivists have been able to include some of the factors raised by constructivists in their own work (Tierney and Weaver 2007).

Methodologically driven progress has significant limits, however. While judicious use of methods improves empirical and theoretical analysis of International Relations problems, methods are the means and not the goal. Over-emphasis on methodological criteria can discourage research in areas that aren't (yet?) amenable to the most advanced techniques. Just as it was valuable to study war before extensive datasets had been developed for quantitative analysis, so it is useful to study problems such as human rights even if we cannot formally model normative action or if our statistical data are limited. Important research questions cannot always wait for method.

A related problem emerges when research is expected to meet the multiple standards of empirics and theory. Research can be first-rate without doing everything. For example, inductive research that improves our knowledge of what the world looks like—and of important relationships that we care about—is useful even before the relationships are well theorized. Indeed, theoretical progress necessarily requires empirical facts even before they are deeply theorized. Conversely, theoretical analysis can improve the quality of International Relations arguments even if they are not yet tested or, in some cases, cannot be tested: Good theory often takes us beyond our current empirical knowledge. In short, there is a virtue in a division of labor where not every article has to do everything—some papers should be largely theoretical with limited empirics, others largely inductive with thin theory, and others mainly normative, or even methodological. The corollary to this division of labor is that no piece of research is fully complete in and of itself. The meaning and value of individual projects depends vitally on their interconnections with International Relations research in general.

How then does progress occur? It is useful to distinguish progress within individual research areas from progress in the field as a whole. When discussing a specific approach or issue, all authors in the *Oxford Handbook of International Relations* report on some type of progress within their area,[11] even if they sometimes express dissatisfaction with the rate or direction of progress. It might seem that if all its areas have advanced, then presumably so has the field. However, there is no consensus that the field has advanced in the sense of moving toward a common and integrated understanding of international politics. International Relations remains a diverse and contested field whose different areas are often claimed to be, and sometimes probably are, incompatible. To reconcile this coexistence of progress within areas with the seeming lack of overall progress, we need to consider the different ways that progress is made within and across areas.

Progress within areas often results from pursing the internal logic of a theoretical argument and/or investigating the empirical realm that it identifies. In some cases, a key theoretical puzzle (for example, why is there cooperation?) or empirical fact (for example, democracies don't fight one another) has motivated enormous research effort and substantial advancement. Thus folk theorem results about the possibility of cooperation in anarchy have developed into a rich analysis of the institutions that surround cooperation; a few empirical facts about the relationship of democracy and war (Doyle 1986) have launched a thousand articles addressing the relation between domestic regimes and international outcomes (for a discussion see Mansfield and Pevehouse 2008). These more inward-looking logics of enquiry can be highly productive but, in isolation, promote relatively narrow specialization within areas sometimes leading to some splintering of the areas itself. A prime example of this is Wohlforth's (2008) discussion of how the development of realist theory has increased the variety of different camps of types of realists.

The opposite extreme is when progress is based on the importation of external ideas. International Relations always has been a deeply interdisciplinary enterprise, and one of its most important sources of progress has been borrowing from outside the field. Various chapters of the *Oxford Handbook of International Relations* document extensive borrowing of theoretical ideas, substantive arguments, and methodological tools from the disciplines of sociology (Hurd 2008; Kratochwil 2008), history (Quirk 2008; Bennett and Elman 2008; Blaney and Inayatullah 2008), economics (Kydd 2008; Stein 2008), philosophy (Burke 2008), psychology (Goldgeier and Tetlock 2008), and political science (Donnelly 2008; Moravcsik, this volume). We also see the incorporation of ideas from theoretical approaches such as feminism, critical theory, and postmodernism that cross over the social science disciplines as well as the humanities. Of particular note in this volume is the reinvigoration of International Relations' borrowing from political theory. This is hardly new since,

---

[11] Despite the obvious selection bias in terms of the criteria by which we solicited authors and that they accepted, the authors generally make compelling cases for progress within their areas—at least by that area's criteria.

as Donnelly notes, many of International Relations' intellectual icons—including Thucydides, Thomas Hobbes, Hugo Grotius, and Immanuel Kant—are theorists of more than international relations. More recently, the field has begun to build on a wide range of more contemporary political theorists such as Jürgen Habermas, Carl Schmidt, Michel Foucault, John Rawls, Giorgio Agamben, Judith Butler, and Axel Honneth.

External borrowing is an important way to advance the field but poses problems of its own. One danger is that International Relations problems will be adapted to fit to the theory rather than the other way round as is appropriate. Theories developed in other contexts may not provide a good match: There is no reason to believe that states are socialized in the same way as individuals, that rational international actors are like marketplace consumers, or that individual psychology transfers to how leaders and bureaucracies act in international crises. Thus external borrowing needs to be carefully tailored to the circumstances of international relations in order to be valuable. Although there is no simple way to measure it, the quality of our intellectual "borrowing," and especially of our adapting it to the specific circumstances of international relations, has significantly improved. The probable reason is that International Relations scholars are increasingly well versed in the particular external intellectual terrains from which they draw. However, this leads to a second danger that such borrowing fragments International Relations as a field by connecting its sub-areas more to their respective external source than to each other. Even if we don't care whether International Relations coheres as a "discipline," the commonality of our questions makes it desirable for different approaches to seek productive engagement with one another. Fortunately, there has also been extensive interaction across various International Relations communities. Some of this has been in the form of borrowing ideas developed in one area to better understand another. In other cases, borrowing has been more competitive or even conflictual in nature. A prominent example is liberal institutionalism's adoption of realist premisses to develop a nonidealist account of cooperation. This has led to competition and even conflict between the two areas on topics such as relative gains or the importance of institutions since they have very different and even opposed explanations for the "same" phenomenon.

Contestation can be both productive and destructive. It is most productive when it is over what questions matter and over the answers to those questions. This type of engagement can reveal shortcomings, challenge presuppositions, sharpen argument, and raise new questions. Debate also reinvigorates the contending theories and challenges the complacency toward which internal research programs sometimes gravitate. Contestation is least productive when it degenerates into defensive discussions that impede communication across areas. Arguments over ontology and epistemology, while sometimes important, are too often deployed in this fashion. Contestation also becomes destructive when vindication of the theory becomes more important than understanding the world—as illustrated by the so-called "paradigm wars" where different International Relations traditions engage in intellectual gladiatorial combat more focused on "victory" for their perspective than on explaining the world.[12] Whether contestation or not is productive depends on how we collectively channel our efforts. Trespassing across sub-areas of International Relations is necessarily treacherous and difficult but the goal is to make it easier, not to raise barriers against it. Bially Mattern (2008) offers an interesting assessment of how contestation of the "power" concept has advanced International Relations. On one hand, it has helped broaden the discipline; on the other hand, it has separated International Relations into niches. As she points out, this contestation can be productive only if it is channeled through enough common ground that diverse elements of the (un)discipline can truly challenge one another.

One of the key questions is whether different International Relations approaches (or which ones) are sufficiently compatible that their competition can be productive. The realist–liberal interchange over relative gains suggests that the possibilities may be limited even among two traditions that share a rationalist underpinning. Perhaps surprisingly, the rationalist–constructivist interaction offers more grounds for optimism. Sometimes the debate has centered on questions of whether the two schools (which are themselves internally quite diverse) are sufficiently compatible in terms of either epistemology or ontology to allow a constructive exchange. Yet recent work has found substantial common ground including successful efforts by each to accommodate key insights from the other. Table 32.1 above shows many points of intersection across ostensibly separate theoretical traditions at a very broad level. Such intersections can also be seen in the specific details of ongoing research. Constructivists have incorporated collective action and principal–agent relations into their analyses (Keck and Sikkink 1998; Nielson, Tierney, and Weaver 2006); rationalists have increased their attention to norms to deepen their analysis of institutions. The second generation of feminist work is much more empirically oriented, perhaps in part due to earlier criticisms, and more attuned to drawing connections to other factors that affect international politics. Sandra Whitworth (2008) illustrates this in terms of looking at the different ways in which various international institutions from the World Bank to the military use gender, while Jacqui True (2008) engages the compatibility of feminist theory with other International Relations theories. Of course, the more radical postmodern and critical theorists suggest that mainstream International Relations "doesn't get it" and hold out little hope that it will. Even here, however, the criticism can still be valuable in raising awareness of hidden assumptions and presumptions and may cause some shift in the other work, although probably not to the satisfaction of the critics who will be viewed as impossible to satisfy from the initial group. Finally, a striking challenge for more integration at an epistemological level is raised in Burke's (2008) endorsement of Lene Hansen's (2006) call "for poststructuralism to take methodology back [from rationalism]." This then is the paradox of International Relations theory—progress in individual areas does not aggregate into progress for the field as a whole—at least in this sense of developing a

---

[12] Hasenclever, Mayer, and Rittberger (1997) provide a useful overview of the interaction among neorealists, neoinstitutionalists, and constructivists that highlight areas where the interaction has been positive (cooperation theory and institutions), where it has been more negative (relative gains), and where the ability of theories to improve each other is still unclear (ideas).

unified and synthetic understanding of the subject matter (cf. Kitcher 1981). Instead of a grand synthesis based on a single logic of enquiry we see the ongoing contestation among many diverse strands of theory using multiple logics. But whereas this has generally been seen as a failure of International Relations, it can also be seen as one reason for its success. Contestation provides vitality to the field that keeps it open to changing questions and provides access points for new ideas. The *Oxford Handbook of International Relations* aimed to further progress by bringing these different points of contention together in a constructive way. In particular by emphasizing the importance of underlying normative arguments to all International Relations theory, we locate common ground among seemingly uncommon approaches and elucidate these more fundamental reasons for our differences.

5 CONCLUSION

A central insight of postmodernism is that actors construct their identities through the construction of radical others—who we are is defined against an other who is everything we are not. Sadly, identity politics has been an all too prominent feature of International Relations scholarship. Our theories have become our social identities, and in constructing these theoretical identities we have reified other theoretical positions to accentuate difference and suppress convergence. Our purpose in this chapter—and in the *Oxford Handbook of International Relations* more generally—has been to cut across these lines wrought by identity politics. We have not ignored genuine points of difference—in fact we have drawn attention to previously under-acknowledged differences. Nor have we downplayed the significance of such differences. Indeed, we have argued that they can be productive. We have, however, highlighted two similarities between all theories: the broad style of theorizing that approaches share, a style that integrates questions, assumptions, and logical argumentation; and the presence of empirical and normative aspects in all theorizing. While these similarities cut across existing theoretical differences, they do not homogenize International Relations theory. Instead, they bring to the fore axes of difference and convergence previously obscured.

The existence of both empirical and normative aspects in all International Relations theories is fundamental to their nature as practical discourses, concerned in their diverse ways with the question of how we should act. Only through practical discourses can International Relations scholars speak to the complex problems of political action in the contemporary global system. And if we embrace this as an objective for the field, then we must accept that the terrain between the empirical and the normative is one that we will need to tread, and to do so systematically. This interaction of empirical and normative considerations is what gives International Relations its vitality. It is the source of the questions the field studies and the reason why it is never satisfied with the answers. The world is changing both because of shifts in international problems and because of shifts in what we care about. The scientific effort to wall off the normative issues is fundamentally misguided, as is normative theorizing that is innocent of empirical research.

This does not mean that the field has to be preoccupied by normative debates any more than it should be preoccupied by epistemological ones. Nor does it mean that every individual research effort need (or can) constantly engage the full panoply of empirical and normative issues. International Relations is sufficiently developed and professionalized as a field that no individual scholar can cover everything and every project must "bracket" important considerations—which is not to say ignore or be unaware of them—for research to proceed. Thus scholarship closer to the empirical end may stipulate their research questions, assumptions about the actors, and the evaluation of the issue outcomes as relatively unproblematic while focusing on developing explanations of how interactions occur. Conversely, a more normatively oriented project might stipulate certain "facts" about how the world works, and what is possible, as a prelude to evaluating prevailing circumstances and what we should do about them. This sort of basic research where scholars pursue the internal logic of their arguments, and competition among arguments is pursued for its own sake, is an important means of advancing the field. Such a division of labor is also inevitable and highly productive in a field where the questions are incredibly complex and always changing.

What is important, however, is that individuals recognize the partial nature of their research, acknowledge that their theorizing is infused with both empirical and normative elements, and accept that the parts must interact and communicate if divisions of labor are not to fragment into separate production lines. This latter task is something that can be implemented by the field as a community even if individual practitioners are not always attentive to the interconnections. Of course, it is important that individual researchers be kept aware of this intermittently— which is exactly what a diverse and interacting International Relations community can achieve, and what this chapter and the *Oxford Handbook of International Relations* more generally aim to highlight.

REFERENCES

ABBOTT, K. W. and SNIDAL, D. 2001. International "standards" and international governance. *Journal of European Public Policy*, 8: 345–70.

ACHARYA, A. and JOHNSTON, A. I. (eds.) 2007. *Crafting Cooperation: Regional International Institutions in Comparative Perspective*. Cambridge: Cambridge University Press.

ARROW, K. J. 1951. *Social Choice and Individual Values*. New York: Wiley.

AYSON, R. 2008. Strategic studies. Ch. 32 in Reus-Smit and Snidal 2008.

BARNETT, M. and DUVALL, R. 2005. Power in global governance. Pp. 1–32 in *Power in Global Governance*, ed. M. Barnett and R. Duvall. Cambridge: Cambridge University Press.

BAYLIS, J. and SMITH, S. 2005. *The Globalization of World Politics: An Introduction to International Relations*, 3rd edn. Oxford: Oxford University Press.

BEITZ, C. R. 1979. *Political Theory and International Relations*. Princeton, NJ: Princeton University Press.

BENNETT, A. and ELMAN, C. 2008. Case study methods. Ch. 29 in Reus-Smit and Snidal 2008.

BIALLY MATTERN, J. 2008. The concept of power and the (un)discipline of international relations. Ch. 40 in Reus-Smit and Snidal 2008.

BLANEY, D. L., and INAYATULLAH, N. 2008. International relations from below. Ch. 38 in Reus-Smit and Snidal 2008.

BLAUG, M. 1985. *Economic Theory in Retrospect*, 4th edn. Cambridge: Cambridge University Press.

BROOKS, S. G. and WOHLFORTH, W. C. 2002. American primacy in perspective. *Foreign Affairs*, 81: 20–33.

BUCHANAN, A. and KEOHANE, R. O. 2004. The preventive use of force: a cosmopolitan institutional proposal. *Ethics and International Affairs*, 18: 1–22.

BURCHILL, S., LINKLATER, A., DEVETAK, R., PATERSON, M., DONNELLY, J., REUS-SMIT, C., and TRUE, J. 2005. *Theories of International Relations*, 3rd edn. New York: Palgrave Macmillan.

BURKE, A. 2008. Postmodernism. Ch. 21 in Reus-Smit and Snidal 2008.

BUZAN, B., WÆVER, O., and DE WILDE, J. 1998. *Security: A New Framework for Analysis*. Boulder, Colo.: Lynne Rienner.

BYERS, M. 2008. International law. Ch. 35 in Reus-Smit and Snidal 2008.

CARLSNAES, W., RISSE, T., and SIMMONS, B. A. (eds.) 2002. *Handbook of International Relations*. London: Sage.

CARR, E. H. 1946. *The Twenty Years' Crisis, 1919–1939: An Introduction to the Study of International Relations*, 2nd edn. London: Macmillan.

CEDERMAN, L.-E. 2003. Modeling the size of wars: from billiard balls to sandpiles. *American Political Science Review*, 97: 135–50.

CHECKEL, J. T. 1999. Social construction and integration. *Journal of European Public Policy*, 6: 545–60.

COCHRAN, M. 2008. The ethics of the English School. Ch. 16 in Reus-Smit and Snidal 2008.

COX, R. 1986. Social forces, states and world orders: beyond international relations theory. Pp. 204–54 in *Neorealism and its Critics*, ed. R. O. Keohane. New York: Columbia University Press.

—— 2008. The point is not just to explain the world but to change it. Ch. 4 in Reus-Smit and Snidal 2008.

DARBY, P. 2008. A disabling discipline? Ch. 5 in Reus-Smit and Snidal 2008.

DONNELLY, J. 2003. *Universal Human Rights in Theory and Practice*, 2nd edn. Ithaca, NY: Cornell University Press.

—— 2008. The ethics of realism. Ch. 8 in Reus-Smit and Snidal 2008.

DOWNS, G. W. and ROCKE, D. M. 1995. *Optimal Imperfection? Domestic Uncertainty and Institutions in International Relations*. Princeton, NJ: Princeton University Press.

DOYLE, M. W. 1986. Liberalism and world politics. *American Political Science Review*, 80: 1151–69.

DREZNER, D. W. 2003. Bargaining, enforcement, and multilateral sanctions: when is cooperation counterproductive? *International Organization*, 54: 73–102.

—— 2007. *All Politics is Global: Explaining International Regulatory Regimes*. Princeton, NJ: Princeton University Press.

ECKERSLEY, R. 2008. The ethics of critical theory. Ch. 20 in Reus-Smit and Snidal 2008.

ERSKINE, T. 2008. Locating responsibility: the problem of moral agency in international relations. Ch. 41 in Reus-Smit and Snidal 2008.

FEARON, J. D. 1995. Rationalist explanations for war. *International Organization*, 49: 379–414.

GEORGE, J. 1994. *Discourses of Global Politics: A Critical (Re)Introduction to International Relations*. Boulder, Colo.: Lynne Rienner.

GILPIN, R. 2001. *Global Political Economy: Understanding the International Economic Order*. Princeton, NJ: Princeton University Press.

GILROY, P. 2006. Multiculturalism and post-colonial theory. Pp. 656–74 in *Oxford Handbook of Political Theory*, ed. J. S. Dryzek, B. Honig, and A. Phillips. Oxford: Oxford University Press.

GOLDGEIER, J. and TETLOCK, P. 2008. Psychological approaches. Ch. 27 in Reus-Smit and Snidal 2008.

GOLDSTEIN, J. and KEOHANE, R. O. 1993. Ideas and foreign policy: an analytical framework. Pp. 3–30 in *Ideas and Foreign Policy: Beliefs, Institutions, and Political Change*, ed. J. Goldstein and R. O. Keohane. Ithaca, NY: Cornell University Press.

GOODIN, R. E., REIN, M., and MORAN, M. 2006. The public and its policies. Pp. 3–35 in *Oxford Handbook of Public Policy*, ed. M. Moran, M. Rein, and R. E. Goodin. Oxford: Oxford University Press.

GRUBER, L. 2000. *Ruling the World: Power Politics and the Rise of Supranational Institutions*. Princeton, NJ: Princeton University Press.

HAFNER-BURTON, E. M. 2005. Trading human rights: how preferential trade agreements influence government repression. *International Organization*, 59: 593–629.

HANSEN, L. 2006. *Security as Practice: Discourse Analysis and the Bosnian War*. London: Routledge.

HASENCLEVER, A., MAYER, P., and RITTBERGER, V. 1997. *Theories of International Regimes*. Cambridge: Cambridge University Press.

HATHAWAY, O. A. 2002. Do human rights treaties make a difference? *Yale Law Journal*, 111: 1935–2042.

HOWELL, W. G. and PEVEHOUSE, J. C. 2007. *While Dangers Gather: Congressional Checks on Presidential War Powers*. Princeton, NJ: Princeton University Press.

HURD, I. 2008. Constructivism. Ch. 17 in Reus-Smit and Snidal 2008.

KAPLAN, M. A. 1957. *System and Process in International Politics*. New York: John Wiley and Sons.

KATZENSTEIN, P. and SIL, R. 2008. Eclectic theorizing in the study and practice of international relations. Ch. 6 in Reus-Smit and Snidal 2008.

KECK, M. and SIKKINK, K. 1998. *Activists beyond Borders: Advocacy Networks in International Politics*. Ithaca, NY: Cornell University Press.

KEOHANE, R. O. 1984. *After Hegemony: Cooperation and Discord in the World Political Economy*. Princeton, NJ: Princeton University Press.

——— 2001. Governance in a partially governed world. *American Political Science Review*, 95: 1–13.

——— and NYE, J. S. 1977. *Power and Interdependence: World Politics in Transition*. Boston: Little, Brown.

KITCHER, P. 1981. Explanatory unification. *Philosophy of Science*, 48: 507–31.

KOREMENOS, B., LIPSON, C., and SNIDAL, D. 2001. The rational design of international institutions. *International Organization*, 55: 761–99.

KRATOCHWIL, F. 2008. Sociological approaches. Ch. 26 in Reus-Smit and Snidal 2008.

KYDD, A. 2008. Methodological individualism and rational choice. Ch. 25 in Reus-Smit and Snidal 2008.

LAKE, D. A. 2008. The state and international relations. Ch. 2 in Reus-Smit and Snidal 2008.

LAPID, Y. 1989. The third debate: on the prospects of international theory in a post-positivist era. *International Studies Quarterly*, 33: 235–54.

LAWLER, P. 2008. The ethics of postmodernism. Ch. 22 in Reus-Smit and Snidal 2008.

LEVY, J. S. 1997. Prospect theory, rational choice, and international relations. *International Studies Quarterly*, 41: 87–112.

LINKLATER, A. 1998. *The Transformation of Political Community: Ethical Foundations of the Post-Westphalian Era*. Cambridge: Polity.

LITTLE, R. 2008. International relations theory from a former hegemon. Ch. 39 in Reus-Smit and Snidal 2008.

MANSFIELD, E. D. and PEVEHOUSE, J. C. 2008. Quantitative approaches. Ch. 28 in Reus-Smit and Snidal 2008.

—— MILNER, H. V., and ROSENDORFF, B. P. 2002. Why democracies cooperate more: electoral control and international trade agreements. *International Organization*, 56: 477–513.

MARTIN, L. L. 2000. *Democratic Commitments: Legislatures and International Cooperation*. Princeton, NJ: Princeton University Press.

MATTLI, W. and BÜTHE, T. 2003. Setting international standards: technological rationality or primacy of power? *World Politics*, 56: 1–42

MEARSHEIMER, J. J. 2001. *The Tragedy of Great Power Politics*. New York: W. W. Norton.

MYERSON, R. B. 1992. On the value of game theory in social science. *Rationality and Society*, 4: 62–73.

NARDIN, T. 2008. International ethics. Ch. 34 in Reus-Smit and Snidal 2008.

NAU, H. R. 2008. Scholarship and policy-making: who speaks truth to whom? Ch. 36 in Reus-Smit and Snidal 2008.

NIELSON, D. L., TIERNEY, M. J., and WEAVER, C. E. 2006. Bridging the rationalist–constructivist divide: re-engineering the culture of the World Bank. *Journal of International Relations and Development*, 9: 107–39.

NYE, J. S., JR. 2008. International relations: the relevance of theory to practice. Ch. 37 in Reus-Smit and Snidal 2008.

OLSON, M. 1965. *The Logic of Collective Action: Public Goods and the Theory of Groups*. Cambridge, Mass.: Harvard University Press.

PEVEHOUSE, J. and RUSSETT, B. 2006. Democratic international governmental organizations promote peace. *International Organization*, 60: 969–1000.

POWELL, R. 1999. *In the Shadow of Power: States and Strategies in International Politics*. Princeton, NJ: Princeton University Press.

PRICE, R. 1997. *The Chemical Weapons Taboo*. Ithaca, NY: Cornell University Press.

—— and REUS-SMIT, C. 1998. Dangerous liaisons? Critical international theory and constructivism. *European Journal of International Relations*, 4: 259–94.

QUIRK, J. 2008. Historical methods. Ch. 30 in Reus-Smit and Snidal 2008.

RAE, H. 2002. *State Identities and the Homogenisation of Peoples*. Cambridge: Cambridge University Press.

RAVENHILL, J. 2008. International political economy. Ch. 31 in Reus-Smit and Snidal 2008.

REUS-SMIT, C. 1999. *The Moral Purpose of the State: Culture, Social Identity, and Institutional Rationality in International Relations*. Princeton, NJ: Princeton University Press.

—— 2005. The constructivist challenge after September 11. Pp. 81–95 in *International Society and its Critics*, ed. A. J. Bellamy. Oxford: Oxford University Press.

—— 2008. Constructivism and the structure of ethical reasoning. Pp. 53–82 in *Moral Limit and Possibility in World Politics*, ed. R. Price. Cambridge: Cambridge University Press.

—— and SNIDAL, D. (eds.) 2008. *Oxford Handbook of International Relations*. Oxford: Oxford University Press.

RICHARDSON, J. L. 2008. The ethics of neoliberal institutionalism. Ch. 12 in Reus-Smit and Snidal 2008.

RISSE, T., ROPP, S. C., and SIKKINK, K. (eds.) 1999. *The Power of Human Rights: International Norms and Domestic Change*. Cambridge: Cambridge University Press.

RISSE-KAPPEN, T. (ed.) 1995. *Bringing Transnational Relations Back In: Non-State Actors, Domestic Structures, and International Institutions*. Cambridge: Cambridge University Press.

RODRIK, D. 1997. *Has Globalization Gone Too Far?* Washington, DC: Institute for International Economics.

ROSECRANCE, R. 2008. The failure of static and the need for dynamic approaches to international relations. Ch. 43 in Reus-Smit and Snidal 2008.

RUGGIE, J. G. 2005. What makes the world hang together? Neo-utilitarianism and the social constructivist challenge. Pp. 120–6 in *Foundations of International Law and Politics*, ed. O. A. Hathaway and H. H. Koh. New York: Foundation Press.

RUSSETT, B. and ONEAL, J. R. 2001. *Triangulating Peace: Democracy, Interdependence, and International Organizations*. New York: Norton.

SCHELLING, T. C. 1960. *The Strategy of Conflict*. Cambridge, Mass.: Harvard University Press.

SCHOLTE, J. A. 2005. *Globalization: A Critical Introduction*, 2nd edn. New York: Palgrave Macmillan.

SHAPCOTT, R. 2008. Critical theory. Ch. 19 in Reus-Smit and Snidal 2008.

SIGNORINO, C. 2002. Strategy and selection in international relations. *International Interactions*, 28: 93–115.

SNIDAL, D. 2002. Rational choice and international relations. Pp. 73–94 in Carlsnaes, Risse, and Simmons 2002.

SNIDAL, D. 2004. Formal models of international politics. Pp. 227–64 in *Models, Numbers, and Cases: Methods for Studying International Relations*, ed. D. F. Sprinz and Y. Wolinsky-Nahmias. Ann Arbor: University of Michigan Press.

SPRINZ, D. F. 2004. Environment meets statistics: quantitative analysis of international environmental policy. Pp. 177–92 in *Models, Numbers, and Cases: Methods for Studying International Relations*, ed. D. F. Sprinz and Y. Wolinsky-Nahmias. Ann Arbor: University of Michigan Press.

SPRUYT, H. 1994. *The Sovereign State and its Competitors: An Analysis of Systems Change*. Princeton, NJ: Princeton University Press.

—— 2007. War, trade, and state formation. Pp. 211–35 in *Oxford Handbook of Comparative Politics*, ed. C. Boix and S. Stokes. Oxford: Oxford University Press.

STEIN, A. A. 2008. Neoliberal institutionalism. Ch. 11 in Reus-Smit and Snidal 2008.

STUART, D. T. 2008. Foreign policy decision-making. Ch. 33 in Reus-Smit and Snidal 2008.

TAYLOR, C. 1979. Interpretation and the sciences of man. Pp. 25–72 in *Interpretive Social Science: A Reader*, ed. P. Rabinow and W. M. Sullivan. Berkeley: University of California Press.

TESCHKE, B. 2008. Marxism. Ch. 9 in Reus-Smit and Snidal 2008.

TIERNEY, M. J. and WEAVER, C. (eds.) 2007. The politics of international organizations: bridging the rationalist–constructivist divide. Unpublished manuscript, University of Kansas.

TOMZ, M. 2007. *Reputation and International Cooperation: Sovereign Debt across Three Centuries*. Princeton, NJ: Princeton University Press.

TRUE, J. 2008. The ethics of feminism. Ch. 24 in Reus-Smit and Snidal 2008.

VON STEIN, J. 2005. Do treaties constrain or screen? Selection bias and treaty compliance. *American Political Science Review*, 99: 611–22.

VREELAND, J. R. 2003. *The IMF and Economic Development*. Cambridge: Cambridge University Press.

WÆVER, O. 1995. Securitization and desecuritization. Pp. 46–86 in *On Security*, ed. R. D. Lipschutz. New York: Columbia University Press.

WALTZ, K. 1979. *Theory of International Politics*. New York: McGraw-Hill.

WENDT, A. 1999. *Social Theory of International Politics*. Cambridge: Cambridge University Press.

WHITWORTH, S. 2008. Feminism. Ch. 23 in Reus-Smit and Snidal 2008.

WOHLFORTH, W. C. 2008. Realism. Ch. 27 in Reus-Smit and Snidal 2008.

CHAPTER 33

....

THE NEW
LIBERALISM

....

ANDREW MORAVCSIK

THE universal condition of world politics is *globalization*. States are, and always have been, embedded in a domestic and transnational society that creates incentives for its members to engage in economic, social, and cultural interactions that transcend borders. Demands from individuals and groups in this society, as transmitted through domestic representative institutions, define "state preferences"—that is, fundamental substantive social purposes that give states an underlying stake in the international issues they face. To motivate conflict, cooperation, or any other costly political foreign policy action, states must possess sufficiently intense state preferences. Without such social concerns that transcend borders, states would have no rational incentive to engage in world politics at all, but would simply devote their resources to an autarkic and isolated existence. This domestic and transnational social context in which states are embedded varies greatly over space and time. The resulting globalization-induced variation in social demands and state preferences is a fundamental cause of state behavior in world politics. This is the central insight of liberal international relations theory.

Three specific variants of liberal theory focus are defined by particular types of state preferences, their variation, and their impact on state behavior. *Ideational* liberal theories link state behavior to varied conceptions of desirable forms of cultural, political, socioeconomic order. *Commercial* liberal theories stress economic interdependence, including many variants of "endogenous policy theory." *Republican* liberal theories stress the role of domestic representative institutions, elites and leadership dynamics, and executive–legislative relations. Such theories were first

* For more detailed analysis and a literature review, see Moravcsik (1997; 2003), on which this chapter draws.

conceived by prescient liberals such as Immanuel Kant, Adam Smith, John Stuart Mill, John Hobson, Woodrow Wilson, and John Maynard Keynes—writing well before the independent variables they stressed (democratization, industrialization, nationalism, and welfare provision) were widespread.[1]

The liberal focus on variation in socially determined state preferences distinguishes liberal theory from other theoretical traditions: realism (focusing on coercive power resources), institutionalism (focusing on information), and most nonrational approaches (focusing on patterns of beliefs about appropriate means–ends relationships).[2] In explaining patterns of war, for example, liberals do not stress inter-state imbalances of power, bargaining failure under incomplete information, or particular nonrational beliefs, but conflicting state preferences derived from hostile nationalist or political ideologies, disputes over appropriable economic resources, or exploitation of unrepresented political constituencies. For liberals, a necessary condition for war is that these factors lead one or more "aggressor" states to possess "revisionist" preferences so extreme that other states are unwilling to submit. Similarly, in explaining trade protectionism, liberals look not to shifts of hegemonic power, suboptimal international institutions, or misguided beliefs about economic theory, but to economic incentives, interest groups, and distributional coalitions opposed to market liberalization.

Liberal theory is a paradigmatic alternative theoretically distinct from, empirically at least coequal with, and in certain respects analytically more fundamental than, existing paradigms such as realism, institutionalism, or constructivism. This chapter presents three core theoretical assumptions underlying liberal theories, elaborates the three variants of liberal theory, and draws some broader implications. Perhaps the most important advantage of liberal theory lies in its capacity to serve as the theoretical foundation for a shared multicausal model of instrumental state behavior— thereby moving the discipline beyond paradigmatic warfare among unicausal claims (Lake and Powell 1999 outline a similar vision).

1 CORE ASSUMPTIONS OF LIBERAL THEORY

Liberal international relations theory's fundamental premise—state preferences derived from the domestic and transnational social pressures critically influence state behavior—can be restated in terms of three core assumptions.

[1] In a Lakatosian sense, this should increase our confidence in liberal predictions (Moravcsik 2003).

[2] Some who engage in the pre-scientific practice of classifying theories according to "optimism" and "pessimism," or political pedigree, classify theories of international organizations as liberal (though in fact, in the nineteenth and early twentieth centuries, international institutions were more often espoused by monied conservatives). For modern international relations theorists, however, what matters are core assumptions, and modern regime theory rests on a distinctively different set of assumptions from the liberal theories discussed here. Regime theory concerns the distribution of information, with state preferences treated as exogenous. The liberal theories discussed here seek to endogenize state preferences. For more discussion, see Moravcsik (1997, 536–8); cf. Keohane (1990).

Assumption 1. *The Nature of Societal Actors.*
Globalization generates differentiated demands from societal individuals and groups with regard to international affairs.

Liberal international relations theory rests on a "bottom-up" or pluralist view of politics. Functionally differentiated individuals and groups define material and ideational goals independently of politics, then seek to advance those ends through political means.[3] Social actors favor some economic, social, cultural, and domestic political arrangements rather than others—that is, particular structures of economic production and exchange, social relations, cultural practice, or domestic political rule. For the purpose of studying world politics, the critical source of social interests is *globalization*—that is, the changing opportunities and incentives to engage in transnational economic, social, and cultural activity—which changes the prospects for realizing domestic objectives. Without globalization, societal actors, like states, would have no rational incentive to attend to world politics. Such incentives vary from individual opportunities for glory or plunder (say, in the epoch of Alexander the Great) to the maintenance of complex networks of transnational production, immigration, and cultural discourse (more often found in our own). The most fundamental theoretical task of liberal international relations theory is to define the impact of the shifting terms of economic, social, and cultural globalization on social actors and the competing demands they will thus place upon states.

A simple analysis starts by assuming that, the stronger the aggregate benefit from social interactions across borders, the greater the demand to engage in such interactions. In pursuing such goals, individuals can be assumed to be, on the average, risk averse—that is, they defend existing private opportunities for investment while remaining more cautious about assuming cost and risk in pursuit of new gains. All this can generate strong incentives for peaceful coexistence and *status quo*-oriented policies. This starting point often leads critics, not least realists, to caricature liberals as espousing a utopian belief in an automatic harmony of interest among social actors.

In fact liberal theory—as reflected in liberal philosophers and social scientists alike—rests on the contrary premise. Societal demands are a variable, shifting with factors such as technology, geography, and culture. A harmonious pattern of interest associated with liberal "utopianism" is no more than one ideal endpoint. In nearly all social situations, shifts in control over material resources, authoritative values, and opportunities for social control have domestic and transnational distributional implications, which almost invariably create winners and losers. Moreover, while the average individual may be risk averse, particular individuals may be willing to risk costly conflict for improbable gain. Any liberal theory must therefore specify

---

[3] The critical distinction here is *not* the "level of analysis"—that is, that liberal theory offers a "domestic" explanation ("level of analysis" is an outmoded and misleading concept; see Fearon 1998; Lake and Powell 1999, ch. 1). Essential is rather that liberals take seriously, rather than arbitrarily suppress, Kenneth Waltz's notion of "functional differentiation," grounding it in domestic and transnational society (Ruggie 1983).

more concrete conditions under which the interests of social actors converge toward particular patterns vis-à-vis other societies.

Broadly speaking, conflictual societal demands about the management of globalization tend to be associated with three factors. First, contradictory or irreconcilable differences in core beliefs about national, political, and social identity promote conflict, whereas complementary beliefs promote harmony and cooperation. Secondly, resources that can be easily appropriated or monopolized tend to exacerbate conflict by increasing the willingness of social actors to assume cost or risk to enrich themselves. Thirdly, large inequalities in domestic social or political influence may permit certain groups to evade the costs of costly conflict or rent-seeking behavior, even if the result is inefficient for society as a whole. These general tendencies are developed in more detail in the next section, where we will link them to the three major strands of liberal theory.

Assumption 2. *The Nature of the State.*
States represent the demands of a subset of domestic individuals and social groups, on the basis of whose interests they define "state preferences" and act instrumentally to manage globalization.

For the purpose of analyzing international politics, an essential characteristic of the state is its set of underlying *preferences*: the rank ordering among potential substantive outcomes or "states of the world" that might result from international political interaction. States act instrumentally in world politics to achieve particular goals on behalf of individuals, whose private behavior is unable to achieve such ends as efficiently. Internationally, the liberal state is a purposive actor, but domestically it is a representative institution constantly subject to capture and recapture, construction and reconstruction, by coalitions of social interests. It constitutes the critical "transmission belt" by which the preferences and social power of individuals and groups are translated into foreign policy. In the liberal conception of domestic politics, state preferences concerning the management of globalization reflect shifting social demands, which in turn reflect the shifting structure of domestic and transnational society. Deriving state preferences from social preferences is thus a central theoretical task of liberal theory.

State preferences, the ultimate ends of foreign policy behavior, are distinct from "strategies"—the specific policy goals, bargaining demands, institutional arrangements, tactical stances, military or diplomatic doctrines that states adopt, advocate, or accept in everyday international politics. From rational choice theorists to constructivists, analysts now recognize such a distinction as a necessary precondition for rigorous analysis of world politics. When a government increases military spending and declares an interest in confronting an adversary, for example, it is essential to distinguish a shift resulting from changing preferences over states of the world (as when confrontation is initiated by a new ruling elite intrinsically committed to territorial aggrandizement) from a shift resulting from changing strategies with preferences fixed (as when two states respond to each other's arms build-ups in a "security dilemma"). Even support for apparently "fundamental" political strategies—say, sovereignty, national defense, open markets—vary considerably depending on under-lying patterns of state preferences concerning "states of the world." Few modern states are Sparta: Most compromise security or sovereignty in order to achieve other ends, or, indeed, just to save money. Nor do modern states seek ideal free markets, but rather strike complex and varied trade-offs among economic goals. To see how consequential the results can be, one need look no further than the implications for international relations of Germany's evolution from Adolf Hitler's preference for mil-itant nationalism, fascist rule, and ruthless exploitation of German *Lebensraum* to the social compromise underlying the postwar *Bundesrepubik* for national reunification, capitalist democracy, and expanding German exports (Katzenstein 1987).

This last example highlights the importance, in the liberal conception, of the selective nature of domestic representative institutions. Representation is a key deter-minant (alongside the basic nature of social demands themselves) of what states want, and therefore what they do. No government rests on universal or unbiased political representation. At one ideal extreme, representation might equally empower everyone equally. At the other, it might empower only an ideal-typical Pol Pot or Josef Stalin. Myriad representative practices exist in between, each privileging different sets of demands. Powerful individuals and groups may be entirely "out-side" the state, bureaucratic clients and officials "within" it, or some combination thereof (for example, a "military-industrial complex"). Representation may be cen-tralized and coordinated or disaggregated, subject to strong or weak rationality con-ditions, socialized to various attitudes toward risk and responsibility, and flanked by various substitutes for direct representation (Achen 1995; Grant and Keohane 2005).

It is important to note one qualification to the assumption that states have pre-strategic preferences. Over the longer term there is, of course, feedback, which makes it more difficult to treat preferences as pre-strategic. The fundamental preferences of states may adapt to strategic circumstances. When, to take a simple example, a conqueror exterminates a linguistic group, imposes a new political order, or reshapes a domestic economy, the preferences of the target state will be different in succeeding iterations. Similarly, the outcomes of economic cooperation agreements often alter economic structure for good—often in a self-reinforcing way that encourages further movement in a similar direction. Indeed, it is often precisely to induce such feedback that individuals engage in international politics. Still, any meaningful analysis of international politics as instrumental behavior requires, at the very least, that we distinguish *within any given iteration* between "pre-strategic" preferences, akin to "tastes" in economics, and strategic calculations. Even in explaining dynamic change over a long period, analysts often neglect at their peril to distinguish change caused by constantly evolving exogenous factors from change that is triggered by policy feedback.[4]

---

[4] A major weakness of neofunctionalist integration theory, for example, was its lack of any strong liberal theory of preferences, which led Ernst Haas consistently to attribute policies to "feedbacks" or "spillovers" that were in fact the result of shifts in exogenous factors (Moravcsik 2005).

Assumption 3. *The Nature of the International System.*
The pattern of interdependence among state preferences shapes state behavior.

The critical theoretical link between state preferences, on the one hand, and state behavior, on the other, is the concept of *policy interdependence*. Policy interdependence refers to the distribution and interaction of preferences—that is, the extent to which the pursuit of state preferences necessarily imposes costs and benefits upon other states, independent of the "transaction costs" imposed by the specific strategic means chosen to obtain them.

Liberals argue that patterns of interdependent preferences belong among the most fundamental structures influencing state behavior. In areas of modern life where policy externalities remain low and unilateral policies remain optimal for most states, there is an incentive for sovereignty to remain the norm and states to coexist with low conflict and politicization. Where policy alignment can generate mutual gains with low distributive consequences, there is an incentive for international policy coordination or convergence. The lower the net gains, and the greater the distributional conflict whereby the realization of interests by a dominant social group in one country *necessarily* imposes costs on dominant social groups in other countries, the greater the potential for inter-state tension and conflict. Where motives are mixed such that coordination of policies generates high benefits but also high benefits from unilateral defection, then strong incentives will exist for precommitment to social cooperation to limit cheating. Games such as coordination, assurance, Prisoner's Dilemma, and suasion have distinctive dynamics, as well as precise costs, benefits, and risks for the parties (Oye 1986). While such strategic incentives can, of course, be influenced by power, information, beliefs, and other nonliberal variables, they are often very fundamentally influenced by the structure of transnational interdependence itself—that is, by the extent to which basic national goals are compatible.

By drawing on the relative intensity or "asymmetrical interdependence" among state preferences, liberalism highlights a distinctive conception of inter-state power (Keohane and Nye 1977). In this view, the willingness of states to expend resources or make concessions in bargaining is a function of preferences, not (as in realism) linkage to an independent set of "political" power resources (Baldwin 1979). Nations are in fact rarely prepared to mortgage their entire economy or military capabilities in pursuit of any single foreign-policy goal. Few wars are total, few peaces Carthaginian. On the margin, the binding constraint is more often "resolve" or "preference intensity"—a view set forth by Albert Hirschman and others, and more fundamentally consistent with conventional Nash bargaining theory than is realist theory (Hirschman 1945; Raiffa 1982). Even in "least-likely" cases, where military means are used to contest political independence and territorial integrity, "preferences for the issues at stake ... can compensate for a disadvantage in capabilities." In the Boer War, Hitler's remilitarization of the Rhineland, Vietnam, and Afghanistan, for example, the relative intensity of state preferences arguably reshaped the outcome to the advantage of a "weaker" party (Mack 1975; Morrow 1988, 83–4). Such examples suggest that the liberal view of power politics, properly understood, generates plausible explanations not just of international cooperation and coexistence, but of the full range of systemic phenomena central to the study of world politics, including war.

2 THEORETICAL VARIANTS OF LIBERALISM

The three core liberal assumptions outlined above, like those of institutionalism, realism, or any other broad paradigm, are relatively "thin" or content free. The focus on variation in preferences, rather than autonomous capabilities, beliefs, or information, does exclude most realist, institutionalist, and nonrational theories. But alone it is insufficient to specify a single sharply defined set of theories or hypotheses. This is as it should be.[5] A paradigm should instead clearly define a theoretical field, and the question is whether a coherent, rich, and focused research program emerges. While the analysis of state preferences over managing globalization might appear in theory to be impossibly unparsimonious, as many have argued, the range of viable liberal theories has proven in practice to be focused and empirically fruitful. Three variants have emerged in recent theorizing, stressing respectively identity, interest, and institutions.

2.1 Identity and Legitimate Social Orders

One source of state preferences is the set of core domestic social identities. In the liberal understanding, social identity stipulates who belongs to the society and what is owed to them. Liberals take no distinct position on the ultimate origins of such identities, which may stem from historical accretion or be constructed through conscious collective or state action, nor on the question of whether they "ultimately" reflect ideational or material factors—just as long as they are not conceived as endogenous to short-term inter-state interaction. (The ultimate origin of preferences "all the way down" is an issue on which international relations theorists, the speculations of constructivists notwithstanding, have little comparative advantage.) But liberals have long argued that identity is essential to state preferences—a tradition reaching back through William Gladstone, Mill, Giuseppe Mazzini, Wilson, and Keynes. More research is required to isolate precise causal mechanisms at work. Liberals focus in

---

[5] The Lakatosian understanding of a "paradigm" leads us to expect that core assumptions and concepts define a paradigm, but auxiliary propositions are required to specify it (Moravcsik 2003).

particular on legitimate domestic order across three dimensions: national identity, political ideology, and socioeconomic order.[6]

The first type of social identity concerns beliefs about the proper scope of the political "nation" and the allocation of citizenship rights within it. Where inconsistencies arise between underlying patterns of political identity and existing borders, liberals argue, the potential for inter-state conflict increases. Where they coincide, peaceful coexistence is more likely. Where identities are more fluid, more complex arrangements may be possible. Empirical evidence supports such claims. From mid-nineteenth-century nationalist uprisings to late-twentieth century national liberation struggles, claims and counterclaims involving national autonomy constitute the most common issue over which wars and interventions have been waged: antinationalist intervention under the Concert of Europe and the Holy Alliance, Balkan conflicts preceding the First World War and following the cold war, and ethnic conflicts today (Van Evera 1990; Holsti 1991).[7] Not by chance is scenario planning for China/United States conflict focused almost exclusively on Taiwan—the one jurisdiction where borders and national identity (as well as political ideology) are subject to competing claims (Christensen 2001). Recent literature on civil wars increasingly focuses on contention over the social identity, political institutions, and the political economy of the state (Walter 1997; Fortna 2004; Kaufman 2006). Ironically, the current era of fixed borders may lead civil wars to proliferate then spill over, rather than being resolved by succession or adjustment (Atzili 2006–7).

A second relevant social identity concerns fundamental political ideology. Where claims of political legitimacy or ideology conflict directly, and the realization of legitimate domestic political order in one jurisdiction is perceived as threatening its realization in others, conflict becomes more likely. Whether during the wars of the French Revolution, the nineteenth-century Concert of Europe, the Second World War, the cold war—or now the post-cold war era—the degree of ideological distance among the domestic systems of the great powers appears to have been a critical determinant of international conflict (Gaddis 1997; Haas 2005; 2007). Some argue a similar dynamic of mutual ideological recognition underlies the "democratic peace" (Doyle 1986; Owen 1994).

More recently, some within modern societies have adopted a more cosmopolitan attitude toward political rights, extending political identity beyond the nation state. To be sure, the most intense concerns remain focused on co-religionists and

---

[6] Here is a point of intersection between traditional liberal arguments and more recent constructivist works, which tend to stress the social rather than inter-state origins of socialization to particular preferences (Risse-Kappen 1996). Yet the concept of preferences across public goods is deliberately more focused than Ruggie's "legitimate social purpose" (1982) or Katzenstein's "collective identity" (1996).

[7] Even those who stress the absence of domestic credible commitment mechanisms or the interaction between ideational and socioeconomic variables in explaining patterns of nationalist conflicts concede the importance of underlying identities (Fearon and Laitin 2000). Dissidents include realist John Mearsheimer (1990, 21), who bravely asserts that nationalism is a "second-order force in world politics," with a "largely...international" cause—namely, multipolarity. Greater problems since 1989 in Eastern Europe and the former Soviet Union, where there are more overlapping national claims than in democratic, capitalist Western Europe, belie Mearsheimer's prediction.

co-nationals abroad, but altruistic campaigns are increasingly organized to defend human rights on behalf of others. Where such goals clash with the goals of foreign governments, they can spark international conflict (Keck and Sikkink 1998). Recent literature on the sources of such concern, the conditions under which states take them up, and the ways in which issue networks can increase their salience, reflect core liberal theoretical concerns.[8]

A third important type of social identity concerns the nature of legitimate domestic socioeconomic regulation and redistribution. In a Polanyian and Keynesian vein, John Ruggie reminds us that legitimate social compromises concerning the provision of regulatory public goods impose limits on markets. Such social compromises, domestic and transnational, underlie variation in state preferences and behavior regarding immigration, social welfare, taxation, religious freedom, families, health and safety, environmental and consumer protection, cultural promotion, and many other issues (Ruggie 1982). Recent research on environmental policy and many other areas reveals the emergence of "Baptist-bootlegger" coalitions around regulatory issues, combining economically self-interested producer groups with those interested in regulatory outputs (Ruggie 1995; Vogel 1995).

2.2 Commercial Liberalism: Economic Assets and Cross-border Transactions

A second source of social demands relevant to foreign policy is the pattern of transnational market incentives—a liberal tradition dating back to Smith, Richard Cobden, and John Bright. This argument is broadly functionalist: Changes in the structure of the domestic and global economy alter the costs and benefits of transnational economic activity, creating pressure on domestic governments to facilitate or block it.[9]

Commercial liberal theory does not predict that economic incentives automatically generate universal free trade and peace, but focuses instead on the interplay between aggregate incentives and distributional consequences. Contemporary trade liberalization generates domestic distributional shifts totaling many times aggregate welfare benefits (Rodrik 1992). Losers generally tend to be better identified and organized than beneficiaries. A major source of protection, liberals predict, lies in uncompetitive, undiversified, and monopolistic sectors or factors of production. Their pressure induces a systematic divergence from laissez-faire policies—a tendency recognized by Smith, who famously complained of mercantilism that "the contrivers of this whole

---

[8] This has spawned an enormous literature on social movements designed to promote the interests of such individuals and groups. Some of this literature involves the construction of international institutions and use of coercive sanctions. But the material on the mobilization of social movements to pressure governments to act is a quintessentially liberal argument—e.g. Carpenter (2007).

[9] Keohane and Milner (1996) provide a review and discussion of the relationship between commercial and republican liberal theories, properly conceptualizing interdependence as a structure of incentives, or potential costs and benefits, not as a pattern of behavior.

mercantile system [are] the producers, whose interest has been so carefully attended to".[10]

This commercial liberal approach to analyzing conflict over foreign economic policy is distinct from those of realism (emphasizing security externalities and relative power), institutionalism (informational and institutional constraints on optimal inter-state collective action), and constructivism (beliefs about "free trade"). Extensive research supports the view that free trade is most likely where strong competitiveness, extensive intra-industry trade or trade in intermediate goods, large foreign investments, and low asset specificity internalize the net benefits of free trade to powerful actors, reducing the influence of net losers from liberalization (Milner 1988; Alt and Gilligan 1994; Keohane and Milner 1996). Similar arguments can be used to analyze issues such as sovereign debt (Stasavage 2007), exchange-rate policy (Frieden 1991), agricultural trade policy (Gawande and Hoekman 2006), European integration (Moravcsik 1998), foreign direct investment (Elkins, Guzman, and Simmons 2006), tax policy (Swank 2006), and migration policy.

The effect of economic interdependence on security affairs varies with market incentives. A simple starting point is that the collateral damage of war disrupts economic activity: the more vulnerable and extensive such activity, the greater the cost. A more sophisticated cost–benefit calculation would take into account the potential economic costs and benefits of war. Where monopolies, sanctions, slavery, plunder of natural resources, and other forms of coercive extraction backed by state power are cost-effective means of elite wealth accumulation—as was true for most of human history—we should expect to see a positive relationship, between transnational economic activity and war. Where, conversely, private trade and investment within complex and well-established transnational markets provide a less costly means of accumulating wealth and one that cannot be cost-effectively appropriated—as is most strikingly the case within modern multinational investment and production networks—the expansion of economic opportunities will have a pacific effect. Along with the spread of democracy and relative absence of nationalist conflict, this distinguishes the current era from the period before the First World War, when high levels of interdependence famously failed to deter war (Van Evera 1990; Brooks 2007; Kirshner 2007). We see in current Western relations with China a very deliberate strategy to encourage the slow evolution of social preferences in a pacific direction by encouraging trade. Eric Gartzke (2000) has recently argued that the "democratic peace" phenomenon can largely be explained in terms of a lack of economic and other motives for war. Even among developed economies, however, circumstances may arise where governments employ coercive means to protect international markets. This may take varied forms, as occurred under nineteenth-century empires or with pressure from business for the United States to enter the First World War to defend trade with the allies (Fordham 2007).

---

[10] *An Inquiry into the Nature and Causes of the Wealth of Nations* (Oxford Edition, 1993), p. 378.

2.3 Republican Liberalism: Representation and Rent-seeking

A final source of fundamental social preferences relevant to international politics is the institutional structure of domestic political representation. While ideational and commercial theories stress, respectively, particular patterns of underlying societal identities and interests related to globalization, republican liberal theory emphasizes the ways in which domestic institutions and practices aggregate such pressures, transforming them into state policy. The key variable in republican liberalism, which dates back to the theories of Kant, Wilson, and others, is the nature of domestic political representation, which helps determine *whose* social preferences dominate state policy (Russett 1993).

A simple consequence is that policy tends to be biased in favor of the governing coalitions or powerful domestic groups favored by representative institutions—whether those groups are administrators (rulers, armies, or bureaucracies) or societal groups that "capture" the state. Costs and risks are passed on to others. When particular groups with outlier preferences are able to formulate policy without providing gains for society as a whole, the result is likely to be inefficient and suboptimal policy. Given that (as we assumed earlier) most individuals and groups in society tend generally to be risk averse, the broader the range of represented groups, the less likely it is that they will support indiscriminate use of policy instruments, like war or autarky, that impose large net costs or risks on society as a whole. Republican liberal theory thereby helps to explain phenomena as diverse as the "democratic peace," modern imperialism, and international trade and monetary cooperation. Given the plausibility of the assumption that major war imposes net costs on society as a whole, it is hardly surprising that the most prominent republican liberal argument concerns the "democratic peace," which one scholar has termed "as close as anything we have to an empirical law in international relations"—one that applies to tribal societies as well as modern states (Levy 1988, 668). From a liberal perspective, the theoretical interest in the "democratic peace" lies not in the greater transparency of democracies (a claim about information), the greater political power of democracies (a realist claim), or norms of appropriate behavior (a constructivist claim), but the distinctive preferences of democracies across states of the world.

This is not, of course, to imply that broad domestic representation *necessarily* generates international cooperation. In specific cases, elite preferences in multiple states may be more convergent than popular ones. Moreover, the extent of bias in representation, not democracy per se, is the theoretically critical point. There exist conditions under which specific governing elites may have an incentive to represent long-term social preferences in a way that is less biased—for example, when they dampen nationalist sentiment, as may be the case in some democratizing regimes, or exclude powerful outlier special interests, as is commonly the case in trade policy.

The theoretical obverse of "democratic peace" theory is a republican liberal theory of war, which stresses risk-acceptant leaders and rent-seeking coalitions (Van Evera 1999; Goemans 2000). There is substantial historical evidence that the aggressors who have provoked modern great-power wars tend either to be extremely risk-acceptant individuals, or individuals well able to insulate themselves from the costs of war, or both. Jack Snyder, for example, has refurbished Hobson's classic left-liberal analysis of imperialism—in which the military, uncompetitive foreign investors and traders, jingoistic political elites, and others who benefit from imperialism are particularly well placed to influence policy—by linking unrepresentative and extreme outcomes to log-rolling coalitions (Snyder 1991).[11] Consistent with this analysis, the highly unrepresentative consequences of partial democratization, combined with the disruption of rapid industrialization and incomplete political socialization, suggest that democratizing states, if subject to these influences, may be particularly war prone (Mansfield and Snyder 1995; Snyder 2000). This offers one answer to the paradox posed by James Fearon—namely, why rational states would ever enter into war rather than negotiate their way out. For war or other costly conflict to break out among rational actors, not only must opposed preferences be intense enough to motivate the acceptance of extremely high cost, but the actors must be risk acceptant in pursuit of those goals.

Parallels to the "democratic peace" exist in political economy. We have seen that illiberal commercial policies—trade protection, monetary instability, and sectoral subsidization that may manifestly undermine the general welfare of the population—reflect pressure from powerful domestic groups. In part this power results from biases within representative institutions, such as the power of money in electoral systems, the absence or presence of insulated institutions (for example, "fast-track" provisions in the United States), and the nature of electoral institutions (for example, proportional representation or majoritarianism) (Haggard 1988; Ehrlich 2007).

3 BROADER IMPLICATIONS OF LIBERAL INTERNATIONAL RELATIONS THEORY

Having considered the core assumptions underlying liberal theory, and three concrete variants of it, we turn now to three broader implications: its unique empirical predictions, its status as systemic theory, and its openness to multitheoretical synthesis.

3.1 Distinctive Predictions of Liberal Theory

Liberal international relations theory, we have seen, generates predictions concerning war and peace, trade liberalization and protection, and other important phenomena

---

[11] It is indicative of the muddled metatheoretical mislabeling that besets the field that arguments by Stephen Van Evera, Stephen Walt, Randall Schweller, and Snyder have been termed "neoclassical realism"—despite their clear liberal intellectual pedigree and theoretical structure. See Legro and Moravcsik (1999).

in world politics—predictions that challenge conventional accounts. It also generates some predictions about broad political phenomena for which other international relations paradigms generate few, if any, plausible explanations.

One such phenomenon is *variation in the substantive content of foreign policy across issues, regions, or hegemonic orders*. Why do we observe such different preferences, levels, and styles of cooperation and conflict across different sorts of issues, such as trade and finance, human rights, and environmental policy? Or within issue areas? Or across different countries and regions? Why, for example, do regions vary from highly war prone to de-facto "security communities?" Why do hegemons and great powers seem to have such different schemes for global order?

From a liberal perspective, with its focus on the issue-specific and country-specific social preferences, there are straightforward explanations for such substantive differences. One can easily see why regimes with ideologies, economies, and governmental systems as different as the United States, UK, Nazi Germany, and Soviet Union should generate such disparate plans for the post-Second World War world. One can see why the United States should care so much more about modest, perhaps nonexistent, North Korean or Iraqi nuclear arsenals, but remain unconcerned about far greater British, Israeli, and French forces. One can explain why the compromise of "embedded liberalism" underlying Bretton Woods was struck on entirely different terms from arrangements under the Gold Standard, or why the European Union and the Council for Mutual Economic Assistance differed, though their hegemonic structure was similar, or why the protectionist agricultural trade policy and the open industrial trade policy of OECD countries today differ so strikingly. Such differences continue to have a decisive effect on world politics today. Theories that treat preferences as exogenous, like realism and institutionalism, like constructivist-inspired theories of ideas and beliefs, have difficulty explaining the extreme substantive and geographical variation we observe in the goals and purposes over which states conflict and cooperate. Abstract political forces—relative power, issue density, transaction costs, or strategic culture—provide similarly little insight.

Another related phenomenon is *long-term historical change in the nature of world politics*. Classic realists like Kenneth Waltz, Robert Gilpin, John Mearsheimer, and Paul Kennedy predict unchanging cycles of rise and decline among the great powers, with little impact on the substantive content or form of international order. Liberal theory, by contrast, forges a direct causal link between long-term economic, political, and social transformations, such as economic and political modernization, and state behavior (Ikenberry 2000). Global economic development over the past 500 years has been closely related to greater per capita wealth, democratization, education systems that reinforce new collective identities, and greater incentives for transborder economic transactions (Huntington 1991). Over the modern period the principles of international order have decoupled from dynastic legitimacy and are increasingly tied to national self-determination and social citizenship, economic prosperity, and democratic legitimacy—factors uniquely highlighted by liberal theory.

One result has been that, among advanced industrial democracies, inter-state politics is increasingly grounded in reliable expectations of peaceful change, domestic rule of law, stable international institutions, and intensive societal interaction. Liberal theory argues that the emergence of a large and expanding bloc of pacific, interdependent, normatively satisfied states has been a precondition for such politics. This is the condition Karl Deutsch terms a "pluralistic security community," Robert Keohane and Joseph Nye call "complex interdependence," and John Ikenberry labels "self-binding" (Keohane and Nye 1977; Ikenberry 2000). Consider, for example, the current state of Europe, in particular the absence of serious conflict among Western powers over a case like Yugoslavia—in contrast to the events that led up to the First World War a century before. For liberals, the spread of democracy, commerce, and national self-determination explain why the geopolitical stakes among democratic governments are low and competitive alliance formation absent from modern Europe—an outcome that baffles realists (Van Evera 1990). Overall, these trends have contributed to historically low levels of warfare across the globe in recent decades.

3.2 Liberalism as Systemic Theory

Another fundamental implication of liberal theory concerns its status as a "systemic" theory. To some, the central liberal claim—in essence, "what states want determines what they do"—may seem commonsensical, even tautological. Yet for the past half-century, mainstream international relations theories, notably realism and institutionalism but also nonrational theories, have defined themselves in opposition to precisely this claim. In his classic postwar redefinition of realism, Hans Morgenthau (1960, 5–7) explicitly points to its assertion of "the autonomy of the political," which he says gives realism its "distinctive intellectual and moral attitude" and which he contrasts with "two popular fallacies: the concern with motives and the concern with ideological preferences." Waltz follows Morgenthau almost *verbatim*: "Neo-realism establishes the autonomy of international politics and thus makes a theory about it possible" (Waltz 1979, 29, also 65–6, 79, 90, 108–12, 196–8, 271).

One basic reason why theorists are often skeptical of variation in state preferences as a fundamental cause is because such a claim appears utopian. It seems to imply states do as they please, unconstrained by others. Realists pride themselves, by contrast, on being hard-headed, which they associate with demonstrations that states are forced to pursue objectives strikingly at variance with their underlying desires. Foreign policy, they insist, has *ironic* consequences: The best is the enemy of the good (Waltz 1979, 60–7, 93–9). Waltz, echoing not just Morgenthau but Max Weber, concludes from this that the preferences of states must be unimportant: "Results achieved seldom correspond to the intentions of actors," he argues, therefore "no valid generalizations can logically be drawn" from an examination of intentions—thus runs Waltz's oft-cited argument for structural and systemic theory (Waltz 1979, 29). Hegemonic stability theory and institutionalist regime theory—a combination that Keohane, a scholar otherwise clearly more open to preference-based theory, initially termed "modified structural realism"—rests on a similar distinction: "even where common interests exist, cooperation often fails...cooperation is evidently not a simple function of interests" (Keohane 1984, 6, 12). As Robert

Powell (1994, 318) observes, such approaches "lack a theory of preferences over outcomes."

These realist criticisms simply misunderstand liberal preference-based theory, which is in fact nonutopian precisely because it is "systemic" in the Waltzian sense. Liberal theory implies neither that states get what they want, nor that they ignore the actions of others. The distribution of state *preferences*, just like the distribution of capabilities, information, or beliefs, is itself an attribute of the state system (that is, in Waltzian terms, of the *distribution* of state characteristics) outside the control of any single state. Every state would *prefer* to act as it pleases, yet each is compelled to realize its ends under a constraint imposed by the *preferences* of others. Liberal theory thereby conforms to Waltz's own understanding of systemic theory, explaining state behavior with reference to how states stand in relation to one another.

Liberal theory is systemic and nonutopian in a second, less Waltzian sense as well. National preferences emerge not from a solely domestic context but from a society that is transnational—at once domestic and international. Foreign policy, liberals argue, is about the management of globalization—that is, it is about managing the results of interaction between societies. This interactive or systemic quality goes all the way down. Commercial liberal analyses, for example, explain the interests of domestic groups by situating their domestic economic assets in the context of international markets. Ideational liberal analyses explain the concerns of domestic groups by situating their values in the context of a transnational cultural field. Liberalism does not draw a strict line between domestic and transnational levels of analysis. Critiques that equate theories of state preferences with "domestic" or "second-image" theorizing are not simply misguided in their criticism, but are conceptually confused in their understanding of international relations theory. Liberals side with those who view the "level of analysis" as a misleading concept best set aside.[12]

3.3 Liberalism and Multicausal Synthesis

We have seen that liberal assumptions generate powerful unicausal explanations based on variation in state preferences alone. Yet complex inter-state behavior is rarely shaped by a single factor. Coercive capabilities, information, beliefs about appropriate means, and other facts often play a role as well. To analyze such situations, theoretical synthesis between different types of theory is required. Perhaps the most attractive characteristic of liberal theory is that it suggests a simple and conceptually coherent way of combining theories—in contrast to biased and incoherent means of theory synthesis often proposed.

The explanation of state preferences must receive analytical priority in any such synthesis. That is, variation in state preferences must be explained using liberal theory

---

[12] In rejecting "levels of analysis," I side with Fearon (1998) and Lake and Powell (1999), as well as Gourevitch (1978); Putnam (1988).

before attempting to apply and assess the role of strategic factors like coercive power resources, information, or strategic culture. This is not a distinctively "liberal" claim; it is the only procedure consistent with the assumption of instrumental (soft rational) behavior shared by realism, institutionalism, liberalism, and even many variants of constructivism.[13] This is because preferences shape the nature and intensity of the game that states are playing; thus they help determine which systemic theory is appropriate and how it should be specified.

The necessary analytical priority of preferences over strategic action is hardly surprising to political scientists. It is the fundamental lesson of Robert Dahl's classic work on political influence: We cannot ascertain whether "A influenced B to do something" (that is, power) unless we first know "what B would otherwise do" (that is, preferences) (Dahl 1969; Baldwin 1989, 4; Coleman 1990, 132–5). It would be inappropriate, for example, to employ realist theory to explain state behavior unless state preferences are arrayed so that substantial inter-state conflict of interest exists and the deployment of capabilities to achieve a marginal gain is cost effective. Similarly, institutionalist explanations of suboptimal cooperation are inappropriate unless states have sufficient interest in resolving particular inter-state collective action problems. Without controlling for preference-based explanations, it is easy to mistake one for the other. As Kenneth Oye (1986, 6) notes: "When you observe conflict, think Deadlock—the absence of mutual interest—before puzzling over why a mutual interest was not realized."

State behavior should thus be modeled multicausally—that is, as a *multi-stage process* of constrained social choice in which variation in state preferences comes first. In modeling the process, however, states nonetheless first define preferences, as liberal theories of state–society relations explain, and *only then* debate, bargain, or fight to particular agreements, and thereafter commit in subsequent stages to institutional solutions, explained by realist and institutionalist (as well as liberal) theories of strategic interaction. *This is not to say, of course, that liberal theory is more powerful or that it explains more.* That is an empirical judgment that will vary across cases (indeed, adopting a standardized procedure for synthesis would help us reach and aggregate such empirical results; for more, see Moravcsik 1997). Hence we increasingly see realists and institutionalists retreating to what Keohane terms a "fall-back position," whereby exogenous variation in the configuration of state interests defines the range of possible outcomes within which capabilities and institutions are used to explain specific state behavior—so-called "neoclassical realism" being a prime example (Keohane 1986, 183).[14] Methodologically, however, we must generally theorize and explain preferences, not just assume them, as a basis for strategic analysis.[15]

[13] Many recent constructivist analyses argue that states act instrumentally on the basis of particular cultural beliefs about ends or appropriate means–ends relationships. These can be synthesized with rationalist accounts, as many constructivists have productively pointed out.

[14] There is an implicit subdisciplinary consensus on this view—e.g. Legro (1996); Schweller (1996); Moravcsik (1997); Lake and Powell (1999).

[15] For a very persuasive argument along these lines, as a basis for a programmatic statement of rational choice theorizing, see Frieden (1999) and more generally Lake and Powell (1999).

Practice speaks louder than theory: We need less doctrinaire and more pragmatic theory syntheses, with analytical priority going to theories that endogenize varying state preferences.

This claim about the priority of preference-based theories of state behavior in a multistage explanation reverses the near-universal presumption among contemporary international relations theorists that "liberalism makes sense as an explanatory theory within the constraints" imposed by other theories (see Waltz 1979; Keohane 1990, 192; Matthew and Zacher 1995).[16] The methodological procedure that follows from this conventional misconception, whereby the analyst tests a realist theory first, then turns to theories of preferences (often wrongly termed "domestic" or "second-image") to explain anomalies, is both conceptually incoherent (because it is inconsistent with rationality) and empirically biased (because it arbitrarily ignores results that might confirm liberal theories; for a more detailed argument, see Moravcsik 1997). Yet this intellectual residue of misguided realist criticism of liberalism remains visible in the subdiscipline to this day.

Much of the most vibrant mid-range theorizing in international relations, we have seen, is distinctively liberal. Yet the paradigmatic language of international relations does not reflect it. Much of the work in this chapter is termed "realist" (even though it violates the core premises of any reasonable definition of that paradigm), "domestic" (even though that term describes no theory at all and little empirical work), or "constructivist" (even though that label describes an ontology not a theory).[17] Indeed, the broad categories of "grand" international relations debates remain almost entirely unchanged since the 1950s, when realists squared off against legalists (today: neoliberal institutionalists) and idealists (today: constructivists) (Legro and Moravcsik 1999). No wonder so many scholars today eschew such labels altogether. Yet this is no solution either. Without a recognized paradigm of its own, theories that stress variation in the preferences of socially embedded states are still too often dismissed in theoretical discussions, ignored in comparative theory testing, and, most importantly, disregarded in multicausal syntheses.

REFERENCES

ACHEN, C. 1995. How could we tell a unitary rational actor when we saw one? Presented at the Midwest Political Science Association annual meeting, Chicago, 16–18 April.

ALT, J. and GILLIGAN, M. 1994. The political economy of trading states: factor specificity, collective action problems, and domestic political institutions. *Journal of Political Philosophy*, 2: 165–92.

[16] There is "something particularly satisfying about systemic explanations and about the structural forms of...explanations" (Keohane 1986, 193). This claim may or may not be true, but is often wrongly conflated with setting preferences aside—since, as we have seen, liberalism is a systemic theory.

[17] For a lucid and exceptionally fair-minded effort to distinguish constructivism from ideational liberalism, see Johnston (2005, ch. 1).

ATZILI, B. 2006–7. When good fences make bad neighbors: fixed borders, state weakness, and international conflict. *International Security*, 31: 139–73.

BALDWIN, D. A. 1979. Power analysis and world politics: new trends versus old tendencies. *World Politics*, 31: 161–94.

—— 1989. *Paradoxes of Power*. Oxford: Basil Blackwell.

BROOKS, S. G. 2007. *Producing Security: Multinational Corporations, Globalization, and the Changing Calculus of Conflict*. Princeton, NJ: Princeton University Press.

CARPENTER, R. C. 2007. Studying issue (non)-adoption in transnational advocacy networks. *International Organization*, 61: 643–67.

CHRISTENSEN, T. J. 2001. Posing problems without catching up: China's rise and challenges for US security policy. *International Security*, 25: 5–40.

COLEMAN, J. S. 1990. *Foundations of Social Theory*. Cambridge, Mass.: Harvard University Press.

DAHL, R. A. 1969. The concept of power. Pp. 79–93 in *Political Power: A Reader in Theory and Research*, ed. R. Bell, D. V. Edwards, and R. Harrison Wagner. New York: Free Press.

DOYLE, M. W. 1986. Liberalism and world politics. *American Political Science Review*, 80: 1151–69.

EHRLICH, S. D. 2007. Access to protection: domestic institutions and trade policy in democracies. *International Organization*, 61: 571–605.

ELKINS, Z., GUZMAN, A. T., and SIMMONS, B. A. 2006. Competing for capital: the diffusion of bilateral investment treaties, 1960–2000. *International Organization*, 60: 811–46.

FEARON, J. 1998. Domestic politics, foreign policy, and theories of international relations. *Annual Review of Political Science*, 1: 289–313.

—— and LAITIN, D. 2000. Violence and the social construction of ethnic identity. *International Organization*, 54: 845–77.

FORDHAM, B. 2007. Revisionism reconsidered: exports and American intervention in World War I. *International Organization*, 61: 277–310.

FORTNA, V. P. 2004. *Peace Time: Cease-Fire Agreements and the Durability of Peace*. Princeton, NJ: Princeton University Press.

FRIEDEN, J. 1991. Invested interests: the politics of national economic policies in a world of global finance. *International Organization*, 45: 425–51.

—— 1999. Actors and preferences in international relations. Pp. 39–76 in Lake and Powell 1999.

GADDIS, J. L. 1997. *We Know Now: Rethinking Cold War History*. Oxford: Oxford University Press.

GARTZKE, E. 2000. Preferences and the democratic peace. *International Studies Quarterly*, 44: 191–212.

GAWANDE, K. and HOEKMAN, B. 2006. Lobbying and agricultural trade policy in the United States. *International Organization*, 60: 527–61.

GOEMANS, H. E. 2000. *War and Punishment: The Causes of War Termination and the First World War*. Princeton, NJ: Princeton University Press.

GOUREVITCH, P. 1978. The second image reversed: the international sources of domestic politics. *International Organization*, 32: 881–912.

GRANT, R. W. and KEOHANE, R. O. 2005. Accountability and abuses of power in world politics. *American Political Science Review*, 99: 29–43.

HAAS, M. L. 2005. *The Ideological Origins of Great Power Politics, 1789–1989*. Ithaca, NY: Cornell University Press.

—— 2007. The United States and the end of the Cold War: reactions to shifts in Soviet power, policies, or domestic politics? *International Organization*, 61: 145–79.

HAGGARD, S. 1988. The institutional foundations of hegemony: explaining the Reciprocal Trade Agreements Act of 1934. *International Organization*, 42: 91–119.

HIRSCHMAN, A. O. 1945. *National Power and the Structure of Foreign Trade*. Berkeley: University of California Press.

HOLSTI, K. J. 1991. *Peace and War: Armed Conflicts and International Order 1648–1989*. Cambridge: Cambridge University Press.

HUNTINGTON, S. P. 1991. *The Third Wave: Democratization in the Late Twentieth Century*. Norman: University of Oklahoma Press.

IKENBERRY, G. J. 2000. *After Victory: Institutions, Strategic Restraint, and the Rebuilding of Order after Major Wars*. Princeton, NJ: Princeton University Press.

JOHNSTON, I. 2005. Social states: China in international institutions, 1980–2000. Unpublished typescript, Harvard University.

KATZENSTEIN, P. J. 1987. *Policy and Politics in West Germany: The Growth of a Semisovereign State*. Ithaca, NY: Cornell University Press.

—— (ed.) 1996. *The Culture of National Security: Norms and Identity in World Politics*. New York: Columbia University Press.

KAUFMAN, S. J. 2006. Symbolic politics or rational choice? Testing theories of extreme ethnic violence. *International Security*, 30: 45–86.

KECK, M. and SIKKINK, K. 1998. *Activists beyond Borders: Advocacy Networks in International Politics*. Ithaca, NY: Cornell University Press.

KEOHANE, R. O. 1984. *After Hegemony: Cooperation and Discord in the World Political Economy*. Princeton, NJ: Princeton University Press.

—— (ed.) 1986. *Neorealism and its Critics*. New York: Columbia University Press.

—— 1990. International liberalism reconsidered. Pp. 165–94 in *The Economic Limits to Modern Politics*, ed. J. Dunn. Cambridge: Cambridge University Press.

—— and MILNER, H. V. (eds.) 1996. *Internationalization and Domestic Politics*. Cambridge: Cambridge University Press.

—— and NYE, J. S. 1977. *Power and Interdependence: World Politics in Transition*. Boston: Little, Brown.

KIRSHNER, J. 2007. *Appeasing Bankers: Financial Caution on the Road to War*. Princeton, NJ: Princeton University Press.

LAKE, D. and POWELL, R. (eds.) 1999. *Strategic Choice and International Relations*. Princeton, NJ: Princeton University Press.

LEGRO, J. W. 1996. Culture and preferences in the international cooperation two-step. *American Political Science Review*, 90: 118–37.

—— and MORAVCSIK, A. 1999. Is anybody still a realist? *International Security*, 24: 5–55.

LEVY, J. S. 1988. Domestic politics and war. *Journal of Interdisciplinary History*, 18: 653–73.

MACK, A. 1975. Why big nations lose small wars: the politics of asymmetric conflict. *World Politics*, 27: 175–200.

MANSFIELD, E. D. and SNYDER, J. 1995. Democratization and the danger of war. *International Security*, 20: 5–38.

MATTHEW, R. A. and ZACHER, M. W. 1995. Liberal international theory: common threads, divergent strands. Pp. 107–50 in *Controversies in International Relations Theory: Realism and the Neoliberal Challenge*, ed. C. Kegley. New York: St Martin's Press.

MEARSHEIMER, J. J. 1990. Back to the future: instability in Europe after the Cold War. *International Security*, 15: 5–56.

MILNER, H. 1988. Trading places: industries for free trade. *World Politics*, 40: 350–76.

MORAVCSIK, A. 1997. Taking preferences seriously: a liberal theory of international politics. *International Organization*, 51: 512–53.

—— 1998. *The Choice for Europe: Social Purpose and State Power from Messina to Maastricht.* Ithaca, NY: Cornell University Press.

—— 2003. Liberal international relations theory: a scientific assessment. Pp. 159–204 in *Progress in International Relations Theory: Appraising the Field*, ed. C. Elman and M. F. Elman. Cambridge, Mass.: MIT Press.

—— 2005. The European constitutional compromise and the neofunctionalist legacy. *Journal of European Public Policy*, 12: 349–86.

MORGENTHAU, H. J. 1960. *Politics among Nations: The Struggle for Power and Peace*, 3rd edn. New York: Alfred Knopf.

MORROW, J. D. 1988. Social choice and system structure in world politics. *World Politics*, 41: 75–97.

OWEN, J. 1994. How liberalism produces democratic peace. *International Security*, 19: 87–125.

OYE, K. (ed.) 1986. *Cooperation under Anarchy.* Princeton, NJ: Princeton University Press.

POWELL, R. 1994. Anarchy in international relations theory: the neorealist–neoliberal debate. *International Organization*, 48: 313–44.

PUTNAM, R. D. 1988. Diplomacy and domestic politics: the logic of two-level games. *International Organization*, 42: 427–60.

RAIFFA, H. 1982. *The Art and Science of Negotiation.* Cambridge, Mass.: Harvard University Press.

RISSE-KAPPEN, T. 1996. Collective identity in a democratic community: the case of NATO. Pp. 357–99 in Katzenstein 1996.

RODRIK, D. 1992. The rush to free trade in the developing world: why so late? why now? will it last? NBER Working Paper No. 3947, National Bureau of Economic Research.

RUGGIE, J. G. 1982. International regimes, transactions, and change: embedded liberalism in the postwar economic order. *International Organization*, 36: 379–415.

—— 1983. Continuity and transformation in the world polity: toward a neorealist synthesis. *World Politics*, 35: 261–85.

—— 1995. At home abroad, abroad at home: international liberalization and domestic stability in the new world economy. Jean Monnet Chair Paper, Robert Schuman Centre, European University Institute.

RUSSETT, B. 1993. *Grasping the Democratic Peace: Principles for a Post-Cold War World.* Princeton, NJ: Princeton University Press.

SCHWELLER, R. L. 1996. Neorealism's status-quo bias: what security dilemma? *Security Studies*, 5: 90–121.

SNYDER, J. 1991. *Myths of Empire: Domestic Politics and International Ambition.* Ithaca, NY: Cornell University Press.

—— 2000. *From Voting to Violence: Democratization and Nationalist Conflict.* New York: Norton.

STASAVAGE, D. 2007. Cities, constitutions, and sovereign borrowing in Europe, 1274–1785. *International Organization*, 61: 489–525.

SWANK, D. 2006. Tax policy in an era of internationalization: explaining the spread of neoliberalism. *International Organization*, 60: 847–82.

VAN EVERA, S. 1990. Primed for peace: Europe after the Cold War. *International Security*, 15: 7–57.

—— 1999. *Causes of War: Power and the Roots of Conflict.* Ithaca, NY: Cornell University Press.

VOGEL, D. 1995. *Trading Up: Consumer and Environmental Regulation in a Global Economy.* Cambridge, Mass.: Harvard University Press.

WALTER, B. F. 1997. The critical barrier to civil war settlement. *International Organization*, 51: 335–64.

WALTZ, K. N. 1979. *Theory of International Politics.* Reading, Mass.: Addison-Wesley.

CHAPTER 34

THE ENGLISH SCHOOL

TIM DUNNE

INTERNATIONAL relations is no longer an American social science, as Stanley Hoffmann (1977) proclaimed. This is true in a literal sense: The subject is taught in universities in dozens of countries and is becoming a global discipline. It is also true insofar as the study of international relations outside the United States is often committed to theoretical orientations that are hostile to the dominant approach encapsulated by the phrase "an American social science." The English School of international relations is the oldest and arguably the most significant rival to the American mainstream. By English School, I mean a group of scholars located mainly in the UK who have a common ontological disposition and are critical of the kind of scientific method advanced by positivists. During the classical period in its evolution (1950s–1980s), the leading figures in the School were Charles Manning, Herbert Butterfield, Hedley Bull, Adam Watson, and R. J. Vincent. In the post-classical phase (1990s onwards), the most prominent writers are Barry Buzan, Andrew Hurrell, Robert Jackson, Edward Keene, Andrew Linklater, Richard Little, James Mayall, Hidemi Suganami, and Nicholas J. Wheeler.

The claim that the English School constitutes a distinctive and systematic approach to international relations is one that is relatively uncontroversial today but would not have been accepted in the 1980s, when the landscape of international relations was carved up into the paradigms of realism, pluralism, and structuralism. Today the English School is not only more confident of its own contribution; it is increasingly being taken seriously by other theoretical approaches. What evidence can be cited in

* I would like to thank Chris Reus-Smit for extremely helpful feedback on an early draft of this chapter.

support of this claim? To begin with, key textbooks surveying international relations theory today include the English School (Burchill et al. 2001; Dunne, Kurki, and Smith 2007). Additionally, the influential Cambridge University Press/British International Studies Association series is consistently publishing books on the School, including Buzan (2004) and Linklater and Suganami (2006). A final indicator is the extent to which international relations researchers—primarily in the United States, Canada, Australia, and Scandinavia—are engaging with the work even though many do not identify themselves as being part of an English School project per se (Finnemore 1996; Epp 1998; Reus-Smit 1999; Wendt 1999; Jackson 2000; Shapcott 2004; Adler 2005).

This geopolitical diversity points to an anomaly with the label "English School" in that even in its heyday some of its leading contributors were not English (though all built their academic reputations at British universities). The empirical deficiencies with the label has generated a great deal of debate and to some extent resentment on the part of those who symphathize with the ideas but not the act of union to a particular place. While recognizing this deficiency, it is probably time to admit that the label has taken hold and is understood by just about every undergraduate studying international relations.

Those who identify with the English School today see it as occupying the middle ground in international relations alongside constructivism: This location is preferable to the dominant mainstream theories of neorealism and neoliberalism and the more radical alternatives (such as critical theory and poststructuralism). They are drawn to an English School perspective because it offers a synthesis of different theories and concepts. In so doing, it avoids the "either/or" framing of realism versus idealism, as set out in the writings of many great figures during the 1930s and 1940s. It also avoids the explanatory versus interpretative dichotomy that generated so much heat during the "fourth debate" in the 1990s. In place of these dichotomies, the English School purports to offer an account of international relations that combines theory *and* history, morality *and* power, agency *and* structure.

One obvious consequence of this level of theoretical ambition is that the boundaries of the English School often appear to be unclear, which in part explains the ongoing debate about who belongs in the School and how it differs from other theoretical accounts of world politics. To shed light on these questions, Section 1 of this chapter will consider in more depth the contextual emergence of the English School, and in particular its determination to develop an original account of interstate order. Section 2 takes its central claim—that the practice of states is shaped by international norms, regulated by international institutions, and guided by moral purposes—and explores this in relation to the countervailing forces of the states system and world society. In the course of this exploration, the argument opens up a number of "axes of difference" within the School (Reus-Smit 2002, 496–9) such as the extent to which ontological primacy is accorded to international society, and, at a deeper level, whether that society is understood in procedural or substantive terms.

In Section 3, the focus shifts away from debates inside the English School and toward a wider reflection on its place within international relations as a whole. What do leading US theorists regard as the contribution of the School, or, putting it more negatively, what do they see as being wrong with the English School? Perhaps the most significant conversation of them all is the one with constructivism. The broadly sociological assumptions shared by both schools generated excitement on the part of adherents to the English School: Suddenly works that had seemed outdated and idiosyncratic were opened up for new critically informed readings. Over a decade later, the initial excitement has waned as the English School has come under "friendly fire" from constructivists. As I argue in this chapter, while the English School has a great deal to learn from constructivism, it should maintain its distinctive voice primarily because it has greater synthetic potential and is more openly committed to certain ethical standpoints.

1 CONTEXT AND EMERGENCE

The English School can claim to be a distinctive theory of international relations because of a shared history and a sense that its approach to the subject was a living tradition. What is apparent from existing accounts of the development of the School is the extent to which the main protagonists believed themselves to be part of a collective enterprise, and consciously sought to carry its debates forward.

The emergence of a self-conscious research program, with an open yet distinct agenda, can be seen in the writings of early post-1945 writers working in leading UK universities. Manning developed a curriculum in which the idea of international society played a prominent role. In the 1950s, his colleague Martin Wight developed an approach to the subject that viewed international society as a middle way between realist accounts of systemic logics and revolutionist accounts that plotted the downfall of the state system as a whole. Wight's most famous protégé was Bull. He too was increasingly dissatisfied with the either/or choice between realism and idealism. The former, Bull believed, was right to puncture the utopian schemes of the idealists but wrong to rule out the idea that the inter-state order was capable of reform.

The search for a new analysis of international relations was what drove Butterfield to set up the British Committee on the Theory of International Politics (Dunne 1998; Vigezzi 2005). The committee met regularly between 1959 and 1984. The chairs of the Committee were the pivotal figures in the classical period: Butterfield (until 1968), Wight (until 1972), Watson (until 1978), and Bull until his death in 1984. By then, the work of the Committee and those sympathetic to it was increasingly seen as being out of step with the emergence of new theories (such as postmodernism and critical theory) and sub-disciplines (such as foreign-policy analysis and international political economy). Unsurprisingly, we find that in reflections on the "state of the discipline" in the 1980s, the English School was nowhere to be seen (Banks 1984; Smith 1987); neither did it figure in early representations of the debate between neorealism and its critics. Yet, within a decade, interest in the English School had begun to rekindle.

Many influential textbooks published in the 1990s began to include it as an alternative approach to the subject, placing it alongside realism, liberalism, and various critical approaches (Der Derian 1995; Brown 1997; Jackson and Sørensen 1999). Added to these, original contributions to the history and theory of international society have proliferated, all taking the English School as their point of departure (*inter alia*, Jackson 1990; 1995; Armstrong 1993; Osiander 1994; Welsh 1995; Buzan and Little 2000; Wheeler 2000; Keene 2002; Keal 2003; Clark 2005; 2007; Gonzalez-Pelaez 2005).

This sense of a resurgent paradigm was prompted in part by the recognition that it represented a distinct position that was inhospitable to the rationalist assumptions underpinning both neorealism and neoliberalism. Moreover, in terms of substantive research questions, the English School had long focused on the kind of cultural questions and normative contestations that were rising to the top of the international agenda in the 1990s. Such momentum prompted Buzan—along with Little—to seek to invigorate English School theorizing. This new phase was marked by the publication of Buzan's agenda-setting paper, "The English School: An Underexploited Resource in IR" (Buzan 2001), developed further in Buzan (2004) and followed by Linklater and Suganami's major reassessment of the School (2006).

The previous paragraphs have provided some historical and sociological context for the emergence of the English School. What follows is a focused discussion of "international society," and how this needs to be situated between the system and world society pillars of the world political system.

2 International Society: Between System and World Society

A feature of the earliest historiographical accounts of the English School is that they refer to their defense of international society being the "distinguishing power" of the School (Wilson 1989). Following Buzan (2004), I now hold the view that the School needs not only to provide a powerful account of how and why states form a society; it must also show how this domain relates to world society. Moreover, going further than Buzan, I argue that the distinguishing power of the English School is its synthetic account of how the three pillars of the world political system hang together: the system, the inter-state society, and world society.

According to Bull, the categories system, society, and world society are "elements" that exist "out there" in world politics but can be known to us only through interpretative designs. They are ideal-types, bundles of properties that highlight certain important features while minimizing that which is thought to be less relevant. By seeking to clarify the concepts that reveal patterns in world history, the English School is working with a very different notion of "theory" to that which is found in the dominant American approaches. Rather than "operationalizing" concepts and formulating "testable" hypotheses, the emphasis upon contending concepts is driven by a search for defining properties that mark the boundaries of different historical and normative orders.

It is necessary, before going any further, to consider one objection to representing English School theory as a conversation between three overlapping domains. In Andrew Linklater's view, although the School talked about international society as only one element in the complex patterns of international interactions, it was nevertheless "its central purpose" (Linklater and Suganami 2006, 119).[1] Therefore, to treat the three as being of equal significance is to misunderstand the distinctive character of English School thought. I do not doubt that one of the intellectual drivers propelling the English School into existence was a defense of a middle way between realism and idealism. I also recognize that many publications by English School advocates in the 1990s continued to privilege the societal domain, in part due to the desire to show that the English School was not just a polite form of realism, as many in the 1980s had assumed. However, neither of these points undermines the claim that the most persuasive case one can make in defense of the English School is that it is potentially more illuminating than mainstream alternatives because it seeks to provide a synthetic account of global politics that avoids the series of false dichotomies thrown up by the alternatives such as power versus norms, materialism versus idealism, anarchy versus hierarchy, reasons versus causes. Such a move requires that we situate the inter-state normative order alongside the other two ideal-types to illustrate its boundaries and constraints.

2.1 International Society: Definition, Properties, Variations

Perhaps the sharpest definition of international society is to be found on the first page of the edited collection *The Expansion of International Society*. By an international society, Bull and Watson (1984, 1) write,

we mean a group of states (or, more generally, a group of independent political communities) which not merely form a system, in the sense that the behaviour of each is a necessary factor in the calculations of the others, but also have established by dialogue and consent common rules and institutions for the conduct of their relations, and recognize their common interest in maintaining these arrangements.

The discussion that follows scrutinizes each component of this definition.

The first key element of international society is the unique character of the membership that is confined to sovereign states. What is significant here is that actors both claim sovereignty and recognize one another's right to the same prerogatives (Wight 1977). Clearly the act of mutual recognition indicates the presence of a social practice: recognition is fundamental to an identity relationship. Recognition is the first step in the construction of an international society. If we were to doubt for

---

[1] Although the Linklater and Suganami book is co-authored, the introduction clearly states which chapters were drafted by which author—hence the reference to Linklater only.

a moment the social nature of the process of recognition, then this would quickly be dispelled by those peoples in history who at some time have been or continue to be denied membership of the society of states. The history of the expansion of international society is a story of a shifting boundary of inclusion and exclusion. China was denied sovereign statehood until January 1942, when Western states finally renounced the unequal treaties. Why was this the case? Membership became defined, particularly in the nineteenth century, by a "standard of civilization" that set conditions for internal governance that corresponded with European values and beliefs. What we see here is how important cultural differentiation has been to the European experience of international society. China was not recognized as a legitimate member of international society, and, therefore, was denied equal membership. If the West and China did not recognize each other as equal members, then how should we characterize their relations? Here we see how the system–society dynamic can usefully capture historical boundaries of inclusion and exclusion. There was a great deal of "interaction" between China and the West during the nineteenth and early twentieth centuries, but this was driven by strategic and economic logics. Crucially, neither side believed itself to be part of the same shared values and institutions: China, for example, long resisted the presence of European diplomats on its soil along with their claim to extraterritorial jurisdiction, which has been a long-standing rule among European powers. In the absence of accepting the rules and institutions of European international society, it makes sense to argue that from the Treaty of Nanking in 1843 to 1942 China was part of the states system but was not a member of international society (Gong 1984).

After rightful membership, the next consideration involves thinking about what it means for a state to "act." Here the English School encounters criticism from empiricists who argue that collective constructs cannot have agency. What does it mean to attribute agency to collectivities like states? One straightforward answer is that states act through the medium of their representatives or office-holders. Every state employs officials who act externally on its behalf, from the lowly consulate dealing with "nationals" who have lost their passports to the "head of state." In a narrowly empirical sense, therefore, the diplomatic and foreign-policy elite are the real agents of international society. This is the original sense in which the term "international society" came into existence in the eighteenth century. In 1736, Antoine Pecquet argued that the corps of ministers formed an "independent society" bound by a "community of privileges" (Frey and Frey 1999, 213). If we are looking for the real agents of international society, then it is to the diplomatic culture that we must look, that realm of ideas and beliefs shared by representatives of states (Der Derian 2003).

Sovereign states are the primary members of international society; however, it is important to note that they are not the *only* members. Historical anomalies have always existed, including the diplomatic network belonging to the Catholic Church and the qualified sovereign powers that were granted to nonstate actors such as the rights to make war and annex territory that were transferred to the great trading companies of the imperial era. One might also argue that influential international nongovernmental organizations (INGOs) are members insofar as they give advice to institutions such as the United Nations and on occasions participate in the drafting of significant multilateral treaties. The other important anomaly with the membership of international society is the fact that sovereign rights are often constrained for economic or security reasons. Robert Jackson (1990), a leading writer in the English School, pointed to the fact that postcolonial states are "quasi" sovereigns in that they are recognized by international society but are unable to maintain an effective government internally. A related development is the temporary suspension of sovereign prerogatives by an international institution or occupying authority, a practice that follows from a period of civil conflict or external military intervention. In the colonial period this was often described as trusteeship (Bain 2003); in contemporary international society it goes under the less politically sensitive label of a "transitional authority."

The element of mutual recognition is highly significant for English School understandings of international society, but it is not a sufficient condition for its existence. The actors must have some minimal common interests, such as trade, freedom of travel, or simply the need for stability. Here we see how aspects of the system impinge on the possibilities for a society to develop. The higher the levels of economic interdependence, the more likely it is that states will develop institutions for realizing common interests and purposes. The independence of sovereign states, however, remains an important limiting factor in the realization of common goals. For this reason, the purposes states agreed upon for most of the Westphalian era have had a fairly minimal character centered upon the survival of the system and the endurance of the dominant units within it. The condition of general war is an example of the breakdown of order, but Bull was quick to point out that, even during the Second World War, certain laws of war were respected and, perhaps more significantly, the period of total war triggered an attempt to construct a new order based largely on the same rules and institutions that had operated in the prewar era. It was this that led him to claim that "the element of society had always existed" in the modern states system (Bull 1977, 41). Such a claim prompted disquiet from constructivists, who rightly argued that, if "society" produces order, how can it continue to exist during historical periods when order has clearly broken down (Finnemore 2001)?

2.2 Types of International Society

One answer to Finnemore's question, which the English School needs to develop more fully, is to provide clearer benchmarks that enable an evaluation of how much "society" is present in the inter-state order. At the more minimal end of the spectrum of international societies, we find an institutional arrangement that is restricted solely to the maintenance of order. In a culturally diverse world, where member states have different traditions and political systems, the only collective venture they could all agree on was the maintenance of international order. Without order, the stability of the system would be thrown into doubt and with it the survival of the units. Yet, the extent to which states formed an international society was limited and constrained by the fact of anarchy. For this reason, international society was to be equated not with a harmonious order but, rather, with a tolerable order that was better than a realist would expect but much worse than a cosmopolitan might wish for (MacMillan and Linklater 1995).

In a pluralist international society, the institutional framework is geared toward the liberty of states and the maintenance of order among them. The rules are complied with because, like rules of the road, fidelity to them is relatively cost free but the collective benefits are enormous. A good example is the elaborate rules to do with ambassadorial and diplomatic privileges. Acceptance that representatives of states were not subject to the laws of their host country is a principle that has received widespread compliance for many centuries. This is one instance among many where the rules of coexistence have come to dominate state practice. Pluralist rules and norms "provide a structure of coexistence, built on the mutual recognition of states as independent and legally equal members of society, on the unavoidable reliance on self-preservation and self-help, and on freedom to promote their own ends subject to minimal constraints" (Alderson and Hurrell 2000, 18). Fully to comprehend the pluralist order, one needs only to be reminded that great powers, limited war, and the balance of power were thought by the English School to be "institutions." By this term, Bull and his colleagues were pointing to the practices that helped to sustain order, practices that evolved over many centuries. For example, if the balance of power was essential to preserve the liberty of states, then status quo powers must be prepared to intervene forcefully to check the growing power of a state that threatens the general balance.

Are pluralist rules and institutions adequate for our contemporary world? This is a question that has provoked differing responses within the English School. On one side, traditionalists like Jackson (2000) believe that a pluralist international society is a practical institutional adaptation to human diversity: The great advantage of a society based on the norms of sovereignty and nonintervention is that such an arrangement is most likely to achieve the moral value of freedom.

Critics of pluralism charge that it is failing to deliver on its promise. The persistence of inter-state wars throughout the twentieth century suggest that sovereignty norms were not sufficient to deter predatory states. Moreover, the rule of nonintervention that was central to pluralism was enabling statist elites to violently abuse their own citizens with impunity. For these reasons, both Bull and Vincent were drawn to a different account of international society in which universal values such as human rights set limits on the exercise of state sovereignty. The guiding thought here, and one that is captured by the term solidarism, is that the ties that bind individuals to the great society of humankind are deeper than the pluralist rules and institutions that separate them.

Bull defined a solidarist international society in terms of the collective enforcement of international rules *and* the guardianship of human rights. It differs from cosmopolitanism in that the latter is agnostic as to the institutional arrangement for delivering universal values: Some cosmopolitans believe a world government is best and others would want to abandon formal political hierarchies altogether. By contrast, solidarism is an *extension* of an international society not its transformation. Like pluralism, it is defined by shared values and institutions and is held together by binding legal rules. Where it differs is in the content of the values and the character of the rules and institutions. In terms of values, in a solidarist international society individuals are entitled to basic rights. This in turn demands that sovereignty norms are modified such that there is a duty on the members of international society to intervene forcibly to protect those rights. At this point, Bull was hesitant about what was implied by solidarism. He believed that there was a danger that the enforcement of human rights principles risked undermining international order. Until there was a greater consensus on the meaning and priority to be accorded to rights claims, attempts to enforce them—what he described as "premature global solidarism"— would do more harm than good.

For much of the post-cold war period, the normative debate within the English School fractured along a pluralist/solidarist divide. On one side of the divide, Jackson (2000) made a forceful case for upholding pluralist norms, while Wheeler (2000) set out a persuasive argument in defense of a solidarist account of rights and duties. Buzan is right to argue that one of the negative consequences of the debate is that it assumed normative density was an issue primarily for the inter-state realm rather than understanding how it shapes and enables the transnational and inter-human domains.

While it is correct to argue that "pluralism versus solidarism" was one of the principal axes of difference in English School thinking after the cold war, from the vantage point of today this dispute looks increasingly like a conversation inside the normative wing of the School. Alongside the normative wing, we have seen the emergence of an analytical wing led by Buzan himself and including the work of Little. The former are drawn toward historical narratives of how the international social structure has evolved/changed (e.g. Armstrong 1993; Wheeler 2000; Bain 2003; Keal 2003; Linklater and Suganami 2006), while the latter search for analytical explanations of the various domains and sectors and how these impinge on each other (Watson 1992; Wæver 1998; Buzan and Little 2000; Little 2000; Buzan 2004).

2.3 The Elements of System and World Society

Both Wight and Bull recognized that a sophisticated analysis of world politics required a systemic component. Yet their discussion of Hobbesian dynamics in the "system" is inconsistent and unpersuasive. In my view, this vital element of the English School's theorization of world politics ought to be refined rather than discarded as Buzan (2004, 106) has argued. Bull defined the system as being an arena where there was interaction between communities but no shared rules or institutions. In order for a system to come into being, there has to be sufficient intensity of interactions to make "the behaviour of each a necessary element in the calculations of the other" (Bull 1977, 12).

The concept of a system plays three important roles in the English School's theory of world politics. First, as discussed above, the system/society distinction provides a normative benchmark for addressing the question of how far international society extends (Wight, Wight, and Porter 1991). Secondly, by looking at the formation of the system, it is possible to discern mechanisms that shape and shove international and world societies. Thirdly, the category of the system can be used to capture the basic material forces in world politics—flows of information and trade, levels of destructive capability, and capacities of actors to affect their environment. Let me examine each of these briefly in turn.

The English School's use of the category international system—or more accurately an inter-state system—shares a great deal with the use of systems theory in realist thought. What sets them apart is that the English School was interested in the system primarily for what it tells us about the history of international society. If one takes Bull's developmental insight into the relationship between system and society, then it is clear that the existence of a society presupposes the existence of a system. This can open up into an intriguing series of discussions as to when a system becomes a society—what level and type of interactions are required in order for the units to treat each other as ends in themselves? And under what circumstances might a society lapse back into a systemic order in which their actions impact upon one another but there is no mutual recognition or acceptance of a common framework of rules and institutions? In the British Committee's writings on decolonization, the emphasis is placed on the gradual inclusion of the non-Western world into a globalized society of sovereign states. It is also important to realize that systemic interactions remain a possible future arrangement if the dominant actors in international society cease to comply with the rules and act in ways that undermine international security. The hypothetical case of a major nuclear confrontation could become a reality only if the great powers acted in ways that were catastrophic for international society. As a result, the society collapses back into the system.

The idea of a states system is also useful to identify the current boundaries between members and those states that find themselves shunned by international society. It is in the dark recesses of the states system that pariah states and failed states find themselves. This does not mean pariahs are outside the framework of the rules and institutions entirely, only that their actions are subjected to far greater scrutiny. Actors in the states system can have structured interactions with members of international society—they may even comply with treaties and other rules—but these interactions remain systemic unless the parties grant each other mutual respect and inclusion into international society.

Thinking about the systemic domain also alerts us to the downward pressure exerted by the distribution of material power. In Bull's work we can find two important instances where the system impinges upon the society. First, he notes how general war is "a basic determinant of the shape the system assumes at any one time" (Bull 1977, 187). Even in the cold war, where the massive nuclear arsenals of the North Atlantic Treaty Organization and Warsaw Pact countries were not unleashed, the presence of these weapons was a crucial constraint on the two superpowers' room for maneuver. If the Soviet Union had only conventional weapons, would the United States and its allies have tolerated the "fall" of central European countries into the Soviet sphere of influence? Closely related to the phenomena of general war and destructive capacities as basic determinants of the system, one can find in the English School the view that there is logic of balancing in the states system. Under conditions of anarchy, where there is no overarching power to disarm the units and police the rules, it is in the interests of all states to prevent the emergence of a dominant or hegemonic power (Watson 1992). Those who take the balance of power seriously point to repeated instances in modern history where states with hegemonic ambition have been repelled by an alliance of powers seeking to prevent a change in the ordering principle of the system. Even if this tendency requires states to "act" in order to uphold the balance of power, it can still be persuasively argued that the survival of the states system *demands* balancing behavior from states such that it becomes an inbuilt feature of the system. This is contrasted with the institution of the balance of power in international society that is not mechanical but is rather the outcome of a deliberate policy of pursuing a strategy of self-preservation in the absence of world government (Wight 1978).

Looking through the systemic lens does not only show the ordering of the units; it also directs our attention to the levels of technology, the distribution of material power, and the interaction capacity of the units. Together, these factors tell us a great deal about the ability of units to act, and particularly their "reach" (are actors local, regional, or global?). Levels of technology can be thought of as attributes of the units; an obvious case in point is whether a state has nuclear weapons technology or not. However, it is also useful to think about technology in systemic terms, particularly in areas such as communication, transportation, and levels of destructive capacity. Compare, for example, a states system in which the dominant mode of transportation is a horse-drawn wagon, as opposed to a system in which individuals and goods can be transported by supersonic jets, high-speed rail, and ships the size of several football fields placed end-to-end. As these technologies spread, "they change the quality and character of what might be called the *interaction capacity* of the system as a whole" (Buzan, Jones, and Little 1993, 70).

What make these attributes "systemic?" They are systemic in that for the most part they fall outside the institutional arrangement developed by states to regulate order and promote justice. By way of illustration, take the place of Britain in the world from the early 1940s to the beginning of the cold war. Throughout the war, Britain was one of the "big three" great powers who were the architects of the postwar order. By 1948, the country was increasingly a policy-taker on the world stage and not a policy-maker, despite the fact that its diplomatic network remained global, its language remained dominant, and its values ascendant. None of these soft power advantages was enough to configure the system in multipolar terms. Without wanting to imply overdetermination, it is nevertheless useful to invoke the system to characterize those factors that appear immovable from the perspective of the actors, such as their geographic location, population base, and technological/economic capacity. Of course they are not immovable over the long term—even geographical "distance" can change over time, as globalization has demonstrated in recent decades.

The third element in the English School triad is world society. This concept runs in parallel to international society albeit with one key difference—it refers to the shared interests and values "linking all parts of the human community" (Bull 1977, 279). Vincent's definition of world society is something of a menu of all those entities whose moral concerns traditionally lay outside international society: the claim of individuals to human rights; the claim of indigenous peoples to autonomy; the needs of transnational corporations to penetrate the shell of sovereign states; and the claim to retrospective justice by those who speak on behalf of the former colonized powers. It is undeniable that human rights are at the center of the classical English School's conception of world society. An account of the development of human rights would need to show how the cosmopolitan culture of late modernity is shaping a new institutional arrangement in world society.

One indicator of an evolving world society is the emergence of international humanitarian law. The United Nations Charter represented an important stage in this evolution, thus indicating the dynamic interplay between the inter-state and the world society domains. Justice, rights, fundamental freedoms, were all given prominence in the Charter, and subsequently universal norms of racial equality, the prohibition on torture, and the right to development have been added (among others). Various changes in international criminal law have significantly restricted the circumstances in which state leaders can claim immunity from humanitarian crimes committed while they were in office. Similarly, the Rome Statute of the International Criminal Court adds another layer of international jurisdiction in which agents of states can be held accountable for alleged war crimes. Taken as a whole, one authority on the English School argued that they "may be interpreted as involving a clear shift from an international society to a world society" (Armstrong 1999, 549). Such a claim, however, understates the extent to which the development of world society institutions is dependent on the ideational and material support of core states in international society.

World society is not just about the growing importance of transnational values grounded in liberal notions of rights and justice. Transnational identities can be based upon ideas of hatred and intolerance. Among a significant body of world public opinion, the strongest identification is to the faith and not to the state. This generates countervailing ideologies of liberation on the part of fundamentalist Christians and holy war on the part of certain Islamist groups. In English School thinking, such dynamics can usefully be considered in the context of earlier "revolts" against Western dominance that were apparent during the struggle for decolonization.

3 THE ENGLISH SCHOOL AND ITS CRITICS

It is not unusual for proponents of a particular international relations theory to claim to be "misunderstood." From the 1970s to the early 1990s, the leading figures of

English School were identified as traditionalists who bought into key realist assumptions about great-power dominance amid international anarchy. Somewhat polemically, a recent intervention by John Mearsheimer suggests the opposite: According to him, Butterfield, Wight, and Bull were "Cold War idealists" (Mearsheimer 2005, 144). This chapter has sought to show that the English School is not reducible either to realism or to idealism even if the focus on systemic forces draws insights from realism just as processes in world society—such as our widening moral sensibility—overlaps with idealism (Bull, in Hurrell and Alderson 1999).

The one theoretical position that has positively engaged with the English School is constructivism. Moreover, in the course of this conversation, constructivists have highlighted significant sources of conceptual confusion and theoretical underdevelopment at the core of the English School's research program. In the paragraphs below, I consider the constructivist challenge and examine the extent to which the English School has the capacity to engage in theoretical modification as well as remaining distinct from constructivism.

Christian Reus-Smit has written a number of articles that set out the terms of the debate between the English School and constructivism (Reus-Smit 2002; 2005). He rightly argues that those who wrote about the convergence in the middle 1990s did it on the basis of a narrow reading of both paradigms. On one side, the work of Alexander Wendt was taken to be representative of the constructivism project overall, while, on the other, there was little effort to engage with the richness of English School thinking beneath the standard claim that states form an international society.

Limitations on space do not permit a lengthy discussion of the faultlines between the English School and constructivism. I nevertheless want to reflect on two significant questions that have emerged from the debate. One immediate contrast with constructivism concerns the importance of metatheoretical correctness. Constructivists are theoretically reflective about the meaning of collective action, the status of norms, the relative priority accorded structures and agents, and causation, and the processes of socialization. The English School, by contrast, are more likely to offer narratives on the evolution and contestation of norms and institutions *without* explicit metatheoretical reflection. Part of the explanation for this divergence is the emergence of constructivism in leading American departments of political science where methodological rigor and epistemological awareness is an expectation for all doctoral candidates and early career researchers. So is the need to identify—in exclusionary ways—with one paradigm or another. Constructivism very much emerged as an alternative to the dominant rationalist approaches to international relations: As rationalism has never been anything other than a minority interest in the UK, there was no need of, or desire for, metatheoretical exceptionalism on the part of the English School.

This is not to say that leading members of the English School have avoided all engagement with disciplinary politics. Indeed, one of the motivating factors behind the relaunch of the English School in 2001 was precisely to take theory-building to a new level. Buzan's agenda setting paper (2001) was published by the *Review of*

International Studies, with several authors from outside the English School asked to comment. Martha Finnemore, writing from a constructivist standpoint, posed a series of penetrating questions about the School's method and its theoretical claims. While American international relations is driven by the search for causal explanations, Finnemore (2001, 513) ruefully notes that "I am not sure that the English School shares this interest."

Linklater and Suganami (2006), in their recent book *The English School of International Relations*, have taken up this challenge. They argue that Bull's classic text *The Anarchical Society* (1977, 74–5) explicitly asks the question whether rules and institutions are a "necessary and sufficient" condition for international order to exist. The problem for Bull is that the answer cannot be clear-cut, as the dependent variable (order) is implicated in the independent variables (institutions). The same rules and institutions that "cause" international order also form part of the shared knowledge that animates social action and makes it intelligible.

What the English School needs to set out more clearly—and Buzan has begun this journey—is the way in which the ideal-types of system, society, and community can elucidate important dynamics in the international system. It is not surprising that constructivists ask for greater clarity about the status of these ideal-types and how they relate to each other. "How do you know," asks Finnemore (2001, 509), "an international society (or international system or world society) when you see one?" As I have argued elsewhere, these are analytical categories rather than entities belonging to the real world. International society "is not something you see, but an idea in light of which we can make sense of an aspect of contemporary international relations" (Linklater and Suganami 2006, 103).

Wight's work (1977) was primarily interested in showing how individuals thought and acted in ways that reinforced or altered the normative order. His project comparing international societies throughout history drew extensively on cults, practical philosophies, rhetoric, propaganda, and whatever other contextual clues he could uncover. Diplomatic treaties and legal judgments have also proved to be rich resources for those writings, revealing the prevailing understandings of the states system at any point in time (Osiander 1994; Keene 2002; Clark 2005; 2007). This attention to meaning and understanding in the history of ideas about international society is not *absent* from constructivism (particularly in Fierke 1998; Rae 2002), but it is perhaps more clearly *present* in English School writings.

The treatment of "norms" within the English School is more avowedly normative than one finds in mainstream constructivist thinking. Take, for example, the treatment of human rights by Vincent (1986) and Thomas Risse, Steve Ropp, and Kathryn Sikkink (1999). Vincent seeks to provide a normative defence of human rights. We ought, he argues, to defend the universal rights of citizens to security and subsistence; delivering this basic right to life requires rethinking the authority and legitimacy of sovereign states. The structure of Vincent's argument is classically identifiable with English School theory. Realism is dismissed for not taking duties to noncitizens seriously, while full-blown cosmopolitanism is rejected because, in the minds of domestic publics, citizens matter *more* than strangers. This leaves him to explore the complexities of human rights within contending normative conceptions of international society.

In the Risse, Ropp, and Sikkink volume, the concern is with the status of human rights norms. What impact have they had on practice? How do we account for variation? And by what processes are actors socialized into compliance with the norms? This latter question is addressed by the application of a "spiral model" that begins with repression and ends with sovereign states fully internalizing human rights norms and practices (Risse and Sikkink 1999). While it is noteworthy that the rightness of moral universalism is not openly discussed, the strength of the Risse, Ropp, and Sikkink collection is in its analysis of how international norms become domestically instantiated.

The retreat of human rights post-September 11 raises important questions for constructivist analysis, not least whether the process of socialization is reversible. An English School take on this question would, as I have suggested above, situate the institutionalization of human rights within the interplay of system, society, and community in international politics. Classical writers such as Wight and Watson believed there to be a centripetal momentum to power such that it concentrates around a single source. Once the centralization reaches a tipping point, the conditions exist to challenge the pluralist rules and institutions upon which the post-Westphalian order has been built. This line of thought goes to the heart of debates about the role of the United States (and its allies in the West) in building a world order in its own image. Aside from the emergence of an unbalanced power with global economic and military reach, the other significant systemic logic is that of "new terrorism." The willingness of coordinated Islamist terror networks to use violence against Western targets undermines international society's claim to monopolize violence and regulate its use.

Weaving together these two tendencies—the appearance of an imperial power seeking to wage pre-emptive war and a nonstate actor wielding violence outside the framework of the laws of war—we might conclude that Bull was right to be concerned that the element of international society was in decline. Set against this, just as the bell has tolled for the inter-state order many times before, it is possible that the element of society is resilient enough to resist the power of US hegemony and the challenge of transnational nihilism.

REFERENCES

ADLER, E. 2005. Barry Buzan's use of constructivism to reconstruct the English School: "not all the way down." *Millennium: Journal of International Studies*, 34: 171–82.

ALDERSON, K. and HURRELL, A. (eds.) 2000. *Hedley Bull on International Society*. Basingstoke: Macmillan.

ARMSTRONG, D. 1993. *Revolution and World Order: The Revolutionary State in International Society*. Oxford: Clarendon Press.

—— 1999. Law, justice and the idea of world society. *International Affairs*, 75: 547–61.

BAIN, W. 2003. *Between Anarchy and Society: Trusteeship and the Obligations of Power*. Oxford: Oxford University Press.

BANKS, M. 1984. The evolution of international relations theory. Pp. 3–21 in *Conflict in World Society: A New Perspective on International Relations*, ed. M. Banks. Brighton: Harvester.

BROWN, C. 1997. *Understanding International Relations*. New York: St Martin's Press.

BULL, H. 1977. *The Anarchical Society: A Study of Order in World Politics*. London: Macmillan.

—— and WATSON, A. (eds.) 1984. *The Expansion of International Society*. Oxford: Clarendon Press.

BURCHILL, S., DEVETAK, R., LINKLATER, A., PATERSON, M., REUS-SMIT, C., and TRUE, J. 2001. *Theories of International Relations*, 2nd edn. Basingstoke: Palgrave.

BUZAN, B. 2001. The English School: an underexploited resource in IR. *Review of International Studies*, 27: 471–88.

—— 2004. *From International to World Society? English School Theory and the Social Structure of Globalisation*. Cambridge: Cambridge University Press.

—— JONES, C. A., and LITTLE, R. 1993. *The Logic of Anarchy: Neorealism to Structural Realism*. New York: Columbia University Press.

—— and LITTLE, R. 2000. *International Systems in World History: Remaking the Study of International Relations*. Oxford: Oxford University Press.

CLARK, I. 2005. *Legitimacy in International Society*. Oxford: Oxford University Press.

—— 2007. *International Legitimacy and World Society*. Oxford: Oxford University Press.

DER DERIAN, J. (ed.) 1995. *International Theory: Critical Investigations*. Basingstoke: Macmillan.

—— 2003. Hedley Bull and the case for a post-classical approach. Pp. 61–94 in *International Relations at LSE: A History of 75 Years*, ed. H. Bauer and E. Brighi. London: Millennium.

DUNNE, T. 1998. *Inventing International Society: A History of the English School*. New York: St Martin's Press in association with St Antony's College.

—— KURKI, M., and SMITH, S. (eds.) 2007. *Theories of International Relations: Discipline and Diversity*. Oxford: Oxford University Press.

EPP, R. 1998. The English School on the frontiers of international society: a hermeneutic recollection. Pp. 47–63 in *The Eighty Years' Crisis: International Relations 1919–1999*, ed. T. Dunne, M. Cox, and K. Booth. Cambridge: Cambridge University Press.

FIERKE, K. 1998. *Changing Games, Changing Strategies: Critical Investigations in Security*. Manchester: Manchester University Press.

FINNEMORE, M. 1996. *National Interests in International Society*. Ithaca, NY: Cornell University Press.

—— 2001. Exporting the English School? *Review of International Studies*, 27: 509–13.

FREY, L. S. and FREY, M. L. 1999. *The History of Diplomatic Immunity*. Columbus: Ohio State University Press.

GONG, G. W. 1984. *The Standard of "Civilization" in International Society*. Oxford: Clarendon Press.

GONZALEZ-PELAEZ, A. 2005. *Human Rights and World Trade: Hunger in International Society*. London: Routledge.

HOFFMANN, S. 1977. An American social science: international relations. *Daedalus*, 106: 41–60.

JACKSON, R. H. 1990. *Quasi-States: Sovereignty, International Relations, and the Third World*. Cambridge: Cambridge University Press.

Jackson, R. H. 1995. The political theory of international society. Pp. 110–28 in *International Relations Theory Today*, ed. K. Booth and S. Smith. Cambridge: Polity.

—— 2000. *The Global Covenant: Human Conduct in a World of States*. Oxford: Oxford University Press.

—— and Sørensen, G. 1999. *Introduction to International Relations*. Oxford: Oxford University Press.

Keal, P. 2003. *European Conquest and the Rights of Indigenous Peoples: The Moral Backwardness of International Society*. Cambridge: Cambridge University Press.

Keene, E. 2002. *Beyond the Anarchical Society: Grotius, Colonialism and Order in World Politics*. Cambridge: Cambridge University Press.

Linklater, A. 2001. Rationalism. Pp. 103–28 in Burchill et al. 2001.

—— and Suganami, H. 2006. *The English School of International Relations: A Contemporary Assessment*. Cambridge: Cambridge University Press.

Little, R. 2000. The English School's contribution to the study of international relations. *European Journal of International Relations*, 6: 395–422.

Mearsheimer, J. J. 2005. E. H. Carr vs. idealism: the battle rages on. *International Relations*, 19: 139–52.

MacMillan, J. and Linklater, A. 1995. *Boundaries in Question: New Directions in International Relations*. London: Continuum.

Osiander, A. 1994. *The States System of Europe, 1640–1990: Peacemaking and the Conditions of International Stability*. Oxford: Oxford University Press.

Rae, H. 2002. *State Identities and the Homogenisation of Peoples*. Cambridge: Cambridge University Press.

Reus-Smit, C. 1999. *The Moral Purpose of the State: Culture, Social Identity, and Institutional Rationality in International Relations*. Princeton, NJ: Princeton University Press.

—— 2002. Imagining society: constructivism and the English School. *British Journal of Politics and International Relations*, 4: 487–509.

—— 2005. The constructivist challenge after September 11. Pp 81–95 in *International Society and its Critics*, ed. A. J. Bellamy. Oxford: Oxford University Press.

Risse, T. and Sikkink, K. 1999. The socialization of human rights norms into domestic practices: introduction. Pp. 1–38 in Risse, Ropp, and Sikkink 1999.

—— Ropp, S. C., and Sikkink, K. (eds.) 1999. *The Power of Human Rights: International Norms and Domestic Change*. Cambridge: Cambridge University Press.

Shapcott, R. 2004. IR as practical philosophy: defining a "classical approach." *British Journal of Politics and International Relations*, 6: 271–91.

Smith, S. 1987. Paradigm dominance in international relations: the development of international relations as a social science. *Millennium: Journal of International Studies*, 16: 189–206.

Vigezzi, B. 2005. *The British Committee on the Theory of International Politics 1945–1985: The Rediscovery of History*. Milan: Edizioni Unicopli.

Vincent, R. J. 1986. *Human Rights and International Relations*. Cambridge: Cambridge University Press.

Wæver, O. 1998. Four meanings of international society: a trans-atlantic dialogue. Pp. 80–144 in *International Society and the Development of International Relations Theory*, ed. B. A. Roberson. London: Pinter.

Watson, A. 1992. *The Evolution of International Society: A Comparative Historical Analysis*. London: Routledge.

Welsh, J. M. 1995. *Edmund Burke and International Relations: The Commonwealth of Europe and the Crusade against the French Revolution*. Basingstoke: Macmillan.

WENDT, A. 1999. *Social Theory of International Politics*. Cambridge: Cambridge University Press.

WHEELER, N. J. 2000. *Saving Strangers: Humanitarian Intervention in International Society*. Oxford: Oxford University Press.

WIGHT, M. 1977. *Systems of States*, ed. H. Bull. Leicester: Leicester University Press for the London School of Economics and Political Science.

——1978. *Power Politics*, ed. H. Bull and C. Holbraad. Leicester: Leicester University Press.

——WIGHT, G., and PORTER, B. 1991. *International Theory: The Three Traditions*. Leicester: Leicester University Press for the Royal Institute of International Affairs.

WILSON, P. 1989. The English School of international relations: a reply to Sheila Grader. *Review of International Studies*, 15: 49–58.

FROM INTERNATIONAL RELATIONS TO GLOBAL SOCIETY

MICHAEL BARNETT

KATHRYN SIKKINK

HISTORICALLY speaking, the study of international relations has largely concerned the study of states and the effects of anarchy on their foreign policies, the patterns of their interactions, and the organization of world politics. Over the last several decades worldly developments and theoretical innovations have slowly but surely eroded the gravitational pull of both anarchy and statism in the study of international relations. Although scholars of international relations continue to recognize that the world is organized as a formal anarchy and that states retain considerable power and privileges, they increasingly highlight an international realm where the international structure is defined by material and normative elements, where states share the stage with a multitude of other actors, and where trends in global politics are shaped not only by states but also by this variety of other actors and forces. Simply put, the discipline is moving away from the study of "international relations" and toward the study of the "global society." We use this shift in the name to symbolize a series of transformations in the last twenty years in the discipline regarding what and whom we study, and how and why we study them.

The cumulative effect of these transformations is that the overarching narrative of the field has changed from one of anarchy in a system of states to governance within a global society. Our notion of a global society parallels the arguments of the English School and its notion of world society, particularly the identification of an increasingly dense fabric of international law, norms, and rules that promote forms of association and solidarity, the growing role of an increasingly dense network of state and nonstate actors that are involved in the production and revision of multilayered governance structures, and the movement toward forms of dialogue that are designed to help identify shared values of "humankind" (Buzan 2004; Linklater and Suganami 2006). This shift from "international relations" to "global society" is reflective of several important developments that are the focus of this chapter.

We open with a discussion of the anarchy thematic and what John Agnew (1994) has called "the territorial trap" and survey some of the critical forces that compelled international relations scholars to free themselves from this trap. We then explore the shifts in the what, who, how, and why of the study of international relations. The assumption of anarchy and the territorial trap helped to define the discipline's agenda, fixating on how survival-seeking and self-interested states produce security and pursue wealth and how these states manage to produce cooperation under anarchy. Although these issues remain on the agenda, they increasingly share space with other topics, including "global" issues such as environmental politics and human rights, the sources of international change, the forces that define the identity, interests, and practices of states, and normative international relations and international ethics. A shift in what we study also has affected whom we study. The ecology of international politics is no longer dominated by states and increasingly includes nonstate actors such as nongovernmental organizations, transnational corporations, international organizations (IOs), and transnational networks of all kinds operating alongside states in a reconstituted "global public domain" (Ruggie 2004). Alterations in the ontology of the world polity have also shifted the epistemology of world politics— that is, *how* we study— encouraging scholars to move beyond a narrow conception of the "scientific" enterprise and adopt a diversity of epistemological positions. There has also been a reconsideration of *why* we study global—and not international— politics, a development driven by various factors, including a growing dissatisfaction with theory- and methods-driven research to the exclusion of puzzle-driven research and practical engagement.

This emerging field of global politics is increasingly focused on the study of global governance. Governance can be generically understood as "the maintenance of collective order, the achievement of collective goals, and the collective processes of rule through which order and goals are sought" (Rosenau 2000, 175). The discipline of international relations has always been concerned with issues of governance, venturing from the early twentieth-century study of IOs to the post-Second World War study of integration, transnationalism, international regimes, international institutions, and "governance without government" (Rosenau and Czempiel 1992). Traditionally the study of international governance has focused on how states have established norms, laws, and institutions to help them engage in collective action and create order. Over the last two decades, though, there has been a terminological shift from the study of *international* governance to the study of *global* governance, justified because the purposes of global governance no longer reflect solely the interests of states but now also include other actors, including IOs, transnational corporations, nongovernmental organizations, and new kinds of networks. Global governance is produced through networked relations among different kinds of actors with different kinds of authority and power that are embedded in both formal and informal arrangements. We need to think in more conceptually creative and intellectually diverse ways to understand the production, maintenance, and transformation of the global rules that define the global ends and the means to achieve them. We conclude by considering how governance, rather than anarchy, might be a candidate for narrating the study of international relations.

Our own work draws on and has contributed to constructivist theories of international relations in part because they gave us greater leverage over the changing and fundamentally social character of global relations. Constructivist theory, though, is not a disciplinary panacea, and we are aware of its limitations, the strengths of alternative theories, and the need for theoretical developments and synthesis to address the ongoing challenges of studying global society. Still, our position is deeply influenced by social constructivism, and we believe that it provides some critical intellectual tools that provide insight into both the central changes that have occurred in global relations over the decades and possible futures.

1 GOING GLOBAL

It is widely accepted that the discipline of international relations has undergone something of a sea change. As Brian Schmidt (2002) has forcefully argued, it was organized around the concept of anarchy, shaping the conceptualization of international relations, the boundaries of the field, and its research agenda.[1] International relations became the study of states. In state-centrism's extreme form, the territorial trap (Agnew 1994), international relations carves up the world into mutually exclusive territorial states and the study of international relations becomes the study of relations between these units. States are assumed to have authority over their political space, radiating power from the center to the territorial border, where it comes to a dead halt. This authority over a geographically defined and (mainly) contiguous space is reinforced and underscored by the principle of sovereignty, wherein states

[1] However, William Wohlforth (in *Oxford Handbook of International Relations*, ed. C. Reus-Smit and D. Snidal 2008. Oxford: Oxford University Press) argues that realism can live without the anarchy assumption.

recognize each other's authority over that space and deny any authoritative claims made by those outside the state. Such matters inform the classic differentiation in international relations theory between anarchy, lawlessness, coercion, and particularism on the outside, and hierarchy, legitimate authority, dialogue, and community on the inside. State, territory, and authority became tightly coupled in international relations theory.

The discipline's anarchy narrative shaped a post-Second World War research agenda focused on how self-interested states pursue their security and welfare under a condition of anarchy that makes cooperation desirable but difficult. Under the shadow of the cold war, international relations scholars focused on patterns of war, how states manage their security relations, the impact of the nuclear age, and crisis management. When the once-neglected study of international political economy finally got the attention it deserved, the anarchy narrative shaped the framework employed and questions addressed by international relations scholars: a defining theme was the tension between the logic of capital and the logic of anarchy, how the state was constantly trying to intervene in markets in order to protect the *national* economy and the *national* security, and how the rise of global corporations could undermine the state's autonomy and sovereignty (Gilpin 2003). In the 1980s scholars began to address the question of "cooperation under anarchy" and the conditions under which states might produce sustained forms of coordination and collaboration in various issue areas (Keohane 1984; Oye 1986).

While the anarchy narrative illuminated some problems and issues, it dismissed and obscured many others. There was little attention paid to domestic politics. Ian Clark (1999) calls this "the great divide" in international relations—the presumption that the domestic and the international are distinct spheres that are defined by distinct organizing principles. There was little appreciation of the increasingly rule-bound nature of the decentralized global governance system and the interpenetration of rules in the domestic and international realm. There was little recognition of forms of authority outside the state—that is, disaggregated authority (Rosenau 2000). There was also little attention to important global trends, including the eye-opening development wherein certain regions were becoming more pacific in part because of developments in domestic politics and other regions were becoming undone from the ground up with horrific effects for civilian populations (however, see Buzan 1983).

Beginning in the 1980s, and picking up steam in the 1990s, various scholars from a range of disciplinary perspectives began to take aim at the territorial trap and those theories that were most closely associated with it, namely neorealism and neoliberal institutionalism. This is not the place to revisit the critiques of these theories or retell the rise of constructivism, but it is worth noting two critical dimensions of this development. One was the desire to find an exit option from the territorial trap, as scholars unpacked anarchy (Wendt 1992), sovereignty (Biersteker and Weber 1996), authority (Rosenau and Czempiel 1992), and the bundling of the state, territory, and authority (Ruggie 1992). The other was the failure of existing theories to explain much less predict important international change. Various global changes generated anomalies between existing theories and world developments—most famously and strikingly the remarkably peaceful end of the cold war and the dissolution of the Soviet Union. As Peter Katzenstein (1996) argued, the failure of existing international relations theories to predict let alone contemplate the end of the cold war was to international relations theory what the sinking of the Titanic was to the profession of naval engineering. The next decade of cascading globalization raised further challenges and agitation for new theoretical creativity.

The combination of new kinds of theorizing and rapid global change called into question the accuracy of the very label of international relations. As is well known, international relations was never inter*national* but instead was inter-*state*, but few challenged this sleight of hand. However, events of the 1990s, including globalization, ethno-national conflict, and identity politics, made scholars more aware that the term international politics obscured more than it illuminated. Scholars became more cognizant of transnational networks, relations, and associations that were both affecting inter-state relations and helping to define the very constitution of global society. For many, the label of international relations was no longer a convenient shorthand but was now a contrivance that hindered analysis. Accordingly, many went in search of labels that were more accurate representations of the subject, including international studies and global studies. Although the label of international relations has had clear staying power, scholars of international relations have gone global as they have become more comfortable with operating outside the territorial trap.

One last point. The territorial trap did not have the same hold on students of the international relations of the Third World as it did on students of the global North because the attending analytical assumptions were so glaringly distant from empirical reality. Hierarchy and not anarchy seemed to be the defining organizing principle. Colonialism's end did not transform North–South relations from hierarchy to anarchy (and equality) as economic, security, and political structures continued to place Third World states in a subordinate position, to challenge their authority in various domains, and to create a major chasm between their formal sovereignty and their effective sovereignty. Relatedly, the state in the global North was an accomplishment, while in the global South it was a project, needing to solidify its territorial base, to monopolize the means of coercion, and to eliminate all other rivals to its authority. In order to capture this reality, scholars began to modify their understandings of Third World states, calling them shadow, alien, weak, artificial, and quasi. Scholars of the global South developed a range of theories—including dependency, postcolonial, world-systems, and empire; for them, international relations was always global. Perhaps because Third World scholars saw international hierarchy instead of anarchy, they remained more committed to strengthening and defending sovereignty as a political project and were less likely to celebrate transnational processes that threatened it. Thus, for example, the benefits of global civil society have often been received with more skepticism in the global South than among critical international relations scholars in the North.

2 THE WHAT, WHO, HOW, AND WHY OF GLOBAL SOCIETY

2.1 What Do We Study?

Once scholars began to relax the assumption of anarchy and move beyond state-centrism, a whole new world became visible. There were two defining developments (a third—whom we study—will be discussed below). The first was the rise of topics other than classical security and international political economy. Scholars began to study a range of other issues, including human rights, the environment, gender, culture, religion, democracy, and law. And, even when scholars remained focused on political economy and security, they tracked very different features. The study of political economy underwent a rapid transformation in response to the growing observation that globalization was producing a qualitative shift in the global organization of capitalism, the character of the state and state–society relations, and international economic relations.

Historically, scholars of security focused on the state and inter-state relations—following the assumption that the object of security was the state (which represented the national community) and that the principal threat to the state's (and thus the "nation's") security was from another state. With the end of the cold war, however, there was a growing willingness by scholars to examine the meaning and practice of security (Katzenstein 1996). Whereas once security meant the security of the state, increasingly the object of security was the group or the individual, captured by the increasing circulation of the concept of human security. Shifting the object of security implied a re-examination of what constituted a threat. The state, once viewed as a unit of protection, was increasingly recognized as a principal source of insecurity in many parts of the world (Buzan 1983). In fact, in the twentieth century more individuals were killed by their own governments than in all international wars combined. The fact that states were failing in their responsibilities to protect their citizens implied that the study of human rights is related to security and not a marginal subfield that is irrelevant to the "real" issues of international relations. Individuals, however, were not only passive victims of their governments; they were also increasingly active participants in the creation of new human rights rules and institutions, including some institutions that allowed these individuals to bring claims against their own government. Scholars and policy-makers called attention to "nontraditional" security threats such as famines, environmental degradation, and health epidemics, in some regions. In other regions, international relations scholars pointed out that states had established pacific relations and, importantly, no longer expected or prepared for war (Adler and Barnett 1998).

Another theoretical and empirical breakthrough was a growing recognition of the presence and impact of international normative structures. The individualism and materialism of the dominant theories presented international life as absent of any sort of sociality. In reaction to these axioms and various global developments, many scholars argued that power and interest did not exhaust explanations for global outcomes and change, and developed conceptions of normative structures that imagined how they might shape the state's identity, interests, and what counts as legitimate action. Now that international relations scholars were recognizing that global politics has a sociality, it was possible to resurrect once-banished concepts that are inextricably bound up with all political orders. Two concepts, in particular, are critical for the study of global society: legitimacy and authority.

Both legitimacy and authority are notoriously slippery concepts, difficult to define and measure, and inextricably related to theories of social control and thus bound up with questions of power. For these reasons international relations scholars have resisted them, only to be forced to wrestle, once again, with their causal importance, especially in the areas of compliance, cooperation, and governance. States and nonstate actors agree to be bound by rules, not only because the powerful impose them or because of self-interest, but also because they believe those rules to be legitimate—that is, they deserve to be obeyed (Kratochwil and Ruggie 1986; Hurd 1999; 2007; Bukovansky 2002; Clark 2005). To the extent that actors confer legitimacy on rules and institutions, they gain authority—thus the oft-heard phrase "legitimate authority." Scholars increasingly recognized that actors other than states have forms of legitimate authority in global society and that such authority derives from a variety of sources, including expertise. The existence of different kinds of authority conferred on different kinds of actors undermines the anarchy narrative and presumption that a distinguishing characteristic of the international sphere is that authority is monopolized by the sovereign state. IOs have become particularly important authorities in their own right, often working with states and nongovernmental actors in new hybridized forms of authority (Barnett and Finnemore 2004; Conca 2005).

A related and somewhat belated development is a growing interest in international normative theory and international ethics. The "scientific" study of international relations and normative international relations went their separate ways decades ago, lived parallel lives, and found little opportunity or incentive to cross-fertilize (Price 2008; Reus-Smit 2008). However, this segregation is beginning to break down for various reasons. Norms are defined as standards of appropriate behavior and thus, to study norms empirically, constructivists had to grapple with how and why actors come to believe certain behavior is appropriate or legitimate (Finnemore and Sikkink 1998). This led to a small and growing empirical investigation of international ethics, including studies of the changing ethical metrics that actors use to judge what counts as legitimate action and of the causes and consequences of the institutionalization of ethics in international arrangements. Constructivist investigations of state policies and of international society argue that they are shaped by deep beliefs, including ethical or moral beliefs about the purpose of the state, humanitarianism, and justice (Lumsdaine 1993; Reus-Smit 1997).

Although some of the constructivist research on norms demonstrated the importance of norms and the possibilities for moral change in world politics, most constructivists did not initially articulate their own normative or prescriptive position of those changes to be advocated (Price 2008). With the exception of a handful of scholars interested in questions of international political theory, including forms of global cosmopolitanism, communitarianism, and responsibility (Held 1995; Linklater 1998), scholars were often more committed to critiquing implicit notions of progress in many processes in global society than in articulating their own ethical or normative visions.

The study of global governance reflects these changes in the study of world politics. Whereas this was once limited to how states with pre-existing interests create norms, rules, laws, and institutions to regulate their relations, there have been a number of critical additions in the recent past. First, there is a greater interest in the social construction of what is to be governed—that is, how a problem becomes defined and gets placed on the agenda. Moreover, there is a growing consideration of how international and domestic structures, working through conceptions of self and logics of appropriateness, shape governance structures. The study of multilateralism, for instance, now includes a consideration of how national identity shapes the emergence of the multilateral form and then how the multilateral form came to be viewed as legitimate (Ruggie 1993). In addition to a rational design of institutions, there can also be a "sociological" design that incorporates logics of legitimation (Wendt 2001). There is also a growing desire to bring classical normative questions such as fairness, justice, accountability, and representation to bear on the study of governance and the sources of legitimacy (Kapstein 2005; 2006). Although political theorists have long worried about democracy in an age of internationalization (Held 1995), they are now joined by many international relations theorists who are focusing attention on questions of accountability, power, and legitimacy (Slaughter 2004; Grant and Keohane 2005; Hurd 2007).

2.2 Whom Do We Study?

What we study obviously relates to whom we study. International relations scholars justify the state-centric focus of the discipline on the grounds that nonstate actors either are captured by states or are causally irrelevant. This position, in our view, is now an embattled orthodoxy because states alone cannot account for important international outcomes or the very fabric of global politics.

Two developments deserve mention. The first is growing attention to domestic politics, and in particular to domestic regime type, as a significant factor for explaining global outcomes. Building on microeconomic analytics, one version of liberal theory examined how individuals form groups to shape the state's foreign policies (Slaughter 1995; Moravcsik 1997). Two-level game models demonstrated the importance of analyzing the interaction between domestic and international politics in order to understand inter-state negotiations, treaties, and policy collaboration. Having established the empirical regularity that democracies do not wage war with other democracies, scholars began to focus on the characteristics of democracies that might generate this unexpected outcome. Neoliberal institutionalists also increasingly turned their attention to domestic politics, both for models of how to study the global and for interactive models that helped incorporate domestic politics in efforts to understand global outcomes (Milner 1991). Constructivists, too, contributed to the growing interest in the relationship between domestic and international structures (Risse-Kappen 1995). We are now far beyond worrying about committing the sin of reductionism and are prepared to pick up the challenge of examining the relationship between these different "levels" (Gourevitch 2002). As scholars answer the challenge, though, they should be wary of falling back into the territorial trap—that is, treating the "domestic" and the "international" as necessarily ontologically distinct realms— and should consider their interrelationship and co-constitution.

Another important development is the growing awareness of the wider range of actors that are shaping global relations. Two kinds of actors are receiving increased attention precisely because of their causal importance and their perceived centrality to global governance—IOs and transnational actors. Although the study of IOs is almost as old as the discipline of international relations, it has fallen in and out of theoretical favor over the decades (this section draws heavily from Barnett and Finnemore 2007). The post-First World War emergence of the discipline of international relations included considerable attention to IOs; after the Second World War there was continuing interest in IOs because of the experiments in regional integration in Europe and postwar IO-building. Although international relations scholars lost interest in IOs during the 1970s and 1980s, a very powerful line of argument emerged concerning the conditions under which states will establish international institutions and the functions that they assign to them (Keohane 1984). Briefly, states create and delegate critical tasks to international institutions because they can provide essential functions such as providing public goods, collecting information, establishing credible commitments, monitoring agreements, and generally helping states overcome problems associated with collective action and enhancing collective welfare.

While this institutionalist perspective generates important insights into issues of international governance, its statism and functionalism obscure important features. First, the functionalist treatment of international institutions and IOs reduced them to technical accomplishments, slighting their political character and the political work they do. It also presumes that the only interesting or important functions that IOs might perform are those that facilitate cooperation and resolve problems of interdependent choice. Secondly, the statism of many contemporary treatments of IOs reduced them to mere tools of states, akin to how pluralists treated the state. IOs are mechanisms or arenas through which others (usually states) act. The regimes literature is particularly clear on this point. Regimes are not purposive actors. IOs are thus passive structures; states are the agents who exercise power in this view.

New studies of IOs argued that they have authority, autonomy, and agency, and are political creatures that have effects similar to the effects of other authority-bearing actors, including states. The impact of IOs is not limited to the functions assigned to them by states and the regulation of already existing state interests. IOs also construct the social world in which cooperation and choice take place. They help to define the issues that need to be governed and propose the means by which governance should occur (Barnett and Finnemore 2004). They help define the interests that states and other actors have, not only as a forum where persuasion takes place, but also as an actor that is engaged in processes of socialization (Checkel 2005). In fact, the growing recognition that IOs might have authority and power has encouraged scholars to worry that runaway IOs might become modern-day Frankensteins, where the inventors are no longer able to control their creation. Consequently, there is now a growing interest in what happens when decisional authority is scaled up to IOs that have more autonomy and more power than ever before; the issue is not only effectiveness but also legitimacy and accountability (Barnett and Finnemore 2004; Grant and Keohane 2005).

There has also been a burgeoning study of transnational relations. Similar to the study of IOs, the study of transnationalism had an earlier moment in the sun, faded in the shadow of state-centrism, and has now returned with a burst of energy. Robert Keohane and Joseph Nye (1972) introduced the study of transnational politics in the early 1970s, but that particular research agenda did not prosper in the short term, with the exception of some increased attention to transnational corporations in world politics. Ernst Haas and John Ruggie explored the role of various kinds of knowledge communities and transnational networks for understanding forms of international change and cooperation (Ruggie et al. 2005). These literatures proved to be ahead of their time.

By the early 1990s, though, international relations scholars began to rediscover transnationalism and transnational actors. One of the first important formulations was the work on epistemic communities, which focused on how transnationally connected experts with shared technical knowledge could influence state policy in situations of high complexity and uncertainty (Adler and Haas 1992; Haas 1992). A new literature on transnational advocacy networks, global civil society, and transnational social movements identified these actors as participants in global politics and documented their ability to create norms and contribute to regime formation and implementation (Sikkink 1993; Keck and Sikkink 1998; Price 1998; 2003; Thomas 2000; Tarrow 2005). In contrast to epistemic communities that were formed around scientific knowledge and expertise, these groups formed primarily around shared principled ideas. In either case, transnational communities could create new issue areas, project these issues into the international arena, prod states to "discover" their interests, identify new policy options, and help to constitute an independent global public sphere or public domain apart from the system of states (Wapner 1995; Ruggie 2004).

There was generally a "liberal" bias in much of the post-1990s research on transnationalism—that is, the assumption that these developments are desirable and help to pluralize power and advance basic human freedoms. A second wave of literatures looked at the "dark side" of transnationalism and pointed to the problematic nature of global civil society, its lack of autonomy from the world-views and funding sources of dominant states in the North, and its problems of accountability and representation. Another strand examines so-called dark networks including terrorist groups and criminal networks around drugs and trafficking (Kahler 2007). Regardless of whether one considers transnationalism, on balance, a good or a problematic development, there is general agreement that transnational actors can influence the course of global affairs.

A distinguishing characteristic of many of these transnational actors is that they are organized in network forms.[2] That is, while states and IOs are organized around hierarchies and have bureaucratic properties, networks are characterized by voluntary, reciprocal, and horizontal patterns of communication and exchange (Keck and Sikkink 1998). Organizational theorist Walter Powell calls them a third mode of organization, distinctly different from markets and hierarchy. "Networks are 'lighter on their feet' than hierarchy," and are "particularly apt for circumstances in which there is a need for efficient, reliable information" (Powell 1990, 303–4). International relations theorists are only now beginning to "see" network as an alternative form of organization, assess its presence, prominence, and causal importance in world affairs, and consider its normative implications. The dominant forms of communication in global politics (email and the World Wide Web) have networked forms that are increasingly beyond the complete control of states. Terrorist organizations are viewed as being organized around networks, making them more difficult for states to monitor, locate, and incarcerate. Global corporations are discovering and adopting network forms of organization.

Networks have various positive and negative attributes. They have flexibility, speed, informality, a greater chance for increasing multiple views, and perhaps even enhanced implementation capacities (Slaughter 2004; Weber 2004). Yet they lack "a legitimate organizational authority to arbitrate and resolve disputes" (Podolny and Page 1998); in short, they cannot provide the legitimate authority necessary for full-fledged global governance. Nevertheless, increasingly hybrid network forms of governance are emerging that may combine state and nonstate actors to carry out key governance tasks.

Finally, there is perhaps no more persuasive evidence of the rise of global society than the ability of nonstate actors and even individuals to participate directly in global politics without being mediated by the state. This ability finds formal recognition in human rights regimes, where increasingly individuals can bring claims against their own state to international human rights institutions, and where individuals can now be held accountable for acts (crimes against humanity or genocide) that previously were attributed to states. The rise of individual criminal accountability in the global system, as evidenced in the increase in human rights trials, can thus be seen as a

---

[2] Not all transnational actors are organized in networks (the Vatican is hierarchical, for example) and not all networks are made up of nonstate actors. As Ann-Marie Slaughter (2004) observes, intergovernmental relations also frequently use network forms of interaction.

broader metaphor for the emergence of individuals as direct participants in global society. Three decades ago Hedley Bull (1977, 152) recognized as much when he wrote that "if the rights of each man can be asserted on the world political stage over and against the claims of the state, and his duties proclaimed irrespective of his position as a servant or citizen of that state ... The way is left open for a subversion of the society of sovereign states on behalf of the alternative organizing principle of cosmopolitan community." Contrary to some scholars of global civil society, we do not argue that a cosmopolitan community has emerged, but we would echo Bull's assertions that such changes imply that we have moved well beyond a global society composed only of sovereign states.

2.3 How Do We Study?

What and whom we study necessarily leads to a consideration of how we study. There is now greater epistemological eclecticism and methodological diversity than ever before. While there are various reasons for growing epistemological diversity, arguably most important was the recognition of the underlying social character of international relations. An important early contribution to this awareness was Friedrich Kratochwil and Ruggie's observation (1986) regarding the disconnect between epistemology and the study of international regimes. They argued that, while the very definition of regimes involves inherently intersubjective norms and principles, the prevailing positivist epistemology of international relations made it impossible to explain, assess, or capture the social aspect of life.

A genuinely *social* science cannot model itself only after the natural sciences; international relations scholars of a global society must embrace epistemologies that are appropriate to the task. There is no single path. Some have gravitated toward interpretative social science, frequently drawing from Max Weber and other classical sociological theorists, to understand how actors give significance and meaning to their actions and the intersubjective understandings that frequently constitute social action. Others have gravitated toward forms of scientific realism and theories of discourse, hoping to identify broad patterns of action and inaction. In this regard, there is an interest in "conditions of possibility," what makes possible certain action, what alternatives are seen as simply correct without any reflection or discussion, and which alternatives are seen as unthinkable (Wight 2006). In this important sense, post-positivist scholars operate with a much broader understanding of causality than do positivist scholars; underlying, unobservable structures that make some action possible, difficult, or unimaginable do important explanatory work.

Alongside an increasing diversity of epistemological positions is an increasing array of methodologies. The use of alternative methodologies to address the same questions has deepened our theoretical understanding and enhanced our empirical analysis. Consider two prominent areas in the study of global governance. The first is compliance. Behavioral approaches to the study of norms typically attempt to measure behavioral conformity with norms that are written in formal treaties and agreements

(Simmons 2000; Raustalia and Slaughter 2002). Instances of compliance or noncompliance, in other words, are defined by the scholar as deviations from some measure developed by the analyst of what constitute behavior consistent with expectations codified in the agreement. Interpretative approaches go beyond behavior. They aspire to recover how actors interpret what counts as compliance and defection; whether there is an intersubjective understanding of what compliance demands in particular social situations; the kinds of justifications that are used for acts of noncompliance; and the motivations and reasons that actors give for compliance and noncompliance (Kratochwil and Ruggie 1986; Koh 1997; Kingsbury 1998).

Another area is the study of legitimacy. Certainly any international order that has a modicum of legitimacy will be reflected in behavior that is consistent with the international norms that define that order. Consequently, there should be behavioral effects, effects that can be observed and captured through comparative statics. In this regard, claims about the increasing or decreasing legitimacy of an IO, treaty, or agreement should be evident not only in rates of compliance but also with changes in the willingness of states to rally to its defense, to punish those who violate its norms, and to provide various kinds of resources (Clark 2005; Clark and Reus-Smit 2007). Yet we should also want to understand why legitimacy is conferred, what are the contests over what constitutes a legitimate international order, and what sorts of practices are considered to be appropriate as a consequence.

Not only are particular substantive areas benefiting from the application of diverse methodological approaches, but individual scholars are demonstrating greater agility as they are using multimethod approaches. Increasingly, some scholars who use quantitative methods are asked to supplement their large-n studies with well-selected cases, while qualitative scholars are also turning to some quantitative approaches or formal models. The reason for this development is the desire to balance the strengths and weaknesses of each approach: Large-n studies are very good at helping to determine broad patterns across space and time, but well-designed case studies can be essential for identifying and exploring the causal mechanisms that account for the relationship between independent and dependent variables.

2.4 Why Do We Study?

The what, who, and how raise fundamental issues regarding the why we study global politics. Or, more precisely, why *should* we study world politics? A vibrant discipline of international relations depends on the presence of a community of scholars who are collectively engaged in providing creative explanations and innovative insights into concerns of global importance that have potential relevance beyond that scholarly community. Theory development and methodological innovation is central to this task, but sometimes international relations theorists have become enamored with theory and method for their own sake, turning means into ends. This can lead to sterile paradigm wars and disengagement from the problems and practices of global relations. As Katzenstein and Rudra Sil (in *Oxford Handbook of International Relations*, ed. C. Reus-Smit and D. Snidal 2008. Oxford: Oxford University Press) argue, we should judge progress in international relations by both the "quality and scope of dialogue among social scientists and the proximity of this dialogue to socially important normative and policy issues."

Most of us got into this business to explore and explain particular puzzles. We are motivated by the need to understand and explain developments and changes in global politics and to keep up with the world that often surprises and shocks us. In particular, we are motivated by the need to understand and explain change in global society. As early as 1983, Ruggie (1983) pointed to realism's inability to explain change as its greatest weakness. He argued that realism was unable to explain key changes in the international system because it was missing both a dimension of change and a determinant of change. Other authors have claimed that realism has likewise been unable to explain the most important changes in the late twentieth and early twenty-first centuries, in particular, the consolidation of the European Union, the end of the cold war, the emergence of the war of terror, and the explosion of IOs, international law, and networks. New theories have made some important contributions to understanding specific changes in global society, but have not yet provided a comprehensive theory of change. An increasingly common position is to reject the possibility of a grand theoretical synthesis. In this respect, we concur with Katzenstein and Sil (in *Oxford Handbook of International Relations*, ed. C. Reus-Smit and D. Snidal 2008. Oxford: Oxford University Press) that a much more promising avenue is to develop eclectic theorizing that can be used to explain worldly problems with an eye toward how such eclecticism might or might not contribute to broader theoretical arguments.

Secondly, many of us decided on a career in international relations not only because we wanted to observe and explain from a cool distance but also because we hoped our knowledge might improve the conduct and character of global politics. The social sciences were founded with the expectation that they could solve societal problems and define the "public good." The field of international relations emerged from this tradition and with the desire to develop a scientific and rigorous study of war in order to help pacify a violent world. There is a long story about how, why, and when the social sciences largely abandoned the idea of practical engagement, a story that revolves around the quest for objectivity and the belief that practical engagement would pollute a pure science, the obsession with theory-building and methods, the desire to train graduate students for life in the academy and to forgo the idea of educating young professionals who might have a career in the public and nonprofit sectors (Anderson 2005). The consequence is that scholars are no longer actively engaged in practical politics. To be sure, there are moments when scholars attempt to comment on the controversies of the day in various forums, but the overall incentive structure is to orient scholars toward the community of scholars rather than toward policy-relevant research.

International relations scholars need to think through how to connect their theories and knowledge to practical action, and one possibility concerns a more substantial interest in marrying international ethics to empirical analysis. Because of its roots in critical theory and critical social science, critical international relations theory has always been attentive to the relationship between theory and praxis, particularly regarding how theory can lead to emancipation. For many, Robert Cox's (1981) distinction between a critical theory that unmasks relations of power with the hopes of changing them and problem-solving theory that takes the world as it is, has been a touchpoint. We are very sympathetic to the importance of attempting to uncover the structures that produce forms of oppression and hinder the ability of individuals to control their fates. However, this formulation has encouraged many who associate themselves with critical international relations theory to dismiss out-of-hand political interventions that are deemed insufficiently radical. But what, precisely, is ethically problematic with an engagement that aspires to make small but consequential changes in the lives of others? Is a practical politics that both makes small improvements and works toward more thoroughgoing change impossible? Where is the evidence that radical change has led to radical emancipation?[3]

The empirical engagement with ethics underscores that moral judgment requires evaluation not just of principles but also of consequences. To answer the question "what to do," we need to ask not just "what is right" but also "what may work" to bring about outcomes consistent with our principles.[4] We study the world in part because we believe that our research does yield information about the consequences of human action that may be important for ethical judgment and for action in the world. Resolving empirical questions about consequences is important for making normative judgments about desirable policies. It is not only a question of determining which policies are good and bad, but rather specifying the conditions under which different policies can lead to better or worse outcomes.

Because the theorizing about consequences is an inherently comparative and empirical enterprise, empirically oriented scholars can make an important contribution (Nye 1986; Sikkink 2008). Thus ethical judgment requires the best empirical research we can do, using all the research tools at our disposal. The research will often involve difficult counterfactuals, complex research designs, and demanding evidence. Well-intentioned researchers will disagree about results. But we can improve our discussions by being more explicit about our processes of ethical reasoning and by relating our research findings more explicitly to their normative implications.

A paradigm-driven or methods-mad discipline is an intellectual and professional dead end because it allows scholars to feel satisfied with the resulting intellectual fragmentation and detachment from the world. There are many possible paths for reattaching these severed ties, and several of the chapters in this volume suggest different possibilities for greater dialogue among scholars and engagement with practical politics. Not every scholar needs to be equally engaged in dialogue or practical politics, and there are reasons to foster an intellectual division of labor. But such a division needs to be situated in the context of a general agreement that

---

[3] We recognize that there are potential links to pragmatism, especially pragmatism's interest in engagement with practical problems and in marrying forms of critical theory with social science methods, but we will leave it to others more conversant with pragmatism to draw the connections.

[4] We are indebted to Richard Price for this particular formulation.

part of the responsibility that members of the community have to each other (and to the pursuit of greater understanding about the world) is to listen carefully and openly to alternative arguments and perspectives and then to consider how such perspectives might foster theoretical development, empirical analysis, and practical action.

3 Conclusion: From Anarchy to Global Governance?

All disciplines, if they are to have any coherence whatsoever, must have an overarching narrative. The anarchy thematic has helped to generate coherence for the discipline of international relations. It provided a common narrative that focused on states as actors that were struggling to maintain their security and generate wealth in an inhospitable environment. It helped to define the boundaries of the field and distinguish the study of international relations from the study of comparative politics. It focused scholarly attention on a manageable set of issues that could be subjected to theoretical emendation and empirical analysis. It provided a coherent account of the discipline that could be passed down from one generation to the next. The anarchy thematic served various useful functions.

Yet this singular narrative also bred theoretical, intellectual, and empirical myopia. Theories that escaped the territorial trap were marginalized or ostracized on various grounds, including the view that they were not contributing to the core debates in the field. Students were advised against certain dissertation topics (for example, human rights, gender) because it would marginalize them in the field. At issue were not only diversity for diversity's sake but also the ability to construct alternative theories that had the capacity to provide new insights into the existing research agendas and identify new topics for research. The pluralization of the discipline did not occur because the mainstream digested the ethos of deliberative democracy, but rather because of theoretical shortcomings, empirical anomalies, and new items on the global agenda that demanded new approaches. Consequently, many scholars who once believed that they were on the outside of the discipline looking in rejoiced at the decline of the anarchy thematic and the demise of the territorial trap.

This growing diversity, however welcome, also risks generating disciplinary fragmentation, because there no longer exists a single, overarching story. We hesitate to propose an alternative narrative precisely because there is no magical formulation that can avoid prematurely foreclosing diverse perspectives and voices. However, the concept of governance has been emerging as a worthy alternative to anarchy because of its ability to interrogate enduring, heretofore neglected, and emerging issues in the theory and practice of international relations. Governance is about how actors work together to maintain order and achieve collective goals. Accordingly, the study of global governance is ultimately concerned with how rules are created, produced, sustained, and refined, how these rules help define the purpose of collective action, and how these rules control the activities of international, transnational, and increasingly domestic action.

A narrative of global governance, then, would have to consider both centralized and decentralized forms of governance. International relations scholars have tended to focus on centralized rules, particularly those that exist in inter-state agreements, treaties, and conventions. But we must become more aware of the different kinds of organizational forms and architectures through which global governance occurs. In particular, we must be attentive to the possibility of governance through decentralized rule, including governance through networks that link the public and private realms (Chimni 2004; Ruggie 2004). This suggests that we focus attention less on specific actors, such as specific IOs, and more on "rule systems" (Rosenau 2000) and often on multilayered structures where governance actually occurs (Conca 2005; Khagram 2005).

Global governance has evolved from a state-dominated affair to include a panoply of actors (even as states retain considerable privileges and prerogatives). Global rule-making is increasingly produced by private authorities such as global corporations and bond-rating agencies, transnational actors such as citizens' movements and indigenous groups, IOs such as the United Nations High Commissioner for Refugees, and nongovernmental organizations such as Doctors without Borders. In general, states do not exhaust the mechanisms of reproduction or transformation, and by stalking states we overlook other suspects that are the source and governor of international change.

Any consideration of global governance must necessarily be concerned not only with collective action and international cooperation but also with questions of power. But to see the power in global governance requires seeing power along its multiple dimensions, including compulsory power, the direct control of one actor over another; institutional power, the control actors exercise indirectly over others through diffuse institutional arrangements; structural power, the structural constitution of subject's capacities; and productive power, the discursive production of subjectivity. These different conceptualizations provide different answers to the fundamental question—when and in what respects are actors able to control their own fate?—and illuminate different forms of power in global governance (Barnett and Duvall 2005).

The narrative of global governance must also marry the theoretical and the normative. Indeed, much of the recent literature on global governance has moved from a consideration of the need for governance in order to enhance collective action and minimize market failures (all implicitly desirable outcomes) to a more thoroughgoing consideration of the relationship between the different forms of governance and their relationship to basic issues such as legitimacy, accountability, representation, and democracy. For instance, some forms of governance might be effective but illegitimate, and, if they are viewed by peoples as illegitimate, then they might be inherently unstable. Other forms may be legitimate but ineffective. This has led scholars to posit the possibility of alternative governance forms that can produce both effective and legitimate outcomes, a sterling instance in which theoretical and empirical analysis is married to practical politics.

In summary, we have argued that international relations is now a discipline focused on the governance of a global society. This has transformed whom, what, how, and why we study international politics. We now study a wider range of both public and private actors, recognizing that such actors both are engaged in governance tasks and, at times, embody legitimate authority. Rather than engaging in sterile struggles over paradigms and methods, we will need to use all the theoretical and methodological tools at our disposal to capture the complex and social nature of global society and global governance. These tools need to be capable of helping scholars understand processes and sources of global change, not only to explain the dynamics of global society, but also to permit scholars to engage more directly in helping shape the direction of that change.

References

ADLER, E. and BARNETT, M. (eds.) 1998. *Security Communities*. Cambridge: Cambridge University Press.

—— and HAAS, P. 1992. Conclusion: epistemic communities, world order, and the creation of a reflective research program. *International Organization*, 46: 367–90.

AGNEW, J. 1994. The territorial trap: the geographical assumptions of international relations theory. *Review of International Political Economy*, 1: 53–80.

ANDERSON, L. 2005. *Pursuing Truth, Exercising Power: Social Science and Public Policy in the Twenty-First Century*. New York: Columbia University Press.

BARNETT, M. and DUVALL, R. (eds.) 2005. *Power in Global Governance*. New York: Cambridge University Press.

—— and FINNEMORE, M. 2004. *Rules for the World: International Organizations in Global Politics*. Ithaca, NY: Cornell University Press.

———— 2007. Political approaches. Pp. 41–57 in *The Oxford Handbook on the United Nations*, ed. T. G. Weiss and S. Daws. Oxford: Oxford University Press.

BIERSTEKER, T. and WEBER, C. (eds.) 1996. *State Sovereignty as Social Construct*. Cambridge: Cambridge University Press.

BUKOVANSKY, M. 2002. *Legitimacy and Power Politics: The American and French Revolutions in International Political Culture*. Princeton, NJ: Princeton University Press.

BULL, H. 1977. *The Anarchical Society: A Study of Order in World Politics*. London: Macmillan.

BUZAN, B. 1983. *People, States, and Fear: The National Security Problem in International Relations*. Columbia: University of South Carolina Press.

—— 2004. *From International to World Society? English School Theory and Social Structure of Globalisation*. Cambridge: Cambridge University Press.

CHECKEL, J. 2005. International institutions and socialization in Europe: introduction and framework. *International Organization*, 59: 801–26.

CHIMNI, B. S. 2004. International institutions today: an imperial global state in the making. *European Journal of International Law*, 15: 1–37.

CLARK, I. 1999. *Globalization and International Relations Theory*. Oxford: Oxford University Press.

—— 2005. *Legitimacy in International Society*. New York: Oxford University Press.

—— and REUS-SMIT, C. (eds.) 2007. Resolving international crises of legitimacy, special issue. *International Politics*, 44: 153–339.

CONCA, K. 2005. Old states in new bottles? The hybridization of authority in global environmental governance. Pp. 181–206 in *The State and the Global Ecological Crisis*, ed. J. Barry and R. Eckersley. Boston: MIT Press.

COX, R. 1981. Social forces, states and world orders: beyond international relations theory. *Millennium: Journal of International Studies*, 10: 126–55.

FINNEMORE, M. and SIKKINK, K. 1998. International norm dynamics and political change. Pp. 247–78 in *Exploration and Contestation in the Study of World Politics*, ed. P. Katzenstein, R. Keohane, and S. Krasner. Cambridge, Mass.: MIT Press.

GILPIN, R. 2003. *Global Political Economy: Understanding the International Economic Order*. Princeton, NJ: Princeton University Press.

GOUREVITCH, P. 2002. Domestic politics and international relations. Pp. 309–28 in *Handbook of International Relations*, ed. W. Carlsnaes, T. Risse, and B. Simmons. Thousand Oaks, Calif.: Sage.

GRANT, R. and KEOHANE, R. O. 2005. Accountability and abuses of power in world politics. *American Political Science Review*, 99: 29–43.

HAAS, P. 1992. Introduction: epistemic communities and international policy coordination. *International Organization*, 46: 1–35.

HELD, D. 1995. *Democracy and the Global Order: From the Modern State to Cosmopolitan Governance*. Stanford, Calif.: Stanford University Press.

HURD, I. 1999. Legitimacy and authority in international politics. *International Organization*, 53: 379–408.

—— 2007. *After Anarchy: Legitimacy and Power in the United Nations Security Council*. Princeton, NJ: Princeton University Press.

KAHLER, M. 2007. Political networks: power, legitimacy and governance. Unpublished typescript.

KAPSTEIN, E. 2005. Power, fairness, and the global economy. Pp. 80–101 in Barnett and Duvall 2005.

—— 2006. *Economic Justice in an Unfair World: Toward a Level Playing Field*. Princeton, NJ: Princeton University Press.

KATZENSTEIN, P. (ed.) 1996. *The Culture of National Security: Norms and Identity in World Politics*. New York: Columbia University Press.

KECK, M. and SIKKINK, K. 1998. *Activists beyond Borders: Advocacy Networks in International Politics*. Ithaca, NY: Cornell University Press.

KEOHANE, R. O. 1984. *After Hegemony: Cooperation and Discord in the World Political Economy*. Princeton, NJ: Princeton University Press.

—— and NYE, J. S. (eds.) 1972. *Transnational Relations and World Politics*. Cambridge, Mass.: Harvard University Press.

KHAGRAM, S. 2005. *Dams and Development: Transnational Struggles for Water and Power*. New York: Oxford University Press.

KOH, H. 1997. Why do nations obey international law? *Yale Law Journal*, 106: 2599–659.

KINGSBURY, B. 1998. The concept of compliance as a function of competing conceptions of international law. *Michigan Journal of International Law*, 19: 345–72.

KRATOCHWIL, F. and RUGGIE, J. 1986. International organization: a state of the art on an art of the state. *International Organization*, 40: 753–75.

LINKLATER, A. 1998. *The Transformation of Political Community: Ethical Foundations of the Post-Westphalian Era*. Cambridge: Polity.

—— and SUGANAMI, H. 2006. *The English School of International Relations: A Contemporary Assessment*. New York: Cambridge University Press.

LUMSDAINE, D. H. 1993. *Moral Vision in International Politics: The Foreign Aid Regime, 1949–1999*. Princeton, NJ: Princeton University Press.

MILNER, H. 1991. The assumption of anarchy in international relations theory: a critique. *Review of International Studies*, 17: 67–85.

MORAVCSIK, A. 1997. Taking preferences seriously: a liberal theory of international politics. *International Organization*, 51: 513–53.

NYE, J. S. 1986. *Nuclear Ethics*. New York: Free Press.

OYE, K. (ed.) 1986. *Cooperation under Anarchy*. Princeton, NJ: Princeton University Press.

PODOLNY, J. M. and PAGE, K. L. 1998. Network forms of organization. *Annual Review of Sociology*, 24: 57–76.

POWELL, W. 1990. Neither market nor hierarchy: network forms of organization. *Research in Organizational Behavior*, 12: 295–336.

PRICE, R. 1998. Reversing the gun sights: transnational civil society targets land mines. *International Organization*, 52: 613–44.

—— 2003. Transnational civil society and advocacy in world politics. *World Politics*, 55: 579–606.

—— (ed.) 2008. *Moral Limit and Possibility in World Politics*. Cambridge: Cambridge University Press.

RAUSTIALA, K. and SLAUGHTER, A.-M. 2002. International law, international relations and compliance. Pp. 538–58 in *Handbook of International Relations*, ed. W. Carlsnaes, T. Risse, and B. Simmons. Thousand Oaks, Calif.: Sage.

REUS-SMIT, C. 1997. The constitutional structure of international society and the nature of fundamental institutions. *International Organization*, 51: 555–89.

—— 2008. Constructivism and the structure of ethical reasoning. In Price 2008.

RISSE-KAPPEN, T. 1995. *Bringing Transnational Relations Back In: Non-State Actors, Domestic Structures, and International Institutions*. Cambridge: Cambridge University Press.

ROSENAU, J. 2000. Change, complexity, and governance in a globalizing space. Pp. 169–200 in *Debating Governance: Authority, Steering, and Democracy*, ed. J. Pierre. Oxford: Oxford University Press.

—— and CZEMPIEL, E.-O. (eds.) 1992. *Governance without Government: Order and Change in World Politics*. New York: Cambridge University Press.

RUGGIE, J. 1983. Continuity and transformation in the world polity: toward a neorealist synthesis. *World Politics*, 35: 261–85.

—— 1992. Territoriality and beyond: problematizing modernity in international relations. *International Organization*, 47: 139–74.

—— 1993. *Multilateralism Matters: The Theory and Praxis of an Institutional Form*. New York: Columbia University Press.

—— 2004. Reconstituting the global public domain: issues, actors, and practices. *European Journal of International Relations*, 10: 499–531.

—— KATZENSTEIN, P., KEOHANE, R., and SCHMITTER, P. 2005. Transformations in world politics: the intellectual contributions of Ernst B. Haas. *Annual Review of Political Science*, 8: 271–96.

SCHMIDT, B. 2002. On the history and historiography of international relations. Pp. 3–22 in *Handbook of International Relations*, ed. W. Carlsnaes, T. Risse, and B. Simmons. Thousand Oaks, Calif.: Sage.

Sikkink, K. 1993. Human rights, principled issue-networks, and sovereignty in Latin America. *International Organization*, 47: 411–41.

—— 2008. The role of consequences, comparison, and counterfactuals in constructivist ethical thought. In Price 2008.

Simmons, B. 2000. International law and state behavior: commitment and compliance in international monetary affairs. *American Political Science Review*, 94: 819–35.

Slaughter, A.-M. 1995. International law in a world of liberal states. *European Journal of International Law*, 6: 503–58.

—— 2004. *A New World Order*. Princeton, NJ: Princeton University Press.

Tarrow, S. 2005. *The New Transnational Activism*. Cambridge: Cambridge University Press.

Thomas, D. 2000. *The Helsinki Effect: International Norms, Human Rights, and the Demise of Communism*. Princeton, NJ: Princeton University Press.

Wapner, P. 1995. Politics beyond the state: environmental activism and world civic politics. *World Politics*, 47: 311–40.

Weber, S. 2004. *The Success of Open Source*. Cambridge, Mass.: Harvard University Press.

Wendt, A. 1992. Anarchy is what states make of it: the social construction of power politics. *International Organization*, 46: 391–425.

—— 2001. Driving with the rearview mirror: on the rational science of institutional design. *International Organization*, 55: 1019–49.

Wight, C. 2006. *Agents, Structures and International Relations: Politics as Ontology*. New York: Cambridge University Press.

CHAPTER 36

....

BIG QUESTIONS IN THE STUDY OF WORLD POLITICS

....

ROBERT O. KEOHANE

WE do not study international relations for aesthetic reasons, since world politics is not beautiful. If we sought scientific rigor, we would have pursued careers in experimental disciplines. Instead we are motivated by normative questions, often asked urgently in the wake of disasters, from the Sicilian Expedition (416 BCE) chronicled by Thucydides to the Anglo-American invasion of Iraq (2003 CE). Recurring failures lead us to try to understand the conditions under which states and other actors can achieve their collective purposes rather than engage in destructive, and often self-destructive, behavior.[1] Our normative purposes infuse our positive analysis. Political economy came alive as a field in the wake of the economic crises of the 1970s, which recalled the Great Depression of the 1930s. Security studies became a site of creativity after the Second World War and during the height of the cold war. Work on the sources of internal war expanded in the wake of post-cold war internal conflicts. And it is predictable that there will be a new wave of work on the problem of terrorism, in the wake of the attacks of 11 September 2001.

Students of world politics have an obligation to democratic publics to help them understand the most pressing problems of the current day. Yet this moral obligation does not imply that we should focus on topical issues or be "policy-relevant" in a narrow sense by speaking to governments in terms that are acceptable to them. Our

---

[1] I use the phrase "world politics" rather than "international relations," since the language of "international relations" leads us to think only about states, which are not central to all interesting questions of world politics.

task is to probe the deeper sources of action in world politics, and to speak truth to power—insofar as we can discern what the truth is.

The study of world politics begins with the study of war. *Why is war a perennial institution of international society and what variable factors affect its incidence?* In understanding this problem, as well as other issues in world politics, realist theory, which identifies power and interests as the central forces in the behavior of rational states, has played a central role (Morgenthau 1967), although it remained unclear for years why, if states behaved rationally, they could engage in mutually destructive warfare. Scholars have recently made substantial progress on this problem, notably by following the lead of Thomas Schelling (1960) in focusing on the role played by information and credibility (Fearon 1995), and by linking the study of institutions to that of war (Fortna 2004).

The analysis of warfare relates directly to broader issues of discord and cooperation. Work on these issues over the last quarter-century has emphasized that cooperation arises more from discord than from harmony, and that, when complementary interests exist, multilateral institutions can facilitate cooperation (Keohane 1984). A productive line of work has stressed the role of reciprocity in creating incentives for cooperative behavior (Axelrod 1984). These theoretical contributions are beginning to be linked to the literature on the democratic peace, which I do not have space to discuss here.

An important contemporary as well as historical puzzle is how to think about the role of sovereignty. Under what conditions does it promote cooperation by limiting intervention and clarifying the actors in world politics, and under what conditions does it generate civil conflict by providing a shield behind which states can abuse groups within their societies? Recent work on sovereignty (Krasner 1999) has clarified various meanings of this concept, which has regained analytical significance with the increased attention to issues of civil war and intervention.

Behind all these issues lurks the concept of power. Material resources are significant not just for war and threat, but also for the politics of economic relationships. The study of political economy can be viewed as "the reciprocal and dynamic interaction in international relations of the pursuit of wealth and the pursuit of power" (Gilpin 1975, 43). But we need to question the equation of power resources with material resources. Joseph Nye (2004) has emphasized the role of "soft power"— attractiveness that inspires emulation and facilitates persuasion—in world politics. Soft power depends on the beliefs that human beings have and how they process information; hence its systematic study will require engagement with cognitive and social psychology, where recent progress has been rapid. Efforts to understand the sources of beliefs are likely to become more urgent for students of world politics as social mobilization and the ability of people to communicate directly with one another, unmediated by large institutions, continue to grow.

Questions about war and cooperation, and concepts such as power and interest, remain central to world politics. The field has recently become more aware, however, of the inferential biases to which students of international relations are subject. Wars and crises are rare events. Quite naturally, scholars seeking to understand them focus much more on these events than on the situations of peace, especially situations lacking crises at all. Insofar as our purposes are descriptive, this emphasis is unproblematic. However, when we seek to put forward explanatory propositions, we are in danger of selecting our cases on the dependent variable, which will bias our inferences (Achen and Snidal 1989; King, Keohane, and Verba 1994). We need continually to be aware of the uncertainty of our inferences—since our data are not generated by experiments, and often the class of relevant events is small and not independent of one another—and to try to account for sources of bias.

Students of world politics have made theoretical progress in recent decades on issues of war, cooperation, and the role of multilateral institutions; and conceptual progress on issues of sovereignty. Impressive empirical work, guided by improved technical and methodological sophistication, has been carried out on a variety of problems, including warfare. However, most of this progress has focused on seeking to establish static conditional generalizations. Although we are living in a period of unprecedented change, our understanding of change is very inferior to our understanding of fundamental long-term regularities.

1 Six Big Questions about Change over Time

Compared to the history of civilization, much less of the human race, the known history of world politics is very short indeed, and the period for which reasonably reliable data exist is less than 200 years. Human nature has not changed during that time, nor has the fact that no world government exists. When students of world politics seek to make generalizations based on state behavior during the last two centuries, they implicitly assume that the actors and processes of the early nineteenth century are essentially the same as those operating now. Much, however, has occurred in those 200 years to change some basic factors at work, including the nature of force and the structure of economic life. Furthermore, change seems to be accelerating, generating several new or newly urgent questions.

1. *How has politics been affected by the expansion of force, through technological change, and its dispersion?*
Scholars have explored in depth the effects of changes in the technology of force on international relations in the West over periods of centuries. Recent changes in warfare, relying on global positioning systems and electronic technology of all kinds, have created huge gaps between the military power of the United States and that of other countries. Some of those who celebrated American military power, however, may have forgotten that ingenious adversaries can create effective "weapons

of the weak," such as terrorism, and that possessing a superior resource may lead states to overuse it, or to attempt to use it for purposes for which it is not well suited.

2. *How has world politics been affected by changes in capitalism?*
Karl Marx and Joseph Schumpeter are the two most famous theorists who saw world politics as fundamentally affected by the nature of capitalist development. Marx, Vladimir Lenin, and their followers viewed war as the result of capitalism, with its limitless demand for markets and investment opportunities. Schumpeter, by contrast, thought that capitalism had peace-inducing effects, limiting imperialism by empha-sizing profit over glory and conquest. But he also viewed capitalism as a relentless process of "creative destruction," implying socially disruptive change. Both Marx and Schumpeter thought that change was the essence of capitalism, which implies that how economic structures affect global conflict and cooperation must change over time. Neither would have accepted the static formulations of how world politics operate implicit in much of the statistical work now appearing in the field.

3. *Is there any plausible sense in which progress has taken place in international rela-tions, and if so, is this progress due to intellectual or moral advances in human thinking?*
Since the Enlightenment, many thinkers in the West have observed fundamental changes in human practices and have concluded, or at least dared to hope, that moral as well as scientific and technical progress was occurring. These hopes peaked in the years before the First World War, when both publicists and practical men of affairs expected economic interdependence to dampen or even prevent wars and sought arbitration and arms limitation treaties to facilitate and institutionalize benign changes. World wars and the Holocaust generated great disillusionment, but in the 1980s and 1990s hopes for progress, through learning or changes in principled ideas, were revived. The effects of changes in the ideas in which people believe are by no means necessarily benign, as illustrated by nuclear weapons and the recent militancy of Islamic fundamentalism. We should expect no simple answer to questions about progress, but they are nevertheless important questions to ask.

4. *What is the impact on world politics of the increasing diversity and complexity of social structures in the most powerful societies of the world?*
It is a platitude that contemporary democratic–capitalist societies are increasingly complex, a complexity that is magnified by the increasing blurring of lines between societies as transnational relations become more dense. Governments themselves are becoming diversified, along with civil society, which has experienced a vast increase at the transnational level of nongovernmental organizations and social movements (Keck and Sikkink 1998). Traditional gender roles have been changing in Western societies, with potential impacts on decision-making and leadership behavior. Anne-Marie Slaughter has recently put forward the vision of a "disaggregated world order," in which, as a result largely of social complexity, hierarchies have weakened and networks have become the dominant form of connection among individuals and groups in society (Slaughter 2004). There is considerable evidence for Slaughter's argument—from peaceful activities such as accounting and securities regulation and

violent ones such as terrorism—but it is largely anecdotal. We need to understand these changes more systematically.

5. *What are the implications of electronic technologies, especially of the Internet, for world politics?*

To exercise influence, sets of individuals with common values or interests need to be able to communicate with each other, to form groups, and to act collectively. Historically, such communication has been very difficult except through formal organizations, including the state; and all but impossible across state boundaries except with the aid of states. This formerly constant reality has been changing with incredible speed during the last two decades, and we have hardly begun to understand the implications of this momentous fact. One implication may be that collective action on a transnational or even global scale, for good or ill, is easier than it has ever been before.

6. *What modes of action can effectively cope with the unprecedented stress that human beings are imposing on the global environment?*

The reality of human-induced climate change has become undeniable, although many uncertainties surround the pace and severity of change and the prospects for relevant technological innovation. The political uncertainties may be even greater, both with respect to the willingness of publics and governments around the world to pay significant costs to mitigate climate change and adapt to it, and with respect to the capacity of existing or feasible institutions to implement measures involving global taxes or tradeable permit schemes (Aldy and Stavins 2007).

2 Issues of Institutional Design

I began this chapter with the argument that the study of world politics is driven heavily by normative concerns, although in our positive research we have an obligation to follow the canons of scientific inference. If we are serious about these normative concerns, we cannot merely pontificate: We need instead to think deeply about these issues so that we can articulate coherent normative points of view, and then to connect these normative issues with practical problems. For me, as a student of institutions, the most pressing practical problems involve institutional design.

The fundamental normative question can be posed as follows: *What is the extent and depth of human obligations to other human beings, extending across political and cultural boundaries?* Do people in Europe and North America have obligations to people in Africa, simply as a result of our common humanity? To what extent are moral obligations limited by shared bonds of historical experience and community? Moral philosophers have reflected profoundly on these issues. Our answers to this question will condition our answers to a related but derivative question: *How should we think about trade-offs among values, such as democracy, liberty, equality (including gender equality), and economic welfare?* It is not obvious that the trade-offs made in wealthy democracies apply fully to developing countries, or to societies with different cultural practices; yet, for liberal cosmopolitans, there is an irreducible core of human rights that must be respected (Okin 1999). What should these rights be considered to be?

The way we think about practical issues such as institutional design will necessarily be shaped by our answers to these fundamental normative questions. I am a cosmopolitan liberal democrat: a cosmopolitan, since I think that basic human rights are universal and not dependent on membership in a particular community; a liberal, because I give priority to liberty as a crucial value for a good society; a democrat, because I believe that elites should not only serve the public good but should be accountable to deliberative public views through institutions that give publics power over leaders. The two basic issues of institutional design that I raise reflect these values.

My first issue of institutional design involves effectiveness. *How can institutions in world politics be designed, or modified, in ways that would make them more effective in attaining collective purposes, from restoring peace in war-torn societies to facilitating nondiscriminatory trade, protecting human rights, and preventing damage to the global environment?* Theoretical and empirical work on institutional design over the last two decades has pointed to the importance of incentives for reaching and complying with international agreements (Koremenos, Lipson, and Snidal 2001). Since institutions vary in the incentives they help to generate, a worthwhile normative project would be to figure out systematically how to get the incentives right in constructing institutions, and what scope global institutions should have in light of the incentives of potential member states and the capacity of domestic and multilateral institutions in a variety of issue areas.

To be worthwhile for a democrat, institutions have to be accountable as well as effective. So the second question can be posed as follows: *How can multilateral institutions be designed, without global government, so that qualified and dedicated leaders are more likely to be chosen, and those leaders who are selected are held accountable to the people whose actions they affect?* Accountability is a basic principle of democracy. Multilateral institutions cannot be fully democratic, since they remain dependent on states. Many states are not democratic, and the connections between multilateral institutions and publics even in democratic states are weak. Yet mechanisms have been devised to make multilateral institutions accountable, and they could be strengthened.

The questions that I have emphasized are necessarily selective. Some issues have been omitted simply for lack of space. But I have deliberately omitted discussion of the alleged incompatibility of broad approaches to the study of international relations such as realism, institutionalism, and constructivism, since I regard these approaches as complementary rather than alternatives. The relevant question is to figure out how they can be combined to address theoretically or practically relevant problems. Nor have I emphasized analytical or statistical tools that are playing an increasing role in scholarship, even though these tools have been valuable both theoretically and empirically. To my taste, there has been an overemphasis recently on tools at the expense of reflection about which questions are most important for the human race and for the ecosystem. Focusing on major problems can help us to figure out which insights from the broad approaches to the field are valuable, and which analytical tools yield genuine insights or evidence. If we then focus on developing testable theories, we can investigate their implications empirically. But if we fail to ask the right questions, there is no hope of getting the answers we need.

References

Achen, C. H. and Snidal, D. 1989. Rational deterrence theory and comparative case studies. *World Politics*, 41: 143–69.

Aldy, J. and Stavins, R. (eds.) 2007. *Architectures for Agreement: Addressing Global Climate Change in the Post-Kyoto World*. Cambridge: Cambridge University Press.

Axelrod, R. 1984. *The Evolution of Cooperation*. New York: Basic Books.

Fearon, J. D. 1995. Rationalist explanations for war. *International Organization*, 49: 379–414.

Fortna, V. P. 2004. *Peace Time: Cease-Fire Agreements and the Durability of Peace*. Princeton, NJ: Princeton University Press.

Gilpin, R. 1975. *US Power and the Multinational Corporation: The Political Economy of Foreign Direct Investment*. New York: Basic Books.

Keck, M. and Sikkink, K. 1998. *Activists beyond Borders: Advocacy Networks in International Politics*. Ithaca, NY: Cornell University Press.

Keohane, R. O. 1984. *After Hegemony: Cooperation and Discord in the World Political Economy*. Princeton, NJ: Princeton University Press.

King, G., Keohane, R. O., and Verba, S. 1994. *Designing Social Inquiry: Scientific Inference in Qualitative Research*. Princeton, NJ: Princeton University Press.

Koremenos, B., Lipson, C., and Snidal, D. 2001. The rational design of international institutions. *International Organization*, special issue, 55: 761–1102.

Krasner, S. D. 1999. *Sovereignty: Organized Hypocrisy*. Princeton, NJ: Princeton University Press.

Morgenthau, H. J. 1967. *Politics among Nations: The Struggle for Power and Peace*, 4th edn. New York: Knopf.

Nye, J. S., Jr. 2004. *Soft Power: The Means to Success in World Politics*. New York: Public Affairs Press.

Okin, S. M. 1999. *Is Multiculturalism Bad for Women?* Princeton, NJ: Princeton University Press.

Schelling, T. C. 1960. *The Strategy of Conflict*. Cambridge, Mass.: Harvard University Press.

Slaughter, A.-M. 2004. *A New World Order*. Princeton, NJ: Princeton University Press.

SIX WISHES FOR A MORE RELEVANT DISCIPLINE OF INTERNATIONAL RELATIONS

STEVE SMITH

THIS chapter looks at how the discipline of international relations should develop over the next twenty years. I start by saying something about the main features of the discipline in the last twenty years. I have previously written on this topic and do not wish to repeat that analysis (see Smith 2000; 2002; 2004; 2007). I follow Ole Wæver's (2007) view of the development of international relations; like him, and following Stanley Hoffmann (1977), I see international relations as an American discipline that dominates by having the largest and best-funded academic community, having the dominant journals, and being able to ignore the work of scholars outside the United States (Wæver 2007, 296). Within international relations, the key journals are almost all US based, and prefer theory testing to the development of new theory (Wæver

* I would like to thank Jodie Anstee for her research assistance on this chapter.

2007, 297). This results in a field that prioritizes publishing in the leading journals, for promotion and status reasons, and leads to a focus on testing and modifying dominant theories rather than confronting them in debates. Despite this generalization, most of the theoretical developments in international relations have come from academics based in the United States; partly this reflects the relative size of the US academic community, but the US community is a varied and diverse one that leads to most innovation in the discipline. Nonetheless, the vast majority of work in the United States focuses on developing existing research paradigms, and the major innovations tend not to come from academics based in the main departments of international politics.

Despite the discipline's fondness for so-called great debates, there have been few; in the main, the differing positions have simply ignored one another. This does not mean that there have not been strong opposing positions within the discipline. Therefore, in this weak sense of the word "debate," there has indeed been a rivalry between competing theoretical frameworks; what there have not been are debates in the strong sense of the word (whereby contrasting positions indicate their superiority over rival positions through explicit debates).

In the period between the late 1980s and the late 1990s the discipline was marked by two key features: first, a coming-together (not debate) of neorealist and neoliberal approaches into a neo-neo synthesis; second, a more general dispute (again, not a debate) between this rationalist core of the field and a group of approaches (feminist, post-structuralist, critical theory, postcolonial, and green theory), collectively known as reflectivism. But these approaches have not debated with rationalism nor have they together constituted a coherent alternative. The contemporary scene is one in which there is a set of debates within broad theoretical positions, and no great debate defining the field. In this sense, the field has a set of powerful theories that almost never touch or confront one another in the major journals. Either the core conversations in international relations are debates within these theoretical positions (for example between offensive and defensive realism, or between the group of theories that comprise neoliberalism), or they are developments of specific aspects of the main theoretical positions.

Importantly, the often-cited concern about theories being divorced from empirical material (the claim that international relations theory is not interested in "real-world" problems) seems not to be the case. Whether the approach is a mainstream one or a reflectivist one, the most common article is one that examines a discrete empirical field through the lens of a specific theory; this is as true of post-structural and gender work as it is of neorealism, neoliberalism, or constructivism. The field, therefore, is not preoccupied with metatheoretical debates, but instead attempts to link theory and empirical domains. Just as the extent of debate involved in the previous four "great debates" has been exaggerated, so it is difficult to find any notion of a fifth "great debate" in the current literature.

1 How should International Relations Develop over the Next Twenty Years?

....

1. *All approaches should be seen as having normative commitments.*

Since this is an explicit position taken by this volume's editors, I need say little here. International relations is unavoidably normative for two related reasons: first there can be no simple separation between "fact" and "values;" second, international relations is a practical discipline, concerned with how we should act. From the inception of international relations as a distinct discipline, neither of these reasons has been commonly accepted; indeed, the opposite positions have dominated international relations. These were particularly powerful when positivism was the dominant methodology. But accepting that all theories contain normative commitments does not necessarily create a more level playing field, since some normative commitments can be seen as more "natural" or acceptable than others. This could be because some practical prescriptions will be seen as more "accurately" fitting the commonsense reality of world politics. Or it could be because of the dominance of statements about the need to separate "facts" from "values" in analysis; this, of course, assumes that such a distinction is indeed possible, whereas I believe that, following Foucault, disciplines and theories constitute the criteria through which we access the "facts" of the social world. Just as there can never be a theory-neutral account of "reality," so there cannot be a theoretical account that does not have normative commitments and assumptions. Particularly good examples of this problem are contained in two recent articles: first, Stefan Elbe's analysis (2006) of whether HIV/AIDS should be securitized. This is a disease that every day kills three times the death toll from the events of 11 September 2001. Elbe shows that, although there might be advantages of securitizing the discourse—for example, by raising awareness and thereby increasing the resources devoted to dealing with the pandemic—there are also ethical dangers; those living with HIV/AIDS could be seen as the problem, and civil society's role could be increasingly taken over by the military and intelligence services. Similarly, Piki Ish-Shalom (2006) has shown how international relations theories play a political, normative role by shaping the reality that they study, since theorists have agency and therefore automatically have a moral responsibility. For Ish-Shalom this moral ethic should replace the dominant academic ethic of objectivity. All theories have normative assumptions flowing through them, and these are never more powerful than when they are hidden, denied, or eschewed.

2. *International relations has to become less of an American discipline.*

Any academic discipline will take particular interest in the policy concerns of its major subjects, but in international relations the US policy agenda, and its dominant methodology, has been so influential that other voices have been either ignored or placed in a position whereby they are of interest or relevance only insofar as they relate to the dominant agenda. US academic journals set the agenda for the discipline and the US policy agenda constructs the world that international relations theory "sees." While this does not mean that the discipline has been uncritical of US foreign policy (indeed many of the key journals are major sites for the criticism of US foreign policy), this has meant that international relations has been unable to deal with the policy issues that preoccupy the vast majority of the world's people. Dealing with this will require more academics outside the United States building their own academic communities and places of publication; but this will be pointless unless the US academic community is prepared to read material in other languages and publish in journals other than the handful that dominate the promotion process in leading universities. If international relations remains a narrow American social science, then the dangers are that it will be irrelevant to the concerns of large parts of the world's population, and more problematically it may become increasingly part of the process of US hegemony.

3. *International relations has to reject its current, and historic, privileging of a specific, and culturally entailed, social scientific approach.*

International relations has been overwhelmingly focused on one version of social science for the last fifty years. Positivism has legitimized international relations, and has served as the benchmark for what counts as acceptable work. This can be contrasted with the much more eclectic intellectual environment in most other academic communities around the world; but, because international relations is an American discipline, this has meant that only a very specific set of answers to questions of method and knowledge generation have been seen as scientifically legitimate. On the other hand, there has been precious little in the way of accepting the deficiencies and limitations of positivism. Recent papers by Friedrich Kratochwil (2006), Milja Kurki (2006), and Colin Wight (2007) have each shown just how limited and historically specific are the core assumptions underlying positivism. Yet the bulk of the papers in the key US academic journals continue to work within this paradigm without an awareness either of the existence of alternative social scientific approaches, or of the major limitations of positivism. It is as if the entire post-positivist movement never happened. Unless the discipline accepts that there is a wide set of legitimate approaches to studying world politics, then it will become more and more restricted in its ability to relate to other disciplines and it will become a besieged academic fortress validated and legitimized only internally.

4. *International relations academics need to reflect on their relation to power and on their social location.*

I raised this issue in my 2003 Presidential Address to the International Studies Association (Smith 2004). More recently the issue has been discussed in a special section in *Millennium: Journal of International Studies*, 35 (2006). In their introduction, Karena Shaw and R. B. J. Walker (2006) ask fundamental questions about the relationship between the academic's research and teaching roles and their political responsibility. Merely teaching the received wisdom of the history of the discipline of international relations is certainly not a neutral act, since it predisposes students to accept the categories of debate as natural or given. Therefore, what we research and teach are choices we make as academics; these choices can be explained as simply studying the "main features" of world politics, but this merely covers up what are at base political and ethical choices. When we research or teach, we either explicitly or implicitly give that topic a status and we also locate it within a view of the world that reflects our cultural/social/economic and political location. Unless we question the assumptions we make when we teach and research, then we will simply be reinforcing the existing distribution of power, and reinforcing the agenda of the powerful.

5. *International relations needs to focus on the relationship between the material and the ideational.*

Because the linkages between ideational and material structures are so complex, international relations needs to develop theories that focus on accounts of the linkages. Whereas rationalism assumes that interests construct identity, reflectivists assume the opposite (yet the idea of them existing as separate realms is problematic). One route would be for the return of more materialist accounts to international relations, albeit with more developed accounts of the *relationship* between the material and the ideational than such accounts have tended to have (since they assumed that the ideational was a function of the material). As Chris Brown (2007) argues, Marxism has been much missed in international relations over the last twenty years; it was a theoretical position that had a clear, if contested, view of how material and ideational worlds interrelated. Critical realism is one such account, although that has tended to be discussed in international relations in relation to questions of epistemology.

6. *International relations should not take the core concerns of the most powerful as the dominant issues for the discipline.*

International relations has historically ignored large sections of humanity. This is most obvious when it focuses on US policy interests, but it also follows from the definition of international relations that the discipline works within. International relations has privileged deaths by politics over deaths by economics (ten times as many children die each day from poverty and easily preventable diseases as died in total in the 11 September attacks). Similarly, women have largely been ignored, and, as Alison Watson (2006) has recently noted, so have children. This is a direct result of the core assumptions of the discipline, which determine what we see and what we think international relations has to explain. In a recent article, Tarak Barkawi and Mark Laffey (2006) claim that security studies is Eurocentric, and is thus unable to develop adequate understandings of the security concerns of the postcolonial world. It contains, they argue, a "taken-for-granted" politics that effectively sides with the strong over the weak. Thus a security studies that was really relevant to postcolonial states would account for how the strong exploit the weak, and would focus on the politics of resistance. Unless international relations is able to deal with agendas outside those of the dominant powers, then it will be completely unable to account for the motivations of all those who fundamentally reject the Western models of development, human rights, and civil society.

Let me summarize my arguments by directly considering the four questions that the editors asked those writing these concluding sections to consider.

2 WHERE SHOULD THE FIELD BE GOING?

The field should be going in no particular direction, since that would assume that there is one thing called international relations. Rather, international relations needs to be pluralistic, in the strong sense of valuing different intellectual approaches; not pluralistic in a weaker sense of "anything goes." International relations should move toward being a truly international field, rather than being a field for one, dominant, part of humanity. It should reject simple dichotomies such as domestic/international, economics/politics, and public/private, and not accept that humanity is moving toward common identities and politics.

1. *What should international relations be about?*
International relations should be about the patterns of international and domestic power, and not assume that those patterns most relevant to dominant powers are those that matter to the rest of the world. International relations should aid the understanding of politics from any social location, and any identity, and not be a discipline written from an Archimedean point of neutrality. It has to be a discipline located in the real lives of real people.

2. *What are the big questions that should animate our scholarship?*
These relate to: identity and how it relates to material interests; how identities are constructed; how they relate to patterns of political, economic, and social power, both between and within societies. How do we categorize our thinking? How do we construct the inside and the outside, or the public and the private realms, and therefore how do we develop the categories within which we "do" international relations?

3. *What are the implications of these questions for how we do research?*
International relations should focus on understanding rather than on assuming a common human identity that can be explained by interest-based models of choice. It needs to understand the world of the powerless as well as the powerful, and be self-reflective as to the relationship between our scholarship, our stated ethical standards, and our location as scholars. Put simply, could our scholarship be part of a pattern of dominance of one set of interests over another, all carried out in the name of academia and scholarship?

Taken together, these comments lead to a simple conclusion: International relations runs the danger of becoming a discourse applicable only to one part of the world, organized by powerful theories, legitimized by a specific and flawed epistemology, and "disciplined" by the structures of the discipline itself. In place of this, international relations needs to become more applicable to politics outside the world of the dominant power, more interested in the security concerns of the powerless, and better able to account for why we focus on some politics rather than others. When we study international relations, we make choices: Throughout most of its history, international relations has chosen to study the politics of the great powers. Yet these are not the "natural" or "given" focal points; they are choices. In the next twenty years the discipline should opt for choices that will make it a truly international relations.

REFERENCES

BARKAWI, T. and LAFFEY, M. 2006. The postcolonial moment in security studies. *Review of International Studies*, 32: 329–52.

BROWN, C. 2007. Situating critical realism. *Millennium: Journal of International Studies*, 35: 409–16.

ELBE, S. 2006. Should HIV/AIDS be securitized? The ethical dilemmas of linking HIV/AIDS and security. *International Studies Quarterly*, 50: 119–44.

HOFFMANN, S. 1977. An American social science: international relations. *Daedalus*, 106: 41–60.

ISH-SHALOM, P. 2006. Theory gets real, and the case for a normative ethic: Rostow, modernization theory, and the alliance for progress. *International Studies Quarterly*, 50: 287–311.

KRATOCHWIL, F. 2006. History, action and identity: revisiting the "second" great debate and assessing its importance for social theory. *European Journal of International Relations*, 12: 5–29.

KURKI, M. 2006. Causes of a divided discipline: rethinking the concept of cause in international relations theory. *Review of International Studies*, 32: 189–216.

SHAW, K. and WALKER, R. B. J. 2006. Situating academic practice: pedagogy, critique and responsibility. *Millennium: Journal of International Studies*, 35: 155–65.

SMITH, S. 2000. The discipline of international relations: still an American social science? *British Journal of Politics and International Relations*, 2: 374–402.

—— 2002. The United States and the discipline of international relations: "hegemonic country, hegemonic discipline." *International Studies Review*, 4: 67–86.

—— 2004. Singing our world into existence: international relations theory and September 11. *International Studies Quarterly*, 48: 499–515.

—— 2007. Introduction: diversity and disciplinarity in international relations theory. Pp. 1–12 in *International Relations Theories: Discipline and Diversity*, ed. T. Dunne, M. Kurki, and S. Smith. Oxford: Oxford University Press.

WATSON, A. 2006. Children and international relations: a new site of knowledge? *Review of International Studies*, 32: 237–50.

WÆVER, O. 2007. Still a discipline after all these debates? Pp. 288–308 in *International Relations Theories: Discipline and Diversity*, ed. T. Dunne, M. Kurki, and S. Smith. Oxford: Oxford University Press.

WIGHT, C. 2007. A manifesto for scientific realism in IR: assuming the can-opener won't work! *Millennium: Journal of International Studies*, 35: 379–98.

PART IX

POLITICAL ECONOMY

CHAPTER 38

OVERVIEW OF POLITICAL ECONOMY

THE REACH OF POLITICAL ECONOMY

BARRY R. WEINGAST
DONALD A. WITTMAN

OVER its long lifetime, the phrase "political economy" has had many different meanings. For Adam Smith, political economy was the science of managing a nation's resources so as to generate wealth. For Marx, it was how the ownership of the means of production influenced historical processes. For much of the twentieth century, the phrase political economy had contradictory meanings. Sometimes it was viewed as an area of study (the interrelationship between economics and politics) while at other times it was viewed as a methodological approach. Even the methodological approach was divided into two parts—the economic approach (sometimes called public choice, sometimes called positive political theory) emphasizing individual rationality and the sociological approach where the level of analysis tended to be institutional.

Here, we view political economy as a grand (if imperfect) synthesis of these various strands. In our view, political economy is the methodology of economics applied to the analysis of political behavior and institutions. As such, it is not a single, unified approach, but a family of approaches. Because institutions are no longer ignored, but instead are themselves the subject matter of the investigation, this approach incorporates many of the issues of concern to political sociologists. Because political behavior and institutions are a subject of study, politics also becomes the subject of political economy. All of this is tied together by a set of methodologies, typically associated with economics, but now part and parcel of political science itself.[1] The unit of analysis is typically the individual. The individual is motivated to achieve goals (usually preference maximization, but in evolutionary games maximization of surviving offspring), the theory is based in mathematics (often game theoretic), and the empirics either use sophisticated statistical techniques or involve experiments where money is used as a motivating force in the experiment (see Palfrey 2006).

In this chapter, we illustrate the intellectual excitement in political economy by covering some important elements on the scholarly frontier.

Rather than providing a shallow survey of the whole field, we discuss a set of approaches and issues that have spawned interesting results and that are likely to spur considerable research in the next decade.

We divide our chapter into five sections. In Section 1, we discuss research on endogenous institutions. The research agenda on institutions follows a natural progression. The first step is to determine how institutions affect behavior. Indeed, this step seems a necessary condition for a theory of endogenous institutions. Having built up a large literature on the effects of institutions, students of political economy have begun to treat institutions as endogenous (thereby incorporating some of the subject matter of sociology and anthropology). We focus our attention on legislative institutions because this is where much of the work originated. The success of institutional analysis of legislatures is not surprising, as scholars have collected a large body of data and evidence (both quantitative and qualitative) on legislatures. For example, votes have been recorded with party affiliations and other attributes noted. These large data-sets allow hypotheses to be tested and theory to be refined. Because the rules of the US Congress are internal to Congress, voting procedures, the type of committees, and committee assignments are all endogenous. So legislatures are fertile ground for exploring institutional choice.

One of the technically most challenging but at the same time one of the most exciting areas of research in political economy concerns the revelation and aggregation of information, the subject of Section 2. This work is exciting because many of the results contradict earlier beliefs based on decision-theoretic models and because this research answers many puzzles. Here, our focus is on voters, particularly voters who are uninformed in one way or another, but are nevertheless rational. Since this research area is still in its infancy, we expect much more to be done in ensuing years.

Section 3 is devoted to evolutionary models of human and political behavior. Political economy is now at the confluence of two related paradigms: utility maximization and evolutionary fitness. Both employ survival arguments in the context

---

[1] See Austen-Smith (2006).

of competitive forces—for example, candidates need to win elections to survive. Further both employ the concept of equilibrium. These two concepts of survival and equilibrium distinguish political economy from other approaches to political behavior. However, these two approaches at times provide contradictory insights. As we will show, some kinds of irrational behavior seem to improve evolutionary fitness. So at the same time that political economy is pushing the envelope of hyper-rationality (as illustrated in Section 2), it is also trying to incorporate elements of emotions and irrationality (Section 3). Furthermore, while political economy has traditionally been based on self-regarding behavior, a considerable body of research in evolutionary politics tries to explain other-regarding behavior, such as altruism and vengeance.

Scientific knowledge depends to a great extent on the interplay between empirical knowledge and theoretical development. Not surprisingly, our most comprehensive knowledge is about the advanced industrial democracies in general and legislatures in particular where the great number of observations (of votes, party affiliation, etc.) allow for an extensive testing of hypotheses and considerable refinement of theory.[2]

Nevertheless, over time, there has been a spread of knowledge from the core areas of research. This spread has occurred for several reasons. First, the same behavioral relations that we observe within democracies may occur across political systems once we account for the divergent institutional constraints on the actors. For example, authoritarians may not face elections, but they too need political support to remain in power (see Bueno de Mesquita 2006; Haber 2006). Second, more information is being collected so that cross-country comparisons can now be done.[3] Finally, the political phenomena in nondemocratic countries raise a host of questions typically ignored in democratic countries, that demand answers: Why is there ethnic conflict? When is democracy a stable political system? What if any is the relationship between democracy and capitalism? And why are so many nations underdeveloped?[4]

In Section 4, we consider the spread of political economy to new areas of research. Here the empirical and theoretical answers are the least certain, but perhaps the most interesting because of their novelty. We use, as our illustrative example, work on the size and wealth of nations. A motivating reason for choosing the size of nations as our prime example of the spread of political economy is that rational choice models have

[2] This disproportionate focus of political economy research has arisen for several reasons. First, the political economy tools were first developed studying democratic countries and are therefore more easily adapted to other democratic countries than to nondemocratic ones. Second, close observation and data are more easily obtained in democratic countries so that theories applying to them have been honed the most. Third, the institutional tools of political economy are more readily applied to the more highly developed institutions of the advanced industrial democracies, in contrast to the less stable and less institutionalized politics in the developing world.

[3] Indeed, another defining characteristic of the political economy approach is the use of large data-sets that enable econometric comparisons across a variety of countries, where the varieties are captured by different independent variables. For examples of cross-country comparisons, see Persson and Tabellini (2006) and Glaeser (2006). The econometric approach is in stark contrast to the older comparative politics literature, which compared two or three countries at a time.

[4] For handbook surveys of these fields see, respectively: Fearon (2006), Przeworski (2006), Iverson (2006), and both Acemoglu and Robinson (2006) and Bates (2006).

often been (unfairly) accused of dealing with "epiphenomena," such as voting, rather than with "deeper and more substantive" issues. The size and wealth of nations clearly passes the gravitas test.

1 ENDOGENOUS INSTITUTIONS: THE STRUCTURE OF CONGRESS

Institutions can be studied at three different levels. First, the most basic and common level takes institutions as given and studies their effects. Second, the first method can be used as a form of comparative institutional analysis to study the implications of different forms of institutions. Third, the deepest level of institutional analysis is to take the institutions themselves as endogenous; here, the analysis attempts to explain how and why institutions are structured in particular ways, and why some types of institutions survive but not others. The third approach is both the newest and least explored of the three approaches to institutions and is therefore likely to be a major frontier over the coming years.

To illustrate the differences in the three approaches to institutions, we focus on legislatures, where scholars have made significant progress on institutional choice. We begin our discussion with models that take legislative institutions as given and study their effects. In a relatively "institution-free" legislature with majority rule voting in one dimension, legislative choice will be the preference of the median legislator. By adding institutional features to this simple spatial model of legislative choice, scholars have studied the implications of a variety of institutional details. For example, several scholars have studied the effect of committee gatekeeping authority (Denzau and MacKay 1983; Shepsle and Weingast 1981) or party gatekeeping authority (Cox and McCubbins 2005) on legislative choice. The idea is that committees (during the mid-twentieth century) or parties (during the late twentieth and early twenty-first century) held the power to keep issues within their jurisdiction from coming up for a vote. In contrast to the median voter model, the gatekeeping models show that some nonmedian status quos can be sustained: The gatekeeper will keep the gates closed for any status quo that she prefers to the median's ideal.

This research agenda has produced a wealth of knowledge about how legislative institutions affect both legislative policy choices and policy decisions by the other branches. For example, Laver and Shepsle (1996) show how parliamentary institutions affect policy choices;[5] Krehbiel (1998; 2006) demonstrates the effects of internal congressional rules (notably, the filibuster) on policy-making, as well as showing the influence of electoral changes on policy; Ferejohn and Shipan (1990) show how potential threats of legislation affect bureaucratic decision-making even without any

---

[5] See also Laver (2006).

legislation passing;[6] and Marks (1988) demonstrates the close relationship between legislative preferences and judicial decisions that interpret the meaning of statutes.[7]

The second type of institutional analysis utilizes the above methodology to make comparative statements about different institutions. For example, pivotal politics models show the differences in behavior between a unicameral majoritarian system, a bicameral system where each chamber uses majority rule, and a bicameral system in which one chamber employs a filibuster rule allowing a minority of legislators to prevent the passage of legislation. The first institution always results in the median legislator's ideal policy. The second institution creates a gridlock range of possible policy choices—the set of points between the ideal policies of the median in each chamber. Any status quo policy in this set is an equilibrium in that there does not exist a majority in both chambers that can overturn it. The third institution widens the set of status quo points that cannot be overturned even further: The possibility of a filibuster means that only policies commanding 60 percent in one chamber and a majority in the other can overturn a policy, so more status quo policies are stable. For a further discussion of these issues see Krehbiel (1998; 2006) and Cutrone and McCarty (2006).

Third, a much smaller set of papers studies the structure of the legislature itself and treats its institutions as endogenous.[8] Four different approaches have been used to explain legislative structure: (1) legislator preferences, (2) committees as commitment devices, (3) parties as transactions cost reducers, and (4) committees as information providers.[9] We will now discuss each in turn.

1.1 Legislator Preferences

The simplest of the approaches bases legislative choice on legislator preferences and relies on the "majoritarian postulate," which holds that legislative policy and procedural choices are made by majorities (Krehbiel 1991). In the context of one-dimensional models of policy choice, the preference-based approach has the following implications (Krehbiel 1993): First, policy choice corresponds to the preference of the median legislator. Second, voting will be polarized according to party lines even though there is no party enforcement.

To illustrate the latter point, suppose that legislators join one of two parties, and, further, that those to the right of the median largely join one party while those to the left of the median largely join the other party. Suppose further that the status quo is to the right of the median and the proposed legislation seeks to move policy left toward the median voter's ideal. The "cutting line" divides the set of voters into those favoring the status quo and those favoring the proposal. In this context, the

---

[6] See also Huber and Shipan (2006).

[7] See also McCubbins and Rodriguez (2006).

[8] Weingast (2002) surveys this mode of analysis in different contexts. Shepsle (2006) provides a variant on these themes.

[9] Laver (2006) covers some of these issues; see also the summary in Shepsle and Weingast (1995).

cutting line is that policy halfway between the status quo and the proposed alternative (assuming that legislator utility functions are symmetric). Since the status quo is to the right of the median, so too will be the cutting line. The proposal makes every legislator to the right of the cutting line worse off, so they vote against the policy, while every legislator to the left of the cutting line is better off under the proposal and will vote for it.

Given the assumption of how legislators choose parties, nearly all legislators from the left party vote for the proposal; while most of those of the right party vote against it. Indeed, if the status quo is not too far to the right relative to the distribution of legislature preferences, then most of the members of the right party will vote against the change. In other words, voting on this legislature will exhibit polarization by party even though the party exerts no pressure on its members to vote one way or another.

A lesson of this model is that polarized party voting can emerge as the combined result of legislative preferences and sorting into parties without being a function of any legislative institutions that advantage parties or that constrain member behavior.

Although this approach rationalizes only minimalist legislative institutions, it provides an important baseline from which to judge other models. While most approaches rely on legislator preferences to some degree, we term this approach a preference-based approach because it relies solely on legislative preferences and the median voter model to explain political phenomena, such as polarized party voting.

1.2 Committees as Commitment Devices

The second approach is exemplified by Weingast and Marshall's (1988) "Industrial organization of Congress." This approach built on previous theoretical and empirical work. Going back to Buchanan and Tullock (1962), many models of legislative choice emphasized logrolling and vote-trading. By logrolling and trading votes, members and the districts they represented were better off. Logrolling can thus be seen as a legislative institution parallel to market institutions in the economic sphere.

Empirically, the substantive literature on Congress long emphasized the central importance of committees, which were seen to dominate the policy-making process, at least in the mid-twentieth century. That literature emphasized committee specialization and self-selection onto committees by members most interested in the committee jurisdiction (Fenno 1966; 1973; Shepsle 1978). Congress scholars argued that this form of committee organization suited members' electoral goals (Mayhew 1974). Committee organization was seen as reflecting the preferences of the legislators and their constituents. In this view, the key to understanding legislative organization was legislative exchange.

Weingast and Marshall sought an explanation of congressional organization that accounted for the fundamental features then found in the substantive literature. They based their approach on two observations. First, the legislature faced many different issues that cannot be combined into a single dimension: agriculture is not commensurate with civil rights, banking, or defense. Second, vote-trading had significant enforcement problems as a means of legislative exchange. For example, suppose that one group of legislators seeks to build dams and bridges, another group seeks regulatory control of some market, and that neither group alone comprises a majority. The two groups could, per logrolling, agree to support one another's legislation. But this raises a problem: Once their dams and bridges are built, what stops those receiving them from joining members locked out of the original trade to renege on the original deal by passing new legislation ending the regulation? Because of the possibility of reneging, some logrolls will fail *ex ante* as legislators fear their deals will ultimately fail.[10]

Enforcement problems imply that direct exchange of votes is not likely to provide a durable means of legislative exchange. Instead, Weingast and Marshall argued that legislators were likely to institutionalize their exchanges in the form of a legislative committee system (LCS) that granted legislators greater powers over policies within the committee's jurisdiction. They showed that, in the context of a mechanism to grant rights to committee seats in combination with self-selection onto committees, the LCS made members with different preferences better off.

Consider the problem of reneging noted above. Self-selection onto committees with gatekeeping power prevents this type of reneging. Suppose the group favoring dams and bridges seek to renege on their original deal and introduce legislation to undo the regulation. This legislation now goes to the committee with jurisdiction. Populated by those who favor maintaining the regulation, committee members prevent the legislation from coming before the legislature. This system preserves both the status quo and the original legislative exchange.

This approach also addresses an important question raised by the majoritarian postulate. This postulate questions why a majority would ever vote to reduce or restrict its own powers in the future. In the context of a single dimension of legislative choice, it is hard to understand why the median (and hence a majority) would vote to restrict itself. In the context of multiple dimensions, however, no median exists. The exchange postulate underlying the LCS provides an answer to the question: A majority votes to restrict itself on a series of different policy issues simultaneously. Although this restricts the majority's actions on each dimension, if each member is assigned to a committee of higher value than the average, this exchange makes each better off (see also Calvert 1995).

In this model, committee organization solves the problem of legislative exchange. Given pervasive enforcement problems of direct exchange of votes, legislators instead choose to organize the legislature in such a way as to institutionalize a pattern of exchange that furthers the goals of all. Of course, that model reflected the substantive literature of studying the textbook Congress of the mid-twentieth century, a world of Congress very different from that more partisan-dominated Congress of the late twentieth and early twenty-first centuries.

---

[10] A second enforcement problem is that exchange of votes over time creates additional opportunities for reneging, especially as bills evolve.

1.3 Legislative Parties as Solutions to Collective Dilemmas

The third approach uses legislative parties to explain legislative organization and behavior. In this view, parties are more than just a collection of people choosing the same party label (Aldrich 1995; Rohde 1991; Sinclair 2006). Cox and McCubbins (1993), for example, argue that legislators face a series of collective action problems that political parties can resolve. For example, individual legislators have trouble passing their own legislation; and without coordinating, legislator activity fails to add up to enough to help each get re-elected. In particular, all legislators face a common-pool problem in which they have incentives to shift costs onto each other. Parties overcome these problems by enforced coordination.[11]

In the face of various coordination and related problems, Cox and McCubbins argue that members have an incentive to use parties to coordinate the behavior of their members for several ends: to produce legislation more attractive to their members; to develop a national reputation or brand name; and, in combination, to use these tools to help re-elect their members (see also Wittman 1989; 1995).

Committees in this view are a tool of the majority party used to further party goals; namely, to propose legislation benefiting party members and to prevent legislation that would make party majorities worse off. The majority party's delegation to each committee, rather than being composed of those most interested in the policy as in the Weingast and Marshall approach, are representative of the party. This particularly holds for gatekeeping committees, such as the budget committee where the members do not self-select. Tests of the representatives of committees tend to support the party view (see, e.g., Cox and McCubbins 1993). Also consistent with this view was the striking partisan aspect of congressional voting, particularly since 1980.

In more recent work, Cox and McCubbins present the negative agenda control model (NAC), which holds that the majority party does not coerce its members to vote anything but their preferences, but does carefully control the *agenda*; that is, the alternatives that arise for a vote. In particular, the majority party uses NAC to prevent any bill from arising that would make a majority of the majority party worse off. This means that any bill seeking to move a status quo located between the floor median and the reflection of the floor median around the party median should never come up for vote. A range of empirical tests provide strong evidence for the proposition based on predicted asymmetries in roll-rates (Cox and McCubbins 2005), direction of movements in bills (Cox and McCubbins 2005), and estimated cutpoints (Stiglitz and Weingast 2008).

However, this party-centric approach has not been without its critics. Krehbiel (1993) presented a major challenge to this perspective by asking, "where's the party?" Relying on the preference-based approach noted above, he showed that many of the findings of the party-centric perspective were consistent with the majoritarian perspective. We have already noted how polarized party voting, rather than being a

---

[11] See also Cox (2006) who shows how legislative parties arise endogenously as a means to resolve the problem of potential over-use of plenary time.

product of the party organization of the legislature, can result from simple preferences in combination with legislator sorting into parties. Another aspect is the representativeness of committees. As noted, the party perspective emphasizes that each party's delegation to a committee is representative of the party; but if both parties do this, then the overall committee will be representative of the chamber, also consistent with the majoritarian perspective.

The debate about parties has spurned a remarkable empirical literature. See for example, Cox and McCubbins (2005), Krehbiel (2006), and Groseclose and Snyder (2001). We do not have time here to cover this literature, but we do want to emphasize that the research in endogenous legislative institutions is empirical, as well.

1.4 Information Explanations for Structure

The final approach to legislative organization, associated with Gilligan and Krehbiel (1989) and Krehbiel (1991), emphasizes that legislators are uncertain about the impact of their choices on actual outcomes. Legislators therefore have an incentive to organize the legislature to reflect the task of gaining expertise and information that reduces this uncertainty. In this world, committees are bodies of legislative experts in the policies of their jurisdiction. Committee expertise allows committee members to reduce the uncertainty between legislation and actual outcomes.

This perspective has significant implications for legislative organization, including the choice of rules governing consideration of legislation on the floor. For example, because expertise requires costly investment, legislators will undertake this costly investment only if the system somehow compensates them for this. Krehbiel argues that restrictive rules that bias legislative choice in favor of committees are the answer. Although restrictive rules prevent legislators from choosing policy associated with the median voter *ex post*, legislators are better off *ex ante* because committee expertise allows committees to reduce the uncertainty associated with the difference between legislation and policy outcomes.

1.5 Concluding Thoughts

The debate about legislative institutions has been lively, and no consensus has yet emerged on the determinants of legislative organization. We cannot yet say whether one perspective will ultimately triumph (as Gilligan and Krehbiel 1995 suggest) or whether a synthesis of perspectives is likely to emerge (as Shepsle and Weingast 1995 suggest).

From a broader perspective, the study of legislative institutions provides a template for how research on institutions is likely to proceed in the future. The first stage is to see how a particular institution affects behavior; next, similar but somewhat different institutions are compared; then in the final stage, institutions are treated as being endogenous. If the history of research on endogenous legislative institutions is any guide, there will be disagreement on which institutions are endogenous to other institutions. These controversies, in turn, help shape our understanding of institutions and provide a deeper understanding of organizations.

2 REVELATION AND AGGREGATION OF INFORMATION: VOTING

In this section, we consider the revelation and aggregation of information. This is a game-theoretic, as opposed to a decision-theoretic, approach to information. An exciting aspect of this research is that it often turns the standard theoretic wisdom on its head. We illustrate by looking at voting behavior.[12]

Traditional democratic theory argues that, for democracy to work, voters should inform themselves about the candidates and the issues. Moreover, voters should be unbiased and rely on unbiased sources of information. Practice in all working democracies differs greatly from this ideal. Voters appear to be notoriously uninformed (and, indeed, have little incentive to become informed). Some voters base their choice of candidate solely on party label, while other voters rely on biased sources of information, including information provided by pressure groups.

Does this apparent lack of information imply that democracy will fall far from its ideal? Possibly not, if the lack of information is more apparent than real. In the following, we show how voters can make logical inferences so that their behavior is similar to perfectly informed voters.

We start with an easy example to illustrate how information revelation arises. A number of articles study the endogenous timing of elections in parliamentary systems.[13] Because it has access to information, the ruling party is able to forecast future economic performance and other events that are likely to impact on voters' welfare. This information is not likely to be available to the voters. The party in power has an incentive to call an election when it is at the height of its popularity.

However, this decision-theoretic analysis does not consider the voter response to an early election call. Voters can infer from an early election call that the ruling party expects to do worse in the future.[14] Voters can therefore infer that there is likely to be bad news in the future. The ruling government realizes that voters will act this way. As a result, governments are less likely to call early elections than they would otherwise; and when they do, voters will take this information into account and be less positively inclined towards the government. Smith (2003; 2004) provides empirical evidence in support of this argument. Polls taken after the announcement of an early election show a decline from polls taken before the announcement. Incorporating the

---

[12] Ansolabehere (2006) reviews the broad topic of voting behavior.

[13] See for example, Cargill and Hutchison (1991) and the long list of citations found in Smith (2003, n. 6).

[14] Here, we ignore other reasons for calling an early election, in particular the desire of the ruling party in a coalition government to strengthen its hand.

voters' response made obsolete much of the earlier research on endogenous timing of elections that did not consider the possibility that voters could make inferences.

Consider another area where earlier research assumed mechanical, uninformed voters, but more recent research assumes uninformed but rational voters, often with starkly differing results. Starting with Ben Zion and Eytan (1974) and continuing on into the recent past (see Baron 1994; Grossman and Helpman 1996), an extensive literature has assumed that the more money a candidate spends on advertising, the more votes the candidate receives from uninformed voters. Sources of money tend to come from interests on the extremes of the political distribution. To get contributions that pay for such advertising, candidates move their policies away from the median voter toward a pressure group's most preferred position.

Let us look at the Grossman and Helpman model in greater detail.[15] Grossman and Helpman assume the following: voters, candidates, and pressure groups are arrayed along a one-dimensional issue space. Each voter has a most preferred position with a concave utility function over policy; this means that voters are risk averse.[16] There are two types of voters: informed voters who know the positions of the candidates and uninformed voters who have no knowledge of the candidates' or pressure group's positions. Informed voters vote for the candidate closest to the voter's most preferred position. Uninformed voters respond only to political advertising—the more money spent on advertising by one of the candidates, the greater the percentage of uninformed voters voting for the candidate.

Each candidate wants to maximize the percentage of votes that he or she receives. There is one pressure group (say, on the extreme right). The pressure group is willing to donate money to one of the candidates if the candidate moves right from the median voter.

The election proceeds as follows:

1. The pressure group makes a one-time take-it-or-leave-it offer to one of the candidates. If the candidate agrees to move right of the median informed voter, then the pressure group provides funds to the candidate for political advertising. If the agreement is accepted, it is binding on both sides.
2. The candidate receiving the offer decides whether to accept or reject it. If the candidate accepts the offer, then the other candidate knows the position of the candidate accepting the offer. The other candidate will then choose a position between the candidate and the median informed voter to capture as many informed voters as possible. If the candidate rejects the offer, then the pressure group is out of the picture. Per the standard Downsian (1957) model, both candidates will then choose to be at the median of the informed voters.
3. The positions of the candidates are then made public to the *informed* voters. The candidate who received the donation then advertises.
4. The voters choose.

---

[15] For heuristic purposes, we simplify their model.
[16] Risk aversion means that voters prefer a sure thing over a lottery having the same expected value as the sure thing.

Given the setup of the model, it is not hard to see that the candidate will be willing to move right from the median of the informed voters as long as the advertising from the campaign funds sufficiently increases the number of uninformed voters to compensate for the loss of informed voters caused by the movement to the right and away from the median informed voter.

The model seems to imply that pressure groups are likely to undermine the political process. But is it rational for uninformed voters to act in the way postulated? Let us consider the model more carefully.

In the above model, the candidates, pressure group, and informed voters are all rational, but not the uninformed voters. As already mentioned, uninformed voters vote mechanically. But being uninformed does not mean being irrational. Suppose instead that the uninformed do not vote mechanically but can make logical inferences. We consider two variants with different characterizations of uninformed voter behavior.

First, let us continue to assume that the uninformed voters know neither the positions of the candidates nor the position of the pressure group (the pressure group being equally likely to be on the left or the right). Campaign advertising is, by its very nature, public so that an ordinary person can infer which candidate received the most contributions by observing which candidate has the most political advertising. The uninformed voters can simply watch television and passively observe the candidate who has the most advertisements. Given the logic of the model, the uninformed can infer that the candidate doing the advertising is further away from the median informed voter than the candidate not doing the advertising.

Given our assumption that the uninformed voter does not even know whether the pressure group is on the left or the right, the uninformed voter faces a greater risk from the candidate who is doing the advertising. Both candidates will on average be at the median informed voter's most preferred position, but the candidate receiving the campaign funds will be more extreme. Thus the risk-averse uninformed voter should vote for the candidate not doing the advertising! The rational voter does not act like the mechanical voter in this case. Of course, if this behavior characterizes uninformed voters, then the candidate will not accept campaign donations from the pressure group in the first place.

Now suppose that the uninformed know something. For example, they may know that the National Rifle Association supports one of the candidates, and as a consequence these voters can infer that the candidate receiving the funds is closer than the median informed voter is to the position of the NRA. More generally, the uninformed voter may know whether the pressure group is on the right. If the uninformed voter also knows where he or she stands relative to the median voter, the uninformed voter to the left of the median voter can infer that he or she should vote for the other candidate, while those uninformed voters to the right will be inclined to vote for the candidate receiving funds from the right-wing pressure group.

Consider two cases: If uninformed voters tend to be to the right of the median informed voter, then the candidate may accept funds from the right-wing pressure group and even advertise this to be the case. This occurs when the candidate gets sufficiently more votes from the uninformed voters on the right than she loses from the uninformed voters on the left to make up for the reduced vote share from informed voters. Alternatively, if there are more uninformed voters to the left of the median informed voter, the candidate would lose if she accepted the deal from the pressure group. Hence she would not do so in the first place.

In this version of the model, pressure group contributions help the uninformed voters. If the mass of uninformed voters is to the right of the median of the informed voters (and hence, the overall median is to the right of the median of the informed voters), then one candidate will accept the funds and the effect of campaign donations will be to move the candidate to the right from the median of the informed voters. On the other hand, if more uninformed voters lie to the left of the median, neither candidate will accept funds from a pressure group on the right.[17] In short, pressure groups aid the political process rather than undermine it!

We have just modeled the case where some voters are uninformed about the candidates' positions. Another possibility is that voters are informed about the candidates' positions but not about their relative quality. Again, assume that voters are rational and the pressure group has private information (in this case, about the relative quality of the candidates). A number of recent papers consider this case but employ differing subsidiary assumptions: advertising has content (see Coate 2004; Wittman 2007); advertising has no content, but expenditures on advertising signal information (see Prat 2002; 2006); pressure groups make the offers (Coate, Prat), candidates make the offers; there is one pressure group, there are multiple pressure groups; the candidates are only interested in winning, and the candidates have policy goals. These various modeling efforts do not all come to the same positive conclusion as the previous paragraph. In general, the results depend on whether the value of the revealed information is outweighed by the loss from inferior candidate positions when the candidates compete for pressure group funds. In turn, this balance depends to a great degree on the number of pressure groups and whether it is the candidates or the pressure groups that make the offer. All these various modeling efforts take into account that information valuable to uninformed voters is revealed by the pressure group's donation or endorsement and all of them assume rationality of the voters. This is the key methodological advance—how voters can incorporate information that others might want to distort or hide (see Prat 2006).

We have shown how uninformed voters can make inferences from behavior and thereby become more informed. Because all of this is embedded in a game, all other players take this behavior and information into account when they make their decisions; and of course the uninformed take the other players' strategies into account when they make their own inferences.[18]

---

[17] The exact result requires more technical specification and can be found in Wittman (forthcoming).

[18] There are other ways in which voters can be informed despite an apparent lack of information. Parties create brand names so that party labels are in fact informative about a candidate's position (Cox and McCubbins 1993; 2005). Relying on biased information can be rational for voters who have strong priors in favor of one of the parties (Calvert 1985). And uninformed voters can learn from polls of informed voters (McKelvey and Ordeshook 1986).

The final example for this section considers aggregation of information in the context of voting. Suppose a set of voters face a decision about how much money to spend. To gain intuition, we begin with an exceedingly simple example. Suppose that there are five voters with identical preferences: three have unbiased estimates of the correct action to take, while two are fully informed. The voters know whether they are informed or not. The uninformed know that informed voters exist, but not how many. Suppose further that the correct action is to spend $7 million and that, with equal probability, the uninformed players receive a signal that it should be 5, 7, or 9 million dollars. Assuming that the voters cannot communicate with each other, how likely is it that the majority rule decision is not 7? The answer is zero if the voters are rational: All the uninformed voters will rationally abstain. By doing so, they know that only informed voters will participate and that these informed voters will make the correct decision.

This example illustrates two important but related issues. First, the more informed people will choose to vote (here, at least, the argument does not go against conventional wisdom). Second, the potential voter asks: Given that he will be pivotal, should he vote, and if he votes, how should he vote? In other words, the decision to vote and how to vote does not just depend on whether the person will be pivotal, but also on the preferences and information structure of all of the voters. Our understanding of the problem is no longer in terms of decision theory but in terms of game theory.

To illustrate this idea in terms of a more complicated (but more realistic) model, assume that there are three voters (or three groups of voters), labeled V_1, V_2, and V_3; and two states of the world, labeled 1 and 2. Assume that voter V_1 votes for candidate D regardless of the state of the world. The second voter, V_2, is independent but informed. This voter knows the state of the world and votes for D when the state of the world is 1 and votes for R when the state of the world is 2: Given V_2's preferences, D makes a better president if the state of the world is 1 while R makes a better president if the state of the world is 2. The third voter, V_3, has the same preference structure as V_2, but is uninformed. However, V_3 knows the preferences and information sets of the other two voters.

How should V_3 vote if the probability of state 1 (where D is V_3's preferred candidate) is more likely than the probability of state 2? The decision-theoretic model, where V_3's vote is based on the most likely state of the world (state 1), suggests that V_3 should vote for D. But the game-theoretic pivot model argues that V_3 should vote for R. The reasoning is as follows. If the state of the world is 1, then both voter V_1 and voter V_2 vote for D, and D will win regardless of V_3's vote. When the state of the world is 2, then the other two voters will split their vote and V_3 will be pivotal. Under such circumstances, V_3 should vote for R since she prefers R to D in state 2. So V_3 always votes for R.[19] Behaving in this way allows the informed voter, V_2, whose preferences are similar to V_3's, to be pivotal in all circumstances. This behavior results in better outcomes for V_3 than that suggested by the decision-theoretic perspective. Because

---

[19] For a more extended discussion see Fedderson and Pesendorfer (1996; 1999).

the latter tells V_3 to always vote for D, V_3 incorrectly votes for D even in the state 2 when she prefers R.

These two examples show that uninformed voters can make inferences about how to behave that make them better off, even when they remain ignorant of critical aspects of the election. Now this particular example requires V_3 to know a lot about the other voters, but the conceptual apparatus can be incorporated into other models where the information requirements are not so high.

To return to our earlier discussion of pressure groups where some voters are uninformed about the candidates' positions, Wittman (2009) shows that the uninformed voters to the right (left) of the median voter should always employ the following rule of thumb: Vote for (against) the candidate endorsed by the right-wing pressure group.[20] Sometimes this could result in some of the uninformed voters on the right voting for the wrong candidate, and at other times this could result in some of the uninformed voters on the left voting for the wrong candidate. However, even if all the mistaken votes for one candidate were reversed this would not change the outcome. So fully rational but uninformed voters consider the effect of their behavior when pivotal even if their likelihood of being pivotal is small. Indeed, in this example, by their rule of thumb, the uninformed make the informed median over all voters the pivot.

To summarize: Democratic theory has long held that ignorant voters harm the operation of democracy. The force of this section is to demonstrate that uninformed voters and uninformed actors more generally can make inferences based on the behavior of others, the structure of their strategic situation, and signals received from other actors. These inferences make uninformed voters better off than predicted by decision-theoretic models; and they improve the workings of democracy more than predicted by traditional democratic theory.[21] We believe that in the next decade the aggregation and revelation of information will continue to be a very important mode of research and that it will continue to overturn received wisdom (see Moulin 2006 and Ledyard 2006 for further examples).

3 Evolutionary Models of Human and Political Behavior

Both economics and evolutionary models of human behavior employ the concepts of survival and equilibrium (Alchian 1950). Nonetheless, the implications of economic and biological models at times conflict. Although people who are capable of achieving

---

[20] The actual model employs additional assumptions that assure that certain pathologies do not arise.

[21] See Ansolabehere (2006) who makes this point. Calvert (1985) makes a similar point, showing that voters with preferences for *biased* information may also be rational, especially if they have strong priors.

their goals either because of their physical or mental prowess are more likely to survive and produce offspring, it is not clear that fitness would accrue to those who maximized utility and were happier. Furthermore, at times evolutionary fitness may be gained by being less rational; for example, the emotional may serve as a useful commitment device (see Hirshleifer 2001).

Humans are preeminently social animals. Political structures are one kind of social structure, and such structures need to be compatible for better or worse with the biology of human behavior. Are people naturally xenophobic, vengeful, or generally limited in their capacity for empathy? Hypotheses about human behavior abound. But economics and/or evolutionary biology demand that the hypothesized behavior survives in a competitive equilibrium. The principle of survival in equilibrium imposes discipline on modeling efforts because not all hypotheses satisfy this criterion.

Models of pure self-regarding preferences have generated considerable insight into the political process; yet such an assumption is not requisite for rational behavior. People may be other-regarding in that they care about their children or feel altruistic or vengeful towards others.[22] How other-regarding behavior survives in equilibrium is a major research question that still has not been fully answered.

Let us start with an easy question. Why are human parents altruistic to their children? Infants and small children need care in order to survive. Parental altruism helps to ensure the genetic transmission. But genetic relatedness rapidly approaches zero as the population increases in size. So this simple explanation for altruism falters when we want to extend it to the population as a whole.

A significant number of researchers seek to understand the role of vengeance. The phenomenon of suicide bombers inspires some of this interest—being a suicide bomber hardly appears to improve genetic fitness. Further interest in vengeance is inspired by experiments demonstrating that the standard income-maximizing model does not work well in certain situations. For example, consider the ultimatum game in which person A is given a certain amount of money (say ten dollars); A then offers a share of this money to B; B then either rejects or accepts the offer. If B rejects the offer, neither gets any of the money and the game is over. A theory that is based on humans being purely self-regarding predicts that A should offer B a trivial amount, say one cent. Because one cent is better than nothing, B is better off accepting the offer than rejecting it. Experiments consistently reveal that B subjects often reject low offers even though this hurts them financially. Further, experiments also reveal that A subjects often offer significant amounts to B to forestall such a rejection.[23]

---

[22] The phrase "other regarding" gets around the problem that altruistic behavior may make the person feel good and therefore altruism could be termed selfish behavior.

[23] The explanation for the rejection is that the person dividing the money has not been "fair." For a further discussion of fairness in experiments and the implications for political behavior see Palfrey (2006).

This vengeful behavior by B is contrary to income maximization. Thus, the key intellectual puzzle to resolve is how vengeful behavior can be evolutionarily stable.

Scholars provide two types of answers. One is that a reputation for vengeful behavior may enhance fitness because others may avoid provoking revenge by avoiding doing harm to the vengeful person in the first place. Following this intuition, some evolutionary models show that, under certain circumstances, two types of people, vengeful and nonvengeful, can survive in equilibrium (Friedman and Singh forthcoming).[24]

Here we will concentrate on the second approach—the co-evolution of memes (social constructs) and genes—because that is more relevant to our understanding of collective choice and social cooperation. Humans are more social than their ancestors, and many argue that this sociability evolved along with the social institutions that made such sociability result in greater reproductive success. Consider the following thought experiment. If chimpanzees had language (which in itself enhances sociability) and could do calculus, would chimpanzee society look like human society if they were able to observe our customs? The co-evolution argument says no. Shame, guilt, the ability to be empathetic or vengeful, and certain conceptual possibilities that make us human would all be much more circumscribed in chimpanzees, which themselves show more of these qualities than marsupials. Without pro-social emotions, all humans (rather than just a few) might be sociopaths, and human society as we know it might not exist despite the institutions of contract, government law enforcement, and reputation.[25]

Groups that overcome prisoner's dilemmas (and other social dilemmas) are likely to be more productive in gathering food and more successful in warfare against other groups. In turn, this leads to greater reproductive success. The central question for evolutionary models is how, if at all, evolutionary pressure keeps individual shirking in check. It seems, for example, that a person who is slightly less brave in battle is more likely to survive and have children than his braver compatriots. Bravery at once increases the risk for the brave while making it more likely that the less brave survive. If bravery/cowardice is genetic, how is a downward spiral of cowardice prevented?

One answer proceeds along the following lines: If the individuals are punished for shirking (in this case, being cowardly), this will keep them in line. But because engaging in punishment is costly (possibly resulting in the would-be punisher's death), who will do the punishing? The evolutionary approach suggests that punishment, a kind of vengeance, will be a successful strategy for the punisher if he gains even a

---

[24] To get this result, Friedman and Singh develop a new equilibrium concept—evolutionary perfect Bayesian equilibrium. Their paper, as is the case for much of the research on the evolutionary stability of vengeance, employs sophisticated mathematical modeling. This illustrates another theme of our chapter—that political economy, unlike other intellectual approaches to political science, emphasizes logical rigor, which often requires considerable mathematics.

[25] For further discussion along these lines see Bowles and Gintis (2006); Friedman and Singh (2000); Boyd et al. (2003); Gintis et al. (2005).

mild fitness advantage (status, more females, etc.). This is because, in equilibrium, the cost to the punisher is relatively small since punishment does not have to be meted out very often. Punishment need not be carried out frequently to be effective. It is the threat that is important. To the degree that shirkers by being punished (possibly by being banished from the tribe) become less fit, the need to engage in punishment decreases even more as there are fewer shirkers. And given that those who punish are more aligned with the interests of the society and therefore may be more likely to survive, there may be enough potential punishers so that the need for any individual to bear the costs of punishment is reduced still further (which of course means that the benefits received will also be reduced). If altruism and vengeance are gene-based rather than meme-based, memes and genes may co-evolve. Over the eons, human society may have encouraged pro-social genetically based emotions.[26]

The force of this argument is that pro-social emotions bypass the cognitive optimizing process that is at the core of rational economic man. This cognitive difference implies that at times we should observe profound differences between the evolutionary model and the economic model. Under certain circumstances, seemingly irrational behavior, such as vengeance or shame, may be evolutionarily stable even if it runs counter to individual utility maximization. Moreover the relatively slow genetic evolution in comparison with meme evolution (especially in the last 100 years) yields a further conclusion: It is quite possible that some of the pro-social emotions whose genetic basis evolved over the last 100,000 or more years are maladapted for the modern world.

At present the evolutionary study of genes and memes has produced very tentative results. Human behavior is part mammalian (possibly even reptilian), part primate, and part hominid. Although some have argued that much of human psychology developed in the savannah, it is not clear what part of human psychology developed then or earlier or, to a lesser degree, later. Also, we have only a rudimentary picture of human life in the savannah so evolutionary models of this period are very speculative. Furthermore, it is not clear whether the transmission of behavior is through memes or genes. Clearly, we have much room for further research on these topics, and we believe that in the coming decade there will be many advances.[27]

---

[26] This just gives the flavor of the argument. Once again, it is worthwhile to emphasize that the research summarized here employs very carefully specified models. The challenge for researchers in the field is to characterize a situation where vengeance survives, but does not become so intense that it undermines social relations. At the same time, the researcher must account for the possibility that nonvengeful types may want to mimic vengeful types. Finally, the researcher must mix the memes and genes so that they are in a stable equilibrium.

[27] Another group of social scientists employs a different strategy for generalizing about human behavior from the standard model of rationality, by drawing on cognitive science and psychology (e.g. North 2005). Space constraints prevent an adequate treatment.

4 PUSHING THE ENVELOPE OF INVESTIGATION

As political economy has matured, it has begun to tackle a wider range of topics. This work includes a series of larger questions, such as the origins of dictatorship and democracy. In this section, we consider one of these frontier topics—the size of nations.

Much of history reflects the expansion and contraction of nations. The conquests of Alexander the Great, the rise and decline of the Roman Empire, the aggressive expansions of Napoleon and Hitler, and the dissolution of the USSR are just a few examples. At the other end of the spectrum, many tiny countries, such as Singapore and Andorra, have survived a considerable length of time.

For over two millennia, historians and philosophers have asked why some nations have expanded, why others have contracted, and what is the optimal size of a polity (Plato, for example, said that the optimal size was 5,040 families). In this section, we discuss recent political economy contributions to this area. In the process, we show how research in political economy builds upon earlier foundations.

The political economy approach to the size of nations starts with the Downsian characterization of voter preferences. In this case, citizen preferences can be placed along a line (or a circle). This line or circle is then divided into n parts (not necessarily equal), each part representing a country. Each country chooses a policy position, X_j, which might be the median or mean of the citizens' preferences. A citizen's utility for her nation's policy is assumed to be decreasing in distance from her own preferred position, x (e.g. $-|x - |X_j$ or $-(x - X_j)^2$). Individuals at the boundary of two countries can choose in which country to reside (see Spolaore 2006; Alesina and Spolaore 2003, for a more complete coverage).[28]

Each citizen would like to have his or her country's policy as closely aligned as possible to her preferred policy. If policy were the only factor, all countries would be composed of only one citizen. But other factors run counter to this extreme decentralization. The most important are economies of scale in production and military power. When barriers to free trade exist between countries, a more populous country achieves greater economies of scale through its larger domestic market. A larger population also allows for greater military power, which may make war against smaller and weaker states more profitable because of the higher probability of success. At the same time greater military power makes predation by other states less profitable to these other states and therefore less likely (see Skaperdas 2006).

These insights yield comparative statics predictions. When barriers to free trade are reduced (so that economies of scale can be achieved within a small country as long as it has sufficient international sales) and the returns to warfare are decreased,

---

[28] Of course, individuals might not be free to migrate. See Friedman (1977) for an explanation for the Iron Curtain and the promotion of linguistic boundaries.

the number of countries will increase and the average country size will decrease. The returns to warfare depend greatly on the nature of the victim country's wealth. If the wealth is in oil, the predating county can expropriate most of the wealth; when the wealth is in human capital, the predating country can expropriate very little. In the latter case, the benefits to predation are reduced, the threat of war is less credible, and the benefits of being a large country are diminished.

In a simple model where wealth is distributed evenly among the citizens, those citizens at the periphery of the country will be most dissatisfied with their country's policy. They are therefore the most likely citizens to exit and join the adjacent country. Because of economies of scale in production and military power, this "migration" is costly to those citizens left behind. In order to forestall such migration, countries might institute a nonlinear transfer scheme that grants citizens on the periphery greater resources. Le Breton and Weber (2001) make this argument and point to a number of cases, such as Quebec in Canada and some of the border states of India, where the center grants special rights to the peripheral states. This extension of the basic model affords a nice illustration of how political economy often grows. Instead of two competing models, the basic model is expanded so that we have a more general theory.

In the basic model, except for the median policy, all of the countries have the same characteristics; and, when population is uniformly distributed on the line or circle, all countries are of the same size. Extensions of the basic model allow countries to have different characteristics. Nations are characterized as a nexus of public goods. A wise public policy choice may significantly increase the overall wealth of the citizenry. Successful countries create conditions for high productivity in the economic sphere by enforcing property rights and providing social overhead capital, while at the same time minimizing political costs by creating a system of rules that reduce influence costs and allow for diverse preferences. Countries also need an effective military apparatus to protect their wealth from predation by other countries. Success in these endeavors may lead to immigration and geographical expansion, while failure to meet these goals may lead to extensive emigration or breakup of a country (see Wittman 2000).

Bolton and Roland (1997) consider another variant of the model. Until now we have assumed that the citizens are similar in all respects except for their preference for public policy, which has been given exogenously. Suppose instead that individuals differ in productivity and income, which determines their preference for redistributive public policy. Suppose further that there are two sections of the country and that each section votes by majority rule. Then two sections of a country may separate because of significant productivity differences. All of this is reflective of Tiebout's (1956) argument that jurisdictions specialize to reflect the preferences and wealth of their constituents.[29]

---

[29] For an extensive discussion of the Tiebout hypothesis, see Wildasin (2006). For ethnic causes of division, see Fearon (2006).

To summarize, these works illustrate how political economy makes use of its basic tools to investigate an ever deepening set of questions. Ultimately, fewer institutions are treated as being exogenously determined and more institutions, including the nation state, are treated as variables to be explained. In this way, anthropology and history become part of political economy.

We conclude this section on pushing the envelope with a final observation. The bulk of political economy research has focused on institutions and behavior within advanced industrial democracies (as the essays in Weingast and Wittman 2006 illustrate). In these settings, the formal institutions of courts, legislatures, executives, bureaucracy, and elections can all be taken as given. Hundreds, if not thousands, of papers have been written on these topics. Not surprisingly, the most progress has been made in these areas.

In contrast, political economy work that studies phenomena in countries outside of the advanced industrial democracies has made far less progress. Nevertheless, there are a number of exciting developments. We briefly mention a few areas of nascent research (posed as questions) that are likely to blossom in the future.

- What do authoritarians maximize and why do they make the decisions they do? In past, many scholars assumed that they maximize their share of rents (e.g. North 1981, ch. 3; Olson 2001). Yet this approach remains inadequate because it takes as given that the authoritarian remains in power, something deeply problematic (as Tullock 1987 observed). Bueno de Mesquita et al. (2003; see Bueno de Mesquita 2006 for a summary) provide a new approach, arguing that authoritarians maximize their likelihood of staying in power. Haber (2006) provides a program for future research on this topic. North, Wallis, and Weingast (2009) criticize models in this category because they assume a single ruler with a monopoly on violence, showing that models of the state must instead take into account how coalitions without a monopoly on violence are able to rule.
- Why does democracy survive in some countries but not others? Przeworski (2006) argues against some common answers and suggests that per capita wealth is an important reason.
- And while we are on the subject of democracy, what is the relationship between democracy and capitalism? Iverson (2006) surveys various political economy models that try to answer this question.
- Why do so many countries remain poor? And why did a handful of countries in the eighteenth and nineteenth centuries manage to rise well above the rest of the world? Here too we have important new political economy models that seek to answer these questions (see, for example, Acemoglu and Robinson 2006; Bates 2006).
- What are the sources and circumstances of ethnic coalitions and violence? Fearon (2006) provides an overview of the political economy approach and an agenda for future research.

In short, the extension of political economy methods beyond the advanced industrial nations is rapidly developing. and we expect significant advances in the near future.

5 The Intellectual Arms Race

Although we have characterized political economy as a set of agreed-upon methodological approaches, the set is large and diverse, and different models and empirical studies frequently come to quite opposing conclusions. Scholarly works tend to play off each other so that there is an ever-increasing level of sophistication. Thus, while we have characterized political economy as a synthesis of fields, the synthesis will nonetheless provide sparks and an exciting research agenda for decades to come.

References

Acemoglu, D. and Robinson, J. 2006. Paths of Economic and Political Development. Ch. 36 in Weingast and Wittman 2006.

Alchian, A. 1950. Uncertainty, evolution, and economic theory. *Journal of Political Economy*, 58: 211–21.

Aldrich, J. H. 1995. *Why Parties? The Origin and Transformation of Party Politics in America*. Chicago: University of Chicago Press.

Alesina, A. and Spolaore, E. 2003. *The Size of Nations*. Cambridge, Mass.: MIT Press.

Ansolabehere, S. 2006. Voters, candidates, and parties. Ch. 2 in Weingast and Wittman 2006.

Austen-Smith, D. 2006. Economic methods in positive political theory. Ch. 49 in Weingast and Wittman 2006.

Baron, D. P. 1994. Electoral competition with informed and uninformed voters. *American Political Science Review*, 88: 33–47.

Bates, R. 2006. The role of the state in development. Ch. 38 in Weingast and Wittman 2006.

Ben-Zion, U. and Eytan, Z. 1974. On money, votes and policy in a democratic society. *Public Choice*, 17: 1–10.

Bolton, E. and Roland, G. 1997. The breakup of nations: a political economy analysis. *Quarterly Journal of Economics*, 112: 1057–89.

Bowles, S. and Gintis, H. 2006. The evolutionary basis of collective action. Ch. 52 in Weingast and Wittman 2006.

Boyd, R., Gintis, H., Bowles, S., and Richerson, P. J. 2003. Evolution of altruistic punishment. *Proceedings of the National Academy of Sciences*, 1100: 3531–5.

Buchanan, J. and Tullock, G. 1962. *Calculus of Consent*. Ann Arbor: University of Michigan Press.

Bueno de Mesquita, B. 2006. Central issues in the study of international conflict. Ch. 45 in Weingast and Wittman 2006.

—— SMITH, A., SIVERSON, R. M., and MORROW, J. D. 2003. *The Logic of Political Survival*. Cambridge, Mass.: MIT Press.

CALVERT, R. L. 1985. The value of biased information: a rational choice model of political advice. *Journal of Politics*, 47: 530–55.

—— 1995. Rational actors, equilibrium, and social institutions. In *Explaining Social Institutions*, ed. J. Knight and I. Sened. Ann Arbor: University of Michigan Press.

CARGILL, T. F. and HUTCHISON, M. 1991. Political business cycles with endogenous election timing: evidence from Japan. *Review of Economics and Statistics*, 73: 733–9.

COATE, S. 2004. Pareto-improving campaign finance policy. *American Economic Review*, 94: 628–5.

COX, G. W. 2006. The organization of democratic legislatures. Ch. 7 in Weingast and Wittman 2006.

—— and McCUBBINS, M. D. 1993. *Legislative Leviathan*. Los Angeles: University of California Press.

—— —— 2005. *Setting the Agenda: Responsible Party Government in the U.S. House of Representatives*. New York: Cambridge University Press.

CUTRONE, M. and McCARTY, N. 2006. Does bicameralism matter. Ch. 10 in Weingast and Wittman 2006.

DENZAU, A. T. and MacKAY, R. J. 1983. Gatekeeping and monopoly power of committees: an analysis of sincere and sophisticated behavior. *American Journal of Political Science*, 27: 740–61.

DOWNS, A. 1957. *An Economic Theory of Democracy*. New York: Harper and Row.

FEARON, J. 2006. Ethnic mobilization and ethnic violence. Ch. 47 in Weingast and Wittman 2006.

FEDDERSEN, T. and PESENDORFER, W. 1996. The swing voter's curse. *American Economic Review*, 86: 408–24.

—— —— 1999. Abstentions in elections with asymmetric information and diverse preferences. *American Political Science Review*, 69: 381–98.

FENNO, R. 1966. *Power of the Purse*. Boston: Little, Brown.

—— 1973. *Congressmen in Committees*. Boston: Little, Brown.

FEREJOHN, J. and SHIPAN, C. 1990. Congressional influence on bureaucracy. *Journal of Law, Economics, and Organization*, 6: 1–20.

FRIEDMAN, D. 1977. A theory of the size and shape of nations. *Journal of Political Economy*, 85: 59–77.

FRIEDMAN, D. and SINGH, N. 2000. Negative reciprocity: the coevolution of memes and genes. *Evolution and Human Behavior*, 25: 155–73.

—— —— forthcoming. Equilibrium vengeance. *Games and Economic Behavior*.

GILLIGAN, T. and KREHBIEL, K. 1989. Asymmetric information and legislative rules with a heterogeneous committee. *American Journal of Political Science*, 33: 459–90.

—— —— 1995 The gains from exchange hypothesis of legislative organization. In *Positive Theories of Congressional Institutions*, ed. K. A. Shepsle and B. R. Weingast. Ann Arbor: University of Michigan Press.

GINTIS, H., BOWLES, S., BOYD, R., and FEHR, E. 2005. *Moral Sentiments and Material Interests: On the Foundations of Cooperation in Economic Life*. Cambridge, Mass.: MIT Press.

GLAESER, E. 2006. Inequality. Ch. 33 in Weingast and Wittman 2006.

GROSECLOSE, T. and SNYDER, J. 2001. Estimating party influence on congressional roll call voting: regression coefficients vs. classification success. *American Political Science Review*, 95: 689–98.

GROSSMAN, G. M. and HELPMAN, E. 1996. Electoral competition and special interest politics. *Review of Economic Studies*, 63: 265–86.

HABER, S. 2006. Authoritarian government. Ch. 38 in Weingast and Wittman 2006.

HIRSHLEIFER, J. 2001. On the emotions as guarantors of threats and promises. In Hirshleifer, *The Dark Side of the Force*. Cambridge: Cambridge University Press.

HUBER, C. and SHIPAN, C. 2006. Politics, delegation, and democracy. Ch. 13 in Weingast and Wittman 2006.

IVERSON, T. 2006. Capitalism and democracy. Ch. 32 in Weingast and Wittman 2006.

KREHBIEL, K. 1991. *Information and Legislative Organization*. Ann Arbor: University of Michigan Press.

—— 1993. Where's the party? *British Journal of Political science*, 23: 235–66.

—— 1998. *Pivotal Politics*. Chicago: University of Chicago Press.

—— 2006. Pivots. Ch. 12 in Weingast and Wittman 2006.

—— and SHEPSLE, K. A. 1996. *Making and Breaking Governments: Cabinets and Legislatures in Parliamentary Democracies*. Cambridge: Cambridge University Press.

LAVER, M. 2006. Legislatures and parliaments in comparative context. Ch. 6 in Weingast and Wittman 2006.

LE BRETON, M. and WEBER, S. 2001. The art of making everybody happy: how to prevent a secession. IMF Staff Papers, Working Paper No. 011176.

LEDYARD, J. 2006. Voting and efficient public good mechanisms. Ch. 26 in Weingast and Wittman 2006.

McCUBBINS, M. and RODRIGUEZ, D. 2006. The judiciary and the role of law. Ch. 14 in Weingast and Wittman 2006.

McKELVEY, R. and ORDESHOOK, P. 1986. Information, electoral equilibria, and the democratic ideal. *Journal of Politics*, 48: 909–37.

MARKS, B. A. 1988. A model of judicial influence on congressional policymaking: *Grove City College v. Bell*. Working Paper 88–7, Hoover Institution, Stanford University.

MAYHEW, D. 1974. *Congress: The Electoral Connection*. New Haven, Conn.: Yale University Press.

MOULIN, H. 2006. Social Choice. Ch. 20 in Weingast and Wittman 2006.

NORTH, D. C. 1981. *Structure and Change in Economic History*. New York: Cambridge University Press.

—— 2005. *Understanding the Process of Economic Change*. Princeton, NJ: Princeton University Press.

—— WALLIS, J. J., and WEINGAST, B. R. 2009. *Violence and Social Orders: A Conceptual Framework for Interpreting Recorded Human History*. New York: Cambridge University Press.

OLSON, M. 2001. *Power and Prosperity: Outgrowing Communist and Capitalist Dictatorships*. New York: Basic Books.

PALFREY, T. 2006. Laboratory experiments. Ch. 50 in Weingast and Wittman 2006.

PERSSON, T. and TABELLINI, G. 2006. Electoral systems and economic policy. Ch. 39 in Weingast and Wittman 2006.

PRAT, A. 2002. Campaign advertising and voter welfare. *Review of Economic Studies*, 69: 997–1017.

—— 2006. Rational voters and political advertising. Ch. 2 in Weingast and Wittman 2006.

PRZEWORSKI, A. 2006. Self-enforcing democracy. Ch. 16 in Weingast and Wittman 2006.

ROHDE, D. W. 1991. *Parties and Leaders in the Postreform House*. University of Chicago Press.

SHEPSLE, K. A. 1978. *Giant Jigsaw Puzzle*. Chicago: University of Chicago Press.

—— and WEINGAST, B. R. 1981. Structure-induced equilibrium and legislative choice. *Public Choice*, 37: 503–19.

———— 1995 Introduction. In *Positive Theories of Congressional Institutions*, ed. K. A. Sheplse and B. R. Weingast. Ann Arbor: University of Michigan Press.

———— 2006. Old questions and new answers. Ch. 57 in Weingast and Wittman 2006.

SINCLAIR, B. 2006. *Party Wars*. Norman: University of Oklahoma Press.

SKAPERDAS, S. 2006. Anarchy. Ch. 49 in Weingast and Wittman 2006.

SMITH, A. 2003. Election timing in majoritarian parliaments. *British Journal of Political Science*, 33: 397–418.

—— 2004. *Election Timing*. Cambridge: Cambridge University Press.

SPOLAORE, E. 2006. National borders and the size of nations. Ch. 42 in Weingast and Wittman 2006.

STIGLITZ, E. and WEINGAST, B. R. 2008. Agenda control in Congress: evidence from cut-point estimates and ideal point uncertainty. Working Paper, Hoover Institution, Stanford University.

TIEBOUT, C. 1956. The pure theory of local expenditures. *Journal of Political Economy*, 64: 16–24.

TULLOCK, G. 1987. *Autocracy*. Hingham, Mass.: Kluwer Academic.

WEINGAST, B. R. 2002. Rational choice institutionalism. In *Political Science: State of the Discipline*, ed. I. Katznelson and H. Milnor. New York: Norton.

—— and MARSHALL, W. J. 1988. The industrial organization of Congress: why legislatures, like firms, are not organized as markets. *Journal of Political Economy*, 96: 132–63.

—— and WITTMAN, D. (eds.) 2006. *Oxford Handbook of Political Economy*. Oxford: Oxford University Press.

WILDASIN, D. 2006. Fiscal competition. Ch. 27 in Weingast and Wittman 2006.

WITTMAN, D. 1989. Why democracies produce efficient results. *Journal of Political Economy*, 97: 1395–424.

—— 1995 *The Myth of Democratic Failure*. Chicago: University of Chicago Press.

—— 2000. The wealth and size of nations. *Journal of Conflict Resolution*, 44: 885–95.

—— 2007. Candidate quality, pressure group endorsements, and the nature of political advertising. *European Journal of Political Economy*, 23: 360–78.

—— forthcoming. How campaign advertising activates uninformed voters. *Economic Journal*.

CHAPTER 39

....

ECONOMIC METHODS IN POSITIVE POLITICAL THEORY

....

DAVID AUSTEN-SMITH

1 INTRODUCTION

....

ECONOMICS and political science share a common ancestry in "political economy" and both are concerned with the decisions of people facing constraints, at the individual level and in the aggregate. But while rational choice theory in some form or other has been a cornerstone of economic reasoning for over a century, with the mathematical development of this theory beginning in the middle of the nineteenth century, its introduction to political science is relatively recent and far from generally accepted within the discipline.[1] Three books proved seminal with respect to the application

[1] A suggestion (first made to me in conversation many years ago by Barry Weingast) as to why the two disciplines differ so markedly with respect to the use of mathematical modeling is that political science has no analogous concept to that of the *margin* in economics. And the importance of the margin in this respect lies less with its substantive content than with the amenability of its logic to elementary diagrammatic representation. Economic theorizing evolved into its contemporary mathematical form through a diagrammatic development of the logic of the margin, whereas positive political theory, almost of necessity, bypassed any such graphical development and jumped directly to applied game theory.

of economic methods in political science, the first of which is Kenneth Arrow's *Social Choice and Individual Values* (1951, 1963).[2]

Although mathematical models of voting can be found at least as far back as the thirteenth century (McLean 1990) and despite Paul Samuelson's claim, in the foreword to the second edition of the book, that the subject of Arrow's contribution was "mathematical politics," an appreciation within political science (as opposed to economics) of the significance of both Arrow's possibility theorem itself or, more importantly for this chapter, the axiomatic method with which it is established was slow in coming. An exception was William Riker, who quickly understood the depth of Arrow's insight and the significance of an axiomatic theory of preference aggregation, both for normative democratic theory and for the positive analysis of agenda-setting and voting.

The remaining two of the three seminal books are Anthony Downs's *An Economic Theory of Democracy* (1957) and William Riker's *The Theory of Political Coalitions* (1962). These books were distinguished for political science by their use of rational choice theory and distinguished for rational choice theory by their explicit concern with politics.

Downs's 1957 volume covers a wide set of issues but is perhaps most noted for his development of the spatial model of electoral competition and for the decision-theoretic argument suggesting rational individuals are unlikely to vote. The spatial model builds on an economic model of retail location due to Hotelling (1929) and Smithies (1941). Approximately a decade after the publication of Downs's book, Davis and Hinich (1966, 1967) and Davis, Hinich, and Ordeshook (1970) described the multidimensional version of the (political) spatial model, the mathematics of which has given rise to a remarkable series of results, exposing the deep structure of a variety of preference aggregation rules, most notably, simple plurality rule (e.g. Plott 1967; McKelvey 1979; Schofield 1983; McKelvey and Schofield 1987; Saari 1997). Similarly, Downs's decision-theoretic approach to turnout elicited a variety of innovations as authors sought variations on the theme to provide a better account of participation in large elections (e.g. Riker and Ordeshook 1968; Ferejohn and Fiorina 1975). But although treating voters as taking decisions independent of any consideration of others' behaviour (as the Downsian decision-theoretic approach surely does) yields some insight, the character of most if not all political behavior is intrinsically strategic, for which the appropriate model is game theoretic.[3]

Riker understood the importance not only of Arrow's theorem and a mathematical theory of preference aggregation, he also recognized that game theory, the quintessential theory of strategic interaction between rational agents, was the natural tool with which to analyze political behaviour. In his 1962 book, Riker exploited a cooperative game-theoretic model, due to von Neumann and Morgenstern (1944), to develop an

---

[2] Duncan Black's *The Theory of Committees and Elections* (1958) has some claim to be included as a fourth such book. However, although Black considers similar issues to those taxing Arrow, his concern was more limited than that of Arrow and his particular contribution to political science was generally recognized only after the importance of Arrow's work had begun to be appreciated.

[3] Palfrey and Rosenthal 1983 and Ledyard 1984 provide the earliest fully strategic models of turnout.

understanding of coalition structure and provide the first thoroughgoing effort to apply game theory to understand politics. Cooperative game theory is distinguished essentially by the presumption that if gains from cooperation or collusion were available to a group of agents, then those gains would surely be realized. As such, it is closely tied to the Arrovian approach to preference aggregation and much of the early work stimulated by Riker's contribution reflected concerns similar to those addressed in the possibility theorem. An important concept here is that of the *core* of a cooperative game.

Loosely speaking, if an alternative x is in the core, then any coalition of individuals who agree on a distinct alternative y that they all strictly prefer, cannot be in a position to replace x with y. For example, the majority rule core contains only alternatives that cannot be defeated under majority voting. Similarly, if we imagine that a group uses a supramajority rule requiring at least 2/3 of the group to approve any change, then x is in the core if there is no alternative y such that at least 2/3 of the group strictly prefer y to x. So if a group involves nine individuals, five of whom strictly prefer x to y and the remaining four strictly prefer y to x, then the majority rule core (when the choice is between x and y) is x alone whereas both x and y are in the 2/3 rule core.

The concept of the core is intuitively appealing as a predictor of what might happen. Given the actions available to individuals under the rules governing any social interaction, and assuming that coalitions can freely form and coordinate on mutually advantageous courses of action, the core describes those outcomes that cannot be overturned: even if a coalition does not like a particular core outcome, the very fact that the outcome is in the core means that the coalition is powerless to overturn it. On the other hand, when the core is empty (that is, fails to contain any alternatives) then its use as a solution concept for a cooperative game-theoretic model is suspect. For example, suppose a group of three persons has to use majority rule to decide how to share a dollar and suppose every individual cares exclusively about their own share. Then every possible outcome (that is, division of the dollar) can be upset by a majority coalition. To see this, suppose a fair division of $(1/3)$ to each individual is proposed; then individuals (say, A and B) can propose and vote to share the dollar evenly between themselves and give nothing to individual C; but then A and C can propose and vote to give $(2/3)$ to A and $(1/3)$ to C. Because A and C care only about their own shares, this proposal upsets the proposal favoring A and B. But by the same token, a division that shares the dollar equally between C and B, giving nothing to A, upsets the outcome that gives B nothing; and so on. In this example, the core offers no guidance about what to expect as a final outcome. Furthermore, it does not follow that the core being empty implies instability or continued change. Rather, core emptiness means only that every possible outcome can in principle be overturned; as such, the model offers *no* prediction at all. It is an unfortunate fact, therefore, that, save in constrained environments, the core of any cooperative game-theoretic model of political behavior is typically empty, attenuating the predictive or explanatory content of the model.

Discovering the extent to which the core failed to exist was disappointing and induced at least some pessimism about the general value of formal economic reasoning as a tool for political science. Things changed with the development of techniques within economics and game theory that greatly extended the scope and power of *non*-cooperative game theory, in which there is no presumption that the existence of gains from cooperation are realized. And at least at the time of writing this chapter, it is non-cooperative game theory that dominates contemporary positive political theory.

This chapter concerns economic methods in political science. It is confined exclusively to positive (formal) political theory, paying no attention to econometric methods for empirical political science. Furthermore, I adopt the perspective that a central task for positive political theory is to understand the relationship between the preferences of individuals comprising a polity and the collective choices from a set of possible alternatives over which the individuals' preferences are defined.[4] The next section sketches the two canonical approaches to developing a positive political theory, collective preference theory and game theory. I briefly argue that despite some clear formal differences, these two techniques are essentially distinguished by the trade-off each makes with respect to a minimal democracy constraint and a demand that well-defined predictions are generally guaranteed. Moreover, the attempt to develop collective preference theory as an explanatory framework for political science reveals two important analytical characteristics, distinctive to political science rather than economics. The subsequent section, therefore, considers some more specific techniques within the game-theoretic approach designed to accommodate these characteristics. A third section concludes.

2 Two Approaches From Economics

Economics is rooted in the choices of individuals, albeit with a broad notion of what counts as an "individual" when useful, as in the theory of markets where firms are often treated as individuals. And the basic economic model of individual choice is decision theoretic: in its simplest variant, individuals are assumed to have preferences over a set of feasible alternatives that are complete (every pair of alternatives can be ranked) and transitive (for any three alternatives, say x, y, z, if x is preferred to y and y is preferred to z, then x must be preferred to z) and to choose an alternative (e.g. purchasing bundles of groceries, cars, education, . . .) that maximizes their preferences, or payoffs, over this set. The predictions of the model, therefore, are given

---

[4] Of course, this understanding itself reflects a largely consequentialist perspective intrinsic to economics. Insofar as there is consideration with any economic process, it is rarely with the process per se but with respect to the outcomes supported or induced by that process. This remains true for normative analysis. For example, axiomatic characterizations of procedures for dispute resolution (such as bargaining or bankruptcy) rarely exclude all references to the consequences of using such procedures: Pareto efficiency and individual rationality are common instances of such consequentialist properties. In contrast, a consequentialist perspective is less well accepted within political science at large, where (*inter alia*) there is widespread concern with, say, the legitimacy of procedures independent of the outcomes they might induce.

by studying how the set of maximal elements varies with changes in the feasible set. Now it is certainly true that individuals make political decisions but those decisions of interest to political science are not primarily individual consumption or investment decisions; rather, they are decisions to vote, to participate in collective action, to adopt a platform on which to run for elected office, and so forth. In contrast to canonical decision-making in economics, therefore, what an individual chooses in politics is not always what an individual obtains (e.g. voting for some electoral candidate does not ensure that the candidate is elected). Thus, the link between an individual's decisions in politics and the consequent payoffs to the individual is attenuated relative to that for economic decisions: the basic political model of individual choice is game theoretic.

The preceding observations suggest two approaches to understanding how individual preferences connect to political, or collective, choices and both are pursued: a *direct* approach through extending the individual decision-theoretic model to the collectivity as a whole, an approach essentially begun with Arrow (1951, 1963) and Black (1958); and an *indirect* approach through exploring the consequences of mutually consistent sets of strategic decisions by instrumentally rational agents, an approach with roots in von Neumann and Morgenstern (1944) and Nash (1951).

Under the direct (*collective preference*) approach to social choice, individuals' *preferences* are directly aggregated into a "social preference" which, as in individual decision theory, is then maximized to yield a set of best (relative to the maximand) alternatives, the collective choices. But although individual preferences surely influence individual decisions such as voting, there is no guarantee that individuals' preferences are revealed by their decisions (for example, an individual may have strict preferences over candidates for electoral office, yet choose to vote strategically or to abstain). Under the indirect (*game-theoretic*) approach to social choice, therefore, it is individuals' *actions* that are aggregated to arrive at collective choices. Faced with a particular decision problem, individuals rarely have to declare their preferences directly but instead have to take some action. For example, in a multicandidate election under plurality rule, individuals must choose the candidate for whom to vote and may abstain; the collective choice from the election is then decided by counting the recorded votes and not by direct observation of all individuals' preferences over the entire list of candidates. It is useful to be a little more precise.

A preference profile is a list of preferences, one for each individual in the society, over a set of alternatives for that society. An abstract collective choice rule is a rule that assigns collective choices to each and every profile; that is, for any list of preferences, a collective choice rule identifies the set of outcomes chosen by society. Similarly, a preference aggregation rule is a rule that aggregates individuals' preferences into a single, complete, "social preference" relation over the set of alternatives; that is, for any profile, the preference aggregation rule collects individual preferences into a social preference relation over alternatives. It is important to note that while the theory (following economics) presumes individual preferences are complete and transitive, the only requirement at this point of a social preference relation is that it is complete. For any profile and preference aggregation rule, we can identify those alternatives (if any) that are ranked best by the social preference relation derived from the profile by the rule. With a slight abuse of the language, this set is known as the *core* of the preference aggregation rule at the particular profile of concern.[5] Taken together, therefore, a preference aggregation rule and its associated core for all possible preference profiles is an instance of an abstract collective choice rule. Thus, the extension of the classical economic decision-theoretic model of individual choice to the problem of collective decision-making, the direct approach mentioned above, can be described as the analysis of the abstract collective choice rules defined by the core of various preference aggregation rules.

The analytical challenge confronted by the direct approach is to find conditions under which preference aggregation relations exist and yield well-defined, that is, non-empty, cores. This approach has focused on two complementary issues: delineating classes of preference aggregation rule that are consistent with various sets of *desiderata* (for instance, Arrow's possibility theorem (1951, 1963) and May's theorem (May 1952) characterizing majority rule) and describing the properties of particular preference aggregation rules in various environments[6] (for instance, Plott's characterization of majority cores (Plott 1967) in the spatial model and the chaos theorems of McKelvey 1976 1979, and Schofield 1978, 1983). Contributions to the first issue rely heavily on axiomatic methods whereas contributions to the second have, for the most part, exploited the spatial voting model in which the feasible set of alternatives is some subset of (typically) k-dimensional Euclidean space and individuals' preferences can be described by continuous quasi-concave (loosely, single peaked in every direction) utility functions.

From the perspective of developing a decision-theoretic approach to prediction and explanation at the collective level, the results from collective preference theory are a little disappointing. There exist aggregation rules that justify treating collective choice in a straightforward decision-theoretic way only if the environment is very simple, having a minimal number of alternatives from which to choose or satisfying severe restrictions on the sorts of preference profiles that can exist (for instance, profiles of single-peaked preferences over a fixed ordering of the alternatives), or if the preferences of all but a very few are ignored in the aggregation (as in dictatorships). Moreover, in the context of the spatial model, most of the aggregation procedures observed in the world are, at least in principle, subject to chronic instability unless politics concerns only a single issue.[7] Nevertheless, a great deal has been learned from the collective preference approach to political decision-making about the properties and implications of preference aggregation and voting rules,

---

[5] The abuse arises since, strictly speaking, the core is defined with respect to a given family of coalitions. To the extent that a preference aggregation rule can be defined in terms of so-called decisive, or winning coalitions, the use of the term is standard. But not all rules can be so defined in which case the set of best elements induced by such a rule is not a core in the strict sense (see, for example, Austen-Smith and Banks 1999, ch. 3). The terminology in these instances is therefore an abuse but a useful and harmless one nevertheless.

[6] That is, various admissible classes of preference profiles and sorts of feasible sets of alternatives.

[7] See Austen-Smith and Banks 1999 for an elaboration of these claims.

and about the normative and descriptive trade-offs inherent in choosing one rule over another.[8]

Unlike the direct collective preference approach, the indirect approach to collective choice through the aggregation of the strategic decisions of instrumentally rational individuals begins by specifying the collection of possible decision, or strategy, profiles that could arise. A strategy for an individual specifies what the individual would do in every possible contingency that could arise in the given setting. A strategy profile is then a list of individual strategies, one for each member of the polity. An outcome function is a rule that identifies a unique alternative in the set of possible social alternatives with every feasible strategy profile. A specification of all possible strategy profiles along with an outcome function is called a *mechanism*. An abstract theory of how individuals make their respective decisions under any mechanism is a rule that associates a strategy profile with every preference profile; that is, for any given preference profile, an abstract decision theory assigns a set of possible strategy profiles consistent with the theory when individuals' preferences are described by the given list of preferences.[9] For any preference profile, mechanism, and decision theory, we can identify those alternatives that could arise as outcomes from strategy profiles consistent with the decision theory at that preference profile. This is the set of *equilibrium outcomes* under the mechanism at the preference profile. Then the indirect approach to preference aggregation can be described as the analysis of the collective choice rules defined by the sets of equilibrium outcomes of various mechanisms and theories of individual decision-making.

There is no effort under the indirect approach to treat collective decision-making as in any way analogous to individual decision-making. Instead, individuals make choices (vote, contribute to collective action, and so forth) taking account of the choices of others and the likely consequences of various combinations of the individuals' decisions. Although such choices are expected to reflect individual preferences, there is no presumption that they do so in any immediately transparent or literal fashion. The approach therefore requires both a theory of how individuals make their decisions (the abstract theory of decision-making considered above) and a description of how the resulting decisions are mapped into collective choices (a specification of the outcome function). Putting these two components together with preferences then yields a model of collective choice through the aggregation of individual decisions.

Unlike the collective preference approach, there is little difficulty with developing coherent predictive models of collective choice within the game-theoretic framework. That is, while the social choice mapping derived from a preference aggregation rule rarely yields maximal elements, the mapping derived from a mechanism and theory of individual behavior is typically well defined. This fact, coupled with the flexibility of the approach with respect to modeling institutional details, uncertainty, and

---

[8] It is worth pointing out here, too, that the typical emptiness of the core has stimulated work on solutions concepts other than the core for collective preference theory (e.g. Schwarz 1972; Miller 1980; McKelvey 1986).

[9] Examples of such decision theories include Nash equilibrium and its refinements. See Fudenberg and Tirole 1991 or Myerson 1991.

incomplete information, has led to game theory dominating contemporary formal theory. Indeed, it has been argued that the adoption of (in particular) non-
cooperative game-theoretic techniques represents a fundamental shift in methodology from those of collective preference theory (e.g. Baron 1994; Diermeier 1997). Yet,
at least from a formal perspective, the difference between the collective preference and
the game-theoretic approaches is not so stark.

Both approaches to collective choice, the direct and the indirect, yield social choice
rules, taking preference profiles into collective choices. Thus any result concerning such rules must apply equally to both. In particular, it is true that a social
choice rule is generally guaranteed to yield a non-empty core only if it violates
a "minimal democracy" property, where "minimal democracy" means that if all
but at most one individuals strictly prefer some alternative x to another y, then y
should not be ranked strictly better than x under the choice rule (Austen-Smith
and Banks 1998). Whence it follows that the indirect approach ensures existence of
well-defined solutions by violating minimal democracy, whereas the direct approach
insists on minimal democracy at the expense of ensuring non-empty cores in any
but the simplest settings. On this account, the direct and the indirect approaches
to understanding collective decision-making are complementary rather than competitive. Which sort of model is most appropriate depends on the problem at hand
and, in some important cases, their respective predictions are intimately related
(Austen-Smith and Banks 1998, 2004). Moreover, the collective preference approach
has revealed two general analytical characteristics of collective decision-making
peculiar to political science relative to economics, characteristics that have stimulated important methodological and substantive innovations in the game-theoretic
approach. It is to these characteristics and the innovations they have induced that I
now turn.

3 TWO ANALYTICAL CHARACTERISTICS

The first characteristic exposed by collective preference theory involves the role of
opportunities for trade. In economics, it is typically the case that, for any given
society, the greater are the opportunities for trade the more likely it is that welfare-
improving trade takes place. The analogue to increasing opportunities for trade in
politics is increasing the dimensionality of the policy space in the spatial model or the
number of alternatives in the finite-alternative model. As the number of alternatives
or issue dimensions on which the preferences of a given population can differ grows,
so too does the number of opportunities for winning coalitions to agree on a change
from any policy; with one dimension, for example, coalitions must agree either to
"move policy to the left" or to "move policy to the right" but, with two dimensions,
there are uncountable directions in which to change policy, and preferences can be
distributed over the plane, permitting more coalitions to form against any given

policy. But it is precisely in such complex settings that preference aggregation rules are most poorly behaved: with one dimension the median voter theorem ensures a well-defined collective choice under majority rule (Black 1958) but, with two dimensions, the existence of such a choice is an extremely rare event and virtually any pair of alternatives can be connected by a finite sequence of majority-preferred steps (McKelvey 1979). Thus increasing "opportunities for trade" in the political setting exacerbate the problems of reaching a collective choice rather than ameliorate them.

The second characteristic concerns large populations. In economics it is the market that aggregates individual decisions into a collective outcome. As the number of individuals grows, the influence of any single agent becomes negligible and, in the limit, instrumentally rational individuals act as price-takers; moreover, large populations tend to smooth over non-convexities and irregularities at the individual level, justifying an approximation that all members of the population act as canonic economic theory presumes. These nice properties do not hold in political settings. Individual decisions are aggregated through voting and although the likelihood that any individual is pivotal vanishes as the electorate grows, for any finite society that likelihood is not zero: under majority rule in the classical Downsian spatial model, the median voter is pivotal whether there are three voters or three billion and three. So not only can the collective choice depend critically on a single person's decision, it is unjustified to treat each agent analogously to a "price-taker" and non-convexities and irregularities can matter a great deal depending on precisely where they are located in the population. The "correct" model of decision-making here is therefore to presume individuals condition their choices on being pivotal and act as if their vote or contribution or whatever tips the balance in favour of one or other collective choice: either they are not in fact pivotal in which case their decision is irrelevant, or they are pivotal in which case their decision determines the collective choice.[10]

The conclusion that rational individuals condition their vote decisions on the event that they are pivotal is a strategic, game-theoretic, perspective and it is within this framework that efforts to tackle the problems raised by each characteristic have been undertaken.

3.1 Institutions and Explanation

A virtue of the collective preference methodology (and, to a large extent, the cooperative game-theoretic methodology exploited by Riker 1962 and others) is that it is essentially "institution free," focusing exclusively on how domains of preference profiles are mapped into collective choices without attention to how the profiles might be recorded, from where the alternatives might arise, and so on. The idea underlying the axiomatic method of collective preference theory is to abstract from empirical and detailed institutional complications and study whole classes of possible institution-

---

[10] While this applies to any large finite electorate, proceeding to the limit in which each voter is infinitessimally small removes even this prescription regarding how strategically rational agents may behave, on which more below.

satisfying particular properties. A limitation of this method for an explanatory theory, however, is the typical emptiness of the core in complex settings, that is, those with many issues or alternatives over which to choose. And although non-cooperative game theory typically requires an exhaustive description of the relevant institutional details in any application, it is rarely hampered by questions of the existence of solutions. This observation prompted a shift in emphasis away from a collective preference methodology tailored to avoid concerns with the details of any application, to a non-cooperative game-theoretic approach that embraces such details as intrinsic to the analysis.

Two illustrations of the role of institutional detail in finessing problems of existence in complex political environments are provided by the use of particular sorts of agenda in committee decision-making from finite sets of alternatives (see Miller 1995 for an overview) and the citizen-candidate approach to electoral competition in the spatial model, whereby the candidates contesting an election are themselves voters who strategically choose whether or not to run for office at some cost (Osborne and Slivinsky 1996; Besley and Coate 1997).

In the classical preference profile to illustrate the instability of majority rule (the Condorcet paradox), three committee members have strict preferences over three alternatives such that each alternative is best in one person's ordering, middle ranked in a second person's ordering, and worst in a third person's ordering. There is no majority core in this example, with every alternative being beaten by one of the others under majority *preference*. However, committee decisions are often governed by rules, such as the amendment agenda. Under the amendment agenda, one alternative is first voted against another and the majority winner of the *vote* (not preference) is then put against the residual alternative in a final majority vote to determine the outcome. It is well known that the unique subgame perfect Nash equilibrium (an instance of a theory of individual decision-making in the earlier language) prescribes that individuals vote with their immediate (sincere) preferences at the final division to yield two conditional outcomes, one for each possible winner at the first division, and then vote sincerely at the first division with respect to these two conditional outcomes. Assuming majority preference is always strict, this backwards induction procedure invariably produces a unique prediction which in general depends on the ordering of the alternatives as well as the distribution of individual preferences per se.[11] Moreover, the set of possible outcomes from amendment agendas (on any given finite set of alternatives and any finite committee) as a function of the preference profiles inducing a strict majority preference relation is now completely characterized (Banks 1985).

Similar to the difficulty with many alternatives illustrated by the Condorcet paradox, the majority rule core in the multidimensional spatial model is typically empty, and core emptiness means the model offers *no* positive predictions beyond the claim that for every policy, there exists an alternative policy and a majority that strictly

---

[11] It is worth noting in this example that the equilibrium outcome surely violates minimal democracy because, for every possible decision, there is an alternative that is strictly preferred by two of the three individuals.

prefers that alternative. But policies are offered by candidates and candidates are themselves members of the electorate. It is natural, therefore, to treat the set of potential candidates as being exactly the set of citizens. Furthermore, since citizens are endowed with policy preferences, other things equal and conditional on being elected, a successful candidate has no incentive to implement any platform other than his or her most preferred policy. In turn, rational voters recognize that whatever a candidate drawn from the electorate might promise in the campaign, should the candidate be elected then that person's ideal policy is the final outcome. When the set of potential candidates coincides with the set of voters, therefore, there is no essential difference between the problem of electoral platform selection and the problem of candidate entry: explaining the distribution of electoral policy platforms in the citizen-candidate model is equivalent to explaining the distribution of citizens who choose to run for electoral office. And assuming that it is costly to run for office, individuals weigh the expected gains (which depend, *inter alia*, on who else is running) from entering an election against this cost when deciding whether to run for office. It follows that alternatives are costly to place on the agenda in the citizen-candidate model and it is not hard to see, then, that these institutional details introduce sufficient stickiness to ensure the existence of equilibria. Moreover, by varying parameters such as the cost of entry, the electoral rule of concern, and so forth, various comparative predictions concerning policy outcomes and electoral system are available.[12]

3.2 Information and Large Populations

Beyond questions of core existence, the application of the collective preference model to environments in which individuals face considerable uncertainty, either about the implications of any collective decision (imperfect information) or about the preferences of others (incomplete information), is awkward. Non-cooperative game theory, however, can readily accommodate uncertainty and informational variations.[13] And whereas uncertainty is unnecessary for developing a coherent theory of economic behavior among large populations (in particular, the theory of perfect competition), it is uncertainty that provides a hook on which to develop a coherent theory of political behavior among large populations.

As remarked above, a peculiarity of political decision-making relative to economic decision-making is that consideration of large populations greatly complicates rather than simplifies the analysis of individual decisions. In markets, each consumer becomes negligible with respect to influencing price as the number of consumers

---

[12] The contemporary literature on game-theoretic models of comparative institutions is large and growing. Examples include Austen-Smith and Banks 1988; Cox 1990; Persson, Roland, and Tabellini 1997; Myerson 1999; and Diermeier, Eraslan, and Merlo 2003.

[13] The theoretical foundations were laid by Harsanyi 1967–8. Two particularly important papers since then for political science are Spence 1973, who introduced the class of signaling games, and Crawford and Sobel 1982, who extended this class to include cheap-talk (costless) signaling.

grows and, therefore, is properly conceived as taking prices as given; in electorates, however, while it remains true that the likelihood that any single vote tips the outcome becomes vanishingly small as the number of voters grows, it is not true (at least for finite electorates) that the behavior of any given voter should be conditioned on the almost sure event that the voter's decision is consequentially irrelevant. This is not usually a problem for classical collective preference theory which, as the name suggests, focuses on aggregating given preference profiles, not vote profiles. Nor is it any problem for Nash equilibrium theory insofar as there are a huge number of equilibrium patterns of voting in any large election (other than with unanimity rule), most of which look empirically silly. But empirical voting patterns are not arbitrary. And once account is taken of the fact that preferring one candidate to another in an election does not imply voting for that candidate (individuals can abstain or vote strategically), there is clearly a severe methodological problem with respect to analysing equilibrium behavior in large electorates.

One line of attack has been by brute force, using combinatorial techniques to compute the probability that a particular vote is pivotal, conditional on the specified (undominated) votes of others (Ledyard 1984; Cox 1994; Palfrey 1989). But this is cumbersome and places considerable demands on exactly what it is that individuals know about the behavior of others. In particular, individuals are assumed to know the exact size of the population. Myerson (1998, 2000, 2002) relaxes this assumption and develops a novel theory of Poisson games to analyse strategic behavior in large populations.

Rather than assume the size of the electorate is known, suppose that the actual number of potential voters is a random variable distributed according to a Poisson distribution with mean n, where n is large. Then the probability that there is any particular number of voters in the society is easily calculated. As a statistical model underlying the true size of any electorate, the Poisson distribution uniquely exhibits a very useful technical property, *environmental equivalence*: under the Poisson distribution, any individual in the realized electorate believes that the number of other individuals in the electorate is also a random variable distributed according to a Poisson distribution with the same mean. And because the number and identity of realized individuals in the electorate is a random variable, it is enough to identify voters by *type* rather than their names, where an individual's type describes all of the strategically relevant characteristics of the individual (for example the individual's preferences over the candidates seeking office in any election). If the list of possible individual types is fixed and known, then the distribution of each type in a realized population of any size is itself given by a Poisson distribution.

The preceding implications of modeling population size as an unobserved draw from a Poisson distribution allow a relatively tractable and appealing strategic theory of elections. Because only types are relevant, individual strategies are appropriately defined as depending only on voter type rather than on voter identity. Thus individuals know only their own types, the distribution of possible types in the population, that the population size is a random draw from a Poisson distribution, and that all individuals of the same type behave in the same way. Call such a strategic model a

Poisson game. An equilibrium to a Poisson game is then a specification of strategies, one for each type, such that, for any individual of any type, the individual is taking a best decision taking as given the strategies of all other types, conditional on his or her beliefs regarding the numbers of individuals of each type in the electorate. Such equilibria exist and have well-defined limits with strictly positive turnout as the mean population size increases. Myerson proposes using these limiting equilibria as the basis of predictions about political behavior in large populations. And to illustrate the relative elegance of the method over the usual combinatoric approach, in Myerson (2000) he provides a version of a theorem on turnout and candidate platform convergence due to Ledyard (1984) and, in Myerson (1998), he establishes a Condorcet jury theorem (see also Myerson 2002 for a comparative analysis of three-candidate elections under scoring rules using a Poisson game framework).[14]

In economics, markets also serve to aggregate information through relative prices. There are no relative prices explicit in elections, yet it is not only implausible to presume voters know the true size of the electorate, it is also implausible that they know the full implications of electing one candidate rather than another. Because the likelihood that any single vote is pivotal in a large election is negligible, the incentives for any one voter in a large electorate to invest in becoming better informed regarding the candidates for election are likewise negligible. Thus Downs (1957) argued that voters in large populations would be "rationally ignorant." But just as is the case with his theory of participation, Downs's argument is decision-theoretic and does not necessarily apply once the strategic character of political behavior is made explicit. In particular, an instrumentally rational voter conditions her vote on the event that she is pivotal; and in the presence of asymmetric information throughout the electorate, conditioning on the event of being pivotal can yield a great deal of information about what others know. To see this, consider an example in which two candidates are competing for a majority of votes in a three-person electorate. Suppose each voter receives a noisy private signal correlated with which of the two candidates would be best and (for simplicity) suppose further that all voters share identical full-information preferences. Now if the first two voters are voting sincerely relative to their signals and the third voter is pivotal, it must be the case that the first two voters have received conflicting information about the candidates, in which case the third voter can base her vote on all of the available information distributed through the electorate, even though that distribution was not publicly known.

Exactly what are the information aggregation properties of various electoral schemes is currently subject to much research. In some settings, the logic sketched above can yield quite perverse results; for example, Ordeshook and Palfrey (1988) provide an example in which an almost sure Condorcet winner (that is, an alternative against which no alternative is preferred by a strict majority) is surely defeated in an amendment agenda with incomplete information. And in other settings, it turns

---

[14] Condorcet jury theorems address the problem of choosing one of two alternatives when voters are uncertain about which is most in their interests. Typically, the theorems connect the size of the electorate (jury) to the probability that majority voting outcomes coincide with the majority choice that would be made under no uncertainty.

out that elections are remarkably efficient at aggregating information; Feddersen and Pesendorfer (1996) prove a striking full-information equivalence theorem for two-candidate elections with costly voting under any majority or super-majority rule shy of unanimity, namely despite the fact that a significant proportion of the electorate might abstain, the limiting outcome as the population grows is almost surely the outcome that would arise if all individuals voted under complete information.[15]

4 CONCLUSION

To all intents and purposes, the methods of contemporary positive political theory coincide with the methods of contemporary economic theory. The most widespread framework for models of campaign contributions at present derives from the common agency problem introduced by Bernheim and Whinston (1986); Rubinstein's model of alternating offer bargaining (Rubinstein 1982) has been developed and extended to ground a general theory of legislative decision-making and coalition formation; Spence's theory of costly signaling games (Spence 1974) and Crawford and Sobel's (1982) extension of this theory to costless (cheap-talk) signaling provide the tools for a theory of legislative committees, delegation, informational lobbying, debate, and so on. More recently, the growth of interest in behavioral economics, experimental research, and so forth is beginning to appear in the political science literature. Rather than sketch these and other applications of economic methods to political science, this chapter attempts to articulate a broader (likely idiosyncratic) view of positive political theory since the importation of formal rational choice theory to politics. After all, political decision-making has at least as much of a claim to being subject to rational choice as economic decision-making; political agents make purposive decisions to promote their interests subject to constraints. It would be odd, then, to discover that the methods of economics are of no value to the study of politics.

REFERENCES

ARROW, K. J. 1951. *Social Choice and Individual Values*. New Haven, Conn.: Yale University Press.
——1963. *Social Choice and Individual Values*, 2nd edn. New Haven, Conn.: Yale University Press.

[15] The logic of this result is that the while, as Downs suggested, the *relative* number of voters voting informatively declines as the electorate grows due to the diminishing likelihood of being pivotal, the *absolute* number of voters voting informatively increases as the electorate grows at a faster rate, and it is the latter that dominates the information aggregation.

AUSTEN-SMITH, D. and BANKS, J. S. 1988. Elections, coalitions and legislative outcomes. *American Political Science Review*, 82: 405–22.

————1998. Social choice theory, game theory and positive political theory. In *Annual Review of Political Science*, vol. i, ed. N. Polsby. Palo Alto, Calif: Annual Reviews.

————1999. *Positive Political Theory*, i: Collective Preference. Ann Arbor: University of Michigan Press.

————2004. *Positive Political Theory*, ii: Strategy and Structure. Ann Arbor: University of Michigan Press.

BANKS, J. S. 1985. Sophisticated voting outcomes and agenda control. *Social Choice and Welfare*, 1: 295–306.

BARON, D. 1994. A sequential choice perspective on legislative organization. *Legislative Studies Quarterly*, 19: 267–96.

BERNHEIM, D. and WHINSTON, M. 1986. Common agency. *Econometrica*, 54: 923–42.

BESLEY, T. and COATE, S. 1997. An economic model of representative democracy. *Quarterly Journal of Economics*, 112: 85–114.

BLACK, D. 1958. *The Theory of Committees and Elections*. Cambridge: Cambridge University Press.

COX, G. W. 1990. Centripetal and centrifugal incentives in electoral systems. *American Journal of Political Science*, 34: 903–935.

——1994. Strategic voting equilibria under the single nontransferable vote. *American Political Science Review*, 88: 608–21.

CRAWFORD, V. and SOBEL, J. 1982. Strategic information transmission. *Econometrica*, 50: 1431–51.

DAVIS, O. A. and HINICH, M. J. 1966. A mathematical model of policy formation in a democratic society. In *Mathematical Applications in Political Science*, ii, ed. J. Bernd. Dallas, Tex. Southern Methodist University Press.

————1967. Some results related to a mathematical model of policy formation in a democratic society. In *Mathematical Applications in Political Science*, iii, ed. J. Bernd. Dallas, Tex. Southern Methodist University Press.

————and ORDESHOOK, P. C. 1970. An expository development of a mathematical model of the electoral process. *American Political Science Review*, 64: 426–48.

DIERMEIER, D. 1997. Explanatory concepts in formal political theory. Mimeo, Stanford University.

——ERASLAN, H., and MERLO, A. 2003. A structural model of government formation. *Econometrica*, 71: 27–70.

DOWNS, A. 1957. *An Economic Theory of Democracy*. New York: Harper.

FEDDERSEN, T. J. and PESENDORFER, W. 1996. The swing voter's curse. *American Economic Review*, 86: 408–424.

FEREJOHN, J. A. and FIORINA, M. P. 1975. Closeness counts only in horseshoes and dancing. *American Political Science Review*, 69: 920–5.

FUDENBERG, D. and TIROLE, J. 1991. *Game Theory*. Cambridge, Mass.: MIT Press.

HARSANYI, J. 1967–8. Games with incomplete information played by "Bayesian" players, parts I, II and III. *Management Science*, 14: 159–82, 320–34, 486–502.

HOTELLING, H. 1929. Stability in competition. *Economic Journal*, 39: 41–57.

LEDYARD, J. 1984. The pure theory of large two-candidate elections. *Public Choice*, 44: 7–43.

McLEAN, I. 1990. The Borda and Condorcet principles: three medieval applications. *Social Choice and Welfare*, 7: 99–108.

McKELVEY, R. D. 1976. Intransitivities in multidimensional voting models and some implications for agenda control. *Journal of Economic Theory*, 12: 472–82.

McKELVEY, R. D. 1979. General conditions for global intransitivities in formal voting models. *Econometrica*, 47: 1086–112.

——1986. Covering, dominance and institution-free properties of social choice. *American Journal of Political Science*, 30: 283–314.

—— and SCHOFIELD, N. J. 1987. Generalized symmetry conditions at a core point. *Econometrica*, 55: 923–34.

MAY, K. O. 1952. A set of independent necessary and sufficient conditions for simple majority decision. *Econometrica*, 20: 680–4.

MILLER, N. R. 1980. A new solution set for tournaments and majority voting. *American Journal of Political Science*, 24: 68–96.

——1995. *Committees, Agendas and Voting*. Chur: Harwood Academic.

MYERSON, R. B. 1991. *Game Theory: Analysis of Conflict*. Cambridge, Mass.: Harvard University Press.

——1998. Population uncertainty and Poisson games. *International Journal of Game Theory*, 27: 375–92.

——1999. Theoretical comparisons of electoral systems. *European Economic Review*, 43: 671–97.

——2000. Large Poisson games. *Journal of Economic Theory*, 94: 7–45.

——2002. Comparison of scoring rules in Poisson voting games. *Journal of Economic Theory*, 103: 217–51.

NASH, J. F. 1951. Noncooperative games. *Annals of Mathematics*, 54: 289–95.

ORDESHOOK, P. and PALFREY, T., 1988. Agendas, strategic voting and signaling with incomplete information. *American Journal of Political Science*, 32: 441–66.

OSBORNE, M. J. and SLIVINSKI, A. 1996. A model of political competition with citizen-candidates. *Quarterly Journal of Economics*, 111: 65–96.

PALFREY, T. R. 1989. A mathematical proof of Duverger's Law. In *Models of Strategic Choice in Politics*, ed. P. C. Ordeshook. Ann Arbor: University of Michigan Press.

—— and ROSENTHAL, H. 1983. A strategic calculus of voting. *Public Choice*, 41: 7–53.

PERSSON, T., ROLAND, G. and TABELLINI, G. 1997. Separation of powers and political accountability. *Quarterly Journal of Economics*, 112: 310–27.

PLOTT, C. R. 1967. A notion of equilibrium and its possibility under majority rule. *American Economic Review*, 57: 787–806.

RIKER, W. H. 1962. *The Theory of Political Coalitions*. New Haven, Conn: Yale University Press.

—— and ORDESHOOK, P. C. 1968. A theory of the calculus of voting. *American Political Science Review*, 62: 25–43.

RUBINSTEIN, A. 1982. Perfect equilibrium in a bargaining model. *Econometrica*, 50: 97–109.

SAARI, D. G. 1997. The generic existence of a core for q-rules. *Economic Theory*, 9: 219–60.

SCHOFIELD, N. J. 1978. Instability of simple dynamic games. *Review of Economic Studies*, 45: 575–94.

——1983. Generic instability of majority rule. *Review of Economic Studies*, 50: 695–705.

SCHWARTZ, T. 1972. Rationality and the myth of the maximum. *Nous*, 7: 97–117.

SMITHIES, A. 1941. Optimum location in spatial competition. *Journal of Political Economy*, 49: 423–39.

SPENCE, A. M. 1974. *Market Signaling: Informational Transfer in Hiring and Related Screening Processes*. Cambridge, Mass.: Harvard University Press.

SPENCE, M. 1973. Job market signaling. *Quarterly Journal of Economics*, 87: 355–79.

VON NEUMANN, J., and MORGENSTERN, O. 1944. *Theory of Games and Economic Behaviour*. Princeton, NJ: Princeton University Press.

CHAPTER 40

CAPITALISM AND DEMOCRACY

TORBEN IVERSEN

1 INTRODUCTION

A QUESTION permeates much comparative political economy from the classics to contemporary scholarship: how it is possible to combine capitalism with democracy? The former produces stark inequalities in the distribution of property and income, while the latter divides power in a manner that is in principle egalitarian (one person, one vote). So why don't the poor soak the rich? And if they do, how can capitalism be viable as an economic system?

The answer to the first question depends a great deal on how economic interests are aggregated into public policies. We know from Arrow's impossibility theorem that getting a well-behaved "social welfare function" when there are multiple dimensions and no dictator is, well, impossible (Arrow 1951). In the case of distributive politics the policy space is inherently multidimensional since there are as many dimensions as there are agents fighting for a piece of the pie. Distributive politics under democratic rules—who gets how much, including whether the poor soak the rich—is therefore anything but straightforward. Like the proverbial elephant in the corner of the room that everyone ignores, most of the existing political economy literature on democracy has skirted the issue. But it cannot be ignored. It is fundamental to how we understand distributive politics under democracy.

Answering the second question requires an understanding of how economic agents respond to the democratic pressures for redistribution. If the state undermines the market, as commonly assumed, how can we explain the economic success of countries that spend well over half their gross domestic products on social protection and redistribution? If the welfare state is built on the shoulders of an unwilling capitalist class, should we not expect capitalists to shun productive investment, stage coups, or move their money abroad? Yet the welfare state has not collapsed, democracy is spreading, and globalization has not resulted in convergence around laissez-faire capitalism. If we want to understand how democracy and capitalism coexist, therefore, we need a model of capitalism that goes beyond a simple dichotomy between state and market.

This chapter discusses three different approaches to the study of democratic redistribution, and then considers the recent literature on capitalism as an economic system and how economic and democratic institutions may relate to each other. The first approach assumes that democratic politics is structured around a single left–right redistributive dimension. The central issue in this literature is how democratic politics affects who sets public policies, and much of the debate centers on the question of partisanship: Does "Who Governs" matter, and if so, in what ways? This is a key question for political economy because it goes to the heart of whether democratic politics makes a difference: Do the poor ever get a chance to try to soak the rich, and how successful are they when they do? In Section 3 I discuss some plausible answers.

The main weakness of this approach is that it largely ignores the question of what happens when several political agents compete in a multidimensional distributive space (the elephant in the corner). It is hard to understand why politicians should limit themselves to pursuing redistribution in a single predetermined policy dimension, and when they do not, opportunities to form distributive coalitions abound. The work that puts coalitional politics at the center of the analysis, which I discuss in Section 4, paints a richer and more realistic picture of the politics of redistribution. But the cost may be theoretical intractability, and much of the coalitional literature falls into the trap of *post hoc* description. Description, no matter how accurate, will not produce explanation. At the end of the section I discuss two recent attempts to move beyond such description.

The third approach explains distributive politics as a function of the specific design of democratic institutions—including electoral rules and federalism. The strategy here is to replace ad hoc model assumptions, such as unidimensionality, with ones that are rooted in careful observation of actual institutional designs. This approach moves beyond the partisan literature by explicitly considering how economic preferences are aggregated into policies, at the same time as it avoids the chaotic world of unconstrained coalitional politics. As I argue in Section 5, this combination has produced a vibrant research program that helps answer key questions such as the conditions under which the poor are more likely to soak the rich.

The modern study of capitalism as an economic system has also taken an institutionalist turn, building on transaction costs economics rather than neoclassical models. The "varieties of capitalism" approach, in particular, illuminates the relationship between redistributive politics and economic performance and helps explain why there is no necessary contradiction between state and market. The work also helps make sense of the observed institutional diversity of modern capitalism, and why such diversity persists in the face of global market integration. But the tradition has thus far produced few insights into the relationship between economic and political institutions, and it has little to say about the political origins of economic institutions—focusing instead on economic-organizational efficiency as a cause.

The lack of a theory of institutional origins also haunts the literature on political institutions. As Riker (1980) argued many years ago, institutions are "congealed tastes" which themselves have to be explained. Some of the latest literature on democracy and capitalism seeks to endogenize institutions, including the institution of democracy itself, by modeling these as a function of class interests. This brings us right back to the elephant in the corner because without institutional constraints, the issues of multidimensionality and preference aggregation re-emerge. In the concluding section I suggest that there is a new structuralist turn in political economy, where the parameters for our models of institutional design are derived from the specific historical conditions that shaped capitalism in different parts of the world. But I start with a brief discussion of some of the most important precursors for the contemporary literature.

2 Precursors for the Contemporary Literature

In a seminal article, Przeworski and Wallerstein (1982) give a simple answer to the question of why the poor don't soak the rich. Any attempt at radical redistribution, or socialism, they argue, would be met by massive disinvestment and possibly violence by the upper classes. So even if the poor would ultimately be better off in a system where private property rights were suspended (itself a big if, of course), the "valley of transition" would dissuade any rational government with a limited time horizon from attempting it. Conversely, the rich might consent to democracy and redistribution because the costs of repression or the threat of revolution would otherwise be too high. "Class compromise," in other words, could be an equilibrium. This model wiped out the notion in the Marxist literature that capitalism could only survive if the lower classes were repressed or misinformed.

Class compromise has survived as a central concept (e.g. Swenson 1991; Garrett 1998; Acemoglu and Robinson 2005), but conceptualizing capitalist democracy as a class compromise does not itself take us very far in explaining the variance in policies and outcomes across countries. Although it is easy to think that democracy—as a particular form of government—and capitalism—as a particular type of economic system—would produce similar policies and outcomes, one of the most striking facts about capitalist democracies is the enormous cross-national variance in inequality, social spending, redistribution, and the structure of social protection. A full-time Norwegian worker in the top decile of the income distribution, for example, earns about twice as much as someone in the bottom decile, whereas in the United States this ratio is well over four (based on 2000 data from the OECD). The extent to which democratic governments redistribute also varies to a surprising degree. According to data from the Luxembourg Income Study the reduction in the poverty rate in the United States as a result of taxation and transfers was 13 per cent in 1994 whereas the comparable figure for Sweden was 82 per cent.

There are two standard approaches to explaining this variance, which frame much of the current debate (even as the literature has moved beyond the original formulations). One is Meltzer and Richard's (1981) model of redistribution, which has been the workhorse in the political economy for two decades (see also Romer 1975). The model is built on the intuitively simple idea that since the median voter tends to have below-average income (assuming a typical right-skewed distribution of income) he or she has an interest in redistribution. With a proportional tax and flat rate benefit, and assuming that there are efficiency costs of taxation, Downs's median voter theorem can be applied to predict the extent of redistribution. The equilibrium is reached when the benefit to the median voter of additional spending is exactly outweighed by the efficiency costs of such spending. This implies two key comparative statics: spending is higher (*a*) the greater the skew in the distribution of income, and (*b*) the greater the number of poor people who vote.

The latter suggests that an expansion of the franchise to the poor, or higher voter turnout among the poor, will shift the decisive voter to the left and therefore raise support for redistribution. Assuming that the median voter's policy preference is implemented, democratization will therefore lead to redistribution. There is some support for this proposition (see Rodrik 1999 on democracy and Franzese 2002, ch. 2 on turnout), although the evidence is contested (see Ross 2005).

The first implication—that inegalitarian societies redistribute more than egalitarian ones—has been soundly rejected by the data (see Bénabou 1996; Perotti 1996; Lindert 1996; Alesina and Glaeser 2004; Moene and Wallerstein 2001). Indeed, the pattern among democracies appears to be precisely the opposite. As noted in the example above, a country with a flat income structure such as Sweden redistributes much more than a country like the USA with a very inegalitarian distribution of income. Sometimes referred to as the "Robin Hood paradox," this is a puzzle that informs much contemporary scholarship.

The other main approach to the study of capitalism and democracy focuses on the role of political power, especially the organizational and political strength of labor. If capitalism is about class conflict, then the organization and relative political strength of classes should affect policies and economic outcomes. There are two variants of the approach. *Power resources theory* focuses on the size and structure of the welfare state, explaining it as a function of the historical strength of the political left, mediated by alliances with the middle classes (Korpi 1983, 1989; Esping-Andersen 1990; Huber and Stephens 2001). *Neo-corporatist theory* focuses on the organization of labor and its relationship to the state—especially the degree of centralization of unions and their incorporation into public decision-making processes (Schmitter 1979; Goldthorpe 1984; Cameron 1984; Katzenstein 1985).

Both variants have come under attack for not paying sufficient attention to the role of employers. Research by Martin (1995), Swenson (2002), and Mares (2003), for example, suggests that employers did not simply oppose social policies, but in fact played a proactive role in the early formation of such policies. Also, if the welfare state is built on the shoulders of employers, we should expect investment and economic performance to suffer. But the remarkable fact is that there is no observed relationship between government spending, investment, and national income across advanced democracies (Lindert 1996). Or if there is one, it is so weak that it does not appear to have imposed much of a constraint on governments' ability to spend and regulate labor markets. The neo-corporatist variant is more satisfactory in this respect because it suggests how encompassing unions may choose wage restraint, which leads to higher profits and investment. But this cannot be the whole story since corporatist arrangements were dismantled in the 1980s, often led by export-oriented employers who presumably care deeply about wage restraint (Pontusson and Swenson 1996; Iversen 1996).

A more fundamental question is why conflict should be organized around class and not, say, around sector or occupational group. When people make investments in specific assets, which may be physical or human capital, their interests will be tied up with those investments rather than the collective interest broader class to which they belong (Frieden 1991; Iversen 2005). There is also no systematic account of how distributive conflict between different groups of wage earners gets worked out politically. Dividing a pie invites the formation of redistributive coalitions, and such coalitions cannot be modeled as simply a function of interests. This is clearly also a problem for the Meltzer–Richard model where the median voter is assumed to be king.

3 DEMOCRACY AND PARTISANSHIP

Median voter models are very simple to use, but as the Robin Hood paradox suggests, they do not provide much leverage on explaining the observed variance in redistributive politics. Power resources theory points to one potential source of such variation that has been subject to much research: government partisanship. If center-left governments *simultaneously* promote pre-fisc income equality and redistribution, partisanship may not only explain distributive outcomes but solve the Robin Hood paradox.[1] If partisanship is important in explaining distributive outcomes, we would expect equality and redistribution to go hand in hand.

Partisanship may also explain why corporatist institutions are not always conducive to good economic performance. In Lange and Garrett's (1985) well-known

---

[1] Governments may affect the primary distribution of income through public education (Boix 1998), through the facilitation corporatist bargains that promote wage equality (Cameron 1984; Katzenstein 1985; Garrett 1998), or through minimum wage legislation.

model of economic growth, "encompassing" unions that organize all or most workers are not likely to restrain wages if right partisan governments are in power that are not attentive to the long-term interests of labor. As I discuss in Section 5, this idea of "congruence" between policies and institutions is an important topic for contemporary models of capitalist institutions.

For partisanship to matter, the median voter theorem must be systematically violated, so there must be some explanation for why this should be the case. It is by no means obvious. Although Downs only applied his argument to majoritarian two-party systems, the median voter theorem also applies to multiparty systems where the median legislator can make take-it-or-leave-it proposals. Since no majority can be formed without the support of the median legislator, those proposals will become government policy. In simple unidimensional models of government formation the government always includes the party with the median legislator and does not even need a majority to govern since no viable alternatives can be formed (Laver and Schofield 1990). Yet, the comparative evidence seems to imply that partisanship matters (see, for example, Hicks and Swank 1992; Iversen 1998; Huber and Stephens 2001; Cusack 1997; Allan and Scruggs 2004; Kelly 2005; Kwon and Pontusson 2005).

One explanation is suggested by Wittman's (1973) model of probabilistic voting.[2] If two parties represent constituencies with distinct interests on any set of issues, and if they face uncertainty about the election outcome, the platforms that maximize the implementation of the parties' preferred policies will be away from the median. Since their expected utility is the product of the probability of winning times the proximity of policies to parties' ideal point, parties trade off a lower probability of winning for a policy that is closer to their preference. The Wittman model has found wide application in the study of two-party systems, where one of its attractive features is that it can handle multidimensional spaces (more on this below).

Another explanation for partisanship is that political parties, to be electorally successful, have to appeal to core constituents who provide the money and activists required to run effective electoral campaigns (Hibbs 1977; Schlesinger 1984; Kitschelt 1994; Aldrich 1993, 1995). Aldrich (1983) has formalized this idea in a Downsian model with party activists in which party leaders exchange policy influence to relatively extreme core constituents for unpaid work during campaigns.[3] The logic is illustrated by the American primary system where successful presidential candidates first have to win the support of the parties' core constituents before they can contest the general election. In the general election they have an incentive to moderate their image to appeal to the median voter, but since they were chosen as candidates on different platforms, the perception among voters of real policy differences is accurate.

Aldrich's amended Downsian model raises a critical issue of commitment in politics—an issue that is also important for understanding partisanship. If the

---

[2] For a more exhaustive discussion of the different possibilities in two-party systems, see Grofman 2004.

[3] An interesting model along these lines has been developed by McGann 2002. In the McGann model voters sort themselves into parties based on their platforms, and the platforms of parties are determined by their members (the median members to be precise). Needless to say, this set-up produces policy divergence.

winning electoral platform in an election is the median voter preference, but candidates represent partisan constituencies, how can their commitment to the median voter be credible? Downs largely skirted this issue by assuming that party platforms had to be consistent over time, but it is now standard to assume that such commitments cannot be credible (Persson and Tabellini 1999, 2000). In modern political macroeconomics, for example, governments have a short-term incentive before elections to make the economy look better by using inflationary policies, even as such policies are unsustainable and have deleterious long-run effects (Alesina, Cohen, and Roubini 1992; Franzese 2002; Adolph 2005; Clark 2003).[4] This creates room for partisan politics.[5]

"Citizen-candidates" models takes this idea to its logical conclusion by assuming that candidates cannot commit to anything other than their own preferred policies (Osborne and Slivinski 1996; Besley and Coate 1997). With two candidates and costs of running, the equilibrium is away from the median voter because otherwise one citizen would not find it worthwhile to enter the race (why run if someone is already representing you?). With strategic voting this divergence can be quite large because voters may not want to switch from an existing candidate to a more moderate entrant in the fear that this may cause the least preferred candidate to win.

Turning from party competition to government formation, new bargaining models also do not bear out the idea that the median legislator can dictate policy. If there is real bargaining taking place, Rubinstein bargaining theory essentially implies that parties will split their policy differences. The threat to break off negotiations and initiate bargaining with another party cannot easily be used by the median party to get its way. The reason is that if there are *any* costs of switching (which may simply be the cost of a delay), the new bargaining partner has no incentive to offer a bargain that is better than the original *minus* the cost of switching.[6] As long as parties have different policy preferences, as in the citizen-candidate model, governments will therefore be away from the median.

But while there are compelling reasons why partisanship matters, a critical issue that has largely been skirted is why some countries are dominated by center-left governments and others by center-right governments. In the absence of such dominance we may get partisan political business cycles, as argued by Alesina and others (Alesina, Cohen, and Roubini 1992), but partisanship could no longer explain persistent cross-national differences in policies and outcomes. Nor could partisanship serve as a credible commitment mechanism as it does in the Lange–Garrett model (since partisanship would change in the future). In fact, government partisanship *does*

---

[4] Stokes 1999 offers an interesting alternative in which parties appeal to the short-term interests of voters in the election only to pursue longer-term group interests after the election.

[5] There is a very large literature on the political economy of macroeconomics that is not discussed here. Much of this literature originates with Hibbs's seminal 1977 article and is discussed by Hibbs in *Oxford Handbook of Political Economy*, ed. B. R. Weingast and D. A. Wittman 2006. Oxford: Oxford University Press.

[6] This can be inferred from the "outside option principle" in bargaining theory (Osborne and Rubinstein 1994, 128), although the only proof I am aware of is in Soskice and Iversen 2005.

vary significantly across democracies (see Powell 2002; Iversen and Soskice 2002), and much of the evidence for the importance of partisanship is cross-national.[7]

Rather surprisingly, most of the literature also fails to distinguish between the preferences of parties and the preferences of voters. Observed policy differences between left and right governments could be due to either. There are methodological fixes to this problem—such as comparing the ideological composition of the government to that of the legislature, or focusing on "natural experiments" where the outcome approximates a random assignment of the partisan "treatment" (say, in very close elections)—but we also need a theory of voter preferences. Since voters have an incentive to be "rationally ignorant," as argued by Downs many years ago, it is not really satisfactory to assume that parties simply reflect the interests of citizens. Partisan models must also explain how interests are defined and become common knowledge—a major agenda for future research.

4 MULTIPLE DIMENSIONS AND COALITIONAL POLITICS

As noted in the introduction, distributive politics is inherently multidimensional because a pie can be divided along as many dimensions as there are political agents vying for a piece. It is therefore hard to understand why politicians should constrain themselves to contest a single policy instrument such as the proportional tax/flat rate benefit in the Meltzer–Richard model. And when alternative tax-benefit schedules are considered the results change. In Snyder and Kramer (1988), for example, the choice is over different—linear and non-linear—tax schedules, and the majority choice is no longer redistribution that benefits the poor. The Snyder–Kramer model is itself restricted to one dimension (because it limits the choice to single-parameter schedules subject to an exogenously given revenue target), but it demonstrates the sensitivity of model predictions to the tax-benefit assumptions they make.[8]

One of the first to recognize the importance of multidimensional distributive politics was Esping-Andersen (1990). He distinguishes three different "worlds" of welfare capitalism—each associated with a distinct tax-benefit structure. In the most redistributive (social democratic) type, progressive taxation is coupled with flat rate benefits; in the "liberal" type means-tested benefits are targeted to the poor; while in the "conservative" type benefits are tied to income and occupation. Esping-Andersen makes a plausible (and interesting) argument that the structure of benefits is associated with, and perhaps causes, different social divisions and political patterns: the

---

[7] Power resource theory implies that this is due to differences in the strength of the labor movement. But unionization, or the size of the industrial working class, are in fact poor predictors of partisanship.

[8] The winner in the Snyder–Kramer model is the middle class—a result that is echoed in some multidimensional models discussed below.

poor against the middle class in the means tested, insiders versus outsiders in the conservative, and public against private sector in the social democratic. To explain redistributive politics, political economy therefore has to endogenize the structure of benefits.

Clearly this task can be accomplished neither with a median voter model, nor with a simple left–right partisan model. Building on the majestic work of Moore (1971), Esping-Andersen instead suggests that the answer lies in historically unique class coalitions. Red-green coalitions in Scandinavia forced socialist parties (which lacked stable majorities) to accept universalism. State-corporatist coalitions in continental Europe were forged by autocrats like Bismarck to stem the rise of the labor movement. In countries such as Britain and the USA, where the state and the left were both relatively weak, social issues were essentially dealt with through an extension of the old poor laws, allying the middle class with higher income groups.

Echoing the recent literature on path dependence (Pierson 2000), Esping-Andersen then suggests that the structure of the benefit system re-produces the political support for each type. But neither the origins of the three worlds, nor their stability, can be said to be *explained* since there is no argument to preclude alternative outcomes. For example, why would it not be possible for liberal welfare states to expand redistribution towards the middle class? Or why does the middle class not try to exclude the poor from sharing in the generous benefits of the social democratic model? Or why can outsiders not offer a deal to a subset of insiders in the conservative model that would cause the coalition to break up? Without any explicit theory, much of Esping-Andersen's analysis comes across as *post hoc* description.

One could make a similar charge against Lowi's (1964) account of public policy-making. Like Esping-Andersen's work, however, it provides a convincing account of the numerous forms that distributive politics can take. Specifically, Lowi distinguishes between distributive, regulatory, and redistributive politics. Distributive politics refers to a situation where narrowly defined groups or constituencies, such as congressional districts, seek to maximize their share of appropriations. Since most of the cost can be externalized, everyone pushes for more spending and no one has a sufficiently strong incentive to prevent others from doing the same: "I agree to spend on your project if you agree to spend on mine." The result is what Olson terms "distributive coalitions," characterized by excessive and wasteful spending.

Unlike the quiet, behind-the-scenes logrolling of distributive politics, regulatory politics pits losers against winners as some are advantaged and others disadvantaged by public policies (public procurement decisions, licensing, and other regulatory decisions). Redistributive politics of the Meltzer–Richard variety is also contentious, but the divisions are now across class instead of sector. In a sense, therefore, the nature of public policy (distributive, regulatory, or redistributive) can be predicted by the policy area. Yet, it is hard to see how "policy area" can be treated as a truly exogenous variable any more than the benefit structure in Esping-Andersen's story can. Sure, we know that the New Deal involved class politics and major redistribution, and it clearly contrasts to Lowi's other types, but to move beyond *post hoc* description needs a theory of why distributive politics takes on particular forms at particular times.

Dixit and Londregan's (1996, 1998) model of transfer spending takes us one step in this direction. Assuming probabilistic voting, if two parties do not know individual voter preferences but do know the distribution of such preferences by groups, and if loyalty to different parties varies across groups, vote-maximizing parties will concentrate transfers on the groups with the most "swing" voters. The principle is to distribute transfers so that the marginal vote gain for each dollar spent is exactly the same across all groups. Not surprisingly, groups that have a lot of swing votes will be advantaged because the returns (in terms of votes) of investing in these groups are higher than in other groups. With the additional assumption that loyalists are concentrated among the rich and the poor (those with "extreme" preferences), the implication is that middle class will receive most of the transfers[9]—a result that is known as "Director's Law".

An assumption that is not explained is why parties cannot compete for the loyalty of ideologically committed voters. For example, if African-Americans are loyal to the Democrats because of the party's position on affirmative action (or for any other reason for that matter), then there is no reason Republicans cannot appeal to these voters by adopting a more pro-affirmative action platform. Yet, if loyalty is endogenous to party strategies we are right back into strange world of multidimensional politics without a core. The same is true if we drop the two-party assumption since the "divide the pie" game then does not predict any stable coalition. What is lost by adopting restrictive model assumptions is therefore the ability to consider more complex patterns of coalition formation, and that limits the usefulness of the model for comparative purposes.

Modeling multidimensional coalitional politics is at the center of several new attempts to understand distribution in democracies. In Roemer's (1997, 2001) model, people have intrinsic preferences on some ascriptive dimension such as race or religion, in addition to preferences over redistribution. If the redistributive dimension was the only one that mattered, the analysis would essentially collapse to a Meltzer–Richard model. When a second dimension is introduced, however, the right party can appeal to poor religious or racist voters, and the left party is forced to respond by attracting more wealthy anticlerical or anti-racist voters. As this "exchange" of voters takes place, the two constituencies will tend to become more similar in terms of income. The original pro-welfare coalition is thus broken apart by appeals to commonalities on another, non-economic, dimension. As Riker (1986) recognized informally many years ago, the (re-)bundling of issues is a critical component of coalitional politics, and it helps explain why the poor often don't soak the rich.[10]

---

[9] Not *necessarily* all because if utility is declining in income, and hence transfers, marginal vote gain of giving to groups with many swing voters will also be declining.

[10] The model is in fact more complicated because, once again, there is no equilibrium with majority voting in a multidimensional space. Roemer solves this problem in two alternative ways. In the first formulation one party gets to select its platform before the other party, producing a Stackelberg equilibrium. In another, different factions of both parties must all agree to the policy platform, and this reduces the feasible policy space to a single point.

Alesina and Glaeser (2004) make a related argument for why racial politics may undermine redistribution. If people feel altruistic only towards people of their own race, they will not redistribute to a minority that constitutes a disproportionate share of the poor. Of course, if solidarity with the poor is a "taste" then we need a theory of why people acquire this taste, and Alesina and Glaeser go on to argue that elites that oppose redistribution can use the "race card" to undermine support for redistribution. This is similar to the logic in Roemer's model.

Austen-Smith and Wallerstein (2003) provide a quite different story about the importance of race. In their model people have "race-blind" preferences and are simply trying to maximize their net income. Yet the mere existence of a second dimension (here affirmative action) can cause a legislative coalition in favor of redistribution to break up. The reason (loosely speaking) is that the rich in the majority can offer a bargain to the minority that strengthens affirmative action but reduces redistribution to the poor. Of course, other coalitions are also feasible, but none that generate as much redistribution as bargaining over a single redistributive policy would.

The Roemer and Austen-Smith models are both very complex, but they suggest that countries with a higher dimensionality of the policy space also tend to have less redistribution. Przeworski and Sprague (1986) proposed a similar idea when they argued that left policies would become less prominent as party competition became more influenced by non-economic issues. Yet, to my knowledge no systematic comparative test of the effect of multidimensionality on redistribution has been carried out. Alesina and Glaeser present cross-national correlations between spending and racial, ethnic, and religious heterogeneity, but this is an area ripe for empirical research.

5 DEMOCRATIC INSTITUTIONS

As we have seen, some of the literature has dealt with the complexity of democratic politics by using highly simplifying model assumptions. The Meltzer–Richard model is a prominent example. Such simplifications lead to clear and deductively valid inferences, but they often come at a considerable cost in terms of realism. Those who believe that this cost is too great have turned to history and "thick description." Much of this work, such as Esping-Andersen's influential book on welfare capitalism, underscores the importance of coalitional politics and leads to compelling accounts of cross-national differences in policy regimes. Yet, *post hoc* description is not explanation and the few attempts to model the complexity of coalitional politics, while promising, are themselves complex and have so far produced little comparative research.

In the view of many scholars, focusing on the role of institutions strikes an attractive middle ground. Instead of ad hoc model assumptions, the constraints on political behavior are derived from observed characteristics of political and economic institutions, and instead of *post hoc* descriptions of behavior, outcomes are predicted from the interaction of purposeful behavior and institutional constraints.[11] The approach has been highly successful in explaining cross-national differences in economic policies and outcomes.

Other contributions to this volume go into considerable detail on the role of particular institutions. Here I pick some prominent examples that focus on either democratic institutions (this section) or economic institutions (the next section).[12] These examples are meant to be illustrative of the institutionalist approach, not an exhaustive discussion of the literature. I begin with a discussion of the role of the electoral system because it is a feature of democracies that varies a great deal *and* covaries with government spending, redistribution, and income equality (Persson and Tabellini 2005). This covariation has become the focus of intense scrutiny in recent work in comparative political economy.

In a path-breaking article, Carey and Shugart (1995) propose one way to understand the effects of electoral rules. They argue that the electoral system shapes the incentives of politicians either to toe the party line or to use their influence over public policies to cultivate a personal following. Confirming a long-standing intuition among students of political parties, the incentives for politicians to campaign on a broad party platform depends on the ability of parties to control politicians' re-election chances. The best-known means to accomplish such control is a closed party list system where a candidate's rank on the list determines that candidate's likelihood of re-election. By contrast, in systems where candidates are chosen through primaries, such as elections to the US Congress, political parties cannot directly control who gets on the ballot and politicians have a stronger incentive to pursue their own agendas and appeal to location-specific interests.

Carey and Shugart do not fully spell out the implications of their argument for economic policy, but an obvious hypothesis is that systems that encourage politicians to cultivate a personal following will lead to a targeting of public money to local projects and narrowly defined groups. An example is the pre-1994 Japanese system where candidates from the same party competed against each other for a single non-transferable vote, and therefore produced strong incentives for politicians to spend on their districts while ignoring the public interest. The consequence was a highly fragmented fiscal policy (Cox and Thies 1998; Rosenbluth and Thies 2001). This resonates with Lowi's notion of distributive politics, but in the Carey–Shugart framework the nature of the policy-making process is a function of the political system, which varies across time and space. Put another way, Carey and Shugart help explain differences in countries with respect to their use of policies across Lowi's categories.

In Persson and Tabellini's (1999, 2000) account, the critical institutional feature is the electoral formula. In majoritarian systems, they argue, if middle-class swing voters are concentrated in particular districts, parties have an incentive to ignore

---

[11] "Institutions" defined broadly as the "rules of the game" (North 1990).
[12] For a comprehensive review of the "new" institutionalist literature see Hall and Taylor 1996.

completely other districts that are leaning one way or the other ideologically. These districts are "safe" and therefore not worth fighting over. Similarly to Dixit and Londregan's model, money therefore flows to swing votes in middle-class districts. In single-district PR systems, by contrast, there are no safe districts so politicians cannot ignore the loss of support among other groups by concentrating transfers on the middle class. The result is greater dispersion of spending across classes (or more spending on broad public goods).

PR systems, however, tend to spend more on *both* transfers and public goods. To explain this Persson and Tabellini point to a "second-order effect" of PR, namely that PR systems tend to have more parties and be ruled by multiparty governments (see Ordeshook and Shvetsova 1994; Neto and Cox 1997 for the evidence). If each party wants to spend on its own group (so that the space is multidimensional), this can lead to a common-pool problem with excessive spending as a result (see also Bawn and Rosenbluth 2002; Crepaz 1998). Again, Lowi's distributive politics is here linked to an institutional feature that varies across countries.

Electoral systems also appear to be systematically related to class politics. Iversen and Soskice (2006) argue that when parties representing different classes have to form coalitions to govern, as is typically the case under PR, the center and left have an incentive to get together to soak the rich. This is not true in two-party majoritarian systems where parties are coalitions of classes. In this situation, middle-class voters can be soaked by the poor if the center-left party deviates from a median voter plat-form. Assuming that the right cannot engage in regressive redistribution, incomplete platform commitment therefore puts the median voter at risk and the center-left at an electoral disadvantage. The implication is that partisanship and redistribution, class politics in Lowi's scheme, systematically covary with electoral system.

Another democratic institution that has generated intense scholarly scrutiny is federalism. Much of the research in this area originates with Brennan and Buchanan's (1980) argument that competition between local governments for mobile sources of revenue undermines the ability of predatory governments to impose excessive taxation. Coupled with the potential ability of states to secede, which restricts the ability of central governments to exploit member states, federalism may also consti-tute a credible commitment to property rights—what Weingast (1995) calls "market-preserving federalism." Viewed from the left, this logic suggests that federalism may undermine the welfare state and lead to under-provision of social welfare or a "race to the bottom" (Pierson 1995).

A related argument is that federalism makes it harder to pass new legislation because it has to be ratified in two legislative assemblies. The implication is a status quo bias, which is sometimes argued to have slowed the expansion of the welfare state (Huber, Ragin, and Stephens 1993). But while federalism does appear to be associated with smaller governments, there is in fact a striking amount of variance across feder-alist states (Obinger, Leibfried, and Castles 2005). Swiss and US federalism seems to be linked to low spending, but this is not true of German or Austrian federalism.

To account for this variation, Rodden (2003, 2005) has proposed to distinguish between federalist systems with different fiscal institutions. If local spending is locally financed, tax competition puts a damper on spending, but if local spending is financed through central or intergovernmental grants, local politicians have little incentive to contain spending. This argument applies more generally to political systems where there is a division of labor between local governments and the center (a unitary system like Sweden, for example, exhibits a lot of local policy autonomy).

Revenue-sharing may be seen as a source of common-pool problems (or Lowi's distributive politics), or it may be seen as a method to reduce the power of those with mobile assets and empowering governments to pursue redistribution. Whatever the normative perspective, if there are two different types of federalism, one with a "soft" and one with a "hard" budget constraint, then a key issue is why some governments have adopted hard budget constraints while others have not (Wibbels 2003; Wildasin, in *Oxford Handbook of Political Economy*, ed. B. R. Weingast and D. A. Wittman 2006. Oxford: Oxford University Press). Alternatively, there is a wealth of interesting variation in revenue-sharing between local governments and states that seems critical to fiscal policy, yet is not treated as an object of explanation. There *is* a literature on fiscal discipline and its consequences (see von Hagen and Harden 1995 and the von Hagen chapter in *Oxford Handbook of Political Economy*, ed. B. R. Weingast and D. A. Wittman 2006. Oxford: Oxford University Press), but budgetary rules are for the most part treated as exogenous.

By anchoring model assumptions in the rich details of actual political institutions, the new institutionalist literature enables the coupling of formal reasoning with the realism of inductive research. It reduces the indeterminism of democratic policy-making and suggests promising ways to endogenize partisanship, coalition formation, and styles of policy-making. Our understanding of fiscal policies and distributive outcomes has been greatly advanced in the process. But by highlighting the critical importance of institutional detail, one cannot help but wonder if the real task is not the explanation of the institutions themselves. I return to this question below. But first I turn to another successful branch of institutionalism that focuses on modern capitalism as an economic system.

6 VARIETIES OF CAPITALISM

It is common to portray democratic capitalism as a system where markets allocate income according to efficiency while governments redistribute income according to political demand. This suggests a convenient intellectual division of labor between economists and political scientists, but it is based on a neoclassical view of the economy that few today believe. Instead, the dominant approach to the study of capitalism as an economic system builds on new institutional economics and is known as the "varieties of capitalism" (or VoC) approach (Hall and Soskice 2001). Just as democracy has been shown to divide into institutional subspecies, so has capitalism. As I discuss at the end of this section, there is in fact a close empirical association between political and economic institutions, although the reasons for this association are not well understood.

The VoC approach assumes that economic institutions are designed to help firms and other economic agents make the best use of their productive assets (Hall and Soskice 2001). As argued by Williamson (1985), North (1990), and others, when an economy is characterized by heavy investment in co-specific assets, economic agents are exposed to risks that make market exchange problematic.[13] A precondition for such an economy to work efficiently is therefore a dense network of institutions that provide information, offer insurance against risk, and permit continuous and impartial enforcement of complex contracts. In the complete absence of such institutions, exchange is possible only at a small scale in local trading communities where repeated face-to-face interactions enable reputational enforcement of contracts. At a larger scale, or with a greater division of labor, markets that are left to their own devices will either be accompanied by costly and continuous haggling, or be restricted to exchanges of very homogeneous goods.

Another central feature of the VoC approach is the idea that an institution has to be understood in relation to other institutions. Institutional complementarity means that the effectiveness of one institution depends on the design of another. Precursors for this idea are Lange and Garrett's (1985) congruence model (that I discussed above), as well as Streeck's (1991) account of the German model and Aoki's (1994) account of the Japanese. The VoC approach generalizes the idea and argues that *all* major institutions of capitalism are complementary to each other: the industrial relations system, the financial and corporate governance system, the training system, and the innovation system. For example, if firms make investments in their workers' skills, unions gain hold-up power that can be levied against the firms. This necessitates an industrial relations system where such hold-up power can be managed. Conversely, workers will be reluctant to acquire firm-specific skills unless firms can make credible long-term commitments, which require a financial system that provide access to "patient" capital, and a corporate governance system where workers are given influence, and so on.

Because of these institutional complementarities, one is not likely to find every logically conceivable combination of institutions in the real world. In fact, Soskice (1999) makes the claim that there are only two dominant types: one called liberal market economies (LMEs) and another called coordinated market economies (CMEs). Each is characterized by the extent to which institutions protect and encourage investment in assets that assist firms in pursuing particular product market strategies. In CMEs where firms and workers have invested heavily in assets that are specific to particular companies, industries, or jobs, institutions are designed to protect those investments.[14] In LMEs where such institutional protection is missing or weak, market

---

[13] Polanyi 1944 is an important precursor for many of these arguments.

[14] For example, unionized workers with specific skills possess very considerable potential hold-up power over firms, and firms will be unlikely to rely on workers with specific skills unless individual unions are constrained through an interfirm collective bargaining system. In turn there is strong evidence that such collective bargaining systems lead to a compression of wages (Rueda and Pontusson 2000; Wallerstein 1999).

competition encourages economic agents to make investments in general assets since, in the absence of protection, mobility is the best insurance against risks. This does not eliminate specific assets, but it will reduce their relative importance.

The VoC argument suggests a very different explanation for the welfare state than power resources theory. Mares (2003), for example, argues that companies and industries that are highly exposed to risk will favor a social insurance system where cost and risk are shared, leading employers to push universalistic unemployment and accident insurance. Although low-risk firms will oppose such spending, it is remarkable that universalism has been promoted by groups of employers since the literature associates it so closely with policies imposed on employers by unions and left governments. Manow (forthcoming) argues that social insurance systems shape the structure of production systems, and Estevez-Abe, Iversen, and Soskice (2001) and Iversen (2005) suggest that social protection (including job protection, unemployment benefits, income protection, and a host of related policies such as public retraining programs and industry subsidies) encourages workers to acquire specific skills, which in turn enhances the ability of firms to compete in certain international market segments.[15] The welfare state is thus linked to the economy in a manner that creates beneficial complementaries. This may help explain the lack of evidence for the deleterious effects of social spending on growth, and why globalization has not spelled the end to the welfare state.

A mostly unexplored topic in the VoC literature is the relationship between economic and political institutions. It is striking, for example, that the distinction between LMEs and CMEs is almost perfectly collinear with the distinction between PR and majoritarian electoral systems. One possible explanation, which goes back to Katzenstein's (1985) work on corporatism, is that PR promotes the representation of specialized interests in the legislature and its committees. At least this would be true if parties have incentives to accommodate each other's specific interests.[16] Majoritarian systems, by contrast, encourage parties to elect strong leaders in order to convince the median voter that they are not beholden to special interests. Such "leadership parties" are consequently not conducive to the protection of specialized interests and therefore encourage economic agents to make investments in more portable assets (say, college degrees as opposed to extensive vocational training).

Another reason for the coupling of electoral and economic systems may be that PR serves as a credible commitment to social protection because of its effect on class coalitions and redistribution. A high level of insurance will encourage investment

[15] The skill argument may also account for some of the variation in labor market segregation between the sexes. Women appear to find it much harder than men to enter into specific skills jobs, and this may have to do with the differential ability of men and women to commit to uninterrupted careers (Estevez-Abe 1999; Iversen and Rosenbluth 2006).

[16] This logic may build on Laver and Shesple's (1996) model of government formation, since policies of multiparty governments in their theory reflect the distinct interests of the participating parties. Parties representing agriculture dominate the agricultural ministry, parties representing industry the industrial ministry, etc. It does require, however, that parties representing significant specific interests are not permanently excluded from policy influence.

in risky assets and hence support a particular type of firm.[17] This is a conjecture that still awaits careful empirical corroboration. In particular, it will need to be shown that the correlation between electoral systems and production regimes is not a historical accident, but the result of a deliberate design of political institutions by representatives of particular economic interests.

The question of institutional origins, of course, is a matter that concerns the entire institutionalist approach to political economy. The more successful political economy is in explaining economic policies and outcomes with reference to the institutional design, the more pressing it is to explain why one design was chosen rather than another (Thelen 1999; Pierson 2000). But the question then is how we can approach this task without being overwhelmed by the complexity of institution-free politics. In the concluding section I ask whether the answer may lie in a structuralist approach.

7 CONCLUSION: TOWARDS A NEW STRUCTURALISM?

A decade ago nearly all comparative political economists would have called themselves institutionalists. Today an increasing number of scholars are convinced that only way forward is by going back—back to the origins of institutions and the conditions that gave rise to them. The questions that are being asked by these scholars are fundamental: under which structural-economic conditions do autocracies move to democracy (Acemoglu and Robinson 2005; Boix 2003)? How do institutions emerge that will protect property rights and produce prosperity (North and Weingast 1989)? What are the origins of modern skill systems (Thelen 2004)? What accounts for differences in the structure of social programs (Mares 2003; Swenson 2002)? What are the origins of federalism (Wibbels 2003) and of electoral institutions (Boix 1999; Cusack, Iversen, and Soskice 2004)?

In a recent paper, Rogowski and MacRay (2003) conjecture that many of the institutional effects that have been documented in painstaking detail by decades of institutional research are in fact epiphenomenal to the structural conditions and interests that gave rise to them. If this is true, it puts a premium on understanding the "pre-strategic" policy preferences of agents and the circumstances that determine them. But if we make this move we need to understand that this could bring us head to head with that elephant in the corner: the chaos of institution-free politics. If we take this path, is there a way to avoid *post hoc* description or ad hoc modeling?

---

[17] Although redistribution and insurance are analytically distinct, in practice they are closely related. The unemployed, the sick, the old, and those with low pre-fisc income more generally, will support redistribution and benefit from it. But for those who are currently employed, healthy, young, and enjoying a high income such redistribution is insurance against many of the vagaries of the capitalist economy.

Take the example of Acemoglu and Robinson's (2005) theory of democratic transitions. This is one of the most sophisticated attempts to model democracy, yet it relies heavily on the simplifying assumptions of the Meltzer–Richard model. Understandably, Acemoglu and Robinson replace the lack of well-defined institutional constraints with the safe familiarity of a model that is easy to understand, but may omit important aspects of the coalitional dynamics.

There is however the outline of an alternative in Acemoglu and Robinson's book that I will loosely refer to as "new structuralism" (to distinguish it from Marxist structuralism, structural functionalism, and other previous uses of the term). In their model, inequality and the size of the middle class powerfully shape the incentives that political agents have to compromise. A sizeable middle class essentially serves as a buffer against radical demands for redistribution under democracy. Or to put the matter in more general terms: the structure of the pre-democratic economy places constraints on political agents that may help to explain their behavior.

This idea of rooting actors in the structure of the capitalist economy can clearly be taken further. Rogowski (1989), who has made one of the most influential structural arguments to date, focuses on variation in trade exposure and relative factor endowments. Others imply that political interests are defined not only by factor endowments, but by the specificity of these factors (e.g. Frieden 1991; Alt et al. 1996; Iversen and Soskice 2001). In a different context, Mares (2003) emphasizes the size of firms and their exposure to risk when explaining preferences over social policy. Swenson (2002) similarly traces employer-driven social policy initiatives to product market conditions. In explaining modern skill and production systems, Thelen (2004) argues that the strength of the guild system at the dawn of the industrial revolution powerfully shaped subsequent developments. Thelen also makes a convincing case that institutions are rarely created *de novo* but grow out of existing institutions, which shape the direction of change even as they are transformed. In other words, institutions often belong on both sides of the causal equation.

These examples do not add up to a single coherent approach to the study of institutional design. The point is simply that as we move "behind" the institutions to explain their genesis, an important task will be to identify the key structural attributes of capitalist economies (including old "obsolete" institutions), and the agents that populate them, so that they can serve as parameters in our models of institutional design and change. Similarly to the institutionalist project, the success of the new structuralism will depend on combining carefully identified historical constraints with rigorous theorizing. If this can be done, we may be able to leave the elephant in peace for a while longer.

References

Acemoglu, D. and Robinson, J. 2005. *Political Origins of Dictatorship and Democracy*. Cambridge: Cambridge University Press.

Adolph, C. 2005. The dilemma of discretion: career ambitions and the politics of central banking. Ph.D. dissertation, Department of Government, Harvard University.

ALDRICH, J. H. 1983. A Downsian spatial model with party activism. *American Political Science Review*, 77: 974–90.

—— 1993. Rational choice and turnout. *American Journal of Political Science*, 37: 246–78.

—— 1995. *Why Parties? The Origins and Transformation of Party Politics in America*. Chicago: University of Chicago Press.

ALESINA, A., COHEN, G., and ROUBINI, N. 1992. Macroeconomic policy and elections in OECD democracies. *Economics and Politics*, 4: 1–30.

—— —— 2004. *Fighting Poverty in the US and Europe: A World of Difference*. Oxford: Oxford University Press.

—— ROSENTHAL, H. 2000. Polarized platforms and moderate policies with checks and balances. *Journal of Public Economics*, 75: 1–20.

ALLAN, J. and SCRUGGS, L. 2004. Political partisanship and welfare state reform in advanced industrial societies. *American Journal of Political Science*, 48: 493–512.

ALT, J. FRIEDEN, J., GILLIGAN, M. J., RODRIK, D., and ROGOWSKI, R. 1996. The political economy of international trade: enduring puzzles and an agenda for inquiry. *Comparative Political Studies*, 29: 689–717.

AOKI, M. 1994. The Japanese firm as a system of attributes: a survey and research agenda. Pp. 11–40 in *The Japanese Firm: Sources of Competitive Strength*, ed. M. Aoki. Oxford: Clarendon Press.

ARROW, K. 1951. *Social Choice and Individual Values*. New York: John Wiley (2nd edn. 1963).

AUSTEN-SMITH, D. and WALLERSTEIN, M. 2003. Redistribution in a divided society. Unpublished paper.

BAWN, K. and ROSENBLUTH, F. 2002. Coalition parties versus coalitions of parties: how electoral agency shapes the political logic of costs and benefits. PIEP Working Paper Series, WCFIA, Harvard University.

BÉNABOU, R. 1996. Inequality and growth. Pp. 11–74 in *National Bureau of Economic Research Macro Annual*, 11, ed. B. S. Bernanke and J. J. Rotemberg. Cambridge, Mass.: MIT Press.

BESLEY, T. and COATE, S. 1997. An economic model of representative democracy. *Quarterly Journal of Economics*, 112: 85–114.

BOIX, C. 1998. *Political Parties, Growth and Equality*. New York: Cambridge University Press.

—— 1999. Setting the rules of the game: the choice of electoral systems in advanced democracies. *American Political Science Review*, 93: 609–24.

—— 2003. *Democracy and Redistribtuion*. Cambridge: Cambridge University Press.

BRENNAN, G. and BUCHANAN, J. 1980. *The Power to Tax: Analytical Foundations of a Fiscal Constitution*. New York: Cambridge University Press.

CAMERON, D. 1984. Social democracy, corporatism, labor quiescence, and the representation of economic interest in advanced capitalist society. Pp. 143–78 in *Order and Conflict in Contemporary Capitalism*, ed. J. Goldthorpe. Oxford: Clarendon Press.

CAREY, J. M. and SHUGART, M. S. 1995. Incentives to cultivate a personal vote: a rank ordering of electoral formulas. *Electoral Studies*, 14: 417–39.

CLARK, W. R. 2003. *Capitalism, Not Globalism: Capital Mobility, Central Bank Independence, and the Political Control of the Economy*. Ann Arbor: University of Michigan Press.

COX, G. 1990. Centripetal and centrifugal incentives in electoral systems. *American Journal of Political Science*, 34: 903–35.

—— and THIES, M. F. 1998. The cost of intraparty competition: the single, non-transferable vote and money politics in Japan. *Comparative Political Studies*, 31: 267–91.

CREPAZ, M. M. L. 1998. Inclusion versus exclusion: political institutions and welfare expenditures. *Comparative Politics*, 31: 61–80.

CUSACK, T. 1997. Partisan politics and public finance: changes in public spending in the industrialized democracies, 1955–1989. *Public Choice*, 91: 375–95.

—— IVERSEN, T., and SOSKICE, D. 2004. Specific interests and the origins of electoral systems. Paper prepared for presentation at the American Political Science Associations Meetings, Chicago, Aug.

DIXIT, A. and LONDREGAN, J. 1996. The determinants of success of special interests in redistributive politics. *Journal of Politics*, 58: 1132–55.

—— —— 1998. Ideology, tactics, and efficiency in redistributive politics. *Quarterly Journal of Economics*, 113: 497–529.

ESPING-ANDERSEN, G. 1990. *The Three Worlds of Welfare Capitalism*. Princeton, NJ: Princeton University Press.

ESTEVEZ-ABE, M. 1999. Comparative political economy of female labor participation. Paper prepared for presentation at the Annual Meetings of the American Political Science Association, Atlanta, 2–5 Sept.

—— IVERSEN, T., and SOSKICE, D. 2001. Social protection and the formation of skills: a reinterpretation of the welfare state. Pp. 145–83 in *Varieties of Capitalism: The Institutional Foundations of Comparative Advantage*, ed. P. A. Hall and D. Soskice. Oxford: Oxford University Press.

FRANZESE, R. 2002. *Macroeconomics of Developed Democracies*. Cambridge: Cambridge University Press.

FRIEDEN, J. 1991. Invested intersts: the politics of national economc policies in a world of global finance. *International Organization*, 45: 425–51.

GARRETT, G. 1998. *Partisan Politics in the Global Economy*. Cambridge: Cambridge University Press.

GOLDTHORPE, J. (ed.). 1984. *Order and Conflict in Contemporary Capitalism*. Oxford: Clarendon Press.

GROFMAN, B. 2004. Downs and two-party convergence. *Annual Review of Political Science*, 7: 25–46.

HALL, P. A. and SOSKICE, D. 2001. An introduction to varieties of capitalism. Pp. 1–68 in *Varieties of Capitalism: The Institutional Foundations of Comparative Advantage*, ed. P. A. Hall and D. Soskice. Oxford: Oxford University Press.

—— and TAYLOR, R. 1996. Political science and the three new institutionalisms. *Political Studies*, 44: 936–57.

HIBBS, D. 1977. Political parties and macroeconomic policy. *American Political Science Review*, 71: 1467–87.

HICKS, A. and SWANK, D. 1992. Politics, institutions, and welfare spending in industrialized democracies, 1960–82. *American Political Science Review*, 86: 649–74.

HUBER, E., RAGIN, C., and STEPHENS, J. 1993. Social democracy, Christian democracy, constitutional structure and the welfare state. *American Journal of Sociology*, 99: 711–49.

—— and STEPHENS, J. D. 2001. *Development and Crisis of the Welfare State: Parties and Policies in Global Markets*. Chicago: University of Chicago Press.

IVERSEN, T. 1996. Power, flexibility and the breakdown of centralized wage bargaining: the cases of Denmark and Sweden in comparative perspective. *Comparative Politics*, 28: 399–436.

—— 1998. Equality, employment, and budgetary restraint: the trilemma of the service economy. *World Politics*, 50: 507–46.

—— 2005. *Capitalism, Democracy and Welfare*. Cambridge: Cambridge University Press.

—— and ROSENBLUTH, F. 2006. The political economy of gender: explaining cross-national variation in the gender division of labor and the gender voting gap. *American Journal of Political Science*, 50: 1–19.

—— and SOSKICE, D. 2001. An asset theory of social policy preferences. *American Political Science Review*, 95: 875–93.

IVERSEN, T. and SOSKICE, D. 2002. Electoral institutions, parties, and the politics of class: why some democracies redistribute more than others. Paper presented at the Annual Meetings of the American Political Science Association.

—— 2005. Why governments diverge from the preferences of the median legislator. Manuscript, Dept. of Government, Harvard University.

KATZENSTEIN, P. 1985. *Small States in World Markets*. Ithaca, NY: Cornell University Press.

KELLY, N. J. 2005. Political choice, public policy, and distributional outcomes. *American Journal of Political Science*, 49: 865–80.

KITSCHELT, H. 1994. *The Transformation of European Social Democracy*. Cambridge: Cambridge University Press.

KORPI, W. 1983. *The Democratic Class Struggle*. London: Routledge and Kegan Paul.

—— 1989. Power, politics, and state autonomy in the development of social citizenship: social rights during sickness in 18 OECD countries since 1930. *American Sociological Review*, 54: 309–28.

KWON, H. Y. and PONTUSSON, J. 2005. The zone of partisanship: parties, unions and welfare spending in OECD countries, 1962–99. Unpublished manuscript, Dept. of Political Science, Cornell University.

LANGE, P. and GARRETT, G. 1985. The politics of growth: strategic interaction and economic performance, 1974–1980. *Journal of Politics*, 47: 792–827.

LAVER, M. and SCHOFIELD, N. 1990. *Multiparty Government: The Politics of Coalition in Western Europe*. Oxford: Oxford University Press.

—— and SHEPSLE, K. 1996. *Making and Breaking Governments: Cabinets and Legislatures in Parliamentary Democracies*. Cambridge: Cambridge University Press.

LINDERT, P. H. 1996. What limits social spending? *Explorations in Economic History*, 33: 1–34.

LOWI, T. 1964. American business, public policy, case studies, and political theory. *World Politics*, 16: 677–715.

McGANN, A. J. 2002. The advantages of ideological cohesion: a model of constituency representation and electoral competition in multiparty democracies. *Journal of Theoretical Politics*, 14: 37–70.

MANOW, P. forthcoming. *Social Protection and Capitalist Production: The Bismarckian Welfare State and the German Political Economy, 1880–1990*. Amesterdam: Amesterdam University Press.

MARES, I. 2003. *The Politics of Social Risk: Business and Welfare State Development*. Cambridge: Cambridge University Press.

MARTIN, C. J. 1995. Nature of Nuture? Source of firm preferences for national health reform. *American Political Science Review*, 89: 898–913.

MELTZER, A. H. and RICHARD, S. F. 1981. A rational theory of the size of government. *Journal of Political Economy*, 89: 914–27.

MOENE, K. O. and WALLERSTEIN, M. 2001. Inequality, social insurance and redistribution. *American Political Science Review*, 95: 859–74.

MOORE, B. 1971. *Social Origins of Democracy and Dictatorship: Lord and Peasant in the Making of the Modern World*. Boston: Beacon Press.

NETO, O. A. and COX, G. W. 1997. Electoral institutions, cleavage structures, and the number of parties. *American Journal of Political Science*, 41: 149–74.

NORTH, D. 1990. *Institutions, Institutional Change and Economic Performance*. Cambridge: Cambridge University Press.

—— and WEINGAST, B. R. 1989. Constitutions and commitment: the evolution of institutions governing public choice in the 17th-century England. *Journal of Economic History*, 49: 803–32.

OBINGER, H., LEIBFRIED, S., and CASTLES, F. G. (eds.). 2005. *Federalism and the Welfare State: New World and European Experiences.* Cambridge: Cambridge University Press.

ORDESHOOK, P. and SHVETSOVA, O. 1994. Ethnic heterogeneity, district magnitude, and the number of parties. *American Journal of Political Science*, 38: 100–23.

OSBORNE, M. J. and RUBINSTEN, A. 1994. *A Course in Game Theory.* Cambridge, Mass.: MIT Press.

OSBORNE, M. J. and SLIVINSKI, A. 1996. A model of political competition with citizen-candidates. *Quarterly Journal of Economics*, 111: 65–96.

PEROTTI, R. 1996. Growth, income distribution and democracy: what the data say. *Journal of Economic Growth*, 1: 149–87.

PERSSON, T. and TABELLINI, G. 1999. The size and scope of government: comparative politics with rational politicians. *European Economic Review*, 43: 699–735.

————2000. *Political Economics: Explaining Economic Policy.* Cambridge, Mass.: MIT Press.

————2005. *The Economic Effects of Constitutions.* Cambridge, Mass.: MIT Press.

PIERSON, P. 1995. Fragmented welfare states: federal institutions and the development of social policy. *Governance*, 8: 449–78.

——2000. Path dependence, increasing returns, and the study of politics. *American Political Science Review*, 94: 251–67.

POLANYI, K. 1944. *The Great Transformation.* New York: Rinehart.

PONTUSSON, J. and SWENSON, P. 1996. Labor markets, production strategies, and wage bargaining institutions: the Swedish employer offensive in comparative perspective. *Comparative Political Studies*, 29: 223–50.

POWELL, B. 2002. PR, the median voter, and economic policy: an exploration. Paper presented at the Annual Meetings of the American Political Science Association, Boston.

PRZEWORSKI, A. and SPRAGUE, J. 1986. *Paper Stones: A History of Electoral Socialism.* Chicago: University of Chicago Press.

——and WALLERSTEIN, M. 1982. Structural dependence of the state on capital. *American Political Science Review*, 82: 11–29.

RIKER, W. H. 1980. Implications for the disequilibrium of majority rule for the study of institutions. *American Political Science Review*, 74: 432–46.

——1986. *The Art of Political Manipulation.* New Haven, Conn.: Yale University Press.

RODDEN, J. 2003. Reviving Leviathan: fiscal federalism and the growth of government. *International Organization*, 57: 695–729.

——2005. *Hamilton's Paradox: The Promise and Peril of Fiscal Federalism.* Cambridge: Cambridge University Press.

RODRIK, D. 1999. Democracies pay higher wages. *Quarterly Journal of Economics*, 114: 707–38.

ROEMER, J. E. 1997. The democratic political economy of progressive taxation. *Econometrica*, 67: 1–19.

——2001. *Political Competition: Theory and Applications.* Cambridge, Mass.: Harvard University Press.

ROGOWSKI, R. 1989. *Commerce and Coalitions: How Trade Affects Domestic Political Alignments.* Princeton, NJ: Princeton University Press.

——and MACRAY, D. 2003. Does inequality determine institutions? What history and (some) data tell us. Paper presented in the Political Institutions and Inequality Study Group, Center for European Studies, Harvard University, Oct.

ROMER, T. 1975. Individual welfare, majority voting, and the properties of a linear income tax. *Journal of Public Economics*, 14: 163–85.

ROSENBLUTH, F. M. and THIES, M. F. 2001. The electoral foundations of Japan's financial politics: the case of *Jusen*. *Policy Studies Journal*, 29: 23–37.

ROSS, M. 2005. Is democracy good for the poor? Unpublished manuscript, UCLA, Dept. of Political Science.

RUEDA, D. and PONTUSSON, J. 2000. Wage inequality and varieties of capitalism. *World Politics*, 52: 350–83.

SCHLESINGER, J. 1984. On the theory of party organization. *Journal of Politics*, 46: 369–400.

SCHMITTER, P. 1979. Modes of interest intermediation and models of societal change. Pp. 43–94 in *Trends toward Corporatist Intermediation*, ed. P. Schmitter and G. Lehmbruch. Beverly Hills, Calif.: Sage.

SNYDER, J. M. and KRAMER, G. H. 1988. Fairness, self-interest, and the politics of the progressive income tax. *Journal of Public Economics*, 36: 197–230.

SOSKICE, D. 1999. Divergent production regimes: coordinated and uncoordinated market economies in the 1980s and 1990s. Pp. 101–34 in *Continuity and Change in Contemporary Capitalism*, ed. H. Kitschelt, P. Lange, G. Marks, and J. D. Stephens. Cambridge: Cambridge University Press.

—— and IVERSON, T. 2005. *Why Governments Diverge from the Prefrences of the Median Voter*. Manuscript. Harvard University.

STOKES, S. 1999. Political parties and democracy. *Annual Review of Political Science*, 2: 243–67.

STREECK, W. 1991. On the institutional conditions of diversified quality production. Pp. 21–61 in *Beyond Keynesianism*, ed. E. Matzner and W. Streeck. Aldershot: Elgar.

SWENSON, P. 1991. Bringing capital back in, or social democracy reconsidered: employer power, cross-class alliances, and centralization of industrial relations in Denmark and Sweden. *World Politics*, 43: 513–44.

—— 2002. *Employers against Markets* Cambridge: Cambridge University Press.

THELEN, K. 1999. Historical institutionalism in comparative politics. *Annual Review of Political Science*, 2: 369–404.

—— 2004. *How Institutions Evolve: The Political Economy of Skills in Germany, Britain, the United States and Japan*. Cambridge: Cambridge University Press.

VON HAGEN, J. and HARDEN, I. 1995. National budget processes and commitment to fiscal discipline. *European Economic Review*, 39: 771–9.

WALLERSTEIN, M. 1999. Wage-setting institutions and pay inequality in advanced industrial societies. *American Journal of Political Science*, 43: 649–80.

WEINGAST, B. R. 1995. The economic role of political institutions: market-preserving federalism and economic development. *Journal of Law, Economics, and Organization*, 1: 1–31.

—— and MARSHALL, W. J. 1988. The industrial organization of Congress: or, why legislatures, like firms, are not organized as markets. *Journal of Political Economy*, 96: 132–63.

WIBBELS, E. 2003. Bailouts, budget constraints, and Leviathans: comparative federalism and lessons from the early United States. *Comparative Political Studies*, 36: 475–508.

WILLIAMSON, O. E. 1985. *The Economic Institutions of Capitalism: Firms, Markets, Relational Contracting*. New York: Free Press.

WITTMAN, D. 1973. Parties as utility maximizers. *American Political Science Review*, 67: 490–8.

CHAPTER 41

....

POLITICS, DELEGATION, AND BUREAUCRACY

....

JOHN D. HUBER

CHARLES R. SHIPAN

MODERN democratic government cannot function without bureaucracy. Given the vast array of policy issues that come before government, the complexity of these issues, and the resources needed to address them, elected politicians have no choice but to delegate at least some responsibility over these issues to bureaucracies. Of course, once politicians delegate, they also face a potential loss of control over the issues that they have delegated. This tension between the necessity of delegation and the potential problems associated with delegation underlines the fundamentally political nature of bureaucracy. Government bureaucracies are surrounded, and affected, by other political actors, including legislators and courts, presidents and governors, prime ministers and cabinet ministers, and interest groups, all of whom attempt to manage this tension. Any analysis of bureaucracies, therefore, needs to view them through the lens of political analysis.

Prior to the 1980s, a dominant theme in the literature on bureaucracy emphasized the "administrative state." The complexity of policy issues and the rapid expansion of government involvement into new policy areas made it very difficult for politicians to make important policy decisions. By contrast, the increasing professionalism and specialization of bureaucracy equipped bureaucrats with the expertise and experience needed to make these decisions. Consequently, the argument went, bureaucrats run

* We are grateful to Mike Ting for helpful comments and to Eduardo Leoni for research assistance.

the show, while politicians essentially have no choice but to sit on the sidelines and watch.

In the early 1980s, scholars began strongly to challenge the administrative dominance perspective. In particular, researchers began to examine the design of rules for bureaucratic decision-making and political oversight of bureaucracy (e.g. McCubbins, Noll, and Weingast 1987, 1989; Moe 1989). With the correct institutions governing agency decision-making, some argued, politicians ensure that bureaucratic actors pursue the goals of politicians. Although researchers disagreed about whether this in fact was true, and, more generally, about which elements of structure and process were central to understanding bureaucratic behavior, these arguments have set the agenda for much research on bureaucracy in the last twenty years. A large number of formal models of delegation have explored the instruments that politicians use to delegate to bureaucrats. These models, which have spawned a rich empirical literature, typically focus on two types of delegation instruments: *ex ante* instruments, which allow politicians to establish the level of discretion bureaucrats have when making policy, and *ex post* instruments, which allow politicians or other political actors to monitor or audit bureaucrats after agents take action.

This chapter reviews some of these recent models and associated empirical research. We begin by describing the four core theoretical arguments that consistently emerge from these models about the circumstances under which politicians should be expected to grant either more or less discretion to bureaucrats. After reviewing these arguments, we describe empirical tests that focus on patterns of delegation strategies. We argue that considerable support is accumulating for these arguments, and that we can therefore use the models on which they are based to make inferences about the circumstances under which administrative dominance is most likely. We conclude by reviewing recent theoretical models that provide insights into the circumstances under which the logic of these theoretical arguments breaks down. By considering questions of theoretical robustness, we are able to describe areas that are ripe for additional theorizing and empirical research.

1 CORE ARGUMENTS ABOUT DELEGATION STRATEGIES

In this section we sketch the four most prominent arguments that have emerged from efforts to model delegation. Two standard assumptions underlie these arguments. First, politicians and bureaucrats often want to achieve different objectives. This is not always true, of course; but when it is not, delegation presents few problems, since politicians can trust bureaucrats to act in their interests. Second, there is asymmetric information about how to achieve policy goals, with bureaucrats typically having more expertise than politicians. The challenge for politicians is how to draw on this

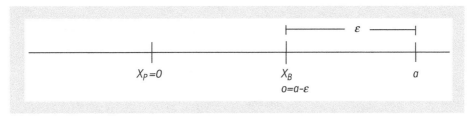

Fig. 41.1. Politicians, bureaucrats, and policy uncertainty

expertise given that bureaucrats want to put it to ends that differ from those desired by politicians.

Many models use a simple, unidimensional spatial framework to implement these two assumptions. A typical model will have a single Politician with ideal point at x_P, and a single Bureaucrat with ideal point at x_B, as illustrated in Figure 41.1. The level of policy conflict between them is simply the distance between x_P and x_B. As this distance grows, the Politician becomes increasingly worried that delegating more authority to the Bureaucrat will lead to a policy outcome that the Politician does not like. In the examples that follow, we assume $x_P = 0 < x_B$ and that both players have quadratic preferences.

The Bureaucrat's informational advantage is often introduced into delegation models by assuming uncertainty about the outcome that will occur if a particular policy is adopted. A common way to model this asymmetry is to assume that after some policy action, a, is taken, the outcome from this policy is $o = a - \varepsilon$. The random variable ε is typically drawn from some well-behaved distribution with finite support, for instance, a uniform distribution. If $\varepsilon \in [-E, E]$, then E is a parameter that measures policy uncertainty. As E gets larger, so too does uncertainty about the outcome that will result from adopting a particular policy a. Both players might know the distribution from which ε is drawn, but the Bureaucrat has more information. Models typically make the information asymmetry as stark as possible by assuming that the Bureaucrat knows the exact value of ε, whereas the Politician knows only the distribution from which ε is drawn. If, for example, the Bureaucrat knows ε and is allowed to implement any policy choice he wants, he can choose a policy a that will produce an outcome equal to his ideal point, as shown in Figure 41.1.

Scholars use the framework described above to explore the strategies that politicians can use to encourage bureaucrats to adopt policies that serve the interests of politicians. The models tell us how different forms of delegation yield different outcomes. One central thrust of the literature is to use these results to understand the factors that influence *how much* authority politicians should delegate to bureaucrats. Politicians can use legal instruments, such as legislative statutes or regulations, to determine the range of policies that bureaucrats can adopt or the types of actions they can take in making policy decisions.

Epstein and O'Halloran (1994) developed a modeling technology that allows one to make explicit the amount of discretion that politicians delegate to bureaucrats. In models of this type, the Politician specifies an interval, such as $[\underline{x}, \overline{x}]$, from which the

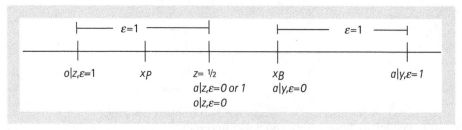

Fig. 41.2. The decision to delegate in spatial models

Bureaucrat must choose his policy action. The lowest discretion law occurs, for example, when $\underline{x} = \overline{x}$—in other words, when the Politician tells the Bureaucrat precisely what to do. As the interval $[\underline{x}, \overline{x}]$ expands, the Bureaucrat has more discretion in the policy space from which to choose his action.

To illustrate the logic of the central results in the literature, we consider a simple example of the type of delegation model originally developed by Epstein and O'Halloran. In this example, the Politician can chose one of two delegation strategies. She can give the Bureaucrat no discretion, instead instructing him to implement some specific policy, z (e.g. $\underline{x} = \overline{x} = z$). Or she adopt some law, y, that gives complete discretion to the Bureaucrat to adopt any policy he wishes (e.g. y is such that $\underline{x} = -\infty$ and $\overline{x} = \infty$). The example also puts the simplest possible structure on policy uncertainty: $\varepsilon \in \{0, 1\}$ and each ε occurs with probability of one-half.

When will the Politician prefer to delegate substantial authority to the Bureaucrat, and when will she prefer to grant minimal discretion? Suppose the Politician delegates policy-making to a Bureaucrat by adopting $y = [-\infty, \infty]$. As shown in Figure 41.2, the Bureaucrat will take action $a = x_B + \varepsilon$, ensuring an outcome at x_B and yielding the Politician an expected utility of $EU_P(y = [-\infty, \infty]) = -x_B^2$. The Politician will compare the utility she receives from a policy at the Bureaucrat's ideal point with the expected utility she receives from her optimal low discretion statute, z. The expected utility of z is $EU_P(z) = -\frac{1}{2}z^2 - \frac{1}{2}(z - 1)^2$, which is maximized when $z = \frac{1}{2}$. As illustrated in Figure 41.2, this yields an outcome at $\frac{1}{2}$ if $\varepsilon = 0$, and an outcome at $-\frac{1}{2}$ if $\varepsilon = 1$. Consequently, the expected utility to the Politician of adopting her optimal z is $-\frac{1}{4}$, and the Politician prefers $z = \frac{1}{2}$ to $y = [-\infty, \infty]$ whenever $x_B > \frac{1}{2}$.

The example illustrates the fundamental tension that bureaucrats' policy expertise can create for politicians. A politician can allow substantial discretion to bureaucrats, but only at the risk that bureaucrats will use their policy expertise against the politician. But if a politician tries to counter this risk by writing a low-discretion statute, the policy expertise of the bureaucrat is wasted, potentially making both politicians and bureaucrats worse off than they could have been. In Figure 41.2, for example, if $z = \frac{1}{2}$, then whenever $\varepsilon = 1$, the outcome is $o = -\frac{1}{2}$. Both the Politician and the Bureaucrat would have preferred $z = 1$, yielding an outcome at x_P.

Given this tension, what factors lead Politicians to delegate more versus less discretion to bureaucrats? One central theme in the literature concerns the effect of *policy uncertainty*. Suppose that there was a higher level of uncertainty than in the previous example. It may be the case, for instance, that $\varepsilon \in \{0, 2\}$, with each ε equally probable. Since the Bureaucrat knows ε, the expected utility to the Politician of delegating to the Bureaucrat is unaffected by this increase in the level of policy uncertainty. The Bureaucrat will still adopt $a = x_B + \varepsilon$, yielding an expected utility to the Politician of $EU_P(y = [-\infty, \infty]) = -x_B^2$. But the Politician's expected utility of setting policy herself is lowered by the increase in policy uncertainty. In this case, $EU_P(z) = -\frac{1}{2}z^2 - \frac{1}{2}(z - 2)^2$ is maximized when $z = 1$, which yields an expected utility of -1. Thus, the Politician would prefer in this case to set policy herself only when $x_B > 1$. A core argument that consistently emerges from models of delegation is that as politicians' *policy uncertainty* increases relative to that of the bureaucracy, it becomes more attractive for the politicians to delegate more policy-making authority to the bureaucrats (e.g. Epstein and O'Halloran 1994, 1999; Bawn 1995).

The level of policy conflict between the Politician and Bureaucrat is also one of the central variables that influences the type of delegation strategy politicians adopt. The core argument about policy conflict, called the *ally principle*, is that all else equal, as the policy preferences of politicians and bureaucrats converge, politicians will delegate more discretion to bureaucrats. Return to the example where $\varepsilon \in \{0, 1\}$. If $x_B \leq \frac{1}{2}$, the Politician can delegate substantial discretion. She need not fear that in so doing she will invite the Bureaucrat to use his expertise against the Politician because the Bureaucrat's interests are more or less aligned with the Politician's. By contrast, if $x_B > \frac{1}{2}$, the Politician must worry that the Bureaucrat will use his expertise against the Politician. The Politician responds to this concern by limiting discretion (and adopting $z = \frac{1}{2}$). Bureaucratic discretion will therefore be largest when the bureaucrat is an ally of the politician.

Politicians influence bureaucratic behavior not only by using the *ex ante* strategies (i.e. actions that are taken before bureaucrats actually implement policies) to limit bureaucratic discretion described above. Following bureaucratic policy actions, politicians—and other political actors, such as courts or auditing agencies—can monitor bureaucratic behavior and attempt to influence their policy-making activities. Because of this second opportunity to influence agency actions, *ex ante* limits on discretion and *ex post* monitoring are often viewed as substitutes. Models generally show that politicians are more likely to prefer low discretion statutes when the monitoring environment is sufficiently weak. When the Politician can rely on *ex post* monitoring, she will have less incentive to pay the cost of writing a low discretion statute, as she'd prefer to rely instead on less costly *ex post* mechanisms. This *substitution effect* frequently recurs in the theoretical literature (e.g. Bawn 1997; Epstein and O'Halloran 1994; Gailmard 2002; Huber and Shipan 2002; Huber and McCarty 2004; Bendor and Meirowitz 2004).

The models discussed thus far have assumed a single politician whose preferences are stable during the play of the game. But a central distinguishing feature of delegating to bureaucrats, as opposed to delegating to employees, is that there typically is substantial uncertainty about the preferences of future politicians, since politicians are often replaced by others who have different policy goals. *Political uncertainty*, then, is uncertainty about the future preferences of politicians, and this variable is central to early theorizing about delegation by Moe (1989), Shepsle (1992), and Horn (1995). More recently, de Figueiredo (2002) explicitly models the effects of political uncertainty on discretion. In his model, politicians have an opportunity to "lock in" policy by limiting bureaucratic autonomy. The model suggests that politicians are most likely to do so when they feel it is unlikely they will control the political process in the future. This allows current politicians to tie the hands of future politicians by constraining bureaucratic autonomy.

2 EMPIRICAL TESTS OF THE FOUR ARGUMENTS

....

After the publication of the early "structure and process" articles in the 1980s, considerable empirical research focused on whether *ex ante* efforts to restrict bureaucratic behavior actually allow effective congressional control over the bureaucracy in the USA.[1] Unfortunately, this empirical literature is highly inconclusive, with some studies finding evidence of such effectiveness (e.g. Bawn 1997; Potoski 1999; Balla and Wright 2001; Potoski and Woods 2001), while others find either mixed support or no support at all (e.g. Hamilton and Schroeder 1994; Balla 1998; Spence 1999; Nixon, Howard, and DeWitt 2002). As we have argued previously (Huber and Shipan 2000, 2002), this lack of conclusiveness is not surprising given the elusiveness of pinning down the quality of control over bureaucracy. In our view, no one has yet been able to solve the very difficult problem of assessing empirical relationships between the preferences of bureaucrats and politicians on the one hand and policy outcomes on the other. Even if accurate measurement were possible, since all theoretical models indicate "control" will never be perfect, one would be left with the difficult task of imposing subjective judgements as to whether particular outcomes indicate sufficient control.

The four theoretical arguments described above, which emerge from a variety of related formal models, have highlighted an alternative pathway for empirical research. The models provide predictions about where final policy outcomes will be located vis-à-vis the preferences of bureaucrats and politicians. But they also provide predictions about the circumstances under which particular delegation strategies—such as more versus less discretion in legislation—should be adopted. Since these strategies are typically easier to observe than are outcomes, the predictions about delegation strategies are easier to test. And if empirical tests support the four arguments from the models, we can have confidence that the models are on the right track, and thus that the model's implications for understanding delegation *outcomes* are worth taking seriously. So how have policy uncertainty, the ally principle, substitution effects, and political uncertainty fared in empirical tests?

One strategy for measuring the amount of discretion politicians give to bureaucrats is to look at the design of bureaucratic agencies. Volden's (2002*b*) study of welfare

[1] Howell and Lewis 2002 and Lewis 2003 provide evidence that presidents successfully use such tools to influence agencies.

boards in state governments provides one of the most impressive sets of empirical tests. Using a variety of dependent variables, including whether the legislature has delegated authority to a welfare board, whether powers are delegated to a policy board or an advisory board, and whether delegation is to independent agencies or those controlled by the executive, he finds robust support for the effects of policy uncertainty: when legislatures face more policy uncertainty in the form of greater demographic changes, they are more likely to delegate authority to agencies and to establish welfare boards. At the same time, he finds mixed support for the ally principle. Like many others, he begins by positing that policy conflict between legislator and bureaucrat will be highest during divided government (i.e. when the governor is of a different party from the legislature), but he finds that in actuality the effects of conflict are more subtle than that. When preferences are aligned, legislatures will delegate to welfare boards and give the government appointment powers. When preferences are *not* aligned, however, they are still willing to delegate; but they limit these grants of delegation by placing checks on the appointment powers of governors.

Wood and Bohte (2004) also focus on the design of administrative agencies. Drawing on the laws that established 141 US administrative agencies, they examine and code a number of design attributes, including the autonomy of leaders, the authority to engage in rule-making, budgetary autonomy, and the existing of reporting requirements. Their analysis provides substantial support for the ally principle, with features that foster independence more common when there are high levels of conflict (as measured by vetoes and overrides) between the legislative and executive branches.

Other tests have focused not on the design of agencies, but on the nature of legislation itself. Epstein and O'Halloran's (1999) book-length treatment of delegation and the use of procedural means to control discretion is seminal. They measure discretion in legislation by coding the nature of procedural provisions in all key regulatory laws passed in the post-Second World War US Congress, identifying, for example, whether agencies are subject to time or spending limits and whether agencies are required to either report to or consult with the legislature about policy decisions and actions. Consistent with the ally principle, they find that preference conflict, measured by divided government, leads to legislation that places greater constraints on agencies. And consistent with the idea of policy uncertainty, they find that Congress delegates the most discretion to agencies in situations that are more informationally demanding.[2]

Huber and Shipan (2002) also focus on discretion levels in legislation. Their study differs from Epstein and O'Halloran in two significant respects. First, their study is broadly comparative, focusing on how variation in the institutional context in which politicians find themselves influences delegation strategies. To this end, they examine differences in delegation processes *on the same issue* across political systems. They therefore cannot test the uncertainty principle because issue type is held constant. Second, based on an analysis of labor laws across parliamentary democracies and health laws across the US states, they argue that the primary way politicians influence

----

[2] Potoski 1999 finds similar effects in US states.

discretion is not by the inclusion of procedural details in legislation, but rather by specifying in more or less detail the substantive policies bureaucrats must implement. They find strong support for the ally principle, with divided government leading to less discretion in the states and coalition or minority government leading to less discretion in parliamentary systems. But they find that the degree to which coalition status or divided government diminishes discretion depends on other variables. Low discretion laws require legislative resources, and thus the ally principle is not robust to situations of low legislative professionalism in the American states, or to high levels of cabinet turnover in parliamentary democracies. And the ally principle depends on there being a clearly identifiable "politician." In the American states, when only one chamber of the legislature is against the governor, while the other supports him or her, the legislature is less able to use legislative details to limit discretion than in cases where there is unified opposition to the governor across the two chambers.

Franchino also finds support for the uncertainty and policy conflict arguments in his studies of delegation in the European Union. He finds that the Council of Ministers delegates more authority to a supranational bureaucracy, the European Commission, in specialized and technical policy areas, as measured by the existence of detailed rules within the laws themselves, the creation of "action programmes," and the use of specialized committees to write the law. He also finds that as conflict between member states increases in the Council, discretion for implementation typically declines (e.g. Franchino 2004, n.d.; see also 2001).

An impressive degree of support, then, is building for the ally principle and policy uncertainty. Scholars have also begun to test for, and find evidence of, substitution effects. For over two decades now, researchers have examined the extent to which *ex post* mechanisms cause bureaucrats to anticipate potential reprisals from legislatures and to modify their actions accordingly (e.g. Weingast and Moran 1983; Wood and Waterman 1991; Olson 1999; Shipan 2004). More recently, scholars have begun to examine the link between *ex ante* and *ex post* strategies (e.g. Aberbach 1990). If little oversight occurs, is this because bureaucrats anticipate what politicians desire, and thus need not be monitored directly, or because bureaucrats have substantial autonomy to do what they want? Bawn (1997) finds evidence of this substitution effect at the level of individual member of Congress: those members who sit on relevant oversight committees are least likely to seek *ex ante* limits on discretion.[3] Looking across systems, Huber and Shipan (2002) find evidence of the substitution effect. In the American states, they find that the presence of a legislative veto over agency actions allows state legislatures to write less detailed statutes. And across parliamentary democracies, they show that countries write less detailed labor laws when the legal system is structured to protect the politicians' interests as *ex post* and when corporatist bargaining arrangements give politicians an *ex post* check on labor policy.

Finally, several studies have begun to examine the effects of political uncertainty (i.e. uncertainty about the identity of future politicians). The Wood and Bohte (2004) study discussed earlier, for example, finds strong evidence that Congress is much

---

[3] See, however, Balla 2000.

more likely to limit agency discretion when political uncertainty is high (e.g. conflict exists within the enacting coalition and levels of electoral turnover are high). At the state level, Volden (2002*b*) finds that legislatures are far more likely to establish policy boards, which are insulated from political winds, if the dominant party in the legislature is in decline.[4] In the cross-national context, Gilardi (2002) examines a range of policy areas and finds that agencies are likely to be most independent when political uncertainty is high. And Huber (2000) reports that politicians in parliamentary systems adopt global budgets for health care departments, thereby limiting discretion, when cabinet turnover is high.[5]

3 Implications of the Formal and Empirical Work on the Four Arguments

As the preceding section illustrates, empirical support is beginning to accumulate for the four arguments about delegation described above. Bureaucrats are granted more discretion when there is policy conflict between politicians and bureaucrats, when policy uncertainty is high, when *ex post* opportunities to influence bureaucratic behavior are limited, and when politicians have more certainty that they will retain power into the future. But these tests focus on patterns of delegation strategies, rather than on the substantive outcomes of political-bureaucratic interactions. If we take the results of the empirical tests to suggest that the models are on the right track, what are the more general lessons about the outcomes of delegation processes?

At the most basic level, one implication of these empirical tests is that some non-trivial level of political control over bureaucrats must exist. It is interesting to observe that these tests to date do not have clear measures of bureaucratic preferences. Instead, the typical approach is to assume that there exists a privileged political actor who exercises non-trivial control over bureaucrats. In studies of Congress, this political actor is the president, and empirical measures of preference conflict between the "Politician" (Congress) and the "Bureaucrat" (president who controls agencies) are usually captured by the presence or absence of divided government. In studies of the US states, divided government is also used, and in parliamentary democracies, scholars have focused on division across parties during coalition and minority government. With these proxies for preference conflict, we find substantial support for the ally principle. If in fact the president (or governor or cabinet minister) is not exercising influence over bureaucracy, it is very difficult to imagine why this support

---

[4] De Figueiredo 2003 also provides evidence about the effects of political uncertainty on policy insulation in US state legislatures.

[5] See also Bernhard 2002 on the political factors that lead to central bank independence.

would exist in the data. To our knowledge, there is no competing theory that assumes the absence of political control and that yields the same prediction that legislators should give less discretion to agencies during periods of divided (or coalition) government.

Second, these results about divided and coalition government also remind us that "bureaucratic politics" is often simply one more arena where standard distributive battles among politicians are waged. Legislators who craft new legislation or design new agencies are not simply worried about how they might motivate recalcitrant bureaucrats. They are also worried about how they can use legislation and agency design to control rival politicians. Delegation, then, is often as much about using bureaucracy to control the actions of other politicians as it is about figuring out strategies to counter administrative dominance. This perspective on bureaucracy is not something one finds in the models themselves, but rather in the results from empirical tests of insights from the models.

Third, these models and empirical tests caution us about making inferences about administrative dominance by simply observing the strategies of politicians. If politicians exercise little *ex post* oversight, is this because they cannot influence bureaucrats? If legislators write vague statutes that give bureaucrats wide scope to fill in the policy details, does this mean that bureaucrats are likely to use their discretion to work against the interests of politicians? The fact that the data support the four arguments suggests a clear "no" to both questions. Politicians are likely to give substantial discretion to bureaucrats precisely in those situations where it is in the interest of politicians to do so, such as when the bureaucrat is an ally, or when the legislative majority can rely on effective *ex post* mechanisms—such as friendly judges—to help ensure desirable policy outcomes even in the presence of considerable bureaucratic discretion.

The fact remains, however, that with existing models and empirical techniques, we do not know how much control over bureaucrats exists. Indeed, the models underline that such control is quite difficult to achieve. In the stark model presented above, for instance, when policy uncertainty is low ($\overline{x} \in \{0, 1\}$), the Politician delegates authority to the Bureaucrat only if policy conflict is relatively low ($x_B \leq \frac{1}{2}$). As policy uncertainty increases, the Bureaucrat's policy expertise becomes more valuable to the Politician, and thus the Politician delegates authority even if policy conflict is larger ($x_B \leq 1$). The model therefore underlines the simple fact that the ability of bureaucrats to usurp the policy-making role of politicians increases as their relative expertise increases.

Since empirical tests support the models with these policy uncertainty assumptions, one clear implication is that administrative dominance is most likely when technical complexity is high. This, of course, has been central to the study of delegation since at least the work of Max Weber. But the more general models go beyond this simple insight to help identify more precisely the conditions under which the ability of politicians to use delegation strategies to control bureaucrats is most limited. Consider models that combine *ex ante* and *ex post* strategies and assume that the politicians must pay a cost to adopt legislation that limits discretion. The models show that the ability of politicians to influence bureaucratic behavior is substantially limited only when several specific conditions exist:

(*a*) Politicians and bureaucrats disagree about which outcome to pursue (such as should exist during divided or coalition government);

(*b*) Politicians must lack the capacity to pay the cost of writing detailed statutes that limit discretion (such as in systems with unprofessionalized legislatures);

(*c*) Politicians must not be able to rely on *ex post* mechanisms (such as auditing or courts) to ensure desirable bureaucratic actions.

Only when these three conditions are simultaneously met can we infer that statutes granting large discretion to bureaucrats are essentially abdicating policy-making authority to them.

4 Theoretical Robustness: How Fragile are the Arguments?

The four arguments—policy uncertainty, the ally principle, substitution effects, and political uncertainty—are robust in two senses. First, they have emerged from a number of different types of models, albeit models that make similar assumptions about policy uncertainty. Second, empirical research is beginning to build support for them. Recent theoretical research, however, has begun to reveal circumstances under which the theoretical predictions falter. What are these circumstances, and what are the implications of these models for future studies of bureaucracy?

As noted above, the models of delegation to bureaucrats that generate the four arguments typically assume that bureaucrats have more expertise than politicians. But what if politicians try to redress this imbalance by investing in information themselves? Gailmard (2002) examines this question, and his model has implications for theoretical arguments about preference divergence and delegation. For reasons similar to those discussed in conjunction with the stark model above, his model illustrates that as the preferences of a Bureaucrat diverge from a Politician's, the value of policy expertise to the Politician increases. But this fact, Gailmard observes, should create incentives for the Politician to invest more in information when these preferences diverge. Since the Politician's policy expertise increases with preference divergence, the Politician has less need to grant the Bureaucrat discretion. Thus, with endogenous specialization by the Politician, discretion can decrease with policy conflict because policy uncertainty can also decrease.

Bendor and Meirowitz (2004) take a different approach to fleshing out the origins of information asymmetries. Like Gailmard, they focus on endogenous investment in expertise, but unlike Gailmard, they focus on incentives for bureaucrats to become informed. In one variant that they analyze, a Bureaucrat cannot pre-commit to becoming informed about ε, but rather must pay a cost to do so *after* the discretion level is announced. In this model, the ally principal can fail. If the Politician does not delegate, the Bureaucrat's expected utility is that associated with the Politician's uninformed policy choice. Since this is a better outcome for an allied Bureaucrat than for one with divergent preferences, the Bureaucrat with divergent preferences has more incentive to pay the cost of specialization. The Politician, recognizing this incentive to specialize, is more likely to delegate to a non-ally bureaucrat under certain levels of policy uncertainty. Both the Gailmard and the Bendor–Meirowitz model suggest, then, that the ally principle may depend a great deal on the assumption of some exogenous source of information asymmetry. If one tries to make this asymmetry endogenous, then the ally principle can be turned on its head, with more discretion going to bureaucrats who are further from the politician's ideal point.

The standard models from which the ally principle emerges also assume that bureaucrats are very good at what they do (i.e. that they have high "capacity")—bureaucrats not only know ε, they can execute whatever policy action they wish. But even if individuals at the top of a bureaucratic hierarchy know which policy consequences will result from adopting a particular policy, they may be unable to execute this policy. Huber and McCarty (2004) explore delegation when bureaucratic capacity is low. Their model distinguishes between policy uncertainty, as described above, and bureaucratic capacity, which is the Bureaucrat's ability to execute his intended action. A Bureaucrat with low capacity has less ability to take the action he intends, even if he knows ε. Low capacity therefore makes it more difficult for the Bureaucrat to comply with a statute—the Bureaucrat may try to comply, but his lack of capacity may push the action he intends out of compliance. Consequently, a low-capacity Bureaucrat with preferences that diverge from the Politician's is less likely to make policy concessions toward the Politician's ideal point because the impact of such efforts on policy compliance is relatively low. In this situation, the Politician must give more discretion to the "enemy" Bureaucrat. This extra discretion induces the "enemy" Bureaucrat to forgo attempting to implement his most preferred policy, and instead to make policy concessions toward the Politician's ideal point. Consequently, the ally Bureaucrat, who pays a much lower policy cost of his unreliable attempts at policy compliance, receives less discretion than the "enemy" Bureaucrat.

The ally principle stems from models where a single Politician delegates to a single Bureaucrat. In many political systems, however, the distribution of agenda power for, say, setting discretion levels is divided among several politicians. If the multiple politicians are making collective decisions by majority rule in a single chamber, then the existence of multiple politicians may not be much of an issue. One could simply assume that the "politician" who seeks an ally in the bureaucracy is the median legislator, or some other pivotal politician. But often institutional separation of powers will create multiple pivotal politicians. In such cases, how does one think about an ally principle?

Studies of this question focus primarily on presidential systems. These studies assume legislatures propose and presidents veto, and typically explore the extent to which discretion levels—which are proposed by the legislature, not the president—are influenced by the extent to which the bureaucracy is an ally of the legislature. Volden (2002a), for example, develops a model where an executive can veto legislation that sets discretion levels. His model suggests that when the executive and legislature have divergent preferences, the ally principle will hold for some configurations of status quos and ideal points, but will fail for others. If the status quo is extreme relative to the preferences of the legislature and executive agent, for instance, then as the ideal points of the legislature and agent diverge, with the agent moving closer to the status quo, more discretion must be given to the agent in order to induce the agent to change the status quo. Similar results are found in Bendor and Meirowitz (2004) and Huber and Shipan (2002).

McCarty (2004) examines the multi-principal issue through the lens of the appointment processes. The politicians who grant discretion, McCarty notes, are often different from those who control appointments, with non-trivial consequences for strategic behavior. In his model, a President, who has the power to appoint a Bureaucrat, is constrained by the Legislature, which grants policy-making discretion to this Bureaucrat by providing budgetary resources to change the policy. If the President appoints a Bureaucrat who is too close to the President's ideal point, then the Legislature, whose preferences diverge from the President, will write laws that limit discretion. Given the Bureaucrat's expertise, both the President and the Legislature can be made better off if the President appoints a Bureaucrat who is between the President's and the Legislature's ideal point rather than at the President's ideal point. To this end, the President must be able to commit to not changing the Bureaucrat's ideal point after the Legislature establishes the discretion level. Constitutional or statutory provisions that limit the power of the President to remove bureaucrats from office are one obvious source of such precommitment.

Ting (2001) examines the possibility that a different sort of commitment problem can be overcome in a repeated-play setting. His model describes why we might expect *ex ante* and *ex post* strategies to be complements rather than substitutes. In Ting's model, the Politician establishes a budget, which determines bureaucratic discretion by constraining the types of policy that the Bureaucrat can implement. After the Bureaucrat implements a policy, the Politician can invest resources in *ex post* monitoring. Without repeated play, the Politician's auditing strategy is independent of the outcome she observes because she cannot *precommit* to conditioning intensity of audits on this outcome. If the game is repeated, with a new ε drawn in each period, the Politician can indirectly condition auditing on outcomes by conditioning future budget levels (which influence audit strategies) on outcomes. This can only occur, however, if the Politician and Bureaucrat have sufficiently similar preferences. In such cases, *ex ante* discretion and *ex post* monitoring are not substitutes, but complements. Larger budgets provide greater discretion, and since without precommitment politicians cannot condition monitoring on observing outcomes, they will increase discretion (i.e. budgets) only when they can increase monitoring.

5 CONCLUSION

Considerable energy has been devoted to developing models of the strategies that politicians use to shape bureaucratic behavior. Central to these models are two assumptions: first, bureaucrats, left to their own devices, will pursue outcomes that are not necessarily in the interest of politicians, and second, bureaucrats have more policy expertise than politicians. From these two assumptions, four theoretical arguments consistently emerge regarding delegation strategies. First, as *policy uncertainty* increases, politicians can achieve better outcomes by giving more discretion to bureaucrats. Second, as the policy preferences of politicians and bureaucrats converge, politicians can achieve better outcomes by giving more discretion to bureaucrats. Third, as *ex post* mechanisms to achieve policy goals become more effective, politicians should give bureaucrats more discretion. And fourth, greater political uncertainty provides current politicians with the incentive to shield bureaucratic actions from future political influence.

Empirical research, much of it on the US Congress or the US states, has begun to build support for these arguments. We can therefore have some confidence that the predictions from these models—not simply about delegation strategies, but also about delegation outcomes—are on the right track. This has allowed us to understand the strategies that politicians can use to create incentives for bureaucrats to act on behalf of politicians, and also to understand the circumstances under which exercising effective control over bureaucrats is most difficult.

As impressive as the research has been at bringing politics and political institutions into the study of bureaucracy, many questions remain unanswered. First, as we noted, the ally principle and the uncertainty principle are foundations for the study of delegation, but recent formal models suggest that both principles are fragile. The models, for example, identify specific conditions that lead to the failure of the ally principle, conditions related to endogenous specialization, low bureaucratic capacity, or separation of powers with extreme status quos. Yet most empirical work focuses on straightforward tests of the two principles, without taking into account the factors that models suggest could lead to their failure. By taking seriously some of the nuances in recent theoretical models, future empirical research could shed new light on the extent to which these two simple but pervasive principles shape delegation processes. One clear domain for testing models where bureaucrats are uninformed or of low capacity is in developing democracies. In any event, these most recent models require empirical scholars to consider carefully the precise circumstances under which it is appropriate to test the four arguments that have largely dominated the literature.

Second, courts represent one of the central yet neglected ways in which politicians can influence policy outcomes and agency actions. Empirical work (e.g. Spriggs 1996; Hanssen 2000; Howard and Nixon 2002; Canes-Wrone 2003) has examined how judges influence bureaucratic actions, or how legal structures influence *ex ante* delegation strategies (e.g. Huber and Shipan 2002). And spatial models have begun to examine similar issues (e.g. Shipan 2000). Yet given the relevance of the legislative–judicial–bureaucratic relationship to political science and to administrative law (e.g. Shapiro 2002), this is clearly an area that is ripe for further research.

Finally, studies of delegation—particularly formal models—typically rest on the premiss that politicians adopt strategies that lead to the best obtainable policy choice by a bureaucrat in some current policy space. But the choices politicians make in delegating today can have ramifications long into the future. As Lewis (2004) points out, for example, a politicized bureaucracy, where politicians can make numerous bureaucratic appointments, might allow politicians to ensure the presence of their allies in the bureaucracy. This benefit, however, could be accompanied by a non-trivial cost, which is that it will be more difficult to attract quality personnel to work in the non-politicized parts of bureaucracies. Similarly, scholars have noted that basic features of bureaucratic organization, such as the existence of meritocratic recruitment, influence corruption levels (Rauch and Evans 2000) or economic growth (Evans and Rauch 1999).

It is clear, then, that there exists considerable variation in such institutions *within* bureaucracies—that is, in the politicization of appointments, pay levels of bureaucrats, rules for hiring and promotion, and so on. But little attention has been paid to explaining the sources or consequences of this variation. Thus, linking studies of the politics of delegation to studies of structures internal to bureaucracies, which have been chiefly the domain of sociology (but see Whitford 2002), represents one of the most important avenues for future research on bureaucracy.

References

ABERBACH, J. D. 1990. *Keeping a Watchful Eye.* Washington, DC: Brookings Institution.

BALLA, S. J. 1998. Administrative procedures and political control of the bureaucracy. *American Political Science Review*, 92: 663–74.

—— 2000. Legislative organization and congressional review of agency regulations. *Journal of Law, Economics, and Organization*, 16: 424–48.

—— and WRIGHT, J. R. 2001. Interest groups, advisory committees, and congressional control of bureaucracy. *American Journal of Political Science*, 45: 799–812.

BAWN, K. 1995. Political control versus expertise: congressional choices about administrative procedures. *American Political Science Review*, 89: 62–73.

—— 1997. Choosing strategies to control the bureaucracy: statutory constraints, oversight, and the committee system. *Journal of Law, Economics, and Organization*, 13: 101–26.

BENDOR, J. and MEIROWITZ, A. 2004. Spatial models of delegation. *American Political Science Review*, 98: 293–310.

BERNHARD, W. 2002. *Banking on Reform.* Ann Arbor: University of Michigan Press.

CANES-WRONE, B. 2003. Bureaucratic decisions and the composition of the lower courts. *American Journal of Political Science*, 47: 205–14.

DE FIGUEIREDO, R. J. P., JR. 2002. Electoral competition, political uncertainty, and policy insulation. *American Political Science Review*, 96: 321–33.

—— 2003. Budget institutions and political insulation: why states adopt the item veto. *Journal of Public Economics*, 87: 2677–701.

EPSTEIN, D. and O'HALLORAN, S. 1994. Administrative procedures, information, and agency discretion. *American Journal of Political Science*, 38: 697–722.

——— 1999. *Delegating Powers*. New York: Cambridge University Press.

EVANS, P. and RAUCH, J. 1999. Bureaucracy and growth: a cross-national analysis of the effects of "Weberian" state structures on economic growth. *American Sociological Review*, 64: 748–65.

FEREJOHN, J. and SHIPAN, C. 1990. Congressional influence on bureaucracy. *Journal of Law, Economics, and Organization*, 6: 1–20.

FRANCHINO, F. 2001. Delegation and constraints in the national execution of the EC policies: a longitudinal and qualitative analysis. *West European Politics*, 24: 169–92.

——— 2004. Delegating powers in the European Community. *British Journal of Political Science*, 34: 269–93.

——— n.d. The powers of the Union: who does what and why in the European Union. Manuscript, University College London.

GAILMARD, S. 2002. Expertise, subversion, and bureaucratic discretion. *Journal of Law, Economics, and Organization*, 18: 536–55.

GILADI, F. 2002. Policy creditility and delegation to independent regulatory agencies: a comparative empirical analysis. *Journal of European Public Policy*, 9: 873–93.

HAMILTON, J. T. and SCHROEDER, C. H. 1994. Strategic regulators and the choice of rulemaking procedures: the selection of formal vs. informal rules in regulating hazardous waste. *Law and Contemporary Problems*, 57: 111–60.

HANSSEN, F. A. 2000. Independent courts and administrative agencies: an empirical analysis of the states. *Journal of Law, Economics, and Organization*, 16: 534–71.

HORN, M. J. 1995. *The Political Economy of Public Administration*. New York: Cambridge University Press.

HOWARD, R. M. and NIXON, D. C. 2002. Regional court influence over bureaucratic policy-making: courts, ideological preferences, and the Internal Revenue Service. *Political Research Quarterly*, 55: 907–22.

HOWELL, W. G. and LEWIS, D. E. 2002. Agencies by presidential design. *Journal of Politics*, 64: 1095–114.

HUBER, J. D. 2000. Delegation to civil servants in parliamentary democracies. *European Journal of Political Research*, 37: 397–413.

——— and McCARTY, N. 2004. Bureaucratic capacity, delegation and political reform. *American Political Science Review*, 98: 481–94.

——— and SHIPAN, C. R. 2000. The costs of control: legislators, agencies, and transaction costs. *Legislative Studies Quarterly*, 25: 25–52.

——— 2002. *Deliberate Discretion: The Institutional Foundations of Bureaucratic Autonomy*. New York: Cambridge University Press.

LEWIS, D. E. 2003. *Presidents and the Politics of Agency Design*. Stanford, Calif.: Stanford University Press.

——— 2004. Presidents and the politicization of the institutional presidency. Working paper, Princeton University.

McCARTY, N. 2004. The appointments dilemma. *American Journal of Political Science*, 48: 413–28.

McCUBBINS, M. D., NOLL, R. G., and WEINGAST, B. R. 1987. Administrative procedures as instruments of political control. *Journal of Law, Economics, and Organization*, 3: 243–77.

——— 1989. Structure and process, politics and policy: administrative arrangements and the political control of agencies. *Virginia Law Review*, 75: 431–82.

Moe, T. M. 1989. The politics of bureaucratic structure. In *Can the Government Govern?* ed. J. E. Chubb and P. E. Peterson. Washington, DC: Brookings Institution.

Nixon, D. C., Howard, R. M., and DeWitt, J. R. 2002. With friends like these: rule-making comment submissions to the Securities and Exchange Commission. *Journal of Public Administration Research and Theory*, 12: 59–76.

Olson, M. K. 1999. Agency rulemaking, political influences, regulation and industry compliance. *Journal of Law, Economics, and Organization*, 15: 573–601.

Potoski, M. 1999. Managing uncertainty through bureaucratic design: administrative procedures and state air pollution control agencies. *Journal of Public Administration Research and Theory*, 9: 623–39.

——and Woods, N. 2001. Designing state clean air agencies: administrative procedures and bureaucratic autonomy. *Journal of Public Administration Research and Theory*, 11: 203–22.

Rauch, J. and Evans, P. 2000. Bureaucratic structure and bureaucratic performance in less developed countries. *Journal of Public Economics*, 74: 49–71.

Shapiro, M. 2002. Judicial delegation doctrines: the US, Britain, and France. *West European Politics*, 25: 173–99.

Shepsle, K. A. 1992. Bureaucratic drift, coalitional drift, and time inconsistency: a comment on Macey. *Journal of Law, Economics, and Organization*, 8: 111–18.

Shipan, C. R. 2000. The legislative design of judicial review: a formal analysis. *Journal of Theoretical Politics*, 12: 269–304.

——2004. Regulatory regimes, agency actions, and the conditional nature of political influence. *American Political Science Review*, 93: 467–80.

Spence, D. B. 1999. Managing delegation ex ante: using law to steer administrative agencies. *Journal of Legal Studies*, 28: 413–59.

Spriggs, J. F. 1996. The Supreme Court and federal administrative agencies: a resource-based theory and analysis of judicial impact. *American Journal of Political Science*, 40: 1122–51.

Ting, M. M. 2001. The "power of the purse" and its implications for bureaucratic policy-making. *Public Choice*, 106: 243–74.

Volden, C. 2002a. A formal model of the politics of delegation in a separation of powers system. *American Journal of Political Science*, 46: 111–33.

——2002b. Delegating power to bureaucracies: evidence from the states. *Journal of Law, Economics, and Organization*, 18: 187–220.

Weingast, B. R. and Moran, M. J. 1983. Bureaucratic discretion or congressional control: regulatory policy-making by the FTC. *Journal of Political Economy*, 91: 765–800.

Whitford, A. B. 2002. Decentralization and political control of the bureaucracy. *Journal of Theoretical Politics*, 14: 167–93.

Wood, B. D. and Bohte, J. 2004. Political transaction costs and the politics of administrative design. *Journal of Politics*, 66: 176–202.

——and Waterman, R. W. 1991. The dynamics of political control of the bureaucracy. *American Political Science Review*, 85: 801–28.

CHAPTER 42

THE EVOLUTIONARY BASIS OF COLLECTIVE ACTION

SAMUEL BOWLES

HERBERT GINTIS

1 INTRODUCTION

MANY aspects of political behavior have been illuminated by standard models in which political actors maximize self-interested preferences. The works of Downs (1957), Buchanan and Tullock (1962), Buchanan, Tollison, and Tullock (1980), and Becker (1983), as well as those inspired by these seminal contributions, have contributed to our understanding of voter, party, and policy preferences, interest group politics, rent-seeking, coalition formation, bargaining, and other aspects of political behavior. Using this framework, works on electoral support for the welfare state (Bénabou and Ok 2001; Moene and Wallerstein 2002), informal enforcement of contracts (Greif 1994; Greif, Milgrom, and Weingast 1994), the efficiency of democratic

* We would like to thank the John D. and Catherine T. MacArthur Foundation and the Behavioral Sciences Program of the Santa Fe Institute for financial support.

governance (Wittman 1989), nationalism (Breton et al. 1995), and ethnic conflict (Varshney 2003) have produced important and sometimes surprising insights.

Yet as Ostrom (1998) and others have pointed out, a number of critical aspects of political behavior remain difficult to explain within this framework. These include the fact that people bother to vote at all, and electoral support for costly redistributive programs from which the voter concerned is unlikely to benefit and for which he will certainly pay additional taxes (Luttmer 2001; Fong 2001; Fong, Bowles, and Gintis 2004), and many forms of political violence (Stern 2003). Among the more striking examples of the shortcomings of the standard model is the large class of political behavior that takes the form of voluntary contribution to public goods. Included is participation in joint political activities and other forms of collective action (Moore 1978; Wood 2003; Scott 1976), the adherence to social norms (Young and Burke 2001; Andreoni, Erard, and Feinstein 1998), and the punishment of those violating social norms (Mahdi 1986; Harding 1978; Boehm 1993; Wiessner 2003).

When one is motivated to bear personal costs to help or to hurt others we say that one has *other-regarding* preferences, meaning that affecting the states experienced by someone other than oneself is part of one's motivations. Unlike the conventional self-regarding preferences of *Homo economicus*, social preferences are other regarding. Generosity towards others and punishing those who violate norms are commonly motivated by other-regarding preferences.

We use the term self-regarding rather than "selfish" to describe the standard assumptions about preferences to avoid the circularity arising from the fact that all uncoerced actions are motivated by preferences and hence might confusingly be termed selfish, leaving only those actions that violate one's preference ordering to be called unselfish (but which would better be called non-rational). To explain behavior, both other-regarding and self-regarding preferences must be transitive, and when they are (as we assume) the actions they motivate are rational in the strict sense typically adopted in economics and decision theory. The common designation of generous behavior as "irrational" is based on a gratuitous conflation of rationality and self-regarding preferences.

We explore two problems in the study of the political behaviors supporting collective action. The first concerns the view frequently advanced by economists and biologists that cooperative behaviors can be fully explained on the basis of self-interested motivations, once one takes account of the repeated nature of interactions and the degree of genetic relatedness among members of a cooperating group. We show that repeated interactions and kin-based altruism, while strong influences on behavior in many settings, do not provide an adequate account of the forms of cooperation observed in natural and experimental settings.

These and other types of political behavior are based on preferences that include a concern for the well-being of others and a taste not only for fairness but also for retribution. We review recent behavioral experiments documenting the variety and extent of these so called social preferences and the manner in which the existence of even a minority of individuals with social preferences can dramatically affect group behavior (see Bowles and Gintis 2005*b*; Gintis et al. 2005; and Henrich et al. 2004 for a more extensive review of this evidence).

The second is the puzzle of how these social preferences could have evolved by means of genetic transmission and natural selection, or cultural learning and socialization, or both. The puzzle arises because the political behaviors motivated by social preferences are often altruistic in the biological sense—of conferring gains on others in one's group while entailing costs—and altruistic behaviors will be disadvantaged in most evolutionary processes that favor higher payoff types. Our treatment of these topics is necessarily cursory, drawing extensively on work presented more fully in Bowles and Gintis (2007), Gintis et al. (2005), and Henrich et al. (2004).

2 THE COOPERATIVE SPECIES

Cooperation among humans is unique in nature, extending to a large number of unrelated individuals and taking a vast array of forms. By cooperation we mean engaging with others in a mutually beneficial activity. Cooperative behavior may confer benefits net of costs on the individual cooperator, and thus may be motivated by entirely self-regarding preferences. In this case, cooperation is a form of what biologists call *mutualism*, namely an activity that confers net benefits both on the actor and on others.

But, cooperation may also incur net costs to the individual. In this case cooperative behavior constitutes a form of *altruism*. In contrast to mutualistic cooperation, altruistic cooperation would not be undertaken by an individual whose motives were entirely self-regarding and thus did not take account of the effects of one's actions on others.

While the high frequency of altruistic cooperation in humans relative to other species could be an evolutionary accident, a more plausible explanation is that altruistic cooperation among humans is the result of capacities that are unique to our species and that strongly promote our relative reproductive fitness. Thus we seek an explanation of cooperation that works for humans, but which, because it involves capacities that are unique to humans, does not work for other species, or works substantially less well.

Central to our explanation will be human cognitive, linguistic, and physical capacities that allow the formulation of general norms of social conduct, the emergence of social institutions regulating this conduct, the psychological capacity to internalize norms, and the capacity to base group membership on such non-kin characteristics as ethnicity and linguistic differences, which in turn facilitates costly conflicts among groups. Also important is the unique human capacity to use projectile weapons, a consequence of which is to lower the cost of punishing norm violators within a group, and to render intergroup conflicts more lethal.

Thus, our account of human sociality and its evolution hinges critically on a reconsideration of the canonical economic model of self-interested behavior. But more than individual motivation is involved. The extraordinary levels of cooperation observed in human society cannot be attributed simply to our generosity towards those with whom we interact or our capacity to favor the advancement of our nation or ethnic group over our individual well-being. The regulation of social interactions by group-level norms and institutions plays no less a role than altruistic individual motives in understanding how the cooperative species came to be. The institutions that regulate behaviors among non-kin affect the rewards and penalties associated with particular behaviors, often favoring the adoption of cooperative actions over others. In the social environments common to human interactions, the self-regarding are often induced to act in the interest of the group. Of course it will not do to posit these rules and institutions a priori. Rather, we show that these could have co-evolved with other human traits in a plausible representation of the relevant ecologies and social environments.

Cooperation is not an end to be valued in its own right, but rather is a means that under some conditions may contribute to human well-being. In other settings, competition plays no less essential a role. Similarly, the individual motives and group-level institutions that account for cooperation among humans include not only the most elevated—a concern for others, fair-mindedness, and democratic accountability of leaders, for example—but also the most venal: vengeance, exclusion of "outsiders," and frequent warfare among groups, for example.

Our reasoning is disciplined in three ways. First, the forms of cooperation we seek to explain are confirmed by natural observation, historical accounts, and behavioral experiments. Second, our account is based on a plausible evolutionary dynamic involving some combination of genetic and cultural transmission, the consistency of which can be demonstrated through formal modeling. Third, agent-based simulations show that our models can account for human cooperation under parameter values consistent with what can be reasonably inferred about the environments in which humans evolved.

3 MUTUALISTIC COOPERATION

Because mutualistic cooperation will be sustained by individuals with entirely self-regarding preferences, it is treated in standard biological and economic models as an expression of self-interest. "Natural selection favors these...behaviors," wrote Robert Trivers in his "The evolution of reciprocal altruism" (1971), "because in the long run they benefit the organism performing them....two individuals who risk their lives to save each other will be selected over those who face drowning on their own" (pp. 34–5). Cooperation, in Trivers's interpretation, is simply symbiosis with a time lag. Trivers's explanation initially found favor among biologists and economists because it is consistent with both the common biological reasoning that natural selection will not favor altruistic behaviors and with the canonical economic assumption of self-interest.

Trivers identified the conditions under which assisting another would be reciprocated in the future with a likelihood sufficient to make mutual assistance a form of mutualism. These conditions favoring reciprocal altruism included an extended lifetime, mutual dependence, and other reasons for limited dispersal so that groups remain together, extended periods of parental care, attenuated dominance hierarchies, and frequent combat with conspecifics and predators. Foraging bands of humans, he pointed out, exhibit all of these conditions. Michael Taylor (1976) and Robert Axelrod and William Hamilton (1981) subsequently formalized Trivers's argument using the theory of repeated games. In economics, analogous reasoning is summarized in the folk theorem, which shows that cooperation among self-regarding individuals can be sustained as long as interactions are expected to be repeated with sufficient frequency and individuals are not too impatient (Fudenberg and Maskin 1986; Fudenberg, Levine, and Maskin 1994).

But, in many important human social environments, Trivers's conditions favoring reciprocal altruism do not hold, yet cooperation among non-kin is commonly observed. These include contributing to common projects when community survival is threatened, and cooperation among very large numbers of people who do not share common knowledge of one another's actions. In fact, the scope of application of the folk theorem is quite restricted, especially in groups of any significant size, once the problem of cooperation is posed in an evolutionary setting and account is taken of "noise" arising from mistaken behaviors and misinformation about the behaviors of others.

A plausible model of cooperation must satisfy the following five conditions. First, it must be *incentive compatible*. In particular, those who provide the rewards and inflict punishments dictated by the rules for cooperation must have the motivation to do so. Second, a model must be *dynamically stable*, in the sense that random fluctuations, errors, and mutations (the emergence of novel strategies) do not disrupt cooperation or entail excessive efficiency losses. Third, the organizational forms and incentive mechanisms deployed in the model must reflect the types of strategic interaction and incentives widely observed in human groups. In particular, the model should work well with group sizes on the order of ten to twenty, and the incentive to punish defectors should reflect those deployed in real-world public goods game settings. Fourth, the model should not require extraordinary *informational requirements*. Finally the model should work with *plausible discount factors*. It is reasonable to suppose that within a group faced by a public goods game, there will be a distribution of discount factors among members, and average discount factors can be high in some periods and low in others, as the probability of group dissolution rises an falls.

A careful analysis shows that all models of cooperation based on tit-for-tat and related repeated game strategies, when played among self-interested individuals violate at least one of these conditions, and hence fail to solve the problem of cooperation among unrelated agents.[1] First, reciprocal altruism fails when a social group is threatened with dissolution, since members who sacrifice now on behalf of group members do not have a high probability of being repaid in the (highly uncertain) future.

Second, many human interactions in the relevant evolutionary context took the form of n-person public goods games—food sharing and other co-insurance, upholding social norms among group members, information sharing, and common defense—rather than dyadic interactions. The difficulty in sustaining cooperation in public goods games by means of the standard tit-for-tat and related repeated game strategies increases exponentially with group size (Boyd and Richerson 1988; Bowles and Gintis 2007), even if interactions are repeated with high probability. The reason is that in groups larger than two, withdrawing cooperation in response to a single defection imposes a blanket punishment on all, defectors and cooperators alike. But, targeting punishment on defectors alone does not work in large groups unless members have unrealistically accurate information about the actions taken by others.

Third, the contemporary study of human behavior has documented a large class of social behaviors inexplicable in terms of reciprocal altruism. For instance, there is extensive support for income redistribution in advanced industrial economies, even among those who cannot expect to be net beneficiaries (Fong, Bowles, and Gintis, 2005). Under some circumstances group incentives for large work teams are effective motivators even when the opportunity for reciprocation is absent and the benefits of cooperation are so widely shared that a self-interested group member would gain from free riding on the effort of others (Ghemawat 1995; Hansen 1997; Knez and Simester 2001). Finally, laboratory and field experiments show that other-regarding motives are frequently robust causes of cooperative behavior, even in one-shot, anonymous settings.

4 STRONG RECIPROCITY: EVIDENCE FROM BEHAVIORAL EXPERIMENTS

A more direct reason for doubting the interpretation that most cooperation is mutualistic is given by the compelling evidence that many (perhaps most) people behave in ways inconsistent with the assumption that they are motivated by self-regarding preferences. A suggestive body of evidence points to the importance of a suite of behaviors that we call *strong reciprocity*. A strong reciprocator comes to a new social situation with a predisposition to cooperate, is predisposed to respond to cooperative

---

[1] This analysis is presented in full in Gintis (2004) and Bowles and Gintis (2007), which also shows that recent game-theoretic extensions of these models using repeated game theory (Fudenberg and Maskin 1986; Fudenberg et al. 1994; Sekiguchi 1997; Piccione 2002; Ely and Välimäki 2002; Bhaskar and Obara 2002; Matsushima 2000; Kandori 2002) do not alter this conclusion. These contributions, while important in their own right, either suffer the same problems discussed in the text, or are not stable in a dynamic setting.

behavior on the part of others by maintaining or increasing his level of cooperation, and responds to antisocial behavior on the part of others by retaliating against the offenders, even at a cost to himself, and even when he cannot not reasonably expect future personal gains from such retaliation. The strong reciprocator is thus both a *conditionally altruistic cooperator* and a *conditionally altruistic punisher* whose actions benefit other group members at a personal cost. We call this "strong reciprocity" to distinguish it from "weak" (i.e. self-regarding) forms of reciprocity, such as Trivers's reciprocal altruism.

Strong reciprocity is an example of a larger class of so-called *social preferences* which describe the motivations of people who care (one way or the other) about the well-being of others, and not only have preferences over the states they and others experience but also care about how the states came about.

In the ultimatum game, under conditions of anonymity, two players are shown a sum of money, say $10. One of the players, called the "proposer," is instructed to offer any number of dollars, from $1 to $10, to the second player, who is called the "responder." The proposer can make only one offer. The responder, again under conditions of anonymity, can either accept or reject this offer. If the responder accepts the offer, the money is shared accordingly. If the responder rejects the offer, both players receive nothing.

Since the game is played only once and the players do not know each other's identity, a self-interested responder will accept any positive amount of money. Knowing this, a self-interested proposer will offer the minimum possible amount, $1, and this will be accepted. However, when actually played, *the self-interested outcome is never attained and never even approximated*. In fact, as many replications of this experiment have documented, under varying conditions and with varying amounts of money, proposers routinely offer respondents very substantial amounts (50 per cent of the total generally being the modal offer), and respondents frequently reject offers below 30 per cent (Camerer and Thaler 1995; Güth and Tietz 1990; Roth et al. 1991).

Strong reciprocity emerges in many other experimental games, some of which are described in Table 42.1 (from Camerer and Fehr 2004). In all cases, given the one-shot, anonymous nature of the game, self-regarding agents would neither contribute to the common good, nor reward others for so contributing. Nor would they punish others for failing to contribute. Yet, in each game, under many different conditions and in different cultures, a considerable fraction of agents contributes, and enough agents punish free riding that even the self-regarding agent often contributes simply to avoid punishment.

5 THE EVOLUTION OF STRONG RECIPROCITY

If preferences were entirely self-regarding, the extent of human cooperation would indeed be puzzling. But if social preferences are common, the puzzle takes a somewhat different form: how might strong reciprocity and other altruistic preferences

Table 42.1. Seven experimental games useful for measuring social preferences

Game	Definition of the game	Real-life example	Predictions with selfish players	Experimental regularities, references	Interpretation
Prisoner's Dilemma Game	Two players, each of whom can either cooperate or defect. Payoffs are as follows: Cooperate / Defect Cooperate H,H S,T Defect T,S L,L $H > L, T > H.$ $L > S$	Production of negative externalities (pollution, loud noise), exchange without binding contracts, status competition.	Defect.	50% choose to cooperate. Communication increases frequency of cooperation. Dawes (1980).[a]	Reciprocate expected cooperation.
Public Goods Game	n players simultaneously decide about their contribution g_i. ($0 \leq g_i \leq y$) where y is players' endowment; each player i earns $\pi_i = y - g_i + mG$ where G is the sum of all contributions and $m < 1 < mn$.	Team compensation, cooperative production in simple societies, over-use of common resources (e.g. water, fishing grounds).	Each player contributes nothing; that is, $g_i = 0$.	Players contribute 50 % of y in the one-short game. Contributions unravel over time. Majority chooses $g_i = 0$ in final period. Communication strongly increases cooperation. Individual punishment opportunities greatly increase contributions. Ledyard (1995).[a]	Reciprocate expected cooperation.
Ultimatum Game	Division of a fixed sum of money S between a proposer and a responder. Proposer offers x. If responder rejects x both earn zero; if x is accepted the proposer earns $S - x$ and the responder earns x.	Monopoly pricing of a perishable good; '11th hour' settlement offers before a time deadline.	Offer $x = \varepsilon$ where ε is the smallest money unit. Any $x > 0$ is accepted.	Most offers are between 0.3 and $0.5S$. $x < 0.2S$ rejected half of the time. Competition among proposers has a strong x-increasing effect; competition among responders strongly decreases x. Güth, Schmittberger, and Schwartze (1982);[b] Camerer (2003).[a]	Responders punish unfair offers; negative reciprocity.

Game	Description	Context	Standard prediction	Findings	Summary
Dictator Game	Like the UG but the responder cannot reject; that is, the "proposer" dictates $(S − x, x)$.	Charitable sharing of a windfall gain (lottery winners giving anonymously to strangers).	No sharing; that is, $x = 0$.	On average "proposers" allocate $x = 0.2S$. Strong variations across experiments and across individuals. Kahneman, Knetsch, and Thaler (1986);[b] Camerer (2003).[a]	Pure altruism.
Trust Game	Investor has endowment S and make a transfer y between 0 and S to the trustee. Trustee receives $3y$ and can send back any x between 0 and $3y$. Investor earns $S − y + x$. Trustee earns $3y − x$.	Sequential exchange without binding contracts (buying from sellers on eBay).	Trustee repays nothing: $x = 0$. Investor invests nothing: $y = 0$.	On average $y = 0.5S$ and trustees repay slightly less than $0.5S$. x is increasing in y. Berg, Dickhaut, and McCabe (1995);[b] Camerer (2003).[a]	Trustees show positive reciprocity.
Gift Exchange Game	"Employer" offers a wage w to the "Worker" and announces a desired effort level $\hat{e}$. If Worker rejects $(w, \hat{e})$ both earn nothing. If worker accepts, he can choose *any* e between 1 and 10. Then Employer earns $10e − w$ and Worker earns $w − c(e)$. $c(e)$ is the effort cost which is strictly increasing in e.	Non-contractibility or non-enforceability of the performance (effort, quality of goods) of workers or sellers.	Worker chooses $e = 1$. Employer pays the minimum wage.	Effort increases with the wage w. Employers pay wages that are far above the minimum. Workers accept offers with low wages but respond with $e = 1$. In contrast to the UG, competition among workers (i.e. responders) has no impact on wage offers. Fehr, Kirchsteiger, and Reidl (1993).[b]	Workers reciprocate generous wage offers. Employers appeal to workers' reciprocity by offering generous wages.
Third-party Punishment Game	A and B play a DG. C observes how much of amount S is allocated to B. C can punish A but the punishment is also costly for C.	Social disapproval of unacceptable treatment of others (scolding neighbors).	A allocates nothing to B. C never punishes A.	Punishment of A is higher, the less A allocates to B. Fehr and Fischbacher (2004).[b]	C sanctions violation of a sharing norm.

[a]Denotes survey papers.
[b]Denotes papers that introduced the respective games.
Source: Camerer and Fair 2004.

that support cooperation have evolved over the course of human history? The puzzle is posed especially clearly if the processes of cultural and genetic evolution favor behavioral traits that on average are associated with higher levels of material success. We think that this assumption of what is called a *payoff monotonic dynamic* is not entirely adequate. But Gintis (2000) and Bowles and Gintis (2004) adopt just such an evolutionary model to show that individuals behaving as strong reciprocators can proliferate in a population in which they were initially rare, and that their presence in a population could sustain high levels of cooperation among group members.

One intuition behind these models is that in groups with strong reciprocators present, group members whose self-regarding preferences lead them to shirk on contributing to common projects will be punished by being ostracized from the group. Strong reciprocators bear the cost not only of contributing to common projects, but also of punishing the shirking of the self-interested members. If reciprocators are common enough, however, the self-interested members will conform to cooperative norms in order to escape punishment, thereby reducing or eliminating the fitness differences between the reciprocators and the self-interested members. A second argument supporting strong reciprocity is that groups with a sufficient proportion of strong reciprocators will be better able to survive such group crises as war, pestilence, and adverse climatic conditions. In such situations, a group of self-regarding agents would simply disband, since each member will do better to bear the personal costs of abandoning the group rather than bearing the even heavier costs of attempting to preserve the group, most of the gains of which would accrue to other group members. Since strong reciprocators enforce cooperation without regard for the possibility of extinction, a sufficient proportion of strong reciprocators can enhance the possibility of group survival.

Group-level characteristics—such as relatively small group size, limited migration, or frequent intergroup conflicts—have co-evolved with cooperative behaviors. Cooperation is thus based in part on the distinctive capacities of humans to construct institutional environments that limit within-group competition and reduce phenotypic variation within groups, thus heightening the relative importance of between-group competition, and hence allowing individually costly but in-group-beneficial behaviors to coevolve with these supporting environments through a process of interdemic selection.

The idea that the suppression of within-group competition may be a strong influence on evolutionary dynamics has been widely recognized in eusocial insects and other species. Alexander (1979), Boehm (1982), and Eibl-Eibesfeldt (1982) first applied this reasoning to human evolution, exploring the role of culturally transmitted practices that reduce phenotypic variation within groups. Group-level institutions thus are constructed environments capable of imparting distinctive direction and pace to the process of biological evolution and cultural change (Friedman and Singh 2001).

Bowles, Choi, and Hopfensitz (2003) models an evolutionary dynamic along these lines. They show that intergroup conflicts may explain the evolutionary success of both altruistic forms of human sociality towards non-kin, and group-level institutional structures such as resource-sharing that have emerged and diffused repeatedly in a wide variety of ecologies during the course of human history.

6 PROXIMATE MOTIVES: INTERNALIZED NORMS AND SOCIAL EMOTIONS

An *internal norm* is a pattern of behavior enforced in part by internal sanctions, including shame and guilt. Individuals follow internal norms when they value certain behaviors for their own sake, in addition to, or despite, the effects these behaviors have on personal fitness and/or perceived well-being. The ability to internalize norms is nearly universal among humans. All successful cultures foster internal norms that enhance personal fitness, such as future orientation, good personal hygiene, positive work habits, and control of emotions. Cultures also widely promote altruistic norms that subordinate the individual to group welfare, fostering such behaviors as bravery, honesty, fairness, willingness to cooperate, and empathy with the distress of others (Brown 1991).

If even a fraction of society internalizes the norms of cooperation and punish free riders and other norm violators, a high degree of cooperation can be maintained in the long run. The puzzles are two: why do we internalize norms, and why do cultures promote cooperative behaviors? Gintis (2003) provides an evolutionary model in which the capacity to internalize norms develops because this capacity enhances individual fitness in a world in which social behavior has become too complex to be learned through personal experience alone. It is not difficult to show that if an internal norm is fitness enhancing, then for plausible patterns of socialization, the allele for internalization of norms is evolutionarily stable. This framework implements the suggestion in Simon (1990) that altruistic norms can "hitchhike" on the general tendency of internal norms to be fitness enhancing.

Pro-social emotions are physiological and psychological reactions that induce agents to engage in cooperative behaviors as we have defined them above. The pro-social emotions include some, such as shame, guilt, empathy, and sensitivity to social sanction, that induce agents to undertake constructive social interactions, and others, such as the desire to punish norm violators, that reduce free riding when the pro-social emotions fail to induce sufficiently cooperative behavior in some fraction of members of the social group (Frank 1987; Hirshleifer 1987). Without the pro-social emotions we would all be sociopaths, and human society would not exist, however strong the institutions of contract, governmental law enforcement, and reputation. Sociopaths have no mental deficit except that their capacity to experience shame, guilt, empathy, and remorse is severely attenuated or absent.

Pro-social emotions function like the basic emotion, "pain," in providing guides for action that bypass the explicit cognitive optimizing process that lies at the core of the standard behavioral model in economics. Antonio Damasio (1994, 173) calls these "somatic markers," that is, a bodily response that "forces attention on the negative outcome to which a given action may lead and functions as an automated alarm signal which says: beware of danger ahead if you choose the option that leads to this outcome.... the automated signal protects you against future losses." Emotions thus contribute to the decision-making process, not simply by clouding reason, but in beneficial ways as well. Damasio continues: "suffering puts us on notice.... it increases the probability that individuals will heed pain signals and act to avert their source or correct their consequences" (p. 264).

Does shame serve a purpose similar to that of pain? If being socially devalued has fitness costs, and if the amount of shame is closely correlated with the level of these fitness costs, then the answer is affirmative. Shame, like pain, is an aversive stimulus that leads the agent experiencing it to repair the situation that led to the stimulus, and to avoid such situations in the future. Shame, like pain, replaces an involved optimization process with a simple message: whatever you did, undo it if possible, and do not do it again.

Since shame is evolutionarily selected and is costly to use, it very likely confers a selective advantage on those who experience it. Two types of selective advantage are at work here. First, shame may raise the fitness of an agent who has incomplete information (e.g. as to how fitness reducing a particular antisocial action is), limited or imperfect information-processing capacity, and/or a tendency to undervalue costs and benefits that accrue in the future. Probably all three conditions conspire to react suboptimally to social disapprobation in the absence of shame, and shame brings us closer to the optimum. Of course the role of shame in alerting us to negative consequences in the future presupposes that society is organized to impose those costs on rule violators. The emotion of shame may have co-evolved with the emotions motivating punishment of antisocial actions (the reciprocity motive in our model).

The second selective advantage to those experiencing shame arises through the effects of group competition. Where the emotion of shame is common, punishment of antisocial actions will be particularly effective and as a result seldom used. Thus groups in which shame is common can sustain high levels of group cooperation at limited cost and will be more likely to spread through interdemic group selection (Bowles and Gintis 2004; Boyd et al. 2003). Shame thus serves as a means of economizing on costly within-group punishment.

While we think the evidence is strong that pro-social emotions account for important forms of human cooperation, there is no universally accepted model of how emotions combine with more cognitive processes to affect behaviors. Nor is there much agreement on how best to represent the pro-social emotions that support cooperative behaviors.

Bowles and Gintis (2005b) considers a public goods game where subjects maximize a utility function that captures five distinct motives: personal material payoffs, one's valuation of the payoffs to others, which depend both on ones' altruism and one's degree of reciprocity, and one's sense of guilt or shame when failing to contribute one's fair share to the collective effort of the group. We have evidence of shame if players who are punished by others respond by behaving more cooperatively than is optimal for a material payoff-maximizing agent. We present indirect empirical evidence suggesting that such emotions play a role in the public goods game.

Direct evidence on the role of emotions in experimental games remains scanty. The forms of arousal associated with emotions are readily measured, but they do not readily allow us to distinguish between, say, fear and anger. Self-reports of emotional states are informative but noisy. Recent advances in brain imaging, however, can identify the areas of the brain that are activated when an experimental subject is confronted with a moral dilemma or unfair treatment by another experimental subject. This use of fMRI and related technology may eventually allow us to distinguish among the emotional responses of subjects in experimental situations.

7 CONCLUSION

The study of collective action and other forms of cooperative behaviors exhibits a curious disparity among social scientists. In the Marxian tradition, and among many historians, sociologists, anthropologists, and political scientists, the fact that people often behave pro-socially in the pursuit of common objectives, even when this involves cooperating in an n-person prisoner's dilemma game, is frequently invoked to explain social structures and their dynamics. Among economists, biologists, and others influenced by their models, by contrast, self-regarding actors will rarely, if ever, cooperate in such a setting.

It may be thought that the key difference accounting for this divergence is the methodological individualism adopted by economists and biologists, in contrast to the more holist or structural approaches adopted by historians and many social scientists outside of economics. According to this view, if anthropologists, sociologists, Marxists, and others were only to ask the obvious question—why would an individual engage in a costly activity to benefit others?—they would agree with the economists. But this is not the case.

The question needs an answer, but in light of what we now know about the nature of social preferences, it is not that altruistic forms of collective ction are likely to be an ephemeral and unimportant aspect of political life and that most forms of seemingly altruistic cooperation are just self-interest in disguise. Like adherence to social norms and punishment of those who violate them, collective action is an essential aspect of political behavior and one which is readily explained by the fact that strong reciprocity and other social preferences are sufficiently common in most human populations to support high levels of cooperation in many social settings.

References

ABREU, D., PEARCE, D., and STACCHETTI, E. 1990. Toward a theory of discounted repeated games with imperfect monitoring. *Econometrica*, 58: 1041–63.

ALEXANDER, R. D. 1979. *Biology and Human Affairs*. Seattle: University of Washington Press.

ANDREONI, J., ERARD, B., and FEINSTEIN, J. 1998. Tax compliance. *Journal of Economic Literature*, 36: 818–60.

AUMANN, R. J. 1987. Correlated equilibrium and an expression of Bayesian rationality. *Econometrica*, 55: 1–18.

AXELROD, R. and HAMILTON, W. D. 1981. The evolution of cooperation. *Science*, 211: 1390–6.

BECKER, G. 1983. A theory of competition among pressure groups for political influence. *Quarterly Journal of Economics*, 98: 71–400.

BÉNABOU, R. and OK, E. A. 2001. Social mobility and the demand for redistribution: the Poum hypothesis. *Quarterly Journal of Economics*, 116: 47–87.

BERG, J., DICKHAUT, J., and McCABE, K. 1995. Trust, reciprocity, and social history. *Games and Economic Behavior*, 10: 122–42.

BHASKAR, V. and OBARA, I. 2002. Belief-based equilibria: the repeated prisoner's dilemma with private monitoring. *Journal of Economic Theory*, 102: 40–69.

BOEHM, C. 1982. The evolutionary development of morality as an effect of dominance behavior and conflict interference. *Journal of Social and Biological Structures*, 5: 413–21.

—— 1993. Egalitarian behavior and reverse dominance hierarchy. *Current Anthropology*, 34: 227–54.

BOWLES, S., CHOI, J. K., and HOPFENSITZ, A. 2003. The co-evolution of individual behaviors and social institutions. *Journal of Theoretical Biology*, 223: 135–47.

—— and GINTIS, H. 2004. The evolution of strong reciprocity: cooperation in heterogeneous populations. *Theoretical Population Biology*, 65: 17–28.

—— —— 2007. *A Cooperative Species: Human Reciprocity and its Evolution*. Manuscript in preparation.

—— —— 2005a. Social preferences, *Homo economicus*, and *zoon politikon*. In *The Oxford Handbook of Contextual Political Analysis*, ed. R. E. Goodin and C. Tilly. Oxford: Oxford University Press.

—— —— 2005b. Prosocial emotions. In *The Economy as an Evolving Complex System III*, ed. L. E. Blume and S. N. Durlauf. Santa Fe, N. Mex.: Santa Fe Institute.

BOYD, R., GINTIS, H., BOWLES, S., and RICHERSON, P. J. 2003. Evolution of altruistic punishment. *Proceedings of the National Academy of Sciences*, 100: 3531–5.

BRETON, A., GALEOTTI, G., SALMON, P., and WINTROBE, R. 1995. *Nationalism and Rationality*. Cambridge: Cambridge University Press.

BROWN, D. E. 1991. *Human Universal*. New York: McGraw-Hill.

—— and TULLOCK, G. 1962. *The Calculus of Consent: Logical Foundations of Constitutional Democracy*. Ann Arbor: University of Michigan Press.

BUCHANAN, J., TOLLISON, R., and TULLOCK, G. 1980. *Toward a Theory of the Rent-Seeking Society*. College Station: Texas A&M University Press.

CAMERER, C. 2003. *Behavioral Game Theory: Experiments in Strategic Interaction*. Princeton, NJ: Princeton University Press.

—— and FEHR, E. 2004. Measuring social norms and preferences using experimental games: a guide for social scientists. Pp. 55–95 in *Foundations of Human Sociality: Economic Experiments and Ethnographic Evidence from Fifteen Small-Scale Societies*, ed. J. Henrich, R. Boyd, S. Bowles, C. F. Camerer, E. Fehr, and H. Gintis. Oxford: Oxford University Press.

—— and THALER, R. 1995. Ultimatums, dictators, and manners. *Journal of Economic Perspectives*, 9: 209–19.

DAMASIO, A. R. 1994. *Descartes' Error: Emotion, Reason, and the Human Brain*. New York: Avon.

DAWES, R. M. 1980. Social dilemmas. *Annual Review of Psychology*, 31: 169–93.

DOWNS, A. 1957. *An Economic Theory of Democracy*. Boston: Harper and Row.

EIBL-EIBESFELDT, I. 1982. Warfare, man's indoctrinability and group selection. *Journal of Comparative Ethnology*, 60: 177–98.

ELY, J. C. and VÄLIMÄKI, J. 2002. A robust folk theorem for the prisoner's dilemma. *Journal of Economic Theory*, 102: 84–105.

FEHR, E. and FISCHBACHER, U. 2004. Third party punishment and social norms. *Evolution and Human Behavior*, 25: 63–87.

—— KIRCHSTEIGER, G., and RIEDL, A. 1993. Does fairness prevent market clearing? *Quarterly Journal of Economics*, 108: 437–59.

FONG, C. M. 2001. Social preferences, self-interest, and the demand for redistribution. *Journal of Public Economics*, 82: 225–46.

—— BOWLES, S., and GINTIS, H. 2004. Reciprocity and the welfare state. In *Moral Sentiments and Material Interests: On the Foundations of Cooperation in Economic Life*, ed. H. Gintis et al. Cambridge, Mass.: MIT Press.

FRANK, R. H. 1987. If *Homo economicus* could choose his own utility function, would he want one with a conscience? *American Economic Review*, 77: 593–604.

FRIEDMAN, D. and SINGH, N. 2001. Negative reciprocity: the coevolution of memes and genes. *Evolution and Human Behavior*, 25: 155–73.

FUDENBERG, D., LEVINE, D. K., and MASKIN, E. 1994. The Folk Theorem with imperfect public information. *Econometrica*, 62: 997–1039.

—— and MASKIN, E. 1986. The folk theorem in repeated games with discounting or with incomplete information. *Econometrica*, 54: 533–54.

GINTIS, H. 2000. Strong reciprocity and human sociality. *Journal of Theoretical Biology*, 206: 169–79.

—— 2003. The Hitchhiker's Guide to altruism: genes, culture, and the internalization of norms. *Journal of Theoretical Biology*, 220: 407–18.

—— 2004. Modeling cooperation among self-interested agents: a critique. Manuscript, Santa Fe Institute.

—— BOWLES, S., BOYD, R., and FEHR, E. 2005. *Moral Sentiments and Material Interests: On the Foundations of Cooperation in Economic Life*. Cambridge, Mass.: MIT Press.

GREIF, A. 1994. Cultural beliefs and the organization of society: an historical and theoretical reflection on collectivist and individualist societies. *Journal of Political Economy*, 102: 912–50.

—— MILGROM, P., and WEINGAST, B. R. 1994. Coordination, commitment, and enforcement: the case of the merchant guild. *Journal of Political Economy*, 104: 745–76.

GÜTH, W., SCHMITTBERGER, R., and SCHWAT, B. 1982. An experimental analysis of ultimatum bargaining. *Journal of Economic Behavior and Organization*, 3: 367–88.

—— and TIETZ, R. 1990. Ultimatum bargaining behavior: a survey and comparison of experimental results. *Journal of Economic Psychology*, 11: 417–49.

HARDING, S. 1978. Street shouting and shunning: conflict between women in a Spanish village. *Frontiers*, 3: 14–18.

HARSANYI, J. C. 1973. Games with randomly distributed payoffs: a new rationale for mixed-strategy equilibrium points. *International Journal of Game Theory*, 2: 1–23.

HENRICH, J., BOYD, R., BOWLES, S., CAMERER, C., FEHR, E., and GINTIS, H. 2004. *Foundations of Human Sociality: Economic Experiments and Ethnographic Evidence from Fifteen Small-Scale Societies*. Oxford: Oxford University Press.

HIRSHLEIFER, J. 1987. Economics from a biological viewpoint. Pp. 319–71 in *Organizational Economics*, ed. J. B. Barney and W. G. Ouchi. San Francisco: Jossey-Bass.

KAHNEMAN, D., KNETSCH, J. L., and THALER, R. H. 1986. Fairness as a constraint on profit seeking: entitlements in the market. *American Economic Review*, 76: 728–41.

KANDORI, M. 2002. Introduction to repeated games with private monitoring. *Journal of Economic Theory*, 102: 1–15.

LEDYARD, J. O. 1995. Public goods: a survey of experimental research. Pp. 111–94 in *The Handbook of Experimental Economics*, ed. J. H. Kagel and A. E. Roth. Princeton, NJ: Princeton University Press.

LUTTMER, E. F. P. 2001. Group loyalty and the taste for redistribution. *Journal of Political Economy*, 109: 500–28.

MAHDI, N. Q. 1986. Pukhtunwali: ostracism and honor among the Pathan hill tribes. *Ethology and Sociobiology*, 7: 295–304.

MATSUSHIMA, H. 2000. The folk theorem with private monitoring and uniform sustainability. CIRJE Discussion Paper F-84, University of Tokyo.

MILGROM, P. R., NORTH, D. C., and WEINGAST, B. R. 1990. The role of institutions in the revival of trade: the Law Merchant, private judges, and the Champagne fairs. *Economics and Politics*, 2: 1–23.

MOENE, K. O. and WALLERSTEIN, M. 2002. Inequality, social insurance and redistribution. *American Political Science Review*, 95: 859–74.

MOORE, B., JR. 1978. *Injustice: The Social Bases of Obedience and Revolt*. White Plains, NY: M. E. Sharpe.

OSTROM, E. 1998. A behavioral approach to the rational choice theory of collective action. *American Political Science Review*, 92: 1–21.

PICCIONE, M. 2002. The repeated prisoner's dilemma with imperfect private monitoring. *Journal of Economic Theory*, 102: 70–83.

ROTH, A. E., PRASNIKAR, V., OKUNO-FUJIWARA, M., and ZAMIR, S. 1991. Bargaining and market behavior in Jerusalem, Ljubljana, Pittsburgh, and Tokyo: an experimental study. *American Economic Review*, 81: 1068–95.

SCOTT, J. C. 1976. *The Moral Economy of the Peasant: Rebellion and Subsistence in Southeast Asia*. New Haven, Conn.: Yale University Press.

SEKIGUCHI, T. 1997. Efficiency in repeated prisoner's dilemma with private monitoring. *Journal of Economic Theory*, 76: 345–61.

SIMON, H. 1990. A mechanism for social selection and successful altruism. *Science*, 250: 1665–8.

STERN, J. 2003. *Terror in the Name of God*. New York: HarperCollins.

TAYLOR, M. 1976. *Anarchy and Cooperation*. London: John Wiley and Sons.

TRIVERS, R. L. 1971. The evolution of reciprocal altruism. *Quarterly Review of Biology*, 46: 35–57.

VARSHNEY, A. 2003. Nationality, ethnic conflict, and rationality. *Perspectives on Politics*, 1: 85–99.

WIESSNER, P. 2005. Norm enforcement among the Ju/'hoansi bushmen: a case of strong reciprocity? *Human Nature*, 16: 115–45.

WITTMAN, D. 1989. Why democracies produce efficient results. *Journal of Political Economy*, 97: 1395–424.

WOOD, E. J. 2003. *Insurgent Collective Action and Civil War in El Salvador*. Cambridge: Cambridge University Press.

YOUNG, P. and BURKE, M. 2001. Competition and custom in economic contracts: a case study of Illinois agriculture. *American Economic Review*, 91: 559–73.

PART X

PUBLIC POLICY

CHAPTER 43

....

OVERVIEW OF
PUBLIC POLICY

THE PUBLIC AND ITS
POLICIES

....

ROBERT E. GOODIN

MARTIN REIN

MICHAEL MORAN

THE *Oxford Handbook of Public Policy* aspires to provide a rounded understanding of what it is to make and to suffer, to study and to critique, the programs and policies by which officers of the state attempt to rule. Ruling is an assertion of the will, an attempt to exercise control, to shape the world. Public policies are instruments of this assertive ambition, and policy studies in the mode that emerged from operations research during the Second World War were originally envisaged as handmaidens in that ambition.[1] There was a distinctly "high modernist" feel to the enterprise, back then: technocratic hubris, married to a sense of mission to make a better world; an

---

* We thank Rod Rhodes for comments on an earlier draft.

[1] In recommending continuation of wartime research and development efforts into the postwar era, Commanding General of the Army Air Force H. H. ("Hap") Arnold had reported to the Secretary of War in the following terms: "During this war the Army, Army Air Forces and the Navy have made unprecedented use of scientific and industrial resources. The conclusion is inescapable that we have not yet established the balance necessary to insure the continuance of teamwork among the military, other government agencies, industry and the universities." Just hear the high-modernist ring in the bold mission statement adopted by Project RAND in 1948, as it split off from the Douglas Aircraft Company:

overwhelming confidence in our ability to measure, monitor, and control that world; and boundless confidence in our capacity actually to pull off the task of control (Scott 1997; Moran 2003).

High modernism in the largest democracies was rule by "the best and the brightest" (Halberstam 1969). It left little room for rhetoric and persuasion, privately much less publicly. Policy problems were technical questions, resolvable by the systematic application of technical expertise. First in the Pentagon, then elsewhere across the wider policy community, the "art of judgment" (Vickers 1983) gave way to the dictates of slide-rule efficiency (Hitch 1958; Hitch and McKean 1960; Haveman and Margolis 1983).

Traces of that technocratic hubris remain, in consulting houses and IMF missions and certain other important corners of the policy universe. But across most of that world there has, over the last half-century, been a gradual chastening of the boldest "high modernist" hopes for the policy sciences.[2] Even in the 1970s, when the high modernist canon still ruled, perceptive social scientists had begun to highlight the limits to implementation, administration, and control.[3] Subsequently, the limits of authority and accountability, of sheer analytic capacity, have borne down upon us.[4] Fiasco has piled upon fiasco in some democratic systems (Henderson 1977; Dunleavy 1981; 1995; Bovens and t'Hart 1996). We have learned that many of the tools in the "high modernist" kit are very powerful indeed, within limits; but they are strictly limited (Hood 1983). We have learned how to supplement those "high modernist" approaches with other "softer" modes for analyzing problems and attempting to solve them.

In trying to convey a sense of these changes in the way we have come to approach public policy over the past half-century, the chapters in our *Handbook* (and still more in this chapter introducing it) focus on the big picture rather than minute details. There are other books to which readers might better turn for fine-grained analyses of current policy debates, policy area by policy area.[5] There are other books providing more fine-grained analyses of public administration.[6] The *Oxford Handbook of Public Policy* offers instead a series of connected stories about what it is like, and what it might alternatively be like, to make and remake public policy in new, more modest modes.

This chapter is offered as a scene-setter, rather than as a systematic overview of the whole field of study, much less a potted summary of the chapters of the *Oxford Handbook of Public Policy*. The authors of those speak most ably for themselves. In this chapter, we simply do likewise. And in doing so we try to tell a particular story: a story about the limits of high ambition in policy studies and policy-making, about the

"to further and promote scientific, educational and charitable purposes, all for the public welfare and security of the United States of America" (RAND 2004).

2   For a remarkable early send-up, see Mackenzie's (1963) "The Plowden Report: a translation."

3   Pressman and Wildavsky 1973; Hood 1976; van Gunsteren 1976.

4   Majone and Quade 1980; Hogwood and Peters 1985; Bovens 1998.

5   The best regular update is probably found in the Brookings Institution's "Setting National Priorities" series; see most recently Aaron and Reischauer 1999.

6   Lynn and Wildavsky 1990; Peters and Pierre 2003.

way those limits have been appreciated, about the way more modest ambitions have been formulated, and about the difficulties in turn of modest learning. Our story, like all stories, is contestable. There is no single intellectually campelting account available of the state of either policy-making or the policy sciences; but the irredeemable fact of contestability is a very part of the argument of the pages that follow.

1 Policy Persuasion

We begin with the most important of all limits to high ambition. All our talk of "making" public policy, of "choosing" and "deciding," loses track of the home truth, taught to President Kennedy by Richard Neustadt (1960), that politics and policy-making is mostly a matter of persuasion. Decide, choose, legislate as they will, policy-makers must carry people with them, if their determinations are to have the full force of policy. That is most commonly demonstrated in systems that attempt to practice liberal democracy; but a wealth of evidence shows that even in the most coercive systems of social organization there are powerful limits to the straightforward power of command (Etzioni 1965).

To make policy in a way that makes it stick, policy-makers cannot merely issue edicts. They need to persuade the people who must follow their edicts if those are to become general public practice. In part, that involves persuasion of the public at large: Teddy Roosevelt's "bully pulpit" is one important lever. In part, the persuasion required is of subordinates who must operationalize and implement the policies handed down to them by nominal superiors. Truman wrongly pitied "Poor Ike," whom he envisaged issuing orders as if he were in the army, only to find that no one would automatically obey: as it turned out, Ike had a clear idea how to persuade up and down the chain of command, even if he had no persuasive presence on television (Greenstein 1982). Indeed Eisenhower's military experience precisely showed that even in nominally hierarchical institutions, persuasion lay at the heart of effective decision.

Not only is the practice of public policy-making largely a matter of persuasion. So too is the discipline of studying policy-making aptly described as itself being a "persuasion" (Reich 1988; Majone 1989). It is a mood more than a science, a loosely organized body of precepts and positions rather than a tightly integrated body of systematic knowledge, more art and craft than genuine "science" (Wildavsky 1979; Goodsell 1992). Its discipline-defining title notwithstanding, Lerner and Lasswell's pioneering book *The Policy Sciences* (1951) never claimed otherwise: quite the contrary, as successive editors of the journal that bears that name continually editorially recall.

The cast of mind characterizing policy studies is marked, above all else, by an aspiration toward "relevance." Policy studies, more than anything, are academic works that attempt to do the real political work: contributing to the betterment of life, offering something that political actors can seize upon and use. From Gunnar Myrdal's *American Dilemma* (1944) through Charles Murray's *Losing Ground* (1984) and William Julius Wilson's *Truly Disadvantaged* (1987), policy-oriented research on race and poverty has informed successive generations of American policy-makers on both ends of the political spectrum, to take only one important example.

Beyond this stress on relevance, policy studies are distinguished from other sorts of political science, secondly, by being unabashedly value laden (Lasswell 1951; Rein 1976; Goodin 1982). They are explicitly normative, in embracing the ineliminable role of value premisses in policy choice—and often in forthrightly stating and defending the value premisses from which the policy prescriptions that they make proceed. They are unapologetically prescriptive, in actually recommending certain programs and policies over others. Policy studies, first and foremost, give *advice* about policy; and they cannot do that (on pain of the "naturalistic fallacy") without basing that advice on some normative ("ought") premisses in the first place.

Policy studies are distinguished from other sorts of political science, thirdly, by their action-orientation. They are organized around questions of what we as a political community should *do*, rather than just around questions of what it should *be*. Whereas other sorts of political studies prescribe designs for our political institutions, as the embodiments or instruments of our collective values, specifically *policy* studies focus less on institutional shells and more on what we collectively *do* in and through those institutional forms. Policy studies embody a bias toward acts, outputs, and outcomes—a concern with consequences—that contrasts with the formal-institutional orientation of much of the rest of political studies.

These apparently commonplace observations—that policy studies is a "persuasion" that aspires to normatively committed intervention in the world of action—pose powerful challenges for the policy analyst. One of the greatest challenges concerns the language that the analyst can sensibly use. The professionalization of political science in the last half-century has been accompanied by a familiar development—the development of a correspondingly professional language. Political scientists know who they are talking to when they report findings: They are talking to each other, and they naturally use language with which other political scientists are familiar. They are talking to each other because the scientific world of political science has a recursive quality: The task is to communicate with, and convince, like-minded professionals in terms that make sense to the professional community. Indeed some powerful traditions in purer forms of academic political science are actually suspicious of "relevance" in scholarly enquiry (Van Evera 2003). The findings and arguments of professional political science may seep into the world of action, but that it not the main point of the activity. Accidental seepage is not good enough for policy studies. It harks back to an older world of committed social enquiry where the precise object is to unify systematic social investigation with normative commitment—and to report both the results and the prescriptions in a language accessible to "nonprofessionals." These can range from engaged—or not very engaged—citizens to the elite of policy-makers. Choosing the language in which to communicate is therefore a tricky, but essential, part of the vocation of policy analysis.

One way of combining all these insights about how policy-making and policy studies are essentially about persuasion is through the "argumentative turn" and the analysis of "discourses" of policy in the "critical policy studies" movement (Fischer and Forrester 1993; Hajer 1995; Hajer and Wagenaar 2003). On this account, a positivist or "high modernist" approach, either to the making of policy or to the understanding of how it is made, that tries to decide what to do or what was done through vaguely mechanical-style causal explanations is bound to fail, or anyway be radically incomplete. Policy analysts are never mere "handmaidens to power." It is part of their job, and a role that the best of them play well, to *advocate* the policies that they think right (Majone 1989). The job of the policy analyst is to "speak truth to power" (Wildavsky 1979), where the truths involved embrace not only the hard facts of positivist science but also the reflexive self-understandings of the community both writ large (the polity) and writ small (the policy community, the community of analysts).

It may well be that this reflexive quality is the main gift of the analyst to the practitioner. In modern government practitioners are often forced to live in an unreflective world: The very pressure of business compresses time horizons, obliterating recollection of the past and foreshortening anticipation of the future (Neustadt and May 1986). There is overwhelming pressure to decide, and then to move on to the next problem. Self-consciousness about the limits of decision, and about the setting, social and historical, of decision, is precisely what the analyst can bring to the policy table, even if its presence at the table often seems unwelcome.

Of course, reason-giving has always been a central requirement of policy application, enforced by administrative law. Courts automatically overrule administrative orders accompanied by no reasons. So, too, will their "rationality review" strike down statutes which cannot be shown to serve a legitimate purpose within the power of the state (Fried 2004, 208–12). The great insight of the argumentative turn in policy analysis is that a robust process of reason-giving runs throughout all stages of public policy. It is not just a matter of legislative and administrative window-dressing.

Frank and fearless advice is not always welcomed by those in positions of power. All organizations find self-evaluation hard, and states find it particularly hard: There is a long and well-documented history of states, democratic and nondemocratic, ignoring or even punishing the conveyor of unwelcome truths (Van Evera 2003). Established administrative structures that used to be designed to generate dispassionate advice are increasingly undermined with the politicization of science and the public service (UCS 2004; Peters and Pierre 2004). Still, insofar as policy analysis constitutes a profession with an ethos of its own, the aspiration to "speak truth to power"—even, or especially, unwelcome truths—must be its prime directive, its equivalent of the Hippocratic Oath (ASPA 1984).

2 ARGUING VERSUS BARGAINING

Our argument thus far involves modest claims for the "persuasion" of policy studies, but even these modest ambitions carry their own hubristic dangers. Persuasion; the encouragement of a reflexive, self-conscious policy culture; an attention to the language used to communicate with the world of policy action: All are important. But all involve the danger of losing sight of a fundamental truth—that policy is not only about arguing, but is also about bargaining. A policy forum is not an academic seminar. The danger is that we replicate the fallacy of a tradition which we began by rejecting.

Policy analysts, particularly those who see themselves as part of a distinct high modernist professional cadre, often take a technocratic approach to their work. They see themselves as possessing a neutral expertise to be put in the service of any political master. They accept that their role as adviser is to advise, not to choose; and they understand that it is in the nature of advice that it is not always taken. Accepting all this as they do, policy advisers of this more professional, technocratic cast of mind inevitably feel certain pangs of regret when good advice is overridden for bad ("purely political") reasons.

Politics may rightly seem disreputable when it is purely a matter of power in the service of interests. When there is nothing more to be said on behalf of the outcome than that people who prefer it have power enough to force it, one might fatalistically accept that outcome as politically inevitable without supposing that there is anything at all to be said for it normatively. Certainly there is not much to be said for it normatively, anyway, without saying lots more about why the satisfaction of those preferences is objectively desirable or why that distribution of power is proper.

Nor is this account necessarily incompatible with some conception of democratic policy-making. Indeed some democratic theorists try to supply the needed normative glue by analogizing political competition to the economic market. The two fundamental theorems of welfare economics prove Adam Smith's early speculation that, at least under certain (pretty unrealistic) conditions, free competition in the marketplace for goods would produce maximum possible satisfaction of people's preferences (Arrow and Hahn 1971). Democratic theorists after the fashion of Schumpeter (1950) say the same about free competition in the political marketplace for ideas and public policies (Coase 1974). "Partisan mutual adjustment"—between parties, between bureaucracies, between social partners—can, bargaining theorists of politics and public administration assure us, produce socially optimal results (Lindblom 1965).

Of course there are myriad assumptions required for the proofs to go through, and they are met even less often in politics than in economics. (Just think of the assumption of "costless entry of new suppliers:" a heroic enough assumption for producers in economic markets, but a fantastically heroic one as applied to new parties in political markets, especially in a world of "cartelized" party markets

(Katz and Mair 1995).) Most importantly, though, the proofs only demonstrate that preferences are maximally satisfied in the Pareto sense: No one can be made better off without someone else being made worse off. Some are inevitably more satisfied than others, and who is most satisfied depends on who has most clout—money in the economic market, or political power in the policy arena. So the classic "proof" of the normative legitimacy of political bargaining is still lacking one crucial leg, which would have to be some justification for the distribution of power that determines "who benefits" (Page 1983). The early policy scientists clearly knew as much, recalling Lasswell's (1950) definition of "politics" in terms of "who gets what, when, how."

The success of that enterprise looks even more unlikely when reflecting, as observers of public policy inevitably must, on the interplay between politics and markets (Lindblom 1977; Dahl 1985). The point of politics is to constrain markets: If markets operated perfectly (according to internal economic criteria, and broader social ones), we would let all social relations be determined by them alone. It is only because markets fail in one or the other of those ways, or because they fail to provide the preconditions for their own success, that we need politics at all (Hirsch 1976; Offe 1984; Esping-Andersen 1985; World Bank 1997). But if politics is to provide these necessary conditions for markets, politics must be independent of markets—whereas the interplay of "political money" and the rules of property in most democracies means that politics is, to a large extent, the captive of markets (Lindblom 1977).

Tainted though the processes of representative democracy might be by political money, they nonetheless remain the principal mechanism of public accountability for the exercise of public power. Accountability through economic markets and informal networks can usefully supplement the political accountability of elected officials to the electorate; but they can never replace it (Day and Klein 1987; Goodin 2003).

Another strand of democratic theory has recently emerged, reacting against the bargaining model that sees politics as simply the vector sum of political forces and the aggregation of votes. It is a strand which is easier to reconcile with the "persuasive" character of policy studies. Deliberative democrats invite us to reflect together on our preferences and what policies might best promote the preferences that we reflectively endorse (Dryzek 2000). There are many arenas in which this might take place. Those range from small-scale fora (such as "citizens' juries," "consensus conferences," or "Deliberative Polls" involving between twenty and 200 citizens) through medium-sized associations (Fung and Wright 2001). Ackerman and Fishkin (2004) even have a proposal for a nationwide "Deliberation Day" before every national election.

Not only might certain features of national legislature make that a more "deliberative" assembly, more in line with the requirements of deliberative democracy (Steiner et al. 2005). And not only are certain features of political culture—traditions of free speech and civic engagement—more conducive to deliberative democracy (Sunstein 1993; 2001; Putnam 1993). Policy itself might be made in a more "deliberative" way, by those charged with the task of developing and implementing policy proposals (Fischer 2003). That is the aim of advocates of critical policy studies, with their multifarious proposals for introducing a "deliberative turn" into the making of policies on everything from water use to urban renewal to toxic waste (Hajer and Wagenaar 2003).

Some might say that this deliberative turn marks a shift from reason to rhetoric in policy discourse. And in a way, advocates of that turn might embrace the description, for part of the insight of the deliberative turn is that reason is inseparable from the *way* we reason: Rhetoric is not decoration but is always engrained in the intellectual content of argument. Certainly they mean to disempower the dogmatic deliverances of technocratic reason, and to make space in the policy-making arena for softer and less hard-edged modes of communication and assessment (Young 2000; Fischer 2003). Reframing the problem is, from this perspective, a legitimate part of the process: It is important to see that the problem looks different from different perspectives, and that different people quite reasonably bring different perspectives to bear (March 1972; Schon and Rein 1994; Allison and Zelikow 1999). Value clarification, and reenvisioning our interests (personal and public), is to be seen as a legitimate and valued outcome of political discussions, rather than as an awkwardness that gets in the way of technocratic fitting of means to pre-given ends. Thus the deliberative turn echoes one of the key features of the "persuasive" conception of policy studies with which we began: Reflexivity is—or should be—at the heart of both advice and decision.

These conceptions, true, are easier to realize in some settings than in others. The place, the institutional site, and the time all matter. National traditions clearly differ in their receptivity to deliberation and argument. The more consultative polities of Scandinavia and continental Europe have always favored more consensual modes of policy-making, compared to the majoritarian polities of the Anglo-American world (Lijphart 1999). Votes are taken, in the end. But the process of policy development and implementation proceeds more according to procedures of "sounding out" stakeholders and interested parties, rather than majorities pressing things to a vote prematurely (Olsen 1972b). Of course, every democratic polity worth the name has some mechanisms for obtaining public input into the policy-making process: letters to Congressmen and congressional hearings, in the USA; Royal Commissions and Green Papers in the UK; and so on. But those seem to be pale shadows of the Scandinavian "remiss" procedures, inviting comment on important policy initiatives and actually taking the feedback seriously, even when it does not necessarily come from powerful political interests capable of blocking the legislation or derailing its implementation (Meijer 1969; Anton 1980).

Sites of governance matter, as well. The high modernist vision was very much one of top-down government: Policies were to be handed down not just from superiors to subordinates down the chain of command, but also from the governing center to the governed peripheries. New, and arguably more democratic, possibilities emerge when looking at governing as a bottom-up process (Tilly 1999). The city or neighborhood suddenly becomes the interesting locus of decision-making, rather than the national legislature. Attempts to increase democratic participation in local decision-making have not met with uniform success, not least because of resistance from politicians nearer the center of power: The resistance of mayors was a major hindrance to the "community action programs" launched as part of the American War on Poverty, for example (Marris and Rein 1982). Still, many of the most encouraging examples of new deliberative processes working to democratize the existing political order operate at very local levels, in local schools or police stations (Fung 2004).

Meshing policy advice and policy decision with deliberation is therefore easier in some nations, and at some levels of government, than others. It also seems easier at some historical moments than others: thus time matters. Until about a quarter of a century ago, for example, policy-making in Britain was highly consensual, based on extensive deliberation about policy options, albeit usually with a relatively narrow range of privileged interests. Indeed, the very necessity of creating accommodation was held to be a source of weakness in the policy process (Dyson 1980; Dyson and Wilks 1983). Since then the system has shifted drastically away from a deliberative, accommodative mode. Many of the characteristic mechanisms associated with consultation and argument—such as Royal Commissions—are neglected; policy is made through tiny, often informally organized cliques in the core executive.

The shift is partly explicable by the great sense of crisis which engulfed British policy-makers at the end of the 1970s, and by the conviction that crisis demanded decisive action free of the encumbrances of debates with special interests. The notion that crisis demands decision, not debate, recurs in many different times and places. Indeed "making a crisis out of a drama" is a familiar rhetorical move when decision-makers want a free hand. Yet here is the paradox of crisis: Critical moments are precisely those when the need is greatest to learn how to make better decisions; yet the construction of crisis as a moment when speed of decision is of the essence precisely makes it the moment when those advocating persuasion and reflexivity are likely to be turned away from the policy table.

All is not gloom even here, however. The analysis of crises—exactly, particular critical events—can be a powerful aid to institutional learning (March, Sproul, and Tamuz 1991). Moreover, there are always multiple "tables"—multiple fora—at which policies are argued out and bargained over. "Jurisdiction shopping" is a familiar complaint, as lawyers look for sympathetic courts to which to bring their cases and polluting industries look for lax regulatory regimes in which to locate. But policy activists face the same suite of choices. Policies are debated, and indeed made, in many different fora. Each operates according to a different set of rules, with a different agenda and on different timelines; each responds to different sets of pressures and urgencies; each has its own norms, language, and professional ethos. So when you cannot get satisfaction in one place, the best advice for a policy activist is to go knocking on some other door (Keck and Sikkink 1998; Risse, Ropp, and Sikkink 1999).

Place, site, and moment often obstruct the "persuasive" practice of the vocation of policy studies. Yet as we show in our next section, there is overwhelming evidence of powerful structural and institutional forces that are dragging policy-makers in a deliberative direction. These powerful forces are encompassed in accounts of networked governance.

3 Networked Governance

Policy-making in the modern state commonly exhibits a contradictory character. Under the press of daily demands for action, often constructed as "crises," decision-makers feel the need to act without delay. Yet powerful forces are pushing systems increasingly in more decentralized and persuasion-based directions.

Of course, even in notionally rigid high modernist hierarchies, the "command theory" of control was never wholly valid. "Orders backed by threats" were never a good way to get things done, in an organization any more than in governing a country. Complex organizations can never be run by coercion alone (Etzioni 1965). An effective authority structure, just as an effective legal system, presupposes that the people operating within it themselves internalize the rules it lays down and critically evaluate their own conduct according to its precepts (Hart 1961). That is true even of the most nominally bureaucratic environments: For instance, Heclo and Wildavsky (1974) characterize the relations among politicians and public officials in the taxing and spending departments of British government as a "village community" full of informal norms and negotiated meanings; an anthropologically "private" way of governing public money.

Thus there have always been limits to command. But the argument that, increasingly, government is giving way to "governance" suggests something more interesting, and something peculiarly relevant to our "persuasive" conception of policy studies: that governing is less and less a matter of ruling through hierarchical authority structures, and more and more a matter of negotiating through a decentralized series of floating alliances. The dominant image is that of "networked governance" (Heclo 1978; Rhodes 1997; Castells 2000). Some actors are more central, others more peripheral, in those networks. But even those actors at the central nodes of networks are not in a position to dictate to the others. Broad cooperation from a great many effectively independent actors is required in order for any of them to accomplish their goals.

To some extent, that has always been the deeper reality underlying constitutional fictions suggesting otherwise. Formally, the Queen in Parliament may be all-powerful; in Dicey's phrase, may "make or unmake any law whatsoever" (Dicey 1960, 39–40). Nonetheless, firm albeit informal constitutional conventions mean there are myriad things that she simply may not do and retain any serious expectation of retaining her royal prerogatives (unlike, apparently, her representative in other parts of her realm) (Marshall 1984). Formally, Britain was long a unitary state and local governments were utterly creatures of the central state; but even in the days of parliamentary triumphalism the political realities were such that the center had to bargain with local governments rather than simply dictate to them, even on purely financial matters (Rhodes 1988).

But increasingly such realities are looming larger and the fictions even smaller. Policy increasingly depends on what economists call "relational contracts:" an agreement to agree, a settled intention to "work together on this," with details left to be specified sometime later (Gibson and Goodin 1999). Some fear a "joint decision trap," in circumstances where there are too many veto players (Scharpf 1988). But Gunnar Myrdal's (1955, 8, 20) description of the workings of the early days of the Economic Commission for Europe is increasingly true not just of intergovernmental negotiations but intragovernmental ones as well:

> If an organization acquires a certain stability and settles down to a tradition of work, one implication is usually that on the whole the same state officials come together at regular intervals. If in addition it becomes repeatedly utilized for reaching inter-governmental agreements in a given field, it may acquire a certain institutional weight and a momentum. Certain substitutes for real political sanctions can then gradually be built up. They are all informal and frail. They assume a commonly shared appreciation of the general usefulness of earlier results reached, the similarly shared pride of, and solidarity towards, the "club" of participants at the meetings, and a considerable influence of the civil servants on the home governments in the particular kind of questions dealt with in the organizations.... Not upholding an agreement is something like a breach of etiquette in a club.

And so it has gone in the later life of the European Community, and now the European Union (Héritier 1999).[7]

Within these networks, none is in command. Bringing others along, preserving the relationship, is all. Persuasion is the way policy gets made, certainly in any literal "institutional void" (Hajer 2003) but even within real institutions, where authority is typically more fictive than real (Heclo and Wildavsky 1974).

If this is bad news for titular heads of notionally policy-making organizations, it is good news for the otherwise disenfranchised. The history of recent successes in protecting human rights internationally is a case in point. Advocacy coalitions are assembled, linking groups of powerless Nigerians whose rights are being abused by the Nigerian government with groups of human rights activists abroad, who bring pressure to bear on their home governments to bring pressure to bear in turn on Nigeria (Risse, Ropp, and Sikkink 1999; Keck and Sikkink 1998). Networking across state borders, as well as across communities and affected interests within state borders, can be an important "weapon of the weak" (Scott 1985).

The change has invaded areas hitherto thought of as the heartland of hierarchy and of authoritative decision by the rich and powerful. Bureaucratic organizations, paradigms of Weberian hierarchy, are yielding to "soft bureaucracy" (Courpasson 2000). And in the world of globally organized business, Braithwaite and Drahos (2000) paint a picture of a decentered world, where networks of bewildering complexity produce regulation often without the formality of any precise moment of decision.

---

[7] For example, "it is rare in [European] Community environmental policy for negotiations to fail.... An important factor seems to be the dynamics of long-lasting negotiations: i.e., the 'entanglement' of the negotiations which ultimately exerts such pressure on the representatives of dissenters (especially where there is only one dissenting state) that a compromise can be reached...[O]n the whole, no member state is willing to assume the responsibility for causing the failure of negotiations that have lasted for years and in which mutual trust in the willingness of all negotiators to contribute to an agreement has been built up" (Rehbinder and Stewart 1985, 265).

The rise of networked governance in turn accounts for a related turn that is central to the practice of the "persuasive" vocation: the self-conscious turn to government as steering.

4 ROWING VERSUS STEERING

High modernist models of policy-making were, first and foremost, models of central control. On those models, policy-makers were supposed to decide what should be done to promote the public good, and then to make it happen.

This ambition became increasingly implausible as problems to which policy was addressed became (or came to be recognized as) increasingly complex. Despite brave talk of ways of "organizing social complexity" (Deutsch 1963; La Porte 1975), a sense soon set in that government was "overloaded" and society was politically ungovernable (King 1975; Crozier, Huntington, and Watanuki 1975). Despite the aspiration of constantly improving social conditions, producing generally good outcomes for people without fail, a sense emerged that society is now characterized by increasingly pervasive risks, both individually and collectively (Beck 1992).

Even when policy-makers thought they had a firm grip on the levers of power at the center, however, they long feared that they had much less of a grip on those responsible for implementing their policies on the ground. "Street-level bureaucrats"—police, caseworkers in social service agencies, and such like—inevitably apply official policies in ways and places at some distance from close scrutiny by superiors (Lipsky 1980). Substantial de facto discretion inevitably follows, however tightly rule bound their actions are formally supposed to be. But it is not just bureaucrats literally on the streets who enjoy such discretion. Organization theorists have developed the general concept of "control loss" to describe the way in which the top boss's power to control subordinates slips away the further down the chain of command the subordinate is (Blau 1963; Deutsch 1963). It can never be taken for granted that policies will be implemented on the ground as intended: Usually they will not (Pressman and Wildavsky 1973; Bardach 1977; 1980).

One early response to appreciation of problems of control loss within a system of public management was to abandon "command-and-control" mechanisms for evoking compliance with public policies, in favor of a system of "incentives" (Kneese and Schultze 1975; Schultze 1977). The thought was that, if you structure the incentives correctly, people will thereby have a reason for doing what you want them to do, without further intrusive intervention from public officials in the day-to-day management of their affairs. This thinking persisted into the 1980s and 1990s: It lay, for instance, behind the mania for "internal markets" in so many of the state-funded health care systems of Europe (Le Grand 1991; Saltman and von Otter 1992).

The trick, of course, lies in setting the incentives just right. Allowing the Nuclear Regulatory Commission to fine unsafe nuclear power plants only $5,000 a day for unsafe practices, when it would cost the power company $300,000 a day to purchase substitute power off the grid, is hardly a deterrent (US Comptroller General 1979).

Appreciation of the incapacity of the center to exercise effective control over what happens on the ground through command-and-control within a hierarchy has also led to increasing "contracting out" of public services, public–private partnerships, and arm's-length government (Smith and Lipsky 1993; Commission on Public– Private Partnerships 2001). The image typically evoked here is one of "steering, not rowing" (Kaufman, Majone, and Ostrom 1985; Bovens 1990).

Twin thoughts motivate this development. The first is that, by divesting itself of responsibility for front-line service delivery, the policy units of government will be in a better position to focus on strategic policy choice (Osborne and Gaebler 1993; Gore 1993). The second thought is that by stipulating "performance standards" in the terms of a contract, and monitoring compliance with them, public servants will be better able to ensure that public services are properly delivered than they would have been had those services been provided within the public service itself.

This is hardly the first time such a thing has happened. In the early history of the modern state, under arrangements that have come to be called "tax farming," rulers used to subcontract tax collections to local nobles, with historically very mixed success. Fix the incentives as the prince tried, the nobles always seemed to be able to figure out some way of diddling the crown (Levi 1988). Those committed to steering, by monitoring others' rowing, would like to think they have learned how better to specify and monitor contract compliance. But so too has always every prince's new adviser.

The history of "steering and rowing" crystallizes the contradictory character of the modern "governance" state, and illuminates also the complex relations between "governance" and the conception of policy studies as a persuasive vocation. On the one hand, powerful, well-documented forces are pushing policy systems in the direction of deliberation, consultation, and accommodation. "High modernism" is accompanied by high complexity, which requires high doses of voluntary coordination. And high modernism has also helped create smart people who cannot simply be ordered around: Rising levels of formal education, notably sharp rises in participation in higher education, have created large social groups with the inclination, and the intellectual resources, to demand a say in policy-making. These are some of the social developments that lie behind the spread of loosely networked advocacy coalitions of the kind noted above.

Modern steering may therefore be conceived as demanding a more democratic mode of statecraft—one where the practice of the persuasive vocation of policy studies is peculiarly important. But as we have also just seen, "steering" can have a less democratic face. It echoes the ambitions of princes, and a world of centralized scrutiny and monitoring prefigured in Bentham's (1787) Panopticon. The earliest images of the steering state, in Plato's *Republic*, are indeed avowedly authoritarian;

and the greatest "helmsman" of the modern era was also one of its most brutal autocrats, Mao Zedong.

As the language of "steering" therefore shows, the legacy of "networked governance" is mixed, indeed contradictory, inscribed with both autocracy and democracy. This helps explain much of the fixation of the new public management on monitoring and control.

For all the borrowing that new public management, with its privatization and outsourcing, has done from economics, the one bit of economics it seems steadfastly to ignore is the one bit that ought presumably to have most relevance to the state as an organized enterprise: the economic theory of the firm (Simon 2000).

Two key works emphasize the point. One is Ronald Coase's (1937) early analysis of why to internalize production within the same firm, rather than just buying the components required from other producers on the open market—the "produce/buy decision." The answer is obvious as soon as the question is asked. You want to internalize production within the firm if, but only if, you have more confidence in your capacity to monitor and control the quality of the inputs into the production process than you do the quality of the outputs (the components you would alternatively have to buy on the open market). You produce in-house only when you are relatively unconfident of your capacity to monitor the quality of the goods that external producers supply to you.

One implication of this analysis for contracting out of public services to private organizations is plain: For the same reason that a private *organization* is formed to provide the service, the public should be hesitant to contract to them. For the same reason the private organization does not buy in the outputs it promises to supply, preferring to produce them in-house, so too should the public organization: Contracts are inevitably incomplete, performance standards underspecified, and the room for maximizing private profits at the cost of the public purposes too great. Indeed this problem of what may summarily be called "opportunism" lies at the heart of the way the new institutional economics addresses the firm (Williamson 1985, 29–32, 281–5). There then follows another obvious implication: If we do contract out public services, it is better to contract them out to nonprofit suppliers who are known to share the goals that the public had in establishing the program than it is to contract them out to for-profit suppliers whose interests clearly diverge from the public purposes (Smith and Lipsky 1993; Rose-Ackerman 1996; Goodin 2003).

The second contribution to the theory of the firm that ought to bear on current practices of outsourcing and privatizing public services is Herbert Simon's (1951) analysis of the "employment relationship." The key to that, too, is the notion of "incomplete contracting." The reason we hire someone as an employee of our firm is that we cannot specify, in detail in advance, exactly what performances will be required. If we could, we would subcontract the services; but not knowing exactly what we want, we cannot write the relevant performance contract. Instead we write an employment contract, of the general form that says: "The employee will do whatever the employer says." Rudely, it is a slavery contract (suitably circumscribed by labor law); politely, it is a "relational contract," an agreement to stand in a relationship the precise terms of which will be specified later (Williamson 1985). Indeed as North points out, there are even elements of the relational in the master–slave relationship (1990, 32). But the basic point, once again, is that we cannot specify in advance what is wanted; and insofar as we cannot, that makes a powerful case for producing in-house rather than contracting out. And that is as true for public organizations as for private, and once again equally for public organizations contracting with private *organizations*. For the same reasons that the private contractors employ people at all, for those very same reasons the state ought not subcontract to those private suppliers.

The more general way in which these insights have been picked up among policy-makers is in the slogan, "privatization entails regulation." A naive reading of the "downsizing government" program of Reagan and Thatcher and their copyists world-wide might lead one to suppose that it would have resulted in "less government:" specifically, among other things, "less regulation" (after all, "deregulation" was one of its first aims). But in truth privatization, outsourcing, and the like actually requires more regulation, not less (Majone 1994; Moran 2003). At a minimum, it requires detailed specification of the terms of the contract and careful monitoring of contract compliance. Thus, we should not be surprised that the sheer number of regulations emanating from privatized polities is an order of magnitude larger (Levi-Faur 2003; Moran 2003).

The paradoxes of privatization and regulation thus just bring us back to the beginning of the growth of government in the nineteenth century. That came as a pragmatic response to practical circumstances, if anything against the ideological current of the day. No political forces were pressing for an expansion of government, particularly. It was just a matter of one disaster after another making obvious the need, across a range of sectors, for tighter public regulation and an inspectorate to enforce it (MacDonagh 1958; 1961; Atiyah 1979). Over the course of the next century, some of those sectors were taken into public hands, only then to be reprivatized. It should come as no surprise, however, that the same sort of regulatory control should be needed over those activities, once reprivatized, as proved necessary before they had been nationalized. There was a "pattern" to government growth identified by Macdonagh (1958; 1961); and there is likely a pattern of regulatory growth under privatization.

5 POLICY, PRACTICE, AND PERSUASION

To do something "as a matter of policy" is to do it as a general rule. That is the distinction between "policy" and "administration" (Wilson 1887), between "legislating" policy and "executing" it (Locke 1690, ch. 12). Policy-makers of the most ambitious sort aspire to "make policy" in that general rule-setting way, envisioning administrators applying those general rules to particular cases in a minimally discretionary fashion (Calvert, McCubbins, and Weingast 1989). That and cognate aspirations toward taut control from the center combine to constitute a central trope of political high modernism.

One aspect of that is the aspiration, or rather illusion, of total central control. All the great management tools of the last century were marshaled in support of that project: linear programming, operations research, cost–benefit analysis, management-by-objectives, case-controlled random experiments, and so on (Rivlin 1971; Self 1975; Stokey and Zeckhauser 1978).

One non-negligible problem with models of central control is that there is never any single, stable central authority that can be in complete control. For would-be totalitarians that is a sad fact; for democratic pluralists it is something to celebrate. But whatever one's attitude toward the fact, it remains a hard fact of political life that the notional "center" is always actually occupied by many competing authorities. A Congressional Budget Office will always spring up to challenge the monolithic power of an Executive Branch General Accounting Office, just as double sets of books will always be kept in all the line departments of the most tightly planned economy.

In any case, total central control is always a fraud or a fiction. In the terms of the old Soviet joke, "They pretend to set quotas, and we pretend to meet them." The illusion of planning was preserved even when producers wildly exceeded their targets, which surely must, in truth, have indicated a failure of planning, just as much as missing their targets in the other direction would have been (Wildavsky 1973). Every bureaucrat, whether on the street or in some branch office, knows well the important gap between "what they think we're doing, back in central office" and "what actually happens around here." And any new recruit incapable of mastering that distinction quickly will not be long for that bureau's world—just as any landless peasant who supposes that some entitlement will be enforced merely because it is written down somewhere in a statute book will soon be sadly disappointed (Galanter 1974).

One solution is of course to abandon central planning altogether and marketize everything (Self 1993). The "shock treatment" to which the formerly planned economies of Central Europe were subjected at the end of the cold war often seemed to amount to something like that (Sacks 1995; World Bank 1996). But as we have seen above, even the more moderate ambitions of privatization and creating managed markets in the established capitalist democracies, led to anything but a more decentralized world: They created their own powerful incentives to monitor and control.

More modestly, there are new modes of more decentralized planning and control that are more sensitive to those realities. "Indicative planning" loosens up the planning process: Instead of setting taut and unchanging targets, it merely points in certain desired directions and recalibrates future targets in light of what past practice has shown to be realistic aspirations (Meade 1970).

More generally, policy-makers can rely more heavily on "loose" laws and regulations. Instead of tightly specifying exact performance requirements (in ways that are bound to leave some things unspecified), the laws and regulations can be written in more general and vaguely aspirational terms (Goodin 1982, 59–72). Hard-headed political realists might think the latter pure folly, trusting too much to people's goodwill (or alternatively, putting too much power in the hands of administrators charged with interpreting and applying loose laws and regulations). But it has been shown that, for example, nursing homes achieve higher levels of performance in countries regulating them in that "looser" way than in countries that try to write the regulations in a more detailed way (Braithwaite et al. 1993).

An interesting variation on these themes is the Open Method of Coordination practiced within the European Union. That consists essentially in "benchmarking." In the first instance, there is merely a process of collecting information on policy performance from all member states on some systematic, comparable basis. But once that has been done, the performance of better-performing states will almost automatically come to serve as a "benchmark" for the others to aspire to—voluntarily initially, but with increasing amounts of informal and formal pressure as time goes by (Atkinson et al. 2002; Offe 2003).

Another aspect of "political high modernism" is the illusion of instrumental rationality completely governing the policy process. That is the illusion that policy-makers begin with a full set of ends (values, goals) that are to be pursued, full information about the means available for pursuing them, and full information about the constraints (material, social, and political resources) available for pursuing them.

"Full information" is always an illusion. Policy, like all human action, is undertaken partly in ignorance; and to a large extent is a matter of "learning-by-doing" (Arrow 1962; Betts 1978). In practice, we never really have all the information we need to "optimize." At best, we "satisfice"—set some standard of what is "good enough," and content ourselves with reaching that (Simon 1955). In the absence of full information about the "best possible," we never really know for certain whether our standard of "good enough" is too ambitious or not ambitious enough. If we set educational standards too high, too many children will be "left behind" as failures; if too low, passing does them little pedagogic good.

The failure of instrumental reason in the "full information" domain is unsurprising. Its failure in the other two domains is perhaps more so. Policy-makers can never be sure exactly what resources are, or will be, available for pursuing any set of aims. It is not only Soviet-style planners who faced "soft budget constraints" (Kornai, Maskin, and Roland 1993). So do policy-makers worldwide. In the literal sense of financial budgets, they often do not know how much they have to spend or how much they are actually committing themselves to spending. Legislating an "entitlement" program is to write a blank check, giving rise to spending that is "uncontrollable"

(Derthick 1975)—uncontrollable, anyway, without a subsequent change in the leg-islation, for which political resources might be lacking, given the political interests coalesced around entitlements thus created (Pierson 1994). In a more diffuse sense of social support, policy-makers again often do not know how much they have or need for any given policy. Sometimes they manage to garner more support for pro-grams once under way than could ever have been imagined, initially; and conversely, programs that began with vast public support sometimes lose it precipitously and unpredictably. In short: perfect means–ends fitters, in "high modernist" mode, would maximize goal satisfaction within the constraints of the resources available to them; but public policy-makers, in practice, often do not have much of a clue what resources really will ultimately be available.

Policy-makers also often do not have a clear sense of the full range of instruments available to them. Policies are intentions, the product of creative human imagination. Policy-making can proceed in a more or less inventive way: by deliberately engag-ing in brainstorming and free association, rather than just rummaging around to see what "solutions looking for problems" are lying at the bottom of the existing "garbage can" of the policy universe (Olsen 1972a; March 1976; March and Olsen 1976). But creative though they may be, policy-makers will always inevitably fail the high modernist ambition to some greater or lesser degree because of their inevitably limited knowledge of all the possible means by which goals might be pursued in policy.

Perhaps most surprising of all, policy-makers fail the "high modernist" ambition of perfect instrumental rationality in not even having any clear, settled idea what all the ends (values, goals) of policy are. Much is inevitably part of the taken-for-granted background in all intentional action. It might never occur to us to specify that we value some outcome that we always enjoyed until some new policy intervention sud-denly threatens it: wilderness and species diversity, or the climate, or stable families, or whatever. We often do not know what we want until we see what we get, not because our preferences are irrationally adaptive (or perhaps counter-adaptive) but merely because our capacities to imagine and catalogue all good things are themselves strictly limited (March 1976).

The limits to instrumental rationality strengthen the case made in this chapter for policy studies as a persuasive vocation, for they strengthen the case that policy is best made, and developed, as a kind of journey of self-discovery, in which we have experientially to learn what we actually want. And what we learn to want is in part a product of what we already have and know—which is to say, is in part a product of what policy has been hitherto. Recognizing the limits to instrumental rationality also strengthens the case for a self-conscious eclecticism in choice of the "tools of government" (Hood 1983; Salamon 2002). These "tools" are social technologies and thus their use and effectiveness are highly contingent on the setting in which they are employed. That setting is also in part a product of what has gone before. In other words, policy legacies are a key factor in policy choice—and to these we now turn.

6 POLICY AS ITS OWN CAUSE

....

It may truly be the case that "policy is its own cause." That is the case not just in the unfortunate sense in which cynics like Wildavsky (1979, ch. 3) originally intended the term: that every attempt to fix one problem creates several more; that every "purposive social action" always carries with it certain "unintended consequences" (Merton 1936). Nor is it simply a matter of issues cycling in and out of fashion, with the costs of solving some problem becoming more visible than the benefits (Downs 1972; Hirschman 1982). It can also be true in more positive senses. As we experiment with some policy interventions, we get new ideas of better ways to pursue old goals and a clearer view of what new goals we collectively also value.

From an organizational point of view, solving problems can be as problematic as not solving them. The March of Dimes had to redefine its mission or close up shop, after its original goal—conquering polio—had been achieved. What Lasswell (1941) called the US "Garrison State" had to find some new *raison d'être* once the cold war had been won. Policy is its own cause in cases of successes as well as failures: In both cases, some new policy has to be found, and found fast, if the organization is to endure.

Policy successes can cause problems in a substantive rather than merely organizational sense. Longevity, increasing disability-free life-years, is a central goal of health policy and one of the great accomplishments of the modern era. But good though it is in other respects, increasing longevity compromises the assumptions upon which "pay as you go" pension systems were predicated, giving rise to the "old age crisis" that has so exercised pension reformers worldwide (World Bank 1994).

Policy can be its own cause both directly as well as indirectly. A policy might successfully change the social world in precisely the ways intended, and then those changes might themselves either prevent or enable certain further policy developments along similar lines. This is the familiar story of "path dependency:" the subsequent moves available to you being a function of previous moves you have taken. Sometimes path dependency works to the advantage of policy-makers: Once village post offices are set up to deliver the Royal Mail across the realm, the same infrastructure is suddenly available also to pay all sorts of social benefits (pensions, family allowances, and such like) over the counter through them; there, the latter policy is easier to implement because of the first (Pierson 2000). Sometimes path dependency works the other way, making subsequent policy developments harder. An example of that is the way in which pensions being paid to Civil War veterans undercut the potential political constituency for universal old-age pensions in the USA for fully a generation or two after the rest of the developed world had adopted them (Skocpol 1992). Policy is its own cause due to such path dependencies, as well.

7 CONSTRAINTS

Policy-making is always a matter of choice under constraint. But not all the constraints are material. Some are social and political, having to do with the willingness of people to do what your policy asks of them or with the willingness of electors to endorse the policies that would-be policy-makers espouse.

Another large source of constraints on policy-making, however, is ideational. Technology is at its most fundamental a set of ideas for how to use a set of resources to achieve certain desired outcomes. The same is true of the "technology of policy" as it is of the more familiar sorts of "technology of production." Ideas of how to pursue important social goals are forever in short supply (Reich 1988).

Occasionally new policy ideas originate with creative policy analysts. Take two examples from the realm of criminology. One idea about why the long, anonymous corridors of public housing complexes were such dangerous places was that common space was everybody's and nobody's: It was nobody's business to monitor, protect and defend that space. If public housing were designed instead in such a way as to create enclaves of "defensible space," crime might be reduced (Newman 1972). Another idea is that "broken windows" might signal that "nobody cares" about this neighborhood, thus relaxing inhibitions on further vandalism and crime. Cracking down on petty misdemeanors might reduce crime by sending the opposite signal (Wilson and Kelling 1982).

More often, however, policy-making is informed by "off the shelf" ideas. Sometimes these are borrowed from other jurisdictions. In times gone by—the times of mimeographed legislative proposals being dropped into the legislative hopper—policy borrowing could be traced by tracking the typographical errors in legislative proposals in one jurisdiction being replicated in the next (Walker 1969). In other cases, the borrowing is from casebooks and classrooms of Public Policy Schools, or under pressure from the World Bank and the International Monetary Fund (Stiglitz 2002).

March and Olsen (1976; Olsen 1972a) famously capture this proposition with their "garbage can model" of public policy-making. Policy choice is there characterized as the confluence of three streams: problems looking for solutions; solutions looking for problems; and people looking for things to do. The first stream, but only that one, lines up with the hyper-rationalism of political high modernism. The latter stream represents the desperation of post-polio March of Dimers and the post-cold war Garrison State, looking for things to do once their original missions had been accomplished. The middle stream—solutions looking for problems—captures the paucity of policy ideas that serves as a major constraint on high modernist policy-making.

High modernist policy-making is supposed to be a matter of instrumentally rationally fitting means to ends. But often the means come first, and they get applied (inevitably imperfectly) to whatever end comes along which they might remotely fit. Take the case of the cruise missile. That technology originally developed as an unarmed decoy to be launched by bombers to confuse enemy radar as they penetrated enemy airspace; but when the Senate insisted that surely some of those missiles should be armed, the air force dropped the scheme rather than acquiesce in the development of unmanned weapons systems. There was a subsequent attempt to adapt the technology jointly by the air force for use on "stand-off bombers" (firing the missiles while still in friendly airspace) and by the navy for use on submarines; but given the differences between launching through an airplane's "short-range attack missile" launcher and a submarine's torpedo tube, that joint venture came to naught. So the original plan was shelved. But the idea was kept on the shelf; and several years later, in a window of strategic opportunity opened up by the SALT I agreements, the cruise missile was suddenly resurrected, this time as a ground-based missile system installed on the edge of the Evil Empire (Levine 1977).

Equally often, certain sorts of means constitute a "good fit" to certain sorts of ends, only under certain conditions which themselves are subject to change. Those often unspoken "background conditions" constitute further constraints to policy-making. Consider, for example, the peculiarly Australian style of "worker's welfare state," which made good sense under the conditions of its introduction at the beginning of the twentieth century but no sense under the conditions prevailing by that century's end: If you have, as Australia initially had, full employment and an industrial arbitration system that ensured that everyone in employment earned enough to support a family, then you need no elaborate scheme of transfer payments to compensate people for inadequacies in their market income; but once you have (as under Thatcherite Labor and even more right-wing conservative governments) eviscerated both full employment and industrial arbitration schemes, and with them any guarantee of a "living wage" from market sources, the traditional absence of any transfer scheme to compensate for inadequacies in market income bites hard (Castles 1985; 2001).

The largest constraint under which public policy operates, of course, is the sheer selfishness of entrenched interests possessed of sufficient power to promote those interests in the most indefensible of ways. Politics, Shapiro (1999) usefully reminds us, is ultimately all about "interests and power." Anyone who has watched the farm lobby at work, anywhere in the world, would not doubt that for a moment (Self and Storing 1962; Smith 1990; Grant 1997). Neither would anyone conversant with the early history of the British National Health Service and the deeply cynical maneuvering of physicians to avoid becoming employees of the state (Marmor and Thomas 1972; Klein 2001).

Moralists hope for more, as do conscientious policy analysts. But at the end of the day, politics may well end up being purely about "who gets what, when, how," as the first self-styled policy scientist long ago taught us (Lasswell 1950).

Even those most political of constraints might be of indeterminate strength, though. Consider for example the growth of "alternative medicine" in the USA. Professional medicine, especially in the USA, is a powerfully organized interest (Marmor 1994). Ordinarily we expect its practitioners to be able to see off any challengers with ease. Certainly they successfully froze chiropractors out, when they tried to horn in on the business of osteopaths, for example. Somehow, however, "alternative medicine" has managed to become sufficiently established—despite the political power of conventional medical practitioners—to appear now as an option in Americans' Health Maintenance Organizations and to be eligible for reimbursement by health insurance schemes. It may just be a case of the political power of the insurance industry, weary of ever-escalating medical costs, having been mobilized against the political power of physicians, with practitioners of alternative medicine being the incidental beneficiaries. But, *ex ante,* that would have been a surprising and unexpected source of political support for the alternative medicine movement: *Ex ante,* one could scarcely have guessed that the power of organized medicine was as fragile as it turned out to be in this respect.

Of course, "constraints" are not immutable. Indeed, one person's constraint may be another person's opportunity. From Kingdon's windows of opportunity (1984) to Hall's political power of economic ideas (1989) we see how the story is more than one about constraints: It is also about opportunities for change. These we now examine.

8 CHANGE, CONSTRAINT, AND DEMOCRATIC POLITICS

The story of policy is in part a story about constraints. But it is also a story about change, and that is what we now examine. Policies change for all sorts of reasons. The problems change; the environments change; technologies improve; alliances alter; key staff come and go; powerful interests weigh in. For those sadly in the know, all those are familiar facts of the policy world.

But for those still inspired by democratic ideals, there is at least sometimes another side to the story: Policies can sometimes change because the people subject to those policies want them to change. There is a mass mobilization of groups pressing for reform—workers pressing for legislation on hours and wages, racial or religious minorities pressing for civil rights, women pressing for gender equity. What is more, there is powerful comparative evidence that social and cultural developments are promoting the spread of these mass groups (Cain, Dalton, and Scarrow 2003).

Advocacy groups are always an important force, even in routine policy-making (Sabatier and Jenkins-Smith 1993). And they are becoming more so, in networked transnational society (Keck and Sikkink 1998; Risse, Ropp, and Sikkink 1999). But they are often treated as "just another interested party"—like physicians vis-à-vis the NHS—speaking for narrow sectoral interests alone, however much they might pretend otherwise. Even (or perhaps especially) self-styled "public interest lobbies" like Common Cause are often said to lack any authority to speak with any authority about what is "in the public interest:" "Self-styled" is importantly different from "duly elected," as members of Congress regularly remind Common Cause lobbyists (Macfarland 1976; Berry 1977).

Social movements are advocacy coalitions writ large. They bring pressure to bear where politically it matters, in terms of democratic theory: on elected officials. Sometimes the pressure succeeds, and Voting Rights Acts are legislated. Other times it fails, and the Equal Rights Amendment gets past Congress but is stymied by political countermobilization in state houses (Mansbridge 1986). Sometimes there is no very precise set of legislative demands in view, as with the "poor people's movement" of the early 1970s (Piven and Cloward 1979), and the aim is mostly just to alter the tone of the national debate.

There is always an element of that, in any social movement. Even social movements ostensibly organized around specific legal texts—the proposed Great Charter or Equal Rights Amendment—were always about much more than merely enacting those texts into law. Still, for social movements to have any impact on policy, they have to have some relatively specific policy implications. Every social movement, if it is to make any material difference, has to have a determinate answer to the question, "What do we want, and when do we want it?"

A full discussion of social movements would take us deep into the territory covered by other *Handbooks* in the series. But there are some things to be said about them, purely from a policy perspective. Consider the question of why social movements seem eventually to run out of steam. Many of the reasons are rooted in their political sociology: They lose touch with their grassroots; they get outmaneuvered in the centers of power; and so on (Tarrow 1994). But another reason, surely, is that they sometimes simply "run out of ideas." They no longer have any clear idea what they want, in policy terms. Winning the sympathies of legislators and their constituents counts for naught, if movements cannot follow up with some specific draft bill to drop into the legislative hopper.

That was at least part of the story behind the waning of the civil rights and feminist movements in the USA as sources of demand for legislative or administrative change. At some point there was a general sense, among policy-makers and mass publics, that there was simply not much more that could be done through legislation and public administration to fix the undeniable problems of racial and sexual injustice that remained. The policy-making garbage can was simply empty of the crucial element of "ideas."

Even more narrowly focused advocacy coalitions experience the same phenomenon of "running out of steam" for the lack of further ideas. Consider the case of the "safety coalition" so prominent in US policy-making in the 1960s (Walker 1977). It first mobilized around the issue of coal mine safety. That was a problem that had been widely discussed both in technical professional journals and in the wider public for some time; everyone had a pretty clear understanding of the nature of the problems and of what might constitute possible solutions. Having successfully enacted coal mine safety legislation, the safety coalition—like any good denizen of the policy-making garbage can—went looking for what to do next. Auto safety emerged. There, the issue was less "ripe," in the sense that there had been less discussion both in technical journals and in the public press. Still, auto safety legislation was enacted. What to do next? The safety coalition then seized upon "occupational health and safety," an issue about which there had been very little public discussion and little technical scientific discussion. A law was passed, but it was a law with little general backing that in effect discredited the safety coalition and inhibited it from playing any serious role in public policy discussions for more than a decade to come. It revived, in a different guise, only after the accident at the Three Mile Island nuclear reactor.

9 PUZZLES, PROBLEMS, AND PERSUASION

Policy gets made in response to problems. But what is perceived as puzzling or problematic is not predetermined or fixed for all time. The public's policy agenda shifts as "personal troubles" shift into and out of the realm of perceived "social problems" (Mills 1959). In part, this is a matter of a gestalt shift to "whose problem it is." And in part it is a matter of transforming sheer "puzzles" into "actionable problems:" If no solution can be envisaged, then for all *practical* purposes there simply is no problem.

The "progressive agenda" had the state assuming increasing responsibility for personal troubles (Rose-Ackerman 1992; Crenson 1998). The catchcry of the opposite agenda is "personal responsibility," with the state washing its own hands of responsibility for "personal troubles" ranging from health to income security (Wikler 1987; Schmidtz and Goodin 1998). "Deinstitutionalization"—the decanting of asylums' inmates into cardboard boxes across America—is perhaps the saddest instance (Dear and Wolch 1987; Mechanic and Rochefort 1990). But in a way this twentieth-century morality play was just a reenactment of the earlier processes by which seventeenth-century poor laws emerged as a solution to the public nuisance of vagrancy, only to be shifted over subsequent centuries to punitive regimes of workhouses in hopes of forcing the undeserving poor to take more responsibility for their own lives (Blaug 1963).

Policy is sometimes simply overtaken by events. Whole swathes of policy regulating obsolete technologies become redundant with technological advances. Military strategies designed to contain one opponent become redundant, or worse, when one's opponent shifts.

Policy disputes are often resolved by reframing. Lincoln's great genius, on one account, was reframing the argument over slavery: not as one over abolitionism, but rather as one over the extension of slavery to new territories, and the dangers for free white men in having to compete there against cheap slave labor (Hofstadter 1948, ch. 5).

Policy proposals gain political traction by "hitching a ride" on other policies more in tune with general social values. Described as "a free lunch," proposals for giving everyone a guaranteed basic income are politically dead in the water (Moynihan 1973). Described as "participation income," paying people for socially useful work—or better still, as a form of "workfare"—the same policies might be real runners, politically (Atkinson 1996; Goodin 2001).

Policy disputes are as often resolved by some telling new fact. The rights and wrongs of policies of nuclear deterrence had been hotly contested, both morally and strategically, for more than a quarter of a century; but the unthinkable became truly unthinkable when Carl Sagan pointed out the risk that any large-scale use of nuclear weapons might initiate a "nuclear winter" destroying all life even in the country initiating the attack (Sagan 1983–4; see also Sagan and Turco 1990). Or again: the rights and wrongs of banning smoking in public places had been hotly contested for years; but once the risks of "passive smoking" became known, it ceased being a matter of moral dispute and became a straightforward issue of preventing public assaults (Goodin 1989).

Issues cease being issues for all sorts of reasons: some good, some bad. "Benign neglect" might have been the best way of treating all sorts of issues, ranging from race to abortion (Luker 1984). Making public policy can often be a mistake. But making an issue of child abuse and neglect was almost certainly not a mistake (Nelson 1984). The difference between those cases is that in the former there was a real risk of countermobilization undoing any good done by making de facto policies more public, whereas in the latter there seems little risk of countermobilization by or even on behalf of child abusers.

Thinking about the way issues become, or fail to become, policy "problems" takes us right back to the heart of the argument about the persuasive vocation of policy studies. We have argued that the grounds for this persuasive conception are formidable. They include the limits of instrumental rationality; the importance of deliberation in policy formation; the overwhelming evidence of the way modern governing conditions demand a style of policy-making that maximizes consultation and voluntary coordination.

"High modernism" is an anachronism. Running modern government by its dictates is like trying to assemble motor cars on a replica of one of Ford's 1920s assembly lines—a recipe for defective production, when interacting components are not fully decomposable (Simon 1981).

But the pursuit of this persuasive vocation is a hard road to follow. It demands a unique combination of skills: the skills of "normal" social science allied to the skills of "rhetoric" in the best sense of that much misused word. And the persuasive vocation must be practiced in a hostile world. There is hostility from pressed decision-makers who feel impelled to make rapid decisions in the face of urgency or even crisis; hostility from the still powerful administrative doctrines associated with the high modernist project; and hostility from entrenched powers and interests threatened by more reflective and inclusive modes of decision. Intellectually anachronistic doctrines continue to flourish in the world of policy practice for a whole range of reasons, and all are applicable to the case of high modernism. Within bureaucracies and in the vastly rewarding consulting industries that have grown up around the New Public Management there is a huge investment—intellectual and financial—in the modernistic drive for measurement and hierarchical control (Power 1997). Individual crazes still sweep across policy worlds because they offer possibilities of evading democratic control: The enthusiasm for evidence-based policy-making in arenas like health care is a case in point (Harrison, Moran, and Wood 2002). And in the promotion of one key variant of high modernism—globalization—key global management institutions like the World Bank and the IMF continue to promote standardized reform packages (Rodrik 1997; Stiglitz 2002; Cammack 2002).

So, in the end, the persuasive appeal comes back to power and interests. Which is to say, politics. Just as the founders of the policy sciences told us from the start.

Policy analysts use the imperfect tools of their trade not only to assist legitimately elected officials in implementing their democratic mandates but also to empower some groups rather than others. Furthermore, policy is never permanent, made once and for all time. Puzzles get transformed into actionable problems, and policies get made on that basis. But that gives rise to further puzzlement, and the quest for ways of acting on those new problems. The persuasive task of policy-making and analysis alike lodges in these dynamics of deciding which puzzle to solve, what counts as a solution, and whose interests to serve.

References

AARON, H. J. and REISCHAUER, R. D. (eds.) 1999. *Setting National Priorities*. Washington, DC: Brookings Institution Press.

ACKERMAN, B. A. and FISHKIN, J. F. 2004. *Deliberation Day*. New Haven, Conn.: Yale University Press.

ALLISON, G. T. and ZELIKOW, P. 1999. *The Essence of Decision*, 2nd edn. Reading, Mass.: Longman.

ANTON, T. J. 1980. *Administered Politics: Elite Political Culture in Sweden*. Boston: Martinus Nijhoff.

ARROW, K. J. 1962. The economic implications of learning by doing. *Review of Economic Studies*, 29: 155–73.

—— and HAHN, F. 1971. *General Competitive Analysis*. San Francisco: Holden-Day.

ASPA (American Society for Public Administration) 1984. *Code of Ethics*. Washington, DC: ASPA.

ATIYAH, P. S. 1979. *The Rise and Fall of Freedom of Contract*. Oxford: Clarendon Press.

ATKINSON, A. B. 1996. The case for a participation income. *Political Quarterly*, 67: 67–70.

ATKINSON, T., CANTILLION, B., MARLIER, E., and NOLAN, B. 2002. *Social Indicators: The EU and Social Inclusion*. Oxford: Oxford University Press.

BARDACH, E. 1977. *The Implementation Game: What Happens After a Bill Becomes a Law*. Cambridge, Mass.: MIT Press.

BARDACH, E. 1980. On desiging implementable programs. Pp. 138–58 in Majone and Quade 1980.

BECK, U. 1992. *The Risk Society*, trans. M. Ritter. London: Sage.

BENTHAM, J. 1787. Panopticon: or, the Inspection-House: Containing the idea of a new principle of construction applicable to penitentiary-houses, prisons, houses of industry, work-houses, poor-houses, manufactories, mad-houses, hospitals, and schools; with a plan of management adapted to the principle. In Volume 4 of *The Works of Jeremy Bentham*, ed. J. Bowring. Edinburgh: William Tait, 1843.

BERRY, J. M. 1977. *Lobbying for the People*. Princeton, NJ: Princeton University Press.

BETTS, R. K. 1978. Analysis, war and decision: why intelligence failures are inevitable. *World Politics*, 31: 61–89.

BLAU, P. M. 1963. *The Dynamics of Bureaucracy*, 2nd edn. Chicago: University of Chicago Press.

BLAUG, M. 1963. The myth of the old poor law and the making of the new. *Journal of Economic History*, 23: 151–84.

BOVENS, M. A. P. 1990. The social steering of complex organizations. *British Journal of Political Science*, 20: 91–117.

——1998. *The Quest for Responsibility: Accountability and Citizenship in Complex Organizations*. Cambridge: Cambridge University Press.

—— and 'T HART, P. 1996. *Understanding Policy Fiascos*. New Brunswick, NJ: Transaction.

BRAITHWAITE, J. and DRAHOS, P. 2000. *Global Business Regulation*. Cambridge: Cambridge University Press.

—— MAKKAI, T., BRAITHWAITE, V., and GIBSON, D. 1993. *Raising the Standard*, Final Report of the Nursing Home Regulation in Action Project to the Department of Health, Housing and Community Services. Canberra: AGPS.

CAIN, B., DALTON, R., and SCARROW, S. (eds.) 2003. *Democracy Transformed? Expanding Political Opportunities in Advanced Industrial Democracies*. Oxford: Oxford University Press.

CALVERT, R., McCUBBINS, M. D., and WEINGAST, B. R. 1989. A theory of political control and agency discretion. *American Journal of Political Science*, 33: 588–61.

CAMMACK, P. 2002. The mother of all governments: the World Bank's matrix for global governance. Pp. 36–53 in *Global Governance: Critical Perspectives*, ed. R. Wilkinson and S. Hughes. London: Routledge.

CASTELLS, M. 2000. Materials for an exploratory theory of the network society. *British Journal of Sociology*, 51: 5–24.

CASTLES, F. G. 1985. *The Working Class and the Welfare State: Reflections on the Political Development of the Welfare State in Australia and New Zealand, 1890–1980*. Sydney: Allen and Unwin.

——2001. A farewell to Australia's welfare state. *International Journal of Health Services*, 31: 537–44.

COASE, R. H. 1937. The nature of the firm. *Economica*, 4: 386–405.

——1974. The market for goods and the market for ideas. *American Economic Review (Papers and Proceedings)*, 64: 384–402.

COMMISSION ON PUBLIC PRIVATE PARTNERSHIPS 2001. *Building Better Partnerships*. London: Institute for Public Policy Research.

COURPASSON, D. 2000. Managerial strategies of domination: power in soft bureaucracies. *Organization Studies*, 21: 141–61.

CRENSON, M. A. 1998. *Building the Invisible Orphanage: A Prehistory of the American Welfare System*. Cambridge, Mass.: Harvard University Press.

CROZIER, M., HUNTINGTON, S., and WATANUKI, J. 1975. *The Crisis of Democracy*. New York: New York University Press.

DAHL, R. A. 1985. *A Preface to Economic Democracy*. Berkeley: University of California Press.

DAY, P. and KLEIN, R. 1987. *Accountabilities: Five Public Services*. London: Tavistock.

DEAR, M. J. and WOLCH, J. R. 1987. *Landscapes of Despair: from Deinstitutionalization to Homelessness*. Princeton, NJ: Princeton University Press.

DERTHICK, M. 1975. *Uncontrollable Spending for Social Services Grants*. Washington, DC: Brookings Institution.

DEUTSCH, K. 1963. *The Nerves of Government*. Glencoe, Ill.: Free Press.

DICEY, A. V. 1960. *Introduction to the Study of the Law of the Constitution*, 10th edn. London: Macmillan. First published 1885.

DOWNS, A. 1972. Up and down with ecology: the issue-attention cycle. *Public Interest*, 28: 38–50.

DRYZEK, J. S. 2000. *Deliberative Democracy and Beyond*. Oxford: Oxford University Press.

DUNLEAVY, P. 1981. *The Politics of Mass Housing 1945–75*. Oxford: Clarendon Press.

—— 1995. Policy disasters: explaining the UK's record. *Public Policy and Administration*, 10: 52–70.

DYSON, K. 1980. *The State Tradition in Western Europe*. Oxford: Martin Robertson.

—— and WILKS, S. (eds.) 1983. *Industrial Crisis: A Comparative Study of the State and Industry*. Oxford: Martin Robertson.

ESPING-ANDERSEN, G. 1985. *Politics against Markets*. Princeton, NJ: Princeton University Press.

ETZIONI, A. 1965. *A Comparative Analysis of Complex Organizations*. New York: Free Press.

FISCHER, F. 2003. *Reframing Public Policy: Discursive Politics and Deliberative Practices*. Oxford: Oxford University Press.

—— and FORESTER, J. (eds.) 1993. *The Argumentative Turn in Policy Analysis and Planning*. Durham, NC: Duke University Press.

FRIED, C. 2004. *Saying What the Law Is*. Cambridge, Mass.: Harvard University Press.

FUNG, A. 2004. *Empowering Democracy*. Chicago: University of Chicago Press.

—— and WRIGHT, E. O. 2001. Deepening democracy: innovations in empowered participatory governance. *Politics and Society*, 29: 5–41.

GALANTER, M. 1974. Why the "haves" come out ahead: speculations on the limits of legal change. *Law and Society Review*, 9: 95–160.

GIBSON, D. M. and GOODIN, R. E. 1999. The veil of vagueness. Pp. 357–85 in *Organizing Political Institutions: Essays for Johan P. Olsen*, ed. M. Egeberg and P. Lægreid. Oslo: Scandinavian University Press.

GOODIN, R. E. 1982. *Political Theory and Public Policy*. Chicago: University of Chicago Press.

—— 1989. *No Smoking*. Chicago: University of Chicago Press.

—— 2001. Something for nothing? Pp. 90–8 in P. Van Parijs et al., *What's Wrong With a Free Lunch?*, ed. J. Cohen and J. Rogers. Boston: Beacon.

—— 2003. Democratic accountability: the distinctiveness of the Third Sector. *Archives européennes de sociologie*, 44: 359–96.

GOODSELL, C. T. 1992. The public administrator as artisan. *Public Administration Review*, 52: 246–53.

GORE, A. 1993. *From Red Tape to Results: Creating a Government that Works Better and Costs Less*. Report of the National Performance Review. Washington, DC: Government Printing Office.

GRANT, W. 1997. *The Common Agricultural Policy*. London: Palgrave Macmillan.

GREENSTEIN, F. I. 1982. *The Hidden-Hand Presidency: Eisenhower as Leader*. New York: Basic Books.

HAJER, M. A. 1995. *The Politics of Environmental Discourse.* Oxford: Clarendon Press.

——2003. Policy without polity? Policy analysis and the institutional void. *Policy Sciences*, 36: 175–95.

——and WAGENAAR, H. (eds.) 2003. *Deliberative Policy Analysis.* Cambridge: Cambridge University Press.

HALBERSTAM, D. 1969. *The Best and the Brightest.* New York: Random House.

HALL, P. (ed.) 1989. *The Political Power of Economic Ideas.* Princeton, NJ: Princeton University Press.

HARRISON, S., MORAN, M., and WOOD, B. 2002. Policy emergence and policy convergence: the case of "scientific-bureaucratic" medicine in the United States and the United Kingdom. *British Journal of Politics and International Relations*, 4: 1–24.

HART, H. L. A. 1961. *The Concept of Law.* Oxford: Clarendon Press.

HAVEMAN, R. H. and MARGOLIS, J. (eds.) 1983. *Public Expenditure and Policy Analysis.* Boston: Houghton-Mifflin.

HECLO, H. 1978. Issue networks and the executive establishment. Pp. 87–124 in *The New American Political System*, ed. A. King. Washington, DC: American Enterprise Institute.

——and WILDAVSKY, A. 1974. *The Private Government of Public Money.* London: Macmillan.

HENDERSON, P. D. 1977. Two British errors: their probable size and some possible lessons. *Oxford Economic Papers*, 29: 159–205.

HÉRITIER, A. 1999. *Public Policymaking and Diversity in Europe: Escaping Deadlock.* Cambridge: Cambridge University Press.

HIRSCH, F. 1976. *Social Limits to Growth.* Cambridge, Mass.: Harvard University Press.

HIRSCHMAN, A. O. 1982. *Shifting Involvements: Private Interest and Public Action.* Oxford: Martin Robertson.

HITCH, C. J. 1958. Economics and military operations research. *Review of Economics and Statistics*, 40: 119–209.

——and McKEAN, R. N. 1960. *The Economics of Defense in the Nuclear Age.* Cambridge, Mass.: Harvard University Press.

HOFSTADTER, R. 1948. *The American Political Tradition and the Men Who Made It.* New York: Knopf.

HOGWOOD, B. and PETERS, B. G. 1985. *The Pathology of Public Policy.* Oxford: Clarendon Press.

HOOD, C. 1976. *The Limits of Administration.* London: Wiley.

——1983. *The Tools of Government.* London: Macmillan.

KATZ, R. and MAIR, P. 1995. Changing models of party organization and party democracy: the emergence of the cartel party. *Party Politics*, 1: 5–28.

KAUFMANN, F.-X., MAJONE, G., and OSTROM, V. (eds.) 1985. *Guidance, Control and Evaluation in the Public Sector.* Berlin: W. de Gruyter.

KECK, M. and SIKKINK, K. 1998. *Activists beyond Borders: Advocacy Networks in International Politics.* Ithaca, NY: Cornell University Press.

KING, A. 1975. Overload. *Political Studies*, 23: 284–96.

KINGDON, J. 1984. *Agendas, Alternatives and Public Policies.* Boston: Little, Brown.

KLEIN, R. 2001. *The New Politics of the NHS*, 4th edn. Harlow: Prentice Hall.

KNEESE, A. V. and SCHULTZE, C. L. 1975. *Pollution, Prices and Public Policy.* Washington, DC: Brookings Institution.

KORNAI, J., MASKIN, E., and ROLAND, G. 2003. Understanding the soft budget constraint. *Journal of Economic Literature*, 41: 1095–136.

LA PORTE, T. R. (ed.) 1975. *Organized Social Complexity.* Princeton, NJ: Princeton University Press.

LASSWELL, H. D. 1941. The garrison state. *American Journal of Sociology*, 46: 455–68.

—— 1950. *Politics: Who Gets What, When, How?* New York: P. Smith.

—— 1951. The policy orientation. Pp. 3–15 in Lerner and Lasswell 1951.

LE GRAND, J. 1991. Quasi-markets and social policy. *Economic Journal*, 101: 1256–67.

LERNER, D. and LASSWELL, H. D. (eds.) 1951. *The Policy Sciences*. Stanford, Calif.: Stanford University Press.

LEVI, M. 1988. *Of Rule and Revenue*. Los Angeles: University of California Press.

LEVI-FAUR, D. 2003. The politics of liberalization: privatization and regulation-for-competition in Europe's and Latin America's telecoms and electric industries. *European Journal of Political Research*, 42: 705–40.

LEVINE, H. D. 1977. Some things to all men: the politics of cruise missile development. *Public Policy*, 25: 117–68.

LIJPHART, A. 1999. *Patterns of Democracy*. New Haven, Conn.: Yale Univeristy Press.

LINDBLOM, C. E. 1965. *The Intelligence of Democracy*. New York: Free Press.

—— 1977. *Politics and Markets*. New York: Basic Books.

—— 1979. Still muddling: not yet through. *Public Administration Review*, 39: 517–26.

LIPSKY, M. 1980. *Street Level Bureaucracy*. New York: Russell Sage.

LOCKE, J. 1690. *Second Treatise of Government*, ed. P. Laslett. Cambridge: Cambridge University Press, 1960.

LUKER, K. 1984. *Abortion and the Politics of Motherhood*. Los Angeles: University of California Press.

LYNN, N. B. and WILDAVSKY, A. (eds.) 1990. *Public Administration: The State of the Discipline*. Chatham, NJ: Chatham House.

MacDONAGH, O. 1958. The nineteenth-century revolution in government: a reappraisal. *Historical Journal*, 1: 52–67.

—— 1961. *A Pattern of Government Growth, 1800–1860*. London: MacGibbon and Kee.

McFARLAND, A. S. 1976. *Public Interest Lobbies*. Washington, DC: American Enterprise Institute.

MACKENZIE, W. J. M. 1963. The Plowden Report: a translation. *Public Administration*. Repr. pp. 238–51 in Mackenzie, *Explorations in Government*. London: Macmillan, 1975.

MAJONE, G. 1989. *Evidence, Argument, and Persuasion in the Policy Process*. New Haven, Conn.: Yale University Press.

—— 1994. Paradoxes of privatization and deregulation. *Journal of European Public Policy*, 1: 53–69.

—— and QUADE, E. S. (eds.) 1980. *Pitfalls of Analysis*. Chichester: Wiley, for International Institute for Applied Systems Analysis.

MANSBRIDGE, J. J. 1986. *Why we Lost the ERA*. Chicago: University of Chicago Press.

MARCH, J. G. 1972. Model bias in social action. *Review of Educational Research*, 42: 413–29.

—— 1976. The technology of foolishness. Pp. 69–81 in March and Olsen 1976.

—— and OLSEN, J. P. 1976. *Ambiguity and Choice in Organizations*. Bergen: Universitetsforlaget.

—— SPROUL, L. S., and TAMUZ, M. 1991. Learning from samples of one or fewer. *Organization Science*, 2: 1–13.

MARMOR, T. R. 1994. *Understanding Health Care Reform*. New Haven, Conn.: Yale University Press.

—— and THOMAS, D. 1972. Doctors, politics and pay disputes: "Pressure Group Politics" revisited. *British Journal of Political Science*, 2: 421–42.

MARRIS, P. and REIN, M. 1982. *Dilemmas of Social Reform*, 2nd edn. Chicago: University of Chicago Press. Originally published 1967.

MARSHALL, G. 1984. *Constitutional Conventions*. Oxford: Clarendon Press.

MEADE, J. E. 1970. *The Theory of Indicative Planning*. Manchester: Manchester University Press.

MECHANIC, D. and ROCHEFORT, D. A. 1990. Deinstitutionalization: an appraisal of reform. *Annual Review of Sociology*, 16: 301–27.

MEIJER, H. 1969. Bureaucracy and policy formulation in Sweden. *Scandinavian Political Studies*, 4: 102–16.

MERTON, R. K. 1936. The unintended consequences of purposive social action. *American Sociological Review*, 1: 894–904.

MILLS, C. W. 1959. *The Sociological Imagination*. New York: Oxford University Press.

MORAN, M. 2003. *The British Regulatory State: High Modernism and Hyper-innovation*. Oxford: Oxford University Press.

MOYNIHAN, D. P. 1973. *The Politics of a Guaranteed Income: The Nixon Administration and the Family Assistance Plan*. New York: Random House.

MURRAY, C. 1984. *Losing Ground: American Social Policy, 1950–80*. New York: Basic.

MYRDAL, G. 1944. *The American Dilemma*. New York: Harper and Row.

——1955. *Realities and Illusions in Regard to Inter-Governmental Organizations*. L. T. Hobhouse Memorial Trust Lecture, No. 24; delivered at Bedford College, London, Feb. 25, 1954. London: Oxford University Press.

NELSON, B. J. 1984. *Making an Issue of Child Abuse: Political Agenda Setting for Social Problems*. Chicago: University of Chicago Press.

NEUSTADT, R. E. 1960. *Presidential Power*. New York: Wiley.

——and MAY, E. R. 1986. *Thinking in Time*. New York: Free Press.

NEWMAN, O. 1972. *Defensible Space: Crime Prevention through Urban Design*. New York: Macmillan.

NORTH, D. 1990. *Institutions, Institutional Change and Economic Performance*. Cambridge: Cambridge University Press.

OFFE, C. 1984. *Contradictions of the Welfare State*. Cambridge, Mass: MIT Press.

——2003. The European model of "social" capitalism: can it survive European integration? *Journal of Political Philosophy*, 12: 437–69.

OLSEN, J. P. 1972a. Public policymaking and theories of organizational choice. *Scandinavian Political Studies*, 7: 45–62.

——1972b. Voting, "sounding out" and the governance of modern organisations. *Acta Sociologica*, 15: 267–84.

OSBORNE, D. and GAEBLER, T. 1993. *Reinventing Government*. New York: Plume/Penguin.

PAGE, B. I. 1983. *Who Gets What from Government?* Berkeley: University of California Press.

PETERS, B. G. and PIERRE, J. (eds.) 2003. *Handbook of Public Administration*. Thousand Oaks, Calif.: Sage.

—— ——2004. *Politicization of the Civil Service in Comparative Perspective: The Quest for Control*. London: Routledge.

PIERSON, P. 1994. *Dismantling the Welfare State? Reagan, Thatcher, and the Politics of Retrenchment*. New York: Cambridge University Press.

——2000. Increasing returns, path dependence and the study of politics. *American Political Science Review*, 94: 251–68.

PIVEN, F. F. and CLOWARD, R. A. 1979. *Poor People's Movements: Why They Succeed, How They Fail*. New York: Vintage.

POWER, M. 1997. *The Audit Society: Rituals of Verification*. Oxford: Oxford University Press.

PRESSMAN, J. L. and WILDAVSKY, A. 1973. *Implementation*. Los Angeles: University of California Press.

PUTNAM, R. D. 1993. *Making Democracy Work: Civic Traditions in Modern Italy*. Princeton, NJ: Princeton University Press.

RAND CORPORATION 2004. History and mission. Available at: <www.rand.org/about/history> (accessed July 10, 2004).

REICH, R. B. (ed.) 1988. *The Power of Public Ideas*. Cambridge, Mass.: Ballinger.

REIN, M. 1976. *Social Science and Public Policy*. Harmondsworth: Penguin.

REHBINDER, E. and STEWART, R. 1985. *Environmental Protection Policy*. Berlin: Walter de Gruyter.

RHODES, R. A. W. 1988. *Beyond Westminster and Whitehall*. London: Unwin Hyman.

—— 1997. *Understanding Governance: Policy Networks, Governance and Accountability*. Buckingham: Open University Press.

RISSE, T., ROPP, S. C., and SIKKINK, K. (ed.) 1999. *The Power of Human Rights: International Norms and Domestic Change*. Cambridge: Cambridge University Press.

RIVLIN, A. M. 1971. *Systematic Thinking for Social Action*. Washington, DC: Brookings Institution.

RODRIK, D. 1997. *Has Globalization Gone Too Far?* Washington, DC: Institution of International Economics.

ROSE-ACKERMAN, S. 1992. *Rethinking the Progressive Agenda*. New York: Free Press.

—— 1996. Altruism, nonprofits and economic theory. *Journal of Economic Literature*, 34: 701–28.

SABATIER, P. A. and JENKINS-SMITH, H. C. (eds.) 1993. *Policy Change and Learning: An Advocacy Coalition Approach*. Boulder, Colo.: Westview.

SACHS, J. 1995. Shock therapy in Poland: perspectives of 5 years. *Tanner Lectures on Human Values*, 16: 265–90.

SAGAN, C. 1983–4. Nuclear war and climate consequence: some policy implications. *Foreign Affairs*, 62: 257–92.

—— and TURCO, R. 1990. *A Path Where No Man Thought: Nuclear Winter and the End of the Arms Race*. New York: Random House.

SALAMON, L. (ed.) 2002. *The Tools of Government: A Guide to the New Governance*. Oxford: Oxford University Press.

SALTMAN, R. and VON OTTER, C. 1992. *Planned Markets and Public Competition: Strategic Reform in Northern European Health Systems*. Buckingham: Open University Press.

SCHARPF, F. W. 1988. The joint decision trap: lessons from German federalism and European integration. *Public Administration*, 66: 239–78.

SCHMIDTZ, D. and GOODIN, R. E. 1998. *Social Welfare and Individual Responsibility*. Cambridge: Cambridge University Press.

SCHON, D. A. and REIN, M. 1994. *Frame Reflection: Toward the Resolution of Intractable Policy Controversies*. New York: Basic.

SCHULTZE, C. L. 1977. *The Public Use of Private Interest*. Washington, DC: Brookings Institution.

SCHUMPETER, J. A. 1950. *Capitalism, Socialism and Democracy*, 3rd edn. New York: Harper and Row.

SCOTT, J. C. 1985. *Weapons of the Weak*. New Haven, Conn.: Yale University Press.

—— 1997. *Seeing Like a State*. New Haven, Conn.: Yale University Press.

SELF, P. 1975. *Econocrats and the Policy Process: The Politics and Philosophy of Cost–Benefit Analysis*. London: Macmillan.

—— 1993. *Government by the Market?* London: Macmillan.

—— and STORING, H. 1962. *The State and the Farmer*. London: Allen and Unwin.

SHAPIRO, I. 1999. Enough of deliberation: politics is about interests and power. Pp. 28–38 in *Deliberative Politics,* ed. S. Macedo. New York: Oxford University Press.

SIMON, H. A. 1951. A formal theory of the employment relationship. *Econometrica*, 19: 293–305.

—— 1955. A behavioral theory of rational choice. *Quarterly Journal of Economics*, 69: 99–118.

—— 1981. *The Sciences of the Artificial*, 2nd edn. Cambridge, Mass.: MIT Press.

—— 2000. Public administration in today's world of organizations and markets. *PS: Political Science and Politics*, 33: 749–56.

SKOCPOL, T. 1992. *Protecting Soldiers and Mothers: The Political Origins of Social Policy in the United States*. Cambridge, Mass.: Harvard University Press.

SMITH, M. 1990. *The Politics of Agricultural Support in Britain: Development of the Agricultural Policy Community*. Aldershot: Dartmouth.

SMITH, S. R. and LIPSKY, M. 1993. *Non-profits for Hire: The Welfare State in an Age of Contracting*. Cambridge, Mass.: Harvard University Press.

STEINER, J., BÄCHTIGER, A. B, SPÖRNDLI, M., and STEENBERGEN, M. R. 2005. *Deliberative Politics in Action: Cross-national Study of Parliamentary Debates*. Cambridge: Cambridge University Press.

STIGLITZ, J. E. 2002. *Globalization and its Discontents*. London: Penguin.

STOKEY, E. and ZECKHAUSER, R. 1978. *A Primer for Policy Analysis*. New York: Norton.

SUNSTEIN, C. R. 1993. *Democracy and the Problem of Free Speech*. New York: Free Press.

—— 2001. *Republic.com*. Princeton, NJ: Princeton University Press.

TARROW, S. G. 1994. *Power in Movement: Social Movements, Collective Action and Politics*. New York: Cambridge University Press.

TILLY, C. 1999. Power: top down and bottom up. *Journal of Political Philosophy*, 7: 330–52.

UCS (Union of Concerned Scientists) 2004. *Scientific Integrity in Policymaking: An Investigation into the Bush Administration's Misuse of Science*. Available at: <www.ucsusa.org/global_environment/rsi/page.cfm?pageID=1322> (accessed July 10, 2004).

US COMPTROLLER GENERAL 1979. *Higher Penalties Could Deter Violations of Nuclear Regulations*. Report to the Congress EMD-79-9. Washington, DC: General Accounting Office.

VAN EVERA, S. 2003. Why states believe foolish ideas: non-self-evaluation by states and societies. In *Perspectives on Structural Realism*, ed. A. Hanami and S. Walt. New York: Palgrave.

VAN GUNSTEREN, H. 1976. *The Quest for Control*. London: Wiley.

VICKERS, G. 1983. *The Art of Judgment: A Study of Policy Making*. London: Harper and Row.

WALKER, J. L. 1969. The diffusion of innovations among the American states. *American Political Science Review*, 63: 880–99.

WALKER, J. L. 1977. Setting the agenda in the U.S. Senate: a theory of problem selection. *British Journal of Political Science*, 7: 423–46.

WIKLER, D. 1987. Personal responsibility for illness. Pp. 326–58 in *Health Care Ethics*, ed. D. van de Veer and T. Regan. Philadelphia: Temple University Press.

WILDAVSKY, A. 1973. If planning is everything, maybe it's nothing. *Policy Sciences*, 4: 127–53.

—— 1979. *Speaking the Truth to Power: The Art and Craft of Policy Analysis*. Boston: Little, Brown.

WILLIAMSON, O. E. 1985. *The Economic Institutions of Capitalism: Firms, Markets, Relational Contracting*. New York: Free Press.

WILSON, J. Q. and KELLING, G. L. 1982. Broken windows. *Atlantic Monthly*, 249: 29–38.

WILSON, W. 1887. The study of administration. *Political Science Quarterly*, 56: 481–506.

WILSON, W. J. 1987. *The Truly Disadvantaged: The Inner City, the Underclass and Public Policy.*
Chicago: University of Chicago Press.

WORLD BANK 1994. *Averting the Old Age Crisis: Policies to Protect the Old and Promote Growth.*
New York: Oxford University Press.

——1996. *World Development Report 1996: From Plan to Market.* Oxford: Oxford University
Press, for the World Bank.

——1997. *The State in a Changing World: World Development Report 1997.* Washington, DC:
World Bank.

YOUNG, I. M. 2000. *Inclusion and Democracy.* Oxford: Oxford University Press.

ZOLBERG, A. 1972. Moments of madness. *Politics and Society,* 2: 183–208.

CHAPTER 44

SOCIAL AND CULTURAL FACTORS

CONSTRAINING AND ENABLING

DAVIS B. BOBROW

When a pickpocket looks at a king all he sees is pockets.

(Senegalese saying)

understanding how it is that men's notions, however implicit, of the "really real" and the dispositions these notions induce in them, color their sense of the reasonable, the practical, the humane, and the moral.

(Clifford Geertz 1973, 124)

1 INTRODUCTION

Public policy never begins with a blank slate whether we are talking about how and why it is made or whether it plays out in terms of wanted or unwanted consequences.

* I am indebted to my two favorite anthropologists, Gail Benjamin and Riall Nolan, for their suggestions.

Policy makers, implementers, target populations, and their audiences already hold and use a complex of "notions" to arrive at choices and evaluations (as Geertz suggests). Those "notions" affect what is treated as more or less relevant, important, and desirable—from information to material assets to institutions to skills to normative judgements. They "load the dice" with regard to public policy indicators, focal situations, issue categories, cause and effect judgements, strategic repertoires, and success criteria. They even define what is for people, public policy and politics (Hudson 1997; Thompson, Grendstad, and Selle 1999). Notions in use amount to constraints on and enablers for public policy.[1]

How well we explain the occurrence and consequences of one or another policy or policy problem depends significantly on how well we understand the notions used by actors involved with it. How effectively we shape policy seldom will be greater than our understanding of the notions used by those who matter for policy adoption and implementation (Elmore 1985). For example, law enforcement attempts to curtail gang-related crime in Chicago ghettos would benefit from recognizing that for the residents, both gangs and the police are sources of protection *and* exploitation (Akerlof and Yellen 1994). How accurately we predict the effects of chosen policies depends on understanding of the notions used by those populations the policies seek to influence. Such understandings often amount to awareness of what is "local knowledge" for the various parties to public policy and policy processes, be they White House staffs or impoverished female heads of households.

Meeting those challenges encounters at least two major complications. One is that of variety: "what men believe is as various as what they are—a proposition that holds with equal force when it is inverted" (Geertz 1973, 124).[2] In the Senegalese saying, what is for some a ruler is for others a set of professional opportunities. A statement or act or material object is then subject to alternative interpretations and thus diverse implications for action and evaluation. The second is a less than total overlap between what people alone and in groups say, what they do, and what they believe (assume, know, or think). There often may be a very substantial difference between what they say to "insiders" (persons they classify as ongoing members of their identity or membership group) and to outsiders. What people actually do can vary as they think their actions are or are not observed by insiders or outsiders. The outsider is faced with the task of seeing behind "veils" and "masks" whether those are worn because of conscious deception or just acceptance of cultural notions—and often less well prepared to do so accurately than are insiders.

---

[1] The premise is not that cultural notions matter *instead* of material and institutional factors (as discussed in Snyder 2002). Rather, it is that such notions lead to important, choice-mediating interpretations of those other sorts of factors, interpretations which provide conditions conducive to their continuity or change.

[2] What level of aggregation is useful or distorting is a recurrent concern, and has raised doubts about looking for and relying on a common characterization of large sets of people categorized by a particular nationality, religion, or even profession (for critical examples of the last, see Kier 1995; Zhang 1992). Charges of excessive aggregation have been leveled at modal personality, national character, and civic culture studies.

Later sections will briefly discuss these complications, and note some ways to cope with them. Those ways feature approaches central in social science fields other than political science—ethnography, sociology, social psychology, cognitive linguistics, and organizational behavior. Yet, as the next section reports, the concepts and methods involved have a substantial history of use by eminent political scientists concerned with public policy. This chapter does not call for doing what is unprecedented in understanding cultural and social constraints and enablers on public policy.[3] It does call for greater attention to the pursuit and application of such understandings, and making such activities as standard a part of the analysis and design of public policies as applied micro- or macroeconomics or law.[4]

2 SOME INTELLECTUAL HISTORY

The sort of political science concerned with public policy in light of cultural and social factors was a feature of the Chicago school which emerged between the First and Second World Wars (Almond 2002, 23–108), and exemplified in the work of Harold Lasswell (e.g. Lasswell 1971, 1951; Lasswell and Fox 1979; Lasswell and Leites 1949). That prominence reflected strong professional relationships with notable sociologists, social psychologists, anthropologists, and linguists. The appeals of policy alternatives and their consequences were shaped by belief systems encoded in symbols. Symbol manipulation was a major part of politics. Political capital included intangible assets such as social status and rectitude as well as material assets such as instruments of coercion and wealth. Indeed the legitimacy and influence of the material was partly a function of the non-material assets accorded by association with and propagation of symbols.

Political appraisals and policy assessments then needed to be informed by three types of inventories of markers for intangibles, and methods to take those inventories. One was of symbol usage and the associations thus invoked. The relevant symbols might be words, but they also might be physical icons and sites used in public rituals. A second was of social memberships and origins (life histories) of policy elites. The premiss was that shares of representation in policy processes served to constrain and enable in one or both of two ways. A predominant share might make some particular set of "notions" prevalent in policy processes. It also might indicate that a broader population viewed those thought to hold certain "notions" as particularly relevant, capable, and normatively sound players of central roles in public policy. A third inventory focused on symbols and complexes of "notions" in and about primary

---

[3] The distinction between social and cultural factors is not useful as the level of modernization distinctions between the sets of people analyzed by sociologists and anthropologists has eroded.

[4] Positively, recent "behavioral economics" innovates by probing relevant populations to get at their "notions" and related actions rather than assuming fit with an assumed model.

social membership groups. That required identifying primary membership groups for actors in the aspect of public policy under consideration.

For Lasswell and his associates, new sorts of knowledge were needed to cope with stunning failures in domestic public policy, and with grave challenges from foreign "others" to favored conceptions about and even the existence of a just and humane world. The inventories would show variety from place to place and time to time. They would be useful for monitoring and countering politically malign actors, and designing strategies to improve and protect a valued political order.

Unsurprisingly, the landmark *The Policy Sciences* (Lerner and Lasswell 1951) included chapters by anthropologists (Kluckhohn on culture and Mead on national character), a sociologist (Shils on primary groups), and a social psychologist (Stouffer on how to discern what is really going on in large organizations). After the Second World War, work by Lasswell's students and their students evolved in several directions with a common intent of arriving at more systematic policy and political system implications. Those efforts sought to organize notions used in official speech by policy elites into operational codes (e.g. Leites 1951; George 1969) and notions expressed by mass populations into profiles of national civic cultures (e.g. Almond and Verba 1963). Subsequent work presented alternative models of political cultures about major policy matters such as budgets and risk management (e.g. Wildavsky 1987, 1988; Thompson, Ellis, and Wildavsky 1990; Douglas and Wildavsky 1982); sweeping characterizations of particular national and regional political systems (e.g. Pye 1988; Pye and Pye 1985); thematic inventories of the notions and related actions of politicians in for them important situations (e.g. Fenno 1990 on US legislators); and reconstructions of the strategic rationales and related actions of ordinary (or even marginal) populations in encounters with public sector policies and institutions (e.g. Scott 1985, 1990 on Malaysian peasants).

It is important to note the scope of this legacy. The actors have ranged from elites to marginal populations, in the USA and abroad. The units have ranged from whole nations to small groups. The methods have ranged from at-a-distance analysis of public documents and interviews with émigrés to large-scale opinion surveys and direct observation (with more or less participation), and sometimes gone further to construct typologies and models. Both quantitative and qualitative tools have been used. To say that policy analysis needs to consider cultural and social factors as constraints and enablers is not to commit to a single methodology or type of data. It is, however, to commit to empirical enquiry, i.e. to beginning if not ending with "thick description" of what people say and do. For those an analyst holds to be of political and public policy interest, "If something is important to them, it becomes important to you. Their view of the world is as important as your view of that world" (Fenno 1990, 113–14).

Work in the Lasswellian tradition does not focus mostly on the texts of a few intellectuals. It does not assume that populations marginal to prevailing systems of power and wealth are especially worthy (or unworthy) of study or of public policy "voice." Priorities should depend on what are crucial roles in the policy process and in its consequences, matters which differ across policy issues, options, and salient events.

Deciding whose notions most call for understanding should not be confounded with moral judgements about who holds meritorious notions. Finally, the Lasswellian tradition recognizes that the cultural and social information it would have us gather can be used for "emancipatory" or oppressive purposes.

3 COMING TO TERMS WITH VARIETY

General laws of political behavior have obvious appeals. Yet public policy in application is less a general than a specific matter in terms of its when and where, who to whom, the options considered, and the consequences of options chosen. Accordingly, most general laws, be they of rational choice utilitarianism, prospect theory anchoring and loss aversion (Levy 1997), or social affiliation and identity (Sen 1977), provide only containers lacking situationally relevant operational content.[5] Applying the containers of utility, costs, and benefits involves imputing what the relevant actors treat as having more or less utility, cost, or benefit. Similar imputations, filling in, are required to get at what anchors are used and losses focused on, or what social affiliations are given great weight.

Policy-relevant applications of such laws involve accurately recognizing what participants pull from their containers to assess cause and effect relations between alternative courses of action in a situation and likely consequences. Excessively general, ahistorical labeling does little to illuminate why some population behaves as it does or what would lead it to act differently. Consider the variety of significations attached in different countries to visits by their heads of state and ordinary citizens to war casualty memorial sites, and even more distinctions between indigenous and foreign interpretations of such commemorative activities (as with domestic and international controversy about Japan's Yasukuni Shinto Shrine; Nelson 2003).

A similar need to specify content in use applies to make informative such broad "classical" cultural and social categories as class, race, ethnicity, religion, nationality, age, or generation. Doing that will often reveal that the category may be a useful summary of aggregate outcomes, but not of much which bears on achieving changes in outcomes. Thus, Thompson and Wildavsky (1986) called for a shift "from economic homogeneity to cultural heterogeneity in the classification of poor people." Suppose the category is being used to anticipate how those placed in it will respond to different policy treatments or interventions. Suppose further that the members of the category have more than one behavioral choice open to them during the time period during which a policy is supposed to accomplish its desired consequences. For example, in the context of US election-related quarantine policies toward Castro's Cuba, it matters

---

[5] To recognize a dimension of possible difference is of course to recognize one of possible similarity. That still leaves a need for content to substantiate contentions about the predominance of similarity or difference (as argued in Johnston 1995).

if relevant voters in Florida think of themselves as primarily Hispanic Americans or as Cuban Americans, and give more weight to ties with relatives in Cuba or to a vision of regime change there.

Realizing the policy maker's anticipations (Cuban-American votes) depends then on the "notions" of the targets with respect to: (*a*) their giving membership or identity primacy to the general category over subdivisions of it and over other categories; and (*b*) their "notions" as they lead them to recognize and evaluate alternatives open to them as category members. The targets are not clay but intentional actors from whom passive compliance and uniform reactions are not givens. Differences in (interpreted) experience with particular public institutions can lead to different general notions of effectiveness in dealing with public institutions and participating in politics more generally (as Soss 1999 found for recipients of two cash-providing US social safety net programs administered in contrasting ways). Specific content will still be needed even if claims are true that we are in an era of new, post-industrial broad categories replacing the "classical" ones (e.g. Clark and Hoffman-Martinot 1998; Inglehart 1990).

Suppose that the use of familiar categories follows less from an intent to shape the ostensible target population and more from judgements about how third parties (e.g. majority populations, taxpayers, allied governments) will react to invocations of a category label—e.g. "welfare cheats" or "the deserving poor," "terrorists" or "liberation fighters." Third-party reactions will depend on their "notions" about the members of the target category in relation to the salient situation. Other policy elites, bureaucrats, or populations which can reward or punish the invoker can use notions far different from those of the ostensible target population. When they do, public policies can produce desired behaviors and interpretations by almost everyone but it. The post 9/11 USA Patriot Act arguably has impacted less on those who would commit terrorist actions than on the general population and a host of government agencies. That bears some resemblance to what Edelman (1977) had in mind when he evaluated American anti-poverty programs as "words that succeed and policies that fail."

Talk about cultures or subcultures in relation to public policy usually follows from an image of a set of people whose relevant notions and actions differ from some historical, existing, or imaginable set of people. Differences get our attention when we think they constrain or enable some relative to other policies and policy processes. What contribution such talk will make to the analysis and conduct of public policy depends on awareness of the multiple dimensions of difference the world offers, and on the breadth and depth of efforts to understand how particular differences get applied to specific situations.

Cultures and subcultures and their members can differ in the dimensions of difference their notions identify. They can differ in the number of distinctions made on a given dimension and the distance between points on a dimension, e.g. about what religious or ethnic differences make a marriage mixed. They can differ in the value they place on being different or even unique. They can differ in how situations determine the importance of some aspect of difference. They can differ in what are key markers (signifiers) of any of these facets of difference. They can differ in what are held to be the correlates of commonly identified aspects of difference in terms of behavior, capability, intent, and normative worth. And, of course, they can differ in the degree to which their beliefs about how they are different from others and others different from them are shared by those others.

Whatever the cultural or subcultural content in these respects, it is not completely fixed if the experience of members is itself changing. Yet, in a context of pre-existing variety of notions and salient material context, populations can view that change as amounting to a very different sort of experience. Thus, the turn in US social policy from "welfare" to "workfare" may for those not participating in such programs appear as a well-intentioned offer of an avenue to a better life. At the same time, some participants view it as an ill-intentioned move to "cram down their throat" harsh choices between child rearing and work, or education and income (as with part-time fast-food jobs for Oakland teenagers of color; Stack 2001).

People come to any particular policy situation with a stock of notions about the degree and nature of relevant variety based on their prior actual or virtual experiences (including socialization, accepted history, academic learning). Thus Grammig (2002, 56) reports that a development assistance project was for experts of different nationalities "an empty shell that each participant filled with his own meaning." What is learned about whom usually results from prior judgements about the importance of a culture or subculture and sufficient curiosity to enquire about it. We are more likely to have elaborated profiles of others we have dealt with before and previously treated as important, and less likely to have such about those rarely encountered or thought lacking in wealth, coercive power, status, or rectitude. Of course players in policy systems and policy issues are a heterogeneous lot in terms of who they have encountered and treated as important. In sum, which and how many differences get recognized (or denied) are political and cultural matters. Public policies shape and are shaped by those recognitions, especially with regard to the processing of actual experiences into notion-related interpretative precedents, maxims, fables, and warnings.

Unfortunately, a number of often thought to be general tendencies for public policy get in the way of facing up to variety, and favor downplaying it. Consider three rather common assumptions: (1) *ceteris paribus* public policy tries to keep things simple to avoid overload; (2) politicians try to stay in good standing with their selectorates; and (3) bureaucratic agents try to look good to those who can affect their careers and agency resources.

Keeping things simple works against attending to a plethora of differences which would cast doubt on "one size fits all" policies. It favors attributing to apparently similar verbal or physical acts a standard meaning, and similar intent and affect. It is far easier to treat all welfare recipients as having similar views of work, or all Muslims as having similar notions of what being a "good Muslim" entails. It is far easier to interpret the reasons for poor grades by African-American males as following from factors which would account for poor grades by Caucasian or Asian males. It is far easier to interpret an audible "yes," smile, or even calls by admirals in different countries for a "strong Navy" (Booth 1979, 80–1) as meaning what they mean for us when we engage in such acts. A determined effort to think and act otherwise would compound the work involved in public policy formation, implementation, and evaluation.

Since public policy seldom is a "unitary actor" phenomenon, it usually involves achieving (or at least assuming) somewhat cooperative and communicative relationships between people and groups with less than identical notions. If it cannot be avoided, it can seemingly be made easier by an emphasis on dealing with persons and groups who seem less different from one's own culture or subculture. For example, a retired director of the CIA profiled for me a desirable replacement leader in an Islamic country as someone who "wears Western clothes, drinks whiskey, speaks English." Political legitimacy with indigenous constituencies can be slighted.

Of course, some stark claims of difference can enable policies which the prevailing notions in the adopting policy culture would otherwise deem morally illegitimate or pragmatically counter-productive. If others are inherently different in ways which threaten our culture and its preferred policies and policy processes, anything (or at least almost anything) goes, e.g. American treatment of some Iraqi and Afghan detainees. In such cases, what becomes constrained are policies which treat members of counter-cultures or clashing "civilizations" as our proclaimed notions would have us treat fellow culture members.[6] In its less culturally stressful and physically harsh versions, this makes for policies which deny existence through constructed invisibility (the Israeli tour leader who said, "the population of Israel is three million Jews"). In its often more culturally stressful and physically brutal versions, it can enable policies of genocide, ethnic cleansing, and state and non-state terrorism (e.g. Sluka 2000).

Selectorate-sensitive politicians (i.e. those particularly likely to gain and hold power) are constrained and enabled by the notions used by their selectorates. They tend to more or less proactively accommodate to them either reflexively when they too hold those notions or by consciously opportunistic acts of symbol manipulation (labeling, exemplification, and association). Policy issues and stances, salient events, political parties/movements/factions, and prominent personalities are then subjects for framing and counter-framing in light of judgements about the selectorate's notions. Informative examples are the testimony of expert witnesses for the prosecution and defense in the Rodney King police brutality trial (Goodwin 1994), and the politics of public school "reform" in Nashville (Pride 1995).

When the selectorate is quite uniform in its notions, the constraints and enablers are rather obvious. Politicians and activists compete to seem to fit best with predominant notions, and "expose" rivals as deviating from them. Given widely held notions of a USA under terrorist attack and of government employees as slackers, it was predictable that politicians would compete for authorship of a Department of Homeland Security. It was also hardly surprising that those of them trying

---

[6] The fact of harsh treatment of some Americans in American prisons is handled by invisibility, at least among much of the white US population.

to make establishment contingent on provision of established civil service protections to its employees would come under partisan attack and for the most part fold.

A selectorate rather evenly divided between clashing sets of notions calls for different strategies and tactics to relax the constraint of dissensus. Imagine a US selectorate split between holders of very different notions about the proper role of government derived from equally different notions about the good family (Lakoff 1996). Public policy practitioners may then seek to couch policies in ways which bundle together seemingly incompatible symbols and labels to appeal simultaneously to several sets of notions (e.g. "compassionate conservative"). They may engage in policy turn taking with respect to serial use of different symbolic packages catering to one or another of the competing sets of notions. They may even seek to create a replacement set of notions based on credible constructions of recent experience which promise to replace notions in mutual tension with a "Third Way" (as did President Clinton and Prime Minister Blair in the 1990s). Politicians, and not just ones in democratic societies, have reasons to be practicing ethnographers, or at least to have staff members who are.

Further complications arise when politicians have to appeal to domestic selectorates with one set of notions and also secure favorable treatment from elites and selectorates embedded in different cultures. That dual agenda may motivate policy elites to develop a repertoire with more than one set of culturally appropriate content. They may metaphorically (and sometimes quite literally) don different wardrobes (or dialects) for dealings with local, domestic, or foreign parties. Cosmopolitan US Southern senators have been known to shift into the regional dialect of their constituency when talking with its members. Flights from non-Arab countries to Saudi Arabia shortly before arrival often have returning citizens of considerable standing covering up modish Euro-American clothes.

In a multicultural polity and an internationalized world, politicians with more than a monocultural repertoire can be advantaged—at least if their practices avoid triggering conclusions that they are not really genuine, sincere members of any of the pertinent cultures. Manifesting some characteristics of another culture can lead its members to expect that actor to manifest others. Disappointment may follow, and accusations of "bad faith."[7] Of course, if selectorates in one policy culture have negative notions about another, there are risks of "guilt by association."[8]

Most public policies and policy processes originate in some bureaucratic agency or professional epistemic community, and most depend for stamps of approval

---

[7] "Governments like individuals, have great expectations of reasonable behaviour from those they think are like themselves. They will naturally expect them to see the world in the same way and to behave sensibly, which in political practice does not mean behaving with 'good sense', but rather means behaving 'like me' or 'in accordance with my wishes'.... When a close associate fails to act in a desired manner, the disappointment is all the greater" (Booth 1979, 56).

[8] For example, that premiss may have underlain Republican attacks on the US Democratic presidential candidate in 2004, John Kerry, as being "too French." The counter unsurprisingly was to display Kerry in association with symbols thought to be central to the selectorate's notions of genuine membership in American culture such as driving a motorcycle and hunting.

(certification) and implementation on one or more bureau or professional communities. Top policy makers and their policies are then enabled and constrained by what members of those groupings hold to be the notions used by their career gatekeepers, and by their convictions about the grounds (notions and situational triggers) which others rely on to determine collective or individual rewards or punishments.[9] When agency is given to a bureau or profession with a distinct set of notions, the chances are that set of notions is privileged *de jure* or de facto. Some policies and policy process routines are then more enabled and some more constrained.

To say that bureaux and professions have "world-views," "standard operating procedures," "folklore," and pantheons of exemplary individuals and events is to say that they have a culture. The centrality of membership in that culture mounts when bureaux and professions have accepted and nearly deterministic cause-and-effect theories, normative criteria of merit, high barriers to entry and exit, and identities framed in terms of contrasts with other bureaux and professions. Consider, for example, the protective "code blue" of silence US policemen sometimes use when challenged by civilians and civilian authorities, or the claims to special turf rights made by "foreign area experts" to keep out international relations "generalists" (Samuels and Weiner 1992). A public health service (e.g. the Centers for Disease Control) is likely to treat the problem of bioterrorism differently from a domestic security service (e.g. the FBI). Economists are likely to treat pollution problems more with an eye to market mechanisms such as permit auctions while lawyers might emphasize regulatory mechanisms such as penalties for breaching emission ceilings.

Suppose an issue is assigned to two bureaux with different established notions, notions which include viewing each other as expansionist, untrustworthy, or less competent rivals. Policies which require generous cooperation are constrained, e.g. think of the FBI and CIA even if both are labeled as belonging to a common membership group (the US "Intelligence Community"). A more subtle form of constraint occurs when some key policy role is assigned to a "subculture" which exists in a low-status way (e.g. civil affairs units in the US military) in a larger organization whose culture centers on quite different missions (e.g. war fighting and deterrence). Unsurprisingly, the assignment is then often followed by resource and promotion starvation (e.g. the fate of enforcement agents in the US Immigration and Naturalization Service or INS; Weissinger 1996).

In any event, for many members of most agencies and bureaux there are widely held views ("conventional wisdom") of what policy-relevant behavior carries high risks. Those views may or may not be transparent to outsiders, especially if they clash with declared norms among members. Privileged bureaux and professions (and indeed "ordinary folks") will go to considerable effort to get around policy emphases and directives which seem to them to pose such risks.

---

[9] Policy systems vary in the extent to which and ways in which they have a common culture across key bureaux, levels of government, and specializations (e.g. as the French try to do with few entry paths into the elite higher civil service or the Chinese Communists used to try to do through party socialization).

4 Finding Variety

The arguments to this point are that: (1) cultural variety matters for public policy; (2) there are chronic tendencies to deny it the attention it ought to have; and (3) denial deprives some policy options and policy process alternatives of a level playing field. A superficial acknowledgement of variety will not help much unless acted on to improve the information provided for and actually used in public policy. Those changes are more likely with increased representation and standing in policy processes of those attentive to variety. What sort of repertoire of enquiry would then get greater emphasis?[10]

One priority would be analyzing two aspects of language used by members with each other. The first is that of metaphors which treat some matter as similar to another, and invoke from such similarities guidance about situational interpretations and warranted action (Lakoff and Johnson 1980). For American public policy, for example, one may note the frequent use of conflict metaphors such as the "war on" or the "fight against" (as with the Johnson administration on poverty, the Carter administration on energy dependence, and the Bush II administration on terrorism). For Americans and Japanese, the sheer volume of talk about sport suggests that it is seen as a source of relevant metaphors for much else (Boswell 1990; Whiting 1990). The more frequently similar metaphors and analogies occur in general writing and speech, the more likely they are to be drawn on with respect to public policies and policy processes.

A second focus would be on thorough elicitation of what members of a relevant population use by way of categories of actors and actions, cues to relevant categories, and expectations about the efficacy of particular actions in relation to actors in some category (e.g. Spradley 1970). Rather than imposing categories (as in closed response survey interviews), the emphasis would be on discovering the categories, cues, and expectations held by those whose behavior we are trying to understand and perhaps influence. Special attention would go to matters elaborated with numerous distinctions suggesting importance in the lives of those whose language is under examination.

Language is only one form of behavior open to observation. A variety-finding orientation calls for as much direct observation as possible of what people do in their natural situations, i.e. what for them are real situations involved with the aspect of public policy of interest, and then seeking their rationales for acting as they have done (e.g. DeWalt and DeWalt 2002). The observation should be conducted as unobtrusively as possible (e.g. along the lines of Webb et al. 1966) with the observer as blended into and neutral in the situation as possible. The observer would try to become a watcher and listener *in situ* whether the subject of interest is the campaign behavior of elected politicians in Hong Kong (Beatty 2003), the processing of issues by local office holders in New York state (Sady 1990), or the inferential process of

---

[10] Brief reviews of pertinent methods and applications appear in Schensul et al. 1999*a*, 1999*b*, 1999*c*.

arriving at US intelligence estimates (Johnston 2003). That may or may not involve participation either as part of blending in or as a way to discern notions used by culture members.

Whether the focus is on language or other behaviors, considerable attention should go to associations and evaluations in terms of cultural propriety and likely pragmatic consequences operating for those being observed. That involves eliciting and recognizing what for the members of the culture under examination are codes of conduct, key historical references and myths, understandings (images) of others who matter to them for dealings with public policy, and prototypically successful or unsuccessful courses of action by those held to be similar to themselves. Those may often be surprisingly elaborated and shared, as with homeless alcoholics in Seattle on dealing with the personnel and institutions of the "criminal justice" system (Spradley 1970).

When the behaviors in question involve physical actions and material objects, the discovery process needs to look contextually at when those actions are taken and the full range of uses made of those objects. If we wish to change practices in India about cows, we should engage in a "functional systems analysis" of how cows are used in and adapted to Hindu society and its economy and ecology (Harris 1966). If we wish to understand the extent to which educational administrators are concerned with student demonstrations and physical disruption, or diplomats with their embassies being attacked, we should examine features of newly constructed facilities (as in "riot renaissance" architecture). If we wish to understand and improve the availability of public recreational space for children in New York City, we should look to see where they play (the street) rather than assuming that only parks and playgrounds are sites for play (e.g. Yin 1972).

Fully understanding variety may not be possible, and faces numerous obstacles of access, evidence, and inference. Yet several "best practices" can at least increase understanding. One is to extend the language mapping and other observations across time and situations. For example, a longitudinal study of an "innovative school" found notions, processes, and roles far different from those stressed in the professional literature on school innovation (Smith et al. 1998). A one-time, few-day, and situationally unusual field trip or site visit may produce a "shock of recognition" that variety exists. It is unlikely to create substantial awareness of the notions used by others. Shortcomings are especially likely when the "visitor" deals primarily with stationed officials from his or her own culture rather than those of another. Deliberate steps to "get out of the bubble" need to be taken to avoid pitfalls of "spurious direct encounters" with other cultures at home and abroad.

It also can be helpful to focus on material practices and talk widespread in the population one wishes to understand. For example, insider jokes among them and what for them are popular mass media products should not be slighted in favor of "serious" talk and highbrow products. If we are interested in young Americans, MTV programs may be more informative than the *New York Review of Books*. If we are interested in US legislators and their staffs, their "neighborhood" newspaper (*Roll Call*) may merit as much attention as the *American Political Science Review*.

If we are interested in the extent to which upper- and middle-class South Africans are preoccupied with crime, we might gain insight by noting the large amount of attention home design and accessory magazines for that market give to residential alarm systems and security barriers, and the consumer demand for "armed response team" services.

Finally, there is the selection and assessment of informants, individual and group sources thought by outsiders to be "insiders" to a culture of interest and relied on to illuminate it. Some use of informants is hard to avoid, but taking what they communicate at face value is not. It is advisable to rely more on informants with substantial recent experience in the culture of interest than on those who have been "in exile" for several decades. It is advisable to weigh what informants tell us in light of their own likely agendas, interests in our holding particular views of their cultures and taking or avoiding certain interventions in it. All of those cautions should enter into decisions about giving informants and their primary membership groups key roles in relationships between our culture and theirs. Prudential lessons might be drawn from the disappointments of US efforts at regime change which drew on unwarrantedly rosy émigré judgements (the Bay of Pigs in the Kennedy administration and the 2003 invasion of Iraq).

This repertoire deserves a far more prominent place than it usually has in programs to prepare future professionals to analyze and participate in public policy.

REFERENCES

AKERLOF, G. and YELLEN, J. L. 1994. Gang behavior, law enforcement and community values. Pp. 173–97 in *Values and Public Policy*, ed. H. J. Aaron, T. E. Mann, and T. Taylor. Washington, DC: Brookings Institution.

ALMOND, G. A. 2002. *Ventures in Political Science*. Boulder, Colo.: Lynne Rienner.

—— and VERBA, S. 1963. *The Civic Culture: Political Attitudes and Democracy in Five Nations*. Princeton, NJ: Princeton University Press.

BEATTY, B. 2003. *Democracy, Asian Values, and Hong Kong: Evaluating Political Elite Beliefs*. Westport, Conn.: Praeger.

BOOTH, K. 1979. *Strategy and Ethnocentrism*. New York: Homes and Meier.

BOSWELL, T. 1990. What we talk about when we talk about sports: it's not just who won or lost—it's how we use the game. *Washington Post Magazine*, 12 Aug.: 23–8.

CLARK, T. N. AND HOFFMANN-MARTINOT, V. 1998. *The New Political Culture*. Boulder, Colo.: Westview.

DEWALT, K. M. and DEWALT, B. R. 2002. *Participant Observation: A Guide for Fieldworkers*. Walnut Creek, Calif.: AltaMira Press.

DOUGLAS, M. and WILDAVSKY, A. 1982. *Risk and Culture: An Essay on the Selection of Technical and Environmental Dangers*. Berkeley: University of California Press.

EDELMAN, M. 1977. *Political Language: Words That Succeed and Policies That Fail*. New York: Academic Press.

ELMORE, R. F. 1985. Forward and backward mapping: reversible logic. Pp. 33–70 in *Policy Implementation in Federal and Unitary Systems*, ed. K. Hanf and T. A. J. Toonen. Boston: Martinus Nijhoff.

FENNO, R. 1990. *Watching Politicians: Essays on Participant Observation*. Berkeley: University of California at Berkeley Institute of Governmental Studies.

GEERTZ, C. M. 1973. *The Interpretation of Cultures*. New York: Basic Books.

GEORGE, A. 1969. "The operational code:" a neglected approach to the study of political leaders and decision-making. *International Studies Quarterly*, 13: 190–222.

GOODWIN, C. 1994. Professional vision. *American Anthropologist*, 96: 606–33.

GRAMMIG, T. 2002. *Technical Knowledge and Development: Observing Aid Projects and Processes*. London: Routledge.

HARRIS, M. 1966. The cultural ecology of India's sacred cattle. *Current Anthropologist*, 7: 51–9.

HUDSON, V. M. (ed.) 1997. *Culture and Foreign Policy*. Boulder, Colo.: Lynne Rienner.

INGLEHART, R. 1990. *Culture Shift in Advanced Industrial Societies*. Princeton, NJ: Princeton University Press.

JOHNSTON, A. I. 1995. Thinking about strategic culture. *International Security*, 19: 32–64.

JOHNSTON, R. 2003. Developing a taxonomy of intelligence analysis variables. *Studies in Intelligence*, 47: 61–72.

KIER, A. 1995. Culture and military doctrine. *International Security*, 19: 65–93.

LAKOFF, G. 1996. *Moral Politics: What Conservatives Know That Liberals Don't*. Chicago: University of Chicago Press.

—— and JOHNSON, M. 1980. *Metaphors We Live By*. Chicago: University of Chicago Press.

LASSWELL, H. D. 1951. *The Political Writings of Harold Lasswell*. Glencoe, Ill.: Free Press.

—— 1971. *Propaganda Technique in World War I*. Cambridge, Mass.: MIT Press.

—— and FOX, M. B. 1979. *The Signature of Power: Buildings, Communication, and Policy*. New Brunswick, NJ: Transaction.

—— and LEITES, N. 1949. *The Language of Politics: Studies in Quantitative Semantics*. New York: George W. Stewart.

LEITES, N. 1951. *The Operational Code of the Politburo*. New York: McGraw-Hill.

LERNER, D. and LASSWELL, H. R. (eds.) 1951. *The Policy Sciences: Recent Developments in Scope and Method*. Stanford, Calif.: Stanford University Press.

LEVY, J. 1997. Prospect theory and the cognitive-rational debate. Pp. 33–50 in *Decisionmaking on War and Peace*, ed. N. Geva and A. Mintz. Boulder, Colo.: Lynne Rienner.

NELSON, J. 2003. Social memory as ritual practice: commemorating spirits of the military dead at Yasukuni Shrine. *Journal of Asian Studies*, 62: 443–67.

PRIDE, R. A. 1995. How activists and media frame social problems. *Political Communication*, 12: 5–26.

PYE, L. 1988. *The Mandarin and the Cadre: China's Political Cultures*. Ann Arbor: Center for Chinese Studies, University of Michigan.

—— and PYE, M. 1985. *Asian Power and Politics: The Cultural Dimensions of Authority*. Cambridge, Mass.: Harvard University Press.

SADY, R. 1990. *District Leaders: A Political Ethnography*. Boulder, Colo.: Westview.

SAMUELS, R. J. and WEINER, M. 1992. *The Political Culture of Foreign Area and International Studies: Essays in Honor of Lucian W. Pye*. Washington, DC: Brassey's.

SCHENSUL, J. J. et al. 1999a. *Using Ethnographic Data: Interventions, Public Programming, and Public Policy*. Walnut Creek, Calif.: AltaMira Press.

—— et al. 1999b. *Enhanced Ethnographic Methods: Audiovisual Techniques, Focused Group Interviews, and Elicitation Techniques*. Walnut Creek, Calif.: AltaMira Press.

SCHENSUL, J. J., et al. 1999c. *Mapping Social Networks, Spatial Data, and Hidden Populations.* Walnut Creek, Calif. AltaMira Press.

SCOTT, J. C. 1985. *Weapons of the Weak: Everyday Forms of Peasant Resistance.* New Haven, Conn.: Yale University Press.

——1990. *Domination and the Arts of Resistance: Hidden Transcripts.* New Haven, Conn.: Yale University Press.

SEN, A. 1977. Rational fools. *Philosophy & Public Affairs*, 6: 317–44.

SLUKA, J. A. (ed.) 2000. *Death Squad: The Anthropology of State Terror.* Philadelphia: University of Pennsylvania Press.

SMITH, L. M., DWYER, D. C., PRUNTY, J. J., and KLEINE, P. F. 1998. *Innovation and Change in Schooling: History, Politics, and Agency.* New York: Falmer Press.

SNYDER, J. 2002. Anarchy and culture: insights from the anthropology of war. *International Organization*, 56: 7–45.

SOSS, J. 1999. Lessons of welfare: policy design, political learning, and political action. *American Political Science Review*, 93: 363–80.

SPRADLEY, J. P. 1970. *You Owe Yourself a Drunk: An Ethnography of Urban Nomads.* Boston: Little, Brown.

——1979. *The Ethnographic Interview.* New York: Holt, Rinehart and Winston.

STACK, C. 2001. Coming of age in Oakland. Pp. 179–98 in *The New Poverty Studies: The Ethnography of Power, Politics, and Impoverished People in the United States*, ed. J. Goode and J. Maskovsky. New York: New York University Press.

THOMPSON, M., ELLIS, R., and WILDAVSKY, A. 1990. *Cultural Theory.* Boulder, Colo.: Westview.

——GRENDSTAD, G., and SELLE, P. (eds.) 1999. *Cultural Theory as Political Science.* New York: Routledge.

——and WILDAVSKY, A. 1986. A poverty of distinction: from economic homogeneity to cultural heterogeneity in the classification of poor people. *Policy Sciences*, 19: 163–99.

WEBB, E. J., CAMPBELL, D. T., SCHWARTZ, R. D., and SECHREST, L. 1966. *Unobtrusive Measures: Nonreactive Research in the Social Sciences.* Chicago: Rand-McNally.

WEISSINGER, G. 1996. *Law Enforcement and the INS: A Participant Observation Study of Control Agents.* Lanham, Md.: University Press of America.

WHITING, R. 1990. *You Gotta Have Wa.* New York: Vintage.

WILDAVSKY, A. 1987. Choosing preferences by constructing institutions: a cultural theory of preference formation. *American Political Science Review*, 81: 3–21.

——1988. A cultural theory of budgeting. *International Journal of Public Administration*, 11: 651–77.

YIN, R. K. 1972. *Participant-Observation and the Development of Urban Neighborhood Policy.* New York: New York City RAND Institute, R-962.

ZHANG, S. G. 1992. *Deterrence and Strategic Culture: Chinese–American Confrontations, 1949–1958.* Ithaca, NY: Cornell University Press.

CHAPTER 45

....

POLICY DYNAMICS

....

EUGENE BARDACH

UNDERSTANDING dynamics is about understanding change, and a concern with policy dynamics has to be, in some measure, about policy change—how to get from here to there in the political process. This concern should be focused on both policy-making and policy-implementing processes. Consider the following questions that call for answers framed at least partially in dynamic terms:

- The federal welfare reform Act[1] of 1996 was something of a backlash against an unpopular program that was seen as encouraging dependency. But was it also:

  - An equilibrating move in a political system that tends to seek the ideological center?
  - An evolutionary move towards economic efficiency that either does or does not have a built-in tropism towards efficiency?
  - A product of successful long-term "learning" processes in the policy-making system?

- Why can't the United States seem to get a rational health care system that provides reasonable quality care at reasonable cost to all Americans? Perhaps one reason is that the dynamics of policy development in this area, begun in the 1930s, have locked us in to a system that depends heavily, but also only partially on employer-based financing.
- Regulatory agencies are often said to become captured by the industries they regulate. How does the process of becoming captured unfold?
- How did the United States Congress come to be such a polarized body? It was not always this way, and the process took place over many years. How did the process

---

[1] Formally known as the Personal Responsibility and Work Opportunity Reconciliation Act (PRWORA).

work? Is the process specific to this institution and its historical context(s), or is the process, at least in part, more generic?

- An entrepreneurial group of legislative staff and legislators with close ties to the powerful Speaker of the California Assembly sought the Speaker's assistance for a major reform in mental health policy only in the closing days of the legislative struggle. Why did they wait? Might they have been better off not waiting so long?

While this chapter does not attempt to answer these questions in particular, it does seek to describe and evaluate a number of conceptual frameworks for answering questions like these.

1 OVERVIEW

This is not a review essay on the status of a mature field. It does not try to summarize comprehensively the works of others. The study of policy dynamics is not a field at all; and, to the best of my knowledge, no one has previously brought together all the phenomena I canvass here. I have scanned for work in which dynamics and policy both happen to be present, even if the authors did not self-consciously intend to make the connection. I have also not aimed to eliminate subjectivity on my part. Scanning is bound to be subjective, perhaps idiosyncratic, as is interpretation of the results.

My main objective is to stimulate research interest in a neglected phenomenon and, by way of doing so, to present concepts and substantive hypotheses that I have found stimulating or that others might find so.

The most important others are the likely readers of this *Handbook*. I assume the average reader to have a generalist's interest in the policy process. Hence, I have favored breadth over depth. Secondly, I have focused more on the institutional dynamics of the policy-making process than on the evolution of substantive policies themselves, though obviously the two subject matters overlap. This focus has naturally led me to look primarily to the work done by political scientists, though I also mention stimulating contributions by economists and other social scientists.[2] Thirdly, I have tried to point to policy-relevant applications of leading ideas in the study of dynamic social systems, even though such applications are often isolated, pioneering, and not necessarily widely cited by students of the policy process. Fourthly, I occasionally refer to studies or bodies of work that, although not closely related to the policy process, suggest the power of certain approaches to the study of dynamic systems.

In Section 2, I explain some key concepts in systems analysis that are necessary for understanding dynamics.

---

[2] I am, of course, indebted to the work of Baumgartner and Jones, who have presented a survey on these topics as well (Baumgartner and Jones 2002).

Section 3 deals with dynamic processes dominated by negative feedback. They are in some sense equilibrating, or balance seeking. However, in most cases equilibrium is not actually achieved, unless one is willing to call oscillating within some broad or narrow range an equilibrium. They all have to do with what one might think of as "the balance of power."

Section 4 discusses processes dominated by positive feedback. These are the more integrative processes of political life, e.g. consensus building, network construction, community mobilization, collective learning, interorganizational collaboration.

Section 5 briefly describes dynamic processes that unfold in only one direction. That is, they do not involve feedback loops. The processes selected here for discussion involve filtering and chain reactions, or "cascades."

Section 6 concludes with a short wish list for future research.

1.1 Do Dynamics Matter Anyway?

As this chapter is devoted exclusively to policy dynamics, it would be easy for both author and reader to be carried away by the putative importance of dynamic processes and process-related tactical skills relative to, say, institutionalized authority or interest group power or interpersonal influence. The conceptual fascination of the subject matter, and some of the exotic models to deal with it, increases the temptation. Not all scholars working in this area have been immune. We should probably believe, though, that in the end, authority, power, and influence all matter more. If you are wrestling Hercules, you will lose eventually, no matter what the sequence of holds and escapes along the way. The assumption behind this chapter is merely that *when* process dynamics are consequential, we need the conceptual tools and empirical knowledge for understanding them.

2 "Systems" and "Dynamics"

Not all systems are dynamic, but all dynamics occur within systems. We must therefore say something at the outset about how to understand systems.

Robert Jervis, in *System Effects: Complexity in Political and Social Life*, provides this useful definition of a system: "We are dealing with a system when (a) a set of units or elements is interconnected so that changes in some elements or their relations produce changes in other parts of the system, and (b) the entire system exhibits properties and behaviors that are different from those of the parts" (Jervis 1997, 6). A closed system is one that is responsive only to changes initiated by its own elements; an open system contains an endogenous core that behaves in many ways like a closed system but can also receive inputs from its environment. In this chapter, I consider only open systems but often focus mainly on the dynamics of their endogenous cores.[3]

To convey the flavor of what counts as what, in Terry Moe's paper on the dynamics of the National Labor Relations Board (NLRB), the endogenous core consists of the Board, the staff, and the millions of employers and workers who are potential complainants, whereas the environment is composed of political officials, judges, and a variety of economic conditions (Moe 1985). In Moe's analysis of who wins and who loses at the NLRB, the workings of the endogenous core have an interesting but minor influence compared to influences from the larger environment. Exogenous influences on the Board, especially by way of presidential appointments, importantly shift its pro- or anti-labor tilt. Then endogenous dynamics take over. Suppose, for instance, the Board shifts its interpretative standards in a direction favorable to labor. This leads to a temporary increase in the win rate. But this increase is only temporary. As the backlog of cases to be settled favorably to labor under the standards diminishes, so too does the average win rate. But the temporarily above-average win rate, in combination with signals about the Board's new interpretative standards, encourages an increase in labor filings. The average quality of the new filings is below the average quality of the old caseload, however, and the win rate at the staff level (as they filter cases up to the board) drops. As staff criteria and labor perceptions of those criteria stabilize, the average merit of cases and the labor win rate converge on some "normal" level. This new level, though, is more pro-labor than it used to be before the shifts in the Board's composition.

2.1 Negative and Positive Feedback Loops

The structure of a system consists of (1) its constituent elements, (2) the rules governing their interactions, and (3) the information required by the system to apply the rules. In virtually all dynamic systems of interest to students of policy, "running" the system creates feedbacks that might alter the structure of the system.

By means of feedback loops certain system outputs (whether intermediate or final) influence certain of the system's inputs. For instance, teachers encourage parents to read to their children, and the children's improved performance encourages parents to keep up the good work. The literature on systems dynamics calls such growth-inducing feedback loops "positive" because in conventional loop diagrams such as Fig. 45.1 the product of the components' polarities is positive. "Negative" feedback loops, on the other hand, have balancing, or equilibrating effects, as the product of the polarities is negative. Figure 45.1 diagrams the well-known arms race model of Lewis Richardson. Richardson's algebraic model is given in equations (1) and (2), with x and y representing stockpiles of arms in two nations, m and n being

---

[3] Richardson usefully distinguishes two meanings, analytical and material, of "closed" system. In a material, or real, sense all systems are open. For analytical purposes, however, it sometimes makes sense to treat certain systems as closed. Jay W. Forrester, a pioneer of at least one wing of contemporary systems analysis, works only on analytically closed systems (Richardson 1991, 297–8).

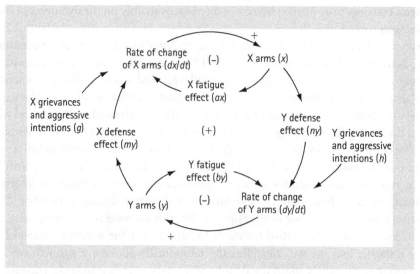

Fig. 45.1. Loop structure of Richardson's linear model of an arms race

positive "defense" coefficients, and g and h representing "grievances" or "aggressive intentions" (Richardson 1991, 40).

$$dx/dt = my - ax + g \tag{1}$$

$$dy/dt = nx - by + h \tag{2}$$

In the NLRB case, a larger gap between cases filed and cases won increased worker realism, while increased realism fed back and decreased the gap.

2.2 "Emergent Properties" and "Developments"

As they run, most complex systems with positive feedback loops create new features, "emergent properties." In the physical world, think of a pot that miraculously emerges from the system of clay, wheel, and potter. In the social world, think of gridlock that emerges from thousands of drivers converging on the same highways or urban streets. As these examples suggest, emergent properties are properties of the system as a whole rather than any of its component parts.

"Emergent properties" can loosely be translated back into more conventional language as "developments." In the course of this chapter I shall refer to many such developments in policy-related systems. I have already mentioned win rates in the NLRB case. Other such examples will be:

- Partial fragmentation of an advocacy coalition following soon after countermobilization by its opponents.

- The emergence of a functioning "interagency collaborative" out of a combination of human and non-human assets hitherto relatively independent of one another.
- A variety of momentum processes that go into the creation of electoral bandwagons, the construction of implementation networks, and the development of legislative consensus.
- The "lock-in effect" that comes to hem in social policy by all the policies previously enacted and with which any new policy must be reconciled.

3 Negative Feedback Processes: The Balancing of Power

I discuss two types of negative feedback, or equilibrating, processes. They are:

- Oscillations occurring within certain—perhaps changeable—limits.[4]
- Efforts being made to maintain a "monopolistic" equilibrium condition, one based on the superior political power of the monopolists. When reformers do manage to succeed, this might be termed a "disequilibrating" process.

I will note preliminarily that I ignore the large domain of processes that either do or might reach a game-theoretical equilibrium. Many of these, such as the Prisoner's Dilemma game, are of great relevance to policy making and implementation and have inspired a large literature. The reason for this omission is that equilibration in these games, if it occurs, is instantaneous; hence, there is no "dynamic" to talk about. For the same reason I also omit effects that compensate for failures to reach an equilibrium, such as discussed in Miller (Miller 1992).

3.1 Oscillating Processes

Before turning to domestic policy processes, our main interest, let us consider the classic oscillating system, balance of power politics in the international arena. At its core, the process features (1) the rise of a countervailing coalition to challenge any emerging coalition of states and (2) fluidity in coalition formation, so that today's enemy may be tomorrow's ally. The system oscillates between relative peace and near-war, sometimes tipping over into actual war when countervailing threat fails to deter.

---

[4] In their generally thorough and insightful work on both positive and negative feedback, Baumgartner and Jones refer occasionally to the "homeostatic" role of negative feedback (Baumgartner and Jones 2002, 8–9). This implies a return to some prior defined state. I do not think this occurs very frequently. All I attribute to negative feedback is system movement in a reactive direction.

However, it also tends to preserve most actors' territorial integrity and bars the way to successful total domination (Jervis 1997, 131–3).

Whether or not one thinks the balance of power actually "works"—in Renaissance Italy or in Europe, say, from the seventeenth century until the Second World War—it is clear that it does not work all the time. When rulers are extremely ambitious or miscalculate, or countervailing forces are slow to mobilize, the system will break down. That is, war will occur. These failures do not arise from the dynamics of the system's endogenous core, however, but from exogenous forces in the system's environment, such as leaders' psychology (Napoleon, Hitler) or the influences of domestic politics (public opinion in Neville Chamberlain's England).

Regulatory agencies. In domestic politics, the oscillation of regulatory policy is the best illustration of negative feedback. As we have seen in the case of Moe's study of the NLRB, the influence of exogenous factors on the dynamics of the core is a point of great importance and general applicability. Of course, one might say that the oscillations in the political environment are themselves the expression of endogenous processes within a larger system. Like the NLRB, risk regulators such as the Occupational Safety and Health Administration (OSHA) and the Environmental Protection Agency (EPA) are more aggressive regulators when Democrats are in power than when Republicans are. This oscillation between parties, and the interest groups that thrive under their protection, is certainly systematic after a fashion. We shall return to this point below.

Politics aside, the very nature of risk regulation probably guarantees a certain amount of endogenous oscillation independent of that induced by the political environment (Hood, Rothstein, and Baldwin 2001; Bardach and Kagan 2002/1982). All that is required is regulators who wish to adhere to norms about making "good public policy" but who work under conditions of great technical uncertainty. This is a standard condition for almost all risk-regulating agencies. Good scientific information is often lacking about what exposures cause how much damage to what kinds of individuals under which circumstances. Nor do regulators know with certainty whether, in the real world of policy and program implementation, particular remedies will be applied effectively or not. Following Jonathan Bendor, suppose that regulators follow heuristics like "If it seemed to work in the past, keep on doing it" and "If it didn't seem to work, tighten (loosen) the regulatory regime." As long as mistakes appear to happen, the agency will not get trapped in a suboptimal regime, but it will not be able to prevent its oscillating away from an optimal regime either (Bendor 2004, 13–14).

Bendor uses the Food and Drug Administration as his primary illustration, following the work of Paul Quirk (Quirk 1980, ch. 6), and plausibly assumes that the point of optimal stringency lies within the limits of oscillatory movement. But of course, it need not do so. Bardach and Kagan (2002/1982) postulate a regulatory dynamic that has regulatory stringency (in its multiple dimensions) oscillating according to political pressures in the short run and the medium run but over the long run, drifting upward. They refer to a "regulatory ratchet." In any given cycle, stringency may be reduced, but it will not be reduced below its lowest level in the previous cycle. If such a ratchet is indeed at work,[5] it would be a fortunate but only tempo-rary happenstance that the optimum point would be located within the oscillatory limits.

Spending. In "The public as thermostat: dynamics of preferences for spending," Christopher Wlezien explicitly tests a negative feedback hypothesis, one based on what he takes to be a theory of democratic accountability, in which the public "would adjust its preferences for 'more' or 'less' policy in response to policy outputs themselves. In effect, the public would behave like a thermostat; when the actual policy 'temperature' differs from the preferred policy temperature, the public would send a signal to adjust policy accordingly, and once sufficiently adjusted, the signal would stop" (Wlezien 1995, 981). Wlezien did find, in regard to defense and to five social programs, that public preferences were a counterweight to budgetary appropri-ations: whatever direction they had moved in, public opinion wanted them to move back.

Elections and parties. Periodic contested elections in a two-party system are, of course, a negative feedback system writ very large. Although in a separation-of-powers system the idea of a "party in power" is sometimes ambiguous, over time grievances build up against whoever is identified as "the party in power," and voters "throw the rascals out." That these grievances may not realistically be attributable to the actions of the party or its standard bearers (Fiorina 1981) is not to the point. The feedback loop from party conduct to voter attributions of responsibility is not the only source of such attributions, and systems can function as smoothly with irrational as rational feedback. The system-like quality of electoral oscillations is not diminished by the lack of uniformity in the intervals between turnovers. The duration of such intervals probably must be explained by exogenous factors, such as business cycles, changing demographics, and random shocks from foreign events or scandals.[6]

Within particular election seasons, negative feedback systems also come into play. Anthony Downs's well-known spatial models of party positioning show that, in a simple single-dimensional (left/right) world of voter preferences, two parties are driven towards the center as they compete for the loyalties of the median voter. This is not a negative but a positive feedback system. However, the process may not move to completion, as the party leaders (candidates) are dragged back from the center by the threat of non-voting (and non-campaigning) from their party's base. Negative feedback arising from moves too far towards the center or back towards the party's enthusiasts leads to an equilibration of candidates' positions short of the median voter (Shepsle and Bonchek 1997, 114).

---

[5] For evidence that the ratchet effect occurs, see Ruhl and Salzman 2003.

[6] The duration of intervals might, however, have a statistical regularity such as Zipf's law, which connects the frequency of an event type with the rank of that type in a population of related events. Zipf's law holds for diverse events like the appearances of words in the English language and the population sizes of cities. See Bak 1996, 24–6. For instance, the tenth most frequently used word appeared 2,653 times in Zipf's sample; the twentieth most used word, 1,311 times; and the 20,000th most used word once. Such data fit a straight line on a logarithmic plot with slope near one.

Reform cycles. Observers have noted episodes of reform—principally anti-corruption, anti-business, and/or anti-government—in American political history. Samuel Huntington speaks of a characteristically American "creedal passion" to create a civic life of democratic and ethical purity erupting every sixty years (Huntington 1981, 147 ff.). This eruption occurs when the "ideals-versus-institutions gap" has grown too large. Although Huntington does claim there is a systematic basis for the sixty-year cycle, he does not explain what it is.

Similarly, McClosky and Zaller, in their much praised *The American Ethos* (1984) postulate that, over decades, there are "swings in the national mood" between support for "a competitive, private economy in which the most enterprising and industrious individuals receive the greatest income" and "a democratic society in which everyone can earn a decent living and has an equal chance to realize his or her full human potential." These values of "capitalism" and "democracy" are in some tension politically and philosophically, they argue. Yet beyond this they do not specify the mechanisms whereby the predominance of one value set begins to retreat in the face of its rival.[7]

In the classic age of interest group theory, David Truman once famously wrote of the "balance wheel" in American politics, which had interest groups who triumphed in one round losing to newly mobilized "potential groups" in the next (Truman 1951, 514). "In a relatively vigorous political system ... unorganized interests are dominant with sufficient frequency ... so that ... both the activity and the methods of organized interest groups are kept within broad limits" (1951: 515). Here indeed is a theory of reform cycles based on negative feedback.

Andrew McFarland has updated Truman and proposed a "reform cycle" theory focused on pro- and anti-business policies and politics from 1890 to at least 1991, the date of his paper (McFarland 1991). His summary:

Economic producer groups have a more stable incentive to participate in issue-area decision making than the reform groups that challenge their control. However, after a few years of the business-control phase of the cycle, unchecked producer groups tend to commit "excesses", violations of widely shared values. This leads to political participation [and policy triumphs] by the reformers [1991, 257]. [But once legislation has been passed, and regulations drawn up] ... the period of high politics is over: the public loses interest, journalistic coverage ceases, Congress and the president turn to other issues ..., but the activity of producer groups remains constant, due to their continuing economic stakes ... After a few years, another period of producer group power is at hand, leading eventually to new excesses, a new reform period and so forth. (1991, 263–4)

One implication of this theory, says McFarland, is that "across the scope of hundreds of issue areas, business control or reform phases tend to occur at the same time" (1991, 257).

That there are indeed waves of "reform" cutting across many issue areas simultaneously is true enough. McFarland points in particular to the Progressive movement

[7] McClosky and Zaller greatly overstate the general case for a tension between these two value sets. Exchanging the highly charged "capitalism" for the more neutral "markets," democratic and market institutions are not only compatible but may be mutually required.

(after 1900), the New Deal (in the 1930s), and the 1960s (the civil rights and anti-Vietnam War movements). Whether these represent true cycles in an oscillating system is questionable, however. In McFarland's theory the stimulus for the reform phase of the cycle is "new excesses" by business, implying that it is an *increase* relative to some accepted or acceptable lower level of misconduct that triggers reform. The basic driver of the system is thus varying and objectively perceived levels of business misconduct. It is just as likely to be the case, however, that the actual levels of business misbehavior do not vary greatly over time and that changing social and cultural conditions trigger collective expressions of outrage and demands for "reform." It is noteworthy that since the 1960s, reformist demands have been directed at *both* business and government, that is, at institutions representing hierarchy (Douglas and Wildavsky 1982; Inglehart 1997).[8]

If there were indeed reform cycles in the past, they might have given way since the 1960s to a world of institutionalized "reform" almost on a par with the institutions of business. Critics would say even stronger than those of business. Reformist interest groups abound. In Washington and in some US state capitals, those representing "good government," environmental, gay, women, and safety interests have solid financial bases, professional staffs, and strategic sophistication.[9] Those representing the poor and various minorities are much weaker. All such interests benefit from the "rights revolution" of the last thirty to forty years, however, and have legal protection, at least in principle, against a great many more impositions than in earlier eras. Actual implementation of these rights is, of course, very patchy.

3.2 Monopolistic Equilibria and Punctuated Equilibria

Frank R. Baumgartner and Bryan D. Jones have taken an important step beyond the imagery and theory of the oscillating equilibrium (Baumgartner and Jones 1993). They postulate a condition of monopolistic control of the agenda in an issue area by established interests. An older imagery describing the same thing is the "iron triangle" (also "subgovernment") of interest group, executive agency, and congressional appropriations and policy committees. If this triad agreed on policy, no one else could get into the game. And even if they disagreed, they had a stake in keeping others out while they settled matters among themselves. Knowing this, few even tried. Baumgartner and Jones call this condition an equilibrium, even though it does not in fact equilibrate anything. It is an "equilibrium" only in the same sense that death is a state of "peace."

Nevertheless, the term is usefully applied here because overturning this system of domination, unlike being resurrected from death, is actually possible. Adopting the language of evolutionary biology, they call the overturning process a "punctuation" of the existing equilibrium. In a useful departure from the oscillation imagery, they

---

[8] Rejecting both cultural and corporate misconduct theories, David Vogel argues that reformist movements flourish when the economy is performing relatively well and become more quiescent when it is deteriorating (Vogel 1989).

[9] See Baumgartner and Jones 1993, 179–89 for useful details.

presume that the forces unleashed by punctuation can start at almost any time and go off in many directions. Once alcohol abuse, for instance, gets on the agenda of social problems that government must somehow attend to, a variety of remedies are considered in a variety of venues. The brewers and distillers lobby cannot suppress all the talk everywhere. Policy approaches run the gamut from supporting research into drunk driving to education against alcohol abuse, to funding treatment. Moreover, institutions are established, such as the National Institute on Alcohol Abuse and Alcoholism, that ensure a continuing level of attention to the issue even after a popular groundswell may have receded (Baumgartner and Jones 1993, 161–4, 84).

Baumgartner and Jones describe two "models of issue expansion." In one case a wave of popular enthusiasm for dealing with a novel problem or opportunity leads to the creation of new policies and institutions. In the other case, there is a "mobilization of criticism," which invades existing monopoly turf and seizes control of the agenda. In both cases, media attention is a central and early developmental catalyst, followed by the attention of elected officials. Although Baumgartner and Jones count both cases as representing "pattern[s] of punctuated change" (1993, 244), the first ought not to count as an instance of "punctuated equilibrium." If there is indeed novelty, there is nothing substantive to punctuate. The punctuated change is only with respect to the pace of change itself.

4 POSITIVE FEEDBACK PROCESSES: ENDOGENOUS DEVELOPMENTS

In a purely technical sense positive feedback processes are more interesting than negative feedback processes. They are more complex and are sometimes counter-intuitive. They are also more interesting substantively, in that they are at the heart of all processes of growth and development.[10]

4.1 Momentum

Momentum affects many political processes, such as electioneering, legislative coalition building, developing interagency collaboratives, implementing complex program designs, energizing social movements, building community consensus, and diffusing innovations. The central structural fact about a momentum process is that

---

[10] It is worth emphasizing that I am referring here to positive and negative feedback *processes* rather than *systems*. Systems often contain both, and which type of feedback dominates is often dictated as much by how an observer defines "the system's" boundaries as by ontological realities, such as they may be.

every step in the process has a dual aspect. On the one hand, it is a movement in the direction of a goal; more indirectly, it creates a stimulus or an opportunity that encourages others to move towards the goal as well. In the simplest case, a bandwagon, every new supporter is an increment towards getting enough support to win according to the rules of the game; but it is also an addition to the signal that observers on the sidelines should regard this as the winning side.

A more complicated dynamic involves not merely signaling but interacting as well. Each new recruit to the cause becomes an asset in the emerging advocacy coalition as well, a potential proselytizer. Thus, in a community consensus-building process, each new recruit is both a confidence-building signal on a broadcast channel, so to speak, and a persuader and reinforcer to those with whom she communicates in a network of narrowcast channels. To take another example, implementing a complex program design, or building an interagency collaborative, is even more complicated. Each new institutional actor that begins to play its required role becomes (1) a bandwagon signal, (2) a persuader and reinforcer for others who are more reluctant, and (3) another node in a communications network that creates more capacity both to mobilize and to work through further implementation details. The constructive role of momentum building and of emergent new communications capacity was underappreciated in the pioneering work on implementation by Pressman and Wildavsky (Pressman and Wildavsky 1979), who assumed that all institutional actors made decisions independently of one another, whereas in most cases positive decisions by some increase the likelihood of positive decisions by others.

Momentum dynamics are at the heart of the very complex phenomenon of revolutions. Susanne Lohmann has postulated a model of "informational cascades" to illuminate mass protest activities leading to regime collapse and applied it persuasively to East Germany in the period 1989–91. The model incorporates: (1) "costly political action" by individuals that expresses dissatisfaction with the regime; (2) the public receiving "informational cues" from the size of the protest movement over time; and (3) loss of support and regime collapse "if the protest activities reveal it to be malign" (Lohmann 1994, 49).

4.2 Selective Retention

From biological evolution, selective retention is familiar as a competitive process. This model obviously applies to the results of electoral competition as well. A less obvious application of the model is to agenda setting. John Kingdon has applied the model, however, to remarkable effect (Kingdon 1995).[11] Separate streams carrying problems, policies, and politics course through a community of political elites, intersecting haphazardly if not exactly randomly. Elements of each stream may combine with one another and flourish ("coupling," for Kingdon) should they be lucky enough to pass through a "window of opportunity," itself created by a confluence of macro and

---

[11] He calls it a "garbage can model," but this counts as a type of evolutionary model.

micro events. The result is that within the relevant subset of political actors, a certain problem, and a certain set of candidate policies, gets to be discussed, that is, treated as an "agenda" issue.[12]

4.3 Path-dependent Shaping of Policy Options

Today's policy options are a product of policy choices made previously—"the path"— sometimes decades previously. Hence the concept of "path dependency." Those earlier choices may have both a constraining, or "lock-in" effect and an opportunity-enhancing effect.

The current health care delivery system in the United States is an example of both such effects. Rationalizing the current system is constrained by the extensive system of employer-financed health insurance for employees plus the tax-exempt status of such insurance for the recipients. If employers could not offer this benefit, to keep employee total compensation at the same level they would have to increase the employee's *after-tax* income. This would cost employers more than they presently pay in insurance premiums. The public treasury also has a stake in the present employer-based system to the extent that any shift from employer financing to government financing would be a budgetary burden. Here we have two serious institutional barriers to shifting away from employer-based and tax-subsidized financing. The scheme overall rose to prominence in the 1930s, following the marketplace's invention of group-based health insurance and employers' perception that offering such insurance as a fringe benefit might foster worker allegiance and retard unionization (Hacker 2002, 199–202).

The evolved system, or the installed base as some would put it, constrains radical departures from it. Hence the lock-in effect. On the other hand, what started as an afterthought in the collective mind evolved into a full-fledged policy system, a very extensive system of health insurance for the working population and their families. As is the case with most tax-expenditure-financed policies, it multiplied by stealth far more than an on-budget financing scheme would probably have done. Hence what I called above the opportunity-enhancing effect.

Policy reforms are a special but nevertheless representative case of policy evolution processes in general, and Eric Patashnik has followed the course of three reforms over the years following adoption: airline deregulation in 1978, the 1986 tax reform (which lowered rates and broadened the base), and the Federal Agricultural Improvement and Reform Act (FAIR) in 1996 (Patashnik 2003). Although the rates have stayed low, the tax base has shrunk again, as special interests never laid to rest, chipped away at it. Similarly, the subsidies ended by FAIR have made a return. But the new flexibility given to farmers over planting decisions has been retained, since farmers made large investments in the expectation of continuation. These investments warded

---

[12] To this model, True, Jones, and Baumgartner add what they call a "serial shift" in attention. This involves both a shift in the object of attention and a self-reinforcing process of attention growth from disparate quarters (True, Jones, and Baumgartner 1999, 103).

off any serious thoughts of diminishing the flexibility. Thus, reform got "locked in." Or perhaps one might better say that would-be meddlers got "locked out" (Schwartz n.d.). What is the difference between reforms that stick and those that don't? Those that stick develop constituencies that will be greatly aggrieved if the reforms don't stick.[13] Airline deregulation was successfully maintained because it created almost overnight a number of winners in the newly competitive airline industry who have resisted—or locked out—efforts to roll back the deregulation.[14]

What is the explanation for path dependency? In an influential line of thinking, nicely expressed in a paper by Paul Pierson (2000), the explanation lies in "increasing returns." In the context of production this means higher returns to the next increment of investment virtually without limit (without the normal process of diminishing returns setting in), as in the case of a software firm that creates larger network economies among its product users the larger the network grows. Pierson applies the idea to policy-making systems: it is easier politically to try to modify something already in place than to set out on a new course even if the new course is believed technically superior; and in any case, preferences endogenously shift towards the current policy configuration, giving it an automatically increasing return. Hence, there is a positive feedback loop. Pierson's conclusions are reasonable, but it is unnecessary and generally misleading to invoke increasing returns as an explanatory model. The imagery behind increasing returns is endogenously expanding opportunity, whereas the appropriate imagery for the policy-making process is typically endogenously increasing constraint (lock-in/out). Even in the case of opportunity-enhancing effects (e.g. tax expenditures facilitating the expansion of subsidized health care), the increasing returns model would still be misleading if in fact the marginal returns function were conventionally shaped (rising and then falling) and the observer accidentally focused only on the rising portion.[15]

The particular paths that policy has taken in certain spheres of regulatory policy bear special mention. Government regulation, market structure, common law rules, and trade and professional association oversight often co-evolve. They are partial functional substitutes for one another in market conditions of information asymmetry combined with high transaction costs in common law enforcement. Thus,

---

[13] On the importance of constituencies as barriers to terminating policies in general, see Bardach 1976.

[14] For other examples of constituency creation that is intended to lock in policies, see Glazer and Rothenberg 2001, especially 78, 114. The 1977 Clean Air Act amendments forced expensive scrubbers on the coal-burning utilities partly because, once the capital investments had been made, the industry would have little incentive to press for revisions in the direction of regulatory leniency. Glazer and Rothenberg also conjecture that military service academies plus minimum years-of-service requirements following graduation is a better way to subsidize officer training than to provide higher salaries during a career. The higher-salaries strategy would be subject to policy reversals down the line; and, unwilling to take this risk, potential recruits might not sign up.

[15] One of the virtues of the "path" metaphor is that it reminds us that the character of the path depends on the distance from which it is observed. The same path that looks full of twists and turns to a pedestrian might look perfectly straight to an airplane passenger passing over it. The federal welfare reform Act of 1996 looks like a revolution close up (end welfare as an entitlement, require work as a condition of receipt, time limits on receipt), but from a distance it looks like a modest recalibration of some of the mutually interdependent terms in a fairly stable social insurance contract (Bardach 2001*b*).

the regulation of milk and dairy products began in the early part of the twentieth century because consumers were uninformed and ill effects sometimes hard to attribute definitively or cheaply. As small retail groceries with open milk bins gave way to large supermarket chains, milk in cartons, better refrigeration, and the ability to monitor the quality of dairy farm conditions, the utility of government regulation declined. Dairy farms have in effect become vertically integrated into the operations of large buyers with a reputation to protect. In California, government inspectors have effectively been made into paid agents of the large buyers in all but name.[16]

4.4 Trial-and-error Learning

The policy process is in some sense a trial-and-error problem-solving process. Problems arise, citizens complain, and policy makers offer a policy solution. The solution works imperfectly (or not at all), the facts become known, and a new policy solution is devised. It too is imperfect, and the process then continues.

Although it is common to conceptualize trial-and-error learning as a negative feedback process (deviations from the goal stimulating adjustments that get closer to the goal), learning in complex and ambiguous problem situations is better thought of as a positive feedback process. The positive feedback element under these conditions has to do with the constantly improving store of information and analytical understanding about both the nature of the problem to be solved and the workability of potential solutions. By what mechanisms does this learning process work? And how well?

System-wide learning. Based on the literature, it is hard to answer these questions. Most of the literature on social and organizational learning refers to the private sector. It therefore assumes substantial goal consensus within the organization (profit maximization, typically). Rational analysis (variously interpreted), open communication, and open-mindedness are thought to be critical (Senge 1990).[17] The policy process, however, institutionalizes value conflict as well as consensus formation. Learning is undoubtedly present, and emerges from the work of advocacy coalitions (Sabatier and Jenkins-Smith 1993). However, it is typically much more effective in policy domains that lend themselves to technical analysis (e.g. worker safety and environmental issues[18] more than child abuse prevention). Learning is also selective. What is learned is smoothed so as not greatly to deform the learner's preconceptions. Learning is also a matter of cultural, not merely cognitive change (Cook and Yanow 1996), and may

---

[16] See Roe 1996 for an interesting evolutionary story about how government regulation of the securities market arose as a functional substitute for oversight by strong national banking firms, which failed to emerge because Andrew Jackson vetoed the rechartering of the Second Bank of the United States.

[17] Even under these conditions, it is hard for learning that occurs in small groups within an organization to diffuse to other units (Roth 1996).

[18] See, for instance, Perez-Enriquez 2003; Taylor, Rubin, and Hounshell 2004. In the latter case, one must think of private sector entities (utilities and technology firms) as part of the relevant policy system.

be inhibited across the cultural communities existing within the borders of advocacy coalitions. If the policy-making *system* learns at all, and learns how to increase overall welfare rather than simply a partisan version of it, how might that happen?

One possibility is that turnover within elites brings to the fore, temporarily, a faction that learned something complementing and/or correcting what its predecessor took for granted. It is the Bendor process of oscillation enacted on a larger scale. Whether the temporary learning survives the next turnover, however, is a different question. In the political process it sometimes happens that new elites cast down the work of their predecessors simply because it was the work of their predecessors. One constraint on such a process is the presence of technically minded professionals in the orbit of the political elites. Nearly any agency or legislative body has at least some such individuals who will be a ballast for technical rationality.[19] And forums that manage to cut across opposed advocacy coalitions may be able to give technical rationality a better hearing than it otherwise might receive (Sabatier and Jenkins-Smith 1999, 145–6).[20]

Interjurisdictional learning. If a technical solution to a problem has been tried somewhere else and seems to work, it should have a leg up on ideas still untried. And if that somewhere else is a nearby jurisdiction, such as a neighboring state or city, so much the better. A momentum effect is likely at work: "the probability that a state will adopt a program is proportional to the number of interactions its officials have had with officials of already-adopting states" (Berry and Berry 1999, 172); and the potential for such interactions goes up as a function of the number of already-adopting states. In any case, there is by now solid evidence for the realism of regional diffusion models (Walker 1969; Berry and Berry 1999, 185–6). In the realm of public administration, a diffuse philosophy called "New Public Management," which is highly results oriented and sympathetic towards competitive outsourcing, entrepreneurial management, and other practices normally associated with business, has picked up momentum across many jurisdictions in the USA and also internationally (Barzelay 2001; Hood 1998; Hood and Peters 2004).[21]

4.5 Complex Systems

Complex systems are hard to predict because they are hard to understand. The primary source of the complexity is the multiplicity of interactions within the system, or as Jervis calls them, "interconnections" (Jervis 1997, 17).[22]

---

[19]   This does not mean they are without flaws and prejudices of their own. But on balance, across all agencies, and in the long run these flaws and prejudices are probably less harmful than those of the political elites whom the technical cadres serve.

[20]   For an interesting exception to all the above—a case where two ideologically opposed legislators set out on what proved to be a successful mission to learn jointly about welfare policy—see Kennedy 1987.

[21]   It started in the UK and in Australia and New Zealand in the early 1980s.

[22]   Robert Axelrod and Michael D. Cohen write, "a system should be called complex when it is hard to predict not because it is random but because the regularities it does have cannot be briefly described" (Axelrod and Cohen 1999, 16).

The creator and guiding spirit of the "system dynamics" school of systems modeling since the early 1960s has been Jay W. Forrester, now emeritus of the Sloan School of Management at MIT. According to Forrester (Forrester 1968) and his interpreter George P. Richardson (Richardson 1991, 300), systems with multiple, non-linear, and high-order feedback loops are "complex." Cause and effect are not closely related in time and space, and are often counter-intuitive. They are also "remarkably insensitive to changes in many system parameters" (Richardson 1991, 301), presumably because their behavior is dominated by the structural interconnections between their components and between components and the emergent system itself.

Compensating feedback. Forrester and his disciples have long been interested in policy issues. They have concluded that "compensating feedback" mechanisms hidden in complex systems would often defeat policy interventions. For instance, in *Urban Dynamics* Forrester argued that government-sponsored low-income housing and a jobs program for the unemployed would create a poverty trap, expand the dependent population within the city, and diminish the city's prospects, while tearing down low-income housing and declining business structures would create jobs and boost the city's overall economy (Forrester 1969).[23] A systems dynamics study of heroin use in a community concluded that a legal heroin maintenance scheme for addicts would not stop heroin addiction because reduced demand from one subgroup would simply induce new users into the market to take up the slack, and pushers would more aggressively recruit new suppliers (Richardson 1991, 307–8).

Such studies are conducted by means of computer simulation. Although the model structure and parameters can be calibrated against reality to some extent, typically model construction requires a lot of guesswork. Hence, although it is quite possible that the models in these and other such cases were sufficiently realistic to give good projections, it is also possible that they were not, as critics have typically alleged. In any case, it is generally accepted that complex systems are indeed hard to predict, and often counter-intuitive and insensitive to their precise parameters.

Agent-based models. The systems dynamics school populates its models with "level" variables, feedback loops connecting these levels, and "rate" variables governing the feedback flows. It is in a sense a "top-down" approach to systems modeling, since the modeler must know, or assume, a lot about the structure and the parameter values. Robert Axelrod has pioneered a "bottom-up" approach to the modeling of systems, populating his models with a variety of independent agents who interact according to certain strategies. He has relied on computer simulation to project the emergence of empires, cultures, cabinets, business alliances, cooperative norms, metanorms, and perhaps everything in between (Axelrod 1984, 1997). In agent-based models, the relative densities of different types in the population change, as do the frequency of different strategies in use. Selection rules then allow these changing densities to propagate still further changes in the population (Axelrod and Cohen 1999, 3–7). When the community of agents seek to adapt to one another (even if that

---

[23] Forrester was inspired to study the problem of the urban economy by a former mayor of Boston, John Collins, who occupied an adjacent office at the Sloan School for a time.

means "try to dominate"), Axelrod and Cohen speak of a "Complex Adaptive System" (1999, 7).

In their 1999 book Axelrod and Cohen sought to give advice to organizational managers (primarily) about how to "harness complexity." Perhaps the most valuable advice, in the authors' view and in mine, was the least specific: get comfortable with "the ideas of perpetual novelty, adaptation as a function of entire populations, the value of variety and experimentation, and the potential of decentralized and overlapping authority" (Axelrod and Cohen 1999, 29).

Simulation as a policy design tool. Almost any policy of significant scope and purchase will be intervening in a complex social, economic, political, and cultural system. Given its record of providing deep insights into the nature of complex systems, computer simulation is plausibly of some value as an aid for projecting the efficacy of alternative policy proposals or designs. The efforts appear to be fragmentary but growing.

One example is the work done, in the Forrester systems analysis tradition, by a group based at the State University of New York at Albany modeling alternative welfare-to-work program designs (Zagonel et al. 2004). For instance, they compared an "Edges" and a "Middle" policy and a Base Case fit to actual 1997 data. The Middle policy was designed to intensify investment in and emphasis on assessment, monitoring, and job finding. The Middle policy was implemented primarily by the social services agency. The Edges policy focused on what happened to clients before and after they entered the social services caseload. The relevant services were prevention, child support enforcement, and self-sufficiency promotion, functions not typically under the direct control of social services. The model contained various agency and other resource stocks. Somewhat surprisingly to the analysts, the Middle policy did not do well at all compared to the Edges policy in terms of reducing caseloads:

To summarize the mechanism at work here, the Middle policy is great at getting people into jobs, but then they lose those jobs and cycle back into the system because there aren't enough resources devoted to help them stay employed. The Edges policy lets them trickle more slowly into jobs but then does a better job of keeping them there.

Another example is climate change models. Robert J. Lempert, Steven W. Popper, and Steven C. Bankes of the RAND Corporation are developing a computer-based tool for projecting the effects of various interventions to manage climate change as well as other such problems of large scale and long duration. They call the project "long-term policy analysis (LTPA)" (Lempert, Popper, and Bankes 2003, xii). Central to the generic LTPA problem is the inevitability of surprise and the consequent "deep uncertainty" about what to model and how to model it. They propose four key elements of a high-quality LTPA:

- Consider large *ensembles* (hundreds to millions) of scenarios.
- Seek *robust*, not optimal strategies.
- Achieve robustness with *adaptivity*.

- Design analysis for *interactive exploration* of the multiplicity of plausible futures. (2003, xiii)

They note that none of the computer models available for modeling climate change were suitable for their own work because the models "strive[d] for validity through as precise as possible a representation of particular phenomenology" (2003, 82). What they chose instead was almost the opposite, a simple systems-dynamics model, Wonderland, which provided the flexibility they needed "for representing crucial aspects of the robust decision approach—e.g., consideration of near-term adaptive policies and the adaptive responses of future generations" (2003, 82).

4.6 Chaos Theory

Even if most complex systems are insensitive to their parameter values, as Forrester contends, this is not true of all of them. System outputs that increase as a multiplicative function of their own growth and of the difference between their actual growth and their potential growth are an important exception. They exhibit four types of behavior depending on how intensively they react to this product, expressed by the parameter w in equation (3):[24]

$$y_{t+1} = wy_t(1 - y_t) \qquad (3)$$

At low levels of reactivity, they approach a point equilibrium; at higher levels they oscillate stably; at still higher levels they are oscillating and explosive; and at the highest levels they show no periodic pattern at all and appear to be random—"chaotic"—even though their behavior is in fact completely determined (Kiel 1993; Baumol and Benhabib 1989). The set of points towards which any such system moves over time is said to be an "attractor."[25]

The time profile of such a system can also shift dramatically as its behavior unfolds. For this reason the behavior of the system will look very different depending on where in its course one first views the behavior, i.e. the first-observed value of y. Hence, the system is said to be sensitive to its "initial condition,"[26] although a more meaningful characterization would usually be "the point at which we choose to start graphing it."

How much of the world really fits? It is still open as to whether chaos models realistically describe many phenomena of interest to students of policy or the policy process. I suspect it will always be difficult to choose between models of endogenously

---

[24] This is "[t]he most widely used mathematical formula for exploring [the] behavioral regimes [of interest] ... a first-order nonlinear difference equation, labeled the logistic map" (Kiel and Elliott 1996a, 20).

[25] For a discussion of the properties of five basic different attractors, see Daneke 1999, 33, and also Guastello 1999, 33–5.

[26] This sensitivity is often called "the butterfly effect" because the flapping of a butterfly's wings in Brazil could, by virtue of its happening within a chaotic system (weather), set off storms in Chicago.

induced chaotic change and more commonsensical models of exogenously induced multivariate but linear change laced with pure randomness.[27] Chaos models can only be applied to substantially closed systems with a relatively long history, and it is not clear that such phenomena exist in great abundance. Macroeconomic systems are the most obvious (Baumol and Benhabib 1989).[28]

Unfortunately, because "chaos" is often used loosely, it may describe *any* non-linear complex process. For instance, Berry and Kim (1999) entitle a paper "Has the Fed reduced chaos?" when they mean by "chaos" a series of changing oscillating equilibria in two historical periods from the end of the Civil War through 1950. An even greater danger is that the "sensitivity to initial conditions" of chaos models will be applied to systems that are merely linear and therefore, in principle, much more manageable. Hamilton and West (1999), for instance, analyze a twenty-seven-year time series of teenage births in Texas and claim to find a pattern behind which lies a non-linear dynamic system, the character of which they do not explicitly define and for which they provide no plausible behavioral theory. Yet they conclude by warning that "a small change in school policy, health care accessibility or welfare eligibility can, due to feedback in the system, result in large changes in teen births." Were it only true in social policy that small changes *could* issue in large results! It is more likely that "compensating feedback" (see above) finds a way to dampen results.

Self-organizing systems. Decentralized systems with rich interactions and good information flow among the components are capable of evolving high degrees of internal coordination and productivity. They are "self-organizing." It is possible that their richest possibilities for attaining a high degree of self-organization occur when their interactions have reached "the edge of chaos" (Kauffman 1995). However, this proposition may apply most effectively to inanimate or at any rate non-human systems. Human beings may be able purposively to create the requisite interaction, variety, and communication in a complex adaptive system without having to push themselves to such a danger point. It is noteworthy that Axelrod and Cohen, in *Harnessing Complexity*, hardly refer to chaos or its edge (Axelrod and Cohen 1999, xv, 72).

4.7 Qualities-based Sequencing

So far we have been discussing what might be called the dynamics of quantities: the feedback loops tell us that the more (or less) of x, then the more (or less) of y. But

---

[27] The interaction of chaotic systems and exogenous disturbances is also possible, of course. The result is "nonlinear amplification that alter[s] the qualitative behavior of the system." These are called "symmetry-breaking" events (Kiel and Elliott 1999, 5).

[28] See also the persuasive efforts by Courtney Brown to apply chaos models to electoral phenomena, particularly to the rise of the Nazi Party in the 1930s (Brown 1995, ch. 5). Less persuasive are the political chapters contained in Kiel and Elliott 1996*b*.

there is no reason to eschew qualitative models where they are appropriate. The basic idea behind these can be summed up as: Sequence Matters.

In an earlier work (Bardach 1998) I have conceptualized the emergence of a well-functioning interagency collaborative—an "ICC"—as the result of a *building* process.[29] The process has a dynamic aspect, in that sequence makes a difference, just as in building a house it is only the erection of a frame that then permits one to install a roof, or the creation of a wall that will then constitute a medium for the making of doors and windows. Considered in feedback loop terms, each step feeds back into the emergence of a new state that affords a previously non-existent opportunity to reach the next-most state.

Opportunities. These states are qualitative. In the ICC case, they are defined by the variety of organizational and political building blocks that have been assembled on the way to building a functional collaborative. These would include, for instance: a workable operating system, a culture of pragmatism, a threshold quantity of real resources, a degree of political latitude, and a number of others. The full set is displayed in Fig. 45.2[30]. The sequence in which these elements are assembled makes a difference to how well the building process works.

Figure 45.2 in effect puts forward a hypothesis: it is more efficient and less risky to put the building blocks in place in the depicted sequence—starting from the bottom and moving upward—than it is to assemble them in any other sequence.[31] Space does not afford the opportunity to explain just why this developmental sequence might be more efficient and less risky than some alternative sequence of interest.[32] One example, concerning just one pairing in the sequence, must suffice, namely the proposition that trust should precede the acceptance of leadership rather than the other way around. Leadership is extremely useful for solving communications and other problems in an emerging collaborative (as indicated by the platforms above it in Fig. 45.2). It can be fragile, though, because the institutional partners in a typical collaborative are moderately suspicious of one another. Thus, leadership will function best if a prior base of trust can be established.[33]

---

[29] "ICC" stands for Interagency Collaborative Capacity. It is a more precise term than "collaborative" because at any given moment in the evolution of the "collaborative" it may not be capable of doing much and the participants may be doing more arguing than collaborating. "Capacity" may be large or small, growing or shrinking; hence it can be construed as a continuous variable, which is analytically useful.

[30] Slightly modified from Bardach 1998, 274.

[31] The process of trying to execute better rather than worse sequences I call "platforming." I leave aside complexities such as the relatively weak but non-trivial interdependence between platforms supporting the two different legs of the structure.

[32] See Bardach 2001a for further details. Nor is it clear which of all the alternative sequences should be held up to comparison. I acknowledge that empirical evidence bearing on the efficiency and risk properties of this sequence matter is fragmentary and merely suggestive (Bardach 1998, ch. 8). The main point, though, is not to assert the truth of this particular developmental hypothesis but to illustrate the nature of reasoning about how sequence might matter.

[33] There is more to the dynamics of ICC construction than platforming, I would note. Building momentum of various kinds is also significant (Bardach 1998, 276–92).

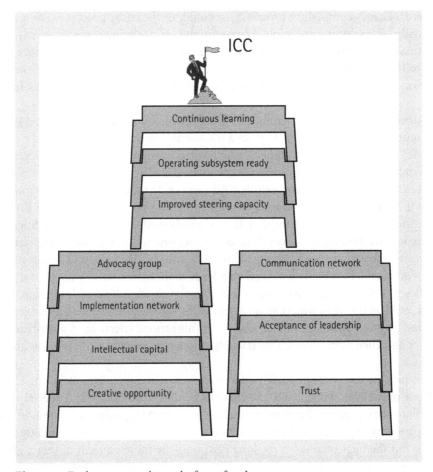

Fig. 45.2. Each new capacity a platform for the next

5 Dynamics without Feedback Loops

Not all dynamics processes involve feedback loops. Some unfold in only one direction.[34]

5.1 Selective Retention and Filtering

We discussed selective retention above, in the section on positive feedback, and offered the example of agenda setting. In the Kingdon model, agendas emerged from the agglutination of policies, politics, and problems as they intersected and

---

[34] Some systems dynamics theorists would question this possibility. They would say that nothing fails to produce feedback of some kind, however indirect. This is true. Nevertheless, as mentioned earlier, to draw the boundaries around a particular system or process is ultimately an analytical, not an ontological decision. There is no analytical barrier to defining a dynamic process as single directional.

survived a chancy competitive process. One could see the entire process as composed essentially of a selective retention subsystem and an agglutination subsystem. The agglutination subsystem is dominated by positive feedback loops and gives its character to the whole system. However, it is also possible to view selective retention as a process that works, in some circumstances, without the benefit of feedback loops at all.

Consider, for instance, the evolution of the common law rules of property, torts, and contracts, which, if not "policy" in a traditional sense, are the functional equivalent of "policy" in their own sphere, which often overlaps with that of policy. One of the most impressive developments in the social sciences in the last quarter-century has been the field of law and economics. And one of its most impressive conclusions is that the rules of the common law evolve in a welfare-maximizing fashion.[35] Briefly, the argument turns on the assumption that relatively inefficient[36] laws will be litigated at a higher rate than efficient laws. This occurs because inefficient laws fail to sustain the wealth-increasing social arrangements that efficient laws do, and a party that loses wealth under an inefficient legal rule loses more than a party who loses under an efficient rule. Facing a larger incentive, more of the first kind of losers sue, and spend more on trying to win, than do losers of the second kind. So long as judges are not biased *against* efficiency in their decisions, this process selects against inefficiency (Cooter and Ulen 1997, 375–6). This is surely a dynamic process, but it is one without feedback.[37]

This process involves not merely passive variation and selective retention. There is also a propulsive element, i.e. the motives behind litigation. It is a special kind of evolutionary process, therefore, a filtering process. Many potential common law rules pass through the filter of judicial consideration, attached, as it were, to litigants' claims; but the filter retains (in the long run) only the more efficient of these, while the rest wash into history. Another such filtering dynamic is the well-known Peter Principle, whereby people "rise to the level of their incompetence." The dynamic involves promotion in a hierarchy based on demonstrated competence in a particular position. Once one demonstrates incompetence in a position, advancement ends and the incumbent just sits there, being incompetent. (Of course, if promotion depends on expected rather than demonstrated competence, the Peter Principle does not apply.) A special case of a filtering process is stranding, e.g. the progressive concentration of less motivated, and perhaps less apt students in certain public schools as the wealthier and more education-oriented families in the catchment area move away or opt for private schools.

[35] Such claims are not generally made about statutory law, however, nor should they be.

[36] "Inefficient" in the technical economic sense of the term.

[37] In fact there is an element of positive feedback, since common law rules do not get transformed overnight. They get eroded and refashioned, at both the extensive and the intensive margin; and each instance of eroding and refashioning feeds into the legal culture to facilitate further change. However, we focus here only on the filtering subsystem.

5.2 Event Cascades

What I shall call "event cascades" are another significant class of one-way dynamic processes. These are sequences of events that have a built-in, or structural dynamic, like the stones in a rockslide that come from above and dislodge stones below, or the workings of a Rube Goldberg machine. Discrete events trigger subsequent discrete, and substantially irreversible events through the medium of a structure that links them. Here is an example in political life from Winston Churchill, describing changes in British naval technology before the First World War (quoted in Jervis 1997, 129, though he does not call this an event cascade): "From the original desire to enlarge the gun we were led on step by step to the Fast Division, and in order to get the Fast Division we were forced to rely for vital units of the Fleet upon fuel oil. This led to the general adoption of oil fuel and to all the provisions which were needed to build up a great oil reserve. This led to enormous expense and to tremendous opposition on the Naval Estimates.... Finally we found our way to the Anglo-Persian Oil agreement and contract which...has led to the acquisition by the Government of a controlling share in oil properties and interests."

No doubt it is a lot easier to describe such an event cascade once it has occurred than to model the process that produces it and to use the model to predict the result beforehand. One could conceptualize the process as the actualization of one chain of events out of a host of potential events probabilistically linked in a Markov matrix. The empirical challenge would entail defining the universe of potential events contained in the Markov matrix and then stipulating each of their contingent probabilities. Most event chains through such a matrix would have close to no probability of being actualized. A few would probably stand out as very likely candidates; and a very few would be intriguing long shots. The event chain from the British decision to enlarge a warship's guns to a transformation of British Middle East policy might not have been apparent to decision makers *ex ante*; but in Churchill's account, it seems *ex post* to have been a near certainty.

6 FUTURE RESEARCH

I conclude with suggestions for future research. If the study of policy dynamics were "a field," these thoughts would be cast as a proposed research agenda. But the phenomena that ought to be studied through a "dynamics" lens are varied and do not congeal as one field. Nor, with the important exception of computer simulation, is there or ought there to be a widely utilized methodology.[38] At the conceptual level,

---

[38] One of several reasons why our understanding of dynamic processes is not far advanced is that their internal behavior is too hard to grasp with language, pictures, or mathematics. Computer simulation is the solution to this problem, as work in the agent-based models and the Forrester-type

our understanding is so rudimentary that it makes sense to let dozens of flowers bloom—agent-based models, systems dynamics models, chaos models, cascade models, punctuated equilibrium models, and path dependency models, to mention only the principal models already discussed. All are promising in their own way, and one can only urge work on all of them.

I am, however, ready to urge particular attention to two phenomena that I take to be of unusual substantive significance and which require a dynamic approach: (1) understanding a process Aaron Wildavsky once labeled "policy as its own cause," and (2) bringing more rigor to the study of what scholars loosely call "stages" or "phases" in various processes, particularly that of legislative coalition building.

6.1 Policy as its Own Cause

Aaron Wildavsky in 1979 wrote of "the growing autonomy of the policy environment" (Wildavsky 1979, 62), because policy "solutions create their own effects, which gradually displace the original difficulty," and "big problems usually generate solutions so large that they become the dominant cause of the consequences with which public policy must contend." His prime example was Medicare and Medicaid, which succeeded in expanding access for the poor and elderly but at the same time made access more difficult for others and increased costs for everyone. The whole system started to behave unpredictably:

> For each additional program that interacts with every other, an exponential increase in consequence follows. These consequences, moreover, affect a broader range of different programs, which in turn, affect others, so that the connection between original cause and later effect is attenuated. One program affects so many others that prediction becomes more important and its prospects more perilous, because effects spread to entire realms of policy.

Social policy. A quarter-century ago, Wildavsky was writing about the *social* effects of policies, and sounding very much like Jay Forrester and his students in his concern over the sheer complexity of things. Today there is a second, if not third generation of problems that arise from the complexity of interactions, and these are the problems of making policy adjustments in an environment already dense with interconnected policies. In social policy, for instance, eligibility for one program is sometimes conditioned on eligibility for another, so that reasonable cutbacks (or expansions) in the latter have unexpected and undesirable effects in the former. As these interdependencies multiply, it becomes more difficult for responsible policy makers to consider adjustments of any kind. The gridlock is worsened when low-level adjustments are also delayed pending higher-level and more comprehensive reforms

"systems dynamics" traditions attests. To be sure, there are uncertainties over how to validate computer models, but computer simulation is a powerful tool that deserves to be wielded more extensively by scholars interested in dynamics.

that policy makers signal are "imminent." This is not just a locked-in or locked-out effect, but a locked-up effect.

The important questions for study here concern just how prevalent these phenomena are and what mechanisms are at work. Of interest also is the question of what exactly happens should one of these cascades actually be set in motion. Do negative feedback loops kick in at some point to dampen the disequilibrating consequences?

Regulatory policy. In the regulatory sphere, J. B. Ruhl and James Salzman have written of "the accretion effect" on emerging bodies of regulatory rules (Ruhl and Salzman 2003). Various mechanisms cause rules to accumulate but only rarely to diminish. Ruhl and Salzman claim, with some evidence, that this accretion has a negative effect on compliance, vastly increases the compliance burden on companies (in the environmental area), and diminishes the legitimacy of the regulatory regime. They present a further claim which is more interesting and more speculative. It concerns what they call "the properties of dynamic conflicting constraints" (2003, 811), which cause improved compliance with one rule to decrease the likelihood of compliance with another. They appeal to the theory of complex dynamic systems to explain why this should happen. Despite a few examples, however, they do not provide evidence of a widespread problem. This is a tantalizing theoretical as well as practical issue, and more systematic research would be welcome.

6.2 "Phases" and "Stages"

There is no shortage of the word "dynamics" in the titles of works about one or another aspect of the policy process.[39] Usually, the implications are that important developments happen in "stages" or "phases," that earlier stages somehow condition later ones, and that later stages have been conditioned by earlier ones. For instance, in conventional accounts of "the dynamics of the legislative process," successive majorities must be sought in subcommittees, committees, and full chambers; and a compromise at one stage may reduce or enhance a bill's prospects at a later stage. In the course of interagency collaboration, to take another example, Barbara Gray has written that there are three phases: problem setting, direction setting, and structuring (Gray 1985, 916–17). A paper on the development of buyer–seller relationships posits that they "evolve through five general phases identified as (1) awareness, (2) exploration, (3) expansion, (4) commitment, and (5) dissolution ... Each phase represents a major transition in how parties regard one another" (Dwyer, Schurr, and Oh 1987, 15). A controversy swirls over whether the idea of "stages of the policy process" is or is not analytically useful (deLeon 1999). The most recent list of candidate stages

---

[39] "Dynamics" is often a virtual synonym for complex phenomena that are slightly mysterious and that may or may not actually be "dynamic" once properly understood.

is: initiation, estimation, selection, implementation, evaluation, and termination (deLeon 1999, 21).[40]

I acknowledge that any such list of phases or stages is bound to be at least in part a product of the observer's theoretical notions, for developments of this sort are in no way "natural kinds." Nevertheless, these developmental categories do not seem to me well enough grounded empirically. The developments in question ought to be expressions of *endogenous* systems processes, and it is not clear to what system these processes might belong. Is it possible to conceptualize developmental phases of this sort that will prove analytically useful?

What is analytically useful? By social scientific standards a conceptual scheme is analytically useful to the extent that it permits one to generate propositions about the world that are insightful, interconnected, explanatory, and realistic. In the case of trying to conceptualize endogenously connected developmental phases, it is hard to know how to apply this standard because the idea of offering a satisfying "explanation" is elusive—a point I shall not elaborate upon here. A satisfactory alternative, however, is to use a practical standard that is in all respects but the demand for explanatory power like the social scientific standard. In place of explanatory power, the practically based standard asks whether the conceptual scheme could produce an *intertemporal map of the foreseeable risks and opportunities that might emerge*; for with such a map anticipatory strategies can be canvassed.

I made an unsophisticated effort to model the endogenous emergence of such risks and opportunities in *The Skill Factor in Politics* (Bardach 1972, 241–60). The generic model tracked "Support" (a continuous variable) through time in a legislative contest over a reformist policy proposal. The time path of Support rose and fell as a function of: (1) mobilization on the part of an advocacy coalition, (2) lagged resistance on the part of opponents, (3) differential adherence by a small pool of neutrals, (4) concessions and sweeteners that alter the evolving shape of the legislative proposal, (5) the emergence of intracoalition tensions and resultant defections in response to the changing shape of the proposal, (6) the uncertainties, and struggles over various arena and scheduling parameters, and (7) the intersection of the current contest, in its endgame phase, with a variety of unrelated issue agendas, actors, and influence patterns. The model was intended to map foreseeable risks and opportunities that a hypothetical entrepreneur would try to anticipate and prepare for.

So far as I am aware, neither this model nor any model aiming to accomplish the same objectives has found a place in the literature on legislative dynamics. I do not hold a particular brief for my own effort. But I do think the objective would be scientifically useful as well as of practical worth to a would-be legislative entrepreneur, and that others should try their hand at the problem.

---

[40] DeLeon credits Garry Brewer with this list. Brewer derived it from Harold Lasswell's seven stages: intelligence, promotion, prescription, invocation, application, termination, and appraisal.

References

Axelrod, R. 1984. *The Evolution of Cooperation*. New York: Basic Books.

—— 1997. *The Complexity of Cooperation: Agent-Based Models of Competition and Collaboration*. Princeton, NJ: Princeton University Press.

—— and Cohen. M. D. 1999. *Harnessing Complexity*. New York: Free Press.

Bak, P. 1996. *How Nature Works: The Science of Self-Organized Criticality*. New York: Copernicus.

Bardach, E. 1972. *The Skill Factor in Politics: Repealing the Mental Commitment Laws in California*. Berkeley: University of California Press.

—— (ed.) 1976. Special issue on termination of policies, programs, and organizations. *Policy Sciences*, 7 (June).

—— 1998. *Getting Agencies to Work Together: The Practice and Theory of Managerial Craftsmanship*. Washington, DC: Brookings Institution.

—— 2001a. Developmental dynamics: interagency collaboration as an emergent phenomenon. *Journal of Public Administration Research and Theory*, 11 (2): 149–64.

—— 2001b. Exit "equality," enter "fairness." In *Seeking the Center: Politics and Policymaking at the New Century*, ed. M. A. Levin, M. K. Landy, and M. Shapiro. Washington, DC: Georgetown University Press.

—— and Kagan. R. A. 2002/1982. *Going by the Book: The Problem of Regulatory Unreasonableness*. Somerset, NJ: Transaction.

Barzelay, M. 2001. *The New Public Management: Improving Research and Policy Dialogue*. Berkeley: University of California Press.

Baumgartner, F. R. and Jones, B. D. 1993. *Agendas and Instability in American Politics*. Chicago: University of Chicago Press.

—— —— 2002. Positive and negative feedback in politics. In *Policy Dynamics*, ed. F. R. Baumgartner and B. D. Jones. Chicago: University of Chicago Press.

Baumol, W. J. and Benhabib, J. 1989. Chaos: significance, mechanism, and economic applications. *Journal of Economic Perspectives*, 3 (1): 77–105.

Bendor, J. 2004. *Bounded Rationality: Theory and Policy Implications*. Berkeley: Goldman School of Public Policy.

Berry, F. S. and Berry, W. D. 1999. Innovation and diffusion models in policy research. In *Theories of the Policy Process*, ed. P. A. Sabatier. Boulder, Colo.: Westview Press.

Berry, J. L. and Kim, H. 1999. Has the Fed reduced chaos? In *Nonlinear Dynamics, Complexity and Public Policy*, ed. E. Elliott and L. D. Kiel. Commack, NY: Nova Science.

Brown, C. 1995. *Serpents in the Sand: Essays on the Nonlinear Nature of Politics and Human Destiny*. Ann Arbor: University of Michigan Press.

Cook, S. D. N. and Yanow, D. 1996. Culture and organizational learning. In *Organizational Learning*, ed. M. D. Cohen and L. S. Sproull. Thousand Oaks, Calif.: Sage.

Cooter, R. and Ulen, T. 1997. *Law and Economics*, 2nd edn. Reading, Mass.: Addison-Wesley.

Daneke, G. A. 1999. *Systemic Choices: Nonlinear Dynamics and Practical Management*. Ann Arbor: University of Michigan Press.

deLeon, P. 1999. The stages approach to the policy process. In *Theories of the Policy Process*, ed. P. A. Sabatier. Boulder, Colo.: Westview Press.

Douglas, M. and Wildavsky. A. 1982. *Risk and Culture: An Essay on the Selection of Technical and Environmental Dangers*. Berkeley: University of California Press.

Dwyer, R. F., Schurr, P. H., and Oh, S. 1987. Developing buyer–seller relationships. *Journal of Marketing*, 51: 11–27.

FIORINA, M. P. 1981. *Retrospective Voting in National Politics*. New Haven, Conn.: Yale University Press.

FORRESTER, J. W. 1968. *Principles of Systems*. Cambridge, Mass.: Wright-Allen Press.

——1969. *Urban Dynamics*. Cambridge, Mass.: MIT Press.

GLAZER, A. and ROTHENBERG, L. S. 2001. *Why Government Succeeds and Why it Fails*. Cambridge, Mass.: Harvard University Press.

GRAY, B. 1985. Conditions facilitating interorganizational collaboration. *Human Relations*, 38 (10): 911–36.

GUASTELLO, S. J. 1999. Hysteresis, bifurcation structure, and the search for the natural rate of unemployment. In *Nonlinear Dynamics, Complexity and Public Policy*, ed. E. Elliott and L. D. Kiel. Commack, NY: Nova Science.

HACKER, J. S. 2002. *The Divided Welfare State: The Battle over Public and Private Social Benefits in the United States*. New York: Cambridge University Press.

HAMILTON, P. and WEST, B. J. 1999. Scaling of complex social phenomena such as births to teens: implications for public policy. In *Nonlinear Dynamics, Complexity and Public Policy*, ed. E. Elliott and L. D. Kiel. Commack, NY: Nova Science.

HOOD, C. 1998. *The Art of the State: Culture, Rhetoric, and Public Management*. Oxford: Oxford University Press.

—— and GUY, P. 2004. The middle aging of new public management: into the age of paradox. *Journal of Public Administration Research and Theory*, 14 (3): 267–82.

——ROTHSTEIN, H. and BALDWIN, R. 2001. *The Government of Risk: Understanding Risk Regulation Regimes*. Oxford: Oxford University Press.

HUNTINGTON, S. P. 1981. *American Politics: The Promise of Disharmony*. Cambridge, Mass.: Harvard University Press.

INGLEHART, R. 1997. Postmaterialist values and the erosion of institutional authority. In *Why People Don't Trust Government*, ed. J. S. J. Nye, P. D. Zelikow, and D. C. King. Cambridge, Mass.: Harvard University Press.

JERVIS, R. 1997. *System Effects: Complexity in Political and Social Life*. Princeton, NJ: Princeton University Press.

KAUFFMAN, S. 1995. *At Home in the Universe: The Search for the Laws of Self-Organization and Complexity*. New York: Oxford University Press.

KENNEDY, D. 1987. California Welfare reform. Kennedy School of Government Case Program, Case # C16-87-782.0.

KIEL, L. D. 1993. Nonlinear dynamical analysis: assessing systems concepts in a government agency. *Public Administration Review*, 53 (2): 143–53.

—— and ELLIOTT, E. 1996a. Exploring nonlinear dynamics with a spreadsheet: a graphical view of chaos for beginners. In *Chaos Theory in the Social Sciences: Foundations and Applications*, ed. L. D. Kiel and E. Elliott. Ann Arbor: University of Michigan Press.

—— —— (eds.) 1996b. *Chaos Theory in the Social Sciences*. Ann Arbor: University of Michigan Press.

—— ——1999. Nonlinear dynamics, complexity and public policy: introduction. In *Nonlinear Dynamics, Complexity and Public Policy*, ed. E. Elliott and L. D. Kiel. Commack, NY: Nova Science.

KINGDON, J. W. 1995. *Agendas, Alternatives, and Public Policies*, 2nd edn. New York: HarperCollins.

LEMPERT, R. J., POPPER, S. W., and BANKES, S. C. 2003. *Shaping the Next One Hundred Years: New Methods for Quantitative, Long-Term Policy Analysis*. Santa Monica, Calif.: RAND Pardee Center.

LOHMANN, S. 1994. The dynamics of informational cascades: the Monday demonstrations in Leipzig, East Germany, 1989–1991. *World Politics*, 47 (1): 42–101.

McCLOSKY, H. and ZALLER, J. 1984. *The American Ethos: Public Attitudes toward Capitalism and Democracy*. Cambridge, Mass.: Harvard University Press.

McFARLAND, A. S. 1991. Interest groups and political time: cycles in America. *British Journal of Political Science*, 21 (3): 257–84.

MILLER, G. J. 1992. *Managerial Dilemmas: The Political Economy of Hierarchy*. New York: Cambridge University Press.

MOE, T. M. 1985. Control and feedback in economic regulation: the case of the NLRB. *American Political Science Review*, 79 (4): 1094–116.

PATASHNIK, E. 2003. After the public interest prevails: the political sustainability of policy reform. *Governance*, 16 (2): 203–34.

PEREZ-ENRIQUEZ, B. 2002. *Economics and Politics of Global Environmental Commodities Market*. Berkeley: University of California Press.

PIERSON, P. 2000. Increasing returns, path dependence and the study of politics. *American Political Science Review*, 94 (2): 251–67.

PRESSMAN, J. L. and WILDAVSKY, A. 1979. *Implementation*, 2nd edn. Los Angeles: University of California Press.

QUIRK, P. J. 1980. Food and drug administration. In *The Politics of Regulation*, ed. J. Q. Wilson. New York: Basic Books.

RICHARDSON, G. P. 1991. *Feedback Thought in Social Science and Systems Theory*. Philadelphia: University of Pennsylvania Press.

ROE, M. J. 1996. Chaos and evolution in law and economics. *Harvard Law Review*, 109: 641–68.

ROTH, G. 1996. From individual and team learning to systems learning. In *Managing in Organizations that Learn*, ed. S. A. Cavaleri and D. S. Fearon. Cambridge, Mass.: Blackwell.

RUHL, J. B. and SALZMAN, J. 2003. Mozart and the Red Queen: the problem of regulatory accretion in the administrative state. *Georgetown Law Journal*, 91 (3): 757–850.

SABATIER, P. A. and JENKINS-SMITH, H. C. (eds.) 1993. *Policy Change and Learning: An Advocacy Coalition Approach*. Boulder, Colo.: Westview Press.

————1999. The advocacy coalition framework: an assessment. In *Theories of the Policy Process*, ed. P. A. Sabatier. Boulder, Colo.: Westview Press.

SCHWARTZ, H. n.d. *Down the Wrong Path: Path Dependence, Increasing Returns, and Historical Institutionalism*. Charlottesville: University of Virginia Department of Politics.

SENGE, P. M. 1990. *The Fifth Discipline: The Art and Practice of the Learning Organization*. New York: Doubleday.

SHEPSLE, K. A. and BONCHEK, M. S. 1997. *Analyzing Politics: Rationality, Behavior, and Institutions*. New York: W. W. Norton.

TAYLOR, M. R., RUBIN, E. S., and HOUNSHELL, D. A. 2005. Regulation as the mother of invention: the case of SO_2 control. *Law and Policy*, 27 (2): 348–78.

TRUE, J. L., JONES, B. D., and BAUMGARTNER, F. R. 1999. Punctuated-equilibrium theory: explaining stability and change in American policymaking. In *Theories of the Policy Process*, ed. P. A. Sabatier. Boulder, Colo.: Westview.

TRUMAN, D. B. 1951. *The Governmental Process*. New York: Knopf.

VOGEL, D. 1989. *Fluctuating Fortunes: The Political Power of Business in America*. New York: Basic Books.

WALKER, J. L. 1969. The diffusion of innovations among the American states. *American Political Science Review*, 63: 880–99.

WILDAVSKY, A. 1979. *Speaking Truth to Power: The Art and Craft of Policy Analysis.* Boston: Little, Brown.

WLEZIEN, C. 1995. The public as thermostat: dynamics of preferences for spending. *American Journal of Political Science*, 39 (4): 981–1000.

ZAGONEL, A. A., ROHRBAUGH, J., RICHARDSON, G. P., and ANDERSEN, D. F. 2004. Using simulation models to address "what if" questions about welfare reform. *Journal of Policy Analysis and Management*, 23(4): 890–901.

CHAPTER 46

....

REFRAMING PROBLEMATIC POLICIES

....

MARTIN REIN

PUBLIC policies are often problematic because the ends they seek are themselves problematic. The defining challenge of public policy lies not in finding the best means to given ends, but rather in reframing ends so as better to cope with unavoidable problems of vagueness and conflicts among the ends themselves. Those problems are largely neglected in the standard instrumentalist approach to policy research.

Two weaknesses of the instrumental conception of policy knowledge are particularly important. First, lopsided attention to instrumental knowledge can have the effect of obscuring the value choices facing public policy, hiding them in the tools of the policy analysts' trade. Instrumentalism cannot completely bypass value choices. Instead it makes those choices silently, in its decisions about what to measure, how to specify models, and how to quantify outcomes (Rein 1976).

Second, instrumentalism has had mixed success on its own terms. Instrumentalism presupposes strong causal reasoning to demonstrate that specific variables lead to particular normatively desirable outcomes. Social science has had very little success establishing that type of relationship. Most evaluative studies simply do not reveal any strong and unambiguous effects and outcomes. The literature is littered with only modest effects, with most of the variance in the dependent variable usually remaining

* I want to extend special thanks to David Thacher and Chris Winship for our discussions about the issues raised in this chapter. Nancy Borofsky and Bob Goodin were especially helpful during the final stages.

unexplained (Rein and Winship 2000). In the meantime, the values themselves, as well as conflicts among them, usually remain unexplored.[1]

I begin by exploring various different types of situations that threaten instrumental means–end rationality. Starting with two of the most familiar—namely, the conflict of values and the ambiguity of ends—I then proceed to extend the list and consider other dynamics that are less well known. The problematic ends thus revealed are not free standing but rather, are interdependent and mutually reinforcing. I end by surveying various ways of socially coping with these problematic ends, concluding with an extended discussion of "secondary reframing" as a way of avoiding problematic ends and unwanted clients. Choice is always choice under some description: institutions frame policy problems and choices in that way; and reframing, looking at the problem through a different frame, can shift how we perceive the policy problem and how we respond to it.[2]

1 PROBLEMATIC ENDS: SIX EXAMPLES

1.1 Conflicting Aims

What does the term "values" mean in practice? "Values" are the ultimate ends of public policy—the goals and obligations that public policy aims to promote as desirable in their own right, rather than as some clear means to some other specific objective. Goals like safety, equality, prosperity, freedom and self-governance, family autonomy (to name a few) can all have this character. Each of these ends can be its own justification, at least to some people at some times.

For example, at some level most of us believe in some form of equality. We cling to it as an ideal, even if only modest instrumental benefits can be claimed for it, or even if these benefits turn out to be an illusion. As Isaiah Berlin (1981, 102) puts it, "Equality is one of the oldest and deepest elements in liberal thought ... Like all human ends it cannot itself be defended or justified, for it is itself that justifies other acts [as] means taken towards its realization."

---

[1] Consider racial integration. *Brown* v. *the Board of Education* was based on the evidence suggesting that segregated schools "damage the personality of minority group children" and "decrease their motivation and thus impair their ability to learn." This established the instrumental case for the desegregation of schools. But thirty years later, experience and further research showed that the benefits were minor and the community opposition among both black and white parents strong. The instrumental argument crowded out the case for desegregation on the grounds it was an important societal value, the right thing to do in a democracy. Most important, it obscured the opposition of the affected groups, who (leaving the less noble values that motivated their opposition aside) did not believe that either goal—desegregation as an end in itself, or the improvement of education for minority children—should outweigh neighborhood autonomy and cohesion (Rein and Winship 2000, 44).

[2] On this see Schön and Rein 1994 and cognate work across a range of disciplines, e.g. March 1972; Axelrod 1976; Sen 1980; Douglas 1986; Kahneman and Tversky 2000; Allison and Zelikow 1999.

Of course, the value of equality still needs specification if it is to serve as a guide for action through public policy. For example, equality has been broadly interpreted as "equal opportunity" rather than "equal outcomes." But even on this interpretation, equality conflicts with other values such as "family autonomy." After all, parents want to give their children an *un*equal opportunity of access to resources, in order that they will be in a better position to compete and to do well in the labor market. The value of equal opportunity is in conflict with the autonomy of the family to protect and to advance their children's career in whatever way they can (Fishkin 1983; Swift 2003).

Another example is the conflict between participation and deliberation, seen in the American attempt, four decades ago, to promote the participation of the poor as a way to reduce poverty. Community Action programs were designed to reduce the apathy of the poor by encouraging participation that challenged the performance of local public institutions. Here, the conflict soon became visible and the program to promote participation dramatically changed. In the *Dilemmas of Social Reform*, Marris and Rein (1982, 1) tersely state the problem as follows: "A reformer in America faces three crucial tasks. He must recruit a coalition of power sufficient for his power; he must respect the democratic tradition which expects every citizen, not merely to be represented, but to play an autonomous part in the determination of his own affairs; his policies must be demonstrably rational." The imperatives for power, participation, and rationality all conflict with each other, in practice.

Participation has evolved over time from an action-oriented concept to a more passive mode. Confrontation, viewed as building power in order to confront inept bureaucrats, has faded as a meaningful public approach to promote participation. Modern-day advocacy takes the different form of collaboration (coalition building, partnerships, building trust, citizen juries); but through this evolution of the meaning of the term, the idea of some form of citizen participation is now widely accepted. Hence, the conflict was mitigated by sanitizing the form of participation and thus, hopefully, reducing the potential conflict between participation and deliberation.

1.2 Ambiguity and Vagueness

Ambiguity is so widespread in the legislative and administrative process that a large body of literature on the subject has emerged (March and Olsen 1976; Goodin 1982, ch. 4). Even the courts sometimes make use of it to reach a decision (Sunstein 1996; White 2002).

But we still seem to be undecided about the virtues of ambiguity in political and legal decision making. The former head of the French government is widely credited with the skeptical comment, "if we extricate ourselves out of ambiguity we do so at our own cost." Thus there is a mixed message in the literature: in some situations clarity can be costly and the only pragmatic course to follow is by the use of ambiguity, viewed as a strong precondition to achieve some measure in building a political coalition to promote collective action.

More than the vagueness of ends and means can be found in the academic public policy literature. There is also an interesting use of ambiguous concepts and theories. Some examples are the use of ideas like "sustainability," the "informal sector," and "organizational learning." These concepts are hard to define but nevertheless can be useful in both mobilizing action and charting a course for research and enquiry. The world of action and research are linked, because once a vague concept is accepted in the field of practice, and resources become available, then the academic community becomes involved in the evaluation of outcomes and in the design of future policy.

1.3 Abstract Ends

Maybe the classic statement can be found in the writing of Selznick (1957), who says: "Means tyrannize when the commitments they build up divert us from our true objectives. Ends are impotent when they are so abstract and unspecified that they offer no principles of criticism and assessment."

1.4 Unwanted Precarious Ends

"Unwanted ends" are ones that are imposed on an organization, requiring that the organization pursue goals that extend beyond the original mandate of the organization. They create an organizational "triple bottom line:" maintaining fiscal solvency; realizing the primary mission; and dealing with the imposed and unwanted mission, which they are obliged to follow, since some regulatory oversight is imposed by an outside agency. These new and imposed values become what Selznick (1965, 126) called "'precarious values', defined as values that are not well integrated into the agency's core mission." It is precisely this loose coupling with the primary mission of the organization that makes those ends "precarious."

David Miller (2001) formulates the problem in more normative terms, as a conflict about "distributive responsibility." This frames the problem at an earlier stage. There can be broad agreement that we should collectively intervene in this situation, but what is unresolved is the distribution of responsibility for that intervention. Who is responsible for covering the financial and organizational costs of the decision to actually do something? We can agree to name a problem as a "humanitarian crisis;" we can collectively agree that the genocide must be stopped. But we can't agree at what cost, to be incurred by whom. We seem willing only to define the problem, not to agree on a principle distributing responsibility for action. Many social welfare problems also take this form.

There are, of course, many other examples of posing issues of how to distribute responsibility. Consider the situation where the government cuts back on the funding of non-profit organizations and these organizations, over time, find that they increasingly lack the necessary funding to carry out their missions. They are then forced to seek other resources if they are to survive. Some turn to the market as a source of income; others seek to pass on the cost to the consumer if the form of co-payment. Weisbrod (1998) offers a telling analysis of the dilemmas of practice that emerge when public policy shifts its distribution of responsibility, by focusing on how non-profit organizations deal with their double bottom line of promoting financial stability and commitment to their mission.

This situation could provide an entrée for government to impose values on the reluctant non-profit agencies. For example, local government might insist that non-profit agencies accept a large portion of the poor welfare mothers or the homeless or prisoners released from incarceration in their caseload. That can then create a Selznick-type problem of "precarious values," depending on how the situation is resolved. Who has the responsibility of caring for prisoners released from incarceration and unable to find their footing in their local community? Organizations eager to maintain clear and simple goals have developed strategies of restructuring to deal with these unwanted, and often alien, imposed ends.

Thacher (2004) ponders one of the serious dilemmas of a strategy of imposing punishment when the law is broken: what if no institutions will take the responsibility for what happens after the sentence is fulfilled? The graduates of these programs, with no place to go, then create a new category of "institutional orphans," who are unwanted clients. Those caught between the punishment and rehabilitation system are often simply ignored, responsibility for them being distributed to no one who effectively accepts it.

1.5 Unattainable Objectives

The child welfare system provides a good example of the pursuit of desirable but unattainable ends. The desirable end is for children to live in "normal" families, defined as ones who accept broad social norms of child rearing. Efforts are made to realize this goal by removing neglected and abused children into alternative care, such as foster care or sometimes adoption.

The experience shows that many of these children in care do not in fact return to their original families. The child welfare system of foster care and adoption has not developed effective means to create a substitute living arrangement for these children. Many of these children spend large parts of their lives moving from one foster home to another, or from adoptions back to foster care. We seem not to be able to return these children to "normalized" living arrangements (Steiner 1981). So normalization is perhaps not an attainable objective, in child welfare organizations that pursue their mission with insufficient resources and periodic shifts in direction.

These children eventually come of age and leave foster care to be absorbed, as best they can, into the community. A recent study of youth aging out of foster care shows that "overall 19% of the study group experienced a stay on Shelters" and the numbers are higher for some subgroups depending on race and gender (Youth Aging Out of Foster Care 2002). The adjustment of many of these children to the community is clearly wanting. But this does not mean that public policy can give up on the self-evident objective of rehabilitation or normalization of these children.

We do not have a viable alternative. Placing unwanted children in institutions seems not to be the way to go forward. The cost of building and maintaining such institutions is alarmingly high and there is no evidence that is a very effective way to go. One can read accounts that date back 100 years to see that we have not made much progress (Rothman 1971; Crenson 1998). Hence we call this a "problematic end," since we have not devised a way to attain that end (a system of normalization) for a substantial portion of this group.

1.6 Missing Ends

An interesting example of "missing ends" is found in an essay by Russell Baker (2004). Here in brief is the argument. Since the end of the cold war, Washington has been suffering from "the sense of pointlessness." "Government is about raising money to get elected and then reelected to service those that put up the money," but it is unclear what form that service should now take. To deal with this problem Washington has invented something called "spinning" which the press converts into what is "spun" by cunning spin doctors who create urgent problems they can then solve.

There are of course other examples in the political science literature on symbolic politics. There, action is taken for show, with little commitment to act on these symbolic intensions. Edelman's work on *The Symbolic Uses of Politics* (1964; see also Edelman 2001) is an early example of this political form.

2 INSTITUTIONAL STRUGGLES TO DEAL WITH PROBLEMATIC ENDS

One might think that the best way to deal with these troublesome "problematic ends" is, at the conceptual level, to clarify the fuzzy ideas. If the ends are confusing, contradictory, and conflicting, then the starting point must surely be first to clarify the muddle and substitute clear, disciplined thinking. What is needed is an intellectual search for more coherent policies that seeks to redefine the goals being sought. Henry Richardson's (1997) writing on practical reasoning develops a compelling argument to support the case for coherence.

We consider next some illustrative examples of an institutional approach to coping with the problematic ends discussed above. The central idea is to approach problematic ends as a puzzle that demands finding a plausible and coherent solution (Winship, in *Oxford Handbook of Public Policy*, ed. R. E. Goodin, M. Rein, and M. Moran 2006. Oxford: Oxford University Press). It is a "practice worry"[3] where the main focus is on the question of action, "What is to be done?" This does not rule out clarification of ends, but it extends the search for coherence and clarity to consider practical and programmatic redesigns of existing practice.

The best way to illustrate this intuition is to provide several concrete examples of these pragmatic institutional approaches. Each is briefly discussed to illustrate different approaches that we find in practice.

Gibson and Goodin (1999) view ambiguity as an ally in policy development. They call their approach "the veil of vagueness," in contrast to Rawls's famous "veil of ignorance." Rawls's idea is that if individual players did not know crucial facts about their identity and place in society, they could devise through a deliberative process a set of fundamental principles of justice as fairness. But real-world political actors cannot do this. The authors propose an alternative model, a "veil of vagueness," which can work in two different ways: the "vagueness of ends" and the "vagueness of means" respectively. First, vagueness can cloak the nature of the agreement: ambiguity or abstraction can facilitate agreement getting; practitioners who disagree at some level can often agree at some higher level of abstraction about what should be done; in broad, vague terms, most members of society can agree what is in the "public interest." Second, vagueness can be used to mask the subsequent steps in the process by which a final agreement will eventually be reached.

Joshua Cohen (1996, 2004) proposes a second, very different approach to the puzzle of how problematic ends can be dealt with in practice. He makes a forceful argument that the values of "deliberation" and "participation," the two foundational pillars on which of theory of democracy rests, not only can in practice pull in different directions; furthermore, improving the quality of participation may come at the cost of public deliberation. In brief, the theory of democracy rests on two potentially conflicting imperatives. Cohen believes that there is no intellectual way to resolve these deep value conflicts by climbing the ladder of abstraction in search of resolution at an abstract level of reasoning. It is an illusion to believe that more thought and deeper conceptual clarification of the sources of the conflict can resolve the conflict. A solution can only be realized through an institutional or a procedural approach. What is called for is "practice experimentation," an idea in the spirit of what Dewey calls "inquiry and institutional innovation." What is needed is thought combined with action, and a willingness to consider doing something different and non-conventional.

Popular devices such as referenda certainly encourage direct citizen participation. But at the same time, "requiring a yes/no vote may discourage reasoned discourse in legislation." A good example of how the referendum can be disruptive is the experience of a small country like Switzerland. A small but determined group can

---

[3] For an elaboration of this concept, see Rein 1983.

undo a legislative initiative that has been the result of a long deliberative process (Neidhart 1970). Something like this occurred in pension policy that eventually led to mandating private pensions rather than increasing the value of pensions in the public sector. This might in the end prove to be a judicious outcome, but the process was created by a referendum designed to block legislative intent.[4]

A theory of practical reasoning must always involve the combination of thought in action and enquiry into the process and the outcomes of this enquiry. This is in fact what we actually do in practice. Consider the third example of, and the institutional approach to, how to deal with value conflicts. Thacher and Rein (2004) identify three practical strategies that societies have used for concretely dealing with them:

1. *casuistry*, which involves seeing how similar conflicts are actually dealt with and resolved in practice;
2. *cycling*, which emphasizes first one value and then another; and
3. the art of *separation* (Walzer 1983, 1984), which assigns responsibilities for each value to different institutional structures.

The principle of casuistry is common practice among legal scholars. Following this approach they ask, "what is this a case of?" They then rely upon the repertoire of case law to see how the case was handled in past practice, letting earlier decisions provide a guide for what to do in the present, on the assumption that the two cases are similar in important ways. The drawback to this approach is that in most fields of public policy no such written record exists and the repertoire of experience is only available in the lived experience of the practitioners, who often cannot fully articulate what the intuition is that guides their action (Neustadt and May 1986; Thacher and Rein 2004; Searle 2001). Cycling and separation can also fail to provide a complete solution. But they do illustrate how, in the real world, institutions cope with value conflict.

Another example of how the legal system makes use of ambiguity in its decisions involves the Environmental Protection Agency (EPA) mandate to implement the Clean Air Act. In *Whitman v. American Trucking Association* (1999), the US Supreme Court decided unanimously that the non-delegation doctrine (Alexander and Prakash 2003) was satisfied so long as the EPA had provided an "intelligible principle" governing the writing of administrative guidelines; there was no danger of passing undue vagueness on to other agencies of government (White 2002).

Another approach to dealing with problematic ends builds on the intuition (Winship, in *Oxford Handbook of Public Policy*, ed. R. E. Goodin, M. Rein, and M. Moran 2006. Oxford: Oxford University Press) that the precondition for dealing with disagreements must also be based on a widely shared agreement as to what are the choices over which we might be disagreeing. Institutionally, the key to acting on this insight is a pre-negotiation stage that creates a template about the naming and framing of what is to be addressed and what is to be ignored in an actual negotiation. The institutional solution is the invention of an "art of convening" that generates a

---

[4] This is of course a one-dimensional account of the effects of referrenda: some can stimulate a national conversation, such as that over the monarchy/republic in Australia, or the series of referenda that eventually radically changed Irish abortion law.

way to map the terrain of what is discussable and non-discussable in the later stage of direct negotiations (Raiffa, Richardson, and Metcalfe 2003).

One can hire an outsider, a trusted person to map actionable terrain. The aim is not to reach a philosophical clarification of what is at issue but rather to define a practical way to deal with this specific situation. It is a case of "learning by monitoring:" "an institutional device for churning, amidst the flux of economic life, the pragmatic trick of simultaneously defining a collective-action problem and a collective actor with a natural interest in solving it" (Sabel 1994, 272).

3 Secondary Reframing: The Case of Offloading Unwanted Clients

While some institutional approaches try to adapt a practical way to cope with the problematic ends that they confront in their practice, other institutions act in ways that exacerbate them. The strategies of offloading and secondary reframing that I review next are not really new, but are much older ideas that can be recognized under different names.[5]

The basic intuition is illustrated by the following example. Suppose a government does not wish to make the level of its unemployment of older workers politically visible, as a problem of "people without jobs sufficient to provide an adequate income to live on." It may try to mask or hide the phenomenon by "renaming" it, and by giving it a somewhat different name shifting the problem a different institutional spheres. I call this the "transfer" from one policy domain to another. One well-known way of dealing with the problem of older workers is to pass it on to another institutional domain as a problem, not of the weakness of the labor market, but of "disability" or where the institutional rules permit, as a problem of "ageing" and "retirement" (Kohli et al. 1991). In Germany the formal retirement age is sixty-five, but the average age of actual entry in the Old Age Pension System was around age fifty-five (Schön and Rein 1994, ch. 4). In the Netherlands, where the pension system had rigid rules of entry by age, in practice flexibility was established by using the disability system as the port of entry into retirement for those below the age of sixty-five, No one seriously believes that a healthy and affluent country of 15 million people also has a population close to one million disabled persons, even though that is the number receiving public and private disability benefits.

This attempt to reframe the mission of a policy domain occurs not only at the national level but also at the local level, where a different dynamic of "offloading" is visible. Consider next the flow across domains of "security" and "services" in the case of prison incarceration, mental illness, or homelessness. In the United States and

---

[5] On framing and reframing more generally, see Schön and Rein 1994.

other advanced industrial societies, we find that the local jail is the largest manager of care for the mentally ill.[6] No one seriously believes that the best way to deal with the mentally ill is to place them in local jails or prisons. Instead, it is an institutional process of "secondary reframing" that leads to such problematic ends.

Some providers of homeless shelters anecdotally report that the proportion of formerly incarcerated people in shelters is as high as 70 per cent. Furthermore, a national survey shows that—judging from the fact that it is now increasingly "people leaving state prisons, as opposed to city jails, who are entering the shelter system"— "the bouts of correctional involvement are no longer the result of vagrancy or the benevolent sheltering function of local jails" (Cho 2004, 1–2). Cho's diagnosis is that this institutional failure derives from "the growing fragmentation of government . . . stemming from isolated policy making." He goes on to argue that homeless shelter is a default category, the last residual institution that manages to provide some care and service when the others have turned away.[7]

The conventional approaches for coping with these problems usually consist of three main ideas: more resources are needed; less organizational fragmentation is needed; or more coordination is needed. Resource scarcity suggests that the problem derives from a passive process that no one intended and no one wanted, but no one noticed or was capable of altering. But this type of reframing can also be a byproduct of an intended process of the administrative classification of individuals based on the "primary cause" of their condition. In other words, secondary reframing can be partly created by a process of categorization (Douglas 1986, ch. 8).

Here I want to stress three less well-known interpretations of the mechanisms in play (Rein 2000):

1. Professional and institutional "creaming."
2. The institutional dynamics of "offloading."
3. A professional commitment to "ideals," in which the commitment to "do good" is not balanced with an equally strong commitment to responsibility in a way that requires a realistic assessment of what is doable (Weber 1919).

3.1 Creaming

"Creaming" is a mechanism whose importance has long been recognized in the administration of professional programs in many domains. Creaming involves both a passive process of drift through indifference and an active process where professionals "pass over" or reject unwanted clients, either at the initial point of contact or intake or

---

[6] "There are now far more mentally ill in the nation's jails and prisons (200,000) than in the state hospitals (61,700). With 3,000 mentally ill inmates, Riker's Island in New York has, in effect, become the state's largest psychiatric facility" (Winship, in *Oxford Handbook of Public Policy*, ed. R. E. Goodin, M. Rein, and M. Moran 2006. Oxford: Oxford University Press).

[7] His paper explores three strategies for dealing with the default: "frame reflection, transformative learning and boundary spanning," categories that he developed from the literature on collaborative learning and policy making, and from his engagement in a program in New York designed to cope with the problem.

some time after some service has begun through a process known as "information and referral." In this process of "creaming," one could identify specific actions of agents that make the phenomenon happen, namely, the passing on clients that they cannot or do not want to handle "on their watch." There is an impressive body of literature which identifies "creaming" as one of the most important keys to understanding how, perversely, those most in need are not served by a program that takes that objective as its main mission.

In one of the earliest sociological studies of creaming, "Creaming the poor," Miller, Roby, and Steenwijh (1970) focus on the dynamics of organizational exclusion, and how it came about organizationally and became normal professional practice. Miller and his colleagues studied a French religious organization called in the 1960s "Aide à Toute Détresse' ("Help for All in Need"); under its new name, the "Fourth World Movement," the organization is still alive and active today with a worldwide agenda. I recently discovered another service organization with a similar mission.

The Alliance for the Mentally Ill is an advocacy group in Boston formed by the families of the mentally ill, whose goal is to challenge the "resource scarcity" view of drift. This is a group of parents who had family members with severe mental illness and which is committed to an alternative, non-creaming agenda. They argued that professional mental health practice is organized to serve the "worried well." The Alliance sponsors propose an alternative frame: mental illness is a brain disease; the condition requires treatment by drugs and not conventional therapy; and the mentally ill require lifelong chronic care, even though the severity of the condition fluctuates periodically. The Alliance strongly objects to the priority allocation of resources to the "worried well," and aspires to become an important political force pressing the mental health community to reform present practice, committing itself to the care of the severely mental ill and eschewing the current professional practice of creaming. The Alliance has had some success in creating "continuity of care" by creating therapeutic teams (consisting of members of several professional groups including nurses, social workers, rehabilitation counselors, and so on), with the same team being available, in principle, to the severely mentally ill for their lifetime.

3.2 Offloading

In this section I want to call attention to "offloading," and its two different types, "diversion" and "shedding," without an explicit organizational commitment to redefine who it services. "Diversion" is illustrated by the professional movement to promote diversion in the criminal justice domain. This example illustrates an active, self-reflective dimension of getting other domains to help in solving a "practice problem." That is in contrast to the other common form of "shedding," or aggressively offloading, which is an only partially visible policy that operates in the twilight, without discussion or debate.

The mechanism of diversion can be seen as an opposite one to that involved in the earlier example of prisons as temporary guardians of the mentally ill. The strategy of diversion involves an explicit decision to divert clients away from the criminal justice system into or back to the mental health system. This is an instance of an intentional rather than passive policy of dealing with clients that overlap both the health and security domains. The difference between offloading and diversion may be difficult to distinguish in the complicated world of practice, with its demands for a quick decision.

Police are almost always accused of excessive use of authority in carrying out their law-enforcement mandate. This antagonism can create community backlash, with the public charge of "police harassment" taking on strong racial overtones. When this occurs in minority communities with a predominately white police force, the charge of harassment can undermine the legitimacy of the police. The police then have a strong incentive to reduce the tension by passing on responsibility and authority to non-police domains.

There is a fundamental, and to a degree inescapable conflict between strategies designed to cut street crime (saturation patrols, close surveillance) and those designed to minimize tensions (avoid "street stops," reduce surveillance, ignore youth groups). Ultimately, the best way to minimize tensions is to find non-police methods for reducing street crime. To the extent that better economic opportunities, speedier court dispositions, more effective sentencing decisions, and improved correctional methods can reduce street crime, the burdens on the police and the tensions between police and citizen can be greatly reduced.[8]

The basic idea is that the domains overlap and are linked in ways that require a broader policy focus, not on the autonomy of a single domain to realize its unique mission, but on the interdependencies and linkage across domains. Accordingly, only some diversion strategies might be an appropriate forum to address problems of professional practice in the criminal justice domain.

While it is difficult to see the general case for actively managing mental illness in prisons and homeless shelters, the case can certainly be made in specific situations. Consider where two very different labels can be aptly applied to describe the same condition. A phenomenon need not be either A or B; it can be, or it can represent the so-called "missing middle" by being both A and B. The behavior of a mentally ill person, in a specific situation, may both signal a deep mental disorder and express itself in law-violating behavior.

The practical question becomes: what is the appropriate strategy for dealing with this person, at this specific time, and in this situation? This way of viewing the process of is as "redefining the case," not as one of offloading or diversion. It is as a more practical matter of "reclassification," based on professional discretion. That does not need to presume that there exists a deliberative forum for a practitioner to make a reflective decision about which is the more appropriate classification and hence which is the more appropriate course of action to follow. Such a system can also be regulated,

---

[8] This is a restatement of the writing of James Q. Wilson (1972, 139).

if there are standards that could be applied in this situation, which has in the legal context been dubbed an "intelligibility principle."

3.3 Idealization

There is a subtle tension between an idealized commitment to goals of "doing good" and an idealized goal of "being responsible." The commitment to the good can have the unintended effect of initiating a dialectic that resulted in its opposite, the creation of "evil." Max Weber creatively transformed this dialectic into an important insight about policy and practice, when he articulated a very useful distinction between the ethics of conviction and the ethics of responsibility in his famous essay on "Politics as a vocation" (1919).[9] The ethics of conviction insists that it is our duty to do certain things that we believe are the right things to do, regardless of whether these right actions actually have the effect of producing good results. "Here I stand, I can do no other." The crucial point is that one must do the right thing regardless of its consequences. The ethic of responsibility contrasts sharply; it insists that "it is irresponsible to settle on what one ought to do apart from what others are likely to do as a result...so this ethic is equivalent to consequentialism." Weber thus argued that doing right things can actually lead to intentional or non-intentional evil, at some later stage in the process.

The challenge then is how to strike a balance between these two ethics. We need to know how to make moral judgements about choice or balance in concrete situations, so that it can actually lead to something constructive. After all, the concrete judgements might be based on the overselling of the idealized vision, or the failure to enquire about the internal contradictions of the two idealized norms, or the inability to take seriously and to reflect on current actual practice and to learn from practice the history of past failures.

Many mental health workers practice within the context of institutional policies that give prominence to their role in the social control of the behavior of the poor (such as protecting public housing from irresponsible tenants who damage property (e.g. continuously clogging toilets), protecting the integrity of the rationing system that is designed to develop queues so as to allocate scarce housing to families that are in greatest need, and discouraging practices like social workers advising their clients to enter a haveless shelter with their children in order to jump the queve). However, in their own view, their everyday practice of mental health can occur in a policy environment that can be antagonistic to their idealized, preferred practice. Not infrequently their practice is guided by the idealized logic of a mental health frame that enjoins them to "help" their clients get what they need, based on need and without attention to actual constraints. This definition of their mission sets the stage for an idealized practice that fails to recognize the conflict between the ethics of commitment and of responsibility.

[9] This interpretation draws freely on the discussion in Larmore (1987, 144–50).

4 Conclusion

Thus, at least three quite different mechanisms might plausibly account for secondary reframing, leading one domain to take on the functions of another. These are, of course, not necessarily alternative interpretations, and the relative importance of each varies depending on the specific domain under consideration.

- The first and most conventional interpretation is that of resource scarcity: drift across domains occurs because the domain lacks the personnel and the material resources to provide the appropriate service within the domain. Since these are largely public programs, the main causal agent becomes the failure of government to allocate the needed resources.
- Secondly, "creaming" occurs when professionals keep the clients they want, especially those that can be most successfully helped, and the unwanted population drifts or is actually pushed into other domains.
- A third mechanism arises from an active process of offloading. The simple case is when behavior poses multiple and overlapping problems, and "naming" the appropriate category requires professional judgement. But there are other cases where "secondary renaming" originates from positive motives, as in the case of diversion programs designed to separate the system to promote security (like courts and prisons) and the system designed to promote mental health. In general, the commitment to prevention is an example of an active design, believed to offer the best chance of reducing a specific problem by moving to a different domain than that of the presenting problem.[10]
- The fourth and perhaps least understood mechanism is that of an idealized practice which neglects to balance the practical consequences of an "ethics of conviction" with an "ethic of responsibility." This occurs, for example, where the risks of offloading are widely understood but seldom acknowledged in the vocabulary of professional practice.

The challenge we now face is how to reduce secondary reframing and the problems it creates by permitting creaming, offloading, and idealization. The problem of idealization may be more ellusive, because we do not yet have any deep understanding of the underlying dynamics at play. But regulatory agencies with oversight responsibility for social policy might be able to take first steps to deal with creaming and offloading by formulating some "intelligible principles" to guide the conduct of those to whom they delegate tasks of service delivery. This chapter is a preliminary attempt to lay the intellectual framework. What is now needed is a detailed, well-documented study of

---

[10] Delinquency prevention offers an example, where a federal anti-delinquency program assumed that apathy and blocked opportunity caused crime. This program allocated Community Action funds to local communities to empower the poor, to overcome apathy, and to create new programs that provided employment and training opportunities as a way of overcoming blocked opportunity. But the responsible outcome can be different from the idealized desire "to do good" and "to help."

practice, which offers concrete examples of how all these processes are actually played out in everyday practice in the administration of social and other public services.

REFERENCES

ALEXANDER, L. and PRAKASH, S. 2003. Reports of the non-delegation doctrine's death are greatly exaggerated. *University of Chicago Law Review*, 70: 1297–329; available at: http://papers.ssrn.com/sol3/papers.cfm?abstract_id=449020 (accessed 10 Dec. 2004).

ALLISON, G. T. and ZELIKOW, P. 1999. *The Essence of Decision*, 2nd edn. Reading, Mass.: Longman.

AXELROD, R. 1976. *Structure of Decision: The Cognitive Maps of Political Elites*. Princeton, NJ: Princeton University Press.

BAKER, R. 2004. In Bush's Washington. *New York Review of Books*, 18 (8: 13 May).

BERLIN, I. 1981. *Concepts and Categories*. London: Penguin.

CHO, R. 2004. Putting the pieces back together: overcoming fragmentation to prevent post-incarceration homelessness. Working paper, Corporation for Supportive Housing; available at: www.csh.org/index.cfm?fuseaction=Page.viewPage&pageId=641&nodeID=81 (accessed 10 Dec. 2004).

COHEN, J. 1996. Procedure and substance in deliberative democracy. Pp. 95–119 in *Democracy and Difference*, ed. S. Benhabib. Princeton, NJ: Princeton University Press.

—— 2004. Participation and deliberation. Available at: http://lawweb.usc.edu/cslp/conferences/democracy_workshops/cohen.pdf.

CRENSON, M. A. 1998. *Building the Invisible Orphanage: A Prehistory of the American Welfare System*. Cambridge, Mass.: Harvard University Press.

DOUGLAS, M. 1986. *How Institutions Think*. Syracuse, NY: Syracuse University Press.

EDELMAN, M. 1964. *The Symbolic Uses of Politics*. Urbana: University of Illinois Press.

—— 2001. *The Politics of Misinformation*. Cambridge: Cambridge University Press.

FISHKIN, J. S. 1983. *Justice, Equal Opportunity and the Family*. New Haven, Conn.: Yale University Press.

GIBSON, D. and GOODIN, R. E. 1999. The veil of vagueness: a model of institutional design. Pp. 357–85 in *Organizing Political Institutions*, ed. M. Egeberg and P. Lægreid. Oslo: Scandinavian University Press.

GOODIN, R. E. 1982. *Political Theory and Public Policy*. Chicago: University of Chicago Press.

KAHNEMAN, D. and TVERSKY, A. (eds.) 2000. *Choices, Values and Frames*. Cambridge: Cambridge University Press.

KOHLI, M., REIN, M., GUILLEMARD, A. M., AND VAN GUNSTEREN, H. (eds.) 1991. *Time for Retirement: Comparative Studies of Early Exit from the Labor Force*. Cambridge: Cambridge University Press.

LARMORE, C. E. 1987. *Patterns of Moral Complexity*. Cambridge: Cambridge University Press.

MARCH, J. G. 1972. Model bias in social action. *Review of Educational Research*, 42: 413–29.

—— and OLSEN, J. P. 1976. *Ambiguity and Choice in Organizations*. Bergen: Universitetsforlaget.

MARRIS, P. and REIN, M. 1982. *Dilemmas of Social Reform: Poverty and Community Action in the United States*, 2nd edn. Chicago: University of Chicago Press.

MILLER, D. 2001. Distributing responsibilities. *Journal of Political Philosophy*, 9: 452–70.

MILLER, S. M., ROBY, P., and STEENWIJH, A. A. V. 1970. Creaming the poor: help to the worse off. *Trans-Action*, 7 (8: June).

NEIDHART, L. 1970. *Direkte Demokratie: Ein Vergleich der Einrichtungen und Verfahren in der Schweiz und Kalifornien, unter Berücksichtigung von Frankreich, Italien, Dänemark, Irland, Österreich und Australia*. Bern: Haupt.

NEUSTADT, R. E. and MAY, E. R. 1986. *Thinking in Time*. New York: Free Press.

RAIFFA, H., RICHARDSON, J., and METCALFE, D. 2003. *Negotiation Analysis: The Science and Art of Collaborative Decision-Making*. Cambridge, Mass.: Harvard University Press.

REIN, M. 1976. *Social Science and Public Policy*. Harmondsworth: Penguin.

—— 1983. *From Policy to Practice*. London: Macmillan.

—— 2000. Primary and secondary reframing. *Cybernetics and Human Knowing*, 7 (2–3): 89–103.

—— and WINSHIP, C. 2000. The dangers of strong causal reasoning. Pp. 26–54 in *Experiencing Poverty*, ed. J. Bradshaw and R. Sainsbury. Aldershot: Ashgate.

RICHARDSON, H. S. 1997. *Practical Reasoning about Final Ends*. Cambridge: Cambridge University Press.

ROTHMAN, D. 1971. *The Discovery of the Asylum: Social Order and Disorder in the New Republic*. Boston: Little, Brown.

SABEL, C. 1994. Learning by monitoring: the institutions of economic development. Pp. 137–65 in *The Handbook of Economic Sociology*, ed. N. J. Smelser and R. Swedberg. Princeton, NJ: Princeton University Press.

SCHÖN, D. A. and REIN, M. 1994. *Frame Reflection: Toward the Resolution of Intractable Policy Controversies*. New York: Basic Books.

SEARLE, J. R. 2001. *Rationality in Action*. Cambridge, Mass.: MIT Press.

SELZNICK, P. 1957. *Leadership in Administration*. Berkeley: University of California Press.

—— 1965. *TVA and the Grassroots*, 2nd edn. Berkeley: University of California Press.

SEN, A. 1980. Description as choice. *Oxford Economic Papers*, 32: 353–69.

STEINER, G. Y. 1981. *The Futility of Family Policy*. Washington, DC: Brookings Institution.

SUNSTEIN, C. R. 1996. Leaving things undecided. *Harvard Law Review*, 110: 4–101.

SWIFT, A. 2003. *How Not to be a Hypocrite*. London: Routledge.

THACHER, D. 2004. Prisoner reentry and the professionalization of housing. Paper presented at the American Society of Criminology, Nov.

—— and REIN, M. 2004. Managing value conflict in public policy. *Governance*, 17: 457–86.

WALZER, M. 1983. *Spheres of Justice*. Oxford: Martin Robertson.

—— 1984. Liberalism and the art of separation. *Political Theory*, 12: 415–30.

WEBER, M. 1919. Politics as a vocation. Pp. 77–128 in *From Max Weber*, ed. H. Gerth and C. W. Mills. New York: Oxford University Press, 1946.

WEISBROD, B. 1998. *To Profit or Not to Profit*. Cambridge: Cambridge University Press.

WHITE, D. J. 2002. The non-delegation doctrine revisited: *Whitman v. American Trucking Associations*. *University of Cincinnati Law Review*, 71: 359–82.

WILSON, J. Q. 1972. *The Police and the Community*. Baltimore: Johns Hopkins University Press.

YOUTH AGING OUT OF FOSTER CARE 2002. *Preventing Homelessness at an Early Stage: Summary*. New York: Youth Aging Out of Foster Care.

CHAPTER 47

REFLECTIONS ON POLICY ANALYSIS

PUTTING IT TOGETHER AGAIN

RUDOLF KLEIN

THEODORE R. MARMOR

THE attempt to pin down a chameleon concept like "public policy" tends all too often to become an exercise in anatomy rather than physiology. The bones are there, right down to joints of the little finger. They can even be put together, rather like an exhibit in a natural history museum. But the creature itself, the sense of what drives it and shapes its actions, remains elusive: a victim of the academic drive to taxonomize everything in sight. To make this point is not to criticize the editors. Their strategy accurately reflects the state of the field and the end product mirrors its diversity. As Robert Goodin has put it in a different context, "theorists are inveterate product-differentiators" (Goodin 2000, 523). Different disciplines, and different sects within disciplines have fought over the body of public policy, all seeking to impose their own definitions of the subject and to patent their own analytic methodology. To set out these varied and competing perspectives is in itself, a valuable pedagogic exercise but risks analyzing the subject out of existence.

In what follows we shall argue for a theoretically less ambitious but (in our view) practically more useful strategy. We define public policy quite simply. It is what governments do and neglect to do. It is about politics, resolving (or at least attenuating) conflicts about resources, rights, and morals. We sideline the issue of whether policy analysis is about understanding or prescribing by claiming that no prescription is worth the paper it is written on if it is not based on an understanding of the world of policy making. If prescription (or advice to policy makers) is not based on such a foundation of understanding, it will either mislead or fall on deaf ears. In turn, understanding depends not just on seeing policy making as a strange form of theater—with the analyst in the first row of the stalls—but on trying to capture the intentions of the authors of the drama, the techniques of the actors, and the workings of the stage machinery. Empathy in the sense of capturing what drives policy actors and entering into their assumptive worlds, is crucial. In adopting this view we place ourselves unapologetically in the tradition of those who see policy analysis as an art and craft, not as a science (to use Wildavsky's 1979 terminology).

By assumptive worlds (Vickers 1965) we mean the "mental models" that "provide both an interpretation of the environment and a prescription as to how that environment should be structured" (Denzau and North 1994, 4). Policy actors have theories about the causes of the problems that confront them. They have theories about the appropriate solutions. To take an obvious example: poverty can be seen as reflecting social factors outside the control of individuals or the result of individual failings, and very different policy responses follow depending on the initial diagnosis made. There is additionally and importantly, a normative component to such mental models. What counts as a problem depends once again on assumptions about the nature of society and the proper role of government. Problems, as the constructivists are the latest to remind us, are not givens but the product of social and political perceptions. If AIDS is seen as a judgement of God punishing sinful behavior, then governments will see this as a matter for the preacher, not for the politician. When such mental model or assumptive worlds are tightly organized, and internally consistent, then traditionally we tend to call them ideologies.

What other fundamental tools of understanding do we need to make sense of what governments do? Parsimoniously, we would suggest only two. First, we need an analysis of the institutions within which governments operate. In contrast to much of the literature, we define "institutions" narrowly: the constitutional arrangements within which governments operate, the rules of the game, and the bureaucratic machinery at their disposal. Self-evidently the process of producing public policy will be very different in a country with a Westminster-type constitution and one with a US-type constitution with its multiple veto points. Second, we need an analysis of the interests operating in the political arena: interests which may be structured around either economic or social concerns (which may be either self or other-regarding) and serve both to organize and articulate demands on governments and to resist measures which are seen to be inimical by those interests.

In what follows, we develop these notions. The first section's starting point is the uncontentious proposition that what (democratic) governments do—that is, the policies they advance and implement—reflect their larger concerns about gaining (and maintaining) office and doing so legitimately. Uncontentious, even banal though this proposition may appear to be, it is much ignored in the more rationalistic conceptions of policy analysis. The second section argues that individual policy outputs need to be interpreted in the context of the overall policy portfolio. That is, governments are almost always engaged in a complex balancing act, given that the demands for policy action usually exceed the supply of the administrative, financial, and political resources required to meet them. The third section explores the importance of taking the historical dimension into account when analysing public policy. The fourth section examines the promise and perils of cross-national analysis, and its role as a check on overdetermined national explanations of why governments do what they do. As a final coda, we briefly restate the case for eclecticism in public policy analysis.

Throughout we illustrate our arguments with examples drawn from history. And even those examples which were contemporary with the writing of this chapter in 2004, will have become history by the time this chapter is read. Accordingly, where appropriate, footnotes provide the necessary background information about the events concerned.

1 THE DOUBLE IMPERATIVE

To define public policy as what governments do may seem a rather simple-minded opening gambit. In fact, much follows from it. It suggests that before analyzing the genesis and life-cycle of specific policies—the focus of most of the public policy literature—we should first consider some of the larger concerns of governments: the context in which specific policy decisions are taken and which helps to shape those decisions. Two such concerns, we would suggest, underlie the actions of all governments (at least in Western-style liberal democracies.) The first is to gain office and, having done so, to maintain their own authority and the legitimacy of the political system within which they operate. The second is to stay in office. We explore each of these points in turn.

The authority of governments, and the legitimacy of political systems tends to be taken for granted in the public policy literature. The centuries-old debate among political philosophers about the nature of, and justification for the exercise of political power is left to another branch of the academic industry. And even the more recent political science literature expressing worries about the decline of active support for democratic regimes and engagement in civic participation (Putnam 2001)—as shown, for example, by the fall in voter turnout at election times—has taken a long time to percolate into the academic analysis of public policies, particularly the economistic variety, with some notable exceptions.

Do they, however, figure in the concerns of policy makers? It would be absurd to suggest that presidents and prime ministers spend sleepless nights worrying explicitly about how to maintain their authority and the legitimacy of the political system, though occasionally there are spasms of interest in such notions as social capital. Indeed it can be argued that it may be in their self-interest to gain short-term advantages for themselves—by deception or concealment—at the price of undermining confidence in the system in the long term. Nevertheless, balancing such incentives, concerns about legitimacy and authority are woven into the fabric of policy making. If they are largely invisible, it is precisely because they are so much part of normal routine. Before governments decide to act, they must first determine whether they are "entitled" to do so: whether a particular course of action conforms to what governments are supposed to do. The fact that their interpretation may be contestable does not detract from the importance of this policy filter. And when they decide to act, they must establish that they are doing so in the right way: whether the proposed policy conforms to contemporary understandings of the requirements of the constitution and the law and whether their implementation has followed the appropriate processes of consultation and legislation.

In short, policy making takes place in a framework of established conventions and normative rules. Governments may at times attempt to stretch those conventions and to sidestep those rules. But governments which are judged to act in an arbitrary fashion, or which threaten the private sphere of the citizen, are rightly seen as undermining the basis of their authority—whose maintenance depends on its exercise conforming to the established rules and conventions. The point is obvious enough. It is emphasized here only because it is so often forgotten—because taken as "read"—in the public policy literature.

There is a further point to note. The legitimacy of any political system depends on its ability to ensure the stability of the social order, as Hobbes (among many others) observed a long time ago. Not only must governments, if they are to justify their authority, be able to defend the state against external enemies. They must also be able to maintain social cohesion at least in the minimal sense of maintaining law and order and protecting the vulnerable. How best to maintain law and order is, of course, another matter, involving disputes about the criteria to be used in framing and judging policies (to which we return later). For example, does it simply require efficient policing and capacious prisons, or does it mean social engineering designed to deal with the sources of crime, disorder, or disaffection? Governments with different assumptive worlds will give different answers to such questions. But however interpreted, the maintenance of social cohesion is surely a fundamental concern of all governments which not only shapes individual policies but also the priorities within any list of candidate policies. And what is more, the apparent responsiveness to these concerns is electorally important in all liberal democracies. Governments face evaluation not only for what they in fact deliver, but whether they do so in ways various publics regard as legitimate.

The other obvious concern of governments once in office, is to keep themselves there: to secure their own re-election. From this perspective, the production of public policy can be seen as an exercise in maximizing their chances of winning office

(Downs 1957). This raises both analytical and normative issues. Normatively, the notion that politicians design their policies (and more often still, the presentation of those policies) in order to win votes prompts criticism. It is often seen as an abuse of politics: a misuse of political authority/power. It can suggest bad faith, manipulative cynicism, and the deceptive use of power (Goodin 1980). Far be it for us to suggest that politicians do not engage in manipulation: there is no shortage of examples of "spin," of misrepresentation of the evidence, and of the selective use of data by governments. There are few better examples in recent history than the case made in 2003 by the United States and British governments for invading Iraq: Subsequently no evidence was found to justify the claim that Iraq had the capacity to use weapons of mass destruction (Butler 2004; Woodward 2004). It also provides a warning: whatever the motives that drove Bush and Blair, their policies were not simple exercises in vote maximization (and if so, they turned out to be a massive miscalculation). But, if we change the wording—if instead of talking about vote chasing, we substitute the assertion that in a democracy politicians should be sensitive and responsive to public concerns—we will get approving nods. Politicians are not necessarily or exclusively vote maximizers. They may, for example, be *maximizers of* moral rectitude (or history book reputation).

Moving one step further, let us take a slightly weaker but more realistic definition of the political imperative from which somewhat different normative conclusions follow. If we assume that one of the tests applied to the production of public policies by governments is their acceptability, then we may conclude that this is a perfectly legitimate concern. Not only are governments that produce policies unacceptable to the public less likely to be re-elected. They will also be condemned as foolish or authoritarian, on the grounds that unacceptable policies will also be either not implementable or in breach of the conventions that delineate the proper role of government (or both). The introduction in the 1980s of the poll tax by Mrs Thatcher's government in Britain would be one example of producing an unacceptable policy that was roundly (and plausibly) condemned and subsequently abandoned;[1] the US example of the repeal of catastrophic coverage for Medicare in the late 1980s is more complicated. It was in fact a perfectly sensible policy that was widely misunderstood as unfair (Oberlander 2003).[2]

---

[1] After decades of discussion about reforming Britain's system for funding local government—a mixture of property taxes and central government grants—the government of Mrs Thatcher decided to replace the former by a poll tax, as from 1988. The decision was widely criticized, led to sometimes violent demonstrations, and prompted widespread evasion. While 8 million people gained as a result of the switch from property taxes to the poll tax, 27 million lost. As one of Mrs Thatcher's ministers subsequently commented: "It was fundamentally flawed and politically incredible. I guess it was the single most unpopular policy any government has introduced since the War" (quoted in the classic account of this episode: Butler, Adonis, and Travers 1994, 1). The poll tax fiasco greatly weakened Mrs Thatcher's position and contributed to her subsequent downfall, and her successor's government promptly dropped the poll tax.

[2] The legislation to add catastrophic health insurance and outpatient prescription drug coverage to Medicare in 1987–8 was and is regarded as a debacle. The legislation, repealed within a year, addressed two serious problems, but was financed exclusively by increased premiums on beneficiaries, which in

There is a fine borderline between on the one hand, the investment of political capital and the use of rhetoric in persuading the public of the necessity and desirability of policies—in rallying support and making them acceptable, in other words—and on the other hand, manipulative cynicism in their presentation. We praise the former as political leadership—only consider Churchill's use of rhetoric in rallying the British people in the dark days of 1940 or Roosevelt's defense of the Lend-Lease policy—while condemning the latter. Modeling governments as prudential, self-regarding actors does not, therefore, capture the complexity of the real world of public policy. It leaves unexplained, for example, why governments take policy decisions that will only benefit their successors. It also creates a puzzle: why do governments address moral or ethical issues which at best are neutral in their impact on voting behavior or at worst may turn out to be stirring up an angry hornet's nest of opposition?

The case of pension policy in the opening years of the twenty-first century illustrates the first point. Across most OECD countries governments were anxiously addressing the problem of aging populations and the expected (and often exaggerated) burden of meeting the consequent pensions' bill. In doing so, they were looking twenty and more years ahead. Why did they do so when, on the face of it, they had little to gain by such a strategy? After all, no government in office in 2000 would have to answer to the electorate of 2030. One reason may of course be that they were using the future as a pretext for pursuing present reform proposals (such as further pension privatization) which otherwise might be regarded as unacceptable.[3] Ideology is there for sure but so is serving their friends in the finance community. This is a fully defensible interpretation of the Bush administration's embrace of social security pension reform as required by the feared insolvency that population aging foreshadows. The argumentative structure and rhetoric is familiar: actuarial forecasts project increasing pension claims and assuming no change in benefits or contributions, "bankruptcy" at some future date is a mathematical certainty. The fact that "trust fund" language originally was meant to communicate political commitment is lost. Instead, the analogy to private trust funds which can go broke, becomes a contemporary source of public fearfulness (Marmor 2004).

turn was neither explained nor justified well by the Reagan administration and the reform's defenders in Congress. In a memorable incident, the then chairman of the House Ways and Means Committee, Congressman Dan Rostenkowski, was pelted with tomatoes by older constituents in Chicago who were outraged by this unorthodox form of financing a social insurance program. The obvious truth was that while the program had merit, the financing means were genuinely a surprise, not well defended, and especially vulnerable to the claim that they had not been legitimized by broad public discussion and understanding.

[3] There is no question that President Bush was hesitant about direct criticism of the US social insurance pension programs. The use of spectres of an aging America was a vehicle for prompting present adjustments in the name of necessity. The change he proposed—using social insurance contributions for investments in individual risk-bearing accounts—was deeply controversial within the policy analytic community, but amplified rather than ridiculed by the media.

However, even conceding this explanation, invoking the interests of yet to be born voters can be seen (like hypocrisy) as the tribute paid by vice to virtue. Governments rightly presume that they are expected to take a long-term view and the fact that policy makers feel obliged to invoke this justification for their policies illustrates the extent to which public policy is shaped by such normative considerations. Which is not to argue, of course, that governments invariably (or even usually) examine the long-term implications of their policies: witness, for example, the problem of nuclear waste that will remain radioactive for generations. Rhetorical long-sightedness can sit alongside policy myopia.

Again, the self-image of policy actors—who want to be seen to be following certain ideal types of behavior—seems to be at least as important as their narrow self-interest when it comes to ethical and moral issues. Only consider President Clinton's ill-fated decision at the very outset of his presidency about how to treat homosexuality in the American armed services. In February 1993, his very first presidential decision on defense matters was to propose that the US military change its long-standing objections to having homosexuals in the services. The presidential suggestion pro- voked sharp criticism within the military, enthusiastic support from the organized homosexual community, and derision among the chattering classes for its timing, content, and presumed insensitivity to military norms. In terms of self-seeking polit- ical behavior this made no sense, as quickly became apparent. But it did make sense in terms of the president's sense of what was right and appropriate in terms of his self-image as a progressive liberal. (It also made Clinton the recipient of substantial financial support from the gay community, which is comparatively rich, ready to spend, and politically active.[4])

The same point could be made about many other governmental "policy outputs." In the case of the UK, for example, successive governments have resisted attempts to restore capital punishment, even though survey evidence suggests that bringing back the hangman would earn them applause from a majority of the population and the tabloids. However, not only would such a move bring them condemnation from the liberal establishment and the broadsheets. But for many legislators opposition to the death penalty is a core value which they are prepared to put before majoritarian- ism. The 2003 controversy over the religious symbolism of attire in French schools— with the state forbidding the wearing of headscarves—obviously involved ideals of secular republicanism as well as prejudice against Islamic fundamentalism. In short, policy actors have moral constituencies, as well as constituencies of material interest, and follow moral imperatives. It is not unknown for policy actors to congratulate themselves on pursuing unpopular policies for what they consider right. Invoking considerations of moral rectitude earns points in this world as well as (possibly) the next. And any convincing analysis of their assumptive worlds must take this into account.

---

[4] The Clinton suggestion ended up with what came to be known as the "don't ask, don't tell" policy. While not what President Clinton called for, this operational policy has no doubt changed military norms substantially.

2 THE POLICY PORTFOLIO

Analyzing the genesis, development, and implementation of individual policies is misleading to the extent that it misses out on an important characteristic of public policy making. This is that demands for public action tend to exceed any government's capacity to supply policy responses. The portfolio of policies that eventually emerges therefore is the product of a complex process of bargaining, negotiation, and political calculation. On the one hand, there is competition between and among interest groups and departments pressing for action on their concerns. Governments are not unitary actors, although for convenience we refer to them as a collectivity in the text (Allison 1971; Allison and Zelikow 1999). Cabinet ministers with different and sometimes conflicting priorities jostle for space in the legislative program. On the one hand, there are judgements about where the investment of administrative capacity and political capital will yield the largest returns—judgements which are filtered through the lenses of the "mental models" of the policy actors whose interests will be affected. In short, the launch of a policy may reflect as much the desire to have a "balanced portfolio" (whether in terms of maintaining the legitimacy of the government or in terms of political expediency) as factors intrinsic to the specific policy arena.

The heterogeneity of such a policy portfolio is illustrated by both the British data in Appendix 44.1 and the American counterpart in Appendix 44.2. The first summarizes the Queen's speech delivered to the UK Parliament in November 2003, outlining the British government's legislative program for the next year. The US example summarizes the State of the Union speech given by President Bush to the Congress in January 2004. Both examples should be seen as illustrative, not representative. The contents of these two speeches are time specific. Under different governments, at different stages in the life-cycle of any administration and in a different global environment, they could have been very different. Our concern here, however, is not so much with the details of the policies involved—which are only discussed to the extent that they need to be comprehensible to the reader—but with the overall style and shape of such policy portfolios at one particular historical moment.

Even the long laundry list that is the 2003 Queen's speech greatly understates the extent and variety of British public policy "outputs" in any given year. Most importantly, it excludes fiscal policies: decisions by the Chancellor of the Exchequer about the level of spending on specific programs and the design of the system of taxes and benefits. And it cannot include, by definition, government policies—whether administrative, legislative, or judicial—prompted by the outbreak of an epidemic, a natural disaster, or an external threat.

Immediately striking is the prominence in this particular portfolio of what might be called social stability concerns. These included: tightening up the appeal system in asylum cases, working towards the introduction of national identity cards, and modernizing the law and system for protecting women and children. All three examples can be understood as public policy in the responsive mode, reacting to external events and perhaps even more importantly, to public perceptions of those events. The tightening up of the appeals system and the incremental development of identity cards can both be seen as part of a strategy for reassuring the public that the government was acting to stop the UK from being flooded by fraudulent asylum seekers and illegal immigrants. These were concerns with high political salience that had attracted much attention in the media in the UK, as in many other European countries. The improvement of services for protecting children was again a response to an issue with a high public and media profile: a series of appalling cases of child abuse had revealed great shortcomings in the existing system of surveillance and protection.

All three examples also, however, underline the importance of distinguishing between *why* a particular issue makes it onto the agenda for action and *how* it is then translated into a specific public policy measure. In all three cases, the government's decision to respond to public worries could be interpreted either as (three cheers) a demonstration of its sensitivity to public concerns or (boos) as a cynical political maneuver designed to prevent the opposition from exploiting these issues. But all three cases had long histories. The UK system for processing asylum seekers had long been recognized as a shambles (not least because of the hardships inflicted on genuine cases). What is more, previous attempts to improve it had produced meager results. The introduction of identity cards had been debated since at least the 1960s, though the debate was given new impetus after 2000 by both developments in technology and increasing concern (whether justified or not) about illegal immigration. Child protection had been an ongoing worry, with recurring scandals despite a succession of attempts to improve the system, for at least as long. As this historical example shows, a raised sensitivity to public concerns (or pejoratively, political expediency) opened the window for the various government agencies who had long been working on these problems to get their ideas onto the agenda for action (Kingdon 1995). The specific measures that eventually emerged reflect as much bureaucratic bargaining and negotiation, organizational routines, and notions of administrative feasibility, as political-electoral considerations. The factors that influence the timing of public policy do not necessarily determine the contents.

There are some other points to note about this particular British policy portfolio. First, little of the proposed legislation involved classic pressure group activity. Like the three examples already discussed, most of the initiatives represented a response to diffuse public concerns rather than to demands from organized interest groups (though in the case of pension reform the government was involved in tough negotiations with employers, the insurance industry, and the trade unions when it came to the details of the legislation). Second, much of it represented the incremental processes of government rather than policy innovation: for example, the proposals to make the planning system faster and to improve traffic flows—a reminder that public policy is as much drudgery as drama, a constant process of tinkering and repairing. The small print of public policy (we all care about traffic flows) matters if governments want to demonstrate their competence in dealing with the day-to-day concerns of their citizens. Most of public policy is as boring as darning old socks. Third, policy may represent a moral commitment, which has little or nothing to do with political expediency. The proposed legislation to allow the registration of civil partnerships between same-sex couples is a case in point. This was symbolism not as a substitute for action but as a signal that the government's heart was in the right place: that it was a liberal, progressive administration. In this sense, it was an important part of a balanced portfolio, a rebuttal of the charges of authoritarianism prompted by some of the Blair government's law and order policies.

Quite different in kind was one of the most contentious measures in the 2004 Queen's speech: reform of the House of Lords. Here the fissures were as much within the governing Labour Party as between the Labour Party and the Conservative opposition. In the case of the House of Lords, there was cross-party agreement that the hereditary element should be eliminated. But divisions existed within all parties about how the new composition of the second chamber should be determined, whether by election or nomination: a series of votes in the House of Commons on various options had failed to produce a consensus about the composition. This, then, can be seen as an example of a government being able to exploit confusion and disagreement to impose its own preferred option: a second chamber appointed by an independent commission, its party composition reflecting voting patterns. It was an unusual and rare form of public policy making worth noting, however, for demonstrating the difficulty of classifying and anatomizing the variety of activities that go under that label.

The State of the Union speech, given 20 January 2004, set out President Bush's legislative aims for 2004 and beyond. The contents of the list range from announcing broad policy aims to proposing legislative action: It is the breadth of the range—and the loose connection to likely legislative action—that most sharply distinguishes the American practice from that of parliamentary leaders like Blair.

Yet, the similarities of the two forms are striking. The Bush speech offered to its audience just the kind of "balanced portfolio" presented to the Commons. In other words, within the heterogeneous legislative proposals and public policy concerns there were a parallel mix of appeals. For example, all of the funding proposals were incremental, with flourishes about "doubling" efforts to encourage sexual abstinence and to make the world safer for democracy, free markets, and free speech. Evident as well were the responses to what we have characterized as diffuse concerns about social stability. So, we find aspirational gestures towards such difficult subjects as how to control medical inflation with policies as weakly connected to the purpose as tax subsidies for catastrophic plans. Likewise, there was top billing for concerns about terrorism, however uncertain the connection between means and ends. And finally, the speech appealed for support of two very controversial legislative actions: the re-enactment of the Patriot Act (and its attendant conflict with civil liberties) as well as the proposal for a temporary workers program (which excites the ire of the labor movement). Very few of the American proposals looked like simple responses to classic pressure group demands. Or put another way, the language suggested responsiveness to diffuse rather than concentrated organizational concerns.

Institutional structures and the policy context of the moment explain much of the remaining differences between our two illustrations. The most obvious feature of the Bush laundry list is its aspirational character, not its predictive accuracy. In the US system of government, the general rule is that administration proposes, but the Congress disposes. And what the Congress does is not usually decided by general elections, as it is in parliamentary regimes. There is no necessary policy majority in the Congress even when controlled by one party, as it was in 2004. As a result, no one could have said with any certainty in January of 2004 whether any of the actions President Bush proposed would become law that year. In the event, the worsening circumstances in Iraq during the spring and summer of 2004 rendered the president's influence in the Congress less decisive. The electoral context increasingly made the Democrats unwilling to cooperate and fissures within the Republican congressional majority made legislative majorities harder to construct.

This brings us back to the most general conclusion of this section: namely, that it is very difficult to classify (or anatomize) public policy. What counts as an issue, or what similar "issues" evoke, depends, as we have argued, on context, which in turn is filtered through the mental models of actors and audiences. So, for instance, the salience of immigration reform in the UK is not reflected in the modest reference by the Bush administration to a temporary worker program. In 2004, immigration had priority on the policy agendas of the EU generally, reflecting domestic conflict over amnesty programs, EU worker mobility policies, and claims of foreigner "misuse" of welfare state programs. Nothing of that kind is evident in the US document, and the reason is largely institutional rather than ideological. American federalism shapes welfare state disputes in the USA so that conflicts over access to medical care programs (like Medicaid) or educational expenses of newcomers (local and state funding issues) are channeled away from national debates. The same range of sentiments that excited debate in the UK during the first years of the twenty-first century did appear in the USA, but not during those years, on the national agenda. California enacted measures limiting the access to social programs by foreign, largely Mexican workers; Texas confronted cross-border concerns in state legislation. And at the national level, the federal Immigration and Naturalization Service increasingly used helicopters to interdict workers crossing deserts and rivers to enter the south-west. But the "face" of immigration policy looked different across the Atlantic, which illustrates our classificatory caution.

3 THE HISTORICAL DIMENSION

Much is made in the literature of path dependency, variously defined. At one level this is simply another way of describing the incremental, adaptive nature of much policy making: that (as we have seen in our case study) public policy consists to a large extent of patching and repairing, building on and learning from experience (Heclo 1974). Again, the fact that policy makers faced with a new problem tend to draw on an established repertory of tools reinforces the bias of public policy against radical innovation, as does dependence on existing organizations for delivery. Initial policy reactions to AIDS were a case in point (Fox, Day, and Klein 1989). More narrowly and rigorously, path dependency is seen as flowing from the structure of interests created by policy (Tuohy 1999; Hacker 2002). Decisions taken at point A in time entrench—sometimes indeed create—interests that come to constrain decisions at point B. Either way, what is interesting and appears to call for explanation is the rare occasion when public policy takes a new turn, whether successfully or not, rather than the sock-darning dimension of public policy.

So history matters. But we would suggest, it matters in a more profound sense still. Not only are policy makers obliged to work within the context of inherited institutions—constitutional arrangements and conventions and the administrative machinery of government—as well as the structure of interests created by previous policies, as noted. But their world of ideas is also the product of history. This is so in a double sense. On the one hand, their notions are likely to be shaped by early experience and the culture of their time, as with all of us. On the other hand, they are likely to use history (or rather their own interpretation of it) as a quarry for policy exemplars or warnings.

From this wider perspective, history can be used to explain change and divergence from existing paths as well as continuity. Consider, for example, the generation of politicians who grew to maturity in the years of slump and mass unemployment of the 1920s and 1930s. The experience persuaded even those in the middle of the political spectrum (Roosevelt in the USA; Macmillan in the UK) to adopt radical social and economic policies. And to underline the importance of ideas, they could draw on Keynesian theory to justify their policies. In short, there was not only a change in what was considered politically important but also in what was considered to be possible in practice. The converse applies to the next generation, who grew up in a period of unprecedented economic growth and full employment. They proved, when in power, less sensitive to unemployment statistics. And again, they could turn for justification to the new economic paradigm (Hall 1993) which challenged Keynesian notions by arguing that there was a natural rate of unemployment about which governments could do little and only at the risk of fueling inflation.

What matters in all this, of course, is not history as written in academic textbooks but the interpretations put on it by policy makers: the lessons they choose to draw from the past (Neustadt and May 1988). So, for example, the nebulous Third Way as espoused by Clinton and Blair in the 1990s—the latest in a long line of attempts to find a middle way (Macmillan 1938)—cannot be understood without taking into account their diagnosis of the mistakes made by their predecessors as party leaders. The interpretation of history need not be correct. Some disastrous policy decisions have flown from the misapplication of supposed historical lessons, largely as a result of mis-specifying the similarity between past and present situations. The conclusion that it never pays to appease dictators drawn from the abject surrender of the Western powers to Hitler at Munich in 1938, plus the equation of Nasser with Hitler, was used to justify Britain's disastrous Suez adventure in 1956. And Bush's initiation of the 2003 Iraq War may also, in part at least, have reflected a misreading of history. Bush's Iraq policy appeared to some a reaction against his father's "failure" to topple Saddam. Whatever the president's motives, the justifications offered—that weapons of mass destruction in the hands of a dictator will be used and therefore must be "taken out" preventively—relied on historical claims. In another sense, the Iraq policy was an earlier conviction searching for an occasion, a commitment to get rid of Saddam by officials from Bush I's presidency acted upon in Bush II's administration (Woodward 2002, 2004; Dean 2004).

Particular readings of history may also persuade policy makers to diverge from the trodden path. Policy change is not only the result of windows of opportunity suddenly opening as the result of some upheaval in the economic or political environment. Policy change itself may open such windows by demonstrating that the previously unthinkable has become doable. A case in point is the repudiation in the 1980s by Mrs Thatcher of the assumption shaping the policies of all post-1945 British governments that they needed the cooperation of the trade union movement to manage the economy. Instead, she was prepared to confront and fight the unions (Young 1989). The skies did not fall in. And Tony Blair, as Labour Prime Minister, shaped his policies accordingly, largely sidelining the unions when he took office in 1997 and making a political virtue of his independence of them.

The Bush II 2004 administration's approach to old-age and retirement policy illustrated similar risk taking. By suggesting that what Americans call social security retirement pensions should be partially privatized, President Bush repeatedly risked identification as an enemy of a public policy "sacred cow." The cliché has been that "social security is the third rail of American politics, electrocuting all those who touch it." Yet, throughout his administration's first term, Bush called for private, individual pension accounts funded by a proportion of the compulsory "contributions" that all Americans pay. This innovation, the president claimed, was the right response to the fiscal strains the aging American society faces. Leaving aside the merits of this view—which are few if any—this bold rhetoric in presidential speeches and proposals did not provoke the public condemnation pundits anticipated on the basis of social security's status as a supposed "sacred cow." In turn, the rhetoric emboldened the interest groups who would gain financially if the American government required some share of social insurance taxes to be invested in the stock and bond markets. As a result, the presidential election of 2004 was replete with references to the differences between the traditional defense of social insurance (largely by Democrats) and the call for private individual accounts (largely by Republicans).

Innovation occurs, but not as commonly as appeals to its possibility (Baumgartner and Jones 1993, 2002). Nonetheless, without history there can therefore be no understanding of public policy. And without history there can also be no realistic evaluation of public policy. For if evaluation does not take into account what policy makers were trying to achieve, if the criteria used in judging the success or otherwise of policies are those of the evaluator rather than those of the originator, the result will at best yield a very partial, perhaps anachronistic verdict. By this we do not claim a historical monopoly on either the understandings or the evaluation of public policy. But we do connect our insistence on the explanatory importance of the assumptive world of policy actors with the truism that all our assumptions incorporate historical understandings, both biographical and cultural.

4 THE COMPARATIVE DIMENSION

This chapter has so far emphasized the importance of context—institutional, ideological, and historical—in the understanding of policy making in modern polities. Here we turn to another important way to understand and to evaluate policy making: namely, the use of cross-national policy studies. There is little doubt such work has mushroomed in recent decades, partly no doubt, because of technological innovations that have speeded up the transfer of information about what is happening abroad. Indeed, none of us can escape the "bombardment of information about what is happening in other countries" (Klein 1995). The pressing question, however, is whether this informational dispersion is a help or a hindrance to understanding what governments do and why.

There are at least three obvious ways in which policy analysis might be improved by cross-national understanding. One is simply to define more clearly what is on the policy agenda by reference to quite similar or quite different formulations elsewhere. The more similar the problems or policy responses, the more likely one can portray the nuanced formulations of any particular country. The more dissimilar, the more striking the contrast with what one takes for granted in one's own policy setting. This is the gift of perspective, which may or may not bring with it explanatory insight or lesson drawing. A second approach is to use cross-national enquiry to check on the adequacy of nation-specific accounts. Let's call that a defense against explanatory provincialism. What precedes policy making in country A includes many things—from legacies of past policy to institutional and temporal features that "seem" decisive. How is one to know how decisive as opposed to simply present? One answer is to look for similar outcomes elsewhere where some of those factors are missing or configured differently. Another is to look for a similar configuration of precedents without a comparable outcome. A third and still different approach is to treat cross-national experience as quasi-experiments. Here one hopes to draw lessons about why some policies seem promising and doable, promising and impossible, or doable but not promising. All of these approaches appear in the comparative literature. And with the growth of such writing, one senses an optimism about the possible improvement of comparative learning and lesson drawing. But is the optimism justified? That question is what interests us here.

The interest, however, is not in addressing the broad topic of the promise and perils of cross-national policy studies (Klein 1991; Marmor, Okma, and Freeman 2005). Rather, it is to offer some illustrations of how comparative understanding can advance the art and craft of policy analysis. This requires some examples of each of these approaches, positive or negative. A useful starting point would be to take a misleading cross-national generalization that upon reflection, helps to clarify differences in how policy problems are in fact posed. A 1995 article on European health reform claimed that "countries everywhere are reforming their health systems." It went on to assert that "what is remarkable about this global movement is that both the diagnosis of the problems and the prescription for them are virtually the same in all health care systems" (Hunter 1995). These globalist claims, it turns out, were mistaken (Jacobs 1998; Marmor 1999). But the process of specifying exactly what counts as health care problems—whether of cost control, of poor quality, or of fragmented organization of services—is helpful. The comparative approach first refutes the generalization, but it also enriches what any one analyst portrays as national "problems." So, for instance, the British health policy researcher coming to investigate Oregon's experiment in rationing would have soon discovered that it was neither restrictive in practice nor a major cost control remedy in the decade 1990–2000 (Jacobs, Marmor, and Oberlander 1999).

Offering new perspectives on problems and making factual adjustments in national portraits are not to be treated as trivial tasks. They are what apprentice policy craftsmen and -women might well spend a good deal of time perfecting. That is because all too many comparative studies are in fact caricatures rather than characterizations of policies in action. A striking illustration of that problem is the 2000 World Health Organization (WHO) report on how one might rank health systems across the globe. Not only was the ambition itself grandiose, but the execution of it would be best regarded as ridiculous (Williams 2001). The WHO posed five good questions about how health systems work: are they fair, responsive, efficient, and so on. But they answered those questions without the faintest attention to the difficulties of describing responsiveness or fairness or efficiency in some universalistic manner. What's more, they used as partial evidence the distant opinions of Geneva-based medical personnel to "verify" what takes place in Australia, Oman, or Canada. With comparativists like that, one can easily understand why some funders of research regard comparative policy studies as excuses for boondoggles. But mistakes should not drive out the impulse for improvement.[5]

***

[5] There are, of course, other interpretations of the WHO action, however unreliable the precise evaluations of national performance. One such interpretation, offered by one of the *Handbook*'s editors, is that the ranking of countries on the basis of specious data surely would provoke local political interest in gathering and presenting more reliable data about health across the globe. In the case of Australia for instance, the civil servant in charge of the federal health department did in fact challenge the WHO report; in other capitals outrage did lead to condemnation and the provision of counter-evidence. This was certainly one result of the exercise, and there is reason to believe this aim was in the mind of the WHO study director, Murray. One of this chapter's authors confronted Murray in London during the spring of 2001 at a conference with the inaccuracies and absurdities of this ranking. Murray responded by invoking the experience of national income accounts. No one, he said, thought GDP measured

The most commonly cited advantage of comparative studies, however, is as an antidote to explanatory provincialism. Once again, a health policy example provides a good illustration of how and how not to proceed. There are those in North America who regard universal health insurance as incompatible with American values. They rest their case in part on the belief that Canada enacted health insurance and the USA has not because North American values are sharply different. In short, these comparativists attribute a different outcome to a different political culture in the USA. In fact, the values of Canada and the United States, while not identical, are quite similar. Canada's distribution of values is closer to that of the United States than any other modern, rich democracy. Like siblings, differences are there. In fact, the value similarities between British Columbia and Washington state are greater than those between either of those jurisdictions and, say, New Brunswick or New Hampshire along the North American east coast. Similar values are compatible with different outcomes, which in turn draw one's attention to other institutional and strategic factors that distinguish Canadian from American experience with financing health care (Maioni 1998; White 1995). One can imagine multiplying examples of such cautionary lessons, but the important point is simply that the lessons are unavailable from national histories alone.

The third category of work is not so directly relevant to our enquiry. But it is worth noting that drawing lessons from the policy experience of other nations is what supports a good deal of the comparative analysis available. The international organizations have this as part of their rationale. WHO, as noted, is firmly in the business of selling "best practices." The OECD regularly produces extensive, hard to gather, statistical portraits of programs as diverse as disability and pensions, trade flows and the movement of professionals, educational levels, and health expenditures. No one can avoid using these efforts, if only because the task of discovering "the facts" in a number of countries is daunting indeed. But the portraiture that emerges requires its own craft review. Does what Germany spends on spas count as health expenditures under public regulation or should it, as with the United States be categorized differently? The same words do not mean the same things. And different words may denote similar phenomena. For now, it is enough to note that learning about the experience of other nations is a precondition for learning from them. A number of comparative studies fail on the first count and thus necessarily on the second. On the other hand, if one were to look for exemplary instances of cross-national learning, one would turn quite quickly to Japan, Taiwan, and Korea. All have sent first-rate civil servants abroad to find promising models, have worried about the barriers to transplantation, and have when using these apparent models, worked carefully on issues of adaptation, transformation, and implementation.

---

income perfectly or did so correctly at the outset. But Murray went on to add, "we would not want to go back on GDP measures, would we?" The notion that producing junk science energizes better science may have some empirical backing, but it is the weakest possible defense of any particular, flawed study.

5 THE CASE FOR ECLECTICISM

One reaction to our chapter may well be to dismiss it as an exercise in trying to have it all ways: eclecticism as a substitute for intellectual rigor. However, we make no apology for this. In practice, no public policy analyst can use all the tools of the trade all the time: a rational choice analyst in the morning, a psycho-biographer in the afternoon, a historian in the evening, and a political theorist in the hours when sleep does not come. However, our contention throughout has been that the attempt to draw on all these disciplines is essential. Trying to understand and explain public policy as a whole—making sense of what governments do, rather than analysing specific election results or policy outputs—has to be in our view, an exercise in synthesis.

The point can be simply illustrated, bringing together many of the issues previously discussed. Central to most public policy analysis (including our own) is the notion of self-interest. We invoke the self-interest of politicians in getting elected and staying in office. We invoke the self-interest of lobbies in pressing for their share of pork or in pursuit of some ideology. Yet as Thomas Macaulay (cited in Wildavsky 1994, 155) pointed out some 150 years ago in his critique of utilitarianism:

One man cuts his father's throat to get possession of his old clothes; another hazards his own life to save that of an enemy. One man volunteers on a forlorn hope; another is drummed out of a regiment for cowardice. Each of these men has no doubt acted from self-interest. But we gain nothing from knowing this, except the pleasure, if it be one, of multiplying useless words.

In short, much of public policy analysis involves giving meaning to what, in the absence of background knowledge, is indeed an empty word. How people define their self-interest (their assumptive worlds) depends on culture and history. How people in turn, act to further that self-interest will depend on the institutions within which they operate. And the definitions, and the way in which they are translated into practice, will vary and evolve over time as the intellectual, social, and economic environment changes. So, for example, no one can understand the evolving history of Britain's National Health Service (Klein 2001) without taking into account the changing environment in which it operates.

In summary then, we have argued that no sensible understanding of what liberal democratic governments should do, have done, or will do is possible without attention to the realities of office seeking and office keeping, and how those realities are perceived by those involved. This theme—stunningly obvious in one sense—is nonetheless all too frequently ignored. The history of efforts to make the analysis of public policy more scientific, rigorous, and thereby more helpful for policy development is a fascinating (and controversial) one, but has not been our concern here. Rather our contribution is to insist that whatever technical improvements are possible—in polling accuracy, in economic modeling, in the simulation of policy options, and so on—it remains essential to emphasize the centrality of the most basic features of governmental policy making in democratic polities. These, we have suggested, include the need to maintain regime legitimacy, the competitive struggle to achieve (and keep) office, and the search for a balanced policy portfolio.

Beyond that we have emphasized the importance of understanding the constellation of ideas, institutions, and interests that converge in any policy activity. Here the focus is, as argued above, on how historical evidence—and evidence about history—shapes the options available to policy makers, their understanding of the material (and other) interests at stake, and their interpretation of what contemporary audiences will make of their ideas. Throughout we have illustrated our claims about historical understanding by citing examples that appear to tell an apt illustrative story—in line with our contention that the analysis of public policy, like policy making itself is an exercise in persuasion (Majone 1989). Hence the importance of examining critically the rhetoric of persuasion used by both policy makers and public policy analysts.

The discussion of comparative policy emphasizes still another element in the art and craft of policy analysis. Comparing formulations of policy problems across national borders illustrated the degree to which the mental worlds of actors are shaped by their distinctive historical understandings and the ideas that stakeholders in particular settings take for granted, as well as being a protection against explanatory provincialism. Finally, we note the complexities of evaluating public policy making once the perspectives of policy makers are taken as central to understanding their options and choices. Put another way, an appreciation of what policy makers believe they are doing is a necessary—albeit far from sufficient—condition for understanding and evaluating their actions.

APPENDIX 44.1 THE QUEEN'S SPEECH, NOVEMBER 2004 THE UK GOVERNMENT'S LEGISLATIVE PROGRAMME

The Queen's speech announced the following planned legislation, for the 2004/5 session of Parliament. The bills announced would:

- Enable young people to people to benefit from higher education and abolish up-front tuition fees.
- Encourage employers to provide good-quality pensions and individuals to save for retirement, and set up a Pension Protection Fund to protect people when companies become insolvent.
- Allow registration of civil partnerships between same-sex couples.
- Establish a single tier of appeal against asylum decisions.
- Take forward work on an incremental approach to a national identity cards scheme.
- Modernize the laws on domestic violence and improve services designed to protect children.

- Remove hereditary peers and set up an independent Appointments Commission.
- Enable a referendum on the single currency, subject to the government's five economic tests being met.
- Make the planning system faster and fairer with greater community participation.
- Improve traffic flows and manage road works more effectively.
- Modernize charity law and allow for the creation of Community Interest Companies.

Source: Adapted from *The Queen' Speech* 2004.

APPENDIX 44.2   BUSH'S 2004 STATE OF THE
UNION ADDRESS

Summary of Contents

- Continue support for the War on Terror; a peaceful, stable, and democratic Iraq; and homeland security.
- Renew the Patriot Act, which is set to expire in 2005.
- Put pressure on regimes that support and harbor terrorists and seek to obtain weapons of mass destruction.
- Double the budget for the National Endowment for Democracy to help it develop free elections, free markets, free press, and free labor unions in the Middle East.
- Give students the skills they need to succeed in the workplace with Jobs for the Twenty-First Century, a series of measures that includes extra help for students falling behind in reading and math, greater access to AP programs in high schools, private sector math and science professionals teaching part-time in high schools, larger Pell grants for college students, and increased support for community colleges.
- Make the temporary tax cuts permanent to keep the economy going strong.
- Help small business owners and employees find relief from excessive federal regulation and frivolous lawsuits.
- Enact energy-related measures to modernize the electricity system, protect the environment, and make America less dependent on foreign oil.
- Create Social Security Personal Retirement Accounts.
- Cut the federal deficit in half over five years with a budget that limits growth in discretionary spending to 4 per cent.
- Reform immigration laws to create a temporary worker program allowing illegal immigrants to obtain temporary legal status.
- Control medical costs and expand access to care by letting small businesses collectively bargain with insurance companies, giving refundable tax credits to low-income Americans so they can buy their own health insurance, computerizing health records to improve quality and reduce cost, reforming medical malpractice law, and making the purchase of catastrophic health care coverage 100 per cent tax deductible.
- Increase funding to combat drug use through education, drug testing in schools, and asking children's role models to set a good example.
- Double federal funding for abstinence programs to reduce the incidence of sexually transmitted diseases.
- Prevent same-sex marriages, using the constitutional process if necessary.

- Codify into law the executive order allowing faith-based charities to compete for federal social service grants.
- Enact a prisoner re-entry program providing better job training and placement, transitional housing, and mentoring.

Source: Adapted from Bush 2004.

REFERENCES

ALLISON, G. 1971. *Essence of Decision: Explaining the Cuban Missile Crisis.* Boston: Little, Brown.

—— and ZELIKOW, P. 1999. *Essence of Decision: Explaining the Cuban Missile Crisis,* 2nd edn. New York: Longman.

BAUMGARTNER, F. and JONES, B. 1993. *Agendas and Instability in American Politics.* Chicago: Chicago University Press.

—— —— 2002. *Policy Dynamics.* Chicago: Chicago University Press.

BUSH, G. W. 2004. State of the Union Address, Jan. 20. Available at: www.whitehouse.gov/news/releases/2004/01/20040120-7.html.

BUTLER, D., ADONIS, A., and TRAVERS, T. 1994 *Failure in British Government: The Politics of the Poll Tax.* Oxford: Oxford University Press.

BUTLER, R. 2004. *Review of Intelligence on Weapons of Mass Destruction.* London: HMSO.

DEAN, J. 2004. *Worse than Watergate: The Secret Presidency of George W. Bush.* New York: Little, Brown.

DENZAU, A. T. and NORTH, D. C. 1994. Shared mental models: ideologies and institutions. *Kyklos,* 47 (1): 3–31.

DOWNS, A. 1957. *An Economic Theory of Democracy.* New York: Harper and Row.

FOX, D., DAY, P., and KLEIN, R. 1989. The power of professionalism: policies for AIDS in Britain, Sweden and the United States. *Daedalus,* 118 (2): 93–112.

GOODIN, R. E. 1980. *Manipulative Politics.* New Haven, Conn.: Yale University Press.

—— 2000. Institutional gaming. *Governance,* 13: 523–33.

HACKER, J. S. 2002. *The Divided Welfare State.* New York: Cambridge University Press.

HALL, P. A. 1993. Policy paradigms, social learning and the state. *Comparative Politics,* 25: 275–96.

HECLO, H. 1974. *Modern Social Politics in Britain and Sweden.* New Haven, Conn.: Yale University Press.

HUNTER, D. 1995. A new focus for dialogue. *European Health Reform: The Bulletin of the European Network and Database,* 1 (Mar.).

JACOBS, A. 1998. Seeing difference: market health reform in Europe. *Journal of Health Politics, Policy and Law,* 23 (1): 1–33.

—— MARMOR, T., and OBERLANDER, J. 1999. The Oregon Health Plan and the political paradox of rationing: what advocates and critic have claimed and what Oregon did. *Journal of Health Politics, Policy and Law,* 24 (1): 161–80.

JACOBS, L. R. and SHAPIRO, R. Y. 2000. *Politicians Don't Pander: Political Manipulation and the Loss of Democratic Responsiveness.* Chicago: University of Chicago Press.

KENNEDY, J. 1964. *Profiles in Courage.* New York: Harper and Row.

KINGDON, J. W. 1995. *Agendas, Alternatives and Public Policies,* 2nd edn. New York: HarperCollins.

KLEIN, R. 1991. Risks and benefits of comparative studies. *Milbank Quarterly*, 69 (2): 275–91.

—— 1995. Learning from others: shall the last be the first? Pp. 95–102 in *Four Country Conference on Health Care Reforms and Health Care Policies in the United States, Canada, Germany and the Netherlands: Report*, ed. K. Okma. The Hague: Ministry of Health.

—— 2001. *The New Politics of the NHS*, 4th edn. Harlow: Prentice Hall.

MACMILLAN, H. 1938. *The Middle Way*. London: Macmillan.

MAIONI, A. 1998. *Parting at the Crossroads: The Emergence of Health Insurance in the United States and Canada*. Princeton, NJ: Princeton University Press.

MAJONE, G. 1989. *Evidence, Argument and Persuasion in the Policy Process*. New Haven, Conn: Yale University Press.

MARMOR, T. 1999. The rage for reform: sense and nonsense in health policy. Pp. 260–72 in *Health Reform: Public Success, Private Failure*, ed. D. Drache and T. Sullivan. London: Routledge.

—— 2000. *The Politics of Medicare*, 2nd edn. New York: Aldine de Gruyter.

—— 2004. The US Medicare programme in political flux. *British Journal of Health Care Management*, 10: 143–7.

—— OKMA, K. G. and FREEMAN, R. 2005. *Health Policy, Comparison and Learning*. New Haven, Conn.: Yale University Press.

NEUSTADT, R. E. and MAY, E. R. 1988. *Thinking in Time: The Uses of History for Decision Makers*. New York: Free Press.

OBERLANDER, J. 2003. *The Political Life of Medicare*. Chicago: University of Chicago Press.

PUTNAM, R. 2001. *Bowling Alone: The Collapse and Revival of American Community*. New York: Simon and Schuster.

The Queen's Speech 2004. *Hansard's Parliamentary Debates* (Lords), 467: cols. 1–4. Available at: www.publications.parliament.uk/id19900/dlhansard/pdvn/ldso4/41123-01.htm.

TUOHY, C. H. 1999. *Accidental Logics*. New York: Oxford University Press.

VICKERS, G. 1965. *The Art of Judgment*. London: Chapman and Hall.

WHITE, J. 1995. *Competing Solutions: American Health Care Proposals and International Experience*. Washington, DC: Brookings Institution.

WILDAVSKY, A. 1979. *The Art and Craft of Policy Analysis*. London: Macmillan.

—— 1994. Why self-interest means less outside of a social context. *Journal of Theoretical Politics*, 6: 131–59.

WILLIAMS, A. 2001. Science or marketing at WHO? A commentary on World Health 2000. *Health Economics*, 10 (2): 93–100.

WOODWARD, B. 2002. *Bush at War*. New York: Simon and Schuster.

—— 2004. *Plan of Attack*. New York: Simon and Schuster.

WORLD HEALTH ORGANIZATION 2000. *The World Health Report 2000, Health Systems: Improving Performance*. Geneva: World Health Organization.

YOUNG, H. 1989. *One of US: A Biography of Margaret Thatcher*. London: Macmillan.

PART XI

POLITICAL METHODOLOGY

CHAPTER 48

OVERVIEW OF POLITICAL METHODOLOGY

POST-BEHAVIORAL MOVEMENTS AND TRENDS

HENRY E. BRADY

DAVID COLLIER

JANET M.
BOX-STEFFENSMEIER

1 OVERVIEW

WITH the ascendancy of "behavioralism" in political science during the mid-twentieth century, an emphasis upon careful conceptualization, precise measurement, and fastidious causal thinking emerged in the study of politics. These tasks have become the hallmarks of political methodology. Assessing the progress of methodology is therefore inextricably bound up with an evaluation of behavioralism.

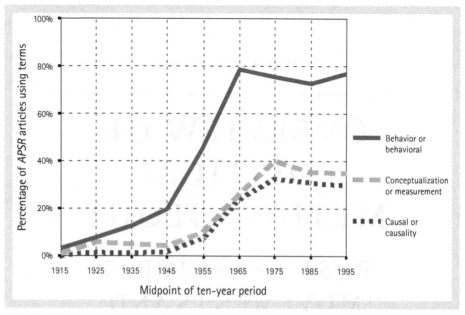

Fig. 48.1. Percentage of *APSR* articles using terms

Behavioralism was a self-consciously "scientific" movement within political science that began in the 1930s and took off in the 1950s.[1] Now it is embedded in the warp and woof of the discipline. The movement pushed political scientists to be more specific and systematic about their methodology—about their concepts, their measures, and their causal arguments concerning the actions and behaviors of political actors. Figure 48.1 depicts the simultaneous development of behavioralism and political methodology by plotting the frequency of articles referring to these perspectives in the *American Political Science Review*, the flagship journal of the American political science profession, between 1910 and 2000. The solid line plots the terms "behavior" or "behavioral," the dashed line the words "conceptualization" or "measurement," and the dotted line the words "causal" or "causality."[2] Behavioralism takes off around 1945 and from 1960 to the present about 80 percent of the articles include the word "behavior" or "behavioral." Concern with causality and with conceptualization and measurement take off soon after 1945, and today about one-third of the articles in the *APSR* use the words "causal" or "causality" and about one-third use the words "conceptualization" or "measurement." Since about 1970, roughly one-half of the articles use one or the other set of terms.

Behavioralism's focus on human actions and its legacy of precision, care, and fastidiousness in studying them (that is, its emphasis upon methodology) is a good one,

---

[1] Behavioralism was a complex phenomenon with many different currents. For proponents see Dahl (1961) and Eulau (1963; 1969); for histories see Farr, Dyrzek, and Leonard (1995), Farr and Seidelman (1993); and for a critique, Bevir (2008).

[2] For a discussion and defense of why we use these specific words see our introduction to the *Oxford Handbook of Political Methodology*.

but its weaknesses included a neglect of theory, an excessive reliance upon the tenets of logical empiricism, and sometimes an emphasis on investigating overt behavior to the exclusion of speech and language. Political methodology must be assessed in part in light of the weaknesses, as well as the strengths, of behavioralism. Political science has moved beyond behavioralism, but different observers see political science going in distinct directions. Some see it moving toward more theory (e.g. game theory) and empirical testing of theories—as with the Empirical Implications of Theoretical Models movement (Aldrich, Alt, and Lupia 2008); others associate it with the recent resurgence of a rigorous concern with qualitative and multimethod research (Collier and Elman 2008); and still others see it moving in the "post-positivist" direction of more narrative and interpretative work (Patterson and Monroe 1998; Yanow and Schwartz-Shea 2006).[3] All these perspectives might see political methodology as too tightly bound to a "positivist" or at least nominalist, operationalist, and inductive approach to political science.

  We agree that political science has moved beyond simple behavioralism, and we also believe that political methodology has done so, in ways that accommodate divergent perspectives on the road to post-behavioralism. We will argue that political methodology has made impressive strides by coming to grips with many of the criticisms of behavioralism, although recondite problems remain such as linking theory to methodology, developing methodologies for understanding speech acts and text, comprehending the role of case-studies and assessing causation for singular events, and developing methods for systematizing and improving qualitative methods. In this chapter, we begin by reviewing how methodologists now deal with conceptualization and measurement, then we discuss causal inference, and we end with a discussion of unresolved problems, the methodology organizations that are considering these problems, and future directions.

2 CONCEPTUALIZATION AND MEASUREMENT

2.1 Introduction: Concepts and Measures

Philosophers, scientists, and political scientists have moved a long way from the Aristotelian notion that the best concepts designate "natural kinds" based upon "natural laws." They have also moved beyond the classical philosophical notion (see Mill 1888, book I, ch. VIII)—developed further by the logical empiricists (Hempel 1952; Cohen and Nagel 1934)—that concepts can be defined by a set of necessary and sufficient conditions—by a set of attributes that the concept must have.

---

[3] As we make clear in the "Introduction" to the stand-alone methods volume (Box-Steffensmeier, Brady, and Collier 2008) in the Oxford series of handbooks, we mostly deferred to the Goodin and Tilly (2006) handbook which made a wide-ranging contribution to this line of investigation.

To illustrate where we are now in our thinking about conceptualization, consider this example. In the social sciences, it was once thought that ethnic groups, nations, and races were natural kinds, but modern social science suggests that these concepts are constructed (Berger and Luckman 1966; Giddens 1986) and not natural. In their manifestation at any point in history, the coherence of ethnic groups may well rest on numerous coinciding cleavages, and the identities and solidarities associated with the groups may well be deeply embedded. But in their origin and evolution, one must consider carefully the role of social construction. At such times, individuals associated with the group may evoke a supposedly primordial characteristic such as language, descent, or territory, but a potential group usually has many possible such characteristics from which to choose and only a few of them are selected— sometimes without a strict adherence to what an outsider might consider the reality of the presumed group (Anderson 1991; Brass 1991).

What standard of conceptualization might be employed here? One option would be that the investigator fully accepted the idea of social construction, but also set an external standard for judging when this process of construction in fact had produced a group. For example, an ethnic group might be understood as really being a group when the following statements are true: There is common agreement among its members that they belong to the group, nonmembers see them as a group, and all of these actors behave as if this is so.

Further, the perspective of social constructivism should not be taken to suggest that just anything is possible, even though some researchers (Tajfel 1970) have concluded that when experimenters bring people together in a laboratory, even the most minimal pretext can serve as the basis for the emergence of ideas about group differences, and hence for the idea that distinct groups have formed. Most discussions of this "minimal group" paradigm ignore the fact that the experimenter brought the people together in the first place. Thus, the creation of a group requires not only a pretext for imagining group differences, but also something powerful enough to bring people together in the first place to get the word out about their supposed differences from other groups. This may, for example, require that elites (sometimes an intelligentsia) deliberately formulate an ethnic identity out of the available histories and character- istics of a people (Hroch 1986). As Anderson puts it, "imagined" communities may thereby be created, involving a creative use of the facts.

We see here a crucial link to issues of measurement and data. For the methodolo- gist, this discussion shows why census, survey, and other data with social categories or concepts must be approached with great caution. As is discussed in much research on racial and ethnic politics in the USA (Lee 1993; Nobles 2000; Lee 2007) the questions on race and ethnicity on the US Census have constantly undergone change. There have been periods when citizens were asked whether they were colored or white, whether colored, quadroons, or octaroons, and whether Negro or White. Most recently, citizens could identify themselves as belonging to multiple races. Similarly, the Soviet Census (Hirsch 2005) defined and redefined nationalities and peoples in ways that fit the needs of the regime. Hence, any notion that census data are based on "hard facts" that can readily be treated as the basis for a rigorous social science must be examined with great care. A student of race and ethnicity must think carefully about measuring the concept in multiple ways (Brady and Kaplan 2000; 2009) and about being sensitive to the history and narratives of the people and the regime.

This example also shows that social science concepts have an additional feature that distinguishes them from concepts in the natural sciences. Because social science concepts routinely reflect the thinking of those being studied, they must take into account those thoughts. This, in turn, calls for criteria to establish the credibility of the concepts being formed. For example, the existence of an ethnic identity requires that people in a group believe that they have the identity, and it requires that others believe that the members of the group have that identity, and it requires that the members of the group believe that others believe that they have that identity, and so forth. Thus, any analysis of a situation must take into account not only what each person thinks about themselves, but what each person thinks about each other person, and what each person thinks each other person thinks about them, and so on. In game theory, the notion that everyone has the same knowledge about everyone is called "common knowledge" (Geanakopols 1992), and studying departures from this common knowledge assumption is a vigorous field of investigation in game theory. The study of these departures links game theory, constructivism, and some ethnographic approaches. Consider, for example, the difficulties that could ensue in an interaction if a man thinks that another person (named Pat) is a woman and he thinks that Pat believes that she is a woman and he believes that Pat thinks that he thinks of her in this way, but suppose Pat does not think of (herself?) as a woman and Pat thinks that people should not think of (her?) in this way at all. Just such confusions are at the root of some of the work of constructivists, symbolic interactionists (Blumer 1969), and the ethnographic work of Erving Goffman (1959) and Harold Garfinkel (1967). Thus, constructivism and game theory are coming together in a common concern with common understandings and misunderstandings.

These examples of race, ethnicity, gender, and identity—while perhaps representing unusually difficult analytic challenges—remind us that in many domains of research, concepts and analytic categories are hard to pin down and refer to human behavior of great complexity. The challenges of conceptualization and measurement well merit our attention as methodologists, and the remainder of this section explores them.

2.2 Three Approaches to Conceptualization and Measurement

This section explores three approaches to conceptualization and measurement which we call the classic syntactic statistical approach, the semantic-pragmatic approach, and the formal modeling approach.

2.2.1 The Classical Syntactic-Statistical Approach

The classical approach to concept formation relied heavily on the tenets of logical empiricism (Hempel 1952) which distinguished between theoretical terms (e.g.

concepts) connected to one another through theoretical axioms and logic (thus forming a theory) and observational terms or empirical statements about the world which were connected to, and provided meaning for, concepts through rules of correspondence. Empirical statements, in turn, were meaningful only if they were verifiable—capable of being assessed as true or false.

To employ, for example, the concept of "utility" would require the truth of both some theoretical and empirical statements. At the theoretical level, the preference relation P must satisfy the crucial transitive axiom that "if alternatives A, B, and C are such that APB (A preferred to B) and BPC, then we also have APC." With this axiom, it can be proved that an "ordinal utility function" exists with meaningful properties. One set of corresponding empirical statements is that when presented with choices A and B, the person chooses A, when presented with B and C, the person chooses B, and when presented with A and C, the person chooses A.

These statements could be verified by simply presenting a person with each pair of choices and observing whether or not each statement were true. If the empirical statements are true, then we can use the theoretical concept of "utility function" to describe the behavior of this person. This simple description hides a spate of difficulties including whether or not axioms and logic are sufficient to describe a theory, how empirical verification actually occurs, and how correspondence rules (between theoretical concepts and empirical observations) actually work. We will not get into those thickets here. Instead, we will briefly review how some early social science methodology relied upon a simplistic version of these tenets which often ignored the need for theory and the importance of meaning by inductively developing concepts from observational statements.

Standard tools of those forming concepts from quantitative data are reliability analysis (Lord and Novick 1968), validity analysis (Campbell and Fiske 1959), and scaling and factor analysis (Jackman 2008). In the 1950s and 1960s, many social science researchers started with a set of survey items or measures of the characteristics of nations (which were certainly empirically true statements) and used factor analysis or related techniques to find their underlying "dimensions" which were treated as theoretical concepts. The primary emphasis was upon discovering the structure of the data, and meaning fell out from the structures that were found.

For example, in a series of papers and books, R. J. Rummel (1963; 1966a; 1966b; 1972) and Raymond Tanter (1966) measured the "dimensions" of nations. Their method was to factor analyze numerous items (empirical statements) coded from various sources about a large number of countries. The resulting dimensions were then treated as theoretical concepts. Sometimes this led to interesting results as in the distinction (Tanter 1966) between "turmoil" (strikes, riots, demonstrations, governmental crises) and "internal war" (guerrilla war, purges, revolts, and domestic deaths from violence) within countries, but sometimes it led to odd and indefensible dimensions (Doran, Pendley, and Atunes 1973). A defender of logical empiricism might note that the failing here is a lack of underlying theory, but a critic might note that the deeper problem is the inattention to meaning and an emphasis upon structure and syntax instead of semantics. This approach was repeated in other areas of political science, with more success, in the scaling of legislative votes (MacRae 1970) and the scaling of attitude items (Stouffer et al. 1950), partly because more attention was paid to the meaning of the resulting concepts. Our take is that these methods can be very useful, but they require substantial attention to both meaning and theory.

2.2.2 *The Semantic-Pragmatic Approach*

This perspective on concepts and measurement systematically explores the diverse meanings of the concepts employed by social scientists, and seeks to develop productive ways—in light of a pragmatic concern with the research tasks at hand—of understanding, coordinating, adapting, and sometimes sharply modifying these meanings. A central idea is that, especially in light of the high degree of technification of much contemporary work on measurement in political science, it is invaluable to maintain a sustained focus on the sometimes contrasting meanings of the concepts used by researchers. This focus is routinely enriched by careful attention to context, which is valuable in its own right, and—to the extent that the scholar is concerned with systematic measurement—can contribute decisively to meeting more adequately the conventional standards of measurement validity.

The semantic-pragmatic perspective has sometimes been seen as the Sartori–Collier tradition of concept analysis (Bevir and Kedar 2008; Goertz 2006, 1, 69). It has been called a tradition of "qualitative concept formation" (Bevir and Kedar 2008, 503, 509). Yet this designation overlooks the interest of many relevant scholars—including Sartori—in linking careful work with concepts not only to qualitative, but also to quantitative, measurement. In addition to the studies by Sartori and Collier discussed below, important work in this tradition includes books and numerous articles by Gerring (e.g. 2001) and Goertz (e.g. 2006), Elman's (2005) analysis of typologies, efforts by Kotowski (1984) and Kurtz (2000) to untangle concepts through a systematic accounting of contrasting meanings, and studies that seek to address dilemmas of causal inference through more careful treatment of concepts (Levitsky 1998; Paxton 2000; Kurtz 2000).

In this tradition, the pragmatic goals that shape choices about concepts are sometimes contradictory. For example, these goals may include a concern with achieving analytic generality, an objective that routinely must be traded off against the priorities of adapting concepts to different spatial and historical contexts and/or working with actor-defined rather than observer-defined sources of meaning. Other central objectives include dealing in a coherent and productive way with the normative valence of concepts; seeking good procedures for linking concepts with observations about the world; and finding appropriate standards for sorting out the interplay between disputes about concepts and alternative choices about observation and measurement.

The wider history of concept analysis in political science certainly extends back to classical political theory, and many of the concerns addressed in the semantic-pragmatic approach have their roots in the work of major figures as different as Weber and Wittgenstein. However, viewing the semantic-pragmatic approach as a component of contemporary political science methodology, we see it as deriving from four analytic currents. The first and most important is the period of intense methodological innovation in the late 1960s and early 1970s in the field of comparative and international studies. For present purposes, this innovation is seen most crucially in the work of Sartori (1970; see also 1975; 1984; 1991) and in the contributions of many other scholars, for example, Przeworski and Teune (1970) and Verba (1967; 1971a). The second current is work in sociology by scholars such as Barton (1955) and Barton and Lazarsfeld (1969; see also McKinney 1966 and Tiryakian 1968), who focused on typologies, classification, and the interplay between theoretical and inductive analysis in concept-formation. A third line of influence can be dated back to the work of the British political scientist W. B. Gallie (1956a; 1956b; see also Collier, Hidalgo, and Maciuceanu 2006), who has stimulated a long trajectory of reflection and writing on conceptual structure, conceptual confusion, and the normative content of concepts. Finally, the fields of linguistics and cognitive science (Lakoff 1987; for recent syntheses see Taylor 2003; Cruse 2004) have contributed important insights into conceptual hierarchies, framing, and questions of the well-boundedness (or otherwise) of concepts.

Several features of the semantic-pragmatic approach should be underscored. First, at the same time that it is rigorous and systematic, it is committed to recognizing diversity of conceptual meanings, both as a potential source of analytic richness to be preserved, and as a source of potential confusion that can lead to analytic disaster. A recurring concern is with choices about when the standardization of meaning is productive, and when it gives up too much.

Second, we find a focus on the specificity of context, involving the challenges of addressing contrasts in the national, subnational, and temporal/historical settings under analysis. Sartori (1970) played a key role in inaugurating the discussion of this challenge with his arguments about how scholars can adapt their concepts to distinct contexts—thereby avoiding conceptual stretching—through movement on the ladder of abstraction. Numerous subsequent discussions have explored tools for the valid conceptualization and measurement of political phenomena across different settings (a brief overview is found in Adcock and Collier 2001, 534–36).

Sartori's concern with the ladder of abstraction has been extended in discussions of two types of conceptual hierarchies: the kind hierarchy (basically the same as Sartori's ladder) and the part–whole hierarchy (Collier and Levitsky 2008). An important aspect of movement on these hierarchies is the creation of subtypes (the concept with adjectives—see Collier and Levitsky 1997; Goertz 2006). With regard to kind hierarchies, Goertz has worked with the idea from cognitive linguistics of the "basic level," which is then a point of departure for his argument about developing two-level theories.

A third focus is on the normative valence of concepts, i.e. how they convey ethical judgements (Gallie 1956a). One need not spend much time reasoning about such standard political science topics as democracy, justice, equality, and the rule of law—as opposed to totalitarianism, war, genocide, torture, and rape—to recognize that each of these concepts has a fundamental evaluative component. An important goal that animates political science as a discipline is indeed to understand and explain the successes and disasters of human politics. Finding dependent variables that are deemed humanly important is thus routinely seen as a high priority. This is certainly the case even in areas of the discipline where advanced quantitative or formal tools are employed.

The point here is not that the normative evaluations entailed in particular concepts will gain universal agreement. There are "just wars," wars that should be avoided, and debates about which is which. Given these debates, scholars should deal frankly with the normative content of concepts. Classic substantive studies—for example Dahl's *Polyarcy* (1971, esp. ch. 2) and O'Donnell and Schmitter's *Transitions from Authoritarian Rule* (1986, esp. ch. 1)—are admirable for many reasons, including their frank attention to normative issues. These issues must be a central focus in the treatment of concepts, and a key ongoing issue is the sharply contrasting degrees of optimism and pessimism about whether normative disputes undermine coherent work with political science concepts (Gallie 1956a).

A further question is whether this approach focused on normative issues— and indeed the semantic-pragmatic approach more broadly—is exclusively concerned with concepts used by scholars. Whereas Gallie (1956a, 183) focused on concepts employed in the academy, subsequent writing in the tradition of Gallie provides a useful reminder that careful work with political science concepts must be alert to the embeddedness of their meanings in a larger context of politics and public discourse (Freeden 1994, 141). And indeed, as one looks at the dramatic evolution over the decades in the concepts used by political scientists, as well as the larger forces that motivate this evolution, it is easy to see that this wider perspective is essential. An excellent example is the evolving meaning of "neoliberalism," which Boas and Gans-Morse (2009) analyze, drawing on Gallie's framework.

A fourth and final issue is the interplay between qualitative and quantitative approaches. Many scholars in the semantic-pragmatic tradition are indeed focused on qualitative methodology. For example, work on typologies—such as that by Elman (2005) and Collier, LaPorte, and Seawright (2008)—explores how careful work with concepts can yield well-crafted categorical variables. Yet many analysts are likewise concerned with quantitative measurement, and Sartori's famous injunction (1970, 1038) that "concept formation stands prior to quantification" does not at all mean that he opposes quantitative work in political science (or mathematical formalization, for that matter). Indeed, he states that ultimately, building on appropriate work with concepts, "the more we measure, the better" (1975, 296). Adcock and Collier (2001) discuss how the complexity and ambiguities of work with concepts can be linked to careful measurement. Among many points, they advocate maintaining a clear separation between dealing with and potentially resolving disputes about conceptual meaning, as opposed to questions of measurement validity. The first must be dealt with before the second can be appropriately addressed. Various approaches have been adopted in building this bridge. Coppedge and Reinicke (1990), as well as Munck and Verkuilen (2002)—among many other studies—link careful work with concepts and the development of indicators. Elkins (2000) uses quantitative tools to address the question, sometimes identified with the qualitative tradition (see Collier and Adcock

1999), of whether it is most productive to view democracy versus nondemocracy as a dichotomy, or in terms of gradations.

To conclude, the semantic-pragmatic approach is not narrowly a tradition of qualitative concept analysis. It is a multimethod tradition in which many scholars are strongly concerned with building bridges to quantitative measurement. However, we find a distinctive focus, which might be thought of as more typical of the qualitative tradition, on sustained attention to concepts, careful reasoning with categorical variables, and attention to crafting concepts (and measures) to accommodate distinctive features of context. During a period in which "multimethod" sometimes becomes a slogan in our discipline that pushes scholars to use multiple tools poorly—rather than one tool with skill—we feel that this semantic-pragmatic approach is an area of multimethod work that points scholarly attention in a productive direction.

2.2.3 *The Formal Modeling Approach*

The simple example of the "utility model" described earlier shows that models can help to clarify, even perhaps define, concepts. Choice-theoretic and game theory modeling have certainly done this for many political science concepts. Consider, for example, the notions of "the general will" and "democracy." One exegesis of Rousseau's idea of the general will is that it is the expression of the public's most preferred policy as determined by democratic voting procedures such as majority rule.[4] But modern social choice theory (Riker 1982) suggests that things are not so simple. Because of "cycling" (Arrow 1951), democratic voting procedures may not lead to any one best choice that could be considered the "most preferred alternative." Social choice theory, therefore, certainly rules out one interpretation of "the general will" as the "most preferred alternative."

Or take the concept of "cleavages," which starts to appear in political science articles around the 1890s and is used casually to mean differences in politically relevant sociodemographic characteristics,[5] in politically relevant issue positions,[6] or in political groups themselves.[7] Initial elaborations of the concept (Rice 1928) were purely statistical and used differences in voting support for party candidates

---

[4] We are vastly simplifying a very complicated topic: see Radcliff (1992).

[5] For example: "lines of social cleavage due to differences in industrial and social status" or "the cleavage line between city and country" (Emerick 1910, 649–50).

[6] For example: "there will not improbably appear a fresh cleavage when 'social' legislation reaches an active phase" (Mavor 1895, 505) or "Socialism seems destined to produce in the near future a perfectly new moral 'line of cleavage' in English society" (Webb 1889, 36).

[7] "A decade of self-government under this liberal and democratic charter [the Weimar Constitution] has rather definitely established the lines of party cleavage and the general features of the party system . . ." (Pollock 1929, 859).

If we think of societies being composed of people with sociodemographic characteristics X, who have issue positions I, and who belong to groups G, then political cleavages were variously described as differences in politically relevant characteristics (South versus North or farmers versus business), differences in political issue positions (pro-slavery versus anti-slavery or pro-silver versus anti-silver), or differences in political groups (Democrats versus Republicans). Neither the considerations for diagnosing a factor as political nor the exact way of measuring this was made clear.

based upon geographic location or type of economic activity to examine cleavages.[8] Rice even noted that "[t]heoretically the electorate might be divided up in well-nigh infinite variety of ways," but he says nothing about how some ways might become paramount for politics.[9] His approach is baldly nominal, operational, and empirical, with no explanation of which cleavages are important or where they come from.

Work by Peter Odegard in 1935 developed a simple model in which cleavages were the result of conflicting "group pressures" based upon interests "which are compounds of economic, historical, traditional, and even ethnic influences" (Odegard 1935, 69). E. E. Schattschneider (1952, 19) extended this model by noting "that an indefinite multiplication of conflicts is extremely unlikely even in a free political system" because "conflicts interfere with each other, because the lines of cleavage never or rarely coincide." In 1960 he expanded on these ideas in a book where he presented simple two-dimensional circles in which each member of the electorate had some position in the circle representing his or her interests. Lines ran across these circles indicating "cleavages" between groups such as Democrats or Republicans of the 1870s who supported different policies for "Civil War Reconstruction" (the North–South cleavage) or the Populists and the Bourbons of the 1890s who supported different agricultural and monetary policies. Schattschneider's work represents the first pictorial description of a cleavage in a multidimensional issue space, but he did not explain the origins of these issue cleavages nor did he explain how the line of cleavage formed, except that it involved political groups such as political parties or movements.

Independently of Schattschneider's work, Duncan Black (1948) and Anthony Downs (1957) introduced a one-dimensional "left–right" issue space in which legislators or voters voted for alternative motions (Black) or parties (Downs) located in this same space. Black's contribution was to show that if individual preferences along this one dimension satisfied the property of "single-peakedness"[10] then in a pairwise consideration of motions at most only one would get a simple majority over all others and this motion would be the one preferred by the median voter—the voter with his or her ideal point at the median. Downs added two more features: the notion that voters would compare distances and vote for the alternative nearest them (which automatically satisfies single-peakedness) and the notion that just two parties would compete in the space by taking up locations in it and obtaining votes depending upon their distance from the voters. In this model, the line of cleavage between those who vote for one party versus those who vote for the other runs perpendicular to

---

[8] In terms of the notation in the previous footnote, Rice showed that given distinct characteristics X_1 and X_2, the value of Prob(Voting for $G|X_1$) was very different from Prob(Voting for $G|X_2$).

[9] In fact, he elides the question by noting that "In reality narrow limits to inquiry are imposed by official models of grouping, recording, and reporting votes and voters, and by the possibilities of statistical analysis of records" (167). Therefore, a substantive problem becomes merely one for which data are available. In effect, Rice presumed that a characteristic X was political if for political parties G1 and G2, we have Prob(Support $G_1|X$) is very different from Prob(Support $G_2|X$).

[10] Defined as having an "ideal point" representing maximum utility from which utilities decline monotonically on each side from this point.

the midpoint of the line drawn between the locations of the two parties in the issue space. The model stipulates very clearly that a cleavage is defined by both individual preferences and the locations of parties.[11] Downs's model was extended to multiple dimensions by Davis, Hinich, and Ordeshook (1970) who generalized his result in a model where cleavage lines continue to be perpendicular to the midpoint of the line drawn between the locations of the two parties.[12]

These models make it clear that a cleavage depends both on the distribution of individual preferences and on the political actors such as parties who help to define them by their position-taking. This elaboration of the concept of political cleavage has implications for their genesis and their alteration. If major historical events (Reformation and Counter-Reformation, French and Democratic Revolutions, Industrial Revolution, or the Russian and Communist Revolutions) cause changes in preferences as in the classic Lipset and Rokkan (1967) paper on "Cleavage structures, party systems, and voter alignments," then lines of cleavage might change but *only* if there are political entrepreneurs who exploit them. Even without any change in preferences, politicians might maneuver and change the lines of cleavage by modifying their positions or by emphasizing one cleavage over another (Riker 1986; Johnston et al. 1992, ch. 3). In this case, formal theory helps to clarify the concept of cleavage by showing that it is the result of the interaction between position-taking by political elites and the preferences of mass publics. More generally, formal theory has helped to clarify many concepts such as utility, deterrence, arms races, party identification, collective action, and many more.

2.3 Data Collection and Measurement

The data available to social scientists have increased dramatically in the past sixty years, partly as a result of the behavioral revolution which emphasized the collection of data of all sorts including quantitative and interview data. It is true that prior to 1950 some political scientists analyzed aggregate election data (e.g. Gosnell and Gill 1935; Key 1949), legislative votes (Rice 1928; Beyle 1931; Brimhall and Otis 1948; Gage and Shimberg 1949), judicial votes (Pritchett 1941; 1945), elite biographical data (Lasswell and Sereno 1937), in-depth interviews (Weeks 1930), or quantitative media data (Lasswell 1941), but there was not much of this kind of research. For example, articles about multiple in-depth interviews do not even appear in the *APSR* until the decade of the 1930s when there were eight articles (six of which used interviews and two of which merely advocated their use). There was no increase in the 1940s with only seven articles (of which four were advocacy), but the number increased

---

[11] Downs went on to argue that if the parties were mobile, then they would both converge to the middle of the space if ideal points were distributed somewhat like a normal distribution. Downs was apparently unaware of Black's work, which would have led him to the stronger conclusion that the parties would converge to the median voter in the space no matter what the distribution of people's ideal points. Hence, the line of cleavage would be at the median voter.

[12] As with the Downsian model, the major concern of this paper was with the possibilities of equilibrium and not with the definition of cleavages.

dramatically in the 1950s with twenty-three articles and the 1960s with forty articles (of which only one was advocacy). We see similar patterns with surveys and legislative voting.[13] We cannot review every mode of data collection here, but we will review a few areas where major advances have been made.

2.3.1 *Surveys*

Scientific surveys first appeared in the 1930s, but they did not take off in political science until two major election studies in 1948—a panel study in Erie County, Ohio by Lazarsfeld and his colleagues at Columbia University (reported in *Voting* 1954) and another national post-election study at Michigan by Campbell and Kahn at the University of Michigan (reported in *The People Elect a President* 1952).[14] Since that time, surveys have been used to study political culture (Almond and Verba 1963), political participation (Verba and Nie 1972), political socialization (Jennings and Niemi 1974; 1981), political parties (Eldersveld 1964), and many other topics. There are many national election studies,[15] single-point-in-time cross-national studies, and ongoing cross national studies such as the World Values Surveys, the International Social Survey Programme, the Comparative Study of Electoral Systems, the Pew Global Attitudes Survey, Gallup's Voice of the People, and many others.[16]

Surveys provided political scientists with the first opportunities to collect micro-data on people's attitudes, beliefs, and behaviors, and they continue to be an important method of data collection. Moreover, they have become much more useful because there are better instruments, better designs, greater comparability over time, and greater comparability over space.

We now know a great deal about how to write better questions (Bradburn, Sudman, and Wansink 2004; Tourangeau, Kips, and Rasinski 2000). We also know how to ask questions about political information, political attitudes (liberalism–conservatism, political issues and agendas, racial attitudes, patriotism, trust, etc.), political and economic values (tolerance, democratic values, civil liberties, economic equality, capitalist values, the Protestant ethic), identity (partisanship, ethnic identity, racial identity), political emotions, candidate and group traits, the use of the news media, and political participation and other behaviors (Robinson, Shaver, and

---

[13] These data are based upon a search of JSTOR for the *APSR* for the periods indicated. The search terms were "interview or interviews or interviewing and not (survey or surveying)." Then each article found was examined by the authors to determine if multiple interviews (but not a survey) were used as the basis for the research or if the article advocated the use of such interviews. In most cases, it was easy to make this determination.

[14] Both of these studies were inspired by Lazarsfeld, Berelson, and Gaudet, *The People's Choice* (1944), which reported on a 1940 panel study in Erie County, Ohio.

[15] The American National Election Studies provides access to many other studies as well: <http://www.electionstudies.org/other_election_studies.htm>.

[16] World Values Surveys: <http://www.worldvaluessurvey.org/>; International Social Survey Programme: <http://www.issp.org/>; Comparative Study of Electoral Systems: <http://www.issp.org/>; Pew Global Attitudes Survey: <http://pewglobal.org/>; Voice of the People: <http://www.voice-of-the-people.net/>. For a listing of many others see: <http://www.gesis.org/EN/data_service/eurobarometer/handbook/index.htm>.

Wrightsman 1993; Abdelal et al. 2009; Marcus and MacKuen 1993; Price and Zaller 1993). We take seriously issues of reliability and validity, and we have better techniques for analyzing batteries of questions (Jackman, in Brady and Collier 2008). We have better techniques for making interpersonal comparisons across places and times using "vignettes" (King et al. 2003). We know a great deal about the problem of social desirability bias and other mechanisms affecting responses and memory, and we have learned a lot about interpreting and improving responses on racial attitudes (Berinsky 2002; Krysan and Couper 2003), religious attendance (Presser and Stinson 1998), voting (Beilli et al. 1999), and welfare spell lengths (Luks and Brady 2003). We have innovative methods for getting at racism such as the "list experiment" (Kuklinski, Cobb, and Gilens 1997) and the Implicit Association Test and its close relatives (Greenwald, McGhee, and Schwartz 1998; Fazio and Olson 2003; but see Arkes and Tetlock 2004). Still, it is frustrating that we cannot reliably (and perhaps not even validly) identify the true extent of racism, the role of emotions, and the extent of social desirability bias and other mechanisms which distort response.

We also have much better designs for surveys along three distinct dimensions. First, experiments embedded within surveys (Sniderman and Grob 1996) have been used to probe general population attitudes and opinions in novel and interesting ways. Second, panel studies in which the same people are interviewed repeatedly and rolling cross-sections in which true daily random samples are repeated day after day over a long period of time such as a political campaign have been used to study change over time (Brady and Johnston 2006). Researchers now combine these approaches into rolling cross-sectional panel designs. Third, researchers now combine experiments, panels, rolling cross-sections, and other designs across the modes of in-person, telephone, Internet, and self-administered mail questionnaires (Johnston, in Brady and Collier 2008). By repeating questions across surveys, across countries, and over time and by building up collections of data, we are able to make interesting descriptive comparisons (e.g. with respect to partisan identification, ethnic and racial attitudes, or concern for economic issues across countries and over time) and we can often make some causal inferences by using differences across countries or over time (or changes in differences) to pin down (technically, "to identify") causes.

2.3.2 Legislative and Judicial Voting Data

Another area where there have been great advances is in the collection and scaling of voting data which has moved considerably beyond the classic books by Rice (1928) and MacRae (1970). Keith Poole (in Brady and Collier 2008) and his collaborator Harold Rosenthal have created the definitive version of American congressional roll-call data which are available (and constantly updated) on the VoteView[17] website, and they have produced the classic interpretation of these data (Poole and Rosenthal 1997) using their widely used "Nominate" method for analyzing legislative votes

---

[17] Search on "Voteview" or go to Poole's website: <http://www.voteview.com/>.

(Poole and Rosenthal 1985).[18] Data from around the world are archived and disseminated on the VoteWorld website,[19] and the VoteWorld project aims to create "open source" software standards for formatting and archiving roll-call data-sets. Judicial data, including votes on every Supreme Court case back to 1953, are available at the "Oyez" website (<www.oyez.org>). The site also includes Martin–Quinn measures of judicial ideology (Martin and Quinn 2007) based upon a dynamic Bayesian ideal-point model.

2.3.3 *Events and Media Data*

Since the pioneering work of Gosnell and Rice in the 1920s, political scientists have used aggregate voting data, survey data, and legislative and judicial voting data. "Content analysis" of the media began in the 1930s and 1940s with the work of Harold Lasswell (1941), but the study of political events has been a more recent innovation. At least five types of events are now regularly studied in political science: political campaign events, agenda-setting actions such as hearings or the introduction of legislation, contentious (protest) events, civil wars and civil strife, and international interactions and transactions. The recording of events can be traced back to the efforts forty years ago to create cross-national data books (Banks and Textor 1963; Russett et al. 1964; Banks 1971; Taylor and Hudson 1972). These compendia contained aggregate data on countries over time on variables such as "domestic group violence deaths" (Russett et al. 1964) or "coups d'etat, assassinations, general strikes, or riots" (Banks 1971). In the past forty years, much more refined data have been produced. Some important publications in the development of specific types of events data are Feierabend and Feierabend (1966) for internal conflict, Gurr (1968; 1970*a*) for protest and civil strife, Azar (1970) for international interactions, Ben-Dak and Azar (1972) with a symposium on Arab–Israeli conflict using mostly events data, Singer and Small (1972) on war and alliances, Tilly, Tilly, and Tilly (1975) for protest ("contentious politics"), Bartels (1987) on primaries as campaign events, Allsop and Weisberg (1988) on campaign events and party identification, Holbrook (1996) and Shaw (1999) on campaign events, and Baumgartner, Jones, and MacLeod (1998) on agenda-setting actions.

Events data are most useful when many different features of the events are coded: For example, it is helpful to know the date (and length) of the protest, its size, its location, the characteristics of its participants, its targets, and any violence associated with it. Or it is helpful to know all participants in an international event (such as a war), its date, its duration, the sizes and economic characteristics of the participants, whether they have other linkages with one another, and the outcome of the interaction. Knowing these things requires having good sources, and events have typically been coded from newspapers, yearbooks, police records, and historical records, which can be problematic. From the very beginning (Azar et al.

---

[18] Other scaling methods include Jackman (2001); Lewis and Poole (2004); and Clinton, Jackman, and Rivers (2004).

[19] Search on "Voteworld" or go to: <http://ucdata.berkeley.edu:7101/new_web/VoteWorld/voteworld/>.

1972) and continuing up to the present day (Schrodt and Gerner 1994; Woolley 2000; Oliver and Maney 2000), there has been a concern with the representativeness and accuracy of these sources. But with good event data, sophisticated event history methods can be used (Golub 2008), and important works can be completed such as Beissinger's (2002) analysis of how protest events contributed to the fall of the Soviet Union, Freeman and Goldstein's (1990) analysis of reciprocity in the international system, and Shaw's (2006) analysis of American political campaigns.

2.3.4 *Other Measurement Methods*

In addition to the improvement of older methods of data collection, some fascinating new methods are available. Game theorists have added to our stock of measurement techniques with simple games that tell us about people's willingness to free-ride, their trust in one another, and many other features of interactive situations (Camerer 2003). Two new methods inform us about the neurological bases of attitudes: fMRI techniques provide real-time brain scans that indicate what parts of the brain are activated when subjects are presented with stimuli (Lieberman, Schreiber, and Ochsner 2003; Phelps and Thomas 2003). ERP or event-related potential methods (Morris et al. 2003) provide another, somewhat less difficult to obtain, measure of brain activity.

2.3.5 *Textual data*

One of the most exciting frontiers in political science research at the present time is developing ways to code and use the enormous bodies of textual data that are now available on the web and through other sources. Human coding of text into categories through "content analysis" has been used to analyze textual data since the 1930s, but the very large bodies of data that are now available and the increasing capabilities of computers make it both feasible and necessary to automate this process (King and Lowe 2003). The possibilities are extraordinary. We have large collections of newspaper texts and books (including biographies) that have been scanned. We also have judicial opinions and briefs, congressional debate and testimony, political advertisements in text and video form, nightly news in text and video, party platforms, and, of course, the entire contents of the web. The challenge is to find ways to code these data and to link them with political surveys, judicial or legislative votes, or events. To take just one example, as part of its Social, Political, and Economic Event Database project, the Cline Center at the University of Illinois has assembled in a machine readable form over 30 million reports dating from the Second World War from the *New York Times*, the *Wall Street Journal*, the BBC's Summary of World Broadcasts, and the Foreign Broadcast Information Service reports, and it intends to use computers to code these data into over 200 event categories. The results will provide researchers with a worldwide, sixty-year record of events in the world.

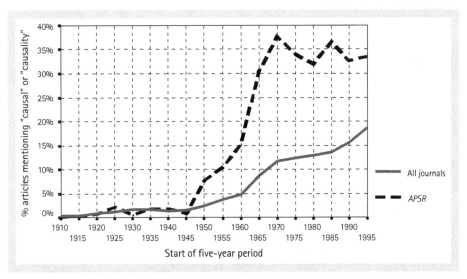

Fig. 48.2. Growth of causal thinking

3 CAUSAL THINKING

Although not all of modern political science is about causation, Figure 48.2 shows that between 1990 and 1999, about one-third of the articles in the *American Political Science Review* included the words "causal" or "causality," and 17 percent of the political science journal articles in JSTOR for this period mentioned them. Moreover, the mentions of these terms grew rapidly from less than 2 percent of the JSTOR articles from 1910 to 1950 to an increasing proportion from 1950 onwards, with the *APSR* leading the way.

In our introductory chapter to the *Handbook of Political Methodology*, we explored the roots of this dramatic increase in mentions of "causal" or "causality." Our discussion of the rise of "causal thinking" was, in many ways, simply a "toy example," meant to show the difficulties of *explaining* anything—even something as prosaic as the rise of causal thinking within political science. In demonstrating these difficulties, we hoped that the example illustrated the problems of making defensible causal claims.

We explored three possible causes of the increased emphasis on causality in political science. Two potential causes involved the availability of new tools such as correlation (Pearson 1909) or regression analysis (Pearson 1896; Yule 1907) that might have fostered causal thinking because they made it easier for scholars to determine causality. A third potential cause, a commitment to behavioralism, might have placed more emphasis within the discipline upon making causal inferences. The growth in the mention of words representing each of these possible explanations ("correlation," "regression," and "behavioralism") is plotted in Figure 48.3, which demonstrates that they grew in tandem with causal thinking as depicted in Figure 48.2. There may be other plausible explanations for the growth of causal thinking, but these three provide

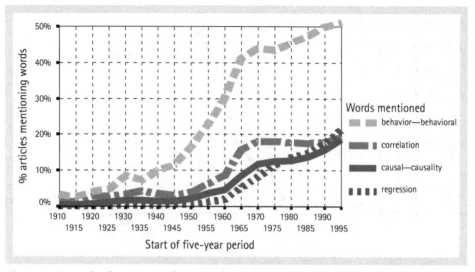

Fig. 48.3. Growth of mentions of words related to causal thinking in political science

us with a trio of interesting possibilities. Indeed, these categories of explanation—
new inventions and new values—crop up again and again in social science. We
concluded, with some trepidation given the incompleteness of our analysis, that
values and inventions both helped to explain the rise of "causal thinking" in political
science. The behavioral movement furthered "scientific values" like causal thinking,
while regression analysis (but not correlation) provided an invention that seemingly
provided political scientists with estimates of causal effects with minimal fuss and
bother.

Despite this long-held presumption that regression could uncover causal relationships, the experiences of the last thirty years have undermined the belief that
regression is the philosopher's stone that can turn base observational studies into
gold-standard experimental studies. Doubts have grown about inferences made from
simple regressions, and increasingly sophisticated methods have been developed to
improve regression analysis and causal inference. Researchers now know that most
regression equations simply provide a multivariate summary of the data—at best a
descriptive inference—not a sure-fire *causal inference* about them (King, Keohane, and
Verba 1994) because the conditions for justifying a causal interpretation of regression
coefficients are not met. Although establishing the Humean conditions of constant
conjunction and temporal precedence with regression-like methods often takes pride
of place when people use these methods, we now know that they seldom deliver
a reliable causal inference. Rather regressions are often more usefully thought of
as ways to describe complex data-sets by estimating parameters that summarize
important things about the data. For example, Auto-Regressive Integrated Moving
Average (ARIMA) models can quickly tell us a lot about a time series through the
standard "p,d,q" parameters, which are the order of the autoregression (p), the level
of differencing (d) required for stationarity, and the order of the moving average

component (q). And a graph of a hazard rate over time derived from an events history model reveals at a glance important facts about the ending of wars or the dissolution of coalition governments. Descriptive inference is often underrated in the social sciences (although survey methodologists proudly focus on this problem), but even more worrisome is the tendency for social scientists to mistakenly assume that a descriptive inference is a valid causal inference. Most regression analyses in the social sciences are probably useful descriptions of the relationships among various variables, but usually they cannot properly be used for causal inferences because they omit variables, fail to deal with selection bias and endogeneity, and lack theoretical grounding. In short, they typically do not establish causal relationships (Freedman 1997).

3.1 Nature of Causality

Why does regression typically fail to provide valid causal inferences? The basic problem is that establishing a causal relationship requires much more than estimating conditional expectations using regression. Brady (2008; and this volume) presents an overview of the challenges of making causal inferences by describing four perspectives on them. The *neo-Humean regularity approach* focuses on "lawlike" constant conjunction and temporal antecedence, and many statistical methods—preeminently regression analysis—are designed to provide just the kind of information to satisfy the requirements of the Humean model. Regression analysis can be used to determine whether a dependent variable is still correlated ("constantly conjoined") with an independent variable when other plausible causes of the dependent variable are held constant by being included in the regression, and time series regressions can look for temporal antecedence by regressing a dependent variable on lagged independent variables. But regression can fail to make valid inferences because researchers typically cannot consider all the plausible alternative explanations that can confound their analysis.

The *counterfactual approach* to causation asks what would have happened had a putative cause not occurred in the most similar possible world without the cause. It requires either finding a similar situation in which the cause is not present or imagining what such a situation would be like. But researchers seldom have a perfect counterfactual situation.

The *manipulation approach* asks what happens when we actively manipulate the cause—does it lead to the putative effect? This approach is what characterizes most laboratory experiments in the natural sciences. Some factors (temperature, pressure, chemicals, DNA, and so forth) are manipulated, and the scientist observes the results. Typically there is no "control" (or "counterfactual") condition because it is thought to be obvious that the manipulation of the factors produces the result. But manipulations of some factors (e.g. party identification, race, or gender) is hard, if not impossible, in the social sciences, and the multitude of confounding factors that can cause a result makes it hard to determine the impact of a manipulation.

Finally, the *mechanism and capacities approach* asks what detailed steps lead from the cause to the effect and what underlying theoretical perspective might explain the causal relationship. When done well, this approach helps to pin down the nature of the cause or treatment, it clarifies the intervening or contextual variables needed for the result to occur, and it helps to generalize to other situations. But social science researchers often have both too many loosely worked-out explanations and too few that are adequately worked out.

These four approaches provide a framework for understanding two successive developments in the study of causality in political science that have changed our understanding of it. First, there has been the realization that regression approaches that (seemingly) satisfy the Humean conditions for causation may suffer from problems of omitted variables, endogeneity, and selection bias. Second, there has been the recognition that researchers must focus on causes that can be manipulated; they must be able to make counterfactual statements about what would occur without the putative cause; and they must be able to describe an explicit causal mechanism (Brady 2008; and this volume). These developments have been accompanied by a growing emphasis on experimentation as an excellent way to deal with many (although not all) of these concerns. The change in our understanding of how to make causal inferences is captured by considering Figure 48.4, which displays the number of *APSR* articles in each decade that mentioned some of these things—endogeneity, selection bias, counterfactuals, and experiments. (During this period, there were roughly 500 *APSR* articles each decade.)

Before 1960, researchers adduced causal inferences from regressions with very little self-consciousness about their limitations. There are essentially no mentions of any of these concerns (omitted variables, endogenity, selection bias, manipulations, counterfactuals, or mechanisms) before 1960. At that point, a nearly exponential growth begins in the use of the terms "endogenous" or "endogeneity." This growth corresponds with the realization that statistical regression models with endogenous regressors are incorrectly estimated by standard (OLS) regression methods. Many of the mentions of endogeneity in these articles are associated with the spread of structural equation modeling methods with their "systems of equations" in which variables appear on both the left- and right-hand sides of equations—thus making it impossible to accept the standard regression assumption of no correlation between the right-hand-side variables and the error term. The growth in the use of the terms "endogenous" or "endogeneity" increases dramatically in 1970 and 1980; and by 1990, 101 articles mention the term and in the five-year period from 2000 to 2004, 75 articles mention it.[20]

However, regression methods were "saved" for a long time by the presumption that instrumental variables could be found (typically within the structural equation model itself) that would provide a statistical fix to the problem of endogeneity (Jackson 2008). It was only when researchers began to realize that instrumental variables

---

[20] In the chart, we double the number of articles for the 2000–4 period to make it comparable to the previous decanal periods. Hence, "endogeneity" or "endogenous" are extrapolated to appear in 150 total articles.

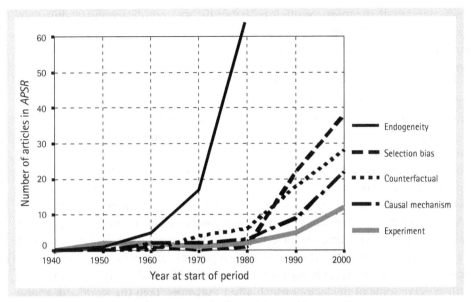

Fig. 48.4. Number of articles in *APSR* dealing with specific causal issues

are hard to justify (that is, statistical identification is hard to come by), and that a supposed "treatment" in a simple regression equation (such as exposure to an advertisement in an equation estimating candidate preference) might be assigned nonrandomly through a "selection" process, that worries arose that regression methods, including structural equation modeling, might not solve the causal inference problem (Achen 1986).

Concern with the problem of selection bias,[21] for example, rises dramatically in the 1990s (see Figure 48.4), which suggests that researchers began to realize that even without the problem of simultaneity, regression models might be incorrectly specified and incorrectly estimated without instruments or some other method of identification. An increase in mentions of the words "counterfactual" and "mechanism" in the 1990s suggests an even more detailed understanding of the problems with causal inference, and the increasing number of experiments described in the *APSR* suggests a modest move toward solving causal inference problems using that method. But there are practically no mentions of the words "manipulation" in the *APSR* or in other journals, suggesting that political scientists have not yet made sufficient use of this approach to causal inference.

In addition to an awakening to the complexity of causal inference involving a single putative cause and effect, political science has also become more attuned to the complexity of causal inference involving many causal factors. Since the beginning of the use of statistical methods within political science, there has been an

[21] Figure 48.4 only includes the data on selection bias, but a search for the words "omitted variable(s)," "confounding variable(s)," or "confounder(s)" yields almost exactly the same pattern. There are no mentions of these terms until the 1960s when there are four, then seven in the 1970s, nine in the 1980s, fifteen in the 1990s, and fourteen in the first half of the 2000s.

understanding that causes are often probabilistic, and not deterministic, but there has been surprisingly little discussion of what this means. Perhaps the most important theoretical question is how a deterministic world might nevertheless lead to a probabilistic social science.[22] One answer is that we observe only part of a complex web of causation. Brady (2008; and this volume), for example, discusses the INUS model of causation which gets beyond simple necessary or sufficient conditions for an effect by arguing that often there are different sufficient pathways (but no pathway is strictly necessary) to causation—each pathway consisting of an *insufficient* but *nonredundant* part of an *unnecessary* but *sufficient* (INUS) condition for the effect. For example, revolutions may occur because of an interaction between state breakdown and peasant revolts (Skocpol 1979) or they may occur because of an interaction between indecisive secular repressive regimes and growing religious fundamentalism (Arjomand 1986). Hence, none of these four conditions (state breakdown, peasant revolts, indecisive repressive regimes, or religious fundamentalism) is either necessary or sufficient for a revolution, but there are two pairs of sufficient conditions. In most situations, we would expect to have multiple causal paths, and Brady shows that if we only observe some of the factors which affect outcomes, then the world will appear probabilistic. Sekhon (2004) concludes from this that the use of Mill's methods and other deterministic approaches is inherently flawed. We would not go so far. In fact, the work on necessary and sufficient conditions (e.g. Goertz and Starr 2002; Goertz and Levy 2007), conjunctural causation (Collier and Collier 1991; Pierson 2000), and Qualitative Comparative Analysis (Ragin 1987) has made political scientists more aware of the complexity of social phenomena (Achen 2002) and the need for exploring multiple pathways and complex interactions.

3.2 Statistical Methods for Establishing Causality: Quantitative Tools for Causal and Descriptive Inference

As noted earlier, regression analysis, much more than correlation analysis, provides a seductive technology for exploring causality. Its inherent asymmetry with a dependent variable that is a function of a number of independent variables lends itself to discussions of causes (independent variables) and effect (dependent variable) whereas correlation (even partial correlation) analysis is essentially symmetrical. The path analysis generalizations of regression make it even more attractive because of the widespread use of "path diagrams" with directed pathways that look just like causal arrows between variables. And social scientists and statisticians provide even more credibility for the method by their proofs that under certain conditions regression coefficients will be an unbiased estimate of the impact of the independent variables on the dependent variables (Simon 1954; Blalock 1964).

---

[22] In effect, the question is how one can reconcile a metaphysically (or ontologically) deterministic world with the need for a probabilistic epistemology. Some authors, however, argue that the world is inherently probabilistic: See Suppes (1984).

Table 48.1. Results of regressing whether "causal thinking" was mentioned on mentions of potential explanatory factors for 1970–9 (all political science journal articles in JSTOR)

Independent variables	Regression coefficient (standard error)	
	One	Two
Behavior	.122 (.006)***	.110 (.006)***
Regression	.169 (.010)***	.061 (.021)**
Correlation	.157 (.008)***	.150 (.015)***
Behavior X regression		.135 (.022)***
Behavior X correlation		.004 (.017)
Regression X correlation		.027 (.021)
Constant	.022 (.008)***	.028 (.004)***
R^2/N	.149/ 12,305	.152/ 12,305

Notes: *** Significant at .001 level; ** significant at .01 level; * significant at .05 level.

Finally, regression analysis provides the striking capacity to predict that if there is a one-unit change in some independent variable, then there will be a change in the dependent variable equal to the value of the independent variable's regression coefficient. In short, regression analysis seems to deliver a great deal whereas correlation analysis appears to deliver much less, so that it seems likely that regression analysis contributed much more to the emphasis on causal thinking than correlations.

We can illustrate these points and test our theories about the rise of causal thinking with some data from JSTOR. The classic regression approach to causality suggests estimating a simple regression equation such as the following for cross-sectional data on all political science articles in JSTOR between 1970 and 1979. For each article, we score a mention of either "causality or causal" as a one and no mention of these terms as a zero. We then regress these zero–one values of the "dependent variable" on zero–one values for "independent variables" measuring whether or not the article mentioned "regression," "correlation," or "behavioralism." When we do this, we get the results in column one in Table 48.1. If we use the causal interpretation of regression analysis to interpret these results, we might conclude that all three factors led to the emphasis on "causal thinking" in political science because each coefficient is substantively large and statistically highly significant. But this interpretation ignores a multitude of problems.

Given the INUS model of causation which emphasizes the complexity of necessary and sufficient conditions, we might suspect that there is some interaction among these variables, so we should include interactions between each pair of variables. These interactions require that both concepts be present in the article so that a "Regression X Correlation" interaction requires that both regression and correlation are mentioned. The results from estimating this model are in column two of the table. Interestingly, of the interaction terms, only the "behavior X regression" interaction is significant, suggesting that the combination of the behavioral revolution and the development of regression analysis helps "explain" the prevalence of causal thinking in political science. (The three-way interaction is not reported and is statistically insignificant.) Descriptively this result is certainly correct—it appears that a mention of behavioralism alone increases the probability of "causal thinking" in an article by about 11 percent, the mention of regression increases the probability by about 6 percent, the mention of correlation increases the probability by about 15 percent, and the mention of both behavioralism and regression together further increases the probability of causal thinking by about 13.5 percent.

But are these causal effects? This analysis is immediately open to the standard criticisms of the regression approach when it is used to infer causation: Maybe some other factor (or factors) causes these measures (especially "behavioral," "regression," and "causality") to cohere during this period. Maybe these are all spurious relationships that appear to be statistically significant because the true cause is omitted from the equation. Or maybe causality goes both ways and all these variables are endogenous. Perhaps "causal thinking" causes mentions of the words "behavioral or behavior" and "regression" and "correlation."

Although the problem of spurious relationships challenged the regression approach from the very beginning (see Yule 1907), many people (including apparently Yule) thought that it could be overcome by simply adding enough variables to cover all potential causes. The endogeneity problem posed a greater challenge, which only became apparent to political scientists in the 1970s. If all variables are endogenous, then there is a serious identification problem with cross-sectional data that cannot be overcome no matter how much data are collected. For example, in the bivariate case where "causal thinking" may influence "behavioralism" as well as "behavioralism" influencing "causal thinking," the researcher only observes a single correlation, which cannot produce the two distinctive coefficients representing the impact of "behavioralism" on "causal thinking" and the impact of "causal thinking" on "behavioralism."

The technical solution to this problem is the use of "instrumental variables" known to be exogenous and known to be correlated with the included endogenous variables, but the search for instruments proved elusive in many situations. The literature on this topic is now vast (Jackson 2008), and it includes tests for exogeneity, dealing with weak instruments, and the theoretical question of when structural equations must be used to understand a phenomenon. Heckman (2008, 5), for example, argues that the statistical models of causality (the Neyman–Rubin–Holland model discussed in more detail below and in Sekhon 2008) are incomplete because "[t]hey do not allow for simultaneity in choices of outcomes and treatment that are at the heart of game theory and models of social interactions and contagion." As a result, statistical models produce parameters that are of limited use.

This perspective suggests that the ongoing generalization of regression models is not just, as some proponents of the experimental model seem to suggest (Gerber, Green, and Kaplan 2004), a fruitless attempt to overcome insoluble problems with statistical tricks. Rather, these more sophisticated methods are needed in conjunction with a better eye toward finding defensible instruments and natural experiments. They are also needed because they often make us think harder about the nature of our data and the types of problems that we must overcome before making inferences. For example, the synthesis of factor analysis and causal modeling that produced what became known as LISREL, covariance structure, or structural equation models has increased our understanding of both measurement and causality. These approaches use factor analysis types of models to develop measures of latent concepts that are then combined with causal models of the underlying latent concepts (Bollen, Rabe-Hesketh, and Skrondal 2008). These techniques have been important at two levels. At one level, they simply provide a way to estimate more complicated statistical models that take into account both causal and measurement issues. At another level, partly through the vivid process of preparing "LISREL diagrams," they provide a metaphor for understanding the relationships between concepts and their measurements, latent variables and causation, and the process of going from theory to empirical estimation. Unfortunately, the models have also sometimes led to baroque modeling adventures and a reliance on linearity and additivity that at the same time complicates and simplifies things too much. Perhaps the biggest problem is the reliance upon "identification" conditions that often require heroic assumptions about instruments.

One way out of the instrumental variables problem is to use time series data. At the very least, time series give us a chance to see whether a putative cause "jumps" before a supposed effect. We can also consider values of variables that occur earlier in time to be "predetermined"—not quite exogenous but not endogenous either. Time series methods such as simple time series regressions, ARIMA models, vector autoregression (VAR) models, and unit root and error correction models (ECM) take this approach (Pevehouse and Brozek 2008). The literature faces two tricky problems. One is the complex but tractable difficulty of autocorrelation, which typically means that time series have less information in them per observation than cross-sectional data and which suggest that some variables have been omitted from the specification (Beck and Katz 1996). The second is the more pernicious problem of unit roots and commonly trending (co-integrated) data which can lead to nonsense correlations. In effect, in time series data, time is almost always an "omitted" variable that can lead to spurious relationships which cannot be easily (or sensibly) disentangled by simply adding time to the regression. Hence the special adaptation of methods designed for these data.

For our exploration of the rise of causal thinking, we can estimate a time series autoregressive model for eighteen five-year periods from 1910 to 1999. The model regresses the proportion of articles mentioning "causal thinking" on the lagged proportions mentioning the words "behavioral or behavior," "regression," or "correlation." Table 48.2 shows that mentions of "correlation" do not seem to matter (the

Table 48.2. Mentions of "causal thinking" for five-year periods regressed on mentions of "behavioral or behavior," "regression," and "correlation" for five-year periods for 1910–99

Independent variables lagged	Regression coefficients (standard errors)
Behavior	.283 (.065)***
Regression	.372 (.098)**
Correlation	−.159 (.174)
AR (1)	.276 (.342)
Constant	−.002 (.005)
N	17 (one dropped for lags)

Note: Significant: .05 (*), .01 (**), .001 (***).

coefficient is negative and the standard error is bigger than the coefficient), but mentions of "regression" or "behavioralism" are substantively large and statistically significant. (Also note that the autoregressive parameter is statistically insignificant.) These results provide further evidence that it might have been the combination of behavioralism and regression that led to an increase in causal thinking in political science.

A time series often throws away lots of cross-sectional data that might be useful in making inferences. Time series Cross-Sectional (TSCS) methods (Beck 2008) and event history models (Golub 2008) try to remedy this problem by using both sorts of information together. These techniques provide both fixes for problems and insights into subtle causal questions. They provide some elegant fixes for omitted variables problems because TSCS methods can use fixed unit effects to control for factors that are constant over time for a given unit, or fixed period effects to control for factors that are constant over units for a given time period. They also raise a host of important methodological questions such as distinguishing the degree of causal heterogeneity in units versus the amount of learning ("duration or state dependence"). This issue is important in many different research areas. In the study of welfare, solutions to these technical problems have implications for welfare policy. If recipients have different length welfare spells because they are heterogeneous (e.g. they might have different skill levels), then liberal job-training programs make sense; but if welfare spell lengths differ because being on welfare leads to welfare dependency (duration dependence), then conservatives are right about the need for time limits and "back-to-work" policies. In the study of party identification, it makes a difference whether people are subject to heterogeneous exogenous forces leading to persistence in identification or whether they are subject to becoming more partisan simply as a result of a past experience as partisans (Bartels et al. 2007; Box-Steffensmeier and Smith 1996).

Other "regression" methods also increase our understanding of measurement and modeling issues. Discrete choice modeling (Glasgow and Alvarez 2008) deals with dichotomous variables, ordered choices, and unordered choices. Ecological regression and its more sophisticated cousins (King 1997; Cho and Manski 2008) can be used whenever scholars are interested in the behavior of individuals but the data are aggregated at the precinct or census tract level (Cho and Manski 2008). Spatial analysis (Franzese and Hays 2008) and hierarchical modeling (Jones 2008; Steenbergen and Jones 2002) take into account the spatial and logical structure of data.

Consider what spatial analysis tells us about causal thinking. "Spatial interdependence" between units of analysis can be thought of as a nuisance just like autocorrelation in time series, but it can also be thought of as a sign that we must explain why the behavior of nearby units might be affected by similar unobserved variables. Spatial interdependence can be represented by a symmetric weighting matrix for the units of observation whose elements reflect the relative connectivity between unit i and unit j. By including this matrix in estimation in much the same way that we include lagged values of the dependent variable in time series, we can discover the impact of different forms of interdependence. But we are still left with questions about why this interdependence exists.

Hierarchical models also challenge our causal thinking. The classic use of multilevel models is in educational research where students are in classrooms situated in schools, which are in turn in school districts that are in states. Students may be affected by factors at all these levels—their own individual characteristics, the teaching in their classrooms, the culture of their schools, the policies of their school districts, and so forth. Many political problems have a similar structure. If we are to understand public opinion, shouldn't we consider more than people's individual characteristics? Shouldn't we consider how they are affected by their organizational affiliations, their communities, their political jurisdictions, and so forth? Don't we expect that two evangelicals with the same individual characteristics will behave differently if one is surrounded by other evangelicals while the other is surrounded by mainstream Protestants, Catholics, or nonbelievers?

In addition to these innovations in statistical methods, there have been important innovations in statistical estimation methods. The classic book by Eric Hanushek and John Jackson (1977) introduced many political scientists to a much broader set of statistical methods. Gary King (1998) made R. A. Fisher's maximum likelihood methods popular in political science. More recently, Bayesian estimation methods (Gill 2007; Martin 2008) have vastly increased our ability to estimate complex models. Before the 1990s, many researchers could write down a plausible model and the likelihood function for what they were studying, but the model presented insuperable estimation problems. Bayesian estimation was often even more daunting because it required not only the evaluation of likelihoods, but the evaluation of posterior distributions that combined likelihoods and prior distributions. In the 1990s, the combination of Bayesian statistics, Markov Chain Monte Carlo (MCMC) methods, and powerful computers provided a technology for overcoming these problems. These methods make it possible to simulate even very complex distributions and to obtain estimates of previously intractable models. Recently, political scientists have also been contributing to the development of computational methods for function maximization (Sekhon and Mebane 1998) and matching methods (Sekhon and Diamond 2005).

3.3 The Neyman–Rubin–Holland Model and Experimentation

In the last twenty years the spread of the Neyman–Rubin–Holland model of causal inference (Neyman 1990; Rubin 1974; Holland 1986) has revolutionized the teaching of causal inference (Brady 2008; Sekhon 2008) by emphasizing the importance of counterfactuals, manipulations, and above all, experimentation. This model also makes one important aspect of testing for a causal relationship a probabilistic one: whether or not the probability of the effect goes up when the cause is present.[23]

Experiments have become the gold standard for establishing causality because of their strong claim to making valid inferences—to what Donald Campbell (Campbell and Stanley 1966; Cook and Campbell 1979) called their "internal validity." Combining R. A. Fisher's notion of randomized experiment (1925) with the Neyman–Rubin model (Neyman 1923; Rubin 1974; 1978; Holland, 1986) provides a recipe for valid causal inference as long as several assumptions are met. At least one of these, the Stable Unit Treatment Value Assumption (SUTVA), is not trivial,[24] but some of the other assumptions are relatively innocuous so that when an experiment can be done, the burden of good inference is to properly implement the experiment.

The number of experiments in political science has increased dramatically in the last thirty-five years (Morton and Williams 2008) because of their power for making causal inferences.[25] At the same time, experiments, especially those in highly controlled situations such as college classrooms, have an Achilles heel—their lack of generalizability across people, places, and things—what Donald Campbell (Campbell and Stanley 1966; Cook and Campbell 1979) labeled "external validity." One of the challenges to modern political science is to find ways to undertake experiments in more general locations, with more representative populations, and with more realistic conditions. Another approach is to use field experiments and natural experiments to overcome the external validity limitations of laboratory experiments (Gerber and Green 2008). Despite early skepticism about what could be done with experiments,

---

[23] Thus if C is cause and E is effect, a necessary condition for causality is that $\text{Prob}(E|C) > \text{Prob}(E|\text{not } C)$. Of course, this also means that the expectation goes up $\text{Exp}(E|C) > \text{Exp}(E|\text{not } C)$.

[24] SUTVA means that a subject's response depends only on that subject's assignment, not the assignment of other subjects. SUTVA will be violated if the number of units getting the treatment versus the control status affects the outcome (as in a general equilibrium situation where many people getting the treatment of more education affects the overall value of education more than when just a few people get education), or if there is more communication of treatment to controls depending on the way assignment is done.

[25] The observant reader will note that these authors make a causal claim about the power of an invention (in this case experimental methods) to further causal discourse.

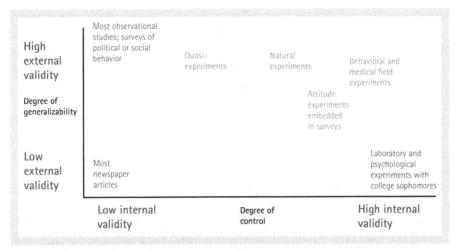

Fig. 48.5. External–internal validity trade-off

social scientists are increasingly finding ways to experiment in areas such as criminal justice, the provision of social welfare, schooling, and even politics. But "there remain important domains of political science that lie beyond the reach of randomized experimentation" (Gerber and Green 2008, 361). Moreover, more realistic experiments also must cope with the real-world problems of "noncompliance" and "attrition." Noncompliance occurs when medical subjects do not take the medicines they are assigned or citizens do not actually get the phone calls that were supposed to encourage their participation in politics. Attrition is a problem for experiments when people are more likely to be "lost" in one condition (typically, but not always, the control condition) than another. These difficulties make it hard to estimate causal impacts (if someone does not take the medicine, it is hard to estimate its impact), but they also present opportunities for making inferences about real-world situations (in the real world, people often do not take their medicine).

Figure 48.5 depicts the basic "external validity" versus "internal validity" inherent in experimentation versus observational studies. Observational studies, especially those using surveys, can make a strong claim to external validity—in fact that is the preeminent goal of the random sample. But it is often very hard to draw valid inferences from observational studies no matter how the sample is drawn. Randomized laboratory experiments can claim substantial internal validity, but often at the cost of external validity. In between are quasi-experiments, natural experiments, field experiments, and attitude experiments embedded in surveys.

3.4 Qualitative Tools for Causal Inference

What, then, is the role of qualitative research? When causal inference was defined solely as satisfying the neo-Humean regularity and antecedence conditions, then causal inference could be compressed into the tasks of showing that the cause preceded the effect and that the probability of the effect increased with the presence (or strength) of the putative cause once all the plausible confounders had been controlled. The ingredients for this recipe for establishing causation were: (1) large numbers of observations to deal with random variation; (2) quantitative measures of causes, effects, and especially "control" variables to rule out confounding explanations; and (3) a computerized regression package to run the data. When randomization was added as a condition for inferring causality, then experiments seemed de rigueur. But when establishing causal relations is broken apart into the requirements for counterfactuals, manipulations, mechanisms, and necessary and sufficient conditions, other, more focused strategies seem plausible in many situations.

David Freedman (2008, 312), for example, has argued that "substantial progress also derives from informal reasoning and qualitative insights" even though he has written extensively on the Neyman–Rubin–Holland (NRH) framework and he believes that it should be employed whenever possible because it sets the gold standard for causal inference. He suggests that another strategy relying upon "causal process observations" (CPOs) can be useful as a complement to the NRH framework (Brady and Collier 2004). CPOs rely upon detailed observations of situations to look for hints and signs that one or another causal process or mechanism might be at work, to look for cases where manipulations seem to have produced some effect, and to be open to natural experiments (where we observe two similar situations, one with and the other without the putative cause). Not just any cases or situations will do, but some provide inferential leverage because of their special qualities.

Thus Edward Jenner used fifteen case studies (involving thirty-one people) to conclude that cowpox inoculations could protect people against smallpox. Ignaz Semmelweis used cases to rule out "atmospheric, cosmic, telluric changes" as the causes for puerperal (also called childbed) fever, and he used the death of his colleague by "cadaveric particles" to identify the disease's mode of transmission. Alexander Fleming observed an anomaly in a bacterial culture in his laboratory that led to the discovery of penicillin. John Snow was led to understand the method by which cholera was transmitted by thinking about the deaths of a poor soul in London who next occupied the same room as a newly arrived and cholera-infected seaman and the death of a lady who had drunk from the cholera-infected "Broad Street Pump" because she liked the taste of the water, even though she lived far from the pump.

This careful use of case study material has been codified in the "process tracing" of Alexander George and Andrew Bennett (George and Bennett 2005; Bennett 2008) and in the CPOs of Brady and Collier (2004). Process tracing is an analytic procedure through which scholars make fine-grained observations to test ideas about causal mechanisms and causal sequences. Bennett (2008) argues that the logic of process tracing has important features in common with Bayesian analysis: It requires clear prior expectations linked to the theory under investigation, examines highly detailed evidence relevant to those expectations, and then considers appropriate revisions to the theory in light of observed evidence. With process tracing, the movement from theoretical expectations to evidence takes diverse forms, and Bennett reviews these alternatives and illustrates them with numerous examples.

A related, but somewhat more theoretically inclined approach, is to try to understand the mechanisms which are the underlying "cogs and wheels," which connect cause and the effect (Hedstrom 2008). The mechanism, for example, which explains how vaccinations work to provide immunity from an illness is the interaction between a weakened form of a virus and the body's immune system which confers longtime immunity. In social science, the rise in a candidate's popularity after an advertisement might be explained by a psychological process that works on a cognitive or emotional level to process messages in the advertisement. Various authors have inventoried stylized mechanisms that underlie social phenomena (Hedstrom 2008; Elster 1998; Mahoney 2001), and game theorists and formal modelers are certainly at the ready with mechanisms to explain almost any phenomena.

For example, Levy (2008)—in a discussion of counterfactuals and case studies–argues that game theory is one (but not the only) approach that provides clear counterfactuals and mechanisms for understanding social phenomena. A game explicitly models all of the actors' options including those possibilities that are not chosen. Game theory assumes that rational actors will choose an equilibrium path through the extensive form of the game, and all other routes are considered "off the equilibrium path"—counterfactual roads not taken. Levy argues that any counterfactual argument requires a detailed and explicit description of the alternative antecedent (i.e. the cause that did not occur in the counterfactual world), which is plausible and involves a minimal rewrite of history, and he suggests that one of the strengths of game theory is its explicitness about alternatives. Levy also argues that any counterfactual argument requires some evidence that the alternative antecedent would have actually led to a world in which the outcome is different from what we observe with the actual antecedent. With these ingredients useful causal arguments can be made.

4 THE FUTURE

4.1 Causal Inference and Interpretation: Bridging Alternative Approaches

Political methodology has become much more sophisticated and nuanced in the past thirty years, and these developments have met some of the challenges from critics of behavioralism. Nevertheless, there are still competing perspectives on political science, and the following data suggest that one of the cleavages is between those who focus on explanation and hypothesis testing and those who are interested in interpretation and narrative. One of the challenges for political methodology is to get beyond this cleavage.

Table 48.3. Two dimensions of political science analysis, 1970–99

	Component	
	Causal	Interpretative
Narrative	.018	.759
Interpretive	.103	.738
Causal/causality	.700	.105
Hypothesis	.750	−.073
Explanation	.701	.131

Notes: Extraction method: principal component analysis. Rotation method: oblimin with Kaiser normalization.

Based upon our qualitative understanding of methodological perspectives in American political science, we searched among all articles in JSTOR from 1970 to 1999 for five words that we suspected might have a two-dimensional structure. The words were "narrative," "interpretive," "causal or causality," "hypothesis," and "explanation." After obtaining their correlations across articles,[26] we used principal components and an oblimin rotation to clarify the structure. We found two eigenvalues with sizes larger than one which suggested the two-dimensional principal components solution reported in Table 48.3. There is clearly a "causal dimension" which applies to roughly one-third of the articles and an "interpretive" dimension which applies to about 6 percent of the articles.[27] Although we expected this two-dimensional structure, we were somewhat surprised to find that the word "explanation" was almost entirely connected with "causal or causality" and with "hypothesis." And we were surprised that the two dimensions were completely distinctive since they are essentially uncorrelated at .077. Moreover, in a separate analysis, we found that whereas the increase in "causal thinking" occurred around 1960 or maybe even 1950 in political science (see Figure 48.1), the rise in the use of the terms "narrative" and "interpretive" came in 1980.[28]

We view these findings not as a "fact" to be accepted, but as a methodological divide to overcome. "Causal thinking" is clearly not the only approach to political analysis. Modern political methodology, as demonstrated in this chapter, has a repertoire that recognizes the interpretative problems inherent in conceptualization, historical narrative (Mahoney and Terrie 2008), intensive interviewing (Rathbun 2008), and other

---

[26] We constructed variables for each word with a zero value if the word was not present in an article and a one if it was mentioned at least once. Then we obtained the ten correlations between pairs of the five variables with articles as the unit of analysis.

[27] Each word appears in a different number of articles, but one or the other or both of the words "narrative" or "interpretive" appear in about 5.9% of the articles and the words "hypothesis" or "causal" or "causality" appear in almost one-third (31.3%). "Explanation" alone appears in 35.4% of the articles.

[28] In 1980–4, the words "narrative" or "interpretive" were mentioned only 4.1% of the time in political science journals; in the succeeding five-year periods, the words increased in use to 6.1%, 8.1%, and finally 10.1% for 1995–9.

methods (Goodin and Tilly 2006, ch. 28). In an effort to come to grips with different conceptions of political research, modern methodology is developing techniques that go beyond simple behavioralism.

4.2 Organizations, Institutions, and Movements in the Field of Methodology

We see strong reasons to believe that political methodology will continue to advance far beyond simple behavioralism. One of the most interesting features of American political science during the last fifty years has been the attention paid to methodology and the creation of organizations devoted to its advancement. The initial step in this direction was the creation in 1962 of the Inter-university Consortium for Political Research (now the Inter-university Consortium for Political and Social Research), which runs an important summer training program in methods and that has become an internationally renowned facility for data archiving (Converse 1964; Franklin 2008). It is hard to over-emphasize the impact of the ICPSR on American political science through its training and archiving of digital data.

In the last twenty-five years, several methodological movements have developed within political science, which involved the present authors at first hand.[29] The two methodology sections of the American Political Science Association are among the largest of the discipline's thirty-eight sections. The Political Methodology Section, formed in 1984, has annual summer meetings that have grown to hundreds of attendees, and the section's journal, *Political Analysis,* publishes some of the best articles on political methodology (Franklin 2008; Lewis-Beck 2008). The APSA organized section for Qualitative Methods (now "Qualitative and Multi-Method Research") became an APSA organized section in 2003, and works in parallel with the Institute for Qualitative and Multi-Method Research (initially at Arizona State University, but now at Syracuse University) that has run a training program since 2002.

Recently, the National Science Foundation, under the leadership of James Granato and Frank Scioli (Granato and Scioli 2004), created the Empirical Implications of Theoretical Models (EITM) initiative to create a new generation of scholars who knew enough formal theory and enough about methods to do two things: (1) build theories that could be tested; and (2) develop methods for testing theories (Aldrich, Alt, and Lupia 2008). Two major EITM summer programs (one that has rotated among Harvard, Duke, Michigan, Berkeley, and UCLA since 2002 and another at Washington

---

[29] Brady was a founding member and early president of the Political Methodology Society. He was a co-principal investigator (with PI Paul Sniderman and Phil Tetlock) of the Multi-Investigator Study which championed the use of experiments in surveys and which provided the base for the Time-sharing Experiments for the Social Sciences (TESS) program. He was present at the meeting convened by Jim Granato at NSF which conceived of the EITM idea, and he is a co-PI of one of the two EITM summer programs. Janet Box-Steffensmeier was an early graduate student member of the Political Methodology Society and a recent president. David Collier was the founding president of the APSA Qualitative Methods section, and the chair of CQRM's Academic Council.

University in St. Louis that has run since 2003) have trained several hundred students and faculty members. NSF has also provided support for the qualitative methods training institute, as well as for a new initiative to explore ways of archiving qualitative data.

Through these various institutes and organizations, the discipline has expanded its ability to train its own graduate students, and there is an increasing capacity to train both graduate and undergraduate students within political science departments. More attention is being paid to the training of undergraduates as a fundamental base needed for the discipline, including discussions of a political methodology Wiki led by Philip Schrodt. Political methodology is also finding more and more connections with theory. Beck (2000) draws the contrast between statisticians and political methodologists in that "statisticians work hard to get the data to speak, whereas political scientists are more interested in testing theory." The focus on theory draws both quantitative and qualitative political scientists into the substance of politics, and it helps unite political methodologists with the political science community. Finally, the range and scope of outlets for publishing work in political methodology has increased dramatically in the last forty years (Lewis-Beck 2008). Based on the vibrancy of these institutions, the future of political methodology looks bright indeed.

4.3 Political Science at the Disciplinary Crossroads

In two different ways, political methodology straddles a disciplinary crossroads with all the hubbub, excitement, and diversity of the traditional bazaar. Within the discipline of political science, methodology serves the many different substantive and methodological interests of political scientists. In doing this, it helps to unite the discipline by focusing on the importance of providing methods that offer conceptual clarity, better interpretations of meanings, inferential leverage, and better explanations. In the words of two of us, it provides "diverse tools, shared standards" (Brady and Collier 2004).

Political methodology is also at the crossroads of other disciplines because it has evolved from borrowing, to welcoming, to creating new wares and new methods. Historically, quantitative methodology borrowed heavily from statistics, sociology, econometrics, psychometrics, statistics again, and most recently, biostatistics. Qualitative methodology borrowed from anthropology, history, and sociology. However, political methodology has recently begun to come into its own. Beck (2000) characterizes the field as one of welcoming methods from other disciplines, while also making important advances tailored to the unique features of political science data and problems. This represents a substantial improvement on Achen's assessment of political methodology as a field that "has so far failed to make serious theoretical progress on any of the major issues facing it" (1983, 69). Achen lamented that a major preoccupation (and limitation) of political methodologists was simply to teach methods developed in other fields.

Bartels and Brady (1993) noted approvingly that beyond describing important methodological developments in other fields, political scientists were routinely applying advanced quantitative techniques in every substantive area of enquiry in political science. Indeed, in looking specifically at the two areas Achen (1983) identified as ripe for methodological contributions (the nature of survey response and economic voting), Bartels and Brady concluded that "political methodologists have made significant progress on both of these problems in the intervening decade" and suggested that "further investment in basic methodological research will continue to pay handsome dividends in terms of our substantive understanding of politics" (1993, 146).

Recent contributions in qualitative methodology, interestingly enough, have been able to draw upon canonical works from within political science. Examples are Sartori (1970), Przeworski and Teune (1970), Verba (1967; 1971a; 1971b), Lijphart (1971; 1975), Eckstein (1975), Almond and Genco (1977), and George (1979). Notwithstanding significant contributions from other disciplines, these studies retained a foundational status for qualitative researchers well into the 1990s, and even with the renaissance of writing on qualitative methods that began slowly in the 1990s, and expanded greatly after 2000 (Collier and Elman 2008), this earlier work by political scientists retains its importance.

While political methodologists should always seek to introduce methodological advances from other fields and to teach the "canon" of well-known methods, it is heartening that the field is beginning to make its own contributions, and that the evolution from borrowing, to welcoming, to a discipline that is welcomed by other social sciences is occurring.

We believe that in doing this, political methodologists should keep in mind three principles.

- Techniques should be the servants of improved data collection, measurement, and conceptualization and of better understanding of meanings and enhanced identification of causal relationships. Methodologists should develop strong research designs that ensure "that the results have internal, external, and ecological validity" (Educational Psychology 2008), and these principles are more important than whether researchers use qualitative or quantitative methods.
- These tasks can be undertaken in diverse ways: description and modeling, case-study and large-n designs, and quantitative and qualitative research.
- Techniques should cut across boundaries and be useful for many different kinds of researchers. Methodologists should ask how their methods can be used by, or at least inform, the work of those outside those areas where they are usually employed. For example, those describing large-n statistical techniques should provide examples of how their methods inform, or even are adopted by, those doing case studies or interpretive work. Similarly, authors explaining how to do comparative historical work or process tracing should reach out to explain how it could inform those doing cross-sectional or time series studies.

From our survey of the literature on qualitative and quantitative methods in the social sciences, these principles seem to be taking hold, and we come to three general conclusions. First, there is a lot of interest in multimethod research—integrating, combining, or mixing methods—however it is termed. Increasing numbers of researchers argue that mixed methods research is an attractive alternative to quantitative-only or qualitative-only research, e.g. Johnson and Onwuegbuzie (2004). Even more quantitatively oriented disciplines, such as counseling psychology, are incorporating what used to be less-favored qualitative methods in their work (Hanson et al. 2005), and some feminist researchers have begun to use more and more quantitative research methods, which in the past have been criticized as associated with masculinity, e.g. Westmarland (2001). In fact, some researchers go so far as to argue that mixed methods should be a separate research movement as opposed to just a fusion of the qualitative and quantitative approaches (Tashakkori and Teddlie 2002).

While there is excitement about multimethod work, not everyone agrees that it is the best way to proceed (see in particular, Symposium: Multi-Method Work, Dispatches from the Front Lines 2007). Bennett (2007) points out that multiple methods might ensure that one method's weaknesses will be offset by the strength of another, but it is also possible that errors might simply accumulate because users might not have had enough time to master all the methods. Indeed, some scholars conclude that it is better to master just one method (see Wittenberg 2007).

Second, "Quantitative versus Qualitative" debates are for the most part over. There are not many quantitative–qualitative "debate" articles. Across the social sciences, this type of article was mostly published in the 1980s and early 1990s. There can be little doubt that research that involves the integration of quantitative and qualitative research has become increasingly common in recent years as a result (Taylor 2006). Recently published articles are generally moving beyond debates (whether one method wins over the other or vice versa) to how to do multimethod research or how to build upon insights or gaps of one or the other.

Third, despite signs of convergence, there still remains an unproductive bifurcation between qualitative and quantitative methods in political science. The *Oxford Handbook of Political Methodology* was designed to help fill that gap, but there are still many instances where researchers pursue one or the other method when a combination would be much more powerful.

4.4 The Future

We end with some speculation about the specific kinds of methods that might be developed in the next thirty years. This exercise is no doubt foolhardy, but it might be amusing to those who read this chapter now and in the future. We organize the possibilities by the two major sections in this review.

4.4.1 *Conceptualization, Measurement, and Data Collection*

1. *Conceptualization.* Just as the last thirty years have seen substantial changes in our understanding of the nature of conceptualization and in our gunny sack of useful concepts, the future should bring innovations in:

    (a) *Our understanding of conceptualization.* Social science concepts still remain mysterious things with their essential contestability, their constructed nature, and their position between political practice and political science research. We expect social theorists to continue to think hard and carefully about concepts and we expect that methodologists will develop new methods that will take us beyond validity, reliability, factor analyses, and our current understandings.

    (b) *Micro-concepts.* We will learn much more about nature of attitudes such as identity, efficacy, liberalism–conservatism, and their roots in neurobiology. We will learn more about the nature of interactions through developments in theoretical and experimental game theory, and the role of social networks through developments in sociology and other fields.

    (c) *Macro-concepts.* We will improve our understanding of democracy, revolutions, transitions, legitimacy, collective action, and many other concepts by having better theories, more data, and better linkages between micro-concepts and macro-concepts (e.g. the role of regime approval, repression, and ignorance in the microfoundations of legitimacy, and the role of context and social networks in collective action or revolutions).

2. *A better understanding of how people conceptualize politics.* The "left–right" and multidimensional conceptualization of politics has been a major innovation in our comprehension of political cleavages, mass politics, and elite politics in organizations, bureaucracies, legislatures, and courts. Cognitive and neurobiological science may tell us more about how people think about politics and about whether our spatial metaphors really make sense at a fundamental level (Gardenfors 2004). The result will be important for how we model and think about politics.

3. *Better measurements.* We expect that there will be better indicators of emotions, values, social networks, racism, ethnic identity, and so forth. Moreover, these methods will increasingly use neurobiological and cognitive science techniques, game theory methods (e.g. "Trust games," Camerer 2003), and the power of the web.

4. *Automatic text, audio, and video coders.* As computer scientists and linguists get better at parsing text, there will be more and better automatic text decoders which will allow researchers to code the vast bodies of data now available on the web in a reproducible and fully documented fashion. These tools will be invaluable for both quantitative and qualitative researchers.

5. *New kinds of large data-sets.* There will be more linking of data over time and space; across modalities of data (video, written, behavioral), and across different sources. There will be continuous sampling of information through modern

telecommunications (e.g. cellphone read-outs of people's locations). Scholars will be increasingly able to analyze large collections of text, audio, and video data, which will greatly extend the horizons of qualitative and quantitative researchers.

6. *World indicators.* We see substantial use of indicators to measure the level of democracy, human rights, corruption, happiness, feelings of efficacy, quality of service delivery, and other features of governments. There will be an increasing use of these indicators, and we hope that there will be greatly expanded attention to their reliability and validity, which at times is problematic.

7. *More use of the web for data collection.* Surveys, experiments, and simulations will be increasingly done on the web (or whatever serves as the system that integrates the web, cellphones, and television) (Berman and Brady 2005).

4.4.2 *Causal Inference*

1. *New techniques for making causal statements.* Statistics courses in the social sciences will increasingly start by studying what is meant by a causal inference. We will see a better understanding of how to use case study and other information, and there will be new statistical techniques that tell us how to establish the inevitably complicated linkages of information across studies (akin to "meta-analysis").

2. *Advances from neurobiology and cognitive sciences.* New methods will be developed for linking political thinking and behavior to the brain. The work using the fMRI will be extended in ways that will provide much more detailed information about what is happening in the brain.

3. *Better linking of formal models to testing procedures.* More sophisticated methods will emerge to link formal models to testing procedures. Often this will involve teams of social scientists with specialties in methods, modeling, or substantive areas of research.

4. *Large-scale field experiments.* Experimental studies of voting turnout and deliberative polls are some of the first-generation work using large-scale field experiments. The next generation will see experiments in countries as they try different public policies and different political systems.

5. *New designs for causal inference.* There will be even more sophisticated ways developed to make causal inferences that combine counterfactuals, manipulations, and interventions in the operation of putative mechanisms. These new methods will make novel uses of temporal and spatial variation.

In sum, we are convinced that political methodologists will continue a vigorous program of innovation on many fronts, and we are convinced that such innovation will make invaluable contributions to the shared goals of our discipline: to advance the substantive understanding of politics.

REFERENCES

ABDELAL, R., HERRERA, Y. M., JOHNSTON, A. I., and McDERMOTT, R. (eds.) 2009. *Measuring Identity*. Cambridge, Mass.: Cambridge University Press.

ACHEN, C. H. 1983. Towards theories of data. In *Political Science: The State of the Discipline*, ed. A. Finifter. Washington, DC: American Political Science Association.

—— 1986. *The Statistical Analysis of Quasi-experiments*. Los Angeles: University of California Press.

—— 2002. Toward a new political methodology: microfoundations and ART. *Annual Review of Political Science*, 5: 423–50.

ADCOCK, R. and COLLIER, D. 2001. Measurement validity: a shared standard for qualitative and quantitative research. *American Political Science Review*, 95: 529–46.

ALDRICH, J. H., ALT, J. E., and LUPIA, A. 2008. The EITM approach: origins and interpretations. Ch. 37 in Box-Steffensmeier, Brady, and Collier 2008.

ALLSOP, D. and WEISBERG, H. 1988. Measuring change in party identification in an election campaign. *American Journal of Political Science*, 32: 996–1017.

ALMOND, G. and GENCO, S. J. 1977. Clouds, clocks, and the study of politics. *World Politics*, 29: 489–522.

—— and VERBA, S. 1963. *The Civic Culture: Political Attitudes and Democracy in Five Nations*. Princeton, NJ: Princeton University Press.

ANDERSON, B. 1991. *Imagined Communities: Reflections on the Origin and Spread of Nationalism*. London: Verso.

ARJOMAND, S. A. 1986. Iran's Islamic revolution in comparative perspective. *World Politics*, 38: 383–414.

ARKES, H. R. and TETLOCK, P. E. 2004. Attributions of implicit prejudice, or "would Jesse Jackson 'fail' the implicit association test?" *Psychological Inquiry*, 15: 257–78.

ARROW, K. J. 1951. *Social Choice and Individual Values*. New York: Wiley.

AZAR, E. E. 1970. The analysis of international events. *Peace Research Reviews*, Nov.: 1–113.

—— COHEN, S. H., JUKAM, T. O., and McCORMICK, J. M. 1972. The problem of source coverage in the use of international events data. *International Studies Quarterly*, 16: 373–88.

BANKS, A. S. *Cross-Polity Time-Series Data*. Cambridge. Mass.: MIT Press.

—— and TEXTOR, R. B. 1963. *A Cross Polity Survey*. Cambridge, Mass.: MIT Press.

BARTELS, B., BOX-STEFFENSMEIER, J. M., SMIDT, C., and SMITH, R. M. 2007. Microfoundations of partisanship. Typescript, Ohio State University.

BARTELS, L. 1987. Candidate choice and the dynamics of the presidential nominating process. *American Journal of Political Science*, 31: 1–30.

—— and BRADY, H. E. 1993. The state of quantitative political methodology. Vol. 2, pp. 121–59, in *Political Science: The State of the Discipline*, ed. A. Finifter. Washington, DC: American Political Science Association.

BARTON, A. H. 1955. The concept of property-space in social research. In *The Language of Social Research: A Reader in the Methodology of Social Research*, ed. P. F. Lazarsfeld and M. Rosenberg. Glencoe, Ill.: Free Press.

—— and LAZARSFELD, P. F. 1969. Some functions of qualitative analysis in social research. In *Issues in Participant Observation*, ed. G. J. McCall and J. L. Simmons. Reading, Mass.: Addison-Wesley.

BAUMGARTNER, F. R., JONES, B. D., and MacLEOD, M. C. 1998. Ensuring quality, reliability, and usability in the creation of a new data source. *Political Methodologist*, 8: 1–10.

BECK, N. 2000. Political science: a welcoming discipline. *Journal of the American Statistical Association*, 95: 651–64.

BECK, N. 2008. Time series cross-sectional methods. Ch. 20 in Box-Steffensmeier, Brady, and Collier 2008.

—— and KATZ, J. N. 1996. Nuisance vs. substance: specifying and estimating time series–cross-section models. *Political Analysis*, 6: 1–36.

BEISSINGER, M. 2002. *Nationalist Mobilization and the Collapse of the Soviet State.* Cambridge, Mass.: Cambridge University Press.

BELLI, R. F., TRAUGOTT, M. W., YOUNG, M., and McGONAGLE, K. A. 1999. Reducing vote overreporting in surveys: social desirability, memory failure, and source monitoring. *Public Opinion Quarterly*, 63: 90–108.

BEN-DAK, J. D. and AZAR, E. 1972. Research perspectives on the Arab–Israeli conflict: introduction to a symposium. *Journal of Conflict Resolution*, 16: 131–4.

BENNETT, A. 2007. Introduction for symposium: "Multi-Method Work, Dispatches from the Front Lines." *Qualitative Methods: Newsletter of the American Political Science Association Organized Section on Qualitative Methods*, 5: 9.

—— 2008. Process tracing: a Bayesian perspective. Ch. 30 in Box-Steffensmeier, Brady, and Collier 2008.

BERGER, P. L. and LUCKMANN, T. 1966. *The Social Construction of Reality: A Treatise in the Sociology of Knowledge.* Garden City, NY: Anchor.

BERINSKY, A. J. 2002. Political context and the survey response: the dynamics of racial policy opinion. *Journal of Politics*, 64: 567–84.

BERMAN, F. and BRADY, H. E. 2005. Final report: NSF SBE-CISE Workshop on Cyberinfrastructure and the Social Sciences. <http://vis.sdsc.edu/sbe/reports/SBE-CISE-FINAL.pdf>

BEVIR, M. 2008. Meta-methodology: clearing the underbrush. Ch. 3 in Box-Steffensmeier, Brady, and Collier 2008.

—— and KEDAR, A. 2008. Concept formation in political science: an anti-naturalist critique of qualitative methodology. *Perspectives on Politics*, 6: 503–17.

BEYLE, H. C. 1931. *Identification and Analysis of Attribute-Cluster-Blocs: A Technique for Use in the Investigation of Behavior in Governance, including Report on Identification and Analysis of Blocs in a Large Non-Partisan Legislative Body, the 1927 Session of the Minnesota State Senate.* Chicago: University of Chicago Press.

BLACK, D. 1948. The decisions of a committee using a special majority. *Econometrica*, 16: 245–61.

BLALOCK, H. M., JR. 1964, *Causal Inference in Nonexperimental Research.* Chapel Hill: University of North Carolina Press.

BLUMER, H. 1969. *Symbolic Interactionism: Perspective and Method.* Englewood Cliffs, NJ: Prentice Hall.

BOAS, T. and GANS-MORSE, J. 2009. Neoliberalism: from new liberal philosophy to anti-liberal slogan. *Studies in Comparative International Development.*

BOLLEN, K. A., RABE-HESKETH, S., and SKRONDAL, A. 2008. Structural equation models. Ch. 18 in Box-Steffensmeier, Brady, and Collier 2008.

BOX-STEFFENSMEIER, J. M., BRADY, H. E., and COLLIER, D. (eds.) 2008. *Oxford Handbook of Political Methodology.* Oxford: Oxford University Press.

—— and SMITH, R. M. 1996. The dynamics of aggregate partisanship. *American Political Science Review*, 90: 567–80.

BRADY, H. E. 2008. Causation and explanation in social science. Ch. 10 in Box-Steffensmeier, Brady, and Collier 2008.

—— and COLLIER, D. 2004. *Rethinking Social Inquiry: Diverse Tools, Shared Standards.* New York: Rowman and Littlefield.

—— and KAPLAN, C. 2000. Categorically wrong? Nominal versus graded measures of ethnic identity. *Studies in Comparative International Development*, 35: 56–91.

—— —— 2009. Conceptualizing and measuring ethnic identity. In Abdelal et al. 2009.

—— and JOHNSTON, R. 2006. The rolling cross-section and causal attribution. Pp. 164–95 in *Capturing Campaign Effects*, ed. H. E. Brady and R. Johnston. Ann Arbor: University of Michigan Press.

BRADBURN, N., SUDMAN, S., and WANSINK, B. 2004. *Asking Questions: The Definitive Guide to Questionnaire Design—For Market Research, Political Polls, and Social Health Questionnaires.* San Francisco: Jossey-Bass.

BRASS, P. 1991. *Ethnicity and Nationalism*. Beverly Hills, Calif.: Sage.

BRIMHALL, D. R. and OTIS, A. S. 1948. Consistency of voting by our Congressmen. *Journal of Applied Psychology*, 32: 1–14.

CAMERER, C. F. 2003. *Behavioral Game Theory*. Princeton, NJ: Princeton University Press.

CAMPBELL, A. and KAHN, R. L. 1952. *The People Elect a President.* Survey Research Center, Institute for Social Research, University of Michigan.

CAMPBELL, D. and FISKE, D. 1959. Convergent and discriminant validation by the multitrait multimethod matrix. *Psychological Bulletin*, 56: 81–105.

CAMPBELL, D. T. and STANLEY, J. C. 1966. *Experimental and Quasi-experimental Designs for Research*. Chicago: Rand-McNally.

CHO, W. K. T. and MANSKI, C. F. 2008. Cross-level/ecological inference. Ch. 24 in Box-Steffensmeier, Brady, and Collier 2008.

CLINTON, J., JACKMAN, S., and RIVERS, D. 2004. The statistical analysis of roll call data. *American Political Science Review*, 98: 355–70.

COHEN, M. R. and NAGEL, E. 1934. *An Introduction to Logic and Scientific Method*. New York: Harcourt, Brace, and Company.

COLLIER, D. 1979. *The New Authoritarianism in Latin America*. Princeton, NJ: Princeton University Press.

—— and ADCOCK, R. 1999. Democracy and dichotomies: a pragmatic approach to choices about concepts. *Annual Review of Political Science*, 2: 537–65.

—— and ELMAN, C. 2008. Qualitative and multimethod research: organizations, publication, and reflections on integration. Ch. 34 in Box-Steffensmeier, Brady, and Collier 2008.

—— and GERRING, J. (eds.) 2008. *Concepts and Method in Social Science: The Tradition of Giovanni Sartori*. Oxford: Routledge.

—— HIDALGO, F. D., and MACIUCEANU, A. O. 2006. Essentially contested concepts: debates and applications. *Journal of Political Ideologies*, 11: 211–46.

—— and LEVITSKY, S. 1997. Democracy with adjectives: conceptual innovation in comparative research. *World Politics*, 49: 430–51.

—— —— 2008. Democracy: conceptual hierarchies in comparative research. Ch. 10 in Collier and Gerring 2008.

—— LAPORTE, J., and SEAWRIGHT, J. 2008. Typologies: forming concepts and creating categorical variables. In Box-Steffensmeier, Brady, and Collier 2008.

—— and MAHON, JR., J. E. 1993. Conceptual stretching revisited: adapting categories in comparative analysis. *American Political Science Review*, 87: 845–55.

COLLIER, R. B. and COLLIER, D. 1979. Inducements versus constraints: disaggregating "corporativism." *American Political Science Review*, 73: 967–86.

—— —— 1991. *Shaping the Political Arena*. Princeton, NJ: Princeton University Press.

CONVERSE, P. E. 1964. The nature of belief systems in mass publics. In *Ideology and Discontent*, ed. D. Apter. New York: Free Press.

COOK, T. D. and CAMPBELL, D. T. 1979. *Quasi-experimentation: Design and Analysis Issues for Field Settings*. Boston: Houghton-Mifflin.

COPPEDGE, M. and REINICKE, W. H. 1990. Measuring polyarchy. *Studies in Comparative International Development*, 25: 51–72.

CRUSE, D. A. 2004. *Meaning and Language: An Introduction to Semantics and Pragmatics*. Oxford: Oxford University Press.

DAHL, R. 1961. The behavioral approach in political science: epitaph for a monument to a successful protest. *American Political Science Review*, 55: 763–72.

——1971. *Polyarchy: Participation and Opposition*. New Haven, Conn.: Yale University Press.

DAVIS, O. A., HINICH, M. J., and ORDESHOOK, P. C 1970. An expository development of a mathematical model of the electoral process. *American Political Science Review*, 64: 426–48.

DONSBACH, W. and TRAUGOTT, M. 2007. *The SAGE Handbook of Public Opinion Research*. Newbury Park, Calif.: Sage.

DORAN, C. F., PENDLEY, R. E., and ATUNES, G. 1973. A test of cross-national event reliability. *International Studies Quarterly*, 17: 175–203.

DOWNS, A. 1957. *An Economic Theory of Democracy*. New York: Harper and Row.

ECKSTEIN, H. 1975. Case study and theory in political science. Pp. 79–138 in *Handbook of Political Science*, ed. F. Greenstein and N. Polsby. Reading, Mass.: Addison-Wesley.

ELDERSVELD, S. J. 1964. *Political Parties: A Behavioral Analysis*. Chicago, Illinois: Rand-McNally.

ELKINS, Z. 2000. Gradations of democracy? Empirical tests of alternative conceptualizations. *American Journal of Political Science*, 44: 293–300.

ELMAN, C. 2005. Explanatory typologies in qualitative studies of international politics. *International Organization*, 59: 293–326.

ELSTER, J. 1998. A plea for mechanisms. In *Social Mechanisms*, ed. P. Hedstrom and R. Swedberg. Cambridge: Cambridge University Press.

EMERICK, C. F. 1910. A neglected factor in race suicide. *Political Science Quarterly*, 25: 638–65.

EULAU, H. 1963. *The Behavioral Persuasion in Politics*. New York: Random House.

——1969. *Behavioralism in Political Science*. New York: Atherton.

FARR, J., DRYZEK, J. S., and LEONARD, S. T. (eds.). 1995. *Political Science in History: Research Programs and Political Traditions*. New York: Cambridge University Press.

—— and SEIDELMAN, R. 1993. *Discipline and History: Political Science in the United States*. Ann Arbor: University of Michigan Press.

FAZIO, R. H. and OLSON, M. A. 2003. Implicit measures in social cognition research: their meaning and use. *Annual Review of Psychology*, 54: 297–327.

FEIERABEND, I. K. and FEIERABEND, R. L. 1966. Aggressive behaviors within polities, 1948–1962: a cross-national study. *Journal of Conflict Resolution*, 10: 149–79.

FISHER, R. A. 1925. *Statistical Methods for Research Workers*. Edinburgh: Oliver and Boyd.

FRANKLIN, C. H. 2008. Quantitative methodology. Ch. 35 in Box-Steffensmeier, Brady, and Collier 2008.

FRANZESE, R. J., JR. and HAYS, J. C. 2008. Empirical models of spatial interdependence. Ch. 25 in Box-Steffensmeier, Brady, and Collier 2008.

FREEDEN, M. 1994. Political concepts and ideological morphology. *Journal of Political Philosophy*, 2: 140–64.

FREEDMAN, D. 1997. From association to causation via regression. *Advances in Applied Mathematics*, 18: 59–110.

——2008. On types of scientific enquiry: the role of qualitative reasoning. Ch. 12 in Box-Steffensmeier, Brady, and Collier 2008.

FREEMAN, J. R. and GOLDSTEIN, J. S. 1990. *Three-Way Street: Strategic Reciprocity in World Politics*. Chicago: University of Chicago Press.

GAGE, N. L. and SHIMBERG, B. 1949. Measuring senatorial "progressivism." *Journal of Abnormal and Social Psychology*, 44: 112.

GALLIE, W. B. 1956a. Essentially contested concepts. *Proceedings of the Aristotelian Society*, 56: 167–98.

——1956b. Art as an essentially contested concept. *Philosophical Quarterly*, 6: 97–114.

GARDENFORS, P. 2004. *Conceptual Spaces: The Geometry of Thought*. Boston: MIT Press.

GARFINKEL, H. 1967. *Studies in Ethnomethodology*. Englewood Cliffs, NJ: Prentice Hall.

GEANAKOPLOS, J. 1992. Common knowledge. *Journal of Economic Perspectives*, 6: 53–82.

GEORGE, A. L. 1979. Case studies and theory development: the method of structured, focused comparison. In *Diplomacy: New Approaches in History, Theory, and Policy*, ed. P. G. Lauren. New York: Free Press.

——and BENNETT, A. 2005. *Case Studies and Theory Development in the Social Sciences*. Boston: MIT Press.

GERBER, A. S. and GREEN, D. P. 2008. Field experiments and natural experiments. Ch. 15 in Box-Steffensmeier, Brady, and Collier 2008.

————and KAPLAN, E. H. 2004. The illusion of learning from observational research. Pp. 251–73 in *Problems and Methods in the Study of Politics*, ed. I. Shapiro, R. Smith, and T. Massoud. New York: Cambridge University Press.

GERRING, J. 2001. *Social Science Methodology: A Criterial Framework*. New York: Cambridge University Press.

GIDDENS, A. 1986. *The Constitution of Society*. Berkeley: University of California Press.

GILL, J. 2007. *Bayesian Methods: A Social and Behavioral Sciences Approach*, 2nd edn. Boca Raton, Fla.: Chapman and Hall.

GLASGOW, G. and ALVAREZ, R. M. 2008. Discrete choice methods. Ch. 22 in Box-Steffensmeier, Brady, and Collier 2008.

GOERTZ, G. 2006. *Social Science Concepts: A User's Guide*. Princeton, NJ: Princeton University Press.

——and LEVY, J. 2007. *Explaining War and Peace: Case Studies and Necessary Condition Counterfactuals*. New York: Routledge.

——and STARR, H. (eds.) 2002. *Necessary Conditions: Theory, Methodology, and Applications*. New York: Rowman and Littlefield.

GOFFMAN, E. 1959. *The Presentation of Self in Everyday Life*. New York: Anchor.

GOLDSTEIN, J. S. and FREEMAN. J. R. 1990. *Three-Way Street: Strategic Reciprocity in World Politics*. Chicago: University of Chicago Press.

GOLUB, J. 2008. Survival analysis. Ch. 23 in Box-Steffensmeier, Brady, and Collier 2008.

GOODIN, R. E. and TILLY, C. (eds.) 2006. *Oxford Handbook of Contextual Political Analysis*. Oxford: Oxford University Press.

GOSNELL, H. F. and GILL, N. N. 1935. An analysis of the 1932 presidential vote in Chicago. *American Political Science Review*, 29: 967–84.

GRANATO, J. and SCIOLI, F. 2004. Puzzles, proverbs, and omega matrices: the scientific and social significance of empirical implications of theoretical models (EITM). *Perspectives on Politics*, 2: 313–23.

GREENWALD, A. G., MCGHEE, D. E., and SCHWARTZ, J. L. K. 1998. Measuring individual differences in implicit cognition: the implicit association test. *Journal of Personality and Social Psychology*, 74: 1464–80.

GURR, T. R. 1968. A casual model of civil strife: a comparative analysis using new indices. *American Political Science Review*, 62: 1104–24.

GURR, T. R. 1970a. Sources of rebellion in Western societies: some quantitative evidence. *Annals of the American Academy of Political and Social Science*, 391: 128–44.

—— 1970b. *Why Men Rebel*. Princeton, NJ: Princeton University Press.

HANSON, W. E., CRESWELL, J. W., CLARK, V. L. P., PETSKA, K. S., and CRESWELL, J. D. 2005. Mixed methods research designs in counseling psychology. *Journal of Counseling Psychology*, 52: 224–35.

HANUSHEK, E. A. and JACKSON, J. E. 1977. *Statistical Methods for Social Scientists*. Orlando, Fla.: Academic Press.

HECKMAN, J. 2008, Econometric causality. NBER Working Paper 13934.

HEDSTROM, P. 2008. Studying mechanisms to strengthen causal inferences in quantitative research. Ch. 13 in Box-Steffensmeier, Brady, and Collier 2008.

HEMPEL, C. G. 1952. *Fundamentals of Concept Formation in Empirical Science*. Chicago: University of Chicago Press.

HIRSCH, F. 2005. *Empire of Nations: Ethnographic Knowledge and the Making of the Soviet Union*. Ithaca, NY: Cornell University Press.

HOLBROOK, T. M. 1996. *Do Campaigns Matter?* Newbury Park, Calif.: Sage.

HOLLAND, P. W. 1986. Statistics and causal inference (in theory and methods). *Journal of the American Statistical Association*, 81: 945–60.

HOPKINS, A. H. and WEBER, R. E. 1976. Dimensions of public policies in the American states. *Polity*, 8: 475–89.

HROCH, M. 1986. *Social Preconditions of National Revival in Europe: A Comparative Analysis of the Social Composition of Patriotic Groups among the Smaller European Nations*. New York: Cambridge University Press.

JACKMAN, S 2001. Multidimensional analysis of roll call data via Bayesian simulation: identification, estimation, inference and model checking. *Political Analysis*, 9: 227–41.

JACKSON, J. E. 2008. Endogeneity and structural equation estimation in political science. Ch. 17 in Box-Steffensmeier, Brady, and Collier 2008.

JENNINGS, M. K. and NIEMI, R. G. 1974. *The Political Character of Adolescence: The Influence of Families and Schools*. Princeton, NJ: Princeton University Press.

—— —— 1981. *A Panel Study of Young Adults and their Parents*. Princeton, NJ: Princeton University Press.

JERIT, J., BARABAS, J., and BOLSEN, T. 2006. Citizens, knowledge, and the information environment. *American Journal of Political Science*, 50: 266–82.

JOHNSON, R. B. and ONWUEGBUZIE, A. J. 2004. Mixed methods research: a research paradigm whose time has come. *Educational Researcher*, 33: 14–26.

JOHNSTON, R., BLAIS, A., BRADY, H. E., and CRETE, J. 1992. *Letting the People Decide: The Dynamics of a Canadian Election*. Stanford, Calif.: Stanford University Press.

JONES, B. S. 2008. Multilevel models. Ch. 26 in Box-Steffensmeier, Brady, and Collier 2008.

KEY, V. O., JR. 1949. *Southern Politics in State and Nation*. New York: Alfred A. Knopf.

KING, G. 1997. *A Solution to the Ecological Inference Problem: Reconstructing Individual Behavior from Aggregate Data*. Princeton, NJ: Princeton University Press.

—— 1998. *Unifying Political Methodology: The Likelihood Theory of Statistical Inference*. New York: Cambridge University Press.

—— KEOHANE, R. O., and VERBA, S. 1994. *Designing Social Inquiry: Scientific Inference in Qualitative Research*. Princeton, NJ: Princeton University Press.

—— and LOWE, W. 2003. An automated information extraction tool for international conflict data with performance as good as human coders: a rare events evaluation design. *International Organization*, 57: 617–42.

——— Murray, C. J. L., Salomon, J. A., and Tandon, A. 2003. Enhancing the validity and cross-cultural comparability of survey research. *American Political Science Review*, 97: 567–83. Reprinted with printing errors corrected February 2004.

Koopmans, R. and Rucht, D. 2002. Protest events analysis. Pp. 231–59 in *Methods of Social Movement Research*, ed. B. Klandermans and S. Staggenborg. Minneapolis: University of Minnesota Press.

Kotowski, C. M. 1984. Revolution. In *Social Science Concepts: A Systematic Analysis*, ed. G. Sartori. Beverly Hills, Calif.: Sage.

Krysan, M. and Couper, M. P. 2003. Race in the live and the virtual interview: racial deference, social desirability, and activation effects in attitude surveys. *Social Psychology Quarterly*, 66: 364–83.

Kuklinski, J. H., Cobb, M. D., and Gilens, M. 1997. Racial attitudes and the "New South." *Journal of Politics*, 59: 323–49.

Kurtz, M. J. 2000. Understanding peasant revolution: from concept to theory to case. *Theory and Society*, 29: 93–124.

Lakoff, G. 1987. *Women, Fire, and Dangerous Things: What Categories Reveal about the Mind*. Chicago: University of Chicago Press.

Lasswell, H. D. 1941. The World Attention Survey. *Public Opinion Quarterly*, 5: 456–62.

——— and Blumenstock, D. 1939. The volume of communist propaganda in Chicago. *Public Opinion Quarterly*, 3: 63–78.

——— and Sereno, R. 1937. Governmental party leaders in Fascist Italy. *American Political Science Review*, 31: 914–29.

Lazarsfeld, P. F. and Barton, A. H. 1951. Qualitative measurement in the social sciences: classification, typologies, and indices. In *The Policy Sciences*, ed. D. Lerner and H. D. Lasswell. Stanford, Calif.: Stanford University Press.

——— Berelson, B., and Gaudet, H. 1944. *The People's Choice: How the Voter Makes up his Mind in a Presidential Campaign*. New York: Duell, Sloan and Pearce.

——— and McPhee, W. N. 1986. *Voting: A Study of Opinion Formation in a Presidential Campaign*. Chicago: University of Chicago Press.

Lee, S. M. 1993. Racial classifications in the U.S. Census, 1890 to 1990. *Ethnic and Racial Studies*, 16: 75–94.

Lee, T. 2007. From shared demographic categories to common political destinies: immigration and the link from racial identity to group politics. *Du Bois Review*, 4: 433–56.

Levitsky, S. 1998. Peronism and institutionalization: the case, the concept, and the case for unpacking the concept. *Party Politics*, 4: 77–92.

Levy, J. S. 2008. Counterfactuals and case studies. Ch. 27 in Box-Steffensmeier, Brady, and Collier 2008.

Lewis, J. and Poole, K. 2004. Measuring bias and uncertainty in ideal point estimates via the parametric bootstrap. *Political Analysis*, 12: 105–27.

Lewis-Beck, M. 2008. Forty years of publishing in quantitative methodology. Ch. 36 in Box-Steffensmeier, Brady, and Collier 2008.

Lieberman, M., Schreiber, D., and Ochsner, K. 2003. Is political cognition like riding a bicycle? How cognitive neuroscience can inform research on political thinking. *Political Psychology*, 24: 681–704.

Lijphart, A. 1971. Comparative politics and comparative method. *American Political Science Review*, 65: 682–93.

——— 1975. The comparable cases strategy in comparative research. *Comparative Political Studies*, 8: 158–77.

LIPSET, S. M. and ROKKAN, S. 1967. Cleavage structures, party systems and voter alignments: an introduction. In *Party Systems and Voter Alignments: Cross-National Perspectives*, ed. S. M. Lipset and S. Rokkan. New York: Free Press.

LORD, F. M. and NOVICK, M. R. 1968. *Statistical Theories of Mental Test Scores*. Reading, Mass.: Addison-Wesley.

LUKS, S. and BRADY, H. E. 2003. Defining welfare spells: coping with problems of survey responses and administrative data. *Evaluation Review*, 27: 395–420.

McKINNEY, J. C. 1966. *Constructive Typology and Social Theory*. New York: Meredith.

MacRAE, D., JR. 1970. *Issues and Parties in Legislative Voting: Methods of Statistical Analysis*. New York: Harper and Row.

MAHONEY, J. 2001. *The Legacies of Liberalism: Path Dependence and Political Regimes in Central America*. Baltimore: Johns Hopkins University Press.

——and TERRIE. P. L. 2008. Comparative-historical analysis in contemporary political science. Ch. 32 in Box-Steffensmeier, Brady, and Collier 2008.

MARCUS, G. E. and MACKUEN, M. B. 1993. Anxiety, enthusiasm, and the vote: the emotional underpinnings of learning and involvement during presidential campaigns. *American Political Science Review*, 87: 672–85.

MARTIN, A. D. 2008. Bayesian analysis. Ch. 21 in Box-Steffensmeier, Brady, and Collier 2008.

——and QUINN, K. M. 2007. Assessing preference change on the US Supreme Court. *Journal of Law, Economics, and Organization Advance Access*, 23: 365–85.

MAVOR, J. 1895. Labor and politics in England. *Political Science Quarterly*, 10: 486–517.

MILL, J. S. 1888. *A System of Logic, Ratiocinative and Inductive*, 8th edn. New York: Harper and Brothers.

MORRIS, J. P., SQUIRES, N., TABER, C. S., and LODGE, M. 2003. Activation of political attitudes: a psychophysiological examination of the hot cognition hypothesis. *Political Psychology*, 24: 727–45.

MORTON, R. B. and WILLIAMS, K. C. 2008. Experimentation in political science. Ch. 14 in Box-Steffensmeier, Brady, and Collier 2008.

MUNCK, G. and VERKUILEN, J. 2002. Conceptualizing and measuring democracy: evaluating alternative indices. *Comparative Political Studies*, 35: 5–34.

NEYMAN, J. 1923. On the application of probability theory to agricultural experiments: essay on principles, trans. D. M. Dabrowska and T. P. Speed. *Statistical Science*, 5 (1990): 463–80.

NOBLES, M. 2000. *Shades of Citizenship: Race and the Census in Modern Politics*. Palo Alto, Calif.: Stanford University Press.

ODEGARD, P. H. 1935. Political parties and group pressures. *Annals of the American Academy of Political and Social Science*, 179: 68–81.

O'DONNELL, G. and SCHMITTER, P. C. 1986. *Transitions from Authoritarian Rule: Tentative Conclusions about Uncertain Democracies*. Baltimore: Johns Hopkins University Press.

OLIVER, P. E. and MANEY, G. M. 2000. Political processes and local newspaper coverage of protest events: from selection bias to triadic interactions. *American Journal of Sociology*, 106: 463–505.

PATTERSON, M. and MONROE, K. R. 1998. Narrative in political science. *Annual Review of Political Science*, 1: 315–31.

PAXTON, P. 2000. Women in the measurement of democracy: problems of operationalization. *Studies in Comparative International Development*, 35: 92–111.

PEARSON, K. 1896. Mathematical contributions to the theory of evolution: III. Regression, heredity, and panmixia. *Philosophical Transactions of the Royal Society of London*, 187: 253–318.

——1909. Determination of the coefficient of correlation. *Science*, 30: 23–5.

PEVEHOUSE, J. C. and BROZEK, J. D. 2008. Time series analysis. Ch. 19 in Box-Steffensmeier, Brady, and Collier 2008.

PHELPS, E. A. and THOMAS, L. A. 2003. Race, behavior, and the brain: the role of neuroimaging in understanding complex social behaviors. *Political Psychology*, 24: 747–58.

PIERSON, P. 2000. Path dependence, increasing returns, and the study of politics. *American Political Science Review*, 94: 251–67.

POLLOCK, J. K., JR. 1929. The German party system. *American Political Science Review*, 23: 859–91.

POOLE, K. and ROSENTHAL, H. 1997. *A Political-economic History of Roll Call Voting*. New York: Oxford University Press.

———— 1985. A spatial model for legislative roll call analysis. *American Journal of Political Science*, 29: 357–84.

PRESSER, S. and STINSON, L. 1998. Data collection mode and social desirability bias in self-reported religious attendance. *American Sociological Review*, 63: 137–45.

PRICE, V. and ZALLER, J. 1993. Who gets the news? Alternative measures of news reception and their implications for research. *Public Opinion Quarterly*, 57: 133–64.

PRITCHETT, C. H. 1941. Divisions of opinion among justices of the U.S. Supreme Court 1939–1941. *American Political Science Review*, 35: 890–8.

———— 1945. Dissent on the Supreme Court, 1943–44. *American Political Science Review*, 3: 42–54.

PRZEWORSKI, A. and TEUNE, H. E. 1970. *The Logic of Comparative Social Inquiry*. New York: Wiley.

RADCLIFF, B. 1992. The general will and social choice theory. *Review of Politics*, 54: 34–49.

RAGIN, C. 1987. *The Comparative Method*. Berkeley: University of California Press.

RAICHLE, M. 2003. Social neuroscience: a role for brain imaging. *Political Psychology*, 24: 759–63.

RATHBUN, B. C. 2008. Interviewing and qualitative field methods: pragmatism and practicialities. Ch. 29 in Box-Steffensmeier, Brady, and Collier 2008.

RICE, S. A. 1928. *Quantitative Methods in Politics*. New York: Alfred A. Knopf.

RIKER, W. H. 1982. *Liberalism against Populism: A Confrontation between the Theory of Democracy and the Theory of Social Choice*. San Francisco: W. H. Freeman.

———— 1986. *The Art of Political Manipulation*. New Haven, Conn.: Yale University Press.

ROBINSON, J. P., SHAVER, P. R., and WRIGHTSMAN, L. S. 1993. *Measures of Political Attitudes*. Volume 2 of *Measures of Social Psychological Attitudes*. San Diego: Academic Press.

RUBIN, D. B. 1974. Estimating causal effects of treatments in randomized and nonrandomized studies. *Journal of Educational Psychology*, 66: 688–701.

———— 1978. Bayesian inference for causal effects: the role of randomization. *Annals of Statistics*, 6: 34–58.

RUMMEL, R. J. 1963. Dimensions of conflict behavior within and between nations. *General Systems Yearbook*, 8: 1–50.

———— 1966. Dimensions of conflict behavior within nations, 1946–59. *Journal of Conflict Resolution*, 10: 65–73.

———— 1966. Some dimensions in the foreign behavior of nations. *Journal of Conflict Resolution*, 10: 201–24.

———— 1972. *The Dimensions of Nations*. Beverly Hills, Calif.: Sage.

RUSSETT, B., ALKER, H., JR., DEUTSCH, K. W., and LASSWELL, H. 1964. *World Handbook of Political and Social Indicators*. New Haven, Conn.: Yale University Press.

SARTORI, G. 1970. Concept misformation in comparative politics. *American Political Science Review*, 64: 1033–53.

—— 1975. The Tower of Babel. In G. Sartori, F. W. Riggs, and H. Teune, *Tower of Babel: On the Definition and Analysis of Concepts in the Social Sciences.* Occasional Paper No. 6, International Studies Association, University of Pittsburgh.

—— (ed.) 1984. *Social Science Concepts: A Systematic Analysis.* Beverly Hills, Calif.: Sage.

—— 1991. Comparing and miscomparing. *Journal of Theoretical Politics*, 3: 243–57.

SCHATTSCHNEIDER, E. E. 1952. Political parties and the public interest. *Annals of the American Academy of Political and Social Science*, 280: 18–26.

—— 1960. *The Semisovereign People: A Realist's View of Democracy in America.* New York: Holt, Rinehart and Winston.

SCHRODT, P. and GERNER, D. J. 1994. Validity assessment of a machine-coded event data set for the Middle East, 1982–92. *American Journal of Political Science*, 38: 825–54.

SEKHON, J. 2004. Quality meets quantity: case studies, conditional probability and counterfactuals. *Perspectives on Politics*, 2: 281–93.

—— 2008. The Neyman–Rubin model of causal inference and estimation via matching methods. Ch. 11 in Box-Steffensmeier, Brady, and Collier 2008.

—— and DIAMOND, A. 2005. Genetic matching for estimating causal effects: a general multivariate matching method for achieving balance in observational studies. Presented at the Political Methodology Summer Conference, Florida State University, July 21–3.

—— and MEBANE, W. 1998. Genetic optimization using derivatives: theory and application to nonlinear models. *Political Analysis*, 7: 189–213.

SHAW, D. R. 1999. The study of presidential campaign event effects from 1952 to 1992. *Journal of Politics*, 61: 387–422.

—— 2006. *The Race to 270: The Electoral College and the Campaign Strategies of 2000 and 2004.* Chicago: University of Chicago Press.

SIMON, H. A. 1954, Spurious correlation: a causal interpretation. *Journal of the American Statistical Association*, 24: 467–74.

SINGER, J. D. and SMALL, M. 1972. *The Wages of War: 1816–1965: A Statistical Handbook.* New York: John Wiley.

SKOCPOL, T. 1979. *States and Social Revolution.* New York: Cambridge University Press.

SNIDERMAN, P. and GROB, D. 1996. Innovations in experimental design in general population attitude surveys. *Annual Review of Sociology*, 22: 377–99.

STEENBERGEN, M. R. and JONES, B. S. 2002. Modeling multilevel data structures. *American Journal of Political Science*, 46: 218–37.

STOUFFER, S., GUTTMAN, L. SUCHMAN, E. A., LAZARFELD, P. F., STAR, S. A., and CLAUSEN, J. A. 1950. *Studies in Social Psychology in World War II: The American Soldier. 4, Measurement and Prediction.* Princeton, NJ: Princeton University Press.

SUPPES, P. 1984. *Probabilistic Metaphysics.* Oxford: Blackwell.

Symposium: Multi-Method Work, Dispatches from the Front Lines 2007. *Qualitative Methods: Newsletter of the American Political Science Association Organized Section on Qualitative Methods*, 5/1.

TAJFEL, H. 1970. Experiments in intergroup discrimination. *Scientific American*, 223: 96–102.

TANTER, R. 1966. Dimensions of conflict behavior within and between nations, 1958–60. *Journal of Conflict Resolution*, 10: 41–64.

TASHAKKORI, A. and TEDDLIE, C. B. (eds.) 2002. *Handbook of Mixed Methods Social and Behavioral Research.* Beverly HIlls, Calif.: Sage.

TAYLOR, G. R. 2006. *Integrating Quantitative and Qualitative Methods in Research*, 2nd edn. Lanham, Md.:University Press of America.

TAYLOR, C. L. and HUDSON, M. C. 1972. *World Handbook of Political and Social Indicators*, 2nd edn. New Haven, Conn.: Yale University Press.

TAYLOR, J. R. 2003. *Linguistic Categorization*, 3rd edn. Oxford: Oxford University Press.

THAGARD, P. 1990. Concepts and conceptual change. *Synthese*, 82: 255–74.

——1992. *Conceptual Revolutions*. Princeton, NJ: Princeton University Press.

TILLY, C., TILLY, L., and TILLY R. 1975. *The Rebellious Century, 1830–1930*. Cambridge, Mass.: Harvard University Press.

TIRYAKIAN, E. A. 1968. Typologies. Pp. 177–86 in *International Encyclopedia of the Social Sciences*, 16. New York: Macmillan Company and the Free Press.

TOURANGEAU, R., KIPS, L. J., and RASINSKI, K. A. 2000. *The Psychology of Survey Response*. Cambridge, Mass.: Cambridge University Press.

VERBA, S. 1967. Some dilemmas in comparative research. *World Politics*, 2: 111–27.

——1971a. Cross-national survey research: the problem of credibility. In *Comparative Methods in Sociology: Essays on Trends and Applications*, ed. I. Vallier. Berkeley: University of California Press.

——1971b. Sequences and development. In *Crises and Sequences in Political Development*, ed. L. Binder et al. Princeton, NJ: Princeton University Press.

——and NIE, N. H. 1972. *Political Participation in America*. Chicago: University of Chicago Press.

WEBB, S. 1889. Socialism in England. *Publications of the American Economic Association*, 4: 7–73.

WEEKS, D. 1930. The Texas-Mexican and the politics of south Texas. *American Political Science Review*, 24: 606–27.

WESTMARLAND, N. 2001. The quantitative/qualitative debate and feminist research. *Forum: Qualitative Social Research*, 2/1, Art. 13. <http://nbn-resolving.de/urn:nbn:de:0114-fqs0101135>

WITTENBERG, J. 2007. Peril and promise: multi-methods research in practice. In Symposium: Multi-Method Work, Dispatches from the Front Lines 2007.

WOOLLEY, J. T. 2000. Using media-based data in studies of politics. *American Journal of Political Science*, 44: 156–73.

YANOW, D. and SCHWARTZ-SHEA, P. 2006. *Interpretation and Method: Empirical Research Methods and the Interpretive Turn*. New York: M. E. Sharpe.

YULE, G. U. 1907. On the theory of correlation for a number of variables, treated by a new system of notation. *Proceedings of the Royal Society of London*, 79: 182–93.

CHAPTER 49

CAUSATION AND EXPLANATION IN SOCIAL SCIENCE

HENRY E. BRADY

1 CAUSALITY

HUMANS depend upon causation all the time to explain what has happened to them, to make realistic predictions about what will happen, and to affect what happens in the future. Not surprisingly, we are inveterate searchers after causes. Almost no one goes through a day without uttering sentences of the form *X caused Y* or *Y occurred because of X*. Causal statements explain events, allow predictions about the future, and make it possible to take actions to affect the future. Knowing more about causality can be useful to social science researchers.

Philosophers and statisticians know something about causality, but entering into the philosophical and statistical thickets is a daunting enterprise for social scientists because it requires technical skills (e.g. knowledge of modal logic) and technical information (e.g. knowledge of probability theory) that is not easily mastered. The net payoff from forays into philosophy or statistics sometimes seems small compared to the investment required. The goal of this chapter is to provide a user-friendly synopsis of philosophical and statistical musings about causation. Some technical issues will be discussed, but the goal will always be to ask about the bottom line—how can this information make us better researchers?

Three types of intellectual questions typically arise in philosophical discussions of causality:

- *Psychological and linguistic*—What do we *mean* by causality when we use the concept?
- *Metaphysical or ontological*—What *is* causality?
- *Epistemological*—How do we *discover* when causality is operative?[1]

Four distinct approaches to causality, summarized in Table 49, provide answers to these and other questions about causality.[2] Philosophers debate which approach is the right one. For our purposes, we embrace them all. Our primary goal is developing better social science methods, and our perspective is that all these approaches capture some aspect of causality. Therefore, practical researchers can profit from drawing lessons from each one of them even though their proponents sometimes treat them as competing or even contradictory. Our standard has been whether or not we could think of concrete examples of research that utilized (or could have utilized) a perspective to some advantage. If we could think of such examples, then we think it is worth drawing lessons from that approach.

A really good causal inference should satisfy the requirements of all four approaches. Causal inferences will be stronger to the extent that they are based upon finding all the following: (1) Constant conjunction of causes and effects required by the neo-Humean approach. (2) No effect when the cause is absent in the most similar world to where the cause is present as required by the counterfactual approach. (3) An effect after a cause is manipulated. (4) Activities and processes linking causes and effects required by the mechanism approach.

The claim that smoking causes lung cancer, for example, first arose in epidemiological studies that found a correlation between smoking and lung cancer. These results were highly suggestive to many, but this correlational evidence was insufficient to others (including one of the founders of modern statistics, R. A. Fisher). These studies were followed by experiments that showed that, at least in animals, the absence of smoking reduced the incidence of cancer compared to the incidence with smoking when similar groups were compared. But animals, some suggested, are not people. Other studies showed that when people stopped smoking (that is, when the putative cause of cancer was manipulated) the incidence of cancer went down as well. Finally, recent studies have uncovered biological mechanisms that explain the link between smoking and lung cancer. Taken together the evidence for a relationship between smoking and lung cancer now seems overwhelming.

---

[1] A fourth question is pragmatic: How do we *convince* others to accept our explanation or causal argument? A leading proponent of this approach is Bas van Fraassen (1980). Kitcher and Salmon (1987, 315) argue that "van Fraassen has offered the best theory of the pragmatics of explanation to date, but ... if his proposal is seen as a pragmatic theory of explanation then it faces serious difficulties" because there is a difference between "a theory of the pragmatics of explanation and a pragmatic theory of explanation." From their perspective, knowing how people convince others of a theory does not solve the ontological or epistemological problems.

[2] Two important books on causality are not covered in this chapter, although the author has profited from their insights. Pearl (2000) provides a comprehensive approach to causality rooted in a Bayesian perspective. Shafer (1996) links decision theory and causal trees in a novel and useful way.

Table 49.1. Four approaches to causality

	Neo-Humean regularity	Counterfactual	Manipulation	Mechanisms and capacities
Major authors associated with the approach	Hume (1739); Mill (1888); Hempel (1965); Beauchamp and Rosenberg (1981)	Weber (1906); Lewis (1973a; 1973b; 1986)	Gasking (1955); Menzies and Price (1993); von Wright (1971)	Harre and Madden (1975); Cartwright (1989); Glennan (1996);
Approach to the symmetric aspect of causality	Observation of constant conjunction and correlation	Truth in otherwise similar worlds of "if the cause occurs then so does the effect" and "if the cause does not occur then the effect does not occur"	Recipe that regularly produces the effect from the cause	Consideration of whether there is a mechanism or capacity that leads from the cause to the effect
Approach to the asymmetric aspect of causality	Temporal precedence	Consideration of the truth of: "if the effect does not occur, then the cause may still occur"	Observation of the effect of the manipulation	An appeal to the operation of the mechanism
Major problems solved	Necessary connection	Singular causation; nature of necessity	Common cause and causal direction	Pre-emption
Emphasis on causes of effects or effects of causes?	Causes of effects (e.g. focus on dependent variable in regressions.)	Effects of causes (e.g. focus on treatment's effects in experiments)	Effects of causes (e.g. focus on treatment's effects in experiments)	Causes of effects (e.g. focus on mechanism that creates effects)
Studies with comparative advantage using this definition	Observational and causal modeling	Experiments; case study comparisons; counterfactual thought experiments	Experiments; natural experiments; quasi-experiments	Analytic models; case studies

2 COUNTERFACTUALS

Causal statements are so useful that most people cannot let an event go by without asking why it happened and offering their own "because." They often enliven these discussions with counterfactual assertions such as "if the cause had not occurred, then the effect would not have happened." A counterfactual is a statement, typically in the subjunctive mood, in which a false or "counter to fact" premise is followed by some assertion about what would have happened if the premise were true. For example, the butterfly ballot was used in Palm Beach County Florida in 2000 and George W. Bush was elected president. A counterfactual assertion might be "if the butterfly ballot had not been used in Palm Beach County in 2000, then George Bush would not have been elected president." The statement uses the subjunctive ("if the butterfly ballot had not been used, . . . then George Bush would not have been elected"), and the premise is counter to the facts. The premise is false because the butterfly ballot was used in Palm Beach County in the real world as it unfolded. The counterfactual claim is that without this ballot, the world would have proceeded differently, and George Bush would not have been president. Is this true?

The truth of counterfactuals is closely related to the existence of causal relationships. The counterfactual claim made above implies that there is a causal link between the butterfly ballot (the cause X) and the election of George Bush (the effect Y). The counterfactual, for example, would be true if the butterfly ballot *caused* Al Gore to lose enough votes so that Bush was elected. Then, if the butterfly ballot had not been used, Al Gore would have gotten more votes and won the election.

Another way to think about this is to simply ask what would have happened in the *most similar world* in which the butterfly ballot was not used. Would George Bush still be president? One way to do this would be to rerun the world with the cause eradicated so that the butterfly ballot was not used. The world would otherwise be the same. If George Bush did not become president, then we would say that the counterfactual is true. Thus, the statement that the butterfly ballot *caused* the election of George W. Bush is essentially the same as saying that in the *most similar world* in which the butterfly ballot did not exist, George Bush would have lost. The existence of a causal connection can be checked by determining whether or not the counterfactual would be true in the most similar possible world where its premise is true. The problem, of course, is defining the most similar world and finding evidence for what would happen in it.

Beyond these definitional questions about most similar worlds, there is the problem of finding evidence for what would happen in the most similar world. We cannot rerun the world so that the butterfly ballot is not used. What can we do? Many philosophers have wrestled with this question, and we discuss the problem in detail later in the section on the counterfactual approach to causation.[3] For now, we merely

---

[3] Standard theories of logic cannot handle counterfactuals because propositions with false premises are automatically considered true which would mean that all counterfactual statements, with their false

note that people act as if they can solve this problem because they assert the truth of counterfactual statements all the time.

3 Exploring Three Basic Questions about Causality

Causality is at the center of explanation and understanding, but what, exactly, is it? And how is it related to counterfactual thinking? Somewhat confusingly, philosophers mingle psychological, ontological, and epistemological arguments when they discuss causality. Those not alerted to the different purposes of these arguments may find philosophical discussions perplexing as they move from one kind of discussion to another. Our primary focus is epistemological. We want to know when causality is truly operative, not just when some psychological process leads people to believe that it is operative. And we do not care much about metaphysical questions regarding what causality really is, although such ontological considerations become interesting to the extent that they might help us discover causal relationships.

3.1 Psychological and Linguistic Analysis

Although our primary focus is epistemological, our everyday understanding, and even our philosophical understanding, of causality is rooted in the psychology of causal inference. Perhaps the most famous psychological analysis is David Hume's investigation of what people mean when they refer to causes and effects. Hume (1711–76) was writing at a time when the pre-eminent theory of causality was the existence of a necessary connection—a kind of "hook" or "force"—between causes and their effects so that a particular cause must be followed by a specific effect. Hume looked for the feature of causes that guaranteed their effects. He argued that there was no evidence for the necessity of causes because all we could ever find in events was the contiguity, precedence, and regularity of cause and effect. There was no evidence for any kind of hook or force. He described his investigations as follows in his *Treatise of Human Nature* (1739):

What is our idea of necessity, when we say that two objects are necessarily connected together?.... I consider in what objects necessity is commonly supposed to lie; and finding that it is always ascribed to causes and effects, I turn my eye to two objects supposed to be placed in that

premises, would be true, regardless of whether or not a causal link existed. Modal logics, which try to capture the nature of necessity, possibility, contingency, and impossibility, have been developed for counterfactuals (Lewis 1973a; 1973b). These logics typically judge the truthfulness of the counterfactual on whether or not the statement would be true in the most similar possible world where the premise is true. Problems arise, however, in defining the most similar world.

relation, and examine them in all the situations of which they are susceptible. I immediately perceive that they are *contiguous* in time and place, and that the object we call cause *precedes* the other we call effect. In no one instance can I go any further, nor is it possible for me to discover any third relation betwixt these objects. I therefore enlarge my view to comprehend several instances, where I find like objects always existing in like relations of contiguity and succession. The reflection on several instances only repeats the same objects; and therefore can never give rise to a new idea. But upon further inquiry, I find that the repetition is not in every particular the same, but produces a new impression, and by that means the idea which I at present examine. For, after a frequent repetition, I find that upon the appearance of one of the objects the mind is *determined* by custom to consider its usual attendant, and to consider it in a stronger light upon account of its relation to the first object. It is this impression, then, or *determination*, which affords me the idea of necessity.   (Hume, 1978 [1739], 155)[4]

Thus for Hume the *idea* of necessary connection is a psychological trick played by the mind that observes repetitions of causes followed by effects and then presumes some connection that goes beyond that regularity. For Hume, the major feature of causation, beyond temporal precedence and contiguity, is simply the regularity of the association of causes with their effects, but there is no evidence for any kind of hook or necessary connection between causes and effects.[5]

The Humean analysis of causation became the predominant perspective in the nineteenth and most of the twentieth century, and it led in two directions, both of which focused upon the logical form of causal statements. Some, such as the physicist Ernst Mach, the philosopher Bertrand Russell, and the statistician/geneticist Karl Pearson, concluded that there was nothing more to causation than regularity so that the entire concept should be abandoned in favor of functional laws or measures of association such as correlation which summarized the regularity.[6] Others, such as the philosophers John Stuart Mill (1888), Karl Hempel (1965), and Tom Beauchamp and

---

[4] In the *Enquiry* (1748, 144–5) which is a later reworking of the *Treatise*, Hume says: "So that, upon the whole, there appears not, throughout all nature, any one instance of connexion, which is conceivable by us. All events seem entirely loose and separate. One event follows another; but we never can observe any tye between them. They seem *conjoined*, but never *connected*. And as we can have no idea of any thing, which never appeared to our outward sense or inward sentiment, the necessary conclusion *seems* to be, that we have no idea of connexion or power at all, and that these words are absolutely without meaning, when employed either in philosophical reasonings, or common life. . . . This connexion, therefore, we feel in the mind, this customary transition of the imagination from one object to its usual attendant, is the sentiment or impression, from which we form the idea of power or necessary connexion."

[5] There are different interpretations of what Hume meant. For a thorough discussion see Beauchamp and Rosenberg (1981).

[6] Bertrand Russell famously wrote that "the word 'cause' is so inextricably bound up with misleading associations as to make its complete extrusion from the philosophical vocabulary desirable. . . . The law of causality, like so much that passes muster among philosophers, is a relic of a bygone age, surviving like the monarchy, only because it is erroneously supposed to do no harm" (Russell 1918). Karl Pearson rejected causation and replaced it with correlation: "Beyond such discarded fundamentals as 'matter' and 'force' lies still another fetish amidst the inscrutable arcana of even modern science, namely the category of cause and effect. Is this category anything but a conceptual limit to experience, and without any basis in perception beyond a statistical approximation?" (Pearson 1911, vi). "It is this conception of correlation between two occurrences embracing all relationship from absolute independence to complete dependence, which is the wider category by which we have to replace the old idea of causation" (Pearson 1911, 157).

Alexander Rosenberg (1981), looked for ways to strengthen the regularity condition so as to go beyond mere accidental regularities. For them, true cause and effect regularities must be unconditional and follow from some lawlike statement. Their neo-Humean approach improved upon Hume's approach, but as we shall see, there appears to be no way to define lawlike statements in a way that captures all that we mean by causality.

What, then, do we typically mean by causality? In their analysis of the fundamental metaphors used to mark the operation of causality, the linguist George Lakoff and the philosopher Mark Johnson (1980a; 1980b; 1999) describe prototypical causation as "the manipulation of objects by force, the volitional use of bodily force to change something physically by direct contact in one's immediate environment" (1999, 177). Causes bring, throw, hurl, propel, lead, drag, pull, push, drive, tear, thrust, or fling the world into new circumstances. These verbs suggest that causation is forced movement, and for Lakoff and Johnson the "Causation Is Forced Movement metaphor is in a crucial way constitutive of the concept of causation" (187). Causation as forceful manipulation differs significantly from causation as the regularity of cause and effect because forceful manipulation emphasizes intervention, agency, and the possibility that the failure to engage in the manipulation will prevent the effect from happening. For Lakoff and Johnson, causes are forces and capacities that entail their effects in ways that go beyond mere regularity and that are reminiscent of the causal "hooks" rejected by Hume, although instead of hooks they emphasize manipulation, mechanisms, forces, and capacities.[7]

"Causation as regularity" and "causation as manipulation" are quite different notions, but each carries with it some essential features of causality. And each is the basis for a different philosophical or everyday understanding of causality. From a psychological perspective, their differences emerge clearly in research done in the last fifteen years on the relationship between causal and counterfactual thinking (Spellman and Mandel 1999). Research on this topic demonstrates that people focus on different factors when they think causally than when they think counterfactually. In experiments, people have been asked to consider causal attributions and counterfactual possibilities in car accidents in which they imagine that they chose a new route to drive home and were hit by a drunk driver. People's *causal attributions* for these accidents tend to "focus on antecedents that general knowledge suggest would covary with, and therefore predict, the outcome (e.g., the drunk driver)," but *counterfactual thinking* focuses on controllable antecedents such as the choice of route (Spellman and Mandel 1999, 123). Roughly speaking, causal attributions are based upon a regularity approach to causation while counterfactual thinking is based upon a manipulation approach to causation. The regularity approach suggests that drunken drivers typically cause accidents but the counterfactual approach suggests that in this

---

[7] As we shall show, two different approaches to causation are conflated here. One approach emphasizes agency and manipulation. The other approach emphasizes mechanisms and capacities. The major difference is the locus of the underlying force that defines causal relationships. Agency and manipulation approaches emphasize human intervention. Mechanism and capacity approaches emphasize processes within nature itself.

instance the person's choice of a new route was the cause of the accident because it was manipulable by the person. The logic of causal and the logic of counterfactual thinking are so closely related that these psychological differences in attributions lead to the suspicion that both the regularity and the manipulation approaches tell us something important about causation.

3.2 Ontological Questions

Knowing how most people think and talk about causality is useful, but we are ultimately more interested in knowing what causality actually is and how we would discover it in the world. These are respectively ontological and epistemological questions.[8] Ontological questions ask about the characteristics of the abstract entities that exist in the world. The study of causality raises a number of fundamental ontological questions regarding the *things that are causally related* and the *nature of the causal relation*.[9]

What are the things, the "causes" and the "effects" that are linked by causation? Whatever they are, they must be the same things because causes can also be effects and vice versa. But what are they? Are they facts, properties, events, or something else?[10] The practicing researcher cannot ignore questions about the definition of events. One of the things that researchers must consider is the proper definition of an event,[11] and a great deal of the effort in doing empirical work is defining events suitably. Not surprisingly, tremendous effort has gone into defining wars, revolutions, firms, organizations, democracies, religions, participatory acts, political campaigns, and many other kinds of events and structures that matter for social science research. Much could be said about defining events, but we shall only emphasize that defining events in a useful fashion is one of the major tasks of good social science research.

A second basic set of ontological questions concern the nature of the causal relationship. Is causality different when it deals with physical phenomena (e.g. billiard

---

[8] Roughly speaking, philosophy is concerned with three kinds of questions regarding "what is" (ontology), "how it can be known" (epistemology), and "what value it has" (ethics and aesthetics). In answering these questions, twentieth-century philosophy has also paid a great deal of attention to logical, linguistic, and even psychological analysis.

[9] Symbolically, we can think of the causal relation as a statement XcY where X is a cause, Y is an effect, and c is a causal relation. X and Y are the things that are causally related and c is the causal relation. As we shall see later, this relationship is usually considered to be incomplete (not all X and Y are causally related), asymmetric for those events that are causally related (either XcY or YcX but not both), and irreflexive (XcX is not possible).

[10] Events are located in space and time (e.g. "the WWI peace settlement at Versailles") but facts are not ("The fact that the WW I peace settlement was at Versailles"). For discussions of causality and events see Bennett (1988) and for causality and facts see Mellors (1995). Many philosophers prefer to speak of "tropes" which are particularized properties (Ehring 1997). Some philosophers reject the idea that the world can be described in terms of distinct events or tropes and argue for events as enduring things (Harre and Madden 1975, ch. 6).

[11] A potpourri of citations that deal with the definition of events and social processes are Abbott (1983; 1992; 1995), Pierson (2004), Riker (1957), Tilly (1984).

balls hitting one another or planets going around stars) than when it deals with social phenomena (democratization, business cycles, cultural change, elections) that are socially constructed?[12] What role do human agency and mental events play in causation?[13] What can we say about the time structure and nature of causal processes?[14] Our attitude is that social science is about the formation of concepts and the identification of causal mechanisms. We believe that social phenomena such as the Protestant ethic, the system of nation states, and culture exist and have causal implications. We also believe that reasons, perceptions, beliefs, and attitudes affect human behavior. Furthermore, we believe that these things can be observed and measured.

Another basic question about the causal relation is whether it is deterministic or probabilistic. The classic model of causation is the deterministic, clockwork Newtonian universe in which the same initial conditions inevitably produce the same outcome. But modern science has produced many examples where causal relationships appear to be probabilistic. The most famous is quantum mechanics where the position and momentum of particles is represented by probability distributions, but many other sciences rely upon probabilistic relationships. Geneticists, for example, do not expect that couples in which all the men have the same height and all the women have the same height will have children of the same height. In this case, the same set of (observed) causal factors produce a probability distribution over possible heights. We now know that even detailed knowledge of the couple's DNA would not lead to exact predictions. Probabilistic causation, therefore, seems possible in the physical sciences, common in the biological sciences, and pervasive in the social sciences. Nevertheless, following the custom of a great deal of philosophical work, we shall start with a discussion of deterministic causation in order not to complicate the analysis.

3.3 Epistemological Questions

Epistemology is concerned with how we can obtain intellectually certain knowledge (what the Greeks called "episteme"). How do we figure out that X really caused Y? At the dinner table, our admonition not to reach across the table might be met with "I didn't break the glass, the table shook," suggesting that our causal explanation for the broken glass was wrong. How do we proceed in this situation? We would probably try to rule out alternatives by investigating whether someone shook the table, whether there was an earthquake, or something else happened to disturb the glass. The problem here is that there are many possibilities that must be ruled out, and what must be ruled out depends, to some extent, on our definition of causality.

---

[12] For representative discussions see Durkheim (1982), Berger and Luckman (1966), von Wright (1971), Searle (1997), Wendt (1999).

[13] See Dilthey (1961), von Wright (1971, ch. 1), Davidson (2001), Searle (1969), Wendt (1999).

[14] In a vivid set of metaphors, Pierson (2004) compares different kinds of social science processes with tornadoes, earthquakes, large meteorites, and global warming in terms of the time horizon of the cause and the time horizon of the impact. He shows that the causal processes in each situation are quite different.

Learning about causality, then, requires that we know what it is and that we know how to recognize it when we see it. The simple Humean approach appears to solve both problems at once. Two events are causally related when they are contiguous, one precedes another, and they occur regularly in constant conjunction with one another. Once we have checked these conditions, we know that we have a causal connection. But upon examination, these conditions are not enough for causality because we would not say that night causes day, even though day and night are contiguous, night precedes day, and day and night are regularly associated. Furthermore, simple regularities like this do not make it easy to distinguish cause from effect—after all, day precedes night as well as night preceding day so that we could just as well, and just as mistakenly, say that day causes night. Something more is needed.[15] It is this something more that causes most of the problems for understanding causation. John Stuart Mill suggested that there had to be an "unconditional" relationship between cause and effect and modern neo-Humeans have required a "lawlike" relationship, but even if we know what this means[16] (which would solve the ontological problem of causation) it is hard to ensure that it is true in particular instances so as to solve the epistemological problem.

In the following sections, we begin with a review of four approaches of what causality might be. We spend most of our time on a counterfactual definition, mostly amounting to a recipe that is now widely used in statistics. We end with a discussion of the limitations of the recipe and how far it goes toward solving the epistemological and ontological problems.

4 The Humean and Neo-Humean Approach to Causation

4.1 Lawlike Generalities and the Humean Regularity Approach to Causation

Humean and neo-Humean approaches propose logical conditions that must hold for the constant conjunction of events to justify the inference that they have a cause–effect relationship. Specifically, Humeans have explored whether a cause must be sufficient for its effects, necessary for its effects, or something more complicated.

---

[15] Something different might also be needed. Hume himself dropped the requirement for contiguity in his 1748 rewrite of his 1738 work, and many philosophers would also drop his requirement for temporal precedence.

[16] Those new to this literature are presented with many statements about the need for lawfulness and unconditionality which seem to promise a recipe that will insure lawfulness. But the conditions that are presented always seem to fall short of the goal.

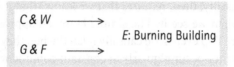

Fig. 49.1. Two sets of INUS conditions

The classic definition shared by Hume, John Stuart Mill, and many others was that "X is a cause of Y if and only if X is sufficient for Y." That is, the cause must always and invariably lead to the effect. Certainly an X that is sufficient for Y can be considered a cause, but what about the many putative causes that are not sufficient for their effect? Striking a match, for example, may be necessary for it to light, but it may not light unless there is enough oxygen in the atmosphere. Is striking a match never a cause of a match lighting? This leads to an alternative definition in which "X is a cause of Y if and only if X is necessary for Y." Under this definition, it is assumed that the cause (such as striking the match) must be present for the effect to occur, but it may not always be enough for the cause to actually occur (because there might not be enough oxygen). But how many causes are even necessary for their effects? If the match does not light after striking it, someone might use a blowtorch to light it so that striking the match is not even necessary for the match to ignite. Do we therefore assume that striking the match is never a cause of its lighting? Necessity and sufficiency seem unequal to the task of defining causation.[17]

These considerations led John Mackie to propose a set of conditions requiring that a cause be an insufficient [I] but necessary [N] part of a condition which is itself unnecessary [U] but exclusively sufficient [S] for the effect. These INUS conditions can be explained by an example. Consider two ways that the effect (E), which is a building burning down, might occur (see Figure 49.1). In one scenario the wiring might short-circuit and overheat, thus causing the wooden framing to burn. In another, a gasoline can might be next to a furnace that ignites and causes the gasoline can to explode. A number of factors here are INUS conditions for the building to burn down. The short circuit (C) and the wooden framing (W) together might cause the building to burn down, or the gasoline can (G) and the furnace (F) might cause the building to burn down. Thus, C and W together are exclusively sufficient [S] to burn the building down, and G and F together are exclusively sufficient [S] to burn the building down. Furthermore, the short circuit and wooden framing (C *and* W) are unnecessary [U], and the gasoline can and the furnace (G *and* F) are unnecessary [U] because the building could have burned down with just one or the other combination of factors. Finally, C, W, G, or F alone is insufficient [I] to burn the building down even though C is necessary [N] in conjunction with W (or vice versa) and G is necessary [N] in conjunction with F (or vice-versa). This formulation allows for the fact that no single cause is sufficient or necessary, but when experts say

[17] And there are problems such as the following favorite of the philosophers: "If two bullets pierce a man's heart simultaneously, it is reasonable to suppose that each is an essential part of a distinct sufficient condition of the death, and that neither bullet is *ceteris paribus* necessary for the death, since in each case the other bullet is sufficient" (Sosa and Tooley 1993, 8–9).

that a short circuit caused the fire they "are saying, in effect that the short-circuit (C) is a condition of this sort, that it occurred, that the other conditions (W) which, conjoined with it, form a sufficient condition were also present, and that no other sufficient condition (such as G *and* F) of the house's catching fire was present on this occasion" (Mackie 1965, 245; letters addded).

From the perspective of a practicing researcher, three lessons follow from the INUS conditions. First a putative cause such as C might not cause the effect E because G *and* F might be responsible. Hence, the burned-down building (E) will not always result from a short circuit (C) even though C could cause the building to burn down. Second, interactions among causes may be necessary for any one cause to be sufficient (C and W require each other and W and G require each other). Third, the relationship between any INUS cause and its effect might appear to be probabilistic because of the other INUS causes. In summary, the INUS conditions suggest the multiplicity of causal pathways and causes, the possibility of conjunctural causation (Ragin 1987), and the likelihood that social science relationships will appear probabilistic even if they are deterministic.[18]

A specific example might help to make these points clearer. Assume that the four INUS factors mentioned above, C, W, G, and F, occur independently of one another and that they are the only factors which cause fires in buildings. Further assume that short circuits (C) occur 10 percent of the time, wooden (W) frame buildings 50 percent of the time, furnaces (F) 90 percent of the time, and gasoline (G) cans near furnaces 10 percent of the time. Because these events are assumed independent of one another, it is easy to calculate that C and W occur 5 percent of the time and that G and F occur 9 percent of the time. (We simply multiply the probability of the two independent events.) All four conditions occur 0.45 percent of the time. (The product of all four percentages.) Thus, fires occur 13.55 percent of the time. This percentage includes the cases where the fire is the result of C and W (5 percent of the time) and where it is the result of G and F (9 percent of the time), and it adjusts downward for double-counting that occurs in the cases where all four INUS conditions occur together (0.45 percent of the time).

Now suppose an experimenter did not know about the role of wooden frame buildings or gasoline cans and furnaces and only looked at the relationship between fires and short circuits. A cross-tabulation of fires with the short circuit factor would yield Table 49.2. As assumed above, short circuits occur 10 percent of the time (see the third column total at the bottom of the table) and as calculated above, fires occur 13.55 percent of the time (see the third row total on the far right). The entries in the interior of the table are calculated in a similar way.[19]

Even though each case occurs because of a deterministic process—either a short circuit and a wooden frame building or a gasoline can and a furnace (or both)—this cross-tabulation suggests a probabilistic relationship between fires and short

[18] These points are made especially forcefully in Marini and Singer (1988).

[19] Thus, the entry for short circuits and fires comes from the cases where there are short circuits and wooden frame buildings (5 percent of the time) and where there are short circuits and no wooden frame buildings but there are gasoline cans and furnaces (5 percent times 9 percent).

Table 49.2. Fires by short circuits in hypothetical example (total percentages of each event)

	Not C—no short circuits	C—short circuits	Row totals
Not E—no fires	81.90	4.55	86.45
E—fires	8.10	5.45	13.55
Column totals	90.00	10.00	100.00

circuits. In 4.55 percent of the cases, short circuits occur but no fires result because the building was not wooden. In 8.10 percent of the cases, there are no short circuits, but a fire occurs because the gasoline can has been placed near the furnace. For this table, a standard measure of association, the Pearson correlation, between the effect and the cause is about .40 which is far short of the 1.0 required for a perfect (positive) relationship. If, however, the correct model is considered in which there are the required interaction effects, the relationship will produce a perfect fit.[20] Thus, a misspecification of a deterministic relationship can easily lead a researcher to think that there is a probabilistic relationship between the cause and effect.

INUS conditions reveal a lot about the complexities of causality, but as a definition of it, they turn out to be too weak—they do not rule out situations where there are common causes, and they do not exclude accidental regularities. The problem of common cause arises in a situation where, for example, lightning strikes (L) the wooden framing (W) and causes it to burn (E) while also causing a short in the circuitry (C). That is, $L \rightarrow E$ and $L \rightarrow C$ (where the arrow indicates causation). If lightning always causes a short in the circuitry, but the short never has anything to do with a fire in these situations because the lightning starts the fire directly through its heating of the wood, we will nevertheless always find that C and E are constantly conjoined through the action of the lightning, suggesting that the short circuit caused the fire even though the truth is that *lightning is the common cause of both*.[21] In some cases of common causes such as the rise in barometric pressure followed by the arrival of a storm, common sense tells us that the putative cause (the rise in barometric pressure) cannot be the real cause of the thunderstorm. But in the situation with the lightning, the fact that short circuits have the capacity to cause fires makes it less likely that we will realize that lightning is the common cause of both the short circuits and the fires. We might be better off in the case where the lightning split some of the wood framing of the house instead of causing a short circuit. In that case,

---

[20] If each variable is scored zero or one depending upon whether the effect or cause is present or absent, then a regression equation of the effect on the product (or interaction) of C and W, the product of G and F, and the product of C, W, G, and F will produce a multiple correlation of one indicating a perfect fit.

[21] It is also possible that the lightning's heating of the wood is (always or sometimes) insufficient to cause the fire (not $L \rightarrow E$), but its creation of a short circuit ($L \rightarrow C$) is (always or sometimes) sufficient for the fire ($C \rightarrow E$). In this case, the *lightning is the indirect cause of the fire* through its creation of the short circuit. That is, $L \rightarrow C \rightarrow E$.

we would probably reject the fantastic theory that split wood caused the fire because split wood does not have the capacity to start a fire, but the Humean approach would be equally confused by both situations because it could not appeal, within the ambit of its understanding, to causal capacities. For a Humean, the constant conjunction of split wood and fires suggests causation as much as the constant conjunction of short circuits and fires. Indeed, the constant conjunction of storks and babies would be treated as probative of a causal connection.

Attempts to fix up these conditions usually focus on trying to require "lawlike" statements that are unconditionally true, not just accidentally true. Since it is not unconditionally true that splitting wood causes fires, the presumption is that some such conditions can be found to rule out this explanation. Unfortunately, no set of conditions seem to be successful.[22] Although the regularity approach identifies a necessary condition for describing causation, it basically fails because association is not causation and there is no reason why purely logical restrictions on lawlike statements should be sufficient to characterize causal relationships. Part of the problem is that there are many different types of causal laws and they do not fit any particular patterns. For example, one restriction that has been proposed to ensure lawfulness is that lawlike statements should either not refer to particular situations or they should be derivable from laws that do not refer to particular situations. This would mean that Kepler's first "law" about all planets moving in elliptical orbits around the sun (a highly specific situation!) was not a causal law before Newton's laws were discovered, but it was a causal law after it was shown that it could be derived from Newton's laws. But Kepler's laws were always considered causal laws, and there seems to be no reason to rest their lawfulness on Newton's laws. Furthermore, by this standard, almost all social science and natural science laws (e.g. plate tectonics) are about particular situations. In short, logical restrictions on the form of laws do not seem sufficient to characterize causality.

4.2 The Asymmetry of Causation

The regularity approach also fails because it does not provide an explanation for the asymmetry of causation. Causes should cause their effects, but INUS conditions are almost always symmetrical such that if C is an INUS cause of E, then E is also an INUS cause of C. It is almost always possible to turn around an INUS condition so that an effect is an INUS for its cause.[23] One of the most famous examples of this problem involves a flagpole, the elevation of the sun, and the flagpole's shadow. The

---

[22] For some representative discussions of the problems see Harre and Madden (1975, ch. 2); Salmon (1990, chs. 1–2); Hausman (1998, ch. 3). Salmon (1990, 15) notes that "Lawfulness, modal import [what is necessary, possible, or impossible], and support of counterfactuals seems to have a common extension; statements either possess all three or lack all three. But it is extraordinarily difficult to find criteria to separate those statements that do from those that do not."

[23] Papineau (1985, 279) provides a demonstration of the symmetry of INUS conditions, and he goes on to suggest a condition for the asymmetry of causation that does not rely on the temporal relationship between causes and effects.

law that light travels in straight lines implies that there is a relationship between the height of the flagpole, the length of its shadow, and the angle of elevation of the sun. When the sun rises, the shadow is long, at midday it is short, and at sunset it is long again. Intuition about causality suggests that the length of the shadow is caused by the height of the flagpole and the elevation of the sun. But, using INUS conditions, we can just as well say that the elevation of the sun is caused by the height of the flagpole and the length of the shadow. There is simply nothing in the conditions that precludes this fantastic possibility.

The only feature of the Humean approach that provides for asymmetry is temporal precedence. If changes in the elevation of the sun precede corresponding changes in the length of the shadow, then we can say that the elevation of the sun causes the length of the shadow. And if changes in the height of the flagpole precede corresponding changes in the length of the shadow, we can say that the height of the flagpole causes the length of the shadow. But many philosophers reject making temporal precedence the determinant of causal asymmetry because it precludes the possibility of *explaining* the direction of time by causal asymmetry and it precludes the possibility of backwards causation. From a practical perspective, it also requires careful measures of timing that may be difficult in a particular situation.

4.3 Summary

This discussion reveals two basic aspects of the causal relation. One is a symmetrical form of association between cause and effect and the other is an asymmetrical relation in which causes produce effects but not the reverse. The Humean regularity approach, in the form of INUS conditions, provides a necessary condition for the existence of the symmetrical relationship,[24] but it does not rule out situations such as common cause and accidental regularities where there is no causal relationship at all. From a methodological standpoint, it can easily lead researchers to presume that all they need to do is to find associations, and it also leads to an underemphasis on the rest of the requirement for a "lawlike" or "unconditional" relationship because it does not operationally define what that would really mean. A great deal of what passes for causal modeling suffers from these defects (Freedman 1987; 1991; 1997; 1999).

The Humean approach does even less well with the asymmetrical feature of the causal relationship because it provides no way to determine asymmetry except temporal precedence. Yet there are many other aspects of the causal relation that seem more fundamental than temporal precedence. Causes not only typically precede their

---

[24] Probabilistic causes do not necessarily satisfy INUS conditions because an INUS factor might only sometimes produce an effect. Thus, the short circuit and the wooden frame of the house might only sometimes lead to a conflagration in which the house is burned down. Introducing probabilistic causes would add still another layer of complexity to our discussion which would only provide more reasons to doubt the Humean regularity approach.

effects, but they also can be used to explain effects or to manipulate effects while effects cannot be used to explain causes or to manipulate them.[25]

Effects also depend upon causes, but causes do not depend upon effects. Thus, if a cause does not occur, then the effect will not occur because effects depend on their causes. The counterfactual, "if the cause did not occur, then the effect would not occur," is true. However, if the effect does not occur, then the cause might still occur because causes can happen without leading to a specific effect if other features of the situation are not propitious for the effect. The counterfactual, "if the effect did not occur, then the cause would not occur," is not necessarily true. For example, where a short circuit causes a wooden frame building to burn down, if the short circuit does not occur, then the building will not burn down. But if the building does not burn down, it is still possible that the short circuit occurred but its capacity for causing fires was neutralized because the building was made of brick. This dependence of effects on causes suggests that an alternative definition of causation might be based upon a proper understanding of counterfactuals.

5 COUNTERFACTUAL DEFINITION OF CAUSATION

In a book *On the Theory and Method of History* published in 1902, Eduard Meyer claimed that it was an "unanswerable and so an idle question" whether the course of history would have been different if Bismarck, then Chancellor of Prussia, had not decided to go to war in 1866. By some accounts, the Austro-Prussian-Italian War of 1866 paved the way for German and Italian unification (see Wawro 1996). In reviewing Meyer's book in 1906, Max Weber agreed that "from the strict 'determinist' point of view" finding out what would have happened if Bismarck had not gone to war "was 'impossible' given the 'determinants' which were in fact present." But he went on to say that "And yet, for all that, it is far from being 'idle' to raise the question what might have happened, if, for example, Bismarck had not decided for war. For it is precisely this question which touches on the decisive element in the historical construction of reality: the causal significance which is properly attributed to this individual decision within the totality of infinitely numerous 'factors' (all of which must be just as they are and not otherwise) if precisely this consequence is to result, and the appropriate position which the decision is to occupy in the historical account" (Weber 1978, 111). Weber's review is an early discussion of the importance of counterfactuals for understanding history and making causal inferences. He argues forcefully that if "history is to raise itself above the level of a mere chronicle of noteworthy events and

---

[25] Hausman (1998, 1) also catalogs other aspects of the asymmetry between causes and effects.

personalities, it can only do so by posing just such questions" as the counterfactual in which Bismarck did not decide for war.[26]

5.1 Lewis's Counterfactual Approach to Causation

The philosopher David Lewis (1973b) has proposed the most elaborately worked out theory of how causality is related to counterfactuals.[27] His approach requires the truth of two statements regarding two distinct events X and Y. Lewis starts from the presumption that X and Y have occurred so that the "counterfactual" statement,[28] "If X were to occur, then Y would occur," is true. The truth of this statement is Lewis's first condition for a causal relationship. Then he considers the truth of a second counterfactual:[29] "If X were not to occur, then Y would not occur either." If this is true as well, then he says that X causes Y. If, for example, Bismarck decided for war in 1866 and, as some historians argue, German unification followed because of his decision, then we must ask: "If Bismarck had not decided for war, would Germany have remained divided?" The heart of Lewis's approach is the set of requirements, described below, that he lays down for the truth of this kind of counterfactual.

Lewis's theory has a number of virtues. It deals directly with singular causal events, and it does not require the examination of a large number of instances of X and Y. At one point in the philosophical debate about causation, it was believed that the individual cases such as "the hammer blow caused the glass to break" or "the assassination of Archduke Ferdinand caused the First World War" could not be analyzed alone because these cases had to be subsumed under a general law ("hammer blows cause glass to break") derived from multiple cases plus some particular facts of the situation in order to meet the requirement for a "lawlike" relationship. The counterfactual approach, however, starts with singular events and proposes that causation can be established without an appeal to a set of similar events and general

---

[26] I am indebted to Richard Swedberg for pointing me towards Weber's extraordinary discussion.

[27] Lewis finds some support for his theory in the work of David Hume. In a famous change of course in a short passage in his *Enquiry Concerning Human Understanding* (1748), Hume first summarized his regularity approach to causation by saying that "we may define a cause to be an object, followed by another, and where all the objects similar to the first, are followed by objects similar to the second," and then he changed to a completely different approach to causation by adding "Or in other words, where if the first object had not been, the second had never existed" (146). As many commentators have noted, these were indeed other words, implying an entirely different notion of causation. The first approach equates causality with the constant conjunction of putative causes and effects across similar circumstances. The second, which is a counterfactual approach, relies upon what would happen in a world where the cause did not occur.

[28] Lewis considers statements like this as part of his theory of counterfactuals by simply assuming that statements in the subjunctive mood with true premises and true conclusions are true. As noted earlier, most theories of counterfactuals have been extended to include statements with true premises by assuming, quite reasonably, that they are true if their conclusion is true and false otherwise.

[29] This is a simplified version of Lewis's theory based upon Lewis (1973a; 1973b; 1986) and Hausman (1998, ch. 6).

laws regarding them.[30] The possibility of analyzing singular causal events is important for all researchers, but especially for those doing case studies who want to be able to say something about the consequences of Stalin succeeding Lenin as head of the Soviet Union or the impact of the butterfly ballot on the 2000 US election.

The counterfactual approach also deals directly with the issue of X's causal "efficacy" with respect to Y by considering what would happen if X did not occur. The problem with the theory is the difficulty of determining the truth or falsity of the counterfactual "If X were not to occur, then Y would not occur either." The statement cannot be evaluated in the real world because X actually occurs so that the premise is false, and there is no evidence about what would happen if X did not occur. It only makes sense to evaluate the counterfactual in a world in which the premise is true. Lewis's approach to this problem is to consider whether the statement is true in the closest possible world to the actual world where X does not occur. Thus, if X is a hammer blow and Y is a glass breaking, then the closest possible world is one in which everything else is the same except that the hammer blow does not occur. If in this world, the glass does not break, then the counterfactual is true, and the hammer blow (X) causes the glass to break (Y). The obvious problem with this approach is identifying the closest possible world. If X is the assassination of Archduke Ferdinand and Y is the First World War, is it true that the First World War would not have occurred in the closest possible world where the bullet shot by the terrorist Gavrilo Princip did not hit the Archduke? Or would some other incident have inevitably precipitated the First World War? And, to add to the difficulty, would this "First World War" be the same as the one that happened in our world?

Lewis's approach substitutes the riddle of determining the similarity of possible worlds for the neo-Humean's problem of determining lawlike relationships. To solve these problems, both approaches must be able to identify similar causes and similar effects. The Humean approach must identify them across various situations in the real world. This aspect of the Humean approach is closely related to John Stuart Mill's "Method of Concomitant Variation" which he described as follows: "Whatever phenomenon varies in any manner, whenever another phenomenon varies in some similar manner, is either a cause or an effect of that phenomenon, or is connected to it through some fact of causation" (Mill 1888, 287).[31] Lewis's theory must also identify similar causes and similar effects in the real world in which the cause does occur and in the many possible worlds in which the cause does not occur. This approach is

---

[30] In fact, many authors now believe that general causation (involving lawlike generalizations) can only be understood in terms of singular causation: "general causation is a generalisation of singular causation. Smoking causes cancer iff (if and only if) smokers' cancers are generally caused by their smoking" (Mellors 1995, 6–7). See also Sosa and Tooley (1993). More generally, whereas explanation was once thought virtually to supersede the need for causal statements, many philosophers now believe that a correct analysis of causality will provide a basis for suitable explanations (see Salmon 1990).

[31] The Humean approach also has affinities with Mill's Method of Agreement which he described as follows: "If two or more instances of the phenomenon under investigation have only one circumstance in common, the circumstance in which alone all the instances agree, is the cause (or effect) of the given phenomenon" (Mill 1888, 280).

closely related to Mill's "Method of Difference" in which: "If an instance in which the phenomenon under investigation occurs, and an instance in which it does not occur, have every circumstance in common save one, that one occurring only in the former; the circumstance in which alone the two instances differ, is the effect, or the cause, or an indispensable part of the cause, of the phenomenon" (Mill 1888, 280).[32]

In addition to identifying similar causes and similar effects, the Humean approach must determine if the conjunction of these similar causes and effects is accidental or lawlike. This task requires understanding what is happening in each situation and comparing the similarities and differences across situations. Lewis's approach must identify the possible world where the cause does not occur that is most similar to the real world. This undertaking requires understanding the facts of the real world and the laws that are operating in it. Consequently, assessing the similarity of a possible world to our own world requires understanding the lawlike regularities that govern our world.[33] It seems as if Lewis has simply substituted one difficult task, that of identifying the most similar world for the job of establishing lawfulness.

5.2 The Virtues of the Counterfactual Definition of Causation

Lewis *has* substituted one difficult problem for another, but the reformulation of the problem has a number of benefits. The counterfactual approach provides new insights into what is required to establish causal connection between causes and effects. The counterfactual approach makes it clear that establishing causation does not require observing the universal conjunction of a cause and an effect.[34] One observation of a cause followed by an effect is sufficient for establishing causation if it can be shown that in a most similar world without the cause, the effect does not occur. The counterfactual approach proposes that causation can be demonstrated by simply finding a most similar world in which the absence of the cause leads to the absence of the effect.

Lewis's theory provides us with a way to think about the causal impact of singular events such as the badly designed butterfly ballot in Palm Beach County, Florida that led some voters in the 2000 presidential election to complain that they mistakenly voted for Reform Party candidate Patrick Buchanan when they meant to vote for Democrat Al Gore. The ballot can be said to be causally associated with these mistakes

---

[32] Mill goes on to note that the Method of Difference is "a method of artificial experiment" (281). Notice that for both the Method of Concomitant Variation and the Method of Difference, Mill emphasizes the association between cause and effect and not the identification of which event is the cause and which is the effect. Mill's methods are designed to detect the symmetric aspect of causality but not its asymmetric aspect.

[33] Nelson Goodman makes this point in a 1947 article on counterfactuals, and James Fearon (1991), in a masterful exposition of the counterfactual approach to research, discusses its implications for counterfactual thought experiments in political science. Also see Tetlock and Belkin (1996).

[34] G. H. von Wright notes that the counterfactual conception of causality shows that the hallmark of a lawlike connection is "*necessity and not universality*" (von Wright 1971, 22).

if in the closest possible world in which the butterfly ballot was not used, the vote for Buchanan was lower than in the real world. Ideally this closest possible world would be a parallel universe in which the same people received a different ballot, but this, of course, is impossible. The next-best thing is a situation where similar people employed a different ballot. In fact, the butterfly ballot was only used for election day voters in Palm Beach County. It was not used by absentee voters. Consequently, the results for the absentee voting can be considered a surrogate for the closest possible world in which the butterfly ballot was not used, and in this absentee voting world, voting for Buchanan was dramatically lower, suggesting that at least 2000 people who preferred Gore—more than enough to give the election to Gore—mistakenly voted for Buchanan on the butterfly ballot.

The difficult question, of course, is whether the absentee voting world can be considered a good enough surrogate for the closest possible world in which the butterfly ballot was not used.[35] The counterfactual approach does not provide us with a clear sense of how to make that judgment.[36] But the framework does suggest that we should consider the similarity of the election day world and the absentee voter world. To do this, we can ask whether election day voters are different in some significant ways from absentee voters, and this question can be answered by considering information on their characteristics and experiences. In summary, the counterfactual perspective allows for analyzing causation in singular instances, and it emphasizes comparison, which seems difficult but possible, rather than the recondite and apparently fruitless investigation of the lawfulness of statements such as "All ballots that place candidate names and punch-holes in confusing arrangements will lead to mistakes in casting votes."

5.3 Controlled Experiments and Closest Possible Worlds

The difficulties with the counterfactual definition are identifying the characteristics of the closest possible world in which the putative cause does not occur and finding an empirical surrogate for this world. For the butterfly ballot, sheer luck led a team of researchers to discover that the absentee ballot did not have the problematic features of the butterfly ballot.[37] But how can we find surrogates in other circumstances?

---

[35] For an argument that the absentee votes are an excellent surrogate, see Wand et al. (1991).

[36] In his book on counterfactuals, Lewis only claims that similarity judgments are possible, but he does not provide any guidance on how to make them. He admits that his notion is vague, but he claims it is not ill-understood. "But comparative similarity is not ill-understood. It is vague—very vague—in a well-understood way. Therefore it is just the sort of primitive that we must use to give a correct analysis of something that is itself undeniably vague" (Lewis 1973a, 91). In later work Lewis (1979; 1986) formulates some rules for similarity judgments, but they do not seem very useful to us and to others (Bennett 1988).

[37] For the story of how the differences between the election day and absentee ballot were discovered, see Brady et al. (2001).

One answer is controlled experiments. Experimenters can create mini-closest-possible worlds by finding two or more situations and assigning putative causes (called "treatments") to some situations but not to others (which get the "control"). If in those cases where the cause C occurs, the effect E occurs, then the first requirement of the counterfactual definition is met: When C occurs, then E occurs. Now, if the situations which receive the control are not different in any significant ways from those that get the treatment, then they can be considered surrogates for the closest possible world in which the cause does not occur. If in these situations where the cause C does not occur, the effect E does not occur either, then the second requirement of the counterfactual definition is confirmed: In the closest possible world where C does not occur, then E does not occur. The crucial part of this argument is that the control situation, in which the cause does not occur, must be a good surrogate for the closest possible world to the treatment.

Two experimental methods have been devised for ensuring closeness between the treatment and control situations. One is classical experimentation in which as many circumstances as possible are physically controlled so that the only significant difference between the treatment and the control is the cause. In a chemical experiment, for example, one beaker holds two chemicals and a substance that might be a catalyst and another beaker of the same type, in the same location, at the same temperature, and so forth contains just the two chemicals in the same proportions without the suspected catalyst. If the reaction occurs only in the first beaker, it is attributed to the catalyst. The second method is random assignment of treatments to situations so that there are no reasons to suspect that the entities that get the treatment are any different, on average, from those that do not. We discuss this approach in detail below.

5.4 Problems with the Counterfactual Definition[38]

Although the counterfactual definition of causation leads to substantial insights about causation, it also leads to two significant problems. Using the counterfactual definition as it has been described so far, the direction of causation cannot be established, and two effects of a common cause can be mistaken for cause and effect. Consider, for example, an experiment as described above. In that case, in the treatment group, when C occurs, E occurs, and when E occurs, C occurs. Similarly, in the control group, when C does not occur, then E does not occur, and when E does not occur, then C does not occur. In fact, there is perfect observational symmetry between cause and effect which means that the counterfactual definition of causation as described so far implies that C causes E *and* that E causes C. The same problem arises with two effects of a common cause because of the perfect symmetry in the situation. Consider, for example, a rise in the mercury in a barometer and thunderstorms. Each is an effect

---

[38] This section relies heavily upon Hausman (1998, especially chs. 4–7) and Lewis (1973*b*).

of high pressure systems, but the counterfactual definition would consider them to be causes of one another.[39]

These problems bedevil Humean and counterfactual approaches. If we accept these approaches in their simplest forms, we must live with a seriously incomplete theory of causation that cannot distinguish causes from effects and that cannot distinguish two effects of a common cause from real cause and effect. That is, although the counterfactual approach can tell whether two factors A and B are causally connected[40] in some way, it cannot tell whether A causes B, B causes A, or A and B are the effects of a common cause (sometimes called spurious correlation). The reason for this is that the truth of the two counterfactual conditions described so far amounts to a particular pattern of the cross-tabulation of the two factors A and B. In the simplest case where the columns are the absence or presence of the first factor (A) and the rows are the absence or the presence of the second factor (B), then the same diagonal pattern is observed for situations where A causes B or B causes A, or for A and B being the effects of a common cause. In all three cases, we either observe the presence of both factors or their absence. It is impossible from this kind of symmetrical information, which amounts to correlational data, to detect causal asymmetry or spurious correlation. The counterfactual approach as elucidated so far, like the Humean regularity approach, only describes a necessary condition, the existence of a causal connection between A and B, for us to say that A causes B.

Requiring temporal precedence can solve the problem of causal direction by simply choosing the phenomenon that occurs first as the cause, but it cannot solve the problem of common cause because it would lead to the ridiculous conclusion that since the mercury rises in barometers before storms, this upward movement in the mercury must cause thunderstorms. For this and other reasons, David Lewis rejects using temporal precedence to determine the direction of causality. Instead, he claims that when C causes E but not the reverse "then it should be possible to claim the falsity of the counterfactual 'If E did not occur, then C would not occur.'" This counterfactual is different from "if C occurs then E occurs" and from "if C does not occur then E does not occur" which, as we have already mentioned, Lewis believes must both be true when C causes E. The required falsity of "If E did not occur, then C would not occur" adds a third condition for causality. This condition amounts to finding situations in which C occurs but E does not—typically because there is some other condition that must occur for C to produce E. Rather than explore this strategy, we describe a much better way of establishing causal priority in the next section.

---

[39] Thus, if barometric pressure rises, thunderstorms occur and vice versa. Furthermore, if barometric pressure does not rise, then thunderstorms do not occur and vice versa. Thus, by the counterfactual definition, each is the cause of the other. (To simplify matters, we have ignored the fact that there is not a perfectly deterministic relationship between high pressure systems and thunderstorms.)

[40] As implied by this paragraph, there is a causal connection between A and B when either A causes B, B causes A, or A and B are the effects of a common cause. See Hausman (1998, 55–63).

6 EXPERIMENTATION AND THE
MANIPULATION APPROACH TO CAUSATION

In an experiment, there is a readily available piece of information that we have overlooked so far because it is not mentioned in the counterfactual approach. The factor that has been manipulated can determine the direction of causality and help to rule out spurious correlation. The manipulated factor must be the cause.[41] It is hard to exaggerate the importance of this insight. Although philosophers are uncomfortable with manipulation and agency approaches to causality because they put people (as the manipulators) at the center of our understanding of causality, there can be little doubt about the power of manipulation for determining causality. Agency and manipulation approaches to causation (Gasking 1955; von Wright 1974; Menzies and Price 1993) elevate this insight into their definition of causation. For Gasking "the notion of causation is essentially connected with our manipulative techniques for producing results" (1955, 483), and for Menzies and Price "events are causally related just in case the situation involving them possesses intrinsic features that *either* support a means-end relation between the events as is, *or* are identical with (or closely similar to) those of another situation involving an analogous pair of means-end related events" (1993, 197). These approaches focus on establishing the direction of causation, but Gasking's metaphor of causation as "recipes" also suggests an approach towards establishing the symmetric, regularity aspect of causation. Causation exists when there is a recipe that regularly produces effects from causes.

Perhaps our ontological definitions of causality should not employ the concept of agency because most of the causes and effects in the universe go their merry way without human intervention, and even our epistemological methods often discover causes, as with Newtonian mechanics or astrophysics, where human manipulation is impossible. Yet our epistemological methods cannot do without agency because human manipulation appears to be the best way to identify causes, and many researchers and methodologists have fastened upon experimental interventions as the way to pin down causation. These authors typically eschew ontological aims and emphasize epistemological goals. After explicitly rejecting ontological objectives, for example, Herbert Simon proceeds to base his initial definition of causality on experimental systems because "in scientific literature the word 'cause' most often occurs in connection with some explicit or implicit notion of an experimenter's intervention in a system" (Simon 1952, 518). When full experimental control is not possible, Thomas Cook and Donald T. Campbell recommend "quasi-experimentation," in which "an abrupt intervention at a known time" in a treatment group makes it

---

[41] It might be more correct to say that the cause is buried somewhere among those things that were manipulated or that are associated with the manipulation. It is not always easy, however, to know what was manipulated as in the famous Hawthorne experiments in which the experimenters thought the treatment was reducing the lighting for workers but the workers apparently thought of the treatment as being treated differently from all other workers. Part of the work required for good causal inference is clearly describing what was manipulated and unpacking it to see what feature caused the effect.

possible to compare the impacts of the treatment over time or across groups (Cook and Campbell 1986, 149). The success of quasi-experimentation depends upon "a world of probabilistic multivariate causal agency in which some manipulable events dependably cause other things to change" (150). John Stuart Mill suggests that the study of phenomena which "we can, by our voluntary agency, modify or control" makes it possible to satisfy the requirements of the Method of Difference ("a method of artificial experiment") even though "by the spontaneous operations of nature those requisitions are seldom fulfilled" (Mill 1888, 281, 282). Sobel champions a manipulation model because it "provides a framework in which the nonexperimental worker can think more clearly about the types of conditions that need to be satisfied in order to make inferences" (Sobel 1995, 32). David Cox claims that quasi-experimentation "with its interventionist emphasis seems to capture a deeper notion" (Cox 1992, 297) of causality than the regularity approach.

As we shall see, there are those who dissent from this perspective, but even they acknowledge that there is "wide agreement that the idea of causation as consequential manipulation is stronger or 'deeper' than that of causation as robust dependence" (Goldthorpe 2001, 5). This account of causality is especially compelling if the manipulation approach and the counterfactual approach are conflated, as they often are, and viewed as one approach. Philosophers seldom combine them into one perspective, but all the methodological writers cited above (Simon, Cook and Campbell, Mill, Sobel, and Cox) conflate them because they draw upon controlled experiments, which combine intervention and control, for their understanding of causality. Through interventions, experiments manipulate one (or more) factor which simplifies the job of establishing causal priority by appeal to the manipulation approach to causation. Through laboratory controls or statistical randomization, experiments also create closest possible worlds that simplify the job of eliminating confounding explanations by appeal to the counterfactual approach to causation.

The combination of intervention and control in experiments makes them especially effective ways to identify causal relationships. If experiments only furnished closest possible worlds, then the direction of causation would be indeterminate without additional information. If experiments only manipulated factors, then accidental correlation would be a serious threat to valid inferences about causality. Both features of experiments do substantial work.

Any approach to determining causation in nonexperimental contexts that tries to achieve the same success as experiments must recognize both these features. The methodologists cited above conflate them, and the psychological literature on counterfactual thinking cited at the beginning of this chapter shows that our natural inclination as human beings is to conflate them. When considering alternative possibilities, people typically consider nearby worlds in which individual agency figures prominently. When asked to consider what could have happened differently in a vignette involving a drunken driver and a new route home from work, subjects focus on having taken the new route home instead of on the factors that led to drunken driving. They choose a cause and a closest possible world in which *their* agency matters. But there is no reason why the counterfactual approach and the manipulation approach should be combined in this way. The counterfactual approach to causation emphasizes possible worlds without considering human agency and the manipulation approach to causation emphasizes human agency without saying anything about possible worlds. Experiments derive their strength from combining both theoretical perspectives, but it is all too easy to overlook one of these two elements in generalizing from experimental to observational studies.[42]

As we shall see in a later section, the best-known statistical theory of causality emphasizes the counterfactual aspects of experiments without giving equal attention to their manipulative aspects. Consequently, when the requirements for causal inference are transferred from the experimental setting to the observational setting, those features of experiments that rest upon manipulation tend to get underplayed.

7 Pre-emption and the Mechanism Approach to Causation

7.1 Pre-emption

Experimentation's amalgamation of the lessons of counterfactual and manipulation approaches to causation produces a powerful technique for identifying the effects of manipulated causes. Yet, in addition to the practical problems of implementing the recipe correctly, the experimental approach does not deal well with two related problems. It does not solve the problem of causal pre-emption which occurs when one cause acts just before and pre-empts another, and it does not so much explain the causes of events as it demonstrates the effects of manipulated causes. In both cases, the experimentalists' focus on the impacts of manipulations in the laboratory instead of on the causes of events in the world, leads to a failure to explain important phenomena, especially those phenomena which cannot be easily manipulated or isolated.

The problem of pre-emption illustrates this point. The following example of pre-emption is often mentioned in the philosophical literature. A man takes a trek across a desert. His enemy puts a hole in his water can. Another enemy, not knowing the action of the first, puts poison in his water. Manipulations have certainly occurred, and the man dies on the trip. The enemy who punctured the water can thinks that she

---

[42] Some physical experiments actually derive most of their strength by employing such powerful manipulations that no controls are needed. At the detonation of the first atom bomb, no one doubted that the explosion was the result of nuclear fission and not some other uncontrolled factor. Similarly, in what might be an apocryphal story, it is said that a Harvard professor who was an expert on criminology once lectured to a class about how all social science evidence suggested that rehabilitating criminals simply did not work. A Chinese student raised his hand and politely disagreed by saying that during the Cultural Revolution, he had observed cases where criminals had been rehabilitated. Once again, a powerful manipulation may need no controls.

caused the man to die, and the enemy who added the poison thinks that he caused the man to die. In fact, the water dripping out of the can pre-empted the poisoning so that the poisoner is wrong. This situation poses problems for the counterfactual approach because one of the basic counterfactual conditions required to establish that the hole in the water can caused the death of the man, namely the truth of the counterfactual "if the hole had not been put in the water can, the man would not have died," is false even though the man did in fact die of thirst. The problem is that the man would have died of poisoning if the hole in the water can had not pre-empted that cause, and the "back-up" possibility of dying by poisoning falsifies the counterfactual.

The pre-emption problem is a serious one, and it can lead to mistakes even in well-designed experiments. Presumably the closest possible world to the one in which the water can has been punctured is one in which the poison has been put in the water can as well. Therefore, even a carefully designed experiment will conclude that the puncturing of the can did not kill the man crossing the desert because the unfortunate subject in the control condition would die (from poisoning) just as the subject in the treatment would die (from the hole in the water can). The experiment alone would not tell us how the man died. A similar problem could arise in medical experiments. Arsenic was once used to cure venereal disease, and it is easy to imagine an experiment in which doses of arsenic "cure" venereal disease but kill the patient while the members of the control group without the arsenic die of venereal disease at the same rate. If the experiment simply looked at the mortality rates of the patients, it would conclude that arsenic had no medicinal value because the same number of people died in the two conditions.

In both these instances, the experimental method focuses on the effects of causes and not on explaining effects by adducing causes. Instead of asking why the man died in his trek across the desert, the experimental approach asks what happens when a hole is put in the man's canteen and everything else remains the same. The method concludes that the hole had no effect. Instead of asking what caused the death of the patients with venereal disease, the experimental method asks whether giving arsenic to those with venereal disease had any net impact on mortality rates. It concludes that it did not. In short, experimental methods do not try to explain events in the world so much as they try to show what would happen if some cause were manipulated. This does not mean that experimental methods are not useful for explaining what happens in the world, but it does mean that they sometimes miss the mark.

7.2 Mechanisms, Capacities, and the Pairing Problem

The pre-emption problem is a vivid example of a more general problem with the Humean account that requires a solution. The general problem is that constant conjunction of events is not enough to "pair-up" particular events even when pre-emption is not present. Even if we know that holes in water cans generally spell trouble for desert travelers, we still have the problem of linking a particular hole in a water can with a particular death of a traveler. Douglas Ehring notes that:

Typically, certain spatial and temporal relations, such as spatial/temporal contiguity, are invoked to do this job. [That is, the hole in the water can used by the traveler is obviously the one that caused his death because it is spatially and temporally contiguous to him.] These singularist relations are intended to solve the residual problem of causally pairing particular events, a problem left over by the generalist core of the Humean account.   (Ehring 1997, 18)

Counterfactual approaches, because they can explain singular causal events, do not suffer so acutely from this "pairing" problem, but the pre-emption problem shows that remnants of the difficulty remain even in counterfactual accounts (Ehring 1997, ch. 1). In both the desert traveler and arsenic examples, the counterfactual account cannot get at the proper pairing of causes and effects because there are two redundant causes to be paired with the same effects. Something more is needed.

The solution in both these cases seems obvious, but it does not follow from the neo-Humean, counterfactual, or manipulation definitions of causality. The solution is to inquire more deeply into what is happening in each situation in order to describe the capacities and mechanisms that are operating. An autopsy of the desert traveler would show that the person died of thirst, and an examination of the water can would show that the water would have run out before the poisoned water could be imbibed. An autopsy of those given arsenic would show that the signs of venereal disease were arrested while other medical problems, associated with arsenic poisoning, were present. Further work might even show that lower doses of arsenic cure the disease without causing death. In both these cases, deeper inquires into the mechanism by which the causes and effects are linked would produce better causal stories.

But what does it mean to explicate mechanisms and capacities?[43] "Mechanisms" we are told by Machamber, Darden, and Craver (2000, 3) "are entities and activities organized such that they are productive of regular changes from start or set-up to finish or termination conditions." The crucial terms in this definition are "entities and activities" which suggest that mechanisms have pieces. Glennan (1996, 52) calls them "parts," and he requires that it should be possible "to take the part out of the mechanism and consider its properties in another context." Entities, or parts, are organized to produce change. For Glennan (52), this change should be produced by "the interaction of a number of parts according to direct causal laws." The biological sciences abound with mechanisms of this sort such as the method of DNA replication, chemical transmission at synapses, and protein synthesis. But there are many mechanisms in the social sciences as well including markets with their methods of transmitting price information and bringing buyers and sellers together, electoral systems with their routines for bringing candidates and voters together in a collective decision-making process, the diffusion of innovation through

---

[43] These approaches are not the same, and those who favor one often reject the other (see, e.g., Cartwright 1989 on capacities and Machamer, Darden, and Craver 2000 on mechanisms). But both emphasize "causal powers" (Harre and Madden 1975, ch. 5) instead of mere regularity or counterfactual association. We focus on mechanisms because we believe that they are a somewhat better way to think about causal powers, but in keeping with our pragmatic approach, we find much that is useful in "capacity" approaches.

social networks, the two-step model of communication flow, weak ties in social networks, dissonance reduction, reference groups, arms races, balance of power, etc. (Hedstrom and Swedberg 1998). As these examples demonstrate, mechanisms are not exclusively mechanical, and their activating principles can range from physical and chemical processes to psychological and social processes. They must be composed of appropriately located, structured, and oriented entities which involve activities that have temporal order and duration, and "an activity is usually designated by a verb or verb form (participles, gerundives, etc.)" (Machamber, Darden, and Craver 2000, 4) which takes us back to the work of Lakoff and Johnson (1999) who identified a "Causation Is Forced Movement metaphor."

Mechanisms provide another way to think about causation. Glennan argues that "two events are causally connected when and only when there is a mechanism connecting them" and "the necessity that distinguishes connections from accidental conjunctions is to be understood as deriving from a underlying mechanism" which can be empirically investigated (64). These mechanisms, in turn, are explained by causal laws, but there is nothing circular in this because these causal laws refer to how the *parts* of the mechanism are connected. The operation of these parts, in turn, can be explained by lower-level mechanisms. Eventually the process gets to a bedrock of fundamental physical laws which Glennan concedes "cannot be explained by the mechanical theory" (65).

Consider explaining social phenomena by examining their mechanisms. Duverger's law, for example, is the observed tendency for just two parties in simple plurality single-member district elections systems (such as the United States). The entities in the mechanisms behind Duverger's law are voters and political parties. These entities face a particular electoral rule (single-district plurality voting) which causes two activities. One is that voters often vote strategically by choosing a candidate other than their most liked because they want to avoid throwing their vote away on a candidate who has no chance of winning and because they want to forestall the election of their least wanted alternative. The other activity is that political parties often decide not to run candidates when there are already two parties in a district because they anticipate that voters will spurn their third party effort.

These mechanisms underlying Duverger's law suggest other things that can be observed beyond the regularity of two-party systems being associated with single-member plurality-vote electoral systems that led to the law in the first place. People's votes should exhibit certain patterns and third parties should exhibit certain behaviors. And a careful examination of the mechanism suggests that in some federal systems that use simple plurality single-member district elections we might have more than two parties, seemingly contrary to Duverger's law. Typically, however, there are just two parties in each province or state, but these parties may differ from one state to another, thus giving the impression, at the national level, of a multiparty system even though Duverger's law holds in each electoral district.[44]

---

[44] This radically simplifies the literature on Duverger's law (see Cox 1997 for more details).

Or consider meterological[45] and physical phenomena. Thunderstorms are not merely the result of cold fronts hitting warm air or being located near mountains; they are the results of parcels of air rising and falling in the atmosphere subject to thermodynamic processes which cause warm humid air to rise, to cool, and to produce condensed water vapor. Among other things, this mechanism helps to explain why thunderstorms are more frequent in areas, such as Denver, Colorado, near mountains because the mountains cause these processes to occur—without the need for a cold air front. Similarly, Boyle's law is not merely a regularity between pressure and volume; it is the result of gas molecules moving within a container and exerting force when they hit the walls of the container. This mechanism for Boyle's law also helps to explain why temperature affects the relationship between the pressure and volume of a gas. When the temperature increases, the molecules move faster and exert more force on the container walls.

Mechanisms like these are midway between general laws on the one hand and specific descriptions on the other hand, and activities can be thought of as causes which are not related to lawlike generalities.[46] Mechanisms typically explicate observed regularities in terms of lower-level processes, and the mechanisms vary from field to field and from time to time. Moreover, these mechanisms "bottom out" relatively quickly—molecular biologists do not seek quantum mechanical explanations and social scientists do not seek chemical explanations of the phenomena they study.

When an unexplained phenomenon is encountered in a science, "Scientists in the field often recognize whether there are known types of entities and activities that can possibly accomplish the hypothesized changes and whether there is empirical evidence that a possible schemata is plausible." They turn to the available types of entities and activities to provide building blocks from which to construct hypothetical mechanisms. "If one knows what kind of activity is needed to do something, then one seeks kinds of entities that can do it, and vice versa" (Machamber, Darden, and Craver 2000, 17).

Mechanisms, therefore, provide a way to solve the pairing problem, and they leave a multitude of traces that can be uncovered if a hypothesized causal relation really exists. For example, those who want to subject Max Weber's hypothesis about the Reformation leading to capitalism do not have to rest content with simply correlating Protestantism with capitalism. They can also look at the detailed mechanism he described for how this came about, and they can look for the traces left by this mechanism (Hedström and Swedberg 1998, 5; Sprinzak 1972).[47]

---

[45] The points in this paragraph, and the thunderstorm example, come from Dessler (1991).

[46] Jon Elster says: "Are there lawlike generalizations in the social sciences? If not, are we thrown back on mere description and narrative? In my opinion, the answer to both questions is No. The main task of this essay is to explain and illustrate the idea of a *mechanism* as intermediate between laws and descriptions" (Elster 1998, 45).

[47] Hedström and Swedberg (1998) and Sorenson (1998) rightfully criticize causal modeling for ignoring mechanisms and treating correlations among variables as theoretical relationships. But it might be worth remarking that causal modelers in political science have been calling for more theoretical thinking (Achen 1983; Bartels and Brady 1993) for at least two decades, and a constant refrain at the annual meetings of the Political Methodology Group has been the need for better "microfoundations."

7.3 Multiple Causes and Mechanisms

Earlier in this chapter, the need to rule out common causes and to determine the direction of causation in the counterfactual approach led us towards a consideration of multiple causes. In this section, the need to solve the problem of pre-emption and the pairing problem led to a consideration of mechanisms. Together, these approaches lead us to consider multiple causes and the mechanisms that tie these causes together. Many different authors have come to a similar conclusion about the need to identify mechanisms (Cox 1992; Simon and Iwasaki 1988; Freedman 1991; Goldthorpe 2001), and this approach seems commonplace in epidemiology (Hill 1965) where debates over smoking and lung cancer or sexual behavior and AIDS have been resolved by the identification of biological mechanisms that link the behaviors with the diseases.

8 Four Approaches to Causality

8.1 What is Causation?

We are now at the end of our review of four causal approaches. We have described two fundamental features of causality. One is the symmetric association between causes and effects. The other is the asymmetric fact that causes produce effects, but not the reverse. Table 10.1 summarizes how each approach identifies these two aspects of causality.

Regularity and counterfactual approaches do better at capturing the symmetric aspect of causation than its asymmetric aspect. The regularity approach relies upon the constant conjunction of events and temporal precedence to identify causes and effects. Its primary tool is essentially the "Method of Concomitant Variation" proposed by John Stuart Mill in which the causes of a phenomenon are sought in other phenomena which vary in a similar manner. The counterfactual approach relies upon elaborations of the "Method of Difference" to find causes by comparing instances where the phenomenon occurs and instances where it does not occur to see in what circumstances the situations differ. The counterfactual approach suggests searching for surrogates for the closest possible worlds where the putative cause does not occur to see how they differ from the situation where the cause did occur. This strategy leads naturally to experimental methods where the likelihood of the independence of assignment and outcome, which ensures one kind of closeness, can be increased by rigid control of conditions or by randomly assigning treatments to cases. None of these methods is foolproof because none solves the pairing problem or gets at the connections between events, but experimental methods typically offer the best chance of achieving closest possible worlds for comparisons.

Causal approaches that emphasize mechanisms and capacities provide guidance on how to solve the pairing problem and how to get at the connections between events.

Brady and Collier's emphasis upon causal process observations is in that spirit (2004, ch. 13; see also Freedman, in *Oxford Handbook of Political Methodology*, ed. J. M. Box-Steffensmeier, H. Brady, and D. Collier 2008. Oxford: Oxford University Press). These observations can be thought of as elucidations and tests of possible mechanisms. And the growing interest in mechanisms in the social sciences (Hedström and Swedberg 1998; Elster 1998) is providing a basis for opening up the black box of the Humean regularity and the counterfactual approaches.

The other major feature of causality, the asymmetry of causes and effects, is captured by temporal priority, manipulated events, and the independence of causes. Each notion takes a somewhat different approach to distinguishing causes from effects once the unconditional association of two events (or sets of events) has been established. Temporal priority simply identifies causes with the events that came first. If growth in the money supply reliably precedes economic growth, then the growth in the money supply is responsible for growth. The manipulation approach identifies the manipulated event as the causally prior one. If a social experiment manipulates work requirements and finds that greater stringency is associated with faster transitions off welfare, then the work requirements are presumed to cause these transitions. Finally, one event is considered the cause of another if a third event can be found that satisfies the INUS conditions for a cause and that varies independently of the putative cause. If short circuits vary independently of wooden frame buildings, and both satisfy INUS conditions for burned-down buildings, then both must be causes of those conflagrations. Or if education levels of voters vary independently of their getting the butterfly ballot, and both satisfy INUS conditions for mistakenly voting for Buchanan instead of Gore, then both must be causes of those mistaken votes.

8.2 Causal Inference with Experimental and Observational Data

Now that we know what causation is, what lessons can we draw for doing empirical research? Table 49.1 shows that each approach provides sustenance for different types of studies and different kinds of questions. Table 49.3 presents a "checklist" based on all of the approaches. Regularity and mechanism approaches tend to ask about the causes of effects while counterfactual and manipulation approaches ask about the effects of imagined or manipulated causes. The counterfactual and manipulation approaches converge on experiments, although counterfactual thought experiments flow naturally from the "possible worlds" perspective of the counterfactual appoach. The regularity approach is at home with observational data, and the mechanism approach thrives on analytical models and case studies.

Which method, however, is the best method? Clearly the gold standard for establishing causality is experimental research, but even that is not without flaws. When they are feasible, well-done experiments can help us construct closest possible worlds and explore counterfactual conditions. But we still have to assume that there is no

Table 49.3. Causality checklist

General Issues

What is the "cause" (C) event? What is the "effect" (E) event?

What is the exact causal statement of how C causes E?

What is the corresponding counterfactual statement about what happens when C does not occur?

What is the causal field? What is the context or universe of cases in which the cause operates?

Is this a physical or social phenomenon or some mixture?

What role, if any, does human agency play?

What role, if any, does social structure play?

Is the relationship deterministic or probabilistic?

Neo-Humean Approach

Is there a constant conjunction (i.e. correlation) of cause and effect?

Is the cause necessary, sufficient, or INUS?

What are other possible causes, i.e. rival explanations?

Is there a constant conjunction after controls for these other causes are introduced?

Does the cause precede the effect? In what sense?

Counterfactual Approach

Is this a singular conjunction of cause and effect?

Can you describe a closest possible (most similar) world to where C causes E but C does not occur? How close are these worlds?

Can you actually observe any cases of this world (or something close to it, at least on average)? Again, how close are these worlds?

In this closest possible world, does E occur in the absence of C?

Are there cases where E occurs but C does not occur? What factor intervenes and what does this tell us about C causing E?

Manipulation Approach

What does it mean to manipulate your cause? Be explicit. How would you describe the cause?

Do you have any cases where C was actually manipulated? How? What was the effect?

Is this manipulation independent of other factors that influence E?

Mechanism and Capacities Approaches

Can you explain, at a lower level, the mechanism(s) by which C causes E?

Do the mechanisms make sense to you?

What other predictions does this mechanism lead to?

Does the mechanism solve the pairing problem?

Can you identify some capacity that explains the way the cause leads to the effect?

Can you observe this capacity when it is present, and measure it?

What other outcomes might be predicted by this capacity?

What are possible pre-empting causes?

---

pre-emption occurring which would make it impossible for us to determine the true impact of the putative cause, and we also have to assume that there are no interactions across units in the treatment and control groups and that treatments can be confined to the treated cases. If, for example, we are studying the impact of a skill training program on the tendency for welfare recipients to get jobs, we should be aware that a very strong economy might pre-empt the program itself and cause those in both the control and treatment conditions to get jobs simply because employers did not care much about skills. As a result, we might conclude that skills do not count for much in getting jobs even though they might matter a lot in a less robust economy. Or if we are studying electoral systems in a set of countries with a strong bimodal distribution of voters, we should know that the voter distribution might pre-empt any impact of the electoral system by fostering two strong parties. Consequently, we might conclude that single-member plurality systems and proportional representation systems both led to two parties, even though this is not generally true. And if we are studying some educational innovation that is widely known, we should know that teachers in the "control" classes might pick up and use this innovation thereby nullifying any effect it might have.

If we add an investigation of mechanisms to our experiments, we might be able to develop safeguards against these problems. For the welfare recipients, we could find out more about their job search efforts, for the party systems we could find out about their relationship to the distribution of voters, and for the teachers we could find out about their adoption of new teaching methods.

Once we go to observational studies, matters get much more complicated. Spurious correlation is a real danger. There is no way to know whether those cases which get the treatment and those which do not differ from one another in other ways. It is very hard to be confident that the requirements for an experiment hold which are outlined in the next section (and in Campbell and Stonley 1966 and Cook and Campbell 1979). Because nothing has been manipulated, there is no surefire way to determine the direction of causation. Temporal precedence provides some information about causal direction, but it is often hard to obtain and interpret it.

9 Going beyond the Neyman–Rubin–Holland Conditions for Causation

9.1 The Neyman–Rubin–Holland (NRH) Theory

Among statisticians, the best-known theory of causality developed out of the experimental tradition. The roots of this perspective are in Fisher (1926) and especially Neyman ([1923] 1990), and it has been most fully articulated by Rubin (1974; 1978) and Holland (1986). In this section, which is more technical than the rest of this chapter, we explain this perspective, and we evaluate it in terms of the four approaches to causality.

There are four aspects of the Neyman–Rubin–Holland (NRH) approach which can be thought of as developing a recipe for solving the causal inference problem by comparing similar possible worlds, if certain assumptions hold. This approach consists of a definition, two assumptions, and a method for satisfying one of the two assumptions:

1. A Counterfactual Definition of Causal Effect—Causal relationships are defined using a counterfactual perspective which focuses on estimating causal effects. This definition alone provides no guidance on how researchers can actually identify causes because it relies upon an unobservable counterfactual. To the extent that the NRH approach considers causal priority, it equates it with temporal priority.

2. An Assumption for Creating Comparable Mini-possible Worlds—Non-interference of Units (SUTVA)—Even if we could observe the outcome for some unit (a person or a country) of both the world with the cause present and without the cause, it is possible that the causal effect would depend upon whether other units received the treatment or did not receive the treatment. For example, the impact of a training program on a child in a family might be different when the child and her sibling received the treatment than when the child alone received the treatment. If this kind of thing happens, then it is very hard to define uniquely what we mean by a "causal effect" because there might be some "interference" across units depending upon which units got the treatment and which did not. The NRH counterfactual possible worlds approach assumes that this kind of interference does not occur by making the Stable Unit Treatment Value Assumption (SUTVA) that treats cases as separate, isolated, closest possible worlds which do not interfere or communicate with one another.

3. An Assumption that Finds a Substitute for Insuring the Identicality of the Counterfactual Situation: The Independence of Assignment and Outcome—The counterfactual possible worlds approach not only assumes that units do not interfere with one another, it also assumes that a world identical to our own, except for the existence of the putative cause, can be imagined. The NHR approach goes on to formulate a set of epistemological assumptions, namely the independence of the assignment of treatment and the outcome or the mean conditional independence of assignment and outcome, that make it possible to be sure that two sets of cases, treatments and controls, only differ on average in whether or not they got the treatment.

4. Methods for Insuring Independence of Assignment and Outcome if SUTVA holds—Finally, the NRH approach describes methods such as unit homogeneity or random assignment for obtaining independence or mean independence of assignment and outcome as long as SUTVA holds.

The definition of a causal effect based upon unobserved counterfactuals was first described in a 1923 paper published in Polish by Jerzy Neyman (1990). Although Neyman's paper was relatively unknown until 1990, similar ideas informed much of the statistical work on experimentation from the 1920s to the present. Rubin (1974; 1978; 1990) and Heckman (1979) were the first to stress the importance of independence of assignment and outcome. A number of experimentalists

identified the need for the SUTVA assumption (e.g. Cox 1958). Random assignment as a method for estimating causal effects was first championed by R. A.
Fisher in 1925 and 1926. Holland (1986) provides the best synthesis of the entire
perspective.

The counterfactual definition of causality rests on the notion of comparing a world
with the treatment to a world without it. The fundamental problem of counterfactual
definitions of causation is the tension between finding a suitable definition of causation that controls for confounding effects and finding a suitable way of detecting
causation given the impossibility of getting perfect counterfactual worlds. As we shall
show, the problem is one of relating a *theoretical* definition of causality to an *empirical*
one.

9.2 Ontological Definition of Causal Effect Based upon Counterfactuals

Consider a situation in which there is one "unit" A which can be manipulated in
some way. Table 10.4 summarizes the situation. Assume that there are two possible
manipulations Z_A of the unit, the "control" which we denote by $Z_A = 0$ and the
"treatment" which we denote by $Z_A = 1$. Outcomes Y_A are a function $Y_A(Z_A)$ of
these manipulations so that the outcome for the control manipulation is $Y_A(0)$ and
the outcome for the treatment manipulation is $Y_A(1)$.

According to the NRH understanding of causation, establishing a causal relationship between a treatment Z_A and an outcome $Y_A(Z_A)$ consists of comparing
outcomes for the case where the case gets the treatment $Z_A = 1$ and where it does
not $Z_A = 0$. Thus we compare:

(a) the value of the outcome variable Y_A for a case that has been exposed to a
treatment $Y_A(1)$ with
(b) the value of the outcome variable *for the same case if that case had not been
exposed to the treatment* $Y_A(0)$.

In this case, we can define causal impact as follows:

$$E_A = \text{Causal Effect on } A = Y_A(1) - Y_A(0). \tag{1}$$

Note that (a) refers to an actual observation in the treatment condition ("a case
that has been exposed to a treatment") so the value $Y_A(1)$ is observed while (b) refers
to a counterfactual observation of the control condition ("if that case had not been
exposed to the treatment").[48] Because the case was exposed to the treatment, it cannot
simultaneously be in the control condition, and the value $Y_A(0)$ is the outcome in the
closest possible world where the case was not exposed to the treatment. Although this

[48] For simplicity, we assume that the treatment case has been observed, but the important point is not
that the treatment is observed but rather that only one of the two conditions can be observed. There is
no reason why the situation could not be reversed with the actual observation of the case in the control
group and the counterfactual involving the unobserved impact of the treatment condition.

Table 49.4. Possible worlds, outcomes, and causal effects from manipulation Z for one unit A

POSSIBLE WORLDS:	Z_A—Manipulation for Unit A	
	0 Control	Treatment 1
	$Y_A(0)$	$Y_A(1)$

Outcomes: $Y_A(Z_A)$
Causal Effect: $Y_A(1) - Y_A(0)$
Problem: Only one world observable.

value cannot be observed, we can still describe the conclusions we would draw if we could observe it.

The causal effect E_A for a particular case is the difference in outcomes, $E_A = Y_A(1) - Y_A(0)$, for the case, and if this difference is zero (i.e. if $E_A = 0$), we say the treatment has no net effect.[49] If this difference is nonzero (i.e. E_A is not 0), then the treatment has a net effect. Then, based on the counterfactual approach of David Lewis, there is a causal connection between the treatment and the outcome if two conditions hold. First, the treatment must be associated with a net effect, and second the absence of the treatment must be associated with no net effect.[50]

Although the satisfaction of these two conditions is enough to demonstrate a causal connection, it is not enough to determine the direction of causation or to rule out a common cause. If the two conditions for a causal connection hold, then the third Lewis condition, which establishes the direction of causation and which rules out common cause, cannot be verified or rejected with the available information. The third Lewis condition requires determining whether or not the cause occurs in the closest possible world in which the net effect does not occur. But the only observed world in which the net effect does not occur in the NRH setup is the control

---

[49] Technically, we mean that the treatment has no effect with respect to that outcome variable.

[50] With a suitable definition of effect, one of these conditions will always hold by definition and the other will be determinative of the causal connection. The NRH approach focuses on the Effect of the Treatment ($E = Y(1) - Y(0)$) in which the control outcome $Y(0)$ is the baseline against which treatment outcome $Y(1)$ is compared. A nonzero E implies the truth of the counterfactual "if the treatment occurs, then the net effect occurs," and a zero E implies that the counterfactual is false. In the NRH setup the Effect for the Control (EC) must always be zero because $EC = (Y(0) - Y(0))$ is always zero. Hence, the counterfactual "if the treatment is absent then there is no net effect" is always true. The focus on the effect of the treatment (E) merely formalizes the fact that in *any* situation one of the two counterfactuals required for a causal connection can always be defined to be true by an appropriate definition of an effect. Philosophers, by custom, tend to focus on the situation where some effect is associated with some putative cause so that it is always true that "if the cause occurs then the effect occurs as well" and the important question is the truth or falsity of "if the cause does not occur then the effect does not occur." Statisticians such as NRH, with their emphasis on the null hypothesis, seem to prefer the equivalent, but reverse, setup where the important question is the truth or falsity of "if the treatment occurs, then the effect occurs." The bottom line is that a suitable definition of effect can always lead to the truth of one of the two counterfactuals so that causal impacts must always be considered comparatively.

condition in which the cause does not occur by *design* so that there is no way to determine whether suppressing the effect would or would not suppress the cause. There is no way to test the third Lewis condition and to show that the treatment causes the net effect.

Alternatively, the direction of causation can be determined (although common cause cannot be ruled out) if the treatment is manipulated to produce the effect. Rubin and his collaborators mention manipulation when they say that "each of the *T* treatments must consist of a series of actions that could be applied to each experimental unit" (Rubin 1978, 39) and "it is critical that each unit be *potentially exposable* to any one of the causes" (Holland 1986, 946), but their use of phrases such as "could be applied" or "potentially exposable" suggests that they are more concerned about limiting the possible types of causes than with distinguishing causes from effects.[51] To the degree that causal priority is mentioned in the NRH literature, it is established by temporal precedence. Rubin (1974, 689), for example, says that the causal effect of one treatment over another "for a particular unit and an interval t_1 to t_2 is the difference between what would have happened at time t_2 if the unit had been exposed to [one treatment] initiated at time t_1 and what would have happened at t_2 if the unit had been exposed to [another treatment] at t_1." Holland (1986, 980) says that "The issue of temporal succession is shamelessly embraced by the model as one of the defining characteristics of a response variable. The idea that an effect might precede a cause in time is regarded as meaningless in the model, and apparently also by Hume." The problem with this approach, of course, is that it does not necessarily rule out common cause and spurious correlation.[52] In fact one of the limitations and possible confusions produced by the NRH approach is its failure to deal with the need for more information to rule out common causes and to determine the direction of causality.

9.3 Finding a Substitute for the Counterfactual Situation: The Independence of Assignment and Outcome

As with the Lewis counterfactual approach, the difficulty with the NRH definition of causal connections is that there is no way to observe both $Y_A(1)$ and $Y_A(0)$ for any particular case. The typical response to this problem is to find two units A and B which are as similar as possible and to consider various possible allocations of the control and the treatment to the two units. (We shall say more about how to ensure this similarity later; for the moment, simply assume that it can be accomplished.) The

[51] Rubin and Holland believe in "NO CAUSATION WITHOUT MANIPULATION" (Holland 1986, 959), which seems to eliminate attributes such as sex or race as possible causes, although Rubin softens this perspective somewhat by describing ways in which sex might be a manipulation (Rubin 1986, 962). Clearly, researchers must consider carefully in what sense some factors can be considered causes.

[52] Consider, for example, an experiment in which randomly assigned special tutoring first causes a rise in self-esteem and then an increase in test scores, but the increase in self-esteem does not cause the increase in test scores. The NRH framework would incorrectly treat self-esteem as the cause of the increased test scores because self esteem is randomly assigned and it precedes and is associated with the rise in test scores. Clearly something more than temporal priority is needed for causal priority.

Table 49.5. Possible worlds, outcomes, and causal effects from manipulations Z for two units A and B

	FOUR POSSIBLE WORLDS			
Manipulations for each unit	$Z_A = 0$, *Control*		$Z_A = 1$, *Treatment*	
	$Z_B = 0$, *Control*	$Z_B = 1$, *Treatment*	$Z_B = 0$, *Control*	$Z_B = 1$, *Treatment*
Outcome value $Y_i(Z_A, Z_B)$, for $i = A$ or B	$Y_A(0,0)$ $Y_B(0,0)$	$Y_A(0,1)$ $Y_B(0,1)$	$Y_A(1,0)$ $Y_B(1,0)$	$Y_A(1,1)$ $Y_B(1,1)$

goal is ultimately to define causal impact as the difference between what happens to A and to B when one of them gets the treatment and the other does not. But, as we shall see, this leads to fundamental problems regarding the definition of causality.

The manipulation for unit A is described by $Z_A = 0$ or $Z_A = 1$ and the manipulation for unit B is described by $Z_B = 0$ or $Z_B = 1$. Table 10.5 illustrates the four possible worlds that could occur based upon the four ways that the manipulations could be allocated. In the first column, both A and B are given the control. In the second column, A gets the control and B gets the treatment. In the third column, A gets the treatment and B gets the control, and in the fourth column, both units get the treatment. The outcomes for these combinations of manipulations are described by $Y_A(Z_A, Z_B)$ and $Y_B(Z_A, Z_B)$.

For each unit, there are then four possible outcome quantities. For example, for A there are $Y_A(0, 0)$, $Y_A(0, 1)$, $Y_A(1, 0)$, and $Y_A(1, 1)$. Similarly for B there are $Y_B(0, 0)$, $Y_B(0, 1)$, $Y_B(1, 0)$, and $Y_B(1, 1)$. For each unit, there are six possible ways to take these four possible outcome quantities two at a time to define a difference that could be considered the causal impact of Z_A, but not all of them make sense as a definition of the causal impact of Z_A. The six possibilities are listed in Table 49.6.

Table 49.6. Six possible definitions of causal impact on unit A

Four observable quantities: $Y_A(0,0)$, $Y_A(0,1)$, $Y_A(1,0)$, $Y_A(1,1)$
Possible definitions:

$Y_A(0,0) - Y_A(0,1)$	Problem: No manipulation
$Y_A(1,0) - Y_A(1,1)$	of A.
$Y_A(1,1) - Y_A(0,0)$	Problem: Different treatments
$Y_A(1,0) - Y_A(0,1)$	for B.
$Y_A(1,0) - Y_A(0,0) = E_A(Z_B = 0)$	Both good.
$Y_A(1,1) - Y_A(0,1) = E_A(Z_B = 1)$	

For example, each of $[Y_A(0, 0) - Y_A(0, 1)]$ and $[Y_A(1, 0) - Y_A(1, 1)]$ involves a difference where Z_A does not even vary—in the first case Z_A is the control manipulation for both states of the world and in the second case Z_A is the treatment manipulation. Neither of these differences makes much sense as a definition of the causal impact of Z_A.

Two other pairs of differences, $[Y_A(1, 1) - Y_A(0, 0)]$ and $[Y_A(1, 0) - Y_A(0, 1)]$, seem better insofar as they each involve differences in which A received the treatment in one case and the control in the other case, but the manipulation of B differs within each pair. In the first difference, for example, we are comparing the outcome for A in the world in which A gets the treatment and B does not with the world in which A does not get the treatment and B gets it. At first blush, it might seem that it doesn't really matter what happens to B, but a moment's reflection suggests that unless A and B *do not interfere* with one another, it might matter a great deal what happens to B.

Suppose, for example, that A and B are siblings, adjacent plots of land, two students in the same class, two people getting a welfare program in the same neighborhood, two nearby countries, or even two countries united by common language and traditions. Then for treatments as diverse as new teaching methods, propaganda, farming techniques, new scientific or medical procedures, new ideas, or new forms of government it might matter for the A member of the pair what happens to the B member because of causal links between them. For example, if a sibling B is given a special educational program designed to increase achievement, it seems possible that some of this impact will be communicated to the other sibling A, even when A does not get the treatment directly. Or if a new religion or religious doctrine is introduced into one country, it seems possible that it will have an impact on the other country. In both cases, it seems foolish to try to compare the impact of different manipulations of A when different things have also been done to B, unless we can be sure that a manipulation of B has no impact on A or unless we define the manipulation of B as part of the manipulation of A.

This second possibility deserves some comment. If the manipulation of B is part of the manipulation of A, then we really have not introduced a new unit when we decided to consider B as well as A. In this situation we can think of the differences listed above, $[Y_A(1, 1) - Y_A(0, 0)]$ and $[Y_A(1, 0) - Y_A(0, 1)]$, as indicating the impact on A of the manipulation of the combined unit $A + B$. For the first difference, $[Y_A(1, 1) - Y_A(0, 0)]$, the manipulation consists of applying $Z_A = 1$ and $Z_B = 1$ as the treatment to $A + B$ and the $Z_A = 0$ and $Z_B = 0$ as the control to $A + B$. Similar reasoning applies to the second difference, $[Y_A(1, 0) - Y_A(0, 1)]$. There are two lessons to be learned from this discussion. First, it is not as easy as it might seem to define isolated units, and the definition of separate units partly depends upon how they will be affected by the manipulation. Second, it does not make much sense to use $[Y_A(1, 1) - Y_A(0, 0)]$ or $[Y_A(1, 0) - Y_A(0, 1)]$ as the definition of the causal impact of the treatment Z_A on A.

This leaves us with the following pairs which are plausible definitions of the causal effect for each unit, depending upon what happens to the other unit. These pairs are

Table 49.7. Theoretical definitions
summarized for units A and B

For unit A:
$$Y_A(1,0) - Y_A(0,0) = E_A(Z_B = 0)$$
$$Y_A(1,1) - Y_A(0,1) = E_A(Z_B = 1)$$
For unit B:
$$Y_B(0,1) - Y_B(0,0) = E_B(Z_A = 0)$$
$$Y_B(1,1) - Y_B(1,0) = E_B(Z_A = 1)$$

summarized in Table 49.7. For example, for A:

$$E_A(Z_B = 0) = Y_A(1, 0) - Y_A(0, 0), \quad \text{and} \tag{2}$$

$$E_A(Z_B = 1) = Y_A(1, 1) - Y_A(0, 1).$$

And for B we have:

$$E_B(Z_A = 0) = Y_B(0, 1) - Y_B(0, 0), \quad \text{and} \tag{3}$$

$$E_B(Z_A = 1) = Y_B(1, 1) - Y_B(1, 0).$$

Consider the definitions for A in (2). Both definitions seem sensible because each one takes the difference between the outcome when A is treated and the outcome when A is not treated, but they differ on what happens to B. In the first case, B is given the control manipulation and in the second case, B is given the treatment manipulation. From the preceding discussion, it should be clear that these might lead to different sizes of effects. The impact of a pesticide on a plot A, for example, might vary dramatically depending upon whether or not the adjacent plot B got the pesticide. The effect of a propaganda campaign might vary dramatically depending upon whether or not a sibling got the propaganda message. As a result, there is no a priori reason why $E_A(Z_B = 0)$ and $E_A(Z_B = 1)$ should be the same thing. The impact on A of a treatment might depend upon what happens to B.

One response to this problem might be simply to agree that $E_A(Z_B = 0)$ and $E_A(Z_B = 1)$ (and $E_B(Z_A = 0)$ and $E_B(Z_A = 1)$) are different and that a careful researcher would want to measure both of them. But how could that be done? Neither can be measured directly because each requires that the unit A both get and not get the treatment, which is clearly impossible. In terms of our notation, the problem is that each difference above involves different values for Z_A and Z_B. For example, $E_A(Z_B = 0)$ which equals $Y_A(1, 0) - Y_A(0, 0)$ involves one state of the world where A gets the treatment and B does not and another state of the world where A does not get the treatment and B does not. Both states of the world cannot occur.

Table 49.8. Observationally feasible definitions of causality

Four states of the world and four possible definitions:
(1) $\{Z_A = 1 \text{ and } Z_B = 1\}$
    Observe $Y_A(1,1)$ and $Y_B(1,1) \rightarrow$ Difference Zero
(2) $\{Z_A = 0 \text{ and } Z_B = 0\}$
    Observe $Y_A(0,0)$ and $Y_B(0,0) \rightarrow$ Difference Zero
(3) $\{Z_A = 1 \text{ and } Z_B = 0\}$
    Observe $Y_A(1,0)$ and $Y_B(1,0) \rightarrow E^*(1,0) = Y_A(1,0) - Y_B(1,0)$
(4) $\{Z_A = 0 \text{ and } Z_B = 1\}$
    Observe $Y_A(0,1)$ and $Y_B(0,1) \rightarrow E^*(0,1) = Y_A(0,1) - Y_B(0,1)$

9.4 Observable Definitions of Causality

As noted earlier, the standard response to this problem is to consider definitions of causal impact that are observable because the relevant quantities can be measured in the same state of the world—thus avoiding the problem of making comparisons across multiple worlds or between the existing world and another, "impossible," world. With two units and a dichotomous treatment, four states of the world are possible: $\{Z_A = 1 \text{ and } Z_B = 1\}$, $\{Z_A = 0 \text{ and } Z_B = 0\}$, $\{Z_A = 1 \text{ and } Z_B = 0\}$, and $\{Z_A = 0 \text{ and } Z_B = 1\}$. These are listed in Table 10.5 along with the two observable quantities, Y_A and Y_B, one for A and one for B, for each state of the world.

The four differences of these two quantities are listed in Table 10.8. Each difference is a candidate to be considered as a measure of causal impact. The differences for the first and second of these four states of the world do not offer much opportunity for detecting the causal impact of Z because there is no variability in the treatment between the two units.[53] Consequently, we consider the differences for the third and fourth cases.

For the state of the world $\{Z_A = 1 \text{ and } Z_B = 0\}$ we can compute the following based upon observable quantities:

$$E^*(1, 0) = Y_A(1, 0) - Y_B(1, 0), \tag{4}$$

where the difference involves terms that occur together in one state of the world. Note that we denote this empirical definition of causality by an asterisk. This difference is computable, but does it represent a causal impact? Intuitively, the problem with using it as an estimate of causal impact is that A and B might be quite different to begin with. Suppose we are trying to estimate the impact of a new teaching method. Person A might be an underachiever while person B might be an overachiever. Hence, even if the method works, person A might score lower on a test after treatment than person B, and the method will be deemed a failure. Or suppose we are trying to determine

[53] Consider, for example, the difference $E^*(1, 1) = Y_A(1, 1) - Y_B(1, 1)$ for state of the world $\{Z_A = 1 \text{ and } Z_B = 1\}$. If we make the very reasonable assumption of identicality described below, then $Y_B(1, 1) = Y_A(1, 1)$ so that $E^*(1, 1)$ is always zero which is not a very interesting "causal effect." The same result applies to the state of the world $\{Z_A = 0 \text{ and } Z_B = 0\}$.

the impact of a new voting machine. County A might be very competent at running elections while county B might not be. Consequently, even if the machine works badly, county A with the new system might perform better than county B without it—once again leading to the wrong inference. Clearly $E^*(1, 0)$ alone is not a very good definition of causal impact. One of the problems is that preexisting differences between the units can confound causal inference.

How, then, can $E^*(1, 0)$ be used to make a better causal inference? Surveying the four definitions of causal impact in equations (2) and (3) above, this definition seems most closely related to two of them:

$$E_A(Z_B = 0) = Y_A(1, 0) - Y_A(0, 0), \quad \text{and} \tag{5a}$$

$$E_B(Z_A = 1) = Y_B(1, 1) - Y_B(1, 0). \tag{5b}$$

Consider the first of these, $E_A(Z_B = 0)$. Obviously, $E^*(1, 0)$ will equal $E_A(Z_B = 0)$ if the second term in the expression for $E^*(1, 0)$ which is $Y_B(1, 0)$ equals the second term in the expression for $E_A(Z_B = 0)$ which is $Y_A(0, 0)$. Thus we require that:

$$Y_B(1, 0) = Y_A(0, 0). \tag{6}$$

What conditions will ensure that this is so?

We shall make the transformation of $Y_B(1, 0)$ into $Y_A(0, 0)$ in two steps which are depicted on Table 49.9. If A and B are identical and Z_A and Z_B are identical as well[54] (although we haven't indicated how this might be brought about yet) it might be reasonable to suppose that:

$$Y_B(1, 0) = Y_A(0, 1) [\textit{Identicality of units and treatment or Unit Homogeneity}]. \tag{7}$$

That is, A and B are mirror images of one another so that the impact of $Z_A = 1$ and $Z_B = 0$ on B is the same as the impact of $Z_A = 0$ and $Z_B = 1$ on A.

This assumption is the same as what Holland (1986) calls "unit homogeneity" in which units are prepared carefully "so that they 'look' identical in all relevant aspects" (Holland 1986, 948). This assumption is commonly made in laboratory work where identical specimens are tested or where the impacts of different manipulations are studied for the identical setup. It obviously requires a great deal of knowledge about what makes things identical to one another and an ability to control these factors. It is typically not a very good assumption in the social sciences.

With this assumption, $E^*(1, 0) = Y_A(1, 0) - Y_A(0, 1)$ which is a definition of causality that we discarded earlier because of the possibility that if B gets the treatment when A does not, then A will be affected even when A does not get the treatment. We discarded this definition because, for example, the impact $Y_A(0, 1)$ of the treatment on Amy when Beatrice gets the treatment might be substantial—perhaps

---

[54] By saying that Z_A and Z_B have to be comparable, we mean that $Z_A = 0$ and $Z_B = 0$ are the same thing and $Z_A = 1$ and $Z_B = 1$ are the same thing.

Table 49.9. Linking observational data to theoretical definitions of causality through unit identicality and noninterference of units

Observational	Unit identicality (unit homogeneity)	Noninterference of units (SUTVA)	Theoretical definition
$E^*(1, 0) = Y_A(1, 0) - Y_B(1, 0)$	$Y_B(1, 0) = Y_A(0, 1) \rightarrow Y_A(1, 0) - Y_A(0, 1)$ $Y_A(1, 0) = Y_B(0, 1) \rightarrow Y_B(0, 1) - Y_B(1, 0)$	$Y_A(0, 1) = Y_A(0, 0) \rightarrow Y_A(1, 0) - Y_A(0, 0)$ $Y_A(1, 0) = Y_A(1, 1) \rightarrow Y_A(1, 1) - Y_A(0, 1)$ $Y_B(1, 0) = Y_B(0, 0) \rightarrow Y_B(0, 1) - Y_B(0, 0)$ $Y_B(0, 1) = Y_B(1, 1) \rightarrow Y_B(1, 1) - Y_B(1, 0)$	$E_A(Z_B = 0)$ $E_A(Z_B = 1)$ $E_B(Z_A = 0)$ $E_B(Z_A = 1)$
$E^*(0, 1) = Y_B(0, 1) - Y_A(0, 1)$	$Y_B(0, 1) = Y_A(1, 0) \rightarrow Y_A(1, 0) - Y_A(0, 1)$ $Y_A(0, 1) = Y_B(1, 0) \rightarrow Y_B(0, 1) - Y_B(1, 0)$	$Y_A(0, 1) = Y_A(0, 0) \rightarrow Y_A(1, 0) - Y_A(0, 0)$ $Y_A(1, 0) = Y_A(1, 1) \rightarrow Y_A(1, 1) - Y_A(0, 1)$ $Y_B(1, 0) = Y_B(0, 0) \rightarrow Y_B(0, 1) - Y_B(0, 0)$ $Y_B(0, 1) = Y_B(1, 1) \rightarrow Y_B(1, 1) - Y_B(1, 0)$	$E_A(Z_B = 0)$ $E_A(Z_B = 1)$ $E_B(Z_A = 0)$ $E_B(Z_A = 1)$

as much as when Amy gets the treatment alone which is $Y_A(1, 0)$. In that case, $E^*(1, 0)$ seems like a poor definition of the causal impact of Z_A when what we really want is the definition in (5a) above. But to get to that definition, we must suppose that:

$$Y_A(0, 1) = Y_A(0, 0) \ [\textit{Non-interference of units or SUTVA}]. \tag{8}$$

In effect, this requires that we believe that the causal impact of manipulation Z_A on A is not affected by whether or not B gets the treatment. Rubin (1990) calls this the "Stable-Unit-Treatment Value Assumption" (SUTVA). As we have already seen, this is a worrisome assumption, and we shall have a great deal to say about it later.

Similarly, $E^*(1, 0)$ will equal the second definition (5b) above, $E_B(Z_A = 1)$, if the first term in the expression for $E^*(1, 0)$ which is $Y_A(1, 0)$ equals the first term in the expression for $E_B(Z_A = 1)$ which is $Y_B(1, 1)$. Once again, if A and B are identical and Z_A and Z_B are identical then we can suppose that:

$$Y_A(1, 0) = Y_B(0, 1) \ [\textit{Identicality of units and treatment or unit homogeneity}]. \tag{9}$$

In addition we need to assume that the causal impact of manipulation Z_A on B is not affected by whether or not A gets the treatment:

$$Y_B(0, 1) = Y_B(1, 1) \ [\textit{Noninterference of Units or SUTVA}]. \tag{10}$$

To summarize, to get a workable operational definition of causality, we need to assume that one of the following holds true:

$$Y_B(1, 0) = Y_A(0, 1) = Y_A(0, 0), \textit{ or} \tag{11a}$$

$$Y_A(1, 0) = Y_B(0, 1) = Y_B(1, 1). \tag{11b}$$

The first equality in each line holds true if we assume identicality and the second holds true if we assume noninterference (SUTVA). Note that if both (11a) and (11b) are true, then the definitions of $E^*(1, 0)$, $E_A(Z_B = 0)$, and $E_B(Z_A = 1)$ all collapse to one another.

Instead of (4) as the operational definition of causal impact, we might consider the following which is the effect for the state of the world $\{Z_A = 0 \text{ and } Z_B = 1\}$:

$$E^*(0, 1) = Y_B(0, 1) - Y_A(0, 1), \tag{12}$$

where the difference involves terms that occur in only one state of the world. Surveying the four theoretical definitions of causal impact in equations (2) and (3) above, this definition seems most closely related to these two:

$$E_A(Z_B = 1) = Y_A(1, 1) - Y_A(0, 1) \tag{13a}$$

$$E_B(Z_A = 0) = Y_B(0, 1) - Y_B(0, 0), \tag{13b}$$

and these two are the remaining two after the ones in (5) are considered. To make these definitions work, we require, analogously to (11) above, that:

$$Y_B(0, 1) = Y_A(1, 0) = Y_A(1, 1), \ or \tag{14a}$$

$$Y_A(0, 1) = Y_B(1, 0) = Y_B(0, 0), \tag{14b}$$

where as before, the first equality in each line comes from identicality and the second comes from assuming noninterference. Once again, with these assumptions, then the definitions of $E^*(0, 1)$, $E_A(Z_B = 1)$, and $E_B(Z_A = 0)$ collapse into the same thing. And if both (11a,b) and (14a,b) hold, then $E^*(1, 0)$ equals $E^*(0, 1)$, and these definitions are all the same. Table 10.9 summarizes this entire argument.

9.5 Getting around Identicality (Unit Homogeneity) through Average Causal Effect

It is clear that the assumptions of noninterference (SUTVA) and identicality are sufficient to define causality unambiguously, but are they necessary? They are very strong assumptions. Can we do without one or the other? Suppose, for example, that we just assume noninterference so that $Y_A(j, k) = Y_A(j, k')$ and $Y_B(j, k) = Y_B(j, k')$ for $j = 1, 2$ and $k \neq k'$. Then we get the comforting result that the two theoretical definitions of causal impact for A (in (2) above) and the two for B (in (3) above) are identical:

$$E_A(Z_B = 0) = Y_A(1, 0) - Y_A(0, 0) = Y_A(1, 1) - Y_A(0, 1) = E_A(Z_B = 1)$$

$$E_B(Z_A = 0) = Y_B(0, 1) - Y_B(0, 0) = Y_B(1, 1) - Y_B(1, 0) = E_B(Z_A = 1).$$

Table 49.10 depicts this argument (moving from the rightmost column in the table to the second to the right column.) Since these equations hold, we denote the common causal effects as simply E_A and E_B:

$$E_A = E_A(Z_B = 0) = E_A(Z_B = 1)$$

$$E_B = E_B(Z_A = 0) = E_B(Z_A = 1).$$

These assumptions alone, however, will not allow us to link these theoretical definitions with the empirical possibilities $E^*(1, 0)$ and $E^*(0, 1)$. We need some additional assumption such as identicality of A and B which would ensure that $E_A = E_B$.

Can we get around identicality? Consider the following maneuver. Although we cannot observe both $E^*(1, 0)$ and $E^*(0, 1)$ at the same time, consider their average which we shall call the Average Causal Effect or ACE:

$$ACE = (1/2)[E^*(1, 0) + E^*(0, 1)]$$

$$= (1/2)\{[Y_A(1, 0) - Y_B(1, 0)] + [Y_B(0, 1) - Y_A(0, 1)]\}$$

$$= (1/2)\{[Y_A(1, 0) - Y_A(0, 1)] + [Y_B(0, 1) - Y_B(1, 0)]\}$$

$$= (1/2)\{[Y_A(1, 0) - Y_A(0, 0)] + [Y_B(0, 1) - Y_B(0, 0)]\}$$

Table 49.10. Linking observational data to theoretical definitions of causality through noninterference of units and average causal effect

Observational →	→ Noninterference →	→ Average Causal Effect ← $ACE = [E^*(1, 0) + E^*(0, 1)]/2$	← Noninterference ←	← Theoretical
$E^*(1, 0) = Y_A(1, 0)$ $- Y_B(1, 0)$	$Y_B(1, 0) = Y_B(0, 0)$ $\to Y_A(1, 0) - Y_B(0, 0)$ $Y_A(1, 0) = Y_A(1,1)$ $\to Y_A(1, 1) - Y_B(1, 0)$	**Take first and third on left:** $ACE = [Y_A(1, 0) - Y_B(0, 0) + Y_B(0, 1) - Y_A(0, 0)]/2$ $= [Y_A(1, 0) - Y_A(0, 0) + Y_B(0, 1) - Y_B(0, 0)]/2$ $= [E_A + E_B]$ (Using results from panels to right)	$Y_A(1, 0) = Y_A(1, 1)$ $Y_A(0, 0) = Y_A(0, 1)$ Hence: $E_A = E_A(Z_B = 0)$ $\quad = E_A(Z_B = 1)$ $\quad = Y_A(1, *) - Y_A(0, *)$	$E_A(Z_B = 0) = Y_A(1, 0)$ $\qquad - Y_A(0, 0)$ $E_A(Z_B = 1) = Y_A(1, 1)$ $\qquad - Y_A(0, 1)$
$E^*(0, 1) = Y_B(0, 1)$ $- Y_A(0, 1)$	$Y_A(0, 1) = Y_A(0, 0)$ $\to Y_B(0, 1) - Y_A(0, 0)$ $Y_B(0, 1) = Y_B(1, 1)$ $\to Y_B(1, 1) - Y_A(0, 1)$	**Take second and fourth on left:** $ACE = [Y_A(1, 1) - Y_B(1, 0) + Y_B(1, 1) - Y_A(0, 1)]/2$ $= [Y_A(1, 1) - Y_A(0, 1) + Y_B(1, 1) - Y_B(1, 0)]/2$ $= [E_A + E_B]$ (Using results from panels to right)	$Y_B(0, 1) = Y_B(1, 1)$ $Y_B(0, 0) = Y_B(1, 0)$ Hence: $E_B = E_B(Z_A = 0)$ $\quad = E_B(Z_A = 1)$ $\quad = Y_B(*, 1) - Y_B(*, 0)$	$E_B(Z_A = 0) = Y_B(0, 1)$ $\qquad - Y_B(0, 0)$ $E_B(Z_A = 1) = Y_B(1, 1)$ $\qquad - Y_B(1, 0)$

where the second line uses the definitions of $E^*(1, 0)$ and $E^*(0, 1)$, the third line is simply algebra, and the last line comes from noninterference. This argument is depicted in Table 49.10 as we move from the first to the second to the third column. As a result, we can write:

$$ACE = (1/2)[E_A + E_B].$$

Therefore, the ACE represents the average causal impact of Z_A on A and Z_B on B. If identicality (of A to B and Z_A to Z_B) held, then ACE would simply be the causal impact of Z.

Unfortunately, we cannot observe ACE, and we do not want to assume identicality. We can observe either $E^*(1, 0)$ or $E^*(0, 1)$, but not both. We can, however, do the following. We can randomly choose the state of the world, either $\{Z_A = 1$ and $Z_B = 0\}$ or $\{Z_A = 0$ and $Z_B = 1\}$. *Randomization in this way ensures that the treatment is assigned at random.* Once we have done this, we can take the observed value of either $E^*(1, 0)$ or $E^*(0, 1)$ as an estimate of ACE. The virtue of this estimate is that it is a statistically unbiased estimate of the average impact of Z_A on A and Z_B on B. That is, in repeated trials of this experiment (assuming that repeated trials make sense), the expected value of ACE will be equal to the true causal effect. Randomization ensures that we don't fall into the trap of confounding because, in repeated trials, there is no relationship between the assignment of treatment and units.

But the measure has two defects. First, it may be problematic to consider the average impact of Z_A on A and Z_B on B if they are not similar kinds of things. Once we drop identicality, it is quite possible that A and B could be quite different kinds of entities, say a sick person (A) and a well person (B). Then one would be randomly chosen to get some medicine, and the subsequent health (Y) of each person would be recorded. If the sick person A got the medicine then the causal effect E_A would be the difference between the health $Y_A(1, 0)$ of the sick person (after taking the medicine) and the health of the well person $Y_B(1, 0)$. If the well person B got the medicine, then the causal effect E_B would be the difference between the health $Y_B(0, 1)$ of the well person (after taking the medicine) and the health of the sick person $Y_A(0, 1)$. If the medicine works all the time and makes people well, then E_A will be zero (giving the medicine to the sick person will make him like the well person) and E_B will be positive (giving the medicine to the well person will not change her but not giving it to the sick person will leave him still sick)—hence the average effect will be to say that the medicine works, half the time. In fact, the medicine works all the time—when the person is sick. More generally, and somewhat ridiculously, A could be a person and B could be a tree, a dog, or anything. Thus, we need some assumption like the identicality of the units in order for our estimates of causal effect to make any sense. One possibility is that they are randomly chosen from some well-defined population to whom the treatment might be applied in the future.

The second defect of the measure is that it is only correct in repeated trials. In the medical experiment described above, if the well person is randomly assigned the medicine, then the experiment will conclude that the medicine does not work. The usual response to this problem is to multiply the number of units so that the random assignment to treatment group and control group creates groups that are, because of the law of large numbers, very similar, on average. This strategy certainly can make it possible to make statistical statements about the likelihood that an observed difference between the treatment and control groups is due to chance or to some underlying true difference. But it relies heavily upon multiplying the number of units, and it seems that multiplying the number of units brings some risks with it.

9.6 Multiplying the Number of Units and the Noninterference (SUTVA) Assumption

We started this section with a very simple problem in what is called singular causation. We asked: How does manipulation $Z = 1$ affect the outcome Y_A for unit A? Equation (1) provided a very simple definition of what we meant by the causal effect. It is simply $E_A = Y_A(1) - Y_A(0)$. This simple definition foundered because we cannot observe both $Y_A(1)$ and $Y_A(0)$. To solve this problem, we multiplied the number of units. Multiplying the number of units makes it possible to obtain an observable estimate of causal effect by either making the noninterference and identicality assumptions or by making the noninterference assumption and using randomization to achieve random assignment. But these assumptions lead us into the difficulties of defining a population of similar things from which the units are chosen and the problem of believing the noninterference assumption. These problems are related because they suggest that ultimately researchers must rely upon some prior knowledge and information in order to be sure that units or cases can be compared. But how much knowledge is needed? Are these assumptions really problematic? Should we, for example, be worried about units affecting one another?

Yes. Suppose people in a treatment condition are punished for poor behavior while those in a control condition are not. Further suppose that those in the control condition who are "near" (i.e. live in the same neighborhood or communicate regularly with one another) those in the treatment condition are not fully aware that they are exempt from punishment or they fear that they might be made subject to it. Wouldn't their behavior change in ways that it would not have changed if there had never been a treatment condition? Doesn't this mean that it would be difficult, if not impossible, to satisfy the noninterference condition?

In the Cal-Learn experiment in California, for example, teenage girls on welfare in the treatment group had their welfare check reduced if they failed to get passing grades in school. Those in the randomly selected control group were not subject to reductions but many thought they were in the treatment group (probably because they knew people who were in the treatment group) and they appear to have worked to get passing grades to avoid cuts in welfare (Mauldon et al. 2000).[55] Their decision

---

[55] Experimental subjects were told which group they were in, but some apparently did not get the message. They may not have gotten the message because the control group was only a small number of people and almost all teenage welfare mothers in the state were in the treatment group. In these

to get better grades, however, may have led to an underestimate of the impact of Cal-Learn because it reduced the difference between the treatment group and the control group. The problem here is that there is interaction between the units. To rule out these possibilities, Rubin (1990) proposed the "Stable-Unit-Treatment-Value-Assumption (SUTVA)" which, as we have seen, asserts that the outcome for a particular case does not depend upon what happens to the other cases or which of the supposedly identical treatments the unit receives.

Researchers using human subjects have worried about the possibility of interference. Cook and Campbell (1986, 148) mention four fundamental threats to randomized experiments. Compensatory rivalry occurs when control units decide that even though they are not getting the treatment, they can do as well as those getting it. Resentful demoralization occurs when those not getting the treatment become demoralized because they are not getting the treatment. Compensatory equalization occurs when those in charge of control units decide to compensate for the perceived inequities between treatment and control units, and treatment diffusion occurs when those in charge of control units mimic the treatment because of its supposed beneficial effects.

SUTVA implies that each supposedly identical treatment really is identical and that each unit is a separate, isolated possible world that is unaffected by what happens to the other units. SUTVA is the master assumption that makes controlled or randomized experiments a suitable solution to the problem of making causal inferences. SUTVA ensures that treatment and control units really do represent the closest possible worlds to one another except for the difference in treatment. In order to believe that SUTVA holds, we must have a very clear picture of the units, treatments, and outcomes in the situation at hand so that we can convince ourselves that experimental (or observational) comparisons really do involve similar worlds. Rubin (1986, 962) notes, for example, that statements such as "If the females at firm f had been male, their starting salaries would have averaged 20% higher" require much more elaboration of the counterfactual possibilities before they can be tested. What kind of treatment, for example, would be required for females to be males? Are individuals or the firm the basic unit of analysis? Is it possible simply to randomly assign men to the women's jobs to see what would happen to salaries? From what pool would these men be chosen? If men were randomly assigned to some jobs formerly held by women, would there be interactions across units that would violate SUTVA?

Not surprisingly, if the SUTVA assumption fails, then it will be at best hard to generalize the results of an experiment and at worst impossible to even interpret its results. Generalization is hard if, for example, imposing a policy of welfare time-limits on a small group of welfare recipients has a much different impact than imposing it upon every recipient. Perhaps the imposition of limits on the larger group generates a negative attitude toward welfare that encourages job seeking which is not generated

circumstances, an inattentive teenager in the control group could have sensibly supposed that the program applied to everyone. Furthermore, getting better grades seemingly had the desired effect because their welfare check was not cut!

when the limits are only imposed on a few people. Or perhaps the random assignment of a "Jewish" culture to one country (such as Israel) is much different than assigning it to a large number of countries in the same area. In both cases, the pattern of assignment to treatments seems to matter as much as the treatments themselves because of interactions among the units, and the interpretation of these experiments might be impossible because of the complex interactions among units. If SUTVA does not hold, then there are no ways such as randomization to construct closest possible worlds, and the difficulty of determining closest possible worlds must be faced directly.

If SUTVA holds and if there is independence of assignment and outcome through randomization, then the degree of causal connection can be estimated.[56] But there is no direct test that can ensure that SUTVA holds and there are only partial tests of "balance" to ensure that randomization has been done properly. Much of the art in experimentation goes into strategies that will increase the likelihood that they do hold. Cases can be isolated from one another to minimize interference, treatments can be made as uniform as possible, and the characteristics and circumstances of each case can be made as uniform as possible, but nothing can absolutely ensure that SUTVA and the independence of assignment and outcome hold.[57]

9.7 Summary of the NRH Approach

If noninterference across units (SUTVA) holds and if independence of assignment and outcome hold, then mini-closest-possible worlds have been created which can be used to compare the effects in a treatment and control condition. If SUTVA holds, then there are three ways to get the conditional independence conditions to hold:

(a) Controlled experiments in which identicality (unit homogeneity) holds.
(b) Statistical experiments in which random assignment holds.
(c) Observational studies in which corrections are made for covariates that ensure mean conditional independence of assignment and outcome.

The mathematical conditions required for the third method to work follow easily from the Neyman–Holland–Rubin setup, but there is no method for identifying the proper covariates. And outside of experimental studies, there is no way to be sure that conditional independence of assignment and outcome holds. Even if we know about *something* that may confound our results, we may not know about *all* things, and without knowing all of them, we cannot be sure that correcting for some of them

---

[56] If SUTVA fails and independence of assignment and outcome obtains, then causal effects can also be estimated, but they will differ depending on the pattern of treatments. Furthermore, the failure of SUTVA may make it impossible to rely on standard methods such as experimental control or randomization to ensure that the independence of assignment and outcome holds because the interaction of units may undermine these methods.

[57] Although good randomization can make it very likely that there is independence of assignment and outcome.

ensures conditional independence. Thus observational studies face the problem of identifying a set of variables that will ensure conditional independence so that the impact of the treatment can be determined. A great deal of research, however, does this in a rather cavalier way.

Even if SUTVA and some form of conditional independence is satisfied, the NRH framework, like Lewis's counterfactual theory to which it is a close relative, can only identify causal connections. Additional information is needed to rule out spurious correlation and to establish the direction of causation. Appeal can be made to temporal precedence or to what was manipulated to pin down the direction of causation, but neither of these approaches provides full protection against common cause. More experiments or observations which study the impact of other variables which suppress supposed causes or effects may be needed, and these have to be undertaken imaginatively in ways that explore different possible worlds.

References

ABBOTT, A. 1983. Sequences of social events. *Historical Methods*, 16: 129–47.
—— 1992. From causes to events. *Sociological Methods and Research*, 20: 428–55.
—— 1995. Sequence analysis: new methods for old ideas. *Annual Review of Sociology*, 21: 93–113.
ACHEN, C. H. 1983. Toward theories of data: the state of political methodology. In *Political Science: The State of the Discipline*, ed. A. Finifter. Washington, DC: American Political Science Association.
BARTELS, L. and BRADY, H. E. 1993. The state of quantitative political methodology. In *Political Science: The State of the Discipline*, 2nd edn., ed. A. Finifter. Washington, DC: American Political Science Association.
BEAUCHAMP, T. L. and ROSENBERG, A. 1981. *Hume and the Problem of Causation*. New York: Oxford University Press.
BENNETT, J. 1988. *Events and Their Names*. Indianapolis: Hackett.
BERGER, P. L. and LUCKMANN, T. 1966. *The Social Construction of Reality: A Treatise in the Sociology of Knowledge*. Garden City, NY: Anchor.
BRADY, H. E. and COLLIER, D. 2004. *Rethinking Social Inquiry: Diverse Tools, Shared Standards*. New York: Rowman and Littlefield.
—— HERRON, M. C., MEBANE, W. R., SEKHON, J. S., SHOTTS, W. S., and WAND, J. 2001. Law and data: the butterfly ballot episode. *PS: Political Science and Politics*, 34: 59–69.
CAMPBELL, D. T. and STANLEY, J. C. 1966. *Experimental and Quasi-Experimental Designs for Research*. Chicago: Rand McNally.
CARTWRIGHT, N. 1989. *Nature's Capacities and Their Measurement*. New York: Oxford University Press.
COOK, T. D. and CAMPBELL, D. T. 1979. *Quasi-Experimentation: Design and Analysis Issues for Field Settings*. Boston: Houghton Mifflin.
—————— 1986. The causal assumptions of quasi-experimental practice. *Synthese*, 68: 141–180.
COX, D. R. 1958. *The Planning of Experiments*. New York: Wiley.
—— 1992. Causality: some statistical aspects. *Journal of the Royal Statistical Society, Series A (Statistics in Society)*, 155: 291–301.

Cox, G. W. 1997. *Making Votes Count: Strategic Coordination in the World's Electoral Systems*, New York: Cambridge University Press.

Davidson, D. 2001. *Essays on Actions and Events*, 2nd edn. Oxford: Clarendon Press.

Dessler, D. 1991. Beyond correlations: toward a causal theory of war. *International Studies Quarterly*, 35: 337–355.

Dilthey, W. 1961. *Pattern and Meaning in History: Thoughts on History and Society*. New York: Harper.

Durkheim, E. 1982 [1895]. *The Rules of Sociological Method*. New York: Free Press.

Elster, J. 1998. A plea for mechanisms. In *Social Mechanisms*, ed. P. Hedström and R. Swedberg. Cambridge: Cambridge University Press.

Ehring, D. 1997. *Causation and Persistence: A Theory of Causation*. New York: Oxford University Press.

Fearon, J. D. 1991. Counterfactuals and hypothesis testing in political science. *World Politics*, 43: 169–95.

Fisher, R. A., Sir 1925. *Statistical Methods for Research Workers*. Edinburgh: Oliver and Boyd.

——1926. The arrangement of field experiments. *Journal of the Ministry of Agriculture*, 33: 503–13.

——1935. *The Design of Experiments*. Edinburgh: Oliver and Boyd.

Freedman, D. A. 1987. As others see us: a case study in path analysis. *Journal of Educational Statistics*, 12: 101–223, with discussion.

——1991. Statistical models and shoe leather. *Sociological Methodology*, 21: 291–313.

——1997. From association to causation via regression. Pp. 113–61 in *Causality in Crisis?* ed. V. R. McKim and S. P. Turner, Notre Dame, Ind.: University of Notre Dame Press.

——1999. From association to causation: some remarks on the history of statistics. *Statistical Science*, 14: 243–58.

Gasking, D. 1955. Causation and recipes. *Mind*, 64: 479–87.

Glennan, S. S. 1996. Mechanisms and the nature of causation. *Erkenntnis*, 44: 49–71.

Goldthorpe, J. H. 2001. Causation, statistics, and sociology. *European Sociological Review*, 17: 1–20.

Goodman, N. 1947. The problem of counterfactual conditionals. *Journal of Philosophy*, 44: 113–28.

Harré, R. and Madden, E. H. *c* 1975. *Causal Powers: A Theory of Natural Necessity*. Oxford: B. Blackwell.

Hausman, D. M. 1998. *Causal Asymmetries*. New York: Cambridge University Press.

Heckman, J. J. 1979. Sample selection bias as a specification error. *Econometrica*, 47: 153–62.

Hedström, P. and Swedberg, R. (eds.) 1998. *Social Mechanisms: An Analytical Approach to Social Theory*. New York: Cambridge University Press.

Hempel, C. G. 1965. *Aspects of Scientific Explanation*. New York: Free Press.

Hill, A. B. 1965. The environment and disease: association or causation? *Proceedings of the Royal Society of Medicine*, 58: 295–300.

Holland, P. W. 1986. Statistics and causal inference (in theory and methods). *Journal of the American Statistical Association*, 81: 945–60.

Hume, D. 1739. *A Treatise of Human Nature*, ed. L. A. Selby-Bigge and P. H. Nidditch. Oxford: Clarendon Press.

——1748. *An Enquiry Concerning Human Understanding*, ed. T. L. Beauchamp. New York: Oxford University Press.

Kitcher, P. and Salmon, W. 1987. Van Fraassen on explanation. *Journal of Philosopy*, 84: 315–30.

LAKOFF, G. and JOHNSON, M. 1980a. Conceptual metaphor in everyday language. *Journal of Philosophy*, 77 (8): 453–86.

——1980b. *Metaphors We Live By*. Chicago: University of Chicago Press.

——1999. *Philosophy in the Flesh: The Embodied Mind and its Challenge to Western Thought*. New York: Basic Books.

LEWIS, D. 1973a. *Counterfactuals*. Cambridge, Mass: Harvard University Press.

——1973b. Causation. *Journal of Philosophy*, 70: 556–67.

——1979. Counterfactual dependence and time's arrow. *Noûs*, Special Issue on Counterfactuals and Laws, 13: 455–76.

——1986. *Philosophical Papers*, vol. ii. New York: Oxford University Press.

MACHAMBER, P., DARDEN, L., and CRAVER, C. F. 2000. Thinking about mechanisms. *Philosophy of Science*, 67: 1–25.

MACKIE, J. L. 1965. Causes and conditions. *American Philosophical Quarterly*, 2: 245–64.

MARINI, M. M., and SINGER, B. 1988. Causality in the social sciences. *Sociological Methodology*, 18: 347–409.

MAULDON, J., MALVIN, J., STILES, J., NICOSIA, N., and SETO, E. 2000. Impact of California's Cal-Learn Demonstration Project: final report. UC DATA Archive and Technical Assistance.

MELLORS, D. H. 1995. *The Facts of Causation*. London: Routledge.

MENZIES, P. and PRICE, H. 1993. Causation as a secondary quality. *British Journal for the Philosophy of Science*, 44: 187–203.

MILL, J. S. 1888 *A System of Logic, Ratiocinative and Inductive*, 8th edn. New York: Harper and Brothers.

NEYMAN, J. 1990. On the application of probability theory to agricultural experiments: essay on principles, trans. D. M. Dabrowska and T. P. Speed. *Statistical Science*, 5: 463–80; first pub. in Polish 1923.

PAPINEAU, D. 1985. Causal asymmetry. *British Journal for the Philosophy of Science*, 36: 273–89.

PEARL, J. 2000. *Causality: Models, Reasoning, and Inference*. Cambridge: Cambridge University Press.

PEARSON, K. 1911. *The Grammar of Science*, 3rd edn. rev. and enlarged, Part 1: *Physical*. London: Adam and Charles Black.

PIERSON, P. 2004. *Politics in Time: History, Institutions, and Social Analysis*. Princeton, NJ: Princeton University Press.

RAGIN, C. C. 1987. *The Comparative Method: Moving beyond Qualitiative and Quantitative Strategies*. Berkeley: University of California Press.

RIKER, W. H. 1957. Events and situations. *Journal of Philosophy*, 54: 57–70.

RUBIN, D. B. 1974. Estimating causal effects of treatments in randomized and nonrandomized studies. *Journal of Educational Psychology*, 66: 688–701.

——1978. Bayesian inference for causal effects: the role of randomization. *Annals of Statistics*, 6: 34–58.

——1986. Statistics and casual inference: comment: which ifs have casual answers. *Journal of the American Statistical Association*, 81: 945–70.

——1990. Comment: Neyman (1923) and causal inference in experiments and observational studies. *Statistical Science*, 5: 472–80.

RUSSELL, B. 1918. On the notion of cause. In *Mysticism and Logic and Other Essays*. New York: Longmans, Green.

SALMON, W. C. 1990. *Four Decades of Scientific Explanation*. Minneapolis: University of Minnesota Press.

SEARLE, J. R. 1969. *Speech Acts: An Essay in the Philosophy of Language*. London: Cambridge University Press.

——1997. *The Construction of Social Reality*. New York: Free Press.

SHAFER, G. 1996. *The Art of Casual Conjecture*. Cambridge, Mass.: MIT Press.

SIMON, H. A. 1952. On the definition of the causal relation. *Journal of Philosophy*, 49: 517–28.

——and IWASAKI, Y. 1988. Causal ordering, comparative statics, and near decomposability. *Journal of Econometrics*, 39: 149–73.

SOBEL, M. E. 1995. Causal inference in the social and behavioral sciences. In *Handbook of Statistical Modeling for the Social and Behavioral Sciences*, ed. G. Arminger, C. C. Clogg, and M. E. Sobel. New York: Plenum.

SORENSON, A. B. 1998. Theoretical mechanisms and the empirical study of social processes. In *Social Mechanisms*, ed. P. Hedström and R. Swedberg. Cambridge: Cambridge University Press.

SOSA, E. and TOOLEY, M. 1993. *Causation*. Oxford: Oxford University Press.

SPELLMAN, B. A. and MANDEL, D. R. 1999. When possibility informs reality: counterfactual thinking as a cue to causality. *Current Directions in Psychological Science*, 8: 120–3.

SPRINZAK, E. 1972. Weber's thesis as an historical explanation. *History and Theory*, 11: 294–320.

TETLOCK, P. E. and BELKIN, A. (eds.) 1996. *Counterfactual Thought Experiments in World Politics: Logical, Methodological, and Psychological Perspectives*. Princeton, NJ: Princeton University Press.

TILLY, C. 1984. *Big Structures, Large Processes, Huge Comparison*. New York: Russell Sage Foundation.

VAN FRAASSEN, B. 1980. *The Scientific Image*. Oxford: Clarendon Press.

VON WRIGHT, G. H. 1971. *Explanation and Understanding*. Ithaca, NY: Cornell University Press.

——1974. *Causality and Determinism*. New York: Columbia University Press.

WAND, J. N., SHOTTS, K. W., SEKHON, J. S., MEBANE, W. R., HERRON, M. C., and BRADY, H. E. 1991. The butterfly did it: the aberrant vote for Buchanan in Palm Beach County, Florida. *American Political Science Review*, 95: 793–810.

WAWRO, G. 1996. *The Austro-Prussian War: Austria's War with Prussia and Italy in 1866*. New York: Cambridge University Press.

WEBER, M. 1906 [1978]. *Selections in Translation*, ed. W. G. Runciman, trans. E. Matthews. Cambridge: Cambridge University Press.

WENDT, A. 1999. *Social Theory of International Politics*. Cambridge: Cambridge University Press.

CHAPTER 50

FIELD EXPERIMENTS AND NATURAL EXPERIMENTS

ALAN S. GERBER
DONALD P. GREEN

THIS chapter assesses the strengths and limitations of field experimentation. The chapter begins by defining field experimentation and describing the many forms that field experiments take. The second section charts the growth and development of field experimentation. Third, we describe in formal terms why experiments are valuable for causal inference. Fourth, we contrast the assumptions of experimental and nonexperimental inference, pointing out that the value accorded to observational research is often inflated by misleading reporting conventions. The fifth section discusses the special methodological role that field experiments play insofar as they lay down benchmarks against which other estimation approaches can be assessed. Sixth, we describe two methodological challenges that field experiments frequently confront, noncompliance and attrition, showing the statistical and design implications of each. Seventh, we discuss the study of natural experiments and discontinuities as alternatives to both randomized interventions and conventional nonexperimental research. Finally, we review a list of methodological issues that arise commonly in connection with experimental design and analysis: the role of covariates, planned vs. unplanned comparisons, and extrapolation. The chapter concludes by discussing the ways in which field experimentation is reshaping the field of political methodology.

1 DEFINITION OF FIELD EXPERIMENTATION

Field experimentation represents the conjunction of two methodological strategies, experimentation and fieldwork. Experimentation is a form of investigation in which units of observation (e.g. individuals, groups, institutions, states) are randomly assigned to treatment and control groups. In other words, experimentation involves a random procedure (such as a coin flip) that ensures that every observation has the same probability of being assigned to the treatment group. Random assignment ensures that in advance of receiving the treatment, the experimental groups have the same expected outcomes, a fundamental requirement for unbiased causal inference. Experimentation represents a deliberate departure from observational investigation, in which researchers attempt to draw causal inferences from naturally occurring variation, as opposed to variation generated through random assignment.

Field experimentation represents a departure from laboratory experimentation. Field experimentation attempts to simulate as closely as possible the conditions under which a causal process occurs, the aim being to enhance the external validity, or generalizability, of experimental findings. When evaluating the external validity of political experiments, it is common to ask whether the stimulus used in the study resembles the stimuli of interest in the political world, whether the participants resemble the actors who are ordinarily confronted with these stimuli, whether the outcome measures resemble the actual political outcomes of theoretical or practical interest, and whether the context within which actors operate resembles the political context of interest.

One cannot apply these criteria in the abstract, because they each depend on the research question that an investigator has posed. If one seeks to understand how college students behave in abstract distributive competitions, laboratory experiments in which undergraduates vie for small economic payoffs may be regarded as field experiments. On the other hand, if one seeks to understand how the general public responds to social cues or political communication, the external validity of lab studies of undergraduates has inspired skepticism (Sears 1986; Benz and Meier 2006). These kinds of external validity concerns may subside in the future if studies demonstrate that lab studies involving undergraduates consistently produce results that are corroborated by experimental studies outside the lab; for now, the degree of correspondence remains an open question.

The same may be said of survey experiments. By varying question wording and order, survey experiments may provide important insights into the factors that shape survey response, and they may also shed light on decisions that closely resemble survey response, such as voting in elections. Whether survey experiments provide externally valid insights about the effects of exposure to media messages or other environmental factors, however, remains unclear. What constitutes a field experiment therefore depends on how "the field" is defined. Early agricultural experiments were called field experiments because they were literally conducted in fields. But if the question were how to maximize agricultural productivity of greenhouses, the appropriate field experiment might be conducted indoors.

Because the term "field experiment" is often used loosely to encompass randomized studies that vary widely in terms of realism, Harrison and List (2004, 1014) offer a more refined classification system. "Artefactual" field experiments are akin to laboratory experiments, except that they involve a "non-standard" subject pool. Habyarimana et al. (2007), for example, conduct experiments in which African subjects win prizes depending on how quickly they can open a combination lock; the random manipulation is whether the person who instructs them on the use of such locks is a co-ethnic or member of a different ethnic group. "Framed" field experiments are artefactual experiments that also involve a realistic task. An example of a framed field experiment is Chin, Bond, and Geva's (2000) study of the way in which sixty-nine congressional staffers made simulated scheduling decisions, an experiment designed to detect whether scheduling preference is given to groups associated with a political action committee. "Natural" field experiments unobtrusively assess the effects of realistic treatments on subjects who would ordinarily be exposed to them, typically using behavioral outcome measures. For example, Gerber, Karlan, and Bergan (2009) randomly assign newspaper subscriptions prior to an election and conduct a survey of recipients in order to gauge the extent to which the ideological tone of different papers manifests itself in the recipients' political opinions. For the purposes of this chapter, we restrict our attention to natural field experiments, which have clear advantages over artefactual and framed experiments in terms of external validity. We will henceforth use the term field experiments to refer to studies in naturalistic settings; although this usage excludes many lab and survey experiments, we recognize that some lab and survey studies may qualify as field experiments, depending on the research question.

2 GROWTH AND DEVELOPMENT OF FIELD EXPERIMENTATION

Despite the allure of random assignment and unobtrusive measurement, field experimentation has, until recently, rarely been used in political science. Although non-randomized field interventions date back to Gosnell (1927), the first randomized field experiment to appear in a political science journal was Eldersveld's (1956) study of voter mobilization in the Ann Arbor elections of 1953 and 1954. Assigning voters to receive phone calls, mail, or personal contact prior to election day, Eldersveld examined the marginal effects of different types of appeals, both separately and in combination with one another, using official records to measure voter turnout. The next field experiments, replications of Eldersveld's study (Adams and Smith 1980; Miller, Bositis, and Baer 1981) and a study of the effects of franked mail on constituent opinions of their congressional representative (Cover and Brumberg 1982), appeared a quarter-century later. Although the number of laboratory and survey experiments grew markedly during the 1980s and 1990s, field experimentation remained quiescent. Not a single such experiment was published in a political science journal during the 1990s.

Nor were field experiments part of discussions about research methodology. Despite the fact that political methodology often draws its inspiration from other disciplines, important experiments on the effects of the negative income tax (Pechman and Timpane 1975) and subsidized health insurance (Newhouse 1993) had very little impact on methodological discussion in political science. The most influential research methods textbook, *Designing Social Inquiry* (King, Keohane, and Verba 1994, 125), scarcely mentions experiments in general, noting in passing that experiments are useful insofar as they "provide a useful model for understanding certain aspects of non-experimental design." Books that champion qualitative methods, such as Mahoney and Reuschemeyer (2003), typically ignore the topic of experimental design, despite the fact that random assignment is compatible with—and arguably an important complement to—qualitative outcome and process measurement.

Field experimentation's low profile in political science may be traced to two prevailing methodological beliefs. The first is that field experiments are infeasible. In every stage in the discipline's development, leading political scientists have dismissed the possibility of experimentation. Lowell (1910, 7) declared, "we are limited by the impossibility of experiment. Politics is an observational, not an experimental, science." After the behavioral revolution, the prospects for experimentation were upgraded from impossible to highly unlikely: "The experimental method is the most nearly ideal method for scientific explanation, but unfortunately it can only rarely be used in political science because of practical and ethical impediments" (Lijphart 1971, 684). Textbook discussions of field experiments reinforce this view. Consider Johnson, Joslyn, and Reynolds's description of the practical problems confronting field experimention in the third edition of their *Political Science Research Methods* text:

Suppose, for example, that a researcher wanted to test the hypothesis that poverty causes people to commit robberies. Following the logic of experimental research, the researcher would have to randomly assign people to two groups prior to the experimental treatment, measure the number of robberies committed by members of the two groups prior to the experimental treatment, force the experimental group to be poor, and then to remeasure the number of robberies committed at some later date.   (2001, 133)

In this particular example, the practical difficulties stem from an insistence on baseline measurement (in fact, baseline measurement is not necessary for unbiased inference, thanks to random assignment), while the ethical concerns arise because the intervention is presumed to involve making people poorer rather than making them richer.

The second methodological view that contributed to the neglect of experimentation is the notion that statistical methods can be used to overcome the infirmities of observational data. Whether the methods in question are maximum likelihood estimation, simultaneous equations and selection models, pooled cross-section time series, ecological inference, vector autoregression, or nonparametric techniques such as matching, the underlying theme in most methodological writing is that proper use of statistical methods generates reliable causal inferences. The typical book or essay in this genre describes a statistical technique that is novel to political scientists and then presents an empirical illustration of how the right method overturns the substantive conclusions generated by the wrong method. The implication is that sophisticated analysis of nonexperimental data provides reliable results. From this vantage point, experimental data look more like a luxury than a necessity. Why contend with the expense and ethical encumbrances of generating experimental data?

Long-standing suppositions about the feasibility and necessity of field experimentation have recently begun to change in a variety of social science disciplines, including political science. A series of ambitious studies have demonstrated that randomized interventions are possible. Criminologists have randomized police raids on crack houses in order to assess the hypothesis that public displays of police power deter other forms of crime in surrounding areas (Sherman and Rogan 1995). Chattopadhyay and Duflo (2004) have examined the effects of randomly assigning India's Village Council head positions to women on the kinds of public goods that these rural administrative bodies provide. Economists and sociologists have examined the effects of randomly moving tenants out of public housing projects into neighborhoods with better schools, less crime, and more job opportunities (Kling, Ludwig, and Katz 2005). Hastings et al. (2005) have examined the effects of a "school choice" policy on the academic achievement of students and the voting behavior of parents. Olken (2005) examined the effects of various forms of administrative oversight, including grass-roots participation, on corruption in Indonesia. In political science, use of field experimentation became more widespread after Gerber and Green's (2000) investigation of the mobilizing effects of various forms of nonpartisan campaign communication, with scholars examining voter mobilization campaigns directed at a range of different ethnic groups, in a variety of electoral contexts, and using an array of different campaign appeals (Cardy 2005; Michelson 2003). Experimentation has begun to spread to other subfields, such as comparative politics (Wantchekon 2003; Guan and Green 2006). Hyde (2006), for example, uses random assignment to study the effects of international monitoring efforts on election fraud.

Nevertheless, there remain important domains of political science that lie beyond the reach of randomized experimentation. Although the practical barriers to field experimentation are frequently overstated, it seems clear that topics such as nuclear deterrence or constitutional design cannot be studied in this manner, at least not directly. As a result, social scientists have increasingly turned to natural experiments (as distinct from "natural" field experiments) in which units of observation receive different treatments in a manner that resembles random assignment. Although there are no formal criteria by which to judge whether naturally occurring variation approximates a random experiment, several recent studies seem to satisfy the requirements of a natural experiment. For example, Miguel, Satyanath, and Sergenti (2004) examine the consequences of weather-induced economic shocks on the violent civil conflicts in sub-Saharan Africa, and Ansolabehere, Snyder, and Stewart (2000) use decennial redistricting to assess the "personal vote" that incumbent legislators receive by comparing voters that legislators retain from their old districts to new voters that they acquire through redistricting.

3 EXPERIMENTS AND INFERENCE

The logic underlying randomized experiments—and research designs that attempt to approximate random assignment—is often explicated in terms of a notational system that has its origins in Neyman (1923) and is usually termed the "Rubin Causal Model," after Rubin (1978; 1990). The notational system is best understood by setting aside, for the time being, the topic of experimentation and focusing solely on the definition of causal influence. For each individual i let Y_0 be the outcome if i is not exposed to the treatment, and Y_1 be the outcome if i is exposed to the treatment. The treatment effect is defined as:

$$\tau_i = Y_{i1} - Y_{i0}. \tag{1}$$

In other words, the treatment effect is the difference between two potential states of the world, one in which the individual receives the treatment, and another in which the individual does not. Extending this logic from a single individual to a set of individuals, we may define the average treatment effect (ATE) as follows:

$$ATE = E(\tau_i) = E(Y_{i1}) - E(Y_{i0}). \tag{2}$$

The concept of the average treatment effect implicitly acknowledges the fact that the treatment effect may vary across individuals in systematic ways. One of the most important patterns of variation in τ_i occurs when the treatment effect is especially large (or small) among those who seek out a given treatment. In such cases, the average treatment effect in the population may be quite different from the average treatment effect among those who actually receive the treatment.

Stated formally, the concept of the average treatment effect among the treated (ATT) may be written

$$ATT = E(\tau_i | T_i = 1) = E(Y_{i1} | T_i = 1) - E(Y_{i0} | T_i = 1), \tag{3}$$

where $T_i = 1$ when a person receives a treatment. To clarify the terminology, $(Y_{i1} | T_i = 1)$ is the outcome resulting from the treatment among those who are actually treated, whereas $Y_{i0}|T_i = 1$ is the outcome that would have been observed in the absence of treatment among those who are actually treated. By comparing equations (2) and (3), it is apparent that the average treatment effect is not in general the same as the treatment effect among the treated.

The basic problem in estimating a causal effect, whether the ATE or the ATT, is that at a given point in time each individual is either treated or not: Either Y_1 or Y_0 is observed, but not both. Random assignment solves this "missing data" problem by creating two groups of individuals that are similar prior to application of the treatment. The randomly assigned control group then can serve as a proxy for the outcome that would have been observed for individuals in the treatment group if the treatment had not been applied to them.

Having now laid out the Rubin potential outcomes framework, we now show how it can be used to explicate the implications of random assignment. When treatments are randomly administered, the group that receives the treatment ($T_i = 1$) has the same expected outcome as the group that does not receive the treatment ($T_i = 0$) would if it were treated:

$$E(Y_{i1}|T_i = 1) = E(Y_{i1}|T_i = 0). \tag{4}$$

Similarly, the group that does not receive the treatment has the same expected outcome, if untreated, as the group that receives the treatment, if it were untreated:

$$E(Y_{i0}|T_i = 0) = E(Y_{i0}|T_i = 1). \tag{5}$$

Equations (4) and (5) are termed the independence assumption by Holland (1986) because the randomly assigned value of T_i conveys no information about the potential values of Y_i. Equations (2), (4), and (5) imply that the average treatment effect may be written

$$ATE = E(\tau_i) = E(Y_{i1}|T_i = 1) - E(Y_{i0}|T_i = 0). \tag{6}$$

Because $E(Y_{i1}|T_i = 1)$ and $E(Y_{i0}|T_i = 0)$ may be estimated directly from the data, this equation suggests a solution to the problem of causal inference. The estimator implied by equation (6) is simply the difference between two sample means: the average outcome in the treatment group minus the average outcome in the control group. In sum, random assignment satisfies the independence assumption, and the independence assumption suggests a way to generate empirical estimates of average treatment effects.

Random assignment further implies that independence will hold not only for Y_i, but for any variable X_i that might be measured prior to the administration of the treatment. For example, subjects' demographic attributes or their scores on a pre-test are presumably independent of randomly assigned treatment groups. Thus, one expects the average value of X_i in the treatment group to be the same as the control group; indeed, the entire distribution of X_i is expected to be the same across experimental groups. This property is known as covariate balance. It is possible to gauge the degree of balance empirically by comparing the sample averages for the treatment and control groups. One may also test for balance statistically by evaluating the null hypothesis that the covariates jointly have no systematic tendency to predict treatment assignment. Regression, for example, may be used to generate an F-test to evaluate the hypothesis that the slopes of all predictors of treatment assignment are zero. A significant test statistic suggests that something may have gone awry in the implementation of random assignment, and the researcher may wish to check his or her procedures. It should be noted, however, that a significant test statistic does not prove that the assignment procedure was nonrandom; nor does an insignificant test statistic prove that treatments were assigned using a random procedure. Balance tests provide useful information, but researchers must be aware of their limitations.

We return to the topic of covariate balance below. For now, we note that random assignment obviates the need for multivariate controls. Although multivariate methods may be helpful as a means to improve the statistical precision with which causal effects are estimated, the estimator implied by equation (6) generates unbiased estimates without such controls.

For ease of presentation, the above discussion of causal effects skipped over two further assumptions that play a subtle but important role in experimental analysis. The first is the idea of an *exclusion restriction*. Embedded in equation (1) is the idea that outcomes vary as a function of receiving the treatment per se. It is assumed that assignment to the treatment group only affects outcomes insofar as subjects receive the treatment. Part of the rationale for using placebo groups in experimental design is the concern that subjects' knowledge of their experimental assignment might affect their outcomes. The same may be said for double-blind procedures: When those who implement experiments are unaware of subjects' experimental assignments, they cannot intentionally or inadvertently alter their measurement of the dependent variable.

A second assumption is known as the Stable Unit Treatment Value Assumption, or SUTVA. In the notation used above, expectations such as $E(Y_{i1}|T_i = t_i)$ are all written as if the expected value of the treatment outcome variable Y_{i1} for unit i only depends upon whether or not the unit gets the treatment (whether t_i equals one or zero). A more complete notation would allow for the consequences of treatments T_1 through T_n administered to other units. It is conceivable that experimental outcomes might depend on the values of $t_1, t_2, \ldots, t_{i-1}, t_{i+1}, \ldots, t_n$ as well as the value of t_i:

$$E(Y_{i1}|T_1 = t_1, T_2 = t_2, \ldots, T_{i-1} = t_{i-1}, T_i = t_i, T_{i+1} = t_{i+1}, \ldots, T_n = t_n).$$

By ignoring the assignments to all other units when we write this as $E(Y_{i1}|T_i = t_i)$ we assume away spillovers from one experimental group to the other. Nickerson (2008) and Miguel and Kremer (2004) provide empirical illustrations of instances in which treatments administered to one person have effects on those around them.

Note that violations of SUTVA may produce biased estimates, but the sign and magnitude of the bias depend on the way in which treatment effects spill over across observations (cf. Nickerson 2008). Suppose an experiment were designed to gauge the ATT of door-to-door canvassing on voter turnout. Suppose that, by generating enthusiasm about the upcoming election, treating one person has the effect of increasing their probability of voting by π and the probability that their next-door neighbors vote by π^* (regardless of whether the neighbors are themselves treated). If treatment subjects are as likely as control subjects to live next to a person who receives the treatment, the difference in voting rates in the treatment and control groups provides an unbiased estimate of π even though SUTVA is violated. On the other hand, suppose that canvassers increase voter turnout by conveying information about where to vote. Under this scenario, treating one person has the effect of increasing their probability of voting by π and the probability that their *untreated* next-door neighbors vote by π^*; there is no effect on treated neighbors. This particular violation of SUTVA will boost the turnout rate in the control group and lead to an underestimation of π. As this example illustrates, the direction and magnitude of SUTVA-related bias are often difficult to know *ex ante*, and experimental researchers may wish to assess the influence of spillover effects empirically by randomly varying the density of treatments within different geographic units. Note that SUTVA, like other core assumptions of experimental inference, in fact applies to both experimental and observational research. The next section comments on the points at which the two modes of research diverge and the consequences of this divergence for the interpretation of experimental and observational findings.

4 CONTRASTING EXPERIMENTAL AND OBSERVATIONAL INFERENCE

Observational studies compare cases that received the "treatment" (through some unknown selection mechanism) with those that did not receive it. Because random assignment is not used, there are no procedural grounds on which to justify the independence assumption. Without independence, equations (4) and (5) do not hold. We cannot assume that the expected value of the outcomes in the "treatment group," $E(Y_{i1}|T_i = 1)$ equals the expected value of treated outcomes for the control group if treated, $E(Y_{i1}|T_i = 0)$, because the treatment group may differ systematically from the control group in advance of the treatment. Nor can we assume that the expected value of the untreated outcomes in the control group, $E(Y_{i0}|T_i = 0)$ equals the expected value of the untreated outcomes for the treatment group, $E(Y_{i0}|T_i = 1)$. Again, the treatment group in its untreated state may not resemble the control group.

There is no foolproof way to solve this problem. In an effort to eliminate potential confounds, a standard approach is to control for *observable* differences between treatment and control. Sometimes regression is used to control for covariates, but suppose one were to take the idea of controlling for observables to its logical extreme and were to match the treatment and control groups exactly on a set of observable characteristics X. For every value of X, one gathers a treatment and control observation.[1] This matching procedure would generate treatment and control groups that are perfectly balanced in terms of the covariates. However, in order to draw unbiased inferences from these exactly matched treatment and control groups, it is necessary to invoke the ignorability assumption described by Heckman et al. (1998), which stipulates that the treatment and potential outcomes are independent conditional on a set of characteristics X.

$$E(Y_{i1}|X_i, T_i = 1) = E(Y_{i1}|X_i, T_i = 0) \tag{7}$$

$$E(Y_{i0}|X_i, T_i = 0) = E(Y_{i0}|X_i, T_i = 1) \tag{8}$$

Note that these two assumptions parallel the two implications of randomization stated in equations (4) and (5), except that these are conditional on X. From these equations, it is easy to generate expressions for average treatment effects, using the same logic as above.

Analysts of observational data reason along these lines when defending their estimation techniques. It is conventional to assume, for example, that conditional on a set of covariates, individuals who receive treatment have the same expected outcomes as those in the control group. Notice, however, the important difference between the assumptions imposed by experimental and observational researchers. The experimental researcher relies on the properties of a procedure—random assignment—to derive unbiased estimates. The observational researcher, on the other hand, relies on substantive assumptions about the properties of covariates. Whereas the properties of the random assignment procedure are verifiable (one can check the random number generator and review the clerical procedures by which numbers were assigned to units of observation), the validity of the substantive assumptions on which observational inferences rest are seldom verifiable in any direct sense.

Even if one believes that the assumptions underlying an observational inference are probably sound, the mere possibility that these assumptions are incorrect alters the statistical attributes of observational results. Gerber, Green, and Kaplan (2004) show formally that an estimate's sampling distribution reflects two sources of variance: the statistical uncertainty that results when a given model is applied to data and additional uncertainty about whether the estimator is biased. Only the first source of uncertainty is accounted for in the standard errors that are generated by conventional statistical software packages. The second source of uncertainty is ignored. In other words, the standard errors associated with observational results are derived using formulas that are appropriate for experimental data but represent lower bounds when applied to observational data. This practice means that observational results

---

[1] This procedure satisfies the auxiliary assumption that cases with the same X values have a positive probability of being in either treated or control group. This assumption would be violated if treatment assignment were perfectly predicted by X.

are conventionally described in ways that are potentially quite misleading. More specifically, they are misleading in ways that exaggerate the value of observational findings.

This point has been demonstrated empirically. Inspired by the pioneering work of LaLonde (1986), which assessed the correspondence between experimental and observational estimates of the effectiveness of job-training programs, Arceneaux, Gerber, and Green (2006) compare experimental and observational estimates of the effects of phone-based voter mobilization campaigns. Using a sample of more than one million observations, they find the actual root mean squared error associated with the observational estimates to be an order of magnitude larger than their nominal standard errors.

LaLonde-type comparisons expose a seldom-noticed deficiency in political methodology research. Heretofore, methodological debate was premised on the assumption that the value of a casual parameter is unknowable; as a result, the terms of debate hinged on the technical attributes of competing approaches. LaLonde's empirical approach radically alters these debates, for it sometimes turns out that cutting-edge statistical techniques perform quite poorly.

That said, experiments are by no means free from methodological concerns. Field experiments in particular are susceptible to noncompliance and attrition, two problems that convinced some early critics of field experimentation to abandon the enterprise in favor of observational research designs (Chapin 1947). The next sections consider in depth the nature and consequences of these two problems.

5 NONCOMPLIANCE

Sometimes only a subset of those who are assigned to the treatment group are actually treated, or a portion of the control group receives the treatment. When those who get the treatment differ from those who are assigned to receive it, an experiment confronts a problem of noncompliance. In experimental studies of get-out-the-vote canvassing, noncompliance occurs when some subjects who were assigned to the treatment group remain untreated because they are not reached. In clinical trials, subjects may choose to stop a treatment. In studies of randomized election monitoring, observers may fail to follow their assignment; consequently, some places assigned to the treatment group go untreated, while places assigned to the control group receive treatment.

How experimenters approach the problem of noncompliance depends on their objectives. Those who wish to gauge the effectiveness of an outreach program may be content to estimate the so-called "intent-to-treat" effect (ITT); that is, the effect of being randomly assigned to the treatment group after "treatment." At the end of the day, a program's effectiveness is a function of both its effects on those who receive

Table 50.1. Summary of notation distinguishing assigned and received treatments

	Experimental assignment	
Actual treatment received	Treatment group $(Z_i = 1)$	Control group $(Z_i = 0)$
Treated $(T_i = 1)$	$D_1 = 1$	$D_0 = 1$
Not treated $(T_i = 0)$	$D_1 = 0$	$D_0 = 0$

the treatment and the extent to which the treatment is actually administered. Other experimenters may be primarily interested in measuring the effects of the treatment on those who are actually treated. For them, the rate at which any specific program reaches the intended treatment group is of secondary interest. The formal discussion below shows how both the intent-to-treat and treatment-on-treated effects may be estimated from data.

When there is noncompliance, a subject's group assignment, Z_i, is not equivalent to T_i, whether the subject gets treated or not. Angrist, Imbens, and Rubin (1996) extend the notation presented in equations (1) through (6) to the case where treatment group assignment and receipt of treatment can diverge. Let $D_1 = 1$ when a subject assigned to the treatement group is treated, and let $D_1 = 0$ when a subject assigned to the treatment group is not treated. Using this notation, which has been summarized in Table 50.1, we can define a subset of the population, called "Compliers," who get the treatment when assigned to the treatment group but not otherwise. "Compliers" are subjects for whom $D_1 = 1$ and $D_0 = 0$. In the simplest experimental design, in which all those in the treatment group get treated and no one in the control group does, every subject is a Complier. Note that whether a subject is a Complier is a function of both subject characteristics and the particular features of the experiment and is not a fixed attribute of a subject.

When treatments are administered exactly according to plan ($Z_i = T_i, \forall\, i$), the average causal effect of a randomly assigned treatment can be estimated simply by comparing mean treatment group outcomes and mean control group outcomes. What can be learned about treatment effects when there is noncompliance? Angrist, Imbens, and Rubin (1996) present a set of sufficient conditions for estimating the average treatment effect for the subgroup of subjects who are Compliers. Here we will first present a description of the assumptions and the formula for estimating the average treatment effect for the Compliers. We then elucidate the assumptions using an example.

In addition to the assumption that treatment group assignment Z is random, Angrist et al.'s result invokes the following four assumptions, the first two of which have been mentioned above:

Exclusion restriction. The outcome for a subject is a function of the treatment they receive but is not otherwise influenced by their assignment to the treatment group. In experiments this assumption may fail if subjects change their behavior in response to the treatment group assignment per se (as opposed to the treatment itself) or are induced to do so by third parties who observe the treatment assignment.

Stable Unit Treatment Value Assumption (SUTVA). Whether a subject is treated depends only on the subject's own treatment assignment and not on the treatment assignment of any other subjects. Also, the subject's outcome is a function of his or her treatment assignment and receipt of treatment, and not affected by the assignment of or treatment received by any other subject.

Monotonicity. For all subjects, the probability the subject is treated is at least as great when the subject is in the treatment group as when the subject is in the control group. This assumption is satisfied by design in experiments where the treatment is only available to the treatment group.

Nonzero causal effects of assignment on treatment. The treatment assignment has an effect on the probability that at least some subjects are treated. This is satisfied if the monotonicity assumption is slightly strengthened to require the inequality to be strong for at least some subjects.

Angrist et al. (1996, proposition 1) show that if assumptions 1–4 are satisfied then the effect of the treatment can be expressed as:

$$\frac{E(Y_1 - Y_0)}{E(D_1 - D_0)} = E\left((Y_1 - Y_0)|D_1 - D_0 = 1\right), \tag{9}$$

where Y_j is the outcome when $Z_i = j$, D_j is the value of D when $Z_i = j$, $E(h)$ is the mean value of h in the subject population, and $E(h|g)$ is the mean value of h in the subset of the subject population for which g holds.

The numerator on the left-hand side of equation (9) is the intent-to-treat (ITT) effect of Z on Y, the average causal effect of Z on Y for the entire treatment group, including those who do not get treated. The ITT may be expressed formally as

$$ITT = E(Y_{i1}|Z_i = 1) - E(Y_{i0}|Z_i = 0). \tag{10}$$

The ITT is often used in program evaluation because it takes into account both the treatment effect and the rate at which the treatment is successfully administered. A program may have a weak intent-to-treat effect because the average treatment effect is weak or because the intervention is actually administered to a small portion of those assigned to receive the treatment.

The denominator of equation (9) is the ITT effect of Z on D, the average effect of being placed in the treatment group on the probability a subject is treated. The ratio of these ITT effects equals the average causal effect of the treatment for the Complier population, which is referred to as the Local Average Treatment Effect (LATE). When the control group is never treated, $D_0 = 0$, the LATE is equal to the ATT defined in equation (3).

This proposition has an intuitive basis. Suppose that p percent of those in the treatment group are converted from untreated to treated by their assignment to the treatment group. Suppose that for those whose treatment status is changed by treatment assignment (the subjects in the treatment group who are Compliers), the average change in Y caused by the treatment is Π. How is the average outcome of those subjects assigned to the treatment group changed by the fact that they were given a random assignment to the treatment, rather than the control group?

The observed average value of Y for the treatment group is altered by $p\Pi$, the share of the treatment group affected by the treatment assignment multiplied by the average treatment effect for compliers. If the control group subjects are not affected by the experiment, and the treatment assignment is random, then the difference between the treatment and control group outcome will be on average $p\Pi$. To recover the average effect of the treatment on compliers, divide this difference by p. The average treatment effect on those who are induced to receive treatment by the experiment is therefore equal to the ratio on the left-hand side of (9): the difference in average group outcomes, inflated by dividing this by the change in the probability the treatment is delivered to a subject.

If treatment groups are formed by random assignment, the left-hand side of (9) can be estimated using the sample analogues for the left-hand side quantities. The ITT effect for Y is estimated by the mean difference in outcomes between the treatment and control group and the ITT for D is estimated by the mean difference in treatment rates in the treatment and control group. Equivalently, the LATE can also be estimated using two-stage least squares (2SLS), where subject outcomes are regressed on a variable for receipt of treatment, and treatment assignment is used as an instrument for receipt of treatment. Note that for the simplest case, where no one in the control group is treated and the treatment rate in the treatment group equals c, the LATE is equal to $\frac{ITT_Y}{c}$, where the numerator is the ITT estimate for Y, which is then inflated by the inverse of the treatment rate.

A basic point of Angrist et al.'s analysis is that while some estimate can always be calculated, the estimate is the causal effect of the treatment only when the set of assumptions listed above are satisfied. These conditions are illustrated using an example in which there is failure to treat the treatment group, but treatment is unavailable to the control group. Suppose that after random assignment to treatment and control groups, investigators attempt to contact and then treat the treatment group. The treatment is unavailable to the control group. Examples of this design are get-out-the-vote canvassing experiments, where there is typically failure to treat some of those assigned to the treatment group. Let us now consider how the assumptions presented above apply to this example.

Exclusion restriction. The exclusion restriction is violated when treatment assignment has a direct effect on a subject's outcome. In the example considered here subjects are not aware of their treatment group status (Z), and so they cannot change their behavior based on Z directly. However, it is possible that third parties can observe the treatment assignment. For example, a campaign worker might observe the list of persons assigned to be contacted for get-out-the-vote and then concentrate persuasive messages on these households. This violation of the exclusion restriction causes bias.

SUTVA. Recall that SUTVA requires that the treatment received by a subject does not alter the outcome for other subjects. The SUTVA assumption will fail if, for example, a subject's probability of voting is affected by the treatment of their neighbors. If an experiment that contains multiple members of a household is analyzed at the individual rather than the household level, SUTVA is violated if a subject's probability of voting is a function of whether another member of the household is treated. More generally, spillover effects are a source of violation of SUTVA. If there are decreasing returns to repeat treatments, spillovers will reduce the difference between the average treatment and control group outcomes without changing the recorded treatment rates. As a result, this violation of SUTVA will bias the estimated treatment effect toward zero.

Monotonicity. In the get-out-the-vote example each subject has a zero chance of getting the treatment when assigned to the control group, and therefore monotonicity is satisfied by the experimental design.

Nonzero effect of treatment assignment on the probability of treatment. This assumption is satisfied by the experimental design so long as some members of the assigned treatment group are successfully contacted.

A few final comments on estimating treatment effects when there is noncompliance:

The population proportion of Compliers is a function of population characteristics and the experimental design. The approach presented above produces an estimate of the average treatment effect for Compliers, but which subjects are Compliers may vary with the experimental design. An implication of this is that if the experimental protocols reach different types of subjects and the treatment rates are low, the treatment effect estimate for the same treatment may change across experiments. In order to detect heterogeneous treatment effects, the experimenter may wish to vary the efforts made to reach those assigned to the treatment group.

Generalization of average treatment effects beyond the Compliers requires additional assumptions. When there is noncompliance, the treatment effect estimate applies to Compliers, not the entire subject population. Statements about the effect of treating the entire population require assumptions about the similarity of treatment effects for Compliers and the rest of the subjects.

There is no assumption of homogeneous treatment effects. While both experimental and observational research often implicitly assumes constant treatment effects, the treatment effect estimated by 2SLS is the average treatment effect for Compliers. If homogeneous treatment effects are assumed, then LATE = ATT = ATE.

Given noncompliance, it is sometimes impossible to determine which particular individuals are Compliers. When no members of the control group can get the treatment, which subjects are Compliers can be directly observed, since they are the subjects in the treatment group who get the treatment. However, in situations where it is possible to be treated regardless of group assignment, the exact subjects who are the Compliers cannot be determined. Angrist et al. (1996) offer as an example the natural experiment produced by the Vietnam draft lottery. Those with low lottery numbers were more likely to enter the military than those with high numbers, but some people with high numbers did get "treated." This suggests that some subjects would have joined the military regardless of their draft number. Subjects who get treated regardless of their group assignment are called "Always Takers;" they are people for whom $D_1 = 1$ and $D_0 = 1$. Since some of the subjects assigned to the treatment group are Always Takers, the set of treated subjects in the treatment group is a mix of Always Takers and Compliers. This mix of subjects cannot be divided into Compliers and Always Takers, since an individual subject's behavior in the counterfactual assignment is never observed.

In sum, problems of noncompliance present a set of design challenges for field experimental researchers. Awareness of these problems leads researchers to gather data on levels of compliance in the treatment and control groups, so that local average treatment effects may be estimated. It also encourages researchers to think about which core assumptions—SUTVA, monotonicity, exclusion, and nonzero assignment effects—are likely to be problematic in any given application and to design experiments so as to minimize these concerns.

6 ATTRITION

Less tractable are the problems associated with attrition. Attrition occurs when outcomes are unobserved for certain observations. Consider a simple example of an intervention designed to encourage political parties in closed-list systems to nominate women candidates as regional representatives. The outcomes for this study are $Y = 1$ (a woman is nominated), $Y = 0$ (no women are nominated), and $Y = ?$ (the investigator does not know whether a woman is nominated). Suppose that the experimental results indicate that 50 percent of the jurisdictions in the treatment group had women nominees, 20 percent did not, and 30 percent remain unknown. The corresponding rates for the control group are 40 percent, 20 percent, and 40 percent. In the absence of any other information about these jurisdictions and the reasons why their outcomes are observed or unobserved, this set of results is open to competing interpretations. One could exclude missing data from the analysis, in which case the estimated treatment effect is $.50/(.50 + .20) - .40/(.40 + .20) = .05$. Alternatively, one could assume that those whose outcomes were not observed failed to field women candidates, in which case the estimated treatment effect is .10. Or, following Manski (1990), one could calculate the bounds around the estimated effect by assuming the most extreme possible outcomes. For example, if none of the treatment group's missing observations fielded women candidates, but all of the missing observations in the control group did so, the treatment effect would be $.50 - .80 = -.30$. Conversely, if the missing observations in the treatment group are assumed to be $Y = 1$, but missing observations in the control group are assumed to be $Y = 0$, the estimated treatment effect becomes $.80 - .40 = .40$. As this example illustrates, the bounds $\{-.30, .40\}$ admit an uncomfortably large range of potential values.

The indeterminacy created by attrition can in principle be reduced by imposing some theoretical structure on the data. Imputation models, for example, attempt to use observed covariates to forecast the outcomes for missing values (Imbens and Rubin 1997; Dunn, Maracy, and Tomenson 2005). This approach will generate unbiased estimates under special conditions that may or may not hold for any given application. In situations where data are missing in a fashion that is random conditional on covariates, this approach will be superior to excluding missing data or substituting the unconditional mean. On the other hand, it is possible to construct examples in which imputation exacerbates the problem of bias, as when missing data arise due to systematic factors that are not captured by observed covariates.

Although the consequences of attrition are always to some degree speculative, certain experimental designs are better able than others to allay concerns about attrition. Consider, for example, Howell and Peterson's (2004) analysis of the effects of school vouchers on students' standardized test scores. From a pool of voucher applicants, a subset of voucher recipients was chosen at random. Outcomes were measured by a test administered privately to both voucher recipients and nonrecipients, but recipients were more likely to take the test than nonrecipients. Thus, Howell and Peterson faced a situation in which attrition rates differed between treatment and control groups. The fact that they administered an academic baseline test prior to random assignment enabled them to assess whether attrition was related to academic ability as gauged in the pre-test. This example provides another instance in which covariates, although not strictly necessary for experimental analysis, play a useful role.

7 NATURAL EXPERIMENTS AND DISCONTINUITY DESIGNS

In contrast to randomized experiments, where a randomization procedure ensures unbiased causal inference, natural experiments and regression discontinuity designs use near-random assignment to approximate experimentation. When evaluating near-random research designs, the key methodological issue is whether the treatment is unrelated to unmeasured determinants of the dependent variable. The plausibility of this claim will depend on substantive assumptions. For example, studies of lottery windfalls on consumption (Imbens, Rubin, and Sacerdote 2001) and political attitudes (Doherty, Gerber, and Green 2006) have invoked assumptions about the comparability of lottery players who win varying amounts in distinct lotteries over time. Although plausible, these assumptions are potentially flawed (lottery players may change over time), resulting in biased estimates. Note that the mere possibility of bias means that the reported standard errors potentially understate the mean squared error associated with the estimates for the reasons spelled out in Gerber, Green, and Kaplan (2004).

Regression discontinuity designs attempt to address concerns about bias by looking at sharp breakpoints that make seemingly random distinctions between units that receive a treatment and those that do not. When, for example, one gauges the effects of legislature size on municipal spending by taking advantage of the fact that Scandinavian countries mandate changes in legislature size as a step function of local population size (Pettersson-Lidbom 2004), the key assumption is that the change in legislature size is effectively random in the immediate vicinity of a population threshold that necessitates a change in legislative size. When the legislature changes in size as the municipal population grows from 4,999 to 5,000, is there an abrupt change in municipal spending? A hypothetical example of this kind of discontinuity is illustrated in Figure 50.1. In the vicinity of the discontinuity in legislative size, there is an abrupt shift in government expenditures.[2] The practical problem with this type of design is that the data are typically sparse in the immediate vicinity of a breakpoint, requiring the analyst to include observations that are farther away and therefore potentially contaminated by other factors. The standard remedy for this problem is to control for these factors through use of covariates, such as polynomial functions of the variable (in this example, population size) on which the discontinuity is based. Pettersson-Lidbom (2004) demonstrates the robustness of his estimates across a variety of specifications, but as always there remains a residuum of uncertainty about whether municipal spending patterns reflect unmeasured aspects of population change.

Even if one isolates a causal effect produced by a discontinuity, problems of interpretation remain. Posner (2004) argues that ethnic groups residing on the border of Zambia and Malawi provide an opportunity to study the effects of party competition and ethnic coalitions. The argument is that Chewa and Tumbuka peoples are more in conflict on the Malawi side of the border than the Zambian side, because they together comprise a much larger proportion of the overall Malawi electorate in a winner-takes-all presidential system. Here the issue is one of internal validity. Conceivably, the observed contrast in inter-group relations could be attributed to any difference between the two countries. In an attempt to bolster his interpretation, Posner attempts to rule out differences in economic status, proximity to roads, and colonial history as potential sources of cross-border variation.

---

[2] Pettersson-Lidbom (2004) actually finds little evidence of a link between legislature size and government expenditures in Scandinavia.

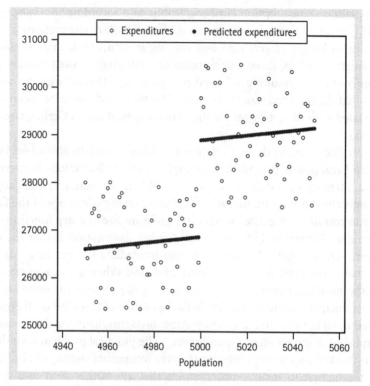

Fig. 50.1. Example of a regression discontinuity

Note: In this hypothetical example, inspired by Pettersson-Lidbom (2004), the number of seats in a local legislature increases abruptly when a town passes the population cutoff of 5,000 residents. The hypothesis tested here is whether local government expenditures (the Y-axis) increase in the vicinity of this breakpoint, presumably due to the exogenous change in legislative size.

8 ASSORTED METHODOLOGICAL ISSUES IN THE DESIGN AND ANALYSIS OF EXPERIMENTS

Various aspects of design, analysis, and inference have important implications for the pursuit of long-term objectives, such as the generation of unbiased research literatures that eventually isolate the causal parameters of interest. This section briefly summarizes several of the leading issues.

8.1 Balance and Stratification

Random assignment is designed to create treatment and control groups that are balanced in terms of both observed and unobserved attributes. As N approaches infinity, the experimental groups become perfectly balanced. In finite samples, random

assignment may create groups that, by chance, are unbalanced. Experimental procedures remain unbiased in small samples, in that there will be no systematic tendency
for imbalance to favor the treatment group. Yet there remains the question of what to
do about the prospect or occurrence of observed imbalances between treatment and
control groups.

If information about covariates is available in advance of an experiment (perhaps
due to the administration of a pre-test), a researcher can potentially reduce sampling
variability of the estimated treatment effect by stratification or blocking. For example,
if gender were thought to be a strong predictor of an experimental outcome, one
might divide the sample into men and women, randomly assigning a certain fraction of each gender group to the treatment condition. This procedure ensures that
gender is uncorrelated with treatment assignment. This procedure may be extended
to include a list of background covariates. Within each type of attribute (e.g. women
over sixty-five years of age, with less than a high school degree), the experimenter
randomly assigns observations to treatment and control groups.

Alternatively, the researcher could stratify after the experiment is conducted by
including the covariates as control variables in a multivariate model. The inclusion
of covariates has the potential to increase the precision with which the treatment
effect is estimated so long as the predictive accuracy of the covariates offsets the loss
of degrees of freedom. The same principle applies also to pre-stratification; adding
the strata-generating covariates as control variables may improve the precision of the
experimental estimates by reducing disturbance variance.

Four practical issues accompany the use of covariates. First, although covariates
potentially make for more precise experimental estimates, the covariates in question
must predict the dependent variable. To the extent that covariates (or nonlinear functions of the covariates or interactions among covariates) have little predictive value,
their inclusion may actually make the treatment estimates less precise. The same goes
for nonparametric methods such as matching, which suspend the usual assumptions
about the linear and additive effects of the covariates, but throw out a certain portion
of the observations for which the correspondence between treatment and control
covariates is deemed to be inadequate. Second, the use of covariates creates the
potential for mischief insofar as researchers have discretion about what covariates to
include in their analysis. The danger is that researchers will pick and choose among
alternative specifications based on how the results turn out. This procedure has the
potential to introduce bias. A third issue concerns potential interactions between the
treatment and one or more covariate. Researchers often find subgroup differences.
Again, the exploration of interactions raises the distinction between planned and
unplanned comparisons. When interactions are specified according to an *ex ante*
plan, the sampling distribution is well defined. When interactions are proposed after
the researcher explores the data, the sampling distribution is no longer well defined.
The results should be regarded as provisional pending confirmation in a new sample.
Fourth, a common use of covariates occurs when the experimenter administers a pre-
test prior to the start of an intervention. Pre-tests, however, may lead subjects to infer
the nature and purpose of the experiment, thereby contaminating the results.

8.2 Publication Bias

An important source of bias that afflicts both observational and experimental research is publication bias. If the size and statistical significance of experimental results determine whether they are reported in the scholarly publications, a synthesis of research findings may produce a grossly misleading estimate of the true causal effect. Consider, for example, the distortions that result when an intervention that is thought to contribute to democratic stability is evaluated using a one-tailed hypothesis test. If statistically insignificant results go unreported, the average reported result will exaggerate the intervention's true effect.

Publication bias in experimental research literatures has several tell-tale symptoms. For one-tailed tests of the sort described above, studies based on small sample sizes should tend to report larger treatment effects than studies based on large sample sizes. The reason is that small-N studies require larger effect sizes in order to achieve statistical significance. A similar diagnostic device applies to two-tailed tests; the relationship between sample size and effect size should resemble a funnel. More generally, the observed sampling distribution of experimental results will not conform to the sampling distribution implied by the nominal standard errors associated with the individual studies. Inconclusive studies will be missing from the sampling distribution. The threat of publication bias underscores the tension between academic norms, which often stress the importance of presenting conclusive results, and scientific progress, which depends on unbiased reporting conventions.

8.3 Extrapolation

Any experiment, whether conducted in the lab or field, raises questions about generalizability. To what extent do the findings hold for other settings? To what extent do they hold for other dosages or types of interventions? These questions raise important epistemological questions about the conditions under which one can safely generalize beyond the confines of a particular intervention and experimental setting. These questions have been the subject of lively, ongoing debate (Heckman and Smith 1995; Moffitt 2004).

Scholars have approached this issue in two complementary ways. The first is to bring to bear theories about the isomorphism of different treatments and contexts. Often, this type of theoretical argument is based on isolating the essential features of a given treatment or context. For example, one might say of the Gerber et al. (2009) study of the effects of newspaper exposure that the key ingredients are the political topics covered by the newspapers, the manner in which they are presented, the care and frequency with which they are read, and the partisanship and political sophistication of the people who are induced to read as a result of the intervention.

The theoretical exercise of isolating what are believed to be the primary characteristics of the treatment, setting, and recipients directs an empirical agenda of experimental extensions. By varying the nature of the treatment, how it is delivered, and to whom, the experimenter gradually assembles a set of empirical propositions about the conditions under which the experimental effect is strong or weak. Note that this empirical agenda potentially unifies various forms of experimental social science by asking whether lab experiments, survey experiments, and natural experiments converge on similar answers and, if not, why the experimental approach generates discrepant results. This process of empirical replication and extension in turn helps refine theory by presenting a set of established facts that it must explain.

8.4 Power and Replication

Often field experiments face practical challenges that limit their size and scope. For example, suppose one were interested in the effects of a political campaign commercial on 100,000 television viewers' voting preferences. Ideally, one would randomly assign small units such as households or blocks to treatment and control groups; as a practical matter, it may only be possible to assign a small number of large geographic units to treatment and control. If individuals living near one another share unobserved attributes that predict their voting preferences, this kind of clustered randomization greatly reduces the power of the study (Raudenbush 1997). Indeed, it is possible to construct examples in which such an experiment has very little chance of rejecting a null hypothesis of no effect.

How should one proceed in this case? Although any given study may have limited diagnostic value, the accumulation of studies generates an informative posterior distribution. Unlike the failure to publish insignificant results, the failure to embark on low-power studies does not lead to bias, but it does slow the process of scientific discovery. In the words of Campbell and Stanley (1963, 3), we must

justify experimentation on more pessimistic grounds—not as a panacea, but rather at the only available route to cumulative progress. We must instill in our students the expectation of tedium and disappointment and the duty of thorough persistence, by now so well achieved in the biological and physical sciences.

9 METHODOLOGICAL VALUE OF EXPERIMENTS

Beyond the substantive knowledge that they generate, field experiments have the potential to make a profound methodological contribution. Rather than evaluate statistical methods in terms of the abstract plausibility of their underlying assumptions, researchers in the wake of LaLonde (1986) have made the performance of statistical methods an empirical question, by comparing estimates based on observational data to experimental benchmarks. Experimentation has been buoyed in part by the lackluster performance of statistical techniques designed to correct the deficiencies of observational data. Arceneaux et al. (2006), for example, find a wide disparity between experimental estimates and estimates obtained using observational methods such as matching or regression. This finding echoes results in labor economics and medicine, where observational methods have enjoyed mixed success in approximating experimental benchmarks (Heckman et al. 1998; Concato, Shah, and Horwitz 2000; Glazerman, Levy, and Myers 2003). By making the performance of observational methods an empirical research question, field experimentation is changing the terms of debate in the field of political methodology.

References

ADAMS, W. C. and SMITH, D. J. 1980. Effects of telephone canvassing on turnout and preferences: a field experiment. *Public Opinion Quarterly*, 44: 53–83.

ANGRIST, J. D., IMBENS, G. W., and RUBIN, D. B. 1996. Identification of casual effects using instrumental variables. *Journal of the American Statistical Association*, 91: 444–55.

ANSOLABEHERE, S., SNYDER, J. M., JR., and STEWART, C., III 2000. Old voters, new voters, and the personal vote: using redistricting to measure the incumbency advantage. *American Journal of Political Science*, 44: 17–34.

ARCENEAUX, K., GERBER, A. S., and GREEN, D. P. 2006. Comparing experimental and matching methods using a large-scale voter mobilization experiment. *Political Analysis*, 14: 1–36.

BENZ, M. and MEIER, S. 2006. Do people behave in experiments as in the field? Evidence from donations. Institute for Empirical Research in Economics Working Paper No. 248.

CAMPBELL, D. T. and STANLEY, J. C. 1963. *Experimental and Quasi-Experimental Designs for Research*. Boston: Houghton-Mifflin.

CARDY, E. A. 2005. An experimental field study of the GOTV and persuasion effects of partisan direct mail and phone calls. *Annals of the American Academy of Political and Social Science*, 601: 28–40.

CHAPIN, F. S. 1947. *Experimental Designs in Sociological Research*. New York: Harper and Brothers.

CHATTOPADHYAY, R. and DUFLO, E. 2004. Women as policy makers: evidence from a randomized policy experiment in India. *Econometrica*, 72: 1409–43.

CHIN, M. L., BOND, J. R., and GEVA, N. 2000. A foot in the door: an experimental study of PAC and constituency effects on access. *Journal of Politics*, 62: 534–49.

CONCATO, J., SHAH, N., and HORWITZ, R. I. 2000. Randomized, controlled trials, observational studies, and the hierarchy of research designs. *New England Journal of Medicine*, 342: 1887–92.

COVER, A. D. and BRUMBERG, B. S. 1982. Baby books and ballots: the impact of congressional mail on constituent opinion. *American Political Science Review*, 76: 347–59.

DOHERTY, D., GERBER, A. S., and GREEN, D. P. 2006. Personal income and attitudes toward redistribution: a study of lottery winners. *Political Psychology*, 27: 441–58.

DUNN, G., MARACY, M., and TOMENSON, B. 2005. Estimating treatment effects from randomized clinical trials with noncompliance and loss to follow-up: the role of instrumental variables methods. *Statistical Methods in Medical Research*, 14: 369–95.

ELDERSVELD, S. J. 1956. Experimental propaganda techniques and voting behavior. *American Political Science Review*, 50: 154–65.

GERBER, A. S. and GREEN, D. P., 2000. The effects of canvassing, direct mail, and telephone contact on voter turnout: a field experiment. *American Political Science Review*, 94: 653–63.

———— and KAPLAN, E. H. 2004. The illusion of learning from observational research. Pp. 251–73 in *Problems and Methods in the Study of Politics*, ed. I. Shapiro, R. Smith, and T. Massoud. New York: Cambridge University Press.

—— KARLAN, D. S., and BERGAN, D. 2009. Does the media matter? A field experiment measuring the effect of newspapers on voting behavior and political opinions. *American Economic Journal: Applied Economics*.

GLAZERMAN, S., LEVY, D. M., and MYERS, D. 2003. Nonexperimental versus experimental estimates of earnings impacts. *Annals of the American Academy of Political and Social Science*, 589: 63–93.

GOSNELL, H. F. 1927. *Getting-out-the-Vote: An Experiment in the Stimulation of Voting*. Chicago: University of Chicago Press.

GUAN, M. and GREEN, D. P. 2006. Non-coercive mobilization in state-controlled elections: an experimental study in Beijing. *Comparative Political Studies*, 39: 1175–93.

HABYARIMANA, J., HUMPHREYS, M., POSNER, D., and WEINSTEIN, J. 2007. *The Co-ethnic Advantage*.

HARRISON, G. W., and LIST, J. A. 2004. Field experiments. *Journal of Economic Literature*, 42: 1009–55.

HASTINGS, J. S., KANE, T. J., STAIGER, D. O., and WEINSTEIN, J. M. 2005. Economic outcomes and the decision to vote: the effect of randomized school admissions on voter participation. Unpublished manuscript, Department of Economics, Yale University.

HECKMAN, J. J. and SMITH, J. A. 1995. Assessing the case for social experiments. *Journal of Economic Perspectives*, 9: 85–110.

—— ICHIMURA, H., SMITH, J., and TODD, P. 1998. Matching as an econometric evaluation estimator. *Review of Economic Studies*, 65: 261–94.

HOLLAND, P. W. 1986. Statistics and causal inference. *Journal of the American Statistical Association*, 81: 945–60.

HOWELL, W. C. and PETERSON, P. E. 2004. Uses of theory in randomized field trials: lessons from school voucher research on disaggregation, missing data, and the generalization of findings. *Anerican Behavioral Scientist*, 47: 634–57.

HYDE, S. D. 2006. Foreign democracy promotion, norm development and democratization: explaining the causes and consequences of internationally monitored elections. Unpublished doctoral thesis, Department of Political Science, University of California, San Diego.

IMBENS, G. W. and RUBIN, D. B. 1997. Bayesian inference for causal effects in randomized experiments with noncompliance. *Annals of Statistics*, 25: 305–27.

———— and SACERDOTE, B. I. 2001. Estimating the effect of unearned income on labor earnings, savings, and consumption: evidence from a survey of lottery winners. *American Economic Review*, 91: 778–94.

JOHNSON, J. B., JOSLYN, R. A., and REYNOLDS, H. T. 2001. *Political Science Research Methods*, 4th edn. Washington, DC: CQ Press.

KING, G., KEOHANE, R. O., and VERBA, S. 1994. *Designing Social Inquiry*. Princeton, NJ: Princeton University Press.

KLING, J. R., LUDWIG, J., and KATZ, L. F. 2005. Neighborhood effects on crime for female and male youth: evidence from a randomized housing voucher experiment. *Quarterly Journal of Economics*, 120: 87–130.

LALONDE, R. J. 1986. Evaluating the econometric evaluations of training programs with experimental data. *American Economic Review*, 76: 604–20.

LIJPHART, A. 1971. Comparative politics and the comparative method. *American Political Science Review*, 65: 682–93.

LOWELL, A. L. 1910. The physiology of politics. *American Political Science Review*, 4: 1–15.

MAHONEY, J. and RUESCHEMEYER, D. (eds.) 2003. *Comparative Historical Analysis in the Social Sciences*. New York: Cambridge University Press.

MANSKI, C. F. 1990. Nonparametric bounds on treatment effects. *American Economic Review Papers and Proceedings*, 80: 319–23.

MICHELSON, M. R. 2003. Getting out the Latino vote: how door-to-door canvassing influences voter turnout in rural central California. *Political Behavior*, 25: 247–63.

MIGUEL, E. and KREMER, M. 2004. Worms: identifying impacts on education and health in the presence of treatment externalities. *Econometrica*, 72: 159–217.

——SATYANATH, S., and SERGENTI, E. 2004. Economic shocks and civil conflict: an instrumental variables approach. *Journal of Political Economy*, 112: 725–53.

MILLER, R. E., BOSITIS, D. A., and BAER, D. L. 1981. Stimulating voter turnout in a primary: field experiment with a precinct committeeman. *International Political Science Review*, 2: 445–60.

MOFFITT, R. A. 2004. The role of randomized field trials in social science research: a perspective from evaluations of reforms of social welfare programs. *American Behavioral Scientist*, 47: 506–40.

NEWHOUSE, J. P. 1993. *Free for All? Lessons from the RAND Health Insurance Experiment*. Boston: Harvard University Press.

NEYMAN, J. 1923. On the application of probability theory to agricultural experiments. Essay on principles. Section 9. *Roczniki Nauk Roiniczych*, 10: 1–51; repr. in English in *Statistical Science*, 5 (1990): 463–80.

NICKERSON, D. W. 2008. Is voting contagious? Evidence from two field experiments. *American Political Science Review*, 102: 49–57.

OLKEN, B. A. 2005. Monitoring corruption: evidence from a field experiment in Indonesia. NBER Working Paper 11753.

PECHMAN, J. A. and TIMPANE, P. M. (eds.) 1975. *Work Incentives and Income Guarantees: The New Jersey Negative Income Tax Experiment*. Washington, DC: Brookings Institution.

PETTERSSON-LIDBOM, P. 2004. Does the size of the legislature affect the size of government? Evidence from two natural experiments. Unpublished manuscript, Department of Economics, Stockholm University.

POSNER, D. N. 2004. The political salience of cultural difference: why Chewas and Tumbukas are allies in Zambia and adversaries in Malawi. *American Political Science Review*, 98: 529–45.

RAUDENBUSH, S. W. 1997. Statistical analysis and optimal design for cluster randomized trials. *Psychological Methods*, 2: 173–85.

RUBIN, D. B. 1978. Bayesian inference for causal effects: the role of randomization. *Annals of Statistics*, 6: 34–58.

——1990. Comment: Neyman (1923) and causal inference in experiments and observational studies. *Statistical Science*, 5 (4): 472–80.

SEARS, D. O. 1986. College sophomores in the laboratory: influences of a narrow database on social-psychology's view of human nature. *Journal of Personality and Social Psychology*, 51: 515–30.

SHERMAN, L. W. and ROGAN, D. P. 1995. Deterrent effects of police raids on crack houses: a randomized, controlled experiment. *Justice Quarterly*, 12: 755–81.

WANTCHEKON, L. 2003. Clientelism and voting behavior: evidence from a field experiment in Benin. *World Politics*, 55: 399–422.

CHAPTER 51

THE CASE STUDY

WHAT IT IS AND WHAT IT DOES

JOHN GERRING

Two centuries after Le Play's pioneering work, the various disciplines of the social sciences continue to produce a vast number of case studies, many of which have entered the pantheon of classic works. Judging by the large volume of recent scholarly output the case study research design plays a central role in anthropology, archeology, business, education, history, medicine, political science, psychology, social work, and sociology (Gerring 2007a, ch. 1). Even in economics and political economy, fields not usually noted for their receptiveness to case-based work, there has been something of a renaissance. Recent studies of economic growth have turned to case studies of unusual countries such as Botswana, Korea, and Mauritius.[1] Debates on the relationship between trade and growth and the IMF and growth have likewise combined cross-national regression evidence with in-depth (quantitative and qualitative) case analysis (Srinivasan and Bhagwati 1999; Vreeland 2003). Work on ethnic politics and ethnic conflict has exploited within-country variation or small-N cross-country comparisons (Abadie and Gardeazabal 2003; Chandra 2004; Posner 2004). By the standard of praxis, therefore, it would appear that the method of the case study is solidly ensconced, perhaps even thriving. Arguably, we are witnessing a movement away from a variable-centered approach to causality in the social sciences and towards a case-based approach.

---

[1] Acemoglu, Johnson, and Robinson (2003), Chernoff and Warner (2002), Rodrik (2003). See also studies focused on particular firms or regions, e.g. Coase (1959; 2000).

Indeed, the statistical analysis of cross-case observational data has been subjected to increasing scrutiny in recent years. It no longer seems self-evident, even to nomothetically inclined scholars, that non-experimental data drawn from nation-states, cities, social movements, civil conflicts, or other complex phenomena should be treated in standard regression formats. The complaints are myriad, and oft-reviewed.[2] They include: (a) the problem of arriving at an adequate specification of the causal model, given a plethora of plausible models, and the associated problem of modeling interactions among these covariates; (b) identification problems, which cannot always be corrected by instrumental variable techniques; (c) the problem of "extreme" counterfactuals, i.e. extrapolating or interpolating results from a general model where the extrapolations extend beyond the observable data points; (d) problems posed by influential cases; (e) the arbitrariness of standard significance tests; (f) the misleading precision of point estimates in the context of "curve-fitting" models; (g) the problem of finding an appropriate estimator and modeling temporal auto-correlation in pooled time series; (h) the difficulty of identifying causal mechanisms; and last, but certainly not least, (i) the ubiquitous problem of faulty data drawn from a variety of questionable sources. Most of these difficulties may be understood as the by-product of causal variables that offer limited variation through time and cases that are extremely heterogeneous.

A principal factor driving the general discontent with cross-case observational research is a new-found interest in experimental models of social scientific research. Following the pioneering work of Donald Campbell (1988; Cook and Campbell 1979) and Donald Rubin (1974), methodologists have taken a hard look at the regression model and discovered something rather obvious but at the same time crucially important: this research bears only a faint relationship to the true experiment, for all the reasons noted above. The current excitement generated by matching estimators, natural experiments, and field experiments may be understood as a move toward a quasi-experimental, and frequently case-based analysis of causal relations. Arguably, this is because the experimental ideal is often better approximated by a small number of cases that are closely related to one another, or by a single case observed over time, than by a large sample of heterogeneous units.

A third factor militating towards case-based analysis is the development of a series of alternatives to the standard linear/additive model of cross-case analysis, thus establishing a more variegated set of tools to capture the complexity of social behavior (see Brady and Collier 2004). Charles Ragin and associates have shown us how to deal with situations where multiple causal paths lead to the same set of outcomes, a series of techniques known as Qualitative Comparative Analysis (QCA) ("Symposium: Qualitative Comparative Analysis" 2004). Andrew Abbott has worked out a method that maps causal sequences across cases, known as optimal sequence matching (Abbott 2001; Abbott and Forrest 1986; Abbott and Tsay 2000). Bear Braumoeller, Gary Goertz, Jack Levy, and Harvey Starr have defended the

---

[2] For general discussion of the following points see Achen (1986), Freedman (1991), Kittel (1999, 2005), Kittel and Winner (2005), Manski (1993), Winship and Morgan (1999), Winship and Sobel (2004).

importance of necessary-condition arguments in the social sciences, and have shown how these arguments might be analyzed (Braumoeller and Goertz 2000; Goertz 2003; Goertz and Levy forthcoming; Goertz and Starr 2003). James Fearon, Ned Lebow, Philip Tetlock, and others have explored the role of counterfactual thought experiments in the analysis of individual case histories (Fearon 1991; Lebow 2000; Tetlock and Belkin 1996). Colin Elman has developed a typological method of analyzing cases (Elman 2005). David Collier, Jack Goldstone, Peter Hall, James Mahoney, and Dietrich Rueschemeyer have worked to revitalize the comparative and comparative-historical methods (Collier 1993; Goldstone 1997; Hall 2003; Mahoney and Rueschemeyer 2003). And scores of researchers have attacked the problem of how to convert the relevant details of a temporally constructed narrative into standardized formats so that cases can be meaningfully compared (Abell 1987, 2004; Abbott 1992; Buthe 2002; Griffin 1993). While not all of these techniques are, strictly speaking, case study techniques—since they sometimes involve a large number of cases—they do move us closer to a case-based understanding of causation insofar as they preserve the texture and detail of individual cases, features that are often lost in large-N cross-case analysis.

A fourth factor concerns the recent marriage of rational choice tools with case study analysis, sometimes referred to as an "analytic narrative" (Bates et al. 1998). Whether the technique is qualitative or quantitative, scholars equipped with economic models are turning, increasingly, to case studies in order to test the theoretical predictions of a general model, investigate causal mechanisms, and/or explain the features of a key case.

Finally, epistemological shifts in recent decades have enhanced the attractiveness of the case study format. The "positivist" model of explanation, which informed work in the social sciences through most of the twentieth century, tended to downplay the importance of causal mechanisms in the analysis of causal relations. Famously, Milton Friedman (1953) argued that the only criterion of a model was to be found in its accurate prediction of outcomes. The verisimilitude of the model, its accurate depiction of reality, was beside the point. In recent years, this explanatory trope has come under challenge from "realists," who claim (among other things) that causal analysis should pay close attention to causal mechanisms (e.g. Bunge 1997; Little 1998). Within political science and sociology, the identification of a specific mechanism—a causal pathway—has come to be seen as integral to causal analysis, regardless of whether the model in question is formal or informal or whether the evidence is qualitative or quantitative (Achen 2002; Elster 1998; George and Bennett 2005; Hedstrom and Swedberg 1998). Given this new-found (or at least newly self-conscious) interest in mechanisms, it is not surprising that social scientists would turn to case studies as a mode of causal investigation.

For all the reasons stated above, one might intuit that social science is moving towards a case-based understanding of causal relations. Yet, this movement, insofar as it exists, has scarcely been acknowledged, and would certainly be challenged by many close observers—including some of those cited in the foregoing passages.

The fact is that the case study research design is still viewed by most methodologists with extreme circumspection. A work that focuses its attention on a single example of a broader phenomenon is apt to be described as a "mere" case study, and is often identified with loosely framed and non-generalizable theories, biased case selection, informal and undisciplined research designs, weak empirical leverage (too many variables and too few cases), subjective conclusions, non-replicability, and causal determinism. To some, the term case study is an ambiguous designation covering a multitude of "inferential felonies."[3]

The quasi-mystical qualities associated with the case study persist to this day. In the field of psychology, a gulf separates "scientists" engaged in cross-case research and "practitioners" engaged in clinical research, usually focused on several cases (Hersen and Barlow 1976, 21). In the fields of political science and sociology, case study researchers are acknowledged to be on the "soft" side of hard disciplines. And across fields, the persisting case study orientations of anthropology, education, law, social work, and various other fields and subfields relegate them to the non-rigorous, non-systematic, non-scientific, non-positivist end of the academic spectrum.

The methodological status of the case study is still, officially, suspect. Even among its defenders there is confusion over the virtues and vices of this ambiguous research design. Practitioners continue to ply their trade but have difficulty articulating what it is they are doing, methodologically speaking. The case study survives in a curious methodological limbo.

This leads to a paradox: although much of what we know about the empirical world has been generated by case studies and case studies continue to constitute a large proportion of work generated by the social science disciplines, the case study *method* is poorly understood.

How can we make sense of the profound disjuncture between the acknowledged contributions of this genre to the various disciplines of social science and its maligned status within these disciplines? If case studies are methodologically flawed, why do they persist? Should they be rehabilitated, or suppressed? How fruitful *is* this style of research?

In this chapter, I provide a reconstructed definition of the case study approach to research with special emphasis on comparative politics, a field that has been closely identified with this method since its birth. Based on this definition, I then explore a series of contrasts between case study and cross-case study research. These contrasts are intended to illuminate the characteristic strengths and weaknesses ("affinities") of these two research designs, not to vindicate one or the other. The effort of this chapter is to understand this persisting methodological debate as a matter of tradeoffs. Case studies and cross-case studies explore the world in different ways. Yet, properly con- stituted, there is no reason that case study results cannot be synthesized with results

---

[3] Achen and Snidal (1989, 160). See also Geddes (1990; 2003), Goldthorpe (1997), King, Keohane, and Verba (1994), Lieberson (1985, 107–15; 1992; 1994), Lijphart (1971, 683–4), Odell (2004), Sekhon (2004), Smelser (1973, 45, 57). It should be noted that these writers, while critical of the case study format, are not necessarily opposed to case studies per se (that is to say, they should not be classified as *opponents* of the case study).

gained from cross-case analysis, and vice versa. My hope, therefore, is that this chapter will contribute to breaking down the boundaries that have separated these rival genres within the subfield of comparative politics.

1 Definitions

The key term of this chapter is, admittedly, a definitional morass. To refer to a work as a "case study" might mean: that its method is qualitative, small-N; that the research is holistic, thick (a more or less comprehensive examination of a phenomenon); that it utilizes a particular type of evidence (e.g. ethnographic, clinical, non-experimental, non-survey based, participant observation, process tracing, historical, textual, or field research); that its method of evidence gathering is naturalistic (a "real-life context"); that the research investigates the properties of a single observation; or that the research investigates the properties of a single phenomenon, instance, or example. Evidently, researchers have many things in mind when they talk about case study research. Confusion is compounded by the existence of a large number of near-synonyms—single unit, single subject, single case, N = 1, case based, case control, case history, case method, case record, case work, clinical research, and so forth. As a result of this profusion of terms and meanings, proponents and opponents of the case study marshal a wide range of arguments but do not seem any closer to agreement than when this debate was first broached several decades ago.

Can we reconstruct this concept in a clearer, more productive fashion? In order to do so we must understand how the key terms—case and case study—are situated within a neighborhood of related terms. In this crowded semantic field, each term is defined in relation to others. And in the context of a specific work or research terrain, they all take their meaning from a specific inference. (The reader should bear in mind that any change in the inference, and the meaning of all the key terms will probably change.) My attempt here will be to provide a single, determinate, definition of these key terms. Of course, researchers may choose to define these terms in many different ways. However, for purposes of methodological discussion it is helpful to enforce a uniform vocabulary.

Let us stipulate that a *case* connotes a spatially delimited phenomenon (a unit) observed at a single point in time or over some period of time. It comprises the sort of phenomena that an inference attempts to explain. Thus, in a study that attempts to explain certain features of nation-states, cases are comprised of nation-states (across some temporal frame). In a study that attempts to explain the behavior of individuals, individuals comprise the cases. And so forth. Each case may provide a single observation or multiple (within-case) observations.

For students of comparative politics, the archetypal case is the dominant political unit of our time, the nation-state. However, the study of smaller social and political units (regions, cities, villages, communities, social groups, families) or specific institutions (political parties, interest groups, businesses) is equally common in other subfields, and perhaps increasingly so in comparative politics. Whatever the chosen unit, the methodological issues attached to the case study have nothing to do with the size of the individual cases. A case may be created out of any phenomenon so long as it has identifiable boundaries and comprises the primary object of an inference.

Note that the spatial boundaries of a case are often more apparent than its temporal boundaries. We know, more or less, where a country begins and ends, even though we may have difficulty explaining *when* a country begins and ends. Yet, some temporal boundaries must be assumed. This is particularly important when cases consist of discrete events—crises, revolutions, legislative acts, and so forth—within a single unit. Occasionally, the temporal boundaries of a case are more obvious than its spatial boundaries. This is true when the phenomena under study are eventful but the unit undergoing the event is amorphous. For example, if one is studying terrorist attacks it may not be clear how the spatial unit of analysis should be understood, but the events themselves may be well bounded.

A *case study* may be understood as the intensive study of a single case for the purpose of understanding a larger class of cases (a population). Case study research may incorporate several cases. However, at a certain point it will no longer be possible to investigate those cases intensively. At the point where the emphasis of a study shifts from the individual case to a sample of cases we shall say that a study is *cross-case*. Evidently, the distinction between a case study and cross-case study is a continuum. The fewer cases there are, and the more intensively they are studied, the more a work merits the appellation case study. Even so, this proves to be a useful distinction, for much follows from it.

A few additional terms will now be formally defined.

An *observation* is the most basic element of any empirical endeavor. Conventionally, the number of observations in an analysis is referred to with the letter N. (Confusingly, N may also be used to designate the number of cases in a study, a usage that I shall try to avoid.) A single observation may be understood as containing several dimensions, each of which may be measured (across disparate observations) as a variable. Where the proposition is causal, these may be subdivided into *dependent* (Y) and *independent* (X) variables. The dependent variable refers to the outcome of an investigation. The independent variable refers to the explanatory (causal) factor, that which the outcome is supposedly dependent on.

Note that a case may consist of a single observation ($N = 1$). This would be true, for example, in a cross-sectional analysis of multiple cases. In a case study, however, the case under study always provides more than one observation. These may be constructed diachronically (by observing the case or some subset of within-case units through time) or synchronically (by observing within-case variation at a single point in time).

This is a clue to the fact that case studies and cross-case usually operate at different levels of analysis. The case study is typically focused on within-case variation (if there a cross-case component it is probably secondary). The cross-case study, as the name suggests, is typically focused on cross-case variation (if there is also within-case variation, it is secondary in importance). They have the same object in view—the explanation of a population of cases—but they go about this task differently.

A *sample* consists of whatever cases are subjected to formal analysis; they are the immediate subject of a study or case study. (Confusingly, the sample may also refer to the observations under study, and will be so used at various points in this narrative. But at present, we treat the sample as consisting of cases.) Technically, one might say that in a case study the sample consists of the case or cases that are subjected to intensive study. However, usually when one uses the term sample one is implying that the number of cases is rather large. Thus, "sample-based work" will be understood as referring to large-N cross-case methods—the opposite of case study work. Again, the only feature distinguishing the case study format from a sample-based (or "cross-case") research design is the number of cases falling within the sample—one or a few versus many. Case studies, like large-N samples, seek to represent, in all ways relevant to the proposition at hand, a population of cases. A series of case studies might therefore be referred to as a sample if they are relatively brief and relatively numerous; it is a matter of emphasis and of degree. The more case studies one has, the less intensively each one is studied, and the more confident one is in their representativeness (of some broader population), the more likely one is to describe them as a sample rather than a series of case studies. For practical reasons—unless, that is, a study is extraordinarily long—the case study research format is usually limited to a dozen cases or less. A single case is not at all unusual.

The sample rests within a *population* of cases to which a given proposition refers. The population of an inference is thus equivalent to the breadth or scope of a proposition. (I use the terms *proposition*, *hypothesis*, *inference*, and *argument* interchangeably.) Note that most samples are not exhaustive; hence the use of the term sample, referring to *sampling* from a population. Occasionally, however, the sample equals the population of an inference; all potential cases are studied.

For those familiar with the rectangular form of a dataset it may be helpful to conceptualize observations as rows, variables as columns, and cases as either groups of observations or individual observations.

2 WHAT IS A CASE STUDY GOOD FOR? CASE STUDY VERSUS CROSS-CASE ANALYSIS

I have argued that the case study approach to research is most usefully defined as the intensive study of a single unit or a small number of units (the cases), for the purpose of understanding a larger class of similar units (a population of cases). This

Table 51.1. Case study and cross-case research designs: affinities and trade-offs

	Affinity	
	Case study	Cross-case study
Research goals		
1. Hypothesis	Generating	Testing
2. Validity	Internal	External
3. Causal insight	Mechanisms	Effects
4. Scope of proposition	Deep	Broad
Empirical factors		
5. Population of cases	Heterogeneous	Homogeneous
6. Causal strength	Strong	Weak
7. Useful variation	Rare	Common
8. Data availability	Concentrated	Dispersed

is put forth as a minimal definition of the topic.[4] I now proceed to discuss the *non-definitional* attributes of the case study—attributes that are often, but not invariably, associated with the case study method. These will be understood as methodological affinities flowing from a minimal definition of the concept.[5]

The case study research design exhibits characteristic strengths and weaknesses relative to its large-N cross-case cousin. These tradeoffs derive, first of all, from basic research goals such as (1) whether the study is oriented toward hypothesis generating or hypothesis testing, (2) whether internal or external validity is prioritized, (3) whether insight into causal mechanisms or causal effects is more valuable, and (4) whether the scope of the causal inference is deep or broad. These tradeoffs also hinge on the shape of the empirical universe, i.e. (5) whether the population of cases under study is heterogeneous or homogeneous, (6) whether the causal relationship of interest is strong or weak, (7) whether useful variation on key parameters within that population is rare or common, and (8) whether available data are concentrated or dispersed.

Along each of these dimensions, case study research has an affinity for the first factor and cross-case research has an affinity for the second, as summarized in Table 51.1. To clarify, these tradeoffs represent methodological *affinities*, not invariant laws. Exceptions can be found to each one. Even so, these general tendencies are often noted in case study research and have been reproduced in multiple disciplines and subdisciplines over the course of many decades.

[4] My intention is to include only those attributes commonly associated with the case study method that are *always* implied by our use of the term, excluding those attributes that are sometimes violated by standard usage. Thus, I chose not to include "ethnography" as a defining feature of the case study, since many case studies (so called) are not ethnographic. For further discussion of minimal definitions see Gerring (2001, ch. 4), Gerring and Barresi (2003), Sartori (1976).

[5] These additional attributes might also be understood as comprising an ideal-type ("maximal") definition of the topic (Gerring 2001, ch. 4; Gerring and Barresi 2003).

It should be stressed that each of these tradeoffs carries a ceteris paribus caveat. Case studies are more useful for generating new hypotheses, *all other things being equal*. The reader must bear in mind that many additional factors also rightly influence a writer's choice of research design, and they may lean in the other direction. Ceteris are not always paribus. One should not jump to conclusions about the research design appropriate to a given setting without considering the entire range of issues involved—some of which may be more important than others.

3 HYPOTHESIS: GENERATING VERSUS TESTING

Social science research involves a quest for new theories as well as a testing of existing theories; it is comprised of both "conjectures" and "refutations."[6] Regrettably, social science methodology has focused almost exclusively on the latter. The conjectural element of social science is usually dismissed as a matter of guesswork, inspiration, or luck—a leap of faith, and hence a poor subject for methodological reflection.[7] Yet, it will readily be granted that many works of social science, including most of the acknowledged classics, are seminal rather than definitive. Their classic status derives from the introduction of a new idea or a new perspective that is subsequently subjected to more rigorous (and refutable) analysis. Indeed, it is difficult to devise a program of falsification the first time a new theory is proposed. Path-breaking research, almost by definition, is protean. Subsequent research on that topic tends to be more definitive insofar as its primary task is limited: to verify or falsify a pre-existing hypothesis. Thus, the world of social science may be usefully divided according to the predominant goal undertaken in a given study, either hypothesis *generating* or hypothesis *testing*. There are two moments of empirical research, a lightbulb moment and a skeptical moment, each of which is essential to the progress of a discipline.[8]

Case studies enjoy a natural advantage in research of an exploratory nature. Several millennia ago, Hippocrates reported what were, arguably, the first case studies ever

---

[6] Popper (1969).

[7] Karl Popper (quoted in King, Keohane, and Verba 1994, 14) writes: "there is no such thing as a logical method of having new ideas ... Discovery contains 'an irrational element,' or a 'creative intuition.'" One recent collection of essays and interviews takes new ideas as its special focus (Munck and Snyder 2007), though it may be doubted whether there are generalizable results.

[8] Gerring (2001, ch. 10). The tradeoff between these two styles of research is implicit in Achen and Snidal (1989), who criticize the case study for its deficits in the latter genre but also acknowledge the benefits of the case study along the former dimension (1989, 167–8). Reichenbach also distinguished between a "context of discovery," and a "context of justification." Likewise, Peirce's concept of *abduction* recognizes the importance of a generative component in science.

conducted. They were fourteen in number.[9] Darwin's insights into the process of human evolution came after his travels to a few select locations, notably Easter Island. Freud's revolutionary work on human psychology was constructed from a close observation of fewer than a dozen clinical cases. Piaget formulated his theory of human cognitive development while watching his own two children as they passed from childhood to adulthood. Lévi-Strauss's structuralist theory of human cultures built on the analysis of several North and South American tribes. Douglass North's neo-institutionalist theory of economic development was constructed largely through a close analysis of a handful of early developing states (primarily England, the Netherlands, and the United States).[10] Many other examples might be cited of seminal ideas that derived from the intensive study of a few key cases.

Evidently, the sheer number of examples of a given phenomenon does not, by itself, produce insight. It may only confuse. How many times did Newton observe apples fall before he recognized the nature of gravity? This is an apocryphal example, but it illustrates a central point: case studies may be more useful than cross-case studies when a subject is being encountered for the first time or is being considered in a fundamentally new way. After reviewing the case study approach to medical research, one researcher finds that although case reports are commonly regarded as the lowest or weakest form of evidence, they are nonetheless understood to comprise "the first line of evidence." The hallmark of case reporting, according to Jan Vandenbroucke, "is to recognize the unexpected." This is where discovery begins.[11]

The advantages that case studies offer in work of an exploratory nature may also serve as impediments in work of a confirmatory/disconfirmatory nature. Let us briefly explore why this might be so.[12]

Traditionally, scientific methodology has been defined by a segregation of conjecture and refutation. One should not be allowed to contaminate the other.[13] Yet, in the real world of social science, inspiration is often associated with perspiration. "Lightbulb" moments arise from a close engagement with the particular facts of a particular case. Inspiration is more likely to occur in the laboratory than in the shower.

The circular quality of conjecture and refutation is particularly apparent in case study research. Charles Ragin notes that case study research is all about "casing"— defining the topic, including the hypothesis(es) of primary interest, the outcome, and the set of cases that offer relevant information vis-à-vis the hypothesis.[14] A study of the French Revolution may be conceptualized as a study of revolution, of social revolution, of revolt, of political violence, and so forth. Each of these topics entails a different population and a different set of causal factors. A good deal of authorial intervention is necessary in the course of defining a case study topic, for there is a great deal of evidentiary leeway. Yet, the "subjectivity" of case study research allows for the generation of a great number of hypotheses, insights that might not be apparent

---

[9] Bonoma (1985, 199). Some of the following examples are discussed in Patton (2002, 245).
[10] North and Weingast (1989); North and Thomas (1973).   [11] Vandenbroucke (2001, 331).
[12] For discussion of this trade-off in the context of economic growth theory see Temple (1999, 120).
[13] Geddes (2003), King, Keohane, and Verba (1994), Popper (1934/1968).   [14] Ragin (1992).

to the cross-case researcher who works with a thinner set of empirical data across a large number of cases and with a more determinate (fixed) definition of cases, variables, and outcomes. It is the very fuzziness of case studies that grants them an advantage in research at the exploratory stage, for the single-case study allows one to test a multitude of hypotheses in a rough-and-ready way. Nor is this an entirely "conjectural" process. The relationships discovered among different elements of a single case have a prima facie causal connection: they are all at the scene of the crime. This is revelatory when one is at an early stage of analysis, for at that point there is no identifiable suspect and the crime itself may be difficult to discern. The fact that A, B, and C are present at the expected times and places (relative to some outcome of interest) is sufficient to establish them as independent variables. Proximal evidence is all that is required. Hence, the common identification of case studies as "plausibility probes," "pilot studies," "heuristic studies," "exploratory" and "theory-building" exercises.[15]

A large-N cross-study, by contrast, generally allows for the testing of only a few hypotheses but does so with a somewhat greater degree of confidence, as is appropriate to work whose primary purpose is to test an extant theory. There is less room for authorial intervention because evidence gathered from a cross-case research design can be interpreted in a limited number of ways. It is therefore more reliable. Another way of stating the point is to say that while case studies lean toward Type 1 errors (falsely rejecting the null hypothesis), cross-case studies lean toward Type 2 errors (failing to reject the false null hypothesis). This explains why case studies are more likely to be paradigm generating, while cross-case studies toil in the prosaic but highly structured field of normal science.

I do not mean to suggest that case studies never serve to confirm or disconfirm hypotheses. Evidence drawn from a single case may falsify a necessary or sufficient hypothesis, as discussed below. Additionally, case studies are often useful for the purpose of elucidating causal mechanisms, and this obviously affects the plausibility of an X/Y relationship. However, general theories rarely offer the kind of detailed and determinate predictions on within-case variation that would allow one to reject a hypothesis through pattern matching (without additional cross-case evidence). Theory testing is not the case study's strong suit. The selection of "crucial" cases is at pains to overcome the fact that the cross-case N is minimal. Thus, one is unlikely to reject a hypothesis, or to consider it definitively proved, on the basis of the study of a single case.

Harry Eckstein himself acknowledges that his argument for case studies as a form of theory confirmation is largely hypothetical. At the time of writing, several decades ago, he could not point to any social science study where a crucial case study had performed the heroic role assigned to it.[16] I suspect that this is still more or less true. Indeed, it is true even of experimental case studies in the natural sciences. "We must recognize," note Donald Campbell and Julian Stanley,

---

[15] Eckstein (1975), Ragin (1992; 1997), Rueschemeyer and Stephens (1997).   [16] Eckstein (1975).

that continuous, multiple experimentation is more typical of science than once-and-for-all definitive experiments. The experiments we do today, if successful, will need replication and cross-validation at other times under other conditions before they can become an established part of science ... [E]ven though we recognize experimentation as the basic language of proof ... we should not expect that "crucial experiments" which pit opposing theories will be likely to have clear-cut outcomes. When one finds, for example, that competent observers advocate strongly divergent points of view, it seems likely on a priori grounds that both have observed something valid about the natural situation, and that both represent a part of the truth. The stronger the controversy, the more likely this is. Thus we might expect in such cases an experimental outcome with mixed results, or with the balance of truth varying subtly from experiment to experiment. The more mature focus ... avoids crucial experiments and instead studies dimensional relationships and interactions along many degrees of the experimental variables.[17]

A single case study is still a single shot—a single example of a larger phenomenon.

The tradeoff between hypothesis generating and hypothesis testing helps us to reconcile the enthusiasm of case study researchers and the skepticism of case study critics. They are both right, for the looseness of case study research is a boon to new conceptualizations just as it is a bane to falsification.

4 VALIDITY: INTERNAL VERSUS EXTERNAL

Questions of validity are often distinguished according to those that are *internal* to the sample under study and those that are *external* (i.e. applying to a broader—unstudied—population). Cross-case research is always more representative of the population of interest than case study research, so long as some sensible procedure of case selection is followed (presumably some version of random sampling). Case study research suffers problems of representativeness because it includes, by definition, only a small number of cases of some more general phenomenon. Are the men chosen by Robert Lane typical of white, immigrant, working-class, American males?[18] Is Middletown representative of other cities in America?[19] These sorts of questions forever haunt case study research. This means that case study research is generally weaker with respect to external validity than its cross-case cousin.

The corresponding virtue of case study research is its internal validity. Often, though not invariably, it is easier to establish the veracity of a causal relationship pertaining to a single case (or a small number of cases) than for a larger set of cases. Case study researchers share the bias of experimentalists in this regard: they tend to be more disturbed by threats to within-sample validity than by threats to out-of-sample validity. Thus, it seems appropriate to regard the tradeoff between external

---

[17] Campbell and Stanley (1963, 3).   [18] Lane (1962).   [19] Lynd and Lynd (1929/1956).

and internal validity, like other tradeoffs, as intrinsic to the cross-case/single-case choice of research design.

5 Causal Insight: Causal Mechanisms versus Causal Effects

A third tradeoff concerns the sort of insight into causation that a researcher intends to achieve. Two goals may be usefully distinguished. The first concerns an estimate of the causal *effect*; the second concerns the investigation of a causal *mechanism* (i.e. pathway from X to Y).

By causal effect I refer to two things: (a) the magnitude of a causal relationship (the expected effect on Y of a given change in X across a population of cases) and (b) the relative precision or uncertainty associated with that point estimate. Evidently, it is difficult to arrive at a reliable estimate of causal effects across a population of cases by looking at only a single case or a small number of cases. (The one exception would be an experiment in which a given case can be tested repeatedly, returning to a virgin condition after each test. But here one faces inevitable questions about the representativeness of that much-studied case.)[20] Thus, the estimate of a causal effect is almost always grounded in cross-case evidence.

It is now well established that causal arguments depend not only on measuring causal effects, but also on the identification of a causal mechanism.[21] X must be connected with Y in a plausible fashion; otherwise, it is unclear whether a pattern of covariation is truly causal in nature, or what the causal interaction might be. Moreover, without a clear understanding of the causal pathway(s) at work in a causal relationship it is impossible to accurately specify the model, to identify possible instruments for the regressor of interest (if there are problems of endogeneity), or to interpret the results.[22] Thus, causal mechanisms are presumed in every estimate of a mean (average) causal effect.

In the task of investigating causal mechanisms, cross-case studies are often not so illuminating. It has become a common criticism of large-N cross-national research—e.g. into the causes of growth, democracy, civil war, and other

---

[20] Note that the intensive study of a single unit may be a perfectly appropriate way to estimate causal effects *within that unit*. Thus, if one is interested in the relationship between welfare benefits and work effort in the United States one might obtain a more accurate assessment by examining data drawn from the USA alone, rather than crossnationally. However, since the resulting generalization does not extend beyond the unit in question it is not a case study in the usual sense.

[21] Achen (2002), Dessler (1991), Elster (1998), George and Bennett (2005), Gerring (2005), Hedstrom and Swedberg (1998), Mahoney (2001), Tilly (2001).

[22] In a discussion of instrumental variables in two-stage least-squares analysis, Angrist and Krueger (2001: 8) note that "good instruments often come from detailed knowledge of the economic mechanism, institutions determining the regressor of interest."

national-level outcomes—that such studies demonstrate correlations between inputs and outputs without clarifying the reasons for those correlations (i.e. clear causal pathways). We learn, for example, that infant mortality is strongly correlated with state failure;[23] but it is quite another matter to interpret this finding, which is consistent with a number of different causal mechanisms. Sudden increases in infant mortality might be the product of famine, of social unrest, of new disease vectors, of government repression, and of countless other factors, some of which might be expected to impact the stability of states, and others of which are more likely to be a result of state instability.

Case studies, if well constructed, may allow one to peer into the box of causality to locate the intermediate factors lying between some structural cause and its purported effect. Ideally, they allow one to "see" X and Y interact—Hume's billiard ball crossing the table and hitting a second ball.[24] Barney Glaser and Anselm Strauss point out that in fieldwork "general relations are often discovered *in vivo*; that is, the field worker literally sees them occur."[25] When studying decisional behavior case study research may offer insight into the intentions, the reasoning capabilities, and the information-processing procedures of the actors involved in a given setting. Thus, Dennis Chong uses in-depth interviews with a very small sample of respondents in order to better understand the process by which people reach decisions about civil liberties issues. Chong comments:

One of the advantages of the in-depth interview over the mass survey is that it records more fully how subjects arrive at their opinions. While we cannot actually observe the underlying mental process that gives rise to their responses, we can witness many of its outward manifestations. The way subjects ramble, hesitate, stumble, and meander as they formulate their answers tips us off to how they are thinking and reasoning through political issues.[26]

Similarly, the investigation of a single case may allow one to test the causal implications of a theory, thus providing corroborating evidence for a causal argument. This is sometimes referred to as pattern matching (Campbell 1988).

Dietrich Rueschemeyer and John Stephens offer an example of how an examination of causal mechanisms may call into question a general theory based on cross-case evidence. The thesis of interest concerns the role of British colonialism in fostering democracy among postcolonial regimes. In particular, the authors investigate the diffusion hypothesis, that democracy was enhanced by "the transfer of British governmental and representative institutions and the tutoring of the colonial people in the ways of British government." On the basis of in-depth analysis of several cases the authors report:

---

[23] Goldstone et al. (2000).

[24] This has something to do with the existence of process-tracing evidence, a matter discussed below. But it is not necessarily predicated on this sort of evidence. Sensitive time-series data, another specialty of the case study, is also relevant to the question of causal mechanisms.

[25] Glaser and Strauss (1967, 40).

[26] Chong (1993, 868). For other examples of in-depth interviewing see Hochschild (1981), Lane (1962).

We did find evidence of this diffusion effect in the British settler colonies of North America and the Antipodes; but in the West Indies, the historical record points to a different connection between British rule and democracy. There the British colonial administration opposed suffrage extension, and only the white elites were "tutored" in the representative institutions. But, critically, we argued on the basis of the contrast with Central America, British colonialism did prevent the local plantation elites from controlling the local state and responding to the labor rebellion of the 1930s with massive repression. Against the adamant opposition of that elite, the British colonial rulers responded with concessions which allowed for the growth of the party–union complexes rooted in the black middle and working classes, which formed the backbone of the later movement for democracy and independence. Thus, the narrative histories of these cases indicate that the robust statistical relation between British colonialism and democracy is produced only in part by diffusion. The interaction of class forces, state power, and colonial policy must be brought in to fully account for the statistical result. [27]

Whether or not Rueschemeyer and Stephens are correct in their conclusions need not concern us here. What is critical, however, is that any attempt to deal with this question of causal mechanisms is heavily reliant on evidence drawn from case studies. In this instance, as in many others, the question of causal pathways is simply too difficult, requiring too many poorly measured or unmeasurable variables, to allow for accurate cross-sectional analysis. [28]

To be sure, causal mechanisms do not always require explicit attention. They may be quite obvious. And in other circumstances, they may be amenable to cross-case investigation. For example, a sizeable literature addresses the causal relationship between trade openness and the welfare state. The usual empirical finding is that more open economies are associated with higher social welfare spending. The question then becomes why such a robust correlation exists. What are the plausible interconnections between trade openness and social welfare spending? One possible causal path, suggested by David Cameron, [29] is that increased trade openness leads to greater domestic economic vulnerability to external shocks (due, for instance, to changing terms of trade). If so, one should find a robust correlation between annual variations in a country's terms of trade (a measure of economic vulnerability) and social welfare spending. As it happens, the correlation is not robust and this leads some commentators to doubt whether the putative causal mechanism proposed by David Cameron and many others is actually at work. [30] Thus, in instances where an intervening variable can be effectively operationalized across a large sample of cases it may be possible to test causal mechanisms without resorting to case study investigation. [31]

Even so, the opportunities for investigating causal pathways are generally more apparent in a case study format. Consider the contrast between formulating a standardized survey for a large group of respondents and formulating an in-depth interview with a single subject or a small set of subjects, such as that undertaken by

[27] Rueschemeyer and Stephens (1997, 62).
[28] Other good examples of within-case research that shed light on a broader theory can be found in Martin (1992); Martin and Swank (2004); Thies (2001); Young (1999).
[29] Cameron (1978).   [30] Alesina, Glaeser, and Sacerdote (2001).
[31] For additional examples of this nature, see Feng (2003); Papyrakis and Gerlagh (2003); Ross (2001).

Dennis Chong in the previous example. In the latter situation, the researcher is able to probe into details that would be impossible to delve into, let alone anticipate, in a standardized survey. She may also be in a better position to make judgements as to the veracity and reliability of the respondent. Tracing causal mechanisms is about cultivating sensitivity to a local context. Often, these local contexts are essential to cross-case testing. Yet, the same factors that render case studies useful for micro-level investigation also make them less useful for measuring mean (average) causal effects. It is a classic tradeoff.

6 SCOPE OF PROPOSITION: DEEP VERSUS BROAD

The utility of a case study mode of analysis is in part a product of the scope of the causal argument that a researcher wishes to prove or demonstrate. Arguments that strive for great breadth are usually in greater need of cross-case evidence; causal arguments restricted to a small set of cases can more plausibly subsist on the basis of a single-case study. The extensive/intensive tradeoff is fairly commonsensical.[32] A case study of France probably offers more useful evidence for an argument about Europe than for an argument about the whole world. Propositional breadth and evidentiary breadth generally go hand in hand.

Granted, there are a variety of ways in which single-case studies can credibly claim to provide evidence for causal propositions of broad reach—e.g. by choosing cases that are especially representative of the phenomenon under study ("typical" cases) or by choosing cases that represent the most difficult scenario for a given proposition and are thus biased against the attainment of certain results ("crucial" cases). Even so, a proposition with a narrow scope is more conducive to case study analysis than a proposition with a broad purview, all other things being equal. The breadth of an inference thus constitutes one factor, among many, in determining the utility of the case study mode of analysis. This is reflected in the hesitancy of many case study researchers to invoke determinate causal propositions with great reach—"covering laws," in the idiom of philosophy of science.

By the same token, one of the primary virtues of the case study method is the depth of analysis that it offers. One may think of depth as referring to the detail, richness, completeness, wholeness, or the degree of variance in an outcome that is accounted for by an explanation. The case study researcher's complaint about the thinness of cross-case analysis is well taken; such studies often have little to say about individual cases. Otherwise stated, cross-case studies are likely to explain only a small portion of the variance with respect to a given outcome. They approach that outcome at a very

---

[32] Eckstein (1975, 122).

general level. Typically, a cross-case study aims only to explain the occurrence/non-occurrence of a revolution, while a case study might also strive to explain specific features of that event—why it occurred when it did and in the way that it did. Case studies are thus rightly identified with "holistic" analysis and with the "thick" description of events.[33]

Whether to strive for breadth or depth is not a question that can be answered in any definitive way. All we can safely conclude is that researchers invariably face a choice between knowing more about less, or less about more. The case study method may be defended, as well as criticized, along these lines.[34] Indeed, arguments about the "contextual sensitivity" of case studies are perhaps more precisely (and fairly) understood as arguments about depth and breadth. The case study researcher who feels that cross-case research on a topic is insensitive to context is usually not arguing that *nothing at all* is consistent across the chosen cases. Rather, the case study researcher's complaint is that much more could be said—accurately—about the phenomenon in question with a reduction in inferential scope.[35]

Indeed, I believe that a number of traditional issues related to case study research can be understood as the product of this basic tradeoff. For example, case study research is often lauded for its holistic approach to the study of social phenomena in which behavior is observed in natural settings. Cross-case research, by contrast, is criticized for its construction of artificial research designs that decontextualize the realm of social behavior by employing abstract variables that seem to bear little relationship to the phenomena of interest.[36] These associated congratulations and critiques may be understood as a conscious choice on the part of case study researchers to privilege depth over breadth.

7 THE POPULATION OF CASES: HETEROGENEOUS VERSUS HOMOGENEOUS

The choice between a case study and cross-case style of analysis is driven not only by the goals of the researcher, as reviewed above, but also by the shape of the empirical universe that the researcher is attempting to understand. Consider, for starters, that the logic of cross-case analysis is premised on some degree of cross-unit comparability (unit homogeneity). Cases must be similar to each other in whatever respects might affect the causal relationship that the writer is investigating, or such differences must be controlled for. Uncontrolled heterogeneity means that cases are "apples and oranges;" one cannot learn anything about underlying causal processes by comparing

---

[33] I am using the term "thick" in a somewhat different way than in Geertz (1973).
[34] See Ragin (2000, 22).
[35] Ragin (1987, ch. 2). Herbert Blumer's (1969, ch. 7) complaints, however, are more far-reaching.
[36] Orum, Feagin, and Sjoberg (1991, 7).

their histories. The underlying factors of interest mean different things in different contexts (conceptual stretching) or the X/Y relationship of interest is different in different contexts (unit heterogeneity).

Case study researchers are often suspicious of large-sample research, which, they suspect, contains heterogeneous cases whose differences cannot easily be modeled. "Variable-oriented" research is said to involve unrealistic "homogenizing assumptions."[37] In the field of international relations, for example, it is common to classify cases according to whether they are deterrence failures or deterrence successes. However, Alexander George and Richard Smoke point out that "the separation of the dependent variable into only two subclasses, deterrence success and deterrence failure," neglects the great variety of ways in which deterrence can fail. Deterrence, in their view, has many independent causal paths (causal equifinality), and these paths may be obscured when a study lumps heterogeneous cases into a common sample.[38]

Another example, drawn from clinical work in psychology, concerns heterogeneity among a sample of individuals. Michel Hersen and David Barlow explain:

Descriptions of results from 50 cases provide a more convincing demonstration of the effectiveness of a given technique than separate descriptions of 50 individual cases. The major difficulty with this approach, however, is that the category in which these clients are classified most always becomes unmanageably heterogeneous. "Neurotics," [for example], ... may have less in common than any group of people one would choose randomly. When cases are described individually, however, a clinician stands a better chance of gleaning some important information, since specific problems and specific procedures are usually described in more detail. When one lumps cases together in broadly defined categories, individual case descriptions are lost and the ensuing report of percentage success becomes meaningless.[39]

Under circumstances of extreme case heterogeneity, the researcher may decide that she is better off focusing on a single case or a small number of relatively homogeneous cases. Within-case evidence, or cross-case evidence drawn from a handful of most-similar cases, may be more useful than cross-case evidence, even though the ultimate interest of the investigator is in a broader population of cases. (Suppose one has a population of very heterogeneous cases, one or two of which undergo quasi-experimental transformations. Probably, one gains greater insight into causal patterns throughout the population by examining these cases in detail than by undertaking some large-N cross-case analysis.) By the same token, if the cases available for study are relatively homogeneous, then the methodological argument for cross-case analysis is correspondingly strong. The inclusion of additional cases is unlikely to compromise the results of the investigation because these additional cases are sufficiently similar to provide useful information.

The issue of population heterogeneity/homogeneity may be understood, therefore, as a tradeoff between N (observations) and K (variables). If, in the quest to explain a particular phenomenon, each potential case offers only one observation and also

[37] Ragin (2000, 35). See also Abbott (1990); Bendix (1963); Meehl (1954); Przeworski and Teune (1970, 8–9); Ragin (1987; 2004, 124); Znaniecki (1934, 250–1).
[38] George and Smoke (1974, 514).   [39] Hersen and Barlow (1976, 11).

requires one control variable (to neutralize heterogeneities in the resulting sample), then one loses degrees of freedom with each additional case. There is no point in using cross-case analysis or in extending a two-case study to further cases. If, on the other hand, each additional case is relatively cheap—if no control variables are needed or if the additional case offers more than one useful observation (through time)—then a cross-case research design may be warranted.[40] To put the matter more simply, when adjacent cases are unit homogeneous the addition of more cases is easy, for there is no (or very little) heterogeneity to model. When adjacent cases are heterogeneous additional cases are expensive, for every added heterogeneous element must be correctly modeled, and each modeling adjustment requires a separate (and probably unverifiable) assumption. The more background assumptions are required in order to make a causal inference, the more tenuous that inference is; it is not simply a question of attaining statistical significance. The ceteris paribus assumption at the core of all causal analysis is brought into question. In any case, the argument between case study and cross-case research designs is not about causal complexity per se (in the sense in which this concept is usually employed), but rather about the tradeoff between N and K in a particular empirical realm, and about the ability to model case heterogeneity through statistical legerdemain.[41]

Before concluding this discussion it is important to point out that researchers' judgements about case comparability are not, strictly speaking, matters that can be empirically verified. To be sure, one can look—and ought to look—for empirical patterns among potential cases. If those patterns are strong then the assumption of case comparability seems reasonably secure, and if they are not then there are grounds for doubt. However, debates about case comparability usually concern borderline instances. Consider that many phenomena of interest to social scientists are not rigidly bounded. If one is studying democracies there is always the question of how to define a democracy, and therefore of determining how high or low the threshold for inclusion in the sample should be. Researchers have different ideas about this, and these ideas can hardly be tested in a rigorous fashion. Similarly, there are long-standing disputes about whether it makes sense to lump poor and rich societies together in a single sample, or whether these constitute distinct populations. Again, the borderline between poor and rich (or "developed" and "undeveloped") is blurry, and the notion of hiving off one from the other for separate analysis questionable, and unresolvable on purely empirical grounds. There is no safe (or "conservative") way to proceed. A final sticking point concerns the cultural/historical component of social phenomena. Many case study researchers feel that to compare societies with vastly different cultures and historical trajectories is meaningless. Yet, many cross-case researchers feel that to restrict one's analytic focus to a single cultural or geographic

---

[40] Shalev (1998).

[41] To be sure, if adjacent cases are *identical*, the phenomenon of interest is *invariant* then the researcher gains nothing at all by studying more examples of a phenomenon, for the results obtained with the first case will simply be replicated. However, virtually all phenomena of interest to social scientists have some degree of heterogeneity (cases are not identical), some stochastic element. Thus, the theoretical possibility of identical, invariant cases is rarely met in practice.

region is highly arbitrary, and equally meaningless. In these situations, it is evidently the choice of the researcher how to understand case homogeneity/heterogeneity across the potential populations of an inference. Where do like cases end and unlike cases begin?

Because this issue is not, strictly speaking, empirical it may be referred to as an *ontological* element of research design. An ontology is a vision of the world as it really is, a more or less coherent set of assumptions about how the world works, a research *Weltanschauung* analogous to a Kuhnian paradigm.[42] While it seems odd to bring ontological issues into a discussion of social science methodology it may be granted that social science research is not a purely empirical endeavor. What one finds is contingent upon what one looks for, and what one looks for is to some extent contingent upon what one expects to find. Stereotypically, case study researchers tend to have a "lumpy" vision of the world; they see countries, communities, and persons as highly individualized phenomena. Cross-case researchers, by contrast, have a less differentiated vision of the world; they are more likely to believe that things are pretty much the same everywhere, at least as respects basic causal processes. These basic assumptions, or ontologies, drive many of the choices made by researchers when scoping out appropriate ground for research.

8 CAUSAL STRENGTH: STRONG VERSUS WEAK

Regardless of whether the population is homogeneous or heterogeneous, causal relationships are easier to study if the causal effect is strong, rather than weak. Causal "strength," as I use the term here, refers to the magnitude and consistency of X's effect on Y across a population of cases. (It invokes both the shape of the evidence at hand and whatever priors might be relevant to an interpretation of that evidence.) Where X has a strong effect on Y it will be relatively easy to study this relationship. Weak relationships, by contrast, are often difficult to discern. This much is commonsensical, and applies to all research designs.

For our purposes, what is significant is that weak causal relationships are particularly opaque when encountered in a case study format. Thus, there is a methodological affinity between weak causal relationships and large-N cross-case analysis, and between strong causal relationships and case study analysis.

This point is clearest at the extremes. The strongest species of causal relationships may be referred to as *deterministic*, where X is assumed to be necessary and/or sufficient for Y's occurrence. A necessary and sufficient cause accounts for all of the variation on Y. A sufficient cause accounts for all of the variation in certain instances of Y. A necessary cause accounts, by itself, for the absence of Y. In all three situations,

---

[42] Gutting (1980); Hall (2003); Kuhn (1962/1970); Wolin (1968).

the relationship is usually assumed to be perfectly consistent, i.e. invariant. There are no exceptions.

It should be clear why case study research designs have an easier time addressing causes of this type. Consider that a deterministic causal proposition can be *disproved* with a single case.[43] For example, the reigning theory of political stability once stipulated that only in countries that were relatively homogeneous, or where existing heterogeneity was mitigated by cross-cutting cleavages, would social peace endure.[44] Arend Lijphart's case study of the Netherlands, a country with reinforcing social cleavages and very little social conflict, disproved this deterministic theory on the basis of a single case.[45] (One may dispute whether the original theory is correctly understood as deterministic. However, if it *is*, then it has been decisively refuted by a single case study.) *Proving* an invariant causal argument generally requires more cases. However, it is not nearly as complicated as proving a probabilistic argument for the simple reason that one assumes invariant relationships; consequently, the single case under study carries more weight.

Magnitude and consistency—the two components of causal strength—are usually matters of degree. It follows that the more tenuous the connection between X and Y, the more difficult it will be to address in a case study format. This is because the causal mechanisms connecting X with Y are less likely to be detectable in a single case when the total impact is slight or highly irregular. It is no surprise, therefore, that the case study research design has, from the very beginning, been associated with causal arguments that are deterministic, while cross-case research has been associated with causal arguments that are assumed to be minimal in strength and "probabilistic" in consistency.[46] (Strictly speaking, causal magnitude and consistency are independent features of a causal relationship. However, because they tend to covary, and because we tend to conceptualize them in tandem, I treat them as components of a single dimension.)

Now, let us now consider an example drawn from the other extreme. There is generally assumed to be a weak relationship between regime type and economic performance. Democracy, if it has any effect on economic growth at all, probably has only a slight effect over the near-to-medium term, and this effect is probably characterized by many exceptions (cases that do not fit the general pattern). This is because many things other than democracy affect a country's growth performance and because there may be a significant stochastic component in economic growth (factors that cannot be modeled in a general way). Because of the diffuse nature of this relationship it will probably be difficult to gain insight by looking at a single case. Weak relationships are difficult to observe in one instance. Note that even if there seems to be a strong relationship between democracy and economic growth

---

[43] Dion (1998).

[44] Almond (1956); Bentley (1908/1967); Lipset (1960/1963); Truman (1951).

[45] Lijphart (1968); see also Lijphart (1969). For additional examples of case studies disconfirming general propositions of a deterministic nature see Allen (1965); Lipset, Trow, and Coleman (1956); Njolstad (1990); discussion in Rogowski (1995).

[46] Znaniecki (1934). See also discussion in Robinson (1951).

in a given country it may be questioned whether this case is actually typical of the larger population of interest, given that we have already stipulated that the typical magnitude of this relationship is diminutive and irregular. Of course, the weakness of democracy's presumed relationship to growth is also a handicap in cross-case analysis. A good deal of criticism has been directed toward studies of this type, where findings are rarely robust.[47] Even so, it seems clear that if there *is* a relationship between democracy and growth it is more likely to be perceptible in a large cross-case setting. The positive hypothesis, as well as the null hypothesis, is better approached in a sample rather than in a case.

9 USEFUL VARIATION: RARE VERSUS COMMON

When analyzing causal relationships we must be concerned not only with the strength of an X/Y relationship but also with the distribution of evidence across available cases. Specifically, we must be concerned with the distribution of *useful variation*— understood as variation (temporal or spatial) on relevant parameters that might yield clues about a causal relationship. It follows that where useful variation is rare—i.e. limited to a few cases—the case study format recommends itself. Where, on the other hand, useful variation is common, a cross-case method of analysis may be more defensible.

Consider a phenomenon like social revolution, an outcome that occurs very rarely. The empirical distribution on this variable, if we count each country-year as an observation, consists of thousands of non-revolutions (0) and just a few revolutions (1). Intuitively, it seems clear that the few "revolutionary" cases are of great interest. We need to know as much as possible about them, for they exemplify all the variation that we have at our disposal. In this circumstance, a case study mode of analysis is difficult to avoid, though it might be combined with a large-N cross-case analysis. As it happens, many outcomes of interest to social scientists are quite rare, so the issue is by no means trivial.[48]

By way of contrast, consider a phenomenon like turnover, understood as a situation where a ruling party or coalition is voted out of office. Turnover occurs within most

---

[47] Kittel (1999; 2005); Kittel and Winner (2005); Levine and Renelt (1992); Temple (1999).

[48] Consider the following topics and their—extremely rare—instances of variation: early industrialization (England, the Netherlands), fascism (Germany, Italy), the use of nuclear weapons (United States), world war (WWI, WWII), single non-transferable vote electoral systems (Jordan, Taiwan, Vanuatu, pre-reform Japan), electoral system reforms within established democracies (France, Italy, Japan, New Zealand, Thailand). The problem of "rareness" is less common where parameters are scalar, rather than dichotomous. But there are still plenty of examples of phenomena whose distributions are skewed by a few outliers, e.g. population (China, India), personal wealth (Bill Gates, Warren Buffett), ethnic heterogeneity (Papua New Guinea).

democratic countries on a regular basis, so the distribution of observations on this variable (incumbency/turnover) is relatively even across the universe of country-years. There are lots of instances of both outcomes. Under these circumstances a cross-case research design seems plausible, for the variation across cases is regularly distributed.

Another sort of variation concerns that which might occur *within* a given case. Suppose that only one or two cases within a large population exhibit quasi-experimental qualities: the factor of special interest varies, and there is no corresponding change in other factors that might affect the outcome. Clearly, we are likely to learn a great deal from studying this particular case—perhaps a lot more than we might learn from studying hundreds of additional cases that deviate from the experimental ideal. But again, if many cases have this experimental quality, there is little point in restricting ourselves to a single example; a cross-case research design may be justified.

A final sort of variation concerns the characteristics exhibited by a case relative to a particular theory that is under investigation. Suppose that a case provides a "crucial" test for a theory: it fits that theory's predictions so perfectly and so precisely that no other explanation could plausibly account for the performance of the case. If no other crucial cases present themselves, then an intensive study of this particular case is de rigueur. Of course, if many such cases lie within the population then it may be possible to study them all at once (with some sort of numeric reduction of the relevant parameters).

The general point here is that the distribution of useful variation across a population of cases matters a great deal in the choice between case study and cross-case research designs.

10 DATA AVAILABILITY: CONCENTRATED VERSUS DISPERSED

I have left the most prosaic factor for last. Sometimes, one's choice of research design is driven by the quality and quantity of information that is currently available, or could be easily gathered, on a given question. This is a practical matter, and is distinct from the actual (ontological) shape of the world. It concerns, rather, what we know about the former at a given point in time.[49] The question of evidence may be posed as follows: How much do we know about the cases at hand that might be relevant to the causal question of interest, and how precise, certain, and case comparable is that data? An evidence-rich environment is one where all relevant factors are measurable, where

---

[49] Of course, what we know about the potential cases is not independent of the underlying reality; it is, nonetheless, not entirely dependent on that reality.

these measurements are relatively precise, where they are rendered in comparable terms across cases, and where one can be relatively confident that the information is, indeed, accurate. An evidence-poor environment is the opposite.

The question of available evidence impinges upon choices in research design when one considers its distribution across a population of cases. If relevant information is concentrated in a single case, or if it is contained in incommensurable formats across a population of cases, then a case study mode of analysis is almost unavoidable. If, on the other hand, it is evenly distributed across the population—i.e. we are equally well informed about all cases—and is case comparable, then there is little to recommend a narrow focus. (I employ data, evidence, and information as synonyms in this section.)

Consider the simplest sort of example, where information is truly limited to one or a few cases. Accurate historical data on infant mortality and other indices of human development are currently available for only a handful of countries (these include Chile, Egypt, India, Jamaica, Mauritius, Sri Lanka, the United States, and several European countries).[50] This data problem is not likely to be rectified in future years, as it is exceedingly difficult to measure infant mortality except by public or private records. Consequently, anyone studying this general subject is likely to rely heavily on these cases, where in-depth analysis is possible and profitable. Indeed, it is not clear whether *any* large-N cross-case analysis is possible prior to the twentieth century. Here, a case study format is virtually prescribed, and a cross-case format proscribed.

Other problems of evidence are more subtle. Let us dwell for the moment on the question of data comparability. In their study of social security spending, Mulligan, Gil, and Sala-i-Martin note that

although our spending and design numbers are of good quality, there are some missing observations and, even with all the observations, it is difficult to reduce the variety of elderly subsidies to one or two numbers. For this reason, case studies are an important part of our analysis, since those studies do not require numbers that are comparable across a large number of countries. Our case study analysis utilizes data from a variety of country-specific sources, so we do not have to reduce "social security" or "democracy" to one single number.[51]

Here, the incommensurability of the evidence militates towards a case study format. In the event that the authors (or subsequent analysts) discover a coding system that provides reasonably valid cross-case measures of social security, democracy, and other relevant concepts then our state of knowledge about the subject is changed, and a cross-case research design is rendered more plausible.

Importantly, the state of evidence on a topic is never entirely fixed. Investigators may gather additional data, recode existing data, or discover new repositories of data. Thus, when discussing the question of evidence one must consider the quality and quantity of evidence that *could* be gathered on a given question, given sufficient time and resources. Here it is appropriate to observe that collecting new data, and correcting existing data, is usually easier in a case study format than in a large-N cross-case format. It will be difficult to rectify data problems if one's cases number in the hundreds or thousands. There are simply too many data points to allow for this.

---

[50] Gerring (2007*b*).   [51] Mulligan, Gil, and Sala-i-Martin (2002, 13).

One might consider this issue in the context of recent work on democracy. There is general skepticism among scholars with respect to the viability of extant global indicators intended to capture this complex concept (e.g. by Freedom House and by the Polity IV data project).[52] Measurement error, aggregation problems, and questions of conceptual validity are rampant. When dealing with a single country or a single continent it is possible to overcome some of these faults by manually recoding the countries of interest.[53] The case study format often gives the researcher an opportunity to fact-check, to consult multiple sources, to go back to primary materials, and to overcome whatever biases may affect the secondary literature. Needless to say, this is not a feasible approach for an individual investigator if one's project encompasses every country in the world. The best one can usually manage, under the circumstances, is some form of convergent validation (by which different indices of the same concept are compared) or small adjustments in the coding intended to correct for aggregation problems or measurement error.[54]

For the same reason, the collection of original data is typically more difficult in cross-case analysis than in case study analysis, involving greater expense, greater difficulties in identifying and coding cases, learning foreign languages, traveling, and so forth. Whatever can be done for a set of cases can usually be done more easily for a single case.

It should be kept in mind that many of the countries of concern to anthropologists, economists, historians, political scientists, and sociologists are still terra incognita. Outside the OECD, and with the exception of a few large countries that have received careful attention from scholars (e.g. India, Brazil, China), most countries of the world are not well covered by the social science literature. Any statement that one might wish to make about, say, Botswana, will be difficult to verify if one has recourse only to secondary materials. And these—very limited—secondary sources are not necessarily of the most reliable sort. Thus, if one wishes to say something about political patterns obtaining in roughly 90 percent of the world's countries and if one wishes to go beyond matters that can be captured in standard statistics collected by the World Bank and the IMF and other agencies (and these can also be very sketchy when lesser-studied countries are concerned) one is more or less obliged to conduct a case study. Of course, one could, in principle, gather similar information across all relevant cases. However, such an enterprise faces formidable logistical difficulties. Thus, for practical reasons, case studies are sometimes the most defensible alternative when the researcher is faced with an information-poor environment.

However, this point is easily turned on its head. Datasets are now available to study many problems of concern to the social sciences. Thus, it may not be necessary to collect original information for one's book, article, or dissertation. Sometimes in-depth single-case analysis is more time consuming than cross-case analysis. If so, there is no informational advantage to a case study format. Indeed, it may be easier to utilize existing information for a cross-case analysis, particularly when a case study

---

[52] Bollen (1993); Bowman, Lehoucq, and Mahoney (2005); Munck and Verkuilen (2002); Treier and Jackman (2005).

[53] Bowman, Lehoucq, and Mahoney (2005).   [54] Bollen (1993); Treier and Jackman (2005).

format imposes hurdles of its own—e.g. travel to distant climes, risk of personal injury, expense, and so forth. It is interesting to note that some observers consider case studies to be "relatively *more* expensive in time and resources."[55]

Whatever the specific logistical hurdles, it is a general truth that the shape of the evidence—that which is currently available and that which might feasibly be collected by an author—often has a strong influence on an investigator's choice of research designs. Where the evidence for particular cases is richer and more accurate there is a strong prima facie argument for a case study format focused on those cases. Where, by contrast, the relevant evidence is equally good for all potential cases, and is comparable across those cases, there is no reason to shy away from cross-case analysis. Indeed, there may be little to gain from case study formats.

11 CONCLUSIONS

At the outset, I took note of the severe disjuncture that has opened up between an often-maligned methodology and a heavily practiced method. The case study is disrespected but nonetheless regularly employed. Indeed, it remains the workhorse of most disciplines and subfields in the social sciences. How, then, can one make sense of this schizophrenia between methodological theory and praxis?

The torment of the case study begins with its definitional penumbra. Frequently, this key term is conflated with a set of disparate methodological traits that are not definitionally entailed. My first objective, therefore, was to craft a narrower and more useful concept for purposes of methodological discussion. The case study, I argued, is best defined as an intensive study of a single case with an aim to generalize across a larger set of cases. It follows from this definition that case studies may be small- or large-N, qualitative or quantitative, experimental or observational, synchronic or diachronic. It also follows that the case study research design comports with any macrotheoretical framework or paradigm—e.g. behavioralism, rational choice, institutionalism, or interpretivism. It is not epistemologically distinct. What differentiates the case study from the cross-case study is simply its way of defining observations, not its analysis of those observations or its method of modeling causal relations. The case study research design constructs its observations from a single case or a small number of cases, while cross-case research designs construct observations across multiple cases. Cross-case and case study research operate, for the most part, at different levels of analysis.

The travails of the case study are not simply definitional. They are also rooted in an insufficient appreciation of the methodological tradeoffs that this method calls forth. At least eight characteristic strengths and weaknesses must be considered. Ceteris

---

[55] Stoecker (1991, 91).

paribus, case studies are more useful when the strategy of research is exploratory rather than confirmatory/disconfirmatory, when internal validity is given preference over external validity, when insight into causal mechanisms is prioritized over insight into causal effects, when propositional depth is prized over breadth, when the population of interest is heterogeneous rather than homogeneous, when causal relationships are strong rather than weak, when useful information about key parameters is available only for a few cases, and when the available data are concentrated rather than dispersed.

Although I do not have the space to discuss other issues in this venue, it is worth mentioning that other considerations may also come into play in a researcher's choice between a case study and cross-case study research format. However, these additional issues—e.g. causal complexity and the state of research on a topic—do not appear to have clear methodological affinities. They may augur one way, or the other.

My objective throughout this chapter is to restore a greater sense of meaning, purpose, and integrity to the case study method. It is hoped that by offering a narrower and more carefully bounded definition of this method the case study may be rescued from some of its most persistent ambiguities. And it is hoped that the characteristic strengths of this method, as well as its limitations, will be more apparent to producers and consumers of case study research. The case study is a useful tool for some research objectives, but not all.

REFERENCES

ABADIE, A. and GARDEAZABAL, J. 2003. The economic costs of conflict: a case study of the Basque Country. *American Economic Review*, 93: 113–32.

ABBOTT, A. 1990. Conceptions of time and events in social science methods: causal and narrative approaches. *Historical Methods*, 23 (4): 140–50.

—— 1992. From causes to events: notes on narrative positivism. *Sociological Methods and Research*, 20 (4): 428–55.

—— 2001. *Time Matters: On Theory and Method*. Chicago: University of Chicago Press.

—— and FORREST, J. 1986. Optimal matching methods for historical sequences. *Journal of Interdisciplinary History*, 16 (3): 471–94.

—— and TSAY, A. 2000. Sequence analysis and optimal matching methods in sociology. *Sociological Methods and Research*, 29: 3–33.

ABELL, P. 1987. *The Syntax of Social Life: The Theory and Method of Comparative Narratives*. Oxford: Clarendon Press.

—— 2004. Narrative explanation: an alternative to variable-centered explanation? *Annual Review of Sociology*, 30: 287–310.

ACEMOGLU, D., JOHNSON, S., and ROBINSON, J. A. 2003. An African success story: Botswana. Pp. 80–122 in *In Search of Prosperity: Analytic Narratives on Economic Growth*, ed. D. Rodrik. Princeton: Princeton University Press.

ACHEN, C. H. 1986. *The Statistical Analysis of Quasi-Experiments*. Berkeley and Los Angeles: University of California Press.

ACHEN, C. H. 2002. Toward a new political methodology: microfoundations and ART. *Annual Review of Political Science*, 5: 423–50.

—— and SNIDAL, D. 1989. Rational deterrence theory and comparative case studies. *World Politics*, 41: 143–69.

ALESINA, A., GLAESER, E., and SACERDOTE, B. 2001. Why doesn't the US have a European-style welfare state? *Brookings Papers on Economic Activity*, 2: 187–277.

ALLEN, W. S. 1965. *The Nazi Seizure of Power: The Experience of a Single German Town, 1930–1935*. New York: Watts.

ALMOND, G. A. 1956. Comparative political systems. *Journal of Politics*, 18: 391–409.

ANGRIST, J. D. and KRUEGER, A. B. 2001. Instrumental variables and the search for identification: from supply and demand to natural experiments. *Journal of Economic Perspectives*, 15 (4): 69–85.

BATES, R. H., GREIF, A., LEVI, M., ROSENTHAL, J.-L. and WEINGAST, B. 1998. *Analytic Narratives*. Princeton: Princeton University Press.

BENDIX, R. 1963. Concepts and generalizations in comparative sociological studies. *American Sociological Review*, 28: 532–9.

BENTLEY, A. 1908/1967. *The Process of Government*. Cambridge, Mass.: Harvard University Press.

BLUMER, H. 1969. *Symbolic Interactionism: Perspective and Method*. Berkeley and Los Angeles: University of California Press.

BOLLEN, K. A. 1993. Liberal democracy: validity and method factors in cross-national measures. *American Journal of Political Science*, 37: 1207–30.

BONOMA, T. V. 1985. Case research in marketing: opportunities, problems, and a process. *Journal of Marketing Research*, 22 (2): 199–208.

BOWMAN, K., LEHOUCQ, F., and MAHONEY, J. 2005. Measuring political democracy: case expertise, data adequacy, and Central America. *Comparative Political Studies*, 38 (8): 939–70.

BRADY, H. E. and COLLIER, D. (eds). 2004. *Rethinking Social Inquiry: Diverse Tools, Shared Standards*. Lanham, Md.: Rowman and Littlefield.

BRAUMOELLER, B. F. and GOERTZ, G. 2000. The methodology of necessary conditions. *American Journal of Political Science*, 44 (3): 844–58.

BUNGE, M. 1997. Mechanism and explanation. *Philosophy of the Social Sciences*, 27: 410–65.

BUTHE, T. 2002. Taking temporality seriously: modeling history and the use of narratives as evidence. *American Political Science Review*, 96 (3): 481–93.

CAMERON, D. 1978. The expansion of the public economy: a comparative analysis. *American Political Science Review*, 72 (4): 1243–61.

CAMPBELL, D. T. 1988. *Methodology and Epistemology for Social Science*, ed. E. S. Overman. Chicago: University of Chicago Press.

—— and STANLEY, J. 1963. *Experimental and Quasi-experimental Designs for Research*. Boston: Houghton Mifflin.

CHANDRA, K. 2004. *Why Ethnic Parties Succeed: Patronage and Ethnic Headcounts in India*. Cambridge: Cambridge University Press.

CHERNOFF, B. and WARNER, A. 2002. Sources of fast growth in Mauritius: 1960–2000. Center for International Development, Harvard University.

CHONG, D. 1993. How people think, reason, and feel about rights and liberties. *American Journal of Political Science*, 37 (3): 867–99.

COASE, R. H. 1959. The Federal Communications Commission. *Journal of Law and Economics*, 2: 1–40.

—— 2000. The acquisition of Fisher Body by General Motors. *Journal of Law and Economics*, 43: 15–31.

COLLIER, D. 1993. The comparative method. Pp. 105–19 in *Political Science: The State of the Discipline II*, ed. A. W. Finifter. Washington, DC: American Political Science Association.

COOK, T. and CAMPBELL, D. 1979. *Quasi-experimentation: Design and Analysis Issues for Field Settings*. Boston: Houghton-Mifflin.

DE SOTO, H. 1989. *The Other Path: The Invisible Revolution in the Third World*. New York: Harper and Row.

DESSLER, D. 1991. Beyond correlations: toward a causal theory of war. *International Studies Quarterly*, 35: 337–55.

DION, D. 1998. Evidence and inference in the comparative case study. *Comparative Politics*, 30: 127–45.

ECKSTEIN, H. 1975. Case studies and theory in political science. Pp. 79–133 in *Handbook of Political Science*, vii: *Political Science: Scope and Theory*, ed. F. I. Greenstein and N. W. Polsby. Reading, Mass.: Addison-Wesley.

——1975/1992. Case studies and theory in political science. In *Regarding Politics: Essays on Political Theory, Stability, and Change*, by H. Eckstein. Berkeley and Los Angeles: University of California Press.

ELMAN, C. 2005. Explanatory typologies in qualitative studies of international politics. *International Organization*, 59 (2): 293–326.

ELSTER, J. 1998. A plea for mechanisms. Pp. 45–73 in *Social Mechanisms: An Analytical Approach to Social Theory*, ed. P. Hedstrom and R. Swedberg. Cambridge: Cambridge University Press.

FEARON, J. 1991. Counter factuals and hypothesis testing in political science. *World Politics*, 43: 169–95.

FENG, Y. 2003. *Democracy, Governance, and Economic Performance: Theory and Evidence*. Cambridge, Mass.: MIT Press.

FREEDMAN, D. A. 1991. Statistical models and shoe leather. *Sociological Methodology*, 21: 291–313.

FRIEDMAN, M. 1953. The methodology of positive economics. Pp. 3–43 in *Essays in Positive Economics*, by M. Friedman. Chicago: University of Chicago Press.

GEDDES, B. 1990. How the cases you choose affect the answers you get: selection bias in comparative politics. Pp. 131–52 in *Political Analysis*, vol. ii, ed. J. A. Stimson. Ann Arbor: University of Michigan Press.

—— 2003. *Paradigms and Sand Castles: Theory Building and Research Design in Comparative Politics*. Ann Arbor: University of Michigan Press.

GEERTZ, C. 1973. Thick description: toward an interpretive theory of culture. Pp. 3–30 in *The Interpretation of Cultures*, by C. Geertz. New York: Basic Books.

GEORGE, A. L. and BENNETT, A. 2005. *Case Studies and Theory Development*. Cambridge, Mass.: MIT Press.

—— and SMOKE, R. 1974. *Deterrence in American Foreign Policy: Theory and Practice*. New York: Columbia University Press.

GERRING, J. 2001. *Social Science Methodology: A Criterial Framework*. Cambridge: Cambridge University Press.

—— 2005. Causation: a unified framework for the social sciences. *Journal of Theoretical Politics*, 17 (2): 163–98.

—— 2007a. *Case Study Research: Principles and Practices*. Cambridge: Cambridge University Press.

—— 2007b. Global justice as an empirical question. *PS: Political Science and Politics*, 40: 67–78.

—— and BARRESI, P. A. 2003. Putting ordinary language to work: a min-max strategy of concept formation in the social sciences. *Journal of Theoretical Politics*, 15 (2): 201–32.

GERRING, J. and THOMAS, C. 2005. Comparability: a key issue in research design. Manuscript.

GLASER, B. G. and STRAUSS, A. L. 1967. *The Discovery of Grounded Theory: Strategies for Qualitative Research*. New York: Aldine de Gruyter.

GOERTZ, G. 2003. The substantive importance of necessary condition hypotheses. Ch. 4 in *Necessary Conditions: Theory, Methodology and Applications*, ed. G. Goertz and H. Starr. New York: Rowman and Littlefield.

——and LEVY, J. (eds.) forthcoming. Causal explanations, necessary conditions, and case studies: World War I and the end of the Cold War. MS.

——and STARR, H. (eds.) 2003. *Necessary Conditions: Theory, Methodology and Applications*. New York: Rowman and Littlefield.

GOLDSTONE, J. A. 1997. Methodological issues in comparative macrosociology. *Comparative Social Research*, 16: 121–32.

——GURR, T. R., HARFF, B., LEVY, M. A., MARSHALL, M. G., BATES, R. H., EPSTEIN, D. L., KAHL, C. H., SURKO, P. T., ULFELDER, J. C., JR., and UNGER, A. N. 2000. State Failure Task Force report: phase III findings. Available at: www.cidcm.umd.edu/inscr/stfail/SFTF%20Phase%20III%20Report%20Final.pdf.

GOLDTHORPE, J. H. 1997. Current issues in comparative macrosociology: a debate on methodological issues. *Comparative Social Research*, 16: 121–32.

GRIFFIN, L. J. 1993. Narrative, event-structure analysis, and causal interpretation in historical sociology. *American Journal of Sociology*, 98: 1094–133.

GUTTING, G. (ed.) 1980. *Paradigms and Revolutions: Appraisals and Applications of Thomas Kuhn's Philosophy of Science*. Notre Dame, Ind.: University of Notre Dame Press.

HALL, P. A. 2003. Aligning ontology and methodology in comparative politics. In *Comparative Historical Analysis in the Social Sciences*, ed. J. Mahoney and D. Rueschemeyer. Cambridge: Cambridge University Press.

HEDSTROM, P. and SWEDBERG, R. (eds.) 1998. *Social Mechanisms: An Analytical Approach to Social Theory*. Cambridge: Cambridge University Press.

HERSEN, M. and BARLOW, D. H. 1976. *Single-Case Experimental Designs: Strategies for Studying Behavior Change*. Oxford: Pergamon Press.

HOCHSCHILD, J. L. 1981. *What's Fair? American Beliefs about Distributive Justice*. Cambridge, Mass.: Harvard University Press.

JERVIS, R. 1989. Rational deterrence: theory and evidence. *World Politics*, 41 (2): 183–207.

KENNEDY, P. 2003. *A Guide to Econometrics*, 5th edn. Cambridge, Mass.: MIT Press.

KING, C. 2004. The micropolitics of social violence. *World Politics*, 56 (3): 431–55.

KING, G., KEOHANE, R. O., and VERBA, S. 1994. *Designing Social Inquiry: Scientific Inference in Qualitative Research*. Princeton: Princeton University Press.

KITTEL, B. 1999. Sense and sensitivity in pooled analysis of political data. *European Journal of Political Research*, 35: 225–53.

——2005. A crazy methodology? On the limits of macroquantitative social science research. Unpublished MS. University of Amsterdam.

KITTEL, B. and WINNER, H. 2005. How reliable is pooled analysis in political economy? The globalization–welfare state nexus revisited. *European Journal of Political Research*, 44 (2): 269–93.

KUHN, T. S. 1962/1970. *The Structure of Scientific Revolutions*. Chicago: University of Chicago Press.

LANE, R. 1962. *Political Ideology: Why the American Common Man Believes What He Does*. New York: Free Press.

LEBOW, R. N. 2000. What's so different about a counterfactual? *World Politics*, 52: 550–85.

LEVINE, R. and RENELT, D. 1992. A sensitivity analysis of cross-country growth regressions. *American Economic Review*, 82 (4): 942–63.

LIBECAP, G. D. 1993. *Contracting for Property Rights*. Cambridge: Cambridge University Press.

LIEBERSON, S. 1985. *Making it Count: The Improvement of Social Research and Theory*. Berkeley: University of California Press.

——1992. Einstein, Renoir, and Greeley: some thoughts about evidence in sociology: 1991 Presidential Address. *American Sociological Review*, 57 (1): 1–15.

——1994. More on the uneasy case for using Mill-type methods in small-N comparative studies. *Social Forces*, 72 (4): 1225–37.

LIJPHART, A. 1968. *The Politics of Accommodation: Pluralism and Democracy in the Netherlands*. Los Angeles: University of California Press.

——1969. Consociational democracy. *World Politics*, 21 (2): 207–25.

——1971. Comparative politics and the comparative method. *American Political Science Review*, 65 (3): 682–93.

LIPSET, S. M. 1960/1963. *Political Man: The Social Bases of Politics*. Garden City, NY: Anchor Books.

——TROW, M. A., and COLEMAN, J. S. 1956. *Union Democracy: The Internal Politics of the International Typographical Union*. New York: Free Press.

LITTLE, D. 1998. *Microfoundations, Method, and Causation*. New Brunswick, NJ: Transaction.

LYND, R. S. and LYND, H. M. 1929/1956. *Middletown: A Study in American Culture*. New York: Harcourt, Brace.

MCKEOWN, T. J. 1983. Hegemonic stability theory and nineteenth-century tariff levels. *International Organization*, 37 (1): 73–91.

MAHONEY, J. 2001. Beyond correlational analysis: recent innovations in theory and method. *Sociological Forum*, 16 (3): 575–93.

——and RUESCHEMEYER, D. (eds.) 2003. *Comparative Historical Analysis in the Social Sciences*. Cambridge: Cambridge University Press.

——and GOERTZ, G. 2004. The possibility principle: choosing negative cases in comparative research. *American Political Science Review*, 98 (4): 653–69.

MANSKI, C. F. 1993. Identification problems in the social sciences. *Sociological Methodology*, 23: 1–56.

MARTIN, C. J. and SWANK, D. 2004. Does the organization of capital matter? Employers and active labor market policy at the national and firm levels. *American Political Science Review*, 98 (4): 593–612.

MARTIN, L. L. 1992. *Coercive Cooperation: Explaining Multilateral Economic Sanctions*. Princeton: Princeton University Press.

MEEHL, P. E. 1954. *Clinical versus Statistical Predictions: A Theoretical Analysis and a Review of the Evidence*. Minneapolis: University of Minnesota Press.

MULLIGAN, C., GIL, R., and SALA-I-MARTIN, X. 2002. Social security and democracy. Manuscript, University of Chicago and Columbia University.

MUNCK, G. L. and SNYDER, R. (eds.) 2007. *Passion, Craft, and Method in Comparative Politics*. Baltimore: Johns Hopkins University Press.

——and VERKUILEN, J. 2002. Measuring democracy: evaluating alternative indices. *Comparative Political Studies*, 35 (1): 5–34.

NJOLSTAD, O. 1990. Learning from history? Case studies and the limits to theory-building. Pp. 220–46 in *Arms Races: Technological and Political Dynamics*, ed. O. Njolstad. Thousand Oaks, Calif.: Sage.

NORTH, D. C., ANDERSON, T. L., and HILL, P. J. 1983. *Growth and Welfare in the American Past: A New American History*, 3rd edn. Englewood Cliffs, NJ: Prentice Hall.

—— and THOMAS, R. P. 1973. *The Rise of the Western World*. Cambridge: Cambridge University Press.

—— and WEINGAST, B. R. 1989. Constitutions and commitment: the evolution of institutions governing public choice in seventeenth-century England. *Journal of Economic History*, 49: 803–32.

ODELL, J. S. 2004. Case study methods in international political economy. Pp. 56–80 in *Models, Numbers and Cases: Methods for Studying International Relations*, ed. D. F. Sprinz and Y. Wolinsky-Nahmias. Ann Arbor: University of Michigan.

ORUM, A. M., FEAGIN, J. R., and SJOBERG, G. 1991. Introduction: the nature of the case study. Pp. 1–26 in *A Case for the Case*, ed. J. R. Feagin, A. M. Orum, and G. Sjoberg. Chapel Hill: University of North Carolina Press.

PAPYRAKIS, E. and GERLAGH, R. 2003. The resource curse hypothesis and its transmission channels. *Journal of Comparative Economics*, 32: 181–93.

PATTON, M. Q. 2002. *Qualitative Evaluation and Research Methods*. Newbury Park, Calif.: Sage.

POPPER, K. 1934/1968. *The Logic of Scientific Discovery*. New York: Harper and Row.

—— 1969. *Conjectures and Refutations*. London: Routledge and Kegan Paul.

POSNER, D. 2004. The political salience of cultural difference: why Chewas and Tumbukas are allies in Zambia and adversaries in Malawi. *American Political Science Review*, 98 (4): 529–46.

PRZEWORSKI, A. and TEUNE, H. 1970. *The Logic of Comparative Social Inquiry*. New York: John Wiley.

RAGIN, C. C. 1987. *The Comparative Method: Moving beyond Qualitative and Quantitative Strategies*. Berkeley: University of California Press.

—— 1992. Cases of "what is a case?" Pp. 1–17 in *What Is a Case? Exploring the Foundations of Social Inquiry*, ed. C. C. Ragin and H. S. Becker. Cambridge: Cambridge University Press.

—— 1997. Turning the tables: how case-oriented research challenges variable-oriented research. *Comparative Social Research*, 16: 27–42.

—— 2000. *Fuzzy-Set Social Science*. Chicago: University of Chicago Press.

—— 2004. Turning the tables. Pp. 123–38 in *Rethinking Social Inquiry: Diverse Tools, Shared Standards*, ed. H. E. Brady and D. Collier. Lanham, Md.: Rowman and Littlefield.

ROBINSON, W. S. 1951. The logical structure of analytic induction. *American Sociological Review*, 16 (6): 812–18.

RODRIK, D. (ed.) 2003. *In Search of Prosperity: Analytic Narratives on Economic Growth*. Princeton, NJ: Princeton University Press.

ROGOWSKI, R. 1995. The role of theory and anomaly in social-scientific inference. *American Political Science Review*, 89 (2): 467–70.

ROSS, M. 2001. Does oil hinder democracy? *World Politics*, 53: 325–61.

RUBIN, D. B. 1974. Estimating causal effects of treatments in randomized and nonrandomized studies. *Journal of Educational Psychology*, 66: 688–701.

RUESCHEMEYER, D. and STEPHENS, J. D. 1997. Comparing historical sequences: a powerful tool for causal analysis. *Comparative Social Research*, 16: 55–72.

SAMBANIS, N. 2004. Using case studies to expand economic models of civil war. *Perspectives on Politics*, 2 (2): 259–79.

SARTORI, G. 1976. *Parties and Party Systems*. Cambridge: Cambridge University Press.

SEKHON, J. S. 2004. Quality meets quantity: case studies, conditional probability and counterfactuals. *Perspectives in Politics*, 2 (2): 281–93.

SHALEV, M. 1998. Limits of and alternatives to multiple regression in macro-comparative research. Paper prepared for presentation at the second conference on The Welfare State at the Crossroads, Stockholm.

SMELSER, N. J. 1973. The methodology of comparative analysis. Pp. 42–86 in *Comparative Research Methods*, ed. D. P. Warwick and S. Osherson. Englewood Cliffs, NJ: Prentice-Hall.

SRINIVASAN, T. N. and BHAGWATI, J. 1999. Outward-orientation and development: are revisionists right? Discussion Paper no. 806, Economic Growth Center, Yale University.

STOECKER, R. 1991. Evaluating and rethinking the case study. *Sociological Review*, 39: 88–112.

Symposium: Qualitative Comparative Analysis (QCA) 2004. *Qualitative Methods: Newsletter of the American Political Science Association Organized Section on Qualitative Methods*, 1 (2): 2–25.

TEMPLE, J. 1999. The new growth evidence. *Journal of Economic Literature*, 37: 112–56.

TETLOCK, P. E. and BELKIN, A. (eds.) 1996. *Counterfactual Thought Experiments in World Politics*. Princeton: Princeton University Press.

THIES, M. F. 2001. Keeping tabs on partners: the logic of delegation in coalition governments. *American Journal of Political Science*, 45 (3): 580–98.

TILLY, C. 2001. Mechanisms in political processes. *Annual Review of Political Science*, 4: 21–41.

TREIER, S. and JACKMAN, S. 2005. Democracy as a latent variable. Department of Political Science, Stanford University.

TRUMAN, D. B. 1951. *The Governmental Process*. New York: Alfred A. Knopf.

VANDENBROUCKE, J. P. 2001. In defense of case reports and case series. *Annals of Internal Medicine*, 134 (4): 330–4.

VREELAND, J. R. 2003. *The IMF and Economic Development*. Cambridge: Cambridge University Press.

WARD, M. D. and BAKKE, K. 2005. Predicting civil conflicts: on the utility of empirical research. Manuscript.

WINSHIP, C. and MORGAN, S. L. 1999. The estimation of causal effects of observational data. *Annual Review of Sociology*, 25: 659–707.

—— and SOBEL, M. 2004. Causal inference in sociological studies. Pp. 481–503 in *Handbook of Data Analysis*, ed. M. Hardy and A. Bryman. London: Sage.

WOLIN, S. S. 1968. Paradigms and political theories. Pp. 125–52 in *Politics and Experience*, ed. P. King and B. C. Parekh. Cambridge: Cambridge University Press.

YOUNG, O. R. (ed.) 1999. *The Effectiveness of International Environmental Regimes: Causal Connections and Behavioral Mechanisms*. Cambridge, Mass.: MIT Press.

ZNANIECKI, F. 1934. *The Method of Sociology*. New York: Rinehart.

CHAPTER 52

....

INTEGRATING QUALITATIVE AND QUANTITATIVE METHODS

....

JAMES D. FEARON

DAVID D. LAITIN

ALMOST by definition, a single case study is a poor method for establishing whether or what empirical regularities exist across cases.[1] To ascertain whether some interesting pattern, or relationship between variables, obtains, the best approach is normally to identify the largest feasible sample of cases relevant to the hypothesis or research question, then to code cases on the variables of interest, and then to assess whether and what sort of patterns or associations appear in the data.

The authors thank the Centro de Estudios Avanzados en Ciencias Sociales at the Juan March Institute in Madrid (and its director, José María Maravall), and the EITM Summer Institute at Berkeley (and its hosts, David Collier, Gary Cox, and Henry Brady) for providing stimulating audiences for earlier versions of this chapter. They thank as well David Freedman for critical commentary. Fearon thanks the Canadian Institute for Advanced Research for its support.

[1] Of course, a single "discrepant" case can disprove a hypothesis asserting a deterministic relationship between two things. But deterministic relationships between variables of interest are at best rare in social science. Eckstein (1975) argues that case studies are, under some conditions, the most efficient method for theory development. But his conditions require theories that make deterministic (i.e. not probabilistic) predictions.

However, with observational data (data not generated by random assignment of presumed causal factors), mere patterns or associations are not enough to allow us to draw inferences about what causes what. The standard approach in large-N statistical work in political and other social sciences is to accompany the presentation of associations (often in the form of regression results) with arguments about (a) why the reader should believe that the variation in an independent variable could cause variation in the dependent variable, and (b) why the reader should believe that the association observed in the data is not due to the independent variable happening to vary with some other, actually causal factor. The latter is usually done by adding "control" variables to the regression model, and arguing that one has not omitted important factors that are correlated with the independent variables of interest.[2]

The arguments for (a) and (b) amount to a sort of *story* the researcher tells about the associations observed in the regression results. The arguments, particularly those for (a), are often referred to as a "theory."[3] To some extent these stories can be evaluated as to whether they are deductively valid; that is, whether the conclusions do indeed follow from the premises, and whether the arguments are consistent. For example, it may be that the argument for why one independent variable matters contradicts the argument made on behalf of some other variable. Or it may be that an argument for a particular independent variable is internally inconsistent, confused, or doesn't follow from the premises on closer inspection. However, while a good analysis tells a valid and internally consistent story about the observed correlations, there may be multiple possible consistent stories about particular independent variables, and in general the reader may not know how much weight to put on the researcher's interpretation. Is the researcher's story capturing "what is really going on" in the cases to generate the observed patterns, or is something else driving the results?

At this point case studies can be extremely useful as a method for assessing whether arguments proposed to explain empirical regularities are plausible. One selects particular cases and examines them in greater depth than was required to code values on the outcome and explanatory variables of interest. When the "cases" are sequences of events in different countries or regions, or years in a particular country, or bills proposed in a legislature, and so on, the case study will entail a narrative account of what led to the outcome, including an assessment of what role the proposed causal factors played. In these narratives one typically uses additional data about the beliefs, intentions, considerations, and reasoning of the people who made the choices that produced the outcome, in order to test whether the "higher-level" general story told about many cases is discernible in particular, concrete cases. One can also ask if

---

[2] With regression analysis, there may be additional assumptions that should be justified in order to warrant a causal inference, such as correct functional form and additional assumptions about error variances.

[3] As Wagner (2007) observes, partisans of quantitative social science sometimes seem to mistake a regression equation itself for a theory.

there were important factors omitted from the large-N analysis that might in fact be driving the results. Finally, one can use the finer-grained analysis possible in a narrative account to ask about the validity and accuracy of measures being used in the large-N analysis.

For these several reasons, so-called "multimethod" research has become increasingly popular in political science in recent years, especially in comparative politics (Laitin 1998; Mares 2003; Iversen 1999; Boix 1998) and international relations (Huth 1998; Martin 1994; Schultz 2001; Goemans 2000; Stone 2002; Walters 2001; Fortna 2004; Mansfield and Snyder 2006; Collier and Sambanis 2005; and Doyle and Sambanis 2006).[4] Done well, multimethod research combines the strength of large-N designs for identifying empirical regularities and patterns, and the strength of case studies for revealing the causal mechanisms that give rise to political outcomes of interest.

An important but neglected problem for this research approach is the question of how to choose the cases for deeper investigation. Most work in this vein adopts the implicit criterion of choosing cases that support (or can be argued to support) the researcher's interpretation of the regression results. This criterion need not yield worthless results, since knowing that there are at least *some* cases that show good evidence of the causal mechanisms proposed by the researcher is something. But "cherry picking" by the researcher, or even the perception of cherry picking when it did not occur, will tend to undermine a reader's confidence that the case-study part of the design demonstrates that the researcher's causal story is on target.

In this article we propose that choosing cases for closer study *at random* is a compelling complement in multimethod research to large-N statistical methods in its ability to assess regularities and specify causal mechanisms. We discuss the advantages of random selection (or random selection within strata) for case studies, as well as problems with other possible criteria. These include choosing cases "on the regression line" that appear to fit the researcher's theory well; cases "off the regression line" that do not; "hard" or "critical" cases that are allegedly "tough tests" for the theory to pass; and choosing cases that have particular values on the explanatory factor of interest.

We illustrate what we will call the "random narratives" approach with work in progress we have been doing on the causes of civil war.[5] In Fearon and Laitin (2003), we report the main results of a cross-national statistical analysis of factors that distinguish countries that have had civil war onsets in the period 1945 to 1999. On the basis of these findings, theoretical arguments, and prior, unsystematic reading of diverse cases, we proposed a story about how to interpret why certain factors (such as low per capita income and high country population) are strongly related

---

[4] To our knowledge survey researchers in American politics do not normally do in-depth, unstructured interviews with or ethnographies of particular respondents to assess their theories based on interpreting regression coefficients. In congressional research, ethnographies produced by scholars such as Richard Fenno inspire quantitative work but rarely combine methods with the goal of making better causal inferences.

[5] Two examples of the random narratives are available in Fearon and Laitin (2005).

to civil war risk, whereas other factors (such as ethnic diversity, autocracy, and broad grievances) are not, once one controls for level of economic development. In order to assess this story we randomly selected twenty-five countries, stratified by region and whether or not the country had at least one civil war, and undertook narrative accounts of these countries' civil war experience (or lack thereof) using secondary sources.

In this chapter, we first summarize the findings of our statistical analysis of civil war onsets. We then in Section 2 look more carefully at different criteria for choosing which narratives to tell. In Section 3, we discuss a method for structuring narratives that is complementary to the statistical work. In Section 4 we illustrate in light of our narrative findings the incompleteness of the statistical models we initially ran. In Section 5, we highlight one narrative as an example of its potential yield. In the conclusion, we underline some surprises and advantages of the random narrative approach.

1 STATISTICAL RESULTS

Cross-national statistically based research by us and several other researchers has tended to find little or no support for two well-entrenched theories of civil war onset. First, our data show that by most measures of broad societal grievance—for example, lack of democracy, lack of religious or linguistic rights, or economic inequality—knowing the *level* of grievances in a country does not help differentiate countries susceptible to a civil war from those that are not.[6] Second, our data show that measures of cultural divides (the level of ethnic heterogeneity or the degree of cultural distance) do not help differentiate countries susceptible to a civil war from those that are not, once one controls for level of economic development.

In their stead, we have advanced an argument that points to the conditions that favor insurgency, a technology of military conflict characterized by small, lightly armed bands practicing guerrilla warfare from rural base areas. This perspective ties together a set of variables that correlate with civil war onset. Our interpretation of all of them is that they point to the relative incapacity of a state to quell insurgencies, which may begin at random and be "selected" for growth in countries with favorable conditions, or may be actively encouraged by signs of state weakness. The key variables that are significant and robust in our statistical models are listed below.

---

[6] This is *not* to say that if a state increases the level of grievance for a set of its citizens it can't provoke an insurgency. It may be that some states aggrieve minority groups as much as they can get away with, but some groups will tolerate higher levels of abuse (perhaps due to their weakness). Therefore increasing grievances can lead to insurgency even if levels of grievance across countries vary without implications for civil war onsets.

- Per capita income—we argue that low per capita income matters primarily because it marks states lacking in financial, bureaucratic, military, and police capability.
- Mountainous terrain—we interpret high degrees of mountainous terrain in a country as a tactical advantage to potential insurgents for hiding from government forces.
- Population—large populations require more layers of principals and agents to govern, making it harder for the regime to competently monitor, police, and respond to security threats at the village level.
- Oil—oil increases per capita income and government revenues and so works against insurgency, but controlling for the level of income we expect that oil producers have weaker governmental institutions, inasmuch as oil revenues make it unnecessary to develop intrusive tax bureaus that need to track individual citizens. Oil revenues can also increase the "prize" value of capturing the state or a region.
- Instability—we interpret rapid shifts in the regime type (a two or more change in a single year in the polity score for democracy) as a proxy for weak or weakening central state institutions.
- New state—in the immediate aftermath of independence, due to withdrawal of colonial forces before indigenous institutions have taken root, states are especially fragile. This provides an opportunity for challengers. They may fear that the leaders of the new state cannot commit not to exploit their region or group in the future after the government consolidates. Or they may see that the government cannot commit to provide state benefits in the future worth as much as their short-run expected value for trying to seize power by force now. Unable to hold as credible such commitments, insurgents can take advantage of a window of opportunity to seek secession or capture of the state.
- Anocracy—regimes that mix autocracy with some democratic features (such as a legislature or partly competitive national elections) suggest the presence of political conflict that weakens its ability to counter an internal threat.

A multivariate analysis thereby helped us to address the question of what factors correlate with higher likelihood of civil war onset. Our selection of variables was motivated by reading the literature on civil war, reading about specific cases, and thinking theoretically about the literature and cases using game-theoretic tools (see for example Fearon 1998; Laitin 1995; Fearon and Laitin 1999; Fearon 2004; 2008). We continue to work on formal models of civil war-related interactions in an effort to clarify and deepen the informal arguments we have proposed (e.g. Fearon and Laitin 2007).

Lacking in both approaches, however, is a clear empirical answer as to whether the variables in our statistical and theoretical arguments are actually "doing the work" in raising a country's susceptibility to a civil war onset. This is where case narratives can play an especially valuable role.

2 CHOOSING NARRATIVES

But which narratives to tell? In statistical work, there are some methodological standards for case selection and analysis. In formal and particularly in game-theoretic analysis, there are well-developed rules and standards for what constitutes a well-posed model and proper analysis of it. There is no intellectual consensus, however, on how to choose cases for narrative exposition in a research design that combines statistical and case study evidence.[7] We consider several criteria that have been used in practice or that might be argued to be desirable.

2.1 "Good Cases" for the Researcher's Theory

In practice, perhaps the most common approach is for the researcher to choose "good cases" that nicely illustrate the causal mechanisms that the researcher proposed to explain the broader empirical regularities found in the statistical analysis. This is not an entirely worthless procedure in terms of producing evidence. It tells us that there exist at least some cases showing plausible evidence of the causal mechanisms hypothesized by the researcher. But selection bias is obviously a problem. "Good cases" have been cherry-picked, so it is not clear that they convey much information about the importance of the proposed causal mechanism in explaining the observed patterns. Even worse, what if these are the very cases that led the researcher to propose the causal mechanisms that she hypothesized to explain the statistical patterns in the first place?

In one version of "good case" selection, the researcher tells the reader that one or more of the cases selected for narrative exposition are, in fact, "hard cases" for her theory. It is then argued that received theories predict that the causal mechanism advanced by the author would be especially unlikely to be found in these "hard cases." Invariably, however, the historical narrative shows that the author's proposed causal mechanism is at play or that it trumps other factors stressed by existing theories ("surprisingly").[8] Selection bias is again a major concern. If the reader's prior belief put a great deal of weight on the existing theories, then there may be some evidentiary value (actual surprise) in learning that in at least one case, the author's favored causal mechanism can be argued to have been as or more important. But the reader can also be confident that the researcher would not present a developed "hard case" narrative unless it could be rendered in a way that seemed to support the claims of the researcher's preferred causal mechanism. So readers may be forgiven for thinking

---

[7] Nor is there a consensus on what, given the choice of a particular case, makes for a methodologically strong narrative. Still, most would agree that factual errors and tendentious interpretation make for a bad narrative or case study. Alex George has been a trailblazer in setting criteria for drawing causal inferences from narrative accounts. For his latest (and alas, his last) statement on this, see George and Bennett (2005).

[8] Though they may exist, we are not aware of any published paper or book in which the author asserts that X is a hard case for the preferred theory, and then finds that the case does not support the theory.

that talk of "hard cases" may be as much a rhetorical as a defensible methodological strategy.

Another version of "good case" selection occurs when the researcher selects "easy cases" for the preferred theory. For example, Schultz (2001) chooses for narrative several international crises involving Britain, in part because Britain's Westminster system most closely approximates the way that his theoretical model of crisis bargaining represents domestic politics, and from which Schultz drew his hypotheses about the role of opposition signaling in international disputes. This makes it easier to evaluate whether the causal mechanism at work in the model is at work in the cases. One downside, however, is that we have less information about whether Schultz's mechanism is more general than the sample of cases that led him to his model in the first place.

2.2 Convenience Samples

Another common approach in practice is to choose cases for narrative exposition that are relatively easy for the analyst to research, due to language skills or data availability, in what is sometimes referred to as a convenience sample. This procedure may be justified in some circumstances. The researcher will have to adjudicate trade-offs between the risk of selecting nonrepresentative cases, the accuracy of the narratives (for example, the validity and reliability of the measurement of the variables in question), and the number of cases that can be studied in depth. Representativeness will often be a significant problem for this approach, however, since the cases that are easy for the analyst to research will often be systematically unrepresentative on important variables. For example, in cross-national studies it is normally easier to find the sort of detailed information necessary for a good political narrative for wealthier countries, or for poor countries that happen to have attracted a lot of OECD attention and money for strategic or other reasons.

2.3 Selecting on Variation in the Dependent or Independent Variables

In principle one might select cases for narrative on the basis of values of the dependent variable, on values of an important independent variable, or on some kind of joint variation in both. For example, if the thing to be explained is the occurrence or absence of a phenomenon like democracy, war, rapid economic growth, or post-conflict peace, the researcher might select for close study a few cases where the phenomenon occurred and a few where it did not. Once again, though, we run into a problem of representativeness. If one is selecting a few cases from a larger set, why this one and not another? Why shouldn't the reader be suspicious about selection of "good cases" if no explanation is given for the choice? If an explanation is given and it amounts to convenience sampling, don't we still need to worry about representativeness? We can probably learn something about the proposed theoretical story from these cases and the contrast between them, but are we maximizing the amount? The same concerns apply for a small sample of cases selected on variation in some independent variable.

Another possibility here would be to select cases that show some particular combination on both the dependent variable and on independent variables of interest. For example, in their large-N analysis Mansfield and Snyder (2005) find that democratizing states with "concentrated" political power have been more likely to initiate interstate wars. They explain this with an argument about the incentives for threatened authoritarian elites to use nationalism and conflict for diversionary purposes. For narrative accounts they choose cases of democratizing states that initiated wars, which they call "easiest" for their theory (p. 169), presumably because these exhibit war and democratization together. As they argue, if they were not able to make a plausible case for the operation of their preferred mechanism in these cases, this would strongly undermine their theoretical claims.

Mansfield and Snyder look at all ten countries that were coded as democratizing when they initiated one or more wars, which protects them against the concern that they might have intentionally or unintentionally cherry-picked within this set. And intuitively, it seems plausible that if one's mechanism links the presence of X to phenomenon Y via such-and-such steps, one can learn more empirically about whether the mechanism matters as hypothesized from cases where X and Y occurred than from cases where one or the other did not. If the empirical question is "How often did democratization lead to war by the specific sequence of events that we have proposed?", then these are obviously the only cases one needs to consult. So here is a strong rationale for selecting cases that are not only "on the regression line," but that show a particular combination of values on Y and X.

If a causal mechanism implies specific sequences of events for more than one value of an independent variable, then the same reasoning leads to the suggestion that cases be sampled that are "on the regression line." For example, we proposed that per capita income proxies for several aspects of a state's capability to conduct effective counterinsurgency, relative to insurgent groups' ability to survive. Thus we would expect to find that in rich states nascent insurgent groups are detected and easily crushed by police (or they stay at the level of small, not very effective terrorist groups), while in poor states we should find would-be insurgent groups surviving and growing due to the states' incompetence (e.g. indiscriminate counter-insurgency) and virtual absence from parts of their territory. One could try to evaluate how much of the empirical relationship between income and civil war this mechanism explains by selecting for narratives poor countries that fell into civil war and rich countries that did not.

Of course, selecting on Y and X in this manner still faces the difficulty of *which* cases among those on the regression line. If it is not feasible to write narratives of all such cases, as Mansfield and Snyder did, we still face the problem of cherry-picking, or appearance of selection bias.

Moreover, there are good reasons to think that cases that are *off* the regression line might hold important, if different, information about the mechanisms in question as well. First, recall that the fundamental threat to causal inference in nonexperimental settings is the risk that there are other causes of Y that happen to be correlated with the proposed cause X. Cases off the regression line are more likely to show these other causal mechanisms at work. Seeing what they are and how they work should increase the ability of the researcher to say whether the observed relationship with X is the result of omitted variable bias. In addition, identifying other causes of the phenomenon in particular cases can lead to new hypotheses about general patterns and explanations, to be evaluated in subsequent rounds of research.

Second, narratives of cases off the regression line improve the researchers' chances of understanding why the proposed causal mechanism sometimes fails to operate as theoretically expected. For example, democratization does not always (or in fact, all that often) lead to interstate war—why not? Were authoritarian elites insufficiently threatened in these cases? Were they threatened but judged that there was no good opportunity for diversionary war? What additional variables determine each of these steps? If we accounted for these as well, would the original relationship hold up? In Snyder and Mansfield's study, answering such questions would require narratives of cases of democratization with concentrated political power that failed to produce interstate war.

Third, cases may fall off the regression not only because of the influence of unmeasured factors, but due to measurement error in Y or X. Particularly with cross-national data, large-N statistical analyses must often employ crude indicators that can be coded for a large number of cases in a reasonable amount of time. Case narratives can then be used to make rough estimates of the validity and reliability of the large-N indicators, and to estimate how often measurement errors are masking instances where the proposed causal mechanism actually did work as predicted, or where it did not work as predicted but mistakenly got credit in the statistical analysis.

2.4 Selecting Randomly

These several considerations and the general concern about selection bias lead us to propose that *randomly choosing a (relatively) small number of cases for narrative analysis will often be a desirable strategy in "multimethod" research.*

With random selection, the investigator is asked to write narratives for cases that were chosen *for* him or her by a random number generator. The investigator goes from the first case on a list ordered by a random series to some number down the list, in each case using the narrative to ask about what connects or fails to connect the statistically significant independent variables to the coded value on the dependent variable. Most importantly, the researcher is protected against the risks caused by (known or unknown) systematic bias in case selection. In addition, with cases both on and off the regression line, the researcher can ask both about whether the proposed causal mechanisms operated in the cases on the line and about why and whether they failed to operate in cases off the line. If there were missing variables previously unexamined that would have improved the initial statistical analysis, they are probably more likely to be found in cases forced upon the investigator than in cases she or he chose, and the investigator has an unbiased, if small, sample of them. Finally, the researcher has the opportunity to estimate the impact of measurement error in both cases that are well predicted by the statistical model and those that are not.

Of course, there are downsides to random selection as well, most resulting from possible trade-offs against the quality and total number of narratives that can be produced. The researcher may be able to write more and better-quality narratives for cases that she already knows well or for which she has language or other skills. On the other hand, this may itself argue against selecting such cases, since it is more likely that they were consciously or unconsciously already used to generate the theoretical arguments that are being tested. Thus, random cases can have the virtue of serving as out-of-sample tests. In addition, case studies of unfamiliar or obscure events may gain from a fresh reading of the standard literature about a country with an eye to how much mileage can be gotten in understanding outcomes through a special focus on significant independent variables validated from cross-national analysis.

Rather than choosing purely at random, it may be more efficient to stratify on particular variables. For example, if one is interested in evaluating whether one's theoretical account for a particular variable in a cross-sectional study is plausible, then it makes sense to sample cases that have a range of values on this particular variable. Or, as we discuss below, it makes sense to stratify on certain variables, for instance region in a cross-national study, to avoid random selection yielding lots of (say) Eastern European cases but almost no Latin American cases. Still, short of doing case studies for every data point, random selection within strata or values of an independent variable will be warranted for the same reasons just advanced.

To construct the sample for our narrative data-set, we took a random sample of countries stratified by region and by whether the country had experienced a civil war in the period under study (1945–99). The rationale for stratifying by region was to ensure an even distribution across a factor that is correlated with common historical experience, culture, religion, and level of economic development.[9] We distinguished between "war" and "no war" countries for a different reason. We initially expected that there was more to be learned by studying a country that had an outbreak of war at some time than one that never did, because a "war country" has periods of both peace and war (variation), whereas a "no war country" has only peace. There is certainly information in the "no war" cases, and we thought it would be wrong to exclude them entirely. But we wanted to make possible the oversampling of countries that experienced a transition from peace to war, as this provides within country variation

[9] If we had not stratified by region, there was a reasonable probability that at least one region would have been significantly underrepresented, and another overrepresented. Since there are so many common and distinguishing features of the politics and economics of states with "regions" as conventionally described, we wanted to have a better chance of distinguishing the impact of our independent variables from unmeasured, region-specific factors.

on the dependent variable in which, in effect, a great many country-specific factors are controlled for.

While this expectation was to some extent borne out, as we note below we were surprised by how theoretically informative and empirically interesting were the narratives for countries that never had a civil war in the period under study.[10]

3 Structuring the Narratives

From our random selection of cases, we created a graph of predicted probabilities of civil onset by year for all chosen countries. The predicted probabilities were generated using the following (logit) model, using coefficients from the estimations using the data discussed in Fearon and Laitin (2003):

Log odds of onset at time t = b0 + b1*Prior war + b2*Per cap Income_t − 1

$$+ b3*\log(Population\_t − 1)$$

$$+ b4*\log(percent\ Mountainous) + b5*Noncontiguous$$

$$+ b6*Oil + b7*New\ state$$

$$+ b8*Instability\ in\ prior\ 3\ years + b9*Anocracy\_t − 1.$$

In other words, we include variables found to be statistically and substantively significant based on that analysis.[11] In generating the predicted probabilities for a given country, we estimate the model *without the data for that country*, so that the experience of the country in question is not being used to shape the predictions for that country.[12] In generating the predicted probabilities, we set "prior war" (which is "1" if there was a civil war in progress in the prior year and zero otherwise) to zero for every year in the country's history, since we did not want to use actual war experience to help predict subsequent war experience. We place a tick on the *x* axis if in fact there was an ongoing civil war in that country for the given year.

---

[10] For countries such as Japan and the United States—both in the data-set—we looked for proto-insurgencies (e.g. the Zengakuren protests against Narita airport in Japan; the Aryan Nation militias at Ruby Ridge) to explain in terms of the model how and why they were successfully marginalized.

[11] Noncontiguous territory—not fully justified statistically—was added to the model for the country graphs. Its effects were minor.

[12] We drop all observations for the country, which can be up to 55, depending on how many years the country has been independent since 1945. Changes in predicted probabilities by this procedure were small, giving us confidence that our results did not turn on any single country. Of course, the country's experience has very indirect influence, since it was used in the earlier data analyses that led to this particular model specification. We are merely trying to avoid saying, in effect, "wow the model does great for country X" if part of the reason is that the model is reflecting the experience of country X.

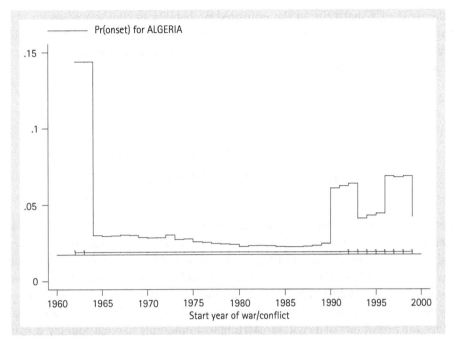

Fig. 52.1. Probability graph for civil war onsets in Algeria

Figure 52.1 illustrates the case of Algeria. Accompanying this graph (Table 52.1) are data on the key variables in comparison to the mean values of the region and the world. Throughout its independent history, Algeria has had a higher predicted probability of onset (.040) than the mean country of the world (.017) and the region as well (.016). We can see that there were two civil war onsets in years that our model predicted heightened susceptibility. Consistent with many other cases, the first civil war coincided with Algeria being a new state and the second civil war coincided with a period of anocracy and instability. Further, there is only one apparent "false positive"

Table 52.1. Key variables for Algeria, and in comparison to regional and world means

Variable	Algeria mean	Regional mean	World mean
Onset probability (predicted)	.040	.016	.017
GDP/capita (in 1985 USD)	2340	5430	3651
Population (in millions)	19.411	11.482	31.787
Mountainous area (as a percentage of total area in country)	15.7	18.6	18.1
Oil (dummy for extensive exports as percentage of total exports)	1	.49	.13
Instability (dummy)	.24	.13	.15
Anocracy (dummy)	.18	.23	.23

in the sense of a sharp rise in the estimated probability of civil war when no war occurred, in 1996–9; and this is fairly excusable given that it occurs during a war in progress, so inclusion of the variable "prior war" in the predictive model would have greatly reduced this "spike."

4 THE INCOMPLETENESS OF STATISTICAL MODELS

How to interpret this graph and how to bring narrative evidence to bear? A first potential concern is that the predicted probabilities from the model are typically very small. Indeed, some 90 percent of the predicted probabilities (for all countries) fall between .0004 and .05. This is probably as it should be—or as it has to be—for two reasons. First, measured by year of onset, civil war starts are extremely rare. We have only about 127 onsets in nearly 7,000 country years. So, not conditioning on any other factors, the probability of a civil war starting in a randomly selected country year in this period was only about .017. Predicting civil war onset in a given country year from factors that can be coded across a large sample of countries and years is a bit like trying to find a needle in a haystack.

Second, it is virtually impossible to identify factors that are codable for a broad cross-section of countries and that can do an excellent job of predicting in *which year* a civil war will break out, if any. The random narratives reinforced our prior belief that a great deal of essentially random historical contingency is involved in determining whether and exactly when a country will "get" a civil war. Bad luck, idiosyncratic choices by leaders, complicated and *ex ante* unpredictable political and social interactions may all factor into explaining why a particular civil war started at a particular time, or even at all, in a particular country. It is an historian's project, and an admirable project at that, to try to understand such particularities and idio-syncrasies for particular cases. Our social science project, implausible though it may be, is to try to identify some factors and mechanisms that do "travel" across countries and years, raising the risk of civil war onset in a consistent and appreciable manner. This is a difficult task and we do not expect that even in the best case it will be possible to come anywhere close to perfect *ex ante* prediction. (Arguably, we could only do this if the participants themselves could do even better, given that they always have access to much more relevant case-specific information. But many examples suggest that it is quite rare for people and even politicians in a country to be able to forecast with confidence, a full year in advance, that a civil war will begin.)

Several of the key explanatory variables in our statistical model do not change much over time within countries. These variables are mountainousness, per capita income, population, and to some extent oil production. This means that while they may contribute a lot to explaining variation in the propensity for civil war outbreaks *across* countries, they are seriously handicapped for explaining in which year a war will start. The four variables that do (or can) change sharply from year to year—prior war, new state, instability, and anocracy—are all quite crude measures. They are relatively easily coded across a broad cross-section of countries and years, but they do not condition in any sophisticated way on political circumstances or events occurring in the country. While they are statistically and substantively significant as predictors of onset, none of them is diagnostic in the sense that they have empirically been followed by onset with a near certainty. Thus, even when several of these time-varying variables are "on," the predicted probability of civil war breaking out in the very next year may only reach .2 or .3.

So, if one had to bet on civil war starting in a particular year using the model's predicted probabilities, even the country years with some of the highest estimated chances of onset are more likely than not to remain peaceful. The highest probability in the data-set is .51 for Indonesia in 1949 and 1950. After that is Pakistan in 1947 and 1948, with a probability of onset at .35. For all but two cases in the entire data-set, for any given country/year, a betting person should bet against a civil war onset occurring that year.

How then to interpret year-to-year changes in predicted probabilities for a given country, like those seen in Figure 52.1? Relatively large jumps or falls in the graph (as seen, for example, for 1961–2, 1989–90, or 1996–7) correspond to changes on one or more of the sharply time-varying explanatory factors. For each such case we can ask: (1) If the change coincides with or shortly precedes a civil war onset, do we see a causal link from the independent variable to the outcome? (2) If there is no onset, do we see signs of strife or other indications of increased conflict that might have become a civil war (and which appear causally related to the change on the independent variable)? And if so, why didn't the violence escalate to the level of civil war? And (3) if there is no onset and no sign of increased violent conflict, why not? For all these cases we can and should also ask if we have miscoded (measured) the dependent variable or an independent variable, giving too much or too little credit to the model and the theory.

Similarly, for years in which we see an onset but no change in predicted probabilities, what occasioned the onset? Is there some new explanatory factor evident that could be coded across cases? Are there miscodings of variables in the model? If the predicted probability of conflict from the model is high on average (relative to the mean for the region or the world), do we see evidence linking any of the slow-moving variables like income or population and the outcome?

In more statistical terms, one way to interpret the graph of predicted onset probabilities for a given country is to interpret the statistical model as a model of an underlying, unobserved *propensity* for civil war in a given country year. The logit transformation scales the estimated propensity index into the $[0, 1]$ interval as predicted probabilities. With narrative analysis we can try to go beyond assessing the fit of the model by looking at 0/1 outcome predictions, as in the standard quantitative approach to binary outcomes. Instead, to some extent we may be able to assess the model's fit by comparing changes in the predicted propensity of civil war to changes in the actual propensity as judged from the narrative evidence.

Despite difficulties in interpreting blunt variables in case analysis, our narratives of particular countries provide a useful complement and comparison to the statistical model. Before summarizing why they are useful, we will draw from the Algeria narrative to give a specific example of this approach.

5 LEARNING FROM THE NARRATIVES

In the case of Algeria's two civil wars, practitioners in the field of comparative politics committed only to the statistical approach might see the nice fit between model and the real world and then let sleeping dogs lie. Algeria, with its poverty, its oil, its large population, and its mountains, was a likely candidate for civil war. This was especially the case for two periods, 1962–3 and 1991–2, when political factors (being a new state in 1962; political instability and the movement toward anocracy beginning in 1990) pushed the expected probability of civil war well above the world average. And in fact, the onsets of civil war took place precisely when our models showed that Algeria was especially prone to such violence.

Why examine with a fine-toothed comb cases for which no explanation is needed? In our method, however, Algeria was chosen through random selection, and so we could not let this sleeping dog lie. Waking him up proved rewarding.[13]

The civil war onset when Algeria was a new state indeed involved a commitment problem like that we theorized in proposing why the variable New State associates with civil war. Berbers who had prospered under French rule feared a loss of status to Arabs who would be the majority group in the new Algerian state. Furthermore, the local guerrilla units that bore the greatest brunt of the fighting for independence feared marginalization once the regular army entered Algeria from Morocco and Tunisia. If these regional militias did not fight for power in the summer of 1962, they feared marginalization as they did not trust the the new leadership to give them as much as they might be able to take by fighting. Indeed some of these units and at least one from the Berber region took part in the 1962 rebellion.

The narrative also made clear that this "weak state" commitment problem stemmed as well from a factor not previously considered, namely the ineffectiveness of France's transfer of power. France left the scene when the independence movement was divided in several ways, with no clearly dominant force and no general commitment to any constitutional mechanism to decide among them or guarantee future, peaceful chances at power. Independence to a new state without a credible commitment by the former metropole to support the leadership to which it transfers

---

[13] The full Algeria narrative is available at <http://www.stanford.edu/group/ethnic>.

power yielded a vacuum that drew in insurgents. It was France's inability to commit to Prime Minister Ben Bella rather than just Ben Bella's inability to commit
to the future security of minorities that accounted for post-independence violence
in 1962.

The civil war coded as beginning in 1992, as our theoretical arguments concerning
anocracy and political instability expected, emerged out of the political opening
granted by the authoritarian regime in 1990. The opening indicated division within
the governing elite and a general sense of weakening in the face of public dissatisfaction and pressure. Clerics in the FIS (Islamic Salvation Front) were emboldened
to exploit an economic crisis to challenge the regime in the name of fundamentalist
ideals. The commitment problem again appears as critical in the explanation for why
there was violence rather than a negotiated or democratic solution—the military
regime feared that the first national election lost to the Islamists would be the last
election held anytime soon. This is consistent with our theoretical account linking
anocracy and political instability (indicated by changed Polity scores) to civil war.

However, a careful look at the civil war that ensued brought into question our
interpretation of the impact of per capita income. We have argued that on average,
country poverty proxies for a weak central government administration and coercive
apparatus, unable to collect information on its own population or to use information
strategically to root out insurgents. In the Algerian case, we find a very strong army,
one that that had learned much from the experience in fighting the French during
the long war of independence. The army was well taken care of and had the resources
and will to develop sophisticated counter-insurgency units. So Algeria's moderately
low per capita income (versus the regional or world averages) is in this case a poor
measure of state coercive capabilities, and civil war occurred despite relatively strong
coercive capability.

The narrative suggested, however, another quite different mechanism linking low
per capita income and civil war. Area experts have pointed to the earlier closing of the
migration outlet to Algerian youth as a causal factor in the onset of the war. Indeed,
the rebellion came shortly after France cut off the immigration spigot. Instead of
further inciting the anti-immigration program of M. Le Pen and his *Front National*
in France, young Algerians that would formerly have been sending back remittances
from France were now unemployed and being recruited into the FIS. And so, the low
GDP and weak economy in Algeria worked through a second mechanism (available
recruits) rather than the first (weak military) to translate high likelihood to actual
onset (consistent in this case with Collier and Hoeffler's 2004 interpretation of the
role of income).

Since the FIS was a religious mobilization, the narrative almost invited us to ask
whether the civil war of 1992 can be explained by some religious factor, even if religion
played no role in our statistical analysis. There can be little doubt that Islamic symbols had a powerful emotional impact on the population. In the late 1970s, Muslim
activists engaged in isolated and relatively small-scale assertions of fundamentalist
principles: harassing women who they felt were inappropriately dressed, smashing
establishments that served alcohol, and evicting official imams from their mosques.

The Islamists escalated their actions in 1982, when they called for the abrogation of the National Charter and for the formation of an Islamic government. Amidst an increasing number of violent incidents on campuses, Islamists killed one student. After police arrested 400 Islamists, about 100,000 demonstrators thronged to Friday prayers at a university mosque. Islamists were also able to mobilize large numbers of supporters successfully to demand that the government abrogate rights given to women in the colonial period. And of course, the Islamist political party shocked and awed the military authorities in their impressive first round electoral victory in December 1991 (Metz 1993). Fundamentalism was popular!

However, it is not clear why Islamic fundamentalists confronted the FLN. Algerian nationalism, consequent on the French denial of citizenship to Muslims in the 1870 Cremieux Decree, was always "Islamic" in sentiment. The FLN was never considered, as many in the army command considered themselves, secular and perhaps even anti-Islam. Some FLN leaders were Islamists. The FIS did not represent a deep cultural cleavage in Algeria. In fact, there is a popular pun among Algerians, "le FIS est le fils du FLN" (Quandt 1998, 96–7). The trump in the FIS hand was not its religious devotion or its sole identification with Islam.

Furthermore, a careful examination of the FIS reveals little about Islam as the source for the Algerian rebellion. For one, the clerics followed the urban proletariat into war rather than led them. There is evidence that in fact the clerics sought in the late 1980s to calm the riots in the streets instigated by the unemployed youth (Pelletiere 1992, 6). To be sure, the GIA (the leading insurgent militia) relied on fundamentalist ideology in order to finance the war through the "Islamic rent" paid by Middle East states (Martinez 2000, 198–206, 240). But this was a strategy of raising funds more than a sign of Islamic devotion.

The narrative suggests that it was not Islamic fundamentalism, but rather state strategies in regard to religion that played a vital role in driving the insurgency. After independence, the Algerian government asserted state control over religious activities for purposes of national consolidation and political control. Islam became the religion of the state in the new constitution and the publicly displayed religion of its leaders. No laws could be enacted that would be contrary to Islamic tenets or that would in any way undermine Islamic beliefs and principles. The state monopolized the building of mosques, and the Ministry of Religious Affairs controlled an estimated 5,000 public mosques by the mid-1980s. Imams were trained, appointed, and paid by the state, and the Friday *khutba*, or sermon, was issued to them by the Ministry of Religious Affairs. That ministry also administered religious property, provided for religious education and training in schools, and created special institutes for Islamic learning.

What is the implication of state control over religion? Our statistical analysis of the whole sample found that religious discrimination could not distinguish countries that experienced civil wars from those that did not. But the narrative suggests a different mechanism. The very act of authorizing and subsidizing religious organizations and leaders automatically politicized religious protest. As religious entrepreneurs sought to capture new audiences for their local mosques, they were in fact challenging state authority. Through its subsidization and promotion of Islam, the Algerian authorities opened themselves up to forms of symbolic attack they could not easily repel. By seeking to suppress religious experimentation, the FLN found itself more vulnerable to attack than if it kept entirely out of religious affairs.

In sum, rather than some deep religious message of FIS that articulated with the religious sentiments of the people, it was the situation in which the state sought to co-opt religious opposition that gave that opposition a chance to articulate a clear anti-regime message through renegade mosques. State sponsorship of religion backfired grievously. The Algerian case could thus suggest that state *sponsorship* of religion (rather than *discrimination* against it) raises the probability of civil war.

6 CONCLUSION

Despite some claims to the contrary in the qualitative methods literature, case studies are not designed to discover or confirm empirical regularities. However they can be quite useful—indeed, essential—for ascertaining and assessing the causal mechanisms that give rise to empirical regularities in politics. We have argued that random selection of cases for narrative development is a principled and productive criterion in studies that mix statistical and case-study methods, using the former for identifying regularities, and the latter to assess (or to develop new) explanations of these.

Using the Algerian example, the narratives suggest a return to large-N analysis with several new ideas. First, the variable "new state" might be productively interacted with the capacity of the metropole to commit to the transitional leadership. The expectation is that a strong metropole would better be able to protect the leaders to whom it transferred authority, and thereby deter (at least for a time) potential insurgents. France, in the wake of occupation in the Second World War, the loss of the colonial war in Vietnam, the collapse of the Fourth Republic, and the long war for Algerian independence, was not in a position to manage the transition to the new leadership in Algiers.

This insight emerging from the narrative of a case that was "on the regression line" illuminated a not-so-obvious pattern in vulnerability of new states to civil war onsets. Many countries that received independence in the immediate postwar era when metropoles were devastated (such as in Indonesia, Vietnam, South Asia, and the Palestine Mandate) fell quickly into civil war. Those countries that became new states when the Soviet metropole disintegrated (Azerbaijan, Georgia, and Moldova are examples) were also highly susceptible to civil war onsets. However, those countries that received independence in the 1960s and 1970s in Africa when the metropoles were strong (except for Belgium and Portugal that could not manage the transitions to new leadership in their colonies) were less likely to suffer immediately rebellion. In several of these cases, "commitment problem" wars started several years later, after the colonial power really did stand back. "New state" is more dangerous the weaker the metropole that grants it independence.

Second, the Algeria narrative suggests that we might develop a coding rule for extent of migration by young men to more productive economies for work. The expectation would be that in countries where young men can relatively easily escape unemployment through migration to industrialized countries, insurgent recruitment will be more difficult than otherwise. (Subsequent narratives reported on the relationship of blocked migration opportunities and civil war in Haiti and near civil war in Jamaica; meanwhile open migration opportunities may have helped save Portugal and the Dominican Republic from joining the list of onsets under revolutionary conditions.)

Third, the Algeria narrative suggested a new way to think about the religious sources of insurgency. Instead of modeling hatreds between people of different religions, or of state discrimination against minority religions, it might be more productive to model the relationship between dominant religious authority and the state. The more the state seeks to regulate the dominant religious organization, the more it is setting up a recruitment base against the state within the religious organization. Preliminary data analysis for our large-N data-set gives support to this narrative-inspired conjecture.

There are several more general lessons as well to be learned from the random narrative exercise. Through narrative, it is possible to point to interactions among individual variables that may not matter in a consistent way by themselves, but that jointly may make for civil war susceptibility. It may then be possible to specify more sharply the conditions when a variable will have some theorized effect. It is possible to point to micro-factors for future coding such as tactical decisions by states and by insurgents that are usually ignored in large-N data collection exercises.

As well, the random narrative method allows us to estimate measurement error for variables that are hard to code reliably across large numbers of cases. In the set of narratives we examined through random selection, we found not insubstantial error in the coding of civil war onset, our dependent variable. To give but one example, northern Thailand has been held by area experts to be a zone of peace compared to the mountainous rebellions in neighboring Burma and Laos. A number of civil war lists have thus ignored the northern troubles in Thailand as a possible civil war. As a result of the research that went into the random narrative, however, we found that the northern insurgency clearly passed the death threshold that our scheme determines as a civil war. In general, we estimate that as many as 5 percent of our initial codings on the dependent variable were erroneous. Statistically, if these errors are random, in a logit analysis this will tend to bias effect estimates towards zero. Of course, the errors may not be random—they are surely more likely for relatively low-level civil wars close to whatever death threshold is employed—so a direct advantage of combining narrative analysis with statistical analysis is better measurement and more accurate effect estimates.

These random narratives, in sum, have already proven both troubling and useful as a complement to, or extension of, a large-N analysis of civil war onsets. They suggest a natural way that qualitative work might be integrated into a research program as a complement to rather than as a rival or substitute for quantitative analysis.

References

BATES, R., et al. 1998. *Analytic Narratives*. Princeton, NJ: Princeton University Press.

BOIX, C. 1998. *Political Parties, Growth and Equality*. Cambridge: Cambridge University Press.

COLLIER, P. and HOEFFLER, A. 2004. Greed and grievance in civil war. *Oxford Economic Papers*, 56: 563–95.

—— and SAMBANIS, N. 2005. *Understanding Civil War*, 2 vols. Washington, DC: World Bank.

DOYLE, M. and SAMBANIS, N. 2006. *Making War and Building Peace*. Princeton, NJ: Princeton University Press.

ECKSTEIN, H. 1975. Case study and theory in political science. Pp. 94–137 in *Handbook of Political Science*, ed. F. Greenstein and N. Polsby. Reading, Mass.: Addison-Wesley.

ELSTER, J. 1998. A plea for mechanisms. In *Social Mechanisms: An Analytical Approach to Social Theory*, ed. P. Hedstrom and R. Swedberg. Cambridge: Cambridge University Press.

FEARON, J. D. 1998. Commitment problems and the spread of ethnic conflict. In *The International Spread of Ethnic Conflict: Fear, Diffusion, and Escalation*, ed. D. Lake and D. Rothchild. Princeton, NJ: Princeton University Press.

—— 2004. Why do some civil wars last so much longer than others? *Journal of Peace Research*, 41: 275–301.

—— 2008. Economic development, insurgency, and civil war. In *Institutions and Economic Performance*, ed. E. Helpman. Cambridge, Mass.: Harvard University Press.

—— and LAITIN, D. D. 1999. Weak states, rough terrain, and large-scale ethnic violence since 1945. Presented at the Annual Meetings of the American Political Science Association, Atlanta, September 2–5.

—— —— 2003. Ethnicity, insurgency and civil war. *American Political Science Review*, 97: 75–90.

—— —— 2005. Civil war narratives. Estudio/Working Paper 2005/218, Centro de Estudios Avanzados en Ciencias Sociales, Instituto Juan March de Estudios e Investigaciones, June.

—— —— 2007. Civil war terminations. Presented at the 103rd Annual Meeting of the American Political Science Association, Chicago, Aug. 30–Sept. 2.

FORTNA, V. P. 2004. *Peace Time: Cease-fire Agreements and the Durability of Peace*. Princeton, NJ: Princeton University Press.

GEORGE, A. and BENNETT, A. 2005. *Case Studies and Theory Development in the Social Sciences*. Cambridge, Mass.: MIT Press.

GERRING, J. 2006. *Case Study Research: Principles and Practices*. Cambridge: Cambridge University Press.

GOEMANS, H. 2000. *War and Punishment*. Princeton, NJ: Princeton University Press.

GOLDTHORPE, J. 2000. *On Sociology*. Oxford: Oxford University Press.

HUTH, P. 1998. *Standing your Ground: Territorial Disputes and International Conflict*. Ann Arbor: University of Michigan Press.

IVERSEN, T. 1999. *Contested Economic Institutions*. Cambridge: Cambridge University Press.

LAITIN, D. 1995. National revivals and violence. *Archives européennes de sociologie*, 36: 3–43.

—— 1998. *Identity in Formation*. Ithaca, NY: Cornell University Press.

MANSFIELD, E., and SNYDER, J. 2005. *Electing to Fight: Why Emerging Democracies Go to War*. Cambridge, Mass.: MIT Press.

MARES, I. 2003. *The Politics of Social Risk*. Cambridge: Cambridge University Press.

MARTIN, L. 1994. *Coercive Cooperation*. Princeton, NJ: Princeton University Press.

MARTINEZ, L. 2000. *The Algerian Civil War 1990–1998*, trans. J. Derrick. London: Hurst.

METZ, H. (ed.) 1993. *Algeria: A Country Study*. Federal Research Division, Library of Congress, <http://memory.loc.gov/cgi-bin/query2/r?frd/cstdy:@field(DOCID+dz0000>), section on Chadli Bendjedid and Afterward.

PELLETIERE, S. C. 1992. *Mass Action and Islamic Fundamentalism: The Revolt of the Brooms*. Carlisle Barracks, Pa.: US Army War College.

QUANDT, W. B. 1998. *Between Ballots and Bullets*. Washington, DC: Brookings.

SCHULTZ, K. 2001. *Democracy and Coercive Diplomacy*. Cambridge: Cambridge University Press.

STONE, R. 2002. *Lending Credibility*. Princeton, NJ: Princeton University Press.

VAN EVERA, S. 1997. *Guide to Methods for Students of Political Science*. Ithaca, NY: Cornell University Press.

WAGNER, R. H. 2007. *War and the State*. Ann Arbor: University of Michigan Press.

WALTERS, B. 2001. *Committing to Peace*. Princeton, NJ: Princeton University Press.

APPENDIX

POLITICAL THEORY

PART IV POLITICAL THEORY IN THE WORLD

PART V STATE AND PEOPLE

POLITICAL INSTITUTIONS

PART IV OLD AND NEW

LAW AND POLITICS

PART IV INTERNATIONAL AND SUPRANATIONAL LAW

PART V FORMS OF LEGAL ORDER

PART VI SOURCES OF LAW AND THEORIES OF JURISPRUDENCE

PART VII THE AMERICAN JUDICIAL CONTEXT

PART VIII THE POLITICAL AND POLICY ENVIRONMENT OF COURTS IN THE UNITED STATES

PART IX INTERDISCIPLINARY APPROACHES TO LAW AND POLITICS

PART X OLD AND NEW

POLITICAL BEHAVIOR

PART IV   POLITICAL VALUES

PART V   NEW DEBATES IN POLITICAL BEHAVIOR

PART VI POLITICAL PARTICIPATION

PART VII DOES PUBLIC OPINION MATTER?

PART VIII THE METHODOLOGY OF COMPARATIVE POLITICAL BEHAVIOR RESEARCH

Contextual Political Analysis

PART IV IDEAS MATTER

PART V CULTURE MATTERS

PART VI HISTORY MATTERS

PART IX TECHNOLOGY MATTERS

PART X OLD AND NEW

COMPARATIVE POLITICS

PART VII   PROCESSING POLITICAL DEMANDS

PART VIII   GOVERNANCE IN COMPARATIVE PERSPECTIVE

International Relations

PART IV THE QUESTION OF METHOD

PART V BRIDGING THE SUBFIELD BOUNDARIES

PART VI THE SCHOLAR AND THE POLICY-MAKER

POLITICAL ECONOMY

PART IV INTERACTION OF THE LEGISLATURE, PRESIDENT, BUREAUCRACY, AND THE COURTS

PART V CONSTITUTIONAL THEORY

PART VI SOCIAL CHOICE

PART X HISTORICAL AND COMPARATIVE DEVELOPMENT AND NONDEMOCRATIC REGIMES

PART XI INTERNATIONAL POLITICAL ECONOMY

PART XII INTERNATIONAL RELATIONS AND CONFLICT

PART XIII METHODOLOGICAL ISSUES

PART XIV OLD AND NEW

PUBLIC POLICY

PART IV PRODUCING PUBLIC POLICY

PART V INSTRUMENTS OF POLICY

PART IX PUBLIC POLICY, OLD AND NEW

POLITICAL METHODOLOGY

PART IV CAUSALITY AND EXPLANATION IN SOCIAL RESEARCH

PART V EXPERIMENTS, QUASI-EXPERIMENTS, AND NATURAL EXPERIMENTS

PART VI QUANTITATIVE TOOLS FOR DESCRIPTIVE AND CAUSAL INFERENCE: GENERAL METHODS

PART IX   ORGANIZATIONS, INSTITUTIONS, AND MOVEMENTS IN THE FIELD OF METHODOLOGY

Name Index

Name Index: includes all referenced authors.

SUBJECT INDEX

Note: all law cases are indexed under 'legal cases'.